P9-BYN-416

2020 EDITION

Best Colleges

University of Pittsburgh
BRETT ZIEGLER FOR USN&WR

CONTENTS

26

52

FROM TOP: PINAR ISTEK FOR USN&WR; BRETT ZIEGLER FOR USN&WR

WHERE
WILLPOWER
MEETS
BRAINPOWER

CALL IT TENACITY. CALL IT GRIT. WE HAVE THE DETERMINATION AND THE INTELLECT. COMBINE THOSE WITH A COMMUNITY THAT HAS THE SAME DRIVE AND SPIRIT, AND WE'VE GOT THE ULTIMATE ADVANTAGE.

Furman is a place where every student is promised a four-year pathway of high-impact engaged learning through research, internships and study away, guided by a team of mentors. The result – a meaningful life and career.

This is **THE FURMAN ADVANTAGE.**

FURMAN.EDU ✦ GREENVILLE, SC

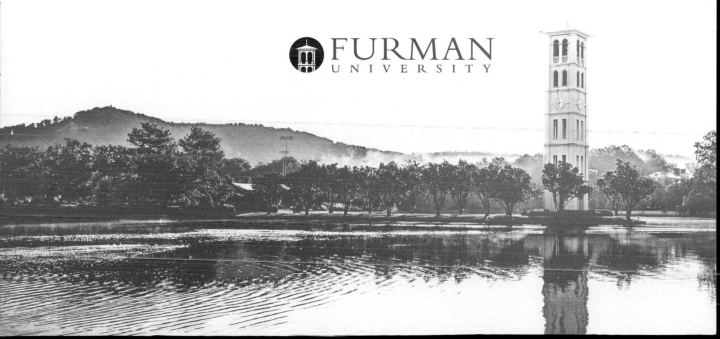

FURMAN
UNIVERSITY

CONTENTS

Boston
University
graduation

 The U.S. News Rankings

CONTENTS

 **GETTING IN**

 **FINDING
THE MONEY**

130

SUDDENLY THE WORLD OPENS

At Seton Hall, we foster those defining moments when passion becomes a profession — when a new idea leads to a deep personal discovery. With rigorous academics that elevate expectations and faculty mentorship that leads to career-shaping discoveries, we help our students live these moments every day. Then they show the world the greatness they can accomplish.

SETON HALL
UNIVERSITY
1856

What great minds can do.
www.shu.edu/greatminds

@ USNEWS.COM

YOUR COLLEGE GAME PLAN
Insider Advice

If you're looking for college advice, you've come to the right place. We provide expert tips to help families research, apply to and pay for college. Our articles and slideshows feature college admissions and financial aid officers, counselors, current students, graduates, parents and more, who all share their insights to help demystify the process.
usnews.com/collegeadvice

GETTING IN
College Admissions Playbook

Get tips from Varsity Tutors, an academic tutoring and test-prep provider. This blog offers advice on mastering the SAT and ACT as well as the college application process.
usnews.com/collegeplaybook

COLLEGE VISITS
Take a Road Trip

We've gone on numerous trips to visit campuses in case you can't. Check out our compendium of more than 30 different trips to 100-plus schools.
usnews.com/roadtrips

RANKINGS INSIGHT
Morse Code Blog

Get the inside scoop on the rankings – and the commentary and controversy surrounding them – from U.S. News' Bob Morse, the mastermind behind our education rankings projects.
usnews.com/morsecode

IN-DEPTH DATA
College Compass

Gain access to the U.S. News College Compass, which offers comprehensive searchable data and tools for high school students starting down the path to campus. To get a 25% discount, subscribe at
usnews.com/compassoffer

PAYING FOR COLLEGE
Researching Aid

Visit our guide to all your possible sources of college funds. Learn about your savings options and which schools meet students' full need.
usnews.com/payforcollege

The Student Loan Ranger

If you're borrowing to finance your degree, don't fall into the trap of taking on too much debt. Experts provide guidance on this blog if you must turn to student loans to pay for college.
usnews.com/studentloanranger

DISTANCE LEARNING
Online Education

Do you need to balance school with work or other obligations? Consult our rankings of the best online degree programs for leads on how to get your diploma without leaving home.
usnews.com/online

FOR SCHOOLS ONLY
Academic Insights

U.S. News Academic Insights is an analytics dashboard intended for use by institutions that comprises all of the undergraduate and graduate historical rankings data we've collected. The dashboard allows for peer group comparisons and includes easy-to-understand visualizations.
ai.usnews.com

Top 10
in the world
for patents

among universities granted U.S. patents

U.S. National Academy of Inventors and the Intellectual Property Owners Association

Cancer-fighting nanobots

ASU Biodesign Institute Center for Molecular Design and Biomimetics

From startups and new technologies to bioscience breakthroughs, our innovation mindset fuels extraordinary outcomes with real-world impact.

Unlimited clean water

ASU startup Zero Mass Water

Arizona State University

innovate.asu.edu

#1 in the U.S.
for innovation
ASU ahead of Stanford and MIT

– U.S. News & World Report 2016, 2017, 2018 and 2019

by **Brian Kelly**
Editorial Director &
Executive Vice President

Welcome to the College Search

FINDING THE RIGHT COLLEGE isn't easy. That's especially true if your family is going through the search for the first time. This is our 35th go-round at U.S. News, so we feel like we've got some experience worth sharing.

Over the years, we've improved our information and sharpened our focus, with our primary objective being to help prospective students and their parents make one of life's most important – and expensive – decisions. Applicants and their families need objective measures that allow them to evaluate and compare schools. The U.S. News rankings are one tool to help them make choices, along with all the other insights and guidance contained in these pages. This sort of assistance is more relevant than ever, with some private colleges now costing more than a quarter of a million dollars for a bachelor's degree. At the same time, many high schools have greatly reduced their college counseling resources, leaving students and parents to educate themselves about the search. And with so many myths and misconceptions swirling around about the admissions process, we take seriously our role in helping consumers understand how it really works (related story, Page 116).

Of course, we have adjusted our rankings methodology over the years to reflect changes in higher education, and we make it clear that we are not doing peer-reviewed social science research, although we do maintain very high survey and data standards. We have strived to be open and transparent. And we have always acknowledged that the rankings are not perfect. Initially, they were based solely on schools' academic reputation among leaders at peer institutions; we later developed a formula in which the opinions of experts and peers account for 20% of a school's score and important quantitative measures such as graduation and retention rates, class size and student-faculty ratios account for the rest. Over time, we have shifted weight from inputs (indicators of the quality of students and resources) to outputs (suc-

cess in graduating students). We operate under this guiding principle: The methodology is altered only if a change will better aid our readers. For example, last year, we incorporated a way to assess schools' commitment to promoting social mobility. We measure how well they're doing graduating Pell Grant recipients. And we've removed college acceptance rates as an indicator of student excellence.

A STARTING POINT. It has helped us a great deal to have these principles to focus on as we have faced the inevitable criticisms from academia about our rankings' growing influence. One main critique remains: that it is impossible to reduce the complexities of a college's offerings and attributes to a single number. It's important to keep in mind that our information is simply a starting point. The next steps in a college search should include careful research on a smaller list of choices, campus visits, and conversations with students, faculty and alumni. Feedback from academia has helped us improve the rankings over time. We meet with our critics, listen to their points of view, debate them on the merits of what we do, and make appropriate changes.

U.S. News is well aware that the higher ed community is also an audience for our rankings. We know how seriously academics, college presidents, trustees and governing boards take our data. They study and use the information for various purposes, including benchmarking against peers, alumni fundraising and advertising.

What does all of this mean in today's global information marketplace? U.S. News has become a respected, unbiased resource that higher education administrators and policymakers and the collegebound public worldwide turn to for reliable guidance. In fact, the Best Colleges rankings have become a key part of the evolving higher education accountability movement. Universities are increasingly being held responsible for their policies, how their funds are spent, the level of student engagement, and how much graduates have learned. The U.S. News rankings have become the annual public benchmark to measure the academic performance of the country's colleges.

We know our role has limits. The rankings should only be used as one factor in the college search. We've long said that there is no single "best college." There is only the best college for you or, more likely, a handful of good options. At usnews.com, you can find thousands of pages of rankings, research, sortable data, info on getting in and getting financial aid, and a personalized tool called College Compass. We know the process of choosing a college is not simple. But our experience tells us the hard work is worth it in the end. ●

BECAUSE SOMEDAY
I'll be the one spending a semester abroad.

Plan for your someday without sacrificing the things you want to do today.

Together, we'll help you achieve what matters most.

- Live the life you want today, and into the future.
- Develop a long-term financial game plan.
- Get, and stay, on track toward your goals.

Talk with Fidelity today about your finances. Because you don't have to know all the answers—that's why we're here to help.

Fidelity INVESTMENTS

Fidelity.com/yoursomeday
866.715.2058

LOOK DEEPER

see a whole other world.

One equally stunning.

Because here, students,

faculty, and researchers

are free to dig as deep as

they like. Ask questions

nobody's asked. Unite

disciplines no one's ever

united. And as a result,

see things no one's ever

seen. This is UC San Diego.

A top 10 public university for

a decade. Enjoy the view.

UC San Diego

lookdeeper.ucsd.edu

Study

the Schools

University of San Diego
PHOTOGRAPHY BY BRETT ZIEGLER FOR USN&WR

A First-Class
First Year

Colleges are doing more to help students transition to campus and thrive

by **Courtney Rubin**

DORM SOCIALS. Intramural sports. So-called enhanced brain breaks (more commonly known as evening snacks). Introductory workshops on how to conduct college-level research. Welcome fetes hosted by student clubs and organizations. During Ramona Park's first year at Harvard, the Santa Fe, New Mexico, native was so inundated with emails and Facebook posts about upcoming events that she is considering creating a platform to organize them all for future students. Each organization would get a profile, she envisions, and then undergrads could go in and save events to their own calendars. "I don't even think I knew everything that was out there," says Park, who expects to either major in computer science or art, film and visual studies.

Harvard is far from the only school to go all-in on the First-Year Experience, as colleges like to call it.

Wittenberg University first-year student orientation

The reason? A growing mountain of research suggests that making students feel connected during their first year means they are more likely to make it to graduation. Before, "students were coming in bright-eyed and they were leaving freshman year much more cynical," says Steven Mintz, a professor of history at the University of Texas–Austin and a senior adviser to the president of Hunter College in New York. "So now it's, 'How can we make the first-year experience seem relevant to students? How can we give them windows into careers or hands-on learning opportunities that students will find meaningful?'"

Southern Utah University, for instance, recently overhauled its first-year experience, ditching randomly assigned orientation groups in favor of ones based on a student's hobbies or interests (everything from "Harry Potter" to hiking to music). Freshman retention rose from 64% in 2015 to 73% in 2018, a record for the school that is due in large part to making first-year programming more personalized, says Eric Kirby, assistant vice president for student affairs focused on completion and student success.

So what should you look for in a first-year experience? Some key questions to consider if you want to set yourself up for success from Day One:

What kind of first-year living-learning programs does the school offer?

First-year seminars have been around for some time, though they often vary in style, and schools are frequently tweaking them – not surprising, when you consider that this type of academic experience has long been spotlighted by the Association of American Colleges and Universities as a practice that makes a big impact on learning. Some 52% of four-year

At UCLA, which offers a range of programs to help freshmen ease into campus life

institutions require such courses, according to data from the U.S. Department of Education.

Christine Harrington, an associate professor in educational leadership at New Jersey City University and author of the book "Student Success in College: Doing What Works," suggests looking for places whose first-year seminars grant more than one credit. That "generally demonstrates a higher level of commitment on the part of the school to student success," she says. A greater number of credits usually means that the class meets more often or for a longer period of time, so there are additional activities and "a deeper experience." Harrington also recommends investigating the syllabi of the courses: Are they more like an extended orientation or do they go above that and help students build important academic skills such as writing and critical thinking?

At Wittenberg University, a private liberal arts college in Ohio, required first-year seminars meet weekly and use documents from the school's 174-year history to engage students and get them to start considering possible majors and careers. "The stories resonate with them, and they don't even realize we're teaching them academic skills at the same time," says Jennifer Oldstone-Moore, a professor of religion and the school's first-year seminar faculty director.

University of New Hampshire

A top-tier research institution

R1 CARNEGIE CLASSIFICATION®

We're the state's flagship public university and one of the nation's top research institutions. We've helped NASA launch satellites for six decades, led efforts to map the world's seafloor and earned the highest rating for sustainability. With state-of-the-art facilities and the nation's largest undergraduate research conference, we prepare our students for success in research and beyond.

One especially effective way of building bonds between students is to turbocharge the experience of academic inquiry through living-learning communities. Cohorts of students live together and explore a common interest (such as social justice at Florida State University) or an academic pursuit (like engineering or the health professions at West Virginia University).

Are there activities for specific groups of students?

For undergrads of color, veterans, first-generation students, those from overseas and others who might be underrepresented on certain campuses, schools are working to ease the transition and provide welcoming support. Some schools offer living-learning communities for women in engineering, for example, or first-gen undergrads. During orientation, incoming students often learn of a particular hub on campus, such as a multicultural, international or women's center, or a group they may wish to connect with, like organizations for black, Latino and LGBTQ students.

First-year students of color at Emory University in Atlanta can be matched with peer mentors in their fall semester to help them get acclimated to the social and academic environment. First-generation undergrads and those from low-income backgrounds are also invited to participate in a program that introduces them to faculty, staff and student mentors, as well as to topics like finding financial success in college.

Since 2010, Vassar College in New York has offered a program called Transitions geared toward students who are from low-income families, are first-gen and/or are living in the U.S. without legal status. Individuals spend a week before orientation getting acquainted with campus and the local community, meeting faculty and administrators, and doing other activities. Then, they can participate in events throughout their four years, such as group meals and professional development programs. Initiatives like these give undergrads a group of peers with whom they can build a sense of community, says program director Capria Berry. About 385 people participated last year.

Many large public universities, including the University of Maryland–College Park, the University of Oregon and Pennsylvania State University, have created honors colleges that aim to provide members with the intimate academic and social community and special activities of, say, a small private school. When she enrolled in 2018, Angelica Olivas, a sophomore at Arizona State University's downtown Phoenix campus, says one of the best things she did was attend "Camp B-Town," an event held after the initial week of classes for incoming Barrett Honors College students. They completed a ropes course and a scavenger hunt, then took part in a lip-syncing competition.

"You're all just laughing at each other, and it brings you together," says Olivas, whose group performed to Bon Jovi's 1986 hit "You Give Love a Bad Name." ASU honors college students are also assigned peer mentors, who organize events and offer guidance.

At certain schools, particularly in urban settings, commuter

INSIDE SCOOP

What's your favorite thing about Morehouse?

The small student body. While it's not for everybody, it really helps you form close relationships with not only your peers, but also your professors. In terms of the HBCU experience, it's a different kind of experience having professors who look like you, who have the same shared experiences as you, and who

Jonathan Epps, '19
Morehouse College • Atlanta

care about you on a very deep level. All that helped me succeed and graduate as co-valedictorian of my class and a Fulbright scholar.

Toward the end of my freshman year, I applied for a program we have here called the UPS Community Service Scholars Program, through which we are assigned to go to an elementary school and tutor at-risk kids. It really gave me a sense of purpose, and it helped me expand my education.

students get special attention. New York University, for example, hosts an overnight retreat for these students prior to the school's Welcome Week, and matches first-years with a "commuter assistant," an already enrolled student who can serve as a guide. UCLA has also begun outreach to first-year commuter students to ensure that they don't feel left out of traditional freshman activities that their peers living on campus attend with their resident assistant, notes La'Tonya Rease Miles, UCLA's director of First Year Experience and Strategic Initiatives. The school

There are Spiders everywhere.

AND THAT'S A GOOD THING.

The moment a new Spider's boundless ambition meets Richmond's programs, an incomparable partnership forms between student and University. Our faculty become accompanists, mentors, and confidants to you in your studies. And when you graduate, you join a global web of successful Spiders who are advancing in fields worldwide.

From here, you can go anywhere — and it all starts within you.

richmond.edu

now hosts commuter breakfasts and meetups, so first-years living at home also have a group to walk in with at welcome events.

Does the college integrate career talk into the first year?

It used to be that students might not make it to their school's career center until senior year. Now these centers have been rebranded at many places, and the focus has shifted away from just mock-interviewing and résumé checks to helping students map out which majors are a match for which careers, and which subject areas and professions suit their academic and other interests (related story, Page 36). Some schools, including Sam Houston State University in Texas, the University of Kansas and the University of Mary Washington in Virginia, offer these services as part of for-credit courses that freshmen can take. The objective, in part, is to get students to graduate on time – something changing a major late in the game can make difficult.

"We want to make sure students are in the best-fit major as early as possible. We do not want our students to incur any more debt than they need to," says Naomi Norman, associate vice president for instruction at the University of Georgia. To that end, UGA recently created an "Exploratory Center" with academic advisers for students who arrive not having declared a major or who might be considering a change.

Meanwhile, at Johns Hopkins University in Baltimore, career prep begins before freshmen even set foot on campus. As part of the school's Launch program, they are linked up with a so-called life design educator in August. Over the course of their first year, undergrads can meet regularly with these staffers, who help them identify their passions and see how they might match up with an academic or career path. Students can also enter one or more industry-focused "Career Academies," where they can find resources in areas like health sciences or nonprofit/government.

What additional support does the school offer?

College students are affected by a host of stressors, from academic challenges to lack of sleep and exposure to alcohol to the prospect of heavy debt and an uncertain job market. Colleges are offering a wide range

of responses, including expanded programming around mental health, sexual health, alcohol abuse and general wellness, plus an increased focus on building stress tolerance and coping strategies (related story, Page 30).

Says Marlene Sandstrom, dean of the college and a professor of psychology at Williams College in Massachusetts: "We really want students to think about how to spend their time doing the things they care about but also taking care of themselves. You can dig yourself into a health hole really quickly if

Making Wellness Matter

DURING AND AFTER freshman year, many colleges and universities are actively working to provide students with mental health touch points. These include a mix of both formal and informal wellness resources, such as drop-in counseling, educational sessions, opportunities to engage with faculty and staff, and 24/7 crisis hotlines for those needing immediate help. In a sense, it's "taking a no-wrong-door approach" and making mental health services "visible in all these places outside of the counseling center," says Chris Brownson, associate vice president for student affairs and director of the Counseling and Mental Health Center at the University of Texas–Austin. At UT, nine Counselors in Academic Residence are embedded across the university's individual colleges, where they can provide more personalized support. According to a 2018 survey released by the Association for University and College

tation wellness event, "realizing how effective a tool writing could be for mental health was a big takeaway," he says.

At Rowan University in New Jersey, incoming undergrads can take a two-credit "Rowan 101: College Success" course focused on the transition to college, with an emphasis on wellness. "We want to really build well-being into the campus culture," says Rory McElwee, vice president for student affairs at Rowan. Through that course and a required first-year seminar, students explore topics like academic integrity, time management and goal-setting, and instructors expose them to key resources across campus, from the academic (libraries) to the health-focused (the counseling center and rec center).

In 2018, Syracuse University in New York for the first time required students to attend a Be Well Expo, where ABC News journalist Dan Harris, author of the book "10% Happier," talked about using meditation to deal with workaholism and other challenges. Afterwards, students could participate in wellness activities like rock climbing or relaxing with a therapy dog. In 2017, UCLA brought in cast members from the popular Netflix show "13 Reasons Why" to discuss mental health.

When it comes to classes, most schools match up incoming students with a faculty adviser who can help them navigate an academic path forward. Some places also link freshmen with peer advisers or mentors who can offer their own insights on classes and the myriad ways to make the most of campus and student life.

Slippery Rock University in Pennsylvania has spent the past 20 years steadily improving its freshman retention rate from 68% to 82%. One recent innovation: During the 2017-2018 academic year, the school began matching new students with success coaches, who act "as a kind of ombudsperson" to help with time management and study skills or to connect undergrads with counseling, says Amanda Yale, associate provost for enrollment services. Coaches are alerted when someone has missed a significant number of classes. That way, they can do their best to make sure everybody makes it to sophomore year. ●

you're not eating well and drinking a lot and not sleeping well. And that's the kind of hole it can take a while to dig your way out of." During orientation in the fall of 2018, Williams for the first time offered a new wellness session that included workshops about self-compassion, managing tough emotions and daily self-care practices, including journaling. "Williams was tough on me during the first semester," says Shreyas Rajesh, a sophomore from New Delhi. Thanks to the orien-

Johns Hopkins gives new undergrads career prep right from the outset.

Counseling Center Directors, nearly 1 in 5 schools reported having counseling resources or centers similarly embedded around campus.

NO ONE METHOD. With mental health services, "it's rarely one-size-fits-all," says Barry A. Schreier, professor of counseling psychology and director of the University Counseling Service at the University of Iowa. Other common ap-

proaches include building peer support programs with undergrads and collaborating with campus chapters of national groups like Active Minds and the National Alliance on Mental Illness. At the University of Michigan, the Wolverine Support Network is a peer-to-peer effort led by trained undergrads who promote wellness and host regular events such as yoga, trivia nights and meditation.

At Pennsylvania State University, every class syllabus includes details about how to access mental health services. Faculty, staff, resident assistants and tour guides are made aware of resources on campus, says Ben Locke, senior director of Counseling and Psychological Services and executive director of the Center for Collegiate Mental Health at Penn State. –*Michael Morella*

A Focus on Student Success

SOME COLLEGES AND UNIVERSITIES are much more determined than others to provide undergrads with the best possible educational experience, recognizing that certain enriched offerings, from learning communities and internships to senior capstone projects, are linked to success. Here, U.S. News highlights schools with outstanding examples of eight programs that education experts, including staff members of the Association of American Colleges and Universities, agree are key. Excellence in such programs isn't directly measured in the Best Colleges overall rankings.

U.S. News surveyed college presidents, chief academic officers and deans of admissions in the spring of 2019, asking them to nominate up to 15 institutions with stellar examples of each program. The colleges ranked here received the most nominations for having especially strong programs.

(*Public)

First-Year Experience

Orientation can go only so far in making freshmen feel connected. Many schools now build into the curriculum first-year seminars or other academic programs that bring small groups of students together with faculty or staff on a regular basis.

1. Agnes Scott College (GA)
2. Elon University (NC)
3. University of South Carolina*
4. Berea College (KY)
5. Georgia State University*
6. Appalachian State University (NC)*
7. Amherst College (MA)
8. Baylor University (TX)
9. Abilene Christian University (TX)
9. Arizona State University-Tempe*
11. Alverno College (WI)
12. Brown University (RI)
13. Butler University (IN)
14. Adrian College (MI)
14. Belmont University (TN)
14. College of William and Mary (VA)*
14. University of Texas-Austin*
14. Yale University (CT)
19. Bard College (NY)
19. Bowdoin College (ME)
19. Princeton University (NJ)

Co-ops/Internships

Schools nominated in this category require or encourage students to apply what they're learning in the classroom to work in the real world through closely supervised internships or practicums, or through cooperative education, in which one period of study typically alternates with one of work.

1. Northeastern University (MA)
2. Drexel University (PA)
3. University of Cincinnati*
4. Elon University (NC)
5. Georgia Institute of Technology*
6. Berea College (KY)
7. Massachusetts Institute of Technology
8. Duke University (NC)
9. Endicott College (MA)
9. Stanford University (CA)
11. Northwestern University (IL)
11. Purdue University-West Lafayette (IN)*
13. Rochester Institute of Technology (NY)
14. Agnes Scott College (GA)
14. Clemson University (SC)*
16. George Washington University (DC)
17. Claremont McKenna College (CA)
18. Cornell University (NY)
19. Carnegie Mellon University (PA)
19. Worcester Polytechnic Institute (MA)

Learning Communities

In these communities, students typically take two or more linked courses as a group and get to know one another and their professors well. Some learning communities are also residential.

1. Elon University (NC)
2. Yale University (CT)
3. Agnes Scott College (GA)
3. Amherst College (MA)
5. Appalachian State University (NC)*
5. Georgia State University*
7. Belmont University (TN)
7. Evergreen State College (WA)*
7. Princeton University (NJ)
10. Michigan State University*
11. Abilene Christian University (TX)
11. University of Michigan-Ann Arbor*
13. Rice University (TX)
13. University of Maryland-College Park*
15. Clemson University (SC)*
16. Vanderbilt University (TN)
17. Dartmouth College (NH)
17. Davidson College (NC)
17. Duke University (NC)
20. Georgia Institute of Technology*
20. Iowa State University*
20. Middlebury College (VT)
20. Purdue University-West Lafayette (IN)*
20. Stanford University (CA)
20. University of Richmond (VA)
20. University of South Carolina*
20. University of Washington*
20. University of Wisconsin-Madison*

Senior Capstone

Whether they're called a senior capstone or go by some other name, these culminating experiences ask students nearing the end of their college years to create a project that integrates and synthesizes what they've learned. The project might be a thesis, a performance or an exhibit of artwork.

1. Princeton University (NJ)
2. College of Wooster (OH)
3. Yale University (CT)
4. Duke University (NC)
5. Elon University (NC)
6. Massachusetts Institute of Technology
7. Agnes Scott College (GA)
7. Stanford University (CA)
9. Brown University (RI)
10. Harvard University (MA)
11. Amherst College (MA)
12. Carleton College (MN)
12. Georgia Institute of Technology*
14. Bates College (ME)

Elon University

Undergraduate Research/ Creative Projects

Independently or in small teams, and mentored by a faculty member, students do intensive and self-directed research or creative work that results in an original scholarly paper or product that can be formally presented on or off campus.

1. Massachusetts Institute of Technology
2. Princeton University (NJ)
3. California Institute of Technology
4. Elon University (NC)
5. College of Wooster (OH)
6. Stanford University (CA)
7. University of Michigan-Ann Arbor*
8. Georgia Institute of Technology^
9. Davidson College (NC)
9. Duke University (NC)
9. Johns Hopkins University (MD)
12. Carnegie Mellon University (PA)
13. College of William and Mary (VA)*
14. Amherst College (MA)
14. Harvard University (MA)
16. University of Texas-Austin*
16. Yale University (CT)
18. Carleton College (MN)
18. Harvey Mudd College (CA)
20. Brown University (RI)

Writing in the Disciplines

These colleges typically make writing a priority at all levels of instruction and across the curriculum. Students are encouraged to produce and refine various forms of writing for a range of audiences in different disciplines.

1. Brown University (RI)
2. Duke University (NC)
3. Princeton University (NJ)
4. Cornell University (NY)
5. Harvard University (MA)
5. Yale University (CT)
7. Stanford University (CA)
8. Carleton College (MN)
8. Hamilton College (NY)
10. Columbia University (NY)
10. Elon University (NC)
10. Middlebury College (VT)
13. Massachusetts Institute of Technology
13. Williams College (MA)
15. Agnes Scott College (GA)
15. University of Iowa^
17. Amherst College (MA)
18. Bowdoin College (ME)
18. Oberlin College (OH)
18. Swarthmore College (PA)
18. Wellesley College (MA)

14. Northeastern University (MA)
14. University of Michigan-Ann Arbor*
14. Worcester Polytechnic Institute (MA)
18. Bard College (NY)
18. Butler University (IN)
20. Adrian College (MI)
20. Allegheny College (PA)
20. Carnegie Mellon University (PA)
20. College of William and Mary (VA)*
20. Dartmouth College (NH)
20. Davidson College (NC)
20. Rice University (TX)
20. Williams College (MA)

Service Learning

Required (or for-credit) volunteer work in the community is an instructional strategy in these programs. What's learned in the field bolsters what happens in class, and vice versa.

1. Berea College (KY)
2. Elon University (NC)
3. Tulane University (LA)
4. Abilene Christian University (TX)
5. Duke University (NC)
5. Seattle University
5. Stanford University (CA)
8. Boston College
9. Fairfield University (CT)
9. Michigan State University^
9. Portland State University (OR)*
9. University of Notre Dame (IN)
9. Warren Wilson College (NC)
14. Appalachian State University (NC)*
14. Creighton University (NE)

16. Brown University (RI)
16. College of the Ozarks (MO)
16. Vanderbilt University (TN)
19. Carleton College (MN)
19. Georgetown University (DC)
19. Loyola University Chicago
19. Northeastern University (MA)

Study Abroad

Programs at these schools involve substantial academic work abroad for credit – a year, a semester or an intensive experience equal to a course – and considerable interaction with the local culture.

1. Elon University (NC)
2. Arcadia University (PA)
3. Kalamazoo College (MI)
4. New York University
5. Goucher College (MD)
6. Middlebury College (VT)
7. American University (DC)
7. Dickinson College (PA)
9. Michigan State University*
10. Agnes Scott College (GA)
11. Pepperdine University (CA)
11. Syracuse University (NY)
13. University of Evansville (IN)
14. Carleton College (MN)
14. St. Olaf College (MN)
16. Dartmouth College (NH)
16. Duke University (NC)
16. Northeastern University (MA)
19. Butler University (IN)
19. Georgetown University (DC)

A Winning
Double
Play

Schools are finding new ways to blend liberal arts
training with skills in tech and entrepreneurship

by **Arlene Weintraub**

CHARLIE YOUNG has been fascinated with both astronomy and computers for as long as he can remember, so when he started applying to colleges, he jumped at the chance to combine the two topics in a blended arts and sciences program at the University of Illinois–Urbana-Champaign. The Naperville, Illinois, native applied and was accepted to the school in 2016, joining its CS+X program, which allows students in various disciplines to earn a single degree that incorporates classes in computer science into their chosen major.

Young, who will graduate in May 2020, plans to use the "CS" portion of his undergraduate training to pursue a career in baseball analytics. While at the U of I, he has secured internships doing everything from web development to data mining for the Houston Astros, Baltimore Orioles and Cincinnati Reds. When school is in session, Young works with the university's Division I baseball team developing a system that uses game outcomes to generate individualized player development plans and reports on competitor teams.

Young believes the liberal arts component has been invaluable to rounding out his skill set. It "helps me stand out, and it makes me a better communicator," he says. Plus, his knowledge of astronomy has proven to be a fantastic icebreaker when he interviews for internships. "The first question is always, 'Oh, tell me more about astronomy,'" he says.

Like a number of colleges across the country, the University of Illinois is ramping up its efforts to equip students with the ideal combination of strong technology acumen and solid creative and interpersonal skills – a combo that many employers say they want in their new hires. To that end, colleges are offering a growing number of cross-disciplinary degrees, such as the CS+X approach, as well as hands-on learning opportunities in sought-after and emerging fields like artificial intelligence and data analytics. And many campuses have also opened innovation and entrepreneurship centers, where students and faculty across many different fields can work together to transform ideas for new technology into full-fledged companies.

Training students to embrace technology is essential for preparing them to enter a rapidly changing workforce, says Phil Bourne, director of the Data Science Institute at the University of Virginia and acting dean of its new School of Data Science. "It doesn't matter what field you're in – energy, retail, health care, you name it – there's a growing need for people with basic skills in using data to make decisions within

organizations," Bourne says. Indeed, people working in the STEM fields of science, technology, engineering and math earn 29% more on average than those in other areas, and STEM job growth jumped to 24% in 2017, compared to just 4% for other occupations, according to a recent report from the nonprofit Strada Institute for the Future of Work.

Dual degrees in computer and data science differ from institution to institution. UVA plans to start by offering students in any of its 70-plus majors the opportunity to earn an undergraduate certificate in data science, which will consist of 12 credits in "core competencies" like statistics and machine learning, Bourne says. The University of Illinois has about a dozen CS+X options, including advertising, crop sciences and linguistics. Each consists of approximately eight classes in computer science and eight in the other discipline. Other schools with CS+X programs include Cornell, Occidental College in Los Angeles and the University of Alabama–Birmingham.

A holistic approach to tech training

Some schools are taking a less structured approach to integrating technology with liberal arts programs, choosing to incorporate tech-focused ma-

Charlie Young does analytics work with the University of Illinois Division I baseball team.

terial directly into their curricula. Northwestern University in Illinois, for example, offers several classes in which undergrads learn how to use the visual arts to present information captured by data analytics. In one class called "Data as Art," art majors worked with computer science students to produce a video showing how the buildup of plastic waste is accelerating over time.

In another class, students learned how to write software that could automatically generate a comedy script from a single prompt, tapping into new AI capabilities. They then beamed the script to student actors via Google Glass – the hands free smart specs – so they could read and perform it in real time. "The drive towards incorporating machine learning is everywhere," says Kristian Hammond, a professor of computer science at Northwestern. "We're crafting new kinds of classes, so undergraduates can be brought into that experience." Other interdisciplinary majors at Northwestern include Mathematical Methods in the Social Sciences and Science in Human Culture, which combines science training with subjects like philosophy and sociology.

Trial and error led Stanford University to its own approach. The school discontinued a pilot CS+X degree program this year after students complained the requirements were so burdensome that they were unable to pursue other opportunities, such as study abroad. Now Stanford offers several alternative options for humanities and technology training, such as its Individually Designed Major in Engineering program, where students work with two or more faculty advisers – one from the engineering school and one from another department – to come up with their own tailored curriculum.

Another way that colleges are fostering connections between techies and humanities-focused students is by building innovation and entrepreneurship programs, both for credit and as extracurricular opportunities. At schools like the University of Michigan, Washington University in St. Louis and Babson College in Massachusetts, students work in cross-disciplinary teams, guided by faculty members, to turn ideas for new mobile apps, software and other technology into products. In the process, they may very well end up creating their own jobs.

That's what happened for Brice Maurice, who graduated with a degree in electrical engineering from Georgia Institute of Technology in May. He gravitated to CREATE-X, an entrepreneurship initiative on campus. He had an idea to create an app that could direct drivers to open spaces in parking lots using data gathered in real time from cameras installed in the lots. Over the course of two semesters, CREATE-X gave Maurice and two other students $1,000 and three credit hours per semester to develop a prototype. In the spring, Maurice was accepted into CREATE-X's Startup Launch program, which awarded him a $4,000 grant plus $30,000 worth of accounting and legal services to get the company off the ground after graduation. During school, Maurice worked with CREATE-X faculty and mentors, many of whom had startup experience, to develop skills he couldn't pick up in his engineering classes. "CREATE-X helped me formalize the business side – how I would identify and talk to customers, and how I would make money," he says.

Even for those who don't launch their own companies, CREATE-X can pay off, says founding director Raghupathy Sivakumar, chair and professor in the School of Electrical and Computer Engineering at Georgia Tech. "Entrepreneurial confidence is a life skill that every student needs," Sivakumar says.

Students can launch their own startups at campus innovation centers.

"We hear from the big companies like Microsoft, Google and Facebook that they're too set in their ways, and they need entrepreneurial-minded students to act as change agents."

Catering to the maker generation

At some campuses, entrepreneurship centers are proving to be powerful magnets for students who consider themselves "makers." That's what drew recent Case Western Reserve University grad Prince Ghosh to Sears think[box], a seven-story, 50,000-square-foot innovation and entrepreneurship center on the school's Cleveland campus that includes 3D printers and other cutting-edge equipment and a business incubator for startups. Ghosh, who graduated in May with a degree in mechanical and aerospace engineering, wandered into Sears think[box] his freshman year and ended up spending much of his free time there. He came up with an idea for a business, Boundary Labs, which would make sensors and software to help factory managers streamline equipment maintenance tasks. Sears think[box] gave him $2,000 in grant funding for basic supplies, plus office space and an introduction to a student at the nearby Cleveland Institute of Art, whom Ghosh hired to design Boundary Labs' sensors.

"Think[box] is a great place to be. There's a talent pipeline of people with the skill sets we need," says Ghosh, who attracted his first customers before he even got his degree.

Malcolm Cooke, associate professor of mechanical and aerospace engineering and executive director of Sears think[box], says about 40% of the people (students, faculty and community members) who use the facility have a humanities, arts or health science background and are curious about what technology can do for them. "They need a resource where they can go and explore that," Cooke says. In fact, 64% of students surveyed recently said think[box] was the reason they chose Case Western Reserve.

Colgate University, a liberal arts college in central New York, also draws nonscience majors to its venture and entrepreneurship incubator, Thought Into Action. That's where 2019 grad Matthew Glick, who majored in peace and conflict studies, spent one Saturday a month trying to develop a sports highlights app he had conceived of in high school. After consulting with mentors and some Colgate alums, Glick pivoted and developed a new app called Gipper, a platform to help schools easily develop engaging content for social media. Computer science students helped build the technology, and Glick's team was accepted into TIA's summer incubator, which provided $13,000 in startup money and office space for six weeks.

Now, Glick has made his startup a full-time job. "When you study liberal arts, you learn a lot about problem-solving, but at TIA, I learned the importance of really listening to customers and finding the right product to fit the market," he says. "Nothing prepared me better for running a business than that." ●

Virginia Tech students claim their role in growing the diversity of ideas, people, and cultures.

WE ALL HAVE A ROLE. CLAIM YOURS...VT.EDU

VIRGINIA TECH™

4 Key Questions to Ask About Safety

Find out how colleges are keeping students well and free from harm on campus

by **Katherine Hobson**

THE SEARCH FOR A COLLEGE will take into account an array of factors, including academics, school size, extracurriculars and campus culture. But as you zero in on your choices, you should also gather info on issues of student safety and wellness and how a university deals with crime, sexual misconduct and assault, substance abuse and mental health. Here are some things to look out for:

1 How does the school support students' mental and emotional health?

According to the American College Health Association's 2018 National College Health Assessment II, nearly two-thirds of students had felt "overwhelming anxiety" at least once in the previous 12 months. About 42% reported feeling "so depressed that it was difficult to function." Young adulthood has always been stressful, but the current generation may feel distinct pressures – including insecurity about getting a job after graduation, a fixation on social media, and 24/7 exposure to a news cycle that often includes tragedies – that are particularly anxiety-provoking, says

Nance Roy, chief clinical officer of The Jed Foundation, a nonprofit that works to improve emotional health and prevent suicide in teens and young adults. Helicopter parenting may also play a role, because it prevents kids from developing life skills they need to operate autonomously. In addition, more students in need of help are likely coming forward, because the stigma of doing so seems to have declined. The bottom line: "Colleges are really struggling to keep up with demand," says Roy.

It's wise to find out how the schools you are considering meet that demand. Many institutions have some kind of triage system through which "they are prioritizing rapid-access care," like an emergency room does, says Ben Locke, executive director of Pennsylvania State University's Center for Collegiate Mental Health. Not everyone in need of help will seek it out, so many schools are being proactive. At the University of Houston, which enrolls about 37,000 undergrads, almost 500 faculty, staff

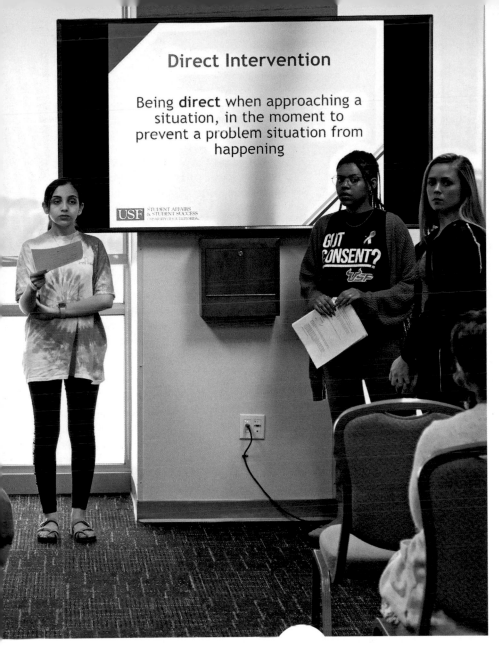

Direct Intervention

Being **direct** when approaching a situation, in the moment to prevent a problem situation from happening

USF STUDENT AFFAIRS & STUDENT SUCCESS
UNIVERSITY OF SOUTH FLORIDA

struggled or is currently in treatment, says Locke. Don't assume that all the necessary services will be available; evaluate possibilities at the school and in the surrounding community, as well as whether fees are involved and how insurance coverage will work.

2 What steps does a campus take to keep students safe?

A good place to look for answers is a college's annual security report, which must be published every year by Oct. 1 by all schools receiving federal funding, as required by the federal Clery Act. You can typically find it on a school's website, and the document can answer many of the questions that students and parents have, including how schools communicate in an emergency and what kind of security resources they employ (some campuses have their own law enforcement officers) and more.

"It's the Cliffs Notes of a campus' safety and community policies," says Abigail Boyer, associate executive director of the Clery Center, a nonprofit focused on promoting campus safety. The report also includes the latest crime statistics, but it's important not to misinterpret those, says Boyer. An increase in reported crime doesn't

and students have been trained in mental health first aid. Once prepared, they know how to look out for signs of depression and anxiety – for example, a hall mate hasn't come to meals in a while – and talk to a student in need about available campus resources, says Patrick Lukingbeal, director of wellness at the school.

For those who are experiencing some stress or problems but don't need intensive or extensive therapy, schools are providing other options. At Penn State, senior counselors are available five days a week for two-hour drop-in periods at a number of locations across campus, including various dining halls and the library. At Wake Forest University in North Carolina, students who need help with issues including time management and getting enough sleep can meet with certified wellbeing coaches.

Asking schools about mental health support is especially important if a student has previously

University of South Florida students take part in bystander intervention training.

necessarily mean a campus is getting less safe; often when schools dedicate more effort toward prevention and response, more people will report problems, she says. So take the stats in context.

The Clery Act stats cover property owned or controlled by the university and recognized student organizations, but only public property that's within or immediately adjacent to campus. So it's also worth checking out what's going on in the broader community and how the school mitigates it. Johns Hopkins University in Baltimore offers community walks early in each academic year to help familiarize students with the surrounding neighborhoods and to discuss safety tips. For off-campus students, university security will do a free home inspection that includes checking locks, lighting levels and smoke detectors.

The good news is that the most recent federal stats show that crime on U.S. campuses generally declined from 2001 to 2015. But campus active shooting incidents, though still relatively rare, have risen nationwide, says Greg Klaiber, director of emergency management at Northwestern University in Illinois. Last year, the school released a new "Run, Hide, Fight" video to show what to do in case of an active shooter. And its emergency notification system, which encompasses text messages, landline phones, Twitter, and digital monitors in 250 campus facilities, can be up and running within one or two minutes of a reported incident.

Ask schools how – and how quickly – students will be notified in the case of an emergency, and whether parents can opt in to also receive alerts. Prevention is also key here, as the final report of the U.S. government's Federal Commission on School Safety, published in December, points out.

3 Is there a comprehensive approach to sexual assault?

In recent years, sexual violence has probably become the most discussed campus crime issue, due to the #MeToo movement and an increase in reporting by victims, as well as federal policy changes. (Under the Obama administration, the Department of Education sought to allow more claims by expanding protections; under the Trump administration, the policy will likely tilt more toward the rights of the accused.) Students and parents should ask how incidents of sexual assault are reported and adjudicated, says B. Ever Hanna, policy manager at the nonprofit End Rape on Campus, who also advises looking for a specific policy forbidding retaliation against survivors and a dedicated rape crisis center or similar space.

On the prevention side, students and parents should look for comprehensive efforts that preferably include in-person programs and an affirmative consent policy, says Hanna. (Familiarize yourself with the specifics of the school's policy; on campuses in California, consent can be verbal or nonverbal but must be affirmative, conscious and voluntary.) Many schools also offer bystander intervention training. At the University of South Florida, for example, students and staffers who go through training

"Heavy drinking is not actually the norm."

learn to employ the three D's if they see someone in a potentially unsafe situation, such as a student at a party leading another up a flight of stairs, explains Dani Smith, violence prevention specialist at the school's Center for Victim Advocacy and Violence Prevention. They can direct (approach the person and ask if he or she is OK), distract (ask the person to come to the bathroom) or delegate (ask a friend of the person to interrupt).

Bystander programs include those that are offered by Green Dot (licensed by the nonprofit Alteristic) and Bringing in the Bystander, which originated at the University of New Hampshire and is now used at more than 500 other schools.

Schools are also looking at new tools to help prevent sexual assault. The uSafeUS app (free for students and campus community users), developed by UNH's Prevention Innovations Research Center, is being rolled out at 22 schools statewide. It includes college-specific resources and safety aids, such as the recipe for an "Angel Drink" to show to a waitress or bartender, that is actually a disguised message for help. "Online dating is a big thing, and you don't always know who the person is. This gives you a perfect excuse to get out of an uncomfortable situation," says Kelsey Higgins, a May graduate of UNH who was a campus ambassador for the app.

4 What steps are being taken to limit alcohol and substance abuse?

Schools should have multipronged education and prevention programs, evidence-based intervention services for those who need help, and recovery services for those committed to sobriety, says Peter Rives, assistant director of wellbeing, alcohol and substance abuse prevention at Wake Forest, where students start getting online prevention education before they arrive on campus. Within the first two months of school, students who have never before experimented with alcohol are more likely to do so, and casual and heavier drinkers are likely to ramp it up, he says. One key element: making clear that heavy drinking is not actually the norm and that plenty of students don't drink at all. According to the NCHA, while almost 62% of students report having used alcohol at least once in the last 30 days, respondents incorrectly perceived that 93% of their peers had. Some schools, including the University of Denver and Texas Tech University, have recovery programs offering support and encouragement – as well as events like sober tailgates before sporting events.

Many college students drink to try to fit in as they enter a new environment, which is why Wake Forest and other schools put resources into getting people engaged in ways that don't involve alcohol. At San Diego State University, the Aztec Nights program presents large-scale social events early in the semester, including DJs, movies, comedy and dance marathons. The events "provide the sense that there's something to do," says James Lange, the coordinator of alcohol and other drug initiatives at SDSU and the executive director of the Higher Education Center for Alcohol and Drug Misuse Prevention and Recovery at Ohio State University.

Marijuana is the most commonly used drug on campus after alcohol, and changes to state laws permitting recreational or medicinal use may confuse students and parents. Regardless of state laws, college campuses are subject to the federal law that makes marijuana illegal. Schools "need to make clear what the policies are and make sure they're enforced," says Jason Kilmer, associate professor of psychiatry & behavioral services and assistant director of health & wellness for alcohol and other drug education at the University of Washington in Seattle. As with alcohol, prevention programming should emphasize that not everyone uses.

Research shows that parents who have a permissive stance toward drinking and drugs are more likely to have a student who uses or uses heavily, says Kilmer. So before heading off to school, parents should explicitly discuss their expectations for their students' behavior. ●

STUDY THE SCHOOLS

Campuses Go Green

Colleges are embracing sustainability in
their classrooms and communities

by **Alison Murtagh**

FOR HER SENIOR ART THESIS at Elon University in North Carolina, Charlotte Murphy made a local farm both the subject of and the source material for her work. The 2019 grad from Essex, Vermont, used red clay soil gathered from a nearby farm to depict maps of the land and the food produced on it. "As an art major, people might think I don't have any connection to sustainability," says Murphy, who created her art "to show the connection the soil makes between farm and fork."

What's more, Murphy has been able to combine her passions for art and the environment by taking interdisciplinary classes and serving as a resident assistant

for Elon's Sustainable Living Learning Community. She and seven other undergrads lived together in a dorm and participated in a range of environmentally focused activities throughout the year, such as hosting lunch discussions with professors and administrators about how to improve sustainability on campus, doing group hikes and making visits to local businesses to see examples of environmental efforts in action. The goal, says Kelly Harer, Elon's assistant director of sustainability for education and outreach, is "to really get the students out to see what sustainability is like in a healthy, thriving community."

Like Elon, many colleges across the country are working to become "greener" and to impart lessons to students about how to care for the natural world around them. Some

Solar panels used for renewable energy research at Arizona State University's Polytechnic campus

are aiming to become "carbon neutral" – meaning any emissions from one activity at the school are offset by removing or producing less carbon elsewhere. In 2006, presidents from 12 schools, including the University of Florida, Ball State University in Indiana and Oberlin College in Ohio, became the first signatories of the American College and University Presidents' Climate Commitment, which sets a goal of reducing greenhouse gas emissions on their campuses. Since then, more than 800 institutions have signed on.

Other institutions are planting sustainable gardens on campus to grow food for their dining halls and local communities. At the same time, many schools have expanded their academic programs to include a more diverse range of classes and full-fledged majors or concentrations in environmental studies, sustainability and other related fields. Often, as part of a class, schools embed students in positions on campus or in the community where they can participate in real-life environmental projects and case studies.

EASING EMISSIONS. Increasingly, as universities are seeing more student demand for such programs, they are acknowledging that "this is part of their obligation as the entity that is preparing students for success in the future," says Julian Dautremont, director of programs for the Association for the Advancement of Sustainability in Higher Education, a nonprofit that promotes social and environmental responsibility at colleges and counts more than 700 campus members.

In addition to curbing carbon emissions, some schools have seen environmental interest and activism translate into initiatives to ban plastic water bottles and build or refurbish campus buildings so that they are LEED certified. (LEED stands for Leadership in Energy and Environmental Design, meaning facilities have met certain energy-efficiency requirements.)

The range of approaches means that many undergrads are gaining experience in both the technical aspects of environmental initiatives and the communication and advocacy that are often a part of driving change. "Students were very involved in writing our first climate action plan" a decade ago, says Keisha Payson, associate director of sustainability at Bowdoin College in Maine, which signed the pledge in 2007. Bowdoin officially became carbon neutral in April of last year, two years ahead of its goal. The college's sustainability implementation committee included several undergrads, and many students helped meet the goal by working to increase outreach and engagement across campus, Payson says. "As a college, we saw that we believed strongly in committing to the common good, and addressing climate change is certainly an issue for the common good," she says. "This is us doing our part of a very large effort."

Elsewhere, the University of Colorado–Boulder introduced a carbon neutrality plan of its own in 2009, with a goal of 20% reduction of greenhouse gas emissions by 2020 and 50% reduction by 2030. The program was put in place after the student government declared its own initiative to move toward carbon neutrality and engage the university's 33,000-plus students, according to Dave Newport, director of the university's environmental center.

At some colleges and universities, students have the option of getting their hands dirty by working at a sustainable garden or farm on or near campus. Dickinson College in Pennsylvania has an 80-acre farm about 6 miles away that supplies food to the school's five eateries and is certified organic by the U.S. Department of Agriculture, meaning it meets a variety of standards such as protecting natural

a small methane digester to convert food waste into fuel used for the farm and to help power stoves for food preparation at two private residences on the land.

HANDS-ON LEARNING. On the academic front, many universities have significantly expanded their environmental programs for undergraduates. Elon, UC–Boulder, Dickinson and Bowdoin all offer bachelor's programs in environmental studies, as do the University of Montana, the University of California–Santa Barbara and Goucher College in Baltimore. Arizona State University's School of Sustainability offers a wide range of undergraduate and graduate programs related to the environment, the economy and society. Students can take courses in "Urban and Environmental Health" and "Sustainable Food and Farms," for example. There are approximately 680 students in ASU's sustainability degree programs at the campuses in Tempe and Mesa and online, says Lisa Murphy, director of academic services for the School of Sustainability.

The school offers a number of community-based and hands-on learning opportunities, and internships are required of all undergrads. After graduation, students have pursued careers as sustainability coordinators or analysts in the private sector or working for a city government or utility agency that oversees waste, energy or sustainability.

Susie Puga, a senior at ASU from Wellton, Arizona, applied her knowledge to help plan a national college residential hall conference hosted at the university in 2018. As the sustainability chair for the conference, she worked to educate more than 2,000 people about how to be environmentally friendly in their own college housing, such as by reducing water and electricity use. "That was an incredible learning experience for me," Puga says.

As at Elon, ASU students can live among like-minded peers in the School of Sustainability Residential Community or join a related student organization, through which they also do field trips together and work on projects around campus – such as zero-waste initiatives at athletic events – and in the local area. Other schools with ecologically minded learning communities include Purdue University in Indiana and Loyola University Chicago.

Brazil native Tatsatom Gonçalves graduated in May from Middlebury College in Vermont, which established its environmental studies program in 1965. On campus, he was treasurer for the Campus Sustainability Coordinators group and a teaching assistant in the geography department. Gonçalves is pursuing a fellowship focused on energy efficiency in cities with the World Resources Institute in Washington, D.C., and he says his college experiences have been "extremely helpful to navigating the job-hunting process." ●

resources and preserving biodiversity. Students can work and volunteer at the farm or tap it as a resource in connection with one of their academic courses. "We're constantly creating opportunities for students to engage in research or engage in technical-skills building that are going to inform their academics but most importantly their professional pathways," says Jenn Halpin, the farm's director.

For instance, environmental classes structure lab sessions around activities at the farm, while some religion courses have visited it to discuss Buddhism and meat consumption. Ceramic classes have used the space for pit firing (a method to finish ceramic pieces by burying them in a pit with wood and lighting it on fire), and other art classes visit to do photography. The farm has its own compost area, as well as

ASU students take part in a gardening class offered through the School of Sustainability.

A Jump on Job Prep

Colleges are doing more to give undergrads a leg up on career planning

by **Mariya Greeley**

YOU'RE STILL CHOOSING a college. Yet if you're like your peers, you're also focused on eventually getting a good job. In 2015, just over 85% of college freshmen reported that getting a better job was a "very important" factor in their decision to go to college, compared to about 72% a decade earlier, according to a report by researchers at UCLA. Especially in the decade since the Great Recession, as the job market struggled back on track and college costs continued to climb, students and families have been "really concerned about what their investment is going towards," observes Mindy Deardurff, dean of the Career Development Center at Macalester College in St. Paul, Minnesota.

As prospective students and parents increasingly assess schools for how well they help undergrads gear up for the job market, colleges are responding. Many are revamping career services programs and curricula, offering help (and money) for internships or hands-on projects, and integrating job prep even in the first year. At the University of Chicago, students can participate in eight programs run by the Office of Career Advancement in the health professions, law or entrepreneurship, among others. By blending both a traditional liberal arts approach and a career-oriented push, "students get the best of both worlds," says Meredith Daw, associate vice president of enrollment and student advancement as well as executive director of career advancement at UChicago. Today, almost 90% of the university's roughly 6,200 undergrads participate in one of these UChicago "Careers In" programs.

Alexa Hanelin, a 2017 political science grad now working as a sales and trading associate at Citigroup in New York, took part in the program with a specialization in markets. She took three courses at the university's Booth School of Business, worked with a specialized adviser, attended weekly talks with industry professionals and enrolled in bootcamps to learn skills in Microsoft Excel and financial accounting. Thanks to these experiences, "I came in and I hit the ground running," she says.

Except for certain fields like engineering, computer science and accounting, employers are becoming "more major-agnostic," says Matthew Brink, assistant executive director for programs and services at the National Association of Colleges and Employers. Instead, they put a premium on competencies and skills, including a balance of technical abilities and strengths in areas like critical thinking, problem-solving, collaboration and communication.

"We take into account a student's educational background or their work or internship experience, but we truly assess on our leadership principles," which include "customer obsession" and an insistence on high standards, says Jamie Kezner, senior manager of student programs at Amazon, which made some 10,000 new hires from colleges and grad schools worldwide in 2018.

To that end, some schools are doing more to stress skills training. For example, at the Center for Career and Professional Development at Clemson University in South Carolina, the focus is on nine core competencies, such as adaptability and analytical abilities, plus revamped career coaching and academic programming that aligns with them. When undergrads do internships, for example, they simultaneously enroll in a course to help them better understand their experiences, the skills they acquire and how to best articulate them effectively to future employers. "All of the homework assignments are really focused on and mapped back to these competencies," says Neil Burton, executive director of the career center.

ENLIVENING THE LIBERAL ARTS. After having long stressed critical thinking and communication skills, liberal arts colleges are answering those who question the value of their degrees with more career-oriented offerings, such as résumé-writing and interviewing workshops and a bigger emphasis on internships and hands-on work.

A recent NACE survey found that internship experience is as

says. And the diversity of experiences paid off in future interviews. He recently began his career as a cloud technical resident at Google in Austin, Texas.

Students at Connecticut College are introduced to their career adviser during a required first-year seminar, the first step along a four-year roadmap preparing them for the working world. To supplement their major, sophomores can opt to join one of 15 pathways organized around a broad theme, such as social justice and sustainability or global capitalism. Once they've developed a narrower focus in the subject, they are required to take courses across the curriculum, complete an off-campus experience and give a senior-year presentation that ties back to their subject of inquiry.

Taking on-campus leadership positions and connecting with alumni are other strategies in students' toolbox. As one of only about 2,100 undergrads at Macalester, Meera Singh got deeply involved with the college's business consulting group and Women in Economics club, and she became president of both by senior year. "I was really able to take charge," says Singh, who graduated in May with an econ major and a job lined up as a business analyst at McKinsey in her hometown of Minneapolis. She also sought out a range of Macalester alumni who offered helpful insights.

CONSIDERING A CO-OP. Some schools offer co-op programs, in which students alternate between semesters in the classroom and semesters working full time in their field. Maddie Coppola, a fourth-year interior design major at the University of Cincinnati, plans to participate in five co-op experiences, including one at a design firm in Zagreb, Croatia. "That's five opportunities to live in a new city and have a real working job where you're making more than minimum wage," she says. Northeastern University in Boston, Drexel University in Philadelphia and Purdue in Indiana are among those that also offer co-ops.

UC also peppers its curricula with career experience in other ways. Students from across academic departments work together in UC Forward classes to help solve a local business's real-world challenges. In one recent class, undergrads teamed up with the Cincinnati Zoo to help create toys that would keep the animals stimulated in their enclosures. Other schools, like Knox College in Illinois and Bennington College in Vermont, offer immersive programs where students are given time, support and mentorship to start a business, say, or to live at and run a fully sustainable community.

Macalester College grad Meera Singh secured a job as a business analyst in Minneapolis.

influential a part of a job application as the school a candidate went to or even his or her GPA. For this reason, an increasing number of liberal arts schools, including Connecticut College, Claremont McKenna College in California and Mount Holyoke College in Massachusetts, have put programs in place to offer financial support to student interns.

Khanh Nghiem, a recent computer science grad from Connecticut College, used the stipend each student receives from the school (up to $3,000) to spend the summer before his senior year doing three different jobs: He developed software to optimize college exam schedules with one of his professors, worked as a product manager at an education technology startup, and served as a lab assistant at a nonprofit research institute affiliated with Yale University. Thanks to the funding, "I could take on part-time jobs and lower-paying opportunities," he

Despite an increased focus on career prep, about 4 in 10 students reported never having visited their career services offices, according to a 2017 Strada-Gallup survey. To change that, many places are making touch points with career centers happen sooner and more frequently. Colgate University in New York spent some $16.4 million to build Benton Hall, which houses a high-tech Center for Career Services that is literally more central to undergrads on the school's main academic quad. First-year students at Johns Hopkins University in Baltimore start exploring "life design" with a career coach and a small cohort during summer orientation.

When Hanelin decided in her junior year that she wanted to go into finance, she worked closely with her adviser at UChicago to get her foot in the door. Today, she says, "I'm exactly where I'm supposed to be." ●

Take a

Bucknell University
PHOTOGRAPHY BY BRETT ZIEGLER FOR USN&WR

Road Trip

PENNSYLVANIA

by **Lindsay Cates**

There are more than 100 four-year colleges and universities in Pennsylvania, so prospective students have no shortage of options. U.S. News zeroed in on a handful: Bucknell, a liberal arts college in Lewisburg; Penn State's main campus near the center of the state; and the University of Pittsburgh and Carnegie Mellon, two schools in the Steel City. Follow along to find out more.

Penn State
University Park

University of Pittsburgh
Pittsburgh

Carnegie Mellon University
Pittsburgh

Bucknell University
Lewisburg

Bucknell University

LEWISBURG

IN HIGH SCHOOL, Tobias Cozzolino of Tewksbury, New Jersey, attended a presentation by Bucknell's student-managed investment fund class in New York City. Hearing undergrads talk about managing a $1.7 million fund gave him a firsthand look at how the liberal arts college blends real-world learning into its curriculum. By his junior year at Bucknell, Cozzolino was a presenter himself as a part of the class and on his way to earning a degree in accounting and financial management. "You not only get the book smarts, but you can put it into practice," says the 2019 grad.

With 3,600 undergraduates, Bucknell "is a small big school," says President John Bravman. The 450-acre campus in central Pennsylvania's Susquehanna River Valley is relatively compact, but students have loads of opportunities. For instance, by graduation, more than half of seniors have worked on research and 87% have completed an internship, student teaching placement or other option for hands-on experience. By nine months after graduation, 96% of the class of 2018 reported they were employed, volunteering or in grad school (or preparing for it).

Dabreon Darby, a 2019 geology and environmental studies and sciences grad from Buffalo, New York, worked with peers from several different disciplines to help a health care communications and marketing firm with research designed to improve specialty care for oncology patients. He welcomed "the opportunity to be involved in different things," he says, and he now works at the National Environmental Education Foundation in Washington, D.C.

Bucknell offers more than 60 majors across its three colleges – arts and sciences, management, and engineering. Arts and sciences students all take a team-taught Integrated Perspectives course, in which they might examine a topic like drug use and consequences or data science through an interdisciplinary lens.

UNDERGRADUATES
Full-time: **3,581**

TOTAL COST*
$72,370

U.S. NEWS RANKING
National Liberal Arts: **#35**

*Tuition, fees and room & board for 2019-20

About 15% of undergrads choose a major in the Freeman College of Management, which offers programs like business analytics and markets, innovation and design.

In the engineering school, students can choose from biomedical, civil, computer and environmental engineering, among others. Megan Grossman, a recent chemical engineering grad from Mechanicsburg, Pennsylvania, enjoyed the liberal arts approach to engineering and "being able as a STEM major to branch out" by filling her schedule with economics and Spanish classes and minoring in both.

BUILDING COMMUNITY. All freshmen take a foundation seminar with about 16 students in a topic that interests them, such as "Global Dress and Fashion Systems" or "Data, Power and Inequality." Several seminar topics correspond to a themed residential college – Environmental College, for instance, or Society and Technology College – and freshmen there live alongside their classmates. "It's a good way to meet people right off the bat," says Julia Shapiro, a 2019 English grad from Holmdel, New Jersey, who lived in the Languages and Cultures College and took "Place, Identity, and Culture."

More than 90% of undergrads live on campus, and Bucknell has a 9:1 student-faculty ratio. "That number comes to life here," says Cozzolino, who appreciated having a lot of one-on-one interaction with his professors in class and in the community.

More than half of sophomores

A campus green at Bucknell, which boasts a 9:1 student-faculty ratio

through seniors join a fraternity or sorority. Greek life has a big presence, undergrads say, but there are not major boundaries between those who join and those who don't. There are also more than 150 other campus organizations. "I was able to put my hands in a lot of different pots," says Alexander M. Jordan, a 2019 political science and sociology grad from Doylestown, Pennsylvania, who worked at the campus radio station and in the athletics and recreation office.

Historic downtown Lewisburg, home to about 5,800 people and a mix of shops, cafes, an art gallery and an art deco movie house, is about a 10-minute walk from campus. The surrounding area brings ample opportunity for hiking, caving, stargazing and kayaking. ●

Penn State

UNIVERSITY PARK

PENNSYLVANIA STATE University is one of the biggest institutions in the country, with some 39,300 undergraduates on a 7,900-acre campus.

It can be overwhelming at first, but there seems to be a widely shared "desire to get to know everyone around you," says Greg Gavazzi, a senior chemical engineering major from Mechanicsburg, Pennsylvania. "While it's a big school, it definitely gives you many opportunities for those smaller, more personal connections."

For instance, everyone starts by choosing a first-year seminar. These classes are capped at 20 undergrads to help ease the transition to college and balance any large intro lectures. The seminars can "open doors" to all Penn State has to offer, says Shannon McClain, a 2019 grad from Warren, Ohio. She chose a seminar related to her advertising and public relations major and built a strong relationship with her professor, often visiting him during office hours and seeking out advice on internships and the industry. Overall, 85% of first-year classes enroll 50 or fewer students, but larger lecture classes can be common early on. Those typically get broken down into smaller recitation periods of about 35, led by a teaching assistant.

There are a number of other resources to help people get acquainted, such as the Student Engagement Network, through which undergrads can get connected with internships, research, study

UNDERGRADUATES
Full-time: 39,321

TOTAL COST*
In-State: $30,334
Out-of-State: $47,398

U.S. NEWS RANKING
National Universities: #57

*Tuition, fees and room & board for 2019-20

While more than half of undergrads come from Pennsylvania, the student body draws from all 50 states and 130 countries. School spirit is a common bond for many. "I love the sense of pride," says Chloe Sokol, a junior political science major from Overland Park, Kansas, who grew up in "a Penn State family," as she puts it. Beaver Stadium brings together more than 107,000 football fans on fall Saturdays to cheer on the Nittany Lions, one of 31 varsity sports teams that compete in the Big Ten Conference.

OPTIONS OVERLAP. In addition to club and intramural sports teams, arts groups and multicultural organizations, about 1 in 6 students joins one of Penn State's 70 fraternities and sororities. Despite all there is to do, "it's amazing how quickly things overlap," says McClain, who was a tour guide and an active member of THON, a 46-hour "no sleeping, no sitting" dance marathon and yearlong fundraising effort benefiting families affected by childhood cancer at Penn State Children's Hospital. Some 16,500 student volunteers participate each year.

Undergrads can choose from more than 275 majors across about a dozen colleges. The university also makes available a range of academic advising resources, career fairs, study abroad programs and the Lion LaunchPad for budding entrepreneurs.

Penn State's campus features a blend of modern and historic buildings, as well as popular sights like the iconic bell tower clock at Old Main (one of the earliest structures) and an oft-photographed Nittany Lion Shrine sculpture. A few steps away is State College, a busy college town full of restaurants, coffee shops and bars. Because of its location at the base of Mount Nittany, the State College area is also known as "Happy Valley" and is in close proximity to hiking and skiing destinations. Penn State has 19 other campuses across Pennsylvania. ●

abroad, clubs or community leadership positions. The Student Minority Advisory and Recruitment Team focuses on bringing more underrepresented individuals to campus and helping undergrads of color build a sense of belonging. (About a third of students are from overseas or represent a race or ethnicity other than white.)

Atlanta native James Dowdy, an economics major who will graduate in December, joined SMART in his first year, and he says that the diverse peers he met through the group and in his residence hall helped give Penn State the "family feel" he needed attending a school far from home. Students say that joining one of the 1,000 or so clubs and organizations can quickly make the place feel smaller.

Carnegie Mellon University

PITTSBURGH

IN 1900, PITTSBURGH steel giant and philanthropist Andrew Carnegie donated money to start the Carnegie Institute of Technology. In 1967, Carnegie Tech merged with the Mellon Institute of Industrial Research (founded by industrial technology investor Andrew W. Mellon) to create Carnegie Mellon University. Today, CMU offers 80 majors and is home to more than 100 research centers in fields including cybersecurity, economic development and energy. Renowned for engineering, it also offers competitive programs in architecture, art, design and drama. Students can even fuse the arts and tech (or other disciplines) through the university's Integrative Design, Arts and Technology (IDeATe) program. Junior David Perry, from New York City, is pursuing a self-defined degree connected to IDeATe that combines mechanical engineering, design, and materials and craft. His work was part of an annual campuswide fashion show focused on infusing technology and complex materials with fashion.

CMU's roughly 6,700 undergraduates are serious about academics, but students say it's not a competitive place. "One thing that runs through our entire campus is passion," says Tess Chan, a senior from New York City majoring in electrical and computer engineering. That attitude

UNDERGRADUATES
Full-time: 6,680

TOTAL COST*
$72,091

U.S. NEWS RANKING
National Universities: #25

*Tuition, fees and room & board for 2019-20

University
PITTSBURGH

LOCATED JUST NORTH of the Monongahela River and next to Carnegie Mellon, the University of Pittsburgh puts students just a few miles from the city's downtown attractions. Just off campus is Schenley Park, a 456-acre green space with a skating rink, golf course, trails and more, providing a nearby dose of nature. "I like having my city life, but sometimes I need time to disconnect," says Adwait Shukla, a winter 2019 finance and marketing grad from North Potomac, Maryland.

Near the center of Pitt's 140-acre campus is the Cathedral of Learning, a 42-story Gothic tower that was built

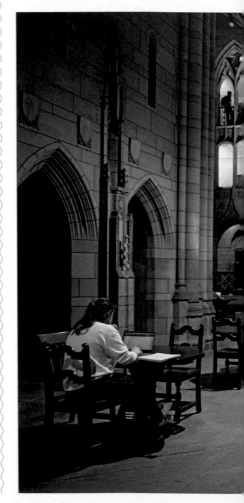

often extends beyond the classroom to extracurricular activities (there are more than 300 clubs) and campus traditions. For instance, for "Booth" and "Buggy" at Spring Carnival, students spend countless hours prepping a booth (a themed fun house) or a buggy (a racing vehicle with a student inside). Nearly 1 in 5 undergrads joins a fraternity or sorority, and the Tartans field 19 NCAA Division III sports teams.

CITY PERKS. CMU's 148-acre campus is 5 miles from downtown in the city's Oakland neighborhood. The University of Pittsburgh is next door, and undergraduates are just a quick walk from the spacious Schenley Park, shops, restaurants and the Carnegie Museums of Art and Natural History. Students can visit or get connected for learning or internship opportunities with Pittsburgh destinations like the Andy Warhol Museum (the pop artist was an alum of Carnegie Tech) or the headquarters of PNC Financial Services Group.

About two-thirds of classes enroll fewer than 20 students, so getting to know and work closely with faculty is possible for those who make the effort. Sung Jun Hong, a senior electrical and computer engineering major from

Working with a robotic arm in class at Carnegie Mellon

Mumbai, India, knocked on a professor's door during his sophomore year to ask about research opportunities and got connected with a project in computer architecture. The Undergraduate Research Office offers individual and group research grants and summer fellowships of $3,500 for full-time work.

Each of the university's six undergraduate schools – humanities, science, fine arts, engineering, business and computer science – has its own set of core and major requirements, and some have first-year seminars or special programming. CMU also enrolls about 7,600 grad students.

Faculty tend to create challenging classes, says Nandini Radhakrishnan, a 2019 business and statistics grad from Centreville, Virginia, who is now pursuing a master's degree at CMU. In her "Business Technology for Consulting" class, for example, groups explored upgrading campus ID door locks to a biometric system that would read fingerprints. "At each iteration, we met with our professor, who challenged us to go a step further," says Radhakrishnan, who was also an academic coach, mentoring her peers to help them achieve success. ●

# of Pittsburgh

UNDERGRADUATES
Full-time: 18,421

TOTAL COST*
In-State: $30,968
Out-of-State: $44,996

U.S. NEWS RANKING
National Universities: #57

*Tuition, fees and room & board
for 2019-20

nearly 100 years ago. Today, it's an academic hub of classrooms, library stacks, study spaces and 30 nationality rooms, each decorated to represent a culture that has had an influence on the city's growth.

With over 18,400 undergraduates and 9,000 grad students, many say that Pitt is the perfect size – not too big, not too small. "I feel like I'm connected to every student by just a few degrees," says senior biological sciences major Luke Persin, who's from Greensburg, about 30 miles from Pitt. Some 43% of undergrads live on campus.

To get connected even further, Persin, who is pursuing the pre-med track, joined the Health Sciences Living Learning Community, one of more than a dozen housing setups

where undergrads live with peers with similar interests and engage in specialized programming. Persin chose Pitt for its opportunities in medicine and the health sciences, including an affiliation with the University of Pittsburgh Medical Center that puts students close to volunteer opportunities and cutting-edge medical research.

First-years in the Kenneth P. Dietrich School of Arts and Sciences, one of five undergraduate schools, can get started with research in their second

semester through the First Experiences in Research program, where they pair with a faculty member and learn the fundamentals of academic inquiry in any discipline. Fiona Eichinger, a 2019 grad in international and area studies and biological sciences from West Chester, Pennsylvania, was linked up with an anthropology professor to help translate and code field notes. Later, she received two fellowships (each with $1,000 in support) through Pitt's honors college to pursue her own research on refugee resettlement in Pittsburgh, Germany and Spain.

Pitt offers more than 100 academic programs, including recently added computational biology and big data analytics. Although there are some large lectures, especially in foundational courses, about 80% of classes enroll fewer than 50 students.

Among the 600-plus campus organizations, students say that coed service and professional fraternities (focused on business or engineering, say) can be a popular way to network with others in your major or discipline. Social fraternities and sororities attract 10% of the student body. The Panthers compete in 19 NCAA Division I sports, a point of pride for many. "I absolutely love the camaraderie," says Shukla of cheering on the Panthers.

STEEL CITY. There's also plenty to do in and around the city. Through PITT ARTS, undergrads receive free access to cultural events like the symphony, concerts, galleries and local museums. A quick bus ride gets students to the Strip District for authentic Pittsburgh cuisine or to the South Side for restaurants and shopping.

Through Pitt's Outside the Classroom Curriculum, anyone can participate in hands-on experiences, leadership development, global awareness events and wellness programs. The Career Center guarantees an internship or other experiential opportunity to those who complete an internship prep program, with students landing positions at local employers like the Pittsburgh Penguins, Google and U.S. Steel. ●

Inside the Cathedral of Learning at Pitt

INDIANA

by **Ilana Kowarski**

U.S. News visited universities big and small all across the Hoosier State. Follow along as we spotlight the public powerhouses of Purdue in West Lafayette and Indiana University in Bloomington; DePauw, a liberal arts college in Greencastle; and Notre Dame, home of the Fighting Irish, in the northern part of the state. Read on to get a sense of how these schools stand out and measure up.

University of Notre Dame
Notre Dame

Purdue University
West Lafayette

DePauw University
Greencastle

Indiana University
Bloomington

Purdue University
WEST LAFAYETTE

PURDUE IS OFTEN called "the cradle of astronauts" because so many of its graduates have ventured into space, including first man on the moon Neil Armstrong. Outside a hall of engineering on campus named after him is a statue of Armstrong alongside a trail of bootprints meant to represent his historic moonwalk. Many students dream of following in those footsteps. "I've always been passionate about space exploration," says junior Kaitlyn Jones, an aeronautical and astronautical engineering major from Nixa, Missouri.

One of her favorite courses so far, in aerospace design, asked students to design an aircraft or a rocket that could save people from zombies in a post-apocalyptic world.

Indeed, from its founding in 1869 until today, Purdue has been a hub for aspiring scientists, engineers and innovators. The university's 31,200-plus undergrads engage in roughly 2,000 research projects yearly, often seeing their work published. They can choose from more than 200 majors, and classes average about 31 students.

MAKING AN IMPACT. Since 2012, the university has been redesigning many of its undergraduate courses to make them as relevant as possible, according to Chantal Levesque-Bristol, executive director of the Center for Instructional Excellence. The IMPACT program, as it's known, encourages professors to create engaging learning environments by teaching students how to apply what they learn in the classroom to solve real-world problems. For instance, one

nursing course includes a "night in the emergency room" simulation where students are asked to make rapid-fire decisions about how to care for imaginary patients. While undergrads are not required to take IMPACT courses, more than 90% complete at least one.

Jessie Searles, a junior from McKinney, Texas, majoring in supply chain, information and analytics, says her courses often include real-life examples,

Purdue students in flight class (left) and at marching band practice (above) which has made them more enjoyable. Her class on spies, lies, intelligence and national security was taught by a former CIA analyst, and students were given a timed challenge for which they were asked to assemble a presidential daily briefing based on mock intelligence. "I've definitely never felt like nonscience, non-STEM majors are put second by any means," she notes. Indeed, campus includes a range of art galleries, performance spaces, music- and arts-related student organizations, and multicultural centers.

West Lafayette is located between Indianapolis and Chicago in northwest Indiana. Just over half of undergrads

come from within the state, and roughly 14% hail from overseas. About 40% of students live on campus in a mix of housing options, including learning communities organized around themes like data science and women in film and video production, for example. About 20% of students join a fraternity, sorority or one of about a dozen cooperative houses.

Purdue's range of Division I sports teams have boasted numerous noteworthy athletes, including eight current or former Boilermakers who competed in the 2016 Summer

Olympics in Rio de Janeiro in such events as rowing and track and field.

One of the university's most popular traditions is its Grand Prix, an annual go-kart race; student teams compete to build the fastest vehicle possible. While they take their studies seriously, students often display a lively sense of fun: Among their recent quirkier extracurricular activities, for example, was a successful effort in 2018 to set a Guinness World Record for the most train whistles sounded at once when precisely 5,527 participants blew their whistles simultaneously. ●

UNDERGRADUATES
Full-time: 31,217

TOTAL COST*
In-State: $20,022
Out-of-State: $38,824

U.S. NEWS RANKING
National Universities: #57

*Tuition, fees and room & board for 2019-20

DePauw University

GREENCASTLE

DEPAUW IS SITUATED in a small town about an hour from Indianapolis, and students say the liberal arts college is both an intellectual haven and a close-knit community. With an undergraduate enrollment of about 2,100 and a student-faculty ratio of 9:1, DePauw's size facilitates close relationships with professors and peers.

"You can find your place here," says Kaela Wright, a 2019 grad from Chicago. She initially found moving from a major metro area to a town of about 10,500 disorienting, but says there was something comforting about attending a school where people tend to recognize each other. The communication major can't recall attending a class of more than 15 students.

Campus resources such as the Center for Diversity and Inclusion are highly accessible, since there aren't an overwhelming number of students competing for them. Wright participated in a variety of extracurriculars, including joining the Alpha Kappa Alpha sorority, serving as an anchor at the campus television station and working as a sports announcer for student radio.

Generally small classes mean that "it's very obvious if you didn't do your work," says Alison Grimm, a 2019 communication and management fellows graduate from Batavia, Illinois. On the other hand, one of the advantages of the school's size is that professors are available, and it's

UNDERGRADUATES
Full-time: 2,138

TOTAL COST*
$64,546

U.S. NEWS RANKING
National Liberal Arts: #46

*Tuition, fees and room & board for 2019-20

relatively easy for students to rise to leadership positions on campus. Grimm worked her way up from news anchor to a marketing leadership role at the student-run TV station.

Some distinguished DePauw alumni include New York Times columnist James B. Stewart, Fox News anchor Bret Baier and author Barbara Kingsolver. The Society of Professional Journalists was established at DePauw 110 years ago, and student media outlets frequently win journalism prizes.

Arman Nazari, a 2019 graduate in economics from Plano, Texas, says he strongly considered attending one

Working on a painting in an art class at DePauw University

of the big public universities in Texas. His sister, though, was a DePauw alum and encouraged him to apply. Nazari eventually realized the school was a great fit because of its friendly student body and cozy atmosphere. He further felt a sense of community through his fraternity, Phi Kappa Psi, where he served as president. Nearly 70% of students participate in Greek life.

LICENSE TO EXPLORE. DePauw has dozens of majors, and the liberal arts curriculum allows students to take a wide range of offerings. Nazari says that one of his favorite courses focused on the ethics of combat and included lessons about Japanese samurai and Roman gladiators. Grimm loved a study abroad program that focused on children's literature and allowed her to see places in London and Paris connected to the works of famous children's authors.

Another aspect of the university that makes it special, according to both students and school officials, is its management fellows honors program for aspiring business leaders. Management fellows complete several business courses, including economics, statistics and accounting. They also have access to a for-credit business internship experience and opportunities to meet high-profile executives. Michael Chen, a management fellow in the class of 2022 who grew up in Taiwan, says the program is helping him to learn the soft skills necessary for success in business. Chen appreciates the school's "family environment," and notes that a professor invited him over for dinner to celebrate Lunar New Year.

In January 2018, DePauw introduced a "Gold Commitment" pledge designed to reassure students (and parents) about career prospects after college. For those who meet certain requirements (graduating in good standing and participating in certain co-curricular and professional development programs, for example), if they are neither employed nor attending grad school within six months of receiving their degree, the school will either provide them with an entry-level professional position or give them an additional semester tuition-free. ●

Indiana University

BLOOMINGTON

MORE THAN 32,100 undergrads are enrolled at Indiana University's campus in Bloomington, which spans 1,900-plus acres and includes an abundance of trees and some 150 buildings. Many of them are made out of limestone milled in the Hoosier State.

With more than 200 undergraduate majors and 750-plus clubs and organizations, it's "impossible to be bored" here, says 2019 grad Nick Kersting, who double-majored in biology and Russian. The vastness of IU was one of its key selling points for Kersting, who was born in Russia and grew up in Downers Grove, Illinois. He got involved with a variety of extracurriculars, including serving as president of a residence hall floor, giving tours to admitted students and participating in the Indiana University Dance Marathon, which raises

In class at IU's School of Informatics, Computing & Engineering

money for Riley Hospital for Children at IU Health in Indianapolis. Kersting also earned a scuba diving certification and took a research trip to the Florida Keys with the university's Center for Underwater Science.

IU offers more than 70 languages as well as 380-plus study abroad programs, which attract over 3,100 students each year. Among IU's 16 colleges and schools are the Jacobs School of Music, which has educated the likes of violinist and conductor Joshua Bell and singer Sylvia McNair. The Kelley School of Business has undergraduate majors in information systems, real estate and professional sales, among others, and is ranked as the No. 10 undergrad business program in the country by U.S. News. Jackson Holforty, an in-state junior

UNDERGRADUATES
Full-time: 32,109

TOTAL COST*
In-State: $21,779
Out-of-State: $47,344

U.S. NEWS RANKING
National Universities: #79

*Tuition, fees and room & board for 2019-20

in the Kelley School, says he has gained an abundance of marketable expertise from his business courses. He also appreciates how the scope and variety of activities at IU allows each undergrad to find his or her own "tightknit community" and pursue a professional calling. "Very rarely have I ever heard of an interest that is not already represented on campus," says Holforty. One of the activities he frequently enjoyed: a recreational club devoted to disc golf, a sport that involves using Frisbees or flying discs on a golf or dedicated course. About 18% of undergrads join a fraternity or sorority.

DEPTH AND BREADTH. The university's rich course offerings and student engagement opportunities are often major selling points, says Sacha Thieme, executive director of admissions. Thieme, who is herself an alumna, says school spirit and an appreciation for tradition are frequently on display, whether it is students camping out for basketball tickets or dressed in IU apparel.

Indeed, IU is home to multiple Division I sports programs, including its famed Hoosiers basketball team, which has won five NCAA men's championships. One of the university's most noteworthy traditions is when students show school pride by becoming part of the Crimson Guard. This group sits together in the student section of the basketball arena to cheer on the teams decked out in the IU colors of crimson and cream.

Another popular university tradition is the Little 500, an annual bicycle event designed to mimic the Indianapolis 500 race car competition. More than 25,000 students, alumni and community members witness the contest each spring.

India Sloan, a junior animal behavior major from Atlanta, says that although the large campus (and cold Midwestern winters) may initially seem intimidating, it is possible to experience a sense of belonging at this Big Ten school, as long as students are willing to seek out support and connections with faculty, advisers and peers. "There's a lot of ways to make a big campus feel small," she says. ●

University of Notre Dame

NOTRE DAME

THE UNIVERSITY OF Notre Dame combines rigorous academics, top-flight athletics and a strong religious heritage. The Catholic school is home to the storied Fighting Irish sports program, whose football team has been depicted in the movies "Knute Rockne: All American" and "Rudy." Notre Dame ranks among the top 15 in both U.S. News' National Universities and undergraduate business program rankings.

Collegiate Gothic architecture and numerous green spaces abound on the 1,261-acre campus, located adjacent to South Bend. Although the university's 8,600 or so undergrads are typically accomplished and ambitious, it's rare that they are "cutthroat and competitive," says Claire Doyle, a 2019 graduate from South Bend who majored

science and the humanities plus subjects like theology and philosophy.

The university was founded by a Catholic priest from the Congregation of Holy Cross in the mid-19th century, and the campus is filled with religious iconography. A mural on the library called "The Word of Life" (affectionately known as "Touchdown Jesus") depicts Christ with arms raised to the heavens, surrounded by notable Christian saints and scholars. The quad at the center of campus includes a basilica and a main administration building topped with a golden dome and statue of the Virgin Mary.

About 83% of undergrads identify as Catholic, and there are more than 50 chapels across campus, including ones in the residence halls that offer weekly services geared towards college students. "A lot of people who don't go to church so often at home really like it because it's so cozy," says Mariah Geary, a senior finance major from Westchester County, New York. Undergrads who come from other (or no) faith traditions note that they still feel a strong sense of belonging, and there's a range of interfaith resources available.

Irla Atanda, a senior American studies major from Jacksonville, Florida, says sports tend to unify everyone on campus. Even when she studied abroad in Santiago, Chile, she made a point of watching Fighting Irish football games with her classmates.

The school does not have any fraternities or sororities, and freshmen are assigned to single-sex residence halls, which are hubs for recreational sports and social activities. Among those: the comedy skit and musical extravaganza performed each February by residents of Keenan Hall, a men's dorm. Notre Dame also has an annual boxing tournament, Bengal Bouts, which raises money to support religious missions in Bangladesh. There are more than 400 student organizations in all. ●

in English. She says the school has a very supportive academic atmosphere. There is a 10:1 student-faculty ratio and ample research opportunities that draw more than a third of undergrads.

SERVICE-MINDED. In addition, the number of undergrads who participate in community service is "astonishing," Doyle says. According to the university, nearly 90% of students undertake service learning projects, many of which are organized by the Center for Social Concerns. Study abroad programs are also extremely popular, with more than 70% of undergrads taking advantage.

Notre Dame tends to attract undergraduates who are eager to make a difference for others and who are "not only interested in cultivating the mind but also the heart," says Erin

Hoffmann Harding, vice president for student affairs. Rev. John I. Jenkins, the university's president, says that the college curriculum is designed to allow students to grapple with big questions about what a good life involves.

All told, students can choose from about 75 degree programs across six colleges and schools, including architecture, business, engineering, global affairs, science, and arts and letters. A core curriculum is required of all, and it includes traditional liberal arts disciplines like

UNDERGRADUATES
Full-time: 8,607

TOTAL COST*
$71,193

U.S. NEWS RANKING
National Universities: #15

*Tuition, fees and room & board for 2019-20

TAKE A
ROAD TRIP

CALIFORNIA

by **Ann Claire Carnahan**

Thanks to its beaches and weather, the Golden State can be an appealing place to spend your college years. U.S. News took a week to visit several campuses in Southern California, starting in Los Angeles at rivals UCLA and USC. Next, we ventured inland to Claremont McKenna before winding south to the University of San Diego.

**University
of Southern
California**
Los Angeles

**Claremont
McKenna College**
Claremont

UCLA
Los Angeles

**University
of San Diego**
San Diego

UCLA
LOS ANGELES

A **S A LARGE PUBLIC** university located in the nation's second largest city, UCLA has a cozy, suburban campus feel but an abundance of opportunities for its 31,000-plus undergraduates to get connected to their city surroundings. Nick Nikoian, a 2019 grad and communication major from nearby Burbank, participated in a mentoring program to help elementary, middle and high school students from high-need area schools along the path to college. Interested in a career in music production, he also interned with Universal Music Group.

Both on campus and off, "there's a sense of community," Nikoian says. And although students are often driven in their academics, "everyone's also well rounded," he adds. About 80%

of undergrads come from within the Golden State, and nearly 1 in 3 are first-generation college students.

UCLA's campus is replete with lush green lawns and a number of buildings that have appeared in films and TV shows like "Legally Blonde," "Angels & Demons" and "The Mindy Project." The arts have a major presence on campus, not only through majors like dance, music, and film and television, but also through seasonal theater productions, the annual Spring Sing talent show and other creative ventures.

The academic

calendar operates on a quarter system, with students typically taking three or four courses per 10-week term. That allows them "to explore a little bit of everything," says Kyle McGourty-Holland, a 2019 sociology graduate from Snohomish, Washington, though the accelerated pace "can be a blessing and a curse," she says.

UCLA has an 18:1 student-faculty ratio, and large classes are common for first-years. The size can feel intimidating at first, students say, but larger lecture courses typically break out into smaller discussion

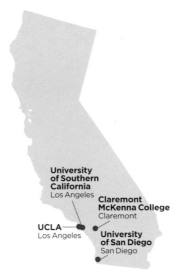

UNDERGRADUATES
Full-time: **31,009**

TOTAL COST*
In-State: **$29,128**
Out-of-State: **$58,120**

U.S. NEWS RANKING
National Universities: **#20**

*Tuition, fees and room & board
for 2019-20

sections to help build bonds between classmates and faculty. Over 50% of undergrads undertake research across a wide range of disciplines. The Undergraduate Research Centers offer guidance and scholarships of up to $3,000 for select students.

It's certainly possible to fly under the radar, students say, but joining one of the more than 1,200 campus groups can help people find their niche. "The organizations I joined gave me a home," says McGourty-Holland, who was a tour guide and a member of the club track and field team and who participated in several health- and service-related activities. About 13% of undergrads get involved in Greek life.

BRUIN PRIDE. Athletics is a popular draw, and UCLA has the second highest number of NCAA Division I championship wins (after Stanford). The Bruins compete in 15 sports, and games are free for students except for football and basketball; those tickets are offered at discounted rates. Buses transport fans the 25 or so miles from campus to the Rose Bowl Stadium in Pasadena for home football games. Traditions like the rivalry week festivities leading up to the game against the University of Southern California spur a sense of camaraderie.

Royce Hall, one of the oldest buildings on campus, was based on a church in Milan, and its 1,800-seat performance hall often hosts prominent speakers and performers. Winding through the center of campus is Bruin Walk, which leads to the bronze

Taking a break on the UCLA campus, which is often featured in films and TV shows

Bruin bear statue and is where students often gather between classes to promote events and extracurricular activities.

Most first-years live in residence halls on "the hill," about a 15-minute walk across campus from the main academic buildings. Those residences also house professors, who lead community programming, and the places have shared dining options.

UCLA's location puts students close to Disneyland and within a short drive of the J. Paul Getty Museum and Santa Monica Beach. Big Bear Mountain Resort, for skiing, is about 120 miles from campus. Students can also take advantage of nearby restaurants and movie theaters in the Westwood neighborhood around the university. ●

University of Southern California

LOS ANGELES

ALTHOUGH LOCATED just south of downtown Los Angeles, the University of Southern California's distinctive brick buildings and wide pedestrian boulevards set it apart from its urban environment. With some 19,200 undergraduates plus more than 27,000 graduate students, the 226-acre campus is almost a city unto itself.

The private university offers more than 150 majors and minors, and some competitive programs have extra requirements. Those wanting to study film, say, can apply to the School of Cinematic Arts, which offers programs such as animation and digital arts or interactive entertainment.

USC's connections to Hollywood run deep. In the popular "Theatrical Film Symposium" class, students watch screenings of popular movies and can discuss the films with their directors and producers. One recent guest: "Black Panther" director Ryan Coogler, a USC alum. Ellie Feinerman, a 2019 grad from Irvine, California, took the class as part of her minor in cinematic arts. She also got connected with internships working for "The Ellen DeGeneres Show," "Jimmy Kimmel Live!" and NBC through her communication major in the USC Annenberg School for Communication and Journalism. "I wouldn't have had that opportunity anywhere else," she says.

USC is very selective, only accepting about 13% of applicants. Nearly two-thirds of undergrads are from California, and about 13% come from abroad.

About a third of all undergraduates live on campus, and the university's residential colleges help establish a sense of community among first-year students. Incoming freshmen apply to live in one of several residence halls focused on academic and cultural interests like arts and humanities or a global college experience. Trenton Stone, a junior from Grand Junction, Colorado, majoring in international relations (with a global business emphasis) and philosophy, credits the residential college system with helping ease his transition to college and providing activities to "find big and small families on campus."

Undergraduates can get involved in research and hands-on learning across USC's schools and academic units. For example, the Bachelor of Science in Arts, Technology and

UNDERGRADUATES
Full-time: **19,194**

TOTAL COST*
$74,107

U.S. NEWS RANKING
National Universities: **#22**

*Tuition, fees and room & board for 2019-20

Students collaborating at USC's Iovine and Young Academy, an art, tech and innovation hub

Studying jazz dance at USC, where the average undergraduate class size is about 26

the Business of Innovation program at the USC Iovine and Young Academy enables small cohorts of students to pursue their individual interests in a multidisciplinary and project-based environment combining those fields. Suraya Shivji, a recent graduate from Fremont, California, teamed up with roommate Jamie Haberman to launch Mello, a "smart" essential oil diffuser for the home. Regardless of their school, all students complete the same core curriculum, with requirements in the arts, humanities and the sciences.

ACTIVE CAMPUS. The menu of extracurricular options is long: Students can join more than 850 campus organizations, such as Peaks & Professors (faculty members lead

hikes and discussions on different topics) and the Trojan Food Pantry (members help people in the community struggling with food insecurity). About 1 in 5 undergrads joins a fraternity or sorority.

One reason Niven Jayanthi, a sophomore majoring in business administration and math from San Bruno, California, chose USC was its sports culture. As a member of the Spirit of Troy marching band (the only collegiate band to have two platinum albums), he enjoys long-standing rituals like leading the pregame march to the coliseum where the football team plays. "You become a part of a family hundreds of thousands of people large," he says. ●

Claremont McKenna College

A **FIXTURE ON THE** west side of Claremont McKenna's 69-acre campus is "the Kube," a glass-walled study space (part of an academic and administrative building) that serves as a sort of living room for the college's 1,300 undergraduates. In addition to exposing them to the Southern California scenery, some see in the facility a symbol of their shared open-minded approach to education and collaboration. Thomas D'Anieri, a senior majoring in philosophy, politics and economics from Wellesley, Massachusetts, found in CMC a supportive "attitude that surrounds this academic excellence," he says.

That core group of undergrads expands to about 6,000 when you figure in the other liberal arts schools in the Claremont Colleges consortium: Scripps, Pomona, Harvey Mudd and Pitzer. Students can take classes – more than 2,000 allow for cross-registration – and sign up for some joint organizations across the so-called 5C schools. The campuses are located side by side, which allows for common dining halls, libraries and other facilities, plus shared social events.

Claremont McKenna teams up with Harvey Mudd and Scripps to compete against Pomona-Pitzer in NCAA Division III sports. The size of the consortium means it's not entirely a fishbowl. The consortium certainly expands one's options and network, but CMC

UNDERGRADUATES
Full-time: 1,321

TOTAL COST*
$73,775

U.S. NEWS RANKING
National Liberal Arts: #7

*Tuition, fees and room & board for 2019-20

is "home base," says Maya Love, a senior from Aurora, Colorado, majoring in international relations and government with a leadership sequence. She has valued being on the women's varsity basketball team as well as serving as president of the Associated Students of Claremont McKenna College, which provides funding to CMC's 70-plus campus organizations.

SHARED PASSION. The school is very selective, with only 9% of applicants accepted each year. "Students definitely have strong passions for their studies," says Connor Bloom, a 2019 science management grad from Whitefish, Montana, and "it's a ton of fun to see students' eyes light up" as they

Undergrads gathered for a meeting at Claremont McKenna

enroll about 2,700 students.

First-years are required to complete a writing and a humanities seminar, and everyone must take "Principles of Economic Analysis" and "Introduction to American Politics." Economics and government are the most popular fields of study, and about a third of undergrads complete a dual or double major. All told, the college offers 32 majors and a dozen "sequences" (similar to minors), such as financial economics and legal studies. CMC does not have majors in art or dance, for example, but students can take those classes at other 5C schools.

Set in the foothills of the San Gabriel Mountains, the city of Claremont (population 36,400) is

explore them. For his senior thesis (required of all), Bloom collaborated with a CMC alum at a blood bank in San Diego to determine whether it makes financial sense for the bank to run a genetic test for each donor, which combined his interests in corporate finance and scientific inquiry.

About 4 in 5 seniors report working on research with faculty, and the college offers 11 research institutes and centers with distinct missions, including human rights, international studies, and innovation and entrepreneurship. The consortium's graduate schools, Claremont Graduate University and the Keck Graduate Institute,

about 35 miles east of Los Angeles. The big city is accessible, but many students stick close to the college on weekends. About 97% of students live on campus, and all freshmen are assigned a first-year guide, an upperclassman who serves as a mentor, easing the transition to college.

The Emett Student Center is a prime gathering spot, with pool tables, TVs and dining destinations. Students also often come together at the Marian Miner Cook Athenaeum (known as the "Ath") to hear speakers four nights a week or on weekday afternoons for free drinks and snacks as a study break during Ath Tea. ●

University of San Diego

SAN DIEGO

L OCATED JUST east of Mission Bay, the University of San Diego's 180-acre campus is dotted with Spanish Renaissance-style buildings and palm trees. Behind the Joan B. Kroc Institute for Peace and Justice, a cross-disciplinary academic and campus center, students can relax by a garden and reflecting pool and take in Instagram-worthy views of the nearby beaches and downtown San Diego. The university enrolls about 5,700 undergrads, and its size and scenic setting allow for a "natural connectedness," says Luke Garrett of Washington, D.C., who will graduate in December with majors in physics and philosophy.

USD was established with the merging of separate men's and women's colleges in 1972, but it is rooted in a Catholic educational tradition that dates back centuries. Today, about half of undergraduates identify as Catholic, but for many, how students experience faith is a "choose your own adventure" process, says Tomy Vettukallel, a senior from Clovis, California, majoring in business administration. The university hosts a range of religiously oriented events and programs that are open to all, such as a weekly Mass for Peace in Founders Chapel and an annual spring All Faith Service that features elements of different faith traditions. All undergrads complete two courses related to theological and religious inquiry.

Freshmen are required to live on campus and join a living-learning community centered around a particular theme, such as Cultivate LLC (focused on sustainability) or Advocate LLC (social justice). As part of the first-year curriculum, students choose a series

of classes with their LLC peers that is often related to their community theme and offers an intro to college-level thinking, discussion and writing. Peer scholastic advisers and faculty mentors are available to help students navigate the transition to college.

CAMPUS COMMUNITY. Overall, USD classes tend to be small, and with a student-faculty ratio of 14:1, undergrads can get to know professors as people to "rely on" and "be comfortable in saying I need more help," says Tiffany Truong, a junior from San Jose, California, double-majoring in biology and history. The university also enrolls about 3,200 graduate students. In January, in between fall and spring terms, students can take part in intersession, enrolling in a single three-week course that might involve a real-world project in the community, for example, or a trip abroad.

Downtown San Diego is just over 5 miles from campus, accessible by

Outside Copley Library on the University of San Diego campus

trolley and bus, though having a car to get around can be an advantage. Students often explore the nearby San Diego Zoo, Balboa Park and the shops, restaurants and live music in the city's Gaslamp Quarter. In addition, there are ample opportunities for "outdoor adventures," Garrett says, from relaxing and surfing on Mission Beach or around La Jolla to taking a weekend hike in Joshua Tree National Park about 160 miles away.

Students can find their niche through the more than 180 different clubs and organizations. The Torero Program Board, for example, plans different events on campus and in and around the Hahn University Center and Student Life Pavilion. The

Division I Toreros compete in football, basketball, swimming and diving and other sports. About 18% of men and 29% of women join fraternities and sororities, which can play a big role on campus, students say, even for those who aren't members.

Nearly 40% of students come from out of state, and 10% are from overseas. The United Front Multicultural Commons offers programs and resources for undergrads of color (more than a third of the student body), women, LGBTQ students and people of different cultures. Events include an annual Multicultural Night featuring performances that represent global cultures and monthly Food for Thought events celebrating different cuisines and their histories. ●

UNDERGRADUATES
Full-time: 5,678

TOTAL COST*
$65,312

U.S. NEWS RANKING
National Universities: #91

*Tuition, fees and room & board for 2019-20

The U.S. News

Rankings

3 THE U.S. NEWS RANKINGS

How We Rank Colleges

Collegebound students can make good use of our statistics

by **Robert J. Morse** *and* **Eric M. Brooks**

DECIDING WHERE TO APPLY IS TOUGH. But the U.S. News Best Colleges rankings, now in their 35th year, are an excellent resource to tap as you begin your search. They can help you compare the academic quality of institutions you're considering based on such widely accepted indicators of excellence as graduation rates and the strength of the faculty. As you learn about colleges already on your shortlist, you may narrow your choices even further or discover unfamiliar new options. Yes, many factors other than those spotlighted here will figure in your decision, including location and the feel of campus life; the range of academic offerings and activities; and the cost. But combined with campus visits, interviews and attention to your own intuition, our rankings can be a powerful tool in your quest for the best fit.

How does the methodology work? The U.S. News ranking system rests on two pillars. The formula uses quantitative and qualitative statistical measures that education experts have proposed as reliable indicators of academic quality, and it is based on our researched view of what matters in education.

First, we categorize regionally accredited institutions by their mission, to establish valid comparisons: National Universities, National Liberal Arts Colleges, Regional Universities and Regional Colleges. The national universities offer a full range of undergraduate majors, plus master's and Ph.D. programs or professional practice doctorates, and emphasize faculty research (Page 64). The national liberal arts colleges focus almost exclusively on undergraduate education (Page 76). They award at least 50% of their degrees in the arts and sciences.

The regional universities (Page 82) offer a broad scope of undergraduate degrees and some master's degree programs but few, if any, doctoral programs. The regional colleges (Page 95) focus on undergraduate education but grant fewer than 50% of their degrees in liberal arts disciplines; this category also includes schools that have small bachelor's degree programs but primarily grant two-year associate degrees. The regional universities and regional colleges are further divided and ranked in four geographical groups: North, South, Midwest and West.

The framework used to group schools is derived from the 2018 update of the Carnegie Classification of Institutions of Higher Education's Basic Classification. The Carnegie classification is used extensively by higher education researchers; the U.S.

A film, TV and theater class at Notre Dame

Weighing What's Important

The U.S. News rankings are based on several categories of quality indicators, listed below. Scores for each group are weighted as shown to arrive at a final overall score.

The Scoring Breakdown

Outcomes*	35%
Faculty Resources	20%
Expert Opinion	20%
Financial Resources	10%
Student Excellence	10%
Alumni Giving	5%

*Graduation, retention, graduation rate performance, social mobility

Department of Education and many higher education associations use the system to organize their data and to determine colleges' eligibility for grant money, for example. Carnegie's 2018 update reclassified many institutions. Most significantly, it added a professional practice doctoral category to its universe of doctoral universities. Consequently, many schools are ranked in different U.S. News categories in the 2020 edition than they were in the previous edition. Indeed, the total number of schools ranked in our national universities category increased by more than 25%, as many former regional universities changed category. It's important to note as you study the rankings tables that you shouldn't compare the rank of a school that is new to its U.S. News ranking category (indicated by a footnote) with its rank in a previous year.

Next, we gather data from each college on 15 indicators of academic excellence. Each ranking factor is assigned a weight that reflects our research about how much a measure matters.

Finally, the schools in each category are ranked against their peers using their overall scores, which are calculated from the sum of their indicators.

Some schools are not ranked and thus do not appear in the tables. The most common reason is that the school does not use ACT or SAT scores in admissions decisions for first-time, first-year, degree-seeking applicants. (Schools with test-optional and test-flexible admission policies are included because they do consider ACT or SAT scores when provided.) In fewer cases, colleges are not ranked because they received too few ratings in the peer assessment survey, had a total enrollment of fewer than 200 students, had a large proportion of nontraditional students, or had no first-year students (as is the case at upper-division schools). As a result of these standards, many for-profit institutions are not ranked. We also did not rank highly specialized schools such as those in arts, health, business and engineering, although eligible specialized schools are included in our separate

rankings of business and engineering programs.

Colleges report most of the data themselves, via the annual U.S. News statistical survey. This year, 91% of the 1,387 ranked colleges and universities returned their statistical information. To ensure the highest possible quality of data, U.S. News compared schools' survey responses to their earlier cohorts' statistics, third-party data, and data reported by other schools. Schools were instructed to review, revise and verify the accuracy of their data, particularly any flagged by U.S. News as requiring a second look. They were also instructed to have a top academic official sign off on the accuracy of the data, a new step this year. Schools that declined to do so could still submit and be ranked but are footnoted. For eligible colleges that declined to complete our survey (identified as nonresponders), we made extensive use of data they reported to the National Center for Education Statistics. Estimates were used in the calculations when schools failed to report data not available from other sources, although missing data are reported in the tables as N/A.

The indicators we use to capture academic quality, described below, include input measures that reflect schools' student bodies, faculties and resources, as well as outcome measures that signal how well institutions are engaging and educating their students. Outcome measures, the most heavily weighted, account for 35% of the overall score. A more detailed explanation of the methodology can be found at usnews.com/collegemeth.

OUTCOMES (weighted at 35%): The higher the proportion of first-year students who return to campus for sophomore year and eventually graduate, the better a school most likely is at offering the classes and services needed to succeed. More than one-third of a school's rank reflects its success at retaining and graduating students within six years.

This measure has several components: six-year graduation and first-year retention rates (together 22% of the score); graduation rate performance, or how well a school performs at graduating students compared to a predicted graduation rate based on student and school characteristics (8%); and a school's record on promoting social mobility by graduating students from low-income backgrounds who received federal Pell Grants (5%).

The average six-year graduation rate (of students entering in fall 2009 through fall 2012) was weighted at 17.6% of the outcomes indicator. Average first-year retention rate (of fall 2014 through fall 2017 entrants) was weighted at 4.4%.

A school's graduation rate performance shows the effect of programs and policies on the graduation rate when controlling for other factors that might influence it. These include spending per student, admissions selectivity, the proportion of undergraduates receiving Pell Grants, the proportion of federal financial aid recipients who were first-generation students, and – for national universities only – the proportion of undergrad degrees awarded in science, technology, engineering and mathematics disciplines. We compare a school's six-year graduation rate for the class that entered in 2012 to the graduation rate we predicted for that class. If the actual graduation rate is higher than the predicted rate, then the college is enhancing achievement. This factor had an 8% weighting.

The social mobility measure assesses a school's performance at supporting students from underserved backgrounds relative to all students and accounts for 5% of the outcomes score. It considers both a school's six-year graduation rate among students entering in the fall of 2011 and 2012 who received Pell

An undergrad at work on campus at UCLA

Grants and how that performance compares with the graduation rate of all other students. Scores were then adjusted by the proportion of the entering class that was awarded Pell Grants, because achieving a higher graduation rate among students from low-income backgrounds is more challenging with a larger proportion of such students.

FACULTY RESOURCES (20%): Research shows that the greater access students have to quality instructors, the more engaged they will be in class, the more they will learn, and the more likely they are to graduate. U.S. News uses five factors from the 2018-2019 academic year to assess commitment to instruction: class size, faculty salary, faculty with the highest degree in their field, student-faculty ratio, and proportion of faculty who are full time.

Class size is the most heavily weighted, at 8% of the faculty resources score. The larger the proportion of fall 2018 classes a school reported as being of a smaller size, the more credit the school receives.

Faculty salary (7%) reflects average pay plus

results from spring 2018 and 2019. Of the 4,815 academics who were sent questionnaires, 43% responded. The high school counselor assessment, formerly part of the National Universities and National Liberal Arts Colleges rankings formulas, was dropped this year because U.S. News had greater confidence in its peer assessment data. The 5 percentage-point weight assigned to that factor previously was added to the peer assessment weight, increasing the weight of that indicator in those two categories from 15% to 20% – equal to the weighting for Regional Universities and Regional Colleges.

FINANCIAL RESOURCES (10%): Generous per-student spending indicates that a college can offer a variety of programs and services. U.S. News measures financial resources by using the average spending per student on instruction, research, student services and related educational expenditures in the 2017 and 2018 fiscal years. Spending on sports, dorms and hospitals does not count.

STUDENT EXCELLENCE (10%): A school's academic atmosphere is influenced by the selectivity of its admissions. Simply put, students who achieved strong grades and test scores during high school have the highest probability of succeeding at college-level coursework, enabling instructors to design classes that have great rigor. Excellence is based on two ranking indicators, standardized tests and high school class standing. The test scores for the fall 2018 entering class used in this year's rankings were weighted at 7.75%. High school class standing for the fall 2018 entering class was weighted at 2.25%. Schools sometimes fail to report SAT and ACT scores for athletes, international students, minority students, legacies, those admitted by special arrangement and those who started in the summer. For any school that did not report all scores (or declined to say whether all scores were reported), U.S. News discounted its test-score value by 15%. Additionally, if test scores reported represented less than 75% of students entering, the value was discounted by 15%.

As for high school class standing, U.S. News incorporates the proportion of first-year students at national universities and national liberal arts colleges who graduated in the top 10% of their high school classes. For regional universities and regional colleges, we used the proportion of those who graduated in the top quarter of their high school classes.

ALUMNI GIVING (5%): This is the average percentage of living alumni with bachelor's degrees who gave to their school during 2016-2017 and 2017-2018. Giving measures student satisfaction and postgraduate engagement.

TO ARRIVE AT A SCHOOL'S RANK, we calculated the weighted sum of its standardized scores. The scores were rescaled so the top college or university in each category received a value of 100 and the other schools' weighted scores were calculated as a proportion of the top score. Final scores were rounded to the nearest whole number and ranked in descending order. Tied schools appear in alphabetical order.

As you mine the tables that follow for insights (a sense of which schools might be impressed enough by your ACT or SAT scores to offer some merit aid, for example, or where you will be apt to get the most attention from professors), keep in mind that the rankings provide a launching pad for more research, not an easy answer. ●

benefits during the 2017-2018 and 2018-2019 academic years. The faculty salary figures were adjusted for regional price differences. The other factors are weighted as follows: proportion of full-time professors with the highest degree in their field (3%), student-faculty ratio (1%), and proportion of faculty who are full time (1%).

EXPERT OPINION (20%): We survey presidents, provosts and deans of admissions, asking them to rate the academic quality of peer institutions with which they are familiar on a scale of 1 (marginal) to 5 (distinguished). An institution known for having innovative approaches to teaching may perform especially well on this indicator, for example, whereas a school struggling to keep its accreditation will likely perform poorly. The peer assessment score is derived from averaging survey

Rank School (State) (*Public)	Overall score	Peer assessment score (5.0=highest)	Graduation and retention rank	Average first-year student retention rate	2018 graduation rate		Over-performance (+) Under-performance (-)	Pell recipient grad rate	Social mobility rank
					Predicted	Actual			
1. Princeton University (NJ)	100	4.9	2	98%	95%	96%	+1	93%	186
2. Harvard University (MA)	96	4.9	2	97%	97%	98%	+1	97%	186
3. Columbia University (NY)	94	4.7	4	99%	94%	96%	+2	93%	138
3. Massachusetts Institute of Technology	94	4.9	10	99%	95%	94%	-1	92%	241
3. Yale University (CT)	94	4.8	1	99%	97%	97%	None	94%	285
6. Stanford University (CA)	93	4.9	10	98%	94%	94%	None	93%	241
6. University of Chicago	93	4.6	10	99%	98%	94%	-4	89%	335
6. University of Pennsylvania	93	4.6	4	98%	98%	95%	-3	92%	241
9. Northwestern University (IL)	92	4.5	10	98%	97%	95%	-2	94%	251
10. Duke University (NC)	91	4.5	8	98%	98%	96%	-2	95%	254
10. Johns Hopkins University (MD)	91	4.7	18	97%	97%	94%	-3	94%	241
12. California Institute of Technology	89	4.7	19	98%	98%	92%	-6	96%	345
12. Dartmouth College (NH)	89	4.4	8	97%	97%	95%	-2	92%	303
14. Brown University (RI)	86	4.5	4	98%	96%	95%	-1	91%	224
15. University of Notre Dame (IN)	84	4.2	4	98%	98%	97%	-1	95%	322
15. Vanderbilt University (TN)	84	4.3	19	97%	98%	94%	-4	90%	291
17. Cornell University (NY)	83	4.6	10	97%	97%	95%	-2	92%	224
17. Rice University (TX)	83	4.2	19	97%	97%	95%	-2	92%	204
19. Washington University in St. Louis	81	4.1	10	97%	98%	95%	-3	91%	381
20. University of California–Los Angeles*	80	4.3	27	97%	87%	90%	+3	88%	13
21. Emory University (GA)	79	4.1	30	94%	91%	90%	-1	88%	200
22. University of California–Berkeley*	78	4.7	23	97%	88%	91%	+3	89%	70
22. University of Southern California	78	3.9	23	96%	92%	92%	None	91%	147
24. Georgetown University (DC)	77	4.2	10	96%	98%	94%	-4	94%	241
25. Carnegie Mellon University (PA)	75	4.3	30	97%	94%	89%	-5	82%	303
25. University of Michigan–Ann Arbor*	75	4.5	23	97%	90%	92%	+2	85%	291
27. Wake Forest University (NC)	74	3.6	33	94%	96%	89%	-7	85%	360
28. University of Virginia*	73	4.2	10	97%	98%	94%	-4	91%	328
29. Georgia Institute of Technology*	72	4.3	40	97%	89%	87%	-2	81%	224
29. New York University	72	4.0	52	93%	84%	85%	+1	84%	115
29. Tufts University (MA)	72	3.8	19	97%	98%	93%	-5	91%	328
29. U. of North Carolina–Chapel Hill*	72	4.1	27	97%	90%	90%	None	86%	165
29. University of Rochester (NY)	72	3.5	40	96%	90%	86%	-4	81%	159
34. University of California–Santa Barbara*	71	3.6	58	93%	84%	87%	+3	84%	9
34. University of Florida*	71	3.8	33	97%	82%	90%	+8	87%	34
36. University of California–Irvine*	70	3.8	46	93%	78%	83%	+5	81%	3
37. Boston College	69	3.7	23	95%	95%	92%	-3	91%	270
37. University of California–San Diego*	69	3.9	40	95%	85%	86%	+1	84%	21
39. University of California–Davis*	68	3.9	48	93%	84%	86%	+2	84%	9
40. Boston University	67	3.7	40	93%	85%	88%	+3	88%	270
40. Brandeis University (MA)	67	3.6	36	93%	87%	88%	+1	84%	138
40. Case Western Reserve Univ. (OH)	67	3.7	58	93%	91%	85%	-6	82%	214
40. College of William & Mary (VA)*	67	3.8	27	95%	95%	91%	-4	88%	354
40. Northeastern University (MA)	67	3.5	36	97%	86%	88%	+2	88%	254
40. Tulane University (LA)	67	3.6	58	93%	81%	85%	+4	77%	365
46. Univ. of Wisconsin–Madison*	65	4.1	40	95%	84%	87%	+3	84%	297
46. Villanova University (PA)	65	3.4	30	96%	85%	91%	+6	94%	214
48. University of Illinois–Urbana-Champaign*	64	3.9	48	93%	79%	84%	+5	81%	186
48. University of Texas–Austin*	64	4.1	58	95%	84%	83%	-1	73%	134
50. Lehigh University (PA)	63	3.3	36	95%	87%	87%	None	84%	270
50. Pepperdine University (CA)	63	3.4	52	91%	80%	83%	+3	84%	96
50. Rensselaer Polytechnic Inst. (NY)	63	3.5	58	93%	88%	86%	-2	80%	270
50. University of Georgia*	63	3.6	46	95%	78%	86%	+8	80%	159

Note: Key to footnotes, Page 75

sities

Faculty resources rank	% of classes under 20 ('18)	% of classes of 50 or more ('18)	Student/ faculty ratio ('18)	Selectivity rank	SAT/ACT 25th-75th percentile ('18)	Freshmen in top 10% of HS class ('18)	Acceptance rate ('18)	Financial resources rank	Average alumni giving rate
7	74%	10%	5/1	11	1440-1570	91%[4]	5%	12	59%
6	72%	10%	6/1	2	1460-1580	94%	5%	8	31%
3	82%	9%	6/1	2	1450-1560	96%	6%	13	30%
9	71%	12%	3/1	2	1500-1570	97%	7%	2	33%
11	73%	9%	6/1	2	1450-1560	95%	6%	1	27%
13	69%	11%	5/1	7	1420-1570	96%	4%	5	30%
1	79%	6%	5/1	1	33-35[2]	99%	7%	7	40%
5	71%	8%	6/1	7	1440-1560	96%	8%	14	38%
3	78%	5%	6/1	11	33-35	92%	8%	9	31%
1	71%	7%	6/1	7	33-35	95%	9%	15	32%
18	74%	9%	7/1	2	33-35	96%	11%	3	37%
9	68%	9%	3/1	18	1530-1580	96%[5]	7%	3	27%
8	62%	7%	7/1	11	1420-1560	95%	9%	16	43%
16	70%	10%	6/1	7	1420-1550	96%	8%	26	31%
14	62%	10%	10/1	11	33-35	89%	18%	27	42%
16	66%	7%	7/1	11	33-35	89%	10%	11	26%
26	57%	17%	9/1	18	1390-1540	83%	11%	18	26%
11	72%	8%	6/1	11	33-35	87%	11%	23	30%
14	64%	12%	7/1	28	32-35	80%[5]	15%	5	24%
27	51%	22%	18/1	23	1270-1520	97%	14%	20	7%
20	60%	13%	9/1	23	1350-1520	84%	19%	16	21%
44	53%	19%	20/1	18	1300-1530	98%	15%	45	8%
39	59%	13%	9/1	30	1350-1530	90%[5]	13%	22	41%
39	61%	6%	11/1	18	1370-1530	89%	15%	33	31%
22	66%	12%	13/1	17	1450-1550	87%	17%	38	14%
48	57%	18%	15/1	40	1330-1510	79%[5]	23%	40	17%
21	57%	1%	10/1	33	29-33[2]	76%	29%	10	24%
39	55%	15%	15/1	23	1330-1500	90%	26%	47	20%
42	45%	14%	21/1	18	1390-1540	89%	23%	58	19%
24	61%	9%	9/1	40	1310-1510[2]	71%	20%	28	11%
27	69%	7%	9/1	23	31-34	78%	15%	31	22%
85	38%	12%	13/1	44	27-33	78%	22%	33	19%
19	74%	9%	10/1	33	1320-1500[2]	75%	29%	23	23%
22	50%	18%	17/1	33	1230-1480	100%	32%	72	17%
77	50%	14%	18/1	47	1280-1440	77%	39%	47	14%
58	53%	23%	18/1	51	1180-1440	99%	29%	61	7%
42	49%	6%	11/1	28	1320-1490	78%	28%	65	24%
147	43%	32%	19/1	30	1250-1470	100%	30%	23	4%
136	36%	29%	20/1	51	1150-1410	100%	41%	31	7%
30	62%	12%	10/1	40	1330-1500[2]	65%	22%	49	10%
48	57%	11%	10/1	48	1280-1500	56%	31%	49	19%
34	59%	13%	11/1	30	30-34	70%	29%	40	19%
54	47%	6%	12/1	33	1310-1490	77%	37%	110	30%
24	67%	6%	14/1	27	32-34	77%	19%	72	11%
27	62%	6%	8/1	33	30-33	63%	17%	33	17%
147	45%	22%	17/1	59	27-32	54%	52%	61	12%
110	42%	2%	11/1	40	1300-1470	72%	29%	110	29%
110	38%	20%	20/1	70	26-32	48%	62%	58	7%
182	38%	26%	19/1	33	1230-1480	85%	39%	76	10%
44	50%	12%	9/1	51	1270-1450	58%	22%	55	17%
36	70%	3%	14/1	65	1220-1420	57%	36%	65	9%
34	52%	10%	13/1	44	1330-1500	64%	43%	69	10%
69	45%	11%	17/1	62	1240-1410	60%	49%	123	13%

What Is a National University?

TO ASSESS MORE than 1,600 of the country's four-year colleges and universities, U.S. News first assigns each to a group of its peers, based on the categories of higher education institutions developed by the Carnegie Foundation for the Advancement of Teaching. The National Universities category consists of 399 institutions (211 public, 180 private and 8 for-profit) that offer a wide range of undergraduate majors as well as master's and doctoral degrees or professional practice doctorates; some institutions emphasize research. A list of the top 30 public national universities appears on Page 75.

Data on 15 indicators of academic quality are gathered from each institution. Schools are ranked by total weighted score; those tied are listed alphabetically. For a description of the methodology, see Page 60. For more on a college, turn to the directory at the back of the book.

Rank School (State) (*Public)	Overall score	Peer assessment score (5.0=highest)	Average first-year student retention rate	2018 graduation rate Predicted	2018 graduation rate Actual	Pell recipient grad rate	% of classes under 20 ('18)	% of classes of 50 or more ('18)	SAT/ACT 25th-75th percentile ('18)	Freshmen in top 10% of HS class ('18)	Accept-ance rate ('18)	Average alumni giving rate
54. Ohio State University–Columbus*	62	3.8	94%	77%	84%	76%	27%	27%	27-32	63%	52%	15%
54. Santa Clara University (CA)†	62	3.1	95%	80%	91%	88%	46%	1%	1270-1440	49%[5]	50%	19%
54. Syracuse University (NY)	62	3.4	91%	74%	83%	80%	57%	9%	1180-1370	39%	50%	11%
57. Florida State University*	61	3.3	93%	70%	83%	79%	57%	12%	1200-1350	39%	37%	19%
57. Pennsylvania State U.–Univ. Park*	61	3.7	93%	73%	85%	77%	31%	17%	1160-1360	43%	56%	13%
57. Purdue University–West Lafayette (IN)*	61	3.8	92%	76%	81%	74%	38%	20%	1180-1410	46%	58%	18%
57. University of Miami (FL)	61	3.5	92%	88%	82%	78%	50%	9%	1250-1430	55%	32%	12%
57. University of Pittsburgh*	61	3.6	93%	80%	83%	76%	45%	18%	1270-1430	55%	59%	7%
62. Rutgers University–New Brunswick (NJ)*	60	3.4	93%	68%	80%	78%	42%	21%	1190-1410	38%	60%	7%
62. University of Washington*	60	3.9	94%	88%	84%	79%	29%	25%	1220-1460	58%	49%	12%
64. Loyola Marymount University (CA)†	59	3.1	90%	75%	84%	80%	53%	1%	1210-1390	44%[5]	47%	20%
64. Southern Methodist University (TX)	59	3.3	91%	80%	78%	67%	59%	9%	29-33	49%	51%	18%
64. University of Connecticut*	59	3.3	93%	76%	85%	78%	52%	16%	1210-1420	50%	49%	9%
64. Univ. of Maryland–College Park*	59	3.7	95%	86%	86%	80%	45%	17%	1290-1480	75%	47%	7%
64. Univ. of Massachusetts–Amherst*	59	3.4	91%	70%	80%	75%	49%	18%	1200-1390	32%	60%	9%
64. Worcester Polytechnic Inst. (MA)	59	3.0	96%	88%	87%	88%	64%	11%	1300-1460[2]	64%	42%	10%
70. Clemson University (SC)*	58	3.4	93%	82%	83%	71%	55%	14%	27-32	56%	47%	23%
70. George Washington University (DC)	58	3.5	92%	86%	82%	78%	53%	11%	1280-1460[2]	56%	42%	8%
70. Texas A&M University–College Station*	58	3.7	91%	78%	82%	76%	21%	27%	1170-1380	63%	67%	17%
70. University of Minnesota–Twin Cities*	58	3.7	93%	78%	80%	72%	38%	20%	26-31	50%	52%	8%
74. Fordham University (NY)	57	3.1	91%	80%	83%	79%	51%	1%	1250-1430	44%	46%	17%
74. Stevens Institute of Technology (NJ)	57	2.9	95%	84%	87%	91%	39%	10%	1330-1480[2]	72%	41%	17%
74. Virginia Tech*	57	3.7	93%	78%	84%	77%	27%	22%	1180-1390	38%	65%	12%
77. American University (DC)	56	3.2	89%	81%	80%	77%	55%	1%	1220-1380[2]	31%	32%	6%
77. Brigham Young Univ.–Provo (UT)	56	3.2	89%	80%	83%	78%	45%	12%	26-31	54%	64%	13%
79. Baylor University (TX)	55	3.2	89%	76%	79%	69%	50%	9%	26-31	40%	52%	14%
79. Binghamton University–SUNY*	55	3.0	92%	77%	82%	79%	46%	14%	1310-1440	54%	40%	6%
79. Gonzaga University (WA)†	55	3.1	94%	78%	86%	78%	37%	1%	1183-1350	41%	66%	14%
79. Indiana University–Bloomington*	55	3.7	91%	74%	78%	66%	37%	17%	1150-1360	35%	77%	11%
79. University at Buffalo–SUNY*	55	3.1	87%	66%	76%	73%	29%	23%	1160-1330	35%	56%	11%
84. Colorado School of Mines*	54	3.5	93%	83%	81%	77%	29%	21%	1290-1450	59%	49%	10%
84. Elon University (NC)†	54	3.0	90%	80%	83%	79%	52%	0%	1150-1330	25%	72%	24%
84. Marquette University (WI)	54	3.1	89%	77%	85%	76%	48%	8%	24-30	36%	82%	14%
84. Michigan State University*	54	3.5	92%	70%	80%	71%	24%	23%	1110-1310	29%	78%	8%
84. North Carolina State U.–Raleigh*	54	3.2	94%	79%	81%	76%	35%	16%	1250-1390	48%	47%	10%
84. University of California–Santa Cruz*	54	3.1	90%	81%	76%	74%	36%	30%	1170-1400	96%	48%	3%
84. University of Iowa*	54	3.5	86%	69%	73%	64%	51%	14%	23-28	30%	83%	8%
91. Clark University (MA)	53	2.8	87%	75%	77%	74%	59%	3%	1200-1390[2]	39%	59%	17%
91. Miami University–Oxford (OH)*	53	3.2	91%	73%	80%	71%	33%	11%	26-31	34%	75%	18%
91. Stony Brook–SUNY*	53	3.3	90%	67%	74%	76%	36%	25%	1230-1420	47%	42%	6%
91. University of California–Riverside*	53	3.1	90%	74%	75%	75%	21%	30%	1110-1330	94%	51%	2%
91. University of Delaware*	53	3.2	91%	78%	82%	75%	34%	16%	1170-1350[2]	34%	62%	9%
91. University of San Diego	53	3.0	89%	78%	80%	75%	42%	0.1%	1190-1360	33%	53%	12%
97. Drexel University (PA)	52	3.1	88%	70%	74%	69%	53%	10%	1170-1380	33%	77%	6%
97. New Jersey Inst. of Technology*	52	2.7	88%	56%	65%	60%	37%	3%	1190-1380	36%	64%	8%
97. Saint Louis University	52	3.0	90%	76%	78%	66%	47%	9%	25-31	48%	58%	10%
97. Texas Christian University	52	2.9	91%	80%	83%	76%	44%	5%	26-30	50%	41%	18%
97. University of Denver	52	3.0	87%	78%	77%	76%	55%	6%	26-31	42%	56%	9%
97. University of San Francisco	52	3.0	84%	66%	75%	79%	44%	2%	1130-1330[2]	38%	65%	7%
97. Yeshiva University (NY)	52	2.8	90%	84%	83%	78%	60%	1%	22-30	N/A	60%	16%
104. Auburn University (AL)*	51	3.3	91%	74%	78%	64%	35%	17%	25-30	32%	75%	13%
104. Creighton University (NE)†	51	3.0	89%	78%	79%	70%	46%	5%	24-30	37%	71%	13%
104. Howard University (DC)	51	3.2	89%	61%	62%	62%	54%	6%	1140-1285	27%	32%	11%
104. Loyola University Chicago	51	3.2	84%	70%	74%	66%	38%	6%	25-30	37%	68%	6%
104. Rochester Inst. of Technology (NY)	51	3.4	89%	71%	70%	67%	49%	5%	1200-1400	37%	66%	6%
104. Temple University (PA)*	51	3.1	90%	59%	73%	67%	39%	8%	1130-1320[2]	23%	59%	6%
104. University of California–Merced*	51	2.7	83%	43%	66%	65%	28%	27%	1000-1190[3]	N/A	66%	13%
104. University of Colorado–Boulder*	51	3.7	87%	71%	71%	59%	44%	17%	1150-1360	29%	82%	6%

Note: Key to footnotes, Page 75

SYRACUSE.EDU

#BEORANGE

BE DRIVEN

Outspoken. Curious. Fiercely committed to advocacy for at-risk schoolchildren. Experiential learning at Syracuse University provides the tools Justine needs to build a future in public policy. A triple major gives her the challenge she craves and the breadth of knowledge her field demands. Exploring Europe on a study abroad trip to France was a lifelong dream fulfilled. Her passion is helping kids build resilience and bridges to success.

Be You. Be Orange.

Syracuse University

JUSTINE '20   **B.A. Political Science, Policy Studies, Citizenship and Civic Engagement**   #BEORANGE

Rank School (State) (*Public)	Overall score	Peer assessment score (5.0=highest)	Average first-year student retention rate	2018 graduation rate		Pell recipient grad rate	% of classes under 20 ('18)	% of classes of 50 or more ('18)	SAT/ACT 25th-75th percentile ('18)	Freshmen in top 10% of HS class ('18)	Accept-ance rate ('18)	Average alumni giving rate
				Predicted	Actual							
104. University of Oregon*	51	3.4	87%	65%	73%	68%	39%	20%	1080-1290	22%[5]	83%	8%
104. Univ. of South Carolina*	51	3.2	88%	71%	77%	69%	37%	17%	1190-1360	29%	63%	14%
104. University of South Florida*	51	2.8	90%	61%	73%	72%	45%	12%	1170-1330	34%	43%	12%
104. University of Tennessee*	51	3.3	86%	76%	73%	64%	30%	15%	25-31	36%	78%	11%
104. University of Utah*	51	3.2	90%	65%	70%	62%	37%	19%	22-29	N/A	67%	11%
117. Arizona State University–Tempe*	50	3.4	87%	62%	69%	62%	38%	18%	1130-1360[2]	33%	85%	10%
117. Clarkson University (NY)	50	2.7	89%	74%	76%	74%	52%	18%	1160-1350	35%	71%	17%
117. Illinois Institute of Technology	50	2.8	92%	71%	72%	66%	46%	9%	1220-1400	49%	58%	7%
117. University of Arizona*	50	3.6	81%	65%	64%	60%	45%	16%	21-28[2]	32%	84%	9%
121. Iowa State University*	49	3.3	88%	70%	75%	67%	29%	20%	22-28	27%	91%	11%
121. SUNY Col. of Envir. Sci. and Forestry*	49	2.6	82%	73%	77%	73%	44%	10%	1120-1310	25%	61%	18%
121. University of Tulsa (OK)	49	2.7	89%	87%	74%	58%	60%	5%	25-32	65%	41%	19%
121. University of Vermont*	49	3.0	86%	79%	76%	72%	49%	13%	1180-1360	37%	68%	9%
125. Chapman University (CA)†	48	2.6	90%	83%	79%	80%	48%	4%	1190-1370	37%	54%	8%
125. DePaul University (IL)	48	3.0	85%	62%	72%	66%	39%	1%	1080-1290[2]	N/A	68%	6%
125. Simmons University (MA)†	48	2.4	83%	69%	80%	75%	69%	2%	1130-1300	29%	70%	13%
125. University of New Hampshire*	48	2.9	86%	66%	77%	73%	41%	12%	1090-1280	20%	77%	7%
125. University of the Pacific (CA)	48	2.6	84%	67%	68%	71%	50%	5%	1120-1350	33%	63%	6%
130. Drake University (IA)†	47	2.8	88%	80%	78%	67%	50%	4%	24-30[2]	39%	68%	10%
130. University of Kansas*	47	3.4	82%	69%	65%	50%	49%	13%	23-29	28%	92%	13%
132. Duquesne University (PA)	46	2.7	86%	72%	78%	69%	40%	9%	1140-1280[2]	26%	72%	7%
132. Rutgers University–Newark (NJ)*	46	2.7	86%	55%	64%	66%	28%	17%	1020-1190	22%	63%	5%
132. University of Dayton (OH)	46	2.7	90%	77%	79%	70%	40%	3%	25-30[3]	25%	72%	13%
132. University of Illinois–Chicago*	46	3.0	80%	54%	59%	57%	35%	20%	1020-1220	28%	76%	2%

BRETT ZIEGLER FOR USN&WR

Northwestern University

Note: Key to footnotes, Page 75

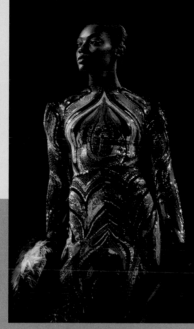

Are You Ready for the Future of Work?

Built for a future that has yet to be defined, Thomas Jefferson University is crossing disciplines to bring unrivaled innovation and discovery to higher education. Through boundary-breaking collaboration, research and hands-on experiential learning, we equip graduates with leadership and analytical skills shaped for an accelerated job market.

Ten colleges and three schools comprise our National Doctoral Research University that offers everything from traditional undergraduate programs to programs for professionals who want to advance their careers.

At Jefferson, we are reshaping education for the 21st century.

College of Architecture and the Built Environment

College of Health Professions

College of Humanities and Sciences

College of Life Sciences

College of Nursing

College of Pharmacy

College of Population Health

College of Rehabilitation Sciences

Kanbar College of Design, Engineering and Commerce
   ~School of Business
   ~School of Design and Engineering

School of Continuing and Professional Studies

Sidney Kimmel Medical College

Jefferson
Thomas Jefferson University
HOME OF SIDNEY KIMMEL MEDICAL COLLEGE

Jefferson.edu
Follow us @Jeffersonuniv

REDEFINING HUMANLY POSSIBLE

BEST NATIONAL UNIVERSITIES

Rank School (State) (*Public)	Overall score	Peer assessment score (5.0=highest)	Average first-year student retention rate	2018 graduation rate Predicted	2018 graduation rate Actual	Pell recipient grad rate	% of classes under 20 ('18)	% of classes of 50 or more ('18)	SAT/ACT 25th-75th percentile ('18)	Freshmen in top 10% of HS class ('18)	Acceptance rate ('18)	Average alumni giving rate
132. University of Kentucky*	46	3.2	83%	70%	66%	53%	37%	15%	23-29	31%	94%	11%
132. University of La Verne (CA)	46	2.0	84%	50%	69%	69%	65%	0.2%	1020-1205	20%	51%	5%
132. University of Oklahoma*	46	3.1	90%	68%	68%	56%	45%	11%	23-29	32%	78%	9%
139. The Catholic University of America (DC)	45	2.8	86%	74%	75%	70%	60%	4%	1140-1320[2]	N/A	84%	10%
139. Oregon State University*	45	3.1	84%	62%	67%	59%	31%	20%	1080-1310	28%	81%	9%
139. Seattle University†	45	2.6	85%	71%	73%	67%	62%	1%	1130-1320	27%	76%	6%
139. Seton Hall University (NJ)	45	3.0	84%	68%	70%	63%	46%	2%	1150-1310	29%	70%	9%
139. University of Cincinnati*	45	2.9	87%	62%	68%	59%	38%	15%	24-29	24%	73%	9%
139. Univ. of Missouri*	45	3.2	87%	71%	69%	55%	39%	17%	23-29	30%	78%	12%
139. Univ. of Nebraska–Lincoln*	45	3.2	83%	70%	69%	59%	35%	18%	22-29	26%	80%	18%
139. University of St. Thomas (MN)	45	2.5	88%	73%	77%	71%	40%	2%	24-29	21%	82%	12%
147. Michigan Technological University*	44	2.7	84%	70%	68%	61%	47%	13%	1170-1360	32%	74%	8%
147. Samford University (AL)†	44	2.6	89%	79%	76%	65%	63%	4%	23-29	33%	82%	8%
147. San Diego State University*	44	3.0	90%	58%	75%	70%	28%	24%	1110-1310	29%	34%	6%
147. University at Albany–SUNY*	44	2.8	83%	59%	64%	64%	42%	14%	1100-1260	20%	52%	6%
147. University of St. Joseph (CT)†	44	2.2	76%	47%	63%	52%	74%	0%	1030-1210[2]	25%	72%	13%
147. University of Texas–Dallas*	44	2.9	87%	68%	75%	74%	22%	25%	1220-1440	37%	81%	3%
153. George Mason University (VA)*	43	3.1	88%	63%	70%	68%	31%	14%	1120-1320[2]	18%	81%	3%
153. Louisiana State University–Baton Rouge*	43	2.9	84%	67%	67%	55%	41%	17%	23-29	23%	74%	13%
153. Mercer University (GA)	43	2.5	88%	68%	66%	57%	55%	5%	1180-1340	37%	72%	11%
153. The New School (NY)	43	2.9	82%	69%	72%	68%	91%	1%	1150-1360[9]	17%[5]	57%	2%
153. Quinnipiac University (CT)†	43	2.6	87%	69%	77%	73%	45%	2%	1090-1260[2]	20%	72%	4%
153. Thomas Jefferson University (PA)†	43	2.4	83%	64%	64%	53%	65%	4%	1060-1240	25%	58%	3%
153. University of Alabama*	43	3.1	87%	75%	72%	58%	34%	23%	23-31	36%	59%	23%
153. University of Arkansas*	43	3.0	83%	67%	66%	52%	46%	18%	23-29	25%	77%	21%
153. Valparaiso University (IN)†	43	2.8	83%	69%	71%	59%	49%	4%	1070-1270	29%	89%	14%
162. Hofstra University (NY)	42	2.8	81%	70%	63%	54%	48%	2%	1150-1330[2]	28%	63%	12%
162. Kansas State University*	42	3.0	85%	66%	64%	48%	46%	12%	22-28	27%	94%	17%[4]
162. University of Mississippi*	42	3.0	86%	64%	64%	48%	51%	14%	21-29[2]	25%	88%	10%
162. Virginia Commonwealth University*	42	2.9	85%	63%	67%	65%	37%	15%	1070-1260[2]	17%	77%	5%
166. Adelphi University (NY)	41	2.3	82%	60%	70%	66%	45%	2%	1080-1270[9]	26%	74%	8%
166. Belmont University (TN)†	41	2.7	83%	77%	73%	63%	45%	0.1%	24-29	30%	82%	8%
166. Colorado State University*	41	3.1	85%	67%	71%	65%	27%	24%	1070-1280	20%	84%	10%
166. Montclair State University (NJ)*	41	2.2	82%	48%	71%	69%	37%	2%	990-1170[2]	11%	71%	3%
166. Rowan University (NJ)*	41	2.4	85%	59%	72%	61%	39%	1%	1005-1225	N/A	73%	3%
166. Rutgers University–Camden (NJ)*†	41	2.7	86%	52%	58%	52%	42%	8%	1000-1180	15%	71%	4%
166. St. John Fisher College (NY)	41	2.1	86%	63%	73%	67%	44%	1%	1080-1250	24%	64%	8%
166. University of Alabama–Birmingham*	41	2.9	82%	62%	58%	48%	41%	17%	21-29	28%	92%	7%
166. University of Central Florida*	41	2.8	90%	62%	73%	70%	26%	25%	1160-1340	34%	43%	3%
166. University of Hawaii–Manoa*	41	2.8	78%	62%	59%	56%	52%	12%	1055-1240	25%	83%	5%
166. Univ. of Maryland–Baltimore County*	41	3.0	87%	66%	68%	67%	36%	13%	1190-1360	23%	58%	4%
166. University of Rhode Island*	41	2.9	84%	62%	67%	61%	45%	10%	1090-1260[3]	18%	71%	5%
166. Washington State University*	41	3.1	79%	60%	59%	51%	33%	21%	1020-1210	38%[4]	77%	12%
179. Gallaudet University (DC)†	40	2.9	71%	51%	47%	46%	97%	0%	15-20	N/A	57%	N/A
179. Missouri Univ. of Science & Tech–Rolla.*	40	2.7	84%	71%	63%	54%	46%	16%	25-31	40%	84%	11%
179. St. John's University (NY)	40	2.8	83%	60%	61%	58%	32%	5%	1070-1270[2]	21%	73%	4%
179. University of Detroit Mercy†	40	2.2	85%	61%	65%	54%	54%	4%	1050-1250	19%	83%	8%
179. University of Idaho*	40	2.8	80%	57%	59%	53%	55%	9%	1010-1220	18%	77%	9%
179. Univ. of Massachusetts–Lowell*	40	2.5	86%	61%	63%	56%	47%	7%	1150-1320[2]	25%	72%	11%
185. Biola University (CA)	39	2.0	86%	70%	73%	69%	54%	5%	1060-1260	47%	87%	6%
185. Chatham University (PA)†	39	2.3	81%	62%	63%	56%	65%	2%	1040-1250[2]	29%	55%	11%
185. Ohio University*	39	3.0	80%	58%	64%	54%	32%	16%	21-26	17%	78%	4%
185. Pacific University (OR)†	39	2.4	79%	62%	65%	52%	58%	3%	1060-1250	N/A	85%	8%
185. Union University (TN)	39	1.9	86%	69%	70%	57%	75%	0%	23-30	34%	57%	3%
185. University of Houston*	39	2.9	85%	59%	59%	56%	25%	24%	1130-1310	32%	62%	12%
185. University of North Carolina–Wilmington*†	39	2.6	85%	67%	73%	69%	32%	8%	23-27	24%	61%	5%
192. Ball State University[1] (IN)*	38	2.6	81%[8]	58%	62%[6]	57%[4]	41%[4]	6%[4]	1080-1240[4]	18%[4]	62%[4]	10%[4]
192. Misericordia University (PA)†	38	1.9	83%	58%	69%	61%	51%	0%	1040-1200	20%	83%	12%

Note: Key to footnotes, Page 75

Rank School (State) (*Public)	Overall score	Peer assessment score (5.0=highest)	Average first-year student retention rate	2018 graduation rate		Pell recipient grad rate	% of classes under 20 ('18)	% of classes of 50 or more ('18)	SAT/ACT 25th-75th percentile ('18)	Freshmen in top 10% of HS class ('18)	Accept-ance rate ('18)	Average alumni giving rate
				Predicted	Actual							
192. Oklahoma State University*	38	2.9	81%	65%	61%	48%	38%	15%	22-28	27%	74%	9%
192. Seattle Pacific University	38	2.4	82%	61%	68%	59%	54%	3%	1030-1240	1%	90%	4%
192. University of Louisville (KY)*	38	2.8	80%	64%	57%	47%	40%	9%	22-29[3]	24%	73%	9%
197. Bellarmine University (KY)†	37	2.2	78%	66%	67%	63%	52%	1%	22-28	N/A	86%	12%
197. Bethel University (MN)†	37	2.0	86%	73%	75%	67%	55%	2%	22-28	25%	71%	9%
197. Illinois State University*	37	2.5	81%	62%	69%	61%	37%	10%	20-26	N/A	89%	6%
197. Loyola University New Orleans†	37	2.7	80%	69%	61%	50%	46%	2%	22-28	25%[5]	75%	6%
197. Towson University (MD)*†	37	2.5	85%	61%	73%	72%	28%	3%	1060-1200	14%	79%	4%
202. Edgewood College (WI)	36	1.7	79%	58%	63%	63%	85%	0%	20-25	17%	73%	6%
202. Florida Institute of Technology	36	2.4	81%	61%	60%	51%	45%	4%	1150-1340	29%	65%	7%
202. Maryville Univ. of St. Louis	36	1.9	86%	63%	72%	69%	72%	1%	20-26[2]	24%	95%	5%
202. Pace University (NY)	36	2.5	79%	59%	56%	53%	51%	3%	1060-1220[2]	15%	76%	4%
202. Regis University (CO)†	36	2.2	80%	64%	68%	67%	59%	0%	1050-1230	25%	60%	4%
202. Robert Morris University (PA)	36	2.2	82%	57%	64%	54%	40%	4%	1030-1200	15%	85%	7%
202. University of Maine*	36	2.8	76%	61%	60%	51%	39%	16%	1050-1250	18%	92%	7%
202. University of St. Francis (IL)†	36	1.9	79%	52%	62%	54%	64%	0.3%	1030-1190	12%[4]	47%	8%
202. Widener University (PA)	36	2.2	80%	54%	63%	58%	57%	2%	1020-1200	N/A	69%	3%
211. California State University–Fresno*	35	2.5	81%	37%	54%	50%	19%	9%	910-1110	15%	58%	3%
211. Georgia State University*	35	2.9	83%	53%	54%	56%	22%	16%	990-1190[3]	17%[4]	57%	4%
211. Immaculata University (PA)	35	1.8	79%	51%	68%	53%	86%	0%	1018-1223[2]	9%	81%	7%
211. Kent State University (OH)*	35	2.6	81%	53%	57%	48%	52%	9%	20-25	15%	85%	4%
211. Mississippi State University*	35	2.7	80%	66%	58%	42%	37%	15%	22-29	29%	57%	15%
211. University of Hartford (CT)	35	2.5	75%	58%	60%	50%	71%	0.2%	1050-1250[2]	N/A	75%	3%
211. Wilkes University (PA)†	35	2.0	76%	56%	60%	51%	58%	4%	1050-1240	23%	75%	13%

Rank School (State) (*Public)	Overall score	Peer assessment score (5.0=highest)	Average first-year student retention rate	2018 graduation rate Predicted	Actual	Pell recipient grad rate	% of classes under 20 ('18)	% of classes of 50 or more ('18)	SAT/ACT 25th-75th percentile ('18)	Freshmen in top 10% of HS class ('18)	Acceptance rate ('18)	Average alumni giving rate
218. Clarke University (IA)†	34	2.1	73%	59%	63%	62%	70%	0.4%	19-23	17%	82%	15%
218. Florida International University*	34	2.5	89%	50%	58%	61%	19%	26%	1090-1260	25%[5]	59%	3%
218. Gannon University (PA)†	34	2.0	83%	61%	67%	54%	49%	0.4%	1020-1220	20%	81%	7%
218. Hampton University (VA)†	34	2.4	77%	60%	58%	53%	60%	3%	19-24[2]	13%	36%	17%
218. Lipscomb University (TN)	34	2.1	82%	68%	65%	55%	55%	5%	22-29	30%	60%	12%
218. Sacred Heart University (CT)†	34	2.4	83%	66%	70%	60%	37%	1%	1100-1240[2]	11%	60%	9%
218. Texas Tech University*	34	2.9	84%	61%	60%	51%	27%	21%	1070-1240	19%	71%	11%
218. Univ. of Massachusetts–Dartmouth*	34	2.6	73%	53%	56%	50%	51%	10%	990-1190	14%	78%	2%
218. University of New Mexico*	34	2.8	78%	57%	49%	45%	60%	9%	19-25[3]	N/A	52%	N/A
218. Western New England University (MA)†	34	2.0	77%	60%	60%	53%	57%	0.1%	1060-1250[2]	19%	85%	4%
228. Azusa Pacific University (CA)	33	2.1	85%[8]	62%	63%	65%	57%	2%	1020-1240	N/A	69%	5%[4]
228. CUNY–City College*†	33	2.9	87%	51%	43%	44%	33%	3%	950-1190[3]	N/A	38%	12%
228. East Carolina University (NC)*	33	2.4	82%	58%	63%	61%	31%	18%	1030-1180	13%	82%	2%
228. Grand Valley State University[7] (MI)*†	33	2.2	84%	61%	65%	58%	25%	5%	1050-1240	20%	83%	4%
228. Indiana University-Purdue U.–Indianapolis*	33	2.9	74%	52%	48%	41%	39%	10%	1000-1200	15%	81%	7%
228. The Sage Colleges (NY)†	33	2.1	78%	49%	62%	59%	53%	0%	940-1140[2]	11%	93%	8%
228. St. Catherine University[7] (MN)†	33	2.1	82%	63%	60%	58%	58%	2%	20-26	24%	70%[4]	12%[4]
228. University of Indianapolis†	33	2.3	75%	54%	60%	50%	56%	1%	990-1180	18%	81%	12%
228. Univ. of Massachusetts–Boston*	33	2.6	78%	52%	48%	47%	38%	6%	1020-1220[2]	15%	78%	4%
228. U. of North Carolina–Charlotte*	33	2.8	83%	58%	59%	55%	26%	24%	21-26	17%[5]	67%	3%
228. University of Wyoming*	33	2.7	77%	65%	57%	45%	38%	11%	22-28[3]	21%	96%	5%
228. West Virginia University*	33	2.8	78%	59%	58%	47%	35%	20%	21-27	23%	82%	10%
240. Central Michigan University*	32	2.4	77%	58%	62%	53%	32%	7%	1000-1200	17%[4]	69%	6%
240. Harding University (AR)†	32	2.0	84%	69%	67%	54%	55%	6%	22-29	23%	68%	10%
240. Long Island University (NY)	32	2.2	80%[8]	N/A	N/A	N/A	66%	1%	1050-1250	15%	76%	2%
240. Oklahoma City University†	32	2.1	82%	70%	63%	60%	71%	1%	23-29[3]	31%	76%	4%
240. University of Findlay (OH)†	32	1.9	80%	69%	62%	61%	60%	1%	21-26	25%	73%	10%
240. University of Nevada–Reno*	32	2.5	81%	59%	58%	49%	37%	21%	21-26	27%	88%	7%
246. Bowling Green State University (OH)*	31	2.6	77%	56%	55%	43%	44%	10%	20-25	15%	72%	6%
246. George Fox University (OR)†	31	2.0	81%	64%	67%	54%	53%	2%	1020-1230[3]	32%	82%	5%
246. Lesley University (MA)	31	2.1	80%	60%	56%[8]	60%[4]	67%	0%	938-1293	13%	76%	N/A
246. Montana State University*	31	2.6	77%	64%	55%	46%	44%	14%	21-28	21%	82%	8%
246. Nova Southeastern University (FL)	31	2.0	78%	54%	50%	43%	75%	2%	1080-1290	32%	79%	2%
246. University of New England (ME)†	31	2.2	78%	68%	64%	56%	56%	6%	1050-1240[2]	N/A	80%	7%
246. Wayne State University (MI)*	31	2.6	80%	55%	47%	37%	50%	8%	1010-1210	18%	71%	5%
246. Western Michigan University*	31	2.5	79%	55%	N/A	45%	38%	10%	990-1190	10%	81%	4%
254. Baker University (KS)†	30	1.8	77%	59%	59%	60%	71%	0.4%	20-25	19%	88%	8%
254. College of St. Scholastica (MN)†	30	1.9	81%	63%	69%	59%	50%	2%	20-26	17%	66%	4%
254. D'Youville College (NY)†	30	1.7	79%	57%	60%	54%	70%	1%	1030-1200	17%[4]	100%	12%
254. Florida A&M University*	30	2.3	83%	43%	51%	49%	33%	14%	1040-1170	11%	39%	5%
254. Lincoln Memorial University (TN)†	30	1.9	71%	53%	60%	51%	55%	4%	19-25[9]	26%	43%	5%
254. Southern Illinois University–Carbondale*	30	2.4	68%	51%	41%	29%	60%	6%	1020-1300	15%	72%	4%
254. University of Colorado–Denver*	30	2.8	70%	60%	48%	43%	36%	9%	1020-1210	22%[5]	64%	3%
254. University of Montana*	30	2.7	70%	58%	50%	43%	51%	9%	20-26	16%	88%	9%
254. Utah State University*	30	2.6	72%	61%	49%	63%	48%	13%	21-28	21%	89%	5%
263. Daemen College (NY)†	29	1.7	78%	53%	57%	50%	64%	0.3%	1040-1230[2]	21%	54%	3%
263. New Mexico State University*	29	2.6	74%	49%	47%	41%	47%	10%	17-23	22%	66%	6%
263. Old Dominion University (VA)*	29	2.6	80%	51%	52%	48%	36%	10%	990-1200[2]	9%	87%	4%
263. Shenandoah University (VA)	29	1.9	81%	59%	58%	46%	66%	2%	980-1190	25%	70%	5%
263. University of Alabama–Huntsville*	29	2.5	82%	63%	52%	42%	26%	21%	25-31	34%	81%	3%
263. University of Alaska–Fairbanks[1]*	29	2.5	76%[8]	55%	40%[6]	33%[4]	70%[4]	3%[4]	17-25[4]	21%[4]	77%[4]	N/A
263. Univ. of Missouri–Kansas City*	29	2.5	75%	63%	48%	40%	51%	11%	21-28	33%	56%	5%
263. University of North Dakota*	29	2.6	81%	66%	55%	42%	38%	11%	21-27	18%	82%	7%
263. University of South Dakota*	29	2.6	76%	60%	58%	47%	43%	8%	20-25	13%	86%	4%
272. Campbell University (NC)†	28	2.1	73%	56%	51%	42%	61%	4%	19-25	26%	76%	6%
272. Keiser University (FL)†	28	1.6	84%	36%	56%	52%	48%	29%	N/A[2]	N/A	100%	1%
272. Louisiana Tech University*	28	2.5	80%	62%	53%	40%	54%	8%	22-28	25%	63%	8%

Note: Key to footnotes, Page 75

Rank	School (State) (*Public)	Overall score	Peer assessment score (5.0=highest)	Average first-year student retention rate	2018 graduation rate Predicted	Actual	Pell recipient grad rate	% of classes under 20 ('18)	% of classes of 50 or more ('18)	SAT/ACT 25th-75th percentile ('18)	Freshmen in top 10% of HS class ('18)	Acceptance rate ('18)	Average alumni giving rate
272.	Mary Baldwin University (VA)†	28	2.0	67%	44%	47%	45%	64%	1%	950-1130	11%	100%	10%
272.	South Dakota State University*	28	2.5	77%	62%	57%	47%	32%	18%	20-26	16%	92%	7%
272.	Tennessee Technological Univ.*	28	2.2	77%	58%	55%	47%	47%	10%	21-27	27%	76%	6%
272.	University of Memphis*	28	2.5	74%	52%	48%	40%	46%	9%	19-26	14%	84%	6%
272.	U. of North Carolina–Greensboro*	28	2.6	76%	56%	51%	48%	23%	24%	990-1160	14%	84%	6%
272.	University of the Incarnate Word (TX)†	28	2.0	76%	46%	49%	45%	65%	2%	950-1140	16%	88%	4%
281.	Concordia University Wisconsin†	27	2.0	77%	57%	58%	49%	58%	2%	20-26[3]	26%	65%	3%
281.	Dallas Baptist University	27	2.0	74%	61%	54%	41%	68%	2%	20-24	18%	88%	1%
281.	Florida Atlantic University*	27	2.4	79%	51%	52%	52%	31%	16%	1080-1240	12%	59%	2%
281.	Gardner-Webb University (NC)	27	2.0	73%	56%	53%	43%	75%	0%	970-1180	17%	48%	3%
281.	North Carolina A&T State Univ.*	27	2.2	77%	44%	53%	48%	25%	7%	950-1110	12%	61%	9%
281.	North Dakota State University*	27	2.5	79%	67%	58%	50%	33%	24%	21-26[3]	16%	93%	5%
281.	Regent University (VA)	27	1.8	78%	49%	58%	50%	61%	2%	950-1170	11%	84%	2%
281.	Sam Houston State University (TX)*	27	2.2	78%	47%	53%	48%	27%	13%	1000-1140	19%[4]	79%	7%
281.	Univ. of Missouri–St. Louis*	27	2.4	76%	63%	52%	45%	50%	9%	21-27	26%	73%	4%
281.	University of North Florida*†	27	2.4	81%	61%	59%	55%	26%	12%	1120-1280	16%	61%	4%
281.	University of North Texas*	27	2.6	79%	55%	55%	50%	25%	22%	1060-1260	19%	71%	4%
281.	William Carey University (MS)†	27	1.8	83%	51%	51%	51%	77%	0%	21-29[3]	27%	68%	5%

School (State) (*Public)	Peer assessment score (5.0=highest)	Average first-year student retention rate	2018 graduation rate Predicted	Actual	Pell recipient grad rate	% of classes under 20 ('18)	% of classes of 50 or more ('18)	SAT/ACT 25th-75th percentile ('18)	Freshmen in top 10% of HS class ('18)	Acceptance rate ('18)	Average alumni giving rate
SCHOOLS RANKED 293 THROUGH 381 ARE LISTED HERE ALPHABETICALLY											
Andrews University (MI)	1.8	84%	68%	57%	34%	69%	4%	21-27	18%	66%	3%
Arkansas State University*†	2.2	75%	54%	47%	36%	54%	4%	21-27[2]	20%	77%	9%
Augusta University[7] (GA)*	2.0	74%	64%	31%	28%	N/A	N/A	20-26[4]	N/A	76%[4]	3%
Aurora University[1] (IL)†	1.8	71%[8]	51%	56%[6]	N/A	N/A	N/A	19-23[4]	N/A	87%[4]	N/A
Barry University (FL)	2.0	63%	43%	36%	33%	69%	0%	940-1100	N/A	91%	1%
Benedictine University (IL)	2.1	70%	53%	47%	45%	64%	0.4%	980-1190	14%	65%	5%
Boise State University (ID)*	2.6	79%	55%	46%	39%	34%	11%	1030-1220[2]	16%	81%	7%
Cardinal Stritch University (WI)	1.8	73%	45%	51%	35%	70%	1%	18-22[2]	8%	71%	3%
Carson-Newman University (TN)†	2.1	67%	60%	51%	46%	59%	1%	20-26	N/A	66%	6%
Clark Atlanta University	2.2	69%	39%	45%	41%	33%	7%	950-1110	11%	52%	7%
Cleveland State University*	2.2	71%	48%	45%	38%	32%	11%	19-25	15%	88%	5%[4]
Delaware State University*†	2.3	72%	39%	40%	34%	45%	4%	840-1010	9%	49%	10%
Eastern Michigan University*	2.3	73%	51%	45%	36%	40%	3%	970-1200	13%	76%	2%
East Tennessee State University[1]*	2.1	73%[8]	52%	41%[8]	32%[4]	43%[4]	9%[4]	19-26[4]	N/A	85%[4]	N/A
Ferris State University (MI)*†	2.1	78%	52%	50%	41%	52%	3%	940-1170[9]	N/A	81%	2%
Georgia Southern University*	2.4	80%	60%	50%	47%	26%[4]	10%[4]	1060-1200	18%	68%	5%[4]
Grand Canyon University[1] (AZ)	1.8	66%[8]	42%	39%[6]	N/A	N/A	N/A	N/A[2]	N/A	67%[4]	N/A
Husson University (ME)†	1.7	75%	44%	55%	47%	51%	0.2%	930-1140	12%	83%	3%
Indiana State University*	2.5	65%	43%	41%	32%	31%	8%	910-1120	11%	90%	6%
Indiana Univ. of Pennsylvania*	2.1	73%	47%	56%	48%	35%	10%	910-1120[3]	8%	93%	5%
Jackson State University (MS)*	2.0	66%	44%	37%[6]	N/A	39%[4]	10%[4]	17-22	N/A	69%	N/A
Kennesaw State University (GA)*	2.4	79%	55%	43%	45%	27%	13%	1080-1270	16%	58%	2%
Lamar University (TX)*	1.9	63%	42%	27%	21%	38%	10%	950-1100	15%	84%	1%
Liberty University (VA)	1.7	83%	48%	55%	41%	33%	4%	980-1180[3]	24%[5]	56%	1%
Lindenwood University (MO)	1.8	70%	54%	50%	46%	65%	0%	20-25[2]	N/A	88%	5%
Marshall University (WV)*†	2.4	73%	51%	46%	36%	48%	3%	19-25	N/A	91%	4%
Metropolitan State University[1] (MN)*†	1.8	72%[0]	48%	33%[6]	N/A	N/A	N/A	N/A[2]	N/A	56%[4]	N/A
Middle Tennessee State Univ.*	2.2	76%	53%	44%	38%	46%	7%	20-26	N/A	94%	3%
Mississippi College†	2.0	79%	69%	53%	33%	59%	3%	21-28[3]	33%	38%	5%
Missouri State University*†	2.4	78%[8]	60%	54%	45%	26%	13%	21-26	22%	85%	5%
Morgan State University (MD)*	2.2	74%	42%	39%	35%	46%	2%	920-1080	7%	66%	16%
National Louis University (IL)	1.9	65%[8]	46%	40%[6]	N/A	70%	0%	15-18[9]	N/A	86%	N/A
Northern Arizona University*	2.5	75%	55%	52%	42%	30%	17%	19-25[2]	21%	83%	3%

School (State) (*Public)	Peer assessment score (5.0=highest)	Average first-year student retention rate	2018 graduation rate		Pell recipient grad rate	% of classes under 20 ('18)	% of classes of 50 or more ('18)	SAT/ACT 25th-75th percentile ('18)	Freshmen in top 10% of HS class ('18)	Accept-ance rate ('18)	Average alumni giving rate
			Predicted	Actual							
CONTINUED (SCHOOLS RANKED 293 THROUGH 381 ARE LISTED HERE ALPHABETICALLY)											
Northern Illinois University*	2.4	73%	50%	46%	32%	49%	8%	940-1170	12%	54%	4%
Northern Kentucky University*†	2.2	71%	50%	44%	33%	38%	4%	20-26	12%[4]	89%	4%
Oakland University (MI)*	2.2	76%	59%	55%	49%	37%	13%	1010-1240	21%	84%	3%
Our Lady of the Lake University (TX)†	1.8	61%	38%	37%	34%	58%	0%	910-1080	14%	93%	12%
Palm Beach Atlantic University (FL)†	1.7	75%	58%	54%	45%	63%	1%	1000-1220	16%[4]	95%	2%
Portland State University (OR)*	2.6	72%	49%	47%	46%	28%	16%	1010-1230[2]	16%	90%	1%
Roosevelt University (IL)†	2.2	67%	46%	39%	33%	65%	2%	1010-1180	N/A[5]	65%	4%
Southern Illinois University–Edwardsville*†	2.1	74%	58%	47%	37%	48%	8%	21-27	19%	87%	3%
Spalding University[1] (KY)	1.8	72%[8]	43%	45%[6]	N/A	N/A	N/A	18-23[4]	N/A	59%[4]	N/A
Stephen F. Austin State University[1] (TX)*†	2.3	71%[8]	50%	43%[8]	N/A	30%[4]	9%[4]	990-1180[4]	13%[4]	65%[4]	3%[4]
Tennessee State University*	2.1	52%[8]	41%	30%	29%	60%	2%	17-21	N/A	52%	N/A
Texas A&M University–Commerce*	2.2	68%	44%	43%	34%	34%	5%	960-1140	16%	34%	3%
Texas A&M University–Corpus Christi*	2.2	58%	44%	37%	30%	27%	16%	980-1160	14%	87%	4%
Texas A&M Univ.–Kingsville*	2.1	69%	34%	37%	31%	31%	5%	940-1130	14%	89%	1%
Texas Southern University*	2.1	52%	30%	21%	21%	34%	13%	830-990	4%	57%	3%
Texas State University*	2.2	78%	52%	55%	50%	28%	16%	1010-1180	13%	78%	4%
Texas Wesleyan University†	2.1	52%	48%	38%	38%	71%	0%	975-1090	10%	36%	7%
Texas Woman's University*	2.3	77%	44%	43%	36%	30%	11%	970-1160[2]	18%	87%	2%
Touro College (NY)†	1.8	71%	61%	45%	33%	86%	1%	1085-1350[2]	N/A	71%	N/A
Trevecca Nazarene University (TN)	1.7	78%[8]	56%	55%	49%	56%	6%	19-25[3]	22%	64%	5%[4]
Trinity International University (IL)	1.8	64%	51%	46%	43%	83%	0%	20-27[4]	N/A	75%[4]	N/A
University of Akron (OH)*	2.2	73%	49%	45%	31%	45%	7%	19-26	16%	69%	3%
University of Arkansas–Little Rock*	2.4	69%	50%	35%	29%	N/A	N/A	18-25	N/A	65%	N/A
University of Bridgeport (CT)†	1.9	65%	36%	42%	36%	71%	1%	900-1090	6%	57%	4%
University of Central Arkansas*†	2.1	73%	55%	41%	32%	48%	2%	21-27	21%	91%	6%
University of Charleston (WV)†	2.3	65%	53%	46%	23%	53%	1%	18-23[2]	N/A	50%	5%
University of Colorado–Colorado Springs*†	2.7	68%	57%	45%	40%	44%	8%	1010-1210	13%	91%	5%
University of Hawaii–Hilo*†	2.5	67%[8]	46%	41%	36%	55%	2%	17-23	22%	79%	N/A
University of Louisiana–Lafayette*	2.2	75%	55%	45%[6]	35%[4]	35%	9%	21-28	20%	56%	5%[4]
University of Louisiana–Monroe*	2.0	73%	52%	43%	34%	44%	12%	20-25	20%	72%	3%
University of Mary (ND)†	1.8	79%[8]	60%	53%	48%	36%	2%	20-26	N/A	88%	N/A
Univ. of Maryland–Eastern Shore*	2.1	64%	40%	39%	35%	62%	2%	870-1050	N/A	54%	2%
University of Michigan–Flint*†	2.3	72%	53%	46%	39%	53%	2%	980-1200	15%	66%	1%
University of Nebraska–Omaha*	2.6	77%	56%	49%	40%	44%	6%	19-26	17%	82%	5%
University of Nevada–Las Vegas*	2.6	75%	52%	43%	38%	37%	14%	19-24	22%	82%	4%
University of New Orleans*	2.2	65%	53%	37%	31%	45%	9%	20-25	17%	57%	4%
University of Northern Colorado*	2.4	71%	54%	47%	40%	39%	10%	990-1190	12%	91%	3%
University of South Alabama*	2.1	75%	59%	43%	33%	49%	7%	21-27[2]	N/A	79%	N/A
Univ. of Southern Mississippi*	2.3	73%	57%	49%	38%	40%	13%	19-26	N/A	98%	8%
University of Tennessee–Chattanooga*†	2.5	73%	58%	48%	44%	40%	10%	21-27	N/A	76%	4%
University of Texas–Arlington*	2.6	71%	55%	49%	48%	34%	26%	1060-1260	28%	80%	1%
University of Texas–El Paso*	2.5	73%	40%	39%	36%	32%	16%	940-1130[2]	18%	100%	3%
University of Texas–Rio Grande Valley*	2.2	75%[8]	36%	42%[6]	N/A	27%	14%	17-22	22%	81%	0.3%
University of Texas–San Antonio*	2.5	72%	50%	40%	39%	16%	32%	1040-1220	18%	79%	6%
University of Texas–Tyler*†	2.1	62%	54%	45%	41%	38%	11%	1080-1280	12%	78%	0.4%
University of the Cumberlands[1] (KY)	1.8	64%[8]	46%	40%[6]	N/A	N/A	N/A	19-25[4]	11%[4]	74%[4]	N/A
University of Toledo (OH)*	2.4	74%	55%	47%	34%	41%	14%	20-26	20%	94%	5%
University of West Georgia*	2.1	72%	45%	42%	39%	35%	7%	920-1080	N/A	58%	1%
Univ. of Wisconsin–Milwaukee*	2.8	73%	54%	44%	35%	42%	12%	20-25[2]	10%	88%	3%
Valdosta State University (GA)*	2.1	69%	47%	42%	35%	54%	3%	1000-1140	N/A	63%	1%
Washburn University (KS)*†	2.2	71%	53%	36%[6]	24%[4]	49%	3%	18-24	13%	100%	9%
Western Kentucky University*†	2.2	72%	56%	53%	40%	49%	5%	20-27	22%	97%	7%
Wichita State University (KS)*	2.4	72%	58%	47%	34%	45%	11%	20-26[2]	19%	75%	7%
William Woods University (MO)†	1.8	74%	56%	60%	53%	83%	0%	19-25	6%	64%	4%
Wingate University (NC)†	2.0	72%	57%	51%	45%	41%	1%	960-1170	15%	85%	10%
Wright State University (OH)*	2.3	65%	51%	39%	26%	N/A	N/A	18-25	17%	95%	N/A

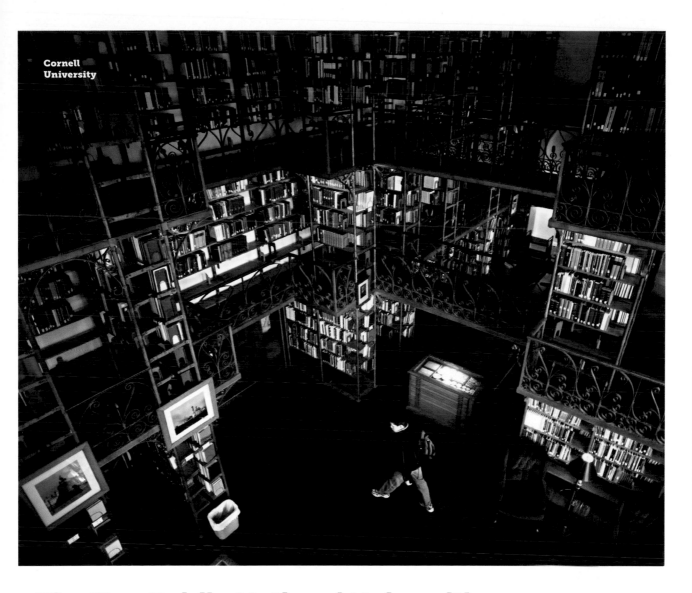

Cornell
University

►The Top Public National Universities

Rank School (State)	Rank School (State)	Rank School (State)	Rank School (State)
1. University of California–Los Angeles	7. University of Florida	16. University of Georgia	24. University of Connecticut
2. University of California–Berkeley	9. University of California–Irvine	17. Ohio State University–Columbus	24. Univ. of Maryland–College Park
3. University of Michigan–Ann Arbor	10. University of California–San Diego	18. Florida State University	24. Univ. of Massachusetts–Amherst
4. University of Virginia	11. University of California–Davis	18. Pennsylvania State U.–Univ. Park	27. Clemson University (SC)
5. Georgia Institute of Technology	12. College of William & Mary (VA)	18. Purdue U.–West Lafayette (IN)	27. Texas A&M University–
5. U. of North Carolina–Chapel Hill	13. Univ. of Wisconsin–Madison	18. University of Pittsburgh	College Station
7. University of California–Santa	14. U. of Illinois–Urbana-Champaign	22. Rutgers U.–New Brunswick (NJ)	27. University of Minnesota–Twin Cities
Barbara	14. University of Texas–Austin	22. University of Washington	30. Virginia Tech"

Footnotes:

1. This school declined to fill out the U.S. News & World Report main statistical survey. Data that appear are from either what the school reported in previous years or from another source, such as the National Center for Education Statistics.
2. SAT and/or ACT not required by school for some or all applicants.
3. In reporting SAT/ACT scores, the school did not include all students for whom it had scores or refused to tell U.S. News whether all students with scores had been included.

4. Data reported to U.S. News in previous years.
5. Data based on fewer than 20% of enrolled freshmen.
6. Some or all data reported to the National Center for Education Statistics.
7. School declined to have a school official verify the accuracy of the information contained in the U.S. News main statistical survey.
8. This rate, normally based on four years of data, is given here for fewer than four years because school didn't report rate for the most recent year or years to U.S. News.

9. SAT and/or ACT may not be required by school for some or all applicants, and in reporting SAT/ACT scores, the school did not include all students for whom it had scores or refused to tell U.S. News whether all students with scores had been included.
N/A means not available.

† School's Carnegie classification has changed. It appeared in a different U.S. News ranking category last year.

Best
National Liberal

Rank School (State) (*Public)	Overall score	Peer assessment score (5.0=highest)	Graduation and retention rank	Average first-year student retention rate	2018 graduation rate			Pell recipient grad rate	Social mobility rank
					Predicted	Actual	Over-performance (+) Under-performance (-)		
1. Williams College (MA)	100	4.7	1	98%	96%	95%	-1	96%	90
2. Amherst College (MA)	96	4.6	3	97%	90%	93%	+3	91%	99
3. Swarthmore College (PA)	93	4.6	3	98%	97%	94%	-3	98%	148
3. Wellesley College (MA)	93	4.5	13	96%	93%	92%	-1	88%	113
5. Pomona College (CA)	92	4.5	1	97%	93%	94%	+1	91%	113
6. Bowdoin College (ME)	91	4.4	3	96%	95%	95%	None	94%	165
7. Carleton College (MN)	90	4.3	6	96%	94%	93%	-1	86%	194
7. Claremont McKenna College (CA)	90	4.3	13	95%	92%	93%	+1	88%	194
7. Middlebury College (VT)	90	4.3	6	96%	95%	91%	-4	89%	185
10. Washington and Lee University (VA)	89	3.9	9	96%	94%	95%	+1	96%	194
11. Colby College (ME)	88	4.1	18	94%	91%	90%	-1	92%	185
11. Haverford College (PA)	88	4.2	13	97%	96%	92%	-4	90%	148
11. Smith College (MA)	88	4.3	30	93%	88%	89%	+1	89%	72
14. Grinnell College (IA)	87	4.2	37	94%	87%	84%	-3	83%	60
14. Hamilton College (NY)	87	3.9	9	94%	93%	93%	None	92%	132
14. Vassar College (NY)	87	4.2	13	96%	88%	92%	+4	92%	34
17. Colgate University (NY)	86	4.1	20	94%	89%	89%	None	92%	179
17. Davidson College (NC)	86	4.2	9	95%	93%	90%	-3	85%	169
17. United States Naval Academy (MD)*	86	4.3	20	97%	89%	91%	+2	N/A	35
17. Wesleyan University (CT)	86	4.1	18	95%	86%	89%	+3	89%	81
21. Bates College (ME)	85	4.1	20	95%	84%	89%	+5	93%	160
21. United States Military Academy[1] (NY)*	85	4.3	37	95%[8]	84%	85%[6]	+1	N/A	35
23. Harvey Mudd College (CA)	84	4.4	6	97%	98%	92%	-6	94%	144
23. University of Richmond (VA)	84	4.0	30	93%	84%	87%	+3	88%	138
25. Barnard College (NY)	82	4.0	13	95%	89%	92%	+3	92%	84
25. Macalester College (MN)	82	4.0	24	94%	89%	90%	+1	85%	144
27. Bryn Mawr College (PA)	81	4.1	42	93%	89%	87%	-2	86%	99
27. College of the Holy Cross (MA)	81	3.6	9	96%	85%	92%	+7	91%	121
27. Colorado College	81	3.9	24	96%	89%	89%	None	88%	200
27. Kenyon College (OH)	81	3.9	24	92%	87%	89%	+2	83%	207
27. Soka University of America (CA)	81	2.6	20	94%	81%	90%	+9	85%	9
32. Mount Holyoke College (MA)	79	3.9	42	91%	83%	83%	None	83%	148
33. Oberlin College (OH)	78	3.9	40	90%	90%	86%	-4	76%	210
33. Scripps College (CA)	78	3.9	32	92%	91%	88%	-3	97%	175
35. Bucknell University (PA)	77	3.9	24	93%	90%	88%	-2	85%	200
35. Pitzer College (CA)	77	3.8	37	93%	81%	84%	+3	78%	185
35. Thomas Aquinas College (CA)	77	2.8	42	92%	72%	86%	+14	80%	14
38. Franklin and Marshall College (PA)	76	3.7	40	92%	86%	83%	-3	86%	137
39. Lafayette College (PA)	75	3.6	24	94%	89%	87%	-2	88%	194
39. Occidental College (CA)	75	3.8	42	91%	83%	85%	+2	87%	90
39. Skidmore College (NY)	75	3.6	32	92%	81%	86%	+5	95%	160
39. United States Air Force Academy (CO)*	75	4.2	57	94%	91%	82%	-9	N/A	35
43. Denison University (OH)	74	3.5	57	89%	79%	85%	+6	83%	99
43. The University of the South (TN)	74	3.6	64	89%	78%	84%	+6	85%	132
45. Union College (NY)	73	3.4	32	93%	87%	87%	None	91%	127
46. Berea College (KY)	72	3.5	135	83%	50%	63%	+13	61%	14
46. Connecticut College	72	3.6	53	90%	85%	81%	-4	95%	148
46. DePauw University (IN)	72	3.5	53	92%	78%	84%	+6	79%	148
46. Dickinson College (PA)	72	3.5	46	91%	84%	84%	None	97%	179
46. Furman University (SC)	72	3.6	57	91%	81%	80%	-1	72%	207
46. Trinity College (CT)	72	3.6	46	90%	90%	84%	-6	87%	194
46. Whitman College (WA)	72	3.5	32	93%	89%	87%	-2	87%	210

Note: Key to footnotes, Page 81.

Arts Colleges

Faculty resources rank	% of classes under 20 ('18)	% of classes of 50 or more ('18)	Student/ faculty ratio ('18)	Selectivity rank	SAT/ACT 25th-75th percentile ('18)	Freshmen in top 10% of HS class ('18)	Acceptance rate ('18)	Financial resources rank	Average alumni giving rate
5	77%	2%	7/1	1	32-35	89%	13%	2	51%
19	71%	4%	7/1	6	31-34	88%	13%	7	47%
16	74%	3%	8/1	1	1380-1550	90%	9%	7	36%
34	67%	0.4%	8/1	8	1330-1520	83%	20%	6	47%
23	70%	1%	8/1	1	1400-1540	91%	8%	7	25%
34	70%	2%	9/1	13	1300-1510[2]	80%	10%	13	48%
7	70%	0.3%	9/1	8	31-34	79%	20%	28	46%
4	81%	2%	8/1	20	31-34	78%[5]	9%	14	35%
13	66%	1%	8/1	8	1330-1500	80%	17%	4	37%
1	75%	0%	8/1	7	31-34	83%	21%	27	43%
5	74%	1%	10/1	8	1350-1510[2]	79%	13%	18	41%
16	78%	1%	9/1	1	1370-1530	95%	19%	18	37%
16	70%	4%	8/1	15	1320-1490[2]	72%	31%	16	30%
10	65%	0%	9/1	15	30-34	68%	24%	20	35%
9	76%	0.2%	9/1	8	1350-1510	81%	21%	25	41%
66	67%	0%	8/1	18	1370-1510	61%	25%	15	27%
13	71%	2%	9/1	13	31-34	77%	25%	28	41%
29	69%	0%	9/1	18	1290-1450	73%	19%	31	42%
86	68%	0%	8/1	38	1150-1370	57%	9%	2	15%
23	73%	3%	8/1	22	1320-1500[2]	57%	17%	42	34%
23	72%	1%	10/1	27	1290-1460[2]	55%	18%	42	40%
56	97%[4]	0%[4]	7/1[4]	68	1185-1400[4]	46%[4]	10%[4]	10	32%[4]
108	57%	5%	8/1	1	1490-1560	87%	14%	16	23%
11	70%	0.1%	8/1	24	1290-1460	56%	30%	20	23%
34	75%	7%	9/1	20	1330-1500	84%[5]	14%	49	22%
43	73%	0%	10/1	22	29-33	63%	41%	51	35%
56	72%	3%	9/1	24	1300-1500[2]	59%	34%	25	31%
73	60%	2%	10/1	31	1270-1420[2]	58%	38%	51	45%
12	73%	0%	10/1	15	29-33[2]	75%	15%	20	22%
19	80%	1%	10/1	24	29-33	55%	36%	33	30%
2	94%	0%	8/1	61	1180-1410	33%	39%	1	24%
29	77%	2%	9/1	31	1290-1500[2]	47%	51%	42	32%
13	78%	1%	9/1	27	1280-1490	53%	36%	42	27%
32	77%	0%	9/1	27	1300-1480	69%[5]	24%	31	18%
86	52%	1%	9/1	31	1250-1420	58%	33%	33	27%
43	69%	0%	10/1	53	30-33[2]	62%	13%	33	23%
23	100%	0%	11/1	64	1220-1400	20%[5]	78%	79	58%
43	68%	1%	9/1	31	1260-1440[2]	59%	35%	33	23%
66	62%	1%	10/1	41	1250-1435	52%	29%	38	29%
73	71%	0%	10/1	31	1270-1450	53%	37%	56	18%
34	75%	1%	8/1	48	1223-1400[2]	38%	27%	47	21%
142	66%	0.1%	8/1	64	28-33[3]	53%	11%	4	13%
34	70%	0.2%	9/1	38	1210-1380[2]	64%	34%	65	17%
66	60%	0.3%	10/1	55	25-31[2]	30%	65%	51	32%
80	58%	1%	10/1	27	1270-1430[2]	61%	39%	49	29%
51	79%	0.4%	10/1	105	22-27	22%	38%	28	16%
51	75%	1%	9/1	68	1290-1430[2]	49%	38%	38	26%
43	68%	0%	9/1	64	1120-1340	45%	63%	62	23%
48	76%	0%	9/1	47	1200-1390[2]	41%	49%	62	25%
34	67%	0%	10/1	43	28-32[2]	41%	61%	56	22%
34	72%	0.4%	9/1	64	1300-1460[2]	46%	34%	33	25%
73	68%	0%	9/1	31	29-32[2]	52%	50%	51	29%

What Is a National Liberal Arts College?

THE COUNTRY'S 223 liberal arts colleges emphasize undergraduate education and award at least half of their degrees in the arts and sciences, which include such disciplines as English, the biological and physical sciences, history, foreign languages, and the visual and performing arts but exclude professional disciplines such as business, education and nursing. There are 199 private and 24 public liberal arts colleges; none are for-profit. The top public colleges appear below.

The Top Public Colleges

Rank School (State)

1. **United States Naval Academy** (MD)
2. **United States Military Academy** (NY)
3. **United States Air Force Academy** (CO)
4. **Virginia Military Institute**
5. **St. Mary's College of Maryland**
6. **New College of Florida**
7. **Massachusetts College of Liberal Arts**
8. **University of Minnesota–Morris**
8. **University of North Carolina–Asheville**

Rank	School (State) (*Public)	Overall score	Peer assessment score (5.0=highest)	Average first-year student retention rate	2018 graduation rate Predicted	2018 graduation rate Actual	Pell recipient grad rate	% of classes under 20 ('18)	% of classes of 50 or more ('18)	SAT/ACT 25th-75th percentile ('18)	Freshmen in top 10% of HS class ('18)	Acceptance rate ('18)	Average alumni giving rate
53.	Centre College (KY)	71	3.5	91%	82%	81%	85%	58%	0%	27-32	55%	73%	43%
53.	Gettysburg College (PA)	71	3.5	91%	90%	82%	86%	70%	0.3%	1270-1420	62%	45%	24%
53.	Rhodes College (TN)	71	3.6	91%	83%	85%	79%	71%	0%	28-31	54%	45%	30%
53.	Wabash College (IN)	71	3.4	88%	72%	71%	65%	76%	1%	1100-1330	29%	65%	40%
57.	Spelman College (GA)	70	3.7	90%	66%	75%	69%	61%	1%	1080-1220	10%	39%	30%
58.	Agnes Scott College (GA)	69	3.4	84%	69%	69%	62%	71%	0%	1090-1320[2]	28%	70%	30%
58.	Lawrence University (WI)	69	3.4	88%	78%	80%	71%	81%	2%	27-31[2]	35%	62%	31%
58.	St. Lawrence University (NY)	69	3.3	90%	80%	82%	72%	62%	1%	1180-1350[2]	36%	46%	24%
58.	Wheaton College (IL)	69	3.2	94%	82%	87%	84%	67%	2%	1210-1420	45%	83%	19%
62.	Bard College (NY)	68	3.5	85%	86%	75%	74%	79%	0%	1248-1420[2]	41%	65%	26%
62.	St. Olaf College (MN)	68	3.7	92%	83%	86%	80%	50%	3%	25-32	41%	50%	21%
64.	Hillsdale College (MI)	67	2.5	93%	84%	87%	N/A	79%	0.4%	29-32	N/A	36%	15%
64.	St. John's College (MD)	67	3.4	85%	81%	76%	76%	86%	1%	1200-1460[2]	22%	58%	21%
66.	College of Wooster (OH)	66	3.4	87%	79%	74%	75%	71%	0.4%	25-30	45%	54%	18%
66.	Knox College (IL)	66	3.2	85%	68%	75%	71%	76%	0%	1090-1350[2]	32%	74%	29%
68.	Cornell College (IA)	65	3.1	81%	70%	74%	78%	77%	0%	23-30[2]	22%	61%	17%
68.	Reed College[1] (OR)	65	3.8	88%[8]	88%	80%[6]	N/A	N/A	N/A	1310-1500[4]	N/A	36%[4]	N/A
68.	Sarah Lawrence College (NY)	65	3.4	84%	80%	73%	75%	95%	1%	1240-1420[2]	33%	56%	17%
68.	Willamette University (OR)	65	3.2	86%	75%	74%	73%	76%	0%	1170-1350[2]	46%	84%	11%
72.	Hobart & William Smith Colleges (NY)	64	3.3	86%	79%	78%	77%	64%	0%	1203-1360[2]	34%	57%	23%
72.	Kalamazoo College (MI)	64	3.4	90%	79%	79%	77%	58%	1%	1140-1370[2]	54%	73%	25%
72.	Lewis & Clark College (OR)	64	3.4	83%	77%	75%	76%	67%	1%	1230-1390[2]	37%	74%	16%
72.	Muhlenberg College (PA)	64	3.1	91%	80%	82%	80%	74%	1%	1170-1360[2]	40%	62%	18%
72.	St. John's College (NM)	64	3.3	77%	70%	63%	56%	98%	0%	1200-1410[2]	27%	67%	14%
72.	Transylvania University (KY)	64	2.9	84%	74%	76%	73%	76%	0%	24-30[2]	30%	89%	29%
72.	Virginia Military Institute*	64	3.2	88%	71%	78%	71%	76%	0.1%	1100-1310[3]	20%	51%	28%
72.	Wofford College (SC)	64	3.2	88%	81%	81%	83%	63%	0%	1180-1350[2]	38%	64%	20%
80.	Earlham College (IN)	63	3.3	83%	71%	64%	55%	78%	2%	1160-1380[2]	40%	65%	23%
80.	Illinois Wesleyan University	63	3.1	92%	78%	79%	71%	70%	2%	24-29	34%	59%	19%
82.	Allegheny College (PA)	62	3.2	82%	75%	74%	70%	68%	1%	1120-1340[2]	28%	64%	22%
82.	Beloit College (WI)	62	3.1	84%	75%	79%	89%	72%	0%	21-29[2]	15%	56%	18%
82.	College of St. Benedict (MN)	62	3.0	88%	74%	80%	75%	62%	1%	22-27	32%	83%	16%
82.	College of the Atlantic (ME)	62	2.8	80%	73%	67%	71%	96%	0%	1210-1400[2]	35%	67%	34%
82.	Juniata College (PA)	62	2.8	84%	73%	78%	68%	75%	1%	1080-1320[2]	31%	70%	23%
82.	Ursinus College (PA)	62	3.0	86%	74%	79%	72%	74%	0.2%	1140-1320[2]	20%	71%	17%
82.	Wheaton College (MA)	62	3.3	87%	76%	78%	85%	65%	1%	1180-1350[2]	21%	70%	17%
89.	Bennington College (VT)	61	2.9	78%	77%	74%	74%	87%	0.4%	1230-1390[2]	55%[5]	57%	18%
89.	Gustavus Adolphus College (MN)	61	3.2	88%	74%	77%	77%	63%	0.2%	24-30[2]	32%	66%	19%
89.	University of Puget Sound (WA)	61	3.3	85%	78%	76%	69%	63%	0.3%	1130-1350[2]	28%	88%	12%
92.	Augustana College (IL)	60	3.1	88%	68%	74%	69%	67%	0.2%	22-29[2]	28%	72%	24%
92.	Hendrix College (AR)	60	3.3	84%	80%	71%	61%	73%	0%	26-32	45%	72%	22%
92.	Lake Forest College (IL)	60	3.0	85%	67%	69%	74%	62%	0%	1110-1310[2]	27%	58%	23%
92.	Ohio Wesleyan University	60	3.1	79%	71%	67%	64%	76%	0%	22-28[2]	25%	69%	21%
92.	Southwestern University (TX)	60	3.0	85%	72%	74%	69%	60%	1%	1130-1330	34%	45%	27%
92.	St. John's University (MN)	60	3.2	87%	72%	75%	62%	62%	1%	22-28	12%	80%	22%
92.	St. Mary's College of Maryland*	60	3.0	86%	72%	80%	84%	75%	0.3%	1060-1290	19%	80%	11%
92.	Washington and Jefferson Col. (PA)	60	3.0	80%	70%	73%	67%	74%	0%	1130-1320[2]	32%	48%[4]	15%
100.	Luther College (IA)	59	3.1	84%	75%	79%	63%	59%	0.4%	23-29	27%	63%	24%
100.	Principia College (IL)	59	2.1	89%	69%	74%	N/A	95%	0%	1028-1300	22%[5]	92%	24%
102.	Hollins University (VA)	58	2.8	77%	60%	55%	54%	88%	0%	1070-1280	23%	64%	27%
102.	New College of Florida*	58	3.1	80%	75%	60%	60%	79%	0%	1220-1420	37%	77%	18%
102.	Saint Mary's College (IN)	58	2.9	86%	75%	78%	79%	54%	0.2%	1050-1260[2]	27%	82%	31%
105.	Elizabethtown College (PA)	57	2.7	86%	66%	73%	68%	70%	0%	1070-1290	30%	76%	16%
105.	Hanover College (IN)	57	2.8	80%	65%	72%	69%	70%	1%	22-27[2]	27%	79%	18%
105.	Hope College (MI)	57	3.0	89%	74%	78%	71%	61%	3%	1110-1330	39%	76%	17%
105.	Ripon College (WI)	57	2.7	79%	60%	68%	63%	66%	2%	20-27[2]	17%	69%	26%

Note: Key to footnotes, Page 81.

Between classes at
Middlebury College

Rank School (State) (*Public)	Overall score	Peer assessment score (5.0=highest)	Average first-year student retention rate	2018 graduation rate Predicted	2018 graduation rate Actual	Pell recipient grad rate	% of classes under 20 ('18)	% of classes of 50 or more ('18)	SAT/ACT 25th-75th percentile ('18)	Freshmen in top 10% of HS class ('18)	Acceptance rate ('18)	Average alumni giving rate
105. Washington College (MD)	57	2.9	85%	75%	68%	66%	81%	0%	1080-1270	33%	64%	16%
105. Whittier College (CA)	57	3.1	78%	58%	66%	62%	58%	0.2%	1030-1213[2]	18%	76%	20%
111. Goucher College (MD)	56	3.1	79%	71%	71%	70%	71%	0%	1040-1290[2]	18%	80%	19%
111. Hampden-Sydney College (VA)	56	3.0	83%	68%	65%	67%	72%	0%	1050-1250	11%	59%	23%
111. Randolph-Macon College (VA)	56	3.0	83%	63%	66%	60%	65%	0%	1020-1240	15%	67%	36%
114. Grove City College (PA)	55	2.5	90%	72%	82%	N/A	55%	3%	1085-1275	33%	79%	19%
114. St. Anselm College (NH)	55	2.7	89%	72%	77%	76%	65%	1%	1120-1310[2]	27%	77%	18%
114. Westminster College (PA)	55	2.7	79%	61%	72%	66%	67%	1%	1000-1225	13%[5]	66%	15%
117. Austin College (TX)	54	3.0	82%	70%	70%	69%	61%	0.3%	1130-1330[2]	24%	55%	N/A
117. College of Idaho	54	2.6	77%	60%	70%	69%	66%	1%	1030-1213[2]	24%[4]	49%	28%
117. Drew University (NJ)	54	2.9	85%	66%	62%	58%	66%	0%	1110-1310[2]	21%	69%	17%
117. Linfield College (OR)	54	2.7	82%	65%	65%	57%	84%	0.3%	1020-1200[2]	30%[4]	81%	12%
117. Lycoming College (PA)	54	2.6	78%	56%	67%	75%	67%	1%	1010-1198[2]	21%	66%	17%
117. Susquehanna University (PA)	54	3.0	85%	65%	70%	74%	53%	1%	1098-1260[2]	21%	72%	12%
117. Westmont College (CA)	54	2.7	82%	78%	74%	81%	67%	2%	1110-1370	28%	62%	13%
124. Houghton College (NY)	53	2.4	87%[8]	67%	71%	70%	71%	1%	1030-1280[2]	29%	95%	17%
124. Millsaps College (MS)	53	3.0	79%	75%	64%	53%	79%	0%	22-28[3]	N/A	59%	16%
124. Monmouth College (IL)	53	2.7	72%	53%	58%	53%	81%	0%	980-1170	22%	69%	18%
124. St. Michael's College (VT)	53	2.8	86%	73%	77%	69%	55%	1%	1140-1320[2]	24%	83%	19%
124. Stonehill College (MA)	53	2.7	88%	74%	79%	69%	51%	0%	1130-1300[2]	20%	70%	15%
124. Wells College (NY)	53	2.6	74%	55%	61%	55%	82%	0%	1000-1230[2]	21%	79%	24%
130. Coe College (IA)	52	2.9	77%	67%	65%	61%	72%	1%	22-28	28%	67%	15%
130. Roanoke College (VA)	52	2.9	81%	66%	67%	63%	59%	0%	1040-1230	18%	72%	16%
132. Concordia College–Moorhead (MN)	51	2.7	83%	74%	75%	66%	53%	0.2%	21-27	22%	61%	16%
132. Randolph College (VA)	51	2.6	71%	65%	59%	50%	86%	0%	960-1190	12%	87%	20%
132. Saint Vincent College (PA)	51	2.3	85%	62%	76%	74%	53%	0%	1030-1230	22%	68%	16%
132. Salem College (NC)	51	2.3	79%[8]	57%	60%	58%	90%	0%	21-28	44%	41%	12%
136. Illinois College	50	2.6	78%	62%	70%	64%	62%	0%	990-1170[2]	15%	76%	20%
136. Marlboro College (VT)	50	2.3	68%[8]	74%	58%	45%	100%	0%	1060-1360[2]	N/A	92%	14%
136. Moravian College (PA)	50	2.5	80%	58%	68%	62%	61%	1%	1050-1200[3]	17%	73%	18%
136. Simpson College (IA)	50	2.5	79%	63%	70%	63%	79%	1%	20-25	22%	84%	13%
140. Albion College (MI)	49	2.8	79%	68%	64%	61%	59%	0%	1010-1240	N/A	68%	12%
140. Birmingham-Southern College (AL)	49	2.8	81%	72%	68%	48%	69%	0.3%	22-28[2]	20%	57%	16%
140. Eckerd College (FL)	49	2.9	81%	68%	68%	56%	52%	0.2%	1080-1280	N/A	68%	N/A
140. Massachusetts Col. of Liberal Arts*	49	2.5	74%	49%	56%	47%	74%	0%	990-1230	23%	74%	6%
140. Presbyterian College (SC)	49	2.8	80%	70%	65%	59%	65%	0.3%	1010-1210[2]	21%	69%	18%
145. Franklin College (IN)	48	2.6	76%	55%	60%	52%	72%	0%	980-1170	13%	75%	17%
145. St. Norbert College (WI)	48	2.6	84%	70%	71%	58%	41%	0%	22-27	26%	78%	16%
145. Wesleyan College (GA)	48	2.9	74%	49%	52%	39%	77%	0%	930-1110	19%	48%	22%
148. Covenant College (GA)	47	2.3	86%	66%	71%	70%	57%	2%	23-30	28%	97%	12%
148. Emory and Henry College (VA)	47	2.7	73%	57%	60%	47%	75%	1%	980-1160	17%	69%	20%
148. Meredith College (NC)	47	2.6	79%	60%	61%	54%	70%	0%	1000-1200	17%	63%	19%
148. University of Minnesota–Morris*	47	2.7	78%	68%	66%	55%	68%	2%	22-27	31%	63%	10%
148. U. of North Carolina–Asheville*	47	3.1	76%	63%	63%	66%	47%	1%	1060-1250	17%	82%	5%
148. Wartburg College (IA)	47	2.7	80%	70%	67%	56%	54%	2%	20-26	22%	76%	21%
154. Guilford College (NC)	46	3.0	69%	54%	59%	53%	72%	0%	17-24[2]	12%	64%	8%
154. Morehouse College (GA)	46	3.4	80%	58%	54%	48%	53%[4]	0.2%[4]	1010-1210	2%	58%	16%[4]
154. Sweet Briar College (VA)	46	2.2	57%	69%	46%	48%	92%	1%	990-1210[2]	22%	76%	34%
157. Centenary College of Louisiana	45	2.4	75%	66%	60%	51%	75%	0%	21-28	23%	60%	11%
157. Georgetown College (KY)	45	2.5	68%	61%	58%	45%	83%	0%	20-26	17%	48%	22%
157. Westminster College (MO)	45	2.5	77%	62%	58%	48%	78%	0%	20-25	20%	94%	17%
160. Central College[1] (IA)	44	2.6	80%[8]	67%	67%[6]	N/A	N/A	N/A	21-26[4]	N/A	70%[4]	N/A
160. Hartwick College (NY)	44	2.6	72%	61%	58%	58%	66%	1%	1070-1190[2]	8%[4]	80%	14%
160. Warren Wilson College (NC)	44	2.7	62%	63%	52%	54%	76%	0%	22-28[2]	13%	83%	12%
160. Wittenberg University (OH)	44	2.8	74%	65%	62%	47%	57%	1%	22-28[2]	16%	90%	14%

School (State) (*Public)	Peer assessment score (5.0=highest)	Average first-year student retention rate	2018 graduation rate		Pell recipient grad rate	% of classes under 20 ('18)	% of classes of 50 or more ('18)	SAT/ACT 25th-75th percentile ('18)	Freshmen in top 10% of HS class ('18)	Acceptance rate ('18)	Average alumni giving rate
			Predicted	Actual							
SCHOOLS RANKED 164 THROUGH 215 ARE LISTED HERE ALPHABETICALLY											
Albright College (PA)	2.5	72%	49%	51%	46%	59%	1%	1023-1200[2]	14%	62%	8%
Allen University[1] (SC)	1.9	41%[8]	25%	20%[6]	N/A	N/A	N/A	N/A[2]	N/A	N/A	N/A
Aquinas College (MI)†	2.4	78%	60%	61%	53%	72%	0.2%	1010-1230	N/A	69%	11%
Ave Maria University (FL)	2.1	70%	65%	57%[6]	N/A	65%	0%	1050-1260[3]	N/A	83%	N/A
Bennett College (NC)†	2.2	49%	31%	32%	32%	66%	1%	800-1000	3%	96%	18%
Bethany College (WV)	2.3	65%	47%	34%	22%	88%	0.4%	890-1130	5%	91%	14%
Bethany Lutheran College (MN)	2.1	80%	63%	55%	47%	67%	1%	19-25	4%	78%	15%
Bethune-Cookman University (FL)	2.3	64%	30%	34%	33%	49%	3%	850-1010	3%	79%	5%
Blackburn College (IL)†	2.2	64%	49%	52%	47%	79%	0.4%	940-1140	10%	54%	12%
Bloomfield College[1] (NJ)	2.1	66%[8]	29%	31%[8]	30%[4]	80%[4]	0%[4]	840-1040[4]	10%[4]	64%[4]	7%[4]
Brewton-Parker College[1] (GA)†	1.9	39%[8]	40%	20%[6]	N/A	N/A	N/A	870-1040[4]	N/A	99%[4]	N/A
Bridgewater College (VA)	2.4	75%	57%	64%	52%	47%	0%	980-1170	14%	66%	13%
Bryn Athyn Col. of New Church (PA)	1.8	66%[8]	54%	46%	50%	88%	0%	996-1203	N/A	89%	N/A
Cheyney U. of Pennsylvania[1]*	1.8	54%[8]	29%	20%[6]	N/A	N/A	N/A	N/A	N/A	39%[4]	N/A
Chowan University (NC)†	2.0	49%	29%	29%	27%	51%	1%	810-1000	2%	59%	10%
Dillard University[1] (LA)	2.6	72%[8]	36%	39%[8]	38%[4]	52%[4]	1%[4]	18-21[4]	12%[4]	41%[4]	21%[4]
East-West University[1] (IL)	1.7	41%[8]	15%	12%[6]	N/A	N/A	N/A	15-19[4]	N/A	41%[4]	N/A
Emmanuel College (MA)	2.4	78%	65%	66%	64%	42%	0%	1100-1280[2]	16%	77%	16%
Fisk University (TN)	2.8	80%	50%	44%	32%	71%	0.4%	17-23	19%	72%	31%
Fort Lewis College (CO)*	2.6	63%	53%	44%	39%	44%	2%	18-24	11%	91%	3%
Gordon College (MA)	2.4	84%	72%	69%	64%	62%	3%	1050-1285[3]	23%	75%	11%
Johnson C. Smith University (NC)	2.3	68%	39%	47%[8]	34%[4]	70%	0%	810-980	N/A	46%	15%[4]
Judson College[1] (AL)	2.1	65%[8]	43%	35%[6]	N/A	N/A	N/A	18-25[4]	N/A	51%[4]	N/A
The King's College (NY)	2.5	74%[8]	65%	51%	49%	41%	3%	1120-1310	N/A	55%	3%[4]
Lane College (TN)†	2.1	55%[8]	19%	22%[6]	N/A	N/A	N/A	N/A[2]	N/A	N/A	N/A
Louisiana State University–Alexandria*	2.1	58%	45%	29%	25%	55%	3%	18-22	9%	73%	3%
Lyon College (AR)	2.5	66%	61%	51%	44%	68%	0%	21-28	24%	50%	8%
Mansfield University of Pennsylvania*†	2.0	73%	44%	52%	51%	53%	3%	950-1130[2]	8%	92%	N/A
Marymount California University	3.0	59%	49%	32%	36%	47%	1%	935-1198[2]	N/A	85%	0.4%
Marymount Manhattan College (NY)	2.5	73%	65%	48%	40%	77%	0%	1030-1220	N/A	78%	6%
Oglethorpe University (GA)	3.0	76%	62%	54%	56%	55%	0%	1110-1290	23%	62%	10%
Pine Manor College (MA)	1.9	54%	39%	46%	50%	84%	0%	740-915[2]	N/A	77%	4%[4]
Providence Christian College[1] (CA)	1.9	66%[8]	60%	65%[6]	N/A	N/A	N/A	2-9[4]	N/A	91%[4]	N/A
Purchase College–SUNY*	2.6	82%	57%	63%	58%	63%	4%	1060-1270[2]	N/A	42%	3%
Rust College (MS)†	2.1	66%	22%	30%	31%	55%	0%	14-15	N/A	53%	N/A
Shepherd University (WV)*	2.3	65%	44%	48%	40%	62%	1%	970-1160	N/A	89%	6%
Southern Virginia University[1]	2.0	75%[8]	50%	30%[6]	N/A	N/A	N/A	14-26[4]	N/A	56%[4]	N/A
Spring Hill College (AL)	2.3	77%	61%	59%	44%	65%	1%	20-25	19%	66%	16%
Stillman College (AL)	2.5	64%[8]	33%	23%[6]	N/A	N/A	N/A	N/A	N/A	40%	13%
Talladega College (AL)†	2.2	63%	21%	24%	24%	46%	12%	20-24	N/A	47%[4]	11%
Tougaloo College (MS)	2.3	71%	38%	35%	37%	75%	0.4%	16-23	28%	91%	25%
University of Pikeville (KY)	2.1	58%	42%	30%	24%	63%	2%	18-24	13%	100%	3%
Univ. of Science and Arts of Okla.[1]*	2.4	75%[8]	50%	37%[6]	N/A	N/A	N/A	19-24[4]	17%[4]	48%[4]	N/A
University of South Carolina–Beaufort[1]*†	2.4	58%[8]	45%	25%[6]	N/A	57%[4]	3%[4]	930-1090[4]	11%[4]	64%[4]	N/A
University of the West[1] (CA)†	2.1	69%[8]	49%	50%[6]	N/A	N/A	N/A	N/A[2]	N/A	N/A	N/A
University of Virginia–Wise*	2.5	68%	46%	50%	50%	78%	1%	950-1130	17%	77%	7%
Univ. of Wisconsin–Parkside*	2.1	72%	45%	38%	31%	43%	5%	18-23[2]	12%	87%	1%
University of Wisconsin–Superior*†	2.0	69%	53%	36%	31%	61%	2%	19-24	8%	74%	4%
Virginia Union University	2.1	61%	30%	33%	33%	45%	1%	782-970[2]	7%	57%	8%
Virginia Wesleyan University	2.5	63%	52%	52%	45%	85%	0.3%	980-1180	10%	70%	7%
Williams Baptist University (AR)†	1.8	58%	42%	35%	28%	64%	0%	18-22	11%	56%	4%
Young Harris College (GA)	2.3	69%	51%	40%	33%	71%	0.3%	930-1130	8%	64%	8%

Footnotes:

1. This school declined to fill out the U.S. News & World Report main statistical survey. Data that appear are from either what the school reported in previous years or from another source, such as the National Center for Education Statistics.
2. SAT and/or ACT not required by school for some or all applicants.
3. In reporting SAT/ACT scores, the school did not include all students for whom it had scores or refused to tell U.S. News whether all students with scores had been included.

4. Data reported to U.S. News in previous years.
5. Data based on fewer than 20% of enrolled freshmen.
6. Some or all data reported to the National Center for Education Statistics.
7. School declined to have a school official verify the accuracy of the information contained in the U.S. News main statistical survey.
8. This rate, normally based on four years of data, is given here for fewer than four years because school didn't report rate for the most recent year or years to U.S. News.

9. SAT and/or ACT may not be required by school for some or all applicants, and in reporting SAT/ACT scores, the school did not include all students for whom it had scores or refused to tell U.S. News whether all students with scores had been included.
N/A means not available.

† School's Carnegie classification has changed. It appeared in a different U.S. News ranking category last year.

Best Regional Universities

What Is a Regional University?

LIKE THE NATIONAL UNIVERSITIES, the institutions that appear here provide a full range of undergraduate majors and master's programs; the difference is that they offer few, if any, doctoral programs. The 605 universities in this category are not ranked nationally but rather against their peer group in one of four regions – North, South, Midwest and West – because in general they tend to draw students most heavily from surrounding states.

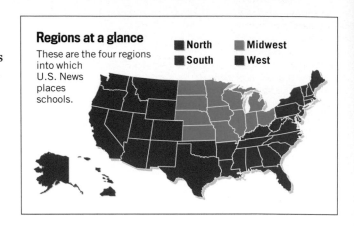

Regions at a glance
These are the four regions into which U.S. News places schools.

■ North   ■ Midwest
■ South   ■ West

NORTH ▶

Rank School (State) (*Public)	Overall score	Peer assessment score (5.0=highest)	Average first-year student retention rate	2018 graduation rate		% of classes under 20 ('18)	% of classes of 50 or more ('18)	Student/ faculty ratio ('18)	SAT/ACT 25th-75th percentile ('18)	Freshmen in top 25% of HS class ('18)	Accept- ance rate ('18)	Average alumni giving rate
				Predicted	Actual							
1. Providence College (RI)	100	3.9	92%	81%	86%	54%	3%	12/1	1210-1360[2]	73%	49%	15%
2. Bentley University (MA)	97	3.6	94%	84%	89%	22%	0%	11/1	1240-1410	86%	43%	6%
3. Fairfield University (CT)	95·	3.6	90%	80%	81%	41%	1%	12/1	1190-1340[2]	77%[5]	60%	17%
4. College of New Jersey*	91	3.5	94%	84%	86%	42%	0.2%	13/1	1160-1350	75%	50%	7%
4. Loyola University Maryland	91	3.7	87%	78%	81%	46%	1%	12/1	1140-1320[2]	61%[5]	79%	11%
6. University of Scranton (PA)	88	3.4	87%	75%	82%	53%	0.2%	13/1	1120-1280	65%	73%	11%
7. Bryant University (RI)	86	3.2	90%	73%	81%	25%	0%	13/1	1130-1300[2]	55%	76%	9%
8. Emerson College (MA)	85	3.4	88%	82%	79%	68%	1%	13/1	1200-1390[2]	70%	36%	5%
8. Ithaca College (NY)	85	3.7	85%	78%	79%	61%	3%	11/1	1160-1338[2]	56%	69%	7%
10. Marist College (NY)	84	3.5	89%	77%	83%	45%	0%	16/1	1140-1320[2]	51%	46%	9%
10. St. Joseph's University (PA)	84	3.4	90%	74%	80%	42%	1%	11/1	1120-1290[2]	50%	76%	11%
12. SUNY Polytechnic Inst.–Albany/Utica*	79	2.7	78%	62%	59%	55%	3%	13/1	1000-1350[3]	68%	65%	2%
13. Manhattan College (NY)	77	3.1	85%	65%	74%	50%	0.2%	13/1	1070-1260[3]	54%	74%	15%
14. Le Moyne College (NY)	76	3.0	86%	67%	75%	53%	1%	13/1	1080-1270[2]	54%	69%	16%
14. SUNY–Geneseo*	76	3.5	87%	78%	81%	33%	9%	18/1	1120-1300	60%	65%	8%
16. CUNY–Baruch College*	75	3.2	90%	57%	69%	20%	16%	18/1	1220-1390	77%	39%	3%
16. Messiah College (PA)†	75	2.9	87%	77%	78%	51%	2%	12/1	1080-1310	61%	79%	9%
16. Siena College (NY)†	75	3.0	88%	72%	74%	37%	0%	13/1	1070-1270[2]	51%	80%	13%
19. Canisius College (NY)	70	2.8	85%	67%	68%	53%	0%	11/1	1050-1270	45%	79%	12%
19. Springfield College (MA)	70	2.9	85%	57%	72%	54%	2%	12/1	1050-1240	48%	63%	8%
19. St. Bonaventure University (NY)	70	3.0	85%	64%	68%	44%	0%	12/1	1040-1240	35%	73%	19%
22. McDaniel College (MD)†	69	2.9	79%	65%	67%	67%	0%	11/1	1050-1230	46%	64%	12%
23. CUNY–Hunter College*	68	3.2	84%	54%	56%	35%	7%	13/1	1090-1260	57%	36%	12%
23. Endicott College (MA)	68	2.8	85%	66%	75%	65%	0%	13/1	1070-1240[2]	40%	80%	13%
23. Molloy College (NY)	68	2.4	88%	64%	76%	65%	2%	10/1	1020-1210	56%	81%	10%
23. Salve Regina University (RI)	68	2.9	84%	68%	72%	47%	0%	13/1	1090-1250[2]	34%	76%	16%
23. St. Francis University (PA)	68	2.6	87%	67%	68%	66%	0%	14/1	1040-1250	60%	75%	16%
28. Lebanon Valley College (PA)	67	2.6	83%	71%	73%	62%	2%	10/1	1068-1280[2]	48%	78%	14%
28. Monmouth University (NJ)	67	3.0	81%	64%	69%	42%	0.1%	13/1	1040-1190	42%	77%	4%
28. Roger Williams University (RI)	67	3.0	81%	72%	70%	49%	0.2%	14/1	1080-1250[2]	35%	86%	4%
28. SUNY–New Paltz*	67	3.0	87%	65%	76%	31%	4%	15/1	1090-1270	61%[5]	41%	3%
32. Assumption College (MA)	66	2.7	83%	68%	75%	49%	0.2%	12/1	1090-1238[2]	39%	81%	13%
32. Nazareth College (NY)	66	2.7	83%	69%	66%	57%	0%	10/1	1090-1270[2]	58%	64%	11%
32. Niagara University (NY)	66	2.8	84%	61%	70%	62%	1%	11/1	1020-1200[2]	40%	87%	9%
32. Ramapo College of New Jersey*	66	2.8	87%	65%	74%	39%	0%	16/1	1050-1230	39%	63%	4%
32. Stockton University (NJ)*	66	2.8	87%	59%	74%	29%	2%	17/1	1000-1190	44%	84%	2%
32. Wagner College (NY)	66	2.8	83%	77%	69%	68%	3%	12/1	1070-1270[2]	49%	70%	7%
38. Alfred University (NY)	65	2.8	73%	65%	60%	71%	2%	10/1	970-1200	34%	63%	12%

Note: Key to footnotes Page 94.

NORTH ▶

Rank School (State) (*Public)	Overall score	Peer assessment score (5.0=highest)	Average first-year student retention rate	2018 graduation rate		% of classes under 20 ('18)	% of classes of 50 or more ('18)	Student/faculty ratio ('18)	SAT/ACT 25th-75th percentile ('18)	Freshmen In top 25% of HS class ('18)	Accept-ance rate ('18)	Average alumni giving rate
				Predicted	Actual							
38. La Salle University (PA)	65	2.9	76%	55%	68%	51%	1%	12/1	970-1160[2]	30%	81%	9%
38. Rider University (NJ)	65	2.8	79%	65%	65%	54%	1%	10/1	1000-1190	38%	70%	7%
38. Suffolk University (MA)†	65	3.0	76%	61%	59%	45%	0.4%	15/1	1030-1220	35%	85%	5%
42. Arcadia University (PA)	64	2.6	78%	63%	71%	72%	0.4%	12/1	1050-1250	50%	64%	9%
42. Marywood University (PA)	64	2.6	85%	59%	67%	57%	1%	12/1	1010-1190	45%	75%	12%
42. Mount St. Mary's University (MD)	64	3.0	75%	65%	64%	54%	0%	12/1	1000-1210	36%	68%	14%
42. New York Inst. of Technology	64	3.1	74%	58%	51%	66%	1%	12/1	1050-1270	N/A	76%	2%
46. Merrimack College (MA)	63	2.9	83%	61%	71%	36%	2%	14/1	1040-1195[2]	24%	83%	8%
46. Wentworth Inst. of Technology (MA)	63	3.1	84%	62%	66%	39%	2%	18/1	1080-1280[2]	40%	76%	6%
48. Hood College (MD)	62	2.8	76%	62%	66%	74%	0%	10/1	990-1270[2]	44%	71%	14%
48. King's College (PA)	62	2.6	74%	56%	63%	55%	0%	14/1	1010-1200[2]	41%	78%	13%
48. Mercyhurst University (PA)	62	2.6	80%	56%	70%	59%	1%	15/1	1020-1210[2]	N/A	87%	11%
48. Seton Hill University (PA)	62	2.7	82%	61%	63%	63%	0.2%	14/1	1020-1240[2]	45%	75%	14%
52. CUNY–Queens College*	61	2.9	84%	54%	57%	38%	8%	16/1	1060-1220	N/A	48%	16%
52. SUNY College–Oneonta[1]*	61	2.9	85%[6]	59%	72%[8]	34%[4]	4%[4]	17/1[4]	1040-1190[4]	39%[4]	60%[4]	N/A
52. SUNY–Oswego*	61	2.9	79%	61%	64%	55%	5%	17/1	1040-1210[3]	50%	54%	6%
55. West Chester Univ. of Pennsylvania*	60	3.0	86%	58%	74%	25%	5%	19/1	1050-1200	32%	74%	4%
56. Fairleigh Dickinson University (NJ)	59	3.1	79%	59%	55%	72%	1%	12/1	1030-1210[2]	46%	87%	3%
56. Iona College (NY)	59	2.8	76%	61%	67%	23%	0%	16/1	990-1170	32%	88%	8%
56. SUNY–Fredonia*	59	2.6	77%	56%	62%	56%	3%	15/1	970-1170	43%	76%	4%
59. CUNY–Brooklyn College*	58	2.9	82%	52%	58%	32%	3%	18/1	1040-1220	N/A	44%	6%
59. DeSales University (PA)	58	2.5	81%	59%	71%	51%	2%	13/1	1010-1230[3]	43%[5]	79%	7%
59. Notre Dame of Maryland University	58	2.7	75%	59%	53%	83%	1%	10/1	930-1140[2]	68%	88%	10%
59. St. Joseph's College New York	58	2.4	83%	56%	68%	64%	0.1%	12/1	1020-1200	N/A	73%	4%
63. Eastern University (PA)	57	2.4	76%	48%	63%	87%	0%	10/1	1030-1190[2]	40%	68%	8%
63. SUNY College–Cortland*	57	2.8	79%	66%	69%	36%	6%	16/1	1060-1200[9]	47%	44%	6%
63. SUNY–Plattsburgh[A]	57	2.6	81%	56%	68%	37%	4%	16/1	1050-1230[3]	43%	54%	6%
66. Albertus Magnus College (CT)	56	2.4	69%	40%	66%	88%	0%	13/1	810-1050[2]	N/A	86%	8%
66. Champlain College (VT)	56	2.6	80%	61%	64%	68%	0%	12/1	1090-1280[2]	35%	75%	3%
66. Norwich University (VT)	56	2.9	77%	63%	62%	49%	1%	14/1	1040-1270[2]	33%[5]	66%	15%
66. SUNY College–Potsdam*	56	2.6	75%	53%	56%	66%	2%	12/1	1040-1230[2]	N/A[5]	64%	6%
66. SUNY Maritime College*	56	2.9	86%	69%	66%	35%	2%	15/1	1075-1260[3]	N/A[5]	72%	5%
66. University of New Haven (CT)	56	2.7	79%	65%	64%	50%	2%	16/1	1030-1220	42%	84%	6%
66. Waynesburg University (PA)	56	2.3	78%	58%	66%	72%	1%	13/1	980-1150	36%	91%	8%
73. Manhattanville College (NY)	55	2.6	75%	58%	59%	76%	0%	10/1	1030-1180[2]	34%	90%	9%
73. Roberts Wesleyan College (NY)	55	2.4	79%	60%	69%	65%	2%	11/1	1010-1230[2]	44%	65%	8%
75. Caldwell University (NJ)	54	2.4	81%	46%	57%	64%	1%	12/1	960-1145	29%	66%	10%
75. Carlow University (PA)	54	2.3	77%	46%	54%	77%	0.3%	12/1	1000-1180	50%	87%	8%
75. Salisbury University (MD)*	54	2.8	83%	64%	68%	37%	4%	15/1	1145-1280[9]	45%	62%	6%
75. Slippery Rock U. of Pennsylvania*	54	2.8	82%	54%	67%	19%	9%	22/1	1010-1170	35%	73%	4%
75. Stevenson University (MD)	54	2.8	79%	59%	56%	65%	0%	14/1	1030-1200	44%	73%	4%
80. College at Brockport–SUNY*	53	2.6	79%	59%	65%	33%	6%	18/1	1020-1180	33%	53%	3%
80. Eastern Connecticut State University*	53	2.5	77%	55%	58%	35%	0%	15/1	1010-1190[2]	40%	66%	6%
80. Johnson & Wales University (RI)	53	2.9	76%	55%	63%	47%	0%	18/1	990-1190[2]	27%	91%	N/A
80. Monroe College (NY)	53	1.8	78%	32%	73%	50%	0.1%	15/1	650-1053[2]	N/A	44%	2%
80. Point Park University (PA)	53	2.5	77%	52%	60%	77%	0.3%	12/1	980-1190	32%	65%	2%
80. York College of Pennsylvania	53	2.5	79%	55%	59%	52%	0.1%	15/1	1020-1220	40%	70%	7%
86. Cedar Crest College (PA)†	52	2.4	80%	55%	46%	78%	2%	10/1	940-1170	43%	57%	11%
86. College of Our Lady of the Elms (MA)	52	2.1	82%	48%	66%	78%	0%	11/1	970-1170	N/A	67%	11%
86. College of Saint Rose (NY)	52	2.3	77%	58%	61%	72%	0.1%	14/1	1010-1190[9]	38%	87%	11%
86. Saint Peter's University (NJ)	52	2.5	82%	43%	50%	58%	0%	13/1	940-1120[2]	42%	74%	9%
86. Utica College (NY)	52	2.5	73%	51%	54%	63%	0%	13/1	1030-1220[2]	35%	84%	7%
86. Westfield State University (MA)[A]	52	2.5	78%	52%	63%	46%	1%	15/1	1000-1160	12%	86%	3%
92. Geneva College (PA)	51	2.2	80%	58%	64%	69%	2%	12/1	1000-1240	43%	63%	9%
92. Southern New Hampshire University	51	2.8	71%	40%	55%[6]	70%	0%	13/1	990-1160[4]	23%	91%	1%
94. Alvernia University (PA)	50	2.5	77%	47%	57%	63%	2%	13/1	950-1130	N/A	68%	8%
94. Bay Path University (MA)	50	2.1	75%	42%	59%	88%	0%	12/1	888-1090[2]	43%	60%	3%
94. Chestnut Hill College (PA)	50	2.3	74%	46%	60%	84%	0%	10/1	940-1120	23%	96%	13%
94. Lock Haven U. of Pennsylvania*	50	2.4	70%	43%	55%	45%	5%	16/1	920-1110	29%	94%	4%
94. Millersville U. of Pennsylvania*	50	2.6	77%	53%	60%	31%	5%	19/1	990-1180	30%	78%	3%

NORTH ▶

Rank School (State) (*Public)	Overall score	Peer assessment score (5.0=highest)	Average first-year student retention rate	2018 graduation rate Predicted	2018 graduation rate Actual	% of classes under 20 ('18)	% of classes of 50 or more ('18)	Student/ faculty ratio ('18)	SAT/ACT 25th-75th percentile ('18)	Freshmen in top 25% of HS class ('18)	Accept-ance rate ('18)	Average alumni giving rate
94. William Paterson Univ. of N.J.*	50	2.6	74%	49%	52%	54%	1%	14/1	890-1090[2]	N/A	93%	4%
100. CUNY–John Jay Col. of Crim. Justice*	49	3.1	78%	41%	46%	30%	1%	17/1	920-1060	N/A	41%	N/A
100. CUNY–Lehman College*	49	2.8	83%	43%	49%	42%	1%	17/1	920-1040	N/A	40%	9%
100. Shippensburg U. of Pennsylvania*	49	2.7	72%	50%	53%	43%	2%	18/1	970-1170	27%	88%	9%
100. Worcester State University (MA)*	49	2.5	79%	51%	57%	57%	0.2%	17/1	1010-1190[2]	N/A	78%	6%
104. Central Connecticut State University*	48	2.4	77%	47%	51%	41%	3%	15/1	980-1170	27%	67%	3%
104. Framingham State University (MA)*	48	2.6	74%	50%	56%	50%	0.2%	14/1	960-1130	21%[4]	73%	5%
104. Gwynedd Mercy University (PA)	48	2.4	83%	44%	61%	58%	5%	10/1	940-1110	32%	92%	4%
104. SUNY Buffalo State*	48	2.8	67%	48%	48%	45%	4%	15/1	860-1130[3]	N/A	61%	2%
108. Bridgewater State University (MA)*	47	2.5	78%	50%	59%[8]	43%	0.1%	18/1	990-1150[2]	N/A	90%	4%[4]
108. College of Mount St. Vincent (NY)	47	2.2	77%	44%	51%	54%	0.2%	13/1	930-1100	29%	78%	14%
108. Fitchburg State University (MA)*	47	2.5	75%	49%	61%	37%	12%	14/1	1000-1150[2]	N/A	87%	2%
108. Frostburg State University (MD)*	47	2.6	76%	49%	54%	50%	3%	16/1	930-1120	29%	78%	5%
108. Georgian Court University (NJ)	47	2.2	77%	45%	54%	80%	0.2%	12/1	935-1130	31%	72%	6%
113. Bloomsburg U. of Pennsylvania*	46	2.5	75%	49%	60%	28%	5%	19/1	990-1150	29%	77%	5%
113. Clarion U. of Pennsylvania*	46	2.3	74%	46%	56%	35%	4%	17/1	950-1130	32%	94%	3%
113. Mount St. Mary College (NY)	46	2.3	80%	52%	57%	51%	1%	14/1	1020-1170	34%	94%	7%
116. Cabrini University (PA)	45	2.3	71%	50%	57%	78%[4]	0.4%[4]	11/1	990-1170[9]	N/A	72%	N/A
116. Lasell College (MA)	45	2.3	74%	54%	61%	69%	0%	14/1	980-1170[2]	30%	80%	7%
116. Rhode Island College*	45	2.6	75%	46%	50%	57%	1%	14/1	890-1100	40%	73%	3%
119. Centenary University (NJ)	44	2.1	78%[8]	47%	55%	88%	0%	14/1	870-1090[3]	N/A	67%	N/A
119. Delaware Valley University (PA)	44	2.4	70%	57%	53%	60%	2%	13/1	970-1160	33%	66%	5%
119. Keuka College (NY)	44	2.3	70%	48%	53%	49%	3%	8/1	980-1140[4]	N/A	86%	10%
119. Lincoln University (PA)*	44	2.1	74%	39%	47%	53%	1%	15/1	860-1020	25%	81%	21%
119. Plymouth State University (NH)*	44	2.5	71%	50%	53%	67%	1%	17/1	815-1203[2]	17%	82%	3%
119. Salem State University (MA)*	44	2.5	78%	50%	58%	46%	0.3%	14/1	980-1140[2]	N/A	85%	3%
119. St. Thomas Aquinas College (NY)	44	2.4	78%	52%	55%	57%	0%	14/1	910-1120[3]	23%[5]	76%	7%
126. Cairn University[7] (PA)	43	2.0	75%	48%	60%	70%[4]	2%[4]	12/1[4]	890-1130	36%[4]	89%	5%
126. Kutztown Univ. of Pennsylvania*	43	2.5	74%	46%	55%	25%	8%	17/1	970-1140	23%	81%	4%
126. Wheelock College[1] (MA)	43	2.4	71%[8]	58%	61%[6]	N/A	N/A	12/1[4]	12-20[4]	N/A	77%[4]	N/A

School (State) (*Public)		Peer assessment score (5.0=highest)	Average first-year student retention rate	2018 graduation rate Predicted	2018 graduation rate Actual	% of classes under 20 ('18)	% of classes of 50 or more ('18)	Student/ faculty ratio ('18)	SAT/ACT 25th-75th percentile ('18)	Freshmen in top 25% of HS class ('18)	Accept-ance rate ('18)	Average alumni giving rate
SCHOOLS RANKED 129 THROUGH 170 ARE LISTED HERE ALPHABETICALLY												
American International College[1] (MA)†		2.0	67%[8]	42%	41%[6]	52%[4]	4%[4]	18/1[4]	902-1090[4]	N/A	72%[4]	4%[4]
Anna Maria College (MA)		1.9	67%[8]	50%	46%	78%[4]	0%[4]	12/1	903-1080[2]	21%	75%	6%
Bowie State University (MD)*		2.4	72%	43%	42%	45%	4%	19/1	860-1020	N/A	33%	4%
California U. of Pennsylvania*		2.3	73%	47%	54%	34%	8%	18/1	900-1100	22%	97%	2%
College of New Rochelle[1] (NY)		1.9	71%[8]	33%	32%[6]	N/A	N/A	15/1[4]	880-1080[4]	N/A	68%[4]	N/A
College of St. Elizabeth[1] (NJ)		2.3	65%[8]	46%	47%[8]	N/A	N/A	9/1[4]	800-1000[4]	N/A	64%[4]	N/A
Concordia College (NY)†		2.2	76%	44%	43%	71%	1%	10/1	950-1118[2]	38%[4]	81%	7%
Coppin State University (MD)*		2.3	65%	36%	24%	60%	0.3%	13/1	880-1030	N/A	38%	N/A
CUNY–College of Staten Island*		2.5	79%	44%	48%	23%	6%	18/1	990-1170	N/A	100%	1%
Curry College (MA)		2.2	67%	54%	53%	64%	0%	12/1	940-1110[2]	16%[5]	93%	3%
Dominican College (NY)		2.2	72%	47%	43%	67%	0%	15/1	940-1120[2]	N/A	77%	2%
East Stroudsburg Univ. of Pa.*		2.6	71%	47%	50%	38%	9%	18/1	910-1120[2]	24%	72%	4%[4]
Edinboro Univ. of Pennsylvania*		2.3	70%	41%	52%	39%	6%	16/1	960-1140	29%	80%	3%
Felician University (NJ)		2.2	80%	45%	46%	67%	0.4%	14/1	920-1080	20%	81%	1%
Franklin Pierce University (NH)		2.4	65%	59%	50%	62%	2%	12/1	970-1160[2]	19%	78%	3%
Harrisburg Univ. of Science and Tech. (PA)		2.3	56%[8]	52%	20%[6]	N/A	N/A	N/A	N/A[2]	N/A	N/A	N/A
Holy Family University[1] (PA)		2.2	77%[8]	47%	58%[6]	62%[4]	0%[4]	15/1[4]	920-1090[4]	28%[4]	71%[4]	4%[4]
Kean University (NJ)*		2.5	74%	44%	49%	41%	1%	17/1	890-1080	N/A	86%	2%
Lancaster Bible College (PA)†		2.0	78%	47%	55%	80%	0.3%	14/1	1000-1200[3]	N/A	57%	4%
La Roche University (PA)†		2.1	71%	45%	55%	66%	0.3%	12/1	910-1110	29%	99%	5%
Medaille College[1] (NY)		2.0	63%[8]	40%	43%[6]	N/A	N/A	12/1[4]	850-1080[4]	N/A	75%[4]	N/A
Mercy College (NY)		2.2	74%	36%	43%	62%	0.3%	17/1	N/A[2]	N/A	79%	2%
Metropolitan College of New York[1]		1.9	46%[8]	32%	28%[6]	94%[4]	0%[4]	11/1[4]	N/A[2]	N/A	91%[4]	N/A
Neumann University (PA)		2.2	72%	45%	47%	65%	2%	14/1	910-1090	N/A	69%	7%[4]

Note: Key to footnotes Page 94.

SMALL CAMPUS & BIG CITY

NORTH ▶

School (State) (*Public)	Peer assessment score (5.0=highest)	Average first-year student retention rate	2018 graduation rate Predicted	Actual	% of classes under 20 ('18)	% of classes of 50 or more ('18)	Student/faculty ratio ('18)	SAT/ACT 25th–75th percentile ('18)	Freshmen in top 25% of HS class ('18)	Acceptance rate ('18)	Average alumni giving rate
CONTINUED (SCHOOLS RANKED 129 THROUGH 170 ARE LISTED HERE ALPHABETICALLY)											
New England College (NH)	2.3	57%	30%	35%	84%	0%	15/1	870-950[2]	34%	100%	6%
New Jersey City University*	2.2	76%	41%	39%	36%	1%	13/1	850-1060[3]	25%	96%	3%[4]
Northern Vermont University[1] (VT)*	2.1	67%[8]	46%	36%[6]	N/A	N/A	14/1[4]	870-1100[4]	N/A	87%[4]	N/A
Nyack College (NY)	2.1	68%	41%	46%	77%	2%	12/1	868-1108[2]	24%	98%	5%
Post University (CT)	2.1	44%	35%	20%	49%	0%	20/1	850-850[9]	N/A	53%	N/A
Rivier University[1] (NH)	2.2	76%[8]	52%	51%[6]	N/A	N/A	13/1[4]	N/A[2]	N/A	68%[4]	N/A
Rosemont College (PA)	2.2	66%	54%	51%	93%	0%	11/1	910-1140	N/A	65%	N/A
Southern Connecticut State University*	2.5	76%	45%	51%	39%	1%	14/1	920-1130	27%	66%	3%
St. Joseph's College[1] (ME)	2.4	83%[8]	54%	56%[6]	N/A	N/A	10/1[4]	N/A[2]	N/A	80%[4]	N/A
SUNY College–Old Westbury*	2.4	80%	47%	48%	21%	0%	21/1	970-1120	N/A	78%	N/A
Thomas College[1] (ME)	2.2	68%[8]	43%	46%[6]	N/A	N/A	21/1[4]	N/A[2]	N/A	N/A	N/A
Trinity Washington University[1] (DC)	2.6	64%[8]	31%	40%[6]	N/A	N/A	11/1[4]	N/A[2]	N/A	92%[4]	N/A
University of Baltimore*	2.5	72%	47%	37%	45%	0%	14/1	910-1115	N/A	79%	4%
University of Southern Maine*	2.6	66%	54%	39%	56%	3%	13/1	940-1060	34%	85%	3%
Univ. of the District of Columbia*	1.9	65%	46%	45%	66%	0%	N/A	N/A	N/A	69%	N/A
Washington Adventist University (MD)	1.8	75%	47%	37%	85%	0%	10/1	860-1070[2]	N/A	52%	1%
Western Connecticut State University*	2.4	74%	49%	49%	36%	2%	13/1	1020-1220[2]	23%	79%	1%
Wilson College (PA)†	2.1	72%	61%	40%	77%	1%	12/1	950-1130[2]	30%	92%	15%

SOUTH ▶

Rank School (State) (*Public)	Overall score	Peer assessment score (5.0=highest)	Average first-year student retention rate	2018 graduation rate Predicted	Actual	% of classes under 20 ('18)	% of classes of 50 or more ('18)	Student/faculty ratio ('18)	SAT/ACT 25th–75th percentile ('18)	Freshmen in top 25% of HS class ('18)	Acceptance rate ('18)	Average alumni giving rate
1. Rollins College (FL)	100	3.9	85%	75%	74%	68%	0%	10/1	1150-1360[2]	62%	67%	6%
2. The Citadel (SC)*	94	4.0	85%	63%	72%	39%	0.4%	12/1	1030-1220	31%	81%	26%
3. James Madison University (VA)*	90	4.1	91%	66%	84%	35%	11%	16/1	1120-1290[2]	36%	71%	7%
4. Berry College (GA)	86	3.4	83%	77%	66%	58%	0%	11/1	23-29	60%	66%	14%
5. Stetson University (FL)	83	3.6	78%	72%	61%	62%	1%	13/1	1120-1300[2]	54%	68%	8%
6. Appalachian State University (NC)*	80	3.7	87%	64%	72%	34%	7%	16/1	22-26	59%	69%	6%
6. Christopher Newport Univ. (VA)*	80	3.3	87%	67%	72%	60%	3%	14/1	1110-1280[2]	51%	68%	20%
8. College of Charleston (SC)*	76	3.8	79%	71%	71%	40%	4%	15/1	1070-1250	51%	79%	4%
9. Asbury University (KY)	74	3.1	82%	64%	62%	71%	0.2%	11/1	21-28[2]	54%	67%	15%
10. Florida Southern College	72	3.1	81%	61%	64%	59%	0%	13/1	1130-1300	61%	50%	11%
11. Embry-Riddle Aeronautical U. (FL)	71	3.7	80%	67%	61%	20%	2%	17/1	1110-1320[2]	49%	65%	2%
11. John Brown University (AR)	71	3.0	82%	66%	65%	56%	0%	13/1	23-30[2]	58%	77%	10%
13. Longwood University (VA)*	68	3.1	79%	57%	69%	55%	1%	14/1	980-1150	28%	89%	10%
13. Milligan College (TN)	68	2.7	76%	64%	70%	75%	1%	10/1	22-28	N/A	83%	17%
13. Queens University of Charlotte (NC)	68	3.2	78%	64%	53%	65%	1%	10/1	1033-1218	46%	79%	21%
16. Univ. of Mary Washington (VA)*	67	3.4	83%	68%	66%	47%	5%	14/1	1050-1269[9]	46%	72%	12%
17. University of Tampa (FL)	66	3.4	76%	63%	60%	37%	3%	17/1	1090-1250	48%	49%	17%
17. Winthrop University (SC)*	66	3.5	76%	59%	56%	52%	2%	14/1	950-1160	42%	67%	5%
17. Xavier University of Louisiana	66	3.3	73%	60%	49%	54%	5%	14/1	20-26	56%	58%	16%
20. Georgia College & State University*	64	3.5	85%	67%	64%	42%	5%	17/1	1110-1280	N/A	78%	3%
20. University of Lynchburg (VA)	64	2.8	78%	58%	61%	68%	1%	11/1	980-1185	22%	97%	12%
22. Converse College (SC)	62	2.7	70%	58%	56%	83%	0.3%	13/1	20-25	45%	59%	11%
23. Western Carolina University (NC)*	60	3.2	80%	53%	61%	30%	5%	17/1	20-25	41%	40%	5%
24. Murray State University (KY)*	59	3.1	75%	54%	56%	62%	3%	15/1	21-27	54%	81%	6%
25. Christian Brothers University (TN)	57	2.8	80%	62%	58%	63%	0%	12/1	22-27	61%	56%	10%
25. Saint Leo University (FL)	57	2.8	72%	37%	50%	48%	0%	12/1	972-1150[2]	30%	84%	5%
25. Tuskegee University (AL)	57	3.1	71%	69%	42%	75%	5%	14/1	17-27[3]	80%	52%	9%
28. Jacksonville University (FL)	55	2.9	71%	59%	53%	73%	0.1%	11/1	21-27[2]	N/A	90%	5%
28. Radford University (VA)*	55	3.1	74%	48%	59%	41%	8%	16/1	940-1130[2]	16%	75%	3%
28. University of Tennessee–Martin*	55	2.9	75%	50%	48%	60%	3%	15/1	21-26	43%	69%	6%
31. Eastern Mennonite University (VA)	54	2.5	74%	60%	60%	70%	1%	9/1	1000-1230	N/A	59%	N/A
31. Freed-Hardeman University (TN)	54	2.7	79%	66%	60%	55%	4%	13/1	21-28	51%	93%	10%
31. University of Montevallo (AL)*	54	3.0	76%	57%	48%[6]	48%	1%	13/1	20-27	N/A	44%	7%
34. Bob Jones University (SC)	52	2.1	82%	58%	63%	63%	9%	13/1	20-27	38%	78%	8%
34. Lee University (TN)	52	2.9	79%	55%	57%	58%	7%	16/1	21-28	49%	83%	7%
34. University of West Florida*†	52	3.1	76%	49%	43%	34%	9%	21/1	22-27	41%	42%	3%

Note: Key to footnotes Page 94.

INTERNSHIPS   **JUNIOR JOURNEY**   **4-YEAR GRADUATION**

OUR GUARANTEES

Florida Southern College goes beyond the conventional college experience, guaranteeing each student an internship, a travel-study experience, and graduation in four years. These signature opportunities, combined with our devoted faculty and stunning historic campus, create a college experience unlike any other.

FLORIDA SOUTHERN COLLEGE

flsouthern.edu/**guarantees**

SOUTH ▶

Rank School (State) (*Public)	Overall score	Peer assessment score (5.0=highest)	Average first-year student retention rate	2018 graduation rate		% of classes under 20 ('18)	% of classes of 50 or more ('18)	Student/ faculty ratio ('18)	SAT/ACT 25th-75th percentile ('18)	Freshmen in top 25% of HS class ('18)	Accept-ance rate ('18)	Average alumni giving rate
				Predicted	Actual							
37. Marymount University (VA)	51	2.9	76%	58%	57%	52%	0.2%	13/1	950-1180[2]	25%	91%	4%
38. Brenau University (GA)	50	2.8	62%	45%	43%	78%	0.4%	9/1	910-1140[2]	32%	65%	5%
38. Columbia International Univ. (SC)	50	2.2	78%	58%	65%	74%	9%	15/1	940-1120	32%	33%	6%
40. University of North Georgia*	49	3.2	80%	57%	54%	32%	3%	20/1	1108-1273	48%	74%	7%
41. Coastal Carolina University (SC)*	48	3.0	68%	51%	44%	39%	2%	16/1	19-24	33%	70%	10%
42. Mississippi Univ. for Women*	47	3.0	64%	55%	47%	64%	5%	13/1	18-24	56%	98%	11%
43. Coker College (SC)†	46	2.8	61%	44%	35%	71%	0%	12/1	17-22	42%	63%	7%[4]
43. Lenoir-Rhyne University (NC)	46	2.7	69%	58%	50%	55%	0%	13/1	960-1180	N/A	74%	12%
43. Morehead State University (KY)*	46	2.9	71%	51%	45%	51%	3%	18/1	20-26	46%	75%	9%
43. University of North Alabama*	46	2.9	76%	48%	46%	51%	4%	19/1	20-25	45%	64%	4%
47. Belhaven University (MS)	45	2.8	66%	48%	46%	84%	2%	10/1	17-24	41%	52%	3%
47. Bryan College (TN)	45	2.5	71%	53%	51%	67%	3%	12/1	21-26[2]	44%	51%	6%
47. Wheeling Jesuit University (WV)	45	2.3	69%	63%	56%	57%	0%	11/1	19-24	32%	91%	6%
50. Anderson University (SC)	44	2.8	76%	63%	59%	42%	9%	14/1	20-26	61%	62%	5%
50. North Greenville University (SC)	44	2.4	72%	51%	54%	74%	0.2%	14/1	21-30[3]	44%	60%	N/A
50. Piedmont College (GA)	44	2.5	65%	52%	50%	74%	0%	10/1	970-1180[3]	28%	60%	4%
50. Southern Adventist University (TN)	44	2.4	76%	60%	53%	64%	5%	13/1	19-26	N/A	93%	10%
54. Columbia College (SC)	43	2.5	72%	52%	53%	80%	0%	11/1	15-19[2]	30%	96%	8%
54. Eastern Kentucky University*	43	2.9	74%	53%	51%	41%	6%	16/1	20-26	43%	87%	3%
54. North Carolina Central Univ.*	43	2.5	80%	41%	46%	39%	4%	15/1	900-1050	21%	47%	10%
54. West Virginia Wesleyan College	43	2.6	72%	59%	49%	52%	0.3%	13/1	19-25	50%	70%	15%
58. Austin Peay State University (TN)*	41	3.0	68%	43%	43%	41%	6%	18/1	19-24[2]	34%	94%	3%
58. Charleston Southern University (SC)	41	2.8	67%	50%	42%	62%	1%	12/1	1020-1190	46%	52%	19%
58. Pfeiffer University (NC)	41	2.4	63%	49%	43%	80%	0%	12/1	900-1130[2]	31%	65%	10%
61. Francis Marion University (SC)*	40	2.7	67%	49%	39%	63%	2%	14/1	17-22	44%	64%	8%
61. Thomas More University (KY)	40	2.5	67%	52%	48%	62%	1%	16/1	19-24	28%	90%	8%
61. Virginia State University[7]*	40	2.6	71%	35%	45%[6]	N/A	N/A	15/1[4]	840-1010[3]	17%	91%	5%[4]
61. Winston-Salem State Univ.[1] (NC)*	40	2.6	76%[8]	46%	47%[6]	N/A	N/A	14/1[4]	890-1020[4]	N/A	67%[4]	N/A
65. King University (TN)	39	2.5	70%	43%	45%	79%	1%	13/1	19-25[2]	26%	58%	5%
65. Lynn University (FL)	39	2.7	71%	59%	54%	49%	0.4%	18/1	990-1170[2]	N/A	70%	3%
65. Troy University (AL)*	39	3.1	74%	52%	44%	55%	5%	18/1	18-24	N/A	88%	5%
65. University of Mount Olive[1] (NC)†	39	2.4	62%[8]	40%	44%[8]	67%[4]	0%[4]	14/1[4]	870-1066[4]	N/A	49%[4]	N/A
69. Florida Gulf Coast University*	38	2.9	79%	50%	48%	17%	15%	22/1	1060-1210	39%	65%	3%
69. University of Holy Cross[1] (LA)†	38	2.7	66%[8]	41%	39%[6]	76%[4]	1%[4]	11/1[4]	18-23[4]	N/A	46%[4]	1%[4]
71. Methodist University (NC)	36	2.6	61%	49%	39%	68%	0.1%	9/1	18-23	37%	55%	10%
72. Jacksonville State University (AL)*	35	2.8	75%	50%	42%	46%	4%	18/1	19-26[3]	51%	54%	5%
73. Midway University (KY)	34	2.1	79%	44%	37%	67%	0%	19/1	19-23	37%	61%	1%
73. St. Thomas University[1] (FL)	34	2.5	65%[8]	49%	41%[8]	61%[4]	0%[4]	11/1[4]	860-1080[4]	40%[4]	49%[4]	2%[4]
75. Arkansas Tech University*	33	2.7	70%	40%	42%	49%	3%	18/1	18-25	36%	90%	3%
75. Columbus State University (GA)*	33	2.8	74%	50%	38%	52%	4%	17/1	870-1100	37%	56%	3%
75. Southern Wesleyan University[1] (SC)	33	2.3	73%[8]	42%	51%[6]	N/A	N/A	17/1[4]	N/A[2]	N/A	53%[4]	N/A
75. West Liberty University (WV)*†	33	2.5	72%	46%	47%	66%	0.4%	13/1	17-23[3]	35%	69%	2%
79. Auburn University–Montgomery (AL)*	32	3.1	67%	51%	34%	44%	2%	17/1	19-23	38%	93%	3%
79. Delta State University (MS)*	32	2.5	67%	49%	39%	65%	1%	12/1	18-24	39%	85%	2%
79. Henderson State University (AR)*	32	2.6	62%	45%	35%	65%	1%	14/1	19-25	22%	91%	4%
82. Alcorn State University (MS)*	31	2.4	74%	37%	38%	48%[4]	2%[4]	19/1	17-22	N/A	89%	9%
82. South Carolina State University[7]*	31	2.3	65%	34%	34%	59%	2%	16/1	15-18	39%	53%	8%
84. Cumberland University (TN)	30	2.6	67%	52%	43%	56%	1%	17/1	19-23	N/A	62%	4%
84. Nicholls State University (LA)*	30	2.6	69%	45%	44%	40%	9%	19/1	20-24	42%	94%	6%
84. Tusculum University[1] (TN)	30	2.5	64%[8]	40%	37%[8]	67%[4]	0.2%[4]	17/1[4]	17-24[4]	N/A	89%[4]	19%[4]
87. Alabama State University*	29	2.4	60%	34%	30%	57%	0.3%	15/1	16-20	12%[5]	98%	5%
87. Fayetteville State University (NC)*	29	2.4	73%	37%	36%	37%	4%	17/1	890-1030	26%	68%	2%
87. Reinhardt University (GA)†	29	2.6	58%	45%	29%	78%	0%	13/1	18-23	31%	90%	4%
87. U. of North Carolina–Pembroke*	29	2.5	69%	46%	38%	47%	2%	18/1	17-21	35%	81%	3%
91. Norfolk State University (VA)*	28	2.4	73%	39%	35%	57%[4]	2%[4]	17/1[4]	860-1030	15%	90%	N/A
92. Campbellsville University (KY)	27	2.6	62%	47%	41%	69%	0.3%	13/1	18-24[2]	36%	83%	8%
92. Lindsey Wilson College (KY)	27	2.3	61%	38%	37%	60%	0%	15/1	19-24	31%	95%	11%
92. McNeese State University (LA)*	27	2.6	68%	49%	44%	46%	7%	20/1	20-25	47%	70%	4%
92. Southeastern University (FL)	27	2.5	68%	50%	42%	57%	5%	20/1	18-24[3]	26%	48%	4%[4]

Note: Key to footnotes Page 94.

SCHOOLS RANKED 96 THROUGH 122 ARE LISTED HERE ALPHABETICALLY

School (State) (*Public)	Peer assessment score (5.0=highest)	Average first-year student retention rate	2018 graduation rate		% of classes under 20 ('18)	% of classes of 50 or more ('18)	Student/ faculty ratio ('18)	SAT/ACT 25th-75th percentile ('18)	Freshmen in top 25% of HS class ('18)	Accept- ance rate ('18)	Average alumni giving rate
			Predicted	Actual							
Alabama Agricultural and Mechanical University[7]*	2.3	58%[8]	38%	27%	48%	3%	20/1	16-19[3]	N/A	90%	12%[4]
Albany State University (GA)*	2.3	66%	39%	35%	46%	1%	18/1	750-900	21%	89%	0.4%
Amridge University (AL)	1.8	25%[8]	29%	29%[6]	N/A	N/A	N/A	N/A	N/A	N/A	N/A
Bethel University (TN)	2.4	58%	36%	27%	67%	1%	17/1	16-25[2]	19%	67%	N/A
Clayton State University (GA)*	2.4	70%	43%	31%	36%	4%	19/1	870-1020	N/A	54%	2%
Concord University (WV)*	2.3	65%	45%	38%	70%	0.4%	15/1	18-23	43%	89%	3%
ECPI University (VA)†	1.8	50%	42%	46%	86%	0.2%	11/1	N/A[2]	N/A	72%	0%[4]
Everglades University[1] (FL)†	1.9	56%[8]	41%	45%[6]	N/A	N/A	15/1[4]	N/A[2]	N/A	73%[4]	N/A
Fairmont State University (WV)*	2.4	67%	43%	35%	62%	2%	16/1	18-23	34%	95%	2%
Faulkner University (AL)	2.5	56%	39%	28%	68%	2%	12/1	18-23	N/A	52%	1%
Fort Valley State University (GA)*	2.3	75%	36%	28%	49%	3%	21/1	833-990	15%	53%	9%
Georgia Southwestern State University*	2.5	68%	48%	29%	56%	1%	17/1	940-1120	39%	69%	2%
Grambling State University (LA)*	2.5	67%	28%	34%	33%	9%	25/1	16-19[2]	14%	96%	4%[4]
Louisiana College	2.3	56%	48%	30%	72%	0.3%	11/1	19-23	30%[4]	78%	1%[4]
Louisiana State University–Shreveport*	2.6	64%[8]	51%	33%	56%	4%	29/1	20-26	N/A	87%	5%
Mississippi Valley State Univ.[1]*	2.3	62%[8]	36%	28%[8]	60%[4]	1%[4]	15/1[4]	16-19[4]	N/A	86%[4]	N/A
Montreat College (NC)	2.3	59%[8]	50%	43%[8]	78%	0.4%	11/1	920-1140	28%[4]	55%	3%
Northwestern State University of Louisiana*	2.5	72%	48%	45%	47%	8%	18/1	19-24	37%	66%	N/A
Savannah State University (GA)*	2.4	60%	33%	28%	43%	0.1%	17/1	870-1030[3]	N/A	57%	5%
Shorter University (GA)†	2.5	59%[8]	47%	41%[6]	N/A	N/A	14/1[4]	17-24[4]	34%[4]	57%	N/A
Southeastern Louisiana University*	2.5	65%	46%	39%	35%	6%	19/1	20-25	34%	90%	3%
Southern Arkansas University*	2.3	65%	44%	38%	44%	4%	17/1	19-24	37%	65%	4%
Southern Univ. and A&M College (LA)*	2.3	64%	39%	32%	39%	7%	18/1	17-20	17%	38%	14%
Southern University–New Orleans[1]*	2.2	52%[8]	36%	17%[6]	46%[4]	0.3%[4]	20/1[4]	15-18[4]	24%[4]	25%[4]	1%[4]
Thomas University[1] (GA)	2.0	57%[8]	45%	33%[6]	N/A	N/A	11/1[4]	N/A[2]	N/A	23%[4]	N/A
Union College[1] (KY)	2.4	60%[8]	45%	31%[6]	N/A	N/A	15/1[4]	17-23[4]	N/A	63%[4]	N/A
University of West Alabama*	2.6	65%	42%	31%	65%	4%	14/1	18-22	N/A	40%	3%

MIDWEST ▶

Rank	School (State) (*Public)	Overall score	Peer assessment score (5.0=highest)	Average first-year student retention rate	2018 graduation rate		% of classes under 20 ('18)	% of classes of 50 or more ('18)	Student/ faculty ratio ('18)	SAT/ACT 25th-75th percentile ('18)	Freshmen in top 25% of HS class ('18)	Accept- ance rate ('18)	Average alumni giving rate
					Predicted	Actual							
1.	Butler University (IN)	100	4.0	90%	83%	82%	45%	3%	11/1	25-30	76%	68%	23%
2.	John Carroll University (OH)	92	3.7	85%	68%	78%	53%	0.1%	13/1	22-28	53%	83%	14%
3.	Calvin University (MI)†	88	3.5	86%	75%	77%	34%	1%	13/1	1150-1370	58%	79%	19%
4.	Bradley University (IL)	87	3.6	86%	74%	78%	58%	3%	12/1	1090-1290	64%	67%	8%
5.	Xavier University (OH)	85	3.9	85%	72%	73%	39%	1%	12/1	22-28[3]	50%[5]	74%	15%
6.	University of Evansville (IN)	84	3.4	85%	73%	74%	70%	1%	11/1	1080-1300[2]	64%	69%	13%
7.	Truman State University (MO)*	82	3.7	86%	74%	72%	46%	2%	16/1	24-30	83%	65%	7%
8.	Milwaukee School of Engineering	81	3.5	86%	71%	74%	43%	0%	15/1	25-30	N/A	63%	6%
9.	Augustana University (SD)†	79	3.3	85%	76%	71%	48%	2%	12/1	23-28	64%	65%	11%
10.	Baldwin Wallace University (OH)	77	3.3	81%	62%	64%	65%	1%	11/1	21-27[2]	46%	74%	7%
11.	Dominican University (IL)	75	3.0	79%	50%	61%	60%	0.2%	10/1	950-1130	52%	64%	14%
11.	Nebraska Wesleyan University	75	3.2	79%	65%	63%	69%	1%	10/1	21-28	55%	72%	14%
13.	Augsburg University (MN)	74	3.3	76%	56%	65%	64%	0%	12/1	19-24[2]	N/A	41%	10%
13.	Kettering University (MI)	74	3.1	93%	75%	63%	50%	0.4%	15/1	1190-1370	71%	70%	7%
13.	North Central College (IL)	74	3.2	80%	67%	68%	41%	0%	13/1	1050-1250	57%	56%	16%
13.	Rockhurst University (MO)	74	3.2	85%	70%	75%	39%	3%	14/1	22-27	60%	66%	12%
17.	Franciscan Univ. of Steubenville (OH)	73	2.6	86%	69%	76%	55%	2%	14/1	1060-1280	59%	77%	11%
17.	Hamline University (MN)	73	3.3	79%	63%	63%	44%	2%	12/1	20-27	49%	67%	9%
17.	Webster University (MO)	73	2.9	78%	57%	59%	89%	0.2%	8/1	21-27	47%	57%	2%
20.	Drury University (MO)	72	3.0	81%	49%	64%	55%	0.2%	13/1	22-29	63%	68%	10%
20.	Lewis University (IL)	72	3.0	81%	55%	63%	65%	0.3%	13/1	1040-1200	46%	58%	6%
20.	Otterbein University (OH)	72	3.3	82%	69%	62%	59%	2%	11/1	21-27	54%	82%	10%
20.	University of Northern Iowa*	72	3.4	83%	64%	65%	34%	7%	18/1	21-26	51%	81%	8%
24.	Elmhurst College (IL)	71	3.3	79%	60%	63%	55%	0.3%	14/1	993-1190	36%	67%	9%
25.	Cedarville University (OH)†	70	2.9	85%	76%	72%	58%	6%	16/1	23-29	60%	79%	9%
25.	Indiana Wesleyan University	70	3.0	80%	51%	66%	58%	6%	13/1	1030-1240	50%	68%	8%

MIDWEST ▶

Rank	School (State) (*Public)	Overall score	Peer assessment score (5.0=highest)	Average first-year student retention rate	2018 graduation rate Predicted	2018 graduation rate Actual	% of classes under 20 ('18)	% of classes of 50 or more ('18)	Student/faculty ratio ('18)	SAT/ACT 25th-75th percentile ('18)	Freshmen in top 25% of HS class ('18)	Acceptance rate ('18)	Average alumni giving rate
27.	St. Ambrose University (IA)	69	3.1	78%	60%	67%	64%	1%	11/1	20-26[3]	44%	63%	7%
28.	Capital University (OH)	67	2.9	77%	62%	58%	67%	1%	11/1	21-26[3]	51%	73%	7%
28.	Univ. of Wisconsin–La Crosse*	67	3.3	85%	72%	71%	25%	12%	19/1	23-27	57%	78%	4%
30.	Bethel University (IN)	66	2.7	76%	55%	71%	65%	5%	12/1	970-1170	41%	92%	8%
30.	Marian University (IN)	66	3.0	78%	60%	57%	69%	1%	13/1	1020-1200	48%	61%	11%
32.	Buena Vista University (IA)†	65	2.8	72%	51%	54%	79%	0.4%	8/1	19-24	42%	58%	5%
33.	Concordia University (NE)	64	2.8	76%	63%	63%	51%	2%	14/1	20-26	48%	68%	20%
33.	Robert Morris University (IL)	64	2.6	48%	40%	76%	54%	0.3%	21/1	810-1030[2]	14%	63%	1%
33.	St. Mary's Univ. of Minnesota	64	2.9	77%	58%	61%	74%	0%	18/1	20-26	N/A	92%	8%
33.	Univ. of Illinois–Springfield*	64	2.9	77%	56%	51%	54%	2%	13/1	990-1218	49%	53%	5%
33.	University of Michigan–Dearborn*	64	2.8	80%	58%	58%	30%	7%	17/1	1080-1290	55%[4]	77%	8%
33.	Univ. of Wisconsin–Eau Claire*	64	3.2	83%	64%	67%	21%	16%	22/1	21-26	48%	86%	6%
39.	University of Minnesota–Duluth*	63	3.1	78%	63%	59%	39%	15%	18/1	21-26	47%	74%	5%
40.	Eastern Illinois University*	62	2.7	73%	52%	58%	56%	1%	13/1	920-1110	34%	55%	3%
40.	Huntington University (IN)†	62	2.6	79%	61%	61%	72%	1%	12/1	990-1180	43%	84%	17%
40.	Mount Mercy University (IA)	62	2.6	73%	56%	71%	59%	1%	15/1	19-25	50%	63%	11%
43.	Lawrence Technological Univ.[1] (MI)	61	2.9	81%[8]	69%	54%[6]	75%[4]	0.3%[4]	11/1[4]	1060-1280[4]	N/A	60%[4]	4%[4]
43.	Spring Arbor University (MI)	61	2.7	79%	52%	56%	71%	1%	12/1	1025-1230	48%	71%	7%
43.	Ursuline College (OH)	61	2.7	68%	51%	44%	84%	0%	8/1	19-24	39%	90%	12%
46.	Madonna University (MI)	60	2.5	78%	53%	61%	77%	2%	12/1	960-1170	24%	78%	2%
46.	Muskingum University (OH)	60	2.7	73%	50%	51%	69%	0%	12/1	19-24	35%	72%	12%
46.	Saint Mary-of-the-Woods Col. (IN)†	60	2.6	71%	49%	59%	84%	0%	9/1	920-1110	N/A	72%	23%
46.	Trine University (IN)†	60	2.8	76%	64%	65%	50%	1%	15/1	1010-1230	46%	73%	10%[4]
46.	Univ. of Nebraska–Kearney*	60	2.8	81%	52%	58%	52%	3%	14/1	19-26	45%	94%	7%
46.	Walsh University (OH)	60	2.7	79%	55%	59%	76%	0.3%	13/1	19-26[2]	N/A	78%	8%
52.	Olivet Nazarene University (IL)	59	2.8	77%	62%	61%	41%	8%	17/1	1000-1220	43%	65%	12%
53.	Alverno College (WI)	58	3.1	70%	40%	41%	85%	0%	9/1	17-21	N/A	67%	9%
53.	Ashland University (OH)†	58	2.6	78%	59%	62%	51%	1%	13/1	20-25	41%	68%	6%
53.	College of St. Mary (NE)	58	2.7	78%	56%	58%	61%	0.4%	10/1	20-25	40%	52%	11%
53.	Fontbonne University (MO)	58	2.5	78%	57%	63%	86%	0%	10/1	18-24	N/A	81%	5%
53.	Malone University (OH)	58	2.6	73%	54%	57%	63%	2%	12/1	19-25	35%	70%	7%
53.	McKendree University (IL)	58	2.6	75%	51%	54%	67%	0%	14/1	960-1270[2]	37%	67%	7%
53.	Univ. of Northwestern–St. Paul (MN)	58	2.5	83%[8]	69%	64%	57%	5%	17/1	21-27	45%	90%	4%
53.	Univ. of Wisconsin–Stevens Point*	58	2.9	74%	56%	63%	33%	9%	18/1	20-25[9]	33%	83%	4%
61.	North Park University (IL)	57	2.9	75%	56%	60%	61%	1%	10/1	950-1167	N/A	47%	N/A
61.	Saint Xavier University (IL)	57	2.9	73%	51%	57%	41%	1%	15/1	950-1130	56%	74%	4%
61.	Univ. of Wisconsin–Whitewater*	57	2.9	81%	51%	58%	33%	5%	20/1	20-24[4]	30%	87%	7%
61.	Viterbo University (WI)	57	2.8	78%[8]	59%	62%	63%	3%	11/1	21-26	51%	76%	7%
61.	Western Illinois University*	57	2.7	68%	48%	46%	59%	2%	13/1	930-1110	32%	59%	4%
66.	Carroll University (WI)	56	3.0	81%	62%	62%	55%	2%	14/1	21-26	47%[4]	69%	8%
66.	Morningside College (IA)	56	2.5	71%	58%	51%	63%	0%	13/1	20-25	36%	56%	20%
66.	Mount Vernon Nazarene U. (OH)	56	2.5	79%	54%	59%	65%	2%	16/1	19-28	48%	76%	6%[4]
66.	Stephens College (MO)	56	2.6	67%	54%	49%	85%	2%	7/1	20-26	37%	53%[4]	7%
66.	University of Saint Francis (IN)	56	2.9	71%	52%	53%	66%	1%	10/1	955-1150	42%	93%	3%
66.	Winona State University (MN)*	56	2.8	78%	56%	64%	33%	7%	19/1	20-24	29%	66%	4%
72.	Concordia University Chicago	55	2.7	67%	49%	49%	78%	0%	10/1	990-1170	45%[4]	76%	7%
72.	Judson University (IL)	55	2.4	73%	55%	63%	78%	0.3%	7/1	950-1180	31%	75%	4%
72.	University of Wisconsin–Stout*	55	2.8	72%	52%	58%	32%	1%	19/1	20-25	28%	92%	2%
75.	Grace College and Seminary[1] (IN)	54	2.3	81%[8]	63%	61%[6]	52%[4]	3%[4]	20/1[4]	990-1220[4]	45%[4]	82%[4]	13%[4]
76.	Concordia University–St. Paul (MN)	53	2.9	71%	51%	60%	69%	0%	18/1	18-24[9]	N/A	97%	4%
76.	Northern Michigan University*	53	3.0	76%	51%	52%	37%	8%	20/1	970-1180[3]	N/A	66%	4%
78.	Central Methodist University (MO)†	52	2.4	68%	50%	40%	67%	1%	12/1	20-24	42%	93%	13%
78.	Cornerstone University (MI)	52	2.4	79%	53%	59%	55%	1%	12/1	950-1180	45%	73%	3%
78.	Mount Mary University (WI)	52	2.7	74%	47%	51%	85%	0%	12/1	16-21	44%	62%	N/A
78.	Southeast Missouri State Univ.*	52	2.7	74%	51%	49%	45%	4%	20/1	20-25	51%	84%	4%
78.	University of Central Missouri*	52	2.8	71%	51%	49%	47%	5%	16/1	19-24[2]	36%	86%	N/A
83.	Mount St. Joseph University (OH)	51	2.3	71%	54%	53%	74%	6%	11/1	20-25	33%	60%	7%
84.	Anderson University[1] (IN)	50	2.9	73%[8]	63%	56%[6]	N/A	N/A	10/1[4]	910-1110[4]	N/A	65%[4]	N/A
84.	Dakota State University (SD)*	50	2.7	71%	53%	43%	55%	1%	18/1	20-26	23%	83%	7%
84.	Minnesota State Univ.–Mankato*	50	2.9	74%	52%	49%	36%	8%	22/1	19-24	26%	61%	3%

Note: Key to footnotes Page 94.

Rank School (State) (*Public)	Overall score	Peer assessment score (5.0=highest)	Average first-year student retention rate	2018 graduation rate Predicted	Actual	% of classes under 20 ('18)	% of classes of 50 or more ('18)	Student/ faculty ratio ('18)	SAT/ACT 25th-75th percentile ('18)	Freshmen in top 25% of HS class ('18)	Accept- ance rate ('18)	Average alumni giving rate
84. Mount Marty College (SD)	50	2.4	72%	56%	51%	66%	0%	12/1	18-24	N/A	69%	8%
84. Northern State University (SD)*	50	2.5	73%	53%	50%	56%	4%	20/1	19-24	29%	88%	10%
84. Ohio Dominican University	50	2.7	67%	52%	50%	51%	0%	14/1	19-24[2]	33%	75%	4%
84. University of St. Mary (KS)	50	2.7	68%	54%	55%	66%	0.4%	11/1	19-23	30%	61%	10%
84. Univ. of Wisconsin–River Falls*	50	2.7	75%	55%	57%	36%	8%	18/1	20-25[3]	34%	75%	6%
92. Bemidji State University (MN)*	49	2.7	69%	50%	46%	41%	8%	20/1	19-24	24%	65%	6%
92. MidAmerica Nazarene University[7] (KS)	49	2.5	68%	55%	42%	69%	4%	9/1	18-26	42%	59%	8%[4]
92. Minnesota State Univ.–Moorhead*	49	2.7	74%	54%	43%[6]	42%	7%	19/1	20-25	31%	60%	4%
95. Emporia State University (KS)*	48	2.8	73%	52%	45%	51%	6%	17/1	19-25[9]	41%	85%	8%
95. Northwest Missouri State Univ.*	48	2.7	73%	53%	48%	43%	7%	22/1	19-24	38%	79%	7%
95. Pittsburg State University (KS)*	48	2.7	75%	49%	52%	53%	6%	17/1	18-24	37%	90%	5%[4]
95. University of Dubuque (IA)	48	2.7	64%	45%	44%	73%	1%	13/1	16-22[3]	20%	73%	9%
95. Univ. of Wisconsin–Green Bay[1]*	48	2.9	74%[8]	57%	49%[6]	30%[4]	9%[4]	23/1[4]	20-25[4]	N/A	95%[4]	4%[4]
95. Univ. of Wisconsin–Platteville[1]*	48	2.7	77%[8]	52%	54%[6]	25%[4]	5%[4]	21/1[4]	20-25[4]	28%[4]	79%[4]	N/A
95. Wayne State College (NE)*	48	2.6	71%	46%	43%	43%	2%	20/1	18-24[2]	28%	100%	10%
102. Greenville University (IL)	47	2.2	69%	55%	68%	61%	1%	13/1	850-1060	N/A	48%	14%
102. Rockford University (IL)	47	2.5	66%	46%	38%	78%	0%	10/1	990-1190	N/A	49%	7%
102. University of Sioux Falls (SD)	47	2.6	72%	59%	46%	55%	2%	16/1	20-25	37%	91%	4%
105. Columbia College Chicago	45	2.6	68%	59%	48%	68%	1%	13/1	1000-1230[2]	35%	87%	0.4%
105. Graceland University (IA)	45	2.3	62%	56%	46%	63%	2%	14/1	18-23	27%	58%	15%
105. Marian University[1] (WI)	45	2.4	68%[8]	48%	45%[8]	74%[4]	0.4%[4]	12/1[4]	17-22[4]	25%[4]	68%[4]	7%[4]
105. Newman University (KS)	45	2.6	76%	63%	53%	67%	1%	11/1	19-25[2]	54%	63%	4%
105. St. Cloud State University (MN)*	45	2.8	70%	50%	44%	41%	4%	19/1	18-24	20%	86%	3%
105. University of Southern Indiana*	45	2.7	71%	47%	46%	40%	4%	16/1	980-1180	34%	95%	3%
111. Davenport University (MI)	44	2.3	72%	45%	55%	52%	0%	15/1	970-1160[2]	N/A	89%	1%
111. Minot State University (ND)*	44	2.6	71%	53%	48%	67%	0.3%	12/1	18-23	20%	60%	3%
111. Siena Heights University (MI)	44	2.7	71%[8]	49%	43%	86%	0%	11/1	870-1090[2]	29%	69%	2%
114. Lake Erie College[1] (OH)	43	2.2	66%[8]	54%	47%[8]	76%[4]	0.3%[4]	14/1[4]	18-23[4]	29%[4]	60%[4]	6%[4]
114. Southwest Minnesota State University*	43	2.4	65%	55%	45%[6]	54%	2%	14/1	17 23	21%	60%	10%[4]
114. Tiffin University (OH)	43	2.6	65%	38%	43%	44%	0%	15/1	17-22[9]	42%[4]	69%	5%

School (State) (*Public)	Peer assessment score (5.0=highest)	Average first-year student retention rate	2018 graduation rate Predicted	Actual	% of classes under 20 ('18)	% of classes of 50 or more ('18)	Student/ faculty ratio ('18)	SAT/ACT 25th-75th percentile ('18)	Freshmen in top 25% of HS class ('18)	Accept- ance rate ('18)	Average alumni giving rate
SCHOOLS RANKED 117 THROUGH 153 ARE LISTED HERE ALPHABETICALLY											
Avila University[1] (MO)	2.6	69%[8]	55%	47%[6]	N/A	N/A	12/1[4]	19-23[4]	N/A	39%[4]	N/A
Black Hills State University (SD)*	2.6	65%[8]	52%	35%[6]	N/A	N/A	N/A	18-24	N/A	88%	N/A
Calumet College of St. Joseph (IN)	2.2	52%	37%	35%	76%	1%	8/1	850-1020[2]	9%	20%	1%
Chicago State University[1]*	1.8	60%[8]	42%	12%[6]	76%[4]	0%[4]	10/1[4]	17-21[4]	N/A	78%[4]	N/A
Crown College[1] (MN)†	2.1	68%[8]	47%	57%[8]	70%[4]	2%[4]	19/1[4]	18-25[4]	17%[4]	51%[4]	2%[4]
DeVry University[1] (IL)	1.5	51%[8]	45%	24%[6]	N/A	N/A	14/1[4]	N/A[2]	N/A	95%[4]	N/A
Evangel University (MO)	2.3	76%	53%	54%[6]	N/A	N/A	14/1[4]	19-25[4]	N/A	79%	N/A
Fort Hays State University (KS)*	2.6	71%[8]	46%	42%	48%	4%	14/1	18-23[2]	34%	92%	10%
Friends University (KS)	2.4	69%	52%	39%	70%	2%	10/1	18-24	37%	47%	7%
Governors State University (IL)*	2.1	53%[8]	N/A	N/A	63%	1%	10/1	860-1045	11%	38%	N/A
Herzing University[1] (WI)	1.7	40%[8]	34%	33%[6]	N/A	N/A	17/1[4]	N/A[2]	N/A	83%[4]	N/A
Indiana Institute of Technology†	2.3	57%[8]	26%	30%	56%	0%	16/1	770 1187	N/A	61%	1%
Indiana University East*	2.3	66%	44%	41%	54%	2%	15/1	920-1120[2]	34%	65%	5%
Indiana University Northwest*	2.3	67%	41%	34%	49%	7%	14/1	910-1100	30%	80%	5%
Indiana University–South Bend*	2.6	65%	42%	32%	37%	3%	13/1	930-1130	29%	82%	5%
Indiana University Southeast*	2.3	61%	44%	33%	48%	1%	14/1	17-23	33%	85%	5%
Lakeland University[1] (WI)	2.1	71%[8]	51%	55%[6]	N/A	N/A	15/1[4]	16-22[4]	N/A	52%[4]	N/A
Lourdes University (OH)	2.4	68%	46%	34%	53%	0%	14/1	18-24	40%	90%	N/A
Marygrove College[1] (MI)	2.1	38%[8]	37%	30%[6]	N/A	N/A	6/1[4]	910-1145[4]	N/A	41%[4]	N/A
Midland University[1] (NE)†	2.3	62%[8]	49%	48%[6]	N/A	N/A	15/1[4]	18-23[4]	N/A	64%[4]	N/A
Missouri Baptist University[1]	2.2	59%[8]	50%	38%[6]	N/A	N/A	19/1[4]	18-23[4]	N/A	55%[4]	N/A
Missouri Western State University[1]*†	2.3	65%[8]	42%	29%[6]	N/A	N/A	16/1[4]	N/A[2]	N/A	N/A	N/A
Northeastern Illinois University*	2.5	53%	41%	21%	62%	0.2%	14/1	770 1170	20%	56%	2%

MIDWEST ▶

CONTINUED (SCHOOLS RANKED 117 THROUGH 153 ARE LISTED HERE ALPHABETICALLY)

School (State) (*Public)	Peer assessment score (5.0=highest)	Average first-year student retention rate	2018 graduation rate Predicted	2018 graduation rate Actual	% of classes under 20 ('18)	% of classes of 50 or more ('18)	Student/ faculty ratio ('18)	SAT/ACT 25th-75th percentile ('18)	Freshmen in top 25% of HS class ('18)	Accept- ance rate ('18)	Average alumni giving rate
Notre Dame College of Ohio[1]	2.4	64%[8]	43%	37%[6]	N/A	N/A	14/1[4]	17-21[4]	N/A	89%[4]	N/A
Ohio Christian University[1]†	2.0	64%[8]	32%	35%[6]	N/A	N/A	11/1[4]	N/A[2]	N/A	N/A	N/A
Purdue University–Fort Wayne*	2.9	61%	51%	37%	48%	4%	16/1	970-1180	28%	97%	3%[4]
Purdue University–Northwest (IN)*	2.8	66%	62%	37%	46%	3%	15/1	930-1150	33%[5]	97%	N/A
Saginaw Valley State Univ. (MI)*	2.6	73%	49%	43%	32%	3%	17/1	990-1200	43%	77%	N/A
Shawnee State University (OH)*†	2.2	69%	37%	29%	58%	1%	14/1	19-24[2]	42%	74%	1%
Silver Lake College[1] (WI)	2.0	72%[8]	53%	48%[6]	N/A	N/A	7/1[4]	N/A[2]	N/A	52%[4]	N/A
Southwest Baptist University (MO)	2.3	67%[8]	49%	47%	77%	1%	12/1	19-26[3]	48%	71%	5%
Southwestern College (KS)	2.2	61%	54%	48%	73%	3%	10/1	18-22	34%	55%	4%
Univ. of Wisconsin–Oshkosh*	2.8	77%	54%	29%	42%	7%	22/1	20-24[3]	33%	69%	2%
Upper Iowa University	2.1	56%[8]	44%	42%	85%	0%	10/1	18-23[3]	15%	81%	4%
Urbana University[1] (OH)†	2.0	52%[8]	49%	30%[6]	N/A	N/A	15/1[4]	17-23[4]	N/A	71%[4]	N/A
Waldorf University[1] (IA)†	1.8	53%[8]	41%	28%[6]	N/A	N/A	19/1[4]	18-22[4]	N/A	72%[4]	N/A
Youngstown State University (OH)*	2.6	76%	40%	37%	38%	6%	17/1	18-24	36%	68%	4%

WEST ▶

Rank School (State) (*Public)	Overall score	Peer assessment score (5.0=highest)	Average first-year student retention rate	2018 graduation rate Predicted	2018 graduation rate Actual	% of classes under 20 ('18)	% of classes of 50 or more ('18)	Student/ faculty ratio ('18)	SAT/ACT 25th-75th percentile ('18)	Freshmen in top 25% of HS class ('18)	Accept- ance rate ('18)	Average alumni giving rate
1. Trinity University (TX)	100	4.2	90%	86%	76%	62%	1%	9/1	1260-1430	77%	34%	13%
2. University of Portland (OR)	84	3.9	90%	77%	82%	35%	1%	12/1	1140-1320	72%	75%	11%
3. Whitworth University (WA)	81	3.9	85%	72%	79%	61%	2%	11/1	1090-1290[2]	64%	91%	11%
4. Calif. Polytechnic State U.–San Luis Obispo*	76	4.1	94%	77%	83%	15%	13%	19/1	1240-1430[3]	89%	30%	4%
5. Mills College (CA)	75	3.4	78%	67%	68%	66%	0.4%	11/1	1008-1240[2]	62%	86%	17%
5. St. Mary's College of California	75	3.6	86%	71%	73%	64%	0.1%	11/1	1060-1250[3]	N/A	77%	6%
7. University of Dallas	74	3.6	82%	77%	66%	60%	2%	11/1	1120-1340	66%	39%	16%
8. St. Edward's University (TX)	72	3.7	81%	64%	63%	49%	0.1%	15/1	1080-1270	55%	86%	9%
9. California Lutheran University	71	3.3	84%	72%	76%	61%	0.3%	16/1	1070-1250	63%	71%	12%
10. Point Loma Nazarene University (CA)	69	3.4	86%	73%	77%	42%	1%	14/1	1140-1300	70%	69%	6%
10. St. Mary's Univ. of San Antonio	69	3.4	75%	58%	56%	61%	0%	11/1	1050-1250	58%	75%	10%
12. Abilene Christian University (TX)	66	3.6	77%	68%	67%	47%	8%	15/1	1040-1230	56%	57%	11%
12. Westminster College (UT)	66	3.3	81%	67%	61%	73%	0%	8/1	21-27	44%	93%	12%
14. Calif. State Polytechnic U.–Pomona*	65	3.8	88%	43%	71%	15%	14%	25/1	1020-1260[3]	N/A	55%	3%
14. Mount Saint Mary's University (CA)	65	3.3	78%	50%	65%	72%	0.1%	10/1	930-1130[2]	43%	84%	9%
16. University of Redlands[1] (CA)	64	3.4	85%[8]	67%	74%[6]	N/A	N/A	12/1[4]	1070-1250[4]	N/A	75%[4]	N/A
17. California State U.–Fullerton*†	63	3.7	88%	52%	68%	22%	9%	24/1	1040-1220	68%	43%	3%
17. Western Washington University*	63	3.5	82%	63%	68%	42%	13%	18/1	1080-1280	56%	88%	5%
19. University of St. Thomas (TX)	62	3.3	83%	63%	57%	56%	1%	11/1	1060-1250	52%	82%	9%
20. California State U.–Long Beach*	61	3.6	89%	58%	69%	25%	8%	26/1	1040-1250	N/A	31%	3%
20. Pacific Lutheran University (WA)	61	3.5	82%	71%	70%	51%	2%	12/1	1070-1270[3]	N/A	80%	8%
22. N.M. Inst. of Mining and Tech.*	60	3.5	75%	73%	56%	55%	8%	11/1	23-29	68%	23%	N/A
23. Dominican University of California	59	3.0	84%	65%	72%	59%	0.3%	9/1	1035-1210	55%	87%	6%
24. San Jose State University (CA)*	57	3.6	86%	45%	65%	24%	10%	26/1	1040-1260[3]	N/A	55%	2%
25. LeTourneau University (TX)	55	3.0	77%	67%	61%	67%	1%	14/1	1090-1320[2]	50%	46%	4%
26. California State U.–Monterey Bay*	53	3.2	81%	51%	61%	20%	4%	27/1	960-1160	46%	59%	1%
27. California State University–Chico*	51	3.1	85%	59%	66%	28%	12%	23/1	990-1170	N/A	65%	4%
27. Montana Technological University*†	51	3.1	75%	60%	53%	62%	6%	13/1	22-27	57%	90%	14%
27. Saint Martin's University (WA)	51	3.0	78%	60%	62%	61%	0.3%	11/1	1020-1220[2]	57%	95%	4%
30. California State U.–Stanislaus*	50	3.0	83%	34%	55%	24%	6%	23/1	900-1090[2]	N/A	86%	1%
31. California State U.–Los Angeles*	49	3.2	81%	20%	49%	23%	7%	25/1	890-1080	5%[4]	42%	2%
31. Fresno Pacific University (CA)	49	2.7	77%	53%	66%	72%	1%	13/1	940-1130	58%	64%	N/A
31. San Francisco State University*†	49	3.5	80%	45%	55%	24%	14%	23/1	950-1160	N/A	72%	1%
34. Chaminade University of Honolulu	48	2.9	76%	49%	58%	58%	0.4%	11/1	970-1130	40%	97%	3%
34. Concordia University (CA)	48	3.0	76%	56%	63%	54%	1%	16/1	1030-1220	48%	62%	5%
34. Oklahoma Christian U.	48	3.2	79%	65%	54%	60%	7%	13/1	20-27	52%	65%	10%
37. Evergreen State College (WA)*	47	3.2	66%	50%	55%	41%	6%	21/1	1000-1220	24%[5]	95%	2%[4]
37. Humboldt State University (CA)*	47	3.0	71%	46%	52%	28%	13%	21/1	970-1180[2]	31%	75%	4%
37. Rocky Mountain College (MT)†	47	3.0	69%	56%	49%	74%	1%	11/1	20-25	46%	58%	6%
37. Sonoma State University (CA)*	47	3.3	79%	51%	63%	24%	19%	23/1	980-1170	N/A	92%	1%[4]

Note: Key to footnotes Page 94.

Rank School (State) (*Public)	Overall score	Peer assessment score (5.0=highest)	Average first-year student retention rate	2018 graduation rate Predicted	2018 graduation rate Actual	% of classes under 20 ('18)	% of classes of 50 or more ('18)	Student/ faculty ratio ('18)	SAT/ACT 25th-75th percentile ('18)	Freshmen in top 25% of HS class ('18)	Accept- ance rate ('18)	Average alumni giving rate
41. California State U.–San Bernardino*	46	3.0	85%	31%	57%	23%	18%	28/1	910-1080[2]	N/A	55%	2%
41. Hardin-Simmons University (TX)	46	3.0	71%	60%	48%	67%	2%	12/1	18-24	38%	84%	7%[4]
43. California Baptist University	45	2.8	76%	51%	55%	50%	5%	14/1	980-1200	38%	80%	1%
43. California State U.,–Channel Islands[1]*	45	3.0	80%[8]	47%	58%[6]	N/A	N/A	23/1[4]	N/A[2]	N/A	78%[4]	N/A
43. Northwest Nazarene University (ID)	45	2.9	77%	59%	57%	61%	3%	16/1	1020-1250	48%	96%	9%[4]
43. University of Houston–Clear Lake*	45	3.0	74%	N/A	N/A	33%[4]	5%[4]	15/1[4]	1030-1200	41%	45%	6%
43. Univ. of Mary Hardin-Baylor (TX)	45	3.2	72%	54%	45%	49%	3%	18/1	1030-1200[3]	45%	87%	4%
43. Vanguard U. of Southern California	45	2.6	75%	57%	64%	61%	5%	15/1	950-1120	41%	40%	7%
49. California State U.–Northridge*	44	3.4	79%	36%	54%	12%	14%	27/1	930-1130	N/A	43%	N/A
49. Walla Walla University[1] (WA)	44	3.0	84%[8]	65%	55%[6]	61%[4]	6%[4]	14/1[4]	1020-1240[4]	N/A	65%[4]	N/A
51. The Master's University & Seminary (CA)	43	2.5	85%	69%	60%	63%	9%	10/1	1010-1240	51%[5]	77%	7%
51. Notre Dame de Namur University (CA)	43	2.8	71%	48%	48%	72%	6%	11/1	870-1060	38%	82%	4%
53. La Sierra University (CA)	42	2.6	80%[8]	51%	51%	61%	3%	14/1	940-1160	38%	49%	1%
53. Woodbury University (CA)	42	2.5	78%	50%	52%	81%	0%	9/1	946-1130[2]	N/A	66%	2%
55. California State University–Sacramento*	41	3.2	82%[8]	38%	48%[6]	23%[4]	15%[4]	25/1[4]	940-1140[4]	N/A	68%[4]	3%[4]
55. Central Washington University*	41	3.0	74%	49%	54%	41%	4%	23/1	930-1130[5]	N/A	78%	2%
55. Northwest University (WA)	41	2.7	81%	53%	53%	54%	4%	12/1	1030-1225	N/A	95%	1%
58. California State Univ.–San Marcos*	40	3.1	82%[8]	43%	55%	16%	8%	25/1	17-22	N/A	58%	N/A
58. Texas A&M International University*	40	3.2	77%	46%	48%	31%	16%	22/1	930-1100	52%	53%	3%
60. Hawaii Pacific University	39	2.9	65%	60%	47%	56%	1%	15/1	1020-1220	46%	75%	1%
61. Houston Baptist University	38	2.9	70%	56%	40%	53%	1%	12/1	1030-1200	54%	70%	3%
62. Eastern Washington University*	37	3.0	75%[8]	47%	47%	41%	9%	21/1	870-1080	N/A	63%	2%
62. Holy Names University (CA)	37	2.5	72%	47%	48%	62%	0%	10/1	713-870	23%	70%	5%
62. University of Alaska–Anchorage*	37	3.3	69%	55%	31%	59%	3%	12/1	1035-1250[2]	33%	81%	2%
62. University of Central Oklahoma*	37	3.2	62%	39%	35%	48%	1%	18/1	19-24	38%	78%	1%
66. California State Univ.–Bakersfield*	36	2.9	74%	33%	42%	32%	8%	21/1	880-1080[2]	N/A	100%	N/A
66. Lubbock Christian University (TX)	36	2.8	69%	52%	47%	68%	1%	13/1	18-25[3]	47%	90%	5%
66. Western Colorado University*	36	2.7	68%	55%	48%	63%	0%	19/1	1000-1170	21%	89%	N/A
66. Western Oregon University*	36	3.0	71%	43%	40%	54%	4%	14/1	940-1150[2]	34%	84%	3%[4]
70. Midwestern State University (TX)*	35	2.7	68%	48%	42%	44%	8%	18/1	940-1140[2]	41%	71%	4%
70. Tarleton State University (TX)*	35	3.0	68%	40%	46%	31%	9%	19/1	970-1150	24%	78%	3%
72. California State U.–Dominguez Hills*	34	2.9	80%	31%	45%	27%	8%	22/1	860-1030[2]	N/A	83%	2%
72. Northwest Christian University (OR)	34	2.5	70%	46%	48%	65%	2%	15/1	935-1170	42%	62%	4%
72. Southern Utah University*	34	2.8	69%	55%	40%	36%	8%	19/1	21-27	47%	79%	5%
75. Texas A&M University–Texarkana[1]*	33	2.9	55%[8]	40%	28%[6]	55%[4]	0%[4]	15/1[4]	19-23[4]	30%[4]	93%[4]	N/A
75. West Texas A&M University*	33	3.0	65%	50%	44%	37%	8%	18/1	19-24	44%	65%	3%
77. Eastern Oregon University*	31	2.9	66%	44%	32%	63%	4%	17/1	940-1133	32%	98%	1%[4]
77. Northeastern State University (OK)*	31	2.9	64%	47%	34%	53%	2%	18/1	18-23	48%	97%	5%
77. University of North Texas–Dallas*	31	3.2	71%	49%	30%[6]	52%	0%	17/1	920-1080	38%	83%	N/A
80. California State University–East Bay*	30	2.9	77%	41%	48%	11%	22%	23/1	890-1090[2]	N/A	72%	N/A
80. Weber State University (UT)*	30	3.2	63%	52%	31%	46%	7%	21/1	18-24[2]	31%	100%	2%
82. Alaska Pacific University[1]	29	2.5	60%[8]	60%	53%[6]	N/A	N/A	9/1[4]	N/A[2]	N/A	86%[4]	N/A
82. Oklahoma Wesleyan University[1]	29	2.6	53%[8]	51%	44%[6]	77%[4]	3%[4]	14/1[4]	18-24[4]	4%[4]	62%[4]	N/A
82. Simpson University[1] (CA)	29	2.4	75%[8]	53%	51%[6]	N/A	N/A	11/1[4]	998-1183[4]	N/A	56%[4]	N/A
82. Southwestern Oklahoma State U.*	29	2.8	67%	51%	40%	50%	5%	19/1	18-24[2]	49%	92%	N/A
82. U. of Texas of the Permian Basin*	29	2.8	64%	58%	41%	39%	10%	22/1	970-1130	52%	83%	1%

School (State) (*Public)	Peer assessment score (5.0=highest)	Average first-year student retention rate	2018 graduation rate Predicted	2018 graduation rate Actual	% of classes under 20 ('18)	% of classes of 50 or more ('18)	Student/ faculty ratio ('18)	SAT/ACT 25th-75th percentile ('18)	Freshmen in top 25% of HS class ('18)	Accept- ance rate ('18)	Average alumni giving rate
SCHOOLS RANKED 87 THROUGH 113 ARE LISTED HERE ALPHABETICALLY											
Adams State University[1] (CO)*	2.4	59%[8]	45%	30%[6]	N/A	N/A	16/1[4]	17-22[4]	N/A	99%[4]	N/A
Angelo State University (TX)*	2.7	66%	47%	34%	28%	8%	20/1	18-24	35%	73%	2%
Cameron University (OK)*	2.6	63%	33%	30%	42%	1%	19/1	16-21[2]	14%	100%	1%
Colorado Christian University[1]	2.7	78%[8]	51%	50%[6]	N/A	N/A	16/1[4]	N/A[2]	N/A	N/A	N/A
Colorado Mesa University*†	2.8	73%	40%	39%	47%	8%	20/1	940-1160	29%	81%	2%
Colorado State University–Pueblo*	2.9	65%	45%	32%	49%	8%	14/1	920-1120	35%	95%	2%
Concordia University Texas[1]	2.8	65%[8]	55%	37%[6]	N/A	N/A	12/1[4]	960-1140[4]	N/A	89%[1]	N/A
East Central University (OK)*	2.5	55%	43%	35%	49%	2%	18/1	18-23	44%	83%	N/A

WEST ▶

School (State) (*Public)	Peer assessment score (5.0=highest)	Average first-year student retention rate	2018 graduation rate		% of classes under 20 ('18)	% of classes of 50 or more ('18)	Student/faculty ratio ('18)	SAT/ACT 25th-75th percentile ('18)	Freshmen in top 25% of HS class ('18)	Acceptance rate ('18)	Average alumni giving rate
			Predicted	Actual							
CONTINUED (SCHOOLS RANKED 87 THROUGH 113 ARE LISTED HERE ALPHABETICALLY)											
Eastern New Mexico University*	2.9	60%	47%	32%	67%	2%	17/1	17-22[3]	32%	60%	2%
Hope International University (CA)	2.5	70%	43%	44%	23%	0%	14/1	930-1090	28%	29%	7%
Langston University (OK)*	2.2	59%	38%	19%[6]	51%	7%	16/1	17-26[3]	N/A	55%	N/A
Metropolitan State University of Denver*	3.2	66%	40%	28%	38%	1%	17/1	900-1110[3]	21%	59%	N/A
Montana State Univ.–Billings*	3.1	55%	45%	28%	54%	2%	13/1	18-23[2]	33%	100%	2%
Northwestern Oklahoma State U.*	2.6	55%	41%	30%	61%	2%	15/1	17-22	30%	74%	4%
Prairie View A&M University (TX)*†	3.0	70%	37%	35%	16%	10%	19/1	890-1050	25%	74%	N/A
Prescott College[1] (AZ)	2.8	71%[8]	51%	35%[6]	N/A	N/A	8/1[4]	19-27[4]	N/A	95%[4]	N/A
Sierra Nevada College[1] (NV)	2.5	65%[8]	52%	38%[6]	88%[4]	0%[4]	10/1[4]	910-1140[4]	20%[4]	69%[4]	N/A
Southeastern Oklahoma State U.[1]*	2.5	60%[8]	44%	27%[6]	53%[4]	3%[4]	18/1[4]	18-23[4]	45%[4]	72%[4]	2%[4]
Southern Nazarene University[1] (OK)	2.8	67%[8]	48%	41%[6]	N/A	N/A	16/1[4]	N/A	N/A	N/A	N/A
Southern Oregon University*	2.9	70%	49%	40%	51%	4%	26/1	920-1150	N/A	76%	1%
Southwestern Assemblies of God University[1] (TX)	2.4	74%[8]	46%	45%[6]	N/A	N/A	16/1[4]	17-24[4]	N/A	28%[4]	N/A
Sul Ross State University[1] (TX)*	2.5	59%[8]	40%	19%[6]	N/A	N/A	12/1[4]	16-20[4]	N/A	100%[4]	N/A
University of Alaska–Southeast[1]*	2.6	63%[8]	64%	22%[6]	N/A	N/A	10/1[4]	N/A[2]	N/A	71%[4]	N/A
University of Houston–Downtown*	3.1	69%	36%	20%	37%	2%	19/1	940-1080	27%	83%	1%
University of Houston–Victoria[1]*	2.8	52%[8]	43%	18%[6]	N/A	N/A	16/1[4]	N/A[2]	N/A	49%[4]	N/A
University of the Southwest[1] (NM)	2.4	51%[8]	44%	14%[6]	N/A	N/A	14/1[4]	N/A	N/A	35%[4]	N/A
Wayland Baptist University (TX)	2.4	49%	46%	24%	85%	0.1%	8/1	16-22	23%	98%	1%

The Top Public Regional Universities ▶

NORTH
Rank School (State)

1. College of New Jersey
2. SUNY Polytechnic Institute–Albany/Utica
3. SUNY–Geneseo
4. CUNY–Baruch College
5. CUNY–Hunter College
6. SUNY–New Paltz
7. Ramapo College of New Jersey
7. Stockton University (NJ)
9. CUNY–Queens College
9. SUNY College–Oneonta
9. SUNY–Oswego
12. West Chester U. of Pennsylvania
13. SUNY–Fredonia
14. CUNY–Brooklyn College
15. SUNY College–Cortland
15. SUNY–Plattsburgh

SOUTH
Rank School (State)

1. The Citadel (SC)
2. James Madison University (VA)
3. Appalachian State University (NC)
3. Christopher Newport Univ. (VA)
5. College of Charleston (SC)
6. Longwood University (VA)
7. University of Mary Washington (VA)
8. Winthrop University (SC)
9. Georgia College & State University
10. Western Carolina University (NC)
11. Murray State University (KY)
12. Radford University (VA)
12. University of Tennessee–Martin
14. University of Montevallo (AL)
15. University of West Florida

MIDWEST
Rank School (State)

1. Truman State University (MO)
2. University of Northern Iowa
3. University of Wisconsin–La Crosse
4. University of Illinois–Springfield
4. University of Michigan–Dearborn
4. University of Wisconsin–Eau Claire
7. University of Minnesota–Duluth
8. Eastern Illinois University
9. University of Nebraska–Kearney
10. U. of Wisconsin–Stevens Point
11. U. of Wisconsin–Whitewater
11. Western Illinois University
13. Winona State University (MN)
14. University of Wisconsin–Stout
15. Northern Michigan University

WEST
Rank School (State)

1. California Polytechnic State University–San Luis Obispo
2. California State Polytechnic University–Pomona
3. California State U.–Fullerton
3. Western Washington University
5. California State U.–Long Beach
6. N.M. Inst. of Mining and Tech.
7. San Jose State University (CA)
8. California State U.–Monterey Bay
9. California State University–Chico
9. Montana Technological University
11. California State U.–Stanislaus
12. California State U.–Los Angeles
12. San Francisco State University
14. Evergreen State College (WA)
14. Humboldt State University (CA)
14. Sonoma State University (CA)

Footnotes:
1. This school declined to fill out the U.S. News & World Report main statistical survey. Data that appear are from either what the school reported in previous years or from another source, such as the National Center for Education Statistics.
2. SAT and/or ACT not required by school for some or all applicants.
3. In reporting SAT/ACT scores, the school did not include all students for whom it had scores or refused to tell U.S. News whether all students with scores had been included.

4. Data reported to U.S. News in previous years.
5. Data based on fewer than 20% of enrolled freshmen.
6. Some or all data reported to the National Center for Education Statistics.
7. School declined to have a school official verify the accuracy of the information contained in the U.S. News main statistical survey.
8. This rate, normally based on four years of data, is given here for fewer than four years because school didn't report rate for the most recent year or years to U.S. News.

9. SAT and/or ACT may not be required by school for some or all applicants, and in reporting SAT/ACT scores, the school did not include all students for whom it had scores or refused to tell U.S. News whether all students with scores had been included.
N/A means not available.

† School's Carnegie classification has changed. It appeared in a different U.S. News ranking category last year.

Best
Regional Colleges

What Is a Regional College?

THESE SCHOOLS FOCUS almost entirely on the undergraduate experience and offer a broad range of programs in the liberal arts (which account for fewer than half of bachelor's degrees granted) and in fields such as business, nursing and education. They grant few graduate degrees. Because most of the 372 colleges in the category draw heavily from nearby states, they are ranked by region: North, South, Midwest, West.

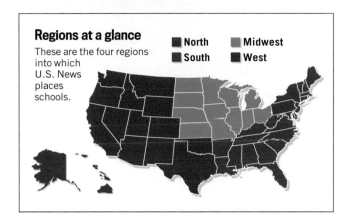

Regions at a glance

These are the four regions into which U.S. News places schools.

- ■ North
- ■ South
- ■ Midwest
- ■ West

NORTH ▶

Rank	School (State) (*Public)	Overall score	Peer assessment score (5.0=highest)	Average first-year student retention rate	2018 graduation rate Predicted	2018 graduation rate Actual	% of classes under 20 ('18)	% of classes of 50 or more ('18)	Student/ faculty ratio ('18)	SAT/ACT 25th-75th percentile ('18)	Freshmen in top 25% of HS class ('18)	Accept-ance rate ('18)	Average alumni giving rate
1.	Cooper Union (NY)	100	4.2	94%	88%	88%	72%	1%	7/1	1283-1510	85%[4]	16%	22%
2.	U.S. Coast Guard Academy (CT)*	89	4.2	94%	80%	84%	56%	0%	7/1	1245-1420	84%	13%	N/A
3.	U.S. Merchant Marine Acad. (NY)*	68	3.8	91%[8]	81%	75%[6]	N/A	N/A	9/1	25-29[4]	66%	15%	N/A
4.	Massachusetts Maritime Academy*†	65	3.6	89%	61%	73%	40%	2%	16/1	1050-1200	N/A	89%	12%
5.	Maine Maritime Academy*	58	3.6	83%	62%	73%	55%	0%	11/1	1000-1180	33%	46%	17%
6.	Elmira College (NY)†	54	2.9	75%	61%	68%	81%	0.4%	10/1	1070-1210[2]	N/A	84%	13%
7.	Bard College at Simon's Rock[1] (MA)†	52	3.2	77%[8]	75%	39%[8]	94%[4]	0%[4]	7/1[4]	1240-1440[4]	72%[4]	55%[4]	14%[4]
8.	Colby-Sawyer College (NH)	51	3.0	75%[8]	54%	61%	68%	1%	15/1	1030-1210[2]	N/A	90%	10%
8.	University of Maine–Farmington*	51	3.2	73%	43%	52%	68%	2%	12/1	970-1180[2]	44%	81%	3%
10.	Keene State College (NH)*†	47	3.1	73%	48%	60%	52%	1%	14/1	960-1140[2]	19%	81%	3%
10.	SUNY College of Technology–Alfred*	47	3.0	73%	42%	70%	53%	2%	18/1	950-1170[2]	N/A	63%	2%
12.	Vaughn Col. of Aeron. and Tech. (NY)	46	3.1	77%	40%	43%	65%	0%	16/1	946-1147[3]	N/A	82%	5%
13.	St. Francis College (NY)	43	2.7	76%	38%	55%	52%	0.2%	15/1	850-1120[2]	N/A	77%	8%
14.	Pennsylvania College of Technology[^]	41	2.9	78%	47%	51%	65%	0%	14/1	980-1180[2]	21%	82%	1%
15.	Cazenovia College (NY)	40	2.7	71%	48%	60%	86%	0%	10/1	935-1142[2]	24%	72%	5%
15.	SUNY College of Technology–Delhi*	40	3.1	73%	33%	52%	48%	2%	15/1	920-1090[2]	16%	64%	3%
17.	Fisher College (MA)	39	2.6	61%	25%	59%	65%	0%	17/1	810-1030[2]	N/A	70%	N/A
17.	Unity College (ME)	39	2.7	68%	48%	65%	48%	0%	15/1	1000-1260[2]	38%	94%	2%
19.	SUNY College of A&T–Cobleskill*	37	2.9	73%	39%	50%	50%	5%	18/1	800-1030[2]	17%	77%	2%
20.	Paul Smith's College (NY)	36	3.0	73%	45%	47%	58%	3%	12/1	N/A[2]	14%[4]	58%	8%
21.	Castleton University (VT)*	35	2.9	73%[8]	45%	49%[6]	N/A	N/A	17/1	930-1170[3]	27%	87%	4%
21.	Farmingdale State College–SUNY*	35	2.9	82%	48%	55%	23%	1%	20/1	1010-1160	31%	46%	0.5%
23.	SUNY Col. of Technology–Canton*	33	3.0	77%	34%	44%	40%	3%	18/1	900-1080[2]	14%	78%	3%
23.	Vermont Technical College[^]	33	2.7	73%	50%	43%	67%	0%	15/1	19-27[2]	26%	69%	1%
25.	Dean College (MA)	32	2.8	72%	42%	47%	43%	0%	17/1	910-1110[2]	N/A	64%	6%
25.	Landmark College (VT)	32	3.0	57%[8]	N/A	N/A	100%	0%	6/1	N/A[2]	N/A	57%	6%
25.	University of Maine–Fort Kent*	32	2.9	67%	35%	45%	77%	1%	15/1	910-1090[2]	23%	97%	4%
28.	University of Maine–Presque Isle*	31	3.0	62%	41%	34%	77%	0%	12/1	880-1100[9]	27%	92%	0.4%
29.	Eastern Nazarene College (MA)†	30	2.7	68%	37%	49%	N/A	N/A	N/A	920-1190	N/A	64%	N/A
29.	SUNY–Morrisville (NY)*	30	2.8	65%	34%	40%	53%	2%	16/1	930-1080[2]	11%	71%	2%
29.	Thiel College (PA)†	30	3.0	66%	45%	43%[6]	N/A	N/A	12/1	860-1080[3]	22%	76%	N/A
32.	Keystone College (PA)	29	2.5	67%	33%	47%	65%	0.3%	12/1	820-1125[2]	N/A	71%	4%
32.	University of Valley Forge (PA)	29	2.5	71%	41%	52%	83%	1%	10/1	960-1148[2]	23%	59%	3%
34.	Mount Aloysius College[^] (PA)	22	2.5	N/A	35%	35%[6]	76%	0%	11/1	943-1120[3]	N/A	46%	N/A
35.	CUNY–New York City Col. of Tech.*	21	3.0	75%	27%	28%[8]	27%[4]	0%[4]	N/A	N/A[2]	N/A	75%	1%[4]

NORTH ►

School (State) (*Public)	Peer assessment score (5.0=highest)	Average first-year student retention rate	2018 graduation rate Predicted	2018 graduation rate Actual	% of classes under 20 ('18)	% of classes of 50 or more ('18)	Student/ faculty ratio ('18)	SAT/ACT 25th-75th percentile ('18)	Freshmen in top 25% of HS class ('18)	Accept-ance rate ('18)	Average alumni giving rate
SCHOOLS RANKED 36 THROUGH 46 ARE LISTED HERE ALPHABETICALLY											
Bay State College (MA)	2.2	56%[8]	36%	46%	88%	0%	14/1	N/A[2]	N/A	70%	N/A
Becker College[1] (MA)	2.4	72%[8]	47%	35%[6]	N/A	N/A	14/1[4]	970-1160[4]	N/A	69%[4]	N/A
Central Penn College	2.5	54%	33%	30%	78%	0%	9/1	N/A[2]	N/A	72%	1%
College of St. Joseph[1] (VT)	2.2	60%[8]	31%	24%[6]	N/A	N/A	9/1[4]	928-1083[4]	N/A	54%[4]	N/A
CUNY–Medgar Evers College*	2.6	66%	25%	9%	5%	1%	17/1	740-920[9]	N/A	99%	N/A
CUNY–York College*	2.6	71%	27%	30%	26%	8%	20/1	880-1040	N/A	53%	N/A
Five Towns College[1] (NY)	2.1	70%[8]	38%	33%[6]	N/A	N/A	15/1[4]	N/A[2]	N/A	91%[4]	N/A
Mitchell College[1] (CT)	2.3	68%[8]	48%	42%[6]	N/A	N/A	13/1[4]	N/A[2]	N/A	78%[4]	N/A
New England Institute of Technology[1] (RI)	2.6	N/A	N/A	N/A	N/A	N/A	13/1[4]	N/A[2]	N/A	N/A	N/A
University of Maine–Augusta[1]*	3.1	55%[8]	31%	14%[6]	65%[4]	5%[4]	15/1[4]	N/A[2]	N/A	97%[4]	0.4%[4]
Wesley College[1] (DE)	2.8	53%[8]	30%	20%[6]	N/A	N/A	11/1[4]	750-1050[4]	N/A	62%[4]	N/A

SOUTH ►

Rank School (State) (*Public)	Overall score	Peer assessment score (5.0=highest)	Average first-year student retention rate	2018 graduation rate Predicted	2018 graduation rate Actual	% of classes under 20 ('18)	% of classes of 50 or more ('18)	Student/ faculty ratio ('18)	SAT/ACT 25th-75th percentile ('18)	Freshmen in top 25% of HS class ('18)	Accept-ance rate ('18)	Average alumni giving rate
1. **High Point University** (NC)	100	3.9	81%	68%	65%	46%	1%	14/1	1090-1250[2]	43%	77%	10%
2. **Ouachita Baptist University** (AR)†	90	3.2	80%	64%	63%	56%	2%	12/1	21-28	55%	64%	16%
3. **Maryville College** (TN)†	89	3.3	72%	54%	55%	63%	0.3%	12/1	21-27	42%	55%	18%
4. **Flagler College** (FL)	84	3.5	71%	54%	56%	56%	0%	17/1	1030-1220[2]	N/A	57%	13%
5. **LaGrange College** (GA)†	79	3.2	65%	59%	46%	72%	0%	11/1	1020-1180	39%	48%	13%
6. **Erskine College** (SC)†	78	3.0	63%	52%	61%	79%	0%	12/1	930-1140	28%	58%	17%
7. **University of the Ozarks** (AR)	76	3.5	70%[8]	56%	50%	51%	0.4%	15/1	19-23[2]	34%	90%	12%
8. **Catawba College** (NC)	73	3.1	75%	46%	46%	70%	0%	12/1	910-1140[9]	36%	52%	11%
9. **Claflin University** (SC)†	72	2.7	78%	35%	50%	65%	1%	13/1	18-20	32%	56%	40%
10. **Barton College** (NC)	71	2.9	69%	44%	52%	61%	1%	11/1	920-1120	34%	40%	6%
11. **University of Mobile** (AL)	70	3.2	73%	46%	50%	69%	0.3%	13/1	18-25[2]	51%	47%	2%
11. **U. of South Carolina–Upstate***	70	3.2	69%	40%	46%	56%	1%	14/1	17-22	35%	51%	1%
13. **Univ. of South Carolina–Aiken***	69	3.3	68%	44%	40%	57%	2%	14/1	950-1140	40%	51%	5%
14. **Blue Mountain College** (MS)	68	2.9	71%	43%	49%	62%	4%	14/1	19-25	47%	93%	6%
15. **Averett University** (VA)	67	3.0	63%	40%	42%	78%	0%	12/1	890-1090	27%	61%	3%
16. **Huntingdon College** (AL)	65	3.0	65%	47%	43%	52%	0%	16/1	19-24	30%	58%	29%
16. **Kentucky Wesleyan College**	65	3.1	66%	48%	42%	74%	0%	13/1	19-26	N/A	64%	10%
16. **Newberry College** (SC)	65	2.8	66%	46%	51%	64%	1%	12/1	17-23	30%	66%	15%
16. **Tennessee Wesleyan University**	65	3.1	68%[8]	39%	40%	76%	2%	13/1	19-24	35%	62%	5%
16. **Welch College** (TN)	65	2.7	75%	48%	49%	85%	2%	8/1	19-24	49%	79%	13%
21. **Alice Lloyd College** (KY)	62	3.0	60%	40%	35%	61%	2%	17/1	18-23	26%	8%	46%
22. **Belmont Abbey College** (NC)	61	3.1	63%	53%	44%	61%	0%	17/1	950-1180[2]	11%	80%	6%
22. **Mars Hill University** (NC)	61	3.0	59%	37%	39%	78%	0%	9/1	16-22	27%	57%	9%
24. **Brevard College** (NC)	60	3.2	56%[8]	49%	39%[6]	78%	0.1%	10/1	18-22[2]	18%	46%	N/A
25. **Toccoa Falls College** (GA)	59	2.5	66%	45%	57%	68%	1%	15/1	960-1160	31%	60%	2%
26. **Elizabeth City State U.** (NC)*†	58	2.4	72%	33%	43%	52%	0.2%	15/1	860-990[3]	5%	59%	N/A
26. **Pensacola State College** (FL)*	58	2.8	79%	34%	62%	74%	0.1%	19/1	18-23[2]	N/A	100%	11%
26. **William Peace University** (NC)†	58	2.9	64%	41%	37%	67%	0.3%	13/1	920-1080	25%	57%	2%
29. **Brescia University** (KY)	57	3.0	62%	42%	33%	86%	0%	13/1	19-25	N/A	39%	10%
29. **Lander University** (SC)*	57	2.9	67%	35%	43%	42%	4%	16/1	930-1120	38%	43%	6%
31. **Florida Memorial University**[7]	54	2.6	67%[8]	23%	38%[6]	N/A	N/A	N/A	N/A[2]	N/A	N/A	N/A
31. **Kentucky State University***	54	2.8	61%	33%	18%	67%	0.2%	10/1	16-26	N/A	45%	N/A
33. **Lees-McRae College**[7] (NC)	53	2.9	63%	36%	39%	79%	0%	12/1	17-23[2]	N/A	57%	6%[4]
34. **Martin Methodist College** (TN)	52	2.7	53%	32%	37%	66%	0%	14/1	18-24	N/A	100%	12%
34. **University of Arkansas–Pine Bluff***	52	2.8	70%	29%	29%	56%	2%	15/1	16-20	35%	44%	11%
36. **Ferrum College** (VA)	51	3.0	53%	35%	27%	70%	0%	14/1	870-1053[2]	1%	75%	6%
36. **Greensboro College** (NC)	51	2.7	61%	37%	31%	69%	0%	11/1	910-1140	20%	44%	15%
36. **South Florida State College***	51	2.8	61%	33%	42%	70%	0%	11/1[4]	400-400[2]	18%	100%	N/A
39. **Alderson Broaddus University** (WV)	50	2.5	55%	46%	35%	70%	2%	14/1	920-1100	19%	43%	23%
39. **Emmanuel College** (GA)	50	2.7	59%	42%	42%	67%	0%	14/1	930-1150	N/A	42%	9%
41. **Davis and Elkins College**[1] (WV)†	49	2.5	68%[8]	42%	44%[6]	N/A	N/A	13/1[4]	17-22[4]	N/A	42%[4]	N/A
41. **Philander Smith College** (AR)†	49	2.6	65%	40%	41%	72%	0.3%	16/1	15-21	42%	41%	6%

Note: Key to footnotes, Page 101.

SOUTH ▶

Rank School (State) (*Public)	Overall score	Peer assessment score (5.0=highest)	Average first-year student retention rate	2018 graduation rate Predicted	2018 graduation rate Actual	% of classes under 20 ('18)	% of classes of 50 or more ('18)	Student/ faculty ratio ('18)	SAT/ACT 25th-75th percentile ('18)	Freshmen in top 25% of HS class ('18)	Accept- ance rate ('18)	Average alumni giving rate
43. North Carolina Wesleyan College	48	2.8	58%	27%	29%	78%	0%	18/1	870-1090[2]	22%	63%	4%
44. Gordon State College[1] (GA)*	47	2.6	55%[8]	23%	50%[6]	N/A	N/A	20/1[4]	840-1030[4]	N/A	84%[4]	1%[4]
44. Ohio Valley University (WV)	47	2.5	55%	50%	43%	81%	0%	11/1	17-24	26%[4]	36%	8%
46. Bluefield College (VA)	46	2.9	55%	32%	29%	75%	0%	14/1	898-1063	16%	94%	7%
46. Oakwood University[1] (AL)	46	2.5	72%[8]	42%	46%[6]	N/A	N/A	12/1[4]	17-22[4]	N/A	47%[4]	N/A
46. West Virginia State University[1]*†	46	2.9	59%[8]	39%	28%[8]	58%[4]	2%[4]	13/1[4]	17-22[4]	N/A	98%[4]	4%[4]
49. Limestone College (SC)	45	2.7	53%	34%	35%	73%	0.4%	14/1	860-1090[2]	N/A	14%	3%
49. Point University (GA)	45	2.6	57%	35%	30%	69%	1%	17/1	880-1085[2]	22%	53%	N/A
51. Truett McConnell University (GA)	43	2.7	64%	42%	43%	53%	6%	20/1	920-1143	29%	93%	2%
52. Bluefield State College (WV)*	42	2.6	63%	27%	28%	89%	0%	12/1	17-22	56%[4]	76%	6%
53. Georgia Gwinnett College*	40	3.1	67%	29%	17%	37%	0%	18/1	930-1110[2]	17%	92%	5%
53. Kentucky Christian University[1]	40	2.7	53%[8]	40%	35%[6]	N/A	N/A	11/1[4]	18-22[4]	N/A	40%[4]	N/A
55. Middle Georgia State University*	39	2.8	65%	35%	33%[8]	49%	1%	19/1	880-1080	N/A	92%	1%
55. St. Augustine's University (NC)	39	2.2	48%[8]	25%	29%[6]	75%	1%	9/1	768-940	N/A	63%	9%
55. Voorhees College (SC)	39	2.3	56%[8]	22%	43%	61%	2%	17/1[4]	17[9]	8%[4]	65%	5%[4]
58. Central Baptist College (AR)	38	2.5	64%	36%	39%	73%	1%	12/1	16-22	22%	60%	7%
58. Warner University (FL)	38	2.6	58%	26%	30%	62%	1%	13/1	880-1080[2]	26%	35%	3%
60. Glenville State College (WV)*	37	2.4	63%	31%	30%	73%	1%	17/1	16-22	23%	71%	5%
61. College of Coastal Georgia*	36	2.8	60%	32%	20%	45%	1%	19/1	910-1100	N/A	93%	0.2%
61. University of Arkansas–Fort Smith[1]*	36	2.8	66%[8]	39%	25%[6]	N/A	N/A	18/1[4]	N/A	N/A	N/A	N/A
63. Atlanta Metropolitan State Col.[1] (GA)*	34	2.0	66%[8]	N/A	N/A	N/A	N/A	16/1[4]	N/A[2]	N/A	N/A	N/A
63. St. Petersburg College (FL)*	34	2.9	71%	35%	32%	32%	1%	21/1	920-1120[2]	N/A	100%	N/A

School (State) (*Public)	Peer assessment score (5.0=highest)	Average first-year student retention rate	2018 graduation rate Predicted	2018 graduation rate Actual	% of classes under 20 ('18)	% of classes of 50 or more ('18)	Student/ faculty ratio ('18)	SAT/ACT 25th-75th percentile ('18)	Freshmen in top 25% of HS class ('18)	Accept- ance rate ('18)	Average alumni giving rate
SCHOOLS RANKED 65 THROUGH 84 ARE LISTED HERE ALPHABETICALLY											
Abraham Baldwin Agricultural College[1] (GA)*	2.6	64%[8]	22%	23%[6]	N/A	N/A	21/1[4]	920-1110[4]	N/A	70%[4]	N/A
Andrew College[7] (GA)	2.3	N/A	N/A	N/A	N/A	N/A	N/A	N/A[2]	N/A	N/A	N/A
Arkansas Baptist College[1]	2.2	44%[8]	18%	3%[6]	N/A	N/A	20/1[4]	N/A[2]	N/A	N/A	N/A
Benedict College[1] (SC)	2.3	57%[8]	24%	25%[6]	N/A	N/A	17/1[4]	N/A[2]	N/A	N/A	N/A
Broward College (FL)*	2.9	N/A	N/A	N/A	34%	0.2%	25/1	N/A[2]	4%[4]	100%	0.2%
Chipola College[1] (FL)*	2.6	N/A	N/A	N/A	N/A	N/A	13/1[4]	N/A[2]	N/A	N/A	N/A
Crowley's Ridge College[1] (AR)	2.1	64%[8]	35%	29%[6]	N/A	N/A	10/1[4]	N/A[2]	N/A	N/A	N/A
East Georgia State College[1]*	2.5	43%[8]	N/A	N/A	N/A	N/A	26/1[4]	N/A[2]	N/A	N/A	N/A
Edward Waters College[1] (FL)	2.4	53%[8]	33%	26%[6]	N/A	N/A	24/1[4]	15-18[4]	N/A	60%[4]	N/A
Florida College[7]	2.5	N/A	51%	22%[6]	68%	8%	13/1	20-26[3]	N/A	74%	N/A
Georgia Highlands College[1]*	2.7	N/A	N/A	N/A	N/A	N/A	21/1[4]	N/A[2]	N/A	N/A	N/A
Hiwassee College[1] (TN)	1.8	69%[8]	N/A	N/A	N/A	N/A	9/1[4]	17-20[4]	N/A	64%[4]	N/A
Indian River State College[1] (FL)*	2.9	N/A	N/A	N/A	33%[4]	1%[4]	27/1[4]	N/A[2]	N/A	100%[4]	N/A
LeMoyne-Owen College (TN)	2.3	51%	21%	14%[8]	78%	0%	13/1	15-17	N/A	93%	N/A
Livingstone College (NC)	2.3	50%	23%	25%[8]	54%	0%	16/1	770-930[3]	6%	42%	8%
Morris College[1] (SC)	2.2	49%[8]	21%	26%[6]	N/A	N/A	16/1[4]	N/A	N/A	79%[4]	N/A
North Florida Community College[7]*	2.6	N/A	N/A	N/A	56%	2%	18/1	N/A[2]	11%	100%	N/A
Paine College[1] (GA)†	1.9	38%[8]	27%	19%[6]	N/A	N/A	10/1[4]	14-18[4]	N/A	32%[4]	N/A
Shaw University (NC)	2.2	46%[8]	24%	15%	55%	0%	16/1	780-910	5%	52%	N/A
Webber International University (FL)	2.6	50%	37%	24%	41%	0%	24/1	876-1060	27%	40%	N/A

MIDWEST ▶

Rank School (State) (*Public)	Overall score	Peer assessment score (5.0=highest)	Average first-year student retention rate	2018 graduation rate Predicted	2018 graduation rate Actual	% of classes under 20 ('18)	% of classes of 50 or more ('18)	Student/ faculty ratio ('18)	SAT/ACT 25th-75th percentile ('18)	Freshmen in top 25% of HS class ('18)	Accept- ance rate ('18)	Average alumni giving rate
1. Taylor University (IN)	100	3.9	87%	70%	82%	62%	4%	13/1	1080-1300	60%	78%	18%
2. Cottey College (MO)	94	3.1	71%	58%	67%	98%	0%	7/1	19-25	53%	97%	6%
3. College of the Ozarks (MO)	92	3.7	74%	51%	66%	51%	2%	15/1	21-26	46%	12%	20%
3. Dordt University (IA)	92	3.6	82%	64%	73%	63%	5%	13/1	19-31[2]	43%	73%	20%
5. Ohio Northern University	91	3.5	85%	67%	70%	61%	1%	11/1	22-27	62%	68%	10%
6. Northwestern College (IA)	87	3.5	79%	63%	69%	72%	1%	11/1	21-27	53%	71%	18%

MIDWEST ▶

Rank School (State) (*Public)	Overall score	Peer assessment score (5.0=highest)	Average first-year student retention rate	2018 graduation rate		% of classes under 20 ('18)	% of classes of 50 or more ('18)	Student/ faculty ratio ('18)	SAT/ACT 25th-75th percentile ('18)	Freshmen in top 25% of HS class ('18)	Accept-ance rate ('18)	Average alumni giving rate
				Predicted	Actual							
7. Goshen College (IN)	86	3.4	78%	56%	68%	62%	2%	11/1	995-1210	70%	66%	19%
8. Alma College (MI)†	83	3.3	80%	65%	64%	66%	2%	12/1	1040-12202	29%	64%	17%
9. William Jewell College (MO)†	81	3.2	78%	68%	65%	76%	0%	10/1	22-292	56%	46%	8%
10. Benedictine College (KS)	79	3.6	80%	62%	64%	69%	1%	13/1	21-28	36%5	97%	21%
10. Marietta College (OH)	79	3.1	69%	64%	56%	85%	0.2%	9/1	20-26	47%5	69%	15%
10. Millikin University (IL)	79	3.5	75%	55%	58%	70%	1%	10/1	960-1210	38%	61%	10%
13. University of Mount Union (OH)	78	3.2	77%	54%	64%	55%	0.2%	13/1	20-26	45%	96%	15%
14. Carthage College (WI)†	76	3.5	78%	62%	64%	59%	0.1%	12/1	21-272	47%	68%	14%
14. Hiram College (OH)†	76	3.1	71%	52%	58%	79%	0%	13/1	18-252	39%	58%	9%
16. Loras College (IA)	73	3.2	79%	65%	68%	46%	0%	13/1	19-25	46%4	93%	17%
17. Wisconsin Lutheran College	71	2.9	77%	61%	63%	62%	1%	11/1	20-26	47%	80%	15%
18. Adrian College (MI)	67	3.2	69%	56%	45%	66%	0.3%	14/1	940-11503	44%	65%	11%
18. Heidelberg University (OH)†	67	3.2	69%	52%	50%	64%4	0%4	13/1	19-25	N/A	67%	16%4
20. Trinity Christian College (IL)	63	2.7	83%	49%	60%	62%	0.4%	10/1	19-26	44%	80%	10%
21. Hastings College (NE)	62	3.0	68%	60%	53%	66%	2%	12/1	19-253	45%	64%	17%
22. Northland College (WI)†	61	2.6	71%	63%	54%	63%	0%	10/1	18-252	30%	51%	12%
23. Bethel College (KS)†	60	2.8	61%	57%	52%	81%	2%	9/1	18-24	37%	44%	15%
24. Dunwoody College of Tech. (MN)	57	2.5	N/A	53%	67%6	86%	0.2%	11/1	N/A2	31%	62%	3%
24. Wilmington College (OH)	57	2.7	68%8	44%	49%	65%	0.4%	15/1	18-23	33%	85%	11%
26. Bluffton University (OH)	56	2.8	67%	49%	54%	70%	0%	11/1	18-253	31%	42%	8%

JESSICA HILL/AP

Graduation at the United States Coast Guard Academy

Note: Key to footnotes, Page 101.

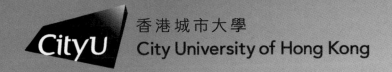

A LEADING GLOBAL UNIVERSITY

Innovation exists in every aspect of our professional education and problem-driven research.

In our world-first discoveries in science and engineering.

In our pioneering integration of teaching and research.

In our academics and students, from Hong Kong and the rest of the world.

In our local, regional and international impact.

That's why we're a leading university.

www.cityu.edu.hk

MIDWEST ▶

Rank	School (State) (*Public)	Overall score	Peer assessment score (5.0=highest)	Average first-year student retention rate	2018 graduation rate Predicted	2018 graduation rate Actual	% of classes under 20 ('18)	% of classes of 50 or more ('18)	Student/faculty ratio ('18)	SAT/ACT 25th-75th percentile ('18)	Freshmen in top 25% of HS class ('18)	Acceptance rate ('18)	Average alumni giving rate
26.	Dakota Wesleyan University (SD)	56	3.1	70%	54%	59%	56%	2%	11/1	19-24	28%	74%	4%
26.	McPherson College (KS)	56	3.0	65%	50%	37%	73%	0%	13/1	19-23[2]	28%	77%	9%
29.	Briar Cliff University (IA)	55	2.8	68%	48%	45%	73%	1%	11/1	19-24	28%	60%	12%
29.	Hesston College (KS)	55	2.8	78%	53%	52%	80%	2%	11/1	18-23[3]	N/A	51%	10%
29.	Holy Cross College (IN)†	55	3.0	54%	46%	41%	74%	0%	14/1	1070-1390	N/A	88%	15%
32.	Union College (NE)	54	2.6	76%	57%	50%	75%	1%	9/1	18-24	N/A	62%	16%[4]
33.	Culver-Stockton College (MO)	53	2.8	67%	47%	50%	62%	0.3%	14/1	18-23	27%	46%	22%
33.	Grand View University (IA)	53	2.8	70%	46%	50%	68%	0.4%	12/1	18-23	37%	92%	3%
35.	Eureka College (IL)	52	2.7	71%	54%	54%	70%	0%	13/1	950-1170	27%	57%	13%
36.	Oakland City University (IN)	51	2.2	69%	39%	54%	85%	0%	12/1	912-1110[2]	34%	50%	4%
36.	Quincy University (IL)†	51	2.7	65%[8]	50%	52%	71%	0%	14/1	18-25	47%	68%	11%
36.	York College (NE)	51	2.5	57%	43%	52%	75%	1%	12/1	17-22	17%	50%	14%
39.	Kansas Wesleyan University	50	2.9	59%	49%	41%	73%	1%	10/1	20-25	36%	47%	12%
39.	University of Jamestown (ND)	50	2.9	72%	54%	43%	62%	1%	10/1	19-24[3]	30%	62%	16%
39.	University of Minnesota–Crookston*	50	2.7	69%	51%	48%	72%	0.4%	16/1	19-24[3]	34%	66%	3%
42.	Olivet College[7] (MI)	48	2.8	63%	44%	48%	69%	2%	16/1	N/A	N/A	71%	N/A
43.	Ottawa University (KS)	46	2.7	63%	42%	49%	63%	1%	12/1	18-22[2]	11%	26%	8%
43.	Valley City State University (ND)*	46	2.7	71%	48%	41%	70%	0.4%	13/1	18-23	N/A	74%	9%
45.	Lake Superior State University (MI)*	45	2.6	69%	50%	51%	56%	6%	16/1	990-1200[2]	36%	63%	1%
46.	Defiance College (OH)	44	2.6	57%	44%	38%	78%	0%	10/1	17-23	21%	52%	7%
46.	Maranatha Baptist University (WI)	44	2.4	71%	54%	54%	77%	2%	11/1	20-26	39%	76%	3%
48.	Dickinson State University (ND)*	43	2.8	62%	47%	35%	81%	1%	11/1	18-23[9]	N/A	66%	3%
49.	Tabor College (KS)	42	2.8	60%	47%	42%	63%	3%	12/1	18-24	32%	58%	6%[4]
50.	Mayville State University (ND)*	41	2.5	58%	46%	30%[6]	78%	1%	16/1	18-23[4]	N/A	48%[4]	18%[4]
51.	Hannibal-LaGrange University[1] (MO)	39	2.7	55%[8]	40%	46%[6]	81%[4]	1%[4]	13/1	N/A	N/A	54%	3%[4]
51.	Kuyper College[1] (MI)	39	2.1	67%[8]	49%	52%[6]	N/A	N/A	10/1[4]	1000-1150[4]	N/A	66%[4]	N/A
53.	Bethany College (KS)	38	2.5	57%	48%	44%[6]	65%	2%	13/1	18-23[4]	25%[4]	70%[4]	N/A
53.	North Central University (MN)	38	2.5	76%	49%	51%	60%	6%	15/1	19-24[3]	45%[4]	63%	4%[4]

School (State) (*Public)	Peer assessment score (5.0=highest)	Average first-year student retention rate	2018 graduation rate Predicted	2018 graduation rate Actual	% of classes under 20 ('18)	% of classes of 50 or more ('18)	Student/faculty ratio ('18)	SAT/ACT 25th-75th percentile ('18)	Freshmen in top 25% of HS class ('18)	Acceptance rate ('18)	Average alumni giving rate
SCHOOLS RANKED 55 THROUGH 70 ARE LISTED HERE ALPHABETICALLY											
Bismarck State College (ND)*	2.6	N/A	N/A	N/A	N/A	N/A	N/A	N/A[2]	N/A	N/A	N/A
Central Christian College (KS)	1.9	58%	25%	31%	87%	2%	14/1	18-22[2]	21%	46%	7%
Central State University (OH)*	1.6	49%	29%	23%	50%	1%	15/1	14-18[2]	23%	57%	33%
Finlandia University[1] (MI)	2.3	44%[8]	40%	26%[6]	N/A	N/A	7/1[4]	790-1040[4]	N/A	36%[4]	N/A
Harris-Stowe State University (MO)*	2.2	53%	25%	9%	N/A	N/A	18/1	15-19	N/A	56%	N/A
Indiana University–Kokomo*	2.4	62%	33%	37%	45%	2%	15/1	950-1130[2]	29%	80%	6%
Iowa Wesleyan University	2.5	55%	47%	23%	70%	0%	11/1	18-22	34%	60%	4%
Lincoln College[1] (IL)	2.2	48%[8]	30%	9%[6]	N/A	N/A	14/1[4]	15-18[4]	N/A	57%[4]	N/A
Lincoln University (MO)*†	2.4	49%	38%	22%	49%	0.3%	18/1	14-19	16%	52%[4]	N/A
MacMurray College[1] (IL)	2.3	67%[8]	41%	33%[6]	N/A	N/A	14/1[4]	18-22[4]	N/A	60%[4]	N/A
Missouri Southern State University*	2.7	63%	37%	33%	46%	2%	18/1	18-24	38%	96%	N/A
Missouri Valley College	2.3	44%[8]	34%	23%	62%	0%	16/1	16-21	21%	59%	N/A
Rochester University (MI)	2.7	63%[8]	41%	35%	72%	0%	10/1	870-1100	N/A	100%	N/A
Sterling College[1] (KS)	2.6	60%[8]	47%	42%[6]	N/A	N/A	12/1[4]	18-22[4]	N/A	52%[4]	N/A
Wilberforce University[1] (OH)	2.3	53%[8]	30%	25%[6]	N/A	N/A	9/1[4]	14-18[4]	N/A	48%[4]	N/A
William Penn University[1] (IA)†	2.5	53%[8]	30%	30%[6]	N/A	N/A	16/1[4]	16-21[4]	N/A	54%[4]	N/A

WEST ▶

Rank	School (State) (*Public)	Overall score	Peer assessment score (5.0=highest)	Average first-year student retention rate	2018 graduation rate Predicted	2018 graduation rate Actual	% of classes under 20 ('18)	% of classes of 50 or more ('18)	Student/faculty ratio ('18)	SAT/ACT 25th-75th percentile ('18)	Freshmen in top 25% of HS class ('18)	Acceptance rate ('18)	Average alumni giving rate
1.	Carroll College (MT)	100	3.8	81%	65%	69%	65%	2%	12/1	22-28	57%	78%	12%
2.	Cal. State U.–Maritime Academy*	91	3.6	81%	60%	62%	34%	0%	14/1	1100-1275	N/A	67%	6%[4]
2.	William Jessup University (CA)	91	3.9	76%	50%	59%	70%	0.3%	12/1	960-1173	48%	59%	5%
4.	Texas Lutheran University	87	3.7	71%	51%	53%	54%	0.2%	14/1	990-1160	42%	54%	12%

WEST ▶

Rank School (State) (*Public)	Overall score	Peer assessment score (5.0=highest)	Average first-year student retention rate	2018 graduation rate		% of classes under 20 ('18)	% of classes of 50 or more ('18)	Student/ faculty ratio ('18)	SAT/ACT 25th-75th percentile ('18)	Freshmen in top 25% of HS class ('18)	Accept- ance rate ('18)	Average alumni giving rate
				Predicted	Actual							
5. Oral Roberts University (OK)†	86	3.6	82%	53%	57%	52%	5%	18/1	19-25	40%	81%	11%
6. Oregon Inst. of Technology*	84	3.6	78%	47%	51%	57%	3%	15/1	1030-1240	57%	96%	5%
7. Corban University[1] (OR)†	79	3.3	80%[8]	57%	55%[6]	53%[4]	1%[4]	14/1[4]	1040-1230[4]	60%[4]	33%[4]	2%[4]
7. Oklahoma Baptist University	79	3.4	75%	58%	60%	68%	3%	13/1	20-26	49%	64%	6%
9. University of Montana–Western*	78	3.7	72%	39%	41%	71%	0%	17/1	17-22[3]	20%	60%	3%
10. Pacific Union College (CA)†	77	3.5	76%	50%	50%	72%	0.3%	11/1	950-1190	N/A	49%	4%
11. Southwestern Adventist Univ. (TX)	72	3.2	73%	44%	45%	79%	0.4%	15/1	900-1145	23%	55%	2%
12. Schreiner University (TX)†	71	3.0	68%	46%	45%	69%	0.3%	13/1	960-1130	33%	91%	7%
12. Warner Pacific University (OR)	71	3.3	65%	51%	45%	78%	1%	9/1	870-1060	17%	97%	3%
14. Howard Payne University (TX)	70	3.3	53%	45%	43%[8]	84%[4]	0%[4]	9/1	950-1100	28%[4]	58%	6%[4]
14. San Diego Christian College[1]	70	3.3	70%[8]	41%	46%[8]	86%[4]	0%[4]	14/1[4]	850-980[4]	28%[4]	62%[4]	N/A
16. John Paul the Great Catholic U. (CA)	69	3.2	75%	56%	64%	53%	11%	15/1	960-1240	27%	90%	4%
17. Brigham Young University–Hawaii[1]	68	3.7	62%[8]	62%	44%[6]	N/A	N/A	17/1[4]	22-26[4]	N/A	37%[4]	N/A
18. McMurry University (TX)	65	3.2	60%	43%	33%	76%	1%	11/1	950-1150	40%	41%	7%
10. East Texas Baptist University	63	3.4	60%	44%	35%	50%	1%	15/1	18-23	36%	54%	3%
20. Brigham Young University–Idaho[1]	61	3.8	70%[8]	50%	47%[6]	N/A	N/A	25/1[4]	20-25[4]	N/A	95%[4]	N/A
21. University of Hawaii–West Oahu*	57	3.1	69%	40%	27%	46%	0%	25/1	16-21	37%	75%	3%
22. Arizona Christian University (AZ)	54	3.1	55%[8]	50%	45%	N/A	N/A	17/1	17-22	N/A	56%	N/A
23. Okla. State U. Inst. of Tech.–Okmulgee*	53	3.3	60%	35%	36%	70%	0%	15/1	16-21	22%	31%	1%
23. Southwestern Christian U. (OK)	53	3.0	52%	31%	28%	80%	0%	12/1	16-21	N/A	58%	N/A
25. Dixie State University (UT)*	51	3.3	56%	35%	22%	39%	4%	20/1	17-24[2]	30%	100%	17%

School (State) (*Public)		Peer assessment score (5.0=highest)	Average first-year student retention rate	2018 graduation rate		% of classes under 20 ('18)	% of classes of 50 or more ('18)	Student/ faculty ratio ('18)	SAT/ACT 25th-75th percentile ('18)	Freshmen in top 25% of HS class ('18)	Accept- ance rate ('18)	Average alumni giving rate
				Predicted	Actual							
SCHOOLS RANKED 26 THROUGH 33 ARE LISTED HERE ALPHABETICALLY												
Bacone College[1] (OK)		1.4	38%[8]	26%	9%[6]	N/A	N/A	21/1[4]	15-18[4]	N/A	73%[4]	N/A
Huston-Tillotson University (TX)		2.8	59%[8]	24%	22%	70%	0%	16/1	810-980	N/A	47%	N/A
Jarvis Christian College (TX)		2.5	50%	26%	18%	56%	2%	20/1	800-980	N/A	14%	6%
Lewis-Clark State College[7] (ID)*		3.2	58%[8]	35%	29%	59%[4]	1%[4]	13/1[4]	930-1100[4]	24%[4]	100%	N/A
Montana State Univ.–Northern[1]*		3.1	60%[8]	37%	24%[6]	N/A	N/A	14/1[4]	N/A[2]	N/A	100%[4]	N/A
Oklahoma Panhandle State Univ.*		2.4	59%[8]	33%	32%[6]	N/A	N/A	N/A	N/A[2]	N/A	N/A	N/A
Rogers State University (OK)*		2.9	68%	32%	34%	56%	1%	19/1	18-19	21%	84%	N/A
Wiley College[1] (TX)		2.3	59%[8]	21%	19%[6]	N/A	N/A	18/1[4]	N/A[2]	N/A	N/A	N/A

The Top Public Regional Colleges ▶

NORTH
Rank School (State)

1. United States Coast Guard Academy (CT)
2. U.S. Merchant Marine Acad. (NY)
3. Massachusetts Maritime Academy
4. Maine Maritime Academy
5. University of Maine–Farmington

SOUTH
Rank School (State)

1. University of South Carolina–Upstate
2. University of South Carolina–Aiken
3. Elizabeth City State University (NC)
3. Pensacola State College (FL)
5. Lander University (SC)

MIDWEST
Rank School (State)

1. University of Minnesota–Crookston
2. Valley City State University (ND)
3. Lake Superior State University (MI)
4. Dickinson State University (ND)
5. Mayville State University (ND)

WEST
Rank School (State)

1. California State University–Maritime Academy
2. Oregon Inst. of Technology
3. University of Montana–Western
4. University of Hawaii–West Oahu
5. Oklahoma State University Institute of Technology–Okmulgee

Footnotes:
1. This school declined to fill out the U.S. News & World Report main statistical survey. Data that appear are from either what the school reported in previous years or from another source, such as the National Center for Education Statistics.
2. SAT and/or ACT not required by school for some or all applicants.
3. In reporting SAT/ACT scores, the school did not include all students for whom it had scores or refused to tell U.S. News whether all students with scores had been included.

4. Data reported to U.S. News in previous years.
5. Data based on fewer than 20% of enrolled freshmen.
6. Some or all data reported to the National Center for Education Statistics.
7. School declined to have a school official verify the accuracy of the information contained in the U.S. News main statistical survey.
8. This rate, normally based on four years of data, is given here for fewer than four years because school didn't report rate for the most recent year or years to U.S. News.

9. SAT and/or ACT may not be required by school for some or all applicants, and in reporting SAT/ACT scores, the school did not include all students for whom it had scores or refused to tell U.S. News whether all students with scores had been included.
N/A means not available.

† School's Carnegie classification has changed. It appeared in a different U.S. News ranking category last year.

Best
Historically Black Colleges

INCREASINGLY, **THE NATION'S TOP** historically black colleges and universities are an appealing option for applicants of all races; many HBCUs, in fact, now actively recruit Hispanic, international and white students in addition to African American high school graduates. Which schools offer the best undergraduate education? U.S. News each year surveys administrators at the HBCUs, asking the president, provost and admissions dean at each to rate the academic quality of all other HBCUs with which they are familiar.

In addition to the two most recent years of survey results reflected in the peer assessment score, the rankings below are based on nearly all the same ranking indicators (although weighted slightly differently) as those used in ranking the regional universities. These include graduation and retention rates,

social mobility, high school class standing, admission test scores, and the strength of the faculty, among others.

To be part of the universe, a school must be designated by the Department of Education as an HBCU, be a baccalaureate-granting institution that enrolls primarily first-year, first-time students, and have been part of this year's Best Colleges survey and ranking process. If an HBCU is unranked in the 2020 Best Colleges rankings, it is also unranked here; reasons that schools are not ranked vary, but include a school's policy not to use test scores in admissions decisions.

There are 80 HBCUs, and 76 were ranked. HBCUs in the top three-quarters are numerically ranked, and those in the bottom quarter are listed alphabetically. For more detail and an explanation of the methodology changes U.S. News made for this ranking, visit **usnews.com/hbcu**.

Key Measures

Outcomes	**30%**
Expert Opinion	**25%**
Faculty Resources	**20%**
Financial Resources	**10%**
Student Excellence	**10%**
Alumni Giving	**5%**

Rank School (State) (*Public)	Overall score	Peer assessment score (5.0=highest)	Average first-year student retention rate	Average graduation rate	% of classes under 20 ('18)	% of classes of 50 or more ('18)	Student/ faculty ratio ('18)	% of faculty who are full time ('18)	SAT/ACT 25th-75th percentile ('18)	Freshmen in top 25% of HS class ('18)	Acceptance rate ('18)	Average alumni giving rate
1. Spelman College (GA)	100	4.8	90%	76%[6]	61%	1%	11/1	88%	1080-1220	25%	39%	30%
2. Howard University (DC)	93	4.4	89%	62%	54%	6%	8/1	93%	1140-1285	59%	32%	11%
3. Xavier University of Louisiana	75	4.3	73%	43%	54%	5%	14/1	95%	20-26	56%	58%	16%
4. Hampton University (VA)	72	4.3	77%	58%[6]	60%	3%	13/1	92%	19-24[2]	22%	36%	17%
4. Morehouse College (GA)	72	4.4	80%	53%	53%[4]	0.2%[4]	14/1	99%	1010-1210	11%	58%	16%[4]
6. North Carolina A&T State Univ.	68	4.5	77%	46%[6]	25%	7%	18/1	80%	950-1110	36%	61%	9%
7. Florida A&M University	67	4.1	83%	45%	33%	14%	16/1	92%	1040-1170	25%	39%	5%
8. Tuskegee University (AL)	63	3.9	71%	46%[6]	75%	5%	14/1	100%	17-27[3]	80%	52%	9%
9. Claflin University (SC)	59	3.9	78%	44%[6]	65%	1%	13/1	80%	18-20	32%	56%	40%
9. Fisk University (TN)	59	3.5	80%	46%	71%	0.4%	11/1	85%	17-23	43%	72%	31%
11. Dillard University[1] (LA)	56	3.6	72%[8]	39%[8]	52%[4]	1%[4]	14/1[4]	80%[4]	18-21[4]	38%[4]	41%[4]	21%[4]
11. North Carolina Central Univ.	56	3.9	80%	44%	39%	4%	15/1	84%	900-1050	21%	47%	10%
13. Clark Atlanta University	52	3.6	69%	40%[6]	33%	7%	19/1	83%	950-1110	37%	52%	7%
13. Delaware State University	52	3.6	72%	41%	45%	4%	15/1	84%	840-1010	26%	49%	10%
15. Morgan State University (MD)	50	3.7	74%	35%[6]	46%	2%	13/1	86%	920-1080	31%	66%	16%
16. Tougaloo College (MS)	48	3.1	71%	42%[6]	75%	0.4%	11/1	87%	16-23	30%	91%	25%
17. Jackson State University (MS)	47	3.6	66%	37%[6]	39%[4]	10%[4]	15/1	85%	17-22	N/A	69%	N/A
17. Winston-Salem State Univ.[1] (NC)	47	3.4	76%[8]	47%[6]	N/A	N/A	14/1[4]	88%[4]	890-1020[4]	N/A	67%[4]	N/A
19. Lincoln University (PA)	46	3.0	74%	45%	53%	1%	15/1	67%	860-1020	25%	81%	21%
19. Univ. of Maryland–Eastern Shore	46	3.3	64%	37%	62%	2%	12/1	88%	870-1050	N/A	54%	2%
21. Prairie View A&M University (TX)	43	3.6	70%	34%	16%	10%	19/1	95%	890-1050	25%	74%	N/A
21. Virginia State University[7]	43	3.4	71%	45%[6]	N/A	N/A	15/1[4]	91%[4]	840-1010[3]	17%	91%	5%[4]
23. Alcorn State University (MS)	42	3.2	74%	34%[6]	48%[4]	2%[4]	19/1	91%	17-22	N/A	89%	9%
23. Fayetteville State University (NC)	42	3.2	73%	33%	37%	4%	17/1	91%	890-1030	26%	68%	2%
25. Bowie State University (MD)	41	3.3	72%	40%	45%	4%	19/1	75%	860-1020	N/A	33%	4%
25. Norfolk State University (VA)	41	3.5	73%	36%	57%[4]	2%[4]	17/1[4]	87%[4]	860-1030	15%	90%	N/A
27. Alabama State University	40	3.3	60%	27%[6]	57%	0.3%	15/1	79%	16-20	12%[5]	98%	5%
28. Elizabeth City State University (NC)	39	2.6	72%	39%[6]	52%	0.2%	15/1	100%	860-990[3]	5%	59%	N/A
29. Johnson C. Smith University (NC)	38	3.0	68%	47%[8]	70%	0%	12/1	77%	810-980	N/A	46%	15%[4]
29. Oakwood University[1] (AL)	38	3.2	72%[8]	46%[6]	N/A	N/A	12/1[4]	87%[4]	17-22[4]	N/A	47%[4]	N/A

Note: Key to footnotes, Page 94.

Rank	School (State) (*Public)	Overall score	Peer assessment score (5.0=highest)	Average first-year student retention rate	Average graduation rate	% of classes under 20 ('18)	% of classes of 50 or more ('18)	Student/faculty ratio ('18)	% of faculty who are full time ('18)	SAT/ACT 25th-75th percentile ('18)	Freshmen in top 25% of HS class ('18)	Acceptance rate ('18)	Average alumni giving rate
29.	South Carolina State University[7]	38	3.1	65%	36%	59%	2%	16/1	84%	15-18	39%	53%	8%
29.	Southern U. and A&M College (LA)	38	3.2	64%	31%	39%	7%	18/1	89%	17-20	17%	38%	14%
29.	Tennessee State University	38	3.6	52%[8]	35%[6]	60%	2%	16/1	69%	17-21	N/A	52%	N/A
29.	Univ. of the District of Columbia	38	3.0	65%	39%	66%	0%	N/A	N/A	N/A	N/A	69%	N/A
35.	Kentucky State University	37	2.9	61%	21%	67%	0.2%	10/1	99%	16-26	N/A	45%	N/A
35.	University of Arkansas–Pine Bluff	37	3.1	70%	27%	56%	2%	15/1	92%	16-20	35%	44%	11%
37.	Alabama Agricultural & Mechanical U.[7]	35	3.6	58%[8]	27%[6]	48%	3%	20/1	89%	16-19[3]	N/A	90%	12%[4]
37.	Talladega College (AL)	35	2.9	63%	39%[6]	46%	12%	22/1	80%	20-24	N/A	47%[4]	11%
39.	Fort Valley State University (GA)	34	3.0	75%	27%[6]	49%	3%	21/1	100%	833-990	15%	53%	9%
39.	West Virginia State University[1]	34	3.0	59%[8]	28%[8]	58%[4]	2%[4]	13/1[4]	79%[4]	17-22[4]	N/A	98%[4]	4%[4]
41.	Bennett College (NC)	33	2.6	49%	39%	66%	1%	11/1	81%	800-1000	32%	96%	18%
41.	Bethune-Cookman University (FL)	33	3.1	64%	34%	49%	3%	17/1	86%	850-1010	16%	79%	5%
41.	Central State University (OH)	33	3.0	49%	22%	50%	1%	15/1	76%	14-18[2]	23%	57%	33%
44.	Mississippi Valley State Univ.[1]	32	2.9	62%[8]	28%[8]	60%[4]	1%[4]	15/1[4]	86%[4]	16-19[4]	N/A	86%[4]	N/A
45.	Albany State University (GA)	31	3.1	66%	33%[6]	46%	1%	18/1	82%	750-900	21%	89%	0.4%
45.	Florida Memorial University[7]	31	2.7	67%[8]	38%[6]	N/A	N/A	N/A	N/A	N/A[2]	N/A	N/A	N/A
47.	Texas Southern University	30	3.3	52%	20%[6]	34%	13%	18/1	76%	830-990	16%	57%	3%
48.	Philander Smith College (AR)	29	2.6	65%	38%	72%	0.3%	16/1	69%	15-21	42%	41%	6%
49.	Coppin State University (MD)	28	2.9	65%	21%[6]	60%	0.3%	13/1	73%	880-1030	N/A	38%	N/A
49.	Grambling State University (LA)	28	3.1	67%	35%[6]	33%	9%	25/1	94%	16-19[2]	14%	96%	4%[4]
51.	Savannah State University (GA)	27	3.1	60%	28%	43%	0.1%	17/1	96%	870-1030[3]	N/A	57%	5%
52.	Cheyney U. of Pennsylvania[1]	26	2.3	54%[8]	20%[6]	N/A	N/A	13/1[4]	82%[4]	N/A	N/A	39%[4]	N/A
53.	Bluefield State College (WV)	24	2.7	63%	23%[6]	89%	0%	12/1	84%	17-22	56%[4]	76%	6%
53.	Stillman College (AL)	24	2.8	64%[8]	23%[6]	N/A	N/A	13/1	87%	N/A	N/A	40%	13%
53.	Virginia Union University	24	2.9	61%	31%	45%	1%	16/1	78%	782-970[2]	15%	57%	8%
56.	Benedict College[1] (SC)	23	2.8	57%[8]	25%[6]	N/A	N/A	17/1[4]	88%[4]	N/A[2]	N/A	N/A	N/A
57.	Langston University (OK)	22	2.7	59%	19%[6]	51%	7%	16/1	94%	17-26[3]	N/A	55%	N/A
57.	St. Augustine's University (NC)	22	2.5	48%[8]	29%[6]	75%	1%	9/1	84%	768-940	N/A	63%	9%

School (State) (*Public)	Peer assessment score (5.0=highest)	Average first-year student retention rate	Average graduation rate	% of classes under 20 ('18)	% of classes of 50 or more ('18)	Student/faculty ratio ('18)	% of faculty who are full time ('18)	SAT/ACT 25th-75th percentile ('18)	Freshmen in top 25% of HS class ('18)	Acceptance rate ('18)	Average alumni giving rate
SCHOOLS RANKED 59 THROUGH 76 ARE LISTED HERE ALPHABETICALLY											
Allen University[1] (SC)	2.4	41%[8]	20%[6]	N/A	N/A	15/1[4]	96%[4]	N/A[2]	N/A	N/A	N/A
Arkansas Baptist College[1]	2.2	44%[8]	3%[6]	N/A	N/A	20/1[4]	75%[4]	N/A[2]	N/A	N/A	N/A
Edward Waters College[1] (FL)	2.4	53%[8]	26%[6]	N/A	N/A	24/1[4]	81%[4]	15-18[4]	N/A	60%[4]	N/A
Harris-Stowe State University (MO)	2.7	53%	7%	N/A	N/A	18/1	34%	15-19	N/A	56%	N/A
Huston-Tillotson University (TX)	2.7	59%[8]	22%[6]	70%	0%	16/1	64%	810-980	N/A	47%	N/A
Jarvis Christian College (TX)	2.4	50%	18%[6]	56%	2%	20/1	72%	800-980	N/A	14%	6%
Lane College (TN)	2.5	55%[8]	22%[6]	N/A	N/A	N/A	N/A	N/A[2]	N/A	N/A	N/A
LeMoyne-Owen College (TN)	2.4	51%	14%[8]	78%	0%	13/1	70%	15-17	N/A	93%	N/A
Lincoln University (MO)	2.8	49%	20%[6]	49%	0.3%	18/1	85%	14-19	16%	52%[4]	N/A
Livingstone College (NC)	2.4	50%	25%[8]	54%	0%	16/1	97%	770-930[3]	6%	42%	8%
Morris College[1] (SC)	2.4	49%[8]	26%[6]	N/A	N/A	16/1[4]	86%[4]	N/A	N/A	79%[4]	N/A
Paine College[1] (GA)	2.2	38%[8]	19%[6]	N/A	N/A	10/1[4]	87%[4]	14-18[4]	N/A	32%[4]	N/A
Rust College (MS)	2.5	66%	34%[6]	55%	0%	19/1	97%	14-15	N/A	53%	N/A
Shaw University (NC)	2.7	46%[8]	20%[6]	55%	0%	16/1	82%	780-910	5%	52%	N/A
Southern University–New Orleans[1]	2.8	52%[8]	17%[6]	46%[4]	0.3%[4]	20/1[4]	87%[4]	15-18[4]	24%[4]	25%[4]	1%[4]
Voorhees College (SC)	2.5	56%[8]	33%[6]	61%	2%	17/1[4]	92%	17[9]	8%[4]	65%	5%[4]
Wilberforce University[1] (OH)	2.5	53%[8]	25%[6]	N/A	N/A	9/1[4]	61%[4]	14-18[4]	N/A	48%[4]	N/A
Wiley College[1] (TX)	2.7	59%[8]	19%[6]	N/A	N/A	18/1[4]	83%[4]	N/A[2]	N/A	N/A	N/A

Sources: Statistical data from the schools. The spring 2019 peer assessment data were collected by U.S. News.

Best
Business Programs

EACH YEAR, U.S. NEWS RANKS undergraduate business programs accredited by AACSB International; the results are based solely on surveys of B-school deans and senior faculty. Participants were asked to rate the quality of business programs with which they're familiar on a scale of 1 (marginal) to 5 (distinguished); 56% of those canvassed responded to the most recent survey conducted in the spring of 2019. Two years of data were used to calculate the peer assessment score. Deans and faculty members also were asked to nominate up to 15 programs they consider best in a number of specialty areas; the five schools receiving the most mentions in the 2019 survey appear on page 106.

▶ Top Programs

Rank School (State) (*Public)	Peer assessment score (5.0=highest)
1. University of Pennsylvania (Wharton)	4.8
2. Massachusetts Inst. of Technology (Sloan)	4.7
3. University of California–Berkeley (Haas)*	4.6
3. University of Michigan–Ann Arbor (Ross)*	4.6
5. Carnegie Mellon University (Tepper) (PA)	4.4
5. New York University (Stern)	4.4
5. University of Texas–Austin (McCombs)*	4.4
8. U. of N. Carolina–Chapel Hill (Kenan-Flagler)*	4.3
8. University of Virginia (McIntire)*	4.3
10. Cornell University (Dyson) (NY)	4.2
10. Indiana University–Bloomington (Kelley)*	4.2
12. University of Notre Dame (Mendoza) (IN)	4.1
12. University of Southern California (Marshall)	4.1
12. Washington University in St. Louis (Olin)	4.1
15. Emory University (Goizueta) (GA)	4.0
15. Georgetown University (McDonough) (DC)	4.0
15. Ohio State University–Columbus (Fisher)*	4.0
15. Univ. of Wisconsin–Madison*	4.0
19. U. of Illinois–Urbana-Champaign (Gies)*	3.9
19. U. of Minnesota–Twin Cities (Carlson)*	3.9
19. University of Washington (Foster)*	3.9
22. Boston College (Carroll)	3.8
22. Georgia Institute of Technology (Scheller)*	3.8
22. Michigan State University (Broad)*	3.8
22. Pennsylvania State U.–Univ. Park (Smeal)*	3.8
22. Purdue U.–West Lafayette (Krannert) (IN)*	3.8
22. Texas A&M U.–College Station (Mays)*	3.8
22. University of Florida (Warrington)*	3.8
22. University of Georgia (Terry)*	3.8
22. Univ. of Maryland–College Park (Smith)*	3.8
31. Arizona State University–Tempe (Carey)*	3.7
31. Babson College (Olin) (MA)	3.7
31. Johns Hopkins University (MD)	3.7
31. University of Arizona (Eller)*	3.7
31. University of Colorado–Boulder (Leeds)*	3.7
31. University of Iowa (Tippie)*	3.7
31. University of Pittsburgh*	3.7
38. Brigham Young Univ.–Provo (Marriott) (UT)	3.6
38. Case Western Reserve U. (Weatherhead) (OH)	3.6
38. University of California–Irvine (Merage)*	3.6
38. Univ. of South Carolina (Moore)*	3.6
38. Wake Forest University (NC)	3.6
43. Boston University (Questrom)	3.5
43. George Washington University (DC)	3.5
43. Tulane University (Freeman) (LA)	3.5
43. University of Alabama (Culverhouse)*	3.5
43. University of Arkansas (Walton)*	3.5
43. University of Utah (Eccles)*	3.5
43. Virginia Tech (Pamplin)*	3.5
50. Bentley University (MA)	3.4
50. College of William & Mary (Mason) (VA)*	3.4
50. Florida State University*	3.4
50. Georgia State University (Robinson)*	3.4
50. Northeastern U. (D'Amore-McKim) (MA)	3.4
50. Pepperdine University (CA)	3.4
50. Southern Methodist University (Cox) (TX)	3.4
50. Syracuse University (Whitman) (NY)	3.4
50. University of California–San Diego (Rady)*	3.4
50. University of Connecticut*	3.4
50. Univ. of Massachusetts–Amherst (Isenberg)*	3.4
50. Univ. of Nebraska–Lincoln*	3.4
50. University of Oklahoma (Price)*	3.4
50. University of Oregon (Lundquist)*	3.4
50. University of Tennessee (Haslam)*	3.4
50. Villanova University (PA)	3.4
66. Auburn University (Harbert) (AL)*	3.3
66. Baylor University (Hankamer) (TX)	3.3
66. Clemson University (SC)*	3.3
66. Fordham University (Gabelli) (NY)	3.3
66. Miami University–Oxford (Farmer) (OH)*	3.3
66. Rochester Inst. of Technology (Saunders) (NY)	3.3
66. Rutgers University–New Brunswick (NJ)*	3.3
66. Santa Clara University (Leavey) (CA)	3.3
66. United States Air Force Academy (CO)*	3.3
66. University of Kansas*	3.3
66. University of Kentucky (Gatton)*	3.3
66. University of Miami (FL)	3.3
66. University of Texas–Dallas (Jindal)*	3.3
79. CUNY–Baruch College (Zicklin)*	3.2
79. George Mason University (VA)*	3.2
79. Iowa State University (Ivy)*	3.2
79. Loyola University Chicago (Quinlan)	3.2
79. Oklahoma State University (Spears)*	3.2
79. Rensselaer Polytechnic Inst. (Lally) (NY)	3.2
79. San Diego State University*	3.2
79. Temple University (Fox) (PA)*	3.2
79. University at Buffalo–SUNY*	3.2
79. Univ. of Missouri (Trulaske)*	3.2
79. Washington State University (Carson)*	3.2
90. American University (Kogod) (DC)	3.1
90. Brandeis University (MA)	3.1
90. Colorado State University*	3.1
90. Creighton University (Heider) (NE)	3.1
90. DePaul University (Driehaus) (IL)	3.1
90. Drexel University (LeBow) (PA)	3.1
90. Lehigh University (PA)	3.1
90. Louisiana State U.–Baton Rouge (Ourso)*	3.1
90. Loyola Marymount University (CA)	3.1
90. Marquette University (WI)	3.1
90. North Carolina State U.–Raleigh (Poole)*	3.1
90. Saint Louis University (Cook)	3.1
90. Texas Christian University (Neeley)	3.1
90. Texas Tech University (Rawls)*	3.1
90. University of California–Riverside*	3.1
90. University of Cincinnati (Lindner)*	3.1
90. University of Delaware (Lerner)*	3.1
90. University of Denver (Daniels)	3.1
90. University of Houston (Bauer)*	3.1
90. University of Illinois–Chicago*	3.1
90. University of Richmond (Robins) (VA)	3.1
90. University of San Diego	3.1
112. Binghamton University–SUNY*	3.0
112. Gonzaga University (WA)	3.0
112. James Madison University (VA)*	3.0
112. Kansas State University*	3.0
112. Loyola University Maryland (Sellinger)	3.0
112. Oregon State University*	3.0
112. Rutgers University–Newark (NJ)*	3.0
112. Seton Hall University (Stillman) (NJ)	3.0
112. United States Coast Guard Academy (CT)*	3.0
112. University of Alabama–Birmingham (Collat)*	3.0
112. University of Hawaii–Manoa (Shidler)*	3.0
112. University of Louisville (KY)*	3.0
112. University of Mississippi*	3.0
112. Univ. of Wisconsin–Milwaukee (Lubar)*	3.0
112. Washington and Lee U. (Williams) (VA)	3.0
112. Xavier University (Williams) (OH)	3.0
128. Bucknell University (PA)	2.9
128. Butler University (IN)	2.9
128. Cal. Poly. State U.–San Luis Obispo (Orfalea)*	2.9
128. California State University–Los Angeles*	2.9
128. Elon University (Love) (NC)	2.9
128. Florida International University*	2.9
128. Hofstra University (Zarb) (NY)	2.9
128. Howard University (DC)	2.9
128. Kennesaw State University (Coles) (GA)*	2.9
128. Mississippi State University*	2.9
128. Ohio University*	2.9
128. Rutgers University–Camden (NJ)*	2.9
128. Seattle University (Albers)	2.9
128. St. Joseph's University (Haub) (PA)	2.9
128. University at Albany–SUNY*	2.9
128. University of Central Florida*	2.9
128. University of Colorado–Denver*	2.9
128. University of Memphis (Fogelman)*	2.9
128. University of Nevada–Las Vegas (Lee)*	2.9
128. University of New Mexico (Anderson)*	2.9

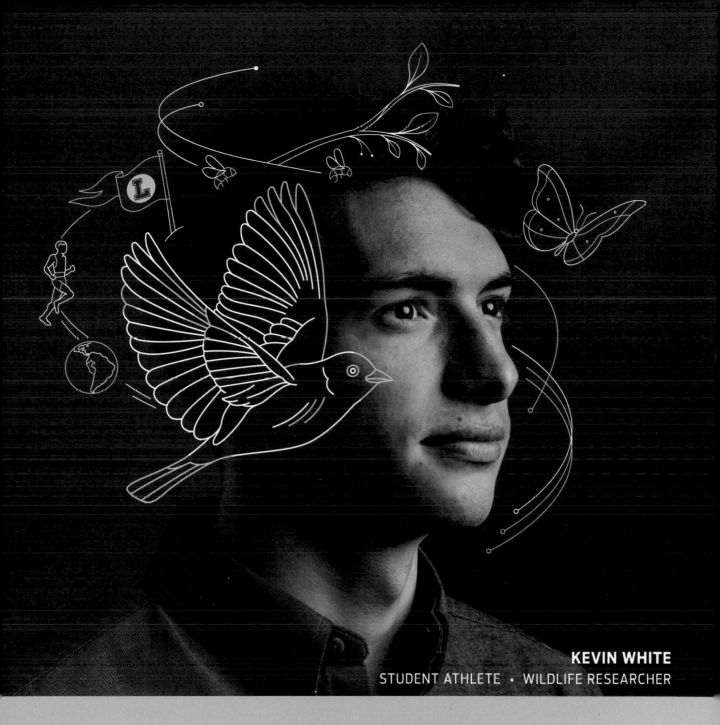

KEVIN WHITE
STUDENT ATHLETE · WILDLIFE RESEARCHER

WE ARE CALLED TO PROTECT

Kevin White came to Loyola to run track, but it was an environmental science class that set him on a new course. Now the triple-major is using science, policy, and politics to solve environmental problems. With the earth as his laboratory, the sky's the limit.

WHAT'S YOUR CALLING? LUC.edu/usnews

LOYOLA
UNIVERSITY CHICAGO
AD · MAJOREM · DEI · GLORIAM
1870

▶Top Programs

Rank School (State) (*Public)	Peer assessment score (5.0=highest)
128. U. of North Carolina–Charlotte (Belk)*	2.9
128. University of San Francisco	2.9
128. University of Texas–Arlington*	2.9
128. University of Vermont*	2.9
128. Virginia Commonwealth University*	2.9
153. Boise State University (ID)*	2.8
153. Quinnipiac University (CT)	2.8
153. San Jose State University (Lucas) (CA)*	2.8
153. University of Alabama–Huntsville*	2.8
153. University of Colorado–Colorado Springs*	2.8
153. University of Idaho*	2.8
153. Univ. of Massachusetts–Boston*	2.8
153. University of Montana*	2.8
153. University of New Hampshire (Paul)*	2.8
153. U. of North Carolina–Greensboro (Bryan)*	2.8
153. University of Rhode Island*	2.8
153. University of South Florida (Muma)*	2.8
153. Utah State University (Huntsman)*	2.8
153. West Virginia University*	2.8
167. Ball State University (Miller) (IN)*	2.7
167. Bowling Green State University (OH)*	2.7
167. Bradley University (Foster) (IL)	2.7
167. California State Polytechnic U.–Pomona*	2.7
167. California State U.–Fullerton (Mihaylo)*	2.7
167. Chapman University (Argyros) (CA)	2.7
167. The Citadel (SC)*	2.7

Rank School (State) (*Public)	Peer assessment score (5.0=highest)
167. Duquesne University (Palumbo) (PA)	2.7
167. Fairfield University (Dolan) (CT)	2.7
167. Florida Atlantic University*	2.7
167. John Carroll University (Boler) (OH)	2.7
167. Kent State University (OH)*	2.7
167. Northern Illinois University*	2.7
167. Pace University (Lubin) (NY)	2.7
167. Rollins College (FL)	2.7
167. San Francisco State University*	2.7
167. Stevens Institute of Technology (NJ)	2.7
167. St. John's University (Tobin) (NY)	2.7
167. University of Dayton (OH)	2.7
167. University of Maine*	2.7
167. University of Minnesota–Duluth (Labovitz)*	2.7
167. Univ. of Missouri–Kansas City (Bloch)*	2.7
167. Univ. of Missouri–St. Louis*	2.7
167. University of Nebraska–Omaha*	2.7
167. University of Portland (Pamplin) (OR)	2.7
167. University of St. Thomas (Opus) (MN)	2.7
167. University of Tampa (Sykes) (FL)	2.7
167. University of Wyoming*	2.7
195. Bryant University (RI)	2.6
195. California State University–Long Beach*	2.6
195. Clark University (MA)	2.6
195. Drake University (IA)	2.6
195. Illinois State University*	2.6

Rank School (State) (*Public)	Peer assessment score (5.0=highest)
195. Ithaca College (NY)	2.6
195. Loyola University New Orleans	2.6
195. Morehouse College (GA)	2.6
195. New Mexico State University*	2.6
195. Northern Arizona University (Franke)*	2.6
195. Old Dominion University (Strome) (VA)*	2.6
195. Portland State University (OR)*	2.6
195. Southern Illinois University–Carbondale*	2.6
195. University of Alaska–Anchorage*	2.6
195. University of Alaska–Fairbanks*	2.6
195. University of Arkansas–Little Rock*	2.6
195. University of Dallas (Gupta)	2.6
195. University of Evansville (Schroeder) (IN)	2.6
195. University of Hartford (Barney) (CT)	2.6
195. U. of Massachusetts–Dartmouth (Charlton)*	2.6
195. U. of Massachusetts–Lowell (Manning)*	2.6
195. University of Michigan–Dearborn*	2.6
195. University of North Texas (Ryan)*	2.6
195. University of Tennessee–Chattanooga*	2.6
195. University of Texas–San Antonio*	2.6
195. Valparaiso University (IN)	2.6
195. Wayne State University (MI)*	2.6
195. Western Michigan University (Haworth)*	2.6
195. Worcester Polytechnic Inst. (MA)	2.6

Note: Peer assessment surveys in 2019 conducted by U.S. News. To be ranked in a specialty, an undergraduate business school may have either a program or course offerings in that subject area. Extended undergraduate business rankings can be found at usnews.com/bestcolleges. U.S. News surveyed 504 business programs.

▶ Best in the Specialties (*Public)

ACCOUNTING
1. **University of Texas–Austin** (McCombs)*
2. **Brigham Young University–Provo** (Marriott) (UT)
2. **University of Illinois–Urbana-Champaign** (Gies)*
4. **Indiana University–Bloomington** (Kelley)*
5. **University of Notre Dame** (Mendoza) (IN)

ENTREPRENEURSHIP
1. **Babson College** (Olin) (MA)
2. **Massachusetts Institute of Technology** (Sloan)
3. **Indiana University–Bloomington** (Kelley)*
4. **University of Michigan–Ann Arbor** (Ross)*
5. **University of California–Berkeley** (Haas)*
5. **University of Pennsylvania** (Wharton)

FINANCE
1. **University of Pennsylvania** (Wharton)
2. **New York University** (Stern)
3. **University of Michigan–Ann Arbor** (Ross)*
4. **University of Texas–Austin** (McCombs)*
5. **Massachusetts Institute of Technology** (Sloan)
5. **University of California–Berkeley** (Haas)*

INSURANCE/RISK MANAGEMENT
1. **University of Wisconsin–Madison***
2. **University of Georgia** (Terry)*
3. **Florida State University***
4. **Georgia State University** (Robinson)*
5. **Temple University** (Fox) (PA)*
5. **University of Pennsylvania** (Wharton)

INTERNATIONAL BUSINESS
1. **University of South Carolina** (Moore)*
2. **Florida International University***
3. **New York University** (Stern)
4. **Georgetown University** (McDonough) (DC)
5. **University of California–Berkeley** (Haas)*

MANAGEMENT
1. **University of Michigan–Ann Arbor** (Ross)*
2. **University of Pennsylvania** (Wharton)
3. **University of California–Berkeley** (Haas)*
4. **University of Texas–Austin** (McCombs)*
5. **University of North Carolina–Chapel Hill** (Kenan-Flagler)*

MANAGEMENT INFORMATION SYSTEMS
1. **Carnegie Mellon University** (Tepper) (PA)
2. **Massachusetts Institute of Technology** (Sloan)
3. **Georgia Institute of Technology** (Scheller)*
4. **University of Arizona** (Eller)*
4. **University of Texas–Austin** (McCombs)*

MARKETING
1. **University of Michigan–Ann Arbor** (Ross)*
2. **University of Pennsylvania** (Wharton)
3. **New York University** (Stern)
4. **University of California–Berkeley** (Haas)*
4. **University of Texas–Austin** (McCombs)*

PRODUCTION/OPERATIONS MANAGEMENT
1. **Massachusetts Institute of Technology** (Sloan)
2. **University of Michigan–Ann Arbor** (Ross)*
3. **University of Pennsylvania** (Wharton)
4. **Ohio State University–Columbus** (Fisher)*
4. **Purdue University–West Lafayette** (Krannert) (IN)*

QUANTITATIVE ANALYSIS/METHODS
1. **Massachusetts Institute of Technology** (Sloan)
2. **Carnegie Mellon University** (Tepper) (PA)
3. **University of Pennsylvania** (Wharton)
4. **Georgia Institute of Technology** (Scheller)*
5. **University of Texas–Austin** (McCombs)*

REAL ESTATE
1. **University of Pennsylvania** (Wharton)
2. **University of Wisconsin–Madison***
3. **University of California–Berkeley** (Haas)*
4. **New York University** (Stern)
5. **University of Southern California** (Marshall)

SUPPLY CHAIN MANAGEMENT/LOGISTICS
1. **Michigan State University** (Broad)*
2. **Arizona State University–Tempe** (Carey)*
2. **Pennsylvania State U.–University Park** (Smeal)*
4. **Ohio State University–Columbus** (Fisher)*
5. **University of Michigan–Ann Arbor** (Ross)*

Best
Engineering Programs

O**N THESE PAGES,** U.S. News ranks undergraduate engineering programs accredited by ABET. Rankings are based solely on surveys of engineering deans and senior faculty at accredited programs. Participants were asked to rate programs with which they're familiar on a scale from 1 (marginal) to 5 (distinguished); the two most recent years' results were used to calculate the peer assessment score. Students who prefer a program focused on its undergrads can use the list of top institutions whose terminal degree is a bachelor's or master's; universities that grant doctorates in engineering, whose programs are ranked separately, may boast more offerings at the undergraduate level. For the spring 2019 surveys, 51.7% of those canvassed returned ratings of schools below; 71.6% did so for the doctorate group. Respondents were also asked to name up to 15 top programs in specialty areas; those mentioned most often in the 2019 survey alone appear here.

Top Programs ▶ AT ENGINEERING SCHOOLS WHOSE HIGHEST DEGREE IS A BACHELOR'S OR MASTER'S

Rank	School (State) (*Public)	Peer assessment score (5.0=highest)	Rank	School (State) (*Public)	Peer assessment score (5.0=highest)	Rank	School (State) (*Public)	Peer assessment score (5.0=highest)
1.	Rose-Hulman Institute of Technology (IN)	4.6	21.	Rowan University (NJ)*	3.4	38.	Purdue University–Fort Wayne*	3.0
2.	Harvey Mudd College (CA)	4.5	25.	Union College (NY)	3.3	38.	Texas Christian University	3.0
3.	Franklin W. Olin Col. of Engineering (MA)	4.4	26.	Bradley University (IL)	3.2	38.	Trinity University (TX)	3.0
4.	United States Military Academy (NY)*	4.2	26.	James Madison University (VA)*	3.2	38.	University of Minnesota–Duluth*	3.0
4.	United States Naval Academy (MD)*	4.2	26.	Seattle University	3.2	38.	University of St. Thomas (MN)	3.0
6.	Bucknell University (PA)	4.1	26.	U.S. Merchant Marine Acad. (NY)*	3.2	38.	University of Wisconsin–Platteville*	3.0
6.	United States Air Force Academy (CO)*	4.1	26.	University of Portland (OR)	3.2	52.	California State University–Sacramento*	2.9
8.	Cal. Poly. State U.–San Luis Obispo*	4.0	26.	Virginia Military Institute*	3.2	52.	Cedarville University (OH)	2.9
9.	Milwaukee School of Engineering	3.9	32.	California State University–Los Angeles*	3.1	52.	Central Michigan University*	2.9
10.	Cooper Union (NY)	3.8	32.	Hofstra University (NY)	3.1	52.	College of New Jersey*	2.9
11.	California State Polytechnic U.–Pomona*	3.7	32.	Miami University–Oxford (OH)*	3.1	52.	Grand Valley State University (MI)*	2.9
11.	United States Coast Guard Academy (CT)*	3.7	32.	Ohio Northern University	3.1	52.	Loyola University Maryland	2.9
13.	Kettering University (MI)	3.6	32.	Oregon Inst. of Technology*	3.1	52.	Massachusetts Maritime Academy*	2.9
13.	Lafayette College (PA)	3.6	32.	Wentworth Inst. of Technology (MA)	3.1	52.	Mercer University (GA)	2.9
13.	University of San Diego	3.6	38.	Brigham Young University–Idaho	3.0	52.	Penn State University–Erie, Behrend Col.*	2.9
13.	Valparaiso University (IN)	3.6	38.	California State University–Fullerton*	3.0	52.	Purdue University–Northwest (IN)*	2.9
17.	Embry-Riddle Aeronautical U.–Prescott (AZ)	3.5	38.	California State University–Northridge*	3.0	52.	SUNY Maritime College*	2.9
17.	San Jose State University (CA)*	3.5	38.	LeTourneau University (TX)	3.0	52.	SUNY Polytechnic Institute–Albany/Utica*	2.9
17.	Smith College (MA)	3.5	38.	Manhattan College (NY)	3.0	52.	Trinity College (CT)	2.9
17.	Swarthmore College (PA)	3.5	38.	New York Inst. of Technology	3.0	52.	University of Alaska–Anchorage*	2.9
21.	The Citadel (SC)*	3.4	38.	Northern Arizona University*	3.0	52.	University of Hartford (CT)	2.9
21.	Gonzaga University (WA)	3.4	38.	Northern Illinois University*	3.0	52.	University of the Pacific (CA)	2.9
21.	Loyola Marymount University (CA)	3.4						

Best in the Specialties ▶

(*Public)

AEROSPACE/AERONAUTICAL/ASTRONAUTICAL
1. Embry-Riddle Aeronautical U.–Prescott (AZ)
2. United States Naval Academy (MD)*

BIOMEDICAL/BIOMEDICAL ENGINEERING
1. Bucknell University (PA)
2. Rose-Hulman Institute of Technology (IN)

CHEMICAL
1. Rose-Hulman Institute of Technology (IN)

CIVIL
1. Rose-Hulman Institute of Technology (IN)
2. Bucknell University (PA)
3. California Polytechnic State University–San Luis Obispo*

4. United States Military Academy (NY)*
5. California State Polytechnic University–Pomona*
5. Harvey Mudd College (CA)

COMPUTER ENGINEERING
1. Rose-Hulman Institute of Technology (IN)
2. California Polytechnic State University–San Luis Obispo*
3. Bucknell University (PA)
3. Harvey Mudd College (CA)
5. California State Polytechnic University–Pomona*

ELECTRICAL/ELECTRONIC/COMMUNICATIONS
1. Rose-Hulman Institute of Technology (IN)
2. California Polytechnic State University–San Luis Obispo*

3. Bucknell University (PA)
4. Harvey Mudd College (CA)
5. Franklin W. Olin College of Engineering (MA)

INDUSTRIAL/MANUFACTURING
1. California Polytechnic State University–San Luis Obispo*

MECHANICAL
1. Rose-Hulman Institute of Technology (IN)
2. California Polytechnic State University–San Luis Obispo*
2. Harvey Mudd College (CA)
4. Bucknell University (PA)
5. Milwaukee School of Engineering

▶ **More @ usnews.com/bestcolleges**

Top Programs ▶ AT ENGINEERING SCHOOLS WHOSE HIGHEST DEGREE IS A DOCTORATE

Rank	School (State) (*Public)	Peer assessment score (5.0=highest)
1.	Massachusetts Institute of Technology	4.9
2.	Stanford University (CA)	4.8
3.	University of California–Berkeley*	4.7
4.	California Institute of Technology	4.6
4.	Georgia Institute of Technology*	4.6
6.	Carnegie Mellon University (PA)	4.4
6.	University of Illinois–Urbana-Champaign*	4.4
6.	University of Michigan–Ann Arbor*	4.4
9.	Cornell University (NY)	4.3
9.	Purdue University–West Lafayette (IN)*	4.3
11.	University of Texas–Austin*	4.2
12.	Princeton University (NJ)	4.1
13.	Northwestern University (IL)	4.0
13.	Virginia Tech*	4.0
15.	Columbia University (NY)	3.9
15.	Johns Hopkins University (MD)	3.9
15.	Texas A&M University–College Station*	3.9
15.	University of California–Los Angeles*	3.9
15.	Univ. of Wisconsin–Madison*	3.9
20.	Duke University (NC)	3.8
20.	Rice University (TX)	3.8
20.	University of California–San Diego*	3.8

Rank	School (State) (*Public)	Peer assessment score (5.0=highest)
20.	University of Pennsylvania	3.8
20.	University of Washington*	3.8
25.	Harvard University (MA)	3.7
25.	Pennsylvania State U.–Univ. Park*	3.7
25.	Univ. of Maryland–College Park*	3.7
25.	University of Minnesota–Twin Cities*	3.7
29.	Ohio State University–Columbus*	3.6
29.	Rensselaer Polytechnic Inst. (NY)	3.6
29.	University of California–Davis*	3.6
29.	University of Colorado–Boulder*	3.6
29.	University of Southern California	3.6
34.	North Carolina State U.–Raleigh*	3.5
34.	University of California–Santa Barbara*	3.5
34.	University of Florida*	3.5
34.	Vanderbilt University (TN)	3.5
34.	Yale University (CT)	3.5
39.	Arizona State University–Tempe*	3.4
39.	Brown University (RI)	3.4
39.	Case Western Reserve Univ. (OH)	3.4
39.	University of California–Irvine*	3.4
39.	University of Notre Dame (IN)	3.4
39.	University of Virginia*	3.4

Rank	School (State) (*Public)	Peer assessment score (5.0=highest)
39.	Washington University in St. Louis	3.4
46.	Colorado School of Mines*	3.3
46.	Iowa State University*	3.3
46.	Northeastern University (MA)	3.3
49.	Boston University	3.2
49.	Dartmouth College (NH)	3.2
49.	Lehigh University (PA)	3.2
49.	Michigan State University*	3.2
49.	Rutgers University–New Brunswick (NJ)*	3.2
54.	Auburn University (AL)*	3.1
54.	Clemson University (SC)*	3.1
54.	Drexel University (PA)	3.1
54.	Tufts University (MA)	3.1
54.	University of Arizona*	3.1
54.	University of Delaware*	3.1
54.	University of Pittsburgh*	3.1
61.	Rochester Inst. of Technology (NY)	3.0
61.	Univ. of Massachusetts–Amherst*	3.0
61.	U. of North Carolina–Chapel Hill*	3.0
61.	University of Utah*	3.0
61.	Worcester Polytechnic Inst. (MA)	3.0

Best in the Specialties ▶

(*Public)

AEROSPACE/AERONAUTICAL/ASTRONAUTICAL
1. Massachusetts Institute of Technology
2. Georgia Institute of Technology*
3. California Institute of Technology
4. Embry-Riddle Aeronautical University (FL)
4. Purdue University–West Lafayette (IN)*

BIOLOGICAL/AGRICULTURAL
1. Purdue University–West Lafayette (IN)*
2. Iowa State University*
3. Cornell University (NY)
3. University of California–Davis*
5. Texas A&M University–College Station*

BIOMEDICAL/BIOMEDICAL ENGINEERING
1. Johns Hopkins University (MD)
2. Massachusetts Institute of Technology
3. Duke University (NC)
4. Georgia Institute of Technology*
5. Stanford University (CA)

CHEMICAL
1. Massachusetts Institute of Technology
2. University of California–Berkeley*
3. Georgia Institute of Technology*
4. University of Texas–Austin*
5. Stanford University (CA)

CIVIL
1. University of California–Berkeley*
2. Georgia Institute of Technology*
3. University of Illinois–Urbana-Champaign*
4. Massachusetts Institute of Technology
5. Purdue University–West Lafayette (IN)*

COMPUTER ENGINEERING
1. Massachusetts Institute of Technology
2. Carnegie Mellon University (PA)
3. University of California–Berkeley*
4. Georgia Institute of Technology*
4. Stanford University (CA)

ELECTRICAL/ELECTRONIC/COMMUNICATIONS
1. Massachusetts Institute of Technology
2. University of California–Berkeley*
3. Stanford University (CA)
4. Georgia Institute of Technology*
5. University of Illinois–Urbana-Champaign*

ENVIRONMENTAL/ENVIRONMENTAL HEALTH
1. University of California–Berkeley*
2. Stanford University (CA)
2. University of Michigan–Ann Arbor*
4. Georgia Institute of Technology*
5. Massachusetts Institute of Technology
5. University of Illinois–Urbana-Champaign*

INDUSTRIAL/MANUFACTURING
1. Georgia Institute of Technology*
2. University of Michigan–Ann Arbor*
3. Purdue University–West Lafayette (IN)*
4. Virginia Tech*
5. University of California–Berkeley*

MATERIALS
1. Massachusetts Institute of Technology
2. Georgia Institute of Technology*
3. University of Illinois–Urbana-Champaign*
4. University of California–Berkeley*
5. Northwestern University (IL)
5. University of Michigan–Ann Arbor*

MECHANICAL
1. Massachusetts Institute of Technology
2. University of California–Berkeley*
3. Georgia Institute of Technology*
4. Stanford University (CA)
5. University of Michigan–Ann Arbor*

PETROLEUM
1. Texas A&M University–College Station*
1. University of Texas–Austin*
3. Louisiana State University–Baton Rouge*
3. Pennsylvania State U.–University Park*
5. Colorado School of Mines*
5. University of Oklahoma*

Note: Peer assessment survey in 2019 conducted by U.S. News. To be ranked in a specialty, a school may have either a program or course offerings in that subject area; ABET accreditation of that program is not needed. Extended rankings can be found at usnews.com/bestcolleges. U.S. News surveyed 206 undergraduate engineering programs at colleges that offer doctoral degrees in engineering and 210 engineering programs at colleges where the terminal degree in engineering is a bachelor's or master's.

CHRIST. CHARACTER.
CONFIDENCE.

These are the things that will guide you throughout life. We know — because at Palm Beach Atlantic University, they're what guide us every day.

CHOOSE FROM OVER 50 MAJORS
at Florida's leading Christian University.

ENJOY MORE THAN
50 student clubs and over 100 performances and events.

AVERAGE CLASS SIZE OF 17
provides students with a world-class educational experience.

FEAR THE FISH
Participate in NCAA Division II Sunshine State Conference athletics.

EARN UP TO $18,000
in scholarships annually.

PALM BEACH ATLANTIC UNIVERSITY

WEST PALM BEACH, FLORIDA

READY TO LAUNCH YOUR CALLING?

PBA.EDU

Best
Online Degree Programs

W HEN WE SURVEYED COLLEGES IN 2018 about their online options, more than 360 schools reported having bachelor's programs that can be completed without showing up in person for class (though attendance may be required for testing, orientations and support services). These offerings, typically degree-completion programs aimed at working adults and community college grads, were evaluated on their success at engaging students, the credentials of their faculty, and the services and technologies made available remotely. The table below features some of the most significant ranking factors, such as the prevalence of faculty holding a Ph.D. or other terminal degree, class size, the percentages of new entrants who stayed enrolled and later graduated, and the debt loads of recent graduates. The top half of programs are listed here. Ranks are determined by the institutions' rounded overall program scores, displayed below. To see the rest of the ranked online bachelor's programs and to read the full details about the methodology, visit usnews.com/online. There you'll also find detail-rich profile pages for each of the schools and (in case you want to plan ahead) rankings of online MBA programs and graduate programs in engineering, nursing, education and more.

(*Public, **For profit)

Rank	School	Overall program score	Average peer assessment score (5.0=highest)	'18 total program enrollment	'18 - '19 tuition[1]	'18 full-time faculty with Ph.D.	'18 average class size	'18 retention rate	'18 graduation rate[2]	% graduates with debt ('18)	Average debt of graduates ('18)
1.	Embry-Riddle Aeronautical U.–Worldwide (FL)	100	3.6	15,752	$390	67%	20	80%	33%	11%	$7,748
2.	Arizona State University*	98	3.9	36,464	$520	72%	43	86%	53%	63%	$19,591
3.	Ohio State University–Columbus*	96	3.7	360	$387	77%	30	100%	89%	43%	$13,486
3.	Oregon State University*	96	3.9	5,948	$297	65%	34	84%	42%	60%	$25,444
5.	Pennsylvania State University–World Campus*	95	4.2	9,273	$555	61%	28	76%	39%	71%	$36,433
5.	University of Florida*	95	3.7	2,823	$500	77%	53	89%	70%	49%	$17,013
5.	University of Illinois–Chicago*	95	3.4	287	$520	39%	20	94%	93%	56%	$16,442
8.	Colorado State University–Global Campus*	93	3.5	12,056	$350	100%	13	79%	48%	67%	$26,234
8.	University at Buffalo–SUNY*	93	3.6	52	$1,023	100%	30	93%	55%	37%	$10,800
8.	University of North Carolina–Wilmington*	93	3.3	2,033	$643	52%	27	98%	98%	39%	$15,988
8.	University of Oklahoma*	93	3.7	1,098	$672	85%	16	80%	46%	54%	$22,783
12.	Loyola University Chicago (IL)	92	3.4	406	$670	76%	13	79%	78%	63%	$23,333
12.	University of Alabama–Birmingham*	92	3.3	1,572	$441	82%	44	80%	87%	50%	$24,294
14.	University of Central Florida*	91	3.8	11,947	$300	70%	71	82%	73%	59%	$21,764
15.	CUNY School of Professional Studies*	89	3.2	2,018	$295	71%	16	62%	39%	33%	$14,119
15.	Utah State University*	89	3.6	1,578	$438	60%	62	71%	42%	48%	$16,877
15.	Western Kentucky University*	89	3.3	3,516	$530	69%	18	81%	48%	63%	$27,770
18.	University of Arkansas*	88	3.3	977	$246	54%	26	99%	23%	59%	$19,487
18.	West Texas A&M University*	88	2.8	1,406	$305	74%	38	80%	77%	52%	$12,600
20.	Colorado State University*	87	3.5	652	$473	65%	12	79%	65%	56%	$26,789
20.	George Washington University (DC)	87	3.6	412	$595	44%	16	64%	50%	36%	$21,453
20.	Indiana University– Online*	87	3.5	2,520	$321	65%	23	82%	62%	75%	$27,551
20.	University of Massachusetts–Amherst*	87	3.6	1,594	$525	67%	24	67%	65%	66%	$24,107
20.	Washington State University*	87	3.6	2,234	$565	74%	33	69%	49%	73%	$26,069
25.	Ball State University* (IN)	86	3.3	1,225	$510	70%	29	76%	46%	68%	$33,516
25.	Charleston Southern University (SC)	86	2.6	338	$490	74%	11	63%	60%	20%	$18,982
25.	University of Georgia* (GA)	86	3.6	134	$481	100%	20	68%	N/A	54%	$28,992
25.	University of Massachusetts–Lowell* (MA)	86	3.4	2,165	$380	83%	26	81%	43%	58%	$24,523
29.	Siena Heights University (MI)	85	2.3	1,343	$530	56%	14	85%	80%	72%	$21,322
29.	University of Arizona*	85	3.3	1,493	$500	75%	23	81%	N/A	59%	$19,553
29.	University of Missouri–St. Louis*	85	3.2	62	$452	71%	20	100%	95%	41%	$18,931
29.	University of Northern Colorado*	85	2.9	475	$420	56%	21	81%	70%	50%	$14,143
33.	City University of Seattle (WA)	84	2.9	2,095	$423	0%	9	70%	51%	14%	$24,292
33.	Creighton University (NE)	84	3.5	114	$456	100%	13	71%	N/A	67%	$27,170
33.	Daytona State College* (FL)	84	2.4	1,716	$550	71%	24	76%	59%	50%	$21,142
33.	University of Illinois–Springfield*	84	3.5	1,047	$359	87%	21	73%	39%	62%	$23,102
37.	Pace University (NY)	83	2.9	280	$680	94%	11	72%	61%	46%	$32,739
37.	Rutgers University–Camden* (NJ)	83	3.5	314	$550	100%	36	78%	N/A	89%	$26,082
37.	Texas A&M University–Commerce*	83	3.0	1,932	$575	68%	23	64%	51%	51%	$18,300
37.	University of North Carolina–Charlotte*	83	3.5	503	$583	63%	26	94%	85%	39%	$13,600
37.	University of North Florida*	83	3.0	244	$285	100%	58	85%	N/A	22%	$6,151
42.	California Baptist University	82	2.9	2,533	$589	79%	21	84%	59%	86%	$35,500

N/A=Data were not provided by the school. **1.** Tuition is reported on a per-credit-hour basis. Out-of-state tuition is listed for public institutions.
2. Displayed here for standardization are six-year graduation rates.

Rank	School	Overall program score	Average peer assessment score (5.0=highest)	'18 total program enrollment	'18 - '19 tuition[1]	'18 full-time faculty with Ph.D.	'18 average class size	'18 retention rate	'18 graduation rate[2]	% graduates with debt ('18)	Average debt of graduates ('18)
42.	Fort Hays State University* (KS)	82	3.0	8,550	$219	56%	24	92%	64%	26%	$24,894
42.	Lee University (TN)	82	3.0	883	$227	96%	9	86%	N/A	75%	$28,122
42.	Maranatha Baptist University (WI)	82	2.3	197	$420	52%	9	82%	83%	47%	$11,253
42.	Regent University (VA)	82	2.7	4,703	$425	77%	17	72%	37%	69%	$27,586
42.	University of Nebraska–Lincoln*	82	3.6	28	$569	71%	21	75%	N/A	57%	$19,166
42.	University of Wisconsin–Whitewater*	82	3.2	312	$389	72%	30	75%	67%	60%	N/A
49.	Marist College (NY)	81	2.8	136	$700	61%	14	92%	56%	65%	$28,256
49.	New England Institute of Technology (RI)	81	3.0	136	$190	100%	13	39%	N/A	88%	$33,097
49.	Robert Morris University (PA)	81	2.6	412	$765	98%	11	66%	N/A	80%	$36,458
49.	University of Massachusetts–Boston*	81	3.4	365	$410	83%	28	73%	70%	56%	$20,546
49.	University of Nebraska–Omaha*	81	3.4	444	$475	79%	30	85%	63%	76%	$23,585
49.	University of Wisconsin–Milwaukee*	81	3.3	3,389	$337	70%	32	84%	31%	71%	$32,329
49.	University of the Incarnate Word (TX)	81	2.5	1,366	$530	100%	18	70%	66%	85%	$24,307
49.	Utica College (NY)	81	3.1	1,023	$475	59%	15	82%	49%	51%	$15,869
49.	Westfield State University* (MA)	81	2.5	227	$315	94%	19	80%	53%	63%	$22,321
58.	Bowling Green State University* (OH)	80	3.1	427	$390	73%	19	85%	49%	51%	$25,710
58.	Clarion University of Pennsylvania*	80	2.4	838	$347	97%	25	74%	60%	56%	$25,344
58.	Florida International University*	80	3.1	4,910	$247	80%	49	84%	39%	63%	$14,616
58.	Illinois State University*	80	3.0	68	$768	0%	13	87%	N/A	69%	$14,024
58.	McKendree University (IL)	80	2.6	434	$390	85%	14	85%	N/A	58%	$23,322
58.	North Carolina State University–Raleigh*	80	3.4	66	$874	100%	19	100%	74%	64%	$26,076
58.	Northern Arizona University*	80	3.2	4,461	$425	56%	30	89%	55%	66%	$19,169
58.	SUNY College of Technology–Delhi*	80	3.0	994	$343	55%	18	80%	52%	49%	$18,311
58.	Sacred Heart University (CT)	80	2.6	328	$590	80%	13	80%	58%	66%	$23,791
58.	University of Memphis* (TN)	80	2.9	1,700	$420	74%	29	80%	44%	67%	$23,785
58.	Western Carolina University* (NC)	80	3.0	1,399	$189	80%	20	80%	65%	N/A	N/A
69.	Concordia University Chicago (IL)	79	2.3	139	$505	85%	7	77%	N/A	88%	$23,809
69.	Saint Leo University (FL)	79	2.8	5,881	$360	83%	19	78%	26%	24%	$37,713
69.	University of Cincinnati* (OH)	79	3.3	2,373	$1,028	67%	33	80%	N/A	69%	$21,170
69.	University of North Dakota*	79	3.4	568	$300	68%	14	68%	36%	61%	N/A
69.	University of North Texas*	79	3.2	1,561	$695	75%	40	78%	70%	61%	$21,790
74.	Old Dominion University* (VA)	78	3.1	7,333	$389	68%	41	83%	63%	N/A	N/A
74.	Savannah College of Art and Design (GA)	78	3.0	535	$814	20%	19	69%	21%	60%	$39,433
76.	Granite State College* (NH)	77	2.6	2,053	$355	25%	12	82%	44%	62%	$17,275
76.	Linfield College (OR)	77	2.6	376	$495	72%	11	80%	63%	55%	$22,320
76.	Missouri State University*	77	3.1	410	$295	63%	27	N/A	N/A	N/A	N/A
76.	Sam Houston State University* (TX)	77	2.7	2,565	$234	N/A	30	81%	57%	72%	$25,070
76.	University of Denver (CO)	77	3.2	130	$647	100%	10	83%	46%	65%	$43,465
76.	University of South Carolina–Aiken*	77	2.7	265	$869	67%	18	83%	81%	58%	$23,588
76.	University of St. Francis (IL)	77	2.7	305	$599	54%	14	76%	57%	53%	$27,823
76.	Western Illinois University*	77	2.9	887	$285	77%	23	78%	53%	61%	$32,968
84.	Anderson University (SC)	76	2.5	398	$460	68%	14	58%	63%	76%	$8,665
84.	Brandman University (CA)	76	2.7	1,473	$500	86%	24	75%	44%	76%	$33,571
84.	California State University–Dominguez Hills*	76	2.6	463	$670	89%	18	85%	62%	36%	$18,898
84.	Cornerstone University (MI)	76	2.5	288	$450	50%	8	65%	90%	82%	$23,732
84.	Drexel University (PA)	76	3.5	1,717	$501	63%	24	76%	35%	66%	$33,061
84.	Eastern Kentucky University*	76	2.9	2,286	$409	69%	18	79%	47%	68%	$31,325
84.	Southeast Missouri State University*	76	2.8	924	$284	97%	16	70%	51%	71%	$26,340
84.	Texas Tech University*	76	3.3	2,430	$261	33%	35	N/A	N/A	37%	$7,883
84.	Union Institute & University (OH)	76	2.4	1,193	$545	57%	8	75%	71%	52%	$36,620
93.	Appalachian State University* (NC)	75	3.0	449	$643	70%	19	85%	58%	46%	$11,978
93.	Dakota Wesleyan University (SD)	75	2.5	103	$350	23%	13	85%	N/A	37%	$24,818
93.	Herzing University (WI)	75	2.2	1,321	$580	43%	16	83%	29%	79%	$19,146
93.	New England Col. of Business and Finance**(MA)	75	2.3	841	$485	50%	17	85%	42%	51%	$28,862
93.	SUNY College of Technology–Canton*	75	3.0	1,106	$343	65%	22	80%	50%	79%	$29,544
93.	University of Houston–Downtown* (TX)	75	2.9	177	$637	100%	22	67%	73%	49%	$11,163
93.	University of Southern Mississippi*	75	N/A	2,683	$360	53%	30	72%	N/A	84%	$26,283
93.	Wayne State University* (MI)	75	3.1	34	$457	67%	21	86%	75%	92%	$27,430
93.	Wentworth Institute of Technology (MA)	75	2.8	232	$475	N/A	12	84%	73%	31%	$4,621
102.	Berkeley College** (NJ)	74	2.5	1,314	$840	63%	20	64%	45%	85%	$31,909
102.	Bluefield College (VA)	74	2.6	506	$365	67%	12	80%	61%	82%	$23,492
102.	Central Michigan University*	74	3.1	1,730	$417	82%	25	64%	37%	73%	$20,794
102.	Central Washington University*	74	N/A	1,396	$700	67%	22	91%	6%	78%	$23,648
102.	Florida Institute of Technology	74	2.9	2,031	$510	78%	18	54%	14%	78%	$41,391
102.	Florida State University*	74	3.5	542	$721	37%	34	N/A	N/A	N/A	N/A

BEST ONLINE DEGREE PROGRAMS

(*Public, **For profit)

Rank	School	Overall program score	Average peer assessment score (5.0=highest)	'18 total program enrollment	'18 - '19 tuition[1]	'18 full-time faculty with Ph.D.	'18 average class size	'18 retention rate	'18 graduation rate[2]	% graduates with debt ('18)	Average debt of graduates ('18)
102.	Graceland University (IA)	74	2.1	168	$414	40%	11	88%	72%	79%	$23,354
102.	Kansas State University*	74	3.5	345	$436	64%	30	85%	N/A	73%	$31,697
102.	Lamar University* (TX)	74	2.5	2,031	$248	59%	26	68%	N/A	7%	$32,259
102.	Lindenwood University (MO)	74	2.4	382	$480	74%	15	62%	N/A	72%	$32,936
102.	Southwestern Oklahoma State University*	74	2.5	624	$434	60%	20	86%	72%	54%	$21,294
102.	University of Louisville* (KY)	74	3.3	404	$497	72%	18	59%	N/A	54%	$24,606
114.	Arkansas State University*	73	2.7	1,115	$210	40%	22	28%	N/A	74%	$25,600
114.	Friends University (KS)	73	2.5	265	$430	45%	12	57%	71%	78%	$21,554
114.	Kentucky Wesleyan College	73	2.3	48	$440	69%	9	15%	74%	89%	$26,850
114.	Moody Bible Institute (IL)	73	2.8	727	$340	42%	14	N/A	44%	19%	$13,142
114.	Pensacola State College* (FL)	73	2.6	182	$420	100%	20	72%	N/A	N/A	N/A
114.	University of Colorado–Colorado Springs*	73	3.3	2,823	$502	74%	23	74%	N/A	60%	$15,455
114.	University of Louisiana–Lafayette*	73	2.8	1,531	$365	47%	34	67%	56%	N/A	N/A
114.	University of Missouri*	73	3.4	419	$370	67%	31	69%	N/A	48%	$18,624
114.	University of Toledo* (OH)	73	2.9	1,592	$746	68%	16	63%	34%	62%	$16,967
123.	Campbell University (NC)	72	N/A	575	$440	88%	11	66%	N/A	48%	$20,612
123.	Champlain College (VT)	72	2.7	2,020	$318	25%	15	88%	44%	47%	$25,035
123.	Chatham University (PA)	72	2.6	92	$880	92%	11	75%	72%	82%	$14,488
123.	College of Coastal Georgia* (GA)	72	2.3	101	$125	72%	23	66%	45%	70%	$14,252
123.	Colorado Technical University**	72	2.6	29,963	$325	72%	31	84%	26%	78%	$21,780
123.	Eastern Oregon University*	72	2.4	1,443	$240	57%	18	81%	47%	69%	$25,661
123.	Frostburg State University* (MD)	72	2.4	564	$570	56%	20	82%	63%	32%	$15,205
123.	Georgia Southern University*	72	2.7	675	$204	76%	37	64%	53%	81%	$27,076
123.	La Salle University (PA)	72	2.9	103	$458	100%	N/A	80%	60%	61%	$31,540
123.	Marian University (IN)	72	2.6	749	$825	31%	26	84%	92%	81%	$46,140
123.	Southwestern College (KS)	72	2.6	1,266	$502	86%	9	85%	44%	27%	$22,811
123.	University of La Verne (CA)	72	2.4	299	$665	91%	18	74%	49%	75%	$33,290
123.	University of Massachusetts–Dartmouth*	72	3.3	377	$332	77%	15	57%	40%	67%	$28,864
123.	Wheeling Jesuit University (WV)	72	2.7	30	$400	100%	7	67%	51%	100%	$36,831
137.	Concordia University Wisconsin & Ann Arbor	71	2.8	347	$483	N/A	9	68%	50%	70%	$6,982
137.	Concordia University–St. Paul (MN)	71	2.5	1,854	$420	73%	14	80%	63%	81%	$23,625
137.	Iowa Wesleyan University	71	2.5	61	$450	73%	7	62%	N/A	64%	$22,159
137.	Johnson & Wales University (RI)	71	2.9	1,173	$330	48%	18	58%	38%	92%	N/A
137.	Northeastern State University* (OK)	71	2.7	841	$453	55%	25	80%	58%	N/A	N/A
137.	Oakland University* (MI)	71	2.7	210	$457	86%	23	59%	41%	55%	$30,099
137.	St. Joseph's College New York	71	3.0	241	$600	77%	14	55%	32%	67%	$20,630
137.	University of Maine–Augusta*	71	2.8	3,010	$291	69%	28	76%	25%	74%	$27,113
137.	University of Maine–Fort Kent*	71	2.7	284	$373	57%	23	84%	44%	N/A	N/A
137.	Valdosta State University* (GA)	71	2.8	958	$250	72%	14	65%	N/A	70%	$28,470
147.	California University of Pennsylvania*	70	2.6	1,663	$328	59%	46	81%	43%	72%	$15,492
147.	Duquesne University (PA)	70	3.1	103	$921	87%	14	60%	N/A	59%	$39,434
147.	Ferris State University* (MI)	70	2.9	989	$447	53%	18	70%	36%	46%	$17,715
150.	Campbellsville University (KY)	69	2.7	439	$399	67%	19	77%	N/A	77%	$25,660

Rank	School	Overall program score	Average peer assessment score (5.0=highest)	'18 total program enrollment	'18 - '19 tuition[1]	'18 full-time faculty with Ph.D.	'18 average class size	'18 retention rate	'18 graduation rate[2]	% graduates with debt ('18)	Average debt of graduates ('18)
	(*Public, **For profit)										
150.	East Carolina University* (NC)	69	3.1	10,182	$700	71%	25	N/A	N/A	63%	$28,724
150.	Houston Baptist University (TX)	69	3.0	232	$550	74%	20	N/A	N/A	60%	$14,904
150.	Indiana State University*	69	3.1	2,221	$695	76%	24	69%	N/A	N/A	N/A
150.	John Brown University (AR)	69	N/A	370	$420	100%	13	82%	69%	79%	$20,856
150.	Lynn University (FL)	69	2.8	246	$295	48%	13	80%	64%	32%	$28,982
150.	Madonna University (MI)	69	2.2	278	$730	50%	N/A	83%	50%	N/A	N/A
150.	National University (CA)	69	2.2	8,213	$370	80%	18	64%	30%	61%	$23,027
150.	Ursuline College (OH)	69	2.8	32	$324	90%	11	93%	N/A	38%	$22,004
159.	Auburn University–Montgomery* (AL)	68	2.9	140	$333	0%	16	95%	N/A	29%	$12,482
159.	Columbia College (MO)	68	2.6	12,283	$320	77%	18	56%	7%	57%	$29,410
159.	Loyola University New Orleans (LA)	68	3.1	71	$450	84%	N/A	29%	N/A	56%	$4,236
159.	North Greenville University (SC)	68	2.5	191	$395	100%	11	10%	N/A	95%	$13,000
159.	Northwest University (WA)	68	2.8	154	$425	0%	10	26%	N/A	90%	$23,677
159.	Portland State University* (OR)	68	3.1	4,328	$605	69%	42	79%	57%	67%	$25,656
159.	Stevenson University (MD)	68	2.5	474	$450	N/A	13	72%	60%	42%	$22,250
166.	Brescia University (KY)	67	2.3	550	$425	46%	14	N/A	43%	63%	$34,980
166.	Gallaudet University (DC)	67	3.1	11	$688	73%	12	60%	N/A	N/A	N/A
166.	Midwestern Baptist Theological Seminary (MO)	67	2.5	250	$350	74%	19	63%	N/A	43%	$11,388
166.	Purdue University–Northwest* (IN)	67	3.1	1,845	$294	0%	30	N/A	90%	36%	$27,860
166.	Slippery Rock University of Pennsylvania*	67	2.5	273	$328	60%	27	68%	74%	57%	$17,110
166.	Tabor College (KS)	67	2.6	84	$491	67%	6	N/A	N/A	N/A	N/A
166.	Upper Iowa University	67	2.6	1,685	$454	53%	15	87%	48%	76%	$30,852
173.	Ashland University (OH)	66	2.4	189	$402	68%	16	63%	75%	60%	$25,014
173.	New England College (NH)	66	2.2	1,334	$405	20%	14	61%	N/A	76%	$28,009
173.	Northwestern College (IA)	66	3.1	28	$400	47%	11	N/A	N/A	75%	$13,559
173.	Northwood University (MI)	66	2.2	2,055	$445	60%	15	82%	65%	70%	$24,984
173.	Purdue University–Fort Wayne* (IN)	66	3.2	170	$676	73%	17	58%	100%	71%	$25,397
173.	Troy University* (AL)	66	2.7	4,401	$338	78%	23	62%	11%	64%	$25,663
173.	University of South Alabama*	66	N/A	50	$482	100%	28	35%	87%	100%	$4,000
173.	University of Texas of the Permian Basin*	66	2.7	1,321	$308	17%	34	63%	44%	67%	$16,523
173.	Valley City State University* (ND)	66	2.4	280	$190	58%	15	N/A	N/A	41%	$21,269
173.	Wichita State University* (KS)	66	2.9	806	$530	70%	45	N/A	N/A	66%	$22,167

▶ Best Online Bachelor's Programs For Veterans

WHICH PROGRAMS OFFER MILITARY VETERANS and active-duty service members the best distance education? To ensure academic quality, all schools included in this ranking had to first qualify for a spot by being in the top half of the Best Online Degree Programs ranking, above. They had to be housed in a regionally accredited institution and were judged on a multitude of factors, including program reputation, faculty credentials, student graduation rate and graduate debt load. Secondly, because veterans and active-duty members often wish to take full advantage of federal benefits designed to make their coursework less expensive, programs also had to be certified for the GI Bill and participate in the Yellow Ribbon Program or charge in-state tuition that can be fully covered by the GI Bill to veterans from out of state. A third criterion for being ranked is that a program must have enrolled a critical mass of students with military backgrounds. The undergraduate-level rankings require a total of 25 veterans and active-duty service members to be included. Qualifying programs were ranked in descending order based on their spot in the overall ranking.

Rank School (State)

1. Embry-Riddle Aeronautical University–Worldwide (FL)
2. Arizona State University*
3. Oregon State University*
4. Pennsylvania State University–World Campus*
4. University of Florida*
6. Colorado State University–Global Campus*
6. University of North Carolina–Wilmington*
6. University of Oklahoma*
9. University of Alabama–Birmingham*
10. University of Central Florida*

Rank School (State)

11. CUNY School of Professional Studies*
11. Western Kentucky University*
13. University of Arkansas*
13. West Texas A&M University*
15. Colorado State University*
15. George Washington University (DC)
15. Indiana University– Online*
15. U. of Massachusetts–Amherst*
15. Washington State University*
20. Ball State University* (IN)
20. Charleston Southern University (SC)
20. U. of Massachusetts–Lowell*
23. Siena Heights University (MI)

Rank School (State)

23. University of Arizona*
25. City University of Seattle
25. Daytona State College* (FL)
25. University of Illinois–Springfield*
28. California Baptist University
28. Fort Hays State University* (KS)
28. Lee University (TN)
28. Regent University (VA)
32. Robert Morris University**,(PA)
32. University of Nebraska–Omaha*
32. University of the Incarnate Word (TX)
32. University of Wisconsin–Milwaukee*

Rank School (State)

32. Utica College (NY)
37. Bowling Green State University* (OH)
37. Florida International University*
37. McKendree University (IL)
37. Northern Arizona University*
37. University of Memphis* (TN)
37. Western Carolina University* (NC)
43. Saint Leo University (FL)
43. University of North Dakota*
45. Old Dominion University* (VA)
45. Savannah College of Art and Design (GA)

Getting In

GETTING IN

How Admissions Really Works

Understanding all that goes into the review can help prospective students maximize their chances

by **Lindsay Cates**

NEWS YOU CAN USE

HIGH SCHOOL SENIORS who have followed the Operation Varsity Blues news may be wondering as they apply to college just how stacked the deck might be. In March 2019, federal prosecutors uncovered a criminal conspiracy to influence admissions at eight universities, including the University of Southern California, Yale, Georgetown University and Stanford. Thirty-three parents had allegedly paid a college prep firm a combined $25 million to falsify their children's standardized test scores or bribe coaches to list them as recruited athletes. Since then, applicants rejected by several of the schools have filed a class-action complaint claiming an unfair admissions process, and more than a dozen parents have pleaded guilty (or agreed to do so) to fraud-related charges.

All of the university employees accused in the scandal worked on athletics staffs, which are often the first to vet student-athletes. College administrators and admissions professionals alike have expressed surprise at the extent of what was uncovered. In interviews with U.S.

News, many such officials stressed that they pride themselves on conducting a careful, fair and transparent process. "The reality is we're paying close attention all the time and constantly reviewing our procedures and protocols," says David Kuskowski, director of admissions at Clemson University in South Carolina.

Still, "there is no doubt the recent college bribery scandal made every president and admissions leader pause and consider checks and balances at their school," says Michael C. Maxey, president of Roanoke College in Virginia and former vice president and dean of admissions at the school. The University of California system has committed to

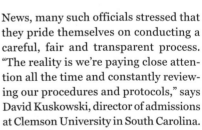

making improvements to its procedures, such as beefing up the verification process for students with "special talents" like athletic ability.

For families just getting started, it's important to grasp that "careful, fair and transparent" doesn't translate to "objective." Choosing a freshman class is actually a very subjective task: Besides good grades and test scores, the admissions office is generally seeking personal characteristics and abilities that will produce a well-rounded student body with diverse talents that fit with the school's mission. That may mean ensuring an even mix of men and women, or a specific balance of in-state vs. out-of-state students. Many schools are especially concerned with enrolling well-qualified applicants of diverse socioeconomic backgrounds, says Julie J. Park, a professor at the University of Maryland–College Park who specializes in racial diversity in higher education. Institutional priorities could also include finding students with exceptional talent in art, music or athletics or filling department-specific needs like encouraging the enrollment of female computer scientists. (Most colleges can't afford to be need-blind, so a family's ability to pay can make a difference in admissions decisions, especially when aid resources run low.) A so-called holistic approach to admissions can work to the advantage of those who understand it and present their strengths accordingly.

EASING THE PRESSURE. Much of the angst students feel about college admission springs from a distorted view of how hard it is to get into a good school. Headlines touting record-low acceptance rates shine a spotlight on the intense competition for spots at the most highly selective schools, but the reality is that the vast majority of places accept at least half of their applicants. "If families knew that

Penn, like most Ivy League schools, accepts fewer than 10% of those who apply.

we're really here to be in their corner, that would take a lot of pressure off," says Sarah Richardson, assistant vice provost for enrollment management and director of admissions and scholarships at Creighton University in Nebraska, which accepts about 71% of applicants on average.

At Roanoke College, which receives around 5,500 applications each year and accepts about 72% of candidates, admissions counselors consider the "whole person," looking beyond grades to evidence of leadership qualities and individual integrity, says Brenda Poggendorf, vice president for enrollment and dean of admissions and financial aid. When Callie Hammer, a junior sociology major from Glen Allen, Virginia, applied to Roanoke, she

But it's the more qualitative factors that help admissions staffers round out a class. Rather than filling spots with well-rounded students, many colleges, particularly selective ones, seek to identify a mix of applicants who show a passion for and very deep talent in an area or two, as well as some smart and accomplished generalists, says Adam Sapp, assistant vice president and director of admissions at Pomona College in California. One way they identify that passion: They look to see if you've taken the initiative to get involved in an interest outside of class. An applicant who claims to love math will stand out if he or she not only has earned good grades in tough courses but also found a way to get involved, say, with math research at a local university, notes Brian Taylor, managing director at Ivy Coach, a college admissions consulting firm.

A good strategy as you move toward senior year is to think about how you might connect the dots about your passion in your application. Someone who loves music might take Advanced Placement Music Theory, list hours spent teaching music lessons to kids among extracurriculars, and write an essay describing a class assignment on how the brain processes music according to neuroscience. For some students, their main commitment will be a job because that's the reality of their life, says Richardson.

Kyle Lee, a senior psychology and theatre major at Pomona, went to a nontraditional high school in New York City, where students didn't get grades and where he could choose his own schedule – a format he loved. Instead of listing sports or clubs on his applications (his school only had a few), he featured his most time-consuming activity: getting to class.

INSIDE SCOOP

What advice do you have for prospective students?

Meet others and make connections, whether that's by introducing yourself to the first professor you meet or knocking on doors in your residence hall. The peers and the classmates that you have surrounding you are the future of today and the future of this world. Make those relationships with professors, advisers, student leaders and anyone else on campus who can really take you to new heights and set you on a path that will help you be successful. This will not only allow you to have an incredible college experience but will also help you establish connections for your future endeavors.

Rachel Ellis, '21
U. of Massachusetts • Amherst

highlighted her experiences competing in triathlons. In her essay she explained how the skills she learned as a triathlete, like good time management, have helped her. "I thrive on a busy schedule," says Hammer, who fills her time outside of class volunteering at afterschool programs and teaching swim lessons at a local YMCA.

No matter how selective a school is, your grades will probably matter most. Admissions officers place a high value on your academic transcript as an indicator of how prepared you are for college work. But straight A's alone don't tell the whole story; reviewers also consider the rigor of your classes and whether you've stretched yourself academically and shown improvement over time. Test scores are typically factored in, too, of course, but experts say they're not driving admissions decisions. Indeed, more than 1,000 universities are now "test-optional," meaning that applicants can choose to withhold scores if they think they don't accurately represent their abilities (related story, Page 124).

After his family moved to Pennsylvania freshman year, Lee commuted two and a half hours each way (by bus and two trains) to stay at his school. He listed that in the activities section of his application, along with the many hours he spent working with young kids as a babysitter and tutor, to prove he was committed to things he cared about. "I didn't have soccer team captain or football team or president of a club, but I feel highlighting the things that were important to me really showed through," he says. Pomona typically admits about 8% of applicants for a class of around 415, says Sapp.

SHOW YOUR VOICE. Your essay is a good place to highlight your unique personality. Topic-wise the essay can be about anything – an ordinary experience, your personal passion, or a common fear,

missions office, says Richardson. The NCAA sets minimum GPA and SAT/ACT scores for prospective athletes to compete at the Division I level (at least a 2.3 GPA in core courses and a corresponding SAT or ACT score; an athlete with a lower score needs a higher GPA), but leaves admissions decisions up to individual schools, many of which require that student-athletes meet or come close to the average grades and scores for the incoming class. In certain cases in the Ivy League or at Division III schools that don't give athletic scholarships, skill at a sport may be considered in a similar light as, say, the initiative of the kid who pursued math research. "It's their 'hook,'" says Taylor, so long as it's demonstrated in the right way. There are checks in place, like the Ivy League's Academic Index (calculated from the athlete's test scores and GPA). All recruited athletes have to meet a minimum index score, and their academic credentials can be no more than one standard deviation below those of the rest of the student body.

ABILITY TO SUCCEED. Coaches and admissions officials say they are looking to admit student-athletes with the ability to succeed academically. Some schools with competitive, high-profile teams have "special admissions programs" to bring in applicants who don't meet a school's typical standards but have exceptional athletic talent. Those are typically decided on a case-by-case basis among top university officials and/or a special committee.

When it comes to donations, a large gift made shortly before a child applies can be seen as a bribe and could potentially hurt one's case for getting in, admissions officers say. However, if an individual with a strong established connection (like a loyal donor who gives every year, or an alum who has donated large sums) is related to an applicant, the prospective student might be flagged by the alumni or development office, even if admissions makes an independent decision.

In a process that may seem mysterious and unpredictable, there are ethical (and smart) steps a prospective student can take to improve his or her odds. Visit the school if you can, experts suggest, and talk to a counselor about how you see yourself contributing to campus. Ask to speak to a faculty member in a department of interest, advises Richardson. Many admissions staffs factor in "demonstrated interest" as a sign of sincerity, particularly if they are on the fence about an applicant. Most importantly, focus on finding the best fit. Your chances of getting in, and thriving, are better at schools where you can most clearly find a sense of belonging. ●

for example – but it should reveal something about your character, your understanding of yourself or your problem-solving skills, say. Many schools pose an essay prompt: Why do you want to attend [insert college name here]? Show how you fit – how you'll contribute and how you'll benefit once you're here.

One effect of the Varsity Blues scandal has been to focus attention on how athletic admits and children of alumni or donors are handled. Schools have policies in place to prevent abuse, admissions deans say, and are constantly making sure those are followed. At Division I schools like Creighton, coaches are typically the ones interacting with prospective athletes first, but recruits also need to meet the requirements of the ad-

Callie Hammer credits triathlon training with helping her get into college.

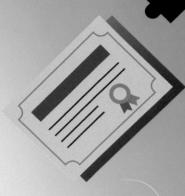

4 GETTING IN

Debunking
6 Myths
About
Admissions

Get a feel for how much grades, tests and your résumé
really matter from those who review the applications

by **Stacey Colino**

WHEN APPLYING TO COLLEGE, many students think they know which strategies will help them attract the attention (in a good way) of admissions officers. But there's often a gap between perception and reality about what actually matters – and what matters most – when it comes to grades, test scores, extracurricular activities and other factors. In fact, the reality can differ from school to school. Many colleges report that they are now taking a multifaceted approach to reviewing applicants, factoring in grades and scores on the SAT or ACT, but also aiming "to evaluate them beyond what is seen on a transcript," says Joe Shields, an admissions counselor at Goucher College in Baltimore. "A holistic admissions review process allows a student to demonstrate their best qualities and discuss how they would be a good fit for that college."

Another promising and often misunderstood fact: It's not as difficult as many students think to get admitted to a college, beyond the most selective schools. On average, nearly two-thirds of first-time, freshman applicants were offered admission to a four-year school in the U.S., according to a 2018 report from the National Association for College Admission Counseling. Some 80% of places accepted 50% or more. "There are many good colleges you may not have heard of," says Hannah Serota, founder and CEO of Creative College Connections, a consulting practice that's dedicated to helping applicants find the right fit.

Here's a look at several other persistent myths about admissions:

MYTH
1

Getting all A's is the most important thing.

OF COURSE, YOUR GRADES MATTER. But what that means depends on a given college's level of selectivity as well as the classes you took, based on the offerings at your high school. After all, some places offer more honors, Advanced Placement or International Baccalaureate courses than others, and an A in one of these more challenging courses can signify mastery of more rigorous content than an A in a grade-level class at a school that offers both. College admissions officers are often well aware of how different high school curricula are because they work with many of the same schools every year and receive detailed profiles of the course offerings, along with context about the student body. "A 3.5 GPA means different things at different schools, and we understand that," says Janine Bissic, director of admission at Whittier College in California.

At Vanderbilt University in Nashville, Tennessee, "we would expect the most rigorous schedule that's appropriate for the student and the highest grades – we would be looking for both," says Douglas Christiansen, vice provost for university enrollment affairs and dean of admissions and financial aid. Being able to handle a challenging course load while maintaining strong marks is a signal that you have the academic grit and discipline to succeed at college.

Balance is also key. Taking a handful of AP or advanced classes can help you look good, but more isn't always better;

the idea is to take the most rigorous course load that makes sense given your abilities. While a B in an AP English lit class may be more impressive than an A in a grade-level English class, a C or D in an advanced class isn't necessarily going to wow anyone. "We want to see students stretching themselves but not too far – if your grades don't show that you're performing at a satisfactory level, it makes us question why you're taking such hard classes or why you're not doing well," says Kevin MacLennan, assistant vice chancellor of enrollment management at the University of Colorado–Boulder. "It makes us wonder if you're ready for college

rigor." If your grades dropped during a semester when you had health problems or personal hardships (such as a death in the family), it's wise to explain the reason somewhere in your application.

But don't be discouraged if your grades aren't where you'd like them to be early in high school. Many admissions officers look for upward trends in grades, improvements over time that enable a student to finish strong. "At the end of the day, we want to feel confident that if we admit a student, they can handle the rigor of the courses here," says Yvonne Romero da Silva, vice president for enrollment at Rice University in Houston.

MYTH

Your test scores can make or break your chances of getting in.

ON THE CONTRARY, THEY'RE JUST ONE element of the application package. "There are many students we've denied with perfect test scores because they didn't have anything else to set them apart," Christiansen says. Different institutions place varying levels of importance on standardized tests, and many colleges have gone test-optional in recent years (related story,

Page 124). This is partly because admissions officers recognize that many applicants may have intellectual abilities and academic strengths that aren't reflected in exam scores.

Taking the test more than once generally improves scores, especially if the testing dates are spaced out appropriately (as in: by months, not weeks) because "the test scores are really a representation of the student's ability at that point in time," Romero da Silva says. Taking the test two or three times can be beneficial, especially if you were nervous or you encountered unfamiliar questions the first time, says Annie Reznik, executive director of the Coalition for College, a group of more than 140 colleges and universities that's dedicated to increasing students' access to higher education. "Exposure to the test does improve the student's score – but beyond two or three times, you're moving into the land of diminishing returns," she adds.

Among colleges that do require the SAT or ACT, many will superscore, which means they use your best section-level scores even if they're from different test dates. In other words, if your SAT reading score was 70 points higher the second time you took the test but your math score was 50 points higher on the first, you can use the better of both attempts.

MYTH

The more clubs and activities you have on your résumé, the better.

THE QUALITY OF YOUR INVOLVEMENT counts more than the quantity of your activities. "Being passionate about key interests is more important than joining a lot of clubs," says Christiansen. "We're looking for depth and progression of leadership, not just participation." David Senter of Oak Ridge, Tennessee, thinks his experience swimming competitively and working his way up to varsity team captain helped demonstrate his dedication and added something important to his strong academic record, along with his participation on the academic quiz bowl team. "You have to show you care," says Senter, now a senior at Rice. "I was never the fastest and I never went to the state championships, but I showed up every day and bonded with the team."

When reviewing extracurricular activities on an application, admissions officers really want to know things like: What did you do in high school that made whatever you participated in better and helped you grow? or What are you doing with your time that would contribute to our campus in a meaningful way if you came here? "Colleges are looking for a well-rounded student body, not necessarily a well-rounded student," says Serota.

These days, college admissions officers are also sensitive to the fact that some students don't have time for extracurricular activities. "If you're taking care of younger siblings after school, be honest about that and focus on the qualities that emerge from that experience," Reznik says. What colleges really want to know is how you spend your nonscheduled time and what you get out of those experiences.

MYTH #5

It's a mistake to get creative with your essay.

ON THE CONTRARY, BEING CLEVER and original can help you stand out from the crowd – but only if you can pull it off. If you're not funny, don't try to be. If you're not impassioned about a controversial subject, don't pretend to be. "You need to make the case for why you care about something and what you're doing about it," advises Serota. But do think carefully about what you choose to share, such as a mental health issue or a gambling or drug problem. "Be careful about revealing things that would make the reader feel a sense of caution about you," Serota says.

An essay's most important quality is that it feels authentic, officials say. Make sure that it addresses the prompt, but also think of your essay as an opportunity to reveal your true voice and to highlight who you really are. Admissions folks are experts at distinguishing between viewpoints that feel genuine and those that don't. "Think about not wearing a mask," Reznik advises. "It's not easy for students to let themselves be vulnerable, but that makes for the best college essay."

Moe de La Viez of Frederick, Maryland, thought her voice and interests would come through most clearly in a visual essay, which she submitted to Goucher when she applied in 2015. "I felt like I could personalize my application more if I did it myself on video," explains de La Viez, who got interested in video production in high school and ultimately crafted an interdisciplinary major at Goucher involving communications, creative writing and studio art under the umbrella of video production.

When it comes to large universities in particular, it may be hard to believe that there are human beings who are actually

MYTH #4

You should only ask for a recommendation from a teacher who gave you an A.

WRONG AGAIN. INSTEAD, IT'S BETTER to consider whether a teacher can help admissions officers get to know a different side of you and understand who you are. It could be from the teacher who taught your most difficult class or a class you thought you wouldn't like but did. "Ideally, you would choose a teacher who knows you very well, likes your work ethic, can speak to your character or has seen you persist in something that's been challenging," Bissic says.

Shields agrees: "If you struggled with a subject and had a good rapport with the teacher, you can get a helpful recommendation if the teacher can talk about how you came for extra help or you were able to advocate for yourself."

INSIDE SCOOP

What advice do you have for prospective students?

My freshman year, I joined a few different clubs to get out of my comfort zone and meet some new people. I definitely used to be super introverted, so I was pushing myself to do things that I wouldn't normally do. I worked for Western's recycling center and also the admissions office as a tour guide.

You might come into college with this idea of who you think you are. I never thought I'd be giving campus tours to large groups of students so comfortably, and now public speaking is no big deal. That was not the case in high school. I find myself telling students don't put yourself in a box. Surprise yourself with things that you're going to discover in college.

Sarah White, '19
Western Washington University, Bellingham, Washington

reading and giving careful consideration to your app, but it's true. "There's no computerization of the admissions process," says MacLennan, whose university reviews more than 36,000 freshman applications per year. "We read every piece of a student's application and essay, and every admissions decision is made by admissions officers and professional educators who care about this process." The essay is your opportunity to connect with them and make an impression.

MYTH
6

To make yourself memorable, you need to visit the campus.

YOU DON'T HAVE TO SHOW UP IN PERSON unless you live near a school, in which case not stopping by might signal a lack of engagement. However, what many competitive colleges look for more generally are applicants who show "demonstrated interest." This can be achieved in various ways: by calling or emailing with questions, requesting a Skype interview, contacting alumni or interacting with a representative on social media or at a local college fair. Indeed, 37% of colleges indicate that demonstrated interest is a moderately or considerably important factor in decisions, according to NACAC.

Admissions officers can track how many contacts you've had with their institution – and they can even see if you've opened or engaged with emails. If you can't visit the campus, show up when an admissions representative comes to town, advises Jamiere Abney, senior assistant dean of admission and coordinator of outreach for opportunity and inclusion at Colgate University in New York. "We remember the interested students we meet at these visits and at college fairs, and we can be a potential advocate for you," he says. Attending a summer program for high schoolers at a college that appeals to you can also help signal interest, and that you might be a good fit, says Marc Harding, vice provost for enrollment at the University of Pittsburgh. "Fit continues to be the most important factor to us – we want students to succeed here." Participating in such a program also shows that you're passionate and curious enough about a subject to take it to the next level, which says a lot about your college readiness. ●

To Test or Not to Test?

Many colleges are giving applicants the option not to share exam scores

by **Ann Claire Carnahan**

THE SAT AND ACT have long been a dreaded staple of the college admissions process. But as of this fall, more than 1,000 schools nationwide – including Bennington College in Vermont, Ohio Wesleyan University, Pitzer College in California, James Madison University in Virginia and the University of Denver – have gone test-optional. To earn admission, prospective students have the opportunity to skip submitting standardized test scores altogether or to share alternate credentials such as Advanced Placement or International Baccalaureate scores, extra essays or creative portfolios in their place. The majority of applicants still take the SAT, ACT or both, but for many, the rise in flexible testing policies offers a welcome option. Students who struggle with tests can now skip them and highlight instead other academic and extracurricular achievements, says Andre Green, executive director of the National Center for Fair and Open Testing, which advocates in favor of test-optional policies.

Specific policies differ from school to school, but "test-optional" typically means that a university will treat standardized test scores as additive to the student's profile rather than required. More consideration is given to the other components – transcript, letters of recommendation and extracurricular involvement. And many admissions

A Social Media Survey

POSTING EMBARRASSING or controversial content on Facebook, Twitter or other social media can have real consequences. More than half of college admissions officers said they consider such info about applicants to be "fair game" when making decisions, though just a quarter of them reported using social media as a tool to learn about applicants, according to a 2018 Kaplan Test Prep survey.

Still, an acceptance can be pulled for an egregious post on a

Only about 10% to 15% of applicants used the test-optional policy, and roughly the same percentage were admitted that way and chose to attend. In part because of the new policy and increased financial aid offerings, the university saw a 20% rise in low-income and first-generation students for its latest admitted class.

Applicants trying to decide whether to submit scores can think about how they'll add to the overall context. If scores support their "academic story," then it's a good idea to include them, says Whitney Soule, dean of admissions and student aid at Bowdoin College in Maine, which has had a test-optional policy since 1969. On the other hand, Soule says, "if they feel that the testing detracts from that, then they should withhold it – and they should withhold it with confidence that we're not looking for it." Nearly 30% of admitted students for Bowdoin's class of 2022 decided not to submit their scores.

Colleges and universities publish the data related to the average test scores of their incoming classes online, so officials suggest that students can use that data to benchmark their own exam results.

Soule cautions that everyone should read the fine print because "test-optional does not look the same everywhere." The University of Delaware, for example, only offers test-optional admissions for in-state students, who accounted for nearly 15% of 27,690 applicants for fall 2018. The pilot program in Delaware was instituted about four years ago "particularly to reach more diverse students" who might not have access to the same kind of test-prep resources as some of their peers, says Doug Zander, director of admissions.

Some public universities offer certain test-optional provisions and caveats, so confirming specific policies with each school is key, admissions officials recommend. You'll also want to know whether test scores factor into financial aid decisions at a particular institution. Typically, scores don't affect need-based aid, but they can be considered when making decisions about merit-based scholarships. When in doubt, ask. ●

counselors look more closely for demonstrated growth over the four years of high school. For many students and counselors, "testing doesn't give the full picture," says Ian Harkness, director of college counseling for Malvern Preparatory School, a private school outside of Philadelphia.

ONE PIECE. Last year, the ultraselective University of Chicago, which admitted just over 6% of applicants for its class of 2023, instituted a test-optional policy. "Testing is one piece. It's not the only piece that determines your admission," says James Nondorf, vice president for enrollment and student advancement. Instead of exam scores, applicants can submit a video profile or additional academic or creative work, be it an artistic portfolio, a business plan, or a scientific research project.

UChicago made the decision to go test-optional because admission is determined by more than test scores, Nondorf says.

personal account. "The things you do now can matter later," says Chris Reeves, a counselor at Beechwood High School in Kentucky, where students start hearing about minding their online footprint in middle school. "We still tell our students better safe than sorry."

TAKING ACTION. At Colby College in Maine, which received 13,500-plus applications for the class of 2023, the admissions office doesn't review applicants' social media in part because "if we were to do that for one student, we'd really feel obligated to do it for all the applicants," says Matt Proto, vice president and dean of admissions and financial aid. However, if they do learn that an applicant's posts have violated laws or Colby's code of

conduct, the school would "take significant action," which could include rescinding admission, Proto notes.

Indeed, the sheer volume of applications at many schools can make it difficult to do exhaustive social searches. "The process of checking social media for that many people is not logistically possible," says Charles Murphy, the director of freshman and international admissions at the University of Florida, which receives more than 40,000 apps each year. However, where you apply can make a difference: A 2017 Inside Higher Ed survey found that private school admissions offices check social media more routinely than do public ones. *–Mariya Greeley*

4 GETTING IN

An **Early Application** Action Plan

Applying in advance of regular decision can give students an edge, but it's best to do so carefully

by **Courtney Rubin**

ONCE UPON A TIME there were only two kinds of "early" options when it came to applying to college, and each school offered only one (if any): early decision, where students applied to one school in November, got a reply by mid-December, and were bound to attend if they were accepted; and early action, where the timing was similar but no commitment was required.

But in the past decade, the permutations have multiplied. Now they include everything from two rounds of early decision (such as at Bates College in Maine and Emory University in Atlanta) to a combination of both early decision and early action (Tulane in New Orleans, the University of Chicago and Fordham in New York City, for example). A number of schools even offer a newer hybrid called restrictive early action, where students typically can only apply early to one institution without having to commit.

Some colleges have even fashioned their own definitions of the terms, which can lead to further confusion – and the oft-repeated suggestion that students and parents always read the fine print. The proliferation of early applications can be a mixed blessing for applicants and schools. In some cases, "students are like, 'Let's apply everywhere,' and it doesn't help them find the right fit, and it doesn't help the college find the right fit," says Grant Gosselin, director of undergraduate admission at Boston College. BC, for example, used to have a nonbinding early action program that barred students from applying to schools with binding early decision policies. Last year, the college switched to nonbinding early action with no bars to other schools, and early apps rose a whopping 53%. Now, beginning in the fall 2019 application cycle, the school will move to binding early decision.

What is clear is that early applications have been rising steadily over the past 15 years – even by double-digit percentages in some years at some colleges. For instance, the University of Georgia received

some 17,000 early action applications for fall 2019 admission, which is a 14% increase from the year before and a 28% increase compared to five years ago. The University of Virginia received more than 25,100 early action apps, about 17% more than last year. Overall, between fall 2016 and fall 2017, colleges reported an average 4% increase in early decision applicants and a 5% increase in early decision admits compared to the previous year, according to a 2018 report from the National Association for College Admission Counseling. Applications through early action were up 9%, with admits rising 10%.

AN EARLY EDGE. Just over a third of colleges say they offer an early action program, according to the NACAC report, compared to only 8% in 2005. In the case of binding early decision, the advantage to the school is clear: locking down great candidates as soon as possible. But colleges with programs that don't require a commitment say the early deadline allows them more time to review all applications, since so many students usually apply at the last minute. (It also gives schools more time to sell those admitted early on committing to attend.)

Thanks in part to the Common Application and other online application portals, so many students are applying early that some high schools are even attempting to impose limits. In many cases, colleges aren't increasing their class sizes, so with the glut of applications, "kids are just making it harder on themselves," says Ellen O'Neill Deitrich, director of college counseling at The Hill School, a private boarding high school in Pottstown, Pennsylvania. At her school, usually at least 85% of each senior class of 150 or so files some kind of early app.

Deitrich counsels students to apply when they're going to look the strongest in the pool – which may not be early. For instance, if you're "a later bloomer" who only by junior or senior year has begun to take your school's most rigorous courses and show strong grades, you may want to wait to apply regular decision and make that clear to the admissions office so the college can see the upward trend in your profile, she says.

Grace Gong chose to attend Princeton after applying early action.

Perhaps the biggest driver of early apps is the widespread notion that applying by November to a highly selective college makes it easier to get in. Many college admissions deans dispute the notion that it's quite that simple, but Gosselin does not. "There will be a benefit – not that we're lowering our academic standards, but in the pool itself," he says. This year, BC predicts 2,500 to 3,000 early decision applications, from which it expects to fill roughly 40% of the incoming class. The rest will come from the regular decision pool, where roughly 25,000 applications are expected. "With regular deci-

can have an impact on financial aid. Some schools say a student receives the same aid offering no matter when they apply. "Ours is need-based, so you get the same package you'd get in March," says Nancy Meislahn, the retiring vice president and dean of admission and financial aid at Wesleyan University in Connecticut, which offers two rounds of binding early decision. At the University of Arkansas, about 85% of merit-based scholarships are awarded to those who apply by the school's Nov. 1 nonbinding "priority application deadline."

Some colleges have little incentive to offer their most attractive financial aid packages to students who apply early and are anything less than "rock stars," says Mark Montgomery, a Denver-based college consultant. Because colleges' aid approaches can differ, Montgomery counsels students that they can use early application to their advantage by picking a school where they fall into the top end of the admissions pool, so the place would be keen to admit them and perhaps sweeten the financial aid offer.

FINE PRINT. As with all things application-related, it pays to confirm the details of each school's policy. Most places with binding early offers of admission have an escape clause only if financial aid is insufficient. Prospective students should keep a record of how aid deadlines compare to application deadlines. When in doubt, ask the school for clarity.

Collegebound students should be careful not to apply early just because it seems like everyone else is, cautions Yelena Shuster, a New York-based independent admissions counselor. She won't work with high school sophomores ("They have a lot more growing to do," she says), and she recommends not diving into the admissions essay until late junior year or the summer before senior

INSIDE SCOOP

What advice do you have for prospective students?

Consider the importance of self-care. I didn't research to really find out what self-care meant. It's not always taking a nap or buying yourself something nice. It's just really assessing what you need to be successful. It's really knowing yourself well, knowing when to say no, knowing when to ask for help. That self-care piece is vital. Because even if you can do everything, maybe you shouldn't do everything. And you can't even attempt to do the things you need to do if you aren't OK.

Najelle Gilmore, '19
Alma College • Alma, Michigan

sion, we're splitting hairs between equally qualified students and not really sure which students actually want to come here," he says. "So yes, the admit rate at the early decision pool will be higher."

At Emory, which offers two rounds of binding early decision, 32% of applicants to the class of 2023 in the first round and 10% of applicants in the second round were admitted, compared to about 14% of those in the regular pool. There were about 3,300 applications in the two early rounds (deadlines of Nov. 1 and Jan. 1, with results in mid-December and mid-February, respectively), while the school saw some 26,700 apps in the regular round. "Honestly, we don't look at early decision applications any differently than we do regular ones," says Giselle Martin, Emory's associate dean of admission.

No matter what a school's options are, applying early

year. That way, "students will have had more experiences that might make good topics," she says, not to mention improved writing skills. Shuster points to a client who wrote an essay about his passion for magic. Only by the fourth revision did he realize that the hobby helped him communicate and made him less shy, she says. He was accepted early to Columbia University's class of 2022.

Keep in mind that applying early is meant to help you focus on the right school for you, not just accelerate the application timeline. Grace Gong from Newark, Delaware, was admitted to Princeton with her early action application (due Nov. 1), so she had time to weigh that early acceptance alongside offers from the University of Southern California and the University of Delaware. Applying this way can give you "more of a chance to find a school you enjoy," says Gong, now a sophomore at Princeton. Plus, "it will give you some peace of mind." ●

Explore Your Passion

The **AP Capstone™ Diploma program** gives you the power to explore topics that inspire you. Develop college-level research and collaboration skills while making your AP® journey unique.

collegeboard.org/apcapstone

We're In!

How 8 Georgia high school seniors got to college

by **Lindsay Cates**

ONE OF THE BEST WAYS to get a handle on the college admissions process is to hear about it from students who have just lived through it. To that end, U.S. News visited Roswell High School, about 25 miles north of Atlanta, in May to see how eight seniors got accepted and made their choices. Of the public high school's 2,242 students, 57% are white, 21% are Hispanic, 14% are African American and 4% are Asian. About 85% continue their education at four-year colleges. Roswell offers 28 Advanced Placement classes, and students can take dual-enrollment courses at local colleges. The high school measures GPA on a scale of 100 rather than 4.0. The Roswell Hornets sports teams, performing arts and an award-winning television broadcast program are popular student activities. Here's how several new college freshmen handled the pressure and made it to campus:

PHOTOGRAPHY BY **LYNSEY WEATHERSPOON** FOR USN&WR

Garvey Goulbourne

Keen on a career at the United Nations or as a foreign ambassador, Goulbourne made academics and strong international relations programs a top priority when he started researching schools sophomore year. A big fan of the University of Virginia (his mom is an alum, and he visited as a freshman), he applied early action there as well as to the University of North Carolina–Chapel Hill and the University of Georgia. He also applied early decision to Columbia in New York. He then added regular decision apps to the University of South Carolina, the University of Denver, and George Washington University and American University in Washington, D.C.

His confidence was shaken when the first letter he opened was a deferral to the regular applicant pool from UGA, but he realized that "one school can't be an indicator for another school because whoever is reading your application is going to have a different take on you." Acceptances followed from everywhere but Columbia (he was denied) and UGA (he was wait-listed). Goulbourne was torn between UVA and UNC, but a second tour of UVA's Charlottesville campus, plus the school's proximity to Washington, D.C., swayed him to stick with the place he had loved from the start.
GPA: 94.09
ACT: 33
Extracurriculars: Varsity lacrosse; Investa Club, where high schoolers learn to invest money; volunteer for a family charity foundation helping to organize 5K and 3K runs
Essay: Goulbourne saw his essays as a chance to distinguish himself. "You really

get to talk about yourself as a person, whereas grades don't really describe your character," he says. For the Common Application essay, he talked about being the only black kid on the lacrosse team for as long as he can remember and how that helped shape his perspective.
Good move: Applying early action. The earlier deadlines forced him to start sooner and not procrastinate.
Regrets: Not doing enough community service. "I cared enough, but wasn't proactive enough in getting out there," he says. He also wishes he'd done more to search for scholarships.
Research: He looked at school websites and at comments from students on Niche. com. Instagram and Twitter also

helped to give him the "rawest perspective" on what students think.
Tip: Follow your passion. Taking AP courses in world history, U.S. history, and government and politics matched up with his interests and prepared him for the workload expected in college.

Sameer Khan

Khan made a last-minute decision to apply to a few small, liberal arts schools – and it paid off. Until late junior year, the senior class valedictorian

thought he would just apply to the Georgia Institute of Technology for computer science, but Reddit and Google searches opened his eyes to other options. With both parents originally from outside the U.S. (his dad is from India and his mom is from London), Khan relied mostly on the internet to guide him as he started leaning toward small and medium-size schools.

All told, he sent nine apps to the University of Chicago, Columbia, Dartmouth, Harvard,

> **Don't let peers' opinions sway you. It could limit your search.**

Garvey
Goulbourne

Swarthmore College in Pennsylvania, Williams College and Amherst College in Massachusetts, Georgia Tech and the Massachusetts Institute of Technology. He scored acceptances to Williams, Georgia Tech and Amherst; was wait-listed at Harvard, Dartmouth and Swarthmore; and was denied at the rest. After visiting Williams, Khan found he loved the sense of community among the 2,000 or so undergrads, plus the likelihood of making close connections with professors.
GPA: 102.85
SAT: 1560
Extracurriculars: Treasurer of Young Democrats Club, captain of the Academic Bowl team, Science Bowl, Science Olympiad, Mu Alpha Theta math honor society, math tutor to young kids
Essay: Khan wrote about how at first he dreaded attending his Saturday morning Quran lessons, but after building a close relationship with his teacher, he eventually found the experience valuable in forming his identity as a Muslim-American and

Indian-American in a predominantly white area.
Music: He's a self-taught musician – guitar, keyboard, bass and banjo – whose playing served as an outlet for relieving school and college application stress. "I showed that I worked pretty hard in school, but at the same time enjoy life outside of school with my music and participating in my community."
Cost: Financial aid will cover the bulk of Williams' $56,970 annual tuition.
Tip: Stay calm. It's important to stop and think about where you will be happy for four years.

> If you stay true to yourself in your essays, they'll turn out better.

Ellie Dover

As a recruited Division I lacrosse player, Dover's application process looked very different from that of her peers. "Once I decided I wanted to try to play in college, it consumed my entire youth," says the goalie, who started seriously thinking about her options in seventh grade. She was also looking for somewhere affordable with a journalism program and not too far from home. In eighth and ninth grades, she started attending lacrosse summer camps and visiting schools that were recruiting her, including UNC–Chapel Hill, Duke University and Elon University in the Tar Heel State; Furman University in South Carolina; Jacksonville University in Florida and the University of Cincinnati.

When the coach at Kennesaw State University (about 20 miles north of Atlanta) saw her play in a tournament and reached out, "it was just the perfect turn of events," Dover says. She was thrilled when she discovered on a visit that the university "checked every box" and felt like home, particularly as it

was the best option financially and was close enough that her parents could attend games. She committed as a sophomore.

"The school I least expected to work out for me was the perfect fit," says Dover, who'll attend KSU's honors college to pursue her dream of being a political analyst on a TV news show.

> Keep an open mind. Pick the college that feels like home to you.

GPA: 94.98
SAT: 1390
Extracurriculars: Varsity lacrosse, secretary of National Honor Society, Young Democrats Club, Will to Live Club, student council representative, sports anchor for "The Buzz" school news broadcast, morning announcements team, Spanish teacher's assistant, worked as a hostess at a restaurant, volunteered at her church
Essay: She wrote about her participation in "The Buzz," learning to work with video, write scripts and edit news broadcasts. She produced weekly segments of filmed sporting events and interviewed coaches and athletes.
Cost: A lacrosse scholarship plus Georgia's Zell Miller Scholarship, awarded to in-state students, will cover tuition. Students in the honors and athletics programs at

Sameer Khan

Ellie Dover

KSU get money toward their housing costs.

Helpful sources: A friend of a friend in the honors program at KSU, plus a KSU athletic academic adviser, have already helped her get questions answered, such as what scores on AP exams would get her credit.

Jacob Brunner

During sophomore year, Brunner's parents had him list some schools he was interested in, but it wasn't until he visited his older sister at the University of Georgia junior year that he realized the public university about 70 miles east of Roswell had everything he wanted in terms of size and college town feel. "I loved Athens and the whole community," he says, and shadowing his sister for a day gave him a "feet on the ground" perspective. He visited several other in-state options, including Kennesaw State, Georgia College & State University, Oglethorpe University and Mercer University, plus the U.S. Naval Academy in Maryland.

He sent applications to all of those schools (except for the Naval Academy) plus the University of Minnesota, where his dad is an alum. He was accepted everywhere except for UGA, where his early action application was initially deferred. When an acceptance letter finally came from UGA, Brunner says it took him just a few minutes to decide he would head to his "dream school," where he'll study marketing.

GPA: 93
ACT: 34
Extracurriculars: Captain of varsity cross-country and track teams; National Honor Society; founder of Cinema Club, whose members watch and discuss movies;

orchestra; intern and bass player at his church

Essay: He wrote several essays about notable life experiences, such as meeting a goat farmer on a mission trip to Africa and collapsing from exhaustion just short of the finish line in a cross-country race.

Big help: His literature teacher gave him keen insights on essay writing. "She helped bring out the 'me' in the essay, instead of it just being words on paper."

Score: Brunner thinks his ACT score helped seal the deal at UGA. He took the test four times before he was happy with his score.

Cost: He'll receive almost $5,000 from Georgia's Zell Miller Scholarship toward his $12,080 in-state tuition and fees. Financial aid, including student

loans, will cover the rest.

Schedule: Having an internship at church, on top of athletics, made for a tough senior year schedule. He kept up with his applications by working on them for 30 minutes a day in the fall.

Rachel Henderson

As a freshman, Henderson reluctantly signed up for Roswell's class in video broadcast when it was all that fit her schedule. Turns out she might have found her calling. Even as she gained skills in reporting, interviewing and film production, she realized she felt most at home in front of the camera anchoring the morning news show. "I could just be myself on camera," she says, "and everybody else could see that, too."

Knowing that she wanted to pursue a career in broadcast journalism, Henderson targeted schools with those programs. She ended up sending 11 regular decision apps to Boston University, Brandeis University (also near Boston), Northwestern University outside Chicago, Syracuse University in New York, UGA, the University of Missouri, Ohio University, the University of Notre Dame in Indiana, Hampton University in Virginia, and Howard University and George Washington University in Washington, D.C. She was accepted to every one except Northwestern. Her final decision came down to costs and the strength of the J-school, and the University of Missouri, where she'll be in the honors college, nailed both.

GPA: 100.5
SAT/ACT: 1360 / 30
Extracurriculars: Co-president of National Honor Society; founder and president of the Black Student Union; senior officer of Chemistry Club; vice president of SkillsUSA, a national organization that trains students and connects them to employers; Congressional Youth Council; viola section leader in orchestra; station

> Start early. The hardest part is managing your time wisely.

Jacob Brunner

manager and co-anchor at Fulton County Schools TV
Essay: She wrote about overcoming an eating disorder in middle school and reflected on the sacrifices her family made to help her get better, such as driving to medical appointments every week. "At the time I didn't realize what it was doing to other people," she says.
Testing: While she did well on the ACT and SAT, she'd have prepped more had she known how important scores were for getting scholarship money. "Really high scores open up opportunities," she says.
Cost: Mizzou issues a waiver for the cost of nonresident tuition (about $16,000) for applicants earning at least a 30 on the ACT or 1360 on the SAT. That perk, plus a scholarship she won for African American students, will cover about half of her $27,090 out-of-state tuition costs. Other local scholarships will add around $6,000 for the first year.

Jiya Fowler

Growing up watching her mom work as a research scientist at the Centers for Disease Control and Prevention in Atlanta, Fowler thought about a career practicing medicine. Then, a summer program helping a team with research on the circadian system at Morehouse School of Medicine caused her to catch the research bug, too. Fowler spent her junior year trying to find a mix of schools where she felt she would fit in, including historically black colleges like Howard University in Washington, D.C., Spelman College in Atlanta, and Hampton University in Virginia.

She was sold on Howard after a visit, but her mom argued that Spelman (her own alma mater) would be the better choice. Upon visiting the Atlanta liberal arts college, Fowler fell in love with the "uplifting environment" and the small size, which she thinks will give her a better chance at finding research opportunities and

> Have a study plan for the tests. High scores open up opportunities.

connecting with professors. She'll pursue a major in chemistry.
GPA: 91.62
SAT/ACT: 1250 / 26
Extracurriculars: Tutor; volunteer at The Drake House for homeless single mothers; Beta Club, a leadership and service group
Essay: Writing about a situation where a teacher made her uncomfortable in class, Fowler used "lots of dialogue and punctuation" to show an "emotional intelligence" in her writing, which she thinks helped her reveal more of her feelings and personality.
Cost: Her parents will shoulder the bulk of the cost, but she'll receive a HOPE Scholarship for $2,150 toward Spelman's $12,970 tuition.
Virtual visits: She didn't get to visit Hamp-

ton or some other schools in person, but she got a sense of those campuses by watching YouTube videos. "It was actually very helpful to see what a day in the life of a student would be like."
Good move: Getting involved in several STEM

Rachel Henderson

and medicine-focused summer camps helped her figure out her interests early, which then gave her a head start in narrowing down schools and a sense of college-level work.

Aaron Wright

Baseball was Wright's focus through much of high school, though he wasn't sure if he would continue on at college. "I knew I'd have to hang up the cleats one day, but you can't hang up an education," says the first baseman. He loved visiting larger Southeastern Conference schools like UGA and the University of Tennessee, but he didn't feel he would be a good fit at either. So he narrowed his search to smaller schools, including several offering a chance to continue playing ball. Military schools were appealing since he plans to join the Navy or Air Force after college.

He sent applications to Knox College in Illinois, Virginia Military Institute, Virginia Commonwealth University, The Citadel in South Carolina, Berry College in Georgia, and Auburn and Samford universities in Alabama. He got into The Citadel, VMI, Berry and Knox, which offered the chance to play baseball for its Division III team. Upon visiting, he decided that the liberal arts college of about 1,400 students was for him. He'll major in international relations to prep for joining the service.
GPA: 89.22
ACT: 27
Extracurriculars: Varsity and travel baseball, youth leader at church, student council representative, volunteer at a baseball camp, worked as an umpire

Essay: He discussed what he feels makes him unique. His family adopted his younger sister from Ethiopia when he was 8, bringing a big

Stay on top of everything. It's easy to fall behind senior year.

State University, Kennesaw State and Gwinnett Technical College if she wasn't accepted. She never needed to. At Oglethorpe, she plans to

study marketing, and she will keep her job as a team leader at Chick-fil-A. She has her sights set on working in marketing at the company's Atlanta headquarters.
GPA: 93.27
SAT: 1130

Explore all your interests, even if it's just to rule things out.

welcome change to his life. He also wrote about the impact of two classmates' suicides and the death of a teammate's brother.
Connections: The Knox baseball coach helped him reach out to current students to find out what life at Knox would be like.
Cost: Financial aid, including grants and loans, will cover a fair amount of Knox's $47,400 annual tuition. Wright's parents will pitch in to pick up the rest.

Alondra Medrano

Medrano was born in Mexico, and she moved to the U.S. at age 9 with her mom and two brothers to join her dad in Georgia. Back in her small hometown of Zacatecas, having a college degree was rare, and both of her older brothers dropped out of Roswell High to work in construction. Although she wanted to go to college, her family had no savings and couldn't give her guidance.

In a conversation with her school counselor senior year, Medrano learned about several schools with diverse student populations near enough that she could likely commute from home. Oglethorpe University immediately caught her attention. She applied early and planned to submit apps to Georgia

Talk to older friends in a similar situation for guidance.

Extracurriculars: Cosmetology pathway in SkillsUSA, Language Fusion Club, worked about 20 hours per week at Chick-fil-A
Essay: When Medrano moved to the U.S., she didn't know any English. She recalled how hard it was to construct her first sentence in a new language, and how now she could write a college essay and complete AP English.
Cost: A $21,000 annual scholarship she got from Oglethorpe will cover about half of the $39,300 tuition cost. Oglethorpe also matches the amount of aid students receive from the HOPE Scholarship, a merit-based award for in-state students attending Georgia schools, so Medrano's $4,000 award gets doubled to $8,000. She and her parents will cover the rest.
Smart move: Seeking out a small school for the community feel and for professors whom she can tap for guidance as a first-generation student. In fact, 40% of Oglethorpe's 1,260 undergraduates are the first in their families to attend college.
Advice: "There is a way, if you really have your mind set, to succeed in life," she says. Two Chick-fil-A co-workers who attend Oglethorpe expressed how much they love the school, and confirmed that the 15-mile commute from Roswell is doable. ●

Jiya Fowler

Aaron Wright

Alondra Medrano

A+ Schools for B Students

SO YOU'RE A SCHOLAR WITH LOTS to offer and the GPA of a B student, and your heart is set on going to a great college. No problem. U.S. News has screened the universe of colleges and universities to identify those where nonsuperstars have a decent shot at being accepted and thriving – where spirit and hard work could make all the difference to the admissions office.

To make this list, which is presented alphabetically, schools had to admit a meaningful proportion of applicants whose test scores and class standing put them in non-A territory (methodology, Page 139). Since many truly seek a broad and engaged student body, be sure to display your individuality and seriousness of purpose as you apply.

▶ National Universities

School (State) (*Public)	SAT/ACT 25th-75th percentile ('18)	Average high school GPA ('18)	Freshmen in top 25% of class ('18)
Adelphi University (NY)	1080-1270[9]	3.5	59%
Auburn University (AL)*	25-30	3.9	62%
Baker University (KS)	20-25	3.5	41%
Belmont University (TN)	24-29	3.8	59%
Bethel University (MN)	22-28	3.6	55%
Biola University (CA)	1060-1260	3.6	71%
Chatham University (PA)	1040-1250[2]	3.6	56%
Clarkson University (NY)	1160-1350	3.7	69%
College of St. Scholastica (MN)	20-26	3.5	47%
Colorado State University*	1070-1280	3.6	46%
Concordia University Wisconsin	20-26[3]	3.4	51%
Creighton University (NE)	24-30	3.7	70%
Daemen College (NY)	1040-1230[2]	3.3	50%
Drake University (IA)	24-30[2]	3.7	68%
Duquesne University (PA)	1140-1280[2]	3.8	57%
Edgewood College (WI)	20-25	3.4	50%
Elon University (NC)	1150-1330	4.0	57%
Florida Atlantic University*	1080-1240	3.9	41%
Florida Institute of Technology	1150-1340	3.7	58%
Florida International University*	1090-1260	4.0	48%[5]
Gannon University (PA)	1020-1220	3.5	48%
George Fox University (OR)	1020-1230[3]	3.6	63%
George Mason University (VA)*	1120-1320[2]	3.7	50%
Gonzaga University (WA)	1183-1350	3.7	76%
Grand Valley State University[7] (MI)*	1050-1240	3.6	47%
Harding University (AR)	22-29	3.6	50%
Hofstra University (NY)	1150-1330[2]	3.6	59%
Howard University (DC)	1140-1285	3.6	59%
Iowa State University*	22-28	3.6	59%
Kansas State University*	22-28	3.6	52%
Lipscomb University (TN)	22-29	3.7	58%
Long Island University (NY)	1050-1250	3.3	42%
Louisiana State University–Baton Rouge*	23-29	3.4	47%
Louisiana Tech University*	22-28	3.5	53%
Loyola University Chicago	25-30	3.7	72%
Loyola University New Orleans	22-28	3.5	51%[5]
Marquette University (WI)	24-30	N/A	69%
Maryville University of St. Louis	20-26[2]	3.6	56%
Mercer University (GA)	1180-1340	3.9	68%
Michigan State University*	1110-1310	3.7	67%
Misericordia University (PA)	1040-1200	3.4	53%
Mississippi State University*	22-29	3.4	55%
Montana State University*	21-28	3.5	46%
North Dakota State University*	21-26[3]	3.4	43%
Nova Southeastern University (FL)	1080-1290	4.0	67%
Ohio University*	21-26	3.5	44%

School (State) (*Public)	SAT/ACT 25th-75th percentile ('18)	Average high school GPA ('18)	Freshmen in top 25% of class ('18)
Oklahoma City University	23-29[3]	3.8	56%
Oklahoma State University*	22-28	3.6	55%
Oregon State University*	1080-1310	3.6	58%
Pace University (NY)	1060-1220[2]	3.4	41%
Quinnipiac University (CT)	1090-1260[2]	3.4	58%
Regis University (CO)	1050-1230	3.6	56%
Robert Morris University (PA)	1030-1200	3.5	42%
Rutgers University–Camden (NJ)*	1000-1180	N/A	43%
Rutgers University–Newark (NJ)*	1020-1190	N/A	48%
Samford University (AL)	23-29	3.8	59%
San Diego State University*	1110-1310	3.7	68%
Seattle University	1130-1320	3.6	64%
Seton Hall University (NJ)	1150-1310	3.6	61%
Shenandoah University (VA)	980-1190	3.5	52%
Simmons University (MA)	1130-1300	3.4	75%
St. Catherine University[7] (MN)	20-26	3.6	66%
St. John Fisher College (NY)	1080-1250	3.5	56%
St. John's University (NY)	1070-1270[2]	3.5	46%
SUNY Col. of Environmental Sci. and Forestry*	1120-1310	3.7	63%
Temple University (PA)*	1130-1320[2]	3.6	56%
Tennessee Technological University*	21-27	3.6	59%
Texas Christian University	26-30	N/A	78%
Texas Tech University*	1070-1240	3.6	51%
Thomas Jefferson University (PA)	1060-1240	3.6	51%
Union University (TN)	23-30	3.8	62%
University at Albany–SUNY*	1100-1260	3.3	55%
University at Buffalo–SUNY*	1160-1330	3.7	70%
University of Alabama–Birmingham*	21-29	3.7	55%
University of Arizona*	21-28[2]	3.3	60%
University of Arkansas*	23-29	3.7	52%
University of Central Florida*	1160-1340	4.0	73%
University of Cincinnati*	24-29	3.7	52%
University of Dayton (OH)	25-30[3]	3.8	60%
University of Delaware*	1170-1350[2]	3.8	69%
University of Detroit Mercy	1050-1250	3.6	47%
University of Findlay (OH)	21-26	N/A	58%
University of Hawaii–Manoa*	1055-1240	3.6	54%
University of Houston*	1130-1310	3.8	66%
University of Idaho*	1010-1220	3.4	40%
University of Illinois–Chicago*	1020-1220	3.4	58%
University of Indianapolis	990-1180	3.5	49%
University of Iowa*	23-28	3.7	62%
University of Kansas*	23-29	3.6	56%
University of Kentucky*	23-29	3.5	59%
University of La Verne (CA)	1020-1205	3.5	48%
University of Louisville (KY)*	22-29[3]	3.6	48%

Note: Key to footnotes, Page 75.

School (State) (*Public)	SAT/ACT 25th-75th percentile ('18)	Average high school GPA ('18)	Freshmen in top 25% of class ('18)
University of Maine*	1050-1250	3.3	40%
University of Massachusetts–Boston*	1020-1220[2]	3.3	44%
University of Massachusetts–Lowell*	1150-1320[2]	3.6	56%
University of Mississippi*	21-29[2]	3.6	52%
University of Missouri*	23-29	N/A	61%
University of Missouri–St. Louis*	21-27	3.5	59%
University of Nebraska–Lincoln*	22-29	3.6	54%
University of Nevada–Reno*	21-26	3.4	58%
University of New Hampshire*	1090-1280	3.5	48%
University of North Carolina–Charlotte*	21-26	3.4	47%[5]
University of North Carolina–Wilmington*	23-27	4.0	60%
University of North Dakota*	21-27	3.4	43%
University of North Florida*	1120-1280	3.9	41%
University of North Texas*	1060-1260	N/A	50%
University of Oklahoma*	23-29	3.6	63%
University of Oregon*	1080-1290	3.6	55%[5]
University of Rhode Island*	1090-1260[3]	3.6	47%
University of San Francisco	1130-1330[2]	3.5	73%
University of South Florida*	1170-1330	3.9	71%
University of St. Joseph (CT)	1030-1210[2]	3.6	40%
University of St. Thomas (MN)	24-29	3.6	51%
University of the Pacific (CA)	1120-1350	3.5	67%
University of Wyoming*	22-28[3]	3.5	48%
Valparaiso University (IN)	1070-1270	3.7	63%
Virginia Commonwealth University*	1070-1260[2]	3.7	44%
Wayne State University (MI)*	1010-1210	3.4	45%
Western New England University (MA)	1060-1250[2]	3.5	47%
West Virginia University*	21-27	3.5	48%
Wilkes University (PA)	1050-1240	3.6	60%
William Carey University (MS)	21-29[3]	3.6	63%

▶ National Liberal Arts Colleges

School (State) (*Public)	SAT/ACT 25th-75th percentile ('18)	Average high school GPA ('18)	Freshmen in top 25% of class ('18)
Agnes Scott College (GA)	1090-1320[2]	3.8	60%
Allegheny College (PA)	1120-1340[2]	3.5	66%
Augustana College (IL)	22-29[2]	3.3	58%
Austin College (TX)	1130-1330[2]	3.6	50%
Beloit College (WI)	21-29[2]	3.3	56%
Berea College (KY)	22-27	3.5	69%
Birmingham-Southern College (AL)	22-28[2]	3.6	49%
Centenary College of Louisiana	21-28	3.5	47%
Coe College (IA)	22-28	3.7	53%
College of St. Benedict (MN)	22-27	3.7	64%
College of Wooster (OH)	25-30	3.7	71%
Concordia College–Moorhead (MN)	21-27	3.5	47%
Cornell College (IA)	23-30[2]	3.5	46%
Covenant College (GA)	23-30	3.7	57%
DePauw University (IN)	1120-1340	3.8	75%
Drew University (NJ)	1110-1310[2]	3.5	47%
Elizabethtown College (PA)	1070-1290	N/A	63%
Franklin College (IN)	980-1170	3.5	44%
Gustavus Adolphus College (MN)	24-30[2]	3.7	61%
Hanover College (IN)	22-27[2]	3.6	54%
Hollins University (VA)	1070-1280	3.7	55%
Hope College (MI)	1110-1330	3.7	67%
Houghton College (NY)	1030-1280[2]	3.4	50%

School (State) (*Public)	SAT/ACT 25th-75th percentile ('18)	Average high school GPA ('18)	Freshmen in top 25% of class ('18)
Illinois College	990-1170[2]	3.5	43%
Illinois Wesleyan University	24-29	3.8	63%
Juniata College (PA)	1080-1320[2]	3.7	67%
Knox College (IL)	1090-1350[2]	3.6	62%
Lake Forest College (IL)	1110-1310[2]	3.6	62%
Luther College (IA)	23-29	3.7	58%
Lycoming College (PA)	1010-1198[2]	N/A	46%
Meredith College (NC)	1000-1200	3.4	48%
Moravian College (PA)	1050-1200[3]	3.5	48%
Ohio Wesleyan University	22-28[2]	3.6	53%
Presbyterian College (SC)	1010-1210[2]	3.3	52%
Principia College (IL)	1028-1300	3.4	50%[5]
Randolph-Macon College (VA)	1020-1240	3.6	40%
Roanoke College (VA)	1040-1230	3.5	41%
Saint Mary's College (IN)	1050-1260[2]	3.7	56%
Salem College (NC)	21-28	4.0	67%
Simpson College (IA)	20-25	3.6	49%
Southwestern University (TX)	1130-1330	N/A	70%
St. Anselm College (NH)	1120-1310[2]	3.3	55%
St. John's University (MN)	22-28	3.5	44%
St. Lawrence University (NY)	1180-1350[2]	3.6	73%
St. Mary's College of Maryland*	1060-1290	3.4	46%
St. Michael's College (VT)	1140-1320[2]	3.3	53%
St. Norbert College (WI)	22-27	3.6	57%
Stonehill College (MA)	1130-1300[2]	3.3	54%
Susquehanna University (PA)	1098-1260[2]	3.6	51%
Transylvania University (KY)	24-30[2]	3.7	67%
University of Minnesota–Morris*	22-27	3.6	57%
University of North Carolina–Asheville*	1060-1250	3.4	42%
University of Puget Sound (WA)	1130-1350[2]	3.5	58%
Ursinus College (PA)	1140-1320[2]	3.3	51%
Virginia Military Institute*	1100-1310[3]	3.7	44%
Wabash College (IN)	1100-1330	3.7	64%
Wartburg College (IA)	20-26	3.6	51%
Washington and Jefferson College (PA)	1130-1320[2]	3.7	62%
Washington College (MD)	1080-1270	3.6	64%
Westminster College (MO)	20-25	3.4	45%
Wheaton College (MA)	1180-1350[2]	3.4	52%
Willamette University (OR)	1170-1350[2]	3.8	73%
Wofford College (SC)	1180-1350[2]	3.6	64%

▶ Regional Universities

School (State) (*Public)	SAT/ACT 25th-75th percentile ('18)	Average high school GPA ('18)	Freshmen in top 25% of class ('18)
NORTH			
Arcadia University (PA)	1050-1250	3.7	50%
Bryant University (RI)	1130-1300[2]	3.3	55%
Canisius College (NY)	1050-1270	3.5	45%
Carlow University (PA)	1000-1180	3.6	50%
College of New Jersey*	1160-1350	N/A	75%
CUNY–Hunter College*	1090-1260	3.5	57%
DeSales University (PA)	1010-1230[3]	3.3	43%[5]
Eastern Connecticut State University*	1010-1190[2]	3.3	40%
Eastern University (PA)	1030-1190[2]	3.5	40%
Endicott College (MA)	1070-1240[2]	3.4	40%
Fairfield University (CT)	1190-1340[2]	3.7	77%[5]
Fairleigh Dickinson University (NJ)	1030-1210[2]	3.4	46%

▶ Regional Universities (continued)

School (State) (*Public)	SAT/ACT 25th-75th percentile ('18)	Average high school GPA ('18)	Freshmen in top 25% of class ('18)
Geneva College (PA)	1000-1240	3.6	43%
Hood College (MD)	990-1270[2]	3.3	44%
Ithaca College (NY)	1160-1338[2]	N/A	56%
Lebanon Valley College (PA)	1068-1280[2]	3.6	48%
Le Moyne College (NY)	1080-1270[2]	3.6	54%
Loyola University Maryland	1140-1320[2]	3.5	61%[5]
Manhattan College (NY)	1070-1260[3]	3.3	54%
Marist College (NY)	1140-1320[2]	3.3	51%
Marywood University (PA)	1010-1190	3.5	45%
McDaniel College (MD)	1050-1230	3.6	46%
Messiah College (PA)	1080-1310	3.8	61%
Molloy College (NY)	1020-1210	3.0	56%
Monmouth University (NJ)	1040-1190	3.4	42%
Nazareth College (NY)	1090-1270[2]	3.6	58%
Niagara University (NY)	1020-1200[2]	3.4	40%
Roberts Wesleyan College (NY)	1010-1230[2]	3.5	44%
Salisbury University (MD)*	1145-1280[9]	3.7	45%
Seton Hill University (PA)	1020-1240[2]	3.7	45%
Siena College (NY)	1070-1270[2]	3.5	51%
Springfield College (MA)	1050-1240	3.5	48%
Stevenson University (MD)	1030-1200	3.1	44%

School (State) (*Public)	SAT/ACT 25th-75th percentile ('18)	Average high school GPA ('18)	Freshmen in top 25% of class ('18)
St. Francis University (PA)	1040-1250	3.5	60%
St. Joseph's University (PA)	1120-1290[2]	3.6	50%
Stockton University (NJ)*	1000-1190	N/A	44%
SUNY College–Cortland*	1060-1200[9]	3.4	47%
SUNY–Geneseo*	1120-1300	3.6	60%
SUNY Maritime College*	1075-1260[3]	3.3	50%[5]
SUNY–New Paltz*	1090-1270	3.6	61%[5]
SUNY–Oswego*	1040-1210[3]	3.5	50%
SUNY–Plattsburgh*	1050-1230[3]	3.2	43%
SUNY Polytechnic Inst.–Albany/Utica*	1000-1350[3]	3.7	68%
University of New Haven (CT)	1030-1220	3.4	42%
University of Scranton (PA)	1120-1280	3.5	65%
Wagner College (NY)	1070-1270[2]	3.5	49%
Wentworth Inst. of Technology (MA)	1080-1280[2]	3.1	40%
York College of Pennsylvania	1020-1220	3.5	40%

SOUTH

School (State) (*Public)	SAT/ACT 25th-75th percentile ('18)	Average high school GPA ('18)	Freshmen in top 25% of class ('18)
Anderson University (SC)	20-26	3.5	61%
Appalachian State University (NC)*	22-26	3.6	59%
Asbury University (KY)	21-28[2]	3.6	54%
Berry College (GA)	23-29	3.7	60%

Colorado State University

JIM LO SCALZO FOR USN&WR

School (State) (*Public)	SAT/ACT 25th-75th percentile ('18)	Average high school GPA ('18)	Freshmen in top 25% of class ('18)
Christian Brothers University (TN)	22-27	3.7	61%
Christopher Newport University (VA)*	1110-1280[2]	3.8	51%
College of Charleston (SC)*	1070-1250	3.9	51%
Embry-Riddle Aeronautical U. (FL)	1110-1320[2]	3.7	49%
Florida Southern College	1130-1300	N/A	61%
Freed-Hardeman University (TN)	21-28	3.6	51%
John Brown University (AR)	23-30[2]	3.7	58%
Lee University (TN)	21-28	3.7	49%
Queens University of Charlotte (NC)	1033-1218	3.3	46%
Stetson University (FL)	1120-1300[2]	3.8	54%
University of Mary Washington (VA)*	1050-1269[9]	3.6	46%
University of North Alabama*	20-25	3.5	45%
University of North Georgia*	1108-1273	3.6	48%
University of Tampa (FL)	1090-1250	3.4	48%
University of Tennessee–Martin*	21-26	3.5	43%
University of West Florida*	22-27	3.8	41%
Western Carolina University (NC)*	20-25	3.4	41%

MIDWEST

School (State) (*Public)	SAT/ACT 25th-75th percentile ('18)	Average high school GPA ('18)	Freshmen in top 25% of class ('18)
Ashland University (OH)	20-25	3.4	41%
Augustana University (SD)	23-28	3.7	64%
Baldwin Wallace University (OH)	21-27[2]	N/A	46%
Bradley University (IL)	1090-1290	3.8	64%
Butler University (IN)	25-30	3.8	76%
Capital University (OH)	21-26[3]	3.6	51%
Cedarville University (OH)	23-29	3.8	60%
College of St. Mary (NE)	20-25	3.0	40%
Concordia University (NE)	20-26	3.6	48%
Drury University (MO)	22-29	3.8	63%
Franciscan U. of Steubenville (OH)	1060-1280	3.7	59%
Hamline University (MN)	20-27	3.5	49%
Huntington University (IN)	990-1180	3.4	43%
Indiana Wesleyan University (Marion)	1030-1240	3.6	50%
John Carroll University (OH)	22-28	3.6	53%
Lewis University (IL)	1040-1200	3.5	46%
Marian University (IN)	1020-1200	3.5	48%
Nebraska Wesleyan University	21-28	3.8	55%
North Central College (IL)	1050-1250	3.6	57%
Olivet Nazarene University (IL)	1000-1220	3.5	43%
Otterbein University (OH)	21-27	3.6	54%
Rockhurst University (MO)	22-27	3.7	60%
Spring Arbor University (MI)	1025-1230	3.6	48%
St. Ambrose University (IA)	20-26[3]	3.3	44%
Trine University (IN)	1010-1230	3.5	46%
University of Evansville (IN)	1080-1300[2]	3.7	64%
University of Illinois–Springfield*	990-1218	3.6	49%
University of Minnesota–Duluth*	21-26	3.6	47%
University of Northern Iowa*	21-26	3.6	51%
U. of Northwestern–St. Paul (MN)	21-27	3.5	45%
University of Wisconsin–Eau Claire*	21-26	N/A	48%
University of Wisconsin–La Crosse*	23-27	N/A	57%
Viterbo University (WI)	21-26	3.6	51%
Webster University (MO)	21-27	3.6	47%
Xavier University (OH)	22-28[3]	3.5	50%[5]

WEST

School (State) (*Public)	SAT/ACT 25th-75th percentile ('18)	Average high school GPA ('18)	Freshmen in top 25% of class ('18)
Abilene Christian University (TX)	1040-1230	3.6	56%
California Lutheran University	1070-1250	3.7	63%
California State University–Fullerton*	1040-1220	3.7	68%

School (State) (*Public)	SAT/ACT 25th-75th percentile ('18)	Average high school GPA ('18)	Freshmen in top 25% of class ('18)
Concordia University (CA)	1030-1220	3.5	48%
Dominican University of California	1035-1210	3.6	55%
LeTourneau University (TX)	1090-1320[2]	3.6	50%
The Master's U. and Seminary (CA)	1010-1240	3.7	51%[5]
Mills College (CA)	1008-1240[2]	3.5	62%
New Mexico Inst. of Mining and Tech.*	23-29	3.8	68%
Northwest Nazarene University (ID)	1020-1250	3.6	48%
Oklahoma Christian University	20-27	3.6	52%
Point Loma Nazarene University (CA)	1140-1300	3.9	70%
Saint Martin's University (WA)	1020-1220[2]	3.4	57%
St. Edward's University (TX)	1080-1270	N/A	55%
St. Mary's University of San Antonio	1050-1250	3.6	58%
University of Dallas	1120-1310	3.8	66%
University of Portland (OR)	1140-1320	3.6	72%
University of St. Thomas (TX)	1060-1250	3.6	52%
Western Washington University*	1080-1280	3.5	56%
Westminster College (UT)	21-27	3.5	44%
Whitworth University (WA)	1090-1290[2]	3.6	64%

▶ Regional Colleges

School (State) (*Public)	SAT/ACT 25th-75th percentile ('18)	Average high school GPA ('18)	Freshmen in top 25% of class ('18)
SOUTH			
High Point University (NC)	1090-1250[2]	3.3	43%
Ouachita Baptist University (AR)	21-28	3.7	55%
MIDWEST			
Carthage College (WI)	21-27[2]	3.3	47%
Goshen College (IN)	995-1210	3.5	70%
Northwestern College (IA)	21-27	3.6	53%
Ohio Northern University	22-27	3.7	62%
Taylor University (IN)	1080-1300	3.7	60%
University of Mount Union (OH)	20-26	3.4	45%
William Jewell College (MO)	22-29[2]	3.6	56%
Wisconsin Lutheran College	20-26	3.4	47%
WEST			
Carroll College (MT)	22-28	3.6	57%
Oregon Institute of Technology*	1030-1240	3.5	57%

Methodology: To be eligible, national universities, liberal arts colleges, regional universities and regional colleges all had to be numerically ranked among the top three-quarters of their peer groups in the 2020 Best Colleges rankings. They had to admit a meaningful proportion of non-A students, as indicated by fall 2018 admissions data on SAT Evidence-based Reading and Writing and Math scores or Composite ACT scores and high school class standing. The cutoffs were: The 75th percentile for the SAT had to be less than or equal to 1,350; the 25th percentile, greater than or equal to 980. The ACT composite range: less than or equal to 30 and greater than or equal to 20. The proportion of freshmen from the top 10% of their high school class had to be less than or equal to 50% (for national universities and liberal arts colleges only); for all schools, the proportion of freshmen from the top 25% of their high school class had to be less than or equal to 80%, and greater than or equal to 40% Average freshman retention rates for all schools had to be greater than or equal to 75%. Average high school GPA itself was not used in the calculations identifying the A-plus schools. N/A means not available.

Your College Search:
A To-Do List

by **Ned Johnson**

PREPARE FOR A GREAT HIGH SCHOOL EXPERIENCE. *You'll be able to grow inside and outside the classroom, while making sure you're ready to apply to college in a few years. Use this list to guide your experience. Careful planning and good choices over time make for strong options later. Ready, set, go!*

Freshman Year

LISTEN AND OBSERVE. Faced with more challenging high school class work, you'll need to pay attention to what your new teachers expect from you and look for ways to work harder and smarter. Grades are important in ninth grade, but seek balance so that you are challenged though not overwhelmed. Ask for help if you need it, and treat a low grade as constructive feedback to help you become a better learner.

☐ **Get involved.** High school is not a four-year audition for college but rather a critical period to develop yourself. Grades are important, but so are social connections and extracurriculars. Use part-time jobs, community service, arts and music, photography, cheer squad, robotics clubs and other activities to pursue your passions. This will also give you an energy boost that will push you through the less exciting parts of school life.

☐ **Read voraciously.** Dive into books, newspapers, magazines and blogs. Explore subjects that engage you. Additionally, check out TED Talks, YouTube videos and other free learning opportunities, such as the massive open online courses known as MOOCs.

☐ **Find mentors.** Look for knowledgeable people who can offer helpful advice: teachers, coaches, counselors and friends. These relationships can pay off in other ways, too: People like to help students they know.

☐ **Schedule downtime.** That means turning off electronic devices. No phones. No screens. We all need time to daydream and think about ourselves and our place in the world.

Sophomore Year

KEEP EVOLVING AS A LEARNER. Focus on better understanding your strengths and passions – and how to develop them.

☐ **Challenge yourself (wisely).** Strive for strong grades and take on new challenges, but ask for help when needed and avoid overtaxing yourself. Balance is your goal.

☐ **Speak up in class.** Colleges look for students who contribute to and elevate class discussions. Down the road, you'll also need to ask for letters of recommendation. Teachers can only write strong ones if they've gotten to know you from hearing your thoughts.

☐ **Sleep.** The typical 15-year-old brain needs eight to 10 hours of sleep to function at 100%, so that should be your goal.

☐ **Refine your route.** Look ahead to the 11th- and 12th-grade courses you might be interested in taking and plan to work any prerequisites into your schedule. Take advantage of special courses, particularly rigorous ones that are in line with your academic interests.

☐ **Learn from the masters.** As you take inventory of your own interests, find people who work in related areas. Listen to their stories and consider opportunities for gaining firsthand experience. A 20-minute conversation with a professional could even turn into a fruitful internship opportunity.

☐ **Put together an activities list.** Start keeping track of your hobbies, jobs, extracurricular activities and accomplishments. This will form the basis of your résumé and will be essential in preparing for college interviews and applications as well as for possible jobs, internships and summer programs.

☐ **Make your summer matter.** Work, volunteer, play sports, travel or take a class. Research summer programs and internships to give yourself the chance to move beyond the scope of your regular high school courses. Plunge into an activity that excites you or one that builds on a special interest.

☐ **Settle on a testing strategy.** Use your PSAT scores and other practice tests to help you identify the right test for you (i.e., SAT vs. ACT). Set up a test-prep plan.

Junior Year

ESSAYS, TESTS AND APs, OH MY! Your grades, test scores and activities this year form a large part of what colleges consider for admission. Prepare for your exams, do your best in class, and stay active and involved.

☐ **Plot out your calendar.** Talk with your parents and guidance counselor about which exams to take and when. If your 10th-grade PSAT scores put you in reach of a National Merit Scholarship, concentrated prep time might be worth it. Then, take the SAT or ACT in winter or early spring. In May or June, the SAT Subject Tests (required by some colleges) are also an option in areas where you shine. If you're enrolled in an AP or honors course now, consider taking a College Board practice test.

☐ **Immerse yourself in activities.** Look for extracurriculars both in and out of school that you enjoy and that show you are dedicated, play well with others, and can assume leadership roles. High school is your time to discover what you like, to grow intellectually and socially, and to sharpen skills you'll use after high school.

☐ **Build your college list in the spring.** Once you get your test scores, talk to a counselor and assemble a list of target, reach and likely schools. Use tools to aid your research. Explore college websites and other resources such as ed.gov/ finaid and usnews. com/bestcolleges.

And clean up social media (e.g., Instagram, Facebook, Twitter) since admissions folks may check it out.

☐ **Visit schools.** Spring break and summer vacation are ideal times to check out a few campuses. Attend college fairs and talk with the people at the tables who can provide information and may serve as future contacts.

☐ **Connect digitally.** Too busy or unable to visit schools? Attend college fairs and information sessions whenever you can. Grab the admissions rep's card at an info session and follow up via email with a thank you note or with questions whose answers aren't already available on the college website.

☐ **Get recommendations.** Right after spring break, ask two teachers with different perspectives on your performance if they will write letters for you. Choose teachers with whom you have a good relationship and who will effectively communicate your academic and personal qualities.

☐ **Write.** Reflect on your experiences and strengths as you prepare to write your college essay. Procrastination causes stress, so aim to have first drafts done by Labor Day of senior year. Share them with an English teacher, parent or counselor.

Senior Year

DON'T SLACK OFF. Colleges look at senior-year transcripts, so keep working hard in your classes.

☐ **Finish testing.** If necessary, you can retake the SAT, ACT or SAT Subject Tests in the early fall. Check deadlines and the admissions testing policies of your schools. Are they test-optional or do they require the SAT

or ACT? If so, do you also need the optional written essays? What about the SAT Subject Tests?

☐ **Know your deadlines.** Many colleges have multiple deadline options. Consider the implications of early action and early, rolling or regular decision – and confirm the rules and deadlines for aid – so you can plan accordingly (related story, Page 126).

☐ **Apply.** Craft your essays with a well-thought-out narrative. Fill out applications carefully. Review a copy of your transcript. Have you displayed an upward trend that should be discussed? Does an anomaly need context? Discuss any issues with your counselor. Leave yourself time to reread essays to clean up any errors.

☐ **Follow up.** Check that your colleges have received records and recs from your high school and your SAT or ACT scores from the testing organization. A month after you submit your application, call the college and confirm that your file is complete.

☐ **Confirm aid rules.** Check with each college for specific financial aid application requirements. Dates and forms may vary.

☐ **Make a choice.** Try to visit or even revisit the colleges where you've been accepted before committing. Talk with alumni; attend an accepted-student reception. Then, make your college choice official by sending in your deposit. Congrats! ●

Ned Johnson is founder of and tutor-geek at PrepMatters (prepmatters.com) where, along with colleagues, he torments teens with test prep, educational counseling and general attempts to help them thrive. He is also co-author with Dr. William Stixrud of "The Self-Driven Child: The Science and Sense of Giving Your Kids More Control Over Their Lives."

CHAPTER

5

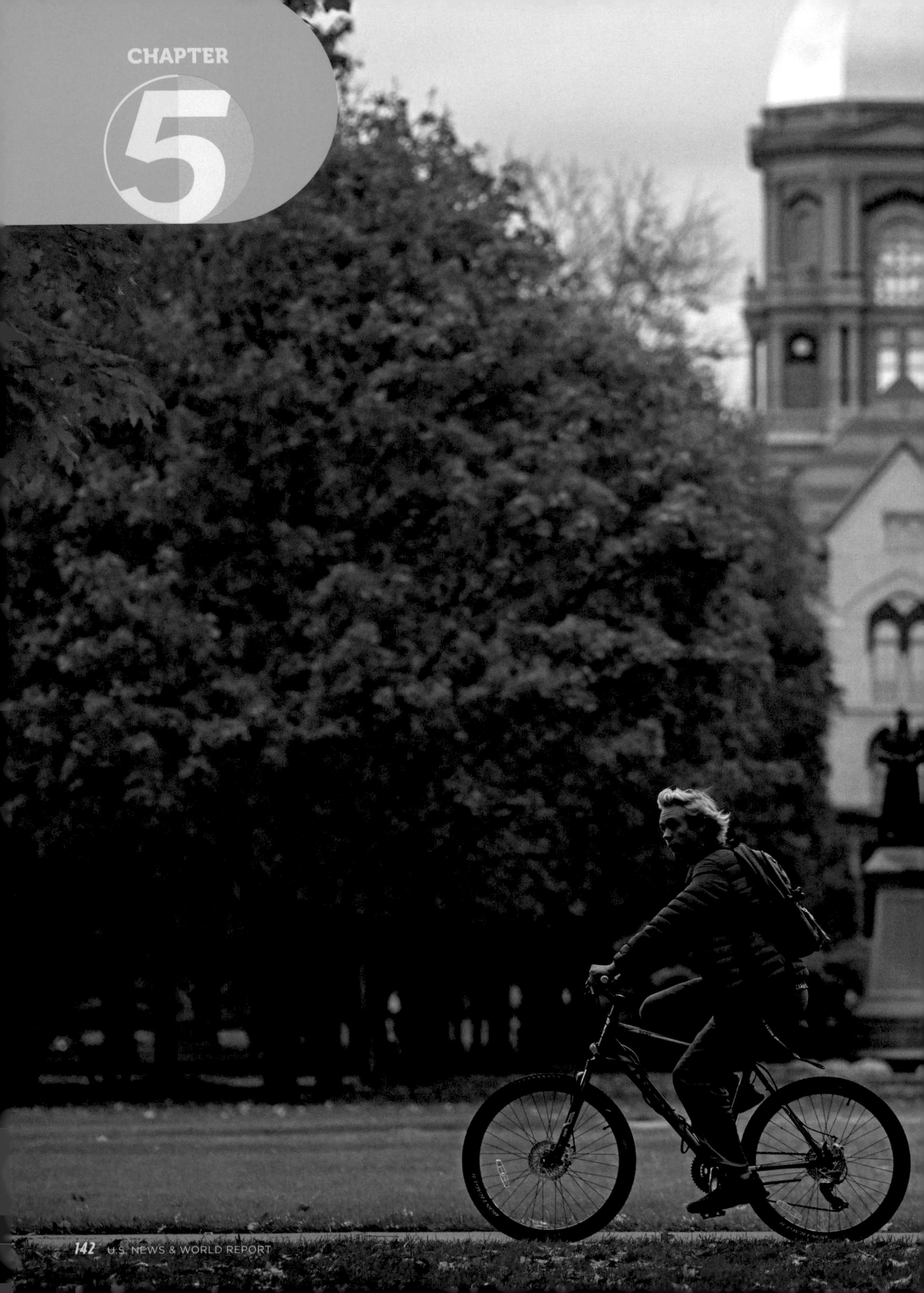

Finding the Money

University of Notre Dame
PHOTOGRAPHY BY BRETT ZIEGLER FOR USN&WR

Map Out Your Money Moves

Doing your homework to identify promising scholarship opportunities can pay off down the line

by **Elizabeth Gardner**

NEWS YOU CAN USE

DEVIN KEENEY'S INTENSE interest in robotics is saving him $25,000 a year off the cost of attending Chicago's Illinois Institute of Technology, where he won a merit scholarship from the school for participating in the FIRST Robotics Competition while he was in high school in Shawnee Mission, Kansas. "At competitions, Illinois Tech was always at the top" of the video showcasing the sponsors, he says, and the scholarship "made me look into the school more." Between the FIRST scholarship and several smaller merit awards, Keeney, now a sophomore computer engineering major, estimates he's paying about 70% less than the school's list price.

Most students hoping to graduate from college with little or no debt will need financial aid in the form of scholarships and grants. There are two categories: need-based and merit aid. To receive need-based awards, families must fill out the Free Application for Federal Student Aid (box, Page 146), which schools use to evaluate a family's ability to contribute to the cost of a student's education. Need-based aid depends

RACHEL PROCTOR
Savannah College of Art and Design

ONE STUDENT'S STRATEGY:
Find other sources of cash

● **AS A KID, RACHEL PROCTOR** was always taking painting, photography or dance classes, but she never considered any of those fields to be a viable career path. "Growing up, there was kind of a stereotype of artists not being successful," she says. Nevertheless, she earned cash before leaving for college

"

Going to college will help me achieve my goals.
It will allow me to get the degree I need to get
the job I want to help other people.

Simone, aspiring social worker

**Free access to 5 million scholarships
worth up to $24 billion**

Register for Scholarship Search at
salliemae.com/scholarship

by snapping photos of her high school peers, marketing her services through Instagram. Once at school, it didn't take long for her to realize that the path she chose – majoring in communications at a small liberal arts college in Illinois – wasn't the right one for her. "I was so unhappy, and I realized that if I work in an office for my whole life I'm going to be really sad," she says.

Halfway through her freshman year, Proctor transferred to Savannah College of Art and Design in Georgia to study commercial photography. The school's $51,000-plus annual price tag was daunting, especially since family finances were tight. But Proctor pays less than half that by being a live-in programming assistant in a dorm, which covers housing and meals, and by having snagged a few scholarships from SCAD for academic achievement and her portfolio. The rest is covered by student loans, which she plans to pay off in part with savings from her growing portrait business.

ENTREPRENEURIAL SPIRIT. Proctor spent her first two college summers back at home in Fort Collins, Colorado, building her photography clientele and banking the income. (In the summer of 2018, she had more than 75 clients.) At SCAD, she works at the school gym and as a nanny to earn spending money, and she also shoots pictures for cash in her free time. "It's so nice because there's no time commitment," she says. Her fees range between $100 and $500, depending on what a client wants.

Now a senior, Proctor knows the move to SCAD was the right one. She spent last summer as an intern at Free People, a clothing and lifestyle brand based in Philadelphia, one step closer to her goal of working in-house for a fashion brand.
–Margaret Loftus

on the gap between the so-called expected family contribution and the cost of attendance, and it doesn't change unless one's financial situation changes. Some middle- and upper-income families may find they don't qualify for these awards.

Merit aid is different. Thousands of students every year score significant discounts off tuition – sometimes even earning a full ride – regardless of their financial need, especially if a school wants them badly enough. These awards may be based strictly on GPA and test scores, but often schools also reward special interests or talents, such as music, leadership or, as with Keeney, robotics.

Jim Franko, a guidance counselor at Riverside Brookfield High School in Riverside, Illinois, recommends students take stock of their value as potential assets to each college they target. A highly selective school might admit you but offer no merit aid, notes Franko, who steers about 80 teens per year through the college application process. Yet there are others, he says, "that would love to have you and be extremely generous with merit scholarships," especially if your GPA and test scores put you at the 75th percentile or higher for students at that school.

CRUNCH THE NUMBERS. The National Center for Education Statistics has a wealth of useful information for families researching financial aid at its College Navigator website (nces.ed.gov/collegenavigator). For each school, it lists (among other things) the total cost of attendance, how many students receive aid and whether it comes from federal or school sources, and the average net cost of attendance for each student (further broken down by household income). You'll want to go through all the numbers and assess what percentage of the typical aid package is made up of grants or scholarships and what amount is composed of loans (related story, Page 151).

For example, while school X might offer higher average awards than school Y, school X's total costs may be higher, so the place with more modest grants may still end up having the lower price tag. Also pay attention to how many incoming students receive aid: It might be 100% at a less selective school and 50% or less at a more selective one. If there are large differences in average cost of attendance based on family income, that's

Cracking the Financial Aid Code

COLLEGE CAN DELIVER A BRUTAL WALLOP to family finances. But with a smart strategy, you can soften the blow and get the best possible deal. Your first move is to tap Uncle Sam's rich resources, including federal grants and loans. For that, you must start by filling out the Free Application for Federal Student Aid – better known as the FAFSA – as early as possible. The deadline for the 2020-21 school year is June 30, but you can file as early as Oct. 1 of senior year. Colleges use the form to allocate their own money, too. They all may have different deadlines, so stay on top of the key dates.

The FAFSA crunches your family's financial data to determine your "expected family contribution," which colleges use to figure out how much a family can pay toward higher ed costs. But schools assemble their aid packages based on multiple factors, including how badly they want you and whether they commit to meeting every student's full demonstrated need, meaning the gap between how much the FAFSA determines you can pay and the total cost of attending. Many colleges resort to "gapping," a practice where they offer a package that falls short of the full need of some applicants, perhaps those who are not in their top tier.

Some schools do have to be "need-aware" when weighing candidates, meaning that they consider how much aid will be required. But to these places, an applicant "may bring other things to the table that outweigh cost," such as geographic diversity or a strong interest in theater, notes Sean Martin, director of financial aid services at Connecticut College. A good tactic is to apply to at least some colleges where you beat the average of previously admitted students on measures like GPA and test scores.

After students are admitted, universities typically bundle a mix of federal grants and need-based loans, plus scholarships from the school based on need, academic merit and/or special talents. Some students will also receive work-study jobs as part of their federal package (related story, Page 152). Many places – particularly those that commit to meeting every student's full need – will expect you to file a supplemental form known as the CSS Profile, available on the College Board's website. Far more detailed than the FAFSA, the CSS collects data about the amount of equity your family has in your home, for example, and how much income is from a family-held business. If one's parents are divorced or separated, financial information about both may be needed – and new spouses, if applicable.

APPLES TO APPLES. When comparing packages, note that some may be more heavily tilted toward loans. To "compare apples to apples, take the cost of each school and subtract the grants and scholarships," says Cindy Deffenbaugh, retired assistant vice president and director of financial aid at the University of Richmond in Virginia. "What's left is the amount you'll pay out of pocket," which may or may not include loans.

Is it OK to negotiate? Yes, in certain circumstances. For example, if your financial situation has changed since you submitted the FAFSA. But make your case with facts and be personable with financial aid officers, suggests Charlie Javice, founder and CEO of Frank, an online tool designed to help college students with the financial aid process. "Schools will work with you," she says, as they're reluctant to lose out on good students once they've made the offer. *–Arlene Weintraub*

Create the future you want

Find free money for college with Sallie Mae® Scholarship Search

 Don't miss out on free money
In academic year 2017 – 18, 20,000 users of Sallie Mae Scholarship Search won at least one scholarship, with a total value of more than $61 million.

 Turn the things you love into scholarships
It's easy. Create a profile and you'll get alerts letting you know which scholarships match your skills, activities, and interests. Plus, new ones are added every day.

 You could win $1,000 for college
When you register, you can enter for a chance to win $1,000 in our monthly sweepstakes.[1]

sallie mae®

a sign that financial need, rather than merit, determines most of the awards. While public institutions generally have lower tuition, private colleges tend to meet more need and have larger scholarship programs. "If you're really at the top of our applicant pool, you'll receive a half-tuition scholarship just in merit aid, and you might receive a need-based award on top of that," says Todd Rinehart, vice chancellor for enrollment at the private University of Denver.

Joe Orsolini, a principal with College Aid Planners in Glen Ellyn, Illinois, recommends applying to six to eight colleges, and paying attention to the relationships between them, to gain maximum leverage for merit aid. "If I know a kid is looking at a school, I will recommend throwing an application to a rival school" in the same general geographic area or in the same athletic conference, he says. "A school might try a little harder when it knows it's competing against a rival."

GRACE WICKERSON
Rice University

ONE STUDENT'S STRATEGY:
Seek out specialized scholarships

● **BY NINTH GRADE,** Grace Wickerson of Englewood, Florida, had set a goal of attending an elite college out of state, and by the next year, she knew she wanted to pursue a career in engineering. Her parents were supportive, but they made it clear they wouldn't be able to help foot the bill.

So began Operation Scholarship Search. "In 11th grade, I made a spreadsheet with every scholarship I could find," she says. "My college counselor helped me with local scholarships, and I did most of the work on the national ones." Her interest in STEM gave her many options, and she landed a Buick Achievers Scholarship, geared toward aspiring engineers and good for $25,000 a year toward tuition and college expenses (renewable for four years).

STACKING AWARDS. After Wickerson was admitted to Rice University in Houston, the school offered her a $27,000 merit scholarship and allowed her to "stack" a handful of other scholarships, including one from the Girl Scouts. All told, the grant money effectively covered the more than $61,000 in annual tuition, fees, plus room and board for her four years there. Wickerson credits her funding success with being extremely organized, and she advises prospective students to create a list of both reach and safe scholarships almost as they might for colleges themselves. "Do as much advance preparation as you can because all the deadlines come up at the same time," she says. That effort also helped her keep straight the different requirements for each award, such as extra essays and interviews.

Wickerson is set to graduate in 2020 debt-free, and she has her sights set on grad school. At Rice, the materials science and nanoengineering major has focused on getting good grades – most of her awards require that she maintain a 3.0 GPA. She also did research in a professor's lab (a paid gig during the summer). "I've been gloriously overwhelmed," she says. *–Margaret Loftus*

BLAKE PLANTE
Pomona College

ONE STUDENT'S STRATEGY: Start at community college

● **BLAKE PLANTE DIDN'T PLAN** on going to community college, but he's glad he did. He first started taking classes at Riverside City College in his hometown of Riverside, California, to get a leg up on earning college credit while he was still a senior at an area charter high school.

After taking part-time classes during high school, Plante ended up doing two years full time at RCC, during which he ultimately earned five associate degrees and several scholarships, all of which could be used toward college-related expenses at community college or a post-transfer institution. He also won a Cal Grant that allowed him to bank additional cash toward tuition and fees at a four-year school in the Golden State. "I was privileged in that I was living nearby, and my family could provide housing and food. All I had to worry about was school," he says. "Community college is an excellent opportunity for saving a lot of money." Enrollment fees for residents at RCC in 2019 are just $46 per credit, for example, and those fees were waived for Plante as a recipient of a California College Promise Grant.

TAKING THE TRANSFER PATH. In 2016, Plante transferred as a second-semester sophomore to Pomona College in Claremont, California, about 30 miles from home. The private liberal arts college offered him the most attractive deal – even compared to state schools — and all told, financial aid underwrote 90% of the college's $71,000-a-year tab. He covered the rest with savings and earnings from a summer job in 2017 teaching debate to middle and high school students.

With no money concerns, Plante flourished during his three years at Pomona – a switch in majors his senior year required he stay an extra semester. He graduated in May with a bachelor's in English and internship experience with the National Endowment for the Humanities in Washington, D.C. He also developed a deep interest in corporeal mime (a type of physical theater that situates expression in the body, rather than substituting gesture for speech), which he's exploring more deeply through a yearlong fellowship. All those years of living at home during community college have paid off: Not only did he graduate without debt, but he's got money in the bank. "I can do pretty much anything," he says. *–Margaret Loftus*

READ THE FINE PRINT. When comparing offers, Rinehart advises students to pay careful attention to detail. For example, when tuition goes up, will your merit- or need-based award go up, too? Often it doesn't, Rinehart says. Keeping a scholarship beyond the first year may require making satisfactory progress toward a degree, maintaining a certain GPA or sticking with an activity or academic area.

As a public institution, the University of Arizona has established set merit scholarship award offers based on high school GPA, test scores and state residency status. There's no wiggle room in that basic amount, says Meghan McKenney, director of counseling in the Office of Scholarships and Financial Aid. But the school created Scholarship Universe (financialaid.arizona.edu/scholarshipuniverse) to help admitted students find and apply for additional scholarships (merit-based and otherwise) both at UA and elsewhere. They include grants from individual academic departments, donors and external scholarships. (UA has also licensed Scholarship Universe to a company to distribute more broadly.)

EXPAND YOUR SEARCH. Besides exhausting aid sources through their chosen school, students can find plenty of other resources online – either free or at modest subscription prices – to search for scholarship money. They include Scholly, a website and mobile app accessible at myscholly.com; Scholarships.com; and Fastweb.com, among many others. Also check with any organizations you're associated with: church, scouting, companies that employ you or your parents, hobby-based organizations (like FIRST Robotics, say, or the Amateur Trapshooting Association), and civic groups like the Benevolent and Protective Order of Elks or a local chamber of commerce.

Opportunities lurk in unexpected places: The Tall Clubs International social organization offers scholarships for tall people, for example, while the Mayflower Society has college money earmarked for proven descendants of families who came to America on the Mayflower. The U.S. Department of Education also offers information and scholarship advice at studentaid.gov.

Bobbi Lehman, director of financial aid compliance at the University of Arizona, urges applicants to go after every scholarship for which they're eligible. She recalls meeting a student who had been particularly determined in his search and won so many awards that he exceeded his cost of attendance. "They were just a few hundred dollars each," Lehman says, "but he treated it like a job and just kept applying." ●

5 FINDING THE MONEY

Be a Smarter Borrower

A savvy student loan strategy can help you keep your debt down

by **Alison Murtagh**

TESS KERKHOF GREW UP working on her family's farm in Wilton, Iowa, and when it came time to apply to college, she was laser-focused on reducing her costs. "Both of my parents are extremely debt-averse," she says, and "the mindset of financial autonomy has always been very important to me." After zeroing in on Grinnell College, a liberal arts school about 90 miles from home, she and her parents met with financial aid counselors to understand how to afford the $54,000 annual tuition plus $12,800 in room and board.

After applying early decision, Kerkhof successfully negotiated with the aid office to boost her initial offer with some additional grant money. She also brought along several scholarships and nabbed a work-study job as a live-in community adviser in a campus residence hall, which covers housing costs. She found work during summers as well, including for Grinnell's campus garden and for a community food justice organization. As a result, Kerkhof expects to graduate in 2021 with less than $20,000 in student loan debt, which she thinks will give her the "freedom to do what I want to do and not to face a huge debt payment."

CONSIDER YOUR SALARY. Thanks to the many undergrads like Kerkhof who borrow to help finance a bachelor's, the total outstanding student loan burden has topped $1.6 trillion; the average graduate who borrows leaves campus owing about $30,000. To avoid taking on such a heavy load, students should start early and plan carefully, financial consultants say.

Tess Kerkhof has worked to keep her student loan debt low.

In general, experts suggest that prospective borrowers consider their future career path and potential earnings. A good rule of thumb is to try to borrow no more than "the amount that you expect to earn in a first-year-out-of-school salary," says Gail Holt, dean of financial aid at Amherst College in Massachusetts. A loan repayment calculator can give you a sense of the potential monthly tab, with interest. For example, borrowing $20,000 at 4.5% interest would mean you pay about $207 per month over 10 years.

Advance planning is key because debt "can really hamper students' plans after college" when it comes to buying a car or a house, for instance, says Andrew Belasco, chief executive officer of College Transitions, an admissions consulting company. It's also worth considering what your midcareer pay might be, as well as whether a graduate degree or additional schooling might be required, Belasco adds.

During college, it can be helpful to do "an annual financial checkup" of where your debt stands, whether you need to borrow the same amount, and if any changes in your financial or family situation might make a difference in your overall aid situation, says Megan Coval, vice president of policy and federal relations at the National Association of Student Financial Aid Administrators.

To start, after exhausting any savings and scholarships, aid specialists recommend exploring federal loan options. Schools use the Free Application for Federal Student Aid to calculate their financial aid awards, and some private lenders also look at the FAFSA when determining loan eligibility (related story, Page 144).

FEDERAL FIRST. Direct loans extended by Uncle Sam allow dependent students to borrow up to $5,500 for their first year, $6,500 for year two, and $7,500 for their third year and beyond, capped at $31,000 total. These loans can either be subsidized (for those with financial need, the government pays interest during school) or unsubsidized (interest starts accruing right away and the borrower must pay it). For 2019-20, direct loans for undergrads have an interest rate of 4.53%; the rate for future loans is readjusted each summer.

If direct loans don't cover the bill, parent PLUS loans are available up to the full cost of attendance (after other aid) as determined by the school. PLUS loans carry an interest rate of 7.08% and are also readjusted each summer for future borrowers.

In addition to fixed interest rates, federal loans carry a number of benefits, such as a six-month grace period after graduation before one has to start paying off debt. There is also a choice of repayment plans. Under income-based repayment, for instance, borrowers can adjust their monthly bills to a percentage of their discretionary income. Those who have worked in a qualifying public sector job, such as for the government or a nonprofit, can apply to have their outstanding balance forgiven after 10 years of payments. Additional details are available at studentaid.gov.

After federal loans, experts suggest exploring private loans, which have their own interest rates and repayment options. Discover, for instance, offers a 1% cash reward per loan for those who maintain a GPA of at least 3.0. Wells Fargo gives a discount to those who have a qualifying checking account with the bank. Some private loans also have grace periods before first payments are due.

These days, many private lenders offer both fixed rates and variable ones, which can swing based on market conditions and other factors. For example, Sallie Mae currently offers loans with fixed rates of between about 4.74% and 11.35% and variable rates from 3.37% to 10.75%. Securing the most favorable option typically requires evidence of creditworthiness, and some lenders insist upon a co-signer. With a wide range in variable rates, borrowers could see their bills fluctuate toward a much higher rate than when they took out a loan. Although protections vary by lender, private loans do not generally have the same safeguards as federal ones, experts say. ●

with Michael Morella

Earn As You Learn

The right work-study job can pay off in more ways than one

by **Barbara Sadick**

AFTER OTHER FORMS OF FINANCIAL AID, a work-study job can be key in helping many undergrads pay college costs and gain valuable career prep along the way. That's been the case for Jessica Gonzalez, a junior at Rollins College in Florida, who has held two different work-study positions: as a career ambassador for the school's Center for Career & Life Planning and as a student assistant in the provost's office. "I've gained data and analytical skills, learned how to network and further developed strengths to bring to the workforce," says Gonzalez, who is considering a career as a clinical psychologist or dance therapist.

Work-study jobs are often included as part of a need-based financial aid package, and they are funded (at least in part) by the government. Money is usually administered by a college financial aid office and paid directly to a student. To be eligible, a student has to

A Glossary of Terms

● **Expected family contribution.** Determined by the info you enter in the FAFSA (see next entry), this is a figure the government provides for schools to determine how much a family should plan to contribute to college costs.

● **FAFSA.** Anyone seeking financial aid must fill out the Free Application for Federal Student Aid, which crunches family income, assets and other personal info. Schools use this to assemble an aid package, and those who wish to receive aid must complete it every year.

● **Federal direct loans.** There are two basic types: subsidized loans (meaning the government covers the interest until after graduation) for undergrads with financial need; or unsubsidized loans, where interest begins accruing immediately. Loans taken out in 2019-20 have a 4.53% interest rate.

● **Fixed- vs. variable-rate loans.** The interest on a fixed-rate loan will never change during its term, whereas a variable rate might rise or fall from year to year based on market conditions. All federal student loans carry fixed rates, while most private loans offer a choice.

● **Grants/scholarships.** This so-called gift aid can come from colleges, the government, foundations and other sources. You don't need to pay it back, though you might owe tax on it and it can come with strings attached, like maintaining a certain GPA or pursuing a major or career in a particular field.

● **Income-based repayment.** A federal government option where

request to be considered on the Free Application for Federal Student Aid. Sometimes aid is awarded on a first-come, first-served basis, and it can be contingent upon the availability of funds and one's financial need.

Work-study positions pay at least the federal minimum wage (currently $7.25 an hour) or the state's minimum, if it's higher. Wages are taxable, and schools typically have a limit on the

Jessica Gonzalez values her work-study job at Rollins.

number of hours one can work (often up to 20 a week). In 2018-19, about 1 in 7 students participated in a work-study gig, earning an average of about $1,800 each, according to a report by consumer bank and educational loan company Sallie Mae.

FINDING A FIT. Many colleges have online job portals that list all available positions, and students often apply directly to a particular office or department. At Rollins, for example, eligible students complete an application that typically includes qualifications, needed skills and a job's "anticipated learning outcomes," says Denisa Metko, assistant director for student employment. All work-study students there complete a career evaluation process at the start of their job, assessing their ex-

isting skills and professional strengths, setting learning goals and making plans for how to meet those goals. Once a job has come to an end, a similar reflection process takes place.

Jobs are typically available on campus, though in some cases colleges have arrangements with outside employers. At the University of Wisconsin–Madison, where about 1,500 students among the university's 44,000 total have work-study jobs, off-campus employers include the Urban League of Greater Madison and the Natural Resources Foundation of Wisconsin, an environmental group. The goal is to give students hands-on experience in areas that interest them, says Justin Mumford, assistant director for student engagement. "If, for example, a student in the computer science program wants to work and is eligible for work-study, we will try our best to connect that student to a computer science job," he says.

APPLIED SKILLS. Indeed, the more real-world and career-applicable skills a position entails, the better, says Tyler Wentworth, director of marketing, communication and engagement for career and professional success at the University of New Hampshire. At UNH, work-studies run the daily operations of the student union (staffing the information desk, managing the cash flow for the mailroom and so on) and help oversee the database of employers who come to campus to recruit, among other positions. Those with an interest in marketing, say, might seek a position that will teach them to use Adobe Creative Suite or other graphic design tools. Think of the positions not "as simply an opportunity to make money, but as a way to create connections, gain references for future employment and learn interviewing skills," says Wentworth.

Some might worry about first-year students taking on a job that could cut into their academic studies, but the reality often is otherwise. In many cases, work-study students can be very successful "because they have to learn early and quickly how to allocate their time," says Mike McLaughlin, director of financial aid operations at Middlebury College in Vermont. ●

---

monthly loan payments are reduced based on salary. This approach will typically extend the time of repayment from the standard 10 years to 20 or 25.
● **Loan forgiveness.** Eligible borrowers' student loan debt may be erased after 10 years of consistent payments if they work for nonprofits, the government or certain public service organizations like the Peace Corps.
● **Meet full need.** The college pledges

to meet 100% of one's "demonstrated financial need," which is the difference between the cost of attendance and the expected family contribution.
● **Need-based vs. merit-based aid.** Need-based aid is given out based on a family's financial circumstances, while merit aid is awarded for academic, extracurricular or other achievements.
● **Need-blind vs. need-aware.** A need-blind college says it does not

consider finances at all when making an admissions decision, while a need-aware school might.
● **Parent PLUS loans.** Parents can take out these loans from the government up to the cost of attendance (minus other aid). The loans are unsubsidized, and for 2019-20, they carry a 7.08% interest rate.
● **Pell Grant.** A federal grant for undergrads who display exceptional

financial need. For 2019-20, the maximum award is $6,195.
● **Subsidized vs. unsubsidized loans.** With subsidized federal loans, the government pays the interest that accumulates while a student is enrolled at least half-time and during a six-month grace period after completing school. Federal student loans have annual limits as to how much of a loan can be subsidized. –*Michael Morella*

Making the Numbers Work

Students can cut thousands from their college costs by making some smart choices

by **Melba Newsome**

WHEN ALEC LUMSDEN OPTED to attend the University of California–Berkeley rather than a less pricey state university in his native North Carolina, his parents pointed out that tuition and fees alone could be at least $30,000 more each year. Lumsden had one big factor on his side, however. He had taken International Baccalaureate classes and graduated in the top 10% of his class, which earned him 20 credits at Berkeley, the equivalent of more than one semester. Those savings plus some of Berkeley's unique offerings finally convinced his parents.

According to the College Board's Trends in College Pricing 2018 report, the cost of tuition and fees for private four-year institutions in 2018-19 was roughly double that of 30 years ago, while the average in-state tuition and fee total for four-year public schools tripled in the same period (adjusting for inflation). And of course, once you factor in housing, meals, textbooks and other expenses, your bill could easily jump thousands more, so savvy students and families are looking for ways to cut costs. Besides taking advantage of Advanced Placement or IB credits, here are some other ways to reduce the price of your degree.

CONSIDER REGIONAL SCHOOLS. Sure, going to a state school can slash your tuition, but the great news is you don't have to stay so close to home to get such breaks. Many institutions belong to one of four regional reciprocity or exchange programs that allow residents to attend a college or university in a nearby state and receive a discount.

The Western Undergraduate Exchange, for example, allows students from 16 Western states and territories to pay a maximum of 150% of resident tuition at over 160 participating two- and four-year institutions. "More than 40,000 current students are benefiting from the program," says Margo Colalancia, director of student access programs (including the WUE) for the Western Interstate Commission for Higher Education. "This past year alone, their savings are estimated at $380.5 million in tuition, with the average tuition savings being $10,100 a year."

By the time Alice Neidiffer graduated from high school in 2018, she was ready to look beyond Petersburg, Alaska. She credits WUE for providing her with more options. "The University of Utah was my first choice," says the political science major, who estimates she will save about $16,000 a year over the standard out-of-state tuition and fees.

Other regional alliances include the 10-state Midwest Student Exchange Program, which offers participating students tuition capped at 150% of in-state rates at public institutions and 10% tuition cuts at private ones; the Southern Regional Education Board's Academic Common Market, encompassing 15 states, which offers in-state tuition rates to out-of-state students at member institutions; and the six-state New England Regional Student Program, which provides tuition discounts at public colleges and universities for out-of-state students enrolling in an approved major or program.

WIDEN YOUR SCHOLARSHIP SEARCH. The College Board estimates that nearly two-thirds of undergraduates rely on

specifically for people like him – Chicago Public Schools students with stellar academic records. Although he knew little about Davidson, a liberal arts institution in North Carolina, he decided to apply and won the scholarship.

"When I received the call, I still didn't believe it," says Cruz, who had his heart set on becoming a teacher. He graduated in May with a bachelor's degree in educational studies. In addition to the roughly $66,000 annual cost of tuition, room and board, the Charles Scholarship covered Cruz's books, and included a personal expense and travel allowance plus funding for special study opportunities. "I tell everyone, 'Don't be afraid,'" he says. "'Just apply, apply, apply for every scholarship.'"

CUT TEXTBOOK COSTS. According to the College Board, undergrads at four-year public institutions paid an average of $1,240 for books and supplies in 2018. But there are ways to save hundreds on your textbook tab each year. Some colleges and universities are offering e-texts as a cost-saving measure. Instead of purchasing a printed copy, students pay a fee per course to access a digital version. Fees vary depending on the type of course, but RedShelf, a firm providing digital course materials to more than 550 colleges and universities, puts the average cost at under $40. That's a huge savings if the printed version runs a not uncommon $200.

If your school doesn't offer that option, you're not out of luck. You can pay a fraction of the campus bookstore cost by shopping online for used books. An older edition might do for subjects in which the course material changes very slowly such as French history or British literature. Don't need the book after the class ends? You can "rent" it at websites like Textbooks.com and CampusBooks.com to save on the purchase price – or sell it back to make some money.

SCRUTINIZE YOUR MEAL PLAN. According to The Hechinger Report, an independent nonprofit that covers education, the average college or university charged around $4,500 per year, or $18.75 per day, for a meal plan in 2017. Most colleges offer different meal plans based on the number of times you eat in the dining facilities. Choosing the wrong option can rob you of hundreds of dollars, either because you're paying for meals you don't eat or adding them to a plan that turned out to be too small. If you have early morning classes or can't drag yourself out of bed before noon, then stocking up on yogurt or granola bars may make more sense than a breakfast plan. If you have a dorm refrigerator and a place to cook, you might forgo a meal plan altogether – assuming you won't end up depending on vending machines or a daily pizza delivery. Bottom line: Pay for a meal plan only if you're going to use it. ●

scholarship and grant money to help pay for school. Competition can be fierce for awards from your chosen institution, but you can tap outside funding sources, too. Online search tools, including Fastweb, Cappex and the Scholarship Finder at the U.S. Department of Labor's careeronestop.org site, can help you find organizations that offer awards targeted at someone with your background, interests, geographic location or other characteristics. Most sites are free to use and operate similarly. Once you complete your profile and answer questions about your background and college interests, a search will return a list of scholarships for which you may qualify.

External scholarships – those not awarded by colleges – are available year-round, but the most common application times are in late summer and early fall, advises Stephanie P. Kennedy, founder of My College Planning Team, a consortium of educational consultants and financial aid specialists. Kennedy says other lesser-known scholarship sources are individual academic departments at colleges. These awards are more commonly available after freshman year and "can be very helpful to upperclass students who need money to continue at the college."

Chicago native Tony Cruz thought college was out of reach because of the high costs. Then he learned about the Charles Scholarship to Davidson College established by a Davidson alum

Great Schools, Great Prices

WHICH COLLEGES AND UNIVERSITIES offer students the best value? The calculation used here takes into account a school's academic quality based on its U.S. News Best Colleges ranking and the 2018-19 net cost of attendance for a student who received the average level of need-based financial aid. The higher the quality of the program and the lower the cost, the better the deal. Only schools in the top half of their U.S. News ranking categories are included because U.S. News considers the most significant values to be among colleges that perform well academically.

▶ National Universities

Rank	School (State) (*Public)	% receiving grants based on need ('18)	Average cost after receiving grants based on need ('18)	Average discount from total cost ('18)
1.	Princeton University (NJ)	61%	$16,438	77%
2.	Harvard University (MA)	55%	$15,972	78%
3.	Yale University (CT)	53%	$17,298	77%
4.	Massachusetts Institute of Technology	60%	$20,234	71%
5.	Stanford University (CA)	48%	$19,787	73%
6.	Columbia University (NY)	50%	$21,195	72%
7.	Vanderbilt University (TN)	49%	$21,142	70%
8.	Duke University (NC)	44%	$22,816	70%
9.	Dartmouth College (NH)	49%	$23,421	69%
10.	U. of North Carolina–Chapel Hill*	39%	$17,934	64%
11.	California Institute of Technology	53%	$24,520	66%
12.	Brigham Young Univ.–Provo (UT)	40%	$13,163	30%
13.	Rice University (TX)	39%	$22,276	66%
14.	Northwestern University (IL)	45%	$26,124	65%
15.	University of Pennsylvania	46%	$26,516	65%
16.	Brown University (RI)	41%	$24,411	67%
17.	University of Chicago	41%	$26,634	66%
18.	Gallaudet University (DC)	89%	$16,680	57%
19.	Johns Hopkins University (MD)	52%	$30,662	58%
20.	Washington University in St. Louis	41%	$27,026	64%
21.	Emory University (GA)	45%	$27,869	60%
22.	University of Rochester (NY)	54%	$27,892	62%
23.	Cornell University (NY)	46%	$30,576	58%
24.	University of Notre Dame (IN)	47%	$31,626	56%
25.	Wake Forest University (NC)	29%	$25,847	65%
26.	Lehigh University (PA)	40%	$24,385	64%
27.	Georgetown University (DC)	36%	$28,829	61%
28.	Tufts University (MA)	34%	$27,813	62%
29.	Valparaiso University (IN)	77%	$24,440	56%
30.	Carnegie Mellon University (PA)	38%	$31,451	57%
31.	University of St. Joseph (CT)	87%	$28,768	46%
32.	University of Virginia*	31%	$29,080	55%
33.	Brandeis University (MA)	45%	$30,606	58%
34.	Boston College	37%	$30,811	58%
35.	Simmons University (MA)	75%	$30,350	49%
36.	Illinois Institute of Technology	66%	$29,540	55%
37.	University of Southern California	34%	$33,512	55%
38.	Clarkson University (NY)	81%	$34,941	49%
39.	Rensselaer Polytechnic Inst. (NY)	58%	$34,761	52%
40.	Mercer University (GA)	70%	$27,582	48%
41.	New Jersey Inst. of Technology*	53%	$27,536	46%
42.	Clark University (MA)	59%	$30,188	47%
43.	Pepperdine University (CA)	52%	$34,749	52%
44.	University of Michigan–Ann Arbor*	28%	$32,507	50%
45.	University of Detroit Mercy	64%	$24,360	41%
46.	St. John Fisher College (NY)	80%	$30,376	38%
47.	Pacific University (OR)	78%	$31,014	48%
48.	Boston University	40%	$34,417	53%
49.	Case Western Reserve Univ. (OH)	46%	$35,655	47%
50.	Rochester Inst. of Technology (NY)	71%	$35,186	41%

▶ National Liberal Arts Colleges

Rank	School (State) (*Public)	% receiving grants based on need ('18)	Average cost after receiving grants based on need ('18)	Average discount from total cost ('18)
1.	Williams College (MA)	52%	$17,579	76%
2.	Pomona College (CA)	55%	$17,483	76%
3.	Amherst College (MA)	56%	$19,251	74%
4.	Swarthmore College (PA)	56%	$20,083	72%
5.	Smith College (MA)	59%	$19,777	73%
6.	Principia College (IL)	72%	$15,015	66%
7.	Soka University of America (CA)	84%	$22,901	55%
8.	Wellesley College (MA)	53%	$23,498	68%
9.	College of the Atlantic (ME)	83%	$18,878	66%
10.	Grinnell College (IA)	66%	$24,119	64%
11.	Vassar College (NY)	62%	$24,110	67%
12.	Bowdoin College (ME)	49%	$23,188	67%
13.	Denison University (OH)	52%	$19,646	71%
14.	Haverford College (PA)	46%	$22,680	69%
15.	Middlebury College (VT)	46%	$23,177	68%
16.	Colby College (ME)	46%	$23,065	68%
17.	Colgate University (NY)	34%	$21,303	71%
18.	Davidson College (NC)	50%	$23,152	66%
19.	Washington and Lee University (VA)	46%	$23,651	66%
20.	Wesleyan University (CT)	42%	$23,768	68%
21.	Wabash College (IN)	77%	$24,271	58%
22.	Gustavus Adolphus College (MN)	72%	$21,063	63%
23.	Claremont McKenna College (CA)	40%	$25,056	66%
24.	University of Richmond (VA)	39%	$23,255	65%
25.	Agnes Scott College (GA)	77%	$24,389	56%
26.	Colorado College	33%	$22,391	69%
27.	Ripon College (WI)	87%	$22,885	58%
28.	Macalester College (MN)	68%	$28,261	59%
29.	Hamilton College (NY)	52%	$27,056	62%
30.	Hollins University (VA)	77%	$22,147	60%
31.	Thomas Aquinas College (CA)	58%	$22,138	40%
32.	Carleton College (MN)	55%	$28,975	59%
33.	St. Olaf College (MN)	75%	$25,754	58%
34.	Earlham College (IN)	87%	$26,673	55%
35.	Franklin and Marshall College (PA)	54%	$25,686	65%
36.	Bryn Mawr College (PA)	53%	$26,721	63%
37.	Lawrence University (WI)	61%	$23,896	60%
38.	Centre College (KY)	57%	$23,478	58%
39.	Bates College (ME)	42%	$26,578	63%
40.	Hendrix College (AR)	75%	$24,434	61%

Methodology: The rankings were based on the following three variables: **1.** Ratio of quality to price: a school's overall score in the latest Best Colleges rankings divided by the net cost to a student receiving the average need-based scholarship or grant. The higher the ratio of rank to the discounted cost (tuition, fees, room and board, and other expenses less average need-based scholarship or grant), the better the value. **2.** Percentage of all undergrads receiving need-based scholarships or grants during the 2018-19 school year. **3.** Average discount: percentage of a school's total costs for 2018-19 school year covered by the average need-based scholarship or grant to undergrads. For public institutions, 2018-19 out-of-state tuition and percentage of out-of-state students receiving need-based scholarships or grants were used. Only those schools ranked in the top half of their U.S. News ranking categories were considered. Ranks were determined by standardizing scores achieved by every school in each of the three variables and weighting those scores. Ratio of quality to price accounted for 60% of the overall score; percentage of undergrads receiving need-based grants, for 25%; and average discount, for 15%. The school with the most total weighted points became No. 1 in its category.

▶ Regional Universities

Rank	School (State) (*Public)	% receiving grants based on need ('18)	Average cost after receiving grants based on need ('18)	Average discount from total cost ('18)
NORTH				
1.	McDaniel College (MD)	79%	$19,988	65%
2.	SUNY Polytechnic Inst.–Albany/Utica*	71%	$25,364	28%
3.	St. Bonaventure University (NY)	73%	$24,456	50%
4.	Le Moyne College (NY)	83%	$28,136	45%
5.	Canisius College (NY)	71%	$25,104	41%
6.	Waynesburg University (PA)	80%	$21,143	43%
7.	Niagara University (NY)	68%	$24,864	49%
8.	Bentley University (MA)	43%	$34,315	50%
9.	Alfred University (NY)	82%	$26,170	47%
10.	Providence College (RI)	47%	$36,978	45%
11.	Ithaca College (NY)	68%	$33,901	46%
12.	Fairfield University (CT)	37%	$34,547	48%
13.	Messiah College (PA)	71%	$29,801	40%
14.	Siena College (NY)	74%	$31,214	44%
15.	Springfield College (MA)	82%	$30,271	43%
SOUTH				
1.	Berry College (GA)	71%	$26,456	50%
2.	Coastal Carolina University (SC)*	21%	$13,430	67%
3.	The Citadel (SC)*	44%	$27,714	48%
4.	Milligan College (TN)	80%	$23,301	48%
5.	Saint Leo University (FL)	73%	$19,428	49%
6.	Bob Jones University (SC)	71%	$17,624	39%
7.	Rollins College (FL)	50%	$32,906	52%
8.	Converse College (SC)	77%	$21,619	37%
9.	University of Lynchburg (VA)	80%	$25,108	51%
10.	Freed-Hardeman University (TN)	73%	$19,949	43%
11.	Stetson University (FL)	67%	$31,243	51%
12.	Columbia International Univ. (SC)	83%	$19,967	45%
13.	Florida Southern College	67%	$27,387	47%
14.	Western Carolina University (NC)*	53%	$19,186	10%
15.	John Brown University (AR)	62%	$25,709	35%
MIDWEST				
1.	Truman State University (MO)*	39%	$21,097	25%
2.	Augustana University (SD)	61%	$23,011	51%
3.	Dominican University (IL)	83%	$24,270	47%
4.	Buena Vista University (IA)	85%	$21,592	54%
5.	Baldwin Wallace University (OH)	75%	$25,123	47%
6.	Bradley University (IL)	71%	$27,827	42%
7.	John Carroll University (OH)	70%	$30,164	48%
8.	Muskingum University (OH)	84%	$21,014	50%
9.	Milwaukee School of Engineering	79%	$27,907	49%
10.	Drury University (MO)	68%	$24,375	44%
11.	Huntington University (IN)	79%	$21,741	43%
12.	Malone University (OH)	84%	$21,634	52%
13.	St. Mary's Univ. of Minnesota	70%	$22,862	52%
14.	Concordia University (NE)	78%	$23,224	47%
15.	Marian University (IN)	78%	$24,489	51%
WEST				
1.	Trinity University (TX)	46%	$26,678	55%
2.	St. Mary's Univ. of San Antonio	70%	$22,516	50%
3.	Mills College (CA)	80%	$25,215	47%
4.	Whitworth University (WA)	70%	$28,733	52%
5.	University of Dallas	61%	$27,099	53%
6.	Westminster College (UT)	63%	$24,639	49%
7.	University of St. Thomas (TX)	68%	$24,373	49%
8.	Abilene Christian University (TX)	66%	$27,650	44%
9.	Rocky Mountain College (MT)	77%	$21,071	49%
10.	Pacific Lutheran University (WA)	75%	$27,819	51%
11.	California State U.–Los Angeles*	96%	$23,254	31%
12.	The Master's U. and Seminary (CA)	68%	$20,621	50%
13.	California Lutheran University	71%	$33,900	45%
14.	LeTourneau University (TX)	69%	$25,902	42%
15.	University of Portland (OR)	47%	$36,613	41%

▶ Regional Colleges

Rank	School (State) (*Public)	% receiving grants based on need ('18)	Average cost after receiving grants based on need ('18)	Average discount from total cost ('18)
NORTH				
1.	Cooper Union (NY)	54%	$22,143	67%
2.	Elmira College (NY)	86%	$26,012	53%
3.	University of Maine–Farmington*	69%	$21,419	33%
4.	Colby-Sawyer College (NH)	79%	$28,694	52%
5.	SUNY College of Technology–Alfred*	65%	$26,842	16%
6.	St. Francis College (NY)	78%	$32,455	27%
7.	Keene State College (NH)*	48%	$29,583	20%
8.	Vaughn Col. of Aeron. and Tech. (NY)	65%	$34,894	24%
9.	Vermont Technical College*	82%	$31,720	23%
10.	Fisher College (MA)	73%	$37,325	28%
SOUTH				
1.	Blue Mountain College (MS)	77%	$13,523	42%
2.	Kentucky State University*	90%	$13,712	51%
3.	Alice Lloyd College (KY)	87%	$15,830	40%
4.	Maryville College (TN)	82%	$23,581	53%
5.	Ouachita Baptist University (AR)	65%	$22,328	42%
6.	Newberry College (SC)	86%	$21,018	49%
7.	Flagler College (FL)	62%	$24,139	30%
8.	Averett University (VA)	86%	$24,281	49%
9.	Barton College (NC)	84%	$26,580	43%
10.	Huntingdon College (AL)	79%	$23,931	39%
MIDWEST				
1.	College of the Ozarks (MO)	57%	$10,615	64%
2.	Cottey College (MO)	76%	$14,631	55%
3.	Ohio Northern University	82%	$23,638	51%
4.	Alma College (MI)	84%	$24,941	54%
5.	Goshen College (IN)	75%	$23,164	51%
6.	Hiram College (OH)	88%	$25,943	48%
7.	Heidelberg University (OH)	87%	$22,800	49%
8.	Marietta College (OH)	69%	$21,613	57%
9.	University of Mount Union (OH)	80%	$23,764	46%
10.	Northland College (WI)	85%	$22,310	54%
WEST				
1.	Oral Roberts University (OK)	70%	$19,538	54%
2.	Texas Lutheran University	81%	$22,337	48%
3.	Carroll College (MT)	64%	$27,671	45%
4.	Pacific Union College (CA)	76%	$23,134	47%
5.	William Jessup University (CA)	78%	$28,264	44%
6.	Howard Payne University (TX)	85%	$23,464	42%
7.	Warner Pacific University (OR)	66%	$21,559	32%
8.	Corban University (OR)	78%	$26,362	43%
9.	University of Montana–Western*	69%	$26,850	17%
10.	Oklahoma Baptist University	63%	$32,266	23%

FINDING THE
Money

The Payback Picture

WITH TUITION RISING and financial aid budgets shrinking, many undergrads have to borrow their way to a degree. U.S. News has compiled a list of the schools whose classes of 2017 graduated with the heaviest and lightest debt loads. The data include loans taken out by students from the federal government – private loans, state and local government loans, and

loans directly to parents are not included. The first column of data indicates what percentage of the class graduated owing money and, by extrapolation, what percentage graduated debt-free. "Median amount of debt" is the 50th percentile amount of cumulative federal borrowing by graduates who incurred debt; it does not reflect all graduates, just those with debt.

MOST DEBT

▶ National Universities

School (State) (*Public)	% of grads with debt	Median amount of debt
Clark Atlanta University	83%	$31,000
Morgan State University (MD)*	68%	$30,727
Texas Southern University*	66%	$29,324
Rensselaer Polytechnic Inst. (NY)	55%	$29,000
Delaware State University*	67%	$28,375
North Carolina A&T State Univ.*	77%	$28,270
Florida A&M University*	64%	$28,002
Barry University (FL)	59%	$28,000
Jackson State University (MS)*	69%	$28,000
Rochester Inst. of Technology (NY)	62%	$28,000
Univ. of Maryland–Eastern Shore*	64%	$27,869
Tennessee State University*	64%	$27,750
University of Michigan–Flint*	54%	$27,500
University of the Incarnate Word (TX)	54%	$27,250

▶ Regional Universities

School (State) (*Public)	% of grads with debt	Median amount of debt
NORTH		
Metropolitan College of New York	84%	$34,500
Lincoln University (PA)*	87%	$31,000
Trinity Washington University (DC)	74%	$31,000
Albertus Magnus College (CT)	84%	$29,253
SOUTH		
Everglades University (FL)	50%	$40,750
Grambling State University (LA)*	86%	$37,543
Fort Valley State University (GA)*	84%	$35,980
Alabama Agricultural and Mechanical University*	77%	$32,750
Tuskegee University (AL)	65%	$32,500
MIDWEST		
DeVry University (IL)	78%	$35,767
Marygrove College (MI)	87%	$34,500
Chicago State University*	87%	$31,862
Alverno College (WI)	80%	$31,000
Lourdes University (OH)	70%	$29,687
WEST		
Woodbury University (CA)	59%	$31,000
La Sierra University (CA)	68%	$30,250
Prairie View A&M University (TX)*	74%	$29,000

▶ National Liberal Arts Colleges

School (State) (*Public)	% of grads with debt	Median amount of debt
Bennett College (NC)	78%	$38,243
Lane College (TN)	86%	$37,909
Chowan University (NC)	90%	$36,222
Dillard University (LA)	87%	$36,000
Tougaloo College (MS)	84%	$35,500
Allen University (SC)	84%	$34,785
Bethune-Cookman University (FL)	84%	$34,750
Stillman College (AL)	86%	$33,500
Bethany College (WV)	71%	$32,500
Johnson C. Smith University (NC)	86%	$32,500
Talladega College (AL)	97%	$31,000
Virginia Union University	88%	$31,000
Bloomfield College (NJ)	78%	$30,967
Rust College (MS)	77%	$29,325
Allegheny College (PA)	66%	$29,000
Coe College (IA)	72%	$28,500
Pine Manor College (MA)	57%	$28,311

▶ Regional Colleges

School (State) (*Public)	% of grads with debt	Median amount of debt
NORTH		
Wesley College (DE)	85%	$30,500
Thiel College (PA)	84%	$28,000
SOUTH		
Benedict College (SC)	87%	$41,750
Livingstone College (NC)	93%	$40,000
Florida Memorial University	72%	$39,500
Shaw University (NC)	89%	$36,500
St. Augustine's University (NC)	93%	$36,500
MIDWEST		
Central State University (OH)*	89%	$35,000
Harris-Stowe State University (MO)*	73%	$29,750
University of Mount Union (OH)	86%	$27,440
Heidelberg University (OH)	92%	$27,388
WEST		
Jarvis Christian College (TX)	93%	$31,226
Oral Roberts University (OK)	59%	$30,402
Bacone College (OK)	75%	$30,315
Wiley College (TX)	74%	$30,059
Pacific Union College (CA)	73%	$29,251

Note: Student debt data are from the U.S. Department of Education College Scorecard

LEAST DEBT

▶ National Universities

School (State) (*Public)	% of grads with debt	Median amount of debt
Harvard University (MA)	2%	$6,100
Princeton University (NJ)	4%	$7,500
Duke University (NC)	36%	$9,200
University of Texas–Rio Grande Valley*	38%	$10,054
Brigham Young Univ.–Provo (UT)	16%	$10,803
Rice University (TX)	16%	$11,200
Stanford University (CA)	10%	$11,447
CUNY–City College*	13%	$11,580
Yale University (CT)	10%	$12,000
California Institute of Technology	4%	$12,179
Thomas Jefferson University (PA)	63%	$12,500
Cornell University (NY)	30%	$12,742
University of Pennsylvania	15%	$12,988
University of California–Berkeley*	24%	$13,200
Utah State University*	31%	$13,491
Johns Hopkins University (MD)	32%	$13,500
University of California–Davis*	36%	$14,000
California State University–Fresno*	29%	$14,367
Touro College (NY)	25%	$14,500
Vanderbilt University (TN)	14%	$14,500
Dartmouth College (NH)	25%	$14,819
Gallaudet University (DC)	40%	$15,000
San Diego State University*	31%	$15,000
University of Alaska–Fairbanks*	22%	$15,000
University of California–Los Angeles*	33%	$15,000
University of the Cumberlands (KY)	40%	$15,000
University of Utah*	33%	$15,000
University of Washington*	27%	$15,000

▶ Regional Universities

School (State) (*Public)	% of grads with debt	Median amount of debt
NORTH		
CUNY–Lehman College*	21%	$9,993
CUNY–John Jay Col. of Crim. Justice*	14%	$10,000
CUNY–Brooklyn College*	15%	$10,500
CUNY–Queens College*	12%	$10,700
CUNY–Baruch College*	11%	$10,724
SOUTH		
Mississippi Univ. for Women*	52%	$14,000
Southern Arkansas University*	77%	$16,750
University of North Georgia*	36%	$17,500
University of West Florida*	65%	$17,750
Bob Jones University (SC)	35%	$17,868
MIDWEST		
Northeastern Illinois University*	32%	$15,000
Central Methodist University (MO)	73%	$16,950
Waldorf University (IA)	53%	$17,187
Siena Heights University (MI)	66%	$17,250
Minot State University (ND)*	37%	$18,349
WEST		
University of North Texas–Dallas*	72%	$10,232
Southern Utah University*	46%	$11,000
California State University–Los Angeles*	33%	$12,500
California State Univ. Bakersfield*	37%	$13,000
Northwestern Oklahoma State U.*	42%	$13,453

▶ National Liberal Arts Colleges

School (State) (*Public)	% of grads with debt	Median amount of debt
Berea College (KY)	16%	$5,300
Wellesley College (MA)	27%	$10,000
Amherst College (MA)	18%	$13,000
Haverford College (PA)	20%	$13,000
Pomona College (CA)	13%	$13,400
Middlebury College (VT)	24%	$13,625
Scripps College (CA)	32%	$13,750
Sarah Lawrence College (NY)	34%	$14,000
Pitzer College (CA)	36%	$14,045
Bates College (ME)	24%	$14,117
Williams College (MA)	24%	$14,489
Claremont McKenna College (CA)	21%	$14,500
New College of Florida*	34%	$15,430
Grinnell College (IA)	40%	$15,600
Reed College (OR)	38%	$16,000
Colgate University (NY)	24%	$16,125
Vassar College (NY)	40%	$16,250
Wesleyan University (CT)	28%	$16,875
Hamilton College (NY)	33%	$17,000
Barnard College (NY)	31%	$18,000
Thomas Aquinas College (CA)	71%	$18,000
Davidson College (NC)	23%	$18,218
Louisiana State University–Alexandria*	42%	$18,454
Kenyon College (OH)	30%	$18,500
Bowdoin College (ME)	19%	$18,647

▶ Regional Colleges

School (State) (*Public)	% of grads with debt	Median amount of debt
NORTH		
CUNY–York College*	8%	$8,163
U.S. Merchant Marine Acad. (NY)*	10%	$9,441
CUNY–Medgar Evers College*	21%	$9,700
CUNY–New York City Col. of Tech.*	9%	$10,266
Landmark College (VT)	39%	$14,500
SOUTH		
Broward College (FL)*	15%	$3,500
Pensacola State College (FL)*	7%	$3,500
Indian River State College (FL)*	9%	$6,333
Georgia Highlands College*	28%	$8,250
Atlanta Metropolitan State College (GA)*	34%	$8,750
MIDWEST		
Bismarck State College (ND)*	31%	$10,500
Cottey College (MO)	53%	$12,000
Lincoln College (IL)	70%	$12,000
Dunwoody College of Tech. (MN)	65%	$15,649
Maranatha Baptist University (WI)	38%	$17,000
WEST		
Brigham Young University–Hawaii	15%	$8,831
Brigham Young University–Idaho	15%	$11,000
Oklahoma State U. Inst. of Technology–Okmulgee*	48%	$12,000
University of Hawaii–West Oahu*	31%	$14,544
Montana State Univ.–Northern*	55%	$15,883

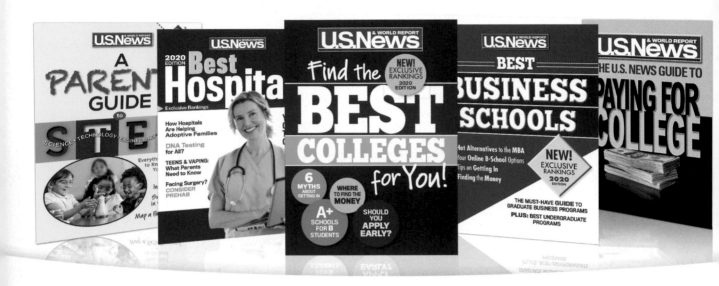

Top Performers on Social Mobility

ECONOMICALLY DISADVANTAGED STUDENTS are less likely than others to finish college. This new ranking reveals which schools stand out among their peers at serving recipients of Pell Grants, federal awards that go to students with exceptional financial need – what U.S. News defines as advancing social mobility. The ranking is based on an average of the six-year graduation rates of students entering in fall 2011 and 2012 (though we show actual data for those entering in 2012 below) and how that performance compares with the rates of all other students. Scores were adjusted by the proportion of the classes awarded Pell Grants, because achieving great results among low-income students is more challenging with a larger proportion of such students. Find additional schools doing a good job at usnews.com, and see page 60 for more on the methodology.

▶ National Universities

Rank	School (State) (*Public)	% of Pell recipients (entering 2012)	Pell graduation rate
1.	University of California–Riverside*	56%	75%
2.	University of California–Santa Cruz*	55%	74%
3.	University of California–Irvine*	48%	81%
4.	Howard University (DC)	47%	62%
4.	Rutgers University–Newark (NJ)*	50%	66%
4.	University of La Verne (CA)	47%	69%
7.	University of California–Merced*	62%	65%
8.	Georgia State University*	66%	56%
9.	University of California–Davis*	37%	84%
9.	University of California–Santa Barbara*	41%	84%
11.	University of South Florida*	40%	72%
12.	Florida International University*	40%	61%
13.	University of California–Los Angeles*	36%	88%
14.	Edgewood College (WI)	39%	63%
14.	University of Illinois–Chicago*	54%	57%
16.	University of Findlay (OH)	43%	61%
17.	CUNY–City College*	69%	44%
17.	University of Texas–Rio Grande Valley*	N/A	N/A
17.	University of the Cumberlands (KY)	N/A	N/A
20.	University of Texas–Arlington*	46%	48%
21.	Mary Baldwin University (VA)	57%	45%
21.	University of California–San Diego*	30%	84%
23.	Montclair State University (NJ)*	40%	69%
24.	The Sage Colleges (NY)	60%	59%
24.	Stony Brook–SUNY*	34%	76%
26.	Portland State University (OR)*	41%	46%
27.	California State University–Fresno*	64%	50%
27.	St. Catherine University (MN)	45%	58%
27.	University at Albany–SUNY*	36%	64%
27.	University of Houston*	40%	56%
27.	Univ. of Massachusetts–Boston*	44%	47%
27.	U. of North Carolina–Greensboro*	48%	48%
27.	University of the Incarnate Word (TX)	49%	45%
34.	Biola University (CA)	35%	69%
34.	Hampton University (VA)	49%	53%
34.	Keiser University (FL)	58%	52%
34.	Pace University (NY)	42%	53%
34.	University of Florida*	30%	87%
39.	East Carolina University (NC)*	39%	61%
39.	St. John's University (NY)	42%	58%
39.	University of the Pacific (CA)	31%	71%
42.	Chatham University (PA)	47%	56%
42.	Grand Canyon University (AZ)	N/A	N/A
42.	New Jersey Inst. of Technology*	36%	60%
45.	Florida A&M University*	68%	49%
45.	Florida Atlantic University*	39%	52%
45.	Gallaudet University (DC)	48%	46%
45.	Virginia Commonwealth University*	35%	65%
49.	Lincoln Memorial University (TN)	40%	51%
49.	Our Lady of the Lake University (TX)	69%	34%
49.	Regent University (VA)	40%	50%
49.	William Carey University (MS)	47%	51%
53.	Ball State University (IN)*	N/A	N/A
53.	Univ. of Maryland–Eastern Shore*	58%	35%
53.	University of West Georgia*	51%	39%
56.	Daemen College (NY)	41%	50%
56.	University of Texas–Dallas*	29%	74%
56.	Utah State University*	38%	63%
59.	Clarkson University (NY)	29%	74%
59.	Rutgers University–New Brunswick (NJ)*	30%	78%
61.	Illinois Institute of Technology	34%	66%
62.	Clarke University (IA)	34%	62%
62.	Rutgers University–Camden (NJ)*	41%	52%
62.	University of New Mexico*	46%	45%
62.	University of Texas–San Antonio*	43%	39%
66.	Benedictine University (IL)	44%	45%
66.	North Carolina A&T State Univ.*	63%	48%
66.	San Diego State University*	35%	70%
66.	University at Buffalo–SUNY*	30%	73%
70.	Husson University (ME)	48%	47%
70.	Simmons University (MA)	25%	75%
70.	University of Arizona*	35%	60%
70.	University of California–Berkeley*	27%	89%
70.	University of Central Florida*	31%	70%
75.	Azusa Pacific University (CA)	30%	65%
75.	Clark Atlanta University	69%	41%
75.	Missouri State University*	49%	45%
78.	Indiana State University*	53%	32%
78.	Western Michigan University*	45%	45%
80.	Florida State University*	27%	79%
80.	George Fox University (OR)	35%	54%
80.	Middle Tennessee State Univ.*	50%	38%
80.	University of Texas–El Paso*	67%	36%
84.	Barry University (FL)	63%	33%
84.	DePaul University (IL)	28%	66%
84.	Loyola University Chicago	28%	66%
84.	Sam Houston State University (TX)*	44%	48%
84.	Univ. of Massachusetts–Dartmouth*	40%	50%
84.	U. of North Carolina–Charlotte*	37%	55%
90.	Adelphi University (NY)	32%	66%
90.	Kennesaw State University (GA)*	42%	45%
90.	Lesley University (MA)	N/A	N/A
90.	Syracuse University (NY)	26%	80%
90.	University of Colorado–Denver*	37%	43%
90.	University of St. Francis (IL)	40%	54%
96.	Delaware State University*	58%	34%

▶ **More** @ usnews.com/bestcolleges

N/A=Data for 2012 were not provided by the school. Rank is based on 2011 data from the school or the federal government or, in some cases, on U.S. News estimates.

161

▶ National Universities (continued)

Rank	School (State) (*Public)	% of Pell recipients (entering 2012)	Pell graduation rate
96.	D'Youville College (NY)	38%	54%
96.	Pepperdine University (CA)	23%	84%
96.	Texas A&M University–College Station*	31%	76%
96.	Union University (TN)	32%	57%
96.	Univ. of Missouri–St. Louis*	42%	45%
96.	University of North Texas*	39%	50%
96.	University of San Francisco	24%	79%
96.	University of St. Joseph (CT)	38%	52%
105.	Jackson State University (MS)*	N/A	N/A
105.	Temple University (PA)*	27%	67%
105.	University of Idaho*	38%	53%
108.	Binghamton University–SUNY*	24%	79%
108.	Morgan State University (MD)*	60%	35%
108.	Rochester Inst. of Technology (NY)	29%	67%
108.	Stevens Institute of Technology (NJ)	21%	91%
108.	Univ. of Missouri–Kansas City*	46%	40%
113.	Georgia Southern University*	38%	47%
113.	Regis University (CO)	29%	67%

▶ National Liberal Arts Colleges

Rank	School (State) (*Public)	% of Pell recipients (entering 2012)	Pell graduation rate
1.	Cornell College (IA)	43%	78%
2.	Agnes Scott College (GA)	65%	62%
3.	Houghton College (NY)	43%	70%
4.	College of Idaho	51%	69%
4.	Salem College (NC)	49%	58%
6.	Spelman College (GA)	46%	69%
7.	Lake Forest College (IL)	40%	74%
7.	Monmouth College (IL)	59%	53%
9.	Soka University of America (CA)	26%	85%
10.	Blackburn College (IL)	59%	47%
11.	Pine Manor College (MA)	69%	50%
12.	Marlboro College (VT)	23%	45%
12.	Morehouse College (GA)	51%	48%
14.	Berea College (KY)	92%	61%
14.	Mansfield University of Pennsylvania*	43%	51%
14.	Thomas Aquinas College (CA)	36%	80%
14.	Wells College (NY)	61%	55%
18.	University of Virginia–Wise*	58%	50%
19.	Westminster College (PA)	41%	66%
20.	The King's College (NY)	39%	49%
21.	U. of North Carolina–Asheville*	34%	66%
22.	Ripon College (WI)	35%	63%
22.	Whittier College (CA)	36%	62%
24.	Hollins University (VA)	41%	54%
25.	Bryn Athyn Col. of New Church (PA)	39%	50%
25.	College of the Atlantic (ME)	43%	71%
25.	Lycoming College (PA)	34%	75%
25.	Oglethorpe University (GA)	33%	56%
29.	Cheyney U. of Pennsylvania*	N/A	N/A
29.	Hartwick College (NY)	34%	58%
31.	Albright College (PA)	47%	46%
31.	Allen University (SC)	N/A	N/A
31.	Warren Wilson College (NC)	39%	54%
34.	Vassar College (NY)	29%	92%
35.	Grove City College (PA)	N/A	N/A
35.	Hillsdale College (MI)	N/A	N/A
35.	United States Air Force Academy (CO)*	N/A	N/A

Rank	School (State) (*Public)	% of Pell recipients (entering 2012)	Pell graduation rate
35.	United States Military Academy (NY)*	N/A	N/A
35.	United States Naval Academy (MD)*	N/A	N/A
40.	Hanover College (IN)	36%	69%
40.	Tougaloo College (MS)	84%	37%
42.	Bethany Lutheran College (MN)	39%	47%
42.	Marymount California University	43%	36%
42.	Virginia Union University	71%	33%
45.	Knox College (IL)	28%	71%
45.	Massachusetts Col. of Liberal Arts*	48%	47%
45.	Williams Baptist University (AR)	53%	28%
48.	Concordia College–Moorhead (MN)	34%	66%
48.	Lewis & Clark College (OR)	21%	76%
50.	Austin College (TX)	28%	69%
50.	Lyon College (AR)	41%	44%
50.	Purchase College–SUNY*	35%	58%
50.	Transylvania University (KY)	31%	73%
50.	Virginia Wesleyan University	40%	45%
55.	College of St. Benedict (MN)	28%	75%
56.	Allegheny College (PA)	26%	70%
56.	Franklin College (IN)	47%	52%
58.	Georgetown College (KY)	37%	45%
58.	Gordon College (MA)	32%	64%
60.	Bethune-Cookman University (FL)	85%	33%
60.	Grinnell College (IA)	22%	83%
60.	Moravian College (PA)	35%	62%
63.	Albion College (MI)	29%	61%
63.	Dillard University (LA)	N/A	N/A
63.	Drew University (NJ)	32%	58%
63.	Illinois College	36%	64%
63.	Southwestern University (TX)	26%	69%
63.	St. John's College (NM)	35%	56%

▶ Regional Universities

Rank	School (State) (*Public)	% of Pell recipients (entering 2012)	Pell graduation rate
NORTH			
1.	Monroe College (NY)	77%	74%
2.	CUNY–Baruch College*	46%	68%
3.	CUNY–Brooklyn College*	52%	58%
3.	Rosemont College (PA)	54%	50%
5.	CUNY–Hunter College*	50%	57%
6.	SUNY College–Old Westbury*	49%	53%
7.	Cedar Crest College (PA)	57%	46%
8.	CUNY–John Jay Col. of Crim. Justice*	64%	46%
8.	Thomas College (ME)	N/A	N/A
10.	CUNY–Queens College*	45%	55%
10.	St. Joseph's College New York	40%	69%
12.	SUNY Buffalo State*	50%	46%
12.	Univ. of the District of Columbia*	57%	45%
14.	Albertus Magnus College (CT)	46%	56%
15.	Bay Path University (MA)	51%	52%
15.	Carlow University (PA)	55%	47%
15.	College of Mount St. Vincent (NY)	61%	48%
15.	SUNY–Fredonia*	41%	60%
19.	Dominican College (NY)	49%	42%
19.	Mercy College (NY)	76%	43%
19.	Saint Peter's University (NJ)	63%	46%
22.	Cairn University (PA)	44%	51%
22.	College of St. Elizabeth (NJ)	N/A	N/A

Rank	School (State) (*Public)	% of Pell recipients (entering 2012)	Pell graduation rate
22.	CUNY–Lehman College*	74%	47%
22.	Felician University (NJ)	69%	46%
22.	Notre Dame of Maryland University	58%	49%
22.	University of Baltimore*	57%	41%
22.	Waynesburg University (PA)	37%	64%
29.	Caldwell University (NJ)	50%	51%
29.	Lancaster Bible College (PA)	43%	50%
29.	Manhattanville College (NY)	44%	59%
32.	Northern Vermont University (VT)*	N/A	N/A
33.	New Jersey City University*	73%	39%
34.	Centenary University (NJ)	37%	55%
34.	College at Brockport–SUNY*	38%	63%
34.	Nyack College (NY)	52%	42%
37.	College of Our Lady of the Elms (MA)	49%	57%
37.	SUNY College–Potsdam*	46%	53%
37.	Trinity Washington University (DC)	N/A	N/A
40.	Keuka College (NY)	48%	48%
41.	Alfred University (NY)	40%	57%
41.	Concordia College (NY)	58%	40%
41.	Fairleigh Dickinson University (NJ)	43%	48%
41.	Kean University (NJ)*	45%	44%
41.	La Salle University (PA)	41%	61%
41.	Lincoln University (PA)*	65%	45%
41.	SUNY–Oswego*	40%	59%
48.	CUNY–College of Staten Island*	52%	46%
48.	Gwynedd Mercy University (PA)	36%	59%
50.	La Roche University (PA)	45%	54%
51.	Fitchburg State University (MA)*	38%	60%
51.	Lock Haven U. of Pennsylvania*	41%	51%
51.	Roberts Wesleyan College (NY)	44%	61%
51.	Stockton University (NJ)*	32%	70%

SOUTH

Rank	School (State) (*Public)	% of Pell recipients (entering 2012)	Pell graduation rate
1.	St. Thomas University (FL)	N/A	N/A
2.	Everglades University (FL)	N/A	N/A
3.	Midway University (KY)	51%	36%
4.	Xavier University of Louisiana	58%	52%
5.	Virginia State University*	N/A	N/A
6.	Converse College (SC)	43%	48%
7.	Bob Jones University (SC)	36%	57%
7.	North Carolina Central Univ.*	76%	44%
9.	Jacksonville University (FL)	42%	56%
10.	Columbia College (SC)	51%	44%
10.	Saint Leo University (FL)	42%	48%
12.	John Brown University (AR)	31%	59%
12.	Tuskegee University (AL)	78%	49%
12.	West Liberty University (WV)*	54%	44%
15.	Winston-Salem State Univ. (NC)*	N/A	N/A
16.	U. of North Carolina–Pembroke*	59%	37%
17.	Mississippi Valley State Univ.*	N/A	N/A
17.	North Greenville University (SC)	39%	50%
19.	Piedmont College (GA)	46%	45%
20.	Western Carolina University (NC)*	39%	57%
21.	University of West Florida*	44%	46%
22.	Winthrop University (SC)*	45%	49%
23.	Brenau University (GA)	59%	42%
23.	Bryan College (TN)	44%	43%
23.	Coker College (SC)	59%	32%
23.	Southern Adventist University (TN)	38%	59%
23.	University of Mount Olive (NC)	N/A	N/A

Rank	School (State) (*Public)	% of Pell recipients (entering 2012)	Pell graduation rate
28.	Grambling State University (LA)*	88%	35%
29.	Fayetteville State University (NC)*	79%	34%
30.	Appalachian State University (NC)*	30%	70%
30.	ECPI University (VA)	62%	41%
30.	Henderson State University (AR)*	57%	32%
33.	Asbury University (KY)	37%	62%
33.	Columbia International Univ. (SC)	41%	56%
35.	Fort Valley State University (GA)*	83%	28%
36.	Stetson University (FL)	34%	56%
36.	University of Tennessee–Martin*	53%	40%

MIDWEST

Rank	School (State) (*Public)	% of Pell recipients (entering 2012)	Pell graduation rate
1.	Dominican University (IL)	59%	62%
1.	Robert Morris University (IL)	52%	70%
3.	Bethel University (IN)	51%	68%
4.	Augsburg University (MN)	45%	64%
5.	Madonna University (MI)	41%	60%
6.	Stephens College (MO)	54%	49%
7.	Spring Arbor University (MI)	47%	54%
8.	Buena Vista University (IA)	39%	52%
9.	Univ. of Northwestern–St. Paul (MN)	44%	64%
10.	Grace College and Seminary (IN)	N/A	N/A
11.	Crown College (MN)	N/A	N/A
12.	Cornerstone University (MI)	33%	58%
12.	Minnesota State Univ.–Moorhead*	N/A	N/A
12.	University of Michigan–Dearborn*	41%	54%
15.	Central Methodist University (MO)	46%	36%
15.	Hamline University (MN)	41%	57%
15.	Mount Mercy University (IA)	26%	88%
18.	MidAmerica Nazarene University (KS)	52%	44%
18.	Muskingum University (OH)	56%	45%
20.	Univ. of Wisconsin–Eau Claire*	33%	65%
21.	Northeastern Illinois University*	63%	21%
22.	Lewis University (IL)	35%	63%
22.	Univ. of Wisconsin–Stevens Point*	39%	59%
22.	Winona State University (MN)*	31%	64%
25.	Concordia University–St. Paul (MN)	49%	46%
25.	Malone University (OH)	44%	50%
25.	Mount Vernon Nazarene U. (OH)	36%	55%
25.	Univ. of Illinois–Springfield*	43%	50%
29.	Baldwin Wallace University (OH)	41%	54%
29.	Ursuline College (OH)	55%	40%
31.	Morningside College (IA)	41%	46%
31.	Southeast Missouri State Univ.*	45%	43%
33.	Bemidji State University (MN)*	42%	45%
33.	Lakeland University (WI)	N/A	N/A
33.	Mount Mary University (WI)	63%	47%
33.	Saint Xavier University (IL)	57%	49%
33.	University of Minnesota–Duluth*	31%	60%
33.	Webster University (MO)	37%	54%
39.	Concordia University Chicago	51%	41%
39.	Franciscan Univ. of Steubenville (OH)	24%	74%
39.	Univ. of Wisconsin–Green Bay*	N/A	N/A
42.	Drury University (MO)	40%	59%
42.	Eastern Illinois University*	41%	50%
42.	Western Illinois University*	48%	37%
45.	Capital University (OH)	37%	51%
45.	Concordia University (NE)	25%	59%
45.	Judson University (IL)	24%	59%
45.	North Park University (IL)	41%	52%
45.	Univ. of Nebraska–Kearney*	35%	53%

▶ Regional Universities (continued)

Rank	School (State) (*Public)	% of Pell recipients (entering 2012)	Pell graduation rate
WEST			
1.	Mount Saint Mary's University (CA)	67%	66%
2.	Southern Nazarene University (OK)	N/A	N/A
3.	California State U.–Monterey Bay*	50%	59%
4.	Fresno Pacific University (CA)	55%	68%
5.	San Jose State University (CA)*	47%	66%
5.	Simpson University (CA)	N/A	N/A
7.	California State University–Long Beach*	51%	66%
8.	California State University–Stanislaus*	62%	56%
9.	California State Polytechnic U.–Pomona*	45%	70%
9.	California State University–San Bernardino*	69%	56%
11.	California State University–Los Angeles*	79%	48%
11.	Mills College (CA)	39%	71%
13.	La Sierra University (CA)	55%	50%
14.	Texas A&M International University*	65%	50%
15.	California State University–Fullerton*	43%	64%
16.	San Francisco State University*	47%	53%
17.	California State University–Northridge*	59%	51%
17.	Holy Names University (CA)	49%	45%
17.	Vanguard University of Southern California	45%	63%
20.	California State University–Channel Islands*	N/A	N/A
20.	California State University–Sacramento*	N/A	N/A
22.	California State Univ.–Bakersfield*	71%	41%
22.	St. Mary's Univ. of San Antonio	54%	49%
24.	California State University–Dominguez Hills*	74%	45%
24.	California State University–East Bay*	55%	46%
26.	California State Univ.–San Marcos*	N/A	N/A
27.	Western Oregon University*	47%	38%
28.	Chaminade University of Honolulu	40%	55%
29.	University of St. Thomas (TX)	38%	56%
29.	U. of Texas of the Permian Basin*	48%	35%
31.	Oklahoma Wesleyan University	N/A	N/A
31.	Univ. of Mary Hardin-Baylor (TX)	49%	41%
31.	Woodbury University (CA)	51%	51%
34.	St. Edward's University (TX)	35%	56%
34.	University of Redlands (CA)	N/A	N/A

▶ Regional Colleges

Rank	School (State) (*Public)	% of Pell recipients (entering 2012)	Pell graduation rate
NORTH			
1.	Fisher College (MA)	66%	65%
2.	St. Francis College (NY)	46%	54%
3.	Five Towns College (NY)	N/A	N/A
4.	SUNY College of A&T–Cobleskill*	47%	43%
5.	Elmira College (NY)	39%	66%
5.	SUNY College of Technology–Alfred*	40%	67%
7.	Keystone College (PA)	50%	50%
8.	Unity College (ME)	44%	67%
9.	Cazenovia College (NY)	47%	51%
9.	SUNY–Morrisville (NY)*	45%	41%
11.	University of Maine–Farmington*	49%	46%
12.	Colby-Sawyer College (NH)	40%	59%
13.	University of Maine–Fort Kent*	52%	36%
14.	U.S. Merchant Marine Acad. (NY)*	N/A	N/A
14.	Vaughn Col. of Aeron. and Tech. (NY)	66%	39%

Rank	School (State) (*Public)	% of Pell recipients (entering 2012)	Pell graduation rate
SOUTH			
1.	Newberry College (SC)	61%	49%
2.	U. of South Carolina–Upstate*	56%	47%
3.	Florida Memorial University	N/A	N/A
4.	Maryville College (TN)	48%	48%
4.	South Florida State College*	N/A	N/A
6.	Toccoa Falls College (GA)	61%	54%
7.	Averett University (VA)	53%	42%
7.	Elizabeth City State University (NC)*	77%	42%
7.	Greensboro College (NC)	52%	37%
10.	Point University (GA)	59%	31%
11.	Claflin University (SC)	72%	45%
12.	Erskine College (SC)	43%	61%
13.	Davis and Elkins College (WV)	N/A	N/A
14.	Alice Lloyd College (KY)	69%	35%
14.	Barton College (NC)	52%	45%
16.	Kentucky Christian University	N/A	N/A
17.	Welch College (TN)	46%	41%
18.	William Peace University (NC)	66%	34%
19.	Blue Mountain College (MS)	49%	35%
20.	Pensacola State College (FL)*	57%	63%
21.	Flagler College (FL)	31%	54%
22.	Emmanuel College (GA)	52%	32%
23.	LaGrange College (GA)	47%	43%
24.	Ohio Valley University (WV)	45%	33%
25.	North Carolina Wesleyan College	60%	23%
MIDWEST			
1.	College of the Ozarks (MO)	67%	66%
2.	Dordt University (IA)	42%	75%
2.	Oakland City University (IN)	52%	54%
4.	York College (NE)	49%	51%
5.	Hiram College (OH)	44%	56%
6.	Wisconsin Lutheran College	36%	68%
7.	Northland College (WI)	47%	49%
8.	Maranatha Baptist University (WI)	55%	51%
8.	Olivet College (MI)	46%	46%
10.	Bethany College (KS)	N/A	N/A
11.	McPherson College (KS)	44%	48%
12.	Heidelberg University (OH)	47%	49%
13.	Central Christian College (KS)	61%	28%
14.	Adrian College (MI)	51%	37%
14.	Central State University (OH)*	81%	24%
14.	Culver-Stockton College (MO)	58%	42%
17.	Sterling College (KS)	N/A	N/A
17.	Wilmington College (OH)	51%	42%
19.	North Central University (MN)	42%	50%
19.	Quincy University (IL)	50%	46%
21.	University of Minnesota–Crookston*	40%	46%
WEST			
1.	Corban University (OR)	N/A	N/A
2.	William Jessup University (CA)	53%	61%
3.	Southwestern Adventist Univ. (TX)	55%	48%
4.	Schreiner University (TX)	44%	40%
5.	Oklahoma Panhandle State Univ.*	N/A	N/A
5.	Texas Lutheran University	41%	47%
7.	Oregon Inst. of Technology*	38%	49%
7.	Southwestern Christian University (OK)	56%	29%
9.	San Diego Christian College	N/A	N/A
9.	University of Montana–Western*	49%	40%

DIRECTORY
OF
COLLEGES
AND
UNIVERSITIES

INSIDE

The latest facts and figures on over
1,600 American colleges and universities,
including schools' U.S. News rankings

New data on tuition, admissions, the
makeup of the undergraduate student body,
popular majors and financial aid

Statistical profiles of freshman classes, including entrance
exam scores and high school class standing

Using the Directory

How to interpret the statistics in the following entries on more than 1,600 American colleges and universities – and how to get the most out of them

THE SNAPSHOTS OF colleges and universities presented here, alphabetized by state, contain a wealth of helpful information on everything from the most popular majors offered to the stats on the freshman class that arrived in the fall of 2018. The statistics were collected in the spring and summer of 2019 and are as of Aug. 26, 2019; they are explained in detail below. A school whose name has been footnoted did not return the U.S. News statistical questionnaire, so limited data appear. If a college did not reply to a particular question, you'll see N/A, for "not available." By tapping our online directory at usnews.com/collegesearch, you can experiment with a customized search of our database that allows you to pick schools based on major, location and other criteria. To find a school of interest in the rankings tables, consult the index at the back of the book.

EXAMPLE

Fairfield University

Fairfield CT
1— (203) 254-4100
2— **U.S. News ranking:** Reg. U. (N), No. 3
3— **Website:** www.fairfield.edu
4— **Admissions email:** admis@fairfield.edu
5— **Private;** founded 1942
Affiliation: Roman Catholic
6— **Freshman admissions:** more selective; 2018-2019: 11,361 applied, 6,851 accepted. Neither SAT nor ACT required. SAT 25/75 percentile: 1190-1340. High school rank: 37% in top tenth, 77% in top quarter, 96% in top half
7— **Early decision deadline:** 11/15, notification date: 12/15
Early action deadline: 11/1, notification date: 12/20
8— **Application deadline (fall):** 1/15
9— **Undergraduate student body:** 3,989 full time, 188 part time; 40% male, 60% female; 0% American Indian, 3% Asian, 2% black, 7% Hispanic, 2% multiracial, 0% Pacific Islander, 77% white, 4% international; 28% from in state; 73% live on campus; N/A of students in fraternities, N/A in sororities
10— **Most popular majors:** 43% Business, Management, Marketing, and Related Support Services, 12% Health Professions and Related Programs, 8% Communication, Journalism, and Related Programs, 8% Social Sciences, 6% Psychology
11— **Expenses:** 2019-2020: $49,830; room/board: $15,150
12— **Financial aid:** (203) 254-4000; 43% of undergrads determined to have financial need; average aid package $33,281

---

1. TELEPHONE NUMBER
This number reaches the admissions office.

2. U.S. NEWS RANKING
The abbreviation indicates which category of institution the school falls into: National Universities (Nat. U.), National Liberal Arts Colleges (Nat. Lib. Arts), Regional Universities (Reg. U.), or Regional Colleges (Reg. Coll.). The regional universities and regional colleges are further divided by region: North (N), South (S), Midwest (Mid. W), and West (W). "Business" refers to business specialty schools, and "Engineering" refers to engineering specialty schools. "Arts" refers to schools devoted to the fine and performing arts.

Next, you'll find the school's 2020 rank within its category. Schools falling in the top three-fourths of their categories are ranked numerically. (Those ranked in the bottom 25% of their category are listed alphabetically in the ranking tables.) You cannot compare ranks of schools in different categories; U.S. News ranks schools only against their peers. Specialty schools that focus on business, engineering and the arts aren't ranked. Also unranked are schools with fewer than 200 students, with a high percentage of older or part-time students, that don't use SAT or ACT test scores for admission decisions, or that have received a very small number of peer assessment votes in a survey conducted in spring 2018 and 2019.

3. WEBSITE
Visit the school's website to research programs, take a virtual tour, or submit an application.

4. ADMISSIONS EMAIL
You can use this email address to request information or to submit an application.

5. TYPE/AFFILIATION
Is the school public, private or for-profit? Affiliated with a religious denomination?

6. FRESHMAN ADMISSIONS
How competitive is the admissions process at this institution? Schools are designated "most selective," "more selective," "selective," "less selective" or "least selective." The more selective a school, the harder it will probably be to get in. All of the admissions statistics reported are for the class that entered in the fall of 2018. The 25/75 percentiles for the SAT Evidence-Based Reading and Writing and Math or ACT Composite scores show the range in which half the students scored: 25% of students scored at or below the lower end, and 75% scored at or below the upper end. If a school reported the averages and not the 25/75 percentiles, the average score is listed. The test score that is published represents the test that the greatest percentage of entering students took.

7. EARLY DECISION/ EARLY ACTION DEADLINES
Applicants who plan to take the early decision route to fall 2020 enrollment will have to meet the deadline listed for the school. If the school offers an early action option, the application deadline and notification date are also shown.

8. APPLICATION DEADLINE
The date shown is the regular admission deadline for the academic year starting in the fall of 2020. "Rolling" means the school makes admissions decisions as applications come in until the class is filled.

9. UNDERGRADUATE STUDENT BODY
This section gives the breakdown of full-time vs. part-time students and male and female enrollment, the ethnic makeup of the student body, proportions of in-state and out-of-state students, percentage living on campus, and percentage in fraternities and sororities. Figures are for 2018-2019.

10. MOST POPULAR MAJORS
The five most popular majors appear, along with the percentage majoring in each among 2018 graduates with a bachelor's degree.

11. EXPENSES
The first figure represents tuition (including required fees); next is total room and board. Figures are for the 2019-2020 academic year; if data are not available, we use figures for the 2018-2019 academic year. For public schools, we list both in-state and out-of-state tuition.

12. FINANCIAL AID
The percentage of undergrads determined to have financial need and the amount of the average package (grants, loans and jobs) in 2018-2019. We also provide the phone number of the financial aid office.

ALABAMA

Alabama Agricultural and Mechanical University[7]
Normal AL
(256) 372-5245
U.S. News ranking: Reg. U. (S), second tier
Website: www.aamu.edu/admissions/undergraduateadmissions/pages/default.aspx
Admissions email: admissions@aamu.edu
Public; founded 1875
Freshman admissions: least selective; 2018-2019: 9,638 applied, 8,661 accepted. Either SAT or ACT required. ACT 25/75 percentile: 16-19. High school rank: N/A
Early decision deadline: N/A, notification date: N/A
Early action deadline: N/A, notification date: N/A
Application deadline (fall): 7/15
Undergraduate student body: 4,842 full time, 301 part time
Most popular majors: Information not available
Expenses: 2018-2019: $9,744 in state, $18,354 out of state; room/board: $9,128
Financial aid: (256) 372-5400

Alabama State University
Montgomery AL
(334) 229-4291
U.S. News ranking: Reg. U. (S), No. 87
Website: www.alasu.edu
Admissions email: admissions@alasu.edu
Public; founded 1867
Freshman admissions: less selective; 2018-2019: 7,783 applied, 7,607 accepted. Either SAT or ACT required. ACT 25/75 percentile: 16-20. High school rank: 1% in top tenth, 12% in top quarter, 40% in top half
Early decision deadline: N/A, notification date: N/A
Early action deadline: N/A, notification date: N/A
Application deadline (fall): 7/30
Undergraduate student body: 3,643 full time, 260 part time; 37% male, 63% female; 0% American Indian, 0% Asian, 94% black, 1% Hispanic, 1% multiracial, 0% Pacific Islander, 2% white, 1% international; 65% from in state; 48% live on campus; 2% of students in fraternities, 3% in sororities
Most popular majors: 18% Health Information/Medical Records Administration/Administrator, 13% Elementary Education and Teaching, 11% Business Administration and Management, General, 9% Speech Communication and Rhetoric, 8% Biology/Biological Sciences, General
Expenses: 2019-2020: $11,068 in state, $19,396 out of state; room/board: $6,050
Financial aid: (334) 229-4712; 96% of undergrads determined to have financial need; average aid package $16,925

Amridge University
Montgomery AL
(888) 790-8080
U.S. News ranking: Reg. U. (S), second tier
Website: www.amridgeuniversity.edu
Admissions email: admissions@amridgeuniversity.edu
Private; founded 1967
Affiliation: Christian Churches and Churches of Christ
Freshman admissions: less selective; 2018-2019: N/A applied, N/A accepted. Either SAT or ACT required. SAT 25/75 percentile: N/A. High school rank: N/A
Early decision deadline: N/A, notification date: N/A
Early action deadline: N/A, notification date: N/A
Application deadline (fall): rolling
Undergraduate student body: 175 full time, 178 part time; 32% male, 68% female, 1% American Indian, 1% Asian, 71% black, 2% Hispanic, 0% multiracial, 0% Pacific Islander, 24% white, 0% international
Most popular majors: 35% Business Administration and Management, General, 30% Organizational Leadership, 15% Human Development and Family Studies, General, 10% Bible/Biblical Studies, 10% Criminal Justice/Law Enforcement Administration
Expenses: 2019-2020: $9,900; room/board: N/A
Financial aid: (334) 387-7523; 93% of undergrads determined to have financial need, average aid package $8,734

Athens State University
Athens AL
(256) 233-8217
U.S. News ranking: Reg. Coll. (S), unranked
Website: www.athens.edu/
Admissions email: N/A
Public; founded 1822
Freshman admissions: least selective; 2018-2019: N/A applied, N/A accepted. Neither SAT nor ACT required. SAT 25/75 percentile: N/A. High school rank: N/A
Early decision deadline: N/A, notification date: N/A
Early action deadline: N/A, notification date: N/A
Application deadline (fall): N/A
Undergraduate student body: 1,205 full time, 1,681 part time; 31% male, 69% female, 1% American Indian, 1% Asian, 13% black, 3% Hispanic, 2% multiracial, 0% Pacific Islander, 77% white, 0% international; 95% from in state; 0% live on campus; N/A of students in fraternities, 0% in sororities
Most popular majors: 45% Business, Management, Marketing, and Related Support Services, 22% Education, 6% Liberal Arts and Sciences, General Studies and Humanities
Expenses: 2019-2020: $7,710 in state, $13,890 out of state; room/board: N/A

Financial aid: (256) 233-8161; 70% of undergrads determined to have financial need; average aid package $10,394

Auburn University
Auburn AL
(334) 844-6425
U.S. News ranking: Nat. U., No. 104
Website: www.auburn.edu
Admissions email: admissions@auburn.edu
Public; founded 1856
Freshman admissions: more selective; 2018-2019: 20,742 applied, 15,645 accepted. Either SAT or ACT required. ACT 25/75 percentile: 25-30. High school rank: 32% in top tenth, 62% in top quarter, 89% in top half
Early decision deadline: N/A, notification date: N/A
Early action deadline: N/A, notification date: N/A
Application deadline (fall): 1/15
Undergraduate student body: 22,460 full time, 2,168 part time; 52% male, 48% female; 0% American Indian, 2% Asian, 5% black, 3% Hispanic, 2% multiracial, 0% Pacific Islander, 81% white, 5% international; 64% from in state; 19% live on campus; 21% of students in fraternities, 43% in sororities
Most popular majors: 23% Business, Management, Marketing, and Related Support Services, 19% Engineering, 11% Biological and Biomedical Sciences, 6% Education, 6% Health Professions and Related Programs
Expenses: 2019-2020: $11,492 in state, $31,124 out of state; room/board: $13,600
Financial aid: (334) 844-4634; 36% of undergrads determined to have financial need; average aid package $11,344

Auburn University–Montgomery
Montgomery AL
(334) 244-3615
U.S. News ranking: Reg. U. (S), No. 79
Website: www.aum.edu
Admissions email: admissions@aum.edu
Public; founded 1967
Freshman admissions: selective; 2018-2019: 5,941 applied, 5,514 accepted. Either SAT or ACT required. ACT 25/75 percentile: 19-23. High school rank: 16% in top tenth, 38% in top quarter, 80% in top half
Early decision deadline: N/A, notification date: N/A
Early action deadline: N/A, notification date: N/A
Application deadline (fall): 8/15
Undergraduate student body: 3,554 full time, 1,078 part time; 35% male, 65% female; 0% American Indian, 2% Asian, 41% black, 1% Hispanic, 4% multiracial, 0% Pacific Islander, 45% white, 5% international; 94% from in state; 25% live on campus; N/A of students in fraternities, 2% in sororities

Most popular majors: 29% Health Professions and Related Programs, 15% Business, Management, Marketing, and Related Support Services, 12% Computer and Information Sciences and Support Services, 9% Education, 5% Parks, Recreation, Leisure, and Fitness Studies
Expenses: 2019-2020: $8,620 in state, $18,292 out of state; room/board: $7,090
Financial aid: (334) 244-3571; 72% of undergrads determined to have financial need; average aid package $9,205

Birmingham-Southern College
Birmingham Al
(205) 226-4696
U.S. News ranking: Nat. Lib. Arts, No. 140
Website: www.bsc.edu
Admissions email: admiss@bsc.edu
Private; founded 1856
Affiliation: United Methodist
Freshman admissions: more selective; 2018-2019: 3,628 applied, 2,069 accepted. Either SAT or ACT required for some. ACT 25/75 percentile: 22-28. High school rank: 20% in top tenth, 49% in top quarter, 75% in top half
Early decision deadline: 11/1, notification date: 12/1
Early action deadline: 11/15, notification date: 12/15
Application deadline (fall): rolling
Undergraduate student body: 1,261 full time, 7 part time; 48% male, 52% female; 0% American Indian, 3% Asian, 14% black, 2% Hispanic, 1% multiracial, 0% Pacific Islander, 79% white, 1% international; 60% from in state; 80% live on campus; 38% of students in fraternities, 52% in sororities
Most popular majors: 15% Biology/Biological Sciences, General, 15% Business Administration and Management, General, 10% Psychology, General, 7% Mathematics, General, 5% Fine/Studio Arts, General
Expenses: 2019-2020: $18,238; room/board: $12,402
Financial aid: (205) 226-4688; 55% of undergrads determined to have financial need; average aid package $16,057

Concordia College[1]
Selma AL
(334) 874-5700
U.S. News ranking: Reg. Coll. (S), unranked
Website: www.ccal.edu/
Admissions email: admission@ccal.edu
Private; founded 1922
Application deadline (fall): N/A
Undergraduate student body: N/A full time, N/A part time
Expenses: N/A
Financial aid: (334) 874-5700

Faulkner University
Montgomery AL
(334) 386-7200
U.S. News ranking: Reg. U. (S), second tier
Website: www.faulkner.edu
Admissions email: admissions@faulkner.edu
Private; founded 1942
Affiliation: Churches of Christ
Freshman admissions: selective; 2018-2019: 2,671 applied, 1,396 accepted. Either SAT or ACT required. ACT 25/75 percentile: 18-23. High school rank: N/A
Early decision deadline: N/A, notification date: N/A
Early action deadline: N/A, notification date: N/A
Application deadline (fall): 8/1
Undergraduate student body: 1,585 full time, 843 part time; 40% male, 60% female; 0% American Indian, 1% Asian, 48% black, 2% Hispanic, 2% multiracial, 0% Pacific Islander, 42% white, 2% international; 86% from in state; 23% live on campus; 11% of students in fraternities, 10% in sororities
Most popular majors: 27% Business Administration and Management, General, 18% Criminal Justice/Safety Studies, 16% Business/Commerce, General, 14% Human Resources Management/Personnel Administration, General, 3% Elementary Education and Teaching
Expenses: 2019-2020: $22,310; room/board: $7,700
Financial aid: (334) 386-7195; 88% of undergrads determined to have financial need; average aid package $12,861

Huntingdon College
Montgomery AL
(334) 833-4497
U.S. News ranking: Reg. Coll. (S), No. 16
Website: www.huntingdon.edu
Admissions email: admiss@hawks.huntingdon.edu
Private; founded 1854
Affiliation: United Methodist
Freshman admissions: selective; 2018-2019: 2,044 applied, 1,194 accepted. Either SAT or ACT required. ACT 25/75 percentile: 19-24. High school rank: 10% in top tenth, 30% in top quarter, 68% in top half
Early decision deadline: N/A, notification date: N/A
Early action deadline: N/A, notification date: N/A
Application deadline (fall): rolling
Undergraduate student body: 881 full time, 200 part time; 50% male, 50% female; 1% American Indian, 1% Asian, 22% black, 6% Hispanic, 4% multiracial, 0% Pacific Islander, 65% white, 0% international
Most popular majors: 45% Business, Management, Marketing, and Related Support Services, 17% Parks, Recreation, Leisure, and Fitness Studies, 13% Biological and Biomedical Sciences, 12% Homeland

Security, Law Enforcement, Firefighting and Related Protective Services, 6% Education
Expenses: 2019-2020: $27,400; room/board: $9,950
Financial aid: (334) 833-4428; 79% of undergrads determined to have financial need; average aid package $18,938

Jacksonville State University
Jacksonville AL
(256) 782-5268
U.S. News ranking: Reg. U. (S), No. 72
Website: www.jsu.edu
Admissions email: info@jsu.edu
Public; founded 1883
Freshman admissions: selective; 2018-2019: 6,033 applied, 3,276 accepted. Either SAT or ACT required. ACT 25/75 percentile: 19-26. High school rank: 22% in top tenth, 51% in top quarter, 83% in top half
Early decision deadline: N/A, notification date: N/A
Early action deadline: N/A, notification date: N/A
Application deadline (fall): rolling
Undergraduate student body: 5,459 full time, 1,862 part time; 42% male, 58% female; 1% American Indian, 1% Asian, 19% black, 1% Hispanic, 0% multiracial, 0% Pacific Islander, 72% white, 2% international; 84% from in state; 20% live on campus; 19% of students in fraternities, 18% in sororities
Most popular majors: 26% Health Professions and Related Programs, 16% Business, Management, Marketing, and Related Support Services, 8% Education, 6% Public Administration and Social Service Professions, 4% Homeland Security, Law Enforcement, Firefighting and Related Protective Services
Expenses: 2019-2020: $10,704 in state, $20,424 out of state; room/board: $7,494
Financial aid: (256) 782-5006; 87% of undergrads determined to have financial need; average aid package $10,349

Judson College[1]
Marion AL
(800) 447-9472
U.S. News ranking: Nat. Lib. Arts, second tier
Website: www.judson.edu/
Admissions email: admissions@judson.edu
Private
Application deadline (fall): N/A
Undergraduate student body: N/A full time, N/A part time
Expenses: N/A
Financial aid: N/A

Miles College[1]
Birmingham AL
(205) 929-1000
U.S. News ranking: Reg. Coll. (S), unranked
Website: www.miles.edu
Admissions email: admissions@mail.miles.edu
Private
Application deadline (fall): N/A

Undergraduate student body: N/A full time, N/A part time
Expenses: N/A
Financial aid: N/A

Oakwood University[1]
Huntsville AL
(256) 726-7356
U.S. News ranking: Reg. Coll. (S), No. 46
Website: www.oakwood.edu
Admissions email: admissions@oakwood.edu
Private; founded 1896
Affiliation: Seventh Day Adventist
Application deadline (fall): N/A
Undergraduate student body: N/A full time, N/A part time
Expenses: N/A
Financial aid: N/A

Samford University
Birmingham AL
(800) 888-7218
U.S. News ranking: Nat. U., No. 147
Website: www.samford.edu
Admissions email: admission@samford.edu
Private; founded 1841
Affiliation: Baptist
Freshman admissions: more selective; 2018-2019: 3,881 applied, 3,185 accepted. Either SAT or ACT required. ACT 25/75 percentile: 23-29. High school rank: 33% in top tenth, 59% in top quarter, 86% in top half
Early decision deadline: N/A, notification date: N/A
Early action deadline: N/A, notification date: N/A
Application deadline (fall): 4/30
Undergraduate student body: 3,453 full time, 82 part time; 33% male, 67% female; 0% American Indian, 1% Asian, 6% black, 3% Hispanic, 2% multiracial, 0% Pacific Islander, 85% white, 1% international; 32% from in state; 67% live on campus; 33% of students in fraternities, 55% in sororities
Most popular majors: 31% Health Professions and Related Programs, 20% Business, Management, Marketing, and Related Support Services, 6% Communication, Journalism, and Related Programs, 6% Family and Consumer Sciences/Human Sciences, 6% Visual and Performing Arts
Expenses: 2019-2020: $32,850; room/board: $10,980
Financial aid: (205) 726-2905; 41% of undergrads determined to have financial need; average aid package $20,861

Spring Hill College
Mobile AL
(251) 380-3030
U.S. News ranking: Nat. Lib. Arts, second tier
Website: www.shc.edu
Admissions email: admit@shc.edu
Private; founded 1830
Freshman admissions: selective; 2018-2019: 8,587 applied, 5,648 accepted. Either SAT or ACT required. ACT 25/75 percentile: 20-25. High school rank: 19% in top tenth, 51% in top quarter, 81% in top half

Early decision deadline: N/A, notification date: N/A
Early action deadline: N/A, notification date: N/A
Application deadline (fall): 7/15
Undergraduate student body: 1,257 full time, 13 part time; 38% male, 62% female; 1% American Indian, 1% Asian, 16% black, 3% Hispanic, 4% multiracial, 0% Pacific Islander, 66% white, 5% international; N/A from in state; 71% live on campus; 0% of students in fraternities, 0% in sororities
Most popular majors: 28% Business, Management, Marketing, and Related Support Services, 12% Health Professions and Related Programs, 12% Psychology, 11% Social Sciences, 9% Biological and Biomedical Sciences
Expenses: 2019-2020: $40,648; room/board: $13,652
Financial aid: (800) 548-7886; 72% of undergrads determined to have financial need; average aid package $35,052

Stillman College
Tuscaloosa AL
(205) 366-8817
U.S. News ranking: Nat. Lib. Arts, second tier
Website: www.stillman.edu
Admissions email: admissions@stillman.edu
Private; founded 1876
Affiliation: Presbyterian Church (USA)
Freshman admissions: less selective; 2018-2019: 3,047 applied, 1,211 accepted. Either SAT or ACT required. SAT 25/75 percentile: N/A. High school rank: N/A
Early decision deadline: N/A, notification date: N/A
Early action deadline: N/A, notification date: N/A
Application deadline (fall): rolling
Undergraduate student body: 660 full time, 137 part time; 43% male, 57% female; 0% American Indian, 0% Asian, 92% black, 0% Hispanic, 0% multiracial, 0% Pacific Islander, 6% white, 0% international
Most popular majors: Information not available
Expenses: 2019-2020: $11,292; room/board: $8,840
Financial aid: (205) 366-8817

Talladega College
Talladega AL
(256) 761-6235
U.S. News ranking: Nat. Lib. Arts, second tier
Website: www.talladega.edu
Admissions email: admissions@talladega.edu
Private; founded 1867
Affiliation: United Church of Christ
Freshman admissions: selective; 2018-2019: N/A applied, N/A accepted. Either SAT or ACT required. ACT 25/75 percentile: 20-24. High school rank: N/A
Early decision deadline: N/A, notification date: N/A
Early action deadline: N/A, notification date: N/A
Application deadline (fall): N/A

Undergraduate student body: 1,088 full time, 120 part time; 51% male, 49% female; 0% American Indian, 0% Asian, 85% black, 4% Hispanic, 2% multiracial, 0% Pacific Islander, 2% white, 4% international
Most popular majors: 29% Business Administration and Management, General, 14% Criminal Justice/Law Enforcement Administration, 11% Psychology, General, 9% Biology/Biological Sciences, General, 8% Mass Communication/Media Studies
Expenses: 2019-2020: $13,571; room/board: $6,704
Financial aid: (256) 761-6237; 68% of undergrads determined to have financial need; average aid package $20,815

Troy University
Troy AL
(334) 670-3179
U.S. News ranking: Reg. U. (S), No. 65
Website: www.troy.edu/
Admissions email: admit@troy.edu
Public; founded 1887
Freshman admissions: selective; 2018-2019: 7,332 applied, 6,428 accepted. Either SAT or ACT required. ACT 25/75 percentile: 18-24. High school rank: N/A
Early decision deadline: N/A, notification date: N/A
Early action deadline: N/A, notification date: N/A
Application deadline (fall): rolling
Undergraduate student body: 9,161 full time, 4,291 part time; 38% male, 62% female; 1% American Indian, 1% Asian, 31% black, 4% Hispanic, 3% multiracial, 0% Pacific Islander, 52% white, 5% international; 71% from in state; 16% live on campus; 10% of students in fraternities, 13% in sororities
Most popular majors: 14% Business Administration and Management, General, 12% Psychology, General, 10% Criminal Justice/Safety Studies, 6% Registered Nursing/Registered Nurse, 5% Computer and Information Sciences, General
Expenses: 2019-2020: $11,110 in state, $20,860 out of state; room/board: $6,804
Financial aid: (334) 670-3182; 63% of undergrads determined to have financial need; average aid package $4,460

Tuskegee University
Tuskegee AL
(334) 727-8500
U.S. News ranking: Reg. U. (S), No. 25
Website: www.tuskegee.edu
Admissions email: admissions@tuskegee.edu
Private; founded 1881
Freshman admissions: selective; 2018-2019: 11,847 applied, 6,162 accepted. Either SAT or ACT required. ACT 25/75 percentile: 17-27. High school rank: 20% in top tenth, 80% in top quarter, 100% in top half
Early decision deadline: N/A, notification date: N/A

Early action deadline: N/A, notification date: N/A
Application deadline (fall): rolling
Undergraduate student body: 2,462 full time, 91 part time; 37% male, 63% female; 0% American Indian, 1% Asian, 85% black, 1% Hispanic, 0% multiracial, 2% Pacific Islander, 0% white, 0% international; 30% from in state; 65% live on campus; 0% of students in fraternities, 0% in sororities
Most popular majors: 18% Aerospace, Aeronautical and Astronautical/Space Engineering, 17% Agribusiness/Agricultural Business Operations, 15% Psychology, General, 11% Marketing/Marketing Management, General, 9% Biology/Biological Sciences, General
Expenses: 2019-2020: $22,679; room/board: $9,844
Financial aid: (334) 727-8088; 88% of undergrads determined to have financial need; average aid package $28,000

University of Alabama
Tuscaloosa AL
(205) 348-5666
U.S. News ranking: Nat. U., No. 153
Website: www.ua.edu
Admissions email: admissions@ua.edu
Public; founded 1831
Freshman admissions: more selective; 2018-2019: 37,302 applied, 22,032 accepted. Either SAT or ACT required. ACT 25/75 percentile: 23-31. High school rank: 36% in top tenth, 58% in top quarter, 82% in top half
Early decision deadline: N/A, notification date: N/A
Early action deadline: N/A, notification date: N/A
Application deadline (fall): rolling
Undergraduate student body: 29,586 full time, 3,442 part time; 44% male, 56% female; 0% American Indian, 1% Asian, 10% black, 5% Hispanic, 3% multiracial, 0% Pacific Islander, 78% white, 2% international; 39% from in state; 23% live on campus; 29% of students in fraternities, 44% in sororities
Most popular majors: 31% Business, Management, Marketing, and Related Support Services, 11% Engineering, 9% Communication, Journalism, and Related Programs, 9% Family and Consumer Sciences/Human Sciences, 8% Health Professions and Related Programs
Expenses: 2019-2020: $10,780 in state, $30,250 out of state; room/board: $10,836
Financial aid: (205) 348-6756; 43% of undergrads determined to have financial need; average aid package $15,003

University of Alabama–Birmingham
Birmingham AL
(205) 934-8221
U.S. News ranking: Nat. U., No. 166
Website: www.uab.edu
Admissions email: chooseuab@uab.edu
Public; founded 1969
Freshman admissions: more selective; 2018-2019: 7,845 applied, 7,226 accepted. Either SAT or ACT required. ACT 25/75 percentile: 21-29. High school rank: 28% in top tenth, 55% in top quarter, 82% in top half
Early decision deadline: N/A; notification date: N/A
Early action deadline: N/A, notification date: N/A
Application deadline (fall): rolling
Undergraduate student body: 10,042 full time, 3,794 part time; 39% male, 61% female; 0% American Indian, 6% Asian, 26% black, 5% Hispanic, 5% multiracial, 0% Pacific Islander, 57% white, 2% international; N/A from in state; 23% live on campus; 6% of students in fraternities, 8% in sororities
Most popular majors: 21% Health Professions and Related Programs, 18% Business, Management, Marketing, and Related Support Services, 9% Biological and Biomedical Sciences, 9% Education, 8% Engineering
Expenses: 2019-2020: $10,710 in state, $25,380 out of state; room/board: $12,307
Financial aid: (205) 934-8223; 60% of undergrads determined to have financial need; average aid package $10,956

University of Alabama–Huntsville
Huntsville AL
(256) 824-6070
U.S. News ranking: Nat. U., No. 263
Website: www.uah.edu/
Admissions email: admissions@uah.edu
Public; founded 1969
Freshman admissions: more selective; 2018-2019: 4,543 applied, 3,674 accepted. Either SAT or ACT required. ACT 25/75 percentile: 25-31. High school rank: 34% in top tenth, 61% in top quarter, 84% in top half
Early decision deadline: N/A, notification date: N/A
Early action deadline: N/A, notification date: N/A
Application deadline (fall): 8/17
Undergraduate student body: 6,393 full time, 1,278 part time; 58% male, 42% female; 1% American Indian, 4% Asian, 10% black, 5% Hispanic, 3% multiracial, 0% Pacific Islander, 72% white, 2% international; 77% from in state; 28% live on campus; 7% of students in fraternities, 7% in sororities
Most popular majors: 28% Engineering, 21% Business, Management, Marketing, and Related Support Services, 15% Health Professions and Related Programs, 6% Computer and Information Sciences and Support Services, 5% Biological and Biomedical Sciences
Expenses: 2019-2020: $10,714 in state, $23,110 out of state; room/board: $10,094
Financial aid: (256) 824-6650; 50% of undergrads determined to have financial need; average aid package $16,187

University of Mobile
Mobile AL
(251) 442-2222
U.S. News ranking: Reg. Coll. (S), No. 11
Website: www.umobile.edu
Admissions email: umenrollment@umobile.edu
Private; founded 1961
Affiliation: Baptist
Freshman admissions: selective; 2018-2019: 1,738 applied, 821 accepted. Either SAT or ACT required for some. ACT 25/75 percentile: 18-25. High school rank: 27% in top tenth, 51% in top quarter, 81% in top half
Early decision deadline: N/A, notification date: N/A
Early action deadline: N/A, notification date: N/A
Application deadline (fall): rolling
Undergraduate student body: 1,150 full time, 530 part time; 35% male, 65% female; 2% American Indian, 1% Asian, 20% black, 2% Hispanic, 3% multiracial, 0% Pacific Islander, 67% white, 4% international; N/A from in state; 35% live on campus; N/A of students in fraternities, N/A in sororities
Most popular majors: 15% Business Administration and Management, General, 12% Registered Nursing/Registered Nurse, 8% Elementary Education and Teaching, 8% Religious/Sacred Music, 6% Psychology, General
Expenses: 2019-2020: $23,220; room/board: $9,700
Financial aid: (251) 442-2222; 80% of undergrads determined to have financial need; average aid package $20,130

University of Montevallo
Montevallo AL
(205) 665 6030
U.S. News ranking: Reg. U. (S), No. 31
Website: www.montevallo.edu
Admissions email: admissions@montevallo.edu
Public; founded 1896
Freshman admissions: selective; 2018-2019: 4,303 applied, 1,894 accepted. Either SAT or ACT required. ACT 25/75 percentile: 20-27. High school rank: N/A
Early decision deadline: N/A, notification date: N/A
Early action deadline: N/A, notification date: N/A
Application deadline (fall): 8/15
Undergraduate student body: 2,063 full time, 222 part time; 33% male, 67% female; 0% American Indian, 1% Asian, 17% black, 5% Hispanic, 4% multiracial, 0% Pacific Islander, 67% white, 3% international
Most popular majors: Information not available
Expenses: 2019-2020: $13,710 in state, $26,730 out of state; room/board: $9,810
Financial aid: (205) 665-6050; 69% of undergrads determined to have financial need; average aid package $12,240

University of North Alabama
Florence AL
(256) 765-4608
U.S. News ranking: Reg. U. (S), No. 43
Website: www.una.edu
Admissions email: admissions@una.edu
Public; founded 1830
Freshman admissions: selective; 2018-2019: 4,450 applied, 2,863 accepted. Either SAT or ACT required. ACT 25/75 percentile: 20-25. High school rank: 18% in top tenth, 45% in top quarter, 76% in top half
Early decision deadline: N/A, notification date: N/A
Early action deadline: N/A, notification date: N/A
Application deadline (fall): rolling
Undergraduate student body: 5,023 full time, 1,173 part time; 40% male, 60% female; 1% American Indian, 1% Asian, 14% black, 3% Hispanic, 3% multiracial, 0% Pacific Islander, 73% white, 4% international; 78% from in state; 25% live on campus; 13% of students in fraternities, 19% in sororities
Most popular majors: 21% Business, Management, Marketing, and Related Support Services, 12% Health Professions and Related Programs, 11% Education, 7% Parks, Recreation, Leisure, and Fitness Studies, 7% Social Sciences
Expenses: 2019-2020: $10,800 in state, $20,400 out of state; room/board: $4,760
Financial aid: (256) 765-4278; 63% of undergrads determined to have financial need; average aid package $9,883

University of South Alabama
Mobile AL
(251) 460-6141
U.S. News ranking: Nat. U., second tier
Website: www.southalabama.edu
Admissions email: recruitment@southalabama.edu
Public; founded 1963
Freshman admissions: selective; 2018-2019: 6,688 applied, 5,259 accepted. Either SAT or ACT required for some. ACT 25/75 percentile: 21-27. High school rank: N/A
Early decision deadline: N/A, notification date: N/A
Early action deadline: N/A, notification date: N/A
Application deadline (fall): 7/15
Undergraduate student body: 8,637 full time, 1,656 part time; 41% male, 59% female; 1% American Indian, 3% Asian, 23% black, 4% Hispanic, 4% multiracial, 0% Pacific Islander, 61% white, 3% international; 82% from in state; 22% live on campus; N/A of students in fraternities, N/A in sororities
Most popular majors: 14% Registered Nursing/Registered Nurse, 6% Health/Medical Preparatory Programs, Other, 5% Elementary Education and Teaching, 5% Multi/Interdisciplinary Studies, 4% Physical Education Teaching and Coaching
Expenses: 2019-2020: $10,294 in state, $20,164 out of state; room/board: $7,620
Financial aid: (251) 460-6231; 63% of undergrads determined to have financial need; average aid package $10,382

University of West Alabama
Livingston AL
(205) 652-3578
U.S. News ranking: Reg. U. (S), second tier
Website: www.uwa.edu
Admissions email: admissions@uwa.edu
Public; founded 1835
Freshman admissions: selective; 2018-2019: 8,870 applied, 3,518 accepted. Either SAT or ACT required. ACT 25/75 percentile: 18-22. High school rank: N/A
Early decision deadline: N/A, notification date: N/A
Early action deadline: N/A, notification date: N/A
Application deadline (fall): rolling
Undergraduate student body: 1,836 full time, 323 part time; 42% male, 58% female; 0% American Indian, 0% Asian, 43% black, 2% Hispanic, 3% multiracial, 0% Pacific Islander, 43% white, 5% international; 81% from in state; 41% live on campus; 10% of students in fraternities, 10% in sororities
Most popular majors: 19% Multi-/Interdisciplinary Studies, Other, 12% Teacher Education, Multiple Levels, 8% Engineering Technologies and Engineering-Related Fields, Other, 7% Kinesiology and Exercise Science, 6% Business Administration and Management, General
Expenses: 2019-2020: $10,040 in state, $18,490 out of state; room/board: $8,116
Financial aid: (205) 652-3576; 77% of undergrads determined to have financial need; average aid package $10,969

ALASKA

Alaska Pacific University[1]
Anchorage AK
(800) 252-7528
U.S. News ranking: Reg. U. (W), No. 82
Website: www.alaskapacific.edu
Admissions email: admissions@alaskapacific.edu
Private; founded 1957
Application deadline (fall): rolling
Undergraduate student body: N/A full time, N/A part time
Expenses: N/A
Financial aid: (907) 564-8342

University of Alaska–Anchorage
Anchorage AK
(907) 786-1480
U.S. News ranking: Reg. U. (W), No. 62
Website: www.uaa.alaska.edu
Admissions email: admissions@alaska.edu
Public; founded 1954
Freshman admissions: selective; 2018-2019: 3,745 applied, 3,039 accepted. Neither SAT nor ACT required. SAT 25/75 percentile: 1035-1250. High school rank: 14% in top tenth, 33% in top quarter, 63% in top half
Early decision deadline: N/A, notification date: N/A
Early action deadline: N/A, notification date: N/A
Application deadline (fall): 7/15
Undergraduate student body: 6,452 full time, 7,552 part time; 42% male, 58% female; 6% American Indian, 8% Asian, 3% black, 8% Hispanic, 13% multiracial, 2% Pacific Islander, 54% white, 2% international; 91% from in state; N/A live on campus; N/A of students in fraternities, N/A in sororities
Most popular majors: 19% Health Professions and Related Programs, 16% Business, Management, Marketing, and Related Support Services, 9% Engineering, 6% Psychology, 6% Social Sciences
Expenses: 2019-2020: $8,088 in state, $25,068 out of state; room/board: $11,878
Financial aid: (907) 786-6170; 42% of undergrads determined to have financial need; average aid package $10,232

University of Alaska–Fairbanks[1]
Fairbanks AK
(800) 478-1823
U.S. News ranking: Nat. U., No. 263
Website: www.uaf.edu
Admissions email: admissions@uaf.edu
Public; founded 1917
Application deadline (fall): 6/15
Undergraduate student body: N/A full time, N/A part time
Expenses: 2018-2019: $8,800 in state, $24,970 out of state; room/board: $8,930
Financial aid: (907) 474-7256

University of Alaska–Southeast[1]
Juneau AK
(907) 465-6457
U.S. News ranking: Reg. U. (W), second tier
Website: www.uas.alaska.edu
Admissions email: admissions@uas.alaska.edu
Public
Application deadline (fall): N/A

Undergraduate student body: N/A full time, N/A part time
Expenses: N/A
Financial aid: N/A

AMERICAN SAMOA

American Samoa Community College

PagoPago AS
(684) 699-9155
U.S. News ranking: Reg. Coll. (W), unranked
Website: www.amsamoa.edu
Admissions email: Admissions@amsamoa.edu
Public; founded 1970
Freshman admissions: least selective; 2018-2019: 321 applied, 321 accepted. Neither SAT nor ACT required. SAT 25/75 percentile: 745-920. High school rank: N/A
Early decision deadline: N/A, notification date: N/A
Early action deadline: N/A, notification date: N/A
Undergraduate student body: 613 full time, 424 part time; 31% male, 69% female; 0% American Indian, 3% Asian, 0% black, 0% Hispanic, 0% multiracial, 96% Pacific Islander, 0% white, 0% international; 100% from in state; 0% live on campus; 0% of students in fraternities, 0% in sororities
Most popular majors: 34% Liberal Arts and Sciences, General Studies and Humanities, 17% Legal Professions and Studies, 8% Business, Management, Marketing, and Related Support Services, 6% Health-Related Knowledge and Skills, 4% Agriculture, Agriculture Operations, and Related Sciences
Expenses: 2018-2019: $3,950 in state, $4,250 out of state; room/board: N/A
Financial aid: N/A

ARIZONA

Arizona Christian University

Phoenix AZ
(602) 386-4100
U.S. News ranking: Reg. Coll. (W), No. 22
Website: arizonachristian.edu/
Admissions email: admissions@arizonachristian.edu
Private; founded 1960
Affiliation: Undenominational
Freshman admissions: less selective; 2018-2019: 404 applied, 228 accepted. Either SAT or ACT required. ACT 25/75 percentile: 17-22. High school rank: N/A
Early decision deadline: N/A, notification date: N/A
Early action deadline: 11/1, notification date: 11/5
Application deadline (fall): 8/15
Undergraduate student body: 642 full time, 134 part time; 56% male, 44% female; 1% American Indian, 1% Asian, 13% black, 21% Hispanic, 7% multiracial, 1% Pacific Islander, 48% white, 4% international; N/A from in state; 32% live on campus; N/A

of students in fraternities, N/A in sororities
Most popular majors: 33% Business, Management, Marketing, and Related Support Services, 19% Psychology, 12% Education, 9% Social Sciences, 8% Theology and Religious Vocations
Expenses: 2019-2020: $27,890; room/board: $11,200
Financial aid: (602) 386-4115; 58% of undergrads determined to have financial need; average aid package $9,685

Arizona State University–Tempe

Tempe AZ
(480) 965-7788
U.S. News ranking: Nat. U., No. 117
Website: www.asu.edu
Admissions email: admissions@asu.edu
Public; founded 1885
Freshman admissions: more selective; 2018-2019: 26,869 applied, 22,779 accepted. Neither SAT nor ACT required. SAT 25/75 percentile: 1130-1360. High school rank: 33% in top tenth, 62% in top quarter, 89% in top half
Early decision deadline: N/A, notification date: N/A
Early action deadline: N/A, notification date: N/A
Application deadline (fall): rolling
Undergraduate student body: 39,396 full time, 3,448 part time; 56% male, 44% female; 1% American Indian, 8% Asian, 4% black, 21% Hispanic, 5% multiracial, 0% Pacific Islander, 50% white, 11% international; 74% from in state; 26% live on campus; 10% of students in fraternities, 16% in sororities
Most popular majors: 27% Business, Management, Marketing, and Related Support Services, 13% Engineering, 9% Social Sciences, 8% Biological and Biomedical Sciences, 7% Visual and Performing Arts
Expenses: 2019-2020: $11,338 in state, $29,428 out of state; room/board: $13,164
Financial aid: (855) 278-5080; 54% of undergrads determined to have financial need; average aid package $16,268

Arizona State University–West

Tempe AZ
(480) 965-7788
U.S. News ranking: Unranked
Website: campus.asu.edu/west
Admissions email: admissions@asu.edu
Public; founded 1984
Freshman admissions: N/A; 2018-2019: 2,610 applied, 2,151 accepted. Neither SAT nor ACT required. ACT 25/75 percentile: 19-25. High school rank: 32% in top tenth, 68% in top quarter, 92% in top half
Early decision deadline: N/A, notification date: N/A
Early action deadline: N/A, notification date: N/A
Application deadline (fall): rolling

Undergraduate student body: 3,521 full time, 526 part time; 40% male, 60% female; 1% American Indian, 6% Asian, 5% black, 36% Hispanic, 3% multiracial, 0% Pacific Islander, 44% white, 4% international; 86% from in state; 15% live on campus; N/A of students in fraternities, N/A in sororities
Most popular majors: 24% Business, Management, Marketing, and Related Support Services, 17% Psychology, 11% Communication, Journalism, and Related Programs, 11% Education, 9% Biological and Biomedical Sciences
Expenses: 2019-2020: $10,803 in state, $27,988 out of state; room/board: $11,914
Financial aid: (855) 278-5080; 74% of undergrads determined to have financial need; average aid package $14,052

Embry-Riddle Aeronautical University–Prescott

Prescott AZ
(928) 777-6600
U.S. News ranking: Unranked
Website: prescott.erau.edu/index.html
Admissions email: Prescott@erau.edu
Private; founded 1926
Freshman admissions: N/A; 2018-2019: 2,859 applied, 1,922 accepted. Neither SAT nor ACT required. ACT 25/75 percentile: 23-30. High school rank: 32% in top tenth, 58% in top quarter, 86% in top half
Early decision deadline: N/A, notification date: N/A
Early action deadline: N/A, notification date: N/A
Application deadline (fall): rolling
Undergraduate student body: 2,592 full time, 134 part time; 75% male, 25% female; 0% American Indian, 6% Asian, 2% black, 13% Hispanic, 6% multiracial, 1% Pacific Islander, 63% white, 6% international; 22% from in state; 44% live on campus; N/A of students in fraternities, N/A in sororities
Most popular majors: 31% Transportation and Materials Moving, 29% Engineering, 18% Social Sciences, 10% Business, Management, Marketing, and Related Support Services, 6% Homeland Security, Law Enforcement, Firefighting and Related Protective Services
Expenses: 2019-2020: $36,708; room/board: $11,718
Financial aid: (800) 888-3728; 59% of undergrads determined to have financial need; average aid package $19,115

Grand Canyon University[1]

Phoenix AZ
(800) 800-9776
U.S. News ranking: Nat. U., second tier
Website: apply.gcu.edu
Admissions email: golopes@gcu.edu

For-profit; founded 1949
Application deadline (fall): rolling
Undergraduate student body: N/A full time, N/A part time
Expenses: N/A
Financial aid: (602) 639-6600

Northcentral University

San Diego AZ
(888) 327-2877
U.S. News ranking: Nat. U., unranked
Website: www.ncu.edu
Admissions email: admissions@ncu.edu
For-profit; founded 1996
Affiliation: Other
Freshman admissions: least selective; 2018-2019: N/A applied, N/A accepted. Neither SAT nor ACT required. SAT 25/75 percentile: N/A. High school rank: N/A
Early decision deadline: N/A, notification date: N/A
Early action deadline: N/A, notification date: N/A
Application deadline (fall): rolling
Undergraduate student body: 10 full time, 60 part time; 20% male, 80% female; 0% American Indian, 1% Asian, 14% black, 12% Hispanic, 7% multiracial, 0% Pacific Islander, 42% white, 0% international
Most popular majors: Information not available
Expenses: 2019-2020: $11,064; room/board: N/A
Financial aid: (888) 896-5112

Northern Arizona University

Flagstaff AZ
(928) 523-5511
U.S. News ranking: Nat. U., second tier
Website: www.nau.edu
Admissions email: admissions@nau.edu
Public; founded 1899
Freshman admissions: selective; 2018-2019: 36,831 applied, 30,428 accepted. Neither SAT nor ACT required. ACT 25/75 percentile: 19-25. High school rank: 21% in top tenth, 52% in top quarter, 84% in top half
Early decision deadline: N/A, notification date: N/A
Early action deadline: N/A, notification date: N/A
Application deadline (fall): rolling
Undergraduate student body: 21,891 full time, 5,187 part time; 39% male, 61% female; 2% American Indian, 2% Asian, 3% black, 25% Hispanic, 6% multiracial, 0% Pacific Islander, 56% white, 4% international; 70% from in state; 36% live on campus; 1% of students in fraternities, 2% in sororities
Most popular majors: 19% Business, Management, Marketing, and Related Support Services, 15% Health Professions and Related Programs, 9% Education, 9% Liberal Arts and Sciences, General Studies and Humanities, 7% Social Sciences
Expenses: 2019-2020: $11,896 in state, $26,516 out of state; room/board: $10,534

Financial aid: (928) 523-4951; 62% of undergrads determined to have financial need; average aid package $12,446

Prescott College[1]

Prescott AZ
(877) 350-2100
U.S. News ranking: Reg. U. (W), second tier
Website: www.prescott.edu/
Admissions email: admissions@prescott.edu
Private; founded 1966
Application deadline (fall): 8/15
Undergraduate student body: N/A full time, N/A part time
Expenses: 2018-2019: $31,485; room/board: $7,700
Financial aid: (928) 350-1104

The School of Architecture at Taliesin[1]

Scottsdale AZ
(480) 627-5345
U.S. News ranking: Arts, unranked
Website: www.taliesin.edu/
Admissions email: admissions@taliesin.edu
Private; founded 1932
Application deadline (fall): 4/1
Undergraduate student body: N/A full time, N/A part time
Expenses: N/A
Financial aid: N/A

Southwest University of Visual Arts[1]

Tucson AZ
(520) 325-0123
U.S. News ranking: Arts, unranked
Website: www.suva.edu/
Admissions email: N/A
For-profit
Application deadline (fall): N/A
Undergraduate student body: N/A full time, N/A part time
Expenses: N/A
Financial aid: N/A

University of Arizona

Tucson AZ
(520) 621-3237
U.S. News ranking: Nat. U., No. 117
Website: www.arizona.edu
Admissions email: admissions@arizona.edu
Public; founded 1885
Freshman admissions: more selective; 2018-2019: 39,941 applied, 33,717 accepted. Neither SAT nor ACT required. ACT 25/75 percentile: 21-28. High school rank: 32% in top tenth, 60% in top quarter, 85% in top half
Early decision deadline: N/A, notification date: N/A
Early action deadline: N/A, notification date: N/A
Application deadline (fall): 5/1
Undergraduate student body: 29,298 full time, 5,935 part time; 47% male, 53% female; 1% American Indian, 5% Asian, 4% black, 27% Hispanic, 5% multiracial, 0% Pacific Islander, 50% white, 6% international; N/A from in state; 19% live on campus; N/A of students in fraternities, N/A in sororities

Most popular majors: 16% Business, Management, Marketing, and Related Support Services, 10% Biological and Biomedical Sciences, 8% Health Professions and Related Programs, 7% Engineering, 7% Multi/Interdisciplinary Studies
Expenses: 2019-2020: $12,467 in state, $36,366 out of state; room/board: $12,550
Financial aid: (520) 621-1858; 52% of undergrads determined to have financial need; average aid package $13,673

University of Phoenix[1]
Phoenix AZ
(866) 766-0766
U.S. News ranking: Nat. U., unranked
Website: www.phoenix.edu
Admissions email: N/A
For-profit
Application deadline (fall): N/A
Undergraduate student body: N/A full time, N/A part time
Expenses: N/A
Financial aid: N/A

Western International University[1]
Tempe AZ
(602) 943-2311
U.S. News ranking: Business, unranked
Website: www.west.edu/
Admissions email: N/A
For-profit; founded 1978
Application deadline (fall): N/A
Undergraduate student body: N/A full time, N/A part time
Expenses: N/A
Financial aid: (602) 943-2311

ARKANSAS

Arkansas Baptist College[1]
Little Rock AR
(501) 420-1234
U.S. News ranking: Reg. Coll. (S), second tier
Website: www.arkansasbaptist.edu
Admissions email: admissions@arkansasbaptist.edu
Private; founded 1884
Affiliation: Baptist
Application deadline (fall): rolling
Undergraduate student body: N/A full time, N/A part time
Expenses: N/A
Financial aid: (501) 420-1223

Arkansas State University
State University AR
(870) 972-2031
U.S. News ranking: Nat. U., second tier
Website: www.astate.edu
Admissions email: admissions@astate.edu
Public; founded 1909
Freshman admissions: selective; 2018-2019: 5,253 applied, 4,056 accepted. Either SAT or ACT required for some. ACT 25/75 percentile: 21-27. High school rank: 20% in top tenth, 56% in top quarter, 89% in top half

Early decision deadline: N/A, notification date: N/A
Early action deadline: N/A, notification date: N/A
Application deadline (fall): 8/22
Undergraduate student body: 6,789 full time, 2,561 part time; 40% male, 60% female; 0% American Indian, 1% Asian, 13% black, 3% Hispanic, 2% multiracial, 0% Pacific Islander, 75% white, 5% international; 81% from in state; 34% live on campus; 12% of students in fraternities, 15% in sororities
Most popular majors: 10% Registered Nursing/Registered Nurse, 8% General Studies, 5% Biology/Biological Sciences, General, 4% Early Childhood Education and Teaching, 4% Kinesiology and Exercise Science
Expenses: 2019-2020: $8,900 in state, $15,860 out of state; room/board: $8,850
Financial aid: (870) 972-2310; 67% of undergrads determined to have financial need; average aid package $12,941

Arkansas Tech University
Russellville AR
(479) 968-0343
U.S. News ranking: Reg. U. (S), No. 75
Website: www.atu.edu
Admissions email: tech.enroll@atu.edu
Public; founded 1909
Freshman admissions: selective; 2018-2019: 5,122 applied, 4,622 accepted. Either SAT or ACT required. ACT 25/75 percentile: 18-25. High school rank: 15% in top tenth, 36% in top quarter, 66% in top half
Early decision deadline: N/A, notification date: N/A
Early action deadline: N/A, notification date: N/A
Application deadline (fall): rolling
Undergraduate student body: 6,396 full time, 4,755 part time; 46% male, 54% female; 1% American Indian, 1% Asian, 7% black, 7% Hispanic, 4% multiracial, 0% Pacific Islander, 75% white, 4% international; N/A from in state; 28% live on campus; 7% of students in fraternities, 7% in sororities
Most popular majors: 16% Multi/Interdisciplinary Studies, 14% Health Professions and Related Programs, 13% Business, Management, Marketing, and Related Support Services, 12% Education, 8% Engineering
Expenses: 2018-2019: $9,068 in state, $15,848 out of state; room/board: $7,870
Financial aid: (479) 968 0399; 70% of undergrads determined to have financial need; average aid package $10,188

Central Baptist College
Conway AR
(501) 329-6873
U.S. News ranking: Reg. Coll. (S), No. 58
Website: www.cbc.edu
Admissions email: admissions@cbc.edu
Private; founded 1952
Affiliation: Baptist
Freshman admissions: less selective; 2018-2019: 555 applied, 334 accepted. Either SAT or ACT required. ACT 25/75 percentile: 16-22. High school rank: 8% in top tenth, 22% in top quarter, 52% in top half
Early decision deadline: N/A, notification date: N/A
Early action deadline: N/A, notification date: N/A
Application deadline (fall): 8/10
Undergraduate student body: 576 full time, 156 part time; 55% male, 45% female; 2% American Indian, 0% Asian, 19% black, 5% Hispanic, 2% multiracial, 0% Pacific Islander, 67% white, 3% international; 78% from in state; 14% live on campus; 0% of students in fraternities, 0% in sororities
Most popular majors: 13% Bible/Biblical Studies, 10% Kinesiology and Exercise Science, 7% Business, Management, Marketing, and Related Support Services, Other, 6% Psychology, General, 6% Psychology, Other
Expenses: 2019-2020: $16,650; room/board: $7,500
Financial aid: (501) 205-8809; 82% of undergrads determined to have financial need; average aid package $11,208

Crowley's Ridge College[1]
Paragould AR
U.S. News ranking: Reg. Coll. (S), second tier
Admissions email: N/A
Private
Application deadline (fall): N/A
Undergraduate student body: N/A full time, N/A part time
Expenses: N/A
Financial aid: N/A

Harding University
Searcy AR
(800) 477-4407
U.S. News ranking: Nat. U., No. 240
Website: www.harding.edu
Admissions email: admissions@harding.edu
Private; founded 1924
Affiliation: Churches of Christ
Freshman admissions: more selective; 2018-2019: 1,927 applied, 1,309 accepted. Either SAT or ACT required. ACT 25/75 percentile: 22-29. High school rank: 23% in top tenth, 50% in top quarter, 77% in top half
Early decision deadline: N/A, notification date: N/A
Early action deadline: N/A, notification date: N/A
Application deadline (fall): rolling
Undergraduate student body: 3,742 full time, 232 part time; 46%

male, 54% female; 0% American Indian, 1% Asian, 4% black, 4% Hispanic, 3% multiracial, 0% Pacific Islander, 81% white, 6% international; 30% from in state; 91% live on campus; 0% of students in fraternities, 0% in sororities
Most popular majors: 18% Business, Management, Marketing, and Related Support Services, 13% Education, 13% Health Professions and Related Programs, 7% Communication, Journalism, and Related Programs, 6% Computer and Information Sciences and Support Services
Expenses: 2019-2020: $20,530; room/board: $7,170
Financial aid: (501) 279-4257; 59% of undergrads determined to have financial need; average aid package $13,119

Henderson State University
Arkadelphia AR
(870) 230-5028
U.S. News ranking: Reg. U. (S), No. 79
Website: www.hsu.edu/pages/future-students/admissions/
Admissions email: admissions@hsu.edu
Public; founded 1890
Freshman admissions: selective; 2018-2019: 2,856 applied, 2,586 accepted. Either SAT or ACT required. ACT 25/75 percentile: 19-25. High school rank: 14% in top tenth, 22% in top quarter, 68% in top half
Early decision deadline: N/A, notification date: N/A
Early action deadline: N/A, notification date: N/A
Application deadline (fall): rolling
Undergraduate student body: 2,726 full time, 274 part time; 43% male, 57% female; 0% American Indian, 1% Asian, 21% black, 5% Hispanic, 4% multiracial, 0% Pacific Islander, 66% white, 1% international; 85% from in state; 56% live on campus; N/A of students in fraternities, N/A in sororities
Most popular majors: 20% Business, Management, Marketing, and Related Support Services, 16% Education, 8% Liberal Arts and Sciences, General Studies and Humanities, 7% Psychology, 7% Public Administration and Social Service Professions
Expenses: 2019-2020: $8,811 in state, $10,521 out of state; room/board: $8,440
Financial aid: (870) 230-5148; 73% of undergrads determined to have financial need; average aid package $10,548

Hendrix College
Conway AR
(800) 277-9017
U.S. News ranking: Nat. Lib. Arts, No. 92
Website: www.hendrix.edu
Admissions email: adm@hendrix.edu
Private; founded 1876
Affiliation: United Methodist

Freshman admissions: more selective; 2018-2019: 1,545 applied, 1,115 accepted. Either SAT or ACT required. ACT 25/75 percentile: 26-32. High school rank: 45% in top tenth, 74% in top quarter, 94% in top half
Early decision deadline: N/A, notification date: N/A
Early action deadline: 11/15, notification date: 12/15
Application deadline (fall): 6/1
Undergraduate student body: 1,193 full time, 9 part time; 48% male, 52% female; 1% American Indian, 5% Asian, 8% black, 6% Hispanic, 4% multiracial, 0% Pacific Islander, 70% white, 1% international; 62% from in state; 92% live on campus; 0% of students in fraternities, 0% in sororities
Most popular majors: Information not available
Expenses: 2019-2020: $47,600; room/board: $12,460
Financial aid: (501) 450-1368; 75% of undergrads determined to have financial need; average aid package $41,587

John Brown University
Siloam Springs AR
(479) 524-9500
U.S. News ranking: Reg. U. (S), No. 11
Website: www.jbu.edu
Admissions email: jbuinfo@jbu.edu
Private; founded 1919
Freshman admissions: more selective; 2018-2019: 1,094 applied, 844 accepted. Either SAT or ACT required for some. ACT 25/75 percentile: 23-30. High school rank: 34% in top tenth, 58% in top quarter, 85% in top half
Early decision deadline: N/A, notification date: N/A
Early action deadline: N/A, notification date: N/A
Application deadline (fall): rolling
Undergraduate student body: 1,430 full time, 473 part time; 44% male, 56% female; 2% American Indian, 1% Asian, 3% black, 7% Hispanic, 4% multiracial, 0% Pacific Islander, 73% white, 6% international; 49% from in state; 58% live on campus; 0% of students in fraternities, 0% in sororities
Most popular majors: 37% Business, Management, Marketing, and Related Support Services, 9% Visual and Performing Arts, 7% Health Professions and Related Programs, 6% Engineering, 6% Theology and Religious Vocations
Expenses: 2019-2020: $27,668; room/board: $9,456
Financial aid: (479) 524-7427; 70% of undergrads determined to have financial need; average aid package $20,064

Lyon College
Batesville AR
(800) 423-2542
U.S. News ranking: Nat. Lib. Arts, second tier
Website: www.lyon.edu
Admissions email: admissions@lyon.edu

Private; founded 1872
Affiliation: Presbyterian Church (USA)
Freshman admissions: more selective; 2018-2019: 1,741 applied, 868 accepted. Either SAT or ACT required. ACT 25/75 percentile: 21-28. High school rank: 24% in top tenth, 51% in top quarter, 80% in top half
Early decision deadline: N/A, notification date: N/A
Early action deadline: 1/15, notification date: 3/15
Application deadline (fall): rolling
Undergraduate student body: 649 full time, 27 part time; 56% male, 44% female; 2% American Indian, 4% Asian, 9% black, 7% Hispanic, 0% multiracial, 0% Pacific Islander, 66% white, 3% international; 67% from in state; 89% live on campus; 17% of students in fraternities, 25% in sororities
Most popular majors: Information not available
Expenses: 2019-2020: $29,140; room/board: $9,810
Financial aid: (870) 307-7250

Ouachita Baptist University

Arkadelphia AR
(870) 245-5110
U.S. News ranking: Reg. Coll. (S), No. 2
Website: www.obu.edu
Admissions email: admissions@obu.edu
Private; founded 1886
Affiliation: Southern Baptist
Freshman admissions: more selective; 2018-2019: 2,162 applied, 1,375 accepted. Either SAT or ACT required. ACT 25/75 percentile: 21-28. High school rank: 33% in top tenth, 55% in top quarter, 84% in top half
Early decision deadline: N/A, notification date: N/A
Early action deadline: N/A, notification date: N/A
Application deadline (fall): rolling
Undergraduate student body: 1,529 full time, 131 part time; 45% male, 55% female; 1% American Indian, 0% Asian, 8% black, 5% Hispanic, 3% multiracial, 0% Pacific Islander, 81% white, 2% international; 64% from in state; 97% live on campus; 23% of students in fraternities, 33% in sororities
Most popular majors: 26% Business, Management, Marketing, and Related Support Services, 13% Biological and Biomedical Sciences, 8% Communication, Journalism, and Related Programs, 8% Visual and Performing Arts, 6% Education
Expenses: 2019-2020: $27,900; room/board: $8,000
Financial aid: (870) 245-5316; 66% of undergrads determined to have financial need; average aid package $24,312

Philander Smith College

Little Rock AR
(501) 370-5221
U.S. News ranking: Reg. Coll. (S), No. 41
Website: www.philander.edu
Admissions email: admissions@philander.edu
Private; founded 1877
Affiliation: United Methodist
Freshman admissions: less selective; 2018-2019: 4,734 applied, 1,924 accepted. Either SAT or ACT required. ACT 25/75 percentile: 15-21. High school rank: 15% in top tenth, 42% in top quarter, 68% in top half
Early decision deadline: N/A, notification date: N/A
Early action deadline: N/A, notification date: N/A
Application deadline (fall): rolling
Undergraduate student body: 955 full time, 45 part time; 34% male, 66% female; 0% American Indian, 0% Asian, 94% black, 2% Hispanic, 2% multiracial, 0% Pacific Islander, 0% white, 2% international; 48% from in state; N/A live on campus; N/A of students in fraternities, N/A in sororities
Most popular majors: 39% Business/Commerce, General, 20% Psychology, General, 8% Biology/Biological Sciences, General, 8% Social Work, 4% Computer Science
Expenses: 2018-2019: $13,014; room/board: $8,250
Financial aid: (501) 370-5380

Southern Arkansas University

Magnolia AR
(870) 235-4040
U.S. News ranking: Reg. U. (S), second tier
Website: www.saumag.edu
Admissions email: muleriders@saumag.edu
Public; founded 1909
Freshman admissions: selective; 2018-2019: 3,910 applied, 2,551 accepted. Either SAT or ACT required. ACT 25/75 percentile: 19-24. High school rank: 16% in top tenth, 37% in top quarter, 71% in top half
Early decision deadline: N/A, notification date: N/A
Early action deadline: N/A, notification date: N/A
Application deadline (fall): 8/27
Undergraduate student body: 3,018 full time, 524 part time; 45% male, 55% female; 1% American Indian, 1% Asian, 26% black, 4% Hispanic, 0% multiracial, 0% Pacific Islander, 66% white, 2% international; 75% from in state; 54% live on campus; 1% of students in fraternities, 1% in sororities
Most popular majors: 23% Business, Management, Marketing, and Related Support Services, 10% Education, 10% Health Professions and Related Programs, 9% Physical Sciences, 8% Psychology
Expenses: 2019-2020: $8,980 in state, $13,480 out of state; room/board: $6,516

Financial aid: (870) 235-4023; 80% of undergrads determined to have financial need; average aid package $12,879

University of Arkansas

Fayetteville AR
(800) 377-8632
U.S. News ranking: Nat. U., No. 153
Website: www.uark.edu
Admissions email: uofa@uark.edu
Public; founded 1871
Freshman admissions: more selective; 2018-2019: 18,732 applied, 14,512 accepted. Either SAT or ACT required. ACT 25/75 percentile: 23-29. High school rank: 25% in top tenth, 52% in top quarter, 84% in top half
Early decision deadline: N/A, notification date: N/A
Early action deadline: 11/1, notification date: 12/15
Application deadline (fall): 8/1
Undergraduate student body: 21,005 full time, 2,381 part time; 47% male, 53% female; 1% American Indian, 2% Asian, 4% black, 9% Hispanic, 4% multiracial, 0% Pacific Islander, 76% white, 3% international; 54% from in state; 25% live on campus; 23% of students in fraternities, 39% in sororities
Most popular majors: 26% Business, Management, Marketing, and Related Support Services, 11% Engineering, 9% Health Professions and Related Programs, 6% Communication, Journalism, and Related Programs, 6% Social Sciences
Expenses: 2019-2020: $9,384 in state, $25,872 out of state; room/board: $11,330
Financial aid: (479) 575-3806; 43% of undergrads determined to have financial need; average aid package $9,896

University of Arkansas–Fort Smith[1]

Fort Smith AR
(479) 788-7120
U.S. News ranking: Reg. Coll. (S), No. 61
Website: www.uafortsmith.edu/Home/Index
Admissions email: N/A
Public; founded 1928
Application deadline (fall): rolling
Undergraduate student body: N/A full time, N/A part time
Expenses: N/A
Financial aid: N/A

University of Arkansas–Little Rock

Little Rock AR
(501) 569-3127
U.S. News ranking: Nat. U., second tier
Website: www.ualr.edu/
Admissions email: admissions@ualr.edu
Public; founded 1927
Freshman admissions: selective; 2018-2019: 2,499 applied, 1,629 accepted. Either SAT

or ACT required. ACT 25/75 percentile: 18-25. High school rank: N/A
Early decision deadline: N/A, notification date: N/A
Early action deadline: N/A, notification date: N/A
Undergraduate student body: 4,059 full time, 4,227 part time; 38% male, 62% female; 0% American Indian, 2% Asian, 28% black, 4% Hispanic, 10% multiracial, 0% Pacific Islander, 50% white, 4% international; 87% from in state; N/A live on campus; N/A of students in fraternities, N/A in sororities
Most popular majors: 15% Business, Management, Marketing, and Related Support Services, 9% Homeland Security, Law Enforcement, Firefighting and Related Protective Services, 7% Psychology, 5% Biological and Biomedical Sciences, 5% Communication, Journalism, and Related Programs
Expenses: 2018-2019: $9,544 in state, $21,754 out of state; room/board: $8,260
Financial aid: (501) 569-3035

University of Arkansas–Monticello[1]

Monticello AR
(870) 367-6811
U.S. News ranking: Reg. U. (S), unranked
Website: www.uamont.edu
Admissions email: admissions@uamont.edu
Public
Application deadline (fall): N/A
Undergraduate student body: N/A full time, N/A part time
Expenses: N/A
Financial aid: N/A

University of Arkansas–Pine Bluff

Pine Bluff AR
(870) 575-8492
U.S. News ranking: Reg. Coll. (S), No. 34
Website: www.uapb.edu/
Admissions email: owasoyop@uapb.edu
Public; founded 1873
Freshman admissions: less selective; 2018-2019: 5,508 applied, 2,443 accepted. Either SAT or ACT required. ACT 25/75 percentile: 16-20. High school rank: 10% in top tenth, 35% in top quarter, 65% in top half
Early decision deadline: N/A, notification date: N/A
Early action deadline: N/A, notification date: N/A
Application deadline (fall): rolling
Undergraduate student body: 2,250 full time, 223 part time; 41% male, 59% female; 0% American Indian, 0% Asian, 91% black, 2% Hispanic, 2% multiracial, 0% Pacific Islander, 3% white, 1% international; 61% from in state; 55% live on campus; 9% of students in fraternities, 10% in sororities
Most popular majors: 12% Business Administration and Management, General, 11% Biology/Biological Sciences, General, 9% Criminal Justice/

Safety Studies, 9% Family and Consumer Sciences/Human Sciences, General, 7% Industrial Technology/Technician
Expenses: 2018-2019: $7,944 in state, $14,304 out of state; room/board: $8,281
Financial aid: (870) 575-8302

University of Central Arkansas

Conway AR
(501) 450-3128
U.S. News ranking: Nat. U., second tier
Website: www.uca.edu
Admissions email: admissions@uca.edu
Public; founded 1907
Freshman admissions: selective; 2018-2019: 5,541 applied, 5,048 accepted. Either SAT or ACT required. ACT 25/75 percentile: 21-27. High school rank: 21% in top tenth, 49% in top quarter, 81% in top half
Early decision deadline: N/A, notification date: N/A
Early action deadline: N/A, notification date: N/A
Application deadline (fall): rolling
Undergraduate student body: 7,863 full time, 1,562 part time; 40% male, 60% female; 1% American Indian, 2% Asian, 17% black, 6% Hispanic, 4% multiracial, 0% Pacific Islander, 66% white, 5% international; 86% from in state; 40% live on campus; 4% of students in fraternities, 9% in sororities
Most popular majors: 19% Business, Management, Marketing, and Related Support Services, 18% Health Professions and Related Programs, 10% Education, 7% Psychology, 6% Visual and Performing Arts
Expenses: 2019-2020: $9,188 in state, $15,998 out of state; room/board: $7,198
Financial aid: (501) 450-3140

University of the Ozarks

Clarksville AR
(479) 979-1227
U.S. News ranking: Reg. Coll. (S), No. 7
Website: www.ozarks.edu
Admissions email: admiss@ozarks.edu
Private; founded 1834
Affiliation: Presbyterian Church (USA)
Freshman admissions: selective; 2018-2019: 1,045 applied, 945 accepted. Neither SAT nor ACT required. ACT 25/75 percentile: 19-23. High school rank: 12% in top tenth, 34% in top quarter, 72% in top half
Early decision deadline: N/A, notification date: N/A
Early action deadline: N/A, notification date: N/A
Application deadline (fall): rolling
Undergraduate student body: 861 full time, 11 part time; 49% male, 51% female; 1% American Indian, 1% Asian, 8% black, 13% Hispanic, 5% multiracial, 0% Pacific Islander, 48% white, 21% international; 43% from in state; 67% live on campus; 0%

More @ usnews.com/bestcolleges

of students in fraternities, 0% in sororities
Most popular majors: 16% Business Administration and Management, General, 14% Public Health Education and Promotion, 11% Biology/Biological Sciences, General, 9% Business Administration and Management, General, 8% Marketing/Marketing Management, General
Expenses: 2019-2020: $25,950; room/board: $7,600
Financial aid: (479) 979-1447; 71% of undergrads determined to have financial need; average aid package $24,455

Williams Baptist University
Walnut Ridge AR
(800) 722-4434
U.S. News ranking: Nat. Lib. Arts, second tier
Website: williamsbu.edu/
Admissions email: admissions@williamsbu.edu
Private; founded 1941
Affiliation: Southern Baptist
Freshman admissions: selective; 2018-2019: 774 applied, 436 accepted. Either SAT or ACT required. ACT 25/75 percentile: 18-22. High school rank: 11% in top tenth, 24% in top quarter, 62% in top half
Early decision deadline: N/A, notification date: N/A
Early action deadline: N/A, notification date: N/A
Application deadline (fall): rolling
Undergraduate student body: 445 full time, 35 part time; 56% male, 44% female; 0% American Indian, 0% Asian, 13% black, 6% Hispanic, 2% multiracial, 1% Pacific Islander, 72% white, 7% international; N/A from in state; 77% live on campus; N/A of students in fraternities, N/A in sororities
Most popular majors: 22% Psychology, General, 21% General Studies, 19% Education, 17% Theology and Religious Vocations, 12% Business Administration and Management, General
Expenses: 2019-2020: $18,058; room/board: $8,026
Financial aid: (870) 759-4112; 87% of undergrads determined to have financial need; average aid package $6,575

CALIFORNIA

Academy of Art University
San Francisco CA
(800) 544-2787
U.S. News ranking: Reg. U. (W), unranked
Website: www.academyart.edu/
Admissions email: admissions@academyart.edu
For-profit; founded 1929
Freshman admissions: least selective; 2018-2019: 2,363 applied, 2,363 accepted. Neither SAT nor ACT required. SAT 25/75 percentile: N/A. High school rank: N/A
Early decision deadline: N/A, notification date: N/A

Early action deadline: N/A, notification date: N/A
Application deadline (fall): rolling
Undergraduate student body: 4,090 full time, 2,961 part time; 44% male, 56% female; 1% American Indian, 6% Asian, 6% black, 11% Hispanic, 3% multiracial, 1% Pacific Islander, 17% white, 28% international; N/A from in state; 14% live on campus; N/A of students in fraternities, N/A in sororities
Most popular majors: 38% Visual and Performing Arts, 21% Computer and Information Sciences and Support Services, 13% Communications Technologies/Technicians and Support Services, 13% Engineering Technologies and Engineering-Related Fields, 6% Family and Consumer Sciences/Human Sciences
Expenses: 2019-2020: $29,190; room/board: $17,510
Financial aid: (415) 618-6190; 43% of undergrads determined to have financial need; average aid package $13,280

Alliant International University
San Diego CA
(858) 635-4772
U.S. News ranking: Nat. U., unranked
Website: www.alliant.edu
Admissions email: admissions@alliant.edu
Private; founded 1969
Freshman admissions: least selective; 2018-2019: N/A applied, N/A accepted. Neither SAT nor ACT required. SAT 25/75 percentile: N/A. High school rank: N/A
Early decision deadline: N/A, notification date: N/A
Early action deadline: N/A, notification date: N/A
Application deadline (fall): rolling
Undergraduate student body: 123 full time, 376 part time; 52% male, 48% female; N/A American Indian, N/A Asian, N/A black, N/A Hispanic, N/A multiracial, N/A Pacific Islander, N/A white, N/A international
Most popular majors: 71% Business Administration and Management, General, 10% Criminal Justice/Law Enforcement Administration
Expenses: 2019-2020: $18,510; room/board: N/A
Financial aid: (858) 635-4700

American Conservatory Theater[1]
San Francisco CA
U.S. News ranking: Arts, unranked
Website: www.act-sf.org
Admissions email: N/A
Private
Application deadline (fall): N/A
Undergraduate student body: N/A full time, N/A part time
Expenses: N/A
Financial aid: N/A

Antelope Valley College[1]
Lancaster CA
(661) 722-6300
U.S. News ranking: Reg. Coll. (W), unranked
Website: www.avc.edu
Admissions email: N/A
Public
Application deadline (fall): N/A
Undergraduate student body: N/A full time, N/A part time
Expenses: N/A
Financial aid: N/A

ArtCenter College of Design
Pasadena CA
(626) 396-2373
U.S. News ranking: Arts, unranked
Website: www.artcenter.edu
Admissions email: admissions@artcenter.edu
Private; founded 1930
Freshman admissions: least selective; 2018-2019: N/A applied, N/A accepted. Neither SAT nor ACT required. SAT 25/75 percentile: N/A. High school rank: N/A
Early decision deadline: N/A, notification date: N/A
Early action deadline: N/A, notification date: N/A
Application deadline (fall): rolling
Undergraduate student body: 1,731 full time, 277 part time; 45% male, 55% female; 0% American Indian, 33% Asian, 1% black, 11% Hispanic, 4% multiracial, 0% Pacific Islander, 14% white, 35% international; N/A from in state; 0% live on campus; 0% of students in fraternities, 0% in sororities
Most popular majors: 68% Visual and Performing Arts, 24% Engineering Technologies and Engineering-Related Fields, 4% Natural Resources and Conservation, 2% Communications Technologies/Technicians and Support Services, 2% Computer and Information Sciences and Support Services
Expenses: N/A
Financial aid: (626) 396-2215

Ashford University[1]
San Diego CA
(866) 711-1700
U.S. News ranking: Reg. U. (W), unranked
Website: www.ashford.edu
Admissions email: admissions@ashford.edu
For-profit
Application deadline (fall): N/A
Undergraduate student body: N/A full time, N/A part time
Expenses: N/A
Financial aid: N/A

Azusa Pacific University
Azusa CA
(800) 825-5278
U.S. News ranking: Nat. U., No. 228
Website: www.apu.edu
Admissions email: admissions@apu.edu
Private; founded 1899

Affiliation: Evangelical Christian
Freshman admissions: selective; 2018-2019: 9,832 applied, 6,736 accepted. Either SAT or ACT required. SAT 25/75 percentile: 1020-1240. High school rank: N/A
Early decision deadline: N/A, notification date: N/A
Early action deadline: 11/15, notification date: 1/15
Application deadline (fall): 6/1
Undergraduate student body: 5,003 full time, 654 part time; 34% male, 66% female; 0% American Indian, 10% Asian, 6% black, 33% Hispanic, 7% multiracial, 1% Pacific Islander, 37% white, 3% international; N/A from in state; 67% live on campus; N/A of students in fraternities, N/A in sororities
Most popular majors: Information not available
Expenses: 2019-2020: $38,880; room/board: $10,076
Financial aid: (800) 825-5278

Bakersfield College[1]
Bakersfield CA
(661) 395-4011
U.S. News ranking: Reg. Coll. (W), unranked
Website: www.bakersfieldcollege.edu/
Admissions email: N/A
Public
Application deadline (fall): N/A
Undergraduate student body: N/A full time, N/A part time
Expenses: N/A
Financial aid: N/A

Biola University
La Mirada CA
(562) 903-4752
U.S. News ranking: Nat. U., No. 185
Website: www.biola.edu
Admissions email: admissions@biola.edu
Private; founded 1908
Affiliation: Multiple Protestant Denominations
Freshman admissions: more selective; 2018-2019: 3,784 applied, 3,295 accepted. Either SAT or ACT required. SAT 25/75 percentile: 1060-1260. High school rank: 47% in top tenth, 71% in top quarter, 88% in top half
Early decision deadline: 11/15, notification date: 1/15
Early action deadline: 11/15, notification date: 1/15
Application deadline (fall): rolling
Undergraduate student body: 3,779 full time, 231 part time; 37% male, 63% female; 0% American Indian, 17% Asian, 3% black, 21% Hispanic, 6% multiracial, 1% Pacific Islander, 45% white, 3% international; 0% from in state; 64% live on campus; 0% of students in fraternities, 0% in sororities
Most popular majors: 14% Business, Management, Marketing, and Related Support Services, 12% Visual and Performing Arts, 11% Communication, Journalism, and

Related Programs, 8% Health Professions and Related Programs, 8% Social Sciences
Expenses: 2019-2020: $41,976; room/board: $11,514
Financial aid: (562) 903-4742; 68% of undergrads determined to have financial need; average aid package $25,186

Brandman University
Irvine CA
(800) 746-0082
U.S. News ranking: Nat. U., unranked
Website: www.brandman.edu
Admissions email: apply@brandman.edu
Private; founded 1958
Affiliation: Other
Freshman admissions: least selective; 2018-2019: 96 applied, 76 accepted. Neither SAT nor ACT required. SAT 25/75 percentile: N/A. High school rank: N/A
Early decision deadline: N/A, notification date: N/A
Early action deadline: N/A, notification date: N/A
Application deadline (fall): rolling
Undergraduate student body: 1,233 full time, 3,013 part time; 39% male, 61% female; 1% American Indian, 2% Asian, 6% black, 53% Hispanic, 1% multiracial, 1% Pacific Islander, 30% white, 0% international; 66% from in state; N/A live on campus; N/A of students in fraternities, N/A in sororities
Most popular majors: 16% Organizational Leadership, 16% Psychology, General, 14% Business Administration and Management, General, 10% Liberal Arts and Sciences/Liberal Studies, 9% Criminal Justice/Safety Studies
Expenses: 2019-2020: $15,440; room/board: N/A
Financial aid: (800) 746-0082; 72% of undergrads determined to have financial need; average aid package $10,495

California Baptist University
Riverside CA
(877) 228-8866
U.S. News ranking: Reg. U. (W), No. 43
Website: www.calbaptist.edu
Admissions email: admissions@calbaptist.edu
Private; founded 1950
Affiliation: Southern Baptist
Freshman admissions: selective; 2018-2019: 6,595 applied, 5,246 accepted. Either SAT or ACT required. SAT 25/75 percentile: 980-1200. High school rank: 13% in top tenth, 38% in top quarter, 74% in top half
Early decision deadline: N/A, notification date: N/A
Early action deadline: 12/15, notification date: 1/31
Application deadline (fall): rolling
Undergraduate student body: 6,859 full time, 996 part time; 38% male, 62% female; 1% American Indian, 5% Asian, 7% black, 36% Hispanic, 6% multiracial, 1% Pacific Islander, 39% white, 2% international; 92% from in

state; 41% live on campus; N/A of students in fraternities, N/A in sororities
Most popular majors: 10% Business/Commerce, General, 10% Psychology, General, 10% Registered Nursing/Registered Nurse, 7% Kinesiology and Exercise Science, 4% Liberal Arts and Sciences/Liberal Studies
Expenses: 2019-2020: $34,922; room/board: $9,660
Financial aid: (951) 343-4235; 82% of undergrads determined to have financial need; average aid package $22,465

California College of the Arts
San Francisco CA
(800) 447-1278
U.S. News ranking: Arts, unranked
Website: www.cca.edu
Admissions email: enroll@cca.edu
Private; founded 1907
Freshman admissions: less selective; 2018-2019: 2,292 applied, 2,021 accepted. Neither SAT nor ACT required. SAT 25/75 percentile: 895-1200. High school rank: N/A
Early decision deadline: N/A, notification date: N/A
Early action deadline: N/A, notification date: N/A
Application deadline (fall): rolling
Undergraduate student body: 1,406 full time, 62 part time; 38% male, 62% female; 0% American Indian, 15% Asian, 5% black, 14% Hispanic, 0% multiracial, 0% Pacific Islander, 20% white, 41% international; 38% from in state; 33% live on campus; 1% of students in fraternities, 1% in sororities
Most popular majors: 65% Visual and Performing Arts, 17% Communications Technologies/Technicians and Support Services, 9% Architecture and Related Services, 6% Multi/Interdisciplinary Studies, 2% Precision Production
Expenses: 2019-2020: $51,092; room/board: $14,071
Financial aid: (415) 703-9573; 43% of undergrads determined to have financial need; average aid package $38,416

California Institute of Integral Studies[1]
San Francisco CA
(415) 575-6100
U.S. News ranking: Nat. U., unranked
Website: www.ciis.edu
Admissions email: N/A
Private; founded 1968
Application deadline (fall): N/A
Undergraduate student body: N/A full time, N/A part time
Expenses: N/A
Financial aid: N/A

California Institute of Technology
Pasadena CA
(626) 395-6341
U.S. News ranking: Nat. U., No. 12
Website: www.caltech.edu
Admissions email: ugadmissions@caltech.edu
Private; founded 1891
Freshman admissions: most selective; 2018-2019: 8,208 applied, 543 accepted. Either SAT or ACT required. SAT 25/75 percentile: 1530-1580. High school rank: 96% in top tenth, 100% in top quarter, 100% in top half
Early decision deadline: N/A, notification date: N/A
Early action deadline: 11/1, notification date: 12/15
Application deadline (fall): 1/3
Undergraduate student body: 948 full time, 0 part time; 55% male, 45% female; 0% American Indian, 40% Asian, 1% black, 14% Hispanic, 8% multiracial, 0% Pacific Islander, 27% white, 9% international; 33% from in state; 86% live on campus; 0% of students in fraternities, 0% in sororities
Most popular majors: 37% Engineering, 26% Physical Sciences, 25% Computer and Information Sciences and Support Services, 5% Biological and Biomedical Sciences, 5% Mathematics and Statistics
Expenses: 2019-2020: $54,600; room/board: $16,644
Financial aid: (626) 395-6280; 53% of undergrads determined to have financial need; average aid package $51,318

California Institute of the Arts[1]
Valencia CA
(661) 255-1050
U.S. News ranking: Arts, unranked
Website: www.calarts.edu
Admissions email: admissions@calarts.edu
Private; founded 1961
Application deadline (fall): N/A
Undergraduate student body: N/A full time, N/A part time
Expenses: N/A
Financial aid: (661) 253-7869

California Lutheran University
Thousand Oaks CA
(877) 258-3678
U.S. News ranking: Reg. U. (W), No. 9
Website: www.callutheran.edu
Admissions email: admissions@callutheran.edu
Private; founded 1959
Affiliation: Evangelical Lutheran Church
Freshman admissions: selective; 2018-2019: 5,752 applied, 4,111 accepted. Either SAT or ACT required. SAT 25/75 percentile: 1070-1250. High school rank: 24% in top tenth, 63% in top quarter, 92% in top half
Early decision deadline: N/A, notification date: N/A

Early action deadline: 11/1, notification date: 1/15
Application deadline (fall): N/A
Undergraduate student body: 2,942 full time, 117 part time; 43% male, 57% female; 0% American Indian, 5% Asian, 4% black, 33% Hispanic, 8% multiracial, 0% Pacific Islander, 43% white, 3% international; N/A from in state; 52% live on campus; N/A of students in fraternities, N/A in sororities
Most popular majors: 24% Business Administration and Management, General, 13% Psychology, General, 13% Speech Communication and Rhetoric, 8% Biology/Biological Sciences, General, 8% Kinesiology and Exercise Science
Expenses: 2019-2020: $44,383; room/board: $14,100
Financial aid: (805) 493-3139; 72% of undergrads determined to have financial need; average aid package $35,700

California Polytechnic State University–San Luis Obispo
San Luis Obispo CA
(805) 756-2311
U.S. News ranking: Reg. U. (W), No. 4
Website: www.calpoly.edu/
Admissions email: admissions@calpoly.edu
Public; founded 1901
Freshman admissions: more selective; 2018-2019: 54,663 applied, 16,491 accepted. Either SAT or ACT required. SAT 25/75 percentile: 1240-1430. High school rank: 59% in top tenth, 89% in top quarter, 99% in top half
Early decision deadline: N/A, notification date: N/A
Early action deadline: N/A, notification date: N/A
Application deadline (fall): 11/30
Undergraduate student body: 20,272 full time, 765 part time; 52% male, 48% female; 0% American Indian, 13% Asian, 1% black, 17% Hispanic, 8% multiracial, 0% Pacific Islander, 54% white, 2% international; N/A from in state; 32% live on campus; 7% of students in fraternities, 11% in sororities
Most popular majors: 27% Engineering, 13% Business, Management, Marketing, and Related Support Services, 12% Agriculture, Agriculture Operations, and Related Sciences, 6% Biological and Biomedical Sciences, 5% Social Sciences
Expenses: 2019-2020: $9,942 in state, $21,822 out of state; room/board: $14,209
Financial aid: (805) 756-2927; 42% of undergrads determined to have financial need; average aid package $10,705

California State Polytechnic University–Pomona
Pomona CA
(909) 869-5299
U.S. News ranking: Reg. U. (W), No. 14
Website: www.cpp.edu
Admissions email: admissions@cpp.edu
Public; founded 1938
Freshman admissions: selective; 2018-2019: 36,660 applied, 20,343 accepted. Either SAT or ACT required. SAT 25/75 percentile: 1020-1260. High school rank: N/A
Early decision deadline: N/A, notification date: N/A
Early action deadline: N/A, notification date: N/A
Application deadline (fall): 11/30
Undergraduate student body: 21,824 full time, 3,109 part time; 53% male, 47% female; 0% American Indian, 21% Asian, 3% black, 46% Hispanic, 4% multiracial, 0% Pacific Islander, 16% white, 6% international; 97% from in state; 10% live on campus; 2% of students in fraternities, 1% in sororities
Most popular majors: 25% Business Administration and Management, General, 6% Hospitality Administration/Management, General, 4% Biology/Biological Sciences, General, 4% Liberal Arts and Sciences/Liberal Studies, 4% Mechanical Engineering
Expenses: 2019-2020: $7,353 in state, $19,233 out of state; room/board: $17,358
Financial aid: (909) 869-3700; 69% of undergrads determined to have financial need; average aid package $10,629

California State University–Bakersfield
Bakersfield CA
(661) 654-3036
U.S. News ranking: Reg. U. (W), No. 66
Website: www.csub.edu
Admissions email: admissions@csub.edu
Public
Freshman admissions: less selective; 2018-2019: 6,888 applied, 6,888 accepted. Either SAT or ACT required for some. SAT 25/75 percentile: 880-1080. High school rank: N/A
Early decision deadline: N/A, notification date: N/A
Early action deadline: N/A, notification date: N/A
Application deadline (fall): 3/1
Undergraduate student body: 7,906 full time, 1,290 part time; 39% male, 61% female; 0% American Indian, 6% Asian, 5% black, 61% Hispanic, 3% multiracial, 0% Pacific Islander, 14% white, 5% international; N/A from in state; 4% live on campus; 1% of students in fraternities, 1% in sororities

Most popular majors: 29% Liberal Arts and Sciences, General Studies and Humanities, 11% Education, 10% Business, Management, Marketing, and Related Support Services, 9% Psychology, 8% Social Sciences
Expenses: 2019-2020: $7,422 in state, $19,500 out of state; room/board: $12,984
Financial aid: (661) 654-3016; 85% of undergrads determined to have financial need; average aid package $11,283

California State University–Channel Islands[1]
Camarillo CA
(805) 437-8500
U.S. News ranking: Reg. U. (W), No. 43
Website: www.csuci.edu
Admissions email: N/A
Public
Application deadline (fall): N/A
Undergraduate student body: N/A full time, N/A part time
Expenses: N/A
Financial aid: N/A

California State University–Chico
Chico CA
(530) 898-6322
U.S. News ranking: Reg. U. (W), No. 27
Website: www.csuchico.edu
Admissions email: info@csuchico.edu
Public; founded 1887
Freshman admissions: selective; 2018-2019: 23,964 applied, 15,639 accepted. Either SAT or ACT required. SAT 25/75 percentile: 990-1170. High school rank: N/A
Early decision deadline: N/A, notification date: N/A
Early action deadline: N/A, notification date: N/A
Application deadline (fall): 11/30
Undergraduate student body: 15,237 full time, 1,183 part time; 47% male, 53% female; 0% American Indian, 5% Asian, 3% black, 34% Hispanic, 5% multiracial, 0% Pacific Islander, 41% white, 3% international; 0% from in state; 2% live on campus; 0% of students in fraternities, 0% in sororities
Most popular majors: 16% Business, Management, Marketing, and Related Support Services, 10% Health Professions and Related Programs, 10% Social Sciences, 8% Parks, Recreation, Leisure, and Fitness Studies, 7% Psychology
Expenses: 2019-2020: $7,578 in state, $19,458 out of state; room/board: $12,390
Financial aid: (530) 898-6451; 67% of undergrads determined to have financial need; average aid package $12,483

California State University–Dominguez Hills

Carson CA
(310) 243-3300
U.S. News ranking: Reg. U. (W), No. 72
Website: www.csudh.edu
Admissions email: info@csudh.edu
Public; founded 1960
Freshman admissions: least selective; 2018-2019: 15,596 applied, 12,939 accepted. Either SAT or ACT required for some. SAT 25/75 percentile: 860-1030. High school rank: N/A
Early decision deadline: N/A, notification date: N/A
Early action deadline: N/A, notification date: N/A
Application deadline (fall): rolling
Undergraduate student body: 10,715 full time, 3,022 part time; 37% male, 63% female; 0% American Indian, 8% Asian, 11% black, 65% Hispanic, 3% multiracial, 0% Pacific Islander, 6% white, 4% international; 99% from in state; 5% live on campus; 1% of students in fraternities, 1% in sororities
Most popular majors: 19% Business, Management, Marketing, and Related Support Services, 11% Health Professions and Related Programs, 11% Psychology, 10% Social Sciences, 8% Homeland Security, Law Enforcement, Firefighting and Related Protective Services
Expenses: 2019-2020: $8,140 in state, $17,644 out of state; room/board: $13,043
Financial aid: (310) 243-3189; 72% of undergrads determined to have financial need; average aid package $6,131

California State University–East Bay

Hayward CA
(510) 885-3500
U.S. News ranking: Reg. U. (W), No. 80
Website: www.csueastbay.edu
Admissions email: admissions@csueastbay.edu
Public; founded 1957
Freshman admissions: less selective; 2018-2019: 16,131 applied, 11,551 accepted. Either SAT or ACT required for some. SAT 25/75 percentile: 890-1090. High school rank: N/A
Early decision deadline: N/A, notification date: N/A
Early action deadline: N/A, notification date: N/A
Application deadline (fall): 11/30
Undergraduate student body: 10,020 full time, 2,296 part time; 39% male, 61% female; 0% American Indian, 23% Asian, 10% black, 36% Hispanic, 5% multiracial, 1% Pacific Islander, 15% white, 6% international; 96% from in state; N/A live on campus; N/A of students in fraternities, N/A in sororities
Most popular majors: 22% Business Administration and Management, General, 15% Health Professions and Related Programs, 9% Social Sciences, 8% Psychology, General, 6%

Public Administration and Social Service Professions
Expenses: 2019-2020: $6,984 in state, $18,864 out of state; room/board: $14,558
Financial aid: (510) 885-2784; 78% of undergrads determined to have financial need; average aid package $15,180

California State University–Fresno

Fresno CA
(559) 278-2191
U.S. News ranking: Nat. U., No. 211
Website: www.csufresno.edu
Admissions email: lyager@csufresno.edu
Public; founded 1911
Freshman admissions: selective; 2018-2019: 18,475 applied, 10,629 accepted. Either SAT or ACT required. SAT 25/75 percentile: 910-1110. High school rank: 15% in top tenth, 80% in top quarter, 100% in top half
Early decision deadline: N/A, notification date: N/A
Early action deadline: N/A, notification date: N/A
Application deadline (fall): 11/30
Undergraduate student body: 19,325 full time, 2,746 part time; 41% male, 59% female; 0% American Indian, 13% Asian, 3% black, 54% Hispanic, 3% multiracial, 0% Pacific Islander, 18% white, 6% international; 99% from in state; 4% live on campus; 7% of students in fraternities, 4% in sororities
Most popular majors: 14% Business, Management, Marketing, and Related Support Services, 10% Health Professions and Related Programs, 8% Homeland Security, Law Enforcement, Firefighting and Related Protective Services, 8% Liberal Arts and Sciences, General Studies and Humanities, 8% Psychology
Expenses: 2019-2020: $6,587 in state, $12,725 out of state; room/board: $10,587
Financial aid: (559) 278-2182; 76% of undergrads determined to have financial need; average aid package $12,843

California State University–Fullerton

Fullerton CA
(657) 278-7788
U.S. News ranking: Reg. U. (W), No. 17
Website: www.fullerton.edu
Admissions email: admissions@fullerton.edu
Public; founded 1957
Freshman admissions: selective; 2018-2019: 51,415 applied, 22,317 accepted. Either SAT or ACT required. SAT 25/75 percentile: 1040-1220. High school rank: 21% in top tenth, 68% in top quarter, 96% in top half
Early decision deadline: N/A, notification date: N/A
Early action deadline: N/A, notification date: N/A
Application deadline (fall): 11/30

Undergraduate student body: 27,907 full time, 6,844 part time; 44% male, 56% female; 0% American Indian, 22% Asian, 2% black, 44% Hispanic, 4% multiracial, 0% Pacific Islander, 19% white, 6% international; N/A from in state; 6% live on campus; 1% of students in fraternities, 2% in sororities
Most popular majors: 24% Business, Management, Marketing, and Related Support Services, 8% Communication, Journalism, and Related Programs, 8% Psychology, 5% Education, 5% Health Professions and Related Programs
Expenses: 2019-2020: $6,922 in state, $16,426 out of state; room/board: $16,296
Financial aid: (657) 278-5256; 70% of undergrads determined to have financial need; average aid package $10,978

California State University–Long Beach

Long Beach CA
(562) 985-5471
U.S. News ranking: Reg. U. (W), No. 20
Website: www.csulb.edu
Admissions email: eslb@csulb.edu
Public; founded 1949
Freshman admissions: selective; 2018-2019: 69,578 applied, 21,725 accepted. Either SAT or ACT required. SAT 25/75 percentile: 1040-1250. High school rank: N/A
Early decision deadline: N/A, notification date: N/A
Early action deadline: N/A, notification date: N/A
Application deadline (fall): rolling
Undergraduate student body: 27,462 full time, 3,985 part time; 43% male, 57% female; 0% American Indian, 22% Asian, 4% black, 43% Hispanic, 5% multiracial, 0% Pacific Islander, 17% white, 6% international; 99% from in state; 4% live on campus; N/A of students in fraternities, N/A in sororities
Most popular majors: 17% Business, Management, Marketing, and Related Support Services, 10% Visual and Performing Arts, 9% Health Professions and Related Programs, 8% Engineering, 8% Social Sciences
Expenses: 2019-2020: $6,798 in state, $17,094 out of state; room/board: $13,158
Financial aid: (562) 985-8403; 79% of undergrads determined to have financial need; average aid package $13,948

California State University–Los Angeles

Los Angeles CA
(323) 343-3901
U.S. News ranking: Reg. U. (W), No. 31
Website: www.calstatela.edu
Admissions email: admission@calstatela.edu
Public; founded 1947

Freshman admissions: less selective; 2018-2019: 39,854 applied, 16,548 accepted. Either SAT or ACT required. SAT 25/75 percentile: 890-1080. High school rank: N/A
Early decision deadline: N/A, notification date: N/A
Early action deadline: N/A, notification date: N/A
Application deadline (fall): 12/15
Undergraduate student body: 20,598 full time, 3,404 part time; 43% male, 57% female; 0% American Indian, 13% Asian, 3% black, 68% Hispanic, 2% multiracial, 0% Pacific Islander, 5% white, 7% international; N/A from in state; 2% live on campus; 1% of students in fraternities, 1% in sororities
Most popular majors: 20% Business, Management, Marketing, and Related Support Services, 12% Social Sciences, 11% Health Professions and Related Programs, 6% English Language and Literature/Letters, 6% Psychology
Expenses: 2019-2020: $6,763 in state, $18,643 out of state; room/board: $12,918
Financial aid: (323) 343-6260; 89% of undergrads determined to have financial need; average aid package $12,239

California State University–Maritime Academy

Vallejo CA
(707) 654-1330
U.S. News ranking: Reg. Coll. (W), No. 2
Website: www.csum.edu
Admissions email: admission@csum.edu
Public; founded 1929
Freshman admissions: selective; 2018-2019: 1,118 applied, 744 accepted. Either SAT or ACT required. SAT 25/75 percentile: 1100-1275. High school rank: N/A
Early decision deadline: N/A, notification date: N/A
Early action deadline: 10/31, notification date: 12/15
Application deadline (fall): 11/30
Undergraduate student body: 975 full time, 42 part time; 83% male, 17% female; 0% American Indian, 10% Asian, 2% black, 20% Hispanic, 11% multiracial, 1% Pacific Islander, 47% white, 0% international; N/A from in state; 72% live on campus; 0% of students in fraternities, 0% in sororities
Most popular majors: 35% Transportation and Materials Moving, 19% Business, Management, Marketing, and Related Support Services, 17% Engineering Technologies and Engineering-Related Fields, 15% Engineering, 14% Multi/Interdisciplinary Studies
Expenses: 2018-2019: $7,056 in state, $18,936 out of state; room/board: $12,322
Financial aid: N/A; 51% of undergrads determined to have financial need; average aid package $11,862

California State University–Monterey Bay

Seaside CA
(831) 582-3783
U.S. News ranking: Reg. U. (W), No. 26
Website: www.csumb.edu
Admissions email: admissions@csumb.edu
Public; founded 1994
Freshman admissions: selective; 2018-2019: 12,423 applied, 7,270 accepted. Either SAT or ACT required. SAT 25/75 percentile: 960-1160. High school rank: 14% in top tenth, 46% in top quarter, 84% in top half
Early decision deadline: N/A, notification date: N/A
Early action deadline: N/A, notification date: N/A
Application deadline (fall): 11/30
Undergraduate student body: 6,051 full time, 665 part time; 38% male, 62% female; 1% American Indian, 6% Asian, 5% black, 41% Hispanic, 8% multiracial, 1% Pacific Islander, 28% white, 6% international; N/A from in state; N/A live on campus; 4% of students in fraternities, 3% in sororities
Most popular majors: 15% Business, Management, Marketing, and Related Support Services, 14% Psychology, 13% Liberal Arts and Sciences, General Studies and Humanities, 10% Parks, Recreation, Leisure, and Fitness Studies, 8% Computer and Information Sciences and Support Services
Expenses: 2019-2020: $7,143 in state, $19,023 out of state; room/board: $12,786
Financial aid: N/A; 70% of undergrads determined to have financial need; average aid package $11,346

California State University–Northridge

Northridge CA
(818) 677-3700
U.S. News ranking: Reg. U. (W), No. 49
Website: www.csun.edu
Admissions email: admissions.records@csun.edu
Public; founded 1958
Freshman admissions: selective; 2018-2019: 62,052 applied, 26,604 accepted. Either SAT or ACT required. SAT 25/75 percentile: 930-1130. High school rank: N/A
Early decision deadline: N/A, notification date: N/A
Early action deadline: N/A, notification date: N/A
Application deadline (fall): 11/30
Undergraduate student body: 29,279 full time, 5,621 part time; 46% male, 54% female; 0% American Indian, 10% Asian, 5% black, 49% Hispanic, 3% multiracial, 0% Pacific Islander, 20% white, 8% international
Most popular majors: 19% Business, Management, Marketing, and Related Support Services, 12% Social Sciences, 10% Health Professions and Related Programs, 10%

Psychology, 7% Communication, Journalism, and Related Programs
Expenses: 2019-2020: $6,972 in state, $17,622 out of state; room/board: N/A
Financial aid: (818) 677-4085; 81% of undergrads determined to have financial need; average aid package $18,744

California State University– Sacramento

Sacramento CA
(916) 278-1000
U.S. News ranking: Reg. U. (W), No. 55
Website: www.csus.edu
Admissions email: admissions@csus.edu
Public; founded 1947
Freshman admissions: less selective; 2018-2019: N/A applied, N/A accepted. Either SAT or ACT required. SAT 25/75 percentile: 940-1140. High school rank: N/A
Early decision deadline: N/A, notification date: N/A
Early action deadline: N/A, notification date: 12/1
Application deadline (fall): 11/30
Undergraduate student body: 23,450 full time, 0 part time; 44% male, 56% female; N/A American Indian, N/A Asian, N/A black, N/A Hispanic, N/A multiracial, N/A Pacific Islander, N/A white, N/A international
Most popular majors: Information not available
Expenses: 2018-2019: $7,204 in state, $19,084 out of state; room/board: $14,396
Financial aid: (916) 278-1000

California State University– San Bernardino

San Bernardino CA
(909) 537-5188
U.S. News ranking: Reg. U. (W), No. 41
Website: www.csusb.edu
Admissions email: moreinfo@csusb.edu
Public; founded 1962
Freshman admissions: less selective; 2018-2019: 16,042 applied, 8,798 accepted. Neither SAT nor ACT required. SAT 25/75 percentile: 910-1080. High school rank: N/A
Early decision deadline: N/A, notification date: N/A
Early action deadline: N/A, notification date: 5/1
Application deadline (fall): rolling
Undergraduate student body: 16,110 full time, 1,744 part time; 39% male, 61% female; 0% American Indian, 5% Asian, 5% black, 65% Hispanic, 2% multiracial, 0% Pacific Islander, 11% white, 7% international; N/A from in state; 6% live on campus; 4% of students in fraternities, 3% in sororities
Most popular majors: 24% Business, Management, Marketing, and Related Support Services, 15% Psychology, 9% Social Sciences, 8% Health

Professions and Related Programs, 5% Parks, Recreation, Leisure, and Fitness Studies
Expenses: 2019-2020: $6,926 in state, $13,064 out of state; room/board: $13,435
Financial aid: (909) 537-5227; 85% of undergrads determined to have financial need; average aid package $9,569

California State University– San Marcos

San Marcos CA
(760) 750-4848
U.S. News ranking: Reg. U. (W), No. 58
Website: www.csusm.edu
Admissions email: apply@csusm.edu
Public; founded 1989
Freshman admissions: less selective; 2018-2019: 17,648 applied, 10,311 accepted. Either SAT or ACT required. ACT 25/75 percentile: 17-22. High school rank: N/A
Early decision deadline: N/A, notification date: N/A
Early action deadline: N/A, notification date: N/A
Application deadline (fall): 11/30
Undergraduate student body: 11,400 full time, 2,562 part time; 39% male, 61% female; 0% American Indian, 9% Asian, 3% black, 47% Hispanic, 5% multiracial, 0% Pacific Islander, 26% white, 5% international
Most popular majors: 19% Health Professions and Related Programs, 17% Social Sciences, 14% Business, Management, Marketing, and Related Support Services, 8% Family and Consumer Sciences/Human Sciences, 7% Psychology
Expenses: 2019-2020: $7,648 in state, $16,576 out of state; room/board: $13,000
Financial aid: (760) 750-4881; 70% of undergrads determined to have financial need; average aid package $11,052

California State University–Stanislaus

Turlock CA
(209) 667-3070
U.S. News ranking: Reg. U. (W), No. 30
Website: www.csustan.edu
Admissions email: Outreach_Help_Desk@csustan.edu
Public; founded 1957
Freshman admissions: less selective; 2018-2019: 7,674 applied, 6,586 accepted. Either SAT or ACT required for some. SAT 25/75 percentile: 900-1090. High school rank: N/A
Early decision deadline: N/A, notification date: N/A
Early action deadline: N/A, notification date: N/A
Application deadline (fall): 11/30
Undergraduate student body: 7,669 full time, 1,418 part time; 34% male, 66% female; 0% American Indian, 9% Asian, 2% black, 55% Hispanic, 3% multiracial, 0% Pacific Islander, 21% white,

4% international; N/A from in state; 7% live on campus; 5% of students in fraternities, 6% in sororities
Most popular majors: 19% Business Administration and Management, General, 14% Psychology, General, 13% Sociology, 8% Criminal Justice/Safety Studies, 8% Liberal Arts and Sciences/Liberal Studies
Expenses: 2019-2020: $7,092 in state, $18,972 out of state; room/board: $8,865
Financial aid: (209) 667-3337; 78% of undergrads determined to have financial need; average aid package $17,568

Chapman University

Orange CA
(888) 282-7759
U.S. News ranking: Nat. U., No. 125
Website: www.chapman.edu
Admissions email: admit@chapman.edu
Private; founded 1861
Affiliation: Christian Church (Disciples of Christ)
Freshman admissions: more selective; 2018-2019: 14,198 applied, 7,605 accepted. Either SAT or ACT required. SAT 25/75 percentile: 1190-1370. High school rank: 37% in top tenth, 81% in top quarter, 96% in top half
Early decision deadline: 11/1, notification date: 12/20
Early action deadline: 11/1, notification date: 12/20
Application deadline (fall): 4/1
Undergraduate student body: 6,785 full time, 491 part time; 39% male, 61% female; 0% American Indian, 13% Asian, 2% black, 16% Hispanic, 7% multiracial, 0% Pacific Islander, 53% white, 4% international; 31% from in state; 39% live on campus; 25% of students in fraternities, 48% in sororities
Most popular majors: 21% Business Administration and Management, General, 10% Cinematography and Film/Video Production, 5% Business/Corporate Communications, 5% Psychology, General, 4% Speech Communication and Rhetoric
Expenses: 2019-2020: $54,924; room/board: $17,818
Financial aid: (714) 997-6741; 56% of undergrads determined to have financial need; average aid package $35,896

Claremont McKenna College

Claremont CA
(909) 621-8088
U.S. News ranking: Nat. Lib. Arts, No. 7
Website: www.claremontmckenna.edu
Admissions email: admission@cmc.edu
Private; founded 1946
Freshman admissions: most selective; 2018-2019: 6,272 applied, 584 accepted. Either SAT or ACT required. ACT 25/75

percentile: 31-34. High school rank: 78% in top tenth, 93% in top quarter, 100% in top half
Early decision deadline: 11/1, notification date: 12/15
Early action deadline: N/A, notification date: N/A
Application deadline (fall): 1/5
Undergraduate student body: 1,321 full time, 3 part time; 52% male, 48% female; 0% American Indian, 11% Asian, 4% black, 15% Hispanic, 6% multiracial, 0% Pacific Islander, 42% white, 16% international; N/A from in state; 96% live on campus; 0% of students in fraternities, 0% in sororities
Most popular majors: 34% Econometrics and Quantitative Economics, 12% Political Science and Government, General, 11% Experimental Psychology, 11% International Relations and Affairs, 7% Accounting
Expenses: 2019-2020: $56,475; room/board: $17,300
Financial aid: (909) 621-8356; 40% of undergrads determined to have financial need; average aid package $52,467

Cogswell Polytechnical College

San Jose CA
(408) 498-5160
U.S. News ranking: Reg. Coll. (W), unranked
Website: www. cogswell.edu
Admissions email: admissions@cogswell.edu
Private; founded 1887
Freshman admissions: selective; 2018-2019: 852 applied, 340 accepted. Neither SAT nor ACT required. SAT 25/75 percentile: 1070-1260. High school rank: N/A
Early decision deadline: N/A, notification date: N/A
Early action deadline: 12/1, notification date: 12/1
Application deadline (fall): rolling
Undergraduate student body: 411 full time, 184 part time; 70% male, 30% female; 1% American Indian, 21% Asian, 6% black, 22% Hispanic, 5% multiracial, 1% Pacific Islander, 33% white, 2% international; 92% from in state; 30% live on campus; N/A of students in fraternities, N/A in sororities
Most popular majors: 34% Animation, Interactive Technology, Video Graphics and Special Effects, 19% Modeling, Virtual Environments and Simulation, 17% Game and Interactive Media Design, 15% Music Technology, 4% Computer Programming/Programmer, General
Expenses: 2019-2020: $20,800; room/board: $11,990
Financial aid: (408) 498-5145; 45% of undergrads determined to have financial need

Columbia College Hollywood

Tarzana CA
(818) 345-8414
U.S. News ranking: Arts, unranked
Website: flashpoint.columbiacollege.edu/
Admissions email: admissions@columbiacollege.edu
Private; founded 1953
Freshman admissions: least selective; 2018-2019: 807 applied, 406 accepted. Neither SAT nor ACT required. SAT 25/75 percentile: N/A. High school rank: N/A
Early decision deadline: N/A, notification date: N/A
Early action deadline: N/A, notification date: N/A
Application deadline (fall): rolling
Undergraduate student body: 781 full time, 131 part time; 63% male, 38% female; N/A American Indian, N/A Asian, N/A black, N/A Hispanic, N/A multiracial, N/A Pacific Islander, N/A white, N/A international; N/A from in state; N/A live on campus; 0% of students in fraternities, 0% in sororities
Most popular majors: Cinematography and Film/Video Production, Digital Arts, Film/Cinema/Video Studies, Graphic Design
Expenses: 2019-2020: $24,495; room/board: N/A
Financial aid: (818) 345-8414

Concordia University

Irvine CA
(949) 214-3010
U.S. News ranking: Reg. U. (W), No. 34
Website: www.cui.edu
Admissions email: admission@cui.edu
Private; founded 1972
Affiliation: Lutheran Church–Missouri Synod
Freshman admissions: selective; 2018-2019: 3,995 applied, 2,468 accepted. Either SAT or ACT required. SAT 25/75 percentile: 1030-1220. High school rank: 20% in top tenth, 48% in top quarter, 84% in top half
Early decision deadline: N/A, notification date: N/A
Early action deadline: 12/1, notification date: 12/15
Application deadline (fall): 8/1
Undergraduate student body: 1,680 full time, 128 part time; 38% male, 62% female; 0% American Indian, 8% Asian, 5% black, 24% Hispanic, 8% multiracial, 0% Pacific Islander, 49% white, 5% international; 81% from in state; 47% live on campus; N/A of students in fraternities, N/A in sororities
Most popular majors: 21% Health Professions and Related Programs, 19% Business, Management, Marketing, and Related Support Services, 11% Psychology, 9% Parks, Recreation, Leisure, and Fitness Studies, 8% Liberal Arts and Sciences, General Studies and Humanities

Expenses: 2019-2020: $36,740; room/board: $11,870
Financial aid: (949) 214-3066; 69% of undergrads determined to have financial need; average aid package $23,750

Cypress College[1]
Cypress CA
(714) 484-7000
U.S. News ranking: Reg. Coll. (W), unranked
Website: www.cypresscollege.edu
Admissions email: N/A
Public
Application deadline (fall): N/A
Undergraduate student body: N/A full time, N/A part time
Expenses: N/A
Financial aid: N/A

Design Institute of San Diego
San Diego CA
(858) 566-1200
U.S. News ranking: Arts, unranked
Website: www.disd.edu
Admissions email: admissions@disd.edu
For-profit; founded 1977
Freshman admissions: least selective; 2018-2019: 40 applied, 23 accepted. Neither SAT nor ACT required. SAT 25/75 percentile: N/A. High school rank: N/A
Early decision deadline: N/A, notification date: N/A
Early action deadline: N/A, notification date: N/A
Application deadline (fall): N/A
Undergraduate student body: 59 full time, 39 part time; 10% male, 90% female; 2% American Indian, 6% Asian, 6% black, 18% Hispanic, 0% multiracial, 2% Pacific Islander, 58% white, 7% international
Most popular majors: 100% Interior Design
Expenses: 2019-2020: $23,999; room/board: $0
Financial aid: (858) 566-1200; 71% of undergrads determined to have financial need; average aid package $9,112

Dominican University of California
San Rafael CA
(888) 323-8763
U.S. News ranking: Reg. U. (W), No. 23
Website: www.dominican.edu
Admissions email: enroll@dominican.edu
Private; founded 1890
Freshman admissions: selective; 2018-2019: 1,909 applied, 1,664 accepted. Either SAT or ACT required. SAT 25/75 percentile: 1035-1210. High school rank: 22% in top tenth, 55% in top quarter, 82% in top half
Early decision deadline: N/A, notification date: N/A
Early action deadline: N/A, notification date: N/A
Application deadline (fall): rolling
Undergraduate student body: 1,135 full time, 220 part time; 27% male, 73% female; 1% American Indian, 28% Asian, 4% black, 24% Hispanic, 6% multiracial, 1% Pacific Islander, 30% white, 1% international; 92% from in state; 42% live on campus; N/A of students in fraternities, N/A in sororities
Most popular majors: 38% Health Professions and Related Programs, 16% Business, Management, Marketing, and Related Support Services, 12% Biological and Biomedical Sciences, 8% Psychology, 6% Visual and Performing Arts
Expenses: 2019-2020: $46,940; room/board: $15,315
Financial aid: (415) 257-1350; 80% of undergrads determined to have financial need; average aid package $32,669

Fashion Institute of Design & Merchandising
Los Angeles CA
(800) 624-1200
U.S. News ranking: Arts, unranked
Website: fidm.edu/
Admissions email: admissions@fidm.edu
Private; founded 1969
Freshman admissions: least selective; 2018-2019: 1,728 applied, 915 accepted. Neither SAT nor ACT required. SAT 25/75 percentile: N/A. High school rank: N/A
Early decision deadline: N/A, notification date: N/A
Early action deadline: N/A, notification date: N/A
Application deadline (fall): rolling
Undergraduate student body: 2,272 full time, 270 part time; 14% male, 86% female; N/A American Indian, N/A Asian, N/A black, N/A Hispanic, N/A multiracial, N/A Pacific Islander, N/A white, N/A international
Most popular majors: 92% Business, Management, Marketing, and Related Support Services, Other, 4% Fashion/Apparel Design, 3% Marketing/Marketing Management, General, 0% Apparel and Textile Marketing Management, 0% Drama and Dramatics/Theatre Arts, General
Expenses: 2019-2020: $31,050; room/board: N/A
Financial aid: (213) 624-1200

Feather River Community College District[1]
Quincy CA
(530) 283-0202
U.S. News ranking: Reg. Coll. (W), unranked
Website: www.frc.edu
Admissions email: N/A
Public
Application deadline (fall): N/A
Undergraduate student body: N/A full time, N/A part time
Expenses: N/A
Financial aid: N/A

Foothill College[1]
Los Altos Hills CA
(650) 949-7777
U.S. News ranking: Reg. Coll. (W), unranked
Website: www.foothill.edu
Admissions email: N/A
Public
Application deadline (fall): N/A
Undergraduate student body: N/A full time, N/A part time
Expenses: N/A
Financial aid: N/A

Fresno Pacific University
Fresno CA
(559) 453-2039
U.S. News ranking: Reg. U. (W), No. 31
Website: www.fresno.edu
Admissions email: ugadmis@fresno.edu
Private; founded 1944
Affiliation: Mennonite Brethren Church
Freshman admissions: selective; 2018-2019: 1,034 applied, 660 accepted. Either SAT or ACT required. SAT 25/75 percentile: 940-1130. High school rank: 24% in top tenth, 58% in top quarter, 87% in top half
Early decision deadline: N/A, notification date: N/A
Early action deadline: N/A, notification date: N/A
Application deadline (fall): 7/31
Undergraduate student body: 2,445 full time, 448 part time; 27% male, 73% female; 1% American Indian, 5% Asian, 5% black, 51% Hispanic, 0% multiracial, 0% Pacific Islander, 28% white, 2% international; N/A from in state; 16% live on campus; 0% of students in fraternities, 0% in sororities
Most popular majors: 25% Liberal Arts and Sciences, General Studies and Humanities, 23% Business, Management, Marketing, and Related Support Services, 11% Family and Consumer Sciences/Human Sciences, 7% Health Professions and Related Programs, 5% Psychology
Expenses: 2019-2020: $32,458; room/board: $8,954
Financial aid: (559) 453-7137; 87% of undergrads determined to have financial need; average aid package $20,626

Golden Gate University
San Francisco CA
(415) 442-7800
U.S. News ranking: Reg. U. (W), unranked
Website: www.ggu.edu/apply
Admissions email: maguilar@ggu.edu
Private; founded 1901
Affiliation: Other
Freshman admissions: least selective; 2018-2019: N/A applied, N/A accepted. Neither SAT nor ACT required. SAT 25/75 percentile: N/A. High school rank: N/A
Early decision deadline: N/A, notification date: N/A

Early action deadline: N/A,
notification date: N/A
Application deadline (fall): N/A
Undergraduate student body: 202 full time, 201 part time; 64% male, 36% female; 1% American Indian, 13% Asian, 10% black, 19% Hispanic, 4% multiracial, 2% Pacific Islander, 28% white, 1% international; 90% from in state; 0% live on campus; 0% of students in fraternities, 0% in sororities
Most popular majors: 93% Business Administration and Management, General, 5% Liberal Arts and Sciences/Liberal Studies, 1% International Business/Trade/Commerce, 1% Marketing/Marketing Management, General
Expenses: 2019-2020: $11,343; room/board: N/A
Financial aid: (415) 442-6632; 42% of undergrads determined to have financial need; average aid package $4,095

Harvey Mudd College
Claremont CA
(909) 621-8011
U.S. News ranking: Nat. Lib. Arts, No. 23
Website: www.hmc.edu
Admissions email: admission@hmc.edu
Private; founded 1955
Freshman admissions: most selective; 2018-2019: 4,101 applied, 594 accepted. Either SAT or ACT required. SAT 25/75 percentile: 1490-1560. High school rank: 87% in top tenth, 98% in top quarter, 100% in top half
Early decision deadline: N/A, notification date: N/A
Early action deadline: N/A, notification date: N/A
Application deadline (fall): 1/5
Undergraduate student body: 887 full time, 2 part time; 51% male, 49% female; 0% American Indian, 19% Asian, 3% black, 20% Hispanic, 11% multiracial, 0% Pacific Islander, 31% white, 9% international; 44% from in state; 98% live on campus; 0% of students in fraternities, 0% in sororities
Most popular majors: 33% Engineering, 23% Computer and Information Sciences and Support Services, 16% Physical Sciences, 13% Multi/Interdisciplinary Studies, 8% Biological and Biomedical Sciences
Expenses: 2019-2020: $58,660; room/board: $18,679
Financial aid: (909) 621-8055; 49% of undergrads determined to have financial need; average aid package $45,484

Holy Names University
Oakland CA
(510) 436-1351
U.S. News ranking: Reg. U. (W), No. 62
Website: www.hnu.edu
Admissions email: admissions@hnu.edu
Private; founded 1868
Affiliation: Roman Catholic

Freshman admissions: least
selective; 2018-2019: 2,076 applied, 1,454 accepted. Either SAT or ACT required. SAT 25/75 percentile: 713-870. High school rank: 5% in top tenth, 23% in top quarter, 52% in top half
Early decision deadline: N/A, notification date: N/A
Early action deadline: N/A, notification date: N/A
Application deadline (fall): rolling
Undergraduate student body: 591 full time, 38 part time; 35% male, 65% female; 0% American Indian, 10% Asian, 18% black, 43% Hispanic, 5% multiracial, 2% Pacific Islander, 16% white, 3% international; N/A from in state; 0% live on campus; 0% of students in fraternities, N/A in sororities
Most popular majors: Information not available
Expenses: 2019-2020: $40,102; room/board: $13,586
Financial aid: (510) 436-1348; 89% of undergrads determined to have financial need; average aid package $35,864

Hope International University
Fullerton CA
(888) 352-4673
U.S. News ranking: Reg. U. (W), second tier
Website: www.hiu.edu
Admissions email: admissions@hiu.edu
Private; founded 1928
Affiliation: Christian Churches and Churches of Christ
Freshman admissions: selective; 2018-2019: 584 applied, 172 accepted. Either SAT or ACT required. SAT 25/75 percentile: 930-1090. High school rank: 12% in top tenth, 28% in top quarter, 81% in top half
Early decision deadline: N/A, notification date: N/A
Early action deadline: N/A, notification date: N/A
Application deadline (fall): rolling
Undergraduate student body: 588 full time, 95 part time; 43% male, 57% female; 1% American Indian, 4% Asian, 8% black, 31% Hispanic, 12% multiracial, 1% Pacific Islander, 35% white, 2% international; 8% from in state; 41% live on campus; N/A of students in fraternities, N/A in sororities
Most popular majors: 21% Business Administration and Management, General, 18% Theological and Ministerial Studies, Other, 16% Social Sciences, General, 13% Psychology, General, 12% Human Development and Family Studies, General
Expenses: 2019-2020: $33,400; room/board: $10,680
Financial aid: (714) 879-3901; 76% of undergrads determined to have financial need; average aid package $19,869

Hult International Business School

Cambridge CA
(617) 746-1990
U.S. News ranking: Business, unranked
Website: www.hult.edu
Admissions email: undergraduate.info@hult.edu
Private; founded 1964
Freshman admissions: least selective; 2018-2019: 4,012 applied, 2,009 accepted. Neither SAT nor ACT required. Average composite ACT score: N/A. High school rank: N/A
Early decision deadline: 11/1, notification date: 12/15
Early action deadline: N/A, notification date: N/A
Application deadline (fall): rolling
Undergraduate student body: 1,487 full time, 0 part time; 64% male, 36% female; 0% American Indian, 0% Asian, 0% black, 1% Hispanic, 0% multiracial, 0% Pacific Islander, 1% white, 93% international
Most popular majors: Information not available
Expenses: 2019-2020: $42,500; room/board: $16,900
Financial aid: N/A; 66% of undergrads determined to have financial need; average aid package $12,979

Humboldt State University

Arcata CA
(707) 826-4402
U.S. News ranking: Reg. U. (W), No. 37
Website: www.humboldt.edu
Admissions email: hsuinfo@humboldt.edu
Public; founded 1913
Freshman admissions: selective; 2018-2019: 10,957 applied, 8,230 accepted. Either SAT or ACT required for some. SAT 25/75 percentile: 970-1180. High school rank: 5% in top tenth, 31% in top quarter, 71% in top half
Early decision deadline: N/A, notification date: N/A
Early action deadline: N/A, notification date: N/A
Application deadline (fall): 11/30
Undergraduate student body: 6,700 full time, 495 part time; 43% male, 57% female; 1% American Indian, 3% Asian, 4% black, 35% Hispanic, 7% multiracial, 0% Pacific Islander, 42% white, 1% international; 93% from in state; 28% live on campus; 1% of students in fraternities, 1% in sororities
Most popular majors: 9% Biology/Biological Sciences, General, 6% Business Administration and Management, General, 8% Psychology, General, 6% Health and Physical Education/Fitness, General, 6% Liberal Arts and Sciences/Liberal Studies
Expenses: 2019-2020: $7,780 in state, $19,660 out of state; room/board: $13,250
Financial aid: (707) 826-4321; 80% of undergrads determined to have financial need; average aid package $13,892

Humphreys College[1]

Stockton CA
(209) 478-0800
U.S. News ranking: Reg. Coll. (W), unranked
Website: www.humphreys.edu
Admissions email: ugadmission@humphreys.edu
Private
Application deadline (fall): N/A
Undergraduate student body: N/A full time, N/A part time
Expenses: N/A
Financial aid: N/A

John F. Kennedy University[1]

Pleasant Hill CA
(925) 969-3300
U.S. News ranking: Nat. U., unranked
Website: www.jfku.edu
Admissions email: proginfo@jfku.edu
Private; founded 1964
Application deadline (fall): N/A
Undergraduate student body: N/A full time, N/A part time
Expenses: N/A
Financial aid: N/A

John Paul the Great Catholic University

Escondido CA
(858) 653-6740
U.S. News ranking: Reg. Coll. (W), No. 16
Website: jpcatholic.edu/
Admissions email: N/A
Private; founded 2006
Affiliation: Roman Catholic
Freshman admissions: selective; 2018-2019: 220 applied, 199 accepted. Either SAT or ACT required. SAT 25/75 percentile: 960-1240. High school rank: 15% in top tenth, 27% in top quarter, 67% in top half
Early decision deadline: N/A, notification date: N/A
Early action deadline: N/A, notification date: N/A
Application deadline (fall): rolling
Undergraduate student body: 268 full time, 18 part time; 57% male, 43% female; 0% American Indian, 3% Asian, 2% black, 26% Hispanic, 4% multiracial, 1% Pacific Islander, 48% white, 3% international; 52% from in state; 77% live on campus; N/A of students in fraternities, N/A in sororities
Most popular majors: 86% Visual and Performing Arts, 14% Business, Management, Marketing, and Related Support Services
Expenses: 2019-2020: $27,000; room/board: $7,710
Financial aid: (858) 653-6740

Laguna College of Art and Design

Laguna Beach CA
(949) 376-6000
U.S. News ranking: Arts, unranked
Website: www.lcad.edu/
Admissions email: admissions@lcad.edu
Private; founded 1961
Freshman admissions: least selective; 2018-2019: N/A

applied, N/A accepted. Neither SAT nor ACT required. SAT 25/75 percentile: N/A. High school rank: N/A
Early decision deadline: N/A, notification date: N/A
Early action deadline: 2/1, notification date: N/A
Application deadline (fall): 8/1
Undergraduate student body: 204 full time, 0 part time; 29% male, 71% female; N/A American Indian, N/A Asian, N/A black, N/A Hispanic, N/A multiracial, N/A Pacific Islander, N/A white, N/A international
Most popular majors: Information not available
Expenses: 2018-2019: $30,700; room/board: $10,000
Financial aid: (949) 376-6000

La Sierra University

Riverside CA
(951) 785-2176
U.S. News ranking: Reg. U. (W), No. 53
Website: lasierra.edu/about/
Admissions email: Admissions@lasierra.edu
Private; founded 1922
Affiliation: Seventh Day Adventist
Freshman admissions: selective; 2018-2019: 4,698 applied, 2,309 accepted. Either SAT or ACT required. SAT 25/75 percentile: 940-1160. High school rank: 11% in top tenth, 38% in top quarter, 77% in top half
Early decision deadline: N/A, notification date: N/A
Early action deadline: N/A, notification date: N/A
Application deadline (fall): 7/15
Undergraduate student body: 1,645 full time, 191 part time; 40% male, 60% female; 0% American Indian, 16% Asian, 7% black, 48% Hispanic, 4% multiracial, 1% Pacific Islander, 12% white, 10% international; 89% from in state; 32% live on campus; 0% of students in fraternities, 0% in sororities
Most popular majors: 15% Criminal Justice/Safety Studies, 12% Kinesiology and Exercise Science, 9% Business Administration and Management, General, 8% Biomedical Sciences, General, 5% Liberal Arts and Sciences/Liberal Studies
Expenses: 2019-2020: $33,570; room/board: $8,625
Financial aid: (951) 785-2175; 78% of undergrads determined to have financial need; average aid package $23,244

Life Pacific College[1]

San Dimas CA
(909) 599-5433
U.S. News ranking: Reg. Coll. (W), unranked
Website: www.lifepacific.edu
Admissions email: adm@lifepacific.edu
Private
Application deadline (fall): N/A
Undergraduate student body: N/A full time, N/A part time
Expenses: N/A
Financial aid: N/A

Loyola Marymount University

Los Angeles CA
(310) 338-2750
U.S. News ranking: Nat. U., No. 64
Website: www.lmu.edu
Admissions email: admission@lmu.edu
Private; founded 1911
Affiliation: Roman Catholic
Freshman admissions: more selective; 2018-2019: 17,846 applied, 8,411 accepted. Either SAT or ACT required. SAT 25/75 percentile: 1210-1390. High school rank: 44% in top tenth, 73% in top quarter, 96% in top half
Early decision deadline: 11/1, notification date: 12/1
Early action deadline: 11/1, notification date: 12/20
Application deadline (fall): 1/15
Undergraduate student body: 6,466 full time, 234 part time; 45% male, 55% female; 0% American Indian, 10% Asian, 7% black, 22% Hispanic, 7% multiracial, 0% Pacific Islander, 44% white, 10% international; 68% from in state; 50% live on campus; 19% of students in fraternities, 25% in sororities
Most popular majors: 24% Business, Management, Marketing, and Related Support Services, 15% Visual and Performing Arts, 14% Social Sciences, 8% Communication, Journalism, and Related Programs, 7% Psychology
Expenses: 2019-2020: $50,283; room/board: $15,610
Financial aid: (310) 338-2753; 52% of undergrads determined to have financial need; average aid package $30,530

Marymount California University

Rancho Palos Verdes CA
(310) 303-7311
U.S. News ranking: Nat. Lib. Arts, second tier
Website: www.marymountcalifornia.edu
Admissions email: admissions@marymountcalifornia.edu
Private; founded 1933
Affiliation: Roman Catholic
Freshman admissions: less selective; 2018-2019: 1,621 applied, 1,378 accepted. Neither SAT nor ACT required. SAT 25/75 percentile: 935-1198. High school rank: N/A
Early decision deadline: N/A, notification date: N/A
Early action deadline: N/A, notification date: N/A
Application deadline (fall): rolling
Undergraduate student body: 721 full time, 14 part time; 51% male, 49% female; 0% American Indian, 5% Asian, 7% black, 40% Hispanic, 3% multiracial, 0% Pacific Islander, 22% white, 18% international; N/A from in state; 34% live on campus; N/A of students in fraternities, N/A in sororities

Most popular majors: 39% Business Administration, Management and Operations, 24% Psychology, General, 18% Liberal Arts and Sciences, General Studies and Humanities, 10% Criminal Justice and Corrections, 9% Visual and Performing Arts, General
Expenses: 2019-2020: $36,134; room/board: $14,666
Financial aid: (310) 303-7217; 79% of undergrads determined to have financial need; average aid package $32,169

The Master's University and Seminary

Santa Clarita CA
(800) 568-6248
U.S. News ranking: Reg. U. (W), No. 51
Website: www.masters.edu
Admissions email: admissions@masters.edu
Private; founded 1927
Affiliation: Other
Freshman admissions: selective; 2018-2019: 718 applied, 552 accepted. Either SAT or ACT required. SAT 25/75 percentile: 1010-1240. High school rank: 33% in top tenth, 51% in top quarter, 86% in top half
Early decision deadline: N/A, notification date: N/A
Early action deadline: 11/15, notification date: 12/22
Application deadline (fall): rolling
Undergraduate student body: 889 full time, 510 part time; 55% male, 45% female; 0% American Indian, 3% Asian, 2% black, 8% Hispanic, 8% multiracial, 0% Pacific Islander, 63% white, 2% international; 67% from in state; 78% live on campus; 0% of students in fraternities, 0% in sororities
Most popular majors: 19% Theology and Religious Vocations, 13% Liberal Arts and Sciences, General Studies and Humanities, 10% Business, Management, Marketing, and Related Support Services, 6% Biological and Biomedical Sciences, 6% Communication, Journalism, and Related Programs
Expenses: 2019-2020: $25,390; room/board: $11,200
Financial aid: (661) 362-2290; 68% of undergrads determined to have financial need; average aid package $25,336

Menlo College[1]

Atherton CA
(800) 556-3656
U.S. News ranking: Business, unranked
Website: www.menlo.edu
Admissions email: admissions@menlo.edu
Private; founded 1927
Application deadline (fall): 4/1
Undergraduate student body: N/A full time, N/A part time
Expenses: 2018-2019: $42,800; room/board: $14,225
Financial aid: N/A

Mills College
Oakland CA
(510) 430-2135
U.S. News ranking: Reg. U. (W), No. 5
Website: www.mills.edu
Admissions email: admission@mills.edu
Private; founded 1852
Freshman admissions: selective; 2018-2019: 1,003 applied, 858 accepted. Neither SAT nor ACT required. SAT 25/75 percentile: 1008-1240. High school rank: 32% in top tenth, 62% in top quarter, 85% in top half
Early decision deadline: N/A, notification date: N/A
Early action deadline: 11/15, notification date: 12/1
Application deadline (fall): rolling
Undergraduate student body: 730 full time, 42 part time; 0% male, 100% female; 1% American Indian, 9% Asian, 10% black, 30% Hispanic, 9% multiracial, 0% Pacific Islander, 37% white, 1% international; 80% from in state; 60% live on campus; 0% of students in fraternities, 0% in sororities
Most popular majors: 14% Psychology, General, 13% English Language and Literature, General, 8% Sociology, 7% Biology/Biological Sciences, General, 5% Economics, General
Expenses: 2019-2020: $30,877; room/board: $13,883
Financial aid: (510) 430-2039; 84% of undergrads determined to have financial need; average aid package $28,449

MiraCosta College[1]
Oceanside CA
(760) 757-2121
U.S. News ranking: Reg. Coll. (W), unranked
Website: www.miracosta.edu
Admissions email: N/A
Public
Application deadline (fall): N/A
Undergraduate student body: N/A full time, N/A part time
Expenses: N/A
Financial aid: N/A

Modesto Junior College[1]
Modesto CA
(209) 575-6550
U.S. News ranking: Reg. Coll. (W), unranked
Website: www.mjc.edu
Admissions email: N/A
Public
Application deadline (fall): N/A
Undergraduate student body: N/A full time, N/A part time
Expenses: N/A
Financial aid: N/A

Mount Saint Mary's University
Los Angeles CA
(310) 954-4250
U.S. News ranking: Reg. U. (W), No. 14
Website: www.msmu.edu
Admissions email: admissions@msmu.edu
Private; founded 1925

Affiliation: Roman Catholic
Freshman admissions: less selective; 2018-2019: 2,169 applied, 1,818 accepted. Either SAT or ACT required for some. SAT 25/75 percentile: 930-1130. High school rank: 13% in top tenth, 43% in top quarter, 79% in top half
Early decision deadline: N/A, notification date: N/A
Early action deadline: 12/1, notification date: 1/30
Application deadline (fall): 8/1
Undergraduate student body: 1,867 full time, 490 part time; 6% male, 94% female; 0% American Indian, 16% Asian, 6% black, 61% Hispanic, 2% multiracial, 1% Pacific Islander, 8% white, 0% international, N/A from in state; 25% live on campus; N/A of students in fraternities, 1% in sororities
Most popular majors: 38% Health Professions and Related Programs, 11% Business, Management, Marketing, and Related Support Services, 11% Psychology, 6% Public Administration and Social Service Professions, 5% Biological and Biomedical Sciences
Expenses: 2019-2020: $42,784; room/board: $12,455
Financial aid: (310) 954-4190; 91% of undergrads determined to have financial need; average aid package $39,155

National University
La Jolla CA
(844) 873-1037
U.S. News ranking: Reg. U. (W), unranked
Website: www.nu.edu/
Admissions email: advisor@nu.edu
Private; founded 1971
Freshman admissions: least selective; 2018-2019: N/A applied, N/A accepted. Neither SAT nor ACT required. SAT 25/75 percentile: N/A. High school rank: N/A
Early decision deadline: N/A, notification date: N/A
Early action deadline: N/A, notification date: N/A
Application deadline (fall): rolling
Undergraduate student body: 2,884 full time, 4,851 part time; 43% male, 57% female; 0% American Indian, 8% Asian, 10% black, 27% Hispanic, 6% multiracial, 1% Pacific Islander, 34% white, 1% international; 88% from in state; N/A live on campus; N/A of students in fraternities, N/A in sororities
Most popular majors: 17% Registered Nursing/Registered Nurse, 14% Business Administration and Management, General, 8% Early Childhood Education and Teaching, 8% Psychology, General, 5% Criminal Justice/Law Enforcement Administration
Expenses: 2019-2020: $13,320; room/board: $0
Financial aid: N/A; 70% of undergrads determined to have financial need; average aid package $6,508

NewSchool of Architecture and Design[1]
San Diego CA
(619) 684-8828
U.S. News ranking: Arts, unranked
Website: newschoolarch.edu/
Admissions email: fguidali@newschoolarch.edu
For-profit; founded 1980
Application deadline (fall): rolling
Undergraduate student body: N/A full time, N/A part time
Expenses: N/A
Financial aid: (619) 684-8803

Notre Dame de Namur University
Belmont CA
(650) 508-3600
U.S. News ranking: Reg. U. (W), No. 51
Website: www.ndnu.edu
Admissions email: admissions@ndnu.edu
Private; founded 1851
Affiliation: Roman Catholic
Freshman admissions: less selective; 2018-2019: 2,062 applied, 1,681 accepted. Either SAT or ACT required. SAT 25/75 percentile: 870-1060. High school rank: 8% in top tenth, 38% in top quarter, 64% in top half
Early decision deadline: N/A, notification date: N/A
Early action deadline: N/A, notification date: N/A
Application deadline (fall): rolling
Undergraduate student body: 669 full time, 202 part time; 34% male, 66% female; 0% American Indian, 11% Asian, 5% black, 45% Hispanic, 6% multiracial, 2% Pacific Islander, 20% white, 5% international; 90% from in state; 46% live on campus; 0% of students in fraternities, 0% in sororities
Most popular majors: 21% Business Administration and Management, General, 16% Biology/Biological Sciences, General, 14% Psychology, General, 11% Public Administration and Social Service Professions, 10% Sociology
Expenses: 2019-2020: $36,596; room/board: $14,766
Financial aid: (650) 508-3741; 79% of undergrads determined to have financial need; average aid package $28,073

Occidental College
Los Angeles CA
(323) 259-2700
U.S. News ranking: Nat. Lib. Arts, No. 39
Website: www.oxy.edu
Admissions email: admission@oxy.edu
Private; founded 1887
Freshman admissions: more selective; 2018-2019: 7,281 applied, 2,716 accepted. Either SAT or ACT required. SAT 25/75 percentile: 1270-1450. High school rank: 53% in top tenth, 85% in top quarter, 97% in top half
Early decision deadline: 11/15, notification date: 12/15

Early action deadline: N/A, notification date: N/A
Application deadline (fall): 1/15
Undergraduate student body: 2,013 full time, 23 part time; 42% male, 58% female; 0% American Indian, 15% Asian, 5% black, 14% Hispanic, 8% multiracial, 0% Pacific Islander, 50% white, 6% international; 48% from in state; 81% live on campus; 16% of students in fraternities, 22% in sororities
Most popular majors: 14% Economics, General, 11% International Relations and Affairs, 8% Biology/Biological Sciences, General, 6% Environmental Studies, 5% Biochemistry
Expenses: 2019-2020: $56,576; room/board: $16,034
Financial aid: (323) 259-2548; 58% of undergrads determined to have financial need; average aid package $51,263

Otis College of Art and Design
Los Angeles CA
(310) 665-6820
U.S. News ranking: Arts, unranked
Website: www.otis.edu
Admissions email: admissions@otis.edu
Private; founded 1918
Freshman admissions: less selective; 2018-2019: 1,806 applied, 1,705 accepted. Neither SAT nor ACT required. SAT 25/75 percentile: 1050-1270. High school rank: N/A
Early decision deadline: N/A, notification date: N/A
Early action deadline: N/A, notification date: N/A
Application deadline (fall): N/A
Undergraduate student body: 1,068 full time, 18 part time; 34% male, 66% female; 1% American Indian, 25% Asian, 4% black, 6% Hispanic, 5% multiracial, 0% Pacific Islander, 29% white, 23% international; 60% from in state; 27% live on campus; N/A of students in fraternities, N/A in sororities
Most popular majors: 33% Digital Arts, 16% Design and Visual Communications, General, 15% Fashion/Apparel Design, 11% Industrial and Product Design, 10% Fine/Studio Arts, General
Expenses: 2019-2020: $45,200; room/board: N/A
Financial aid: (310) 665-6999

Pacific Union College
Angwin CA
(707) 965-6336
U.S. News ranking: Reg. Coll. (W), No. 10
Website: www.puc.edu
Admissions email: admissions@puc.edu
Private; founded 1882
Affiliation: Seventh Day Adventist
Freshman admissions: selective; 2018-2019: 1,782 applied, 878 accepted. Either SAT or ACT required. SAT 25/75 percentile: 950-1190. High school rank: N/A
Early decision deadline: N/A, notification date: N/A

Early action deadline: 12/15, notification date: 11/15
Application deadline (fall): rolling
Undergraduate student body: 964 full time, 94 part time; 39% male, 61% female; 0% American Indian, 19% Asian, 7% black, 26% Hispanic, 9% multiracial, 1% Pacific Islander, 23% white, 3% international; 88% from in state; 72% live on campus; 0% of students in fraternities, 0% in sororities
Most popular majors: 37% Registered Nursing/Registered Nurse, 10% Business/Commerce, General, 8% Health and Wellness, General, 6% Biology/Biological Sciences, General, 4% Emergency Medical Technology/Technician (EMT Paramedic)
Expenses: 2019-2020: $30,813; room/board: $8,310
Financial aid: (707) 965-7200; 77% of undergrads determined to have financial need; average aid package $24,866

Pepperdine University
Malibu CA
(310) 506-4392
U.S. News ranking: Nat. U., No. 50
Website: www.pepperdine.edu
Admissions email: admission-seaver@pepperdine.edu
Private; founded 1937
Affiliation: Churches of Christ
Freshman admissions: more selective; 2018-2019: 11,265 applied, 4,016 accepted. Either SAT or ACT required. SAT 25/75 percentile: 1220-1420. High school rank: 57% in top tenth, 85% in top quarter, 96% in top half
Early decision deadline: N/A, notification date: N/A
Early action deadline: 11/1, notification date: 1/10
Application deadline (fall): 1/15
Undergraduate student body: 3,336 full time, 291 part time; 41% male, 59% female; 0% American Indian, 10% Asian, 5% black, 14% Hispanic, 6% multiracial, 0% Pacific Islander, 49% white, 13% international; 55% from in state; 57% live on campus; 17% of students in fraternities, 27% in sororities
Most popular majors: 28% Business, Management, Marketing, and Related Support Services, 22% Communication, Journalism, and Related Programs, 11% Social Sciences, 7% Parks, Recreation, Leisure, and Fitness Studies, 7% Psychology
Expenses: 2019-2020: $55,892; room/board: $15,670
Financial aid: (310) 506-4301; 52% of undergrads determined to have financial need; average aid package $41,842

Pitzer College
Claremont CA
(909) 621-8129
U.S. News ranking: Nat. Lib. Arts, No. 35
Website: www.pitzer.edu
Admissions email: admission@pitzer.edu
Private; founded 1963

Freshman admissions: more selective; 2018-2019: 4,358 applied, 581 accepted. Either SAT or ACT required for some. ACT 25/75 percentile: 30-33. High school rank: 62% in top tenth, 83% in top quarter, 98% in top half
Early decision deadline: 11/15, notification date: 12/18
Early action deadline: N/A, notification date: N/A
Application deadline (fall): 1/1
Undergraduate student body: 1,083 full time, 23 part time; 44% male, 56% female; 0% American Indian, 10% Asian, 6% black, 14% Hispanic, 7% multiracial, 0% Pacific Islander, 47% white, 10% international; 42% from in state; 73% live on campus; 0% of students in fraternities, 0% in sororities
Most popular majors: 22% Social Sciences, 14% Multi/Interdisciplinary Studies, 9% Natural Resources and Conservation, 8% Business, Management, Marketing, and Related Support Services, 6% Biological and Biomedical Sciences
Expenses: 2018-2019: $54,056; room/board: $16,844
Financial aid: (909) 621-8208

Point Loma Nazarene University
San Diego CA
(619) 849-2273
U.S. News ranking: Reg. U. (W), No. 10
Website: www.pointloma.edu
Admissions email: admissions@pointloma.edu
Private; founded 1902
Affiliation: Church of the Nazarene
Freshman admissions: more selective; 2018-2019: 3,473 applied, 2,394 accepted. Either SAT or ACT required. SAT 25/75 percentile: 1140-1300. High school rank: 39% in top tenth, 70% in top quarter, 91% in top half
Early decision deadline: N/A, notification date: N/A
Early action deadline: 11/15, notification date: 12/21
Application deadline (fall): 2/15
Undergraduate student body: 2,656 full time, 540 part time; 35% male, 65% female; 0% American Indian, 7% Asian, 2% black, 27% Hispanic, 8% multiracial, 1% Pacific Islander, 52% white, 1% international; N/A from in state; 56% live on campus; N/A of students in fraternities, N/A in sororities
Most popular majors: 31% Health Professions and Related Programs, 22% Business, Management, Marketing, and Related Support Services, 7% Psychology, 7% Social Sciences, 6% Family and Consumer Sciences/Human Sciences
Expenses: 2019-2020: $36,950; room/board: $10,650
Financial aid: (619) 849-2538; 66% of undergrads determined to have financial need; average aid package $24,518

Pomona College
Claremont CA
(909) 621-8134
U.S. News ranking: Nat. Lib. Arts, No. 5
Website: www.pomona.edu
Admissions email: admissions@pomona.edu
Private; founded 1887
Freshman admissions: most selective; 2018-2019: 10,245 applied, 780 accepted. Either SAT or ACT required. SAT 25/75 percentile: 1400-1540. High school rank: 91% in top tenth, 100% in top quarter, 100% in top half
Early decision deadline: 11/1, notification date: 12/15
Early action deadline: N/A, notification date: N/A
Application deadline (fall): 1/1
Undergraduate student body: 1,665 full time, 14 part time; 48% male, 52% female; 0% American Indian, 15% Asian, 10% black, 17% Hispanic, 7% multiracial, 0% Pacific Islander, 35% white, 11% international; N/A from in state; 98% live on campus; 5% of students in fraternities, 0% in sororities
Most popular majors: 20% Social Sciences, 12% Mathematics and Statistics, 10% Computer and Information Sciences and Support Services, 9% Multi/Interdisciplinary Studies, 9% Physical Sciences
Expenses: 2019-2020: $54,762; room/board: $17,218
Financial aid: (909) 621-8205; 55% of undergrads determined to have financial need; average aid package $57,450

Providence Christian College[1]
Pasadena CA
(866) 323-0233
U.S. News ranking: Nat. Lib. Arts, second tier
Website: www.providencecc.net/
Admissions email: N/A
Private; founded 2003
Application deadline (fall): rolling
Undergraduate student body: N/A full time, N/A part time
Expenses: N/A
Financial aid: N/A

Rio Hondo College[1]
Whittier CA
(562) 692-0921
U.S. News ranking: Reg. Coll. (W), unranked
Website: www.riohondo.edu
Admissions email: N/A
Public
Application deadline (fall): N/A
Undergraduate student body: N/A full time, N/A part time
Expenses: N/A
Financial aid: N/A

San Diego Christian College[1]
Santee CA
(800) 676-2242
U.S. News ranking: Reg. Coll. (W), No. 14
Website: www.sdcc.edu/
Admissions email: admissions@sdcc.edu
Private; founded 1970
Affiliation: Undenominational
Application deadline (fall): rolling
Undergraduate student body: N/A full time, N/A part time
Expenses: N/A
Financial aid: N/A

San Diego Mesa College[1]
San Diego CA
(619) 388-2604
U.S. News ranking: Reg. Coll. (W), unranked
Website: www.sdmesa.edu/
Admissions email: N/A
Public
Application deadline (fall): N/A
Undergraduate student body: N/A full time, N/A part time
Expenses: N/A
Financial aid: N/A

San Diego State University
San Diego CA
(619) 594-6336
U.S. News ranking: Nat. U., No. 147
Website: www.sdsu.edu
Admissions email: admissions@sdsu.edu
Public; founded 1897
Freshman admissions: more selective; 2018-2019: 69,043 applied, 23,766 accepted. Either SAT or ACT required. SAT 25/75 percentile: 1110-1310. High school rank: 29% in top tenth, 68% in top quarter, 93% in top half
Early decision deadline: N/A, notification date: N/A
Early action deadline: N/A, notification date: N/A
Application deadline (fall): 11/30
Undergraduate student body: 27,398 full time, 2,995 part time; 45% male, 55% female; 0% American Indian, 13% Asian, 4% black, 31% Hispanic, 7% multiracial, 0% Pacific Islander, 33% white, 7% international; 84% from in state; 19% live on campus; 11% of students in fraternities, 13% in sororities
Most popular majors: 19% Business Administration and Management, General, 7% Psychology, General, 5% Criminal Justice/Safety Studies, 5% Health and Physical Education/Fitness, General, 4% Biology/Biological Sciences, General
Expenses: 2019-2020: $7,510 in state, $19,390 out of state; room/board: $17,752
Financial aid: (619) 594-6323; 53% of undergrads determined to have financial need; average aid package $10,100

San Francisco Art Institute
San Francisco CA
(800) 345-7324
U.S. News ranking: Arts, unranked
Website: www.sfai.edu
Admissions email: admissions@sfai.edu
Private; founded 1871
Freshman admissions: selective; 2018-2019: 351 applied, 333 accepted. Neither SAT nor ACT required. SAT 25/75 percentile: 1020-1290. High school rank: N/A
Early decision deadline: N/A, notification date: N/A
Early action deadline: 11/15, notification date: 12/12
Application deadline (fall): rolling
Undergraduate student body: 267 full time, 8 part time; 40% male, 60% female; 1% American Indian, 6% Asian, 3% black, 18% Hispanic, 6% multiracial, 0% Pacific Islander, 38% white, 23% international; 61% from in state; 35% live on campus; 0% of students in fraternities, 0% in sororities
Most popular majors: 33% Photography, 25% Painting, 15% Cinematography and Film/Video Production, 9% Visual and Performing Arts, Other, 8% Printmaking
Expenses: 2019-2020: $46,614; room/board: $13,630
Financial aid: (415) 749-4520; 55% of undergrads determined to have financial need; average aid package $17,954

San Francisco Conservatory of Music[1]
San Francisco CA
(800) 899-7326
U.S. News ranking: Arts, unranked
Website: www.sfcm.edu
Admissions email: admit@sfcm.edu
Private; founded 1917
Affiliation: Other
Application deadline (fall): 12/1
Undergraduate student body: N/A full time, N/A part time
Expenses: 2018-2019: $46,110; room/board: $14,510
Financial aid: (415) 503-6214

San Francisco State University
San Francisco CA
(415) 338-6486
U.S. News ranking: Reg. U. (W), No. 31
Website: www.sfsu.edu
Admissions email: ugadmit@sfsu.edu
Public; founded 1899
Freshman admissions: selective; 2018-2019: 35,606 applied, 25,550 accepted. Either SAT or ACT required. SAT 25/75 percentile: 950-1160. High school rank: N/A
Early decision deadline: N/A, notification date: N/A
Early action deadline: N/A, notification date: N/A
Application deadline (fall): 11/30

Undergraduate student body: 22,159 full time, 4,339 part time; 44% male, 56% female; 0% American Indian, 26% Asian, 6% black, 34% Hispanic, 6% multiracial, 0% Pacific Islander, 17% white, 7% international; N/A from in state; 15% live on campus; N/A of students in fraternities, N/A in sororities
Most popular majors: 28% Business, Management, Marketing, and Related Support Services, 9% Communication, Journalism, and Related Programs, 8% Social Sciences, 7% Visual and Performing Arts, 6% Biological and Biomedical Sciences
Expenses: 2019-2020: $7,266 in state, $19,146 out of state; room/board: $14,384
Financial aid: (415) 338-7000; 72% of undergrads determined to have financial need; average aid package $14,770

San Joaquin Valley College–Visalia[1]
Visalia CA
(559) 734-9000
U.S. News ranking: Reg. Coll. (W), unranked
Website: www.sjvc.edu
Admissions email: N/A
For-profit
Application deadline (fall): N/A
Undergraduate student body: N/A full time, N/A part time
Expenses: N/A
Financial aid: N/A

San Jose State University
San Jose CA
(408) 283-7500
U.S. News ranking: Reg. U. (W), No. 24
Website: www.sjsu.edu/Admissions/
Admissions email: admissions@sjsu.edu
Public; founded 1857
Freshman admissions: selective; 2018-2019: 36,243 applied, 19,811 accepted. Either SAT or ACT required. SAT 25/75 percentile: 1040-1260. High school rank: N/A
Early decision deadline: N/A, notification date: N/A
Early action deadline: N/A, notification date: N/A
Application deadline (fall): 12/15
Undergraduate student body: 23,099 full time, 4,228 part time; 51% male, 49% female; 0% American Indian, 36% Asian, 3% black, 28% Hispanic, 5% multiracial, 0% Pacific Islander, 15% white, 8% international; 99% from in state; 14% live on campus; N/A of students in fraternities, N/A in sororities
Most popular majors: 26% Business, Management, Marketing, and Related Support Services, 13% Engineering, 8% Visual and Performing Arts, 7% Communication, Journalism, and Related Programs, 7% Psychology

Expenses: 2019-2020: $7,852 in state, $19,466 out of state; room/board: $16,946
Financial aid: (408) 924-6086; 66% of undergrads determined to have financial need; average aid package $18,757

Santa Ana College[1]
Santa Ana CA
(714) 564-6000
U.S. News ranking: Reg. Coll. (W), unranked
Website: www.sac.edu
Admissions email: N/A
Public
Application deadline (fall): N/A
Undergraduate student body: N/A full time, N/A part time
Expenses: N/A
Financial aid: N/A

Santa Clara University
Santa Clara CA
(408) 554-4700
U.S. News ranking: Nat. U., No. 54
Website: www.scu.edu
Admissions email: Admission@scu.edu
Private; founded 1851
Affiliation: Roman Catholic
Freshman admissions: more selective; 2018-2019: 16,242 applied, 8,107 accepted. Either SAT or ACT required. SAT 25/75 percentile: 1270-1440. High school rank: 49% in top tenth, 82% in top quarter, 97% in top half
Early decision deadline: 11/1, notification date: 12/31
Early action deadline: 11/1, notification date: 12/31
Application deadline (fall): 1/7
Undergraduate student body: 5,440 full time, 80 part time; 51% male, 49% female; 0% American Indian, 16% Asian, 3% black, 18% Hispanic, 7% multiracial, 0% Pacific Islander, 49% white, 4% international; 72% from in state; 56% live on campus; 0% of students in fraternities, 0% in sororities
Most popular majors: 23% Business, Management, Marketing, and Related Support Services, 16% Engineering, 13% Social Sciences, 9% Communication, Journalism, and Related Programs, 8% Psychology
Expenses: 2019-2020: $53,634; room/board: $15,507
Financial aid: (408) 551-1000; 45% of undergrads determined to have financial need; average aid package $37,858

Santa Monica College[1]
Santa Monica CA
(310) 434-4000
U.S. News ranking: Reg. Coll. (W), unranked
Website: www.smc.edu
Admissions email: N/A
Public
Application deadline (fall): N/A
Undergraduate student body: N/A full time, N/A part time
Expenses: N/A
Financial aid: N/A

Scripps College
Claremont CA
(909) 621-8149
U.S. News ranking: Nat. Lib. Arts, No. 33
Website: www.scrippscollege.edu/
Admissions email: admission@scrippscollege.edu
Private; founded 1926
Freshman admissions: more selective; 2018-2019: 3,160 applied, 766 accepted. Either SAT or ACT required. SAT 25/75 percentile: 1300-1480. High school rank: 69% in top tenth, 98% in top quarter, 100% in top half
Early decision deadline: 11/15, notification date: 12/15
Early action deadline: N/A, notification date: N/A
Application deadline (fall): 1/4
Undergraduate student body: 1,042 full time, 6 part time; 0% male, 100% female; 0% American Indian, 17% Asian, 4% black, 14% Hispanic, 5% multiracial, 0% Pacific Islander, 53% white, 5% international; N/A from in state; 94% live on campus; N/A of students in fraternities, N/A in sororities
Most popular majors: 20% Biological and Biomedical Sciences, 19% Social Sciences, 8% Psychology, 8% Visual and Performing Arts, 7% Area, Ethnic, Cultural, Gender, and Group Studies
Expenses: 2019-2020: $57,188; room/board: $17,600
Financial aid: (909) 621-8275; 38% of undergrads determined to have financial need; average aid package $43,980

Shasta College[1]
Redding CA
(530) 242-7500
U.S. News ranking: Reg. Coll. (W), unranked
Website: www.shastacollege.edu
Admissions email: N/A
Public
Application deadline (fall): N/A
Undergraduate student body: N/A full time, N/A part time
Expenses: N/A
Financial aid: N/A

Simpson University[1]
Redding CA
(530) 226-4606
U.S. News ranking: Reg. U. (W), No. 82
Website: www.simpsonu.edu
Admissions email: admissions@simpsonu.edu
Private; founded 1921
Affiliation: Christ and Missionary Alliance Church
Application deadline (fall): 8/1
Undergraduate student body: N/A full time, N/A part time
Expenses: N/A
Financial aid: (530) 226-4621

Skyline College[1]
San Bruno CA
(650) 738-4100
U.S. News ranking: Reg. Coll. (W), unranked
Website: skylinecollege.edu
Admissions email: N/A
Public
Application deadline (fall): N/A
Undergraduate student body: N/A full time, N/A part time
Expenses: N/A
Financial aid: N/A

Soka University of America
Aliso Viejo CA
(888) 600-7652
U.S. News ranking: Nat. Lib. Arts, No. 27
Website: www.soka.edu
Admissions email: admission@soka.edu
Private; founded 1987
Freshman admissions: more selective; 2018-2019: 464 applied, 180 accepted. Either SAT or ACT required. SAT 25/75 percentile: 1180-1410. High school rank: 33% in top tenth, 81% in top quarter, 100% in top half
Early decision deadline: N/A, notification date: N/A
Early action deadline: 11/1, notification date: 12/1
Application deadline (fall): 1/15
Undergraduate student body: 428 full time, 0 part time; 34% male, 66% female; 0% American Indian, 13% Asian, 4% black, 12% Hispanic, 6% multiracial, 0% Pacific Islander, 19% white, 44% international; 48% from in state; 99% live on campus; 0% of students in fraternities, 0% in sororities
Most popular majors: 100% Liberal Arts and Sciences/Liberal Studies
Expenses: 2019-2020: $34,086; room/board: $13,032
Financial aid: (949) 480-4000; 84% of undergrads determined to have financial need; average aid package $35,117

Solano Community College[1]
Fairfield CA
(707) 864 7000
U.S. News ranking: Reg. Coll. (W), unranked
Website: www.solano.edu
Admissions email: N/A
Public
Application deadline (fall): N/A
Undergraduate student body: N/A full time, N/A part time
Expenses: N/A
Financial aid: N/A

Sonoma State University
Rohnert Park CA
(707) 664-2778
U.S. News ranking: Reg. U. (W), No. 37
Website: www.sonoma.edu
Admissions email: student.outreach@sonoma.edu
Public; founded 1960

Freshman admissions: selective; 2018-2019: 14,129 applied, 13,036 accepted. Either SAT or ACT required. SAT 25/75 percentile: 980-1170. High school rank: N/A
Early decision deadline: N/A, notification date: N/A
Early action deadline: N/A, notification date: N/A
Application deadline (fall): 11/30
Undergraduate student body: 7,855 full time, 710 part time; 39% male, 61% female; 0% American Indian, 5% Asian, 2% black, 33% Hispanic, 6% multiracial, 0% Pacific Islander, 43% white, 3% international; N/A from in state; 32% live on campus; N/A of students in fraternities, N/A in sororities
Most popular majors: Information not available
Expenses: 2019-2020: $7,880 in state, $19,760 out of state; room/board: $15,210
Financial aid: (707) 664-2389; 63% of undergrads determined to have financial need; average aid package $10,713

Southern California Institute of Architecture[1]
Los Angeles CA
(213) 613-2200
U.S. News ranking: Arts, unranked
Website: www.sciarc.edu
Admissions email: admissions@sciarc.edu
Private
Application deadline (fall): N/A
Undergraduate student body: N/A full time, N/A part time
Expenses: N/A
Financial aid: N/A

Stanford University
Stanford CA
(650) 723-2091
U.S. News ranking: Nat. U., No. 6
Website: www.stanford.edu
Admissions email: admission@stanford.edu
Private; founded 1885
Freshman admissions: most selective; 2018-2019: 47,452 applied, 2,071 accepted. Either SAT or ACT required. SAT 25/75 percentile: 1420-1570. High school rank: 96% in top tenth, 100% in top quarter, 100% in top half
Early decision deadline: N/A, notification date: N/A
Early action deadline: 11/1, notification date: 12/15
Application deadline (fall): 1/2
Undergraduate student body: 7,086 full time, 1 part time; 50% male, 50% female; 1% American Indian, 22% Asian, 6% black, 16% Hispanic, 9% multiracial, 0% Pacific Islander, 34% white, 10% international; N/A from in state; 93% live on campus; 18% of students in fraternities, 24% in sororities
Most popular majors: 18% Computer and Information Sciences and Support Services, 18% Engineering, 15% Multi/Interdisciplinary Studies, 12% Social Sciences, 5% Physical Sciences

Expenses: 2019-2020: $53,529; room/board: $16,433
Financial aid: (650) 723-3058; 49% of undergrads determined to have financial need; average aid package $55,500

St. Mary's College of California
Moraga CA
(925) 631-4224
U.S. News ranking: Reg. U. (W), No. 5
Website: www.stmarys-ca.edu
Admissions email: smcadmit@stmarys-ca.edu
Private; founded 1863
Affiliation: Roman Catholic
Freshman admissions: selective; 2018-2019: 5,770 applied, 4,437 accepted. Either SAT or ACT required. SAT 25/75 percentile: 1060-1250. High school rank: N/A
Early decision deadline: N/A, notification date: N/A
Early action deadline: 11/15, notification date: 1/1
Application deadline (fall): 2/1
Undergraduate student body: 2,619 full time, 70 part time; 43% male, 57% female; 0% American Indian, 11% Asian, 4% black, 28% Hispanic, 7% multiracial, 1% Pacific Islander, 43% white, 3% international; 85% from in state; 60% live on campus; 0% of students in fraternities, 0% in sororities
Most popular majors: 30% Business, Management, Marketing, and Related Support Services, 11% Social Sciences, 10% Liberal Arts and Sciences, General Studies and Humanities, 8% Psychology, 7% Parks, Recreation, Leisure, and Fitness Studies
Expenses: 2019-2020: $49,188; room/board: $15,524
Financial aid: (925) 631-4370; 65% of undergrads determined to have financial need; average aid package $34,296

Thomas Aquinas College
Santa Paula CA
(800) 634-9797
U.S. News ranking: Nat. Lib. Arts, No. 35
Website: www.thomasaquinas.edu
Admissions email: admissions@thomasaquinas.edu
Private; founded 1971
Affiliation: Roman Catholic
Freshman admissions: more selective; 2018-2019: 211 applied, 164 accepted. Either SAT or ACT required. SAT 25/75 percentile: 1220-1400. High school rank: 20% in top tenth, 40% in top quarter, 90% in top half
Early decision deadline: N/A, notification date: N/A
Early action deadline: N/A, notification date: N/A
Application deadline (fall): rolling
Undergraduate student body: 407 full time, 0 part time; 49% male, 51% female; 0% American Indian, 3% Asian, 1% black, 14% Hispanic, 5% multiracial, 0% Pacific Islander, 74% white,

1% international; 36% from in state; 99% live on campus; 0% of students in fraternities, 0% in sororities
Most popular majors: Information not available
Expenses: 2019-2020: $25,600; room/board: $8,800
Financial aid: (805) 421-5936; 71% of undergrads determined to have financial need; average aid package $21,064

Trident University International[1]
Cypress CA
(800) 375-9878
U.S. News ranking: Nat. U., unranked
Website: www.trident.edu
Admissions email: N/A
For-profit
Application deadline (fall): N/A
Undergraduate student body: N/A full time, N/A part time
Expenses: N/A
Financial aid: N/A

United States University[1]
Chula Vista CA
U.S. News ranking: Reg. U. (W), unranked
Admissions email: N/A
For-profit
Application deadline (fall): N/A
Undergraduate student body: N/A full time, N/A part time
Expenses: N/A
Financial aid: N/A

University of Antelope Valley[1]
Lancaster CA
U.S. News ranking: Reg. Coll. (W), unranked
Website: www.uav.edu
Admissions email: N/A
Public
Application deadline (fall): N/A
Undergraduate student body: N/A full time, N/A part time
Expenses: N/A
Financial aid: N/A

University of California–Berkeley
Berkeley CA
(510) 642-3175
U.S. News ranking: Nat. U., No. 22
Website: www.berkeley.edu
Admissions email: N/A
Public; founded 1868
Freshman admissions: most selective; 2018-2019: 89,621 applied, 13,308 accepted. Either SAT or ACT required. SAT 25/75 percentile: 1300-1530. High school rank: 98% in top tenth, 100% in top quarter, 100% in top half
Early decision deadline: N/A, notification date: N/A
Early action deadline: N/A, notification date: N/A
Application deadline (fall): 11/30
Undergraduate student body: 29,337 full time, 1,272 part time; 47% male, 53% female; 0% American Indian, 35% Asian, 2% black, 15% Hispanic, 6% multiracial, 0% Pacific Islander,

25% white, 13% international; 84% from in state; 27% live on campus; 10% of students in fraternities, 10% in sororities
Most popular majors: 20% Social Sciences, 11% Engineering, 10% Biological and Biomedical Sciences, 7% Multi/Interdisciplinary Studies, 6% Natural Resources and Conservation
Expenses: 2019-2020: $14,184 in state, $43,176 out of state; room/board: $18,754
Financial aid: (510) 642-7117; 47% of undergrads determined to have financial need; average aid package $25,566

University of California–Davis
Davis CA
(530) 752-2971
U.S. News ranking: Nat. U., No. 39
Website: www.ucdavis.edu
Admissions email: undergraduateadmissions@ucdavis.edu
Public; founded 1905
Freshman admissions: more selective; 2018-2019: 76,647 applied, 31,564 accepted. Either SAT or ACT required. SAT 25/75 percentile: 1150-1410. High school rank: 100% in top tenth, 100% in top quarter, 100% in top half
Early decision deadline: N/A, notification date: N/A
Early action deadline: N/A, notification date: N/A
Application deadline (fall): 11/30
Undergraduate student body: 30,058 full time, 752 part time; 39% male, 61% female; 0% American Indian, 27% Asian, 2% black, 22% Hispanic, 5% multiracial, 0% Pacific Islander, 24% white, 17% international; N/A from in state; 25% live on campus; N/A of students in fraternities, N/A in sororities
Most popular majors: 17% Biological and Biomedical Sciences, 17% Social Sciences, 13% Psychology, 11% Engineering, 7% Agriculture, Agriculture Operations, and Related Sciences
Expenses: 2019-2020: $14,492 in state, $43,484 out of state; room/board: $15,863
Financial aid: (530) 752-2396; 59% of undergrads determined to have financial need; average aid package $22,044

University of California–Irvine
Irvine CA
(949) 824-6703
U.S. News ranking: Nat. U., No. 36
Website: www.uci.edu
Admissions email: admissions@uci.edu
Public; founded 1965
Freshman admissions: most selective; 2018-2019: 95,065 applied, 27,339 accepted. Either SAT or ACT required. SAT 25/75 percentile: 1180-1440. High school rank: 99% in top tenth, 100% in top quarter, 100% in top half

Early decision deadline: N/A, notification date: N/A
Early action deadline: N/A, notification date: N/A
Application deadline (fall): 11/30
Undergraduate student body: 29,250 full time, 486 part time; 49% male, 51% female; 0% American Indian, 36% Asian, 2% black, 26% Hispanic, 4% multiracial, 0% Pacific Islander, 13% white, 17% international; N/A from in state; 38% live on campus; 8% of students in fraternities, 9% in sororities
Most popular majors: 8% Social Psychology, 7% Biology/Biological Sciences, General, 7% Business/Managerial Economics, 7% Computer Science, 7% Public Health, Other
Expenses: 2019-2020: $13,727 in state, $43,481 out of state; room/board: $16,135
Financial aid: (949) 824-5337; 61% of undergrads determined to have financial need; average aid package $23,096

University of California–Los Angeles
Los Angeles CA
(310) 825-3101
U.S. News ranking: Nat. U., No. 20
Website: www.ucla.edu/
Admissions email: ugadm@saonet.ucla.edu
Public; founded 1919
Freshman admissions: most selective; 2018-2019: 113,761 applied, 15,970 accepted. Either SAT or ACT required. SAT 25/75 percentile: 1270-1520. High school rank: 97% in top tenth, 100% in top quarter, 100% in top half
Early decision deadline: N/A, notification date: N/A
Early action deadline: N/A, notification date: N/A
Application deadline (fall): 11/30
Undergraduate student body: 30,937 full time, 568 part time; 42% male, 58% female; 0% American Indian, 28% Asian, 3% black, 22% Hispanic, 6% multiracial, 0% Pacific Islander, 27% white, 12% international
Most popular majors: 27% Social Sciences, 15% Biological and Biomedical Sciences, 11% Psychology, 7% Engineering, 6% Mathematics and Statistics
Expenses: 2019-2020: $13,226 in state, $42,218 out of state; room/board: $15,902
Financial aid: (310) 206-0401; 52% of undergrads determined to have financial need; average aid package $23,990

University of California–Merced
Merced CA
(866) 270-7301
U.S. News ranking: Nat. U., No. 104
Website: www.ucmerced.edu
Admissions email: admissions@ucmerced.edu
Public; founded 2005

Freshman admissions: selective; 2018-2019: 25,123 applied, 16,623 accepted. Either SAT or ACT required. SAT 25/75 percentile: 1000-1190. High school rank: N/A
Early decision deadline: N/A, notification date: N/A
Early action deadline: N/A, notification date: N/A
Application deadline (fall): 11/30
Undergraduate student body: 7,813 full time, 68 part time; 48% male, 52% female; 0% American Indian, 19% Asian, 5% black, 55% Hispanic, 3% multiracial, 1% Pacific Islander, 10% white, 7% international; 99% from in state; 44% live on campus; N/A of students in fraternities, N/A in sororities
Most popular majors: 24% Biological and Biomedical Sciences, 20% Engineering, 16% Psychology, 13% Business, Management, Marketing, and Related Support Services, 10% Social Sciences
Expenses: 2019-2020: $13,538 in state, $42,530 out of state; room/board: $17,046
Financial aid: (209) 228-7178; 90% of undergrads determined to have financial need; average aid package $25,491

University of California–Riverside
Riverside CA
(951) 827-3411
U.S. News ranking: Nat. U., No. 91
Website: www.ucr.edu
Admissions email: admissions@ucr.edu
Public; founded 1954
Freshman admissions: more selective; 2018-2019: 49,082 applied, 25,259 accepted. Either SAT or ACT required. SAT 25/75 percentile: 1110-1330. High school rank: 94% in top tenth, 100% in top quarter, 100% in top half
Early decision deadline: N/A, notification date: N/A
Early action deadline: N/A, notification date: N/A
Application deadline (fall): 11/30
Undergraduate student body: 19,966 full time, 366 part time; 45% male, 55% female; 0% American Indian, 34% Asian, 3% black, 42% Hispanic, 6% multiracial, 0% Pacific Islander, 11% white, 3% international; 99% from in state; 30% live on campus; 4% of students in fraternities, 7% in sororities
Most popular majors: 20% Social Sciences, 16% Biological and Biomedical Sciences, 16% Business, Management, Marketing, and Related Support Services, 10% Engineering, 10% Psychology
Expenses: 2019-2020: $13,827 in state, $42,819 out of state; room/board: $16,485
Financial aid: (951) 827-7249; 78% of undergrads determined to have financial need; average aid package $22,268

University of California–San Diego
La Jolla CA
(858) 534-4831
U.S. News ranking: Nat. U., No. 37
Website: www.ucsd.edu/
Admissions email: admissionsinfo@ucsd.edu
Public; founded 1960
Freshman admissions: most selective; 2018-2019: 97,901 applied, 29,602 accepted. Either SAT or ACT required. SAT 25/75 percentile: 1250-1470. High school rank: 100% in top tenth, 100% in top quarter, 100% in top half
Early decision deadline: N/A, notification date: N/A
Early action deadline: N/A, notification date: N/A
Application deadline (fall): 11/30
Undergraduate student body: 29,674 full time, 491 part time; 50% male, 50% female; 0% American Indian, 37% Asian, 3% black, 19% Hispanic, 0% multiracial, 0% Pacific Islander, 19% white, 19% international; 76% from in state; 38% live on campus; 10% of students in fraternities, 10% in sororities
Most popular majors: 21% Biology, General, 11% Economics, 8% Computer Engineering, 8% Mathematics, 5% Psychology, General
Expenses: 2019-2020: $14,170 in state, $43,162 out of state; room/board: $14,286
Financial aid: (858) 534-3800; 56% of undergrads determined to have financial need; average aid package $23,550

University of California–Santa Barbara
Santa Barbara CA
(805) 893-2881
U.S. News ranking: Nat. U., No. 34
Website: www.ucsb.edu/
Admissions email: admissions@sa.ucsb.edu
Public; founded 1909
Freshman admissions: most selective; 2018-2019: 92,314 applied, 29,725 accepted. Either SAT or ACT required. SAT 25/75 percentile: 1230-1480. High school rank: 100% in top tenth, 100% in top quarter, 100% in top half
Early decision deadline: N/A, notification date: N/A
Early action deadline: N/A, notification date: N/A
Application deadline (fall): 11/30
Undergraduate student body: 22,553 full time, 468 part time; 45% male, 55% female; 0% American Indian, 20% Asian, 2% black, 27% Hispanic, 6% multiracial, 0% Pacific Islander, 32% white, 12% international; 86% from in state; 38% live on campus; 9% of students in fraternities, 14% in sororities
Most popular majors: 26% Social Sciences, 10% Biological and Biomedical Sciences, 10% Multi/Interdisciplinary Studies, 8% Mathematics and Statistics, 8% Psychology

Expenses: 2019-2020: $14,391 in state, $43,383 out of state; room/board: $15,520
Financial aid: (805) 893-2432; 57% of undergrads determined to have financial need; average aid package $23,998

University of California–Santa Cruz

Santa Cruz CA
(831) 459-4008
U.S. News ranking: Nat. U., No. 84
Website: www.ucsc.edu
Admissions email: admissions@ucsc.edu
Public; founded 1965
Freshman admissions: more selective, 2018-2019: 56,634 applied, 27,014 accepted. Either SAT or ACT required. SAT 25/75 percentile: 1170-1400. High school rank: 96% in top tenth, 100% in top quarter, 100% in top half
Early decision deadline: N/A, notification date: N/A
Early action deadline: N/A, notification date: N/A
Application deadline (fall): 11/30
Undergraduate student body: 17,255 full time, 537 part time; 52% male, 48% female; 0% American Indian, 22% Asian, 2% black, 28% Hispanic, 8% multiracial, 0% Pacific Islander, 30% white, 8% international; 4% from in state; 51% live on campus; 7% of students in fraternities, 8% in sororities
Most popular majors: 10% Psychology, General, 8% Computer and Information Sciences, General, 6% Business/Managerial Economics, 5% Cell/Cellular and Molecular Biology, 5% Sociology
Expenses: 2019-2020: $14,054 in state, $43,046 out of state; room/board: $16,916
Financial aid: (831) 459-2963; 60% of undergrads determined to have financial need; average aid package $25,395

University of La Verne

La Verne CA
(800) 876-4858
U.S. News ranking: Nat. U., No. 132
Website: www.laverne.edu
Admissions email: admission@laverne.edu
Private; founded 1891
Freshman admissions: selective; 2018-2019: 7,276 applied, 3,703 accepted. Either SAT or ACT required. SAT 25/75 percentile: 1020-1205. High school rank: 20% in top tenth, 48% in top quarter, 84% in top half
Early decision deadline: N/A, notification date: N/A
Early action deadline: N/A, notification date: N/A
Application deadline (fall): rolling
Undergraduate student body: 2,721 full time, 77 part time, 42% male, 58% female; 0% American Indian, 5% Asian, 5% black, 57% Hispanic, 5% multiracial, 0% Pacific Islander, 18% white, 7% international; 89% from in state; 32% live on campus; 3% of students in fraternities, 6% in sororities
Most popular majors: 24% Business, Management, Marketing, and Related Support Services, 12% Education, 12% Social Sciences, 10% Psychology, 8% Biological and Biomedical Sciences
Expenses: 2019-2020: $44,500; room/board: $13,190
Financial aid: (800) 649-0160; 83% of undergrads determined to have financial need; average aid package $29,047

University of Redlands[1]

Redlands CA
(800) 455-5064
U.S. News ranking: Reg. U. (W), No. 16
Website: www.redlands.edu
Admissions email: admissions@redlands.edu
Private; founded 1907
Application deadline (fall): 1/15
Undergraduate student body: N/A full time, N/A part time
Expenses: N/A
Financial aid: (909) 748-8266

University of San Diego

San Diego CA
(619) 260-4506
U.S. News ranking: Nat. U., No. 91
Website: www.SanDiego.edu
Admissions email: admissions@SanDiego.edu
Private; founded 1949
Affiliation: Roman Catholic
Freshman admissions: more selective; 2018-2019: 13,287 applied, 7,031 accepted. Either SAT or ACT required. SAT 25/75 percentile: 1190-1360. High school rank: 33% in top tenth, 69% in top quarter, 97% in top half
Early decision deadline: N/A, notification date: N/A
Early action deadline: N/A, notification date: N/A
Application deadline (fall): 12/15
Undergraduate student body: 5,678 full time, 177 part time; 45% male, 55% female; 0% American Indian, 7% Asian, 4% black, 20% Hispanic, 6% multiracial, 0% Pacific Islander, 50% white, 9% international; 44% from in state; 46% live on campus; 18% of students in fraternities, 29% in sororities
Most popular majors: 42% Business, Management, Marketing, and Related Support Services, 13% Biological and Biomedical Sciences, 9% Engineering, 8% Social Sciences, 7% Communication, Journalism, and Related Programs
Expenses: 2019-2020: $51,186; room/board: $14,126
Financial aid: (619) 260-2700; 52% of undergrads determined to have financial need; average aid package $38,359

University of San Francisco

San Francisco CA
(415) 422-6563
U.S. News ranking: Nat. U., No. 97
Website: www.usfca.edu
Admissions email: admission@usfca.edu
Private; founded 1855
Affiliation: Roman Catholic
Freshman admissions: more selective; 2018-2019: 18,411 applied, 11,885 accepted. Neither SAT nor ACT required. SAT 25/75 percentile: 1130-1330. High school rank: 38% in top tenth, 73% in top quarter, 95% in top half
Early decision deadline: 11/1, notification date: 12/1
Early action deadline: 11/1, notification date: 12/14
Application deadline (fall): 1/15
Undergraduate student body: 6,435 full time, 269 part time; 37% male, 63% female; 0% American Indian, 24% Asian, 4% black, 21% Hispanic, 8% multiracial, 1% Pacific Islander, 25% white, 14% international; 69% from in state; 36% live on campus; 4% of students in fraternities, 9% in sororities
Most popular majors: 10% Finance, General, 10% Registered Nursing/Registered Nurse, 9% Psychology, General, 7% Business Administration and Management, General, 6% Marketing/Marketing Management, General
Expenses: 2019-2020: $50,282; room/board: $15,410
Financial aid: (415) 422-3387; 60% of undergrads determined to have financial need; average aid package $35,749

University of Southern California

Los Angeles CA
(213) 740-1111
U.S. News ranking: Nat. U., No. 22
Website: www.usc.edu/
Admissions email: admitusc@usc.edu
Private; founded 1880
Freshman admissions: most selective; 2018-2019: 64,352 applied, 8,339 accepted. Either SAT or ACT required. SAT 25/75 percentile: 1350-1530. High school rank: 90% in top tenth, 97% in top quarter, 100% in top half
Early decision deadline: N/A, notification date: N/A
Early action deadline: N/A, notification date: N/A
Application deadline (fall): 1/15
Undergraduate student body: 19,194 full time, 713 part time; 49% male, 51% female; 0% American Indian, 21% Asian, 5% black, 15% Hispanic, 6% multiracial, 0% Pacific Islander, 39% white, 13% international; 61% from in state; 30% live on campus; 26% of students in fraternities, 27% in sororities
Most popular majors: 24% Business, Management, Marketing, and Related Support Services, 12% Social Sciences, 12% Visual and Performing Arts, 10% Engineering, 9% Communication, Journalism, and Related Programs
Expenses: 2019-2020: $58,195; room/board: $15,912
Financial aid: (213) 740-4444; 38% of undergrads determined to have financial need; average aid package $53,683

University of the Pacific

Stockton CA
(209) 946-2011
U.S. News ranking: Nat. U., No. 125
Website: www.pacific.edu
Admissions email: admissions@pacific.edu
Private; founded 1851
Freshman admissions: more selective; 2018-2019: 13,545 applied, 8,598 accepted. Either SAT or ACT required. SAT 25/75 percentile: 1120-1350. High school rank: 33% in top tenth, 67% in top quarter, 91% in top half
Early decision deadline: N/A, notification date: N/A
Early action deadline: 11/15, notification date: 1/15
Application deadline (fall): 1/15
Undergraduate student body: 3,584 full time, 117 part time; 48% male, 52% female; 0% American Indian, 37% Asian, 3% black, 21% Hispanic, 6% multiracial, 0% Pacific Islander, 22% white, 6% international; N/A from in state; 47% live on campus; 4% of students in fraternities, 5% in sororities
Most popular majors: 20% Business, Management, Marketing, and Related Support Services, 12% Biological and Biomedical Sciences, 8% Engineering, 8% Multi/Interdisciplinary Studies, 6% Parks, Recreation, Leisure, and Fitness Studies
Expenses: 2019-2020: $49,588; room/board: $13,740
Financial aid: (209) 946-2421; 72% of undergrads determined to have financial need; average aid package $36,515

University of the West[1]

Rosemead CA
(855) 468-9378
U.S. News ranking: Nat. Lib. Arts, second tier
Website: www.uwest.edu
Admissions email: admission@uwest.edu
Private; founded 1991
Application deadline (fall): 5/1
Undergraduate student body: N/A full time, N/A part time
Expenses: N/A
Financial aid: (626) 571-8811

Vanguard University of Southern California

Costa Mesa CA
(800) 722-6279
U.S. News ranking: Reg. U. (W), No. 43
Website: www.vanguard.edu
Admissions email: admissions@vanguard.edu
Private; founded 1920
Affiliation: Assemblies of God Church
Freshman admissions: selective; 2018-2019: 4,414 applied, 1,773 accepted. Either SAT or ACT required. SAT 25/75 percentile: 950-1120. High school rank: 13% in top tenth, 41% in top quarter, 78% in top half
Early decision deadline: N/A, notification date: N/A
Early action deadline: 12/1, notification date: 1/15
Application deadline (fall): 8/1
Undergraduate student body: 1,588 full time, 260 part time; 33% male, 67% female; 0% American Indian, 4% Asian, 5% black, 42% Hispanic, 3% multiracial, 1% Pacific Islander, 38% white, 2% international; 90% from in state; 50% live on campus; 0% of students in fraternities, 0% in sororities
Most popular majors: 19% Psychology, General, 17% Business Administration and Management, General, 9% Kinesiology and Exercise Science, 9% Nursing Administration, 9% Religion/Religious Studies
Expenses: 2019-2020: $35,100, room/board: $9,430
Financial aid: (714) 966-5490; 89% of undergrads determined to have financial need; average aid package $15,671

West Los Angeles College[1]

Culver City CA
(310) 287-4501
U.S. News ranking: Reg. Coll. (W), unranked
Website: www.wlac.edu
Admissions email: N/A
Public; founded 1969
Application deadline (fall): N/A
Undergraduate student body: N/A full time, N/A part time
Expenses: N/A
Financial aid: N/A

Westmont College

Santa Barbara CA
(805) 565-6000
U.S. News ranking: Nat. Lib. Arts, No. 117
Website: www.westmont.edu
Admissions email: admissions@westmont.edu
Private; founded 1937
Affiliation: Undenominational
Freshman admissions: more selective; 2018-2019: 2,937 applied, 1,833 accepted. Either SAT or ACT required. SAT 25/75 percentile: 1110-1370. High school rank: 28% in top tenth, 63% in top quarter, 89% in top half

Early decision deadline: N/A, notification date: N/A
Early action deadline: 11/1, notification date: 1/1
Application deadline (fall): rolling
Undergraduate student body: 1,266 full time, 11 part time; 39% male, 61% female; 0% American Indian, 8% Asian, 2% black, 18% Hispanic, 6% multiracial, 1% Pacific Islander, 58% white, 2% international; 70% from in state; 94% live on campus; 0% of students in fraternities, 0% in sororities
Most popular majors: 15% Business, Management, Marketing, and Related Support Services, 13% Parks, Recreation, Leisure, and Fitness Studies, 9% Biological and Biomedical Sciences, 9% Communication, Journalism, and Related Programs, 8% English Language and Literature/Letters
Expenses: 2019-2020: $46,594; room/board: $14,646
Financial aid: (805) 565-6063; 69% of undergrads determined to have financial need; average aid package $36,098

Whittier College
Whittier CA
(562) 907-4238
U.S. News ranking: Nat. Lib. Arts, No. 105
Website: www.whittier.edu
Admissions email: admission@whittier.edu
Private; founded 1887
Freshman admissions: selective; 2018-2019: 6,220 applied, 4,724 accepted. Either SAT or ACT required for some. SAT 25/75 percentile: 1030-1213. High school rank: 18% in top tenth, 34% in top quarter, 93% in top half
Early decision deadline: N/A, notification date: N/A
Early action deadline: 11/15, notification date: 12/30
Application deadline (fall): rolling
Undergraduate student body: 1,699 full time, 33 part time; 42% male, 58% female; 0% American Indian, 7% Asian, 5% black, 51% Hispanic, 7% multiracial, 0% Pacific Islander, 26% white, 3% international
Most popular majors: 17% Social Sciences, 16% Business, Management, Marketing, and Related Support Services, 13% Parks, Recreation, Leisure, and Fitness Studies, 10% Biological and Biomedical Sciences, 10% Psychology
Expenses: 2019-2020: $49,314; room/board: $14,154
Financial aid: (562) 907-4285; 77% of undergrads determined to have financial need; average aid package $38,799

William Jessup University
Rocklin CA
(916) 577-2222
U.S. News ranking: Reg. Coll. (W), No. 2
Website: www.jessup.edu
Admissions email: admissions@jessup.edu

Private; founded 1939
Affiliation: Protestant, not specified
Freshman admissions: selective; 2018-2019: 933 applied, 551 accepted. Either SAT or ACT required. SAT 25/75 percentile: 960-1173. High school rank: 26% in top tenth, 48% in top quarter, 76% in top half
Early decision deadline: N/A, notification date: N/A
Early action deadline: N/A, notification date: N/A
Application deadline (fall): rolling
Undergraduate student body: 1,030 full time, 227 part time; 40% male, 60% female; 2% American Indian, 4% Asian, 5% black, 20% Hispanic, 1% multiracial, 1% Pacific Islander, 52% white, 4% international; 89% from in state; 55% live on campus; N/A of students in fraternities, N/A in sororities
Most popular majors: 26% Business, Management, Marketing, and Related Support Services, 26% Psychology, 12% Theology and Religious Vocations, 9% Education, 5% Parks, Recreation, Leisure, and Fitness Studies
Expenses: 2019-2020: $34,950; room/board: $11,700
Financial aid: (916) 577-2232; 79% of undergrads determined to have financial need; average aid package $24,939

Woodbury University
Burbank CA
(818) 252-5221
U.S. News ranking: Reg. U. (W), No. 53
Website: woodbury.edu/
Admissions email: info@woodbury.edu
Private; founded 1884
Freshman admissions: less selective; 2018-2019: 2,120 applied, 1,392 accepted. Neither SAT nor ACT required. SAT 25/75 percentile: 946-1130. High school rank: N/A
Early decision deadline: N/A, notification date: N/A
Early action deadline: N/A, notification date: N/A
Application deadline (fall): rolling
Undergraduate student body: 993 full time, 66 part time; 49% male, 51% female; 0% American Indian, 9% Asian, 3% black, 35% Hispanic, 3% multiracial, 0% Pacific Islander, 34% white, 15% international; N/A from in state; 21% live on campus; N/A of students in fraternities, N/A in sororities
Most popular majors: Information not available
Expenses: 2019-2020: $41,182; room/board: $12,068
Financial aid: (818) 252-5273; 72% of undergrads determined to have financial need; average aid package $32,188

COLORADO

Adams State University[1]
Alamosa CO
(800) 824-6494
U.S. News ranking: Reg. U. (W), second tier
Website: www.adams.edu
Admissions email: ascadmit@adams.edu
Public
Application deadline (fall): N/A
Undergraduate student body: N/A full time, N/A part time
Expenses: N/A
Financial aid: N/A

Art Institute of Colorado[1]
Denver CO
(303) 837-0825
U.S. News ranking: Arts, unranked
Website: www.artinstitutes.edu/denver/
Admissions email: N/A
For-profit
Application deadline (fall): N/A
Undergraduate student body: N/A full time, N/A part time
Expenses: N/A
Financial aid: N/A

Colorado Christian University[1]
Lakewood CO
(303) 963-3200
U.S. News ranking: Reg. U. (W), second tier
Website: www.ccu.edu
Admissions email: admission@ccu.edu
Private
Application deadline (fall): N/A
Undergraduate student body: N/A full time, N/A part time
Expenses: N/A
Financial aid: N/A

Colorado College
Colorado Springs CO
(719) 389-6344
U.S. News ranking: Nat. Lib. Arts, No. 27
Website: www.ColoradoCollege.edu
Admissions email: admission@ColoradoCollege.edu
Private; founded 1874
Freshman admissions: most selective; 2018-2019: 8,552 applied, 1,283 accepted. Either SAT or ACT required for some. ACT 25/75 percentile: 29-33. High school rank: 75% in top tenth, 97% in top quarter, 99% in top half
Early decision deadline: 11/10, notification date: 12/20
Early action deadline: 11/10, notification date: 12/20
Application deadline (fall): 1/15
Undergraduate student body: 2,098 full time, 16 part time; 45% male, 55% female; 1% American Indian, 5% Asian, 2% black, 9% Hispanic, 8% multiracial, 0% Pacific Islander, 66% white, 9% international; 17% from in state; 80% live on campus; N/A of students in fraternities, N/A in sororities

Most popular majors: 10% Economics, General, 7% Political Science and Government, General, 6% Ecology and Evolutionary Biology, 6% Sociology, 5% Environmental Science
Expenses: 2019-2020: $58,086; room/board: $12,956
Financial aid: (719) 389-6651; 34% of undergrads determined to have financial need; average aid package $51,054

Colorado Mesa University
Grand Junction CO
(970) 248-1875
U.S. News ranking: Reg. U. (W), second tier
Website: www.coloradomesa.edu/
Admissions email: admissions@coloradomesa.edu
Public; founded 1925
Freshman admissions: selective; 2018-2019: 7,087 applied, 5,726 accepted. Either SAT or ACT required. SAT 25/75 percentile: 940-1160. High school rank: 11% in top tenth, 29% in top quarter, 60% in top half
Early decision deadline: N/A, notification date: N/A
Early action deadline: N/A, notification date: N/A
Application deadline (fall): rolling
Undergraduate student body: 7,079 full time, 2,286 part time; 46% male, 54% female; 1% American Indian, 2% Asian, 2% black, 19% Hispanic, 4% multiracial, 0% Pacific Islander, 68% white, 1% international; N/A from in state; 25% live on campus; 3% of students in fraternities, 3% in sororities
Most popular majors: 16% Business/Commerce, General, 16% Registered Nursing/Registered Nurse, 9% Kinesiology and Exercise Science, 5% Biology/Biological Sciences, General, 5% Criminal Justice/Safety Studies
Expenses: 2019-2020: $9,306 in state, $23,163 out of state; room/board: $11,168
Financial aid: (970) 248-1396; 64% of undergrads determined to have financial need; average aid package $9,757

Colorado Mountain College
Glenwood Springs CO
(970) 945-8691
U.S. News ranking: Reg. Coll. (W), unranked
Admissions email: joinus@coloradomtn.edu
Public; founded 1967
Freshman admissions: least selective; 2018-2019: N/A applied, N/A accepted. Neither SAT nor ACT required. SAT 25/75 percentile: N/A. High school rank: N/A
Early decision deadline: N/A, notification date: N/A
Early action deadline: N/A, notification date: N/A
Application deadline (fall): rolling
Undergraduate student body: 1,644 full time, 3,530 part time; 42% male, 58% female; 0% American

Indian, 1% Asian, 1% black, 27% Hispanic, 4% multiracial, 0% Pacific Islander, 62% white, 0% international; N/A from in state; 13% live on campus; N/A of students in fraternities, N/A in sororities
Most popular majors: Information not available
Expenses: 2019-2020: $4,620 in state, $11,172 out of state; room/board: $9,658
Financial aid: N/A

Colorado School of Mines
Golden CO
(303) 273-3220
U.S. News ranking: Nat. U., No. 84
Website: www.mines.edu
Admissions email: admissions@mines.edu
Public; founded 1874
Freshman admissions: more selective; 2018-2019: 12,661 applied, 6,228 accepted. Either SAT or ACT required. SAT 25/75 percentile: 1290-1450. High school rank: 59% in top tenth, 85% in top quarter, 100% in top half
Early decision deadline: N/A, notification date: N/A
Early action deadline: N/A, notification date: N/A
Application deadline (fall): 5/1
Undergraduate student body: 4,707 full time, 247 part time; 70% male, 30% female; 0% American Indian, 4% Asian, 1% black, 9% Hispanic, 6% multiracial, 0% Pacific Islander, 72% white, 5% international; 59% from in state; 30% live on campus; 14% of students in fraternities, 21% in sororities
Most popular majors: 86% Engineering, 8% Computer and Information Sciences and Support Services, 3% Mathematics and Statistics, 2% Physical Sciences, 1% Social Sciences
Expenses: 2019-2020: $19,062 in state, $39,762 out of state; room/board: $14,211
Financial aid: (303) 273-3301; 48% of undergrads determined to have financial need; average aid package $15,736

Colorado State University
Fort Collins CO
(970) 491-6909
U.S. News ranking: Nat. U., No. 166
Website: www.colostate.edu
Admissions email: admissions@colostate.edu
Public; founded 1870
Freshman admissions: selective; 2018-2019: 24,496 applied, 20,508 accepted. Either SAT or ACT required. SAT 25/75 percentile: 1070-1280. High school rank: 20% in top tenth, 46% in top quarter, 81% in top half
Early decision deadline: N/A, notification date: N/A
Early action deadline: 12/1, notification date: 2/1
Application deadline (fall): 7/1

Undergraduate student body:
22,310 full time, 4,090 part
time; 48% male, 52% female;
0% American Indian, 3% Asian,
2% black, 14% Hispanic, 4%
multiracial, 0% Pacific Islander,
71% white, 4% international;
70% from in state; 30% live
on campus; 9% of students in
fraternities, 7% in sororities
Most popular majors: 14%
Business, Management,
Marketing, and Related Support
Services, 12% Biological and
Biomedical Sciences, 10%
Engineering, 8% Social Sciences,
6% Parks, Recreation, Leisure,
and Fitness Studies
Expenses: 2019-2020: $12,058
in state, $30,780 out of state;
room/board: $12,078
Financial aid: (970) 491-6321;
48% of undergrads determined to
have financial need; average aid
package $11,511

Colorado State University–Pueblo
Pueblo CO
(719) 549-2462
U.S. News ranking: Reg. U. (W),
second tier
Website: www.csupueblo.edu
Admissions email:
info@colostate-pueblo.edu
Public; founded 1933
Freshman admissions: less
selective; 2018-2019: 2,435
applied, 2,318 accepted. Either
SAT or ACT required. SAT 25/75
percentile: 920-1120. High school
rank: 13% in top tenth, 35% in
top quarter, 67% in top half
Early decision deadline: N/A,
notification date: N/A
Early action deadline: N/A,
notification date: N/A
Application deadline (fall): 8/1
Undergraduate student body: 3,134
full time, 1,251 part time; 48%
male, 52% female; 1% American
Indian, 1% Asian, 6% black,
35% Hispanic, 5% multiracial,
0% Pacific Islander, 46% white,
2% international; 86% from in
state; 16% live on campus; 1%
of students in fraternities, 1% in
sororities
Most popular majors: 11%
Registered Nursing/Registered
Nurse, 10% Sociology, 9%
Kinesiology and Exercise Science,
9% Psychology, General, 8%
Business/Commerce, General
Expenses: 2019-2020: $10,509
in state, $27,146 out of state;
room/board: $10,784
Financial aid: (719) 549-2753;
76% of undergrads determined to
have financial need; average aid
package $12,101

Colorado Technical University[1]
Colorado Springs CO
(888) 404-7555
U.S. News ranking: Nat. U.,
unranked
Website: www.coloradotech.edu
Admissions email:
info@ctuonline.edu
For-profit

Application deadline (fall): N/A
Undergraduate student body: N/A
full time, N/A part time
Expenses: N/A
Financial aid: N/A

Community College of Denver[1]
Denver CO
(303) 556-2600
U.S. News ranking: Reg. Coll. (W),
unranked
Website: www.ccd.edu
Admissions email: N/A
Public
Application deadline (fall): N/A
Undergraduate student body: N/A
full time, N/A part time
Expenses: N/A
Financial aid: N/A

Fort Lewis College
Durango CO
(970) 247-7184
U.S. News ranking: Nat. Lib. Arts,
second tier
Website: www.fortlewis.edu
Admissions email:
admission@fortlewis.edu
Public; founded 1911
Freshman admissions: selective;
2018-2019: 4,198 applied,
3,817 accepted. Either SAT
or ACT required. ACT 25/75
percentile: 18-24. High school
rank: 11% in top tenth, 22% in
top quarter, 68% in top half
Early decision deadline: N/A,
notification date: N/A
Early action deadline: N/A,
notification date: N/A
Application deadline (fall): 8/1
Undergraduate student body: 2,879
full time, 391 part time; 48%
male, 52% female; 27% American
Indian, 1% Asian, 1% black,
11% Hispanic, 11% multiracial,
0% Pacific Islander, 45% white,
1% international; N/A from in
state; 42% live on campus; 0%
of students in fraternities, 0% in
sororities
Most popular majors: 10%
Business, Management,
Marketing, and Related Support
Services, 8% Biological
and Biomedical Sciences,
8% Engineering, 8% Parks,
Recreation, Leisure, and Fitness
Studies, 7% Psychology
Expenses: 2019-2020: $10,688
in state, $21,344 out of state;
room/board: $9,878
Financial aid: (970) 247-7142;
55% of undergrads determined to
have financial need; average aid
package $18,404

Metropolitan State University of Denver
Denver CO
(303) 556-3058
U.S. News ranking: Reg. U. (W),
second tier
Website: www.msudenver.edu
Admissions email:
askmetro@msudenver.edu
Public; founded 1963
Freshman admissions: less
selective; 2018-2019: 13,442
applied, 7,992 accepted. Either
SAT or ACT required. SAT 25/75

percentile: 900-1110. High
school rank: 6% in top tenth, 21%
in top quarter, 53% in top half
Early decision deadline: N/A,
notification date: N/A
Early action deadline: N/A,
notification date: N/A
Application deadline (fall): 7/1
Undergraduate student body:
12,673 full time, 6,764 part
time; 47% male, 53% female;
0% American Indian, 4% Asian,
7% black, 29% Hispanic, 5%
multiracial, 0% Pacific Islander,
51% white, 1% international;
96% from in state; N/A live
on campus; N/A of students in
fraternities, N/A in sororities
Most popular majors: 20%
Business, Management,
Marketing, and Related Support
Services, 9% Health Professions
and Related Programs, 8% Multi/
Interdisciplinary Studies, 8%
Psychology, 7% Biological and
Biomedical Sciences
Expenses: 2019-2020: $7,666 in
state, $20,847 out of state; room/
board: N/A
Financial aid: (303) 605-5504;
69% of undergrads determined to
have financial need; average aid
package $9,249

Naropa University[1]
Boulder CO
(303) 546-3572
U.S. News ranking: Reg. U. (W),
unranked
Website: www.naropa.edu
Admissions email:
admissions@naropa.edu
Private; founded 1974
Application deadline (fall): rolling
Undergraduate student body: N/A
full time, N/A part time
Expenses: 2018-2019: $31,790;
room/board: $12,849
Financial aid: (303) 546-3509

Pueblo Community College
Pueblo CO
(719) 549-3200
U.S. News ranking: Reg. Coll. (W),
unranked
Website: www.pueblocc.edu
Admissions email: N/A
Public
Freshman admissions: least
selective; 2018-2019: N/A
applied, N/A accepted. Neither
SAT nor ACT required. SAT 25/75
percentile: N/A. High school
rank: N/A
Early decision deadline: N/A,
notification date: N/A
Early action deadline: N/A,
notification date: N/A
Application deadline (fall): N/A
Undergraduate student body: 1,669
full time, 4,511 part time; 44%
male, 56% female; N/A American
Indian, N/A Asian, N/A black, N/A
Hispanic, N/A multiracial, N/A
Pacific Islander, N/A white, N/A
international
Most popular majors: Information
not available
Expenses: 2018-2019: $5,179 in
state, $16,262 out of state; room/
board: N/A
Financial aid: N/A

Red Rocks Community College[1]
Lakewood CO
(303) 914-6600
U.S. News ranking: Reg. Coll. (W),
unranked
Website: www.rrcc.edu
Admissions email: N/A
Public
Application deadline (fall): N/A
Undergraduate student body: N/A
full time, N/A part time
Expenses: N/A
Financial aid: N/A

Regis University
Denver CO
(303) 458-4900
U.S. News ranking: Nat. U.,
No. 202
Website: www.regis.edu
Admissions email:
ruadmissions@regis.edu
Private; founded 1877
Affiliation: Roman Catholic
Freshman admissions: selective;
2018-2019: 7,295 applied,
4,399 accepted. Either SAT
or ACT required. SAT 25/75
percentile: 1050-1230. High
school rank: 25% in top tenth,
56% in top quarter, 86% in
top half
Early decision deadline: N/A,
notification date: N/A
Early action deadline: N/A,
notification date: N/A
Application deadline (fall): 8/1
Undergraduate student body: 2,373
full time, 1,588 part time; 40%
male, 60% female; 0% American
Indian, 5% Asian, 4% black,
22% Hispanic, 4% multiracial,
0% Pacific Islander, 55% white,
2% international; 40% from in
state; N/A live on campus; 0%
of students in fraternities, N/A in
sororities
Most popular majors: 33% Health
Professions and Related Programs,
24% Business, Management,
Marketing, and Related Support
Services, 8% Computer and
Information Sciences and
Support Services, 5% Biological
and Biomedical Sciences, 5%
Psychology
Expenses: 2019-2020: $38,180;
room/board: $12,460
Financial aid: (303) 458-4126;
69% of undergrads determined to
have financial need; average aid
package $29,824

Rocky Mountain College of Art and Design[1]
Lakewood CO
(303) 753-6046
U.S. News ranking: Arts, unranked
Website: www.rmcad.edu/
Admissions email:
admissions@rmcad.edu
For-profit; founded 1963
Application deadline (fall): N/A
Undergraduate student body: N/A
full time, N/A part time
Expenses: N/A
Financial aid: (303) 225-8551

United States Air Force Academy
USAF Academy CO
(800) 443-9266
U.S. News ranking: Nat. Lib. Arts,
No. 39
Website: academyadmissions.com
Admissions email:
rr_webmail@usafa.edu
Public; founded 1954
Freshman admissions: more
selective; 2018-2019: 10,376
applied, 1,182 accepted. Either
SAT or ACT required. ACT 25/75
percentile: 28-33. High school
rank: 53% in top tenth, 82% in
top quarter, 98% in top half
Early decision deadline: N/A,
notification date: N/A
Early action deadline: N/A,
notification date: N/A
Application deadline (fall): 12/31
Undergraduate student body:
4,336 full time, 0 part time; 73%
male, 27% female; 0% American
Indian, 6% Asian, 6% black,
11% Hispanic, 8% multiracial,
1% Pacific Islander, 63% white,
1% international; 7% from in
state; 100% live on campus; 0%
of students in fraternities, 0% in
sororities
Most popular majors: 30%
Engineering, 24% Business,
Management, Marketing, and
Related Support Services, 17%
Social Sciences, 6% Biological
and Biomedical Sciences, 5%
Multi/Interdisciplinary Studies
Expenses: N/A
Financial aid: N/A

University of Colorado–Boulder
Boulder CO
(303) 492-6301
U.S. News ranking: Nat. U.,
No. 104
Website: www.colorado.edu
Admissions email:
apply@colorado.edu
Public; founded 1876
Freshman admissions: more
selective; 2018-2019: 36,604
applied, 29,848 accepted. Either
SAT or ACT required. SAT 25/75
percentile: 1150-1360. High
school rank: 29% in top tenth,
58% in top quarter, 88% in
top half
Early decision deadline: N/A,
notification date: N/A
Early action deadline: 11/15,
notification date: 2/1
Application deadline (fall): 1/15
Undergraduate student body:
27,931 full time, 2,221 part
time; 55% male, 45% female;
0% American Indian, 6% Asian,
2% black, 12% Hispanic, 6%
multiracial, 0% Pacific Islander,
67% white, 6% international;
57% from in state; 27% live
on campus; 12% of students in
fraternities, 22% in sororities
Most popular majors: 14%
Business, Management,
Marketing, and Related Support
Services, 13% Biological and
Biomedical Sciences, 13%
Engineering, 13% Social
Sciences, 10% Communication,
Journalism, and Related Programs

Expenses: 2019-2020: $12,500 in state, $38,318 out of state; room/board: $14,778
Financial aid: (303) 492-5091; 36% of undergrads determined to have financial need; average aid package $16,972

University of Colorado–Colorado Springs
Colorado Springs CO
(719) 255-3084
U.S. News ranking: Nat. U., second tier
Website: www.uccs.edu
Admissions email: go@uccs.edu
Public; founded 1965
Freshman admissions: selective; 2018-2019: 10,087 applied, 9,197 accepted. Either SAT or ACT required. SAT 25/75 percentile: 1010-1210. High school rank: 13% in top tenth, 35% in top quarter, 71% in top half
Early decision deadline: N/A, notification date: N/A
Early action deadline: N/A, notification date: N/A
Application deadline (fall): rolling
Undergraduate student body: 8,318 full time, 2,425 part time; 48% male, 52% female; 0% American Indian, 3% Asian, 4% black, 19% Hispanic, 8% multiracial, 0% Pacific Islander, 63% white, 1% international; 87% from in state; 16% live on campus; N/A of students in fraternities, N/A in sororities
Most popular majors: 19% Business, Management, Marketing, and Related Support Services, 14% Health Professions and Related Programs, 10% Social Sciences, 9% Psychology, 8% Biological and Biomedical Sciences
Expenses: 2019-2020: $10,463 in state, $25,593 out of state; room/board: $10,500
Financial aid: (719) 255-3460; 61% of undergrads determined to have financial need; average aid package $9,145

University of Colorado–Denver
Denver CO
(303) 556-2704
U.S. News ranking: Nat. U., No. 254
Website: www.ucdenver.edu
Admissions email: admissions@ucdenver.edu
Public; founded 1912
Freshman admissions: selective; 2018-2019: 11,315 applied, 7,200 accepted. Either SAT or ACT required. SAT 25/75 percentile: 1020-1210. High school rank: 22% in top tenth, 48% in top quarter, 79% in top half
Early decision deadline: N/A, notification date: N/A
Early action deadline: N/A, notification date: N/A
Application deadline (fall): rolling
Undergraduate student body: 8,952 full time, 7,433 part time; 45% male, 55% female; 0% American Indian, 10% Asian, 5% black,

24% Hispanic, 6% multiracial, 0% Pacific Islander, 46% white, 8% international; 91% from in state; 0% live on campus; N/A of students in fraternities, N/A in sororities
Most popular majors: 17% Business, Management, Marketing, and Related Support Services, 14% Health Professions and Related Programs, 13% Social Sciences, 11% Biological and Biomedical Sciences, 8% Visual and Performing Arts
Expenses: 2019-2020: $11,395 in state, $32,005 out of state; room/board: $11,547
Financial aid: (303) 315-1850; 62% of undergrads determined to have financial need; average aid package $10,546

University of Denver
Denver CO
(303) 871-2036
U.S. News ranking: Nat. U., No. 97
Website: www.du.edu
Admissions email: admission@du.edu
Private; founded 1864
Freshman admissions: more selective; 2018-2019: 20,475 applied, 11,563 accepted. Either SAT or ACT required. ACT 25/75 percentile: 26-31. High school rank: 42% in top tenth, 74% in top quarter, 95% in top half
Early decision deadline: 11/1, notification date: 12/15
Early action deadline: 11/1, notification date: 1/15
Application deadline (fall): 1/15
Undergraduate student body: 5,563 full time, 238 part time; 46% male, 54% female; 0% American Indian, 4% Asian, 2% black, 11% Hispanic, 5% multiracial, 0% Pacific Islander, 68% white, 7% international; 63% from in state; 48% live on campus; 21% of students in fraternities, 26% in sororities
Most popular majors: 36% Business, Management, Marketing, and Related Support Services, 17% Social Sciences, 9% Psychology, 8% Biological and Biomedical Sciences, 5% Communication, Journalism, and Related Programs
Expenses: 2019-2020: $52,515; room/board: $13,437
Financial aid: (303) 871-4020; 42% of undergrads determined to have financial need; average aid package $40,907

University of Northern Colorado
Greeley CO
(970) 351-2881
U.S. News ranking: Nat. U., second tier
Website: www.unco.edu
Admissions email: admissions@unco.edu
Public; founded 1890
Freshman admissions: selective; 2018-2019: 8,294 applied, 7,527 accepted. Either SAT or ACT required. SAT 25/75

percentile: 990-1190. High school rank: 12% in top tenth, 36% in top quarter, 72% in top half
Early decision deadline: N/A, notification date: N/A
Early action deadline: N/A, notification date: N/A
Application deadline (fall): 8/1
Undergraduate student body: 8,047 full time, 1,829 part time; 35% male, 65% female; 0% American Indian, 2% Asian, 4% black, 22% Hispanic, 4% multiracial, 0% Pacific Islander, 63% white, 1% international; 86% from in state; 34% live on campus; 6% of students in fraternities, 5% in sororities
Most popular majors: 16% Health Professions and Related Programs, 12% Education, 10% Business, Management, Marketing, and Related Support Services, 10% Parks, Recreation, Leisure, and Fitness Studies, 8% Visual and Performing Arts
Expenses: 2019-2020: $10,188 in state, $21,876 out of state; room/board: $11,204
Financial aid: (970) 351-2502; 66% of undergrads determined to have financial need; average aid package $14,905

Western Colorado University
Gunnison CO
(970) 943-2119
U.S. News ranking: Reg. U. (W), No. 66
Website: www.western.edu
Admissions email: admissions@western.edu
Public; founded 1901
Freshman admissions: selective; 2018-2019: 1,972 applied, 1,755 accepted. Either SAT or ACT required. SAT 25/75 percentile: 1000-1170. High school rank: 7% in top tenth, 21% in top quarter, 46% in top half
Early decision deadline: N/A, notification date: N/A
Early action deadline: N/A, notification date: N/A
Application deadline (fall): rolling
Undergraduate student body: 1,883 full time, 729 part time; 56% male, 44% female; 1% American Indian, 1% Asian, 3% black, 11% Hispanic, 4% multiracial, 0% Pacific Islander, 71% white, 1% international; N/A from in state; 47% live on campus; N/A of students in fraternities, N/A in sororities
Most popular majors: 21% Business, Management, Marketing, and Related Support Services, 14% Parks, Recreation, Leisure, and Fitness Studies, 11% Biological and Biomedical Sciences, 11% Social Sciences, 8% Psychology
Expenses: 2019-2020: $10,437 in state, $21,909 out of state; room/board: $9,704
Financial aid: (970) 943-7015; 58% of undergrads determined to have financial need; average aid package $11,482

CONNECTICUT

Albertus Magnus College
New Haven CT
(800) 578-9160
U.S. News ranking: Reg. U. (N), No. 66
Website: www.albertus.edu
Admissions email: admissions@albertus.edu
Private; founded 1925
Affiliation: Roman Catholic
Freshman admissions: least selective; 2018-2019: 929 applied, 802 accepted. Neither SAT nor ACT required. SAT 25/75 percentile: 810-1050. High school rank: N/A
Early decision deadline: N/A, notification date: N/A
Early action deadline: N/A, notification date: N/A
Application deadline (fall): rolling
Undergraduate student body: 954 full time, 162 part time; 33% male, 67% female; 1% American Indian, 1% Asian, 33% black, 19% Hispanic, 1% multiracial, 0% Pacific Islander, 35% white, 1% international; N/A from in state; 20% live on campus; N/A of students in fraternities, N/A in sororities
Most popular majors: 44% Business, Management, Marketing, and Related Support Services, 10% Psychology, 8% Health Professions and Related Programs, 7% Homeland Security, Law Enforcement, Firefighting and Related Protective Services, 7% Social Sciences
Expenses: 2019-2020: $33,260; room/board: $13,910
Financial aid: (203) 773-8508; 91% of undergrads determined to have financial need; average aid package $18,321

Central Connecticut State University
New Britain CT
(860) 832-2278
U.S. News ranking: Reg. U. (N), No. 104
Website: www.ccsu.edu
Admissions email: admissions@ccsu.edu
Public; founded 1849
Freshman admissions: selective; 2018-2019: 7,903 applied, 5,314 accepted. Either SAT or ACT required. SAT 25/75 percentile: 980-1170. High school rank: 10% in top tenth, 27% in top quarter, 61% in top half
Early decision deadline: N/A, notification date: N/A
Early action deadline: N/A, notification date: N/A
Application deadline (fall): 5/1
Undergraduate student body: 7,576 full time, 1,970 part time; 53% male, 47% female; 0% American Indian, 5% Asian, 12% black, 16% Hispanic, 3% multiracial, 0% Pacific Islander, 59% white, 1% international; 96% from in state; 25% live on campus; N/A of students in fraternities, N/A in sororities

Most popular majors: 26% Business, Management, Marketing, and Related Support Services, 14% Social Sciences, 8% Psychology, 6% Biological and Biomedical Sciences, 6% Communication, Journalism, and Related Programs
Expenses: 2019-2020: $11,068 in state, $22,870 out of state; room/board: $12,528
Financial aid: (860) 832-2203; 79% of undergrads determined to have financial need; average aid package $8,824

Charter Oak State College
New Britain CT
(860) 515-3701
U.S. News ranking: Nat. Lib. Arts, unranked
Website: www.charteroak.edu
Admissions email: admissions@charteroak.edu
Public; founded 1973
Freshman admissions: least selective; 2018-2019: N/A applied, N/A accepted. Neither SAT nor ACT required. SAT 25/75 percentile: N/A. High school rank: N/A
Early decision deadline: N/A, notification date: N/A
Early action deadline: N/A, notification date: N/A
Application deadline (fall): rolling
Undergraduate student body: 296 full time, 1,253 part time; 31% male, 69% female; 0% American Indian, 3% Asian, 18% black, 17% Hispanic, 3% multiracial, 0% Pacific Islander, 54% white, 0% international; 82% from in state; N/A live on campus; N/A of students in fraternities, N/A in sororities
Most popular majors: 62% Liberal Arts and Sciences/Liberal Studies, 15% Business Administration and Management, General, 7% Health/Health Care Administration/Management, 7% Psychology, General, 4% Health Information/Medical Records Administration/Administrator
Expenses: 2019-2020: $10,467 in state, $13,467 out of state; room/board: N/A
Financial aid: (860) 515-3703

Connecticut College
New London CT
(860) 439-2200
U.S. News ranking: Nat. Lib. Arts, No. 46
Website: www.conncoll.edu
Admissions email: admission@conncoll.edu
Private; founded 1911
Freshman admissions: more selective; 2018-2019: 6,433 applied, 2,429 accepted. Neither SAT nor ACT required. SAT 25/75 percentile: 1290-1430. High school rank: 49% in top tenth, 80% in top quarter, 98% in top half
Early decision deadline: 11/15, notification date: 12/15
Early action deadline: N/A, notification date: N/A
Application deadline (fall): 1/1

Undergraduate student body: 1,798 full time, 46 part time; 39% male, 61% female; 0% American Indian, 5% Asian, 4% black, 9% Hispanic, 4% multiracial, 0% Pacific Islander, 70% white, 7% international; 19% from in state; 99% live on campus; 0% of students in fraternities, 0% in sororities

Most popular majors: 16% Economics, General, 9% Psychology, General, 7% English Language and Literature, General, 7% Neuroscience, 7% Political Science and Government, General

Expenses: 2019-2020: $56,870; room/board: $15,720

Financial aid: (860) 439-2058; 58% of undergrads determined to have financial need; average aid package $45,149

Eastern Connecticut State University

Willimantic CT
(860) 465-5286
U.S. News ranking: Reg. U. (N), No. 80
Website: www.easternct.edu
Admissions email: admissions@easternct.edu
Public; founded 1889
Freshman admissions: selective; 2018-2019: 5,580 applied, 3,668 accepted. Neither SAT nor ACT required. SAT 25/75 percentile: 1010-1190. High school rank: 13% in top tenth, 40% in top quarter, 75% in top half
Early decision deadline: N/A, notification date: N/A
Early action deadline: N/A, notification date: N/A
Application deadline (fall): rolling
Undergraduate student body: 4,247 full time, 764 part time; 42% male, 58% female; 0% American Indian, 3% Asian, 10% black, 12% Hispanic, 4% multiracial, 0% Pacific Islander, 64% white, 1% international
Most popular majors: 11% Business, Management, Marketing, and Related Support Services, 11% Liberal Arts and Sciences, General Studies and Humanities, 9% Psychology, 7% Communication, Journalism, and Related Programs, 5% Health Professions and Related Programs
Expenses: 2019-2020: $11,846 in state, $23,648 out of state; room/board: $13,908
Financial aid: (860) 465-5775; 66% of undergrads determined to have financial need; average aid package $11,074

Fairfield University

Fairfield CT
(203) 254-4100
U.S. News ranking: Reg. U. (N), No. 3
Website: www.fairfield.edu
Admissions email: admis@fairfield.edu
Private; founded 1942
Affiliation: Roman Catholic
Freshman admissions: more selective; 2018-2019: 11,361 applied, 6,851 accepted. Neither SAT nor ACT required. SAT 25/75 percentile: 1190-1340.

High school rank: 37% in top tenth, 77% in top quarter, 96% in top half
Early decision deadline: 11/15, notification date: 12/15
Early action deadline: 11/1, notification date: 12/20
Application deadline (fall): 1/15
Undergraduate student body: 3,989 full time, 188 part time; 40% male, 60% female; 0% American Indian, 3% Asian, 2% black, 7% Hispanic, 2% multiracial, 0% Pacific Islander, 77% white, 4% international; 28% from in state; 73% live on campus; N/A of students in fraternities, N/A in sororities
Most popular majors: 43% Business, Management, Marketing, and Related Support Services, 12% Health Professions and Related Programs, 8% Communication, Journalism, and Related Programs, 8% Social Sciences, 6% Psychology
Expenses: 2019-2020: $49,830; room/board: $15,150
Financial aid: (203) 254-4000; 43% of undergrads determined to have financial need; average aid package $33,281

Lincoln College of New England– Southington[1]

Southington CT
U.S. News ranking: Reg. Coll. (N), unranked
Admissions email: N/A
For-profit
Application deadline (fall): N/A
Undergraduate student body: N/A full time, N/A part time
Expenses: N/A
Financial aid: N/A

Mitchell College[1]

New London CT
(860) 701-5000
U.S. News ranking: Reg. Coll. (N), second tier
Website: www.mitchell.edu
Admissions email: admissions@mitchell.edu
Private
Application deadline (fall): N/A
Undergraduate student body: N/A full time, N/A part time
Expenses: N/A
Financial aid: N/A

Post University

Waterbury CT
(800) 660-6615
U.S. News ranking: Reg. U. (N), second tier
Website: www.post.edu
Admissions email: admissions@post.edu
For-profit, founded 1890
Freshman admissions: least selective; 2018-2019: 6,425 applied, 3,406 accepted. Either SAT or ACT required for some. SAT 25/75 percentile: 850-850. High school rank: N/A
Early decision deadline: N/A, notification date: N/A
Early action deadline: N/A, notification date: N/A
Application deadline (fall): rolling

Undergraduate student body: 2,564 full time, 6,485 part time; 31% male, 69% female; 1% American Indian, 1% Asian, 26% black, 8% Hispanic, 4% multiracial, 0% Pacific Islander, 38% white, 1% international; 21% from in state; 3% live on campus; 0% of students in fraternities, 0% in sororities
Most popular majors: 59% Business Administration and Management, General, 14% Criminal Justice/Safety Studies, 10% Public Administration and Social Service Professions, 9% Accounting, 8% Psychology, General
Expenses: 2019-2020: $17,810; room/board: $11,600
Financial aid: (800) 345-2562; 81% of undergrads determined to have financial need; average aid package $16,049

Quinnipiac University

Hamden CT
(203) 582-8600
U.S. News ranking: Nat. U., No. 153
Website: www.qu.edu
Admissions email: admissions@qu.edu
Private; founded 1929
Affiliation: Undenominational
Freshman admissions: selective; 2018-2019: 22,753 applied, 16,492 accepted. Either SAT or ACT required for some. SAT 25/75 percentile: 1090-1260. High school rank: 20% in top tenth, 58% in top quarter, 92% in top half
Early decision deadline: 11/1, notification date: 12/1
Early action deadline: N/A, notification date: N/A
Application deadline (fall): 2/1
Undergraduate student body: 7,051 full time, 374 part time; 39% male, 61% female; 0% American Indian, 3% Asian, 4% black, 9% Hispanic, 2% multiracial, 0% Pacific Islander, 77% white, 2% international; 30% from in state; N/A live on campus; N/A of students in fraternities, N/A in sororities
Most popular majors: 38% Health Professions and Related Programs, 23% Business, Management, Marketing, and Related Support Services, 10% Communication, Journalism, and Related Programs, 5% Psychology, 4% Computer and Information Sciences and Support Services
Expenses: 2019-2020: $49,280; room/board: $15,140
Financial aid: (203) 582-8750; 63% of undergrads determined to have financial need; average aid package $29,097

Sacred Heart University

Fairfield CT
(203) 371-7880
U.S. News ranking: Nat. U., No. 218
Website: www.sacredheart.edu
Admissions email: enroll@sacredheart.edu
Private; founded 1963
Affiliation: Roman Catholic

Freshman admissions: selective; 2018-2019: 10,739 applied, 6,492 accepted. Neither SAT nor ACT required. SAT 25/75 percentile: 1100-1240. High school rank: 11% in top tenth, 35% in top quarter, 71% in top half
Early decision deadline: 12/1, notification date: 12/15
Early action deadline: 12/15, notification date: 1/31
Application deadline (fall): rolling
Undergraduate student body: 5,130 full time, 844 part time; 35% male, 65% female; 0% American Indian, 2% Asian, 5% black, 12% Hispanic, 2% multiracial, 0% Pacific Islander, 72% white, 1% international; 38% from in state; 48% live on campus; 27% of students in fraternities, 47% in sororities
Most popular majors: 33% Health Professions and Related Programs, 28% Business, Management, Marketing, and Related Support Services, 9% Psychology, 7% Communication, Journalism, and Related Programs, 4% Homeland Security, Law Enforcement, Firefighting and Related Protective Services
Expenses: 2019-2020: $43,070; room/board: $15,960
Financial aid: (203) 371-7980; 65% of undergrads determined to have financial need; average aid package $21,553

Southern Connecticut State University

New Haven CT
(203) 392-5644
U.S. News ranking: Reg. U. (N), second tier
Website: www.southernct.edu/
Admissions email: admissions@southernct.edu
Public; founded 1893
Freshman admissions: less selective; 2018-2019: 8,983 applied, 5,949 accepted. Either SAT or ACT required. SAT 25/75 percentile: 920-1130. High school rank: 8% in top tenth, 27% in top quarter, 61% in top half
Early decision deadline: N/A, notification date: N/A
Early action deadline: N/A, notification date: N/A
Application deadline (fall): 8/16
Undergraduate student body: 6,877 full time, 1,245 part time; 39% male, 61% female; 0% American Indian, 3% Asian, 19% black, 10% Hispanic, 4% multiracial, 0% Pacific Islander, 56% white, 0% international; N/A from in state; 31% live on campus; 4% of students in fraternities, 4% in sororities
Most popular majors: 18% Liberal Arts and Sciences/Liberal Studies, 12% Business Administration and Management, General, 9% Psychology, General, 6% Registered Nursing/Registered Nurse, 5% Public Health, General
Expenses: 2019-2020: $11,446 in state, $23,248 out of state; room/board: $13,270
Financial aid: N/A; 76% of undergrads determined to have financial need; average aid package $8,400

Trinity College

Hartford CT
(860) 297-2180
U.S. News ranking: Nat. Lib. Arts, No. 46
Website: www.trincoll.edu
Admissions email: admissions.office@trincoll.edu
Private; founded 1823
Affiliation: Undenominational
Freshman admissions: more selective; 2018-2019: 6,096 applied, 2,045 accepted. Neither SAT nor ACT required. SAT 25/75 percentile: 1300-1460. High school rank: 46% in top tenth, 76% in top quarter, 95% in top half
Early decision deadline: 11/15, notification date: 12/15
Early action deadline: N/A, notification date: N/A
Application deadline (fall): 1/15
Undergraduate student body: 2,112 full time, 70 part time; 50% male, 50% female; 0% American Indian, 4% Asian, 6% black, 9% Hispanic, 3% multiracial, 0% Pacific Islander, 63% white, 13% international; 18% from in state; 86% live on campus; 29% of students in fraternities, 17% in sororities
Most popular majors: 27% Social Sciences, 10% Biological and Biomedical Sciences, 9% Psychology, 8% Area, Ethnic, Cultural, Gender, and Group Studies, 6% English Language and Literature/Letters
Expenses: 2019-2020: $59,050; room/board: $15,300
Financial aid: (860) 297-2048; 54% of undergrads determined to have financial need; average aid package $51,112

United States Coast Guard Academy

New London CT
(800) 883-8724
U.S. News ranking: Reg. Coll. (N), No. 2
Website: www.uscga.edu
Admissions email: admissions@uscga.edu
Public; founded 1932
Freshman admissions: more selective; 2018-2019: 2,274 applied, 290 accepted. Either SAT or ACT required. SAT 25/75 percentile: 1245-1420. High school rank: 47% in top tenth, 84% in top quarter, 100% in top half
Early decision deadline: N/A, notification date: N/A
Early action deadline: 10/15, notification date: 2/1
Application deadline (fall): 1/15
Undergraduate student body: 1,072 full time, 0 part time; 64% male, 36% female; N/A American Indian, N/A Asian, N/A black, N/A Hispanic, N/A multiracial, N/A Pacific Islander, N/A white, N/A international; 5% from in state; 100% live on campus; N/A of students in fraternities, N/A in sororities
Most popular majors: 43% Engineering, 19% Social Sciences, 16% Biological and Biomedical Sciences,

12% Business, Management, Marketing, and Related Support Services, 10% Computer and Information Sciences and Support Services
Expenses: 2019-2020: $0 in state, $0 out of state; room/board: $0
Financial aid: N/A

University of Bridgeport
Bridgeport CT
(203) 576-4552
U.S. News ranking: Nat. U., second tier
Website: www.bridgeport.edu
Admissions email: admit@bridgeport.edu
Private; founded 1927
Freshman admissions: less selective; 2018-2019: 7,404 applied, 4,238 accepted. Either SAT or ACT required. SAT 25/75 percentile: 900-1090. High school rank: 6% in top tenth, 38% in top quarter, 60% in top half
Early decision deadline: N/A, notification date: N/A
Early action deadline: N/A, notification date: N/A
Application deadline (fall): rolling
Undergraduate student body: 2,311 full time, 1,104 part time; 36% male, 64% female; 1% American Indian, 4% Asian, 33% black, 24% Hispanic, 3% multiracial, 0% Pacific Islander, 25% white, 12% international
Most popular majors: 14% Psychology, General, 10% General Studies, 8% Public Administration and Social Service Professions, 7% Dental Hygiene/Hygienist, 6% Finance, General
Expenses: 2019-2020: $34,100; room/board: $15,950
Financial aid: (203) 576-4568; 82% of undergrads determined to have financial need; average aid package $31,000

University of Connecticut
Storrs CT
(860) 486-3137
U.S. News ranking: Nat. U., No. 64
Website: www.uconn.edu
Admissions email: beahusky@uconn.edu
Public; founded 1881
Freshman admissions: more selective; 2018-2019: 34,886 applied, 17,015 accepted. Either SAT or ACT required. SAT 25/75 percentile: 1210-1420. High school rank: 50% in top tenth, 84% in top quarter, 98% in top half
Early decision deadline: N/A, notification date: N/A
Early action deadline: N/A, notification date: N/A
Application deadline (fall): 1/15
Undergraduate student body: 18,478 full time, 655 part time; 49% male, 51% female; 0% American Indian, 11% Asian, 6% black, 11% Hispanic, 3% multiracial, 0% Pacific Islander, 56% white, 9% international; 79% from in state; 65% live on campus; 10% of students in fraternities, 14% in sororities

Most popular majors: 7% Economics, General, 7% Psychology, General, 5% Speech Communication and Rhetoric, 4% Biology/Biological Sciences, General, 4% Registered Nursing/Registered Nurse
Expenses: 2019-2020: $17,226 in state, $39,894 out of state; room/board: $13,258
Financial aid: (860) 486-2819; 53% of undergrads determined to have financial need; average aid package $15,269

University of Hartford
West Hartford CT
(860) 768-4296
U.S. News ranking: Nat. U., No. 211
Website: www.hartford.edu
Admissions email: admission@hartford.edu
Private; founded 1877
Freshman admissions: selective; 2018-2019: 15,115 applied, 11,295 accepted. Neither SAT nor ACT required. SAT 25/75 percentile: 1050-1250. High school rank: N/A
Early decision deadline: N/A, notification date: N/A
Early action deadline: 11/15, notification date: 12/1
Application deadline (fall): rolling
Undergraduate student body: 4,428 full time, 572 part time; 49% male, 51% female; 0% American Indian, 4% Asian, 15% black, 14% Hispanic, 4% multiracial, 0% Pacific Islander, 54% white, 5% international; 49% from in state; 63% live on campus; N/A of students in fraternities, N/A in sororities
Most popular majors: 19% Visual and Performing Arts, 15% Engineering, 14% Business, Management, Marketing, and Related Support Services, 13% Health Professions and Related Programs, 7% Psychology
Expenses: 2019-2020: $42,182; room/board: $12,968
Financial aid: (860) 768-4296; 74% of undergrads determined to have financial need; average aid package $29,084

University of New Haven
West Haven CT
(203) 932-7319
U.S. News ranking: Reg. U. (N), No. 66
Website: www.newhaven.edu
Admissions email: admissions@newhaven.edu
Private; founded 1920
Freshman admissions: selective; 2018-2019: 10,426 applied, 8,744 accepted. Either SAT or ACT required. SAT 25/75 percentile: 1030-1220. High school rank: 13% in top tenth, 42% in top quarter, 78% in top half
Early decision deadline: 12/1, notification date: 12/15
Early action deadline: 12/15, notification date: 1/15
Application deadline (fall): rolling

Undergraduate student body: 4,768 full time, 324 part time; 46% male, 54% female; 0% American Indian, 3% Asian, 12% black, 12% Hispanic, 1% multiracial, 0% Pacific Islander, 62% white, 4% international; 45% from in state; 53% live on campus; N/A of students in fraternities, N/A in sororities
Most popular majors: 40% Homeland Security, Law Enforcement, Firefighting and Related Protective Services, 10% Business, Management, Marketing, and Related Support Services, 9% Engineering, 8% Biological and Biomedical Sciences, 8% Visual and Performing Arts
Expenses: 2019-2020: $40,440; room/board: $16,360
Financial aid: (203) 932-7315

University of St. Joseph
West Hartford CT
(860) 231-5216
U.S. News ranking: Nat. U., No. 147
Website: www.usj.edu
Admissions email: admissions@usj.edu
Private; founded 1932
Affiliation: Roman Catholic
Freshman admissions: selective; 2018-2019: 1,414 applied, 1,022 accepted. Either SAT or ACT required for some. SAT 25/75 percentile: 1030-1210. High school rank: 25% in top tenth, 40% in top quarter, 78% in top half
Early decision deadline: N/A, notification date: N/A
Early action deadline: N/A, notification date: N/A
Application deadline (fall): rolling
Undergraduate student body: 765 full time, 138 part time; 12% male, 88% female; 0% American Indian, 6% Asian, 14% black, 16% Hispanic, 2% multiracial, 0% Pacific Islander, 57% white, 2% international
Most popular majors: 46% Health Professions and Related Programs, 15% Public Administration and Social Service Professions, 9% Biological and Biomedical Sciences, 8% Family and Consumer Sciences/Human Sciences, 8% Psychology
Expenses: 2019-2020: $40,286; room/board: $11,317
Financial aid: (860) 231-5223; 91% of undergrads determined to have financial need; average aid package $29,622

Wesleyan University
Middletown CT
(860) 685-3000
U.S. News ranking: Nat. Lib. Arts, No. 17
Website: www.wesleyan.edu
Admissions email: admissions@wesleyan.edu
Private; founded 1831
Freshman admissions: most selective; 2018-2019: 12,706 applied, 2,218 accepted. Neither SAT nor ACT required. SAT 25/75 percentile: 1320-1500. High school rank: 57% in top

tenth, 85% in top quarter, 98% in top half
Early decision deadline: 11/15, notification date: 12/15
Early action deadline: N/A, notification date: N/A
Application deadline (fall): 1/1
Undergraduate student body: 2,928 full time, 81 part time; 45% male, 55% female; 0% American Indian, 7% Asian, 6% black, 12% Hispanic, 6% multiracial, 0% Pacific Islander, 54% white, 12% international; 7% from in state; 99% live on campus; 4% of students in fraternities, 1% in sororities
Most popular majors: 24% Social Sciences, 13% Psychology, 12% Area, Ethnic, Cultural, Gender, and Group Studies, 11% Visual and Performing Arts, 8% Biological and Biomedical Sciences
Expenses: 2019-2020: $57,004; room/board: $16,799
Financial aid: (860) 685-2800; 42% of undergrads determined to have financial need; average aid package $56,471

Western Connecticut State University
Danbury CT
(203) 837-9000
U.S. News ranking: Reg. U. (N), second tier
Website: www.wcsu.edu
Admissions email: admissions@wcsu.edu
Public; founded 1903
Freshman admissions: selective; 2018-2019: 5,375 applied, 4,259 accepted. Neither SAT nor ACT required. SAT 25/75 percentile: 1020-1220. High school rank: 7% in top tenth, 23% in top quarter, 59% in top half
Early decision deadline: N/A, notification date: N/A
Early action deadline: N/A, notification date: N/A
Application deadline (fall): rolling
Undergraduate student body: 4,128 full time, 900 part time; 48% male, 52% female; 0% American Indian, 4% Asian, 10% black, 19% Hispanic, 3% multiracial, 0% Pacific Islander, 60% white, 0% international; 85% from in state; 30% live on campus; 3% of students in fraternities, 5% in sororities
Most popular majors: 23% Business, Management, Marketing, and Related Support Services, 14% Health Professions and Related Programs, 11% Homeland Security, Law Enforcement, Firefighting and Related Protective Services, 8% Psychology, 7% Communication, Journalism, and Related Programs
Expenses: 2019-2020: $11,344 in state, $23,146 out of state; room/board: $13,452
Financial aid: (203) 837-8580; 64% of undergrads determined to have financial need; average aid package $9,666

Yale University
New Haven CT
(203) 432-9300
U.S. News ranking: Nat. U., No. 3
Website: www.yale.edu/
Admissions email: student.questions@yale.edu
Private; founded 1701
Freshman admissions: most selective; 2018-2019: 35,307 applied, 2,241 accepted. Either SAT or ACT required. SAT 25/75 percentile: 1450-1560. High school rank: 95% in top tenth, 99% in top quarter, 100% in top half
Early decision deadline: N/A, notification date: N/A
Early action deadline: 11/1, notification date: 12/15
Application deadline (fall): 1/2
Undergraduate student body: 5,939 full time, 25 part time; 50% male, 50% female; 0% American Indian, 19% Asian, 8% black, 13% Hispanic, 6% multiracial, 0% Pacific Islander, 42% white, 11% international; 8% from in state; 84% live on campus; N/A of students in fraternities, N/A in sororities
Most popular majors: 27% Social Sciences, 10% Biological and Biomedical Sciences, 10% History, 7% Mathematics and Statistics, 6% Engineering
Expenses: 2019-2020: $55,500; room/board: $16,600
Financial aid: (203) 432-2700; 53% of undergrads determined to have financial need; average aid package $59,070

DELAWARE

Delaware State University
Dover DE
(302) 857-6353
U.S. News ranking: Nat. U., second tier
Website: www.desu.edu
Admissions email: admissions@desu.edu
Public; founded 1891
Freshman admissions: less selective; 2018-2019: 7,000 applied, 3,442 accepted. Either SAT or ACT required. SAT 25/75 percentile: 840-1010. High school rank: 9% in top tenth, 26% in top quarter, 64% in top half
Early decision deadline: N/A, notification date: N/A
Early action deadline: N/A, notification date: N/A
Application deadline (fall): rolling
Undergraduate student body: 3,678 full time, 530 part time; 34% male, 66% female; 0% American Indian, 1% Asian, 74% black, 7% Hispanic, 6% multiracial, 0% Pacific Islander, 8% white, 4% international; 47% from in state; 63% live on campus; N/A of students in fraternities, N/A in sororities
Most popular majors: 14% Parks, Recreation, Leisure, and Fitness Studies, 13% Social Sciences, 12% Business, Management, Marketing, and Related Support Services, 9% Communication, Journalism, and Related Programs, 7% Psychology

Expenses: 2019-2020: $9,088 in state, $18,124 out of state; room/board: $13,068
Financial aid: (302) 857-6250; 81% of undergrads determined to have financial need; average aid package $20,858

Delaware Technical Community College–Terry[1]
Dover DE
(302) 857-1000
U.S. News ranking: Reg. Coll. (N), unranked
Website: www.dtcc.edu/our-campuses/dover
Admissions email: N/A
Public
Application deadline (fall): N/A
Undergraduate student body: N/A full time, N/A part time
Expenses: N/A
Financial aid: N/A

Goldey-Beacom College[1]
Wilmington DE
(302) 998-8814
U.S. News ranking: Business, unranked
Website: www.gbc.edu
Admissions email: admissions@gbc.edu
Private; founded 1886
Application deadline (fall): N/A
Undergraduate student body: N/A full time, N/A part time
Expenses: N/A
Financial aid: (302) 225-6265

University of Delaware
Newark DE
(302) 831-8123
U.S. News ranking: Nat. U., No. 91
Website: www.udel.edu/
Admissions email: admissions@udel.edu
Public; founded 1743
Freshman admissions: more selective; 2018-2019: 27,691 applied, 17,277 accepted. Either SAT or ACT required for some. SAT 25/75 percentile: 1170-1350. High school rank: 34% in top tenth, 69% in top quarter, 94% in top half
Early decision deadline: N/A, notification date: N/A
Early action deadline: N/A, notification date: N/A
Application deadline (fall): 1/15
Undergraduate student body: 17,571 full time, 1,546 part time; 43% male, 57% female; 0% American Indian, 5% Asian, 5% black, 8% Hispanic, 3% multiracial, 0% Pacific Islander, 71% white, 5% international; 38% from in state, 41% live on campus; 18% of students in fraternities, 23% in sororities
Most popular majors: 23% Business, Management, Marketing, and Related Support Services, 12% Health Professions and Related Programs, 10% Engineering, 10% Social Sciences, 6% Biological and Biomedical Sciences

Expenses: 2019-2020: $13,680 in state, $34,310 out of state; room/board: $12,862
Financial aid: (302) 831-0520; 50% of undergrads determined to have financial need; average aid package $13,375

Wesley College[1]
Dover DE
(302) 736-2400
U.S. News ranking: Reg. Coll. (N), second tier
Website: www.wesley.edu
Admissions email: admissions@wesley.edu
Private; founded 1873
Affiliation: United Methodist
Application deadline (fall): 4/30
Undergraduate student body: N/A full time, N/A part time
Expenses: N/A
Financial aid: (302) 736-2483

Wilmington University
New Castle DE
(302) 328-9407
U.S. News ranking: Nat. U., unranked
Website: www.wilmu.edu
Admissions email: undergradadmissions@wilmu.edu
Private; founded 1968
Freshman admissions: least selective; 2018-2019: 3,162 applied, 3,162 accepted. Neither SAT nor ACT required. SAT 25/75 percentile: N/A. High school rank: N/A
Early decision deadline: N/A, notification date: N/A
Early action deadline: N/A, notification date: N/A
Application deadline (fall): rolling
Undergraduate student body: 3,433 full time, 5,609 part time; 35% male, 65% female; 1% American Indian, 2% Asian, 25% black, 8% Hispanic, 1% multiracial, 0% Pacific Islander, 52% white, 3% international
Most popular majors: 26% Nursing Practice, 11% Behavioral Sciences, 10% Business Administration and Management, General, 6% Criminal Justice/Law Enforcement Administration, 6% Psychology, General
Expenses: 2018-2019: $11,210; room/board: N/A
Financial aid: (302) 356-4636

DISTRICT OF COLUMBIA

American University
Washington DC
(202) 885-6000
U.S. News ranking: Nat. U., No. 77
Website: www.american.edu
Admissions email: admissions@american.edu
Private; founded 1893
Affiliation: United Methodist
Freshman admissions: more selective; 2018-2019: 18,984 applied, 5,988 accepted. Neither SAT nor ACT required. SAT 25/75 percentile: 1220-1380. High school rank: 31% in top tenth, 70% in top quarter, 93% in top half

Early decision deadline: 11/15, notification date: 12/31
Early action deadline: N/A, notification date: N/A
Application deadline (fall): 1/15
Undergraduate student body: 7,952 full time, 335 part time; 38% male, 62% female; 0% American Indian, 7% Asian, 7% black, 13% Hispanic, 4% multiracial, 0% Pacific Islander, 56% white, 9% international; N/A from in state; N/A live on campus; 9% of students in fraternities, 11% in sororities
Most popular majors: 23% International Relations and Affairs, 11% Business Administration and Management, General, 8% Political Science and Government, General, 7% Public Relations/Image Management, 6% Multi-/Interdisciplinary Studies, Other
Expenses: 2019-2020: $49,889; room/board: $14,880
Financial aid: (202) 885-6500; 50% of undergrads determined to have financial need; average aid package $33,952

The Catholic University of America
Washington DC
(800) 673-2772
U.S. News ranking: Nat. U., No. 139
Website: www.catholic.edu/
Admissions email: cua-admissions@cua.edu
Private; founded 1887
Affiliation: Roman Catholic
Freshman admissions: selective; 2018-2019: 6,096 applied, 5,101 accepted. Neither SAT nor ACT required. SAT 25/75 percentile: 1140-1320. High school rank: N/A
Early decision deadline: 11/15, notification date: 12/20
Early action deadline: 11/1, notification date: 12/20
Application deadline (fall): 1/15
Undergraduate student body: 3,198 full time, 134 part time; 47% male, 53% female; 0% American Indian, 4% Asian, 4% black, 14% Hispanic, 5% multiracial, 0% Pacific Islander, 65% white, 6% international; 4% from in state; N/A live on campus; N/A of students in fraternities, N/A in sororities
Most popular majors: 10% Registered Nursing/Registered Nurse, 9% Political Science and Government, General, 8% Psychology, General, 6% Architecture, 6% Mechanical Engineering
Expenses: 2019-2020: $47,746; room/board: $15,260
Financial aid: (202) 319-5307; 55% of undergrads determined to have financial need; average aid package $31,789

Gallaudet University
Washington DC
(202) 651-5750
U.S. News ranking: Nat. U., No. 179
Website: www.gallaudet.edu
Admissions email: admissions.office@gallaudet.edu
Private; founded 1864
Freshman admissions: less selective; 2018-2019: 496 applied, 283 accepted. Either SAT or ACT required. ACT 25/75 percentile: 15-20. High school rank: N/A
Early decision deadline: N/A, notification date: N/A
Early action deadline: N/A, notification date: N/A
Application deadline (fall): rolling
Undergraduate student body: 1,066 full time, 72 part time; 46% male, 54% female; 1% American Indian, 4% Asian, 16% black, 12% Hispanic, 4% multiracial, 1% Pacific Islander, 51% white, 4% international; N/A from in state; 83% live on campus; 15% of students in fraternities, 9% in sororities
Most popular majors: 16% Foreign Languages, Literatures, and Linguistics, 10% Business, Management, Marketing, and Related Support Services, 9% Communication, Journalism, and Related Programs, 9% Psychology, 8% Public Administration and Social Service Professions
Expenses: 2019-2020: $17,038; room/board: $14,800
Financial aid: (202) 651-5290; 91% of undergrads determined to have financial need; average aid package $23,724

Georgetown University
Washington DC
(202) 687-3600
U.S. News ranking: Nat. U., No. 24
Website: www.georgetown.edu
Admissions email: guadmiss@georgetown.edu
Private; founded 1789
Affiliation: Roman Catholic
Freshman admissions: most selective; 2018-2019: 22,872 applied, 3,320 accepted. Either SAT or ACT required. SAT 25/75 percentile: 1370-1530. High school rank: 89% in top tenth, 97% in top quarter, 99% in top half
Early decision deadline: N/A, notification date: N/A
Early action deadline: 11/1, notification date: 12/15
Application deadline (fall): 1/10
Undergraduate student body: 6,990 full time, 469 part time; 44% male, 56% female; 0% American Indian, 10% Asian, 7% black, 10% Hispanic, 5% multiracial, 0% Pacific Islander, 52% white, 14% international; N/A from in state; 77% live on campus; N/A of students in fraternities, N/A in sororities

Most popular majors: 35% Social Sciences, 26% Business, Management, Marketing, and Related Support Services, 6% Multi/Interdisciplinary Studies, 5% Biological and Biomedical Sciences, 5% Foreign Languages, Literatures, and Linguistics
Expenses: 2019-2020: $56,058; room/board: $17,047
Financial aid: (202) 687-4547; 38% of undergrads determined to have financial need; average aid package $48,279

George Washington University
Washington DC
(202) 994-6040
U.S. News ranking: Nat. U., No. 70
Website: www.gwu.edu
Admissions email: gwadm@gwu.edu
Private; founded 1821
Freshman admissions: more selective; 2018-2019: 26,512 applied, 11,101 accepted. Either SAT or ACT required for some. SAT 25/75 percentile: 1280-1460. High school rank: 56% in top tenth, 88% in top quarter, 98% in top half
Early decision deadline: 11/1, notification date: 12/15
Early action deadline: N/A, notification date: N/A
Application deadline (fall): 1/1
Undergraduate student body: 11,334 full time, 1,212 part time; 39% male, 61% female; 0% American Indian, 11% Asian, 7% black, 10% Hispanic, 4% multiracial, 0% Pacific Islander, 51% white, 11% international; 3% from in state; 60% live on campus; 14% of students in fraternities, 17% in sororities
Most popular majors: 34% Social Sciences, 17% Business, Management, Marketing, and Related Support Services, 12% Health Professions and Related Programs, 5% Communication, Journalism, and Related Programs, 5% Engineering
Expenses: 2019-2020: $56,935; room/board: $14,300
Financial aid: (202) 994-6620; 48% of undergrads determined to have financial need; average aid package $47,368

Howard University
Washington DC
(202) 806-2755
U.S. News ranking: Nat. U., No. 104
Website: www.howard.edu
Admissions email: admission@howard.edu
Private; founded 1867
Freshman admissions: more selective; 2018-2019: 20,946 applied, 6,617 accepted. Either SAT or ACT required. SAT 25/75 percentile: 1140-1285. High school rank: 27% in top tenth, 59% in top quarter, 89% in top half
Early decision deadline: N/A, notification date: N/A
Early action deadline: 11/1, notification date: 12/20
Application deadline (fall): 2/15

Undergraduate student body: 5,991 full time, 252 part time; 31% male, 69% female; 0% American Indian, 1% Asian, 89% black, 1% Hispanic, 0% multiracial, 1% Pacific Islander, 2% white, 6% international; 3% from in state; 62% live on campus; 3% of students in fraternities, 5% in sororities
Most popular majors: 16% Communication, Journalism, and Related Programs, 15% Business, Management, Marketing, and Related Support Services, 12% Biological and Biomedical Sciences, 10% Social Sciences, 9% Health Professions and Related Programs
Expenses: 2019-2020: $27,206; room/board: $14,374
Financial aid: (202) 806-2747; 78% of undergrads determined to have financial need; average aid package $7,739

Strayer University[1]
Washington DC
(202) 408-2400
U.S. News ranking: Reg. U. (N), unranked
Website: www.strayer.edu
Admissions email: mzm@strayer.edu
For-profit; founded 1892
Application deadline (fall): N/A
Undergraduate student body: N/A full time, N/A part time
Expenses: N/A
Financial aid: N/A

Trinity Washington University[1]
Washington DC
(202) 884-9400
U.S. News ranking: Reg. U. (N), second tier
Website: www.trinitydc.edu
Admissions email: admissions@trinitydc.edu
Private
Application deadline (fall): N/A
Undergraduate student body: N/A full time, N/A part time
Expenses: N/A
Financial aid: N/A

University of the District of Columbia
Washington DC
(202) 274-5010
U.S. News ranking: Reg. U. (N), second tier
Website: www.udc.edu/
Admissions email: N/A
Public; founded 1976
Freshman admissions: less selective; 2018-2019: 3,276 applied, 2,275 accepted. Either SAT or ACT required. SAT 25/75 percentile: N/A. High school rank: N/A
Early decision deadline: N/A, notification date: N/A
Early action deadline: N/A, notification date: N/A
Application deadline (fall): rolling
Undergraduate student body: 1,848 full time, 2,019 part time; 42% male, 58% female; 0% American Indian, 1% Asian, 35% black,

5% Hispanic, 0% multiracial, 0% Pacific Islander, 2% white, 10% international
Most popular majors: 13% Business Administration, Management and Operations, 12% Political Science and Government, 8% Accounting and Related Services, 8% Criminal Justice and Corrections, 5% Social Work
Expenses: 2019-2020: $6,020 in state, $12,704 out of state; room/board: $16,781
Financial aid: (202) 274-6053; 62% of undergrads determined to have financial need; average aid package $9,171

University of the Potomac[1]
Washington DC
(202) 274-2303
U.S. News ranking: Business, unranked
Website: www.potomac.edu
Admissions email: admissions@potomac.edu
For-profit; founded 1991
Application deadline (fall): rolling
Undergraduate student body: N/A full time, N/A part time
Expenses: N/A
Financial aid: N/A

FLORIDA

Ave Maria University
Ave Maria FL
(877) 283-8648
U.S. News ranking: Nat. Lib. Arts, second tier
Website: www.avemaria.edu
Admissions email: N/A
Private; founded 2003
Freshman admissions: selective; 2018-2019: 1,378 applied, 1,143 accepted. Either SAT or ACT required. SAT 25/75 percentile: 1050-1260. High school rank: N/A
Early decision deadline: N/A, notification date: N/A
Early action deadline: N/A, notification date: N/A
Application deadline (fall): rolling
Undergraduate student body: 1,066 full time, 22 part time; 48% male, 52% female; 0% American Indian, 3% Asian, 5% black, 15% Hispanic, 0% multiracial, 0% Pacific Islander, 64% white, 2% international; N/A from in state; N/A live on campus; 0% of students in fraternities, 0% in sororities
Most popular majors: 10% Business Administration and Management, General, 10% Psychology, General, 6% Biochemistry, 6% Health Professions and Related Programs, 6% Kinesiology and Exercise Science
Expenses: 2019-2020: $21,850; room/board: $11,990
Financial aid: (239) 280-1669; 61% of undergrads determined to have financial need; average aid package $21,301

Barry University
Miami Shores FL
(305) 899-3100
U.S. News ranking: Nat. U., second tier
Website: www.barry.edu
Admissions email: admissions@barry.edu
Private; founded 1940
Affiliation: Roman Catholic
Freshman admissions: less selective; 2018-2019: 5,255 applied, 4,795 accepted. Either SAT or ACT required. SAT 25/75 percentile: 940-1100. High school rank: N/A
Early decision deadline: N/A, notification date: N/A
Early action deadline: N/A, notification date: N/A
Application deadline (fall): rolling
Undergraduate student body: 2,968 full time, 515 part time; 39% male, 61% female; 0% American Indian, 1% Asian, 33% black, 34% Hispanic, 2% multiracial, 0% Pacific Islander, 17% white, 8% international; 72% from in state; 32% live on campus; N/A of students in fraternities, N/A in sororities
Most popular majors: 33% Business, Management, Marketing, and Related Support Services, 15% Health Professions and Related Programs, 11% Public Administration and Social Service Professions, 9% Biological and Biomedical Sciences, 5% Liberal Arts and Sciences, General Studies and Humanities
Expenses: 2019-2020: $29,850; room/board: $11,224
Financial aid: (305) 899-3673; 76% of undergrads determined to have financial need; average aid package $22,982

Beacon College[1]
Leesburg FL
(352) 787-7660
U.S. News ranking: Reg. Coll. (S), unranked
Website: www.beaconcollege.edu/
Admissions email: admissions@beaconcollege.edu
Private
Application deadline (fall): N/A
Undergraduate student body: N/A full time, N/A part time
Expenses: N/A
Financial aid: N/A

Bethune-Cookman University
Daytona Beach FL
(800) 448-0228
U.S. News ranking: Nat. Lib. Arts, second tier
Website: www.bethune.cookman.edu
Admissions email: admissions@cookman.edu
Private; founded 1904
Freshman admissions: least selective; 2018-2019: 11,166 applied, 8,838 accepted. Either SAT or ACT required. SAT 25/75 percentile: 850-1010. High school rank: 3% in top tenth, 16% in top quarter, 46% in top half
Early decision deadline: N/A, notification date: N/A

Chipola College[1]
Marianna FL
(850) 718-2211
U.S. News ranking: Reg. Coll. (S), second tier
Website: www.chipola.edu
Admissions email: N/A
Public
Application deadline (fall): N/A

Early action deadline: N/A, notification date: N/A
Application deadline (fall): rolling
Undergraduate student body: 3,483 full time, 137 part time; 38% male, 62% female; 0% American Indian, 0% Asian, 80% black, 3% Hispanic, 2% multiracial, 0% Pacific Islander, 1% white, 3% international; N/A from in state; 68% live on campus; N/A of students in fraternities, N/A in sororities
Most popular majors: 22% Liberal Arts and Sciences, General Studies and Humanities, 19% Business, Management, Marketing, and Related Support Services, 13% Homeland Security, Law Enforcement, Firefighting and Related Protective Services, 12% Psychology, 7% Communication, Journalism, and Related Programs
Expenses: 2019-2020: $14,814; room/board: $9,462
Financial aid: (386) 481-2620; 95% of undergrads determined to have financial need; average aid package $15,089

Broward College
Fort Lauderdale FL
(954) 201-7350
U.S. News ranking: Reg. Coll. (S), second tier
Website: www.broward.edu
Admissions email: N/A
Public; founded 1960
Freshman admissions: least selective; 2018-2019: 6,777 applied, 6,777 accepted. Neither SAT nor ACT required. SAT 25/75 percentile: N/A. High school rank: N/A
Early decision deadline: N/A, notification date: N/A
Early action deadline: N/A, notification date: N/A
Application deadline (fall): rolling
Undergraduate student body: 11,749 full time, 29,035 part time; 40% male, 60% female; 0% American Indian, 3% Asian, 32% black, 37% Hispanic, 4% multiracial, 0% Pacific Islander, 16% white, 5% international; 95% from in state; 0% live on campus; 0% of students in fraternities, 0% in sororities
Most popular majors: 43% Business Administration, Management and Operations, Other, 20% Registered Nursing/Registered Nurse, 11% Information Technology, 8% Logistics, Materials, and Supply Chain Management, 8% Special Education and Teaching, General
Expenses: 2019-2020: $3,537 in state, $10,779 out of state; room/board: N/A
Financial aid: (954) 201-2330; 23% of undergrads determined to have financial need; average aid package $3,881

Undergraduate student body: N/A full time, N/A part time
Expenses: 2018-2019: $8,308 in state, $19,526 out of state; room/board: N/A
Financial aid: N/A

College of Central Florida[1]
Ocala FL
(352) 854-2322
U.S. News ranking: Reg. Coll. (S), unranked
Website: www.cf.edu
Admissions email: admissions@cf.edu
Public; founded 1957
Application deadline (fall): 8/12
Undergraduate student body: N/A full time, N/A part time
Expenses: N/A
Financial aid: (352) 854-2322

Daytona State College[1]
Daytona Beach FL
(386) 506-3000
U.S. News ranking: Reg. Coll. (S), unranked
Website: www.daytonastate.edu
Admissions email: N/A
Public; founded 1957
Application deadline (fall): N/A
Undergraduate student body: N/A full time, N/A part time
Expenses: N/A
Financial aid: N/A

Eastern Florida State College[1]
Cocoa FL
(321) 633-1111
U.S. News ranking: Reg. Coll. (S), unranked
Website: www.easternflorida.edu
Admissions email: N/A
Public; founded 1960
Application deadline (fall): rolling
Undergraduate student body: N/A full time, N/A part time
Expenses: N/A
Financial aid: N/A

Eckerd College
St. Petersburg FL
(727) 864-8331
U.S. News ranking: Nat. Lib. Arts, No. 140
Website: www.eckerd.edu
Admissions email: admissions@eckerd.edu
Private; founded 1958
Freshman admissions: selective; 2018-2019: 4,830 applied, 3,268 accepted. Either SAT or ACT required. SAT 25/75 percentile: 1080-1280. High school rank: N/A
Early decision deadline: N/A, notification date: N/A
Early action deadline: 11/15, notification date: 12/15
Application deadline (fall): rolling
Undergraduate student body: 1,939 full time, 60 part time; 34% male, 66% female; 0% American Indian, 3% Asian, 3% black, 8% Hispanic, 4% multiracial, 0% Pacific Islander, 78% white, 4% international; 79% from in-

state; 88% live on campus; N/A of students in fraternities, N/A in sororities
Most popular majors: 26% Biology/Biological Sciences, General, 15% Natural Resources/Conservation, General, 15% Psychology, General, 11% International Business/Trade/Commerce, 10% Social Sciences, General
Expenses: 2019-2020: $46,096; room/board: $13,026
Financial aid: (727) 864-8334; 60% of undergrads determined to have financial need; average aid package $38,454

Edward Waters College[1]
Jacksonville FL
(904) 470-8200
U.S. News ranking: Reg. Coll. (S), second tier
Website: www.ewc.edu
Admissions email: admissions@ewc.edu
Private
Application deadline (fall): N/A
Undergraduate student body: N/A full time, N/A part time
Expenses: N/A
Financial aid: N/A

Embry-Riddle Aeronautical University
Daytona Beach FL
(800) 862-2416
U.S. News ranking: Reg. U. (S), No. 11
Website: www.embryriddle.edu
Admissions email: dbadmit@erau.edu
Private; founded 1926
Freshman admissions: more selective; 2018-2019: 6,017 applied, 3,941 accepted. Neither SAT nor ACT required. SAT 25/75 percentile: 1110-1320. High school rank: 20% in top tenth, 49% in top quarter, 82% in top half
Early decision deadline: N/A, notification date: N/A
Early action deadline: N/A, notification date: N/A
Application deadline (fall): rolling
Undergraduate student body: 5,601 full time, 383 part time; 77% male, 23% female; 0% American Indian, 5% Asian, 5% black, 14% Hispanic, 4% multiracial, 0% Pacific Islander, 56% white, 13% international; 34% from in state; 39% live on campus; N/A of students in fraternities, N/A in sororities
Most popular majors: 42% Transportation and Materials Moving, 32% Engineering, 8% Business, Management, Marketing, and Related Support Services, 7% Homeland Security, Law Enforcement, Firefighting and Related Protective Services, 3% Psychology
Expenses: 2019-2020: $36,868; room/board: $11,746
Financial aid: (386) 226-6300; 61% of undergrads determined to have financial need; average aid package $18,528

Everglades University[1]
Boca Raton FL
(888) 772-6077
U.S. News ranking: Reg. U. (S), second tier
Website: www.evergladesuniversity.edu
Admissions email: N/A
Private; founded 2002
Application deadline (fall): rolling
Undergraduate student body: N/A full time, N/A part time
Expenses: N/A
Financial aid: (561) 912-1211

Flagler College
St. Augustine FL
(800) 304 4208
U.S. News ranking: Reg. Coll. (S), No. 4
Website: www.flagler.edu
Admissions email: admissions@flagler.edu
Private; founded 1968
Freshman admissions: selective; 2018 2019: 4,858 applied, 2,752 accepted. Neither SAT nor ACT required. SAT 25/75 percentile: 1030-1220. High school rank: N/A
Early decision deadline: 11/1, notification date: 12/15
Early action deadline: N/A, notification date: N/A
Application deadline (fall): 3/1
Undergraduate student body: 2,562 full time, 38 part time; 34% male, 66% female; 0% American Indian, 1% Asian, 4% black, 8% Hispanic, 3% multiracial, 0% Pacific Islander, 75% white, 4% international; 56% from in state; 43% live on campus; N/A of students in fraternities, N/A in sororities
Most popular majors: 23% Business, Management, Marketing, and Related Support Services, 14% Social Sciences, 13% Communication, Journalism, and Related Programs, 10% Psychology, 10% Visual and Performing Arts
Expenses: 2019-2020: $19,500; room/board: $12,060
Financial aid: (904) 819-6225; 64% of undergrads determined to have financial need; average aid package $13,806

Florida A&M University
Tallahassee FL
(850) 599-3796
U.S. News ranking: Nat. U., No. 254
Website: www.famu.edu
Admissions email: ugradmissions@famu.edu
Public; founded 1887
Freshman admissions: selective; 2018-2019: 8,976 applied, 3,488 accepted. Either SAT or ACT required. SAT 25/75 percentile: 1040-1170. High school rank: 11% in top tenth, 25% in top quarter, 73% in top half
Early decision deadline: N/A, notification date: N/A
Early action deadline: N/A, notification date: N/A

Application deadline (fall): 5/15
Undergraduate student body: 6,958 full time, 1,179 part time; 35% male, 65% female; 0% American Indian, 1% Asian, 88% black, 4% Hispanic, 4% multiracial, 0% Pacific Islander, 3% white, 1% international; 86% from in state; N/A live on campus; N/A of students in fraternities, N/A in sororities
Most popular majors: 22% Health Professions and Related Programs, 18% Multi/Interdisciplinary Studies, 8% Business, Management, Marketing, and Related Support Services, 8% Homeland Security, Law Enforcement, Firefighting and Related Protective Services, 7% Social Sciences
Expenses: 2019-2020: $5,785 in state, $17,725 out of state; room/board: $10,986
Financial aid: (850) 599-3730, 85% of undergrads determined to have financial need; average aid package $13,709

Florida Atlantic University
Boca Raton FL
(561) 297-3040
U.S. News ranking: Nat. U., No. 281
Website: www.fau.edu
Admissions email: Admissions@fau.edu
Public; founded 1961
Freshman admissions: selective; 2018-2019: 17,120 applied, 10,156 accepted. Either SAT or ACT required. SAT 25/75 percentile: 1080-1240. High school rank: 12% in top tenth, 41% in top quarter, 81% in top half
Early decision deadline: N/A, notification date: N/A
Early action deadline: N/A, notification date: N/A
Application deadline (fall): 5/1
Undergraduate student body: 16,443 full time, 8,126 part time; 44% male, 56% female; 0% American Indian, 4% Asian, 20% black, 28% Hispanic, 4% multiracial, 0% Pacific Islander, 40% white, 3% international
Most popular majors: Information not available
Expenses: 2019-2020: $6,039 in state, $21,595 out of state; room/board: $11,950
Financial aid: (561) 297-3531; 61% of undergrads determined to have financial need; average aid package $13,887

Florida College[7]
Temple Terrace FL
(800) 326-7655
U.S. News ranking: Reg. Coll. (S), second tier
Website: www.floridacollege.edu/
Admissions email: admissions@floridacollege.edu
Private; founded 1946
Freshman admissions: selective; 2018-2019: 331 applied, 244 accepted. Either SAT or ACT required. ACT 25/75 percentile: 20-26. High school rank: N/A

Early decision deadline: N/A, notification date: N/A
Early action deadline: N/A, notification date: N/A
Application deadline (fall): 8/25
Undergraduate student body: 494 full time, 14 part time
Most popular majors: Information not available
Expenses: 2018-2019: $17,142; room/board: $8,420
Financial aid: (813) 988-5131

Florida Gateway College[7]
Lake City FL
(386) 754-4581
U.S. News ranking: Reg. Coll. (S), unranked
Website: www.fgc.edu
Admissions email: enrollment.services@fgc.edu
Public
Freshman admissions: least selective; 2018-2019: N/A applied, N/A accepted. Neither SAT nor ACT required. SAT 25/75 percentile: N/A. High school rank: N/A
Early decision deadline: N/A, notification date: N/A
Early action deadline: N/A, notification date: N/A
Application deadline (fall): N/A
Undergraduate student body: 1,218 full time, 2,563 part time
Most popular majors: Information not available
Expenses: 2018-2019: $3,100 in state, $11,747 out of state; room/board: $5,400
Financial aid: N/A

Florida Gulf Coast University
Fort Myers FL
(239) 590-7878
U.S. News ranking: Reg. U. (S), No. 69
Website: www.fgcu.edu
Admissions email: admissions@fgcu.edu
Public; founded 1991
Freshman admissions: selective; 2018-2019: 14,702 applied, 9,545 accepted. Either SAT or ACT required. SAT 25/75 percentile: 1060-1210. High school rank: 14% in top tenth, 39% in top quarter, 74% in top half
Early decision deadline: N/A, notification date: N/A
Early action deadline: N/A, notification date: N/A
Application deadline (fall): 7/1
Undergraduate student body: 11,184 full time, 2,687 part time; 44% male, 56% female; 0% American Indian, 2% Asian, 7% black, 21% Hispanic, 3% multiracial, 0% Pacific Islander, 63% white, 2% international; 8% from in state; 35% live on campus; 11% of students in fraternities, 12% in sororities
Most popular majors: 8% Business Administration and Management, General, 8% Speech Communication and Rhetoric, 7% Criminal Justice/Safety Studies, 6% Psychology, General, 6% Resort Management

Expenses: 2019-2020: $6,118 in state, $25,162 out of state; room/board: $9,672
Financial aid: (239) 590-1210; 46% of undergrads determined to have financial need; average aid package $8,364

Florida Institute of Technology
Melbourne FL
(800) 888-4348
U.S. News ranking: Nat. U., No. 202
Website: www.fit.edu
Admissions email: admission@fit.edu
Private; founded 1958
Freshman admissions: more selective; 2018-2019: 9,313 applied, 6,057 accepted. Either SAT or ACT required. SAT 25/75 percentile: 1150-1340. High school rank: 29% in top tenth, 58% in top quarter, 87% in top half
Early decision deadline: N/A, notification date: N/A
Early action deadline: N/A, notification date: N/A
Application deadline (fall): rolling
Undergraduate student body: 3,271 full time, 409 part time; 71% male, 29% female; 0% American Indian, 2% Asian, 6% black, 9% Hispanic, 3% multiracial, 0% Pacific Islander, 49% white, 28% international; 34% from in state; 47% live on campus; 4% of students in fraternities, 3% in sororities
Most popular majors: 12% Mechanical Engineering, 8% Aviation/Airway Management and Operations, 7% Aerospace, Aeronautical and Astronautical/Space Engineering, 5% Chemical Engineering, 5% Civil Engineering, General
Expenses: 2019-2020: $42,470; room/board: $12,880
Financial aid: (321) 674-8070; 55% of undergrads determined to have financial need; average aid package $39,736

Florida International University
Miami FL
(305) 348-2363
U.S. News ranking: Nat. U., No. 218
Website: www.fiu.edu
Admissions email: admiss@fiu.edu
Public; founded 1972
Freshman admissions: selective; 2018-2019: 19,410 applied, 11,366 accepted. Either SAT or ACT required. SAT 25/75 percentile: 1090-1260. High school rank: 25% in top tenth, 48% in top quarter, 85% in top half
Early decision deadline: N/A, notification date: N/A
Early action deadline: N/A, notification date: N/A
Undergraduate student body: 27,934 full time, 20,505 part time; 44% male, 56% female; 0% American Indian, 2% Asian, 12% black, 67% Hispanic,

2% multiracial, 0% Pacific Islander, 9% white, 7% international; 96% from in state; 6% live on campus; N/A of students in fraternities, N/A in sororities
Most popular majors: 25% Business, Management, Marketing, and Related Support Services, 12% Psychology, 8% Multi/Interdisciplinary Studies, 7% Social Sciences, 6% Communication, Journalism, and Related Programs
Expenses: 2019-2020: $6,558 in state, $18,956 out of state; room/board: $10,882
Financial aid: (305) 348-2333; 68% of undergrads determined to have financial need; average aid package $9,512

Florida Keys Community College[1]
Key West FL
(305) 296-9081
U.S. News ranking: Reg. Coll. (S), unranked
Website: www.fkcc.edu
Admissions email: N/A
Public
Application deadline (fall): N/A
Undergraduate student body: N/A full time, N/A part time
Expenses: N/A
Financial aid: N/A

Florida Memorial University[7]
Miami FL
(305) 626-3750
U.S. News ranking: Reg. Coll. (S), No. 31
Website: www.fmuniv.edu/
Admissions email: admit@fmuniv.edu
Private; founded 1879
Affiliation: Baptist
Freshman admissions: less selective; 2018-2019: N/A applied, N/A accepted. Neither SAT nor ACT required. SAT 25/75 percentile: N/A. High school rank: N/A
Early decision deadline: 4/1, notification date: 4/1
Early action deadline: N/A, notification date: N/A
Application deadline (fall): rolling
Undergraduate student body: 1,081 full time, 57 part time
Most popular majors: Information not available
Expenses: 2018-2019: $15,536; room/board: $7,776
Financial aid: (305) 626-3745

Florida National University–Main Campus
Hialeah FL
(305) 821-3333
U.S. News ranking: Reg. Coll. (S), unranked
Website: www.fnu.edu/
Admissions email: rlopez@fnu.edu
For-profit; founded 1988
Freshman admissions: least selective; 2018-2019: 1,545 applied, 1,506 accepted. Neither

SAT nor ACT required. SAT 25/75 percentile: N/A. High school rank: N/A
Early decision deadline: N/A, notification date: N/A
Early action deadline: N/A, notification date: N/A
Application deadline (fall): N/A
Undergraduate student body: 2,641 full time, 1,178 part time; 27% male, 73% female; 0% American Indian, 0% Asian, 3% black, 87% Hispanic, 1% multiracial, 0% Pacific Islander, 1% white, 7% international; 98% from in state; 0% live on campus; 0% of students in fraternities, 0% in sororities
Most popular majors: 65% Registered Nursing/Registered Nurse, 17% Health Services Administration, 11% Business Administration and Management, General, 5% Accounting, 2% Psychology, General
Expenses: 2019-2020: $13,688; room/board: N/A
Financial aid: (305) 821-3333; 90% of undergrads determined to have financial need; average aid package $7,164

Florida Polytechnic University
Lakeland FL
(863) 874-4774
U.S. News ranking: Reg. Coll. (S), unranked
Website: floridapoly.edu/
Admissions email: admissions@floridapoly.edu
Public; founded 2012
Freshman admissions: more selective; 2018-2019: 1,431 applied, 729 accepted. Either SAT or ACT required. SAT 25/75 percentile: 1220-1368. High school rank: 25% in top tenth, 45% in top quarter, 87% in top half
Early decision deadline: N/A, notification date: N/A
Early action deadline: N/A, notification date: N/A
Application deadline (fall): 4/1
Undergraduate student body: 1,251 full time, 141 part time; 87% male, 13% female; 1% American Indian, 5% Asian, 5% black, 19% Hispanic, 3% multiracial, 0% Pacific Islander, 64% white, 3% international
Most popular majors: 30% Mechanical Engineering, 28% Computer Software and Media Applications, Other, 14% Electrical and Electronics Engineering, 7% Data Modeling/Warehousing and Database Administration, 6% Logistics, Materials, and Supply Chain Management
Expenses: 2019-2020: $4,940 in state, $21,005 out of state; room/board: $11,471
Financial aid: (863) 874-4774; 43% of undergrads determined to have financial need; average aid package $8,133

Florida Southern College
Lakeland FL
(863) 680-4131
U.S. News ranking: Reg. U. (S), No. 10
Website: www.flsouthern.edu
Admissions email: fscadm@flsouthern.edu
Private; founded 1883
Freshman admissions: more selective; 2018-2019: 7,254 applied, 3,644 accepted. Either SAT or ACT required. SAT 25/75 percentile: 1130-1300. High school rank: 30% in top tenth, 61% in top quarter, 87% in top half
Early decision deadline: 11/1, notification date: 12/1
Early action deadline: N/A, notification date: N/A
Application deadline (fall): rolling
Undergraduate student body: 2,502 full time, 221 part time; 35% male, 65% female; 1% American Indian, 3% Asian, 6% black, 12% Hispanic, 1% multiracial, 0% Pacific Islander, 71% white, 3% international; 63% from in state; 79% live on campus; 29% of students in fraternities, 35% in sororities
Most popular majors: 17% Business Administration and Management, General, 13% Registered Nursing/Registered Nurse, 8% Psychology, General, 7% Biology/Biological Sciences, General, 5% Elementary Education and Teaching
Expenses: 2019-2020: $37,640; room/board: $11,860
Financial aid: (863) 680-4140; 68% of undergrads determined to have financial need; average aid package $31,099

Florida SouthWestern State College
Fort Myers FL
(239) 489-9094
U.S. News ranking: Reg. Coll. (S), unranked
Website: www.fsw.edu
Admissions email: admissions@fsw.edu
Public; founded 1962
Freshman admissions: least selective; 2018-2019: 5,672 applied, 4,584 accepted. Neither SAT nor ACT required. SAT 25/75 percentile: N/A. High school rank: N/A
Early decision deadline: N/A, notification date: N/A
Early action deadline: N/A, notification date: N/A
Application deadline (fall): 7/31
Undergraduate student body: 6,056 full time, 10,520 part time; 37% male, 63% female; 0% American Indian, 2% Asian, 12% black, 32% Hispanic, 2% multiracial, 0% Pacific Islander, 43% white, 2% international; 96% from in state; 2% live on campus; 0% of students in fraternities, 0% in sororities

Most popular majors: 38% Business, Management, Marketing, and Related Support Services, 34% Health Professions and Related Programs, 19% Education, 8% Homeland Security, Law Enforcement, Firefighting and Related Protective Services
Expenses: 2018-2019: $3,400 in state, $12,978 out of state; room/board: $8,000
Financial aid: (239) 489-9336

Florida State College–Jacksonville[1]
Jacksonville FL
(904) 359-5433
U.S. News ranking: Reg. Coll. (S), unranked
Website: www.fscj.edu
Admissions email: N/A
Public
Application deadline (fall): N/A
Undergraduate student body: N/A full time, N/A part time
Expenses: N/A
Financial aid: N/A

Florida State University
Tallahassee FL
(850) 644-6200
U.S. News ranking: Nat. U., No. 57
Website: www.fsu.edu
Admissions email: admissions@admin.fsu.edu
Public; founded 1851
Freshman admissions: more selective; 2018-2019: 50,314 applied, 18,504 accepted. Either SAT or ACT required. SAT 25/75 percentile: 1200-1350. High school rank: 39% in top tenth, 84% in top quarter, 98% in top half
Early decision deadline: N/A, notification date: N/A
Early action deadline: N/A, notification date: N/A
Application deadline (fall): 3/1
Undergraduate student body: 29,040 full time, 3,432 part time; 43% male, 57% female; 0% American Indian, 2% Asian, 9% black, 21% Hispanic, 4% multiracial, 0% Pacific Islander, 60% white, 2% international; 89% from in state; 21% live on campus; 14% of students in fraternities, 23% in sororities
Most popular majors: 7% Psychology, General, 6% Criminal Justice/Safety Studies, 6% Finance, General, 5% English Language and Literature, General, 5% Marketing/Marketing Management, General
Expenses: 2019-2020: $6,507 in state, $21,673 out of state; room/board: $10,780
Financial aid: (850) 644-5716; 48% of undergrads determined to have financial need; average aid package $17,760

Gulf Coast State College[1]
Panama City FL
U.S. News ranking: Reg. Coll. (S), unranked
Admissions email: N/A
Public
Application deadline (fall): N/A
Undergraduate student body: N/A full time, N/A part time
Expenses: 2019-2020: $2,370 in state, $7,685 out of state; room/board: N/A
Financial aid: (850) 873-3543

Hodges University[1]
Naples FL
(239) 513-1122
U.S. News ranking: Reg. U. (S), unranked
Website: www.hodges.edu
Admissions email: admit@hodges.edu
Private; founded 1990
Application deadline (fall): rolling
Undergraduate student body: N/A full time, N/A part time
Expenses: N/A
Financial aid: (239) 938-7765

Indian River State College[1]
Fort Pierce FL
(772) 462-7460
U.S. News ranking: Reg. Coll. (S), second tier
Website: www.irsc.edu
Admissions email: N/A
Public
Application deadline (fall): rolling
Undergraduate student body: N/A full time, N/A part time
Expenses: 2018-2019: $2,640 in state, $9,890 out of state; room/board: $5,700
Financial aid: (772) 462-7450

Jacksonville University
Jacksonville FL
(800) 225-2027
U.S. News ranking: Reg. U. (S), No. 28
Website: www.ju.edu/index.php
Admissions email: admiss@ju.edu
Private; founded 1934
Freshman admissions: selective; 2018-2019: 4,298 applied, 3,865 accepted. Neither SAT nor ACT required. ACT 25/75 percentile: 21-27. High school rank: N/A
Early decision deadline: N/A, notification date: N/A
Early action deadline: N/A, notification date: N/A
Application deadline (fall): 7/1
Undergraduate student body: 2,292 full time, 628 part time; 39% male, 61% female; 0% American Indian, 3% Asian, 21% black, 12% Hispanic, 3% multiracial, 0% Pacific Islander, 53% white, 7% international; 58% from in state; 47% live on campus; 1% of students in fraternities, 2% in sororities

Most popular majors: 53% Health Professions and Related Programs, 12% Business, Management, Marketing, and Related Support Services, 8% Social Sciences, 7% Visual and Performing Arts, 5% Parks, Recreation, Leisure, and Fitness Studies
Expenses: 2019-2020: $38,620; room/board: $14,330
Financial aid: (904) 256-7062; 74% of undergrads determined to have financial need; average aid package $28,599

Keiser University
Ft. Lauderdale FL
(954) 776-4456
U.S. News ranking: Nat. U., No. 272
Website: www.keiseruniversity.edu/admissions/
Admissions email: N/A
Private; founded 1977
Freshman admissions: less selective; 2018-2019: 5,322 applied, 5,297 accepted. Neither SAT nor ACT required. SAT 25/75 percentile: N/A. High school rank: N/A
Early decision deadline: N/A, notification date: N/A
Early action deadline: N/A, notification date: N/A
Application deadline (fall): rolling
Undergraduate student body: 11,399 full time, 6,493 part time; 31% male, 69% female; 1% American Indian, 2% Asian, 20% black, 34% Hispanic, 3% multiracial, 0% Pacific Islander, 33% white, 1% international
Most popular majors: 22% Business Administration and Management, General, 12% Multi/Interdisciplinary Studies, 9% Psychology, General, 6% Registered Nursing/Registered Nurse, 6% Sport and Fitness Administration/Management
Expenses: 2019-2020: $33,120; room/board: $11,720
Financial aid: (954) 776-4476; 85% of undergrads determined to have financial need; average aid package $8,074

Lake-Sumter State College
Leesburg FL
(352) 323-3665
U.S. News ranking: Reg. Coll. (S), unranked
Website: www.lssc.edu/future-students/admissions/
Admissions email: AdmissionsOffice@lssc.edu
Public; founded 1962
Freshman admissions: least selective; 2018-2019: 1,939 applied, 1,939 accepted. Neither SAT nor ACT required. SAT 25/75 percentile: N/A. High school rank: N/A
Early decision deadline: N/A, notification date: N/A
Early action deadline: N/A, notification date: N/A
Application deadline (fall): 8/5
Undergraduate student body: 1,673 full time, 3,141 part time; 38% male, 62% female; 1% American

Indian, 4% Asian, 9% black, 22% Hispanic, 3% multiracial, 0% Pacific Islander, 57% white, 1% international
Most popular majors: 73% Liberal Arts and Sciences/Liberal Studies, 7% Massage Therapy/Therapeutic Massage, 4% Business Administration, Management and Operations, Other, 2% Electrical and Power Transmission Installation/Installer, General, 2% Information Technology
Expenses: 2018-2019: $9,024 in state, $19,128 out of state; room/board: N/A
Financial aid: (352) 365-3567

Lynn University
Boca Raton FL
(561) 237-7900
U.S. News ranking: Reg. U. (S), No. 65
Website: www.lynn.edu
Admissions email: admission@lynn.edu
Private; founded 1962
Freshman admissions: less selective; 2018-2019: 7,577 applied, 5,338 accepted. Neither SAT nor ACT required. SAT 25/75 percentile: 990-1170. High school rank: N/A
Early decision deadline: N/A, notification date: N/A
Early action deadline: 11/15, notification date: 12/15
Application deadline (fall): 3/1
Undergraduate student body: 2,049 full time, 183 part time; 51% male, 49% female; 0% American Indian, 1% Asian, 11% black, 16% Hispanic, 1% multiracial, 0% Pacific Islander, 47% white, 18% international; 59% from in state; 46% live on campus; 5% of students in fraternities, 4% in sororities
Most popular majors: 45% Business, Management, Marketing, and Related Support Services, 14% Communication, Journalism, and Related Programs, 8% Visual and Performing Arts, 5% Homeland Security, Law Enforcement, Firefighting and Related Protective Services, 5% Psychology
Expenses: 2019-2020: $38,930; room/board: $12,370
Financial aid: (561) 237-7973; 47% of undergrads determined to have financial need; average aid package $23,053

Miami Dade College[1]
Miami FL
(305) 237-8888
U.S. News ranking: Reg. Coll. (S), unranked
Website: www.mdc.edu/
Admissions email: mdcinfo@mdc.edu
Public
Application deadline (fall): N/A
Undergraduate student body: N/A full time, N/A part time
Expenses: N/A
Financial aid: N/A

Miami International University of Art & Design[1]
Miami FL
(305) 428-5700
U.S. News ranking: Arts, unranked
Website: www.aimiu.aii.edu/
Admissions email: N/A
For-profit
Application deadline (fall): 9/14
Undergraduate student body: N/A full time, N/A part time
Expenses: N/A
Financial aid: N/A

New College of Florida
Sarasota FL
(941) 487-5000
U.S. News ranking: Nat. Lib. Arts, No. 102
Website: www.ncf.edu
Admissions email: admissions@ncf.edu
Public; founded 1960
Freshman admissions: more selective; 2018-2019: 1,340 applied, 1,029 accepted. Either SAT or ACT required. SAT 25/75 percentile: 1220-1420. High school rank: 37% in top tenth, 66% in top quarter, 93% in top half
Early decision deadline: N/A, notification date: N/A
Early action deadline: 11/1, notification date: 12/15
Application deadline (fall): 4/15
Undergraduate student body: 808 full time, 0 part time; 38% male, 62% female; 0% American Indian, 3% Asian, 3% black, 17% Hispanic, 3% multiracial, 0% Pacific Islander, 69% white, 2% international; 83% from in state; 79% live on campus; 0% of students in fraternities, 0% in sororities
Most popular majors: 52% Liberal Arts and Sciences, General Studies and Humanities, Other, 33% Biological and Physical Sciences, 6% Environmental Studies, 5% Foreign Languages and Literatures, General, 3% International/Global Studies
Expenses: 2019-2020: $6,916 in state, $29,944 out of state; room/board: $9,529
Financial aid: (941) 487-5000; 53% of undergrads determined to have financial need; average aid package $14,877

North Florida Community College[7]
Madison FL
(850) 973-2288
U.S. News ranking: Reg. Coll. (S), second tier
Admissions email: N/A
Public
Freshman admissions: least selective; 2018-2019: 220 applied, 220 accepted. Neither SAT nor ACT required. SAT 25/75 percentile: N/A. High school rank: 3% in top tenth, 11% in top quarter, 59% in top half
Early decision deadline: N/A, notification date: N/A
Early action deadline: N/A, notification date: N/A

Application deadline (fall): rolling
Undergraduate student body: 369 full time, 860 part time
Most popular majors: 41% Liberal Arts and Sciences/Liberal Studies, 10% Emergency Medical Technology/Technician (EMT Paramedic), 8% Emergency Medical Technology/Technician (EMT Paramedic), 6% Child Care and Support Services Management, 5% Licensed Practical/Vocational Nurse Training
Expenses: 2018-2019: $3,054 in state, $11,400 out of state; room/board: N/A
Financial aid: N/A

Northwest Florida State College[1]
Niceville FL
(850) 678-5111
U.S. News ranking: Reg. Coll. (S), unranked
Website: www.owcc.cc.fl.us/
Admissions email: N/A
Public
Application deadline (fall): rolling
Undergraduate student body: N/A full time, N/A part time
Expenses: N/A
Financial aid: (850) 729-5370

Nova Southeastern University
Ft. Lauderdale FL
(954) 262-8000
U.S. News ranking: Nat. U., No. 246
Website: www.nova.edu
Admissions email: admissions@nova.edu
Private; founded 1964
Freshman admissions: more selective; 2018-2019: 8,946 applied, 7,026 accepted. Either SAT or ACT required. SAT 25/75 percentile: 1080-1290. High school rank: 32% in top tenth, 67% in top quarter, 90% in top half
Early decision deadline: 11/1, notification date: N/A
Early action deadline: 11/1, notification date: N/A
Application deadline (fall): 2/1
Undergraduate student body: 3,685 full time, 1,219 part time; 29% male, 71% female; 0% American Indian, 10% Asian, 14% black, 34% Hispanic, 4% multiracial, 0% Pacific Islander, 28% white, 6% international; 67% from in state; 26% live on campus; 10% of students in fraternities, 9% in sororities
Most popular majors: 45% Health Professions and Related Programs, 21% Biological and Biomedical Sciences, 12% Business, Management, Marketing, and Related Support Services, 5% Psychology, 2% Education
Expenses: 2019-2020: $32,150; room/board: $12,940
Financial aid: (800) 806-3680; 72% of undergrads determined to have financial need; average aid package $32,151

Palm Beach Atlantic University
West Palm Beach FL
(888) 468-6722
U.S. News ranking: Nat. U., second tier
Website: www.pba.edu
Admissions email: admit@pba.edu
Private; founded 1968
Affiliation: Interdenominational
Freshman admissions: selective; 2018-2019: 1,444 applied, 1,376 accepted. Either SAT or ACT required. SAT 25/75 percentile: 1000-1220. High school rank: N/A
Early decision deadline: N/A, notification date: N/A
Early action deadline: 5/1, notification date: 6/1
Application deadline (fall): rolling
Undergraduate student body: 2,269 full time, 586 part time; 37% male, 63% female; 0% American Indian, 2% Asian, 9% black, 16% Hispanic, 3% multiracial, 0% Pacific Islander, 63% white, 5% international; N/A from in state; 48% live on campus; N/A of students in fraternities, N/A in sororities
Most popular majors: 23% Business, Management, Marketing, and Related Support Services, 12% Health Professions and Related Programs, 12% Psychology, 9% Theology and Religious Vocations, 8% Biological and Biomedical Sciences
Expenses: 2019-2020: $32,500; room/board: $10,410
Financial aid: (561) 803-2629; 74% of undergrads determined to have financial need; average aid package $22,570

Palm Beach State College[1]
Lake Worth FL
U.S. News ranking: Reg. Coll. (S), unranked
Admissions email: N/A
Public
Application deadline (fall): N/A
Undergraduate student body: N/A full time, N/A part time
Expenses: N/A
Financial aid: N/A

Pasco-Hernando State College[1]
New Port Richey FL
(727) 847-2727
U.S. News ranking: Reg. Coll. (S), unranked
Website: www.phsc.edu
Admissions email: N/A
Public
Application deadline (fall): N/A
Undergraduate student body: N/A full time, N/A part time
Expenses: N/A
Financial aid: N/A

Pensacola State College

Pensacola FL
(850) 484-2544
U.S. News ranking: Reg. Coll. (S), No. 26
Website: www.pensacolastate.edu
Admissions email: askus@pensacolastate.edu
Public; founded 1948
Freshman admissions: less selective; 2018-2019: 2,362 applied, 2,362 accepted. Neither SAT nor ACT required. ACT 25/75 percentile: 18-23. High school rank: N/A
Early decision deadline: N/A, notification date: N/A
Early action deadline: N/A, notification date: N/A
Application deadline (fall): rolling
Undergraduate student body: 3,785 full time, 5,988 part time; 38% male, 62% female; 1% American Indian, 3% Asian, 17% black, 8% Hispanic, 6% multiracial, 0% Pacific Islander, 62% white, 0% international
Most popular majors: 52% Liberal Arts and Sciences, General Studies and Humanities, 18% Health Professions and Related Programs, 12% Business, Management, Marketing, and Related Support Services, 7% Personal and Culinary Services, 3% Computer and Information Sciences and Support Services
Expenses: 2019-2020: $13,393 in state, $20,958 out of state; room/board: N/A
Financial aid: (850) 484-1708; 45% of undergrads determined to have financial need; average aid package $1,304

Polk State College[1]

Winter Haven FL
U.S. News ranking: Reg. Coll. (S), unranked
Admissions email: N/A
Public
Application deadline (fall): N/A
Undergraduate student body: N/A full time, N/A part time
Expenses: N/A
Financial aid: N/A

Ringling College of Art and Design

Sarasota FL
(800) 255-7695
U.S. News ranking: Arts, unranked
Website: www.ringling.edu
Admissions email: admissions@ringling.edu
Private; founded 1931
Freshman admissions: least selective; 2018-2019: 2,306 applied, 1,543 accepted. Neither SAT nor ACT required. SAT 25/75 percentile: N/A. High school rank: N/A
Early decision deadline: N/A, notification date: N/A
Early action deadline: 11/1, notification date: 12/15
Application deadline (fall): rolling
Undergraduate student body: 1,519 full time, 42 part time; 31% male, 69% female; 0% American Indian, 9% Asian, 3% black,

16% Hispanic, 4% multiracial, 0% Pacific Islander, 47% white, 17% international; 37% from in state; 73% live on campus; 0% of students in fraternities, 0% in sororities
Most popular majors: 37% Animation, Interactive Technology, Video Graphics and Special Effects, 27% Illustration, 9% Cinematography and Film/Video Production, 8% Art/Art Studies, General, 4% Graphic Design
Expenses: 2019-2020: $47,970; room/board: $15,580
Financial aid: (941) 359-7532; 66% of undergrads determined to have financial need; average aid package $27,112

Rollins College

Winter Park FL
(407) 646-2161
U.S. News ranking: Reg. U. (S), No. 1
Website: www.rollins.edu
Admissions email: admission@rollins.edu
Private; founded 1885
Freshman admissions: more selective; 2018-2019: 5,455 applied, 3,635 accepted. Either SAT or ACT required for some. SAT 25/75 percentile: 1150-1360. High school rank: 29% in top tenth, 62% in top quarter, 90% in top half
Early decision deadline: 11/15, notification date: 12/15
Early action deadline: N/A, notification date: N/A
Application deadline (fall): 2/1
Undergraduate student body: 2,027 full time, 7 part time; 40% male, 60% female; 0% American Indian, 3% Asian, 4% black, 18% Hispanic, 5% multiracial, 0% Pacific Islander, 59% white, 8% international; 56% from in state; 63% live on campus; 36% of students in fraternities, 36% in sororities
Most popular majors: 31% Business, Management, Marketing, and Related Support Services, 13% Communication, Journalism, and Related Programs, 12% Social Sciences, 8% Psychology, 7% Visual and Performing Arts
Expenses: 2019-2020: $51,700; room/board: $15,034
Financial aid: (407) 646-2395; 54% of undergrads determined to have financial need; average aid package $40,450

Saint Johns River State College[1]

Palatka FL
U.S. News ranking: Reg. Coll. (S), unranked
Admissions email: N/A
Public
Application deadline (fall): N/A
Undergraduate student body: N/A full time, N/A part time
Expenses: N/A
Financial aid: N/A

Saint Leo University

Saint Leo FL
(800) 334-5532
U.S. News ranking: Reg. U. (S), No. 25
Website: www.saintleo.edu
Admissions email: admission@saintleo.edu
Private; founded 1889
Affiliation: Roman Catholic
Freshman admissions: less selective; 2018-2019: 3,507 applied, 2,950 accepted. Neither SAT nor ACT required. SAT 25/75 percentile: 972-1150. High school rank: 15% in top tenth, 30% in top quarter, 69% in top half
Early decision deadline: N/A, notification date: N/A
Early action deadline: N/A, notification date: N/A
Application deadline (fall): rolling
Undergraduate student body: 2,022 full time, 64 part time; 44% male, 56% female; 1% American Indian, 2% Asian, 14% black, 21% Hispanic, 2% multiracial, 0% Pacific Islander, 40% white, 12% international; 74% from in state; 67% live on campus; 11% of students in fraternities, 14% in sororities
Most popular majors: 23% Business, Management, Marketing, and Related Support Services, 13% Homeland Security, Law Enforcement, Firefighting and Related Protective Services, 11% Computer and Information Sciences and Support Services, 9% Parks, Recreation, Leisure, and Fitness Studies, 8% Psychology
Expenses: 2019-2020: $23,750; room/board: $11,250
Financial aid: (800) 240-7658; 73% of undergrads determined to have financial need; average aid package $24,320

Santa Fe College[1]

Gainesville FL
U.S. News ranking: Reg. Coll. (S), unranked
Admissions email: N/A
Public
Application deadline (fall): N/A
Undergraduate student body: N/A full time, N/A part time
Expenses: N/A
Financial aid: N/A

Seminole State College of Florida[1]

Sanford FL
(407) 708-2380
U.S. News ranking: Reg. Coll. (S), unranked
Website: www.seminolestate.edu
Admissions email: admissions@seminolestate.edu
Public; founded 1965
Application deadline (fall): N/A
Undergraduate student body: N/A full time, N/A part time
Expenses: N/A
Financial aid: N/A

Southeastern University

Lakeland FL
(800) 500-8760
U.S. News ranking: Reg. U. (S), No. 92
Website: www.seu.edu
Admissions email: admission@seu.edu
Private; founded 1935
Affiliation: Assemblies of God Church
Freshman admissions: less selective; 2018-2019: 4,996 applied, 2,405 accepted. Either SAT or ACT required. ACT 25/75 percentile: 18-24. High school rank: 9% in top tenth, 26% in top quarter, 58% in top half
Early decision deadline: N/A, notification date: N/A
Early action deadline: N/A, notification date: N/A
Application deadline (fall): 5/1
Undergraduate student body: 4,909 full time, 2,799 part time; 43% male, 57% female; 0% American Indian, 1% Asian, 14% black, 21% Hispanic, 1% multiracial, 1% Pacific Islander, 58% white, 1% international; 51% from in state; 31% live on campus; N/A of students in fraternities, N/A in sororities
Most popular majors: 21% Theology and Religious Vocations, 17% Business, Management, Marketing, and Related Support Services, 8% Education, 7% Public Administration and Social Service Professions, 6% Communication, Journalism, and Related Programs
Expenses: 2019-2020: $25,870; room/board: $9,832
Financial aid: (863) 667-5306; 76% of undergrads determined to have financial need; average aid package $15,641

South Florida State College

Avon Park FL
(863) 453-6661
U.S. News ranking: Reg. Coll. (S), No. 36
Website: www.southflorida.edu
Admissions email: jonathan.stern@southflorida.edu
Public; founded 1966
Freshman admissions: least selective; 2018-2019: 297 applied, 297 accepted. Neither SAT nor ACT required. SAT 25/75 percentile: 400-400. High school rank: 17% in top tenth, 18% in top quarter, 39% in top half
Early decision deadline: N/A, notification date: N/A
Early action deadline: N/A, notification date: N/A
Application deadline (fall): rolling
Undergraduate student body: 976 full time, 1,934 part time; 37% male, 63% female; 0% American Indian, 2% Asian, 12% black, 37% Hispanic, 2% multiracial, 0% Pacific Islander, 44% white, 2% international; 100% from in state; N/A live on campus; N/A of students in fraternities, N/A in sororities

Most popular majors: 53% Registered Nursing/Registered Nurse, 45% Business Administration, Management and Operations, Other, 2% Elementary Education and Teaching
Expenses: 2018-2019: $3,165 in state, $11,859 out of state; room/board: N/A
Financial aid: (863) 784-7108

State College of Florida—Manatee-Sarasota[1]

Bradenton FL
U.S. News ranking: Reg. Coll. (S), unranked
Admissions email: N/A
Public
Application deadline (fall): N/A
Undergraduate student body: N/A full time, N/A part time
Expenses: N/A
Financial aid: N/A

Stetson University

DeLand FL
(800) 688-0101
U.S. News ranking: Reg. U. (S), No. 5
Website: www.stetson.edu
Admissions email: admissions@stetson.edu
Private; founded 1883
Freshman admissions: more selective; 2018-2019: 13,330 applied, 9,121 accepted. Either SAT or ACT required for some. SAT 25/75 percentile: 1120-1300. High school rank: 22% in top tenth, 54% in top quarter, 86% in top half
Early decision deadline: N/A, notification date: N/A
Early action deadline: 11/1, notification date: N/A
Application deadline (fall): rolling
Undergraduate student body: 3,111 full time, 39 part time; 44% male, 56% female; 0% American Indian, 2% Asian, 8% black, 17% Hispanic, 5% multiracial, 0% Pacific Islander, 60% white, 6% international; 74% from in state; 64% live on campus; 23% of students in fraternities, 27% in sororities
Most popular majors: 30% Business, Management, Marketing, and Related Support Services, 10% Social Sciences, 9% Visual and Performing Arts, 8% Biological and Biomedical Sciences, 8% Psychology
Expenses: 2019-2020: $47,630; room/board: $13,868
Financial aid: (386) 822-7120; 68% of undergrads determined to have financial need; average aid package $38,914

St. Petersburg College

St. Petersburg FL
(727) 341-3400
U.S. News ranking: Reg. Coll. (S), No. 63
Website: www.spcollege.edu/
Admissions email: Admissions@SPC.edu
Public; founded 1927
Freshman admissions: less selective; 2018-2019: 4,114

applied, 4,114 accepted. Either SAT or ACT required for some. SAT 25/75 percentile: 920-1120. High school rank: N/A
Early decision deadline: N/A, notification date: N/A
Early action deadline: N/A, notification date: N/A
Application deadline (fall): rolling
Undergraduate student body: 8,758 full time, 20,425 part time; 38% male, 62% female; 0% American Indian, 4% Asian, 14% black, 16% Hispanic, 3% multiracial, 0% Pacific Islander, 60% white, 1% international
Most popular majors: 49% Liberal Arts and Sciences, General Studies and Humanities, 19% Health Professions and Related Programs, 8% Business, Management, Marketing, and Related Support Services, 7% Computer and Information Sciences and Support Services, 6% Homeland Security, Law Enforcement, Firefighting and Related Protective Services
Expenses: 2019-2020: $2,682 in state, $8,513 out of state; room/ board: N/A
Financial aid: (727) 791-2485; 88% of undergrads determined to have financial need; average aid package $7,344

St. Thomas University[1]
Miami Gardens FL
(305) 628-6546
U.S. News ranking: Reg. U. (S), No. 73
Website: www.stu.edu
Admissions email: signup@stu.edu
Private; founded 1961
Affiliation: Roman Catholic
Application deadline (fall): rolling
Undergraduate student body: N/A full time, N/A part time
Expenses: N/A
Financial aid: (305) 474-6960

Tallahassee Community College[1]
Tallahassee FL
(850) 201-6200
U.S. News ranking: Reg. Coll. (S), unranked
Website: www.tcc.fl.edu
Admissions email: N/A
Public
Application deadline (fall): N/A
Undergraduate student body: N/A full time, N/A part time
Expenses: N/A
Financial aid: N/A

University of Central Florida
Orlando FL
(407) 823-3000
U.S. News ranking: Nat. U., No. 166
Website: www.ucf.edu
Admissions email: admission@ucf.edu
Public; founded 1963
Freshman admissions: more selective; 2018-2019: 41,816 applied, 17,786 accepted. Either SAT or ACT required. SAT 25/75 percentile: 1160-1340. High school rank: 34% in top tenth,

73% in top quarter, 97% in top half
Early decision deadline: N/A, notification date: N/A
Early action deadline: N/A, notification date: N/A
Application deadline (fall): 5/1
Undergraduate student body: 41,852 full time, 17,061 part time; 46% male, 54% female; 0% American Indian, 6% Asian, 11% black, 28% Hispanic, 4% multiracial, 0% Pacific Islander, 48% white, 2% international; 93% from in state; 17% live on campus; 5% of students in fraternities, 17% in sororities
Most popular majors: 21% Business, Management, Marketing, and Related Support Services, 17% Health Professions and Related Programs, 9% Psychology, 7% Education, 7% Engineering
Expenses: 2019-2020: $6,368 in state, $22,467 out of state; room/ board: $9,852
Financial aid: (407) 823-2827; 62% of undergrads determined to have financial need; average aid package $9,982

University of Florida
Gainesville FL
(352) 392-1365
U.S. News ranking: Nat. U., No. 34
Website: www.ufl.edu
Admissions email: webrequests@admissions.ufl.edu
Public; founded 1853
Freshman admissions: most selective; 2018-2019: 38,905 applied, 15,077 accepted. Either SAT or ACT required. SAT 25/75 percentile: 1280-1440. High school rank: 77% in top tenth, 97% in top quarter, 100% in top half
Early decision deadline: N/A, notification date: N/A
Early action deadline: N/A, notification date: N/A
Application deadline (fall): 3/1
Undergraduate student body: 32,209 full time, 3,282 part time; 44% male, 56% female; 0% American Indian, 9% Asian, 6% black, 22% Hispanic, 4% multiracial, 0% Pacific Islander, 53% white, 2% international; 93% from in state; 22% live on campus; 17% of students in fraternities, 22% in sororities
Most popular majors: 13% Engineering, 12% Business, Management, Marketing, and Related Support Services, 11% Biological and Biomedical Sciences, 11% Social Sciences, 8% Communication, Journalism, and Related Programs
Expenses: 2019-2020: $6,380 in state, $28,658 out of state; room/ board: $10,220
Financial aid: (352) 294-3226; 43% of undergrads determined to have financial need; average aid package $13,728

University of Miami
Coral Gables FL
(305) 284-4323
U.S. News ranking: Nat. U., No. 57
Website: www.miami.edu
Admissions email: admission@miami.edu
Private; founded 1925
Freshman admissions: more selective; 2018-2019: 34,279 applied, 11,020 accepted. Either SAT or ACT required. SAT 25/75 percentile: 1250-1430. High school rank: 55% in top tenth, 83% in top quarter, 95% in top half
Early decision deadline: 11/1, notification date: 12/15
Early action deadline: 11/1, notification date: 1/31
Application deadline (fall): 1/1
Undergraduate student body: 10,484 full time, 633 part time; 47% male, 53% female; 0% American Indian, 5% Asian, 8% black, 22% Hispanic, 3% multiracial, 0% Pacific Islander, 42% white, 15% international; 40% from in state; 38% live on campus; 17% of students in fraternities, 18% in sororities
Most popular majors: 21% Business, Management, Marketing, and Related Support Services, 15% Biological and Biomedical Sciences, 11% Health Professions and Related Programs, 10% Engineering, 10% Social Sciences
Expenses: 2019-2020: $51,930; room/board: $14,658
Financial aid: (305) 284-2270; 41% of undergrads determined to have financial need; average aid package $40,813

University of North Florida
Jacksonville FL
(904) 620-2624
U.S. News ranking: Nat. U., No. 281
Website: www.unf.edu
Admissions email: admissions@unf.edu
Public; founded 1965
Freshman admissions: selective; 2018-2019: 14,330 applied, 8,753 accepted. Either SAT or ACT required. SAT 25/75 percentile: 1120-1280. High school rank: 16% in top tenth, 41% in top quarter, 76% in top half
Early decision deadline: N/A, notification date: N/A
Early action deadline: N/A, notification date: N/A
Application deadline (fall): rolling
Undergraduate student body: 10,457 full time, 4,037 part time; 44% male, 56% female; 0% American Indian, 5% Asian, 9% black, 13% Hispanic, 5% multiracial, 0% Pacific Islander, 65% white, 1% international; 96% from in state; 22% live on campus; N/A of students in fraternities, N/A in sororities

Most popular majors: 19% Health Professions and Related Programs, 18% Business, Management, Marketing, and Related Support Services, 8% Psychology, 7% Communication, Journalism, and Related Programs, 6% Social Sciences
Expenses: 2018-2019: $6,394 in state, $20,112 out of state; room/ board: $9,772
Financial aid: (904) 620-5555; 52% of undergrads determined to have financial need; average aid package $10,079

University of South Florida
Tampa FL
(813) 974-3350
U.S. News ranking: Nat. U., No. 104
Website: www.usf.edu
Admissions email: admission@admin.usf.edu
Public; founded 1956
Freshman admissions: more selective; 2018-2019: 35,043 applied, 14,940 accepted. Either SAT or ACT required. SAT 25/75 percentile: 1170-1330. High school rank: 34% in top tenth, 71% in top quarter, 94% in top half
Early decision deadline: N/A, notification date: N/A
Early action deadline: N/A, notification date: N/A
Application deadline (fall): 3/15
Undergraduate student body: 24,833 full time, 7,405 part time; 45% male, 55% female; 0% American Indian, 7% Asian, 10% black, 21% Hispanic, 4% multiracial, 0% Pacific Islander, 47% white, 7% international; N/A from in state; 18% live on campus; 6% of students in fraternities, 7% in sororities
Most popular majors: 20% Health Professions and Related Programs, 16% Business, Management, Marketing, and Related Support Services, 11% Biological and Biomedical Sciences, 11% Social Sciences, 8% Engineering
Expenses: 2019-2020: $6,410 in state, $17,324 out of state; room/ board: $11,610
Financial aid: (813) 974-4700; 62% of undergrads determined to have financial need; average aid package $11,365

University of Tampa
Tampa FL
(888) 646-2738
U.S. News ranking: Reg. U. (S), No. 17
Website: www.ut.edu
Admissions email: admissions@ut.edu
Private; founded 1931
Freshman admissions: more selective; 2018-2019: 22,310 applied, 10,862 accepted. Either SAT or ACT required. SAT 25/75 percentile: 1090-1250. High school rank: 17% in top tenth, 48% in top quarter, 82% in top half
Early decision deadline: N/A, notification date: N/A
Early action deadline: 11/15, notification date: 12/15

Application deadline (fall): rolling
Undergraduate student body: 8,146 full time, 297 part time; 42% male, 58% female; 0% American Indian, 2% Asian, 5% black, 13% Hispanic, 3% multiracial, 0% Pacific Islander, 62% white, 9% international; 33% from in state; 51% live on campus; 6% of students in fraternities, 11% in sororities
Most popular majors: 7% Criminology, 6% Business Administration and Management, General, 6% Finance, General, 6% Marketing/Marketing Management, General, 5% Accounting
Expenses: 2019-2020: $29,992; room/board: $11,136
Financial aid: (813) 253-6219; 59% of undergrads determined to have financial need; average aid package $17,880

University of West Florida
Pensacola FL
(850) 474-2230
U.S. News ranking: Reg. U. (S), No. 34
Website: uwf.edu
Admissions email: admissions@uwf.edu
Public; founded 1963
Freshman admissions: selective; 2018-2019: 5,642 applied, 2,357 accepted. Either SAT or ACT required. ACT 25/75 percentile: 22-27. High school rank: 14% in top tenth, 41% in top quarter, 80% in top half
Early decision deadline: N/A, notification date: N/A
Early action deadline: N/A, notification date: N/A
Application deadline (fall): 6/30
Undergraduate student body: 6,761 full time, 2,972 part time; 43% male, 57% female; 1% American Indian, 3% Asian, 12% black, 10% Hispanic, 6% multiracial, 0% Pacific Islander, 65% white, 2% international; 90% from in state; 13% live on campus; N/A of students in fraternities, N/A in sororities
Most popular majors: 18% Registered Nursing/Registered Nurse, 6% Health and Physical Education/Fitness, General, 6% Mass Communication/Media Studies, 6% Psychology, General, 5% Health Professions and Related Programs
Expenses: 2019-2020: $6,360 in state, $18,628 out of state; room/ board: $10,248
Financial aid: (850) 474-2398; 31% of undergrads determined to have financial need; average aid package $10,852

Valencia College[1]
Orlando FL
U.S. News ranking: Reg. Coll. (S), unranked
Admissions email: N/A
Public
Application deadline (fall): N/A
Undergraduate student body: N/A full time, N/A part time
Expenses: N/A
Financial aid: N/A

Warner University
Lake Wales FL
(800) 309-9563
U.S. News ranking: Reg. Coll. (S), No. 58
Website: www.warner.edu
Admissions email: admissions@warner.edu
Private; founded 1964
Affiliation: Church of God
Freshman admissions: less selective; 2018-2019: 1,375 applied, 487 accepted. Neither SAT nor ACT required. SAT 25/75 percentile: 880-1080. High school rank: 6% in top tenth, 26% in top quarter, 52% in top half
Early decision deadline: N/A, notification date: N/A
Early action deadline: N/A, notification date: N/A
Application deadline (fall): rolling
Undergraduate student body: 818 full time, 92 part time; 54% male, 46% female; 0% American Indian, 0% Asian, 37% black, 12% Hispanic, 1% multiracial, 0% Pacific Islander, 44% white, 5% international; 89% from in state; 38% live on campus; 0% of students in fraternities, 0% in sororities
Most popular majors: 33% Business, Management, Marketing, and Related Support Services, 25% Education, 10% Parks, Recreation, Leisure, and Fitness Studies, 7% Agriculture, Agriculture Operations, and Related Sciences, 5% Public Administration and Social Service Professions
Expenses: 2019-2020: $22,850; room/board: $8,856
Financial aid: (863) 638-7202; 89% of undergrads determined to have financial need; average aid package $18,252

Webber International University
Babson Park FL
(800) 741-1844
U.S. News ranking: Reg. Coll. (S), second tier
Website: www.webber.edu
Admissions email: admissions@webber.edu
Private; founded 1927
Freshman admissions: less selective; 2018-2019: 1,022 applied, 410 accepted. Either SAT or ACT required. SAT 25/75 percentile: 876-1060. High school rank: 6% in top tenth, 27% in top quarter, 61% in top half
Early decision deadline: N/A, notification date: N/A
Early action deadline: N/A, notification date: N/A
Application deadline (fall): 8/1
Undergraduate student body: 587 full time, 28 part time; 74% male, 26% female; 1% American Indian, 0% Asian, 32% black, 13% Hispanic, 1% multiracial, 1% Pacific Islander, 34% white, 17% international; N/A from in state; 50% live on campus; 0% of students in fraternities, 0% in sororities

Most popular majors: 57% Business, Management, Marketing, and Related Support Services, 22% Parks, Recreation, Leisure, and Fitness Studies, 17% Homeland Security, Law Enforcement, Firefighting and Related Protective Services, 2% Computer and Information Sciences and Support Services, 2% Legal Professions and Studies
Expenses: 2019-2020: $27,674; room/board: $9,430
Financial aid: (863) 638-2930; 75% of undergrads determined to have financial need; average aid package $21,206

GEORGIA

Abraham Baldwin Agricultural College[1]
Tifton GA
(800) 733-3653
U.S. News ranking: Reg. Coll. (S), second tier
Website: www.abac.edu/
Admissions email: N/A
Public; founded 1908
Application deadline (fall): 8/1
Undergraduate student body: N/A full time, N/A part time
Expenses: N/A
Financial aid: (229) 391-4985

Agnes Scott College
Decatur GA
(800) 868-8602
U.S. News ranking: Nat. Lib. Arts, No. 58
Website: www.agnesscott.edu
Admissions email: admission@agnesscott.edu
Private; founded 1889
Affiliation: Presbyterian Church (USA)
Freshman admissions: more selective; 2018-2019: 1,625 applied, 1,144 accepted. Either SAT or ACT required for some. SAT 25/75 percentile: 1090-1320. High school rank: 28% in top tenth, 60% in top quarter, 85% in top half
Early decision deadline: 11/1, notification date: 12/1
Early action deadline: 11/15, notification date: 12/15
Application deadline (fall): 5/1
Undergraduate student body: 985 full time, 11 part time; 1% male, 99% female; 0% American Indian, 7% Asian, 32% black, 13% Hispanic, 6% multiracial, 0% Pacific Islander, 33% white, 7% international; 58% from in state; 84% live on campus; N/A of students in fraternities, N/A in sororities
Most popular majors: 12% Psychology, General, 8% Business Administration and Management, General, 8% Neuroscience, 7% Public Health, General, 6% History, General
Expenses: 2019-2020: $42,690; room/board: $12,670
Financial aid: (404) 471-6395; 77% of undergrads determined to have financial need; average aid package $37,199

Albany State University
Albany GA
(229) 500-4358
U.S. News ranking: Reg. U. (S), second tier
Website: www.asurams.edu/
Admissions email: admissions@asurams.edu
Public; founded 1903
Freshman admissions: least selective; 2018-2019: 4,199 applied, 3,758 accepted. Either SAT or ACT required. SAT 25/75 percentile: 750-900. High school rank: 6% in top tenth, 21% in top quarter, 52% in top half
Early decision deadline: N/A, notification date: N/A
Early action deadline: N/A, notification date: N/A
Application deadline (fall): 7/1
Undergraduate student body: 4,190 full time, 1,811 part time; 28% male, 72% female; 0% American Indian, 0% Asian, 74% black, 5% Hispanic, 2% multiracial, 0% Pacific Islander, 14% white, 1% international; 94% from in state; 40% live on campus; N/A of students in fraternities, 0% in sororities
Most popular majors: 21% Business, Management, Marketing, and Related Support Services, 16% Education, 15% Homeland Security, Law Enforcement, Firefighting and Related Protective Services, 14% Health Professions and Related Programs, 7% Biological and Biomedical Sciences
Expenses: 2019-2020: $6,950 in state, $20,352 out of state; room/board: $8,980
Financial aid: (229) 500-4358

Andrew College[7]
Cuthbert GA
(229) 732-5938
U.S. News ranking: Reg. Coll. (S), second tier
Website: www.andrewcollege.edu/
Admissions email: admissions@andrewcollege.edu
Private; founded 1854
Affiliation: United Methodist
Freshman admissions: less selective; 2018-2019: N/A applied, N/A accepted. Neither SAT nor ACT required. SAT 25/75 percentile: N/A. High school rank: N/A
Early decision deadline: N/A, notification date: N/A
Early action deadline: N/A, notification date: N/A
Application deadline (fall): N/A
Undergraduate student body: 205 full time, 88 part time
Most popular majors: Information not available
Expenses: 2018-2019: $17,388; room/board: $10,636
Financial aid: N/A

Art Institute of Atlanta[1]
Atlanta GA
(770) 394-8300
U.S. News ranking: Arts, unranked
Website: www.artinstitutes.edu/atlanta/
Admissions email: aiaadm@aii.edu
For-profit
Application deadline (fall): N/A
Undergraduate student body: N/A full time, N/A part time
Expenses: N/A
Financial aid: N/A

Atlanta Metropolitan State College[1]
Atlanta GA
(404) 756-4004
U.S. News ranking: Reg. Coll. (S), No. 63
Website: www.Atlm.edu
Admissions email: admissions@atlm.edu
Public; founded 1974
Application deadline (fall): rolling
Undergraduate student body: N/A full time, N/A part time
Expenses: N/A
Financial aid: N/A

Augusta University[7]
Augusta GA
(706) 721-2725
U.S. News ranking: Nat. U., second tier
Website: www.augusta.edu/
Admissions email: admissions@augusta.edu
Public; founded 1828
Freshman admissions: less selective; 2018-2019: N/A applied, N/A accepted. Either SAT or ACT required. ACT 25/75 percentile: 20-26. High school rank: N/A
Early decision deadline: N/A, notification date: N/A
Early action deadline: N/A, notification date: N/A
Application deadline (fall): N/A
Undergraduate student body: 4,419 full time, 1,044 part time
Most popular majors: 18% Registered Nursing/Registered Nurse, 8% Kinesiology and Exercise Science, 8% Psychology, General, 5% Marketing/Marketing Management, General, 5% Speech Communication and Rhetoric
Expenses: 2018-2019: $8,604 in state, $23,156 out of state; room/board: $8,850
Financial aid: (706) 737-1524

Berry College
Mount Berry GA
(706) 236-2215
U.S. News ranking: Reg. U. (S), No. 4
Website: www.berry.edu/
Admissions email: admissions@berry.edu
Private; founded 1902
Freshman admissions: more selective; 2018-2019: 3,970 applied, 2,625 accepted. Either SAT or ACT required. ACT 25/75 percentile: 23-29. High school rank: 29% in top tenth, 60% in top quarter, 89% in top half

Early decision deadline: 11/1, notification date: 12/1
Early action deadline: 11/1, notification date: 12/15
Application deadline (fall): 7/26
Undergraduate student body: 1,902 full time, 34 part time; 39% male, 61% female; 0% American Indian, 2% Asian, 6% black, 7% Hispanic, 4% multiracial, 0% Pacific Islander, 79% white, 1% international; 67% from in state; 88% live on campus; 0% of students in fraternities, 0% in sororities
Most popular majors: 18% Biological and Biomedical Sciences, 17% Business, Management, Marketing, and Related Support Services, 9% Parks, Recreation, Leisure, and Fitness Studies, 9% Psychology, 7% Communication, Journalism, and Related Programs
Expenses: 2019-2020: $37,246; room/board: $13,070
Financial aid: (706) 236-1714; 71% of undergrads determined to have financial need; average aid package $31,114

Brenau University
Gainesville GA
(770) 534-6100
U.S. News ranking: Reg. U. (S), No. 38
Website: www.brenau.edu
Admissions email: admissions@brenau.edu
Private; founded 1878
Freshman admissions: selective; 2018-2019: 1,902 applied, 1,230 accepted. Neither SAT nor ACT required. SAT 25/75 percentile: 910-1140. High school rank: 10% in top tenth, 32% in top quarter, 67% in top half
Early decision deadline: N/A, notification date: N/A
Early action deadline: N/A, notification date: N/A
Application deadline (fall): rolling
Undergraduate student body: 1,090 full time, 664 part time; 10% male, 90% female; 0% American Indian, 2% Asian, 29% black, 10% Hispanic, 2% multiracial, 0% Pacific Islander, 48% white, 5% international; 93% from in state; 23% live on campus; N/A of students in fraternities, 9% in sororities
Most popular majors: 38% Health Professions and Related Programs, 22% Business, Management, and Related Support Services, 12% Education, 11% Visual and Performing Arts, 4% Biological and Biomedical Sciences
Expenses: 2019-2020: $31,084; room/board: $12,500
Financial aid: (770) 534-6176; 82% of undergrads determined to have financial need; average aid package $22,109

Brewton-Parker College[1]
Mount Vernon GA
(912) 583-3265
U.S. News ranking: Nat. Lib. Arts, second tier
Website: www.bpc.edu
Admissions email: admissions@bpc.edu
Private; founded 1904
Application deadline (fall): rolling
Undergraduate student body: N/A full time, N/A part time
Expenses: N/A
Financial aid: N/A

Clark Atlanta University
Atlanta GA
(800) 688-3220
U.S. News ranking: Nat. U., second tier
Website: www.cau.edu
Admissions email: cauadmissions@cau.edu
Private; founded 1988
Affiliation: United Methodist
Freshman admissions: selective; 2018-2019: 14,942 applied, 7,747 accepted. Either SAT or ACT required. SAT 25/75 percentile: 950-1110. High school rank: 11% in top tenth, 37% in top quarter, 72% in top half
Early decision deadline: N/A, notification date: N/A
Early action deadline: N/A, notification date: N/A
Application deadline (fall): 6/1
Undergraduate student body: 3,234 full time, 91 part time; 25% male, 75% female; 0% American Indian, 0% Asian, 89% black, 0% Hispanic, 0% multiracial, 0% Pacific Islander, 0% white, 4% international; 38% from in state; 61% live on campus; 2% of students in fraternities, 3% in sororities
Most popular majors: 20% Communication, Journalism, and Related Programs, 18% Business, Management, Marketing, and Related Support Services, 12% Psychology, 11% Visual and Performing Arts, 9% Biological and Biomedical Sciences
Expenses: 2019-2020: $23,672; room/board: $11,238
Financial aid: (404) 880-8992; 60% of undergrads determined to have financial need; average aid package $7,803

Clayton State University
Morrow GA
(678) 466-4115
U.S. News ranking: Reg. U. (S), second tier
Website: www.clayton.edu
Admissions email: ccsu-info@mail.clayton.edu
Public; founded 1969
Freshman admissions: less selective; 2018-2019: 1,974 applied, 1,073 accepted. Either SAT or ACT required. SAT 25/75 percentile: 870-1020. High school rank: N/A
Early decision deadline: N/A, notification date: N/A

Early action deadline: N/A, notification date: N/A
Application deadline (fall): 7/1
Undergraduate student body: 3,870 full time, 2,727 part time; 31% male, 69% female; 0% American Indian, 5% Asian, 66% black, 7% Hispanic, 3% multiracial, 0% Pacific Islander, 15% white, 2% international; 97% from in state; 16% live on campus; N/A of students in fraternities, N/A in sororities
Most popular majors: 13% Liberal Arts and Sciences/Liberal Studies, 10% Community Psychology, 8% Hospital and Health Care Facilities Administration/Management, 8% Registered Nursing/Registered Nurse, 7% Office Management and Supervision
Expenses: 2019-2020: $6,554 in state, $19,956 out of state; room/board: $10,397
Financial aid: (678) 466-4181; 86% of undergrads determined to have financial need; average aid package $10,823

College of Coastal Georgia
Brunswick GA
(912) 279-5730
U.S. News ranking: Reg. Coll. (S), No. 61
Website: www.ccga.edu
Admissions email: admiss@ccga.edu
Public; founded 1961
Freshman admissions: less selective; 2018-2019: 1,611 applied, 1,494 accepted. Either SAT or ACT required. SAT 25/75 percentile: 910-1100. High school rank: N/A
Early decision deadline: N/A, notification date: N/A
Early action deadline: N/A, notification date: N/A
Application deadline (fall): 8/5
Undergraduate student body: 2,078 full time, 1,468 part time; 32% male, 68% female; 0% American Indian, 2% Asian, 21% black, 6% Hispanic, 4% multiracial, 0% Pacific Islander, 64% white, 1% international; 92% from in state; 19% live on campus; 0% of students in fraternities, 0% in sororities
Most popular majors: 24% Business/Commerce, General, 16% Registered Nursing/Registered Nurse, 14% Psychology, General, 10% Biology/Biological Sciences, General, 8% Early Childhood Education and Teaching
Expenses: 2019-2020: $4,774 in state, $13,406 out of state; room/board: $10,328
Financial aid: (912) 279-5726; 63% of undergrads determined to have financial need; average aid package $10,843

Columbus State University
Columbus GA
(706) 507-8800
U.S. News ranking: Reg. U. (S), No. 75
Website: www.columbusstate.edu
Admissions email: admissions@columbusstate.edu
Public; founded 1958
Freshman admissions: selective; 2018-2019: 3,841 applied, 2,166 accepted. Either SAT or ACT required. SAT 25/75 percentile: 870-1100. High school rank: 13% in top tenth, 37% in top quarter, 70% in top half
Early decision deadline: N/A, notification date: N/A
Early action deadline: N/A, notification date: N/A
Application deadline (fall): 6/30
Undergraduate student body: 4,702 full time, 1,938 part time; 40% male, 60% female; 0% American Indian, 2% Asian, 39% black, 7% Hispanic, 2% multiracial, 0% Pacific Islander, 49% white, 1% international; N/A from in state; 22% live on campus; 5% of students in fraternities, 5% in sororities
Most popular majors: 25% Health Professions and Related Programs, 17% Business, Management, Marketing, and Related Support Services, 7% Computer and Information Sciences and Support Services, 7% Education, 7% Visual and Performing Arts
Expenses: 2019-2020: $7,334 in state, $21,152 out of state; room/board: $10,150
Financial aid: (706) 507-8800; 73% of undergrads determined to have financial need; average aid package $9,881

Covenant College
Lookout Mountain GA
(706) 820-2398
U.S. News ranking: Nat. Lib. Arts, No. 148
Website: www.covenant.edu
Admissions email: admissions@covenant.edu
Private; founded 1955
Affiliation: The Presbyterian Church in America
Freshman admissions: more selective; 2018-2019: 672 applied, 653 accepted. Either SAT or ACT required. ACT 25/75 percentile: 23-30. High school rank: 28% in top tenth, 57% in top quarter, 85% in top half
Early decision deadline: N/A, notification date: N/A
Early action deadline: 11/15, notification date: 12/1
Application deadline (fall): 2/1
Undergraduate student body: 969 full time, 33 part time; 48% male, 52% female; 0% American Indian, 1% Asian, 3% black, 2% Hispanic, 5% multiracial, 0% Pacific Islander, 84% white, 4% international; 30% from in state; 83% live on campus; 0% of students in fraternities, 0% in sororities
Most popular majors: 20% Business, Management, Marketing, and Related Support Services, 17% Parks, Recreation, Leisure, and Fitness Studies,

12% Education, 11% Communication, Journalism, and Related Programs, 6% Homeland Security, Law Enforcement, Firefighting and Related Protective Services
Expenses: 2019-2020: $20,712; room/board: $7,994
Financial aid: (706) 245-2844; 76% of undergrads determined to have financial need; average aid package $16,817

Dalton State College[1]
Dalton GA
(706) 272-4436
U.S. News ranking: Reg. Coll. (S), unranked
Website: www.daltonstate.edu/
Admissions email: N/A
Public
Application deadline (fall): N/A
Undergraduate student body: N/A full time, N/A part time
Expenses: N/A
Financial aid: N/A

East Georgia State College[1]
Swainsboro GA
(478) 289-2017
U.S. News ranking: Reg. Coll. (S), second tier
Website: www.ega.edu/admissions
Admissions email: Ask_EGSC@ega.edu
Public; founded 1973
Application deadline (fall): 8/15
Undergraduate student body: N/A full time, N/A part time
Expenses: N/A
Financial aid: N/A

Emmanuel College
Franklin Springs GA
(800) 860-8800
U.S. News ranking: Reg. Coll. (S), No. 39
Website: www.ec.edu
Admissions email: admissions@ec.edu
Private; founded 1919
Affiliation: Pentecostal Holiness Church
Freshman admissions: selective; 2018-2019: 1,089 applied, 457 accepted. Either SAT or ACT required. SAT 25/75 percentile: 930-1150. High school rank: N/A
Early decision deadline: N/A, notification date: N/A
Early action deadline: N/A, notification date: N/A
Application deadline (fall): 8/1
Undergraduate student body: 811 full time, 109 part time; 50% male, 50% female; 0% American Indian, 0% Asian, 16% black, 7% Hispanic, 3% multiracial, 1% Pacific Islander, 64% white, 9% international; 69% from in state; 60% live on campus; 0% of students in fraternities, 0% in sororities
Most popular majors: 20% Business, Management, Marketing, and Related Support Services, 17% Parks, Recreation, Leisure, and Fitness Studies,

Most popular majors: 17% Social Sciences, 10% English Language and Literature/Letters, 10% Visual and Performing Arts, 8% Biological and Biomedical Sciences, 7% Education
Expenses: 2019-2020: $35,640; room/board: $10,660
Financial aid: (706) 419-1447; 67% of undergrads determined to have financial need; average aid package $29,291

Emory University
Atlanta GA
(404) 727-6036
U.S. News ranking: Nat. U., No. 21
Website: www.emory.edu
Admissions email: admission@emory.edu
Private; founded 1836
Affiliation: United Methodist
Freshman admissions: most selective; 2018-2019: 27,559 applied, 5,104 accepted. Either SAT or ACT required. SAT 25/75 percentile: 1350-1520. High school rank: 84% in top tenth, 98% in top quarter, 100% in top half
Early decision deadline: 11/1, notification date: 12/15
Early action deadline: N/A, notification date: N/A
Application deadline (fall): 1/1
Undergraduate student body: 6,985 full time, 101 part time; 40% male, 60% female; 0% American Indian, 21% Asian, 8% black, 10% Hispanic, 4% multiracial, 0% Pacific Islander, 40% white, 16% international; 21% from in state; 63% live on campus; 28% of students in fraternities, 25% in sororities
Most popular majors: 14% Business Administration and Management, General, 10% Biology/Biological Sciences, General, 8% Registered Nursing/Registered Nurse, 6% Economics, General, 5% Psychology, General
Expenses: 2019-2020: $53,804; room/board: $14,972
Financial aid: (404) 727-6039; 48% of undergrads determined to have financial need; average aid package $44,968

Fort Valley State University
Fort Valley GA
(478) 825-6307
U.S. News ranking: Reg. U. (S), second tier
Website: www.fvsu.edu
Admissions email: admissap@mail.fvsu.edu
Public; founded 1895
Freshman admissions: least selective; 2018-2019: 3,684 applied, 1,950 accepted. Either SAT or ACT required. SAT 25/75 percentile: 833-990. High school rank: 4% in top tenth, 15% in top quarter, 46% in top half
Early decision deadline: N/A, notification date: N/A
Early action deadline: N/A, notification date: N/A
Application deadline (fall): 7/19

Undergraduate student body: 2,148 full time, 211 part time; 40% male, 60% female; 0% American Indian, 0% Asian, 92% black, 2% Hispanic, 3% multiracial, 0% Pacific Islander, 3% white, 0% international; 94% from in state; 34% live on campus; N/A of students in fraternities, N/A in sororities
Most popular majors: 40% Psychology, 17% Health Professions and Related Programs, 16% Homeland Security, Law Enforcement, Firefighting and Related Protective Services, 8% Biological and Biomedical Sciences, 6% Physical Sciences
Expenses: 2019-2020: $6,664 in state, $19,740 out of state; room/board: $8,372
Financial aid: (478) 825-6363; 95% of undergrads determined to have financial need; average aid package $7,960

Georgia College & State University

Milledgeville GA
(478) 445-1283
U.S. News ranking: Reg. U. (S), No. 20
Website: www.gcsu.edu
Admissions email: admissions@gcsu.edu
Public; founded 1889
Freshman admissions: selective; 2018-2019: 4,328 applied, 3,366 accepted. Either SAT or ACT required. SAT 25/75 percentile: 1110-1280. High school rank: N/A
Early decision deadline: N/A, notification date: N/A
Early action deadline: 11/1, notification date: 1/1
Application deadline (fall): 4/1
Undergraduate student body: 5,410 full time, 548 part time; 37% male, 63% female; 0% American Indian, 1% Asian, 5% black, 6% Hispanic, 3% multiracial, 0% Pacific Islander, 84% white, 0% international; 99% from in state; 36% live on campus; 7% of students in fraternities, 13% in sororities
Most popular majors: 9% Business Administration and Management, General, 9% Marketing/Marketing Management, General, 8% Kinesiology and Exercise Science, 8% Registered Nursing/Registered Nurse, 6% Biology/Biological Sciences, General
Expenses: 2019-2020: $9,530 in state, $28,710 out of state; room/board: $13,052
Financial aid: (478) 445-5149; 51% of undergrads determined to have financial need; average aid package $11,052

Georgia Gwinnett College

Lawrenceville GA
(678) 407-5313
U.S. News ranking: Reg. Coll. (S), No. 53
Website: www.ggc.edu
Admissions email: ggcadmissions@ggc.edu
Public; founded 2005

Freshman admissions: less selective; 2018-2019: 3,958 applied, 3,625 accepted. Neither SAT nor ACT required. SAT 25/75 percentile: 930-1110. High school rank: 5% in top tenth, 17% in top quarter, 46% in top half
Early decision deadline: N/A, notification date: N/A
Early action deadline: N/A, notification date: N/A
Application deadline (fall): 5/1
Undergraduate student body: 8,203 full time, 4,305 part time; 43% male, 57% female; 0% American Indian, 10% Asian, 33% black, 21% Hispanic, 4% multiracial, 0% Pacific Islander, 29% white, 3% international; 99% from in state; 7% live on campus; N/A of students in fraternities, N/A in sororities
Most popular majors: 35% Business/Commerce, General, 12% Information Technology, 10% Biology/Biological Sciences, General, 10% Psychology, General, 6% Criminal Justice/Safety Studies
Expenses: 2019-2020: $5,762 in state, $16,744 out of state; room/board: $13,346
Financial aid: (678) 407-5701; 74% of undergrads determined to have financial need; average aid package $17,655

Georgia Highlands College[1]

Rome GA
U.S. News ranking: Reg. Coll. (S), second tier
Admissions email: N/A
Public
Application deadline (fall): N/A
Undergraduate student body: N/A full time, N/A part time
Expenses: N/A
Financial aid: N/A

Georgia Institute of Technology

Atlanta GA
(404) 894-4154
U.S. News ranking: Nat. U., No. 29
Website: admission.gatech.edu
Admissions email: admission@gatech.edu
Public; founded 1885
Freshman admissions: most selective; 2018-2019: 35,612 applied, 8,037 accepted. Either SAT or ACT required. SAT 25/75 percentile: 1390-1540. High school rank: 89% in top tenth, 97% in top quarter, 99% in top half
Early decision deadline: N/A, notification date: N/A
Early action deadline: 10/15, notification date: 1/12
Application deadline (fall): 1/1
Undergraduate student body: 14,318 full time, 1,731 part time; 62% male, 38% female; 0% American Indian, 21% Asian, 7% black, 7% Hispanic, 4% multiracial, 0% Pacific Islander, 48% white, 9% international; 61% from in state; 43% live on campus; 28% of students in fraternities, 33% in sororities

Most popular majors: 59% Engineering, 17% Computer and Information Sciences and Support Services, 10% Business, Management, Marketing, and Related Support Services, 3% Biological and Biomedical Sciences, 2% Physical Sciences
Expenses: 2019-2020: $12,682 in state, $33,794 out of state; room/board: $14,830
Financial aid: (404) 894-4160; 40% of undergrads determined to have financial need; average aid package $14,856

Georgia Military College[1]

Milledgeville GA
(478) 387-4900
U.S. News ranking: Reg. Coll. (S), unranked
Website: www.hfcc.edu
Admissions email: N/A
Public
Application deadline (fall): N/A
Undergraduate student body: N/A full time, N/A part time
Expenses: N/A
Financial aid: N/A

Georgia Southern University

Statesboro GA
(912) 478-5391
U.S. News ranking: Nat. U., second tier
Website: www.georgiasouthern.edu/
Admissions email: admissions@georgiasouthern.edu
Public; founded 1906
Freshman admissions: selective; 2018-2019: 11,522 applied, 7,797 accepted. Either SAT or ACT required. SAT 25/75 percentile: 1060-1200. High school rank: 18% in top tenth, 44% in top quarter, 77% in top half
Early decision deadline: N/A, notification date: N/A
Early action deadline: N/A, notification date: N/A
Application deadline (fall): 5/1
Undergraduate student body: 19,483 full time, 3,651 part time; 45% male, 55% female; 0% American Indian, 2% Asian, 25% black, 7% Hispanic, 4% multiracial, 0% Pacific Islander, 59% white, 1% international; 6% from in state; 26% live on campus; 11% of students in fraternities, 14% in sororities
Most popular majors: 18% Business, Management, Marketing, and Related Support Services, 15% Health Professions and Related Programs, 7% Parks, Recreation, Leisure, and Fitness Studies, 6% Biological and Biomedical Sciences, 6% Education
Expenses: 2019-2020: $7,556 in state, $21,374 out of state; room/board: $10,070
Financial aid: (912) 478-5413; 65% of undergrads determined to have financial need; average aid package $10,766

Georgia Southwestern State University

Americus GA
(229) 928-1273
U.S. News ranking: Reg. U. (S), second tier
Website: www.gsw.edu
Admissions email: admissions@gsw.edu
Public; founded 1906
Freshman admissions: selective; 2018-2019: 1,283 applied, 889 accepted. Either SAT or ACT required. SAT 25/75 percentile: 940-1120. High school rank: 12% in top tenth, 39% in top quarter, 76% in top half
Early decision deadline: N/A, notification date: N/A
Early action deadline: N/A, notification date: N/A
Application deadline (fall): 7/21
Undergraduate student body: 1,674 full time, 793 part time; 36% male, 64% female; 0% American Indian, 1% Asian, 26% black, 5% Hispanic, 3% multiracial, 0% Pacific Islander, 62% white, 2% international; N/A from in state; 31% live on campus; 11% of students in fraternities, 10% in sororities
Most popular majors: 18% Registered Nursing/Registered Nurse, 14% Accounting, 14% Business Administration and Management, General, 10% Elementary Education and Teaching, 7% Psychology, General
Expenses: 2019-2020: $6,516 in state, $19,918 out of state; room/board: $8,280
Financial aid: (229) 928-1378; 73% of undergrads determined to have financial need; average aid package $9,897

Georgia State University

Atlanta GA
(404) 413-2500
U.S. News ranking: Nat. U., No. 211
Website: www.gsu.edu
Admissions email: admissions@gsu.edu
Public; founded 1913
Freshman admissions: selective; 2018-2019: 19,838 applied, 11,393 accepted. Either SAT or ACT required. SAT 25/75 percentile: 990-1190. High school rank: N/A
Early decision deadline: N/A, notification date: N/A
Early action deadline: 11/15, notification date: 12/15
Application deadline (fall): 6/1
Undergraduate student body: 21,041 full time, 6,149 part time; 41% male, 59% female; 0% American Indian, 14% Asian, 41% black, 12% Hispanic, 6% multiracial, 0% Pacific Islander, 23% white, 3% international; 96% from in state; 21% live on campus; N/A of students in fraternities, N/A in sororities
Most popular majors: 24% Business, Management, Marketing, and Related Support

Services, 10% Social Sciences, 8% Computer and Information Sciences and Support Services, 8% Psychology, 7% Biological and Biomedical Sciences
Expenses: 2019-2020: $11,076 in state, $30,114 out of state; room/board: $14,908
Financial aid: (404) 413-2600; 76% of undergrads determined to have financial need; average aid package $10,739

Gordon State College[1]

Barnesville GA
(678) 359-5021
U.S. News ranking: Reg. Coll. (S), No. 44
Website: www.gordonstate.edu/
Admissions email: admissions@gordonstate.edu
Public; founded 1852
Application deadline (fall): rolling
Undergraduate student body: N/A full time, N/A part time
Expenses: 2018-2019: $4,164 in state, $12,422 out of state; room/board: $8,101
Financial aid: (678) 359-5990

Kennesaw State University

Kennesaw GA
(770) 423-6300
U.S. News ranking: Nat. U., second tier
Website: www.kennesaw.edu
Admissions email: KSUAdmit@kennesaw.edu
Public; founded 1963
Freshman admissions: selective; 2018-2019: 13,427 applied, 7,779 accepted. Either SAT or ACT required. SAT 25/75 percentile: 1080-1270. High school rank: 16% in top tenth, 45% in top quarter, 80% in top half
Early decision deadline: N/A, notification date: N/A
Early action deadline: 11/1, notification date: 12/8
Application deadline (fall): 5/3
Undergraduate student body: 24,150 full time, 8,124 part time; 52% male, 48% female; 0% American Indian, 5% Asian, 21% black, 10% Hispanic, 5% multiracial, 0% Pacific Islander, 55% white, 2% international; N/A from in state; 16% live on campus; 4% of students in fraternities, 7% in sororities
Most popular majors: 18% Business, Management, Marketing, and Related Support Services, 10% Computer and Information Sciences and Support Services, 9% Engineering, 8% Communication, Journalism, and Related Programs, 7% Psychology
Expenses: 2019-2020: $7,568 in state, $21,636 out of state; room/board: $11,467
Financial aid: (770) 423-6074; 71% of undergrads determined to have financial need; average aid package $11,593

LaGrange College
LaGrange GA
(706) 880-8005
U.S. News ranking: Reg. Coll. (S), No. 5
Website: www.lagrange.edu
Admissions email: admissions@lagrange.edu
Private; founded 1831
Affiliation: United Methodist
Freshman admissions: selective; 2018-2019: 1,511 applied, 728 accepted. Either SAT or ACT required. SAT 25/75 percentile: 1020-1180. High school rank: 17% in top tenth, 39% in top quarter, 84% in top half
Early decision deadline: N/A, notification date: N/A
Early action deadline: N/A, notification date: N/A
Application deadline (fall): 8/31
Undergraduate student body: 831 full time, 46 part time; 48% male, 52% female; 1% American Indian, 1% Asian, 20% black, 1% Hispanic, 2% multiracial, 0% Pacific Islander, 74% white, 1% international; 83% from in state; 58% live on campus; 22% of students in fraternities, 33% in sororities
Most popular majors: 24% Registered Nursing/Registered Nurse, 13% Kinesiology and Exercise Science, 9% Business Administration and Management, General, 6% Biology/Biological Sciences, General, 6% Psychology, General
Expenses: 2019-2020: $31,500; room/board: $11,770
Financial aid: (706) 880-8249; 88% of undergrads determined to have financial need; average aid package $28,416

Mercer University
Macon GA
(478) 301-2650
U.S. News ranking: Nat. U., No. 153
Website: www.mercer.edu
Admissions email: admissions@mercer.edu
Private; founded 1833
Freshman admissions: more selective; 2018-2019: 5,454 applied, 3,927 accepted. Either SAT or ACT required. SAT 25/75 percentile: 1180-1340. High school rank: 37% in top tenth, 68% in top quarter, 92% in top half
Early decision deadline: N/A, notification date: N/A
Early action deadline: 10/15, notification date: 11/8
Application deadline (fall): 7/1
Undergraduate student body: 4,259 full time, 538 part time; 38% male, 62% female; 0% American Indian, 7% Asian, 28% black, 6% Hispanic, 4% multiracial, 0% Pacific Islander, 48% white, 2% international; 84% from in state; 76% live on campus; 27% of students in fraternities, 29% in sororities
Most popular majors: 19% Business, Management, Marketing, and Related Support Services, 19% Engineering, 12% Biological and Biomedical Sciences, 9% Social Sciences, 6% Psychology
Expenses: 2019-2020: $37,808; room/board: $12,968
Financial aid: (478) 301-2670; 70% of undergrads determined to have financial need; average aid package $36,740

Middle Georgia State University
Macon GA
(877) 238-8664
U.S. News ranking: Reg. Coll. (S), No. 55
Website: www.mga.edu/
Admissions email: admissions@mga.edu
Public; founded 2013
Freshman admissions: less selective; 2018-2019: 2,314 applied, 2,128 accepted. Either SAT or ACT required. SAT 25/75 percentile: 880-1080. High school rank: N/A
Early decision deadline: N/A, notification date: N/A
Early action deadline: N/A, notification date: N/A
Application deadline (fall): rolling
Undergraduate student body: 4,788 full time, 2,796 part time; 42% male, 58% female; 0% American Indian, 2% Asian, 36% black, 5% Hispanic, 4% multiracial, 0% Pacific Islander, 50% white, 1% international; 97% from in state; 21% live on campus; N/A of students in fraternities, N/A in sororities
Most popular majors: 11% Business Administration and Management, General, 9% Registered Nursing/Registered Nurse, 5% Computer and Information Sciences, General, 4% Aviation/Airway Management and Operations, 4% Psychology, General
Expenses: 2019-2020: $4,742 in state, $13,926 out of state; room/board: $8,260
Financial aid: (877) 238-8664; 70% of undergrads determined to have financial need; average aid package $8,213

Morehouse College
Atlanta GA
(844) 512-6672
U.S. News ranking: Nat. Lib. Arts, No. 154
Website: www.morehouse.edu
Admissions email: admissions@morehouse.edu
Private; founded 1867
Freshman admissions: selective; 2018-2019: 3,555 applied, 2,057 accepted. Either SAT or ACT required. SAT 25/75 percentile: 1010-1210. High school rank: 2% in top tenth, 11% in top quarter, 28% in top half
Early decision deadline: 11/1, notification date: 12/15
Early action deadline: 11/1, notification date: 12/15
Application deadline (fall): 2/15
Undergraduate student body: 2,146 full time, 60 part time; 100% male, 0% female; 0% American Indian, 0% Asian, 94% black, 0% Hispanic, 3% multiracial,

0% Pacific Islander, 0% white, 1% international; N/A from in state; N/A live on campus; 3% of students in fraternities, 0% in sororities
Most popular majors: 28% Business, Management, Marketing, and Related Support Services, 17% Social Sciences, 9% Biological and Biomedical Sciences, 8% Visual and Performing Arts, 6% Parks, Recreation, Leisure, and Fitness Studies
Expenses: 2019-2020: $27,576; room/board: $13,438
Financial aid: (844) 512-6672

Oglethorpe University
Atlanta GA
(404) 364-8307
U.S. News ranking: Nat. Lib. Arts, second tier
Website: oglethorpe.edu
Admissions email: admission@oglethorpe.edu
Private; founded 1835
Freshman admissions: more selective; 2018-2019: 2,207 applied, 1,367 accepted. Either SAT or ACT required. SAT 25/75 percentile: 1110-1290. High school rank: 23% in top tenth, 47% in top quarter, 85% in top half
Early decision deadline: N/A, notification date: N/A
Early action deadline: 11/15, notification date: N/A
Application deadline (fall): 11/15
Undergraduate student body: 1,212 full time, 52 part time; 43% male, 57% female; 1% American Indian, 5% Asian, 24% black, 11% Hispanic, 1% multiracial, 0% Pacific Islander, 41% white, 8% international; 79% from in state; 53% live on campus; 20% of students in fraternities, 17% in sororities
Most popular majors: 26% Business, Management, Marketing, and Related Support Services, 15% Social Sciences, 13% English Language and Literature/Letters, 10% Psychology, 10% Visual and Performing Arts
Expenses: 2019-2020: $39,580; room/board: $13,400
Financial aid: (404) 504-1500; 72% of undergrads determined to have financial need; average aid package $30,835

Paine College[1]
Augusta GA
(706) 821-8320
U.S. News ranking: Reg. Coll. (S), second tier
Website: www.paine.edu
Admissions email: admissions@paine.edu
Private; founded 1882
Application deadline (fall): 7/15
Undergraduate student body: N/A full time, N/A part time
Expenses: N/A
Financial aid: N/A

Piedmont College
Demorest GA
(800) 277-7020
U.S. News ranking: Reg. U. (S), No. 50
Website: www.piedmont.edu
Admissions email: ugrad@piedmont.edu
Private; founded 1897
Affiliation: United Church of Christ
Freshman admissions: selective; 2018-2019: 1,379 applied, 822 accepted. Either SAT or ACT required. SAT 25/75 percentile: 970-1180. High school rank: 6% in top tenth, 28% in top quarter, 67% in top half
Early decision deadline: N/A, notification date: N/A
Early action deadline: N/A, notification date: N/A
Application deadline (fall): rolling
Undergraduate student body: 1,153 full time, 110 part time; 35% male, 65% female; 0% American Indian, 1% Asian, 10% black, 6% Hispanic, 0% multiracial, 0% Pacific Islander, 69% white, 1% international; 89% from in state; 74% live on campus; 2% of students in fraternities, 7% in sororities
Most popular majors: 28% Health Professions and Related Programs, 19% Education, 16% Business, Management, Marketing, and Related Support Services, 7% Visual and Performing Arts, 4% Psychology
Expenses: 2019-2020: $26,692; room/board: $10,524
Financial aid: (706) 776-0114; 83% of undergrads determined to have financial need; average aid package $20,870

Point University
West Point GA
(706) 385-1202
U.S. News ranking: Reg. Coll. (S), No. 49
Website: www.point.edu
Admissions email: admissions@point.edu
Private; founded 1937
Affiliation: Christian Churches and Churches of Christ
Freshman admissions: less selective; 2018-2019: 1,228 applied, 653 accepted. Neither SAT nor ACT required. SAT 25/75 percentile: 880-1085. High school rank: 9% in top tenth, 22% in top quarter, 63% in top half
Early decision deadline: N/A, notification date: N/A
Early action deadline: N/A, notification date: N/A
Application deadline (fall): 8/1
Undergraduate student body: 1,108 full time, 1,105 part time; 45% male, 55% female; 0% American Indian, 1% Asian, 32% black, 5% Hispanic, 7% multiracial, 0% Pacific Islander, 45% white, 4% international; 72% from in state; 56% live on campus; N/A of students in fraternities, N/A in sororities
Most popular majors: 25% Theology and Religious Vocations, 23% Business, Management, Marketing, and Related Support

Services, 21% Psychology, 9% Philosophy and Religious Studies, 6% Homeland Security, Law Enforcement, Firefighting and Related Protective Services
Expenses: 2018-2019: $20,600; room/board: $7,900
Financial aid: (706) 385-1462

Reinhardt University
Waleska GA
(770) 720-5526
U.S. News ranking: Reg. U. (S), No. 87
Website: www.reinhardt.edu/
Admissions email: admissions@reinhardt.edu
Private; founded 1883
Affiliation: United Methodist
Freshman admissions: selective; 2018-2019: 1,216 applied, 1,092 accepted. Either SAT or ACT required. ACT 25/75 percentile: 18-23. High school rank: 11% in top tenth, 31% in top quarter, 70% in top half
Early decision deadline: N/A, notification date: N/A
Early action deadline: N/A, notification date: N/A
Application deadline (fall): 8/20
Undergraduate student body: 1,307 full time, 166 part time; 51% male, 49% female; 0% American Indian, 1% Asian, 18% black, 8% Hispanic, 3% multiracial, 0% Pacific Islander, 63% white, 0% international; 93% from in state; 47% live on campus; 1% of students in fraternities, 2% in sororities
Most popular majors: 27% Business, Management, Marketing, and Related Support Services, 12% Health Professions and Related Programs, 10% Homeland Security, Law Enforcement, Firefighting and Related Protective Services, 9% Education, 7% Parks, Recreation, Leisure, and Fitness Studies
Expenses: 2019-2020: $24,300; room/board: $10,500
Financial aid: (770) 720-5667; 41% of undergrads determined to have financial need; average aid package $17,817

Savannah College of Art and Design
Savannah GA
(912) 525-5100
U.S. News ranking: Arts, unranked
Website: www.scad.edu
Admissions email: admission@scad.edu
Private; founded 1978
Freshman admissions: selective; 2018-2019: 14,797 applied, 10,605 accepted. Either SAT or ACT required. SAT 25/75 percentile: 1050-1240. High school rank: N/A
Early decision deadline: N/A, notification date: N/A
Early action deadline: N/A, notification date: N/A
Application deadline (fall): rolling
Undergraduate student body: 10,305 full time, 1,912 part time; 32% male, 68% female; 1% American Indian, 5% Asian,

10% black, 7% Hispanic, 0% multiracial, 0% Pacific Islander, 52% white, 21% international; 80% from in state; 44% live on campus; N/A of students in fraternities, N/A in sororities
Most popular majors: 56% Visual and Performing Arts, 15% Communication, Journalism, and Related Programs, 14% Communications Technologies/ Technicians and Support Services, 8% Engineering, 3% Architecture and Related Services
Expenses: 2019-2020: $37,575; room/board: $15,162
Financial aid: (912) 525-5100; 49% of undergrads determined to have financial need; average aid package $16,165

Savannah State University
Savannah GA
(912) 358-4338
U.S. News ranking: Reg. U. (S), second tier
Website: www. savannahstate.edu
Admissions email: admissions@savannahstate.edu
Public; founded 1890
Freshman admissions: least selective; 2018-2019: 5,405 applied, 3,078 accepted. Either SAT or ACT required. SAT 25/75 percentile: 870-1030. High school rank: N/A.
Early decision deadline: N/A, notification date: N/A
Early action deadline: N/A, notification date: N/A
Application deadline (fall): 7/15
Undergraduate student body: 3,319 full time, 576 part time; 40% male, 60% female; 0% American Indian, 0% Asian, 80% black, 9% Hispanic, 4% multiracial, 0% Pacific Islander, 4% white, 2% international; 87% from in state; 56% live on campus; N/A of students in fraternities, N/A in sororities
Most popular majors: 16% Biology/ Biological Sciences, General, 15% Business Administration and Management, General, 13% Social Work, 11% Corrections and Criminal Justice, Other, 11% Journalism
Expenses: 2019-2020: $5,999 in state, $19,401 out of state; room/ board: $7,762
Financial aid: (912) 358-4162

Shorter University
Rome GA
(800) 868-6980
U.S. News ranking: Reg. U. (S), second tier
Website: www.shorter.edu/
Admissions email: admissions@shorter.edu
Private; founded 1873
Affiliation: Baptist
Freshman admissions: less selective; 2018-2019: 1,780 applied, 1,006 accepted. Either SAT or ACT required. ACT 25/75 percentile: 17-24. High school rank: N/A
Early decision deadline: N/A, notification date: N/A
Early action deadline: N/A, notification date: N/A

Application deadline (fall): N/A
Undergraduate student body: 1,078 full time, 274 part time; 42% male, 58% female; N/A American Indian, N/A Asian, N/A black, N/A Hispanic, N/A multiracial, N/A Pacific Islander, N/A white, N/A international
Most popular majors: Information not available
Expenses: 2018-2019: $22,370; room/board: $9,400
Financial aid: (706) 233-7227

South Georgia State College[1]
Douglas GA
(912) 260-4206
U.S. News ranking: Reg. Coll. (S), unranked
Website: www.sgsc.edu
Admissions email: admissions@sgsc.edu
Private
Application deadline (fall): rolling
Undergraduate student body: N/A full time, N/A part time
Expenses: N/A
Financial aid: N/A

Spelman College
Atlanta GA
(800) 982-2411
U.S. News ranking: Nat. Lib. Arts, No. 57
Website: www.spelman.edu
Admissions email: admiss@spelman.edu
Private; founded 1881
Freshman admissions: selective; 2018-2019: 9,451 applied, 3,718 accepted. Either SAT or ACT required. SAT 25/75 percentile: 1080-1220. High school rank: 10% in top tenth, 25% in top quarter, 50% in top half
Early decision deadline: 11/1, notification date: 12/15
Early action deadline: 11/15, notification date: 12/31
Application deadline (fall): 2/1
Undergraduate student body: 2,123 full time, 48 part time; 0% male, 100% female; 2% American Indian, 0% Asian, 97% black, 0% Hispanic, 0% multiracial, 0% Pacific Islander, 0% white, 1% international; 26% from in state; 65% live on campus; N/A of students in fraternities, 3% in sororities
Most popular majors: 17% Psychology, General, 16% Biology/ Biological Sciences, General, 13% Political Science and Government, General, 7% Economics, General, 7% English Language and Literature, General
Expenses: 2019-2020: $29,972; room/board: $14,338
Financial aid: (404) 270-5209; 81% of undergrads determined to have financial need; average aid package $17,630

Thomas University[1]
Thomasville GA
(229) 227-6934
U.S. News ranking: Reg. U. (S), second tier
Website: www.thomasu.edu
Admissions email: rgagliano@thomasu.edu
Private; founded 1950
Application deadline (fall): rolling
Undergraduate student body: N/A full time, N/A part time
Expenses: N/A
Financial aid: (229) 226-1621

Toccoa Falls College
Toccoa Falls GA
(888) 785-5624
U.S. News ranking: Reg. Coll. (S), No. 25
Website: www.tfc.edu
Admissions email: admissions@tfc.edu
Private; founded 1907
Affiliation: Christ and Missionary Alliance Church
Freshman admissions: selective; 2018-2019: 939 applied, 566 accepted. Either SAT or ACT required. SAT 25/75 percentile: 960-1160. High school rank: 13% in top tenth, 31% in top quarter, 64% in top half
Early decision deadline: N/A, notification date: N/A
Early action deadline: N/A, notification date: N/A
Application deadline (fall): rolling
Undergraduate student body: 890 full time, 766 part time; 43% male, 57% female; 0% American Indian, 6% Asian, 8% black, 5% Hispanic, 3% multiracial, 0% Pacific Islander, 76% white, 1% international; N/A from in state; 51% live on campus; 0% of students in fraternities, 0% in sororities
Most popular majors: 31% Bible/ Biblical Studies, 17% Business Administration, Management and Operations, 11% Counseling Psychology, 8% Music, 8% Outdoor Education
Expenses: 2019-2020: $23,184; room/board: $8,496
Financial aid: (706) 886-7299; 89% of undergrads determined to have financial need; average aid package $17,835

Truett McConnell University
Cleveland GA
(706) 865-2134
U.S. News ranking: Reg. Coll. (S), No. 51
Website: truett.edu/
Admissions email: admissions@truett.edu
Private; founded 1946
Affiliation: Southern Baptist
Freshman admissions: less selective; 2018-2019: 677 applied, 630 accepted. Either SAT or ACT required. SAT 25/75 percentile: 920-1143. High school rank: 12% in top tenth, 29% in top quarter, 66% in top half
Early decision deadline: N/A, notification date: N/A
Early action deadline: N/A, notification date: N/A

Application deadline (fall): 8/1
Undergraduate student body: 888 full time, 2,031 part time; 45% male, 55% female; 0% American Indian, 0% Asian, 8% black, 5% Hispanic, 0% multiracial, 0% Pacific Islander, 79% white, 3% international; 89% from in state; 85% live on campus; N/A of students in fraternities, N/A in sororities
Most popular majors: 20% Business, Management, Marketing, and Related Support Services, 20% Health Professions and Related Programs, 15% Psychology, 15% Theology and Religious Vocations, 14% Education
Expenses: 2019-2020: $21,122; room/board: $7,852
Financial aid: (706) 865-2134; 79% of undergrads determined to have financial need; average aid package $16,398

University of Georgia
Athens GA
(706) 542-8776
U.S. News ranking: Nat. U., No. 50
Website: www.admissions.uga.edu
Admissions email: adm-info@uga.edu
Public; founded 1785
Freshman admissions: more selective; 2018-2019: 26,027 applied, 12,659 accepted. Either SAT or ACT required. SAT 25/75 percentile: 1240-1410. High school rank: 60% in top tenth, 92% in top quarter, 99% in top half
Early decision deadline: N/A, notification date: N/A
Early action deadline: 10/15, notification date: 12/1
Application deadline (fall): 1/1
Undergraduate student body: 27,910 full time, 1,648 part time; 43% male, 57% female; 0% American Indian, 10% Asian, 8% black, 6% Hispanic, 4% multiracial, 0% Pacific Islander, 69% white, 1% international; 87% from in state; 34% live on campus; 20% of students in fraternities, 31% in sororities
Most popular majors: 7% Finance, General, 6% Biology/Biological Sciences, General, 6% Psychology, General, 5% Marketing/Marketing Management, General, 3% Business Administration and Management, General
Expenses: 2019-2020: $12,080 in state, $31,120 out of state; room/board: $10,314
Financial aid: (706) 542-6147; 43% of undergrads determined to have financial need; average aid package $12,562

University of North Georgia
Dahlonega GA
(706) 864-1800
U.S. News ranking: Reg. U. (S), No. 40
Website: ung.edu/
Admissions email: admissions-dah@ung.edu
Public; founded 1873

Freshman admissions: selective; 2018-2019: 6,498 applied, 4,792 accepted. Either SAT or ACT required. SAT 25/75 percentile: 1108-1273. High school rank: 14% in top tenth, 48% in top quarter, 87% in top half
Early decision deadline: N/A, notification date: N/A
Early action deadline: 11/15, notification date: 12/15
Application deadline (fall): 2/15
Undergraduate student body: 13,243 full time, 5,798 part time; 43% male, 57% female; 0% American Indian, 3% Asian, 4% black, 13% Hispanic, 4% multiracial, 0% Pacific Islander, 73% white, 2% international; 95% from in state; 22% live on campus; 5% of students in fraternities, 10% in sororities
Most popular majors: 22% Business, Management, Marketing, and Related Support Services, 11% Education, 10% Health Professions and Related Programs, 7% Psychology, 6% Social Sciences
Expenses: 2019-2020: $7,472 in state, $21,630 out of state; room/ board: $10,800
Financial aid: (706) 864-1412; 60% of undergrads determined to have financial need; average aid package $6,815

University of West Georgia
Carrollton GA
(678) 839-5600
U.S. News ranking: Nat. U., second tier
Website: www.westga.edu
Admissions email: admiss@westga.edu
Public; founded 1906
Freshman admissions: less selective; 2018-2019: 8,154 applied, 4,745 accepted. Either SAT or ACT required. SAT 25/75 percentile: 920-1080. High school rank: N/A
Early decision deadline: N/A, notification date: N/A
Early action deadline: N/A, notification date: N/A
Application deadline (fall): 6/1
Undergraduate student body: 8,728 full time, 2,407 part time; 37% male, 63% female; 0% American Indian, 1% Asian, 37% black, 8% Hispanic, 4% multiracial, 0% Pacific Islander, 47% white, 1% international; 93% from in state; 28% live on campus; 3% of students in fraternities, 2% in sororities
Most popular majors: 22% Business, Management, Marketing, and Related Support Services, 16% Social Sciences, 15% Health Professions and Related Programs, 9% Psychology, 8% Education
Expenses: 2019-2020: $7,354 in state, $20,836 out of state; room/ board: $10,488
Financial aid: (678) 839-6421; 68% of undergrads determined to have financial need; average aid package $8,610

Valdosta State University

Valdosta GA
(229) 333-5791
U.S. News ranking: Nat. U., second tier
Website: www.valdosta.edu
Admissions email: admissions@valdosta.edu
Public; founded 1906
Freshman admissions: selective; 2018-2019: 6,557 applied, 4,105 accepted. Either SAT or ACT required. SAT 25/75 percentile: 1000-1140. High school rank: N/A
Early decision deadline: N/A, notification date: N/A
Early action deadline: N/A, notification date: N/A
Application deadline (fall): 6/15
Undergraduate student body: 6,984 full time, 1,716 part time; 37% male, 63% female; 0% American Indian, 1% Asian, 38% black, 7% Hispanic, 4% multiracial, 0% Pacific Islander, 47% white, 2% international; 84% from in state; 29% live on campus; 3% of students in fraternities, 4% in sororities
Most popular majors: 26% Business, Management, Marketing, and Related Support Services, 14% Health Professions and Related Programs, 9% Communication, Journalism, and Related Programs, 7% Education, 7% Psychology
Expenses: 2019-2020: $6,410 in state, $17,196 out of state; room/board: $8,110
Financial aid: (229) 333-5935; 75% of undergrads determined to have financial need; average aid package $15,919

Wesleyan College

Macon GA
(800) 447-6610
U.S. News ranking: Nat. Lib. Arts, No. 145
Website: www.wesleyancollege.edu
Admissions email: admissions@wesleyancollege.edu
Private; founded 1836
Affiliation: United Methodist
Freshman admissions: selective; 2018-2019: 890 applied, 426 accepted. Either SAT or ACT required. SAT 25/75 percentile: 930-1110. High school rank: 19% in top tenth, 49% in top quarter, 73% in top half
Early decision deadline: N/A, notification date: N/A
Early action deadline: N/A, notification date: N/A
Application deadline (fall): rolling
Undergraduate student body: 490 full time, 235 part time; 8% male, 92% female; 0% American Indian, 2% Asian, 34% black, 6% Hispanic, 4% multiracial, 0% Pacific Islander, 44% white, 9% international; N/A from in state; 60% live on campus; 0% of students in fraternities, 0% in sororities
Most popular majors: 24% Business Administration and Management, General, 21% Registered Nursing/Registered

Nurse, 12% Accounting, 7% Psychology, General, 6% Biology/Biological Sciences, General
Expenses: 2019-2020: $23,770; room/board: $10,060
Financial aid: (478) 757-5146; 79% of undergrads determined to have financial need; average aid package $22,184

Young Harris College

Young Harris GA
(706) 379-3111
U.S. News ranking: Nat. Lib. Arts, second tier
Website: www.yhc.edu
Admissions email: cpdaniels@yhc.edu
Private; founded 1886
Affiliation: United Methodist
Freshman admissions: selective; 2018-2019: 1,485 applied, 945 accepted. Either SAT or ACT required. SAT 25/75 percentile: 930-1130. High school rank: 8% in top tenth, 28% in top quarter, 62% in top half
Early decision deadline: N/A, notification date: N/A
Early action deadline: N/A, notification date: N/A
Application deadline (fall): rolling
Undergraduate student body: 984 full time, 441 part time; 45% male, 55% female; 0% American Indian, 1% Asian, 10% black, 4% Hispanic, 3% multiracial, 0% Pacific Islander, 70% white, 7% international; 88% from in state; 85% live on campus; 4% of students in fraternities, 9% in sororities
Most popular majors: 20% Business, Management, Marketing, and Related Support Services, 13% Biological and Biomedical Sciences, 13% Psychology, 11% Communication, Journalism, and Related Programs, 9% Visual and Performing Arts
Expenses: 2019-2020: $29,067; room/board: N/A
Financial aid: N/A; 75% of undergrads determined to have financial need; average aid package $25,610

GUAM

University of Guam

Mangilao GU
(671) 735-2201
U.S. News ranking: Reg. U. (W), unranked
Website: www.uog.edu
Admissions email: admitme@triton.uog.edu
Public; founded 1952
Freshman admissions: least selective; 2018-2019: 645 applied, 597 accepted. Neither SAT nor ACT required. SAT 25/75 percentile: N/A. High school rank: 24% in top tenth, 48% in top quarter, 74% in top half
Early decision deadline: N/A, notification date: N/A
Early action deadline: N/A, notification date: N/A
Application deadline (fall): 6/1
Undergraduate student body: 2,708 full time, 713 part time; 43% male, 57% female; 0% American

Indian, 46% Asian, 1% black, 1% Hispanic, 0% multiracial, 46% Pacific Islander, 2% white, 1% international; 99% from in state; 4% live on campus; 0% of students in fraternities, 0% in sororities
Most popular majors: 21% Business Administration and Management, General, 9% Criminal Justice/Safety Studies, 8% Biology/Biological Sciences, General, 7% English Language and Literature, General, 6% Elementary Education and Teaching
Expenses: 2019-2020: $5,804 in state, $12,860 out of state; room/board: $3,850
Financial aid: (671) 735-2288

HAWAII

Brigham Young University–Hawaii[1]

Laie Oahu HI
(808) 293-3738
U.S. News ranking: Reg. Coll. (W), No. 17
Website: www.byuh.edu
Admissions email: admissions@byuh.edu
Private
Application deadline (fall): N/A
Undergraduate student body: N/A full time, N/A part time
Expenses: N/A
Financial aid: N/A

Chaminade University of Honolulu

Honolulu HI
(808) 735-8340
U.S. News ranking: Reg. U. (W), No. 34
Website: chaminade.edu/
Admissions email: admissions@chaminade.edu
Private; founded 1955
Affiliation: Roman Catholic
Freshman admissions: selective; 2018-2019: 764 applied, 742 accepted. Either SAT or ACT required. SAT 25/75 percentile: 970-1130. High school rank: 21% in top tenth, 40% in top quarter, 82% in top half
Early decision deadline: N/A, notification date: N/A
Early action deadline: N/A, notification date: N/A
Application deadline (fall): rolling
Undergraduate student body: 1,062 full time, 37 part time; 26% male, 74% female; 0% American Indian, 38% Asian, 3% black, 4% Hispanic, 8% multiracial, 28% Pacific Islander, 3% white, 1% international; 74% from in state; 24% live on campus; N/A of students in fraternities, N/A in sororities
Most popular majors: 21% Registered Nursing/Registered Nurse, 15% Criminal Justice/Safety Studies, 11% Psychology, General, 7% Business Administration and Management, General, 7% Forensic Science and Technology
Expenses: 2019-2020: $26,134; room/board: $14,184

Financial aid: (808) 735-4780; 68% of undergrads determined to have financial need; average aid package $20,566

Hawaii Pacific University

Honolulu HI
(808) 544-0238
U.S. News ranking: Reg. U. (W), No. 60
Website: www.hpu.edu/
Admissions email: admissions@hpu.edu
Private; founded 1965
Freshman admissions: selective; 2018-2019: 6,168 applied, 4,634 accepted. Either SAT or ACT required. SAT 25/75 percentile: 1020-1220. High school rank: 4% in top tenth, 46% in top quarter, 85% in top half
Early decision deadline: N/A, notification date: N/A
Early action deadline: 11/15, notification date: 12/31
Application deadline (fall): 8/15
Undergraduate student body: 2,384 full time, 1,161 part time; 41% male, 59% female; 0% American Indian, 15% Asian, 7% black, 16% Hispanic, 19% multiracial, 2% Pacific Islander, 25% white, 11% international
Most popular majors: 27% Business, Management, Marketing, and Related Support Services, 16% Health Professions and Related Programs, 7% Psychology, 5% Biological and Biomedical Sciences, 4% Computer and Information Sciences and Support Services
Expenses: 2019-2020: $27,350; room/board: $19,200
Financial aid: (808) 544-0253; 59% of undergrads determined to have financial need; average aid package $14,116

University of Hawaii–Hilo

Hilo HI
(800) 897-4456
U.S. News ranking: Nat. U., second tier
Website: www.uhh.hawaii.edu
Admissions email: uhhadm@hawaii.edu
Public; founded 1947
Freshman admissions: selective; 2018-2019: 1,816 applied, 1,428 accepted. Either SAT or ACT required. ACT 25/75 percentile: 17-23. High school rank: 22% in top tenth, 52% in top quarter, 67% in top half
Early decision deadline: N/A, notification date: N/A
Early action deadline: N/A, notification date: N/A
Application deadline (fall): 7/1
Undergraduate student body: 2,233 full time, 583 part time; 35% male, 65% female; 0% American Indian, 16% Asian, 1% black, 16% Hispanic, 34% multiracial, 9% Pacific Islander, 19% white, 4% international; N/A from in state; 27% live on campus; N/A of students in fraternities, N/A in sororities

Most popular majors: 16% Health Professions and Related Programs, 10% Parks, Recreation, Leisure, and Fitness Studies, 10% Social Sciences, 9% Biological and Biomedical Sciences, 8% Business, Management, Marketing, and Related Support Services
Expenses: 2018-2019: $7,720 in state, $20,680 out of state; room/board: $8,248
Financial aid: (808) 932-7449

University of Hawaii–Manoa

Honolulu HI
(808) 956-8975
U.S. News ranking: Nat. U., No. 166
Website: www.manoa.hawaii.edu/
Admissions email: manoa.admissions@hawaii.edu
Public; founded 1907
Freshman admissions: selective; 2018-2019: 9,350 applied, 7,805 accepted. Either SAT or ACT required. SAT 25/75 percentile: 1055-1240. High school rank: 25% in top tenth, 54% in top quarter, 86% in top half
Early decision deadline: N/A, notification date: N/A
Early action deadline: N/A, notification date: N/A
Application deadline (fall): 3/1
Undergraduate student body: 10,739 full time, 2,229 part time; 43% male, 57% female; 0% American Indian, 40% Asian, 2% black, 2% Hispanic, 16% multiracial, 17% Pacific Islander, 20% white, 3% international; N/A from in state; 23% live on campus; 1% of students in fraternities, 1% in sororities
Most popular majors: 21% Business, Management, Marketing, and Related Support Services, 9% Engineering, 9% Social Sciences, 7% Biological and Biomedical Sciences, 7% Health Professions and Related Programs
Expenses: 2019-2020: $11,970 in state, $34,002 out of state; room/board: $12,686
Financial aid: (808) 956-7251; 56% of undergrads determined to have financial need; average aid package $14,801

University of Hawaii– Maui College[1]

Kahului HI
(808) 984-3267
U.S. News ranking: Reg. Coll. (W), unranked
Website: www.maui.hawaii.edu/
Admissions email: N/A
Public
Application deadline (fall): N/A
Undergraduate student body: N/A full time, N/A part time
Expenses: N/A
Financial aid: N/A

University of Hawaii–West Oahu

Kapolei HI
(808) 689-2900
U.S. News ranking: Reg. Coll. (W), No. 21
Website: westoahu.hawaii.edu/
Admissions email: uhwo.admissions@hawaii.edu
Public; founded 1976
Freshman admissions: less selective; 2018-2019: 891 applied, 669 accepted. Either SAT or ACT required. ACT 25/75 percentile: 16-21. High school rank: 12% in top tenth, 37% in top quarter, 77% in top half
Early decision deadline: N/A, notification date: N/A
Early action deadline: N/A, notification date: N/A
Application deadline (fall): 7/1
Undergraduate student body: 1,698 full time, 1,405 part time; 33% male, 67% female; 1% American Indian, 39% Asian, 2% black, 1% Hispanic, 16% multiracial, 30% Pacific Islander, 11% white, 1% international; 97% from in state; 2% live on campus; 2% of students in fraternities, 2% in sororities
Most popular majors: 37% Business, Management, Marketing, and Related Support Services, 24% Public Administration and Social Service Professions, 19% Social Sciences, 10% Multi/Interdisciplinary Studies, 5% Liberal Arts and Sciences, General Studies and Humanities
Expenses: 2019-2020: $7,584 in state, $20,544 out of state; room/board: $8,339
Financial aid: (808) 689-2900; 41% of undergrads determined to have financial need; average aid package $8,339

IDAHO

Boise State University

Boise ID
(208) 426-1156
U.S. News ranking: Nat. U., second tier
Website: www.boisestate.edu
Admissions email: admissions@boisestate.edu
Public; founded 1932
Freshman admissions: selective; 2018-2019: 10,788 applied, 8,712 accepted. Either SAT or ACT required for some. SAT 25/75 percentile: 1030-1220. High school rank: 16% in top tenth, 39% in top quarter, 74% in top half
Early decision deadline: N/A, notification date: N/A
Early action deadline: N/A, notification date: N/A
Application deadline (fall): 8/1
Undergraduate student body: 12,787 full time, 9,277 part time; 43% male, 57% female; 0% American Indian, 2% Asian, 2% black, 14% Hispanic, 5% multiracial, 1% Pacific Islander,

73% white, 2% international; N/A from in state; 14% live on campus; N/A of students in fraternities, N/A in sororities
Most popular majors: 23% Health Professions and Related Programs, 17% Business, Management, Marketing, and Related Support Services, 6% Communication, Journalism, and Related Programs, 6% Engineering, 5% Social Sciences
Expenses: 2019-2020: $8,068 in state, $24,988 out of state; room/board: $11,246
Financial aid: (208) 426-1664; 58% of undergrads determined to have financial need; average aid package $10,453

Brigham Young University–Idaho[1]

Rexburg ID
(208) 496-1036
U.S. News ranking: Reg. Coll. (W), No. 20
Website: www.byui.edu
Admissions email: admissions@byui.edu
Private
Application deadline (fall): N/A
Undergraduate student body: N/A full time, N/A part time
Expenses: N/A
Financial aid: N/A

College of Idaho

Caldwell ID
(208) 459-5011
U.S. News ranking: Nat. Lib. Arts, No. 117
Website: www.collegeofidaho.edu
Admissions email: admissions@collegeofidaho.edu
Private; founded 1891
Freshman admissions: selective; 2018-2019: 2,754 applied, 1,355 accepted. Either SAT or ACT required for some. SAT 25/75 percentile: 1030-1213. High school rank: N/A
Early decision deadline: N/A, notification date: N/A
Early action deadline: 11/16, notification date: 12/21
Application deadline (fall): 2/16
Undergraduate student body: 919 full time, 27 part time; 48% male, 52% female; 0% American Indian, 2% Asian, 2% black, 14% Hispanic, 5% multiracial, 1% Pacific Islander, 60% white, 13% international; 64% from in state; 68% live on campus; 12% of students in fraternities, 16% in sororities
Most popular majors: 19% Health Professions and Related Programs, 15% Business, Management, Marketing, and Related Support Services, 13% Psychology, 10% Biological and Biomedical Sciences, 6% Social Sciences
Expenses: 2019-2020: $31,755; room/board: $9,788
Financial aid: (208) 459-5307; 63% of undergrads determined to have financial need; average aid package $29,430

Idaho State University[1]

Pocatello ID
(208) 282-0211
U.S. News ranking: Nat. U., unranked
Website: www.isu.edu
Admissions email: info@isu.edu
Public
Application deadline (fall): N/A
Undergraduate student body: N/A full time, N/A part time
Expenses: N/A
Financial aid: N/A

Lewis-Clark State College[7]

Lewiston ID
(208) 792-2210
U.S. News ranking: Reg. Coll. (W), second tier
Website: www.lcsc.edu
Admissions email: admissions@lcsc.edu
Public; founded 1893
Freshman admissions: less selective; 2018-2019: 1,760 applied, 1,753 accepted. Either SAT or ACT required for some. SAT 25/75 percentile: 930-1100. High school rank: N/A
Early decision deadline: N/A, notification date: N/A
Early action deadline: N/A, notification date: N/A
Application deadline (fall): 8/8
Undergraduate student body: 2,215 full time, 1,531 part time
Most popular majors: Information not available
Expenses: 2019-2020: $6,982 in state, $19,978 out of state; room/board: $7,680
Financial aid: (208) 792-2224; 50% of undergrads determined to have financial need; average aid package $8,632

Northwest Nazarene University

Nampa ID
(208) 467-8000
U.S. News ranking: Reg. U. (W), No. 43
Website: www.nnu.edu
Admissions email: Admissions@nnu.edu
Private; founded 1913
Freshman admissions: selective; 2018-2019: 769 applied, 742 accepted. Either SAT or ACT required. SAT 25/75 percentile: 1020-1250. High school rank: 23% in top tenth, 48% in top quarter, 78% in top half
Early decision deadline: N/A, notification date: N/A
Early action deadline: 1/15, notification date: 9/15
Application deadline (fall): 8/15
Undergraduate student body: 1,089 full time, 374 part time; 42% male, 58% female; 0% American Indian, 2% Asian, 2% black, 7% Hispanic, 6% multiracial, 0% Pacific Islander, 78% white, 2% international; N/A from in state; 68% live on campus; 0% of students in fraternities, 0% in sororities

Most popular majors: 21% Business, Management, Marketing, and Related Support Services, 17% Health Professions and Related Programs, 10% Education, 7% Biological and Biomedical Sciences, 6% Communication, Journalism, and Related Programs
Expenses: 2019-2020: $31,050; room/board: $7,990
Financial aid: (208) 467-8347; 77% of undergrads determined to have financial need; average aid package $25,613

University of Idaho

Moscow ID
(888) 884-3246
U.S. News ranking: Nat. U., No. 179
Website: www.uidaho.edu/admissions
Admissions email: admissions@uidaho.edu
Public; founded 1889
Freshman admissions: selective; 2018-2019: 7,938 applied, 6,132 accepted. Either SAT or ACT required. SAT 25/75 percentile: 1010-1220. High school rank: 18% in top tenth, 40% in top quarter, 72% in top half
Early decision deadline: N/A, notification date: N/A
Early action deadline: N/A, notification date: N/A
Application deadline (fall): 8/1
Undergraduate student body: 7,039 full time, 2,529 part time; 50% male, 50% female; 1% American Indian, 1% Asian, 1% black, 11% Hispanic, 4% multiracial, 0% Pacific Islander, 74% white, 5% international; 74% from in state; 37% live on campus; 18% of students in fraternities, 21% in sororities
Most popular majors: 6% Psychology, General, 4% Marketing/Marketing Management, General, 4% Mechanical Engineering, 3% Business Administration and Management, General, 3% Finance, General
Expenses: 2019-2020: $8,304 in state, $27,540 out of state; room/board: $9,080
Financial aid: (208) 885-6312; 58% of undergrads determined to have financial need; average aid package $14,071

ILLINOIS

American Academy of Art[1]

Chicago IL
(312) 461-0600
U.S. News ranking: Arts, unranked
Website: www.aaart.edu
Admissions email: N/A
For-profit
Application deadline (fall): N/A
Undergraduate student body: N/A full time, N/A part time
Expenses: N/A
Financial aid: N/A

American InterContinental University[1]

Hoffman Estates IL
(877) 701-3800
U.S. News ranking: Reg. U. (Mid. W), unranked
Website: www.aiuniv.edu
Admissions email: N/A
For-profit
Application deadline (fall): N/A
Undergraduate student body: N/A full time, N/A part time
Expenses: N/A
Financial aid: N/A

Augustana College

Rock Island IL
(800) 798-8100
U.S. News ranking: Nat. Lib. Arts, No. 92
Website: www.augustana.edu
Admissions email: admissions@augustana.edu
Private; founded 1860
Affiliation: Evangelical Lutheran Church
Freshman admissions: more selective; 2018-2019: 6,181 applied, 4,463 accepted. Neither SAT nor ACT required. ACT 25/75 percentile: 22-29. High school rank: 28% in top tenth, 58% in top quarter, 90% in top half
Early decision deadline: 11/1, notification date: 11/15
Early action deadline: 11/1, notification date: 12/20
Application deadline (fall): rolling
Undergraduate student body: 2,534 full time, 9 part time; 43% male, 57% female; 0% American Indian, 2% Asian, 4% black, 10% Hispanic, 3% multiracial, 0% Pacific Islander, 70% white, 10% international; 78% from in state; 70% live on campus; 23% of students in fraternities, 39% in sororities
Most popular majors: 17% Biology/Biological Sciences, General, 13% Business Administration and Management, General, 7% Psychology, General, 6% Accounting, 6% Communication Sciences and Disorders, General
Expenses: 2019-2020: $43,610; room/board: $10,890
Financial aid: (309) 794-7207; 75% of undergrads determined to have financial need; average aid package $33,177

Aurora University[1]

Aurora IL
(800) 742-5281
U.S. News ranking: Nat. U., second tier
Website: www.aurora.edu
Admissions email: admission@aurora.edu
Private
Application deadline (fall): N/A
Undergraduate student body: N/A full time, N/A part time
Expenses: N/A
Financial aid: N/A

Benedictine University

Lisle IL
(630) 829-6300
U.S. News ranking: Nat. U., second tier
Website: www.ben.edu
Admissions email: admissions@ben.edu
Private; founded 1887
Affiliation: Roman Catholic
Freshman admissions: selective; 2018-2019: 5,257 applied, 3,435 accepted. Either SAT or ACT required. SAT 25/75 percentile: 980-1190. High school rank: 14% in top tenth, 40% in top quarter, 74% in top half
Early decision deadline: N/A, notification date: N/A
Early action deadline: N/A, notification date: N/A
Application deadline (fall): rolling
Undergraduate student body: 2,372 full time, 346 part time; 46% male, 54% female; 1% American Indian, 15% Asian, 9% black, 17% Hispanic, 0% multiracial, 0% Pacific Islander, 42% white, 1% international; N/A from in state; 19% live on campus; 0% of students in fraternities, 2% in sororities
Most popular majors: 33% Business, Management, Marketing, and Related Support Services, 21% Health Professions and Related Programs, 9% Psychology, 7% Biological and Biomedical Sciences, 5% Homeland Security, Law Enforcement, Firefighting and Related Protective Services
Expenses: 2019-2020: $34,290; room/board: $9,480
Financial aid: (630) 829-6100; 78% of undergrads determined to have financial need; average aid package $24,713

Blackburn College

Carlinville IL
(800) 233-3550
U.S. News ranking: Nat. Lib. Arts, second tier
Website: www.blackburn.edu
Admissions email: justin.norwood@blackburn.edu
Private; founded 1837
Affiliation: Presbyterian Church (USA)
Freshman admissions: selective; 2018-2019: 869 applied, 466 accepted. Either SAT or ACT required. SAT 25/75 percentile: 940-1140. High school rank: 10% in top tenth, 32% in top quarter, 67% in top half
Early decision deadline: N/A, notification date: N/A
Early action deadline: N/A, notification date: N/A
Application deadline (fall): rolling
Undergraduate student body: 548 full time, 18 part time; 40% male, 60% female; 0% American Indian, 1% Asian, 12% black, 4% Hispanic, 2% multiracial, 0% Pacific Islander, 76% white, 2% international; 88% from in state; 68% live on campus; 0% of students in fraternities, 0% in sororities

Most popular majors: 21% Biological and Biomedical Sciences, 21% Business, Management, Marketing, and Related Support Services, 9% Education, 9% Homeland Security, Law Enforcement, Firefighting and Related Protective Services, 9% Psychology
Expenses: 2019-2020: $23,510; room/board: $8,100
Financial aid: (217) 854-5774; 90% of undergrads determined to have financial need; average aid package $19,123

Bradley University

Peoria IL
(309) 677-1000
U.S. News ranking: Reg. U. (Mid. W), No. 4
Website: www.bradley.edu
Admissions email: admissions@bradley.edu
Private; founded 1897
Freshman admissions: more selective; 2018-2019: 11,229 applied, 7,489 accepted. Either SAT or ACT required. SAT 25/75 percentile: 1090-1290. High school rank: 32% in top tenth, 64% in top quarter, 92% in top half
Early decision deadline: N/A, notification date: N/A
Early action deadline: 10/15, notification date: N/A
Application deadline (fall): rolling
Undergraduate student body: 4,462 full time, 144 part time; 49% male, 51% female; 0% American Indian, 3% Asian, 7% black, 10% Hispanic, 3% multiracial, 0% Pacific Islander, 73% white, 2% international; 82% from in state; 67% live on campus; 29% of students in fraternities, 29% in sororities
Most popular majors: 23% Business, Management, Marketing, and Related Support Services, 18% Engineering, 13% Health Professions and Related Programs, 9% Communication, Journalism, and Related Programs, 6% Education
Expenses: 2019-2020: $34,610; room/board: $10,940
Financial aid: (309) 677-3089; 73% of undergrads determined to have financial need; average aid package $24,915

Chicago State University[1]

Chicago IL
(773) 995-2513
U.S. News ranking: Reg. U. (Mid. W), second tier
Website: www.csu.edu
Admissions email: ug-admissions@csu.edu
Public; founded 1867
Application deadline (fall): rolling
Undergraduate student body: N/A full time, N/A part time
Expenses: N/A
Financial aid: N/A

Columbia College Chicago

Chicago IL
(312) 369-7130
U.S. News ranking: Reg. U. (Mid. W), No. 105
Website: www.colum.edu
Admissions email: admissions@colum.edu
Private; founded 1890
Freshman admissions: selective; 2018-2019: 8,121 applied, 7,045 accepted. Neither SAT nor ACT required. SAT 25/75 percentile: 1000-1230. High school rank: 12% in top tenth, 35% in top quarter, 72% in top half
Early decision deadline: N/A, notification date: N/A
Early action deadline: N/A, notification date: N/A
Application deadline (fall): 8/15
Undergraduate student body: 6,073 full time, 495 part time; 42% male, 58% female; 0% American Indian, 4% Asian, 13% black, 16% Hispanic, 5% multiracial, 0% Pacific Islander, 53% white, 5% international; 56% from in state; 34% live on campus; N/A of students in fraternities, N/A in sororities
Most popular majors: 18% Cinematography and Film/Video Production, 6% Retail Management, 5% Graphic Design, 5% Radio and Television, 4% Recording Arts Technology/Technician
Expenses: 2019-2020: $27,756; room/board: $16,000
Financial aid: (312) 369-7140; 65% of undergrads determined to have financial need; average aid package $14,956

Concordia University Chicago

River Forest IL
(877) 282-4422
U.S. News ranking: Reg. U. (Mid. W), No. 72
Website: www.cuchicago.edu/
Admissions email: admission@cuchicago.edu
Private; founded 1864
Affiliation: Lutheran Church–Missouri Synod
Freshman admissions: selective; 2018-2019: 5,024 applied, 3,818 accepted. Either SAT or ACT required. SAT 25/75 percentile: 990-1170. High school rank: N/A
Early decision deadline: N/A, notification date: N/A
Early action deadline: N/A, notification date: N/A
Application deadline (fall): rolling
Undergraduate student body: 1,366 full time, 111 part time; 41% male, 59% female; 0% American Indian, 2% Asian, 13% black, 32% Hispanic, 3% multiracial, 0% Pacific Islander, 45% white, 3% international; 73% from in state; 38% live on campus; N/A of students in fraternities, N/A in sororities

Most popular majors: 21% Business, Management, Marketing, and Related Support Services, 14% Education, 14% Parks, Recreation, Leisure, and Fitness Studies, 11% Health Professions and Related Programs, 7% Psychology
Expenses: 2019-2020: $32,880; room/board: $9,996
Financial aid: (708) 209-3113; 85% of undergrads determined to have financial need; average aid package $24,863

DePaul University

Chicago IL
(312) 362-8300
U.S. News ranking: Nat. U., No. 125
Website: www.depaul.edu
Admissions email: admission@depaul.edu
Private; founded 1898
Affiliation: Roman Catholic
Freshman admissions: selective; 2018-2019: 26,169 applied, 17,673 accepted. Neither SAT nor ACT required. SAT 25/75 percentile: 1080-1290. High school rank: N/A
Early decision deadline: N/A, notification date: N/A
Early action deadline: 11/15, notification date: 1/15
Application deadline (fall): 2/1
Undergraduate student body: 12,795 full time, 1,712 part time; 47% male, 53% female; 0% American Indian, 10% Asian, 8% black, 19% Hispanic, 5% multiracial, 0% Pacific Islander, 52% white, 3% international; 75% from in state; 19% live on campus; 5% of students in fraternities, 10% in sororities
Most popular majors: 30% Business, Management, Marketing, and Related Support Services, 13% Communication, Journalism, and Related Programs, 9% Liberal Arts and Sciences, General Studies and Humanities, 9% Visual and Performing Arts, 7% Computer and Information Sciences and Support Services
Expenses: 2019-2020: $41,202; room/board: $14,736
Financial aid: (312) 362-8520; 71% of undergrads determined to have financial need; average aid package $25,216

DeVry University[1]

Downers Grove IL
(630) 515-3000
U.S. News ranking: Reg. U. (Mid. W), second tier
Website: www.devry.edu
Admissions email: N/A
For-profit; founded 1931
Application deadline (fall): rolling
Undergraduate student body: N/A full time, N/A part time
Expenses: N/A
Financial aid: N/A

Dominican University

River Forest IL
(708) 524-6800
U.S. News ranking: Reg. U. (Mid. W), No. 11
Website: www.dom.edu/
Admissions email: domadmis@dom.edu
Private; founded 1901
Affiliation: Roman Catholic
Freshman admissions: selective; 2018-2019: 4,813 applied, 3,070 accepted. Either SAT or ACT required. SAT 25/75 percentile: 950-1130. High school rank: 22% in top tenth, 52% in top quarter, 86% in top half
Early decision deadline: N/A, notification date: N/A
Early action deadline: N/A, notification date: N/A
Application deadline (fall): 8/26
Undergraduate student body: 1,974 full time, 132 part time; 32% male, 68% female; 0% American Indian, 3% Asian, 6% black, 56% Hispanic, 1% multiracial, 0% Pacific Islander, 30% white, 2% international; 93% from in state; 26% live on campus; 0% of students in fraternities, 0% in sororities
Most popular majors: 16% Business Administration and Management, General, 8% Psychology, General, 8% Registered Nursing/Registered Nurse, 7% Nutrition Sciences, 5% Pre-Medicine/Pre-Medical Studies
Expenses: 2019-2020: $34,420; room/board: $10,549
Financial aid: (708) 524-6950; 85% of undergrads determined to have financial need; average aid package $26,129

Eastern Illinois University

Charleston IL
(877) 581-2348
U.S. News ranking: Reg. U. (Mid. W), No. 40
Website: www.eiu.edu
Admissions email: admissions@eiu.edu
Public; founded 1895
Freshman admissions: selective; 2018-2019: 8,580 applied, 4,746 accepted. Either SAT or ACT required. SAT 25/75 percentile: 920-1110. High school rank: 11% in top tenth, 34% in top quarter, 71% in top half
Early decision deadline: N/A, notification date: N/A
Early action deadline: N/A, notification date: N/A
Application deadline (fall): 8/15
Undergraduate student body: 4,091 full time, 1,921 part time; 43% male, 57% female; 0% American Indian, 1% Asian, 21% black, 8% Hispanic, 3% multiracial, 0% Pacific Islander, 61% white, 2% international; 93% from in state; 30% live on campus; 16% of students in fraternities, 14% in sororities
Most popular majors: 14% Business, Management, Marketing, and Related Support Services, 10% Liberal Arts and Sciences, General Studies and Humanities, 10% Parks,

Recreation, Leisure, and Fitness Studies, 9% Communication, Journalism, and Related Programs, 8% Family and Consumer Sciences/Human Sciences
Expenses: 2019-2020: $11,989 in state, $14,269 out of state; room/board: $10,030
Financial aid: (217) 581-6405; 73% of undergrads determined to have financial need; average aid package $13,272

East-West University[1]

Chicago IL
(312) 939-0111
U.S. News ranking: Nat. Lib. Arts, second tier
Website: www.eastwest.edu
Admissions email: seeyou@eastwest.edu
Private; founded 1980
Application deadline (fall): rolling
Undergraduate student body: N/A full time, N/A part time
Expenses: N/A
Financial aid: N/A

Elmhurst College

Elmhurst IL
(630) 617-3400
U.S. News ranking: Reg. U. (Mid. W), No. 24
Website: www.elmhurst.edu
Admissions email: admit@elmhurst.edu
Private; founded 1871
Affiliation: United Church of Christ
Freshman admissions: selective; 2018-2019: 4,219 applied, 2,842 accepted. Either SAT or ACT required. SAT 25/75 percentile: 993-1190. High school rank: 12% in top tenth, 36% in top quarter, 73% in top half
Early decision deadline: N/A, notification date: N/A
Early action deadline: 11/1, notification date: 12/1
Application deadline (fall): rolling
Undergraduate student body: 2,710 full time, 138 part time; 40% male, 60% female; 0% American Indian, 5% Asian, 5% black, 23% Hispanic, 3% multiracial, 0% Pacific Islander, 60% white, 0% international; 91% from in state; 30% live on campus; 9% of students in fraternities, 13% in sororities
Most popular majors: 22% Business, Management, Marketing, and Related Support Services, 14% Health Professions and Related Programs, 12% Psychology, 9% Parks, Recreation, Leisure, and Fitness Studies, 8% Education
Expenses: 2019-2020: $37,754; room/board: $10,710
Financial aid: (630) 617-3015; 79% of undergrads determined to have financial need; average aid package $28,465

Eureka College

Eureka IL
(309) 467-6350
U.S. News ranking: Reg. Coll. (Mid. W), No. 35
Website: www.eureka.edu
Admissions email: admissions@eureka.edu
Private; founded 1855

Affiliation: Christian Church (Disciples of Christ)
Freshman admissions: selective; 2018-2019: 817 applied, 468 accepted. Either SAT or ACT required. SAT 25/75 percentile: 950-1170. High school rank: 7% in top tenth, 27% in top quarter, 60% in top half
Early decision deadline: N/A, notification date: N/A
Early action deadline: N/A, notification date: N/A
Application deadline (fall): 8/15
Undergraduate student body: 548 full time, 19 part time; 52% male, 48% female; 1% American Indian, 0% Asian, 9% black, 3% Hispanic, 4% multiracial, 0% Pacific Islander, 82% white, 1% international; 95% from in state; 66% live on campus; 18% of students in fraternities, 21% in sororities
Most popular majors: 25% Business, Management, Marketing, and Related Support Services, 11% Education, 10% Psychology, 9% Homeland Security, Law Enforcement, Firefighting and Related Protective Services, 7% Visual and Performing Arts
Expenses: 2019-2020: $26,890; room/board: $9,860
Financial aid: (309) 467-6310; 72% of undergrads determined to have financial need; average aid package $16,742

Governors State University

University Park IL
(708) 534-4490
U.S. News ranking: Reg. U. (Mid. W), second tier
Website: www.govst.edu/
Admissions email: admissions@govst.edu
Public; founded 1969
Freshman admissions: less selective; 2018-2019: 1,504 applied, 568 accepted. Either SAT or ACT required. SAT 25/75 percentile: 860-1045. High school rank: 3% in top tenth, 11% in top quarter, 34% in top half
Early decision deadline: 11/15, notification date: 12/15
Early action deadline: N/A, notification date: N/A
Application deadline (fall): 4/1
Undergraduate student body: 1,882 full time, 1,380 part time; 38% male, 62% female; 0% American Indian, 2% Asian, 39% black, 15% Hispanic, 3% multiracial, 0% Pacific Islander, 31% white, 1% international; 98% from in state; 8% live on campus; 0% of students in fraternities, 0% in sororities
Most popular majors: 18% Liberal Arts and Sciences, General Studies and Humanities, 16% Business, Management, Marketing, and Related Support Services, 16% Health Professions and Related Programs, 12% Psychology, 8% Homeland Security, Law Enforcement, Firefighting and Related Protective Services

Expenses: 2019-2020: $12,616 in state, $22,006 out of state; room/board: $10,181
Financial aid: (708) 534-4480

Greenville University

Greenville IL
(618) 664-7100
U.S. News ranking: Reg. U. (Mid. W), No. 102
Website: www.greenville.edu
Admissions email: admissions@greenville.edu
Private; founded 1892
Affiliation: Free Methodist
Freshman admissions: selective; 2018-2019: 2,245 applied, 1,069 accepted. Either SAT or ACT required. SAT 25/75 percentile: 850-1060. High school rank: N/A
Early decision deadline: N/A, notification date: N/A
Early action deadline: N/A, notification date: N/A
Application deadline (fall): rolling
Undergraduate student body: 872 full time, 92 part time; 53% male, 47% female; 0% American Indian, 0% Asian, 15% black, 6% Hispanic, 2% multiracial, 0% Pacific Islander, 66% white, 5% international; 65% from in state; 85% live on campus; 0% of students in fraternities, 0% in sororities
Most popular majors: 14% Organizational Behavior Studies, 7% Health/Medical Psychology, 6% Biology/Biological Sciences, General, 5% Elementary Education and Teaching, 4% Social Work
Expenses: 2019-2020: $27,954; room/board: $9,348
Financial aid: (618) 664-7108; 81% of undergrads determined to have financial need; average aid package $23,812

Illinois College

Jacksonville IL
(217) 245-3030
U.S. News ranking: Nat. Lib. Arts, No. 136
Website: www.ic.edu
Admissions email: admissions@mail.ic.edu
Private; founded 1829
Freshman admissions: selective; 2018-2019: 3,378 applied, 2,565 accepted. Neither SAT nor ACT required. SAT 25/75 percentile: 990-1170. High school rank: 15% in top tenth, 43% in top quarter, 78% in top half
Early decision deadline: N/A, notification date: N/A
Early action deadline: 12/1, notification date: 12/23
Application deadline (fall): rolling
Undergraduate student body: 976 full time, 7 part time; 49% male, 51% female; 0% American Indian, 1% Asian, 10% black, 7% Hispanic, 4% multiracial, 0% Pacific Islander, 72% white, 6% international; N/A from in state; 84% live on campus; 0% of students in fraternities, 0% in sororities

Most popular majors: 23% Business, Management, Marketing, and Related Support Services, 17% Biological and Biomedical Sciences, 8% English Language and Literature/Letters, 7% Psychology, 5% Multi/Interdisciplinary Studies
Expenses: 2019-2020: $33,740; room/board: $9,374
Financial aid: (217) 245-3035; 84% of undergrads determined to have financial need; average aid package $27,921

Illinois Institute of Art–Chicago[1]

Chicago IL
(312) 280-3500
U.S. News ranking: Arts, unranked
Website: www.artinstitutes.edu/chicago/
Admissions email: N/A
For-profit
Application deadline (fall): N/A
Undergraduate student body: N/A full time, N/A part time
Expenses: N/A
Financial aid: N/A

Illinois Institute of Technology

Chicago IL
(800) 448-2329
U.S. News ranking: Nat. U., No. 117
Website: admissions.iit.edu/undergraduate/apply
Admissions email: admission@iit.edu
Private; founded 1890
Freshman admissions: more selective; 2018-2019: 4,958 applied, 2,885 accepted. Either SAT or ACT required. SAT 25/75 percentile: 1220-1400. High school rank: 49% in top tenth, 80% in top quarter, 96% in top half
Early decision deadline: N/A, notification date: N/A
Early action deadline: N/A, notification date: N/A
Application deadline (fall): 8/1
Undergraduate student body: 2,792 full time, 234 part time; 69% male, 31% female; 0% American Indian, 15% Asian, 5% black, 17% Hispanic, 4% multiracial, 0% Pacific Islander, 37% white, 18% international; 60% from in state; 43% live on campus; 7% of students in fraternities, 6% in sororities
Most popular majors: 51% Engineering, 17% Computer and Information Sciences and Support Services, 14% Architecture and Related Services, 5% Engineering Technologies and Engineering-Related Fields, 3% Psychology
Expenses: 2019-2020: $49,280; room/board: $13,582
Financial aid: (312) 567-7219; 66% of undergrads determined to have financial need; average aid package $41,568

Illinois State University

Normal IL
(309) 438-2181
U.S. News ranking: Nat. U., No. 197
Website: illinoisstate.edu/
Admissions email: admissions@ilstu.edu
Public; founded 1857
Freshman admissions: selective; 2018-2019: 12,886 applied, 11,492 accepted. Either SAT or ACT required. ACT 25/75 percentile: 20-26. High school rank: N/A
Early decision deadline: N/A, notification date: N/A
Early action deadline: N/A, notification date: N/A
Application deadline (fall): 4/1
Undergraduate student body: 16,917 full time, 1,190 part time; 45% male, 55% female; 0% American Indian, 2% Asian, 9% black, 11% Hispanic, 3% multiracial, 0% Pacific Islander, 73% white, 1% international; 97% from in state; 34% live on campus; 3% of students in fraternities, 6% in sororities
Most popular majors: 23% Business, Management, Marketing, and Related Support Services, 12% Education, 10% Health Professions and Related Programs, 7% Communication, Journalism, and Related Programs, 6% Social Sciences
Expenses: 2019-2020: $14,516 in state, $26,040 out of state; room/board: $9,850
Financial aid: (309) 438-2231; 63% of undergrads determined to have financial need; average aid package $11,506

Illinois Wesleyan University

Bloomington IL
(800) 332-2498
U.S. News ranking: Nat. Lib. Arts, No. 80
Website: www.iwu.edu
Admissions email: iwuadmit@iwu.edu
Private; founded 1850
Freshman admissions: more selective; 2018-2019: 3,785 applied, 2,216 accepted. Either SAT or ACT required. ACT 25/75 percentile: 24-29. High school rank: 34% in top tenth, 63% in top quarter, 90% in top half
Early decision deadline: N/A, notification date: N/A
Early action deadline: 11/15, notification date: 12/15
Application deadline (fall): rolling
Undergraduate student body: 1,689 full time, 4 part time; 48% male, 52% female; 0% American Indian, 6% Asian, 6% black, 9% Hispanic, 3% multiracial, 0% Pacific Islander, 70% white, 6% international; 84% from in state; 82% live on campus; 31% of students in fraternities, 34% in sororities

Most popular majors: 14% Accounting, 11% Business/ Commerce, General, 10% Psychology, General, 10% Registered Nursing/Registered Nurse, 9% Biology/Biological Sciences, General
Expenses: 2019-2020: $50,026; room/board: $11,412
Financial aid: (309) 556-3096; 69% of undergrads determined to have financial need; average aid package $36,743

Judson University
Elgin IL
(847) 628-2510
U.S. News ranking: Reg. U. (Mid. W), No. 72
Website: www.judsonu.edu
Admissions email: admissions@judsonu.edu
Private; founded 1963
Affiliation: American Baptist
Freshman admissions: selective; 2018-2019: 512 applied, 385 accepted. Either SAT or ACT required. SAT 25/75 percentile: 950-1180. High school rank: 14% in top tenth, 31% in top quarter, 62% in top half
Early decision deadline: N/A, notification date: N/A
Early action deadline: N/A, notification date: N/A
Application deadline (fall): rolling
Undergraduate student body: 679 full time, 355 part time; 41% male, 59% female; 0% American Indian, 2% Asian, 12% black, 21% Hispanic, 2% multiracial, 0% Pacific Islander, 48% white, 5% international; 83% from in state; 60% live on campus; 0% of students in fraternities, 0% in sororities
Most popular majors: 14% Business Administration, Management and Operations, Other, 8% Architecture, 8% Psychology, General, 7% Business Administration and Management, General, 6% Sport and Fitness Administration/Management
Expenses: 2019-2020: $29,870; room/board: $10,290
Financial aid: (847) 628-2531; 76% of undergrads determined to have financial need; average aid package $20,982

Knox College
Galesburg IL
(800) 678-5669
U.S. News ranking: Nat. Lib. Arts, No. 66
Website: www.knox.edu
Admissions email: admission@knox.edu
Private; founded 1837
Freshman admissions: more selective; 2018-2019: 2,738 applied, 2,032 accepted. Either SAT or ACT required for some. SAT 25/75 percentile: 1090-1350. High school rank: 32% in top tenth, 62% in top quarter, 90% in top half
Early decision deadline: 11/1, notification date: 11/15
Early action deadline: 11/1, notification date: 12/15
Application deadline (fall): 1/15

Undergraduate student body: 1,310 full time, 23 part time; 43% male, 57% female; 0% American Indian, 5% Asian, 8% black, 15% Hispanic, 5% multiracial, 0% Pacific Islander, 48% white, 17% international; 55% from in state; 86% live on campus; 19% of students in fraternities, 12% in sororities
Most popular majors: 11% Economics, General, 9% Biology/ Biological Sciences, General, 8% Creative Writing, 7% Psychology, General, 5% Elementary Education and Teaching
Expenses: 2019-2020: $48,168; room/board: $10,068
Financial aid: (309) 341-7149; 72% of undergrads determined to have financial need; average aid package $38,817

Lake Forest College
Lake Forest IL
(847) 735-5000
U.S. News ranking: Nat. Lib. Arts, No. 92
Website: www.lakeforest.edu
Admissions email: admissions@lakeforest.edu
Private; founded 1857
Freshman admissions: more selective; 2018-2019: 4,147 applied, 2,402 accepted. Neither SAT nor ACT required. SAT 25/75 percentile: 1110-1310. High school rank: 27% in top tenth, 62% in top quarter, 89% in top half
Early decision deadline: 11/1, notification date: 12/15
Early action deadline: 11/1, notification date: 12/15
Application deadline (fall): 2/15
Undergraduate student body: 1,472 full time, 20 part time; 43% male, 57% female; 0% American Indian, 5% Asian, 5% black, 14% Hispanic, 4% multiracial, 0% Pacific Islander, 58% white, 10% international; 62% from in state; 78% live on campus; 15% of students in fraternities, 15% in sororities
Most popular majors: 23% Business, Management, Marketing, and Related Support Services, 16% Social Sciences, 11% Biological and Biomedical Sciences, 7% Communication, Journalism, and Related Programs, 6% Psychology
Expenses: 2019-2020: $48,424; room/board: $10,676
Financial aid: (847) 735-5104; 73% of undergrads determined to have financial need; average aid package $40,534

Lewis University
Romeoville IL
(800) 897-9000
U.S. News ranking: Reg. U. (Mid. W), No. 20
Website: www.lewisu.edu
Admissions email: admissions@lewisu.edu
Private; founded 1932
Affiliation: Roman Catholic
Freshman admissions: selective, 2018-2019: 5,876 applied, 3,394 accepted. Either SAT or ACT required. SAT 25/75 percentile: 1040-1200. High

school rank: 16% in top tenth, 46% in top quarter, 81% in top half
Early decision deadline: N/A, notification date: N/A
Early action deadline: N/A, notification date: N/A
Application deadline (fall): rolling
Undergraduate student body: 3,575 full time, 776 part time; 49% male, 51% female; 0% American Indian, 5% Asian, 6% black, 21% Hispanic, 3% multiracial, 0% Pacific Islander, 59% white, 2% international; 91% from in state; 24% live on campus; 2% of students in fraternities, 4% in sororities
Most popular majors: 12% Registered Nursing/Registered Nurse, 11% Criminal Justice/ Safety Studies, 7% Business Administration and Management, General, 7% Computer Science, 7% Psychology, General
Expenses: 2019-2020: $33,420; room/board: $10,820
Financial aid: (815) 836-5263; 75% of undergrads determined to have financial need; average aid package $27,329

Lincoln College[1]
Lincoln IL
(800) 569-0556
U.S. News ranking: Reg. Coll. (Mid. W), second tier
Website: www.lincolncollege.edu
Admissions email: admission@lincolncollege.edu
Private; founded 1865
Application deadline (fall): rolling
Undergraduate student body: N/A full time, N/A part time
Expenses: N/A
Financial aid: (217) 732-3155

Loyola University Chicago
Chicago IL
(800) 262-2373
U.S. News ranking: Nat. U., No. 104
Website: www.luc.edu
Admissions email: admission@luc.edu
Private; founded 1870
Affiliation: Roman Catholic
Freshman admissions: more selective; 2018-2019: 25,122 applied, 17,064 accepted. Either SAT or ACT required. ACT 25/75 percentile: 25-30. High school rank: 37% in top tenth, 72% in top quarter, 95% in top half
Early decision deadline: N/A, notification date: N/A
Early action deadline: N/A, notification date: N/A
Application deadline (fall): rolling
Undergraduate student body: 11,189 full time, 730 part time; 33% male, 67% female; 0% American Indian, 13% Asian, 5% black, 16% Hispanic, 4% multiracial, 0% Pacific Islander, 55% white, 5% international; 63% from in state; 40% live on campus; 10% of students in fraternities, 20% in sororities

Most popular majors: 12% Biology/ Biological Sciences, General, 10% Registered Nursing/ Registered Nurse, 9% Psychology, General, 4% Marketing/Marketing Management, General, 4% Public Relations, Advertising, and Applied Communication, Other
Expenses: 2019-2020: $45,543; room/board: $14,780
Financial aid: (773) 508-7704; 65% of undergrads determined to have financial need; average aid package $35,671

MacMurray College[1]
Jacksonville IL
(217) 479-7056
U.S. News ranking: Reg. Coll. (Mid. W), second tier
Website: www.mac.edu
Admissions email: admissions@mac.edu
Private; founded 1846
Affiliation: United Methodist
Application deadline (fall): 8/15
Undergraduate student body: N/A full time, N/A part time
Expenses: N/A
Financial aid: (217) 479-7041

McKendree University
Lebanon IL
(618) 537-6831
U.S. News ranking: Reg. U. (Mid. W), No. 53
Website: www.mckendree.edu
Admissions email: inquiry@mckendree.edu
Private; founded 1828
Affiliation: United Methodist
Freshman admissions: selective; 2018-2019: 1,750 applied, 1,166 accepted. Either SAT or ACT required for some. SAT 25/75 percentile: 960-1270. High school rank: 10% in top tenth, 37% in top quarter, 73% in top half
Early decision deadline: N/A, notification date: N/A
Early action deadline: N/A, notification date: N/A
Application deadline (fall): rolling
Undergraduate student body: 1,631 full time, 325 part time; 47% male, 53% female; 0% American Indian, 0% Asian, 13% black, 5% Hispanic, 3% multiracial, 0% Pacific Islander, 62% white, 4% international; N/A from in state; 72% live on campus; 2% of students in fraternities, 17% in sororities
Most popular majors: 15% Registered Nursing/Registered Nurse, 11% Business Administration and Management, General, 9% Psychology, General, 5% Human Resources Management/Personnel Administration, General, 5% Sociology
Expenses: 2019-2020: $31,640; room/board: $10,370
Financial aid: (618) 537-6532; 78% of undergrads determined to have financial need; average aid package $22,642

Midstate College[1]
Peoria IL
(309) 692-4092
U.S. News ranking: Reg. Coll. (Mid. W), unranked
Website: www.midstate.edu/
Admissions email: dprandle@midstate.edu
For-profit
Application deadline (fall): N/A
Undergraduate student body: N/A full time, N/A part time
Expenses: N/A
Financial aid: N/A

Millikin University
Decatur IL
(217) 424-6210
U.S. News ranking: Reg. Coll. (Mid. W), No. 10
Website: millikin.edu
Admissions email: admis@millikin.edu
Private; founded 1901
Freshman admissions: selective; 2018-2019: 4,512 applied, 2,764 accepted. Either SAT or ACT required. SAT 25/75 percentile: 960-1210. High school rank: 14% in top tenth, 38% in top quarter, 71% in top half
Early decision deadline: N/A, notification date: N/A
Early action deadline: N/A, notification date: N/A
Application deadline (fall): rolling
Undergraduate student body: 1,894 full time, 91 part time; 43% male, 57% female; 0% American Indian, 1% Asian, 14% black, 7% Hispanic, 5% multiracial, 0% Pacific Islander, 69% white, 3% international; 80% from in state; 58% live on campus; 19% of students in fraternities, 23% in sororities
Most popular majors: 24% Business, Management, Marketing, and Related Support Services, 22% Visual and Performing Arts, 10% Health Professions and Related Programs, 9% Education, 8% Parks, Recreation, Leisure, and Fitness Studies
Expenses: 2019-2020: $37,054; room/board: $11,794
Financial aid: (217) 424-6317; 83% of undergrads determined to have financial need; average aid package $27,359

Monmouth College
Monmouth IL
(800) 747-2687
U.S. News ranking: Nat. Lib. Arts, No. 124
Website: www.monmouthcollege.edu/admissions
Admissions email: admissions@monmouthcollege.edu
Private; founded 1853
Freshman admissions: selective; 2018-2019: 1,948 applied, 1,352 accepted. Either SAT or ACT required. SAT 25/75 percentile: 980-1170. High school rank: 22% in top tenth, 46% in top quarter, 78% in top half
Early decision deadline: N/A, notification date: N/A
Early action deadline: N/A, notification date: N/A

percentile: 1050-1250. High school rank: 25% in top tenth, 57% in top quarter, 85% in top half
Early decision deadline: N/A, notification date: N/A
Early action deadline: N/A, notification date: N/A
Application deadline (fall): rolling
Undergraduate student body: 2,596 full time, 85 part time; 46% male, 54% female; 0% American Indian, 3% Asian, 4% black, 16% Hispanic, 4% multiracial, 0% Pacific Islander, 65% white, 3% international; N/A from in state; 46% live on campus; N/A of students in fraternities, N/A in sororities
Most popular majors: 10% Psychology, General, 8% Marketing/Marketing Management, General, 6% Business Administration, Management and Operations, Other, 5% Accounting, 5% Economics, General
Expenses: 2019-2020: $40,040; room/board: $11,456
Financial aid: (630) 637-5600; 77% of undergrads determined to have financial need; average aid package $28,786

Northeastern Illinois University
Chicago IL
(773) 442-4000
U.S. News ranking: Reg. U. (Mid. W), second tier
Website: www.neiu.edu
Admissions email: admrec@neiu.edu
Public; founded 1867
Affiliation: Other
Freshman admissions: less selective; 2018-2019: 5,968 applied, 3,320 accepted. Either SAT or ACT required. SAT 25/75 percentile: 770-1170. High school rank: 5% in top tenth, 20% in top quarter, 58% in top half
Early decision deadline: N/A, notification date: N/A
Early action deadline: N/A, notification date: N/A
Application deadline (fall): 7/15
Undergraduate student body: 3,640 full time, 2,750 part time; 44% male, 56% female; 0% American Indian, 8% Asian, 11% black, 38% Hispanic, 2% multiracial, 0% Pacific Islander, 28% white, 2% international; 97% from in state; 3% live on campus; 1% of students in fraternities, 1% in sororities
Most popular majors: 25% Business, Management, Marketing, and Related Support Services, 11% Liberal Arts and Sciences, General Studies and Humanities, 10% Public Administration and Social Service Professions, 7% Psychology, 7% Social Sciences
Expenses: 2019-2020: $11,462 in state, $21,161 out of state; room/board: $9,458
Financial aid: (773) 442-5010; 66% of undergrads determined to have financial need; average aid package $10,075

Northern Illinois University
DeKalb IL
(815) 753-0446
U.S. News ranking: Nat. U., second tier
Website: www.niu.edu/
Admissions email: admissions@niu.edu
Public; founded 1895
Freshman admissions: selective; 2018-2019: 14,157 applied, 7,698 accepted. Either SAT or ACT required. SAT 25/75 percentile: 940-1170. High school rank: 12% in top tenth, 38% in top quarter, 75% in top half
Early decision deadline: N/A, notification date: N/A
Early action deadline: N/A, notification date: N/A
Application deadline (fall): 8/1
Undergraduate student body: 11,190 full time, 1,598 part time; 50% male, 50% female; 0% American Indian, 6% Asian, 17% black, 19% Hispanic, 4% multiracial, 0% Pacific Islander, 53% white, 2% international; 97% from in state; 28% live on campus; 2% of students in fraternities, 2% in sororities
Most popular majors: 6% Accounting, 6% Psychology, General, 6% Speech Communication and Rhetoric, 5% Health/Medical Preparatory Programs, Other, 5% Registered Nursing/Registered Nurse
Expenses: 2019-2020: $14,610 in state, $14,610 out of state; room/board: $10,880
Financial aid: (815) 753-1300; 72% of undergrads determined to have financial need; average aid package $13,217

North Park University
Chicago IL
(773) 244-5500
U.S. News ranking: Reg. U. (Mid. W), No. 61
Website: www.northpark.edu
Admissions email: admissions@northpark.edu
Private; founded 1891
Affiliation: Evangelical Covenant Church of America
Freshman admissions: selective; 2018-2019: 4,528 applied, 2,109 accepted. Either SAT or ACT required. SAT 25/75 percentile: 950-1167. High school rank: N/A
Early decision deadline: N/A, notification date: N/A
Early action deadline: N/A, notification date: N/A
Application deadline (fall): 7/1
Undergraduate student body: 1,783 full time, 193 part time; 38% male, 62% female; 0% American Indian, 8% Asian, 8% black, 30% Hispanic, 4% multiracial, 1% Pacific Islander, 39% white, 6% international; 76% from in state; 39% live on campus; 0% of students in fraternities, 0% in sororities
Most popular majors: 20% Registered Nursing/Registered Nurse, 19% Business Administration and Management,

General, 9% Biology/Biological Sciences, General, 5% Health and Physical Education/Fitness, General, 5% Psychology, General
Expenses: 2018-2019: $29,860; room/board: $9,445
Financial aid: N/A

Northwestern University
Evanston IL
(847) 491-7271
U.S. News ranking: Nat. U., No. 9
Website: www.northwestern.edu
Admissions email: ug-admission@northwestern.edu
Private; founded 1851
Freshman admissions: most selective; 2018-2019: 40,425 applied, 3,422 accepted. Either SAT or ACT required. ACT 25/75 percentile: 33-35. High school rank: 92% in top tenth, 100% in top quarter, 100% in top half
Early decision deadline: 11/1, notification date: 12/15
Early action deadline: N/A, notification date: N/A
Application deadline (fall): 1/1
Undergraduate student body: 8,077 full time, 154 part time; 49% male, 51% female; 0% American Indian, 18% Asian, 6% black, 13% Hispanic, 6% multiracial, 0% Pacific Islander, 45% white, 9% international; 32% from in state; 60% live on campus; 30% of students in fraternities, 35% in sororities
Most popular majors: 15% Econometrics and Quantitative Economics, 6% Biology/Biological Sciences, General, 6% Journalism, 6% Psychology, General, 4% Political Science and Government, General
Expenses: 2019-2020: $56,691; room/board: $17,019
Financial aid: (847) 491-7400; 46% of undergrads determined to have financial need; average aid package $51,913

Olivet Nazarene University
Bourbonnais IL
(815) 939-5011
U.S. News ranking: Reg. U. (Mid. W), No. 52
Website: www.olivet.edu
Admissions email: admissions@olivet.edu
Private; founded 1907
Affiliation: Church of the Nazarene
Freshman admissions: selective; 2018-2019: 4,054 applied, 2,638 accepted. Either SAT or ACT required. SAT 25/75 percentile: 1000-1220. High school rank: 19% in top tenth, 43% in top quarter, 73% in top half
Early decision deadline: N/A, notification date: N/A
Early action deadline: N/A, notification date: N/A
Application deadline (fall): 8/1
Undergraduate student body: 2,946 full time, 285 part time; 41% male, 59% female; N/A American Indian, N/A Asian, N/A black, N/A Hispanic, N/A multiracial, N/A Pacific Islander, N/A white,

N/A international; 65% from in state; 73% live on campus; 0% of students in fraternities, 0% in sororities
Most popular majors: 22% Registered Nursing/Registered Nurse, 11% Business Administration and Management, General, 7% Engineering, General, 4% Biology/Biological Sciences, General, 4% Marketing/Marketing Management, General
Expenses: 2019-2020: $37,070; room/board: $8,000
Financial aid: (815) 939-5249; 82% of undergrads determined to have financial need; average aid package $29,996

Principia College
Elsah IL
(618) 374-5181
U.S. News ranking: Nat. Lib. Arts, No. 100
Website: www.principiacollege.edu
Admissions email: collegeadmissions@principia.edu
Private; founded 1910
Affiliation: Other
Freshman admissions: selective; 2018-2019: 149 applied, 137 accepted. Either SAT or ACT required. SAT 25/75 percentile: 1028-1300. High school rank: 22% in top tenth, 50% in top quarter, 89% in top half
Early decision deadline: N/A, notification date: N/A
Early action deadline: N/A, notification date: N/A
Application deadline (fall): 6/1
Undergraduate student body: 430 full time, 18 part time; 54% male, 46% female; 0% American Indian, 3% Asian, 3% black, 3% Hispanic, 1% multiracial, 0% Pacific Islander, 70% white, 18% international; 86% from in state; 98% live on campus; 0% of students in fraternities, 0% in sororities
Most popular majors: 15% Education, Other, 15% Fine/Studio Arts, General, 12% Business Administration and Management, General, 9% Communication and Media Studies, 9% Computer and Information Sciences, General
Expenses: 2019-2020: $30,190; room/board: $11,960
Financial aid: (618) 374-5187; 72% of undergrads determined to have financial need; average aid package $32,875

Quincy University
Quincy IL
(217) 228-5210
U.S. News ranking: Reg. Coll. (Mid. W), No. 36
Website: www.quincy.edu
Admissions email: admissions@quincy.edu
Private; founded 1860
Affiliation: Roman Catholic
Freshman admissions: selective; 2018-2019: 1,212 applied, 826 accepted. Either SAT or ACT required. ACT 25/75 percentile: 18-25. High school rank: 23% in top tenth, 47% in top quarter, 77% in top half

Application deadline (fall): rolling
Undergraduate student body: 905 full time, 9 part time; 50% male, 50% female; 0% American Indian, 1% Asian, 10% black, 10% Hispanic, 4% multiracial, 0% Pacific Islander, 65% white, 4% international; 78% from in state; 91% live on campus; 17% of students in fraternities, 32% in sororities
Most popular majors: 22% Business, Management, Marketing, and Related Support Services, 12% Parks, Recreation, Leisure, and Fitness Studies, 9% Communication, Journalism, and Related Programs, 9% Psychology, 9% Social Sciences
Expenses: 2019-2020: $38,990; room/board: $9,330
Financial aid: (309) 457-2129; 86% of undergrads determined to have financial need; average aid package $34,502

National Louis University
Chicago IL
(888) 658-8632
U.S. News ranking: Nat. U., second tier
Website: www.nl.edu
Admissions email: nluinfo@nl.edu
Private
Freshman admissions: least selective; 2018-2019: 3,423 applied, 2,938 accepted. Either SAT or ACT required for some. ACT 25/75 percentile: 15-18. High school rank: N/A
Early decision deadline: N/A, notification date: N/A
Early action deadline: N/A, notification date: N/A
Application deadline (fall): N/A
Undergraduate student body: 2,047 full time, 1,004 part time; 27% male, 73% female; 0% American Indian, 2% Asian, 24% black, 41% Hispanic, 1% multiracial, 0% Pacific Islander, 21% white, 6% international; 92% from in state; N/A live on campus; N/A of students in fraternities, N/A in sororities
Most popular majors: 18% Multi-/Interdisciplinary Studies, Other, 17% Hospitality Administration/Management, General, 16% Management Science, 11% Early Childhood Education and Teaching, 7% Health and Medical Administrative Services, Other
Expenses: 2019-2020: $11,010; room/board: $3,500
Financial aid: N/A; 63% of undergrads determined to have financial need

North Central College
Naperville IL
(630) 637-5800
U.S. News ranking: Reg. U. (Mid. W), No. 13
Website: www.northcentralcollege.edu
Admissions email: admissions@noctrl.edu
Private; founded 1861
Affiliation: United Methodist
Freshman admissions: selective; 2018-2019: 6,625 applied, 3,689 accepted. Either SAT or ACT required. SAT 25/75

Early decision deadline: N/A,
notification date: N/A
Early action deadline: N/A,
notification date: N/A
Application deadline (fall): rolling
Undergraduate student body: 976
full time, 111 part time; 49%
male, 51% female; 0% American
Indian, 0% Asian, 10% black,
5% Hispanic, 0% multiracial, 0%
Pacific Islander, 56% white, 2%
international
Most popular majors: 27%
Business, Management,
Marketing, and Related Support
Services, 20% Health Professions
and Related Programs, 8%
Biological and Biomedical
Sciences, 7% Parks, Recreation,
Leisure, and Fitness Studies, 5%
Education
Expenses: 2019-2020: $30,450;
room/board: $10,500
Financial aid: (217) 228-5260;
81% of undergrads determined to
have financial need; average aid
package $24,898

Robert Morris University

Chicago IL
(800) 762-5960
U.S. News ranking: Reg. U.
(Mid. W), No. 33
Website: www.robertmorris.edu/
Admissions email:
enroll@robertmorris.edu
Private; founded 1913
Freshman admissions: least
selective; 2018-2019: 2,749
applied, 1,743 accepted. Either
SAT or ACT required for some.
SAT 25/75 percentile: 810-1030.
High school rank: 3% in top
tenth, 14% in top quarter, 39%
in top half
Early decision deadline: N/A,
notification date: N/A
Early action deadline: N/A,
notification date: N/A
Application deadline (fall): rolling
Undergraduate student body: 1,594
full time, 105 part time; 55%
male, 45% female; 0% American
Indian, 3% Asian, 27% black,
32% Hispanic, 2% multiracial,
0% Pacific Islander, 31% white,
1% international; 87% from in
state; 13% live on campus; 0%
of students in fraternities, 0% in
sororities
Most popular majors: 64%
Business, Management,
Marketing, and Related
Support Services, 25% Multi/
Interdisciplinary Studies, 5%
Computer and Information
Sciences and Support Services,
3% Health Professions and
Related Programs, 3% Visual and
Performing Arts
Expenses: 2019-2020: $29,880;
room/board: $13,965
Financial aid: (312) 935 6260;
91% of undergrads determined to
have financial need; average aid
package $21,132

Rockford University

Rockford IL
(815) 226-4050
U.S. News ranking: Reg. U.
(Mid. W), No. 102
Website: www.rockford.edu
Admissions email:
Admissions@Rockford.edu
Private; founded 1847
Freshman admissions: selective;
2018-2019: 2,682 applied,
1,315 accepted. Either SAT
or ACT required. SAT 25/75
percentile: 990-1190. High
school rank: N/A
Early decision deadline: N/A,
notification date: N/A
Early action deadline: N/A,
notification date: N/A
Application deadline (fall): 8/15
Undergraduate student body: 888
full time, 114 part time; 45%
male, 55% female; 0% American
Indian, 2% Asian, 10% black,
17% Hispanic, 3% multiracial,
0% Pacific Islander, 60% white,
7% international; N/A from in
state; 35% live on campus; N/A
of students in fraternities, N/A in
sororities
Most popular majors: Information
not available
Expenses: 2019-2020: $32,100;
room/board: $9,494
Financial aid: (815) 226-3385;
90% of undergrads determined to
have financial need; average aid
package $21,702

Roosevelt University

Chicago IL
(877) 277-5978
U.S. News ranking: Nat. U.,
second tier
Website: www.roosevelt.edu
Admissions email:
admission@roosevelt.edu
Private; founded 1945
Freshman admissions: selective;
2018-2019: 3,943 applied,
2,557 accepted. Either SAT
or ACT required. SAT 25/75
percentile: 1010-1180. High
school rank: 8% in top tenth, 46%
in top quarter, 62% in top half
Early decision deadline: N/A,
notification date: N/A
Early action deadline: N/A,
notification date: N/A
Application deadline (fall): rolling
Undergraduate student body: 2,061
full time, 358 part time; 34%
male, 66% female; 0% American
Indian, 6% Asian, 15% black,
24% Hispanic, 3% multiracial,
0% Pacific Islander, 44% white,
4% international; 79% from in
state; 22% live on campus; 0%
of students in fraternities, 2% in
sororities
Most popular majors: 15%
Psychology, General, 8% Biology/
Biological Sciences, General,
7% Hospitality Administration/
Management, General, 6%
Accounting, 6% Management
Science
Expenses: 2019-2020: $30,876;
room/board: $13,223
Financial aid: (312) 341-3868;
89% of undergrads determined to
have financial need; average aid
package $24,000

Saint Xavier University

Chicago IL
(773) 298-3050
U.S. News ranking: Reg. U.
(Mid. W), No. 61
Website: www.sxu.edu/admissions/
Admissions email:
admission@sxu.edu
Private; founded 1846
Affiliation: Roman Catholic
Freshman admissions: selective;
2018-2019: 7,920 applied,
5,851 accepted. Either SAT
or ACT required. SAT 25/75
percentile: 950-1130. High school
rank: 19% in top tenth, 56% in
top quarter, 86% in top half
Early decision deadline: N/A,
notification date: N/A
Early action deadline: N/A,
notification date: N/A
Application deadline (fall): rolling
Undergraduate student body: 2,713
full time, 242 part time; 37%
male, 63% female; 0% American
Indian, 3% Asian, 12% black,
39% Hispanic, 2% multiracial,
0% Pacific Islander, 41% white,
0% international; 96% from in
state; 17% live on campus; 0%
of students in fraternities, 0% in
sororities
Most popular majors: 24%
Business, Management,
Marketing, and Related Support
Services, 19% Health Professions
and Related Programs, 11%
Psychology, 7% Biological
and Biomedical Sciences, 7%
Education
Expenses: 2019-2020: $34,390;
room/board: $11,430
Financial aid: (773) 298-3073;
88% of undergrads determined to
have financial need; average aid
package $28,048

School of the Art Institute of Chicago

Chicago IL
(312) 629-6100
U.S. News ranking: Arts, unranked
Website: www.saic.edu
Admissions email:
admiss@saic.edu
Private; founded 1866
Freshman admissions: more
selective; 2018-2019: 5,993
applied, 3,503 accepted. Either
SAT or ACT required. SAT 25/75
percentile: 1120-1340. High
school rank: N/A
Early decision deadline: N/A,
notification date: N/A
Early action deadline: 11/15,
notification date: 12/25
Application deadline (fall): 4/15
Undergraduate student body: 2,746
full time, 147 part time; 25%
male, 75% female; 0% American
Indian, 10% Asian, 4% black,
11% Hispanic, 3% multiracial,
0% Pacific Islander, 34% white,
33% international
Most popular majors: 93% Fine/
Studio Arts, General, 5% Visual
and Performing Arts, General,
1% Creative Writing, 1% Interior
Architecture
Expenses: 2019-2020: $51,875;
room/board: $14,810
Financial aid: (312) 629-6600

Southern Illinois University–Carbondale

Carbondale IL
(618) 536-4405
U.S. News ranking: Nat. U.,
No. 254
Website: www.siu.edu
Admissions email:
admissions@siu.edu
Public; founded 1869
Freshman admissions: more
selective; 2018-2019: 6,232
applied, 4,478 accepted. Either
SAT or ACT required. SAT 25/75
percentile: 1020-1300. High
school rank: 15% in top tenth,
44% in top quarter, 74% in
top half
Early decision deadline: N/A,
notification date: N/A
Early action deadline: N/A,
notification date: N/A
Application deadline (fall): rolling
Undergraduate student body: 8,070
full time, 1,442 part time; 54%
male, 46% female; 0% American
Indian, 2% Asian, 15% black,
9% Hispanic, 3% multiracial,
0% Pacific Islander, 66% white,
4% international; 80% from in
state; 22% live on campus; 8%
of students in fraternities, 8% in
sororities
Most popular majors: 11%
Business, Management,
Marketing, and Related Support
Services, 9% Education, 9%
Engineering Technologies and
Engineering-Related Fields, 8%
Health Professions and Related
Programs, 6% Agriculture,
Agriculture Operations, and
Related Sciences
Expenses: 2019-2020: $14,904
in state, $14,904 out of state;
room/board: $10,622
Financial aid: (618) 453-4613;
69% of undergrads determined to
have financial need; average aid
package $15,514

Southern Illinois University–Edwardsville

Edwardsville IL
(618) 650-3705
U.S. News ranking: Nat. U.,
second tier
Website: www.siue.edu
Admissions email:
admissions@siue.edu
Public; founded 1957
Affiliation: Undenominational
Freshman admissions: selective;
2018-2019: 6,410 applied,
5,605 accepted. Either SAT
or ACT required. ACT 25/75
percentile: 21-27. High school
rank: 19% in top tenth, 44% in
top quarter, 76% in top half
Early decision deadline: N/A,
notification date: N/A
Early action deadline: N/A,
notification date: N/A
Application deadline (fall): 5/1
Undergraduate student body: 8,979
full time, 1,854 part time; 47%
male, 53% female; 0% American
Indian, 2% Asian, 13% black,
5% Hispanic, 4% multiracial,
0% Pacific Islander, 73% white,
1% international; 86% from in
state; 25% live on campus; N/A
of students in fraternities, N/A in
sororities
Most popular majors: 18%
Registered Nursing/Registered
Nurse, 11% Business
Administration and Management,
General, 6% Psychology, General,
5% Biology/Biological Sciences,
General, 5% Criminal Justice/
Safety Studies
Expenses: 2019-2020: $12,219
in state, $12,219 out of state;
room/board: $9,881
Financial aid: (618) 650-3880;
65% of undergrads determined to
have financial need; average aid
package $12,576

St. Augustine College[1]

Chicago IL
(773) 878-8756
U.S. News ranking: Reg. Coll.
(Mid. W), unranked
Website: www.
staugustinecollege.edu/index.asp
Admissions email:
info@staugustine.edu
Private
Application deadline (fall): N/A
Undergraduate student body: N/A
full time, N/A part time
Expenses: N/A
Financial aid: N/A

Trinity Christian College

Palos Heights IL
(800) 748-0085
U.S. News ranking: Reg. Coll.
(Mid. W), No. 20
Website: www.trnty.edu
Admissions email:
admissions@trnty.edu
Private; founded 1959
Affiliation: Other
Freshman admissions: selective;
2018-2019: 768 applied, 616
accepted. Either SAT or ACT
required. ACT 25/75 percentile:
19-26. High school rank: 15%
in top tenth, 44% in top quarter,
73% in top half
Early decision deadline: N/A,
notification date: N/A
Early action deadline: N/A,
notification date: N/A
Application deadline (fall): rolling
Undergraduate student body: 883
full time, 180 part time; 33%
male, 67% female; 0% American
Indian, 1% Asian, 9% black,
12% Hispanic, 1% multiracial,
0% Pacific Islander, 60% white,
13% international; 30% from in
state; 52% live on campus; 0%
of students in fraternities, 0% in
sororities
Most popular majors: 24%
Business, Management,
Marketing, and Related Support
Services, 20% Education,
9% Psychology, 8% Health
Professions and Related Programs,
7% Communication, Journalism,
and Related Programs
Expenses: 2019-2020: $30,950;
room/board: $9,950
Financial aid: (708) 239-4872;
79% of undergrads determined to
have financial need; average aid
package $22,451

Trinity International University

Deerfield IL
(800) 822-3225
U.S. News ranking: Nat. U., second tier
Website: www.tiu.edu
Admissions email: tcadmissions@tiu.edu
Private; founded 1897
Affiliation: Evangelical Free Church of America
Freshman admissions: selective; 2018-2019: N/A applied, N/A accepted. Either SAT or ACT required. ACT 25/75 percentile: 20-27. High school rank: N/A
Early decision deadline: N/A, notification date: N/A
Early action deadline: N/A, notification date: N/A
Application deadline (fall): rolling
Undergraduate student body: 597 full time, 399 part time; 52% male, 48% female; 0% American Indian, 3% Asian, 15% black, 7% Hispanic, 5% multiracial, 0% Pacific Islander, 51% white, 3% international
Most popular majors: Information not available
Expenses: 2019-2020: $33,028; room/board: $10,200
Financial aid: (847) 317-4200; 79% of undergrads determined to have financial need; average aid package $26,806

University of Chicago

Chicago IL
(773) 702-8650
U.S. News ranking: Nat. U., No. 6
Website: www.uchicago.edu
Admissions email: collegeadmissions@uchicago.edu
Private; founded 1890
Freshman admissions: most selective; 2018-2019: 32,283 applied, 2,345 accepted. Neither SAT nor ACT required. ACT 25/75 percentile: 33-35. High school rank: 99% in top tenth, 100% in top quarter, 100% in top half
Early decision deadline: 11/1, notification date: 12/18
Early action deadline: 11/1, notification date: 12/18
Application deadline (fall): 1/2
Undergraduate student body: 6,551 full time, 1 part time; 51% male, 49% female; 0% American Indian, 19% Asian, 5% black, 14% Hispanic, 6% multiracial, 0% Pacific Islander, 39% white, 14% international; N/A from in state; 55% live on campus; N/A of students in fraternities, N/A in sororities
Most popular majors: 31% Homeland Security, Law Enforcement, Firefighting and Related Protective Services, 11% Mathematics and Statistics, 8% Biological and Biomedical Sciences, 7% Physical Sciences, 6% Foreign Languages, Literatures, and Linguistics
Expenses: 2019-2020: $59,298; room/board: $17,004
Financial aid: (773) 702-8666; 42% of undergrads determined to have financial need; average aid package $57,011

University of Illinois–Chicago

Chicago IL
(312) 996-4350
U.S. News ranking: Nat. U., No. 132
Website: www.uic.edu
Admissions email: admissions@uic.edu
Public; founded 1965
Freshman admissions: selective; 2018-2019: 21,106 applied, 15,945 accepted. Either SAT or ACT required. SAT 25/75 percentile: 1020-1220. High school rank: 28% in top tenth, 58% in top quarter, 88% in top half
Early decision deadline: N/A, notification date: N/A
Early action deadline: 11/1, notification date: 12/1
Application deadline (fall): 1/15
Undergraduate student body: 19,254 full time, 1,529 part time; 49% male, 51% female; 0% American Indian, 21% Asian, 8% black, 34% Hispanic, 3% multiracial, 0% Pacific Islander, 28% white, 5% international; 91% from in state; 15% live on campus; 6% of students in fraternities, 6% in sororities
Most popular majors: 15% Business, Management, Marketing, and Related Support Services, 14% Biological and Biomedical Sciences, 13% Engineering, 12% Psychology, 9% Health Professions and Related Programs
Expenses: 2019-2020: $14,816 in state, $27,672 out of state; room/board: $10,882
Financial aid: (312) 996-5563; 74% of undergrads determined to have financial need; average aid package $15,196

University of Illinois–Springfield

Springfield IL
(217) 206-4847
U.S. News ranking: Reg. U. (Mid. W), No. 33
Website: www.uis.edu
Admissions email: admissions@uis.edu
Public; founded 1969
Freshman admissions: selective; 2018-2019: 2,374 applied, 1,254 accepted. Either SAT or ACT required. SAT 25/75 percentile: 990-1218. High school rank: 24% in top tenth, 49% in top quarter, 78% in top half
Early decision deadline: N/A, notification date: N/A
Early action deadline: N/A, notification date: N/A
Application deadline (fall): 5/1
Undergraduate student body: 1,799 full time, 1,015 part time; 50% male, 50% female; 0% American Indian, 3% Asian, 15% black, 9% Hispanic, 3% multiracial, 0% Pacific Islander, 65% white, 3% international; 85% from in state; 31% live on campus; 2% of students in fraternities, 2% in sororities

Most popular majors: 18% Computer Science, 16% Business Administration and Management, General, 9% Psychology, General, 8% Accounting, 6% Communication and Media Studies
Expenses: 2019-2020: $11,813 in state, $21,338 out of state; room/board: $9,760
Financial aid: (217) 206-6724; 68% of undergrads determined to have financial need; average aid package $13,943

University of Illinois–Urbana-Champaign

Champaign IL
(217) 333-0302
U.S. News ranking: Nat. U., No. 48
Website: illinois.edu
Admissions email: ugradadmissions@illinois.edu
Public; founded 1867
Freshman admissions: more selective; 2018-2019: 39,406 applied, 24,496 accepted. Either SAT or ACT required. ACT 25/75 percentile: 26-32. High school rank: 48% in top tenth, 81% in top quarter, 98% in top half
Early decision deadline: N/A, notification date: N/A
Early action deadline: 11/1, notification date: 12/14
Application deadline (fall): 1/5
Undergraduate student body: 32,757 full time, 1,158 part time; 54% male, 46% female; 0% American Indian, 19% Asian, 6% black, 12% Hispanic, 3% multiracial, 0% Pacific Islander, 44% white, 15% international; 73% from in state; 50% live on campus; 20% of students in fraternities, 25% in sororities
Most popular majors: Information not available
Expenses: 2019-2020: $16,210 in state, $33,352 out of state; room/board: $11,480
Financial aid: (217) 333-0100; 47% of undergrads determined to have financial need; average aid package $17,504

University of St. Francis

Joliet IL
(800) 735-7500
U.S. News ranking: Nat. U., No. 202
Website: www.stfrancis.edu
Admissions email: admissions@stfrancis.edu
Private; founded 1920
Affiliation: Roman Catholic
Freshman admissions: selective; 2018-2019: 1,847 applied, 864 accepted. Either SAT or ACT required. SAT 25/75 percentile: 1030-1190. High school rank: N/A
Early decision deadline: N/A, notification date: N/A
Early action deadline: N/A, notification date: N/A
Application deadline (fall): 8/1
Undergraduate student body: 1,362 full time, 267 part time; 33% male, 67% female; 0% American Indian, 3% Asian, 10% black, 20% Hispanic, 3% multiracial,

0% Pacific Islander, 60% white, 3% international; N/A from in state; 22% live on campus; 1% of students in fraternities, 3% in sororities
Most popular majors: 42% Health Professions and Related Programs, 22% Business, Management, Marketing, and Related Support Services, 5% Biological and Biomedical Sciences, 5% Homeland Security, Law Enforcement, Firefighting and Related Protective Services, 4% Public Administration and Social Service Professions
Expenses: 2019-2020: $34,000; room/board: $10,010
Financial aid: (815) 740-3403; 84% of undergrads determined to have financial need; average aid package $23,367

Western Illinois University

Macomb IL
(309) 298-3157
U.S. News ranking: Reg. U. (Mid. W), No. 61
Website: www.wiu.edu
Admissions email: admissions@wiu.edu
Public; founded 1899
Freshman admissions: selective; 2018-2019: 9,151 applied, 5,379 accepted. Either SAT or ACT required. SAT 25/75 percentile: 930-1110. High school rank: 11% in top tenth, 32% in top quarter, 69% in top half
Early decision deadline: N/A, notification date: N/A
Early action deadline: N/A, notification date: N/A
Application deadline (fall): rolling
Undergraduate student body: 5,949 full time, 805 part time; 48% male, 52% female; 0% American Indian, 1% Asian, 21% black, 13% Hispanic, 3% multiracial, 0% Pacific Islander, 59% white, 1% international; 88% from in state; 43% live on campus; 19% of students in fraternities, 15% in sororities
Most popular majors: 20% Criminal Justice/Law Enforcement Administration, 13% Business Administration and Management, General, 11% Liberal Arts and Sciences, General Studies and Humanities, Other, 6% Parks, Recreation and Leisure Facilities Management, General, 6% Speech Communication and Rhetoric
Expenses: 2019-2020: $11,666 in state, $11,666 out of state; room/board: $10,010
Financial aid: (309) 298-2446; 77% of undergrads determined to have financial need; average aid package $12,684

Wheaton College

Wheaton IL
(800) 222-2419
U.S. News ranking: Nat. Lib. Arts, No. 58
Website: www.wheaton.edu
Admissions email: admissions@wheaton.edu
Private; founded 1860
Affiliation: Protestant, not specified
Freshman admissions: more selective; 2018-2019: 1,850

applied, 1,529 accepted. Either SAT or ACT required. SAT 25/75 percentile: 1210-1420. High school rank: 45% in top tenth, 77% in top quarter, 94% in top half
Early decision deadline: N/A, notification date: N/A
Early action deadline: 11/1, notification date: 12/31
Application deadline (fall): 1/10
Undergraduate student body: 2,326 full time, 75 part time; 45% male, 55% female; 0% American Indian, 9% Asian, 3% black, 6% Hispanic, 5% multiracial, 0% Pacific Islander, 73% white, 3% international; 27% from in state; 89% live on campus; N/A of students in fraternities, N/A in sororities
Most popular majors: 16% Social Sciences, 12% Business, Management, Marketing, and Related Support Services, 8% Communication, Journalism, and Related Programs, 8% Visual and Performing Arts, 7% Health Professions and Related Programs
Expenses: 2019-2020: $37,700; room/board: $10,630
Financial aid: (630) 752-5021; 59% of undergrads determined to have financial need; average aid package $24,887

INDIANA

Anderson University[1]

Anderson IN
(765) 641-4080
U.S. News ranking: Reg. U. (Mid. W), No. 84
Website: anderson.edu
Admissions email: info@anderson.edu
Private; founded 1917
Affiliation: Church of God
Application deadline (fall): rolling
Undergraduate student body: N/A full time, N/A part time
Expenses: N/A
Financial aid: (765) 641-4180

Ball State University[1]

Muncie IN
(765) 285-8300
U.S. News ranking: Nat. U., No. 192
Website: www.bsu.edu
Admissions email: askus@bsu.edu
Public; founded 1918
Application deadline (fall): 8/10
Undergraduate student body: N/A full time, N/A part time
Expenses: 2019-2020: $10,080 in state, $26,984 out of state; room/board: $10,534
Financial aid: (765) 285-5600; 68% of undergrads determined to have financial need; average aid package $13,785

Bethel University

Mishawaka IN
(800) 422-4101
U.S. News ranking: Reg. U. (Mid. W), No. 30
Website: www.betheluniversity.edu
Admissions email: admissions@betheluniversity.edu
Private; founded 1947
Affiliation: Missionary Church Inc

Freshman admissions: selective;
2018-2019: 1,187 applied,
1,096 accepted. Either SAT
or ACT required. SAT 25/75
percentile: 970-1170. High school
rank: 13% in top tenth, 41% in
top quarter, 78% in top half
Early decision deadline: N/A,
notification date: N/A
Early action deadline: N/A,
notification date: N/A
Application deadline (fall): rolling
Undergraduate student body: 1,059
full time, 226 part time; 36%
male, 64% female; 0% American
Indian, 1% Asian, 10% black,
10% Hispanic, 9% multiracial,
0% Pacific Islander, 67% white,
3% international; 73% from in
state; 54% live on campus; 0%
of students in fraternities, 0% in
sororities
Most popular majors: 22%
Business, Management,
Marketing, and Related Support
Services, 14% Health Professions
and Related Programs, 14% Multi/
Interdisciplinary Studies, 11%
Education, 7% Theology and
Religious Vocations
Expenses: 2019-2020: $29,170;
room/board: $9,160
Financial aid: (574) 807-7415;
81% of undergrads determined to
have financial need; average aid
package $22,836

Butler University
Indianapolis IN
(317) 940-8150
U.S. News ranking: Reg. U.
(Mid. W), No. 1
Website: www.butler.edu
Admissions email:
admission@butler.edu
Private; founded 1855
Freshman admissions: more
selective; 2018-2019: 16,418
applied, 11,137 accepted. Either
SAT or ACT required. ACT 25/75
percentile: 25-30. High school
rank: 45% in top tenth, 76% in
top quarter, 96% in top half
Early decision deadline: N/A,
notification date: N/A
Early action deadline: 11/1,
notification date: 12/20
Application deadline (fall): 2/1
Undergraduate student body: 4,519
full time, 167 part time; 40%
male, 60% female; 0% American
Indian, 3% Asian, 4% black, 4%
Hispanic, 3% multiracial, 0%
Pacific Islander, 82% white, 1%
international; 45% from in state;
67% live on campus; 21% of
students in fraternities, 36% in
sororities
Most popular majors: 34%
Business, Management,
Marketing, and Related Support
Services, 8% Communication,
Journalism, and Related Programs,
8% Education, 7% Health
Professions and Related Programs,
7% Social Sciences
Expenses: 2019-2020: $42,360;
room/board: $15,540
Financial aid: (317) 940-8200;
58% of undergrads determined to
have financial need; average aid
package $26,085

Calumet College
of St. Joseph
Whiting IN
(219) 473-4295
U.S. News ranking: Reg. U.
(Mid. W), second tier
Website: www.ccsj.edu
Admissions email:
admissions@ccsj.edu
Private; founded 1951
Freshman admissions: less
selective; 2018-2019: 693
applied, 142 accepted. Neither
SAT nor ACT required. SAT 25/75
percentile: 850-1020. High
school rank: 1% in top tenth, 9%
in top quarter, 46% in top half
Early decision deadline: N/A,
notification date: N/A
Early action deadline: N/A,
notification date: N/A
Application deadline (fall): rolling
Undergraduate student body: 285
full time, 299 part time; 58%
male, 42% female; 0% American
Indian, 1% Asian, 23% black,
28% Hispanic, 3% multiracial,
0% Pacific Islander, 33% white,
0% international; 51% from in
state; 0% live on campus; N/A
of students in fraternities, N/A in
sororities
Most popular majors: 39%
Criminal Justice/Safety Studies,
27% Business Administration
and Management, General, 9%
Biology/Biological Sciences,
General, 5% Elementary
Education and Teaching, 5%
Liberal Arts and Sciences, General
Studies and Humanities, Other
Expenses: 2019-2020: $20,370;
room/board: N/A
Financial aid: (219) 473-4296;
87% of undergrads determined to
have financial need; average aid
package $16,931

DePauw University
Greencastle IN
(765) 658-4006
U.S. News ranking: Nat. Lib. Arts,
No. 46
Website: www.depauw.edu
Admissions email:
admission@depauw.edu
Private; founded 1837
Freshman admissions: more
selective; 2018-2019: 5,493
applied, 3,435 accepted. Either
SAT or ACT required. SAT 25/75
percentile: 1120-1340. High
school rank: 45% in top tenth,
75% in top quarter, 97% in
top half
Early decision deadline: 11/1,
notification date: 12/1
Early action deadline: 12/1,
notification date: 1/15
Application deadline (fall): 2/1
Undergraduate student body: 2,138
full time, 18 part time; 47%
male, 53% female; 0% American
Indian, 4% Asian, 5% black, 8%
Hispanic, 4% multiracial, 0%
Pacific Islander, 66% white, 11%
international; 43% from in state;
96% live on campus, 67% of
students in fraternities, 60% in
sororities
Most popular majors: 21% Social
Sciences, 12% Communication,
Journalism, and Related Programs,
9% Biological and Biomedical

Sciences, 9% Visual and
Performing Arts, 8% English
Language and Literature/Letters
Expenses: 2019-2020: $51,146;
room/board: $13,400
Financial aid: (765) 658-4030;
58% of undergrads determined to
have financial need; average aid
package $43,827

Earlham College
Richmond IN
(765) 983-1600
U.S. News ranking: Nat. Lib. Arts,
No. 80
Website: www.earlham.edu/
admissions
Admissions email:
admission@earlham.edu
Private; founded 1847
Affiliation: Friends
Freshman admissions: more
selective; 2018-2019: 2,119
applied, 1,382 accepted. Either
SAT or ACT required for some.
SAT 25/75 percentile: 1160-
1380. High school rank: 40% in
top tenth, 70% in top quarter,
91% in top half
Early decision deadline: 11/1,
notification date: 12/15
Early action deadline: 12/1,
notification date: 1/15
Application deadline (fall): 2/15.
Undergraduate student body:
1,043 full time, 7 part time; 46%
male, 54% female; 0% American
Indian, 4% Asian, 9% black,
7% Hispanic, 2% multiracial,
0% Pacific Islander, 52% white,
22% international; 19% from in
state; 95% live on campus; 0%
of students in fraternities, 0% in
sororities
Most popular majors: 14%
Biological and Biomedical
Sciences, 14% Multi/
Interdisciplinary Studies, 10%
Visual and Performing Arts, 9%
Social Sciences, 8% Psychology
Expenses: 2019-2020: $47,380;
room/board: $10,885
Financial aid: (765) 983-1217;
87% of undergrads determined to
have financial need; average aid
package $40,486

Franklin College
Franklin IN
(317) 738-8062
U.S. News ranking: Nat. Lib. Arts,
No. 145
Website: www.franklincollege.edu
Admissions email:
admissions@franklincollege.edu
Private; founded 1834
Freshman admissions: selective;
2018-2019: 1,869 applied,
1,410 accepted. Either SAT
or ACT required. SAT 25/75
percentile: 980-1170. High school
rank: 13% in top tenth, 44% in
top quarter, 84% in top half
Early decision deadline: N/A,
notification date: N/A
Early action deadline: N/A,
notification date: N/A
Application deadline (fall): rolling
Undergraduate student body: 911
full time, 49 part time; 49% male,
51% female; 0% American
Indian, 1% Asian, 3% black,
3% Hispanic, 4% multiracial,

0% Pacific Islander, 87% white,
0% international; 93% from in
state; 63% live on campus; 39%
of students in fraternities, 48%
in sororities
Most popular majors: 15%
Business, Management,
Marketing, and Related Support
Services, 13% Communication,
Journalism, and Related Programs,
11% Parks, Recreation, Leisure,
and Fitness Studies, 8% Biological
and Biomedical Sciences, 8%
Education
Expenses: 2019-2020: $32,970;
room/board: $10,244
Financial aid: (317) 738-8073;
83% of undergrads determined to
have financial need; average aid
package $25,726

Goshen College
Goshen IN
(574) 535-7535
U.S. News ranking: Reg. Coll.
(Mid. W), No. 7
Website: www.goshen.edu
Admissions email:
admissions@goshen.edu
Private; founded 1894
Affiliation: Mennonite Church
Freshman admissions: selective;
2018-2019: 1,248 applied, 825
accepted. Either SAT or ACT
required. SAT 25/75 percentile:
995-1210. High school rank:
32% in top tenth, 70% in top
quarter, 90% in top half
Early decision deadline: N/A,
notification date: N/A
Early action deadline: N/A,
notification date: N/A
Application deadline (fall): 7/1
Undergraduate student body: 798
full time, 47 part time; 38%
male, 62% female; 0% American
Indian, 2% Asian, 4% black,
24% Hispanic, 2% multiracial,
0% Pacific Islander, 59% white,
8% international; 59% from in
state; 57% live on campus; N/A
of students in fraternities, N/A in
sororities
Most popular majors:
25% Registered Nursing/
Registered Nurse, 8% Social
Work, 6% Accounting, 6%
Molecular Biology, 5% Multi-/
Interdisciplinary Studies, Other
Expenses: 2019-2020: $34,540;
room/board: $10,760
Financial aid: (574) 535-7525;
77% of undergrads determined to
have financial need; average aid
package $28,162

Grace College
and Seminary[1]
Winona Lake IN
(574) 372-5100
U.S. News ranking: Reg. U.
(Mid. W), No. 75
Website: www.grace.edu
Admissions email:
enroll@grace.edu
Private; founded 1948
Affiliation: Other
Application deadline (fall): 3/1
Undergraduate student body: N/A
full time, N/A part time
Expenses: 2018-2019: $24,768;
room/board: $9,134
Financial aid: (574) 372-5100

Hanover College
Hanover IN
(812) 866-7021
U.S. News ranking: Nat. Lib. Arts,
No. 105
Website: www.hanover.edu
Admissions email:
admission@hanover.edu
Private; founded 1827
Affiliation: Presbyterian Church
(USA)
Freshman admissions: selective;
2018-2019: 3,229 applied,
2,562 accepted. Neither SAT
nor ACT required. ACT 25/75
percentile: 22-27. High school
rank: 27% in top tenth, 54% in
top quarter, 88% in top half
Early decision deadline: N/A,
notification date: N/A
Early action deadline: 12/1,
notification date: 12/1
Application deadline (fall): rolling
Undergraduate student body:
1,097 full time, 7 part time; 45%
male, 55% female; 0% American
Indian, 1% Asian, 6% black, 3%
Hispanic, 2% multiracial, 0%
Pacific Islander, 74% white, 3%
international; 67% from in state;
93% live on campus; 41% of
students in fraternities, 26% in
sororities
Most popular majors: 13% Biology/
Biological Sciences, General,
13% Speech Communication and
Rhetoric, 9% Psychology, General,
8% Economics, General, 7%
Kinesiology and Exercise Science
Expenses: 2019-2020: $38,750;
room/board: $11,950
Financial aid: (812) 866-7029;
78% of undergrads determined to
have financial need; average aid
package $32,910

Holy Cross College
Notre Dame IN
(574) 239-8400
U.S. News ranking: Reg. Coll.
(Mid. W), No. 29
Website: www.hcc-nd.edu/home
Admissions email:
admissions@hcc-nd.edu
Private; founded 1966
Affiliation: Roman Catholic
Freshman admissions: selective;
2018-2019: 597 applied, 527
accepted. Either SAT or ACT
required. SAT 25/75 percentile:
1070-1390. High school rank:
N/A
Early decision deadline: N/A,
notification date: N/A
Early action deadline: 11/1,
notification date: 11/15
Application deadline (fall): 7/28
Undergraduate student body: 469
full time, 30 part time; 61%
male, 39% female; 1% American
Indian, 1% Asian, 8% black,
15% Hispanic, 3% multiracial,
0% Pacific Islander, 63% white,
2% international; 47% from in
state; 49% live on campus; 0%
of students in fraternities, 0% in
sororities
Most popular majors: 42%
Business/Commerce, General,
18% Psychology, General, 11%
Communication and Media
Studies, 7% Theology/Theological
Studies, 6% Elementary Education
and Teaching

Expenses: 2019-2020: $32,000; room/board: $11,650
Financial aid: (574) 239-8400; 65% of undergrads determined to have financial need; average aid package $4,397

Huntington University
Huntington IN
(800) 642-6493
U.S. News ranking: Reg. U. (Mid. W), No. 40
Website: www.huntington.edu
Admissions email: admissions@huntington.edu
Private; founded 1897.
Affiliation: Other
Freshman admissions: selective; 2018-2019: 988 applied, 830 accepted. Either SAT or ACT required. SAT 25/75 percentile: 990-1180. High school rank: 16% in top tenth, 43% in top quarter, 77% in top half
Early decision deadline: N/A, notification date: N/A
Early action deadline: N/A, notification date: N/A
Application deadline (fall): 8/1
Undergraduate student body: 907 full time, 194 part time; 43% male, 57% female; 0% American Indian, 0% Asian, 3% black, 7% Hispanic, 4% multiracial, 0% Pacific Islander, 82% white, 4% international; 66% from in state; 73% live on campus; N/A of students in fraternities, N/A in sororities
Most popular majors: 20% Business, Management, Marketing, and Related Support Services, 13% Visual and Performing Arts, 10% Education, 9% Health Professions and Related Programs, 7% Theology and Religious Vocations
Expenses: 2019-2020: $26,846; room/board: $8,754
Financial aid: (260) 359-4326; 79% of undergrads determined to have financial need; average aid package $19,964

Indiana Institute of Technology
Fort Wayne IN
(800) 937-2448
U.S. News ranking: Reg. U. (Mid. W), second tier
Website: www.indianatech.edu
Admissions email: admissions@indianatech.edu
Private; founded 1930
Freshman admissions: selective; 2018-2019: 4,244 applied, 2,569 accepted. Either SAT or ACT required. SAT 25/75 percentile: 770-1187. High school rank: N/A
Early decision deadline: N/A, notification date: N/A
Early action deadline: N/A, notification date: N/A
Application deadline (fall): 8/1
Undergraduate student body: 1,463 full time, 61 part time; 67% male, 33% female; 0% American Indian, 2% Asian, 17% black, 6% Hispanic, 4% multiracial, 0% Pacific Islander, 48% white, 18% international

Most popular majors: 24% Business Administration and Management, General, 10% Mechanical Engineering, 10% Petroleum Engineering, 6% Environmental/Environmental Health Engineering, 5% Psychology, General
Expenses: 2018-2019: $26,900; room/board: $12,660
Financial aid: (260) 422-5561

Indiana State University
Terre Haute IN
(812) 237-2121
U.S. News ranking: Nat. U., second tier
Website: www.indstate.edu/
Admissions email: admissions@indstate.edu
Public; founded 1865
Freshman admissions: less selective; 2018-2019: 12,861 applied, 11,563 accepted. Either SAT or ACT required. SAT 25/75 percentile: 910-1120. High school rank: 11% in top tenth, 28% in top quarter, 62% in top half
Early decision deadline: N/A, notification date: N/A
Early action deadline: N/A, notification date: N/A
Application deadline (fall): 8/15
Undergraduate student body: 8,891 full time, 2,060 part time; 44% male, 56% female; 0% American Indian, 1% Asian, 19% black, 5% Hispanic, 4% multiracial, 0% Pacific Islander, 67% white, 3% international; 75% from in state; 32% live on campus; 12% of students in fraternities, 11% in sororities
Most popular majors: 18% Health Professions and Related Programs, 16% Business, Management, Marketing, and Related Support Services, 11% Engineering Technologies and Engineering-Related Fields, 10% Social Sciences, 8% Parks, Recreation, Leisure, and Fitness Studies
Expenses: 2019-2020: $9,268 in state, $20,228 out of state; room/board: $10,802
Financial aid: (800) 841-4744; 75% of undergrads determined to have financial need; average aid package $10,944

Indiana University–Bloomington
Bloomington IN
(812) 855-0661
U.S. News ranking: Nat. U., No. 79
Website: www.indiana.edu
Admissions email: iuadmit@indiana.edu
Public; founded 1820
Freshman admissions: more selective; 2018-2019: 44,169 applied, 33,970 accepted. Either SAT or ACT required. SAT 25/75 percentile: 1150-1360. High school rank: 35% in top tenth, 69% in top quarter, 95% in top half
Early decision deadline: N/A, notification date: N/A
Early action deadline: 11/1, notification date: 1/15
Application deadline (fall): rolling

Undergraduate student body: 32,109 full time, 1,192 part time; 50% male, 50% female; 0% American Indian, 6% Asian, 5% black, 6% Hispanic, 4% multiracial, 0% Pacific Islander, 69% white, 9% international; 65% from in state; 37% live on campus; 23% of students in fraternities, 20% in sororities
Most popular majors: 25% Business, Management, Marketing, and Related Support Services, 9% Computer and Information Sciences and Support Services, 8% Parks, Recreation, Leisure, and Fitness Studies, 8% Public Administration and Social Service Professions, 7% Biological and Biomedical Sciences
Expenses: 2019-2020: $10,949 in state, $36,514 out of state; room/board: $10,830
Financial aid: (812) 855-6500; 41% of undergrads determined to have financial need; average aid package $14,185

Indiana University East
Richmond IN
(765) 973-8208
U.S. News ranking: Reg. U. (Mid. W), second tier
Website: www.iue.edu
Admissions email: applynow@iue.edu
Public; founded 1971
Freshman admissions: selective; 2018-2019: 1,979 applied, 1,284 accepted. Either SAT or ACT required for some. SAT 25/75 percentile: 920-1120. High school rank: 11% in top tenth, 34% in top quarter, 67% in top half
Early decision deadline: N/A, notification date: N/A
Early action deadline: N/A, notification date: N/A
Application deadline (fall): rolling
Undergraduate student body: 1,986 full time, 1,393 part time; 36% male, 64% female; 0% American Indian, 1% Asian, 5% black, 4% Hispanic, 3% multiracial, 0% Pacific Islander, 78% white, 2% international; 73% from in state; 0% live on campus; 0% of students in fraternities, 0% in sororities
Most popular majors: 25% Business, Management, Marketing, and Related Support Services, 15% Health Professions and Related Programs, 13% Psychology, 7% Education, 7% Liberal Arts and Sciences, General Studies and Humanities
Expenses: 2019-2020: $7,527 in state, $19,978 out of state; room/board: N/A
Financial aid: (765) 973-8206; 75% of undergrads determined to have financial need; average aid package $9,420

Indiana University–Kokomo
Kokomo IN
(765) 455-9217
U.S. News ranking: Reg. Coll. (Mid. W), second tier
Website: www.iuk.edu
Admissions email: iuadmis@iuk.edu
Public; founded 1945
Freshman admissions: less selective; 2018-2019: 2,499 applied, 1,999 accepted. Either SAT or ACT required for some. SAT 25/75 percentile: 950-1130. High school rank: 6% in top tenth, 29% in top quarter, 69% in top half
Early decision deadline: N/A, notification date: N/A
Early action deadline: N/A, notification date: N/A
Application deadline (fall): rolling
Undergraduate student body: 2,259 full time, 653 part time; 36% male, 64% female; 0% American Indian, 1% Asian, 4% black, 5% Hispanic, 4% multiracial, 0% Pacific Islander, 82% white, 1% international; 98% from in state; 0% live on campus; 0% of students in fraternities, 0% in sororities
Most popular majors: 36% Health Professions and Related Programs, 13% Business, Management, Marketing, and Related Support Services, 11% Liberal Arts and Sciences, General Studies and Humanities, 7% Education, 6% Homeland Security, Law Enforcement, Firefighting and Related Protective Services
Expenses: 2019-2020: $7,527 in state, $19,978 out of state; room/board: N/A
Financial aid: (765) 455-9216; 69% of undergrads determined to have financial need; average aid package $8,992

Indiana University Northwest
Gary IN
(219) 980-6991
U.S. News ranking: Reg. U. (Mid. W), second tier
Website: www.iun.edu
Admissions email: admit@iun.edu
Public; founded 1948
Freshman admissions: less selective; 2018-2019: 2,182 applied, 1,737 accepted. Either SAT or ACT required. SAT 25/75 percentile: 910-1100. High school rank: 10% in top tenth, 30% in top quarter, 64% in top half
Early decision deadline: N/A, notification date: N/A
Early action deadline: N/A, notification date: N/A
Application deadline (fall): rolling
Undergraduate student body: 2,515 full time, 1,019 part time; 30% male, 70% female; 0% American Indian, 3% Asian, 15% black, 24% Hispanic, 3% multiracial, 0% Pacific Islander, 53% white, 0% international; 97% from in state; 0% live on campus; 1% of students in fraternities, 1% in sororities

Most popular majors: 27% Health Professions and Related Programs, 16% Business, Management, Marketing, and Related Support Services, 10% Liberal Arts and Sciences, General Studies and Humanities, 9% Homeland Security, Law Enforcement, Firefighting and Related Protective Services, 7% Public Administration and Social Service Professions
Expenses: 2019-2020: $7,526 in state, $19,977 out of state; room/board: N/A
Financial aid: (219) 980-6778; 69% of undergrads determined to have financial need; average aid package $8,865

Indiana University–Purdue University–Indianapolis
Indianapolis IN
(317) 274-4591
U.S. News ranking: Nat. U., No. 228
Website: www.iupui.edu
Admissions email: apply@iupui.edu
Public; founded 1969
Freshman admissions: selective; 2018-2019: 13,339 applied, 10,820 accepted. Either SAT or ACT required. SAT 25/75 percentile: 1000-1200. High school rank: 15% in top tenth, 42% in top quarter, 85% in top half
Early decision deadline: N/A, notification date: N/A
Early action deadline: N/A, notification date: N/A
Application deadline (fall): rolling
Undergraduate student body: 17,555 full time, 3,691 part time; 42% male, 58% female; 0% American Indian, 5% Asian, 9% black, 8% Hispanic, 5% multiracial, 0% Pacific Islander, 68% white, 4% international; 95% from in state; 12% live on campus; 1% of students in fraternities, 2% in sororities
Most popular majors: 18% Business, Management, Marketing, and Related Support Services, 17% Health Professions and Related Programs, 7% Engineering, 6% Liberal Arts and Sciences, General Studies and Humanities, 5% Computer and Information Sciences and Support Services
Expenses: 2019-2020: $9,703 in state, $30,712 out of state; room/board: $9,104
Financial aid: (317) 274-4162; 66% of undergrads determined to have financial need; average aid package $11,936

Indiana University–South Bend
South Bend IN
(574) 520-4839
U.S. News ranking: Reg. U. (Mid. W), second tier
Website: www.iusb.edu
Admissions email: admissions@iusb.edu
Public; founded 1961
Freshman admissions: less selective; 2018-2019: 3,011 applied, 2,466 accepted. Either

SAT or ACT required. SAT 25/75 percentile: 930-1130. High school rank: 7% in top tenth, 29% in top quarter, 65% in top half
Early decision deadline: N/A, notification date: N/A
Early action deadline: N/A, notification date: N/A
Application deadline (fall): rolling
Undergraduate student body: 3,614 full time, 1,093 part time; 37% male, 63% female; 0% American Indian, 2% Asian, 8% black, 12% Hispanic, 4% multiracial, 0% Pacific Islander, 69% white, 3% international; 95% from in state; 8% live on campus; N/A of students in fraternities, N/A in sororities
Most popular majors: 21% Health Professions and Related Programs, 18% Business, Management, Marketing, and Related Support Services, 10% Education, 9% Liberal Arts and Sciences, General Studies and Humanities, 8% Communication, Journalism, and Related Programs
Expenses: 2019-2020: $7,527 in state, $19,978 out of state; room/board: $7,346
Financial aid: (574) 520-4357; 72% of undergrads determined to have financial need; average aid package $9,474

Indiana University Southeast
New Albany IN
(812) 941-2212
U.S. News ranking: Reg. U. (Mid. W), second tier
Website: www.ius.edu
Admissions email: admissions@ius.edu
Public; founded 1941
Freshman admissions: selective; 2018-2019: 2,794 applied, 2,377 accepted. Either SAT or ACT required. ACT 25/75 percentile: 17-23. High school rank: 8% in top tenth, 33% in top quarter, 68% in top half
Early decision deadline: N/A, notification date: N/A
Early action deadline: N/A, notification date: N/A
Application deadline (fall): rolling
Undergraduate student body: 3,204 full time, 1,455 part time; 39% male, 61% female; 0% American Indian, 2% Asian, 7% black, 5% Hispanic, 4% multiracial, 0% Pacific Islander, 82% white, 1% international; 70% from in state; 8% live on campus; 6% of students in fraternities, 5% in sororities
Most popular majors: 22% Business, Management, Marketing, and Related Support Services, 12% Health Professions and Related Programs, 10% Education, 9% Psychology, 8% Liberal Arts and Sciences, General Studies and Humanities
Expenses: 2019-2020: $7,527 in state, $19,978 out of state; room/board: $6,920
Financial aid: (812) 941-2246; 66% of undergrads determined to have financial need; average aid package $8,816

Indiana Wesleyan University
Marion IN
(866) 468-6498
U.S. News ranking: Reg. U. (Mid. W), No. 25
Website: www.indwes.edu
Admissions email: admissions@indwes.edu
Private; founded 1920
Affiliation: Wesleyan
Freshman admissions: selective; 2018-2019: 4,733 applied, 3,232 accepted. Either SAT or ACT required. SAT 25/75 percentile: 1030-1240. High school rank: 22% in top tenth, 50% in top quarter, 83% in top half
Early decision deadline: N/A, notification date: N/A
Early action deadline: N/A, notification date: N/A
Application deadline (fall): rolling
Undergraduate student body: 2,598 full time, 255 part time; 35% male, 65% female; 0% American Indian, 2% Asian, 3% black, 4% Hispanic, 4% multiracial, 0% Pacific Islander, 84% white, 1% international; N/A from in state; 85% live on campus; N/A of students in fraternities, N/A in sororities
Most popular majors: 32% Health Professions and Related Programs, 11% Business, Management, Marketing, and Related Support Services, 10% Education, 7% Theology and Religious Vocations, 5% Biological and Biomedical Sciences
Expenses: 2018-2019: $25,980; room/board: $8,312
Financial aid: (765) 677-2116

Manchester University
North Manchester IN
(800) 852-3648
U.S. News ranking: Reg. Coll. (Mid. W), unranked
Website: www.manchester.edu
Admissions email: admitinfo@manchester.edu
Private; founded 1889
Affiliation: Church of Brethren
Freshman admissions: less selective; 2018-2019: 4,253 applied, 2,523 accepted. Neither SAT nor ACT required. SAT 25/75 percentile: 850-1100. High school rank: 13% in top tenth, 40% in top quarter, 77% in top half
Early decision deadline: N/A, notification date: N/A
Early action deadline: N/A, notification date: N/A
Application deadline (fall): rolling
Undergraduate student body: 1,176 full time, 15 part time; 47% male, 53% female; 0% American Indian, 1% Asian, 9% black, 7% Hispanic, 4% multiracial, 0% Pacific Islander, 72% white, 3% international; 83% from in state; 74% live on campus; 0% of students in fraternities, 0% in sororities

Most popular majors:
24% Business, Management, Marketing, and Related Support Services, 13% Health Professions and Related Programs, 13% Parks, Recreation, Leisure, and Fitness Studies, 10% Education, 6% Psychology
Expenses: 2019-2020: $33,624; room/board: $10,050
Financial aid: (260) 982-5237; 83% of undergrads determined to have financial need; average aid package $30,801

Marian University
Indianapolis IN
(317) 955-6300
U.S. News ranking: Reg. U. (Mid. W), No. 30
Website: www.marian.edu
Admissions email: admissions@marian.edu
Private; founded 1851
Affiliation: Roman Catholic
Freshman admissions: selective; 2018-2019: 2,325 applied, 1,427 accepted. Either SAT or ACT required. SAT 25/75 percentile: 1020-1200. High school rank: 20% in top tenth, 48% in top quarter, 76% in top half
Early decision deadline: N/A, notification date: N/A
Early action deadline: N/A, notification date: N/A
Application deadline (fall): 8/1
Undergraduate student body: 1,995 full time, 434 part time; 37% male, 63% female; 0% American Indian, 3% Asian, 11% black, 6% Hispanic, 3% multiracial, 0% Pacific Islander, 73% white, 1% international; 75% from in state; 49% live on campus; 0% of students in fraternities, 0% in sororities
Most popular majors: 44% Health Professions and Related Programs, 22% Business, Management, Marketing, and Related Support Services, 6% Parks, Recreation, Leisure, and Fitness Studies, 5% Biological and Biomedical Sciences, 3% Education
Expenses: 2019-2020: $35,000; room/board: $10,960
Financial aid: (317) 955-6040; 79% of undergrads determined to have financial need; average aid package $28,312

Martin University[1]
Indianapolis IN
(317) 543-3235
U.S. News ranking: Reg. Coll. (Mid. W), unranked
Website: www.martin.edu
Admissions email: admissions@martin.edu
Private
Application deadline (fall): N/A
Undergraduate student body: N/A full time, N/A part time
Expenses: N/A
Financial aid: N/A

Oakland City University
Oakland City IN
(800) 737-5125
U.S. News ranking: Reg. Coll. (Mid. W), No. 36
Website: www.oak.edu
Admissions email: admission@oak.edu
Private; founded 1885
Affiliation: General Baptist
Freshman admissions: less selective; 2018-2019: 1,010 applied, 502 accepted. Either SAT or ACT required for some. SAT 25/75 percentile: 912-1110. High school rank: 5% in top tenth, 34% in top quarter, 55% in top half
Early decision deadline: N/A, notification date: N/A
Early action deadline: N/A, notification date: N/A
Application deadline (fall): rolling
Undergraduate student body: 597 full time, 634 part time; 47% male, 53% female; 1% American Indian, 0% Asian, 7% black, 4% Hispanic, 3% multiracial, 0% Pacific Islander, 75% white, 3% international; 81% from in state; 61% live on campus; N/A of students in fraternities, N/A in sororities
Most popular majors: 44% Business, Management, Marketing, and Related Support Services, 19% Homeland Security, Law Enforcement, Firefighting and Related Protective Services, 7% Biological and Biomedical Sciences, 7% Education, 6% Psychology
Expenses: 2019-2020: $24,300; room/board: $10,400
Financial aid: (812) 749-1225; 72% of undergrads determined to have financial need; average aid package $13,420

Purdue University– Fort Wayne
Fort Wayne IN
(260) 481-6812
U.S. News ranking: Reg. U. (Mid. W), second tier
Website: www.pfw.edu
Admissions email: ask@pfw.edu
Public; founded 1964
Freshman admissions: selective; 2018-2019: 4,777 applied, 4,615 accepted. Either SAT or ACT required. SAT 25/75 percentile: 970-1180. High school rank: 9% in top tenth, 28% in top quarter, 66% in top half
Early decision deadline: N/A, notification date: N/A
Early action deadline: N/A, notification date: N/A
Application deadline (fall): 8/1
Undergraduate student body: 5,702 full time, 3,962 part time; 46% male, 54% female; 0% American Indian, 3% Asian, 7% black, 8% Hispanic, 4% multiracial, 0% Pacific Islander, 76% white, 3% international; 92% from in state; 10% live on campus; 0% of students in fraternities, 1% in sororities
Most popular majors: 20% Health Professions and Related Programs, 16% Business, Management,

Marketing, and Related Support Services, 11% Liberal Arts and Sciences, General Studies and Humanities, 8% Education, 6% Visual and Performing Arts
Expenses: 2018-2019: $8,450 in state, $20,288 out of state; room/board: $9,242
Financial aid: (260) 481-6820

Purdue University– Northwest
Hammond IN
(219) 989-2213
U.S. News ranking: Reg. U. (Mid. W), second tier
Website: www.pnw.edu/
Admissions email: admissons@pnw.edu
Public; founded 2016
Freshman admissions: selective; 2018-2019: 1,686 applied, 1,631 accepted. Either SAT or ACT required. SAT 25/75 percentile: 930-1150. High school rank: 10% in top tenth, 33% in top quarter, 53% in top half
Early decision deadline: N/A, notification date: N/A
Early action deadline: N/A, notification date: N/A
Application deadline (fall): 8/1
Undergraduate student body: 5,806 full time, 3,767 part time; 44% male, 56% female; 0% American Indian, 3% Asian, 10% black, 20% Hispanic, 3% multiracial, 0% Pacific Islander, 60% white, 3% international; 90% from in state; 7% live on campus; N/A of students in fraternities, N/A in sororities
Most popular majors: 34% Health Professions and Related Programs, 18% Business, Management, Marketing, and Related Support Services, 8% Engineering, 7% Engineering Technologies and Engineering-Related Fields, 5% Education
Expenses: 2019-2020: $7,813 in state, $11,337 out of state; room/board: $7,765
Financial aid: (855) 608-4600; 69% of undergrads determined to have financial need; average aid package $2,631

Purdue University– West Lafayette
West Lafayette IN
(765) 494-1776
U.S. News ranking: Nat. U., No. 57
Website: www.purdue.edu
Admissions email: admissions@purdue.edu
Public; founded 1869
Freshman admissions: more selective; 2018-2019: 53,439 applied, 30,965 accepted. Either SAT or ACT required. SAT 25/75 percentile: 1180-1410. High school rank: 46% in top tenth, 79% in top quarter, 97% in top half
Early decision deadline: N/A, notification date: N/A
Early action deadline: 11/1, notification date: 12/12
Application deadline (fall): rolling
Undergraduate student body: 31,217 full time, 1,455 part time; 57% male, 43% female;

0% American Indian, 9% Asian, 3% black, 5% Hispanic, 4% multiracial, 0% Pacific Islander, 63% white, 14% international; 61% from in state; 41% live on campus; 18% of students in fraternities, 20% in sororities
Most popular majors: 26% Engineering, 16% Business, Management, Marketing, and Related Support Services, 9% Agriculture, Agriculture Operations, and Related Sciences, 9% Liberal Arts and Sciences, General Studies and Humanities, 6% Engineering Technologies and Engineering-Related Fields
Expenses: 2019-2020: $9,992 in state, $28,794 out of state; room/board: $10,030
Financial aid: (765) 494-5050; 39% of undergrads determined to have financial need; average aid package $14,138

Rose-Hulman Institute of Technology
Terre Haute IN
(812) 877-8213
U.S. News ranking: Engineering, unranked
Website: www.rose-hulman.edu
Admissions email: admissions@rose-hulman.edu
Private; founded 1874
Freshman admissions: more selective; 2018-2019: 4,471 applied, 3,049 accepted. Either SAT or ACT required. SAT 25/75 percentile: 1270-1480. High school rank: 64% in top tenth, 93% in top quarter, 100% in top half
Early decision deadline: N/A, notification date: N/A
Early action deadline: 11/1, notification date: 12/15
Application deadline (fall): 2/1
Undergraduate student body: 2,063 full time, 22 part time; 75% male, 25% female; 0% American Indian, 6% Asian, 3% black, 5% Hispanic, 5% multiracial, 0% Pacific Islander, 66% white, 15% international; 29% from in state; 55% live on campus; 37% of students in fraternities, 26% in sororities
Most popular majors: 32% Mechanical Engineering, 12% Chemical Engineering, 12% Computer Science, 9% Electrical and Electronics Engineering, 8% Bioengineering and Biomedical Engineering
Expenses: 2019-2020: $49,527; room/board: $15,414
Financial aid: (812) 877-8672; 56% of undergrads determined to have financial need; average aid package $30,803

Saint Mary-of-the-Woods College
St. Mary-of-the-Woods IN
(800) 926-7692
U.S. News ranking: Reg. U. (Mid. W), No. 46
Website: www.smwc.edu
Admissions email: admission@smwc.edu
Private; founded 1840

Affiliation: Roman Catholic
Freshman admissions: less selective; 2018-2019: 637 applied, 460 accepted. SAT or ACT required. SAT 25/75 percentile: 920-1110. High school rank: N/A
Early decision deadline: N/A, notification date: N/A
Early action deadline: N/A, notification date: N/A
Application deadline (fall): rolling
Undergraduate student body: 550 full time, 269 part time; 14% male, 86% female; 0% American Indian, 1% Asian, 5% black, 3% Hispanic, 6% multiracial, 0% Pacific Islander, 79% white, 1% international; 77% from in state; 51% live on campus; 0% of students in fraternities, 0% in sororities
Most popular majors: 20% Health Professions and Related Programs, 17% Business, Management, Marketing, and Related Support Services, 17% Education, 16% Psychology, 8% Public Administration and Social Service Professions
Expenses: 2019-2020: $30,500; room/board: $11,240
Financial aid: (812) 535-5110; 98% of undergrads determined to have financial need; average aid package $26,216

Saint Mary's College
Notre Dame IN
(574) 284-4587
U.S. News ranking: Nat. Lib. Arts, No. 102
Website: www.saintmarys.edu
Admissions email: admission@saintmarys.edu
Private; founded 1844
Affiliation: Roman Catholic
Freshman admissions: selective; 2018-2019: 1,862 applied, 1,525 accepted. Either SAT or ACT required for some. SAT 25/75 percentile: 1050-1260. High school rank: 27% in top tenth, 56% in top quarter, 90% in top half
Early decision deadline: 11/15, notification date: 12/15
Early action deadline: N/A, notification date: N/A
Application deadline (fall): rolling
Undergraduate student body: 1,470 full time, 49 part time; 1% male, 99% female; 0% American Indian, 2% Asian, 2% black, 13% Hispanic, 3% multiracial, 0% Pacific Islander, 77% white, 1% international; 31% from in state; 84% live on campus; 0% of students in fraternities, 0% in sororities
Most popular majors: 10% Psychology, General, 9% Business Administration and Management, General, 9% Registered Nursing/Registered Nurse, 8% Biology/Biological Sciences, General, 7% Communication and Media Studies
Expenses: 2019-2020: $43,900; room/board: $13,020
Financial aid: (574) 284-4557; 74% of undergrads determined to have financial need; average aid package $37,254

Taylor University
Upland IN
(765) 998-5134
U.S. News ranking: Reg. Coll. (Mid. W), No. 1
Website: www.taylor.edu
Admissions email: admissions_u@taylor.edu
Private; founded 1846
Affiliation: Interdenominational
Freshman admissions: more selective; 2018-2019: 2,165 applied, 1,681 accepted. Either SAT or ACT required. SAT 25/75 percentile: 1080-1300. High school rank: 36% in top tenth, 60% in top quarter, 87% in top half
Early decision deadline: N/A, notification date: N/A
Early action deadline: N/A, notification date: N/A
Application deadline (fall): 8/1
Undergraduate student body: 1,846 full time, 321 part time; 45% male, 55% female; 1% American Indian, 3% Asian, 4% black, 4% Hispanic, 1% multiracial, 0% Pacific Islander, 83% white, 5% international; 42% from in state; 89% live on campus; N/A of students in fraternities, N/A in sororities
Most popular majors: 15% Education, 14% Biological and Biomedical Sciences, 14% Business, Management, Marketing, and Related Support Services, 10% Visual and Performing Arts, 8% Communication, Journalism, and Related Programs
Expenses: 2019-2020: $35,305; room/board: $9,950
Financial aid: (765) 998-5358; 62% of undergrads determined to have financial need; average aid package $24,925

Trine University
Angola IN
(260) 665-4100
U.S. News ranking: Reg. U. (Mid. W), No. 46
Website: www.trine.edu
Admissions email: admit@trine.edu
Private; founded 1884
Freshman admissions: selective; 2018-2019: 3,993 applied, 2,931 accepted. Either SAT or ACT required. SAT 25/75 percentile: 1010-1230. High school rank: 18% in top tenth, 46% in top quarter, 79% in top half
Early decision deadline: N/A, notification date: N/A
Early action deadline: N/A, notification date: N/A
Application deadline (fall): 8/1
Undergraduate student body: 2,054 full time, 99 part time; 67% male, 33% female; 0% American Indian, 1% Asian, 4% black, 5% Hispanic, 3% multiracial, 0% Pacific Islander, 80% white, 4% international; N/A from in state; 70% live on campus; N/A of students in fraternities, N/A in sororities
Most popular majors: 29% Engineering, 17% Parks, Recreation, Leisure, and Fitness Studies, 12% Engineering

Technologies and Engineering-Related Fields, 11% Business, Management, Marketing, and Related Support Services, 8% Homeland Security, Law Enforcement, Firefighting and Related Protective Services
Expenses: 2019-2020: $32,810; room/board: $10,810
Financial aid: (260) 665-4438; 85% of undergrads determined to have financial need; average aid package $28,164

University of Evansville
Evansville IN
(812) 488-2468
U.S. News ranking: Reg. U. (Mid. W), No. 6
Website: www.evansville.edu
Admissions email: admission@evansville.edu
Private; founded 1854
Affiliation: United Methodist
Freshman admissions: more selective; 2018-2019: 4,580 applied, 3,182 accepted. Either SAT or ACT required for some. SAT 25/75 percentile: 1080-1300. High school rank: 28% in top tenth, 64% in top quarter, 89% in top half
Early decision deadline: N/A, notification date: N/A
Early action deadline: 12/1, notification date: 12/15
Application deadline (fall): rolling
Undergraduate student body: 1,992 full time, 251 part time; 42% male, 58% female; 0% American Indian, 3% Asian, 4% black, 4% Hispanic, 3% multiracial, 0% Pacific Islander, 74% white, 11% international; 56% from in state; 57% live on campus; 28% of students in fraternities, 25% in sororities
Most popular majors: 18% Business, Management, Marketing, and Related Support Services, 14% Engineering, 14% Health Professions and Related Programs, 8% Parks, Recreation, Leisure, and Fitness Studies, 8% Visual and Performing Arts
Expenses: 2018-2019: $36,416; room/board: $12,460
Financial aid: (812) 488-2364

University of Indianapolis
Indianapolis IN
(317) 788-3216
U.S. News ranking: Nat. U., No. 228
Website: www.uindy.edu
Admissions email: admissions@uindy.edu
Private; founded 1902
Affiliation: United Methodist
Freshman admissions: selective; 2018-2019: 8,626 applied, 7,030 accepted. Either SAT or ACT required. SAT 25/75 percentile: 990-1180. High school rank: 18% in top tenth, 49% in top quarter, 84% in top half
Early decision deadline: N/A, notification date: N/A
Early action deadline: N/A, notification date: N/A

Application deadline (fall): rolling
Undergraduate student body: 4,065 full time, 443 part time; 36% male, 64% female; 0% American Indian, 2% Asian, 10% black, 6% Hispanic, 3% multiracial, 0% Pacific Islander, 68% white, 7% international; 80% from in state; 47% live on campus; 0% of students in fraternities, 0% in sororities
Most popular majors: 21% Registered Nursing/Registered Nurse, 11% Psychology, General, 10% Business Administration and Management, General, 5% Biology/Biological Sciences, General, 5% Kinesiology and Exercise Science
Expenses: 2019-2020: $30,976; room/board: $11,576
Financial aid: (317) 788-3217; 77% of undergrads determined to have financial need; average aid package $24,063

University of Notre Dame
Notre Dame IN
(574) 631-7505
U.S. News ranking: Nat. U., No. 15
Website: www.nd.edu
Admissions email: admissions@nd.edu
Private; founded 1842
Affiliation: Roman Catholic
Freshman admissions: most selective; 2018-2019: 20,371 applied, 3,608 accepted. Either SAT or ACT required. ACT 25/75 percentile: 33-35. High school rank: 89% in top tenth, 98% in top quarter, 100% in top half
Early decision deadline: N/A, notification date: N/A
Early action deadline: 11/1, notification date: 12/15
Application deadline (fall): 1/1
Undergraduate student body: 8,607 full time, 10 part time; 52% male, 48% female; 0% American Indian, 5% Asian, 4% black, 11% Hispanic, 5% multiracial, 0% Pacific Islander, 68% white, 6% international; 7% from in state; 74% live on campus; N/A of students in fraternities, N/A in sororities
Most popular majors: 13% Finance, General, 8% Economics, General, 6% Accounting, 6% Mechanical Engineering, 6% Political Science and Government, General
Expenses: 2019-2020: $55,553; room/board: $15,640
Financial aid: (574) 631-6436; 48% of undergrads determined to have financial need; average aid package $51,128

University of Saint Francis
Fort Wayne IN
(260) 399-8000
U.S. News ranking: Reg. U. (Mid. W), No. 66
Website: www.sf.edu
Admissions email: admis@sf.edu
Private; founded 1890
Affiliation: Roman Catholic
Freshman admissions: selective; 2018-2019: 1,490 applied, 1,392 accepted. Either SAT

or ACT required. SAT 25/75 percentile: 955-1150. High school rank: 22% in top tenth, 42% in top quarter, 75% in top half **Early decision deadline:** N/A, notification date: N/A **Early action deadline:** N/A, notification date: N/A **Application deadline (fall):** rolling **Undergraduate student body:** 1,511 full time, 267 part time; 28% male, 72% female; 0% American Indian, 2% Asian, 7% black, 8% Hispanic, 3% multiracial, 0% Pacific Islander, 77% white, 1% international; N/A from in state; 23% live on campus; N/A of students in fraternities, N/A in sororities **Most popular majors:** 55% Health Professions and Related Programs, 8% Business, Management, Marketing, and Related Support Services, 8% Visual and Performing Arts, 5% Biological and Biomedical Sciences, 5% Education **Expenses:** 2019-2020: $31,480; room/board: $10,180 **Financial aid:** (260) 399-8003; 86% of undergrads determined to have financial need; average aid package $22,775

University of Southern Indiana

Evansville IN
(812) 464-1765
U.S. News ranking: Reg. U. (Mid. W), No. 105
Website: www.usi.edu
Admissions email: enroll@usi.edu
Public; founded 1965
Freshman admissions: selective; 2018-2019: 4,461 applied, 4,220 accepted. Either SAT or ACT required. SAT 25/75 percentile: 980-1180. High school rank: 14% in top tenth, 34% in top quarter, 69% in top half **Early decision deadline:** N/A, notification date: N/A **Early action deadline:** N/A, notification date: N/A **Application deadline (fall):** 8/15 **Undergraduate student body:** 6,422 full time, 1,091 part time; 38% male, 62% female; 0% American Indian, 1% Asian, 4% black, 4% Hispanic, 3% multiracial, 0% Pacific Islander, 86% white, 2% international; N/A from in state; 32% live on campus; 7% of students in fraternities, 9% in sororities **Most popular majors:** 22% Health Professions and Related Programs, 18% Business, Management, Marketing, and Related Support Services, 7% Education, 7% Parks, Recreation, Leisure, and Fitness Studies, 6% Psychology **Expenses:** 2019-2020: $8,869 in state, $19,957 out of state; room/board: $9,102 **Financial aid:** (812) 464-1767; 66% of undergrads determined to have financial need; average aid package $10,556

Valparaiso University

Valparaiso IN
(888) 468-2576
U.S. News ranking: Nat. U., No. 153
Website: www.valpo.edu
Admissions email: undergrad.admission@valpo.edu
Private; founded 1859
Freshman admissions: more selective; 2018-2019: 7,062 applied, 6,307 accepted. Either SAT or ACT required. SAT 25/75 percentile: 1070-1270. High school rank: 29% in top tenth, 63% in top quarter, 93% in top half **Early decision deadline:** N/A, notification date: N/A **Early action deadline:** N/A, notification date: N/A **Application deadline (fall):** rolling **Undergraduate student body:** 3,138 full time, 79 part time; 44% male, 56% female; 0% American Indian, 2% Asian, 6% black, 10% Hispanic, 4% multiracial, 0% Pacific Islander, 72% white, 4% international; 46% from in state; 62% live on campus; 28% of students in fraternities, 27% in sororities **Most popular majors:** 18% Health Professions and Related Programs, 14% Business, Management, Marketing, and Related Support Services, 14% Engineering, 7% Education, 7% Physical Sciences **Expenses:** 2019-2020: $41,820; room/board: $12,260 **Financial aid:** (219) 464-5015; 77% of undergrads determined to have financial need; average aid package $34,200

Vincennes University

Vincennes IN
(800) 742-9198
U.S. News ranking: Reg. Coll. (Mid. W), unranked
Website: www.vinu.edu
Admissions email: N/A
Public; founded 1801
Freshman admissions: least selective; 2018-2019: 4,728 applied, 3,656 accepted. Neither SAT nor ACT required. SAT 25/75 percentile: N/A. High school rank: N/A **Early decision deadline:** N/A, notification date: N/A **Early action deadline:** N/A, notification date: N/A **Application deadline (fall):** rolling **Undergraduate student body:** 4,970 full time, 12,511 part time; 54% male, 46% female; 0% American Indian, 1% Asian, 10% black, 11% Hispanic, 2% multiracial, 0% Pacific Islander, 71% white, 1% international; N/A from in state; 37% live on campus; N/A of students in fraternities, N/A in sororities **Most popular majors:** 32% Health Professions and Related Programs, 32% Homeland Security, Law Enforcement, Firefighting and Related Protective Services, 22% Engineering Technologies and Engineering-Related Fields, 14% Education

Wabash College

Crawfordsville IN
(765) 361-6225
U.S. News ranking: Nat. Lib. Arts, No. 53
Website: www.wabash.edu
Admissions email: admissions@wabash.edu
Private; founded 1832
Freshman admissions: more selective; 2018-2019: 1,334 applied, 868 accepted. Either SAT or ACT required. SAT 25/75 percentile: 1100-1330. High school rank: 29% in top tenth, 64% in top quarter, 92% in top half **Early decision deadline:** 11/1, notification date: 12/5 **Early action deadline:** 12/1, notification date: 12/31 **Application deadline (fall):** rolling **Undergraduate student body:** 881 full time, 1 part time; 100% male, 0% female; 0% American Indian, 1% Asian, 6% black, 9% Hispanic, 3% multiracial, 0% Pacific Islander, 74% white, 6% international; 73% from in state; 99% live on campus; 64% of students in fraternities, N/A in sororities **Most popular majors:** 15% Economics, General, 12% Biology/Biological Sciences, General, 11% Political Science and Government, General, 10% Mathematics, General, 7% History, General **Expenses:** 2019-2020: $44,720; room/board: $10,500 **Financial aid:** (765) 361-6370; 77% of undergrads determined to have financial need; average aid package $40,744

IOWA

Briar Cliff University

Sioux City IA
(712) 279-5200
U.S. News ranking: Reg. Coll. (Mid. W), No. 29
Website: www.briarcliff.edu
Admissions email: admissions@briarcliff.edu
Private; founded 1930
Affiliation: Roman Catholic
Freshman admissions: selective; 2018-2019: 1,251 applied, 751 accepted. Either SAT or ACT required. ACT 25/75 percentile: 19-24. High school rank: 13% in top tenth, 28% in top quarter, 59% in top half **Early decision deadline:** N/A, notification date: N/A **Early action deadline:** N/A, notification date: N/A **Application deadline (fall):** rolling **Undergraduate student body:** 731 full time, 245 part time; 45% male, 55% female; 2% American Indian, 2% Asian, 12% black, 16% Hispanic, 1% multiracial, 1% Pacific Islander, 60% white, 7% international; 48% from in state; 48% live on campus; 0% of students in fraternities, 0% in sororities

Most popular majors: 23% Registered Nursing/Registered Nurse, 15% Business Administration and Management, General, 8% Criminology, 7% Kinesiology and Exercise Science, 6% Social Work **Expenses:** 2018-2019: $30,970; room/board: $8,896 **Financial aid:** N/A

Buena Vista University

Storm Lake IA
(800) 383-9600
U.S. News ranking: Reg. U. (Mid. W), No. 32
Website: www.bvu.edu
Admissions email: admissions@bvu.edu
Private; founded 1891
Affiliation: Presbyterian Church (USA)
Freshman admissions: selective; 2018-2019: 2,132 applied, 1,228 accepted. Either SAT or ACT required. ACT 25/75 percentile: 19-24. High school rank: 11% in top tenth, 42% in top quarter, 75% in top half **Early decision deadline:** N/A, notification date: N/A **Early action deadline:** N/A, notification date: N/A **Application deadline (fall):** rolling **Undergraduate student body:** 1,394 full time, 225 part time; 35% male, 65% female; 1% American Indian, 1% Asian, 4% black, 5% Hispanic, 2% multiracial, 0% Pacific Islander, 74% white, 1% international; 69% from in state; 90% live on campus; 0% of students in fraternities, 0% in sororities **Most popular majors:** 24% Business, Management, Marketing, and Related Support Services, 15% Education, 10% Communication, Journalism, and Related Programs, 8% Biological and Biomedical Sciences, 7% Parks, Recreation, Leisure, and Fitness Studies **Expenses:** 2019-2020: $35,194; room/board: $9,872 **Financial aid:** (712) 749-2164; 85% of undergrads determined to have financial need; average aid package $30,243

Central College[1]

Pella IA
(641) 628-5286
U.S. News ranking: Nat. Lib. Arts, No. 160
Website: www.central.edu
Admissions email: admission@central.edu
Private; founded 1853
Application deadline (fall): 8/15
Undergraduate student body: N/A full time, N/A part time
Expenses: N/A
Financial aid: (641) 628-5336

Clarke University

Dubuque IA
(563) 588-6316
U.S. News ranking: Nat. U., No. 218
Website: www.clarke.edu
Admissions email: admissions@clarke.edu
Private; founded 1843
Affiliation: Roman Catholic
Freshman admissions: selective; 2018-2019: 1,301 applied, 1,073 accepted. Either SAT or ACT required. ACT 25/75 percentile: 19-23. High school rank: 17% in top tenth, 37% in top quarter, 78% in top half **Early decision deadline:** N/A, notification date: N/A **Early action deadline:** N/A, notification date: N/A **Application deadline (fall):** rolling **Undergraduate student body:** 710 full time, 34 part time; 41% male, 59% female; 0% American Indian, 1% Asian, 8% black, 9% Hispanic, 2% multiracial, 1% Pacific Islander, 74% white, 3% international; N/A from in state; 60% live on campus; N/A of students in fraternities, N/A in sororities **Most popular majors:** 30% Registered Nursing/Registered Nurse, 15% Psychology, General, 14% Business Administration and Management, General, 11% Elementary Education and Teaching, 8% Biology/Biological Sciences, General **Expenses:** 2019-2020: $34,670; room/board: $10,000 **Financial aid:** (563) 588-6327; 84% of undergrads determined to have financial need; average aid package $28,747

Coe College

Cedar Rapids IA
(319) 399-8500
U.S. News ranking: Nat. Lib. Arts, No. 130
Website: www.coe.edu
Admissions email: admission@coe.edu
Private; founded 1851
Freshman admissions: more selective; 2018-2019: 7,795 applied, 5,217 accepted. Either SAT or ACT required. ACT 25/75 percentile: 22-28. High school rank: 28% in top tenth, 53% in top quarter, 84% in top half **Early decision deadline:** N/A, notification date: N/A **Early action deadline:** 12/10, notification date: 1/20 **Application deadline (fall):** 3/1 **Undergraduate student body:** 1,378 full time, 44 part time; 44% male, 56% female; 0% American Indian, 5% Asian, 8% black, 11% Hispanic, 3% multiracial, 0% Pacific Islander, 68% white, 2% international; 43% from in state; 86% live on campus; 18% of students in fraternities, 28% in sororities **Most popular majors:** 19% Biological and Biomedical Sciences, 13% Business, Management, Marketing, and Related Support Services, 9% Psychology, 7% Social Sciences, 6% Visual and Performing Arts

Expenses: 2019-2020: $45,580; room/board: $9,820
Financial aid: (319) 399-8540; 82% of undergrads determined to have financial need; average aid package $37,350

Cornell College

Mount Vernon IA
(800) 747-1112
U.S. News ranking: Nat. Lib. Arts, No. 68
Website: www.cornellcollege.edu
Admissions email: admissions@cornellcollege.edu
Private; founded 1853
Affiliation: United Methodist
Freshman admissions: more selective; 2018-2019: 2,532 applied, 1,545 accepted. Neither SAT nor ACT required. ACT 25/75 percentile: 23-30. High school rank: 22% in top tenth, 46% in top quarter, 82% in top half
Early decision deadline: N/A, notification date: N/A
Early action deadline: 11/1, notification date: N/A
Application deadline (fall): rolling
Undergraduate student body: 1,017 full time, 9 part time; 52% male, 48% female; 2% American Indian, 4% Asian, 6% black, 8% Hispanic, 1% multiracial, 0% Pacific Islander, 68% white, 7% international; 22% from in state; 92% live on campus; 18% of students in fraternities, 30% in sororities
Most popular majors: 12% Biological and Biomedical Sciences, 11% Education, 10% Social Sciences, 10% Visual and Performing Arts, 7% Business, Management, Marketing, and Related Support Services
Expenses: 2019-2020: $43,976; room/board: $9,760
Financial aid: (319) 895-4216; 69% of undergrads determined to have financial need; average aid package $32,475

Dordt University

Sioux Center IA
(800) 343-6738
U.S. News ranking: Reg. Coll. (Mid. W), No. 3
Website: www.dordt.edu
Admissions email: admissions@dordt.edu
Private; founded 1955
Affiliation: Christian Reformed Church
Freshman admissions: selective; 2018-2019: 1,483 applied, 1,082 accepted. Either SAT or ACT required for some. ACT 25/75 percentile: 19-31. High school rank: 18% in top tenth, 43% in top quarter, 71% in top half
Early decision deadline: N/A, notification date: N/A
Early action deadline: N/A, notification date: N/A
Application deadline (fall): 8/16
Undergraduate student body: 1,342 full time, 84 part time; 53% male, 47% female; 1% American Indian, 1% Asian, 3% black, 1% Hispanic, 1% multiracial, 0% Pacific Islander, 82% white,

9% international; 42% from in state; 90% live on campus; 0% of students in fraternities, 0% in sororities
Most popular majors: 23% Elementary Education and Teaching, 19% Business/Commerce, General, 9% Agricultural Business and Management, General, 8% Engineering, General, 5% Health and Physical Education/Fitness, General
Expenses: 2019-2020: $31,770; room/board: $10,020
Financial aid: (712) 722-6082; 67% of undergrads determined to have financial need; average aid package $26,575

Drake University

Des Moines IA
(800) 443-7253
U.S. News ranking: Nat. U., No. 130
Website: www.drake.edu
Admissions email: admission@drake.edu
Private; founded 1881
Freshman admissions: more selective; 2018-2019: 6,886 applied, 4,659 accepted. Either SAT or ACT required for some. ACT 25/75 percentile: 24-30. High school rank: 39% in top tenth, 68% in top quarter, 92% in top half
Early decision deadline: N/A, notification date: N/A
Early action deadline: N/A, notification date: N/A
Application deadline (fall): rolling
Undergraduate student body: 2,834 full time, 181 part time; 42% male, 58% female; 0% American Indian, 4% Asian, 5% black, 6% Hispanic, 3% multiracial, 0% Pacific Islander, 77% white, 4% international; N/A from in state; 70% live on campus; 36% of students in fraternities, 29% in sororities
Most popular majors: 34% Business, Management, Marketing, and Related Support Services, 12% Communication, Journalism, and Related Programs, 8% Social Sciences, 7% Biological and Biomedical Sciences, 7% Visual and Performing Arts
Expenses: 2019-2020: $42,840; room/board: $10,848
Financial aid: (515) 271-2905; 61% of undergrads determined to have financial need; average aid package $29,286

Graceland University

Lamoni IA
(866) 472-2352
U.S. News ranking: Reg. U. (Mid. W), No. 105
Website: www.graceland.edu
Admissions email: admissions@graceland.edu
Private; founded 1895
Affiliation: Other
Freshman admissions: selective; 2018-2019: 3,004 applied, 1,744 accepted. Either SAT or ACT required. ACT 25/75 percentile: 18-23. High school

rank: 12% in top tenth, 27% in top quarter, 65% in top half
Early decision deadline: N/A, notification date: N/A
Early action deadline: N/A, notification date: N/A
Application deadline (fall): rolling
Undergraduate student body: 1,023 full time, 157 part time; 42% male, 58% female; 1% American Indian, 1% Asian, 10% black, 10% Hispanic, 5% multiracial, 2% Pacific Islander, 64% white, 5% international; 27% from in state; 74% live on campus; N/A of students in fraternities, N/A in sororities
Most popular majors: 26% Health Professions and Related Programs, 20% Library Science, 11% Education, 11% Parks, Recreation, Leisure, and Fitness Studies, 4% Psychology
Expenses: 2019-2020: $30,420; room/board: $9,100
Financial aid: (641) 784-5117; 84% of undergrads determined to have financial need; average aid package $24,742

Grand View University

Des Moines IA
(515) 263-2810
U.S. News ranking: Reg. Coll. (Mid. W), No. 33
Website: www.grandview.edu
Admissions email: admissions@grandview.edu
Private; founded 1896
Affiliation: Evangelical Lutheran Church
Freshman admissions: selective; 2018-2019: 1,597 applied, 1,469 accepted. Either SAT or ACT required. ACT 25/75 percentile: 18-23. High school rank: 15% in top tenth, 37% in top quarter, 71% in top half
Early decision deadline: N/A, notification date: N/A
Early action deadline: N/A, notification date: N/A
Application deadline (fall): 8/15
Undergraduate student body: 1,589 full time, 171 part time; 45% male, 55% female; 0% American Indian, 3% Asian, 8% black, 5% Hispanic, 7% multiracial, 0% Pacific Islander, 66% white, 3% international; N/A from in state; 48% live on campus; 0% of students in fraternities, 0% in sororities
Most popular majors: 28% Business, Management, Marketing, and Related Support Services, 9% Health Professions and Related Programs, 9% Public Administration and Social Service Professions, 7% Biological and Biomedical Sciences, 7% Parks, Recreation, Leisure, and Fitness Studies
Expenses: 2019-2020: $28,678; room/board: $9,336
Financial aid: (515) 263-2853; 80% of undergrads determined to have financial need; average aid package $21,187

Grinnell College

Grinnell IA
(800) 247-0113
U.S. News ranking: Nat. Lib. Arts, No. 14
Website: www.grinnell.edu
Admissions email: admission@grinnell.edu
Private; founded 1846
Freshman admissions: most selective; 2018-2019: 7,349 applied, 1,792 accepted. Either SAT or ACT required. ACT 25/75 percentile: 30-34. High school rank: 68% in top tenth, 90% in top quarter, 99% in top half
Early decision deadline: 11/15, notification date: 12/15
Early action deadline: N/A, notification date: N/A
Application deadline (fall): 1/15
Undergraduate student body: 1,679 full time, 37 part time; 46% male, 54% female; 0% American Indian, 8% Asian, 5% black, 8% Hispanic, 5% multiracial, 0% Pacific Islander, 50% white, 19% international; 7% from in state; 88% live on campus; 0% of students in fraternities, 0% in sororities
Most popular majors: 28% Social Sciences, 10% Biological and Biomedical Sciences, 10% Computer and Information Sciences and Support Services, 9% Foreign Languages, Literatures, and Linguistics, 8% Physical Sciences
Expenses: 2019-2020: $54,354; room/board: $13,292
Financial aid: (641) 269-3250; 66% of undergrads determined to have financial need; average aid package $49,880

Iowa State University

Ames IA
(515) 294-2592
U.S. News ranking: Nat. U., No. 121
Website: www.iastate.edu
Admissions email: admissions@iastate.edu
Public; founded 1858
Freshman admissions: more selective; 2018-2019: 18,855 applied, 17,082 accepted. Either SAT or ACT required. ACT 25/75 percentile: 22-28. High school rank: 27% in top tenth, 59% in top quarter, 91% in top half
Early decision deadline: N/A, notification date: N/A
Early action deadline: N/A, notification date: N/A
Application deadline (fall): rolling
Undergraduate student body: 27,929 full time, 1,692 part time; 58% male, 42% female; 0% American Indian, 3% Asian, 3% black, 6% Hispanic, 2% multiracial, 0% Pacific Islander, 75% white, 6% international; 59% from in state; 23% live on campus; 12% of students in fraternities, 20% in sororities
Most popular majors: 21% Engineering, 20% Business, Management, Marketing, and Related Support Services, 11% Agriculture, Agriculture Operations, and Related Sciences,

6% Biological and Biomedical Sciences, 4% Communication, Journalism, and Related Programs
Expenses: 2019-2020: $9,320 in state, $24,508 out of state; room/board: $9,149
Financial aid: (515) 294-2223; 52% of undergrads determined to have financial need; average aid package $13,006

Iowa Wesleyan University

Mount Pleasant IA
(319) 385-6231
U.S. News ranking: Reg. Coll. (Mid. W), second tier
Website: www.iw.edu
Admissions email: admit@iw.edu
Private; founded 1842
Affiliation: United Methodist
Freshman admissions: selective; 2018-2019: 3,742 applied, 2,239 accepted. Either SAT or ACT required. ACT 25/75 percentile: 18-22. High school rank: 8% in top tenth, 34% in top quarter, 55% in top half
Early decision deadline: N/A, notification date: N/A
Early action deadline: N/A, notification date: N/A
Application deadline (fall): rolling
Undergraduate student body: 565 full time, 33 part time; 48% male, 52% female; 0% American Indian, 1% Asian, 16% black, 8% Hispanic, 6% multiracial, 0% Pacific Islander, 41% white, 17% international; 33% from in state; 77% live on campus; 4% of students in fraternities, 5% in sororities
Most popular majors: 30% Business, Management, and Related Support Services, 15% Health Professions and Related Programs, 12% Biological and Biomedical Sciences, 7% Homeland Security, Law Enforcement, Firefighting and Related Protective Services, 7% Parks, Recreation, Leisure, and Fitness Studies
Expenses: 2019-2020: $31,530; room/board: $10,865
Financial aid: (319) 385-6242; 96% of undergrads determined to have financial need; average aid package $26,476

Loras College

Dubuque IA
(800) 245-6727
U.S. News ranking: Reg. Coll. (Mid. W), No. 16
Website: www.loras.edu
Admissions email: admission@loras.edu
Private; founded 1839
Affiliation: Roman Catholic
Freshman admissions: selective; 2018-2019: 1,312 applied, 1,216 accepted. Either SAT or ACT required. ACT 25/75 percentile: 19-25. High school rank: N/A
Early decision deadline: N/A, notification date: N/A
Early action deadline: N/A, notification date: N/A
Application deadline (fall): rolling

Undergraduate student body: 1,345 full time, 48 part time; 55% male, 45% female; 0% American Indian, 1% Asian, 3% black, 8% Hispanic, 2% multiracial, 0% Pacific Islander, 81% white, 2% international; 42% from in state; 65% live on campus; N/A of students in fraternities, N/A in sororities

Most popular majors: 6% Business Administration and Management, General, 4% Elementary Education and Teaching, 4% Psychology, General, 3% Criminal Justice/Safety Studies, 3% Social Work

Expenses: 2019-2020: $35,218; room/board: $8,425

Financial aid: (563) 588-7817; 80% of undergrads determined to have financial need; average aid package $27,972

Luther College

Decorah IA
(563) 387-1287
U.S. News ranking: Nat. Lib. Arts, No. 100
Website: www.luther.edu
Admissions email: admissions@luther.edu
Private; founded 1861
Affiliation: Evangelical Lutheran Church
Freshman admissions: more selective; 2018-2019: 4,422 applied, 2,767 accepted. Either SAT or ACT required. ACT 25/75 percentile: 23-29. High school rank: 27% in top tenth, 58% in top quarter, 87% in top half
Early decision deadline: N/A, notification date: N/A
Early action deadline: N/A, notification date: N/A
Application deadline (fall): rolling
Undergraduate student body: 1,977 full time, 28 part time; 43% male, 57% female; 0% American Indian, 1% Asian, 2% black, 6% Hispanic, 2% multiracial, 0% Pacific Islander, 79% white, 9% international; 29% from in state; 93% live on campus; 1% of students in fraternities, 2% in sororities

Most popular majors: 12% Biology/ Biological Sciences, General, 10% Music, General, 9% Business Administration and Management, General, 8% Registered Nursing/ Registered Nurse, 7% English Language and Literature, General
Expenses: 2019-2020: $44,070; room/board: $9,760
Financial aid: (563) 387-1018; 78% of undergrads determined to have financial need; average aid package $37,623

Maharishi University of Management[1]

Fairfield IA
(641) 472-7000
U.S. News ranking: Reg. U. (Mid. W), unranked
Website: www.mum.edu
Admissions email: admissions@mum.edu
Private
Application deadline (fall): N/A

Undergraduate student body: N/A full time, N/A part time
Expenses: N/A
Financial aid: N/A

Morningside College

Sioux City IA
(712) 274-5111
U.S. News ranking: Reg. U. (Mid. W), No. 66
Website: www.morningside.edu
Admissions email: admissions@morningside.edu
Private; founded 1894
Affiliation: United Methodist
Freshman admissions: selective; 2018-2019: 4,375 applied, 2,459 accepted. Either SAT or ACT required. ACT 25/75 percentile: 20-25. High school rank: 14% in top tenth, 36% in top quarter, 69% in top half
Early decision deadline: N/A, notification date: N/A
Early action deadline: N/A, notification date: N/A
Application deadline (fall): rolling
Undergraduate student body: 1,212 full time, 70 part time; 50% male, 50% female; 0% American Indian, 1% Asian, 2% black, 7% Hispanic, 4% multiracial, 0% Pacific Islander, 73% white, 5% international; 55% from in state; 46% live on campus; 5% of students in fraternities, 2% in sororities

Most popular majors: 20% Business, Management, Marketing, and Related Support Services, 14% Education, 12% Biological and Biomedical Sciences, 10% Psychology, 7% Health Professions and Related Programs
Expenses: 2019-2020: $32,720; room/board: $9,840
Financial aid: (712) 274-5159; 80% of undergrads determined to have financial need; average aid package $26,519

Mount Mercy University

Cedar Rapids IA
(319) 368-6460
U.S. News ranking: Reg. U. (Mid. W), No. 40
Website: www.mtmercy.edu
Admissions email: admission@mtmercy.edu
Private; founded 1928
Affiliation: Roman Catholic
Freshman admissions: selective; 2018-2019: 1,409 applied, 885 accepted. Either SAT or ACT required. ACT 25/75 percentile: 19-25. High school rank: 23% in top tenth, 50% in top quarter, 79% in top half
Early decision deadline: N/A, notification date: N/A
Early action deadline: N/A, notification date: N/A
Application deadline (fall): rolling
Undergraduate student body: 1,074 full time, 427 part time; 31% male, 69% female; 1% American Indian, 2% Asian, 8% black, 1% Hispanic, 2% multiracial, 0% Pacific Islander, 78% white, 4% international; 92% from in

state; 43% live on campus; N/A of students in fraternities, N/A in sororities
Most popular majors: 28% Registered Nursing/Registered Nurse, 11% Business/Commerce, General, 5% Accounting, 5% Psychology, General, 4% Business Administration and Management, General
Expenses: 2019-2020: $33,930; room/board: $9,915
Financial aid: (319) 368-6467; 69% of undergrads determined to have financial need; average aid package $25,140

Northwestern College

Orange City IA
(800) 747-4757
U.S. News ranking: Reg. Coll. (Mid. W), No. 6
Website: www.nwciowa.edu
Admissions email: admissions@nwciowa.edu
Private; founded 1882
Affiliation: Reformed Church in America
Freshman admissions: selective; 2018-2019: 1,310 applied, 934 accepted. Either SAT or ACT required. ACT 25/75 percentile: 21-27. High school rank: 28% in top tenth, 53% in top quarter, 81% in top half
Early decision deadline: N/A, notification date: N/A
Early action deadline: N/A, notification date: N/A
Application deadline (fall): rolling
Undergraduate student body: 949 full time, 83 part time; 44% male, 56% female; 0% American Indian, 1% Asian, 2% black, 4% Hispanic, 2% multiracial, 0% Pacific Islander, 83% white, 3% international; 54% from in state; 88% live on campus; 0% of students in fraternities, 0% in sororities
Most popular majors: 21% Business Administration and Management, General, 12% Elementary Education and Teaching, 8% Registered Nursing/ Registered Nurse, 7% Biology/ Biological Sciences, General, 5% Kinesiology and Exercise Science
Expenses: 2019-2020: $32,300; room/board: $9,600
Financial aid: (712) 707-7131; 72% of undergrads determined to have financial need; average aid package $25,458

Simpson College

Indianola IA
(515) 961-1624
U.S. News ranking: Nat. Lib. Arts, No. 136
Website: www.simpson.edu
Admissions email: admiss@simpson.edu
Private; founded 1860
Affiliation: United Methodist
Freshman admissions: selective; 2018-2019: 1,401 applied, 1,180 accepted. Either SAT or ACT required. ACT 25/75 percentile: 20-25. High school rank: 22% in top tenth, 49% in top quarter, 82% in top half
Early decision deadline: N/A, notification date: N/A

Early action deadline: N/A, notification date: N/A
Application deadline (fall): rolling
Undergraduate student body: 1,198 full time, 193 part time; 47% male, 53% female; 0% American Indian, 1% Asian, 3% black, 5% Hispanic, 3% multiracial, 0% Pacific Islander, 82% white, 1% international; 82% from in state; 77% live on campus; 23% of students in fraternities, 27% in sororities
Most popular majors: 16% Business Administration and Management, General, 9% Elementary Education and Teaching, 8% Accounting, 8% Criminal Justice/Safety Studies, 6% Psychology, General
Expenses: 2019-2020: $40,666; room/board: $8,820
Financial aid: (515) 961-1596; 84% of undergrads determined to have financial need; average aid package $31,822

St. Ambrose University

Davenport IA
(563) 333-6300
U.S. News ranking: Reg. U. (Mid. W), No. 27
Website: www.sau.edu
Admissions email: admit@sau.edu
Private; founded 1882
Affiliation: Roman Catholic
Freshman admissions: selective; 2018-2019: 5,232 applied, 3,280 accepted. Either SAT or ACT required. ACT 25/75 percentile: 20-26. High school rank: 23% in top tenth, 44% in top quarter, 76% in top half
Early decision deadline: N/A, notification date: N/A
Early action deadline: N/A, notification date: N/A
Application deadline (fall): rolling
Undergraduate student body: 2,140 full time, 171 part time; 45% male, 55% female; 0% American Indian, 2% Asian, 4% black, 8% Hispanic, 3% multiracial, 0% Pacific Islander, 73% white, 5% international; 37% from in state; 68% live on campus; 0% of students in fraternities, 0% in sororities
Most popular majors: 24% Business, Management, Marketing, and Related Support Services, 15% Parks, Recreation, Leisure, and Fitness Studies, 11% Health Professions and Related Programs, 10% Psychology, 7% Education
Expenses: 2019-2020: $31,812; room/board: $11,024
Financial aid: (563) 333-6318; 76% of undergrads determined to have financial need; average aid package $22,923

University of Dubuque

Dubuque IA
(563) 589-3200
U.S. News ranking: Reg. U. (Mid. W), No. 95
Website: www.dbq.edu
Admissions email: admssns@dbq.edu
Private; founded 1852

Affiliation: Presbyterian Church (USA)
Freshman admissions: less selective; 2018-2019: 2,666 applied, 1,947 accepted. Either SAT or ACT required. ACT 25/75 percentile: 16-22. High school rank: 6% in top tenth, 20% in top quarter, 49% in top half
Early decision deadline: N/A, notification date: N/A
Early action deadline: N/A, notification date: N/A
Application deadline (fall): rolling
Undergraduate student body: 1,674 full time, 291 part time; 56% male, 44% female; 0% American Indian, 1% Asian, 16% black, 9% Hispanic, 3% multiracial, 0% Pacific Islander, 61% white, 6% international; 42% from in state; 46% live on campus; N/A of students in fraternities, N/A in sororities
Most popular majors: 26% Business, Management, Marketing, and Related Support Services, 13% Transportation and Materials Moving, 8% Education, 8% Health Professions and Related Programs, 8% Homeland Security, Law Enforcement, Firefighting and Related Protective Services
Expenses: 2019-2020: $35,570; room/board: $10,210
Financial aid: (563) 589-3125; 81% of undergrads determined to have financial need; average aid package $30,833

University of Iowa

Iowa City IA
(319) 335-3847
U.S. News ranking: Nat. U., No. 84
Website: www.uiowa.edu
Admissions email: admissions@uiowa.edu
Public; founded 1847
Freshman admissions: more selective; 2018-2019: 26,706 applied, 22,077 accepted. Either SAT or ACT required. ACT 25/75 percentile: 23-28. High school rank: 30% in top tenth, 62% in top quarter, 92% in top half
Early decision deadline: N/A, notification date: N/A
Early action deadline: N/A, notification date: N/A
Application deadline (fall): 5/1
Undergraduate student body: 21,690 full time, 2,299 part time; 47% male, 53% female; 0% American Indian, 4% Asian, 3% black, 8% Hispanic, 3% multiracial, 0% Pacific Islander, 72% white, 7% international; 61% from in state; 27% live on campus, 13% of students in fraternities, 16% in sororities
Most popular majors: 21% Business, Management, Marketing, and Related Support Services, 12% Parks, Recreation, Leisure, and Fitness Studies, 8% Engineering, 8% Social Sciences, 7% Communication, Journalism, and Related Programs
Expenses: 2019-2020: N/A in state, N/A out of state; room/board: $11,400
Financial aid: (319) 335-1450; 48% of undergrads determined to have financial need; average aid package $15,045

University of Northern Iowa

Cedar Falls IA
(800) 772-2037
U.S. News ranking: Reg. U. (Mid. W), No. 20
Website: uni.edu/
Admissions email: admissions@uni.edu
Public; founded 1876
Affiliation: Undenominational
Freshman admissions: selective; 2018-2019: 5,217 applied, 4,212 accepted. Either SAT or ACT required. ACT 25/75 percentile: 21-26. High school rank: 20% in top tenth, 51% in top quarter, 86% in top half
Early decision deadline: N/A, notification date: N/A
Early action deadline: N/A, notification date: N/A
Application deadline (fall): 8/15
Undergraduate student body: 8,745 full time, 816 part time; 42% male, 58% female; 0% American Indian, 1% Asian, 3% black, 4% Hispanic, 2% multiracial, 0% Pacific Islander, 82% white, 3% international; 94% from in state; 36% live on campus; 4% of students in fraternities, 7% in sororities
Most popular majors: 20% Business, Management, Marketing, and Related Support Services, 17% Education, 8% Communication, Journalism, and Related Programs, 6% Parks, Recreation, Leisure, and Fitness Studies, 5% Social Sciences
Expenses: 2019-2020: $8,938 in state, $19,480 out of state; room/board: $9,160
Financial aid: (319) 273-2722; 61% of undergrads determined to have financial need; average aid package $8,237

Upper Iowa University

Fayette IA
(800) 553-4150
U.S. News ranking: Reg. U. (Mid. W), second tier
Website: uiu.edu/
Admissions email: admission@uiu.edu
Private; founded 1857
Freshman admissions: less selective; 2018-2019: 1,261 applied, 1,022 accepted. Either SAT or ACT required. ACT 25/75 percentile: 18-23. High school rank: 1% in top tenth, 15% in top quarter, 41% in top half
Early decision deadline: N/A, notification date: N/A
Early action deadline: N/A, notification date: N/A
Application deadline (fall): rolling
Undergraduate student body: 1,970 full time, 2,024 part time; 39% male, 61% female; 0% American Indian, 2% Asian, 19% black, 6% Hispanic, 2% multiracial, 0% Pacific Islander, 58% white, 7% international; 2% from in state; N/A live on campus; N/A of students in fraternities, N/A in sororities
Most popular majors: 18% Psychology, General, 16% Business Administration and Management, General, 9% Public

Administration and Social Service Professions, 8% Registered Nursing/Registered Nurse, 6% Accounting
Expenses: 2019-2020: $31,685; room/board: $8,706
Financial aid: (563) 425-5299; 89% of undergrads determined to have financial need; average aid package $16,313

Waldorf University[1]

Forest City IA
(641) 585-8112
U.S. News ranking: Reg. U. (Mid. W), second tier
Website: www.waldorf.edu
Admissions email: admissions@waldorf.edu
For-profit
Application deadline (fall): N/A
Undergraduate student body: N/A full time, N/A part time
Expenses: N/A
Financial aid: N/A

Wartburg College

Waverly IA
(319) 352-8264
U.S. News ranking: Nat. Lib. Arts, No. 148
Website: www.wartburg.edu/
Admissions email: admissions@wartburg.edu
Private; founded 1852
Affiliation: Evangelical Lutheran Church
Freshman admissions: selective; 2018-2019: 4,298 applied, 3,254 accepted. Either SAT or ACT required. ACT 25/75 percentile: 20-26. High school rank: 22% in top tenth, 51% in top quarter, 79% in top half
Early decision deadline: N/A, notification date: N/A
Early action deadline: 12/1, notification date: N/A
Application deadline (fall): rolling
Undergraduate student body: 1,456 full time, 42 part time; 47% male, 53% female; 0% American Indian, 1% Asian, 4% black, 5% Hispanic, 3% multiracial, 0% Pacific Islander, 76% white, 8% international; 69% from in state; 87% live on campus; N/A of students in fraternities, N/A in sororities
Most popular majors: 17% Business/Commerce, General, 10% Biology/Biological Sciences, General, 6% Elementary Education and Teaching, 6% Engineering Science, 6% Mass Communication/Media Studies
Expenses: 2019-2020: $43,930; room/board: $9,280
Financial aid: (319) 352-8262; 77% of undergrads determined to have financial need; average aid package $33,393

William Penn University[1]

Oskaloosa IA
(641) 673-1012
U.S. News ranking: Reg. Coll. (Mid. W), second tier
Website: www.wmpenn.edu
Admissions email: admissions@wmpenn.edu
Private

Application deadline (fall): N/A
Undergraduate student body: N/A full time, N/A part time
Expenses: N/A
Financial aid: N/A

KANSAS

Baker University

Baldwin City KS
(800) 873-4282
U.S. News ranking: Nat. U., No. 254
Website: www.bakeru.edu
Admissions email: admission@bakeru.edu
Private; founded 1858
Affiliation: United Methodist
Freshman admissions: selective; 2018-2019: 807 applied, 707 accepted. Either SAT or ACT required. ACT 25/75 percentile: 20-25. High school rank: 19% in top tenth, 41% in top quarter, 83% in top half
Early decision deadline: N/A, notification date: N/A
Early action deadline: N/A, notification date: N/A
Application deadline (fall): rolling
Undergraduate student body: 850 full time, 364 part time; 50% male, 50% female; 1% American Indian, 1% Asian, 9% black, 9% Hispanic, 6% multiracial, 1% Pacific Islander, 70% white, 3% international; 71% from in state; 83% live on campus; 36% of students in fraternities, 45% in sororities
Most popular majors: 22% Business Administration and Management, General, 12% Kinesiology and Exercise Science, 10% Sport and Fitness Administration/Management, 8% Psychology, General, 5% Accounting
Expenses: 2019-2020: $29,800; room/board: $8,350
Financial aid: (785) 594-4595; 79% of undergrads determined to have financial need; average aid package $24,639

Benedictine College

Atchison KS
(800) 467-5340
U.S. News ranking: Reg. Coll. (Mid. W), No. 10
Website: www.benedictine.edu
Admissions email: bcadmiss@benedictine.edu
Private; founded 1858
Affiliation: Roman Catholic
Freshman admissions: selective; 2018-2019: 2,534 applied, 2,457 accepted. Either SAT or ACT required. ACT 25/75 percentile: 21-28. High school rank: 21% in top tenth, 36% in top quarter, 77% in top half
Early decision deadline: N/A, notification date: N/A
Early action deadline: N/A, notification date: N/A
Application deadline (fall): rolling
Undergraduate student body: 1,929 full time, 128 part time; 48% male, 52% female; 1% American Indian, 1% Asian, 3% black, 8% Hispanic, 5% multiracial, 0% Pacific Islander, 80% white,

2% international; 23% from in state; 79% live on campus; 0% of students in fraternities, 0% in sororities
Most popular majors: 23% Business, Management, Marketing, and Related Support Services, 10% Education, 6% Social Sciences, 6% Theology and Religious Vocations, 5% Psychology
Expenses: 2019-2020: $30,530; room/board: $10,500
Financial aid: (913) 360-7484; 66% of undergrads determined to have financial need; average aid package $24,088

Bethany College

Lindsborg KS
(800) 826-2281
U.S. News ranking: Reg. Coll. (Mid. W), No. 53
Website: www.bethanylb.edu
Admissions email: admissions@bethanylb.edu
Private; founded 1881
Affiliation: Evangelical Lutheran Church
Freshman admissions: selective; 2018-2019: N/A applied, N/A accepted. Either SAT or ACT required. ACT 25/75 percentile: 18-23. High school rank: N/A
Early decision deadline: N/A, notification date: N/A
Early action deadline: N/A, notification date: N/A
Application deadline (fall): rolling
Undergraduate student body: 752 full time, 54 part time; 54% male, 46% female; 1% American Indian, 1% Asian, 15% black, 18% Hispanic, 6% multiracial, 1% Pacific Islander, 59% white, 0% international
Most popular majors: Information not available
Expenses: 2019-2020: $29,565; room/board: $11,070
Financial aid: (785) 227-3380

Bethel College

North Newton KS
(800) 522-1887
U.S. News ranking: Reg. Coll. (Mid. W), No. 23
Website: www.bethelks.edu
Admissions email: admissions@bethelks.edu
Private; founded 1887
Affiliation: Mennonite Church
Freshman admissions: selective; 2018-2019: 1,093 applied, 482 accepted. Either SAT or ACT required. ACT 25/75 percentile: 18-24. High school rank: 18% in top tenth, 37% in top quarter, 78% in top half
Early decision deadline: N/A, notification date: N/A
Early action deadline: N/A, notification date: N/A
Application deadline (fall): N/A
Undergraduate student body: 430 full time, 14 part time; 46% male, 54% female; 1% American Indian, 2% Asian, 15% black, 9% Hispanic, 2% multiracial, 0% Pacific Islander, 70% white, 2% international; 65% from in state; 66% live on campus; 0% of students in fraternities, 0% in sororities

Most popular majors: 22% Business, Management, Marketing, and Related Support Services, 21% Health Professions and Related Programs, 11% Parks, Recreation, Leisure, and Fitness Studies, 8% Public Administration and Social Service Professions, 6% Biological and Biomedical Sciences
Expenses: 2019-2020: $29,390; room/board: $9,530
Financial aid: (316) 284-5232; 89% of undergrads determined to have financial need; average aid package $28,449

Central Christian College

McPherson KS
(620) 241-0723
U.S. News ranking: Reg. Coll. (Mid. W), second tier
Website: www.centralchristian.edu
Admissions email: admissions@centralchristian.edu
Private; founded 2004
Affiliation: Free Methodist
Freshman admissions: less selective; 2018-2019: 584 applied, 269 accepted. Neither SAT nor ACT required. ACT 25/75 percentile: 18-22. High school rank: 5% in top tenth, 21% in top quarter, 52% in top half
Early decision deadline: N/A, notification date: N/A
Early action deadline: N/A, notification date: N/A
Application deadline (fall): rolling
Undergraduate student body: 639 full time, 83 part time; 50% male, 50% female; 2% American Indian, 1% Asian, 19% black, 14% Hispanic, 3% multiracial, 0% Pacific Islander, 55% white, 3% international; 27% from in state; 90% live on campus; 0% of students in fraternities, 0% in sororities
Most popular majors: 37% Homeland Security, Law Enforcement, Firefighting and Related Protective Services, 24% Business, Management, Marketing, and Related Support Services, 10% Parks, Recreation, Leisure, and Fitness Studies, 8% Health Professions and Related Programs, 7% Psychology
Expenses: 2019-2020: $28,700; room/board: $7,160
Financial aid: (620) 241-0723; 87% of undergrads determined to have financial need; average aid package $17,858

Donnelly College

Kansas City KS
(913) 621-8700
U.S. News ranking: Reg. Coll. (Mid. W), unranked
Website: donnelly.edu
Admissions email: admissions@donnelly.edu
Private; founded 1949
Affiliation: Roman Catholic
Freshman admissions: least selective; 2018-2019: N/A applied, N/A accepted. Neither SAT nor ACT required. SAT 25/75 percentile: N/A. High school rank: N/A

Early decision deadline: N/A, notification date: N/A
Early action deadline: N/A, notification date: N/A
Application deadline (fall): rolling
Undergraduate student body: 189 full time, 116 part time; 28% male, 72% female; 1% American Indian, 9% Asian, 33% black, 35% Hispanic, 8% multiracial, 0% Pacific Islander, 13% white, 1% international
Most popular majors: Information not available
Expenses: 2018-2019: $7,260; room/board: N/A
Financial aid: N/A

Emporia State University
Emporia KS
(620) 341-5465
U.S. News ranking: Reg. U. (Mid. W), No. 95
Website: www.emporia.edu
Admissions email: go2esu@emporia.edu
Public; founded 1863
Freshman admissions: selective; 2018-2019: 1,648 applied, 1,406 accepted. Neither SAT nor ACT required. ACT 25/75 percentile: 19-25. High school rank: 13% in top tenth, 41% in top quarter, 75% in top half
Early decision deadline: N/A, notification date: N/A
Early action deadline: N/A, notification date: N/A
Application deadline (fall): rolling
Undergraduate student body: 3,293 full time, 276 part time; 37% male, 63% female; 0% American Indian, 1% Asian, 4% black, 7% Hispanic, 10% multiracial, 0% Pacific Islander, 69% white, 7% international; 87% from in state; 22% live on campus; 13% of students in fraternities, 11% in sororities
Most popular majors: 26% Education, 18% Business, Management, Marketing, and Related Support Services, 13% Health Professions and Related Programs, 5% Liberal Arts and Sciences, General Studies and Humanities, 5% Social Sciences
Expenses: 2019-2020: $6,799 in state, $20,715 out of state; room/board: $9,412
Financial aid: (620) 341-5457; 61% of undergrads determined to have financial need; average aid package $9,377

Fort Hays State University
Hays KS
(800) 628-3478
U.S. News ranking: Reg. U. (Mid. W), second tier
Website: www.fhsu.edu
Admissions email: tigers@fhsu.edu
Public; founded 1902
Freshman admissions: selective; 2018-2019: 2,191 applied, 2,022 accepted. Either SAT or ACT required for some. ACT 25/75 percentile: 18-23. High school rank: 15% in top tenth, 34% in top quarter, 66% in top half
Early decision deadline: N/A, notification date: N/A

Early action deadline: N/A, notification date: N/A
Application deadline (fall): rolling
Undergraduate student body: 5,863 full time, 6,917 part time; 41% male, 59% female; 0% American Indian, 1% Asian, 3% black, 8% Hispanic, 2% multiracial, 0% Pacific Islander, 52% white, 33% international; N/A from in state; 11% live on campus; 2% of students in fraternities, 2% in sororities
Most popular majors: 40% Business, Management, Marketing, and Related Support Services, 11% Education, 10% Liberal Arts and Sciences, General Studies and Humanities, 9% Social Sciences, 5% Psychology
Expenses: 2018-2019: $5,130 in state, $15,210 out of state; room/board: $8,034
Financial aid: (785) 628-4408

Friends University
Wichita KS
(316) 295-5100
U.S. News ranking: Reg. U. (Mid. W), second tier
Website: www.friends.edu
Admissions email: admission@friends.edu
Private; founded 1898
Freshman admissions: selective; 2018-2019: 792 applied, 375 accepted. Either SAT or ACT required. ACT 25/75 percentile: 18-24. High school rank: 18% in top tenth, 37% in top quarter, 65% in top half
Early decision deadline: N/A, notification date: N/A
Early action deadline: N/A, notification date: N/A
Application deadline (fall): rolling
Undergraduate student body: 886 full time, 470 part time; 42% male, 58% female; 1% American Indian, 2% Asian, 8% black, 8% Hispanic, 2% multiracial, 0% Pacific Islander, 62% white, 0% international; 78% from in state; 30% live on campus; 0% of students in fraternities, 0% in sororities
Most popular majors: 40% Business, Management, Marketing, and Related Support Services, 12% Education, 8% Psychology, 7% Biological and Biomedical Sciences, 6% Computer and Information Sciences and Support Services
Expenses: 2019-2020: $29,394; room/board: $7,980
Financial aid: (316) 295-5200; 84% of undergrads determined to have financial need; average aid package $18,619

Hesston College
Hesston KS
(620) 327-4221
U.S. News ranking: Reg. Coll. (Mid. W), No. 29
Admissions email: N/A
Private; founded 1909
Affiliation: Mennonite Church
Freshman admissions: less selective; 2018-2019: 861 applied, 441 accepted. Either SAT or ACT required. ACT 25/75 percentile: 18-23. High school rank: N/A

Early decision deadline: N/A, notification date: N/A
Early action deadline: N/A, notification date: N/A
Application deadline (fall): rolling
Undergraduate student body: 377 full time, 42 part time; 40% male, 60% female; 1% American Indian, 1% Asian, 6% black, 12% Hispanic, 3% multiracial, 0% Pacific Islander, 62% white, 14% international
Most popular majors: 100% Registered Nursing/Registered Nurse
Expenses: 2019-2020: $27,690; room/board: $9,140
Financial aid: (620) 327-8220; 70% of undergrads determined to have financial need; average aid package $22,499

Kansas State University
Manhattan KS
(785) 532-6250
U.S. News ranking: Nat. U., No. 162
Website: www.k-state.edu
Admissions email: k-state@k-state.edu
Public; founded 1863
Freshman admissions: selective; 2018-2019: 8,488 applied, 7,990 accepted. Either SAT or ACT required. ACT 25/75 percentile: 22-28. High school rank: 27% in top tenth, 52% in top quarter, 81% in top half
Early decision deadline: N/A, notification date: N/A
Early action deadline: N/A, notification date: N/A
Application deadline (fall): rolling
Undergraduate student body: 16,230 full time, 1,639 part time; 53% male, 47% female; 0% American Indian, 2% Asian, 3% black, 8% Hispanic, 4% multiracial, 0% Pacific Islander, 78% white, 4% international; N/A from in state; 24% live on campus; N/A of students in fraternities, N/A in sororities
Most popular majors: 18% Business, Management, Marketing, and Related Support Services, 12% Agriculture, Agriculture Operations, and Related Sciences, 12% Engineering, 8% Education, 8% Social Sciences
Expenses: 2018-2019: $10,383 in state, $25,887 out of state; room/board: $9,680
Financial aid: (785) 532-7626; 51% of undergrads determined to have financial need; average aid package $13,583

Kansas Wesleyan University
Salina KS
(785) 833-4305
U.S. News ranking: Reg. Coll. (Mid. W), No. 39
Website: www.kwu.edu
Admissions email: admissions@kwu.edu
Private; founded 1886
Affiliation: United Methodist

Freshman admissions: selective; 2018-2019: 891 applied, 423 accepted. Either SAT or ACT required. ACT 25/75 percentile: 20-25. High school rank: 17% in top tenth, 36% in top quarter, 73% in top half
Early decision deadline: N/A, notification date: N/A
Early action deadline: N/A, notification date: N/A
Application deadline (fall): rolling
Undergraduate student body: 606 full time, 62 part time; 60% male, 40% female; 0% American Indian, 1% Asian, 14% black, 17% Hispanic, 0% multiracial, 0% Pacific Islander, 62% white, 2% international; 43% from in state; 62% live on campus; 0% of students in fraternities, 0% in sororities
Most popular majors: 26% Business, Management, Marketing, and Related Support Services, 12% Parks, Recreation, Leisure, and Fitness Studies, 10% Health Professions and Related Programs, 9% Education, 8% Homeland Security, Law Enforcement, Firefighting and Related Protective Services
Expenses: 2019-2020: $30,020; room/board: $9,800
Financial aid: (785) 833-4316; 88% of undergrads determined to have financial need; average aid package $23,050

McPherson College
McPherson KS
(800) 365-7402
U.S. News ranking: Reg. Coll. (Mid. W), No. 26
Website: www.mcpherson.edu
Admissions email: admissions@mcpherson.edu
Private; founded 1887
Affiliation: Church of Brethren
Freshman admissions: selective; 2018-2019: 1,222 applied, 942 accepted. Either SAT or ACT required for some. ACT 25/75 percentile: 19-23. High school rank: 10% in top tenth, 28% in top quarter, 61% in top half
Early decision deadline: N/A, notification date: N/A
Early action deadline: N/A, notification date: N/A
Application deadline (fall): rolling
Undergraduate student body: 706 full time, 10 part time; 67% male, 33% female; 2% American Indian, 1% Asian, 13% black, 15% Hispanic, 2% multiracial, 0% Pacific Islander, 63% white, 1% international; 35% from in state; 71% live on campus; 0% of students in fraternities, 0% in sororities
Most popular majors: 25% Mechanical Engineering Related Technologies/Technicians, 19% Business Administration, Management and Operations, 15% Health and Physical Education/Fitness, 7% Psychology, General, 6% Biology, General
Expenses: 2019-2020: $30,077; room/board: $9,063
Financial aid: (620) 242-0400; 85% of undergrads determined to have financial need; average aid package $28,575

MidAmerica Nazarene University[7]
Olathe KS
(913) 971-3380
U.S. News ranking: Reg. U. (Mid. W), No. 92
Website: www.mnu.edu
Admissions email: admissions@mnu.edu
Private; founded 1966
Affiliation: Church of the Nazarene
Freshman admissions: selective; 2018-2019: 926 applied, 542 accepted. Either SAT or ACT required. ACT 25/75 percentile: 18-26. High school rank: 18% in top tenth, 42% in top quarter, 68% in top half
Early decision deadline: N/A, notification date: N/A
Early action deadline: N/A, notification date: N/A
Application deadline (fall): N/A
Undergraduate student body: 982 full time, 322 part time
Most popular majors: Information not available
Expenses: 2019-2020: $31,786; room/board: $9,012
Financial aid: (913) 971-3298

Newman University
Wichita KS
(877) 639-6268
U.S. News ranking: Reg. U. (Mid. W), No. 105
Website: www.newmanu.edu
Admissions email: admissions@newmanu.edu
Private; founded 1933
Affiliation: Roman Catholic
Freshman admissions: selective; 2018-2019: 1,105 applied, 699 accepted. Either SAT or ACT required for some. ACT 25/75 percentile: 19-25. High school rank: 26% in top tenth, 54% in top quarter, 84% in top half
Early decision deadline: N/A, notification date: N/A
Early action deadline: N/A, notification date: N/A
Application deadline (fall): rolling
Undergraduate student body: 1,029 full time, 1,735 part time; 38% male, 62% female; 1% American Indian, 7% Asian, 5% black, 13% Hispanic, 3% multiracial, 0% Pacific Islander, 63% white, 7% international; 84% from in state; 27% live on campus; 0% of students in fraternities, 0% in sororities
Most popular majors: 14% Education, 11% Biological and Biomedical Sciences, 8% Psychology, 6% Homeland Security, Law Enforcement, Firefighting and Related Protective Services, 5% Communication, Journalism, and Related Programs
Expenses: 2019-2020: $31,774; room/board: $9,930
Financial aid: (316) 942-4291; 77% of undergrads determined to have financial need; average aid package $22,352

Ottawa University

Ottawa KS
(785) 242-5200
U.S. News ranking: Reg. Coll. (Mid. W), No. 43
Website: www.ottawa.edu
Admissions email: admiss@ottawa.edu
Private; founded 1865
Affiliation: American Baptist
Freshman admissions: selective; 2018-2019: 1,168 applied, 302 accepted. Neither SAT nor ACT required. ACT 25/75 percentile: 18-22. High school rank: 4% in top tenth, 11% in top quarter, 52% in top half
Early decision deadline: N/A, notification date: N/A
Early action deadline: N/A, notification date: N/A
Application deadline (fall): 8/15
Undergraduate student body: 671 full time, 35 part time; 58% male, 42% female; 3% American Indian, 1% Asian, 14% black, 12% Hispanic, 3% multiracial, 1% Pacific Islander, 54% white, 0% international; 48% from in state; 69% live on campus; 0% of students in fraternities, 0% in sororities
Most popular majors: 15% Kinesiology and Exercise Science, 10% Biology/Biological Sciences, General, 10% Business Administration and Management, General, 9% Psychology, General, 8% History, General
Expenses: 2019-2020: $30,580; room/board: $11,478
Financial aid: (602) 749-5120; 88% of undergrads determined to have financial need; average aid package $12,466

Pittsburg State University

Pittsburg KS
(800) 854-7488
U.S. News ranking: Reg. U. (Mid. W), No. 95
Website: www.pittstate.edu
Admissions email: psuadmit@pittstate.edu
Public; founded 1903
Freshman admissions: selective; 2018-2019: 2,418 applied, 2,166 accepted. ACT required. ACT 25/75 percentile: 18-24. High school rank: 16% in top tenth, 37% in top quarter, 71% in top half
Early decision deadline: N/A, notification date: N/A
Early action deadline: N/A, notification date: N/A
Application deadline (fall): N/A
Undergraduate student body: 4,865 full time, 537 part time; 51% male, 49% female; 1% American Indian, 1% Asian, 4% black, 6% Hispanic, 7% multiracial, 0% Pacific Islander, 79% white, 2% international
Most popular majors: 21% Business, Management, Marketing, and Related Support Services, 15% Engineering Technologies and Engineering-Related Fields, 13% Education, 9% Health Professions and Related Programs, 6% Psychology

Expenses: 2019-2020: $7,338 in state, $18,682 out of state; room/board: $7,996
Financial aid: (620) 235-4240; 88% of undergrads determined to have financial need; average aid package $7,073

Southwestern College

Winfield KS
(620) 229-6236
U.S. News ranking: Reg. U. (Mid. W), second tier
Website: www.sckans.edu
Admissions email: scadmit@sckans.edu
Private; founded 1885
Affiliation: United Methodist
Freshman admissions: selective; 2018-2019: 846 applied, 468 accepted. Either SAT or ACT required. ACT 25/75 percentile: 18-22. High school rank: 11% in top tenth, 34% in top quarter, 64% in top half
Early decision deadline: N/A, notification date: N/A
Early action deadline: N/A, notification date: N/A
Application deadline (fall): 8/25
Undergraduate student body: 681 full time, 650 part time; 64% male, 36% female; 1% American Indian, 2% Asian, 11% black, 9% Hispanic, 3% multiracial, 1% Pacific Islander, 42% white, 4% international; 34% from in state; 32% live on campus; N/A of students in fraternities, N/A in sororities
Most popular majors: 11% Business, Management, Marketing, and Related Support Services, Other, 11% Operations Management and Supervision, 8% Securities Services Administration/Management, 6% Business Administration and Management, General, 6% Computer Programming/Programmer, General
Expenses: 2019-2020: $31,650; room/board: $8,110
Financial aid: (620) 229-6215; 81% of undergrads determined to have financial need; average aid package $23,923

Sterling College[1]

Sterling KS
(800) 346-1017
U.S. News ranking: Reg. Coll. (Mid. W), second tier
Website: www.sterling.edu
Admissions email: admissions@sterling.edu
Private; founded 1887
Application deadline (fall): rolling
Undergraduate student body: N/A full time, N/A part time
Expenses: 2018-2019: $26,300; room/board: $7,426
Financial aid: (620) 278-4226

Tabor College

Hillsboro KS
(620) 947-3121
U.S. News ranking: Reg. Coll. (Mid. W), No. 49
Website: www.tabor.edu
Admissions email: admissions@tabor.edu
Private; founded 1908

Affiliation: Mennonite Brethren Church
Freshman admissions: selective; 2018-2019: 937 applied, 539 accepted. Either SAT or ACT required. ACT 25/75 percentile: 18-24. High school rank: 11% in top tenth, 32% in top quarter, 63% in top half
Early decision deadline: N/A, notification date: N/A
Early action deadline: N/A, notification date: N/A
Application deadline (fall): rolling
Undergraduate student body: 541 full time, 114 part time; 56% male, 44% female; 1% American Indian, 0% Asian, 11% black, 14% Hispanic, 6% multiracial, 1% Pacific Islander, 63% white, 3% international; 46% from in state; 93% live on campus; N/A of students in fraternities, N/A in sororities
Most popular majors: 24% Business, Management, Marketing, and Related Support Services, 18% Health Professions and Related Programs, 14% Parks, Recreation, Leisure, and Fitness Studies, 8% Education, 7% Psychology
Expenses: 2018-2019: $27,220; room/board: $9,577
Financial aid: (620) 947-3121

University of Kansas

Lawrence KS
(785) 864-3911
U.S. News ranking: Nat. U., No. 130
Website: ku.edu
Admissions email: adm@ku.edu
Public; founded 1865
Freshman admissions: more selective; 2018-2019: 14,752 applied, 13,529 accepted. Either SAT or ACT required. ACT 25/75 percentile: 23-29. High school rank: 28% in top tenth, 56% in top quarter, 86% in top half
Early decision deadline: N/A, notification date: N/A
Early action deadline: N/A, notification date: N/A
Application deadline (fall): 8/19
Undergraduate student body: 17,333 full time, 2,263 part time; 48% male, 52% female; 0% American Indian, 5% Asian, 4% black, 8% Hispanic, 5% multiracial, 0% Pacific Islander, 71% white, 6% international; 66% from in state; 25% live on campus; 18% of students in fraternities, 26% in sororities
Most popular majors: 16% Business, Management, Marketing, and Related Support Services, 12% Health Professions and Related Programs, 11% Engineering, 9% Communication, Journalism, and Related Programs, 6% Visual and Performing Arts
Expenses: 2019-2020: $11,148 in state, $27,358 out of state; room/board: $10,350
Financial aid: (785) 864-4700; 47% of undergrads determined to have financial need; average aid package $16,575

University of St. Mary

Leavenworth KS
(913) 758-5151
U.S. News ranking: Reg. U. (Mid. W), No. 84
Website: www.stmary.edu
Admissions email: admiss@stmary.edu
Private; founded 1923
Affiliation: Roman Catholic
Freshman admissions: selective; 2018-2019: 996 applied, 611 accepted. Either SAT or ACT required. ACT 25/75 percentile: 19-23. High school rank: 9% in top tenth, 30% in top quarter, 63% in top half
Early decision deadline: N/A, notification date: N/A
Early action deadline: N/A, notification date: N/A
Application deadline (fall): rolling
Undergraduate student body: 675 full time, 57 part time; 52% male, 48% female; 1% American Indian, 1% Asian, 12% black, 16% Hispanic, 5% multiracial, 1% Pacific Islander, 49% white, 1% international; 50% from in state; 39% live on campus; 0% of students in fraternities, 0% in sororities
Most popular majors: 55% Health Professions and Related Programs, 8% Psychology, 7% Biological and Biomedical Sciences, 6% Business, Management, Marketing, and Related Support Services, 6% Education
Expenses: 2019-2020: $29,880; room/board: $8,140
Financial aid: (913) 758-6172; 86% of undergrads determined to have financial need; average aid package $31,040

Washburn University

Topeka KS
(785) 670-1030
U.S. News ranking: Nat. U., second tier
Website: www.washburn.edu
Admissions email: admissions@washburn.edu
Public; founded 1865
Freshman admissions: selective; 2018-2019: 1,581 applied, 1,581 accepted. ACT required. ACT 25/75 percentile: 18-24. High school rank: 13% in top tenth, 33% in top quarter, 65% in top half
Early decision deadline: N/A, notification date: N/A
Early action deadline: N/A, notification date: N/A
Application deadline (fall): 8/1
Undergraduate student body: 3,793 full time, 1,918 part time; 39% male, 61% female; 1% American Indian, 1% Asian, 6% black, 12% Hispanic, 5% multiracial, 0% Pacific Islander, 65% white, 4% international; 93% from in state; 13% live on campus; 7% of students in fraternities, 8% in sororities
Most popular majors: 31% Health Professions and Related Programs, 14% Business, Management, Marketing, and Related Support Services, 7% Homeland Security,

Law Enforcement, Firefighting and Related Protective Services, 6% Education, 5% Communication, Journalism, and Related Programs
Expenses: 2018-2019: $8,312 in state, $18,560 out of state; room/board: N/A
Financial aid: (785) 670-2770

Wichita State University

Wichita KS
(316) 978-3085
U.S. News ranking: Nat. U., second tier
Website: www.wichita.edu
Admissions email: admissions@wichita.edu
Public; founded 1895
Freshman admissions: selective; 2018-2019: 5,674 applied, 4,237 accepted. Either SAT or ACT required for some. ACT 25/75 percentile: 20-26. High school rank: 19% in top tenth, 46% in top quarter, 80% in top half
Early decision deadline: N/A, notification date: N/A
Early action deadline: N/A, notification date: N/A
Application deadline (fall): rolling
Undergraduate student body: 8,855 full time, 4,151 part time; 45% male, 55% female; 1% American Indian, 7% Asian, 6% black, 13% Hispanic, 5% multiracial, 0% Pacific Islander, 60% white, 6% international; 91% from in state; 9% live on campus; 7% of students in fraternities, 7% in sororities
Most popular majors: 18% Business, Management, Marketing, and Related Support Services, 18% Health Professions and Related Programs, 13% Engineering, 8% Education, 6% Psychology
Expenses: 2019-2020: $8,272 in state, $17,453 out of state; room/board: $11,053
Financial aid: (316) 978-3430; 61% of undergrads determined to have financial need; average aid package $7,963

KENTUCKY

Alice Lloyd College

Pippa Passes KY
(888) 280-4252
U.S. News ranking: Reg. Coll. (S), No. 21
Website: www.alc.edu
Admissions email: admissions@alc.edu
Private; founded 1923
Freshman admissions: selective; 2018-2019: 4,720 applied, 365 accepted. Either SAT or ACT required. ACT 25/75 percentile: 18-23. High school rank: 13% in top tenth, 26% in top quarter, 37% in top half
Early decision deadline: N/A, notification date: N/A
Early action deadline: N/A, notification date: N/A
Application deadline (fall): 7/1
Undergraduate student body: 573 full time, 19 part time; 47% male, 53% female; 0% American

Indian, 0% Asian, 2% black, 1% Hispanic, 0% multiracial, 0% Pacific Islander, 95% white, 1% international; 67% from in state; N/A live on campus; N/A of students in fraternities, N/A in sororities
Most popular majors: 17% Biological and Biomedical Sciences, 17% Education, 17% Social Sciences, 11% Parks, Recreation, Leisure, and Fitness Studies, 8% Parks, Recreation, Leisure, and Fitness Studies
Expenses: 2019-2020: $12,230; room/board: $7,160
Financial aid: (606) 368-6058; 88% of undergrads determined to have financial need; average aid package $15,148

Asbury University
Wilmore KY
(800) 888-1818
U.S. News ranking: Reg. U. (S), No. 9
Website: www.asbury.edu
Admissions email: admissions@asbury.edu
Private; founded 1890
Affiliation: Other Protestant
Freshman admissions: more selective; 2018-2019: 1,366 applied, 912 accepted. Neither SAT nor ACT required. ACT 25/75 percentile: 21-28. High school rank: 28% in top tenth, 54% in top quarter, 80% in top half
Early decision deadline: N/A, notification date: N/A
Early action deadline: N/A, notification date: N/A
Application deadline (fall): rolling
Undergraduate student body: 1,292 full time, 405 part time; 41% male, 59% female; 0% American Indian, 2% Asian, 4% black, 7% Hispanic, 2% multiracial, 0% Pacific Islander, 77% white, 5% international
Most popular majors: 14% Business/Commerce, General, 13% Radio, Television, and Digital Communication, Other, 11% Elementary Education and Teaching, 8% Educational Leadership and Administration, General, 7% Equestrian/Equine Studies
Expenses: 2019-2020: $30,952; room/board: $7,536
Financial aid: (859) 858-3511; 77% of undergrads determined to have financial need; average aid package $21,820

Bellarmine University
Louisville KY
(502) 272-7100
U.S. News ranking: Nat. U., No. 197
Website: www.bellarmine.edu
Admissions email: admissions@bellarmine.edu
Private; founded 1950
Affiliation: Roman Catholic
Freshman admissions: selective; 2018-2019: 5,535 applied, 4,751 accepted. Either SAT or ACT required. ACT 25/75 percentile: 22-28. High school rank: N/A
Early decision deadline: N/A, notification date: N/A

Early action deadline: 11/1, notification date: 11/15
Application deadline (fall): 8/15
Undergraduate student body: 2,401 full time, 151 part time; 36% male, 64% female; 0% American Indian, 2% Asian, 5% black, 4% Hispanic, 4% multiracial, 0% Pacific Islander, 80% white, 1% international; 71% from in state; 40% live on campus; 1% of students in fraternities, 1% in sororities
Most popular majors: 26% Health Professions and Related Programs, 13% Business, Management, Marketing, and Related Support Services, 10% Parks, Recreation, Leisure, and Fitness Studies, 7% Communication, Journalism, and Related Programs, 7% Psychology
Expenses: 2019-2020: $42,430; room/board: $9,420
Financial aid: (502) 272-7300; 79% of undergrads determined to have financial need; average aid package $35,031

Berea College
Berea KY
(859) 985-3500
U.S. News ranking: Nat. Lib. Arts, No. 46
Website: www.berea.edu
Admissions email: admissions@berea.edu
Private; founded 1855
Freshman admissions: more selective; 2018-2019: 1,576 applied, 602 accepted. Either SAT or ACT required. ACT 25/75 percentile: 22-27. High school rank: 22% in top tenth, 69% in top quarter, 96% in top half
Early decision deadline: N/A, notification date: N/A
Early action deadline: N/A, notification date: N/A
Application deadline (fall): 3/31
Undergraduate student body: 1,631 full time, 42 part time; 42% male, 58% female; 0% American Indian, 3% Asian, 16% black, 12% Hispanic, 7% multiracial, 0% Pacific Islander, 54% white, 8% international; 42% from in state; 87% live on campus, 0% of students in fraternities, 0% in sororities
Most popular majors: 9% Biological and Biomedical Sciences, 8% Business, Management, Marketing, and Related Support Services, 8% Social Sciences, 7% Computer and Information Sciences and Support Services, 7% Visual and Performing Arts
Expenses: 2019-2020: $600; room/board: $6,966
Financial aid: (859) 985 3313; 100% of undergrads determined to have financial need; average aid package $47,527

Brescia University
Owensboro KY
(270) 686-4241
U.S. News ranking: Reg. Coll. (S), No. 29
Website: www.brescia.edu
Admissions email: admissions@brescia.edu
Private; founded 1950
Affiliation: Roman Catholic

Freshman admissions: selective; 2018-2019: 7,654 applied, 2,971 accepted. Either SAT or ACT required. ACT 25/75 percentile: 19-25. High school rank: N/A
Early decision deadline: N/A, notification date: N/A
Early action deadline: N/A, notification date: N/A
Application deadline (fall): rolling
Undergraduate student body: 783 full time, 206 part time; 30% male, 70% female; 1% American Indian, 1% Asian, 13% black, 7% Hispanic, 1% multiracial, 0% Pacific Islander, 61% white, 1% international; 50% from in state; 50% live on campus; 0% of students in fraternities, 0% in sororities
Most popular majors: 50% Social Work, 8% Psychology, General, 7% Accounting, 7% Liberal Arts and Sciences/Liberal Studies, 6% Audiology/Audiologist and Speech-Language Pathology/Pathologist
Expenses: 2019-2020: $23,500; room/board: $9,940
Financial aid: (270) 686-4253; 90% of undergrads determined to have financial need; average aid package $15,728

Campbellsville University
Campbellsville KY
(270) 789-5220
U.S. News ranking: Reg. U. (S), No. 92
Website: www.campbellsville.edu
Admissions email: admissions@campbellsville.edu
Private; founded 1906
Freshman admissions: selective; 2018-2019: 3,542 applied, 2,952 accepted. Neither SAT nor ACT required. ACT 25/75 percentile: 18-24. High school rank: 15% in top tenth, 36% in top quarter, 67% in top half
Early decision deadline: N/A, notification date: N/A
Early action deadline: N/A, notification date: N/A
Application deadline (fall): rolling
Undergraduate student body: 2,263 full time, 2,876 part time; 40% male, 60% female; 0% American Indian, 0% Asian, 13% black, 3% Hispanic, 2% multiracial, 0% Pacific Islander, 69% white, 6% international; 84% from in state; 56% live on campus; 0% of students in fraternities, 0% in sororities
Most popular majors: 17% Business/Commerce, General, 9% Criminal Justice/Law Enforcement Administration, 8% Social Work, 6% Sport and Fitness Administration/Management, 5% Child Care Provider/Assistant
Expenses: 2019-2020: $25,400; room/board: $8,900
Financial aid: (270) 789-5013; 83% of undergrads determined to have financial need; average aid package $19,749

Centre College
Danville KY
(859) 238-5350
U.S. News ranking: Nat. Lib. Arts, No. 53
Website: www.centre.edu
Admissions email: admission@centre.edu
Private; founded 1819
Affiliation: Presbyterian
Freshman admissions: more selective; 2018-2019: 2,457 applied, 1,795 accepted. Either SAT or ACT required. ACT 25/75 percentile: 27-32. High school rank: 55% in top tenth, 85% in top quarter, 99% in top half
Early decision deadline: 11/15, notification date: 12/15
Early action deadline: 12/1, notification date: 1/15
Application deadline (fall): 1/15
Undergraduate student body: 1,433 full time, 1 part time; 49% male, 51% female; 0% American Indian, 5% Asian, 5% black, 7% Hispanic, 3% multiracial, 0% Pacific Islander, 73% white, 6% international; 53% from in state; 77% live on campus; 50% of students in fraternities, 52% in sororities
Most popular majors: 17% Economics, Other, 11% International/Global Studies, 8% Biology/Biological Sciences, General, 8% History, General, 8% Psychology, General
Expenses: 2019-2020: $43,000; room/board: $10,740
Financial aid: (859) 238 5365; 57% of undergrads determined to have financial need; average aid package $35,122

Eastern Kentucky University
Richmond KY
(800) 465-9191
U.S. News ranking: Reg. U. (S), No. 54
Website: www.eku.edu
Admissions email: admissions@eku.edu
Public; founded 1906
Freshman admissions: selective; 2018-2019: 9,116 applied, 7,957 accepted. Either SAT or ACT required. ACT 25/75 percentile: 20-26. High school rank: 17% in top tenth, 43% in top quarter, 74% in top half
Early decision deadline: N/A, notification date: N/A
Early action deadline: N/A, notification date: N/A
Application deadline (fall): 8/1
Undergraduate student body: 10,452 full time, 2,947 part time; 42% male, 58% female; 0% American Indian, 1% Asian, 6% black, 3% Hispanic, 3% multiracial, 0% Pacific Islander, 84% white, 1% international; 87% from in state; N/A live on campus; 11% of students in fraternities, 9% in sororities
Most popular majors: 20% Health Professions and Related Programs, 15% Homeland Security, Law Enforcement, Firefighting and Related Protective Services, 10% Business, Management,

Marketing, and Related Support Services, 8% Liberal Arts and Sciences, General Studies and Humanities, 7% Psychology
Expenses: 2019-2020: $9,566 in state, $19,638 out of state; room/board: $10,364
Financial aid: (859) 622-2361; 72% of undergrads determined to have financial need; average aid package $11,677

Georgetown College
Georgetown KY
(502) 863-8009
U.S. News ranking: Nat. Lib. Arts, No. 157
Website: www.georgetowncollege.edu
Admissions email: admissions@georgetowncollege.edu
Private; founded 1829
Freshman admissions: selective; 2018-2019: 3,629 applied, 1,740 accepted. Either SAT or ACT required. ACT 25/75 percentile: 20-26. High school rank: 17% in top tenth, 40% in top quarter, 68% in top half
Early decision deadline: N/A, notification date: N/A
Early action deadline: N/A, notification date: N/A
Application deadline (fall): 8/22
Undergraduate student body: 912 full time, 49 part time; 45% male, 55% female; 0% American Indian, 1% Asian, 10% black, 4% Hispanic, 4% multiracial, 0% Pacific Islander, 77% white, 0% international
Most popular majors: 10% Biology/Biological Sciences, General, 8% Communication and Media Studies, Other, 8% Elementary Education and Teaching, 7% Kinesiology and Exercise Science, 7% Psychology, General
Expenses: 2019-2020: $39,810; room/board: $10,160
Financial aid: (502) 863-8027; 87% of undergrads determined to have financial need; average aid package $34,952

Kentucky Christian University[1]
Grayson KY
(800) 522-3181
U.S. News ranking: Reg. Coll. (S), No. 53
Website: www.kcu.edu
Admissions email: knights@kcu.edu
Private; founded 1919
Application deadline (fall): 8/1
Undergraduate student body: N/A full time, N/A part time
Expenses: N/A
Financial aid: (606) 474-3226

Kentucky State University
Frankfort KY
(877) 367-5978
U.S. News ranking: Reg. Coll. (S), No. 31
Website: www.kysu.edu
Admissions email: admissions@kysu.edu
Public; founded 1886

Freshman admissions: less selective; 2018-2019: 3,689 applied, 1,673 accepted. Either SAT or ACT required. ACT 25/75 percentile: 16-26. High school rank: N/A
Early decision deadline: N/A, notification date: N/A
Early action deadline: N/A, notification date: N/A
Application deadline (fall): 7/31
Undergraduate student body: 1,081 full time, 585 part time; 40% male, 60% female; 0% American Indian, 1% Asian, 45% black, 2% Hispanic, 3% multiracial, 2% Pacific Islander, 17% white, 0% international
Most popular majors: 16% Registered Nursing/Registered Nurse, 11% Business Administration and Management, General, 10% Health and Physical Education/Fitness, Other, 8% Mass Communication/Media Studies, 6% Social Work
Expenses: 2019-2020: $7,796 in state, $18,704 out of state; room/board: $6,690
Financial aid: (502) 597-5759; 91% of undergrads determined to have financial need; average aid package $14,443

Kentucky Wesleyan College

Owensboro KY
(800) 999-0592
U.S. News ranking: Reg. Coll. (S), No. 16
Website: kwc.edu/
Admissions email: admissions@kwc.edu
Private; founded 1858
Affiliation: United Methodist
Freshman admissions: selective; 2018-2019: 1,607 applied, 1,031 accepted. Either SAT or ACT required. ACT 25/75 percentile: 19-26. High school rank: N/A
Early decision deadline: N/A, notification date: N/A
Early action deadline: N/A, notification date: N/A
Application deadline (fall): 9/3
Undergraduate student body: 753 full time, 77 part time; 51% male, 49% female; 1% American Indian, 1% Asian, 13% black, 2% Hispanic, 1% multiracial, 0% Pacific Islander, 67% white, 1% international
Most popular majors: 13% Business/Commerce, General, 9% Criminal Justice/Safety Studies, 9% Psychology, General, 7% Kinesiology and Exercise Science, 6% Art/Art Studies, General
Expenses: 2019-2020: $26,440; room/board: $9,764
Financial aid: (270) 852-3130

Lindsey Wilson College

Columbia KY
(800) 264-0138
U.S. News ranking: Reg. U. (S), No. 92
Website: www.lindsey.edu
Admissions email: admissions@lindsey.edu
Private; founded 1903
Affiliation: United Methodist

Freshman admissions: selective; 2018-2019: 1,989 applied, 1,893 accepted. Either SAT or ACT required. ACT 25/75 percentile: 19-24. High school rank: 12% in top tenth, 31% in top quarter, 66% in top half
Early decision deadline: N/A, notification date: N/A
Early action deadline: N/A, notification date: N/A
Application deadline (fall): rolling
Undergraduate student body: 1,902 full time, 145 part time; 39% male, 61% female; 0% American Indian, 0% Asian, 10% black, 0% Hispanic, 2% multiracial, 0% Pacific Islander, 61% white, 4% international; 82% from in state; 52% live on campus; 0% of students in fraternities, 0% in sororities
Most popular majors: 49% Clinical, Counseling and Applied Psychology, Other, 11% Business Administration and Management, General, 6% Registered Nursing/Registered Nurse, 5% Criminal Justice/Safety Studies, 5% Speech Communication and Rhetoric
Expenses: 2019-2020: $25,350; room/board: $9,425
Financial aid: (270) 384-8022; 93% of undergrads determined to have financial need; average aid package $22,227

Midway University

Midway KY
(800) 952-4122
U.S. News ranking: Reg. U. (S), No. 73
Website: www.midway.edu
Admissions email: admissions@midway.edu
Private; founded 1847
Affiliation: Christian Church (Disciples of Christ)
Freshman admissions: selective; 2018-2019: 1,256 applied, 761 accepted. Either SAT or ACT required. ACT 25/75 percentile: 19-23. High school rank: 13% in top tenth, 37% in top quarter, 71% in top half
Early decision deadline: N/A, notification date: N/A
Early action deadline: N/A, notification date: N/A
Application deadline (fall): 8/28
Undergraduate student body: 820 full time, 636 part time; 30% male, 70% female; 0% American Indian, 1% Asian, 7% black, 8% Hispanic, 3% multiracial, 0% Pacific Islander, 76% white, 0% international; 85% from in state; N/A live on campus; 0% of students in fraternities, 0% in sororities
Most popular majors: 27% Business/Commerce, General, 14% Education, General, 12% Health/Health Care Administration/Management, 8% Psychology, General, 7% Criminal Justice/Police Science
Expenses: 2019-2020: $24,850; room/board: $8,480
Financial aid: (859) 846-5304; 45% of undergrads determined to have financial need; average aid package $18,283

Morehead State University

Morehead KY
(606) 783-2000
U.S. News ranking: Reg. U. (S), No. 43
Website: www.moreheadstate.edu
Admissions email: admissions@moreheadstate.edu
Public; founded 1887
Freshman admissions: selective; 2018-2019: 8,119 applied, 6,125 accepted. Either SAT or ACT required. ACT 25/75 percentile: 20-26. High school rank: 19% in top tenth, 46% in top quarter, 83% in top half
Early decision deadline: N/A, notification date: N/A
Early action deadline: N/A, notification date: N/A
Application deadline (fall): rolling
Undergraduate student body: 5,751 full time, 3,649 part time; 39% male, 61% female; 0% American Indian, 0% Asian, 4% black, 2% Hispanic, 2% multiracial, 0% Pacific Islander, 88% white, 2% international; N/A from in state; 44% live on campus; 6% of students in fraternities, 7% in sororities
Most popular majors: 14% Business, Management, Marketing, and Related Support Services, 12% Liberal Arts and Sciences, General Studies and Humanities, 11% Health Professions and Related Programs, 9% Education, 7% Public Administration and Social Service Professions
Expenses: 2019-2020: $9,290 in state, $13,876 out of state; room/board: $9,490
Financial aid: (606) 783-2011; 77% of undergrads determined to have financial need; average aid package $12,113

Murray State University

Murray KY
(270) 809-3741
U.S. News ranking: Reg. U. (S), No. 24
Website: www.murraystate.edu
Admissions email: msu.admissions@murraystate.edu
Public; founded 1922
Freshman admissions: selective; 2018-2019: 8,256 applied, 6,722 accepted. Either SAT or ACT required. ACT 25/75 percentile: 21-27. High school rank: 27% in top tenth, 54% in top quarter, 82% in top half
Early decision deadline: N/A, notification date: N/A
Early action deadline: N/A, notification date: N/A
Application deadline (fall): rolling
Undergraduate student body: 6,275 full time, 1,867 part time; 40% male, 60% female; 0% American Indian, 1% Asian, 6% black, 2% Hispanic, 3% multiracial, 0% Pacific Islander, 82% white, 3% international; 68% from in state; 33% live on campus; 16% of students in fraternities, 15% in sororities

Most popular majors: 15% Health Professions and Related Programs, 12% Business, Management, Marketing, and Related Support Services, 10% Education, 10% Engineering Technologies and Engineering-Related Fields, 7% Agriculture, Agriculture Operations, and Related Sciences
Expenses: 2019-2020: $9,168 in state, $24,792 out of state; room/board: $9,894
Financial aid: (270) 809-2546; 68% of undergrads determined to have financial need; average aid package $12,988

Northern Kentucky University

Highland Heights KY
(859) 572-5220
U.S. News ranking: Nat. U., second tier
Website: www.nku.edu/
Admissions email: beanorse@nku.edu
Public; founded 1968
Freshman admissions: selective; 2018-2019: 5,995 applied, 5,351 accepted. Either SAT or ACT required. ACT 25/75 percentile: 20-26. High school rank: N/A
Early decision deadline: N/A, notification date: N/A
Early action deadline: N/A, notification date: N/A
Application deadline (fall): 8/15
Undergraduate student body: 8,570 full time, 3,363 part time; 42% male, 58% female; 0% American Indian, 1% Asian, 7% black, 3% Hispanic, 3% multiracial, 0% Pacific Islander, 81% white, 3% international; 70% from in state; 15% live on campus; 9% of students in fraternities, 12% in sororities
Most popular majors: 6% Organizational Behavior Studies, 6% Registered Nursing/Registered Nurse, 4% Information Technology, 4% Psychology, General, 4% Social Work
Expenses: 2019-2020: $10,296 in state, $20,256 out of state; room/board: $10,212
Financial aid: (859) 572-5143; 64% of undergrads determined to have financial need; average aid package $12,149

Spalding University[1]

Louisville KY
(502) 585-7111
U.S. News ranking: Nat. U., second tier
Website: www.spalding.edu
Admissions email: admissions@spalding.edu
Private; founded 1814
Application deadline (fall): rolling
Undergraduate student body: N/A full time, N/A part time
Expenses: N/A
Financial aid: N/A

Sullivan University[1]

Louisville KY
(502) 456-6504
U.S. News ranking: Reg. U. (S), unranked
Website: www.sullivan.edu
Admissions email: admissions@sullivan.edu
Private
Application deadline (fall): N/A
Undergraduate student body: N/A full time, N/A part time
Expenses: N/A
Financial aid: N/A

Thomas More University

Crestview Hills KY
(800) 825-4557
U.S. News ranking: Reg. U. (S), No. 61
Website: www.thomasmore.edu
Admissions email: admissions@thomasmore.edu
Private; founded 1921
Affiliation: Roman Catholic
Freshman admissions: selective; 2018-2019: 2,698 applied, 2,429 accepted. Either SAT or ACT required. ACT 25/75 percentile: 19-24. High school rank: 10% in top tenth, 28% in top quarter, 65% in top half
Early decision deadline: N/A, notification date: N/A
Early action deadline: N/A, notification date: N/A
Application deadline (fall): rolling
Undergraduate student body: 1,400 full time, 647 part time; 48% male, 52% female; 0% American Indian, 1% Asian, 9% black, 3% Hispanic, 6% multiracial, 0% Pacific Islander, 77% white, 1% international; 57% from in state; 28% live on campus; 1% of students in fraternities, 0% in sororities
Most popular majors: 33% Business Administration and Management, General, 18% Registered Nursing/Registered Nurse, 7% Biology/Biological Sciences, General, 6% Communication and Media Studies, 6% Education
Expenses: 2019-2020: $32,090; room/board: $8,890
Financial aid: (859) 344-3319; 80% of undergrads determined to have financial need; average aid package $22,304

Transylvania University

Lexington KY
(859) 233-8242
U.S. News ranking: Nat. Lib. Arts, No. 72
Website: www.transy.edu
Admissions email: admissions@transy.edu
Private; founded 1780
Affiliation: Christian Church (Disciples of Christ)
Freshman admissions: more selective; 2018-2019: 1,702 applied, 1,509 accepted. Neither SAT nor ACT required. ACT 25/75 percentile: 24-30. High school rank: 30% in top tenth, 67% in top quarter, 90% in top half

Early decision deadline: N/A, notification date: N/A
Early action deadline: 10/15, notification date: 11/1
Application deadline (fall): rolling
Undergraduate student body: 978 full time, 11 part time; 40% male, 60% female; 0% American Indian, 2% Asian, 5% black, 4% Hispanic, 5% multiracial, 0% Pacific Islander, 80% white, 0% international; N/A from in state; 70% live on campus; 44% of students in fraternities, 42% in sororities
Most popular majors: 20% Business, Management, Marketing, and Related Support Services, 14% Biological and Biomedical Sciences, 11% Social Sciences, 9% Psychology, 8% Foreign Languages, Literatures, and Linguistics
Expenses: 2019-2020: $40,210; room/board: $11,140
Financial aid: (859) 233-8239, 71% of undergrads determined to have financial need; average aid package $29,205

Union College[1]
Barbourville KY
(606) 546-4151
U.S. News ranking: Reg. U. (S), second tier
Website: www.unionky.edu
Admissions email: enroll@unionky.edu
Private
Application deadline (fall): N/A
Undergraduate student body: N/A full time, N/A part time
Expenses: 2019-2020: $27,950; room/board: $7,575
Financial aid: (606) 546-1224; 83% of undergrads determined to have financial need; average aid package $23,238

University of Kentucky
Lexington KY
(859) 257-2000
U.S. News ranking: Nat. U., No. 132
Website: www.uky.edu
Admissions email: admissions@uky.edu
Public; founded 1865
Freshman admissions: more selective; 2018-2019: 19,324 applied, 18,258 accepted. Either SAT or ACT required. ACT 25/75 percentile: 23-29. High school rank: 31% in top tenth, 59% in top quarter, 86% in top half
Early decision deadline: N/A, notification date: N/A
Early action deadline: 12/1, notification date: N/A
Application deadline (fall): 2/15
Undergraduate student body: 20,484 full time, 1,652 part time; 45% male, 55% female; 0% American Indian, 3% Asian, 8% black, 5% Hispanic, 4% multiracial, 0% Pacific Islander, 75% white, 2% international; 66% from in state; 31% live on campus; 19% of students in fraternities, 32% in sororities

Most popular majors: 18% Business, Management, Marketing, and Related Support Services, 9% Education, 8% Communication, Journalism, and Related Programs, 8% Health Professions and Related Programs, 7% Engineering
Expenses: 2019-2020: $12,360 in state, $30,680 out of state; room/board: $13,210
Financial aid: (859) 257-3172; 52% of undergrads determined to have financial need; average aid package $13,720

University of Louisville
Louisville KY
(502) 852-6531
U.S. News ranking: Nat. U., No. 192
Website: www.louisville.edu
Admissions email: admitme@louisville.edu
Public; founded 1798
Affiliation: Undenominational
Freshman admissions: selective; 2018-2019: 13,570 applied, 9,890 accepted. Either SAT or ACT required. ACT 25/75 percentile: 22-29. High school rank: 24% in top tenth, 48% in top quarter, 74% in top half
Early decision deadline: N/A, notification date: N/A
Early action deadline: N/A, notification date: N/A
Application deadline (fall): 8/1
Undergraduate student body: 11,930 full time, 3,712 part time; 48% male, 52% female; 0% American Indian, 4% Asian, 12% black, 5% Hispanic, 6% multiracial, 0% Pacific Islander, 72% white, 1% international; 79% from in state; 23% live on campus; 16% of students in fraternities, 14% in sororities
Most popular majors: 12% Engineering, 9% Parks, Recreation, Leisure, and Fitness Studies, 8% Communication, Journalism, and Related Programs, 8% Education, 7% Social Sciences
Expenses: 2019-2020: $12,458 in state, $26,958 out of state; room/board: $9,452
Financial aid: (502) 852-5511; 63% of undergrads determined to have financial need; average aid package $12,848

University of Pikeville
Pikeville KY
(606) 218-5251
U.S. News ranking: Nat. Lib. Arts, second tier
Website: www.upike.edu/
Admissions email: wewantyou@upike.edu
Private; founded 1889
Affiliation: Presbyterian Church (USA)
Freshman admissions: selective; 2018-2019: 1,867 applied, 1,867 accepted. Either SAT or ACT required. ACT 25/75 percentile: 18-24. High school rank: 13% in top tenth, 33% in top quarter, 61% in top half
Early decision deadline: N/A, notification date: N/A

Early action deadline: N/A, notification date: N/A
Application deadline (fall): rolling
Undergraduate student body: 1,056 full time, 443 part time; 47% male, 53% female; 0% American Indian, 1% Asian, 10% black, 1% Hispanic, 0% multiracial, 0% Pacific Islander, 84% white, 3% international; 80% from in state; 53% live on campus; N/A of students in fraternities, N/A in sororities
Most popular majors: 18% Business, Management, Marketing, and Related Support Services, 17% Biological and Biomedical Sciences, 13% Psychology, 10% Homeland Security, Law Enforcement, Firefighting and Related Protective Services, 8% Education
Expenses: 2019-2020: $21,550; room/board: $7,950
Financial aid: (606) 218-5254; 99% of undergrads determined to have financial need; average aid package $21,563

University of the Cumberlands[1]
Williamsburg KY
(800) 343-1609
U.S. News ranking: Nat. U., second tier
Website: www.ucumberlands.edu
Admissions email: admiss@ucumberlands.edu
Private; founded 1888
Affiliation: Baptist
Application deadline (fall): 8/31
Undergraduate student body: N/A full time, N/A part time
Expenses: N/A
Financial aid: (606) 539-4239

Western Kentucky University
Bowling Green KY
(270) 745-2551
U.S. News ranking: Nat. U., second tier
Website: www.wku.edu
Admissions email: admission@wku.edu
Public; founded 1906
Freshman admissions: selective; 2018-2019: 9,250 applied, 8,992 accepted. Either SAT or ACT required. ACT 25/75 percentile: 20-27. High school rank: 22% in top tenth, 46% in top quarter, 75% in top half
Early decision deadline: N/A, notification date: N/A
Early action deadline: N/A, notification date: N/A
Application deadline (fall): 8/1
Undergraduate student body: 12,393 full time, 4,637 part time; 41% male, 59% female; 0% American Indian, 2% Asian, 9% black, 3% Hispanic, 3% multiracial, 0% Pacific Islander, 78% white, 3% international; 78% from in state; 35% live on campus; 15% of students in fraternities, 18% in sororities
Most popular majors: 9% General Studies, 8% Registered Nursing/Registered Nurse, 5% Business Administration and Management,

General, 4% Psychology, General, 3% Elementary Education and Teaching
Expenses: 2019-2020: $10,802 in state, $26,496 out of state; room/board: $8,432
Financial aid: (270) 745-2051; 64% of undergrads determined to have financial need; average aid package $14,809

LOUISIANA

Centenary College of Louisiana
Shreveport LA
(318) 869-5011
U.S. News ranking: Nat. Lib. Arts, No. 157
Website: www.centenary.edu/
Admissions email: admission@centenary.edu
Private; founded 1825
Affiliation: United Methodist
Freshman admissions: more selective; 2018-2019: 893 applied, 533 accepted. Either SAT or ACT required. ACT 25/75 percentile: 21-28. High school rank: 23% in top tenth, 47% in top quarter, 84% in top half
Early decision deadline: N/A, notification date: N/A
Early action deadline: 12/1, notification date: 1/15
Application deadline (fall): rolling
Undergraduate student body: 539 full time, 13 part time; 43% male, 57% female; 1% American Indian, 2% Asian, 14% black, 10% Hispanic, 6% multiracial, 0% Pacific Islander, 65% white, 1% international
Most popular majors: 17% Biology/Biological Sciences, General, 15% Business Administration and Management, General, 12% Psychology, General, 6% Music, General, 5% Accounting
Expenses: 2019-2020: $37,310; room/board: $13,670
Financial aid: (318) 869-5137; 82% of undergrads determined to have financial need; average aid package $31,379

Dillard University[1]
New Orleans LA
(800) 216-6637
U.S. News ranking: Nat. Lib. Arts, second tier
Website: www.dillard.edu
Admissions email: admissions@dillard.edu
Private; founded 1869
Affiliation: United Methodist
Application deadline (fall): 8/1
Undergraduate student body: N/A full time, N/A part time
Expenses: N/A
Financial aid: (504) 816-4864

Grambling State University
Grambling LA
(318) 274-6183
U.S. News ranking: Reg. U. (S), second tier
Website: www.gram.edu/
Admissions email: admissions@gram.edu
Public; founded 1901

Freshman admissions: least selective; 2018-2019: 3,147 applied, 3,008 accepted. Neither SAT nor ACT required. ACT 25/75 percentile: 16-19. High school rank: 8% in top tenth, 14% in top quarter, 53% in top half
Early decision deadline: N/A, notification date: N/A
Early action deadline: N/A, notification date: N/A
Application deadline (fall): rolling
Undergraduate student body: 3,805 full time, 305 part time; 40% male, 60% female; 0% American Indian, 0% Asian, 90% black, 2% Hispanic, 2% multiracial, 0% Pacific Islander, 1% white, 5% international
Most popular majors: 20% Business Administration and Management, General, 17% Criminal Justice/Safety Studies, 9% Psychology, General, 8% Social Work, General, 6% Biology/Biological Sciences, General
Expenses: 2019-2020: $7,683 in state, $7,683 out of state; room/board: $10,306
Financial aid: (318) 274-6328; 77% of undergrads determined to have financial need; average aid package $3,868

Louisiana College
Pineville LA
(318) 487-7259
U.S. News ranking: Reg. U. (S), second tier
Website: www.lacollege.edu
Admissions email: admissions@lacollege.edu
Private; founded 1906
Affiliation: Southern Baptist
Freshman admissions: selective; 2018-2019: 808 applied, 634 accepted. Either SAT or ACT required. ACT 25/75 percentile: 19-23. High school rank: N/A
Early decision deadline: N/A, notification date: N/A
Early action deadline: N/A, notification date: N/A
Application deadline (fall): rolling
Undergraduate student body: 893 full time, 111 part time; 53% male, 47% female; 1% American Indian, 1% Asian, 25% black, 3% Hispanic, 3% multiracial, 0% Pacific Islander, 64% white, 2% international; 89% from in state; 54% live on campus; 0% of students in fraternities, 0% in sororities
Most popular majors: 22% Registered Nursing/Registered Nurse, 13% Health and Physical Education/Fitness, General, 11% Business Administration and Management, General, 8% Biology/Biological Sciences, General, 6% Elementary Education and Teaching
Expenses: 2018-2019: $17,000; room/board: $5,518
Financial aid: (318) 487-7387

Louisiana State University–Alexandria
Alexandria LA
(318) 473-6417
U.S. News ranking: Nat. Lib. Arts, second tier
Website: www.lsua.edu
Admissions email: admissions@lsua.edu
Public; founded 1960
Freshman admissions: selective; 2018-2019: 1,833 applied, 1,332 accepted. Either SAT or ACT required. ACT 25/75 percentile: 18-22. High school rank: 9% in top tenth, 28% in top quarter, 54% in top half
Early decision deadline: N/A, notification date: N/A
Early action deadline: N/A, notification date: N/A
Application deadline (fall): 8/1
Undergraduate student body: 1,823 full time, 1,422 part time; 30% male, 70% female; 6% American Indian, 1% Asian, 21% black, 2% Hispanic, 2% multiracial, 0% Pacific Islander, 63% white, 2% international; 89% from in state; 7% live on campus; N/A of students in fraternities, N/A in sororities
Most popular majors: 15% Business Administration and Management, General, 10% General Studies, 8% Registered Nursing/Registered Nurse, 7% Criminal Justice/Safety Studies, 7% Psychology, General
Expenses: 2018-2019: $6,669 in state, $14,024 out of state; room/board: $7,950
Financial aid: (318) 473-6477

Louisiana State University–Baton Rouge
Baton Rouge LA
(225) 578-1175
U.S. News ranking: Nat. U., No. 153
Website: www.lsu.edu
Admissions email: admissions@lsu.edu
Public; founded 1860
Freshman admissions: more selective; 2018-2019: 24,303 applied, 18,035 accepted. Either SAT or ACT required. ACT 25/75 percentile: 23-29. High school rank: 23% in top tenth, 47% in top quarter, 77% in top half
Early decision deadline: N/A, notification date: N/A
Early action deadline: N/A, notification date: N/A
Application deadline (fall): 4/15
Undergraduate student body: 22,433 full time, 2,928 part time; 47% male, 53% female; 0% American Indian, 4% Asian, 13% black, 7% Hispanic, 2% multiracial, 0% Pacific Islander, 71% white, 2% international; 82% from in state; 30% live on campus; 16% of students in fraternities, 27% in sororities
Most popular majors: 24% Business, Management, Marketing, and Related Support Services, 16% Engineering, 9% Education, 7% Biological

and Biomedical Sciences, 6% Communication, Journalism, and Related Programs
Expenses: 2019-2020: $11,962 in state, $28,639 out of state; room/board: $12,276
Financial aid: (225) 578-3103; 53% of undergrads determined to have financial need; average aid package $15,905

Louisiana State University–Shreveport
Shreveport LA
(318) 797-5061
U.S. News ranking: Reg. U. (S), second tier
Website: www.lsus.edu
Admissions email: admissions@lsus.edu
Public; founded 1967
Freshman admissions: selective; 2018-2019: 712 applied, 616 accepted. Either SAT or ACT required. ACT 25/75 percentile: 20-25. High school rank: N/A
Early decision deadline: N/A, notification date: N/A
Early action deadline: N/A, notification date: N/A
Application deadline (fall): rolling
Undergraduate student body: 1,610 full time, 901 part time; 40% male, 60% female; 0% American Indian, 2% Asian, 22% black, 5% Hispanic, 5% multiracial, 0% Pacific Islander, 52% white, 4% international; 90% from in state; 3% live on campus; 1% of students in fraternities, 1% in sororities
Most popular majors: 20% Business, Management, Marketing, and Related Support Services, 14% Liberal Arts and Sciences, General Studies and Humanities, 11% Health Professions and Related Programs, 10% Psychology, 9% Biological and Biomedical Sciences
Expenses: 2018-2019: $7,519 in state, $20,673 out of state; room/board: N/A
Financial aid: (318) 797-5363

Louisiana Tech University
Ruston LA
(318) 257-3036
U.S. News ranking: Nat. U., No. 272
Website: www.latech.edu
Admissions email: bulldog@latech.edu
Public; founded 1894
Freshman admissions: more selective; 2018-2019: 7,297 applied, 4,602 accepted. Either SAT or ACT required. ACT 25/75 percentile: 22-28. High school rank: 25% in top tenth, 53% in top quarter, 80% in top half
Early decision deadline: N/A, notification date: N/A
Early action deadline: N/A, notification date: N/A
Application deadline (fall): rolling
Undergraduate student body: 8,147 full time, 3,038 part time; 52% male, 48% female; 0% American Indian, 1% Asian, 13% black,

4% Hispanic, 3% multiracial, 0% Pacific Islander, 71% white, 2% international; N/A from in state; 15% live on campus; 11% of students in fraternities, 22% in sororities
Most popular majors: 6% Biological and Biomedical Sciences, 6% Engineering, 6% Parks, Recreation, Leisure, and Fitness Studies, 4% Business, Management, Marketing, and Related Support Services, 4% Engineering Technologies and Engineering-Related Fields
Expenses: 2019-2020: $10,185 in state, $19,098 out of state; room/board: $8,577
Financial aid: (318) 257-2641; 61% of undergrads determined to have financial need; average aid package $11,534

Loyola University New Orleans
New Orleans LA
(800) 456-9652
U.S. News ranking: Nat. U., No. 197
Website: www.loyno.edu
Admissions email: admit@loyno.edu
Private; founded 1912
Affiliation: Roman Catholic
Freshman admissions: selective; 2018-2019: 5,598 applied, 4,218 accepted. Either SAT or ACT required. ACT 25/75 percentile: 22-28. High school rank: 25% in top tenth, 51% in top quarter, 76% in top half
Early decision deadline: N/A, notification date: N/A
Early action deadline: 11/15, notification date: 12/1
Application deadline (fall): rolling
Undergraduate student body: 2,691 full time, 291 part time; 36% male, 64% female; 0% American Indian, 3% Asian, 17% black, 18% Hispanic, 4% multiracial, 0% Pacific Islander, 47% white, 2% international; 43% from in state; 54% live on campus; 6% of students in fraternities, 20% in sororities
Most popular majors: 13% Music Management, 7% Psychology, General, 5% Business Administration and Management, General, 5% Public Relations, Advertising, and Applied Communication, 4% Finance, General
Expenses: 2019-2020: $40,592; room/board: $13,548
Financial aid: (504) 865-3231; 74% of undergrads determined to have financial need; average aid package $33,225

McNeese State University
Lake Charles LA
(337) 475-5504
U.S. News ranking: Reg. U. (S), No. 92
Website: www.mcneese.edu
Admissions email: admissions@mcneese.edu
Public; founded 1939
Freshman admissions: selective; 2018-2019: 3,224 applied,

2,267 accepted. Either SAT or ACT required. ACT 25/75 percentile: 20-25. High school rank: 21% in top tenth, 47% in top quarter, 76% in top half
Early decision deadline: N/A, notification date: N/A
Early action deadline: N/A, notification date: N/A
Application deadline (fall): 8/13
Undergraduate student body: 5,656 full time, 1,377 part time; 41% male, 59% female; 1% American Indian, 2% Asian, 17% black, 4% Hispanic, 4% multiracial, 0% Pacific Islander, 68% white, 6% international
Most popular majors: Information not available
Expenses: 2018-2019: $7,860 in state, $15,898 out of state; room/board: $8,326
Financial aid: (337) 475-5065

Nicholls State University
Thibodaux LA
(985) 448-4507
U.S. News ranking: Reg. U. (S), No. 84
Website: www.nicholls.edu
Admissions email: nicholls@nicholls.edu
Public; founded 1948
Freshman admissions: selective; 2018-2019: 2,651 applied, 2,484 accepted. Either SAT or ACT required. ACT 25/75 percentile: 20-24. High school rank: 18% in top tenth, 42% in top quarter, 72% in top half
Early decision deadline: N/A, notification date: N/A
Early action deadline: N/A, notification date: N/A
Application deadline (fall): 8/1
Undergraduate student body: 4,893 full time, 1,003 part time; 36% male, 64% female; 2% American Indian, 1% Asian, 19% black, 4% Hispanic, 3% multiracial, 0% Pacific Islander, 69% white, 2% international
Most popular majors: 22% Business, Management, Marketing, and Related Support Services, 18% Health Professions and Related Programs, 14% Multi/Interdisciplinary Studies, 9% Education, 6% Engineering Technologies and Engineering-Related Fields
Expenses: 2019-2020: $7,952 in state, $9,045 out of state; room/board: $7,200
Financial aid: (985) 448-4047; 64% of undergrads determined to have financial need; average aid package $10,597

Northwestern State University of Louisiana
Natchitoches LA
(800) 426-3754
U.S. News ranking: Reg. U. (S), second tier
Website: www.nsula.edu
Admissions email: applications@nsula.edu
Public; founded 1884
Freshman admissions: selective; 2018-2019: 4,339 applied,

2,871 accepted. Either SAT or ACT required. ACT 25/75 percentile: 19-24. High school rank: 14% in top tenth, 37% in top quarter, 72% in top half
Early decision deadline: N/A, notification date: N/A
Early action deadline: N/A, notification date: N/A
Application deadline (fall): 10/15
Undergraduate student body: 5,705 full time, 4,199 part time; 30% male, 70% female; 1% American Indian, 1% Asian, 32% black, 6% Hispanic, 4% multiracial, 0% Pacific Islander, 53% white, 2% international; N/A from in state; 15% live on campus; N/A of students in fraternities, N/A in sororities
Most popular majors: 23% Health Professions and Related Programs, 15% Business, Management, Marketing, and Related Support Services, 12% Liberal Arts and Sciences, General Studies and Humanities, 8% Psychology, 6% Homeland Security, Law Enforcement, Firefighting and Related Protective Services
Expenses: 2018-2019: $8,580 in state, $19,368 out of state; room/board: $8,684
Financial aid: (318) 357-5961; 76% of undergrads determined to have financial need; average aid package $15,181

Southeastern Louisiana University
Hammond LA
(985) 549-5637
U.S. News ranking: Reg. U. (S), second tier
Website: www.southeastern.edu
Admissions email: admissions@southeastern.edu
Public; founded 1925
Freshman admissions: selective; 2018-2019: 4,248 applied, 3,828 accepted. Either SAT or ACT required. ACT 25/75 percentile: 20-25. High school rank: 12% in top tenth, 34% in top quarter, 68% in top half
Early decision deadline: N/A, notification date: N/A
Early action deadline: N/A, notification date: N/A
Application deadline (fall): 8/1
Undergraduate student body: 9,194 full time, 4,166 part time; 38% male, 62% female; 0% American Indian, 1% Asian, 22% black, 7% Hispanic, 5% multiracial, 0% Pacific Islander, 63% white, 1% international; 96% from in state; 24% live on campus; 8% of students in fraternities, 8% in sororities
Most popular majors: 19% Business, Management, Marketing, and Related Support Services, 12% Health Professions and Related Programs, 12% Liberal Arts and Sciences, General Studies and Humanities, 7% Education, 7% Parks, Recreation, Leisure, and Fitness Studies
Expenses: 2018-2019: $8,165 in state, $20,643 out of state; room/board: $8,420
Financial aid: (985) 549-2244; 68% of undergrads determined to have financial need; average aid package $10,190

Southern University and A&M College

Baton Rouge LA
(225) 771-2430
U.S. News ranking: Reg. U. (S), second tier
Website: www.subr.edu/
Admissions email: admit@subr.edu
Public; founded 1880
Freshman admissions: less selective; 2018-2019: 7,396 applied, 2,802 accepted. Either SAT or ACT required. ACT 25/75 percentile: 17-20. High school rank: 3% in top tenth, 17% in top quarter, 41% in top half
Early decision deadline: N/A, notification date: N/A
Early action deadline: N/A, notification date: N/A
Application deadline (fall): 7/1
Undergraduate student body: 4,868 full time, 970 part time; 36% male, 64% female; 0% American Indian, 0% Asian, 93% black, 1% Hispanic, 2% multiracial, 0% Pacific Islander, 2% white, 1% international
Most popular majors: 22% Health Professions and Related Programs, 16% Business, Management, Marketing, and Related Support Services, 10% Homeland Security, Law Enforcement, Firefighting and Related Protective Services, 8% Psychology, 5% Engineering
Expenses: 2019-2020: $43,374 in state, $53,816 out of state; room/board: $11,053
Financial aid: (225) 771-4530; 90% of undergrads determined to have financial need

Southern University– New Orleans[1]

New Orleans LA
(504) 286-5314
U.S. News ranking: Reg. U. (S), second tier
Website: www.suno.edu
Admissions email: N/A
Public; founded 1956
Application deadline (fall): N/A
Undergraduate student body: N/A full time, N/A part time
Expenses: N/A
Financial aid: (504) 286-5263

Tulane University

New Orleans LA
(504) 865-5731
U.S. News ranking: Nat. U., No. 40
Website: www.tulane.edu
Admissions email: undergrad.admission@tulane.edu
Private; founded 1834
Freshman admissions: most selective; 2018-2019: 38,816 applied, 6,724 accepted. Either SAT or ACT required. ACT 25/75 percentile: 30-33. High school rank: 63% in top tenth, 88% in top quarter, 96% in top half
Early decision deadline: 11/1, notification date: 12/15
Early action deadline: 11/15, notification date: 1/15
Application deadline (fall): 11/15
Undergraduate student body: 6,747 full time, 26 part time; 40% male, 60% female; 0% American Indian, 5% Asian, 4% black,

7% Hispanic, 4% multiracial, 0% Pacific Islander, 73% white, 5% international; 21% from in state; 48% live on campus; 24% of students in fraternities, 46% in sororities
Most popular majors: 24% Business, Management, Marketing, and Related Support Services, 16% Social Sciences, 10% Biological and Biomedical Sciences, 9% Health Professions and Related Programs, 7% Communication, Journalism, and Related Programs
Expenses: 2019-2020: $56,800; room/board: $15,774
Financial aid: (504) 865-5723; 31% of undergrads determined to have financial need; average aid package $47,129

University of Holy Cross[1]

New Orleans LA
(504) 398-2175
U.S. News ranking: Reg. U. (S), No. 69
Website: www.uhcno.edu/
Admissions email: admissions@UHCNO.edu
Private; founded 1916
Affiliation: Roman Catholic
Application deadline (fall): rolling
Undergraduate student body: N/A full time, N/A part time
Expenses: 2018-2019: $14,372; room/board: $12,400
Financial aid: (504) 398-2133

University of Louisiana–Lafayette

Lafayette LA
(337) 482-6553
U.S. News ranking: Nat. U., second tier
Website: www.louisiana.edu
Admissions email: enroll@louisiana.edu
Public; founded 1898
Freshman admissions: more selective; 2018-2019: 9,467 applied, 5,301 accepted. Either SAT or ACT required. ACT 25/75 percentile: 21-28. High school rank: 20% in top tenth, 44% in top quarter, 73% in top half
Early decision deadline: N/A, notification date: N/A
Early action deadline: N/A, notification date: N/A
Application deadline (fall): rolling
Undergraduate student body: 12,423 full time, 2,650 part time; 43% male, 57% female; 0% American Indian, 2% Asian, 20% black, 6% Hispanic, 2% multiracial, 0% Pacific Islander, 65% white, 1% international
Most popular majors: Information not available
Expenses: 2018-2019: $9,912 in state, $23,640 out of state; room/board: $10,604
Financial aid: (337) 482-6506; 68% of undergrads determined to have financial need; average aid package $12,622

University of Louisiana–Monroe

Monroe LA
(318) 342-7777
U.S. News ranking: Nat. U., second tier
Website: www.ulm.edu
Admissions email: admissions@ulm.edu
Public; founded 1931
Freshman admissions: selective; 2018-2019: 4,156 applied, 2,981 accepted. Either SAT or ACT required. ACT 25/75 percentile: 20-25. High school rank: 20% in top tenth, 47% in top quarter, 77% in top half
Early decision deadline: N/A, notification date: N/A
Early action deadline: N/A, notification date: N/A
Application deadline (fall): rolling
Undergraduate student body: 5,035 full time, 2,441 part time; 37% male, 63% female; 0% American Indian, 2% Asian, 25% black, 3% Hispanic, 3% multiracial, 0% Pacific Islander, 60% white, 5% international; 90% from in state; 26% live on campus; N/A of students in fraternities, N/A in sororities
Most popular majors: 9% Psychology, General, 8% Kinesiology and Exercise Science, 7% General Studies, 6% Business Administration and Management, General, 6% Registered Nursing/Registered Nurse
Expenses: 2018-2019: $8,734 in state, $20,834 out of state; room/board: $7,868
Financial aid: (318) 342-5329; 66% of undergrads determined to have financial need; average aid package $6,731

University of New Orleans

New Orleans LA
(504) 280-6595
U.S. News ranking: Nat. U., second tier
Website: www.uno.edu
Admissions email: admissions@uno.edu
Public; founded 1958
Freshman admissions: selective; 2018-2019: 4,715 applied, 2,700 accepted. Either SAT or ACT required. ACT 25/75 percentile: 20-25. High school rank: 17% in top tenth, 38% in top quarter, 69% in top half
Early decision deadline: N/A, notification date: N/A
Early action deadline: N/A, notification date: N/A
Application deadline (fall): 8/20
Undergraduate student body: 4,833 full time, 1,755 part time; 50% male, 50% female; 0% American Indian, 9% Asian, 18% black, 14% Hispanic, 5% multiracial, 0% Pacific Islander, 50% white, 4% international; 90% from in state; 9% live on campus; 3% of students in fraternities, 5% in sororities
Most popular majors: 28% Business, Management, Marketing, and Related Support Services, 13% Engineering,

12% Multi/Interdisciplinary Studies, 10% Biological and Biomedical Sciences, 8% Visual and Performing Arts
Expenses: 2019-2020: $11,542 in state, $16,378 out of state; room/board: $18,650
Financial aid: (504) 280-6603; 67% of undergrads determined to have financial need; average aid package $9,787

Xavier University of Louisiana

New Orleans LA
(504) 520-7388
U.S. News ranking: Reg. U. (S), No. 17
Website: www.xula.edu
Admissions email: apply@xula.edu
Private; founded 1915
Affiliation: Roman Catholic
Freshman admissions: selective; 2018-2019: 8,352 applied, 4,834 accepted. Either SAT or ACT required. ACT 25/75 percentile: 20-26. High school rank: 29% in top tenth, 56% in top quarter, 85% in top half
Early decision deadline: N/A, notification date: N/A
Early action deadline: N/A, notification date: N/A
Application deadline (fall): 7/1
Undergraduate student body: 2,447 full time, 121 part time; 25% male, 75% female; 0% American Indian, 6% Asian, 78% black, 4% Hispanic, 4% multiracial, 0% Pacific Islander, 3% white, 1% international; 46% from in state; 48% live on campus; 1% of students in fraternities, 2% in sororities
Most popular majors: 41% Biological and Biomedical Sciences, 13% Physical Sciences, 13% Psychology, 8% Business, Management, Marketing, and Related Support Services, 7% Health Professions and Related Programs
Expenses: 2019-2020: $25,006; room/board: $9,047
Financial aid: (504) 520-7835; 76% of undergrads determined to have financial need; average aid package $9,897

MAINE

Bates College

Lewiston ME
(855) 228-3755
U.S. News ranking: Nat. Lib. Arts, No. 21
Website: www.bates.edu
Admissions email: admission@bates.edu
Private; founded 1855
Freshman admissions: most selective; 2018-2019: 7,685 applied, 1,367 accepted. Neither SAT nor ACT required. SAT 25/75 percentile: 1290-1460. High school rank: 55% in top tenth, 89% in top quarter, 98% in top half
Early decision deadline: 11/15, notification date: 12/20
Early action deadline: N/A, notification date: N/A
Application deadline (fall): 1/1

Undergraduate student body: 1,832 full time, 0 part time; 50% male, 50% female; 0% American Indian, 4% Asian, 5% black, 8% Hispanic, 4% multiracial, 0% Pacific Islander, 71% white, 8% international
Most popular majors: 28% Social Sciences, 15% Biological and Biomedical Sciences, 8% English Language and Literature/Letters, 8% Psychology, 6% Visual and Performing Arts
Expenses: 2019-2020: $55,683; room/board: $15,705
Financial aid: (207) 786-6096; 42% of undergrads determined to have financial need; average aid package $48,512

Bowdoin College

Brunswick ME
(207) 725-3100
U.S. News ranking: Nat. Lib. Arts, No. 6
Website: www.bowdoin.edu
Admissions email: admissions@bowdoin.edu
Private; founded 1794
Affiliation: Other
Freshman admissions: most selective; 2018-2019: 9,081 applied, 932 accepted. Neither SAT nor ACT required. SAT 25/75 percentile: 1300-1510. High school rank: 80% in top tenth, 96% in top quarter, 100% in top half
Early decision deadline: 11/15, notification date: 12/15
Early action deadline: N/A, notification date: N/A
Application deadline (fall): 1/1
Undergraduate student body: 1,825 full time, 3 part time; 49% male, 51% female; 0% American Indian, 8% Asian, 8% black, 10% Hispanic, 6% multiracial, 0% Pacific Islander, 61% white, 6% international; 11% from in state; 90% live on campus; N/A of students in fraternities, N/A in sororities
Most popular majors: 21% Political Science and Government, General, 14% Economics, General, 10% Mathematics, General, 7% Biology/Biological Sciences, General, 7% History, General
Expenses: 2019-2020: $56,350; room/board: $15,360
Financial aid: (207) 725-3146; 49% of undergrads determined to have financial need; average aid package $49,337

Colby College

Waterville ME
(800) 723-3032
U.S. News ranking: Nat. Lib. Arts, No. 11
Website: www.colby.edu
Admissions email: admissions@colby.edu
Private; founded 1813
Freshman admissions: most selective; 2018-2019: 12,313 applied, 1,608 accepted. Neither SAT nor ACT required. SAT 25/75 percentile: 1350-1510. High school rank: 79% in top tenth, 94% in top quarter, 100% in top half

Early decision deadline: 11/15, notification date: 12/15
Early action deadline: N/A, notification date: N/A
Application deadline (fall): 1/1
Undergraduate student body: 2,000 full time, 0 part time; 48% male, 52% female; 0% American Indian, 8% Asian, 4% black, 7% Hispanic, 5% multiracial, 0% Pacific Islander, 63% white, 10% international; 11% from in state; 97% live on campus; 0% of students in fraternities, 0% in sororities
Most popular majors: 28% Social Sciences, 13% Biological and Biomedical Sciences, 8% Natural Resources and Conservation, 8% Psychology, 6% Multi/Interdisciplinary Studies
Expenses: 2019-2020: $57,280; room/board: $14,720
Financial aid: (800) 723-4033; 46% of undergrads determined to have financial need; average aid package $49,439

College of the Atlantic
Bar Harbor ME
(800) 528-0025
U.S. News ranking: Nat. Lib. Arts, No. 82
Website: www.coa.edu/
Admissions email: inquiry@coa.edu
Private; founded 1969
Freshman admissions: more selective; 2018-2019: 459 applied, 309 accepted. Neither SAT nor ACT required. SAT 25/75 percentile: 1210-1400. High school rank: 35% in top tenth, 59% in top quarter, 82% in top half
Early decision deadline: 12/1, notification date: 12/15
Early action deadline: N/A, notification date: N/A
Application deadline (fall): 2/1
Undergraduate student body: 317 full time, 15 part time; 24% male, 76% female; 0% American Indian, 1% Asian, 1% black, 5% Hispanic, 2% multiracial, 0% Pacific Islander, 65% white, 25% international; 23% from in state; 48% live on campus; 0% of students in fraternities, 0% in sororities
Most popular majors: Information not available
Expenses: 2019-2020: $43,542; room/board: $9,747
Financial aid: (207) 801-5645; 84% of undergrads determined to have financial need; average aid package $41,564

Husson University
Bangor ME
(207) 941-7100
U.S. News ranking: Nat. U., second tier
Website: www.husson.edu
Admissions email: admit@husson.edu
Private; founded 1898
Freshman admissions: less selective; 2018-2019: 2,893 applied, 2,396 accepted. Either SAT or ACT required. SAT 25/75

percentile: 930-1140. High school rank: 12% in top tenth, 30% in top quarter, 70% in top half
Early decision deadline: N/A, notification date: N/A
Early action deadline: N/A, notification date: N/A
Application deadline (fall): rolling
Undergraduate student body: 2,408 full time, 504 part time; 41% male, 59% female; 0% American Indian, 1% Asian, 4% black, 1% Hispanic, 2% multiracial, 0% Pacific Islander, 84% white, 3% international; 77% from in state; 42% live on campus; 3% of students in fraternities, 5% in sororities
Most popular majors: 31% Health Professions and Related Programs, 26% Business, Management, Marketing, and Related Support Services, 10% Communications Technologies/Technicians and Support Services, 8% Homeland Security, Law Enforcement, Firefighting and Related Protective Services, 6% Psychology
Expenses: 2019-2020: $18,940; room/board: $10,223
Financial aid: (207) 941-7156; 85% of undergrads determined to have financial need; average aid package $15,746

Maine College of Art[1]
Portland ME
(800) 699-1509
U.S. News ranking: Arts, unranked
Website: www.meca.edu
Admissions email: admissions@meca.edu
Private; founded 1882
Application deadline (fall): rolling
Undergraduate student body: N/A full time, N/A part time
Expenses: N/A
Financial aid: (207) 699-5073

Maine Maritime Academy
Castine ME
(207) 326-2206
U.S. News ranking: Reg. Coll. (N), No. 5
Website: www.mainemaritime.edu
Admissions email: admissions@mma.edu
Public; founded 1941
Freshman admissions: selective; 2018-2019: 1,056 applied, 481 accepted. Either SAT or ACT required. SAT 25/75 percentile: 1000-1180. High school rank: 10% in top tenth, 33% in top quarter, 69% in top half
Early decision deadline: N/A, notification date: N/A
Early action deadline: 11/30, notification date: 2/1
Application deadline (fall): 3/1
Undergraduate student body: 958 full time, 21 part time; 84% male, 16% female; 1% American Indian, 1% Asian, 1% black, 3% Hispanic, 0% multiracial, 0% Pacific Islander, 85% white, 0% international; 70% from in state; 70% live on campus; 0% of students in fraternities, 0% in sororities

Most popular majors: 41% Naval Architecture and Marine Engineering, 27% Marine Science/Merchant Marine Officer, 12% Engineering Technologies and Engineering-Related Fields, Other, 11% International Business/Trade/Commerce, 5% Systems Engineering
Expenses: 2019-2020: $13,792 in state, $27,820 out of state; room/board: $10,516
Financial aid: (207) 326-2339; 82% of undergrads determined to have financial need; average aid package $10,215

St. Joseph's College[1]
Standish ME
(207) 893-7746
U.S. News ranking: Reg. U. (N), second tier
Website: www.sjcme.edu
Admissions email: admission@sjcme.edu
Private
Application deadline (fall): N/A
Undergraduate student body: N/A full time, N/A part time
Expenses: N/A
Financial aid: N/A

Thomas College[1]
Waterville ME
(800) 339-7001
U.S. News ranking: Reg. U. (N), second tier
Website: www.thomas.edu
Admissions email: admiss@thomas.edu
Private; founded 1894
Application deadline (fall): rolling
Undergraduate student body: N/A full time, N/A part time
Expenses: 2019-2020: $27,720; room/board: $12,650
Financial aid: (207) 859-1105; 87% of undergrads determined to have financial need; average aid package $21,746

Unity College
Unity ME
(800) 624-1024
U.S. News ranking: Reg. Coll. (N), No. 17
Website: www.unity.edu
Admissions email: admissions@unity.edu
Private; founded 1965
Freshman admissions: selective; 2018-2019: 959 applied, 904 accepted. Neither SAT nor ACT required. SAT 25/75 percentile: 1000-1260. High school rank: 8% in top tenth, 38% in top quarter, 72% in top half
Early decision deadline: N/A, notification date: N/A
Early action deadline: 12/15, notification date: 9/1
Application deadline (fall): rolling
Undergraduate student body: 715 full time, 20 part time; 48% male, 52% female; 2% American Indian, 1% Asian, 0% black, 1% Hispanic, 3% multiracial, 0% Pacific Islander, 86% white, 0% international
Most popular majors: 25% Wildlife, Fish and Wildlands Science and Management, 19% Natural

Resources Law Enforcement and Protective Services, 13% Wildlife Biology, 9% Natural Resource Recreation and Tourism, 8% Therapeutic Recreation/Recreational Therapy
Expenses: 2018-2019: $28,660; room/board: $10,710
Financial aid: (207) 509-7235

University of Maine
Orono ME
(877) 486-2364
U.S. News ranking: Nat. U., No. 202
Website: www.umaine.edu
Admissions email: umaineadmissions@maine.edu
Public; founded 1865
Freshman admissions: selective; 2018-2019: 12,457 applied, 11,503 accepted. Either SAT or ACT required. SAT 25/75 percentile: 1050-1250. High school rank: 18% in top tenth, 40% in top quarter, 73% in top half
Early decision deadline: N/A, notification date: N/A
Early action deadline: 12/1, notification date: 1/15
Application deadline (fall): 2/1
Undergraduate student body: 8,158 full time, 1,207 part time; 53% male, 47% female; 1% American Indian, 1% Asian, 2% black, 4% Hispanic, 3% multiracial, 0% Pacific Islander, 84% white, 2% international; 63% from in state; 38% live on campus; N/A of students in fraternities, N/A in sororities
Most popular majors: 17% Business, Management, Marketing, and Related Support Services, 13% Engineering, 8% Education, 7% Engineering Technologies and Engineering-Related Fields, 7% Health Professions and Related Programs
Expenses: 2019-2020: $11,438 in state, $31,748 out of state; room/board: $10,984
Financial aid: (207) 581-1324; 68% of undergrads determined to have financial need; average aid package $13,716

University of Maine–Augusta[1]
Augusta ME
(207) 621-3465
U.S. News ranking: Reg. Coll. (N), second tier
Website: www.uma.edu
Admissions email: umaadm@maine.edu
Public; founded 1965
Application deadline (fall): 9/1
Undergraduate student body: N/A full time, N/A part time
Expenses: 2018-2019: $7,988 in state, $17,918 out of state; room/board: N/A
Financial aid: (207) 621-3141

University of Maine–Farmington
Farmington ME
(207) 778-7050
U.S. News ranking: Reg. Coll. (N), No. 8
Website: www.farmington.edu
Admissions email: umfadmit@maine.edu
Public; founded 1864
Freshman admissions: selective; 2018-2019: 1,905 applied, 1,547 accepted. Neither SAT nor ACT required. SAT 25/75 percentile: 970-1180. High school rank: 16% in top tenth, 44% in top quarter, 74% in top half
Early decision deadline: N/A, notification date: N/A
Early action deadline: 11/15, notification date: 12/15
Application deadline (fall): rolling
Undergraduate student body: 1,564 full time, 172 part time; 34% male, 66% female; 1% American Indian, 1% Asian, 2% black, 3% Hispanic, 2% multiracial, 0% Pacific Islander, 88% white, 0% international; 83% from in state; 51% live on campus; 0% of students in fraternities, 0% in sororities
Most popular majors: 33% Education, 13% Health Professions and Related Programs, 12% Business, Management, Marketing, and Related Support Services, 10% English Language and Literature/Letters, 9% Psychology
Expenses: 2019-2020: $9,344 in state, $19,514 out of state; room/board: $9,902
Financial aid: (207) 778-7100; 78% of undergrads determined to have financial need; average aid package $14,936

University of Maine–Fort Kent
Fort Kent ME
(207) 834-7600
U.S. News ranking: Reg. Coll. (N), No. 25
Website: www.umfk.edu
Admissions email: umfkadm@maine.edu
Public; founded 1878
Freshman admissions: less selective; 2018-2019: 856 applied, 830 accepted. SAT required for some. SAT 25/75 percentile: 910-1090. High school rank: 5% in top tenth, 23% in top quarter, 56% in top half
Early decision deadline: N/A, notification date: N/A
Early action deadline: N/A, notification date: N/A
Application deadline (fall): rolling
Undergraduate student body: 579 full time, 793 part time; 28% male, 72% female; 1% American Indian, 1% Asian, 4% black, 3% Hispanic, 3% multiracial, 0% Pacific Islander, 78% white, 7% international; 86% from in state; 19% live on campus; 0% of students in fraternities, 0% in sororities

Most popular majors: 60% Health Professions and Related Programs, 11% Business, Management, Marketing, and Related Support Services, 7% Social Sciences, 6% Public Administration and Social Service Professions, 3% Biological and Biomedical Sciences
Expenses: 2019-2020: $8,295 in state, $12,585 out of state; room/board: $8,360
Financial aid: (207) 834-7607; 66% of undergrads determined to have financial need; average aid package $11,946

University of Maine–Machias
Machias ME
(888) 468-6866
U.S. News ranking: Nat. Lib. Arts, unranked
Website: machias.edu/
Admissions email: ummadmissions@maine.edu
Public; founded 1909
Freshman admissions: less selective; 2018-2019: 596 applied, 584 accepted. Neither SAT nor ACT required. SAT 25/75 percentile: 875-1090. High school rank: N/A
Early decision deadline: N/A, notification date: N/A
Early action deadline: 12/15, notification date: N/A
Application deadline (fall): 8/15
Undergraduate student body: 345 full time, 330 part time; 29% male, 71% female; 4% American Indian, 1% Asian, 3% black, 4% Hispanic, 2% multiracial, 0% Pacific Islander, 84% white, 0% international; 89% from in state; 24% live on campus; N/A of students in fraternities, N/A in sororities
Most popular majors: 21% Biological and Biomedical Sciences, 15% Liberal Arts and Sciences, General Studies and Humanities, 15% Psychology, 14% Business, Management, Marketing, and Related Support Services, 13% Parks, Recreation, Leisure, and Fitness Studies
Expenses: 2019-2020: $8,966 in state, $16,046 out of state; room/board: $9,180
Financial aid: (207) 255-1203; 88% of undergrads determined to have financial need; average aid package $12,716

University of Maine–Presque Isle
Presque Isle ME
(207) 768-9532
U.S. News ranking: Reg. Coll. (N), No. 28
Website: www.umpi.edu/admissions/
Admissions email: umpi-admissions@maine.edu
Public; founded 1903
Freshman admissions: least selective; 2018-2019: 801 applied, 734 accepted. Neither SAT nor ACT required. SAT 25/75 percentile: 880-1100. High

school rank: 7% in top tenth, 27% in top quarter, 57% in top half
Early decision deadline: N/A, notification date: N/A
Early action deadline: N/A, notification date: N/A
Application deadline (fall): rolling
Undergraduate student body: 673 full time, 881 part time; 39% male, 61% female; 2% American Indian, 1% Asian, 4% black, 3% Hispanic, 2% multiracial, 0% Pacific Islander, 82% white, 4% international; 86% from in state; 34% live on campus; 0% of students in fraternities, 0% in sororities
Most popular majors: 24% Business Administration and Management, General, 13% Liberal Arts and Sciences/Liberal Studies, 12% Multicultural Education, 9% Psychology, General, 9% Social Work
Expenses: 2019-2020: $8,364 in state, $12,654 out of state; room/board: $8,496
Financial aid: (207) 768-9510; 74% of undergrads determined to have financial need; average aid package $12,482

University of New England
Biddeford ME
(800) 477-4863
U.S. News ranking: Nat. U., No. 246
Website: www.une.edu
Admissions email: admissions@une.edu
Private; founded 1831
Freshman admissions: selective; 2018-2019: 4,985 applied, 3,979 accepted. Either SAT or ACT required for some. SAT 25/75 percentile: 1050-1240. High school rank: N/A
Early decision deadline: N/A, notification date: N/A
Early action deadline: 12/1, notification date: 12/15
Application deadline (fall): 2/15
Undergraduate student body: 2,367 full time, 2,082 part time; 30% male, 70% female; 0% American Indian, 3% Asian, 1% black, 0% Hispanic, 2% multiracial, 0% Pacific Islander, 89% white, 0% international; 29% from in state; 63% live on campus; N/A of students in fraternities, N/A in sororities
Most popular majors: 41% Health Professions and Related Programs, 29% Biological and Biomedical Sciences, 9% Parks, Recreation, Leisure, and Fitness Studies, 5% Social Sciences, 4% Psychology
Expenses: 2019-2020: $38,750; room/board: $14,410
Financial aid: (207) 602-2342; 83% of undergrads determined to have financial need; average aid package $24,047

University of Southern Maine
Portland ME
(207) 780-5670
U.S. News ranking: Reg. U. (N), second tier
Website: www.usm.maine.edu
Admissions email: admitusm@maine.edu
Public; founded 1878
Freshman admissions: less selective; 2018-2019: 4,254 applied, 3,634 accepted. Either SAT or ACT required. SAT 25/75 percentile: 940-1060. High school rank: 10% in top tenth, 34% in top quarter, 72% in top half
Early decision deadline: N/A, notification date: N/A
Early action deadline: N/A, notification date: N/A
Application deadline (fall): rolling
Undergraduate student body: 4,022 full time, 2,368 part time; 42% male, 58% female; 1% American Indian, 2% Asian, 7% black, 3% Hispanic, 4% multiracial, 0% Pacific Islander, 79% white, 1% international
Most popular majors: 22% Business, Management, Marketing, and Related Support Services, 20% Health Professions and Related Programs, 13% Social Sciences, 5% Biological and Biomedical Sciences, 5% Communication, Journalism, and Related Programs
Expenses: 2019-2020: $9,850 in state, $23,590 out of state; room/board: $9,826
Financial aid: (207) 780-5250; 72% of undergrads determined to have financial need; average aid package $14,321

MARYLAND

Bowie State University
Bowie MD
(301) 860-3415
U.S. News ranking: Reg. U. (N), second tier
Website: www.bowiestate.edu
Admissions email: ugradadmissions@bowiestate.edu
Public; founded 1865
Freshman admissions: less selective; 2018-2019: 12,830 applied, 4,204 accepted. Either SAT or ACT required. SAT 25/75 percentile: 860-1020. High school rank: N/A
Early decision deadline: N/A, notification date: N/A
Early action deadline: N/A, notification date: N/A
Application deadline (fall): 5/15
Undergraduate student body: 4,421 full time, 887 part time; 39% male, 61% female; 0% American Indian, 1% Asian, 83% black, 4% Hispanic, 4% multiracial, 0% Pacific Islander, 2% white, 3% international; 89% from in state; 19% live on campus; 37% of students in fraternities, 64% in sororities
Most popular majors: 14% Business Administration and Management, General, 14%

Radio and Television Broadcasting Technology/Technician, 11% Criminal Justice/Safety Studies, 9% Psychology, General, 8% Biology/Biological Sciences, General
Expenses: 2019-2020: $8,444 in state, $19,136 out of state; room/board: $11,444
Financial aid: (301) 860-3540; 86% of undergrads determined to have financial need; average aid package $8,789

Coppin State University
Baltimore MD
(410) 951-3600
U.S. News ranking: Reg. U. (N), second tier
Website: www.coppin.edu
Admissions email: admissions@coppin.edu
Public; founded 1900
Freshman admissions: less selective; 2018-2019: 6,156 applied, 2,352 accepted. Either SAT or ACT required. SAT 25/75 percentile: 880-1030. High school rank: N/A
Early decision deadline: N/A, notification date: N/A
Early action deadline: N/A, notification date: N/A
Application deadline (fall): rolling
Undergraduate student body: 1,765 full time, 597 part time; 22% male, 78% female; 0% American Indian, 0% Asian, 81% black, 3% Hispanic, 2% multiracial, 0% Pacific Islander, 2% white, 9% international
Most popular majors: 16% Registered Nursing/Registered Nurse, 11% Criminal Justice/Safety Studies, 10% Psychology, General, 10% Social Work, 6% Health Information/Medical Records Administration/Administrator
Expenses: 2019-2020: $6,716 in state, $13,113 out of state; room/board: $10,654
Financial aid: (410) 951-3636

Frostburg State University
Frostburg MD
(301) 687-4201
U.S. News ranking: Reg. U. (N), No. 108
Website: www.frostburg.edu
Admissions email: fsuadmissions@frostburg.edu
Public; founded 1898
Freshman admissions: less selective; 2018-2019: 3,061 applied, 2,397 accepted. Either SAT or ACT required. SAT 25/75 percentile: 930-1120. High school rank: 10% in top tenth, 29% in top quarter, 61% in top half
Early decision deadline: 12/15, notification date: N/A
Early action deadline: N/A, notification date: N/A
Application deadline (fall): rolling
Undergraduate student body: 3,805 full time, 833 part time; 48% male, 52% female; 0% American Indian, 2% Asian, 33% black, 5% Hispanic, 4% multiracial,

0% Pacific Islander, 52% white, 2% international; 91% from in state; 27% live on campus; N/A of students in fraternities, N/A in sororities
Most popular majors: 15% Registered Nursing/Registered Nurse, 10% Business Administration and Management, General, 6% Early Childhood Education and Teaching, 6% Psychology, General, 5% Liberal Arts and Sciences/Liberal Studies
Expenses: 2019-2020: $9,410 in state, $23,510 out of state; room/board: $10,788
Financial aid: (301) 687-4301; 66% of undergrads determined to have financial need; average aid package $10,060

Goucher College
Baltimore MD
(410) 337-6100
U.S. News ranking: Nat. Lib. Arts, No. 111
Website: www.goucher.edu
Admissions email: admissions@goucher.edu
Private; founded 1885
Freshman admissions: selective; 2018-2019: 3,154 applied, 2,536 accepted. Neither SAT nor ACT required. SAT 25/75 percentile: 1040-1290. High school rank: 18% in top tenth, 36% in top quarter, 79% in top half
Early decision deadline: 11/15, notification date: 12/15
Early action deadline: 12/1, notification date: 2/1
Application deadline (fall): 1/15
Undergraduate student body: 1,403 full time, 22 part time; 31% male, 69% female; 0% American Indian, 4% Asian, 16% black, 11% Hispanic, 5% multiracial, 0% Pacific Islander, 56% white, 3% international; N/A from in state; 87% live on campus; 0% of students in fraternities, 0% in sororities
Most popular majors: 15% Social Sciences, 11% Psychology, 10% Business, Management, Marketing, and Related Support Services, 10% Health Professions and Related Programs, 8% Natural Resources and Conservation
Expenses: 2019-2020: $45,250; room/board: $14,900
Financial aid: (410) 337-6141; 72% of undergrads determined to have financial need; average aid package $39,160

Hood College
Frederick MD
(800) 922-1599
U.S. News ranking: Reg. U. (N), No. 48
Website: www.hood.edu
Admissions email: admission@hood.edu
Private; founded 1893
Affiliation: United Church of Christ
Freshman admissions: selective; 2018-2019: 1,562 applied, 1,115 accepted. Neither SAT nor ACT required. SAT 25/75 percentile: 990-1270. High school rank: 24% in top tenth, 44% in top quarter, 76% in top half

Early decision deadline: N/A, notification date: N/A
Early action deadline: N/A, notification date: N/A
Application deadline (fall): rolling
Undergraduate student body: 1,014 full time, 78 part time; 37% male, 63% female; 0% American Indian, 3% Asian, 18% black, 11% Hispanic, 6% multiracial, 0% Pacific Islander, 58% white, 2% international; 74% from in state; 51% live on campus; 0% of students in fraternities, 0% in sororities
Most popular majors: 23% Business, Management, Marketing, and Related Support Services, 10% Education, 9% Communication, Journalism, and Related Programs, 8% Social Sciences, 7% Biological and Biomedical Sciences
Expenses: 2019-2020: $41,060; room/board: $12,880
Financial aid: (301) 696-3411; 81% of undergrads determined to have financial need; average aid package $31,926

Johns Hopkins University
Baltimore MD
(410) 516-8171
U.S. News ranking: Nat. U., No. 10
Website: www.jhu.edu
Admissions email: gotojhu@jhu.edu
Private; founded 1876
Freshman admissions: most selective; 2018-2019: 29,127 applied, 3,089 accepted. Either SAT or ACT required. ACT 25/75 percentile: 33-35. High school rank: 96% in top tenth, 98% in top quarter, 100% in top half
Early decision deadline: 11/1, notification date: 12/15
Early action deadline: N/A, notification date: N/A
Application deadline (fall): 1/2
Undergraduate student body: 5,504 full time, 560 part time; 46% male, 54% female; 0% American Indian, 26% Asian, 7% black, 14% Hispanic, 6% multiracial, 0% Pacific Islander, 31% white, 11% international; 11% from in state; 49% live on campus; 20% of students in fraternities, 29% in sororities
Most popular majors: 9% Neuroscience, 9% Public Health, General, 8% Bioengineering and Biomedical Engineering, 7% Cell/Cellular and Molecular Biology, 6% Computer and Information Sciences, General
Expenses: 2019-2020: $55,350; room/board: $16,310
Financial aid: (410) 516-8028; 53% of undergrads determined to have financial need; average aid package $44,147

Loyola University Maryland
Baltimore MD
(410) 617-5012
U.S. News ranking: Reg. U. (N), No. 4
Website: www.loyola.edu
Admissions email: admissions@loyola.edu
Private; founded 1852

Affiliation: Roman Catholic
Freshman admissions: more selective; 2018-2019: 10,251 applied, 8,072 accepted. Neither SAT nor ACT required. SAT 25/75 percentile: 1140-1320. High school rank: 28% in top tenth, 61% in top quarter, 90% in top half
Early decision deadline: N/A, notification date: N/A
Early action deadline: 11/15, notification date: 1/15
Application deadline (fall): 1/15
Undergraduate student body: 3,833 full time, 46 part time; 42% male, 58% female; 0% American Indian, 4% Asian, 6% black, 10% Hispanic, 3% multiracial, 0% Pacific Islander, 76% white, 1% international; 20% from in state; 82% live on campus; 0% of students in fraternities, 0% in sororities
Most popular majors: 39% Business, Management, Marketing, and Related Support Services, 10% Communication, Journalism, and Related Programs, 8% Social Sciences, 7% Health Professions and Related Programs, 7% Psychology
Expenses: 2019-2020: $50,265; room/board: $16,040
Financial aid: (410) 617-2576; 53% of undergrads determined to have financial need; average aid package $32,093

Maryland Institute College of Art
Baltimore MD
(410) 225-2222
U.S. News ranking: Arts, unranked
Website: www.mica.edu
Admissions email: admissions@mica.edu
Private; founded 1826
Freshman admissions: selective; 2018-2019: 3,702 applied, 2,379 accepted. Either SAT or ACT required. SAT 25/75 percentile: 1030-1290. High school rank: N/A
Early decision deadline: 11/1, notification date: 12/1
Early action deadline: 12/1, notification date: 1/11
Application deadline (fall): 2/1
Undergraduate student body: 1,689 full time, 25 part time; 25% male, 75% female; 0% American Indian, 11% Asian, 8% black, 3% Hispanic, 13% multiracial, 0% Pacific Islander, 37% white, 27% international; N/A from in state; 88% live on campus; N/A of students in fraternities, N/A in sororities
Most popular majors: 20% Illustration, 19% Graphic Design, 13% Intermedia/Multimedia, 11% Painting, 8% Fine Arts and Art Studies, Other
Expenses: 2019-2020: $50,330; room/board: $13,720
Financial aid: (410) 225-2285

McDaniel College
Westminster MD
(800) 638-5005
U.S. News ranking: Reg. U. (N), No. 22
Website: www.mcdaniel.edu
Admissions email: admissions@mcdaniel.edu
Private; founded 1867
Freshman admissions: selective; 2018-2019: 3,682 applied, 2,368 accepted. Either SAT or ACT required. SAT 25/75 percentile: 1050-1230. High school rank: 21% in top tenth, 46% in top quarter, 79% in top half
Early decision deadline: 11/1, notification date: 12/1
Early action deadline: 12/15, notification date: 1/15
Application deadline (fall): rolling
Undergraduate student body: 1,529 full time, 29 part time; 49% male, 51% female; 0% American Indian, 2% Asian, 16% black, 7% Hispanic, 3% multiracial, 0% Pacific Islander, 62% white, 3% international; 67% from in state; 83% live on campus; 14% of students in fraternities, 16% in sororities
Most popular majors: 15% Social Sciences, 14% Business, Management, Marketing, and Related Support Services, 10% Psychology, 9% Visual and Performing Arts, 8% Parks, Recreation, Leisure, and Fitness Studies
Expenses: 2019-2020: $44,540; room/board: $11,772
Financial aid: (410) 857-2233; 79% of undergrads determined to have financial need; average aid package $41,454

Morgan State University
Baltimore MD
(800) 332-6674
U.S. News ranking: Nat. U., second tier
Website: www.morgan.edu
Admissions email: admissions@morgan.edu
Public; founded 1867
Freshman admissions: less selective; 2018-2019: 8,613 applied, 5,720 accepted. Either SAT or ACT required. SAT 25/75 percentile: 920-1080. High school rank: 7% in top tenth, 31% in top quarter, 56% in top half
Early decision deadline: 11/15, notification date: 2/15
Early action deadline: 11/15, notification date: 2/15
Application deadline (fall): 2/15
Undergraduate student body: 5,830 full time, 589 part time; 45% male, 55% female; 0% American Indian, 1% Asian, 80% black, 3% Hispanic, 3% multiracial, 0% Pacific Islander, 2% white, 9% international; 76% from in state; 55% live on campus; N/A of students in fraternities, N/A in sororities
Most popular majors: 22% Business, Management, Marketing, and Related Support Services, 15% Engineering, 8%

Education, 7% Communication, Journalism, and Related Programs, 7% Social Sciences
Expenses: 2019-2020: $8,008 in state, $18,480 out of state; room/board: $10,994
Financial aid: (443) 885-3170; 77% of undergrads determined to have financial need; average aid package $11,239

Mount St. Mary's University
Emmitsburg MD
(800) 448-4347
U.S. News ranking: Reg. U. (N), No. 42
Website: www.msmary.edu
Admissions email: admissions@msmary.edu
Private; founded 1808
Affiliation: Roman Catholic
Freshman admissions: selective; 2018-2019: 5,462 applied, 3,721 accepted. Either SAT or ACT required. SAT 25/75 percentile: 1000-1210. High school rank: 14% in top tenth, 36% in top quarter, 69% in top half
Early decision deadline: N/A, notification date: N/A
Early action deadline: 12/1, notification date: 12/25
Application deadline (fall): 3/1
Undergraduate student body: 1,727 full time, 162 part time; 49% male, 51% female; 0% American Indian, 3% Asian, 16% black, 12% Hispanic, 5% multiracial, 0% Pacific Islander, 61% white, 1% international; 58% from in state; 77% live on campus; 0% of students in fraternities, 0% in sororities
Most popular majors: 27% Business, Management, Marketing, and Related Support Services, 8% Biological and Biomedical Sciences, 8% Homeland Security, Law Enforcement, Firefighting and Related Protective Services, 6% Communication, Journalism, and Related Programs, 6% Psychology
Expenses: 2019-2020: $42,590; room/board: $13,330
Financial aid: (301) 447-8364; 74% of undergrads determined to have financial need; average aid package $30,494

Notre Dame of Maryland University
Baltimore MD
(410) 532-5330
U.S. News ranking: Reg. U. (N), No. 59
Website: www.ndm.edu
Admissions email: admiss@ndm.edu
Private; founded 1895
Affiliation: Roman Catholic
Freshman admissions: selective; 2018-2019: 1,310 applied, 1,148 accepted. Neither SAT nor ACT required. SAT 25/75 percentile: 930-1140. High school rank: 40% in top tenth, 68% in top quarter, 92% in top half
Early decision deadline: N/A, notification date: N/A
Early action deadline: N/A, notification date: N/A

Application deadline (fall): rolling
Undergraduate student body: 598 full time, 243 part time; 4% male, 96% female; 0% American Indian, 8% Asian, 29% black, 13% Hispanic, 5% multiracial, 0% Pacific Islander, 39% white, 1% international; 88% from in state; 61% live on campus; 0% of students in fraternities, 0% in sororities
Most popular majors: 44% Registered Nursing/Registered Nurse, 15% Liberal Arts and Sciences, General Studies and Humanities, Other, 10% Multi-/Interdisciplinary Studies, Other, 5% Business Administration and Management, General, 4% Medical Radiologic Technology/Science - Radiation Therapist
Expenses: 2019-2020: $38,340; room/board: $12,200
Financial aid: (410) 532-5369; 72% of undergrads determined to have financial need; average aid package $6,854

Salisbury University
Salisbury MD
(410) 543-6161
U.S. News ranking: Reg. U. (N), No. 75
Website: www.salisbury.edu/
Admissions email: admissions@salisbury.edu
Public; founded 1925
Freshman admissions: selective; 2018-2019: 8,983 applied, 5,585 accepted. Either SAT or ACT required for some. SAT 25/75 percentile: 1145-1280. High school rank: 15% in top tenth, 45% in top quarter, 85% in top half
Early decision deadline: 11/15, notification date: 12/15
Early action deadline: 12/1, notification date: 1/15
Application deadline (fall): 1/15
Undergraduate student body: 7,081 full time, 569 part time; 44% male, 56% female; 1% American Indian, 4% Asian, 14% black, 4% Hispanic, 3% multiracial, 0% Pacific Islander, 71% white, 1% international; 87% from in state; 29% live on campus; N/A of students in fraternities, N/A in sororities
Most popular majors: 16% Business, Management, Marketing, and Related Support Services, 10% Education, 8% Communication, Journalism, and Related Programs, 8% Parks, Recreation, Leisure, and Fitness Studies, 7% Health Professions and Related Programs
Expenses: 2019-2020: $10,046 in state, $20,112 out of state; room/board: $12,360
Financial aid: (410) 543-6165; 54% of undergrads determined to have financial need; average aid package $8,726

Stevenson University

Stevenson MD
(877) 468-6852
U.S. News ranking: Reg. U. (N), No. 75
Website: www.stevenson.edu/
Admissions email: admissions@stevenson.edu
Private; founded 1947
Freshman admissions: selective; 2018-2019: 4,352 applied, 3,184 accepted. Either SAT or ACT required. SAT 25/75 percentile: 1030-1200. High school rank: 18% in top tenth, 44% in top quarter, 79% in top half
Early decision deadline: N/A, notification date: N/A
Early action deadline: N/A, notification date: N/A
Application deadline (fall): rolling
Undergraduate student body: 2,708 full time, 405 part time; 35% male, 65% female; 0% American Indian, 4% Asian, 26% black, 6% Hispanic, 5% multiracial, 0% Pacific Islander, 56% white, 1% international; 77% from in state; 53% live on campus; 3% of students in fraternities, 1% in sororities
Most popular majors: 25% Health Professions and Related Programs, 22% Business, Management, Marketing, and Related Support Services, 8% Education, 7% Computer and Information Sciences and Support Services, 6% Homeland Security, Law Enforcement, Firefighting and Related Protective Services
Expenses: 2019-2020: $37,082; room/board: $13,624
Financial aid: (443) 334-3200; 78% of undergrads determined to have financial need; average aid package $25,047

St. John's College

Annapolis MD
(410) 626-2522
U.S. News ranking: Nat. Lib. Arts, No. 64
Website: www.sjc.edu
Admissions email: annapolis.admissions@sjc.edu
Private; founded 1696
Freshman admissions: more selective; 2018-2019: 913 applied, 526 accepted. Either SAT or ACT required for some. SAT 25/75 percentile: 1200-1460. High school rank: 22% in top tenth, 44% in top quarter, 67% in top half
Early decision deadline: 11/1, notification date: 12/1
Early action deadline: 11/15, notification date: 12/15
Application deadline (fall): rolling
Undergraduate student body: 4/4 full time, 0 part time; 52% male, 48% female; 0% American Indian, 4% Asian, 2% black, 5% Hispanic, 5% multiracial, 0% Pacific Islander, 62% white, 23% international; 23% from in state; 70% live on campus; 0% of students in fraternities, 0% in sororities
Most popular majors: 100% Liberal Arts and Sciences/Liberal Studies

Expenses: 2019-2020: $35,635; room/board: $13,636
Financial aid: (410) 626-2502; 76% of undergrads determined to have financial need; average aid package $44,219

St. Mary's College of Maryland

St. Marys City MD
(800) 492-7181
U.S. News ranking: Nat. Lib. Arts, No. 92
Website: www.smcm.edu
Admissions email: admissions@smcm.edu
Public; founded 1840
Freshman admissions: selective; 2018-2019: 1,700 applied, 1,361 accepted. Either SAT or ACT required. SAT 25/75 percentile: 1060-1290. High school rank: 19% in top tenth, 46% in top quarter, 80% in top half
Early decision deadline: 11/1, notification date: 12/1
Early action deadline: 11/1, notification date: 1/1
Application deadline (fall): 1/15
Undergraduate student body: 1,521 full time, 51 part time; 42% male, 58% female; 0% American Indian, 4% Asian, 9% black, 7% Hispanic, 5% multiracial, 0% Pacific Islander, 72% white, 0% international; 94% from in state; 81% live on campus; 0% of students in fraternities, 0% in sororities
Most popular majors: 23% Social Sciences, 14% Biological and Biomedical Sciences, 12% Psychology, 7% Computer and Information Sciences and Support Services, 7% Visual and Performing Arts
Expenses: 2019-2020: $15,124 in state, $31,200 out of state; room/board: $13,595
Financial aid: (240) 895-3000; 54% of undergrads determined to have financial need; average aid package $14,218

Towson University

Towson MD
(410) 704-2113
U.S. News ranking: Nat. U., No. 197
Website: www.towson.edu
Admissions email: admissions@towson.edu
Public; founded 1866
Freshman admissions: selective; 2018-2019: 11,933 applied, 9,427 accepted. Either SAT or ACT required. SAT 25/75 percentile: 1060-1200. High school rank: 14% in top tenth, 39% in top quarter, 78% in top half
Early decision deadline: N/A, notification date: N/A
Early action deadline: 12/1, notification date: 12/31
Application deadline (fall): 1/15
Undergraduate student body: 17,350 full time, 2,468 part time; 41% male, 59% female; 0% American Indian, 6% Asian, 23% black, 8% Hispanic,

5% multiracial, 0% Pacific Islander, 54% white, 2% international; N/A from in state; 28% live on campus; 10% of students in fraternities, 11% in sororities
Most popular majors: 15% Business, Management, Marketing, and Related Support Services, 13% Health Professions and Related Programs, 10% Social Sciences, 9% Communication, Journalism, and Related Programs, 9% Education
Expenses: 2019-2020: $10,198 in state, $24,334 out of state; room/board: $13,446
Financial aid: (410) 704-4236; 58% of undergrads determined to have financial need; average aid package $10,734

United States Naval Academy

Annapolis MD
(410) 293-1858
U.S. News ranking: Nat. Lib. Arts, No. 17
Website: www.usna.edu
Admissions email: inquire@usna.edu
Public; founded 1845
Freshman admissions: more selective; 2018-2019: 16,086 applied, 1,374 accepted. Either SAT or ACT required. SAT 25/75 percentile: 1150-1370. High school rank: 57% in top tenth, 81% in top quarter, 96% in top half
Early decision deadline: N/A, notification date: N/A
Early action deadline: N/A, notification date: N/A
Application deadline (fall): 1/31
Undergraduate student body: 4,512 full time, 0 part time; 72% male, 28% female; 0% American Indian, 7% Asian, 7% black, 12% Hispanic, 9% multiracial, 1% Pacific Islander, 63% white, 1% international; 6% from in state; 100% live on campus; 0% of students in fraternities, 0% in sororities
Most popular majors: 27% Social Sciences, 8% Physical Sciences, 5% Computer and Information Sciences and Support Services, 5% English Language and Literature/Letters, 5% History
Expenses: 2019-2020: $0 in state, $0 out of state; room/board: N/A
Financial aid: N/A; 0% of undergrads determined to have financial need

University of Baltimore

Baltimore MD
(410) 837-4777
U.S. News ranking: Reg. U. (N), second tier
Website: www.ubalt.edu
Admissions email: admissions@ubalt.edu
Public; founded 1925
Freshman admissions: less selective; 2018-2019: 329 applied, 260 accepted. Either SAT or ACT required. SAT 25/75 percentile: 910-1115. High school rank: N/A

Early decision deadline: N/A, notification date: N/A
Early action deadline: N/A, notification date: N/A
Application deadline (fall): rolling
Undergraduate student body: 1,402 full time, 1,040 part time; 40% male, 60% female; 1% American Indian, 5% Asian, 47% black, 4% Hispanic, 4% multiracial, 1% Pacific Islander, 32% white, 2% international; 95% from in state; N/A live on campus; N/A of students in fraternities, N/A in sororities
Most popular majors: 34% Business/Commerce, General, 12% Criminal Justice/Police Science, 7% Health Services Administration, 5% Animation, Interactive Technology, Video Graphics and Special Effects, 5% Digital Communication and Media/Multimedia
Expenses: 2018-2019: $8,958 in state, $21,076 out of state; room/board: N/A
Financial aid: (410) 837-4772; 76% of undergrads determined to have financial need; average aid package $13,278

University of Maryland– Baltimore County

Baltimore MD
(410) 455-2292
U.S. News ranking: Nat. U., No. 166
Website: www.umbc.edu
Admissions email: admissions@umbc.edu
Public; founded 1966
Freshman admissions: more selective; 2018-2019: 11,720 applied, 6,790 accepted. Either SAT or ACT required. SAT 25/75 percentile: 1190-1360. High school rank: 23% in top tenth, 50% in top quarter, 84% in top half
Early decision deadline: N/A, notification date: N/A
Early action deadline: 11/1, notification date: 12/15
Application deadline (fall): 2/1
Undergraduate student body: 9,623 full time, 1,637 part time; 56% male, 44% female; 0% American Indian, 22% Asian, 18% black, 8% Hispanic, 5% multiracial, 0% Pacific Islander, 40% white, 4% international; 91% from in state; 35% live on campus; 3% of students in fraternities, 5% in sororities
Most popular majors: 20% Computer and Information Sciences and Support Services, 16% Biological and Biomedical Sciences, 12% Psychology, 10% Social Sciences, 9% Engineering
Expenses: 2019-2020: $12,028 in state, $27,062 out of state; room/board: $12,350
Financial aid: (410) 455-2538; 54% of undergrads determined to have financial need; average aid package $11,686

University of Maryland– College Park

College Park MD
(301) 314-8385
U.S. News ranking: Nat. U., No. 64
Website: www.maryland.edu
Admissions email: ApplyMaryland@umd.edu
Public; founded 1856
Freshman admissions: more selective; 2018-2019: 33,461 applied, 15,760 accepted. Either SAT or ACT required. SAT 25/75 percentile: 1290-1480. High school rank: 75% in top tenth, 93% in top quarter, 99% in top half
Early decision deadline: N/A, notification date: N/A
Early action deadline: 11/1, notification date: 1/31
Application deadline (fall): 1/20
Undergraduate student body: 28,501 full time, 2,261 part time; 53% male, 47% female; 0% American Indian, 17% Asian, 12% black, 10% Hispanic, 4% multiracial, 0% Pacific Islander, 50% white, 5% international; 77% from in state; 41% live on campus; 15% of students in fraternities, 19% in sororities
Most popular majors: 7% Economics, General, 6% Biology/Biological Sciences, General, 6% Computer Science, 5% Criminology, 4% Speech Communication and Rhetoric
Expenses: 2019-2020: $10,778 in state, $36,890 out of state; room/board: $12,874
Financial aid: (301) 314-9000; 41% of undergrads determined to have financial need; average aid package $12,364

University of Maryland– Eastern Shore

Princess Anne MD
(410) 651-6410
U.S. News ranking: Nat. U., second tier
Website: www.umes.edu
Admissions email: umesadmissions@umes.edu
Public; founded 1886
Freshman admissions: less selective; 2018-2019: 4,923 applied, 2,664 accepted. Either SAT or ACT required. SAT 25/75 percentile: 870-1050. High school rank: N/A
Early decision deadline: N/A, notification date: N/A
Early action deadline: N/A, notification date: N/A
Application deadline (fall): 6/30
Undergraduate student body: 2,360 full time, 243 part time; 45% male, 55% female; 0% American Indian, 2% Asian, 71% black, 4% Hispanic, 4% multiracial, 0% Pacific Islander, 9% white, 3% international; 81% from in state; 58% live on campus; N/A of students in fraternities, N/A in sororities
Most popular majors: 15% Criminal Justice/Police Science, 10% Kinesiology and Exercise Science,

9% Hotel/Motel Administration/ Management, 7% Sociology, 6% Family and Consumer Sciences/ Human Sciences, General
Expenses: 2018-2019: $8,302 in state, $18,508 out of state; room/ board: $9,864
Financial aid: (410) 651-6172

University of Maryland University College
Adelphi MD
(800) 888-8682
U.S. News ranking: Reg. U. (N), unranked
Website: www.umuc.edu/
Admissions email: enroll@umuc.edu
Public; founded 1947
Freshman admissions: least selective; 2018-2019: 2,592 applied, 2,592 accepted. Neither SAT nor ACT required. SAT 25/75 percentile: N/A. High school rank: N/A
Early decision deadline: N/A, notification date: N/A
Early action deadline: N/A, notification date: N/A
Application deadline (fall): rolling
Undergraduate student body: 9,607 full time, 37,646 part time; 55% male, 45% female; 0% American Indian, 5% Asian, 27% black, 14% Hispanic, 4% multiracial, 1% Pacific Islander, 38% white, 1% international
Most popular majors: 34% Computer and Information Sciences and Support Services, 32% Business, Management, Marketing, and Related Support Services, 8% Psychology, 7% Homeland Security, Law Enforcement, Firefighting and Related Protective Services, 5% Health Professions and Related Programs
Expenses: 2019-2020: $7,416 in state, $12,336 out of state; room/ board: N/A
Financial aid: (301) 985-7510; 58% of undergrads determined to have financial need; average aid package $7,274

Washington Adventist University
Takoma Park MD
(301) 891-4000
U.S. News ranking: Reg. U. (N), second tier
Website: www.wau.edu
Admissions email: enroll@wau.edu
Private; founded 1904
Affiliation: Seventh Day Adventist
Freshman admissions: least selective; 2018-2019: 3,063 applied, 1,591 accepted. Neither SAT nor ACT required. SAT 25/75 percentile: 860-1070. High school rank: N/A
Early decision deadline: N/A, notification date: N/A
Early action deadline: N/A, notification date: N/A
Application deadline (fall): 8/1
Undergraduate student body: 749 full time, 211 part time; 37% male, 63% female; 0% American Indian, 3% Asian, 50% black,

19% Hispanic, 2% multiracial, 0% Pacific Islander, 5% white, 13% international
Most popular majors: Information not available
Expenses: 2019-2020: $24,800; room/board: $9,616
Financial aid: (301) 891-4005; 90% of undergrads determined to have financial need; average aid package $10,500

Washington College
Chestertown MD
(410) 778-7700
U.S. News ranking: Nat. Lib. Arts, No. 105
Website: www.washcoll.edu
Admissions email: wc_admissions@washcoll.edu
Private; founded 1782
Freshman admissions: more selective; 2018-2019: 3,637 applied, 2,312 accepted. Either SAT or ACT required. SAT 25/75 percentile: 1080-1270. High school rank: 33% in top tenth, 64% in top quarter, 84% in top half
Early decision deadline: 11/15, notification date: 12/15
Early action deadline: 12/1, notification date: 1/15
Application deadline (fall): 2/15
Undergraduate student body: 1,346 full time, 21 part time; 41% male, 59% female; 1% American Indian, 3% Asian, 9% black, 6% Hispanic, 0% multiracial, 0% Pacific Islander, 71% white, 7% international; 45% from in state; 83% live on campus; 6% of students in fraternities, 11% in sororities
Most popular majors: 19% Business, Management, Marketing, and Related Support Services, 18% Social Sciences, 14% Biological and Biomedical Sciences, 10% Psychology, 7% Natural Resources and Conservation
Expenses: 2019-2020: $48,814; room/board: $12,722
Financial aid: (410) 778-7214; 69% of undergrads determined to have financial need; average aid package $35,342

MASSACHUSETTS

American International College[1]
Springfield MA
(413) 205-3201
U.S. News ranking: Reg. U. (N), second tier
Website: www.aic.edu
Admissions email: admissions@aic.edu
Private; founded 1885
Application deadline (fall): 9/7
Undergraduate student body: N/A full time, N/A part time
Expenses: 2018-2019: $35,680; room/board: $14,300
Financial aid: (413) 205-3521

Amherst College
Amherst MA
(413) 542-2328
U.S. News ranking: Nat. Lib. Arts, No. 2
Website: www.amherst.edu
Admissions email: admission@amherst.edu
Private; founded 1821
Freshman admissions: most selective; 2018-2019: 9,724 applied, 1,246 accepted. Either SAT or ACT required. ACT 25/75 percentile: 31-34. High school rank: 88% in top tenth, 96% in top quarter, 100% in top half
Early decision deadline: 11/1, notification date: 12/15
Early action deadline: N/A, notification date: N/A
Application deadline (fall): 1/1
Undergraduate student body: 1,855 full time, 0 part time; 50% male, 50% female; 0% American Indian, 15% Asian, 11% black, 13% Hispanic, 7% multiracial, 0% Pacific Islander, 44% white, 8% international; 13% from in state; 98% live on campus; 0% of students in fraternities, 0% in sororities
Most popular majors: 16% Mathematics, General, 14% Econometrics and Quantitative Economics, 11% English Language and Literature, General, 10% Research and Experimental Psychology, Other, 8% Political Science and Government, General
Expenses: 2019-2020: $58,640; room/board: $15,310
Financial aid: (413) 542-2296; 56% of undergrads determined to have financial need; average aid package $55,908

Anna Maria College
Paxton MA
(508) 849-3360
U.S. News ranking: Reg. U. (N), second tier
Website: www.annamaria.edu
Admissions email: admissions@annamaria.edu
Private; founded 1946
Affiliation: Roman Catholic
Freshman admissions: less selective; 2018-2019: 3,285 applied, 2,448 accepted. Either SAT or ACT required for some. SAT 25/75 percentile: 903-1080. High school rank: 8% in top tenth, 21% in top quarter, 53% in top half
Early decision deadline: N/A, notification date: N/A
Early action deadline: N/A, notification date: N/A
Application deadline (fall): rolling
Undergraduate student body: 937 full time, 197 part time; 48% male, 52% female; 1% American Indian, 2% Asian, 14% black, 12% Hispanic, 2% multiracial, 0% Pacific Islander, 64% white, 0% international
Most popular majors: 24% Registered Nursing/ Registered Nurse, 21% Public Administration, 14% Fire Science/ Fire-fighting, 8% Business Administration and Management, General, 3% Social Work

Expenses: 2019-2020: $38,630; room/board: $14,580
Financial aid: (508) 849-3363

Assumption College
Worcester MA
(866) 477-7776
U.S. News ranking: Reg. U. (N), No. 32
Website: www.assumption.edu
Admissions email: admiss@assumption.edu
Private; founded 1904
Affiliation: Roman Catholic
Freshman admissions: selective; 2018-2019: 4,178 applied, 3,387 accepted. Neither SAT nor ACT required. SAT 25/75 percentile: 1090-1238. High school rank: 12% in top tenth, 39% in top quarter, 73% in top half
Early decision deadline: 11/1, notification date: 12/1
Early action deadline: 11/1, notification date: 12/15
Application deadline (fall): 2/15
Undergraduate student body: 1,917 full time, 21 part time; 43% male, 57% female; 0% American Indian, 3% Asian, 5% black, 8% Hispanic, 2% multiracial, 0% Pacific Islander, 77% white, 2% international; N/A from in state; 84% live on campus; N/A of students in fraternities, N/A in sororities
Most popular majors: 23% Business, Management, Marketing, and Related Support Services, 15% Health Professions and Related Programs, 14% Social Sciences, 10% Biological and Biomedical Sciences, 7% Communication, Journalism, and Related Programs
Expenses: 2019-2020: $42,316; room/board: $13,128
Financial aid: (508) 767-7158; 74% of undergrads determined to have financial need; average aid package $27,598

Babson College
Babson Park MA
(781) 239-4006
U.S. News ranking: Business, unranked
Website: www.babson.edu
Admissions email: ugradadmission@babson.edu
Private; founded 1919
Freshman admissions: more selective; 2018-2019: 6,383 applied, 1,558 accepted. Either SAT or ACT required. SAT 25/75 percentile: 1270-1450. High school rank: N/A
Early decision deadline: 11/1, notification date: 12/15
Early action deadline: 11/1, notification date: 1/1
Application deadline (fall): 1/2
Undergraduate student body: 2,361 full time, 0 part time; 52% male, 48% female; 0% American Indian, 12% Asian, 4% black, 11% Hispanic, 2% multiracial, 0% Pacific Islander, 36% white, 28% international; 21% from in state; 82% live on campus; 13% of students in fraternities, 26% in sororities

Most popular majors: Economics, General, Entrepreneurship/ Entrepreneurial Studies, Finance, General, Management Sciences and Quantitative Methods, Marketing/Marketing Management, General
Expenses: 2019-2020: $52,608; room/board: $16,776
Financial aid: (781) 239-4015; 41% of undergrads determined to have financial need; average aid package $44,121

Bard College at Simon's Rock[1]
Great Barrington MA
(800) 234-7186
U.S. News ranking: Reg. Coll. (N), No. 7
Website: www.simons-rock.edu
Admissions email: admit@simons-rock.edu
Private; founded 1966
Application deadline (fall): rolling
Undergraduate student body: N/A full time, N/A part time
Expenses: 2018-2019: $55,732; room/board: $14,916
Financial aid: (413) 528-7297

Bay Path University
Longmeadow MA
(413) 565-1331
U.S. News ranking: Reg. U. (N), No. 94
Website: www.baypath.edu
Admissions email: admiss@baypath.edu
Private; founded 1897
Freshman admissions: less selective; 2018-2019: 1,513 applied, 914 accepted. Neither SAT nor ACT required. SAT 25/75 percentile: 888-1090. High school rank: 29% in top tenth, 43% in top quarter, 57% in top half
Early decision deadline: N/A, notification date: N/A
Early action deadline: 12/15, notification date: 1/2
Application deadline (fall): 8/1
Undergraduate student body: 1,364 full time, 560 part time; 0% male, 100% female; N/A American Indian, N/A Asian, N/A black, N/A Hispanic, N/A multiracial, N/A Pacific Islander, N/A white, N/A international
Most popular majors: Information not available
Expenses: 2019-2020: $35,080; room/board: $12,799
Financial aid: (413) 565-1256; 93% of undergrads determined to have financial need; average aid package $27,453

Bay State College
Boston MA
(617) 217-9000
U.S. News ranking: Reg. Coll. (N), second tier
Website: www.baystate.edu/
Admissions email: admissions@baystate.edu
For-profit; founded 1946
Affiliation: Undenominational
Freshman admissions: less selective; 2018-2019: 180 applied, 126 accepted. Neither

SAT nor ACT required. SAT 25/75 percentile: N/A. High school rank: N/A
Early decision deadline: N/A, notification date: N/A
Early action deadline: N/A, notification date: N/A
Application deadline (fall): rolling
Undergraduate student body: 368 full time, 332 part time; 29% male, 71% female; 0% American Indian, 5% Asian, 25% black, 17% Hispanic, 3% multiracial, 0% Pacific Islander, 43% white, 2% international; 91% from in state; 7% live on campus; 0% of students in fraternities, 0% in sororities
Most popular majors: 43% Business Administration and Management, General, 22% Registered Nursing/Registered Nurse, 14% Criminal Justice/Safety Studies, 11% Fashion Merchandising, 8% Arts, Entertainment,and Media Management, General
Expenses: 2018-2019: $22,320; room/board: $13,300
Financial aid: (617) 217-9003

Becker College[1]
Worcester MA
(877) 523-2537
U.S. News ranking: Reg. Coll. (N), second tier
Website: www.beckercollege.edu
Admissions email: admissions@beckercollege.edu
Private; founded 1784
Application deadline (fall): rolling
Undergraduate student body: N/A full time, N/A part time
Expenses: N/A
Financial aid: (508) 373-9430

Bentley University
Waltham MA
(781) 891-2244
U.S. News ranking: Reg. U. (N), No. 2
Website: www.bentley.edu
Admissions email: ugadmission@bentley.edu
Private; founded 1917
Freshman admissions: more selective; 2018-2019: 9,252 applied, 3,998 accepted. Either SAT or ACT required. SAT 25/75 percentile: 1240-1410. High school rank: 51% in top tenth, 86% in top quarter, 97% in top half
Early decision deadline: 11/15, notification date: 12/31
Early action deadline: N/A, notification date: N/A
Application deadline (fall): 1/7
Undergraduate student body: 4,185 full time, 68 part time; 60% male, 40% female; 0% American Indian, 9% Asian, 4% black, 7% Hispanic, 2% multiracial, 0% Pacific Islander, 59% white, 15% international; 42% from in state; 78% live on campus; 4% of students in fraternities, 7% in sororities
Most popular majors: 20% Finance, General, 14% Business, Management, Marketing, and Related Support Services, Other,

13% Accounting, 12% Marketing/Marketing Management, General, 11% Business Administration and Management, General
Expenses: 2019-2020: $51,830; room/board: $16,960
Financial aid: (781) 891-3441; 44% of undergrads determined to have financial need; average aid package $39,159

Berklee College of Music
Boston MA
(800) 237-5533
U.S. News ranking: Arts, unranked
Website: www.berklee.edu
Admissions email: admissions@berklee.edu
Private; founded 1945
Freshman admissions: least selective; 2018-2019: 6,280 applied, 3,249 accepted. Neither SAT nor ACT required. SAT 25/75 percentile: N/A. High school rank: N/A
Early decision deadline: N/A, notification date: N/A
Early action deadline: 11/1, notification date: 1/31
Application deadline (fall): 1/15
Undergraduate student body: 4,962 full time, 1,438 part time; 60% male, 40% female; 0% American Indian, 5% Asian, 7% black, 10% Hispanic, 4% multiracial, 0% Pacific Islander, 43% white, 28% international; N/A from in state; 26% live on campus; N/A of students in fraternities, N/A in sororities
Most popular majors: 95% Visual and Performing Arts, 3% Health Professions and Related Programs, 1% Education, 1% Engineering Technologies and Engineering-Related Fields
Expenses: 2019-2020: $45,660; room/board: $18,640
Financial aid: (617) 747-2274; 40% of undergrads determined to have financial need; average aid package $23,532

Boston Architectural College
Boston MA
(617) 585-0123
U.S. News ranking: Arts, unranked
Website: www.the-bac.edu
Admissions email: admissions@the-bac.edu
Private; founded 1889
Freshman admissions: least selective; 2018-2019: 61 applied, 61 accepted. Neither SAT nor ACT required. SAT 25/75 percentile: N/A. High school rank: N/A
Early decision deadline: N/A, notification date: N/A
Early action deadline: N/A, notification date: N/A
Application deadline (fall): rolling
Undergraduate student body: 266 full time, 6 part time; 56% male, 44% female; 0% American Indian, 7% Asian, 8% black, 16% Hispanic, 3% multiracial, 0% Pacific Islander, 33% white, 27% international; N/A from in

state; 5% live on campus; 0% of students in fraternities, 0% in sororities
Most popular majors: 56% Architecture, 18% Interior Architecture, 17% Environmental Design/Architecture, 9% Landscape Architecture
Expenses: 2019-2020: $21,894; room/board: $14,750
Financial aid: (617) 585-0183

Boston College
Chestnut Hill MA
(617) 552-3100
U.S. News ranking: Nat. U., No. 37
Website: www.bc.edu
Admissions email: admission@bc.edu
Private; founded 1863
Affiliation: Roman Catholic
Freshman admissions: most selective; 2018-2019: 31,084 applied, 8,669 accepted. Either SAT or ACT required. SAT 25/75 percentile: 1320-1490. High school rank: 78% in top tenth, 94% in top quarter, 98% in top half
Early decision deadline: 11/1, notification date: 12/15
Early action deadline: N/A, notification date: N/A
Application deadline (fall): 1/1
Undergraduate student body: 9,377 full time, 0 part time; 47% male, 53% female; 0% American Indian, 10% Asian, 4% black, 11% Hispanic, 3% multiracial, 0% Pacific Islander, 60% white, 8% international; 28% from in state; 84% live on campus; 0% of students in fraternities, 0% in sororities
Most popular majors: 14% Economics, General, 13% Finance, General, 8% Biology/Biological Sciences, General, 6% Psychology, General, 6% Speech Communication and Rhetoric
Expenses: 2019-2020: $57,910; room/board: $14,826
Financial aid: (617) 552-3300; 42% of undergrads determined to have financial need; average aid package $45,952

Boston University
Boston MA
(617) 353-2300
U.S. News ranking: Nat. U., No. 40
Website: www.bu.edu
Admissions email: admissions@bu.edu
Private; founded 1839
Freshman admissions: most selective; 2018-2019: 64,481 applied, 14,247 accepted. Either SAT or ACT required for some. SAT 25/75 percentile: 1330-1500. High school rank: 65% in top tenth, 93% in top quarter, 100% in top half
Early decision deadline: 11/1, notification date: 12/15
Early action deadline: N/A, notification date: N/A
Application deadline (fall): 1/6
Undergraduate student body: 17,396 full time, 1,119 part time; 40% male, 60% female; 0% American Indian, 16% Asian, 4% black, 11% Hispanic,

4% multiracial, 0% Pacific Islander, 37% white, 21% international; 28% from in state; 75% live on campus; N/A of students in fraternities, 2% in sororities
Most popular majors: 21% Business, Management, Marketing, and Related Support Services, 14% Communication, Journalism, and Related Programs, 14% Social Sciences, 10% Biological and Biomedical Sciences, 9% Engineering
Expenses: 2019-2020: $55,892; room/board: $16,160
Financial aid: (617) 353-2965; 42% of undergrads determined to have financial need; average aid package $43,571

Brandeis University
Waltham MA
(781) 736-3500
U.S. News ranking: Nat. U., No. 40
Website: www.brandeis.edu
Admissions email: admissions@brandeis.edu
Private; founded 1948
Freshman admissions: most selective; 2018-2019: 11,798 applied, 3,675 accepted. Either SAT or ACT required. SAT 25/75 percentile: 1280-1500. High school rank: 56% in top tenth, 91% in top quarter, 99% in top half
Early decision deadline: 11/1, notification date: 12/15
Early action deadline: N/A, notification date: N/A
Application deadline (fall): 1/1
Undergraduate student body: 3,619 full time, 20 part time; 39% male, 61% female; 0% American Indian, 14% Asian, 5% black, 8% Hispanic, 3% multiracial, 0% Pacific Islander, 46% white, 20% international; 30% from in state; 76% live on campus; 0% of students in fraternities, 0% in sororities
Most popular majors: 12% Economics, General, 10% Biology/Biological Sciences, General, 9% Business/Commerce, General, 7% Computer Science, 7% Experimental Psychology
Expenses: 2019-2020: $57,561, room/board: $16,080
Financial aid: (781) 736-3700; 47% of undergrads determined to have financial need; average aid package $46,796

Bridgewater State University
Bridgewater MA
(508) 531-1237
U.S. News ranking: Reg. U. (N), No. 108
Website: www.bridgew.edu/admissions
Admissions email: admission@bridgew.edu
Public; founded 1840
Freshman admissions: selective; 2018-2019: 6,806 applied, 6,135 accepted. Neither SAT nor ACT required. SAT 25/75 percentile: 990-1150. High school rank: N/A
Early decision deadline: N/A, notification date: N/A

Early action deadline: 11/15, notification date: 12/15
Application deadline (fall): rolling
Undergraduate student body: 7,877 full time, 1,627 part time; 41% male, 59% female; 0% American Indian, 2% Asian, 11% black, 7% Hispanic, 5% multiracial, 0% Pacific Islander, 73% white, 0% international; N/A from in state; 40% live on campus; N/A of students in fraternities, N/A in sororities
Most popular majors: 19% Education, 15% Business, Management, Marketing, and Related Support Services, 13% Psychology, 9% Homeland Security, Law Enforcement, Firefighting and Related Protective Services, 7% Social Sciences
Expenses: 2019-2020: $10,500 in state, $16,640 out of state; room/board: $13,300
Financial aid: (508) 531-1341; 71% of undergrads determined to have financial need; average aid package $8,502

Cambridge College[1]
Cambridge MA
(617) 868-1000
U.S. News ranking: Reg. U. (N), unranked
Website: www.cambridgecollege.edu
Admissions email: N/A
Private; founded 1971
Application deadline (fall): N/A
Undergraduate student body: N/A full time, N/A part time
Expenses: N/A
Financial aid: (617) 873-0440

Clark University
Worcester MA
(508) 793-7431
U.S. News ranking: Nat. U., No. 91
Website: www.clarku.edu
Admissions email: admissions@clarku.edu
Private; founded 1887
Freshman admissions: more selective; 2018-2019: 7,687 applied, 4,565 accepted. Neither SAT nor ACT required. SAT 25/75 percentile: 1200-1390. High school rank: 39% in top tenth, 71% in top quarter, 95% in top half
Early decision deadline: 11/1, notification date: 12/15
Early action deadline: 11/1, notification date: 12/15
Application deadline (fall): 1/15
Undergraduate student body: 2,263 full time, 41 part time; 39% male, 61% female; 0% American Indian, 8% Asian, 4% black, 9% Hispanic, 3% multiracial, 0% Pacific Islander, 59% white, 12% international; 39% from in state; 66% live on campus; 0% of students in fraternities, 0% in sororities
Most popular majors: 28% Social Sciences, 18% Psychology, 10% Biological and Biomedical Sciences, 8% Visual and Performing Arts, 6% Business, Management, Marketing, and Related Support Services
Expenses: 2019-2020: $47,200; room/board: $9,480

Financial aid: (508) 793-7478; 60% of undergrads determined to have financial need; average aid package $32,377

College of Our Lady of the Elms

Chicopee MA
(800) 255-3567
U.S. News ranking: Reg. U. (N), No. 86
Website: www.elms.edu
Admissions email: admissions@elms.edu
Private; founded 1928
Affiliation: Roman Catholic
Freshman admissions: selective; 2018-2019: 1,085 applied, 732 accepted. Either SAT or ACT required. SAT 25/75 percentile: 970-1170. High school rank: N/A
Early decision deadline: N/A, notification date: N/A
Early action deadline: N/A, notification date: N/A
Application deadline (fall): rolling
Undergraduate student body: 1,003 full time, 148 part time; 25% male, 75% female; 0% American Indian, 2% Asian, 10% black, 14% Hispanic, 0% multiracial, 0% Pacific Islander, 55% white, 0% international; 75% from in state; 32% live on campus; 0% of students in fraternities, 0% in sororities
Most popular majors: 43% Health Professions and Related Programs, 13% Business, Management, Marketing, and Related Support Services, 10% Education, 9% Psychology, 9% Public Administration and Social Service Professions
Expenses: 2019-2020: $37,000; room/board: $13,600
Financial aid: (413) 265-2303; 88% of undergrads determined to have financial need; average aid package $22,241

College of the Holy Cross

Worcester MA
(508) 793-2443
U.S. News ranking: Nat. Lib. Arts, No. 27
Website: www.holycross.edu
Admissions email: admissions@holycross.edu
Private; founded 1843
Affiliation: Roman Catholic
Freshman admissions: more selective; 2018-2019: 7,054 applied, 2,681 accepted. Neither SAT nor ACT required. SAT 25/75 percentile: 1270-1420. High school rank: 58% in top tenth, 88% in top quarter, 100% in top half
Early decision deadline: 12/15, notification date: N/A
Early action deadline: N/A, notification date: N/A
Application deadline (fall): 1/15
Undergraduate student body: 3,102 full time, 26 part time; 48% male, 52% female; 0% American Indian, 4% Asian, 4% black, 10% Hispanic, 3% multiracial, 0% Pacific Islander, 72% white,

3% international; 42% from in state; 90% live on campus; N/A of students in fraternities, N/A in sororities
Most popular majors: 14% Economics, General, 12% Psychology, General, 11% Political Science and Government, General, 7% English Language and Literature, General, 7% History, General
Expenses: 2019-2020: $54,740; room/board: $15,070
Financial aid: (508) 793-2265; 53% of undergrads determined to have financial need; average aid package $40,533

Curry College

Milton MA
(800) 669-0686
U.S. News ranking: Reg. U. (N), second tier
Website: www.curry.edu
Admissions email: adm@curry.edu
Private; founded 1879
Freshman admissions: less selective; 2018-2019: 5,733 applied, 5,315 accepted. Either SAT or ACT required for some. SAT 25/75 percentile: 940-1110. High school rank: 3% in top tenth, 16% in top quarter, 40% in top half
Early decision deadline: N/A, notification date: N/A
Early action deadline: 12/1, notification date: 12/15
Application deadline (fall): rolling
Undergraduate student body: 1,989 full time, 367 part time; 42% male, 58% female; 0% American Indian, 3% Asian, 12% black, 8% Hispanic, 3% multiracial, 0% Pacific Islander, 65% white, 2% international; 73% from in state; 59% live on campus; 0% of students in fraternities, 0% in sororities
Most popular majors: 42% Health Professions and Related Programs, 13% Business, Management, Marketing, and Related Support Services, 13% Homeland Security, Law Enforcement, Firefighting and Related Protective Services, 9% Communication, Journalism, and Related Programs, 8% Psychology
Expenses: 2019-2020: $40,870; room/board: $16,340
Financial aid: (617) 333-2354; 74% of undergrads determined to have financial need; average aid package $29,931

Dean College

Franklin MA
(508) 541-1508
U.S. News ranking: Reg. Coll. (N), No. 25
Website: www.dean.edu
Admissions email: admissions@dean.edu
Private; founded 1865
Freshman admissions: less selective; 2018-2019: 6,609 applied, 4,220 accepted. Neither SAT nor ACT required. SAT 25/75 percentile: 910-1110. High school rank: N/A
Early decision deadline: N/A, notification date: N/A
Early action deadline: 12/1, notification date: 1/15

Application deadline (fall): rolling
Undergraduate student body: 1,152 full time, 171 part time; 48% male, 52% female; 0% American Indian, 1% Asian, 14% black, 10% Hispanic, 4% multiracial, 0% Pacific Islander, 56% white, 5% international; 47% from in state; 88% live on campus; 0% of students in fraternities, 0% in sororities
Most popular majors: 24% Dance, General, 23% Business Administration and Management, General, 14% Psychology, General, 13% Drama and Dramatics/Theatre Arts, General, 7% Arts, Entertainment,and Media Management, General
Expenses: 2019-2020: $40,414; room/board: $17,258
Financial aid: (508) 541-1518; 76% of undergrads determined to have financial need; average aid package $30,249

Eastern Nazarene College

Quincy MA
(617) 745-3711
U.S. News ranking: Reg. Coll. (N), No. 29
Website: www.enc.edu
Admissions email: admissions@enc.edu
Private; founded 1918
Affiliation: Church of the Nazarene
Freshman admissions: selective; 2018-2019: 950 applied, 605 accepted. Either SAT or ACT required. SAT 25/75 percentile: 920-1190. High school rank: N/A
Early decision deadline: N/A, notification date: N/A
Early action deadline: N/A, notification date: N/A
Application deadline (fall): rolling
Undergraduate student body: 578 full time, 82 part time; 47% male, 53% female; 1% American Indian, 3% Asian, 21% black, 14% Hispanic, 4% multiracial, 0% Pacific Islander, 51% white, 5% international
Most popular majors: Information not available
Expenses: 2019-2020: $26,568; room/board: $9,870
Financial aid: (617) 745-3712

Emerson College

Boston MA
(617) 824-8600
U.S. News ranking: Reg. U. (N), No. 8
Website: www.emerson.edu
Admissions email: admission@emerson.edu
Private; founded 1880
Freshman admissions: more selective; 2018-2019: 12,941 applied, 4,612 accepted. Neither SAT nor ACT required. SAT 25/75 percentile: 1200-1390. High school rank: 29% in top tenth, 70% in top quarter, 94% in top half
Early decision deadline: N/A, notification date: N/A
Early action deadline: 11/1, notification date: 12/15
Application deadline (fall): 1/15

Undergraduate student body: 3,779 full time, 76 part time; 40% male, 60% female; 0% American Indian, 5% Asian, 3% black, 13% Hispanic, 4% multiracial, 0% Pacific Islander, 62% white, 11% international; 22% from in state; 52% live on campus; 2% of students in fraternities, 3% in sororities
Most popular majors: Information not available
Expenses: 2019-2020: $48,728; room/board: $18,400
Financial aid: (617) 824-8655; 54% of undergrads determined to have financial need; average aid package $23,479

Emmanuel College

Boston MA
(617) 735-9715
U.S. News ranking: Nat. Lib. Arts, second tier
Website: www.emmanuel.edu
Admissions email: enroll@emmanuel.edu
Private; founded 1919
Affiliation: Roman Catholic
Freshman admissions: selective; 2018-2019: 5,770 applied, 4,443 accepted. Neither SAT nor ACT required. SAT 25/75 percentile: 1100-1280. High school rank: 16% in top tenth, 27% in top quarter, 77% in top half
Early decision deadline: N/A, notification date: N/A
Early action deadline: 11/1, notification date: 12/15
Application deadline (fall): 2/15
Undergraduate student body: 1,935 full time, 154 part time; 25% male, 75% female; 0% American Indian, 5% Asian, 7% black, 12% Hispanic, 3% multiracial, 0% Pacific Islander, 69% white, 2% international; 59% from in state; 72% live on campus; N/A of students in fraternities, N/A in sororities
Most popular majors: 20% Biological and Biomedical Sciences, 14% Psychology, 13% Business, Management, Marketing, and Related Support Services, 8% Social Sciences, 6% Education
Expenses: 2019-2020: $41,448; room/board: $15,444
Financial aid: (617) 735-9938; 80% of undergrads determined to have financial need; average aid package $31,268

Endicott College

Beverly MA
(978) 921-1000
U.S. News ranking: Reg. U. (N), No. 23
Website: www.endicott.edu
Admissions email: admission@endicott.edu
Private; founded 1939
Freshman admissions: selective; 2018-2019: 3,598 applied, 2,896 accepted. Either SAT or ACT required for some. SAT 25/75 percentile: 1070-1240. High school rank: 16% in top tenth, 40% in top quarter, 78% in top half

Early decision deadline: N/A, notification date: N/A
Early action deadline: N/A, notification date: N/A
Application deadline (fall): 2/15
Undergraduate student body: 3,029 full time, 356 part time; 38% male, 62% female; 0% American Indian, 1% Asian, 2% black, 5% Hispanic, 2% multiracial, 0% Pacific Islander, 81% white, 2% international; 53% from in state; 91% live on campus; 0% of students in fraternities, 0% in sororities
Most popular majors: 13% Registered Nursing/Registered Nurse, 12% Business Administration and Management, General, 6% Marketing/Marketing Management, General, 6% Psychology, General, 6% Sport and Fitness Administration/Management
Expenses: 2019-2020: $34,154; room/board: $15,660
Financial aid: (978) 232-2060; 63% of undergrads determined to have financial need; average aid package $21,861

Fisher College

Boston MA
(617) 236-8818
U.S. News ranking: Reg. Coll. (N), No. 17
Website: www.fisher.edu
Admissions email: admissions@fisher.edu
Private; founded 1903
Freshman admissions: least selective; 2018-2019: 2,326 applied, 1,617 accepted. Either SAT or ACT required for some. SAT 25/75 percentile: 810-1030. High school rank: N/A
Early decision deadline: N/A, notification date: N/A
Early action deadline: N/A, notification date: N/A
Application deadline (fall): rolling
Undergraduate student body: 657 full time, 898 part time
Most popular majors: 31% Business, Management, Marketing, and Related Support Services, 13% Public Administration and Social Service Professions, 8% Health Professions and Related Programs, 7% Homeland Security, Law Enforcement, Firefighting and Related Protective Services, 5% Psychology
Expenses: 2019-2020: $31,992; room/board: $16,244
Financial aid: (617) 236-8821; 89% of undergrads determined to have financial need; average aid package $28,235

Fitchburg State University

Fitchburg MA
(978) 665-3144
U.S. News ranking: Reg. U. (N), No. 108
Website: www.fitchburgstate.edu
Admissions email: admissions@fitchburgstate.edu
Public; founded 1894
Freshman admissions: selective; 2018-2019: 3,234 applied, 2,810 accepted. Either SAT or

ACT required for some. SAT 25/75 percentile: 1000-1150. High school rank: N/A
Early decision deadline: N/A, notification date: N/A
Early action deadline: N/A, notification date: N/A
Application deadline (fall): rolling
Undergraduate student body: 3,320 full time, 844 part time; 47% male, 53% female; 0% American Indian, 2% Asian, 11% black, 13% Hispanic, 3% multiracial, 0% Pacific Islander, 68% white, 0% international
Most popular majors: 14% Visual and Performing Arts, 12% Business, Management, Marketing, and Related Support Services, 11% Biological and Biomedical Sciences, 11% Health Professions and Related Programs, 10% Multi/Interdisciplinary Studies
Expenses: 2018-2019: $10,410 in state, $16,490 out of state; room/board: $10,780
Financial aid: (978) 665-3302; 70% of undergrads determined to have financial need; average aid package $9,957

Framingham State University
Framingham MA
(508) 626-4500
U.S. News ranking: Reg. U. (N), No. 104
Website: www.framingham.edu
Admissions email: admissions@framingham.edu
Public; founded 1839
Freshman admissions: less selective; 2018-2019: 5,706 applied, 4,182 accepted. Either SAT or ACT required. SAT 25/75 percentile: 960-1130. High school rank: N/A
Early decision deadline: N/A, notification date: N/A
Early action deadline: 11/15, notification date: 12/15
Application deadline (fall): rolling
Undergraduate student body: 3,421 full time, 516 part time; 42% male, 58% female; 0% American Indian, 3% Asian, 12% black, 16% Hispanic, 4% multiracial, 0% Pacific Islander, 63% white, 0% international; N/A from in state; 47% live on campus; N/A of students in fraternities, N/A in sororities
Most popular majors: 20% Business, Management, Marketing, and Related Support Services, 17% Social Sciences, 12% Family and Consumer Sciences/Human Sciences, 10% Psychology, 7% Communications Technologies/Technicians and Support Services
Expenses: 2018-2019: $10,520 in state, $16,600 out of state; room/board: $12,210
Financial aid: N/A

Franklin W. Olin College of Engineering
Needham MA
(781) 292-2222
U.S. News ranking: Engineering, unranked
Website: www.olin.edu/
Admissions email: info@olin.edu
Private; founded 1997
Freshman admissions: more selective; 2018-2019: 878 applied, 138 accepted. Either SAT or ACT required. SAT 25/75 percentile: 1460-1550. High school rank: N/A
Early decision deadline: N/A, notification date: N/A
Early action deadline: N/A, notification date: N/A
Application deadline (fall): 1/1
Undergraduate student body: 347 full time, 43 part time; 50% male, 50% female; 0% American Indian, 14% Asian, 2% black, 11% Hispanic, 8% multiracial, 0% Pacific Islander, 50% white, 8% international; 11% from in state; 100% live on campus; 0% of students in fraternities, 0% in sororities
Most popular majors: 51% Engineering, General, 28% Mechanical Engineering, 21% Electrical and Electronics Engineering
Expenses: 2019-2020: $52,844; room/board: $16,872
Financial aid: (781) 292-2215; 44% of undergrads determined to have financial need; average aid package $49,873

Gordon College
Wenham MA
(866) 464-6736
U.S. News ranking: Nat. Lib. Arts, second tier
Website: www.gordon.edu
Admissions email: admissions@gordon.edu
Private; founded 1889
Affiliation: Other
Freshman admissions: selective; 2018-2019: 3,062 applied, 2,311 accepted. Either SAT or ACT required. SAT 25/75 percentile: 1050-1285. High school rank: 23% in top tenth, 51% in top quarter, 83% in top half
Early decision deadline: N/A, notification date: N/A
Early action deadline: 12/1, notification date: 12/15
Application deadline (fall): 8/1
Undergraduate student body: 1,555 full time, 63 part time; 37% male, 63% female; 0% American Indian, 5% Asian, 5% black, 9% Hispanic, 3% multiracial, 0% Pacific Islander, 68% white, 9% international; 33% from in state; 89% live on campus; 0% of students in fraternities, 0% in sororities
Most popular majors: 10% Business Administration and Management, General, 6% English Language and Literature, General, 6% Linguistics, 6% Psychology, General, 5% Finance, General

Expenses: 2019-2020: $38,650; room/board: $11,250
Financial aid: (800) 343-1379; 66% of undergrads determined to have financial need; average aid package $27,298

Hampshire College[1]
Amherst MA
(413) 549-4600
U.S. News ranking: Nat. Lib. Arts, unranked
Website: www.hampshire.edu
Admissions email: admissions@hampshire.edu
Private; founded 1965
Application deadline (fall): N/A
Undergraduate student body: N/A full time, N/A part time
Expenses: N/A
Financial aid: (413) 559-5739

Harvard University
Cambridge MA
(617) 495-1551
U.S. News ranking: Nat. U., No. 2
Website: www.harvard.edu/
Admissions email: college@fas.harvard.edu
Private; founded 1636
Freshman admissions: most selective; 2018-2019: 42,749 applied, 2,024 accepted. Either SAT or ACT required. SAT 25/75 percentile: 1460-1580. High school rank: 94% in top tenth, 99% in top quarter, 100% in top half
Early decision deadline: N/A, notification date: N/A
Early action deadline: 11/1, notification date: 12/15
Application deadline (fall): 1/1
Undergraduate student body: 6,785 full time, 3 part time; 51% male, 49% female; 0% American Indian, 21% Asian, 9% black, 11% Hispanic, 7% multiracial, 0% Pacific Islander, 39% white, 12% international
Most popular majors: 27% Social Sciences, General, 13% Biology/Biological Sciences, General, 11% Mathematics, General, 9% Physical Sciences, 8% History, General
Expenses: 2019-2020: $51,925; room/board: $17,682
Financial aid: (617) 495-1581; 55% of undergrads determined to have financial need; average aid package $58,403

Lasell College
Newton MA
(617) 243-2225
U.S. News ranking: Reg. U. (N), No. 116
Website: www.lasell.edu
Admissions email: info@lasell.edu
Private; founded 1851
Freshman admissions: less selective; 2018-2019: 3,180 applied, 2,537 accepted. Either SAT or ACT required for some. SAT 25/75 percentile: 980-1170. High school rank: 10% in top tenth, 30% in top quarter, 67% in top half
Early decision deadline: N/A, notification date: N/A
Early action deadline: 11/15, notification date: 12/1

Application deadline (fall): rolling
Undergraduate student body: 1,624 full time, 50 part time; 36% male, 64% female; 0% American Indian, 2% Asian, 8% black, 10% Hispanic, 2% multiracial, 0% Pacific Islander, 67% white, 6% international; 60% from in state; 73% live on campus; 0% of students in fraternities, 0% in sororities
Most popular majors: 12% Communication and Media Studies, 10% Fashion Merchandising, 8% Psychology, General, 6% Communication and Media Studies, Other, 6% Sport and Fitness Administration/Management
Expenses: 2019-2020: $37,000; room/board: $16,000
Financial aid: (617) 243-2227; 81% of undergrads determined to have financial need; average aid package $28,800

Lesley University
Cambridge MA
(617) 349-8800
U.S. News ranking: Nat. U., No. 246
Website: www.lesley.edu
Admissions email: admissions@lesley.edu
Private; founded 1909
Freshman admissions: selective; 2018-2019: 3,171 applied, 2,401 accepted. Either SAT or ACT required. SAT 25/75 percentile: 938-1293. High school rank: 13% in top tenth, 39% in top quarter, 74% in top half
Early decision deadline: N/A, notification date: N/A
Early action deadline: 12/1, notification date: 12/23
Application deadline (fall): 7/15
Undergraduate student body: 1,678 full time, 449 part time; 20% male, 80% female; 0% American Indian, 5% Asian, 7% black, 15% Hispanic, 4% multiracial, 0% Pacific Islander, 59% white, 4% international; N/A from in state; 43% live on campus; N/A of students in fraternities, N/A in sororities
Most popular majors: 26% Psychology, 19% Visual and Performing Arts, 10% Health Professions and Related Programs, 10% Liberal Arts and Sciences, General Studies and Humanities, 8% Business, Management, Marketing, and Related Support Services
Expenses: 2019-2020: $28,750; room/board: $16,200
Financial aid: (617) 349-8760; 69% of undergrads determined to have financial need; average aid package $17,832

Massachusetts College of Art and Design
Boston MA
(617) 879-7222
U.S. News ranking: Arts, unranked
Website: www.massart.edu
Admissions email: admissions@massart.edu
Public; founded 1873

Freshman admissions: least selective; 2018-2019: 2,566 applied, 1,724 accepted. Neither SAT nor ACT required. SAT 25/75 percentile: N/A. High school rank: N/A
Early decision deadline: N/A, notification date: N/A
Early action deadline: 12/1, notification date: 1/5
Application deadline (fall): 2/1
Undergraduate student body: 1,650 full time, 295 part time; 28% male, 72% female; 0% American Indian, 8% Asian, 5% black, 10% Hispanic, 2% multiracial, 0% Pacific Islander, 61% white, 5% international; 67% from in state; 41% live on campus; N/A of students in fraternities, N/A in sororities
Most popular majors: 17% Illustration, 12% Film/Video and Photographic Arts, Other, 12% Graphic Design, 8% Art Teacher Education, 8% Fashion/Apparel Design
Expenses: 2019-2020: $13,700 in state, $38,500 out of state; room/board: $13,700
Financial aid: (617) 879-7849; 65% of undergrads determined to have financial need; average aid package $7,948

Massachusetts College of Liberal Arts
North Adams MA
(413) 662-5410
U.S. News ranking: Nat. Lib. Arts, No. 140
Website: www.mcla.edu
Admissions email: admissions@mcla.edu
Public; founded 1894
Freshman admissions: selective; 2018-2019: 1,931 applied, 1,423 accepted. Either SAT or ACT required. SAT 25/75 percentile: 990-1230. High school rank: 23% in top tenth, 48% in top quarter, 80% in top half
Early decision deadline: N/A, notification date: N/A
Early action deadline: 12/1, notification date: 12/15
Application deadline (fall): rolling
Undergraduate student body: 1,109 full time, 168 part time; 38% male, 62% female; 0% American Indian, 2% Asian, 8% black, 10% Hispanic, 3% multiracial, 0% Pacific Islander, 71% white, 0% international; 75% from in state; 58% live on campus; N/A of students in fraternities, N/A in sororities
Most popular majors: 18% Business, Management, Marketing, and Related Support Services, 16% Multi/Interdisciplinary Studies, 15% English Language and Literature/Letters, 12% Psychology, 11% Social Sciences
Expenses: 2019-2020: $11,105 in state, $20,050 out of state; room/board: $11,430
Financial aid: (413) 662-5219; 79% of undergrads determined to have financial need; average aid package $16,322

Massachusetts Institute of Technology
Cambridge MA
(617) 253-3400
U.S. News ranking: Nat. U., No. 3
Website: web.mit.edu/
Admissions email: admissions@mit.edu
Private; founded 1861
Freshman admissions: most selective; 2018-2019: 21,706 applied, 1,464 accepted. Either SAT or ACT required. SAT 25/75 percentile: 1500-1570. High school rank: 97% in top tenth, 100% in top quarter, 100% in top half
Early decision deadline: N/A, notification date: N/A
Early action deadline: 11/1, notification date: 12/20
Application deadline (fall): 1/1
Undergraduate student body: 4,557 full time, 45 part time; 54% male, 46% female; 0% American Indian, 28% Asian, 6% black, 15% Hispanic, 7% multiracial, 0% Pacific Islander, 32% white, 10% international; 9% from in state; 92% live on campus; 43% of students in fraternities, 28% in sororities
Most popular majors: 35% Engineering, 31% Computer and Information Sciences and Support Services, 10% Mathematics and Statistics, 7% Physical Sciences, 6% Biological and Biomedical Sciences
Expenses: 2019-2020: $53,790; room/board: $16,390
Financial aid: (617) 258-8600; 61% of undergrads determined to have financial need; average aid package $51,974

Massachusetts Maritime Academy
Buzzards Bay MA
(800) 544-3411
U.S. News ranking: Reg. Coll. (N), No. 4
Website: www.maritime.edu
Admissions email: admissions@maritime.edu
Public; founded 1891
Freshman admissions: selective; 2018-2019: 758 applied, 675 accepted. Either SAT or ACT required. SAT 25/75 percentile: 1050-1200. High school rank: N/A
Early decision deadline: N/A, notification date: N/A
Early action deadline: 11/1, notification date: 12/31
Application deadline (fall): rolling
Undergraduate student body: 1,614 full time, 91 part time; 86% male, 14% female; 0% American Indian, 1% Asian, 1% black, 4% Hispanic, 2% multiracial, 0% Pacific Islander, 87% white, 1% international; 81% from in state; 97% live on campus; 0% of students in fraternities, 0% in sororities
Most popular majors: 49% Engineering, 23% Transportation and Materials Moving, 13% Business, Management, Marketing, and Related Support Services,

8% Homeland Security, Law Enforcement, Firefighting and Related Protective Services, 7% Natural Resources and Conservation
Expenses: 2019-2020: $10,018 in state, $25,752 out of state; room/board: $13,034
Financial aid: (508) 830-5087; 57% of undergrads determined to have financial need; average aid package $13,236

Merrimack College
North Andover MA
(978) 837-5100
U.S. News ranking: Reg. U. (N), No. 46
Website: www.merrimack.edu
Admissions email: Admission@Merrimack.edu
Private; founded 1947
Affiliation: Roman Catholic
Freshman admissions: selective; 2018-2019: 8,668 applied, 7,174 accepted. Neither SAT nor ACT required. SAT 25/75 percentile: 1040-1195. High school rank: 6% in top tenth, 24% in top quarter, 58% in top half
Early decision deadline: 11/15, notification date: 12/15
Early action deadline: 1/15, notification date: 2/15
Application deadline (fall): 2/15
Undergraduate student body: 3,587 full time, 139 part time; 50% male, 50% female; 0% American Indian, 2% Asian, 3% black, 7% Hispanic, 2% multiracial, 0% Pacific Islander, 77% white, 2% international; 69% from in state; 71% live on campus; 4% of students in fraternities, 10% in sororities
Most popular majors: 25% Business, Management, Marketing, and Related Support Services, 16% Family and Consumer Sciences/Human Sciences, 12% Health Professions and Related Programs, 7% Education, 6% Communication, Journalism, and Related Programs
Expenses: 2019-2020: $43,340; room/board: $16,320
Financial aid: (978) 837-5186; 71% of undergrads determined to have financial need; average aid package $25,192

Montserrat College of Art[1]
Beverly MA
(978) 922-8222
U.S. News ranking: Arts, unranked
Website: www.montserrat.edu
Admissions email: admissions@montserrrat.edu
Private; founded 1970
Application deadline (fall): N/A
Undergraduate student body: N/A full time, N/A part time
Expenses: N/A
Financial aid: (978) 921-4242

Mount Holyoke College
South Hadley MA
(413) 538-2023
U.S. News ranking: Nat. Lib. Arts, No. 32
Website: www.mtholyoke.edu
Admissions email: admission@mtholyoke.edu
Private; founded 1837
Freshman admissions: more selective; 2018-2019: 3,699 applied, 1,883 accepted. Neither SAT nor ACT required. SAT 25/75 percentile: 1290-1500. High school rank: 47% in top tenth, 83% in top quarter, 98% in top half
Early decision deadline: 11/15, notification date: 1/1
Early action deadline: N/A, notification date: N/A
Application deadline (fall): 1/15
Undergraduate student body: 2,177 full time, 31 part time; 0% male, 100% female; 0% American Indian, 10% Asian, 5% black, 7% Hispanic, 4% multiracial, 0% Pacific Islander, 45% white, 27% international; 19% from in state; 96% live on campus; 0% of students in fraternities, 0% in sororities
Most popular majors: 11% Economics, General, 9% Computer Science, 8% Biology/Biological Sciences, General, 7% English Language and Literature, General, 7% Psychology, General
Expenses: 2019-2020: $52,258; room/board: $15,320
Financial aid: (413) 538-2291; 63% of undergrads determined to have financial need; average aid package $40,576

National Graduate School of Quality Management[1]
Falmouth MA
(800) 838-2580
U.S. News ranking: Business, unranked
Website: www.ngs.edu
Admissions email: N/A
Private; founded 1993
Application deadline (fall): N/A
Undergraduate student body: N/A full time, N/A part time
Expenses: N/A
Financial aid: N/A

New England College of Business and Finance[1]
Boston MA
(617) 951-2350
U.S. News ranking: Business, unranked
Website: www.necb.edu/
Admissions email: N/A
For-profit; founded 1909
Application deadline (fall): N/A
Undergraduate student body: N/A full time, N/A part time
Expenses: N/A
Financial aid: N/A

New England Conservatory of Music[7]
Boston MA
(617) 585-1101
U.S. News ranking: Arts, unranked
Website: www. newenglandconservatory.edu
Admissions email: admission@ newenglandconservatory.edu
Private; founded 1867
Freshman admissions: least selective; 2018-2019: N/A applied, N/A accepted. Neither SAT nor ACT required. SAT 25/75 percentile: N/A. High school rank: N/A
Early decision deadline: N/A, notification date: N/A
Early action deadline: N/A, notification date: N/A
Application deadline (fall): 12/1
Undergraduate student body: 438 full time, 30 part time
Most popular majors: Information not available
Expenses: 2019-2020: $50,460; room/board: $16,500
Financial aid: (617) 585-1110; 40% of undergrads determined to have financial need; average aid package $28,975

New England Institute of Art[1]
Brookline MA
(800) 903-4425
U.S. News ranking: Arts, unranked
Website: www.artinstitutes.edu/boston/
Admissions email: N/A
For-profit
Application deadline (fall): N/A
Undergraduate student body: N/A full time, N/A part time
Expenses: N/A
Financial aid: N/A

Nichols College
Dudley MA
(800) 470-3379
U.S. News ranking: Business, unranked
Website: www.nichols.edu/
Admissions email: admissions@nichols.edu
Private; founded 1815
Freshman admissions: less selective; 2018-2019: 2,435 applied, 2,003 accepted. Neither SAT nor ACT required. SAT 25/75 percentile: 940-1140. High school rank: N/A
Early decision deadline: N/A, notification date: N/A
Early action deadline: 12/1, notification date: N/A
Application deadline (fall): rolling
Undergraduate student body: 1,224 full time, 98 part time; 62% male, 38% female; 0% American Indian, 1% Asian, 7% black, 8% Hispanic, 3% multiracial, 0% Pacific Islander, 77% white, 2% international; 59% from in state; 70% live on campus; 0% of students in fraternities, 0% in sororities
Most popular majors: 24% Business/Commerce, General, 13% Sport and Fitness Administration/Management,

12% Criminal Justice/Law Enforcement Administration, 9% Accounting, 8% Finance, General
Expenses: 2019-2020: $35,615; room/board: $14,250
Financial aid: (508) 213-2288; 80% of undergrads determined to have financial need; average aid package $29,083

Northeastern University
Boston MA
(617) 373-2200
U.S. News ranking: Nat. U., No. 40
Website: www.northeastern.edu/
Admissions email: admissions@northeastern.edu
Private; founded 1898
Freshman admissions: most selective; 2018-2019: 62,272 applied, 12,042 accepted. Either SAT or ACT required. ACT 25/75 percentile: 32-34. High school rank: 77% in top tenth, 95% in top quarter, 99% in top half
Early decision deadline: 11/1, notification date: 12/15
Early action deadline: 11/1, notification date: 2/1
Application deadline (fall): 1/1
Undergraduate student body: 13,864 full time, 45 part time; 48% male, 52% female; 0% American Indian, 14% Asian, 4% black, 8% Hispanic, 4% multiracial, 0% Pacific Islander, 45% white, 18% international; 27% from in state; 49% live on campus; 10% of students in fraternities, 17% in sororities
Most popular majors: 25% Business, Management, Marketing, and Related Support Services, 17% Engineering, 12% Social Sciences, 11% Health Professions and Related Programs, 8% Biological and Biomedical Sciences
Expenses: 2019-2020: $53,506; room/board: $16,930
Financial aid: (617) 373-3190; 32% of undergrads determined to have financial need; average aid package $30,981

Pine Manor College
Chestnut Hill MA
(617) 731-7111
U.S. News ranking: Nat. Lib. Arts, second tier
Website: www.pmc.edu
Admissions email: admission@pmc.edu
Private; founded 1911
Freshman admissions: least selective; 2018-2019: 183 applied, 140 accepted. Neither SAT nor ACT required. SAT 25/75 percentile: 740-915. High school rank: N/A
Early decision deadline: N/A, notification date: N/A
Early action deadline: N/A, notification date: N/A
Application deadline (fall): rolling
Undergraduate student body: 371 full time, 2 part time; 56% male, 44% female; 1% American Indian, 5% Asian, 29% black, 24% Hispanic, 9% multiracial, 0% Pacific Islander, 9% white, 2% international

Most popular majors: 28% Business Administration and Management, General, 23% Social Sciences, General, 20% Biology/Biological Sciences, General, 20% Early Childhood Education and Teaching, 9% Psychology, General
Expenses: 2019-2020: $31,660; room/board: $13,830
Financial aid: (617) 731-7628; 91% of undergrads determined to have financial need; average aid package $31,630

Salem State University

Salem MA
(978) 542-6200
U.S. News ranking: Reg. U. (N), No. 119
Website: www.salemstate.edu
Admissions email: admissions@salemstate.edu
Public; founded 1854
Freshman admissions: less selective; 2018-2019: 6,562 applied, 5,558 accepted. Either SAT or ACT required for some. SAT 25/75 percentile: 980-1140. High school rank: N/A
Early decision deadline: N/A, notification date: N/A
Early action deadline: 11/15, notification date: 1/1
Application deadline (fall): rolling
Undergraduate student body: 5,434 full time, 1,377 part time; 38% male, 62% female; 0% American Indian, 3% Asian, 10% black, 17% Hispanic, 3% multiracial, 0% Pacific Islander, 62% white, 3% international; 96% from in state; 33% live on campus; N/A of students in fraternities, N/A in sororities
Most popular majors: 23% Business, Management, Marketing, and Related Support Services, 15% Health Professions and Related Programs, 9% Psychology, 8% Education, 7% Biological and Biomedical Sciences
Expenses: 2018-2019: $10,642 in state, $17,082 out of state; room/board: $13,778
Financial aid: N/A

Simmons University

Boston MA
(617) 521-2051
U.S. News ranking: Nat. U., No. 125
Website: www.simmons.edu
Admissions email: ugadm@simmons.edu
Private; founded 1899
Freshman admissions: more selective; 2018-2019: 3,444 applied, 2,401 accepted. Either SAT or ACT required. SAT 25/75 percentile: 1130-1300. High school rank: 29% in top tenth, 75% in top quarter, 76% in top half
Early decision deadline: N/A, notification date: N/A
Early action deadline: 11/1, notification date: 12/15
Application deadline (fall): 2/1
Undergraduate student body: 1,631 full time, 206 part time; 0% male, 100% female; 0% American Indian, 11% Asian, 7% black,

6% Hispanic, 4% multiracial, 0% Pacific Islander, 63% white, 5% international; 60% from in state; 59% live on campus; 0% of students in fraternities, 0% in sororities
Most popular majors: 33% Registered Nursing/Registered Nurse, 7% Kinesiology and Exercise Science, 4% Nutrition Sciences, 4% Psychology, General, 4% Public Health Education and Promotion
Expenses: 2019-2020: $42,066; room/board: $15,656
Financial aid: (617) 521-2037; 76% of undergrads determined to have financial need; average aid package $33,067

Smith College

Northampton MA
(413) 585-2500
U.S. News ranking: Nat. Lib. Arts, No. 11
Website: www.smith.edu
Admissions email: admission@smith.edu
Private; founded 1871
Freshman admissions: most selective; 2018-2019: 5,780 applied, 1,789 accepted. Either SAT or ACT required for some. SAT 25/75 percentile: 1320-1490. High school rank: 72% in top tenth, 96% in top quarter, 100% in top half
Early decision deadline: 11/15, notification date: 12/15
Early action deadline: N/A, notification date: N/A
Application deadline (fall): 1/15
Undergraduate student body: 2,490 full time, 12 part time; 0% male, 100% female; 0% American Indian, 9% Asian, 7% black, 12% Hispanic, 5% multiracial, 0% Pacific Islander, 48% white, 14% international; 19% from in state; 95% live on campus; 0% of students in fraternities, 0% in sororities
Most popular majors: 9% Political Science and Government, General, 8% Research and Experimental Psychology, Other, 7% Economics, General, 6% Biology/Biological Sciences, General, 6% English Language and Literature, General
Expenses: 2019-2020: $54,224; room/board: $18,130
Financial aid: (413) 585-2530; 61% of undergrads determined to have financial need; average aid package $53,790

Springfield College

Springfield MA
(413) 748-3136
U.S. News ranking: Reg. U. (N), No. 19
Website: springfield.edu/
Admissions email: admissions@springfieldcollege.edu
Private; founded 1885
Freshman admissions: selective; 2018-2019: 3,367 applied, 2,127 accepted. Either SAT or ACT required. SAT 25/75 percentile: 1050-1240. High school rank: 18% in top tenth, 48% in top quarter, 74% in top half

Early decision deadline: 12/1, notification date: 2/1
Early action deadline: N/A, notification date: N/A
Application deadline (fall): 8/1
Undergraduate student body: 2,102 full time, 27 part time; 50% male, 50% female; 0% American Indian, 2% Asian, 6% black, 9% Hispanic, 2% multiracial, 0% Pacific Islander, 73% white, 2% international; 62% from in state; 87% live on campus; N/A of students in fraternities, N/A in sororities
Most popular majors: 8% Physical Therapy/Therapist, 8% Physician Assistant, 7% Kinesiology and Exercise Science, 7% Sport and Fitness Administration/Management, 6% Physical Education Teaching and Coaching
Expenses: 2019-2020: $38,565; room/board: $12,930
Financial aid: (413) 748-3108; 82% of undergrads determined to have financial need; average aid package $27,793

Stonehill College

Easton MA
(508) 565-1373
U.S. News ranking: Nat. Lib. Arts, No. 124
Website: www.stonehill.edu
Admissions email: admission@stonehill.edu
Private; founded 1948
Affiliation: Roman Catholic
Freshman admissions: selective; 2018-2019: 6,609 applied, 4,598 accepted. Neither SAT nor ACT required. SAT 25/75 percentile: 1130-1300. High school rank: 20% in top tenth, 54% in top quarter, 87% in top half
Early decision deadline: 12/1, notification date: 12/31
Early action deadline: 11/1, notification date: 12/31
Application deadline (fall): 1/15
Undergraduate student body: 2,513 full time, 22 part time; 40% male, 60% female; 0% American Indian, 2% Asian, 4% black, 5% Hispanic, 2% multiracial, 0% Pacific Islander, 84% white, 1% international; 63% from in state; 86% live on campus; 0% of students in fraternities, 0% in sororities
Most popular majors: 9% Psychology, General, 8% Finance, General, 8% Marketing/Marketing Management, General, 7% Biology/Biological Sciences, General
Expenses: 2019-2020: $44,420; room/board: $16,620
Financial aid: (508) 565-1088; 63% of undergrads determined to have financial need; average aid package $30,952

Suffolk University

Boston MA
(617) 573-8460
U.S. News ranking: Reg. U. (N), No. 38
Website: www.suffolk.edu
Admissions email: admission@suffolk.edu
Private; founded 1906

Freshman admissions: selective; 2018-2019: 8,477 applied, 7,223 accepted. Either SAT or ACT required. SAT 25/75 percentile: 1030-1220. High school rank: 14% in top tenth, 35% in top quarter, 71% in top half
Early decision deadline: N/A, notification date: N/A
Early action deadline: 11/15, notification date: 12/15
Application deadline (fall): rolling
Undergraduate student body: 4,981 full time, 209 part time; 44% male, 56% female; 0% American Indian, 7% Asian, 5% black, 13% Hispanic, 3% multiracial, 0% Pacific Islander, 48% white, 21% international; 67% from in state; 27% live on campus; N/A of students in fraternities, N/A in sororities
Most popular majors: 47% Business, Management, Marketing, and Related Support Services, 13% Social Sciences, 11% Communication, Journalism, and Related Programs, 5% Biological and Biomedical Sciences, 5% Psychology
Expenses: 2019-2020: $40,104; room/board: $18,062
Financial aid: (617) 573-8470; 60% of undergrads determined to have financial need; average aid package $27,407

Tufts University

Medford MA
(617) 627-3170
U.S. News ranking: Nat. U., No. 29
Website: www.tufts.edu
Admissions email: undergraduate.admissions@tufts.edu
Private; founded 1852
Freshman admissions: most selective; 2018-2019: 21,501 applied, 3,143 accepted. Either SAT or ACT required. ACT 25/75 percentile: 31-34. High school rank: 78% in top tenth, 93% in top quarter, 100% in top half
Early decision deadline: 11/1, notification date: 12/15
Early action deadline: N/A, notification date: N/A
Application deadline (fall): 1/1
Undergraduate student body: 5,508 full time, 135 part time; 48% male, 52% female; 0% American Indian, 13% Asian, 4% black, 7% Hispanic, 5% multiracial, 0% Pacific Islander, 55% white, 11% international
Most popular majors: 25% Social Sciences, 10% Biological and Biomedical Sciences, 10% Engineering, 9% Computer and Information Sciences and Support Services
Expenses: 2019-2020: $58,578; room/board: $15,086
Financial aid: (617) 627-2000; 37% of undergrads determined to have financial need; average aid package $47,195

University of Massachusetts–Amherst

Amherst MA
(413) 545-0222
U.S. News ranking: Nat. U., No. 64
Website: www.umass.edu
Admissions email: mail@admissions.umass.edu
Public; founded 1863
Freshman admissions: more selective; 2018-2019: 41,612 applied, 24,911 accepted. Either SAT or ACT required. SAT 25/75 percentile: 1200-1390. High school rank: 32% in top tenth, 71% in top quarter, 97% in top half
Early decision deadline: N/A, notification date: N/A
Early action deadline: 11/4, notification date: 12/31
Application deadline (fall): 1/15
Undergraduate student body: 21,784 full time, 1,731 part time; 50% male, 50% female; 0% American Indian, 10% Asian, 5% black, 7% Hispanic, 3% multiracial, 0% Pacific Islander, 62% white, 7% international; 76% from in state; 62% live on campus; 8% of students in fraternities, 8% in sororities
Most popular majors: 14% Business, Management, Marketing, and Related Support Services, 12% Social Sciences, 10% Biological and Biomedical Sciences, 9% Health Professions and Related Programs, 8% Psychology
Expenses: 2019-2020: $16,389 in state, $35,710 out of state; room/board: $13,598
Financial aid: (413) 545-0801; 56% of undergrads determined to have financial need; average aid package $17,799

University of Massachusetts–Boston

Boston MA
(617) 287-6100
U.S. News ranking: Nat. U., No. 228
Website: www.umb.edu
Admissions email: undergrad.admissions@umb.edu
Public; founded 1964
Freshman admissions: selective; 2018-2019: 11,907 applied, 9,241 accepted. Either SAT or ACT required for some. SAT 25/75 percentile: 1020-1220. High school rank: 15% in top tenth, 44% in top quarter, 82% in top half
Early decision deadline: N/A, notification date: N/A
Early action deadline: 11/1, notification date: 12/31
Application deadline (fall): 3/1
Undergraduate student body: 10,017 full time, 2,697 part time; 46% male, 54% female; 0% American Indian, 14% Asian, 17% black, 17% Hispanic, 3% multiracial, 0% Pacific Islander, 34% white, 11% international; 95% from in state; 9% live on campus; N/A of students in fraternities, N/A in sororities

Most popular majors: 19% Business, Management, Marketing, and Related Support Services, 12% Health Professions and Related Programs, 12% Social Sciences, 10% Psychology, 9% Biological and Biomedical Sciences
Expenses: 2019-2020: $14,613 in state, $35,075 out of state; room/board: $16,902
Financial aid: (617) 297-6300; 68% of undergrads determined to have financial need; average aid package $16,480

University of Massachusetts–Dartmouth

North Dartmouth MA
(508) 999-8605
U.S. News ranking: Nat. U., No. 218
Website: www.umassd.edu
Admissions email: admissions@umassd.edu
Public; founded 1895
Freshman admissions: selective; 2018-2019: 8,697 applied, 6,744 accepted. Either SAT or ACT required. SAT 25/75 percentile: 990-1190. High school rank: 14% in top tenth, 34% in top quarter, 68% in top half
Early decision deadline: N/A, notification date: N/A
Early action deadline: 11/18, notification date: 12/15
Application deadline (fall): rolling
Undergraduate student body: 5,895 full time, 946 part time; 51% male, 49% female; 0% American Indian, 4% Asian, 16% black, 10% Hispanic, 4% multiracial, 0% Pacific Islander, 59% white, 2% international; 89% from in state; 52% live on campus; N/A of students in fraternities, N/A in sororities
Most popular majors: 28% Business, Management, Marketing, and Related Support Services, 14% Health Professions and Related Programs, 12% Engineering, 11% Social Sciences, 8% Psychology
Expenses: 2019-2020: $14,358 in state, $30,103 out of state; room/board: $14,064
Financial aid: (508) 999-8643; 74% of undergrads determined to have financial need; average aid package $18,405

University of Massachusetts–Lowell

Lowell MA
(978) 934-3931
U.S. News ranking: Nat. U., No. 179
Website: www.uml.edu
Admissions email: admissions@uml.edu
Public; founded 1894
Freshman admissions: more selective; 2018-2019: 12,117 applied, 8,688 accepted. Either SAT or ACT required for some. SAT 25/75 percentile: 1150-1320. High school rank: 25% in top tenth, 56% in top quarter, 88% in top half

Early decision deadline: N/A, notification date: N/A
Early action deadline: 11/1, notification date: 12/10
Application deadline (fall): 2/1
Undergraduate student body: 10,651 full time, 3,354 part time; 61% male, 39% female; 0% American Indian, 11% Asian, 6% black, 12% Hispanic, 3% multiracial, 0% Pacific Islander, 60% white, 4% international; 92% from in state; 39% live on campus; N/A of students in fraternities, N/A in sororities
Most popular majors: 20% Business, Management, Marketing, and Related Support Services, 19% Engineering, 11% Computer and Information Sciences and Support Services, 10% Health Professions and Related Programs, 9% Homeland Security, Law Enforcement, Firefighting and Related Protective Services
Expenses: 2019-2020: $15,180 in state, $32,827 out of state; room/board: $12,748
Financial aid: (978) 934-4220; 62% of undergrads determined to have financial need; average aid package $17,085

Wellesley College

Wellesley MA
(781) 283-2270
U.S. News ranking: Nat. Lib. Arts, No. 3
Website: www.wellesley.edu
Admissions email: admission@wellesley.edu
Private; founded 1870
Freshman admissions: most selective; 2018-2019: 6,631 applied, 1,296 accepted. Either SAT or ACT required. SAT 25/75 percentile: 1330-1520. High school rank: 83% in top tenth, 96% in top quarter, 99% in top half
Early decision deadline: 11/1, notification date: 12/15
Early action deadline: N/A, notification date: N/A
Application deadline (fall): 1/15
Undergraduate student body: 2,391 full time, 143 part time; 2% male, 98% female; 0% American Indian, 22% Asian, 7% black, 13% Hispanic, 6% multiracial, 0% Pacific Islander, 38% white, 14% international; N/A from in state; 97% live on campus; N/A of students in fraternities, N/A in sororities
Most popular majors: 25% Social Sciences, 13% Biological and Biomedical Sciences, 11% Computer and Information Sciences and Support Services, 7% Psychology, 5% Foreign Languages, Literatures, and Linguistics
Expenses: 2019-2020: $56,052; room/board: $17,096
Financial aid: (781) 283-2360; 56% of undergrads determined to have financial need; average aid package $53,776

Wentworth Institute of Technology

Boston MA
(617) 989-4000
U.S. News ranking: Reg. U. (N), No. 46
Website: www.wit.edu
Admissions email: admissions@wit.edu
Private; founded 1904
Freshman admissions: selective; 2018-2019: 7,312 applied, 5,560 accepted. Either SAT or ACT required for some. SAT 25/75 percentile: 1080-1280. High school rank: 16% in top tenth, 40% in top quarter, 73% in top half
Early decision deadline: N/A, notification date: N/A
Early action deadline: N/A, notification date: N/A
Application deadline (fall): rolling
Undergraduate student body: 3,940 full time, 401 part time; 78% male, 22% female; 0% American Indian, 8% Asian, 6% black, 7% Hispanic, 4% multiracial, 0% Pacific Islander, 63% white, 7% international; 67% from in state; 48% live on campus; 0% of students in fraternities, 0% in sororities
Most popular majors: 40% Engineering, 22% Business, Management, Marketing, and Related Support Services, 15% Computer and Information Sciences and Support Services, 10% Architecture and Related Services, 8% Visual and Performing Arts
Expenses: 2019-2020: $34,970; room/board: $14,526
Financial aid: (617) 989-4020; 69% of undergrads determined to have financial need; average aid package $20,615

Western New England University

Springfield MA
(413) 782-1321
U.S. News ranking: Nat. U., No. 218
Website: www.wne.edu
Admissions email: learn@wne.edu
Private; founded 1919
Freshman admissions: selective; 2018-2019: 6,458 applied, 5,513 accepted. Either SAT or ACT required for some. SAT 25/75 percentile: 1060-1250. High school rank: 19% in top tenth, 47% in top quarter, 84% in top half
Early decision deadline: N/A, notification date: N/A
Early action deadline: N/A, notification date: N/A
Application deadline (fall): rolling
Undergraduate student body: 2,629 full time, 122 part time; 63% male, 37% female; 0% American Indian, 3% Asian, 4% black, 9% Hispanic, 2% multiracial, 0% Pacific Islander, 74% white, 3% international; 51% from in state; 59% live on campus; N/A of students in fraternities, N/A in sororities

Most popular majors: 23% Business, Management, Marketing, and Related Support Services, 23% Engineering, 11% Health Professions and Related Programs, 8% Homeland Security, Law Enforcement, Firefighting and Related Protective Services, 6% Psychology
Expenses: 2019-2020: $37,992; room/board: $14,034
Financial aid: (413) 796-2080; 79% of undergrads determined to have financial need; average aid package $26,824

Westfield State University

Westfield MA
(413) 572-5218
U.S. News ranking: Reg. U. (N), No. 86
Website: www.westfield.ma.edu
Admissions email: admissions@westfield.ma.edu
Public; founded 1839
Freshman admissions: selective; 2018-2019: 4,302 applied, 3,701 accepted. Either SAT or ACT required. SAT 25/75 percentile: 1000-1160. High school rank: 1% in top tenth, 12% in top quarter, 45% in top half
Early decision deadline: N/A, notification date: N/A
Early action deadline: N/A, notification date: N/A
Application deadline (fall): 3/1
Undergraduate student body: 4,562 full time, 787 part time; 45% male, 55% female; 0% American Indian, 1% Asian, 5% black, 10% Hispanic, 4% multiracial, 0% Pacific Islander, 75% white, 0% international; 92% from in state; 48% live on campus; 0% of students in fraternities, 0% in sororities
Most popular majors: 14% Business, Management, Marketing, and Related Support Services, 14% Homeland Security, Law Enforcement, Firefighting and Related Protective Services, 13% Liberal Arts and Sciences, General Studies and Humanities, 10% Education, 7% Psychology
Expenses: 2018-2019: $10,155 in state, $16,235 out of state; room/board: $10,968
Financial aid: (413) 572-8530

Wheaton College

Norton MA
(508) 286-8251
U.S. News ranking: Nat. Lib. Arts, No. 82
Website: www.wheatoncollege.edu
Admissions email: admission@wheatoncollege.edu
Private; founded 1834
Freshman admissions: selective; 2018-2019: 3,674 applied, 2,566 accepted. Neither SAT nor ACT required. SAT 25/75 percentile: 1180-1350. High school rank: 21% in top tenth, 52% in top quarter, 84% in top half
Early decision deadline: 11/1, notification date: 12/1
Early action deadline: 11/1, notification date: 1/15
Application deadline (fall): 1/1

Undergraduate student body: 1,751 full time, 9 part time; 39% male, 61% female; 0% American Indian, 5% Asian, 5% black, 8% Hispanic, 4% multiracial, 0% Pacific Islander, 65% white, 10% international; 34% from in state; 96% live on campus; N/A of students in fraternities, N/A in sororities
Most popular majors: 18% Social Sciences, 14% Visual and Performing Arts, 13% Business, Management, Marketing, and Related Support Services, 12% Psychology, 11% Biological and Biomedical Sciences
Expenses: 2019-2020: $54,568; room/board: $14,096
Financial aid: (508) 286-8232; 70% of undergrads determined to have financial need; average aid package $43,984

Wheelock College[1]

Boston MA
(617) 879-2206
U.S. News ranking: Reg. U. (N), No. 126
Website: www.wheelock.edu
Admissions email: undergrad@wheelock.edu
Private; founded 1888
Application deadline (fall): 5/1
Undergraduate student body: N/A full time, N/A part time
Expenses: N/A
Financial aid: N/A

Williams College

Williamstown MA
(413) 597-2211
U.S. News ranking: Nat. Lib. Arts, No. 1
Website: www.williams.edu
Admissions email: admission@williams.edu
Private; founded 1793
Freshman admissions: most selective; 2018-2019: 9,560 applied, 1,240 accepted. Either SAT or ACT required. ACT 25/75 percentile: 32-35. High school rank: 89% in top tenth, 97% in top quarter, 100% in top half
Early decision deadline: 11/15, notification date: 12/15
Early action deadline: N/A, notification date: N/A
Application deadline (fall): 1/1
Undergraduate student body: 2,020 full time, 53 part time; 52% male, 48% female; 0% American Indian, 13% Asian, 8% black, 13% Hispanic, 5% multiracial, 0% Pacific Islander, 50% white, 8% international; 14% from in state; 93% live on campus; N/A of students in fraternities, N/A in sororities
Most popular majors: 18% Econometrics and Quantitative Economics, 14% Mathematics, General, 13% Biology/Biological Sciences, General, 11% Political Science and Government, General, 10% History, General
Expenses: 2019-2020: $57,280; room/board: $14,990
Financial aid: (413) 597-4181; 52% of undergrads determined to have financial need; average aid package $58,728

Worcester Polytechnic Institute
Worcester MA
(508) 831-5286
U.S. News ranking: Nat. U., No. 64
Website: www.wpi.edu/admissions/undergraduate
Admissions email: admissions@wpi.edu
Private; founded 1865
Freshman admissions: more selective; 2018-2019: 10,584 applied, 4,402 accepted. Neither SAT nor ACT required. SAT 25/75 percentile: 1300-1460. High school rank: 64% in top tenth, 93% in top quarter, 100% in top half
Early decision deadline: N/A, notification date: N/A
Early action deadline: 11/1, notification date: 12/20
Application deadline (fall): 2/1
Undergraduate student body: 4,527 full time, 141 part time; 62% male, 38% female; 0% American Indian, 5% Asian, 3% black, 9% Hispanic, 2% multiracial, 0% Pacific Islander, 63% white, 9% international; 45% from in state; 49% live on campus; 33% of students in fraternities, 36% in sororities
Most popular majors: 22% Mechanical Engineering, 14% Computer Science, 10% Chemical Engineering, 9% Bioengineering and Biomedical Engineering, 8% Electrical and Electronics Engineering
Expenses: 2019-2020: $52,322; room/board: $15,302
Financial aid: (508) 831-5469; 61% of undergrads determined to have financial need; average aid package $38,694

Worcester State University
Worcester MA
(508) 929-8040
U.S. News ranking: Reg. U. (N), No. 100
Website: www.worcester.edu
Admissions email: admissions@worcester.edu
Public; founded 1874
Freshman admissions: selective; 2018-2019: 4,076 applied, 3,173 accepted. Either SAT or ACT required for some. SAT 25/75 percentile: 1010-1190. High school rank: N/A
Early decision deadline: N/A, notification date: N/A
Early action deadline: 11/15, notification date: 12/15
Application deadline (fall): 5/1
Undergraduate student body: 4,164 full time, 1,216 part time; 40% male, 60% female; 0% American Indian, 5% Asian, 9% black, 13% Hispanic, 3% multiracial, 0% Pacific Islander, 65% white, 1% international; 96% from in state; 31% live on campus; N/A of students in fraternities, N/A in sororities
Most popular majors: 21% Health Professions and Related Programs, 18% Business, Management, Marketing, and Related Support Services, 11% Homeland Security, Law Enforcement, Firefighting and Related Protective Services, 9% Biological and Biomedical Sciences, 9% Psychology
Expenses: 2018-2019: $10,161 in state, $16,241 out of state; room/board: $12,262
Financial aid: (508) 929-8056; 64% of undergrads determined to have financial need; average aid package $19,226

MICHIGAN

Adrian College
Adrian MI
(800) 877-2246
U.S. News ranking: Reg. Coll. (Mid. W), No. 18
Website: www.adrian.edu
Admissions email: admissions@adrian.edu
Private; founded 1859
Affiliation: United Methodist
Freshman admissions: selective; 2018-2019: 5,133 applied, 3,327 accepted. Either SAT or ACT required. SAT 25/75 percentile: 940-1150. High school rank: 30% in top tenth, 44% in top quarter, 74% in top half
Early decision deadline: N/A, notification date: N/A
Early action deadline: N/A, notification date: N/A
Application deadline (fall): rolling
Undergraduate student body: 1,751 full time, 66 part time; 52% male, 48% female; 0% American Indian, 0% Asian, 7% black, 5% Hispanic, 3% multiracial, 0% Pacific Islander, 68% white, 0% international; 77% from in state; 83% live on campus; 17% of students in fraternities, 19% in sororities
Most popular majors: 26% Business, Management, Marketing, and Related Support Services, 17% Parks, Recreation, Leisure, and Fitness Studies, 9% Biological and Biomedical Sciences, 8% Homeland Security, Law Enforcement, Firefighting and Related Protective Services, 7% Visual and Performing Arts
Expenses: 2019-2020: $37,809; room/board: $11,720
Financial aid: (888) 876-0194; 84% of undergrads determined to have financial need; average aid package $30,250

Albion College
Albion MI
(800) 858-6770
U.S. News ranking: Nat. Lib. Arts, No. 140
Website: www.albion.edu/
Admissions email: admission@albion.edu
Private; founded 1835
Affiliation: United Methodist
Freshman admissions: selective; 2018-2019: 4,226 applied, 2,884 accepted. Either SAT or ACT required. SAT 25/75 percentile: 1010-1240. High school rank: N/A
Early decision deadline: N/A, notification date: N/A
Early action deadline: 12/1, notification date: N/A
Application deadline (fall): rolling

Alma College
Alma MI
(800) 321-2562
U.S. News ranking: Reg. Coll. (Mid. W), No. 8
Website: www.alma.edu
Admissions email: admissions@alma.edu
Private; founded 1886
Affiliation: Presbyterian Church (USA)
Freshman admissions: selective; 2018-2019: 4,833 applied, 3,070 accepted. Neither SAT nor ACT required. SAT 25/75 percentile: 1040-1220. High school rank: 20% in top tenth, 29% in top quarter, 83% in top half
Early decision deadline: N/A, notification date: N/A
Early action deadline: N/A, notification date: N/A
Application deadline (fall): rolling
Undergraduate student body: 1,386 full time, 47 part time; 41% male, 59% female; 1% American Indian, 1% Asian, 3% black, 5% Hispanic, 4% multiracial, 0% Pacific Islander, 79% white, 1% international; 89% from in state; 91% live on campus; 21% of students in fraternities, 20% in sororities
Most popular majors: 19% Health Professions and Related Programs, 16% Business, Management, Marketing, and Related Support Services, 12% Education, 9% Social Sciences, 8% Biological and Biomedical Sciences
Expenses: 2019-2020: $41,398; room/board: $11,384
Financial aid: (989) 463-7347; 84% of undergrads determined to have financial need; average aid package $30,376

Alpena Community College[1]
Alpena MI
(989) 356-9021
U.S. News ranking: Reg. Coll. (Mid. W), unranked
Website: www.lakemichigancollege.edu
Admissions email: N/A
Public

Undergraduate student body: 1,509 full time, 24 part time; 46% male, 54% female; 0% American Indian, 2% Asian, 15% black, 10% Hispanic, 3% multiracial, 0% Pacific Islander, 63% white, 2% international; 73% from in state; 95% live on campus; 35% of students in fraternities, 28% in sororities
Most popular majors: 16% Social Sciences, 14% Business, Management, Marketing, and Related Support Services, 13% Biological and Biomedical Sciences, 7% Communication, Journalism, and Related Programs, 7% Psychology
Expenses: 2019-2020: $48,090; room/board: $12,380
Financial aid: (517) 629-0440; 80% of undergrads determined to have financial need; average aid package $43,146

Andrews University
Berrien Springs MI
(800) 253-2874
U.S. News ranking: Nat. U., second tier
Website: www.andrews.edu
Admissions email: enroll@andrews.edu
Private; founded 1874
Affiliation: Seventh Day Adventist
Freshman admissions: selective; 2018-2019: 1,445 applied, 947 accepted. Either SAT or ACT required. ACT 25/75 percentile: 21-27. High school rank: 18% in top tenth, 47% in top quarter, 78% in top half
Early decision deadline: N/A, notification date: N/A
Early action deadline: N/A, notification date: N/A
Application deadline (fall): rolling
Undergraduate student body: 1,346 full time, 356 part time; 44% male, 56% female; 0% American Indian, 14% Asian, 19% black, 15% Hispanic, 5% multiracial, 0% Pacific Islander, 27% white, 18% international; 36% from in state; 59% live on campus; N/A of students in fraternities, N/A in sororities
Most popular majors: 21% Health Professions and Related Programs, 11% Biological and Biomedical Sciences, 11% Business, Management, Marketing, and Related Support Services, 7% Liberal Arts and Sciences, General Studies and Humanities, 6% Psychology
Expenses: 2019-2020: $30,158; room/board: $9,300
Financial aid: (269) 471-3334; 57% of undergrads determined to have financial need; average aid package $31,065

Aquinas College
Grand Rapids MI
(616) 632-2900
U.S. News ranking: Nat. Lib. Arts, second tier
Website: www.aquinas.edu
Admissions email: admissions@aquinas.edu
Private; founded 1886
Affiliation: Roman Catholic
Freshman admissions: selective; 2018-2019: 2,171 applied, 1,499 accepted. Either SAT or ACT required. SAT 25/75 percentile: 1010-1230. High school rank: N/A
Early decision deadline: N/A, notification date: N/A
Early action deadline: N/A, notification date: N/A
Application deadline (fall): rolling
Undergraduate student body: 1,299 full time, 279 part time; 41% male, 59% female; 1% American Indian, 2% Asian, 4% black, 7% Hispanic, 2% multiracial, 0% Pacific Islander, 69% white, 3% international; 92% from in state; 51% live on campus; N/A of students in fraternities, N/A in sororities

Application deadline (fall): N/A
Undergraduate student body: N/A full time, N/A part time
Expenses: N/A
Financial aid: N/A

Most popular majors: 21% Business, Management, Marketing, and Related Support Services, 9% Parks, Recreation, Leisure, and Fitness Studies, 8% Social Sciences, 8% Visual and Performing Arts, 6% Biological and Biomedical Sciences
Expenses: 2019-2020: $33,854; room/board: $9,598
Financial aid: (616) 632-2893; 75% of undergrads determined to have financial need; average aid package $25,507

Baker College of Flint[1]
Flint MI
(810) 767-7600
U.S. News ranking: Reg. U. (Mid. W), unranked
Website: www.baker.edu
Admissions email: troy.crowe@baker.edu
Private
Application deadline (fall): N/A
Undergraduate student body: N/A full time, N/A part time
Expenses: N/A
Financial aid: N/A

Calvin University
Grand Rapids MI
(800) 688-0122
U.S. News ranking: Reg. U. (Mid. W), No. 3
Website: calvin.edu
Admissions email: admissions@calvin.edu
Private; founded 1876
Affiliation: Christian Reformed Church
Freshman admissions: more selective; 2018-2019: 3,847 applied, 3,038 accepted. Either SAT or ACT required. SAT 25/75 percentile: 1150-1370. High school rank: 31% in top tenth, 58% in top quarter, 83% in top half
Early decision deadline: N/A, notification date: N/A
Early action deadline: N/A, notification date: N/A
Application deadline (fall): 8/15
Undergraduate student body: 3,417 full time, 208 part time; 47% male, 53% female; 0% American Indian, 5% Asian, 4% black, 5% Hispanic, 3% multiracial, 0% Pacific Islander, 69% white, 13% international; 58% from in state; 61% live on campus; 0% of students in fraternities, 0% in sororities
Most popular majors: 9% Engineering, General, 8% Business/Commerce, General, 6% Registered Nursing/Registered Nurse, 5% Psychology, General, 4% Elementary Education and Teaching
Expenses: 2019-2020: $36,300; room/board: $10,600
Financial aid: (616) 526-6134; 60% of undergrads determined to have financial need; average aid package $24,606

Central Michigan University

Mount Pleasant MI
(989) 774-3076
U.S. News ranking: Nat. U., No. 240
Website: www.cmich.edu
Admissions email: cmuadmit@cmich.edu
Public; founded 1892
Freshman admissions: selective; 2018-2019: 17,858 applied, 12,293 accepted. Either SAT or ACT required. SAT 25/75 percentile: 1000-1200. High school rank: N/A
Early decision deadline: N/A, notification date: N/A
Early action deadline: N/A, notification date: N/A
Application deadline (fall): 7/28
Undergraduate student body: 14,270 full time, 2,162 part time; 42% male, 58% female; 1% American Indian, 1% Asian, 10% black, 5% Hispanic, 4% multiracial, 0% Pacific Islander, 77% white, 2% international; 93% from in state; 36% live on campus; 8% of students in fraternities, 9% in sororities
Most popular majors: 28% Business, Management, Marketing, and Related Support Services, 8% Communication, Journalism, and Related Programs, 7% Health Professions and Related Programs, 7% Parks, Recreation, Leisure, and Fitness Studies, 7% Psychology
Expenses: 2018-2019: $12,960 in state, $12,960 out of state; room/board: $9,736
Financial aid: (989) 774-3674; 61% of undergrads determined to have financial need; average aid package $14,145

Cleary University[1]

Howell MI
(800) 686-1883
U.S. News ranking: Business, unranked
Website: www.cleary.edu
Admissions email: admissions@cleary.edu
Private; founded 1883
Application deadline (fall): 8/24
Undergraduate student body: N/A full time, N/A part time
Expenses: N/A
Financial aid: (517) 338-3015

College for Creative Studies[1]

Detroit MI
(313) 664-7425
U.S. News ranking: Arts, unranked
Website: www.collegeforcreativestudies.edu
Admissions email: admissions@collegeforcreativestudies.edu
Private; founded 1906
Application deadline (fall): N/A
Undergraduate student body: N/A full time, N/A part time
Expenses: N/A
Financial aid: (313) 664-7495

Cornerstone University

Grand Rapids MI
(616) 222-1426
U.S. News ranking: Reg. U. (Mid. W), No. 78
Website: www.cornerstone.edu
Admissions email: admissions@cornerstone.edu
Private; founded 1941
Affiliation: Interdenominational
Freshman admissions: selective; 2018-2019: 2,732 applied, 2,005 accepted. Either SAT or ACT required. SAT 25/75 percentile: 950-1180. High school rank: 12% in top tenth, 45% in top quarter, 75% in top half
Early decision deadline: N/A, notification date: N/A
Early action deadline: N/A, notification date: N/A
Application deadline (fall): rolling
Undergraduate student body: 1,288 full time, 262 part time; 38% male, 62% female; 0% American Indian, 2% Asian, 9% black, 5% Hispanic, 1% multiracial, 0% Pacific Islander, 78% white, 5% international; N/A from in state; 63% live on campus; N/A of students in fraternities, N/A in sororities
Most popular majors: 40% Business, Management, Marketing, and Related Support Services, 12% Psychology, 9% Theology and Religious Vocations, 7% Communication, Journalism, and Related Programs, 7% Education
Expenses: 2019-2020: $25,360; room/board: $9,630
Financial aid: (616) 222-1424; 75% of undergrads determined to have financial need; average aid package $19,315

Davenport University

Grand Rapids MI
(866) 925-3884
U.S. News ranking: Reg. U. (Mid. W), No. 111
Website: www.davenport.edu
Admissions email: Davenport.Admissions@davenport.edu
Private; founded 1866
Freshman admissions: selective; 2018-2019: 2,184 applied, 1,951 accepted. Neither SAT nor ACT required. SAT 25/75 percentile: 970-1160. High school rank: N/A
Early decision deadline: N/A, notification date: N/A
Early action deadline: N/A, notification date: N/A
Application deadline (fall): rolling
Undergraduate student body: 2,518 full time, 2,648 part time; 45% male, 55% female; 1% American Indian, 3% Asian, 11% black, 5% Hispanic, 3% multiracial, 0% Pacific Islander, 70% white, 2% international; N/A from in state; 15% live on campus; N/A of students in fraternities, N/A in sororities
Most popular majors: 21% Business Administration and Management, General, 12% Business/Commerce, General, 9% Health/Health Care Administration/Management,

9% Registered Nursing/Registered Nurse, 8% Accounting
Expenses: 2018-2019: $18,414; room/board: $9,928
Financial aid: (616) 732-1132

Eastern Michigan University

Ypsilanti MI
(734) 487-3060
U.S. News ranking: Nat. U., second tier
Website: www.emich.edu/
Admissions email: admissions@emich.edu
Public; founded 1849
Freshman admissions: selective; 2018-2019: 14,461 applied, 10,995 accepted. Either SAT or ACT required. SAT 25/75 percentile: 970-1200. High school rank: 13% in top tenth, 38% in top quarter, 72% in top half
Early decision deadline: N/A, notification date: N/A
Early action deadline: N/A, notification date: N/A
Application deadline (fall): rolling
Undergraduate student body: 11,403 full time, 4,327 part time; 40% male, 60% female; 0% American Indian, 3% Asian, 18% black, 5% Hispanic, 4% multiracial, 0% Pacific Islander, 63% white, 2% international; N/A from in state; 21% live on campus; N/A of students in fraternities, N/A in sororities
Most popular majors: 20% Business, Management, Marketing, and Related Support Services, 18% Health Professions and Related Programs, 7% Education, 6% Psychology, 6% Social Sciences
Expenses: 2019-2020: $12,940 in state, $12,940 out of state; room/board: $10,486
Financial aid: (734) 487-1048; 68% of undergrads determined to have financial need; average aid package $10,251

Ferris State University

Big Rapids MI
(231) 591-2100
U.S. News ranking: Nat. U., second tier
Website: www.ferris.edu
Admissions email: admissions@ferris.edu
Public; founded 1884
Freshman admissions: less selective; 2018-2019: 10,284 applied, 8,320 accepted. Either SAT or ACT required for some. SAT 25/75 percentile: 940-1170. High school rank: N/A
Early decision deadline: N/A, notification date: N/A
Early action deadline: N/A, notification date: N/A
Application deadline (fall): rolling
Undergraduate student body: 8,079 full time, 3,806 part time; 47% male, 53% female; 0% American Indian, 2% Asian, 8% black, 6% Hispanic, 4% multiracial, 0% Pacific Islander, 78% white, 2% international; 92% from in state; 28% live on campus; 1% of students in fraternities, 1% in sororities
Most popular majors: 8% Criminal Justice/Law Enforcement Administration, 6% Business Administration and Management, General, 6% Pharmacy, 5% Health Professions and Related Clinical Sciences, Other, 4% Registered Nursing/Registered Nurse
Expenses: 2019-2020: $13,469 in state, $13,469 out of state; room/board: $10,042
Financial aid: (231) 591-2110; 70% of undergrads determined to have financial need; average aid package $11,820

Finlandia University[1]

Hancock MI
(906) 487-7274
U.S. News ranking: Reg. Coll. (Mid. W), second tier
Website: www.finlandia.edu
Admissions email: admissions@finlandia.edu
Private; founded 1896
Affiliation: Evangelical Lutheran Church
Application deadline (fall): N/A
Undergraduate student body: N/A full time, N/A part time
Expenses: N/A
Financial aid: N/A

Grand Valley State University[7]

Allendale MI
(800) 748-0246
U.S. News ranking: Nat. U., No. 228
Website: www.gvsu.edu
Admissions email: admissions@gvsu.edu
Public; founded 1960
Freshman admissions: selective; 2018-2019: 17,133 applied, 14,178 accepted. Either SAT or ACT required. SAT 25/75 percentile: 1050-1240. High school rank: 20% in top tenth, 47% in top quarter, 83% in top half
Early decision deadline: N/A, notification date: N/A
Early action deadline: N/A, notification date: N/A
Application deadline (fall): 5/1
Undergraduate student body: 19,214 full time, 2,445 part time
Most popular majors: 21% Business, Management, Marketing, and Related Support Services, 19% Health Professions and Related Programs, 7% Communication, Journalism, and Related Programs, 6% Parks, Recreation, Leisure, and Fitness Studies, 6% Psychology
Expenses: 2019-2020: $12,860 in state, $18,296 out of state; room/board: $8,820
Financial aid: (616) 331-3234; 59% of undergrads determined to have financial need; average aid package $10,404

Henry Ford College[1]

Dearborn MI
(313) 845-9600
U.S. News ranking: Reg. Coll. (Mid. W), unranked
Website: www.schoolcraft.edu
Admissions email: N/A
Public
Application deadline (fall): N/A
Undergraduate student body: N/A full time, N/A part time
Expenses: N/A
Financial aid: N/A

Hillsdale College

Hillsdale MI
(517) 607-2327
U.S. News ranking: Nat. Lib. Arts, No. 64
Website: www.hillsdale.edu
Admissions email: admissions@hillsdale.edu
Private; founded 1844
Affiliation: Undenominational
Freshman admissions: more selective; 2018-2019: 2,208 applied, 795 accepted. Either SAT or ACT required. ACT 25/75 percentile: 29-32. High school rank: N/A
Early decision deadline: 11/1, notification date: 12/1
Early action deadline: N/A, notification date: N/A
Application deadline (fall): 4/1
Undergraduate student body: 1,434 full time, 34 part time; 52% male, 48% female; 0% American Indian, 0% Asian, 0% black, 0% Hispanic, 0% multiracial, 0% Pacific Islander, 0% white, 0% international; 33% from in state; 66% live on campus; 21% of students in fraternities, 33% in sororities
Most popular majors: 12% Economics, General, 11% English Language and Literature, General, 10% History, General, 8% Political Science and Government, General, 7% Finance, General
Expenses: 2019-2020: $28,368; room/board: $11,390
Financial aid: (517) 607-2350; 53% of undergrads determined to have financial need; average aid package $18,932

Hope College

Holland MI
(616) 395-7850
U.S. News ranking: Nat. Lib. Arts, No. 105
Website: www.hope.edu
Admissions email: admissions@hope.edu
Private; founded 1866
Affiliation: Reformed Church in America
Freshman admissions: more selective; 2018-2019: 4,362 applied, 3,298 accepted. Either SAT or ACT required. SAT 25/75 percentile: 1110-1330. High school rank: 39% in top tenth, 67% in top quarter, 92% in top half
Early decision deadline: N/A, notification date: N/A
Early action deadline: 11/2, notification date: 11/23
Application deadline (fall): rolling

Undergraduate student body: 3,032 full time, 117 part time; 38% male, 62% female; 0% American Indian, 2% Asian, 3% black, 7% Hispanic, 3% multiracial, 0% Pacific Islander, 82% white, 2% international; N/A from in state; 79% live on campus; 14% of students in fraternities, 18% in sororities
Most popular majors: 19% Business Administration and Management, General, 11% Education/Teaching of Individuals with Specific Learning Disabilities, 8% Engineering, General, 7% Biology/Biological Sciences, General, 7% Kinesiology and Exercise Science
Expenses: 2019-2020: $35,330; room/board: $10,630
Financial aid: (616) 395-7765; 50% of undergrads determined to have financial need; average aid package $27,356

Jackson College[1]
Jackson MI
U.S. News ranking: Reg. Coll. (Mid. W), unranked
Admissions email: N/A
Public
Application deadline (fall): N/A
Undergraduate student body: N/A full time, N/A part time
Expenses: N/A
Financial aid: N/A

Kalamazoo College
Kalamazoo MI
(800) 253-3602
U.S. News ranking: Nat. Lib. Arts, No. 72
Website: www.kzoo.edu
Admissions email: admission@kzoo.edu
Private; founded 1833
Freshman admissions: more selective; 2018-2019: 3,371 applied, 2,454 accepted. Neither SAT nor ACT required. SAT 25/75 percentile: 1140-1370. High school rank: 54% in top tenth, 84% in top quarter, 99% in top half
Early decision deadline: 11/1, notification date: 12/1
Early action deadline: 11/1, notification date: 12/20
Application deadline (fall): 1/15
Undergraduate student body: 1,457 full time, 10 part time; 43% male, 57% female; 0% American Indian, 7% Asian, 8% black, 14% Hispanic, 4% multiracial, 0% Pacific Islander, 58% white, 6% international; 63% from in state; 60% live on campus; 0% of students in fraternities, 0% in sororities
Most popular majors: 14% Biological and Biomedical Sciences, 14% Social Sciences, 11% Business, Management, Marketing, and Related Support Services, 10% Physical Sciences, 10% Psychology
Expenses: 2019-2020: $50,412; room/board: $10,134
Financial aid: (269) 337-7192; 70% of undergrads determined to have financial need; average aid package $42,134

Kettering University
Flint MI
(800) 955-4464
U.S. News ranking: Reg. U. (Mid. W), No. 13
Website: www.kettering.edu
Admissions email: admissions@kettering.edu
Private; founded 1919
Freshman admissions: more selective; 2018-2019: 2,234 applied, 1,574 accepted. Either SAT or ACT required. SAT 25/75 percentile: 1190-1370. High school rank: 48% in top tenth, 71% in top quarter, 94% in top half
Early decision deadline: N/A, notification date: N/A
Early action deadline: 11/15, notification date: 12/15
Application deadline (fall): rolling
Undergraduate student body: 1,825 full time, 55 part time; 80% male, 20% female; 0% American Indian, 4% Asian, 2% black, 5% Hispanic, 3% multiracial, 0% Pacific Islander, 76% white, 4% international; N/A from in state; 6% live on campus; 6% of students in fraternities, 9% in sororities
Most popular majors: 83% Engineering, 7% Computer and Information Sciences and Support Services, 4% Biological and Biomedical Sciences, 4% Business, Management, Marketing, and Related Support Services, 2% Physical Sciences
Expenses: 2019-2020: $44,380; room/board: $8,400
Financial aid: (810) 762-7859; 71% of undergrads determined to have financial need; average aid package $22,631

Kuyper College[1]
Grand Rapids MI
(800) 511-3749
U.S. News ranking: Reg. Coll. (Mid. W), No. 51
Website: www.kuyper.edu
Admissions email: admissions@kuyper.edu
Private
Application deadline (fall): N/A
Undergraduate student body: N/A full time, N/A part time
Expenses: 2019-2020: $22,886; room/board: $7,570
Financial aid: (616) 988-3656; 85% of undergrads determined to have financial need; average aid package $17,268

Lake Michigan College[1]
Benton Harbor MI
(269) 927-8100
U.S. News ranking: Reg. Coll. (Mid. W), unranked
Website: www.theamericancollege.edu
Admissions email: N/A
Public
Application deadline (fall): N/A
Undergraduate student body: N/A full time, N/A part time
Expenses: N/A
Financial aid: N/A

Lake Superior State University
Sault Ste. Marie MI
(906) 635-2231
U.S. News ranking: Reg. Coll. (Mid. W), No. 45
Website: www.lssu.edu
Admissions email: admissions@lssu.edu
Public; founded 1946
Freshman admissions: selective; 2018-2019: 2,846 applied, 1,785 accepted. Either SAT or ACT required for some. SAT 25/75 percentile: 990-1200. High school rank: 13% in top tenth, 36% in top quarter, 70% in top half
Early decision deadline: N/A, notification date: N/A
Early action deadline: N/A, notification date: N/A
Application deadline (fall): rolling
Undergraduate student body: 1,669 full time, 322 part time; 48% male, 52% female; 8% American Indian, 1% Asian, 3% black, 2% Hispanic, 0% multiracial, 0% Pacific Islander, 81% white, 5% international; 7% from in state; 43% live on campus; N/A of students in fraternities, N/A in sororities
Most popular majors: 19% Homeland Security, Law Enforcement, Firefighting and Related Protective Services, 16% Business, Management, Marketing, and Related Support Services, 14% Health Professions and Related Programs, 8% Natural Resources and Conservation, 7% Engineering
Expenses: 2019-2020: $12,450 in state, $12,450 out of state; room/board: $10,230
Financial aid: (906) 635-2678; 69% of undergrads determined to have financial need; average aid package $11,745

Lawrence Technological University[1]
Southfield MI
(248) 204-3160
U.S. News ranking: Reg. U. (Mid. W), No. 43
Website: www.ltu.edu
Admissions email: admissions@ltu.edu
Private; founded 1932
Application deadline (fall): rolling
Undergraduate student body: N/A full time, N/A part time
Expenses: 2019-2020: $35,280; room/board: $10,540
Financial aid: (248) 204-2280; 65% of undergrads determined to have financial need; average aid package $24,859

Madonna University
Livonia MI
(734) 432-5339
U.S. News ranking: Reg. U. (Mid. W), No. 46
Website: www.madonna.edu
Admissions email: admissions@madonna.edu
Private; founded 1937
Affiliation: Roman Catholic

Freshman admissions: selective; 2018-2019: 985 applied, 771 accepted. Either SAT or ACT required. SAT 25/75 percentile: 960-1170. High school rank: 8% in top tenth, 24% in top quarter, 42% in top half
Early decision deadline: 12/1, notification date: 1/15
Early action deadline: N/A, notification date: N/A
Application deadline (fall): rolling
Undergraduate student body: 1,431 full time, 1,009 part time; 35% male, 65% female; 0% American Indian, 2% Asian, 12% black, 5% Hispanic, 3% multiracial, 0% Pacific Islander, 62% white, 12% international; 86% from in state; 12% live on campus; N/A of students in fraternities, N/A in sororities
Most popular majors: 22% Business, Management, Marketing, and Related Support Services, 22% Health Professions and Related Programs, 16% Homeland Security, Law Enforcement, Firefighting and Related Protective Services, 5% Public Administration and Social Service Professions, 4% Biological and Biomedical Sciences
Expenses: 2019-2020: $23,100; room/board: $11,450
Financial aid: (734) 432-5662; 80% of undergrads determined to have financial need; average aid package $13,562

Marygrove College[1]
Detroit MI
(313) 927-1240
U.S. News ranking: Reg. U. (Mid. W), second tier
Website: www.marygrove.edu
Admissions email: info@marygrove.edu
Private
Application deadline (fall): rolling
Undergraduate student body: N/A full time, N/A part time
Expenses: N/A
Financial aid: N/A

Michigan State University
East Lansing MI
(517) 355-8332
U.S. News ranking: Nat. U., No. 84
Website: www.msu.edu
Admissions email: admis@msu.edu
Public; founded 1855
Freshman admissions: more selective; 2018-2019: 33,129 applied, 25,733 accepted. Either SAT or ACT required. SAT 25/75 percentile: 1110-1310. High school rank: 29% in top tenth, 67% in top quarter, 95% in top half
Early decision deadline: N/A, notification date: N/A
Early action deadline: N/A, notification date: N/A
Application deadline (fall): rolling
Undergraduate student body: 35,744 full time, 3,679 part time; 49% male, 51% female; 0% American Indian, 6% Asian, 7% black, 5% Hispanic, 3% multiracial, 0% Pacific Islander, 68% white, 10% international; N/A from in state; 39% live on campus; 12% of students in fraternities, 11% in sororities
Most popular majors: 18% Business, Management, Marketing, and Related Support Services, 12% Communication, Journalism, and Related Programs, 10% Biological and Biomedical Sciences, 10% Social Sciences, 9% Engineering
Expenses: 2019-2020: $14,460 in state, $39,766 out of state; room/board: $10,472
Financial aid: (517) 353-5940; 47% of undergrads determined to have financial need; average aid package $15,505

Michigan Technological University
Houghton MI
(906) 487-2335
U.S. News ranking: Nat. U., No. 147
Website: www.mtu.edu
Admissions email: mtu4u@mtu.edu
Public; founded 1885
Freshman admissions: more selective; 2018-2019: 5,838 applied, 4,313 accepted. Either SAT or ACT required. SAT 25/75 percentile: 1170-1360. High school rank: 32% in top tenth, 65% in top quarter, 90% in top half
Early decision deadline: N/A, notification date: N/A
Early action deadline: N/A, notification date: N/A
Application deadline (fall): rolling
Undergraduate student body: 5,493 full time, 335 part time; 72% male, 28% female; 0% American Indian, 2% Asian, 1% black, 2% Hispanic, 3% multiracial, 0% Pacific Islander, 88% white, 2% international; 76% from in state; 43% live on campus; 8% of students in fraternities, 11% in sororities
Most popular majors: 65% Engineering, 6% Business, Management, Marketing, and Related Support Services, 6% Computer and Information Sciences and Support Services, 5% Engineering Technologies and Engineering-Related Fields, 4% Natural Resources and Conservation
Expenses: 2019-2020: $15,960 in state, $35,196 out of state; room/board: $11,004
Financial aid: (906) 487-2622; 65% of undergrads determined to have financial need; average aid package $15,585

Northern Michigan University
Marquette MI
(906) 227-2650
U.S. News ranking: Reg. U. (Mid. W), No. 76
Website: www.nmu.edu
Admissions email: admissions@nmu.edu
Public; founded 1899
Freshman admissions: selective; 2018-2019: 7,607 applied, 5,001 accepted. Either SAT

or ACT required. SAT 25/75 percentile: 970-1180. High school rank: N/A
Early decision deadline: N/A, notification date: N/A
Early action deadline: N/A, notification date: N/A
Application deadline (fall): rolling
Undergraduate student body: 6,184 full time, 905 part time; 44% male, 56% female; 1% American Indian, 1% Asian, 2% black, 4% Hispanic, 5% multiracial, 0% Pacific Islander, 86% white, 1% international; 79% from in state; 45% live on campus; N/A of students in fraternities, N/A in sororities
Most popular majors: 16% Business, Management, Marketing, and Related Support Services, 15% Health Professions and Related Programs, 9% Biological and Biomedical Sciences, 8% Visual and Performing Arts, 6% Natural Resources and Conservation
Expenses: 2019-2020: $10,944 in state, $16,550 out of state; room/board: $10,774
Financial aid: (906) 227-2327; 69% of undergrads determined to have financial need; average aid package $11,189

Northwestern Michigan College[1]
Traverse City MI
U.S. News ranking: Reg. Coll. (Mid. W), unranked
Admissions email: N/A
Public
Application deadline (fall): N/A
Undergraduate student body: N/A full time, N/A part time
Expenses: N/A
Financial aid: N/A

Northwood University
Midland MI
(989) 837-4273
U.S. News ranking: Business, unranked
Website: www.northwood.edu
Admissions email: miadmit@northwood.edu
Private; founded 1959
Freshman admissions: selective; 2018-2019: 1,445 applied, 976 accepted. Either SAT or ACT required. SAT 25/75 percentile: 990-1180. High school rank: 7% in top tenth, 20% in top quarter, 52% in top half
Early decision deadline: N/A, notification date: N/A
Early action deadline: N/A, notification date: N/A
Application deadline (fall): rolling
Undergraduate student body: 1,177 full time, 67 part time; 66% male, 34% female; 0% American Indian, 0% Asian, 6% black, 4% Hispanic, 3% multiracial, 0% Pacific Islander, 73% white, 6% international; 83% from in state; 43% live on campus; 9% of students in fraternities, 11% in sororities
Most popular majors: 16% Business Administration and Management, General, 16% Marketing/Marketing Management, General, 15% Vehicle and Vehicle

Parts and Accessories Marketing Operations, 13% Accounting, 9% Hospitality Administration/Management, General
Expenses: 2019-2020: $28,080; room/board: $10,790
Financial aid: (989) 837-4230; 64% of undergrads determined to have financial need; average aid package $20,857

Oakland University
Rochester MI
(248) 370-3360
U.S. News ranking: Nat. U., second tier
Website: www.oakland.edu
Admissions email: visit@oakland.edu
Public; founded 1957
Freshman admissions: selective; 2018-2019: 12,309 applied, 10,328 accepted. Either SAT or ACT required. SAT 25/75 percentile: 1010-1240. High school rank: 21% in top tenth, 50% in top quarter, 81% in top half
Early decision deadline: N/A, notification date: N/A
Early action deadline: N/A, notification date: N/A
Application deadline (fall): 8/1
Undergraduate student body: 12,656 full time, 3,143 part time; 44% male, 56% female; 0% American Indian, 5% Asian, 8% black, 4% Hispanic, 3% multiracial, 0% Pacific Islander, 74% white, 2% international; 98% from in state; 19% live on campus; N/A of students in fraternities, N/A in sororities
Most popular majors: 22% Health Professions and Related Programs, 18% Business, Management, Marketing, and Related Support Services, 10% Education, 10% Engineering, 6% Biological and Biomedical Sciences
Expenses: 2019-2020: $13,346 in state, $24,710 out of state; room/board: $10,806
Financial aid: (248) 370-2550; 63% of undergrads determined to have financial need; average aid package $10,129

Olivet College[7]
Olivet MI
(800) 456-7189
U.S. News ranking: Reg. Coll. (Mid. W), No. 42
Website: www.olivetcollege.edu
Admissions email: admissions@olivetcollege.edu
Private; founded 1844
Affiliation: United Church of Christ
Freshman admissions: less selective; 2018-2019: 1,401 applied, 999 accepted. Either SAT or ACT required. SAT 25/75 percentile: N/A. High school rank: N/A
Early decision deadline: N/A, notification date: N/A
Early action deadline: N/A, notification date: N/A
Application deadline (fall): 8/31
Undergraduate student body: 933 full time, 122 part time
Most popular majors: 22% Insurance, 13% Business Administration and Management,

General, 11% Health and Physical Education/Fitness, General, 10% Biology/Biological Sciences, General, 10% Criminal Justice/Safety Studies
Expenses: 2019-2020: $28,692; room/board: $10,100
Financial aid: (269) 749-7645; 93% of undergrads determined to have financial need; average aid package $20,450

Rochester University
Rochester Hills MI
(248) 218-2222
U.S. News ranking: Reg. Coll. (Mid. W), second tier
Website: www.rc.edu
Admissions email: admissions@rc.edu
Private; founded 1959
Affiliation: Churches of Christ
Freshman admissions: less selective; 2018-2019: 361 applied, 361 accepted. Either SAT or ACT required. SAT 25/75 percentile: 870-1100. High school rank: N/A
Early decision deadline: N/A, notification date: N/A
Early action deadline: N/A, notification date: N/A
Application deadline (fall): rolling
Undergraduate student body: 697 full time, 368 part time; 37% male, 63% female; 0% American Indian, 1% Asian, 19% black, 2% Hispanic, 3% multiracial, 0% Pacific Islander, 72% white, 2% international; 93% from in state; 24% live on campus; N/A of students in fraternities, N/A in sororities
Most popular majors: 24% Business, Management, Marketing, and Related Support Services, 19% Education, 12% Health Professions and Related Programs, 12% Psychology, 11% Communication, Journalism, and Related Programs
Expenses: 2018-2019: $53,909; room/board: $16,122
Financial aid: (248) 218-2038

Saginaw Valley State University
University Center MI
(989) 964-4200
U.S. News ranking: Reg. U. (Mid. W), second tier
Website: www.svsu.edu
Admissions email: admissions@svsu.edu
Public; founded 1963
Freshman admissions: selective; 2018-2019: 7,329 applied, 5,672 accepted. Either SAT or ACT required. SAT 25/75 percentile: 990-1200. High school rank: 18% in top tenth, 43% in top quarter, 76% in top half
Early decision deadline: N/A, notification date: N/A
Early action deadline: N/A, notification date: N/A
Application deadline (fall): rolling
Undergraduate student body: 6,483 full time, 1,256 part time; 40% male, 60% female; 0% American Indian, 1% Asian, 8% black, 5% Hispanic, 3% multiracial, 0% Pacific Islander, 74% white,

6% international; N/A from in state; 31% live on campus; 3% of students in fraternities, 3% in sororities
Most popular majors: 22% Health Professions and Related Programs, 19% Business, Management, Marketing, and Related Support Services, 8% Public Administration and Social Service Professions, 5% Education, 5% Parks, Recreation, Leisure, and Fitness Studies
Expenses: 2019-2020: $10,814 in state, $25,401 out of state; room/board: $10,440
Financial aid: (989) 964-4900; 69% of undergrads determined to have financial need

Schoolcraft College[1]
Livonia MI
(734) 462-4400
U.S. News ranking: Reg. Coll. (Mid. W), unranked
Website: www.ptcollege.edu
Admissions email: N/A
Public
Application deadline (fall): N/A
Undergraduate student body: N/A full time, N/A part time
Expenses: N/A
Financial aid: N/A

Siena Heights University
Adrian MI
(517) 264-7180
U.S. News ranking: Reg. U. (Mid. W), No. 111
Website: www.sienaheights.edu
Admissions email: admissions@sienaheights.edu
Private; founded 1919
Affiliation: Roman Catholic
Freshman admissions: less selective; 2018-2019: 1,777 applied, 1,219 accepted. Either SAT or ACT required for some. SAT 25/75 percentile: 870-1090. High school rank: 7% in top tenth, 29% in top quarter, 67% in top half
Early decision deadline: N/A, notification date: N/A
Early action deadline: N/A, notification date: N/A
Application deadline (fall): 8/1
Undergraduate student body: 1,246 full time, 962 part time; 42% male, 58% female; 1% American Indian, 1% Asian, 10% black, 7% Hispanic, 3% multiracial, 0% Pacific Islander, 63% white, 1% international; 86% from in state; 27% live on campus; 2% of students in fraternities, 0% in sororities
Most popular majors: 12% Business Administration and Management, General, 6% Community Organization and Advocacy, 6% Criminal Justice/Safety Studies, 6% Registered Nursing/Registered Nurse, 5% Radiologic Technology/Science - Radiographer
Expenses: 2018-2019: $27,124; room/board: $10,620
Financial aid: (517) 264-7110

Spring Arbor University
Spring Arbor MI
(800) 968-0011
U.S. News ranking: Reg. U. (Mid. W), No. 43
Website: www.arbor.edu/
Admissions email: admissions@arbor.edu
Private; founded 1873
Affiliation: Free Methodist
Freshman admissions: selective; 2018-2019: 1,173 applied, 832 accepted. Either SAT or ACT required. SAT 25/75 percentile: 1025-1230. High school rank: 18% in top tenth, 48% in top quarter, 75% in top half
Early decision deadline: N/A, notification date: N/A
Early action deadline: N/A, notification date: N/A
Application deadline (fall): 8/1
Undergraduate student body: 1,181 full time, 626 part time; 32% male, 68% female; 0% American Indian, 1% Asian, 11% black, 4% Hispanic, 3% multiracial, 0% Pacific Islander, 75% white, 0% international; 84% from in state; 75% live on campus; 0% of students in fraternities, 0% in sororities
Most popular majors: 14% Teacher Education and Professional Development, Specific Subject Areas, 13% Business Administration and Management, General, 10% Religion/Religious Studies, 9% Psychology, General, 9% Social Work
Expenses: 2019-2020: $29,630; room/board: $10,260
Financial aid: (517) 750-6463; 83% of undergrads determined to have financial need; average aid package $24,730

University of Detroit Mercy
Detroit MI
(313) 993-1245
U.S. News ranking: Nat. U., No. 179
Website: www.udmercy.edu
Admissions email: admissions@udmercy.edu
Private; founded 1877
Affiliation: Roman Catholic
Freshman admissions: selective; 2018-2019: 3,760 applied, 3,120 accepted. Either SAT or ACT required. SAT 25/75 percentile: 1050-1250. High school rank: 19% in top tenth, 47% in top quarter, 81% in top half
Early decision deadline: 11/1, notification date: 12/1
Early action deadline: N/A, notification date: N/A
Application deadline (fall): 3/1
Undergraduate student body: 2,494 full time, 386 part time; 38% male, 62% female; 0% American Indian, 6% Asian, 13% black, 6% Hispanic, 2% multiracial, 0% Pacific Islander, 60% white, 8% international; 87% from in state; 30% live on campus; 9% of students in fraternities, 5% in sororities

Most popular majors: 40% Registered Nursing/Registered Nurse, 9% Biology/Biological Sciences, General, 6% Business Administration and Management, General, 5% Engineering, General, 4% Dental Hygiene/Hygienist
Expenses: 2019-2020: $28,840; room/board: $9,990
Financial aid: (313) 993-3354; 65% of undergrads determined to have financial need; average aid package $21,954

University of Michigan–Ann Arbor
Ann Arbor MI
(734) 764-7433
U.S. News ranking: Nat. U., No. 25
Website: umich.edu
Admissions email: N/A
Public; founded 1817
Freshman admissions: most selective; 2018-2019: 64,917 applied, 14,818 accepted. Either SAT or ACT required. SAT 25/75 percentile: 1330-1510. High school rank: 79% in top tenth, 96% in top quarter, 99% in top half
Early decision deadline: N/A, notification date: N/A
Early action deadline: 11/1, notification date: 12/24
Application deadline (fall): 2/1
Undergraduate student body: 29,245 full time, 1,073 part time; 50% male, 50% female; 0% American Indian, 15% Asian, 4% black, 6% Hispanic, 4% multiracial, 0% Pacific Islander, 59% white, 7% international; 59% from in state; 31% live on campus; 12% of students in fraternities, 25% in sororities
Most popular majors: 8% Business Administration and Management, General, 8% Computer and Information Sciences, General, 3% Economics, General, 3% Experimental Psychology, 3% Physiological Psychology/Psychobiology
Expenses: 2019-2020: $15,558 in state, $51,200 out of state; room/board: $11,996
Financial aid: (734) 763-6600; 39% of undergrads determined to have financial need; average aid package $27,695

University of Michigan–Dearborn
Dearborn MI
(313) 593-5100
U.S. News ranking: Reg. U. (Mid. W), No. 33
Website: umdearborn.edu/
Admissions email: umd-admissions@umich.edu
Public; founded 1959
Freshman admissions: selective; 2018-2019: 7,740 applied, 5,997 accepted. Either SAT or ACT required. SAT 25/75 percentile: 1080-1290. High school rank: N/A.
Early decision deadline: N/A, notification date: N/A
Early action deadline: N/A, notification date: N/A

Application deadline (fall): 9/4
Undergraduate student body: 5,238 full time, 1,947 part time; 54% male, 46% female; 0% American Indian, 8% Asian, 8% black, 6% Hispanic, 3% multiracial, 0% Pacific Islander, 69% white, 2% international; 97% from in state; N/A live on campus; N/A of students in fraternities, N/A in sororities
Most popular majors: 23% Business, Management, Marketing, and Related Support Services, 18% Engineering, 9% Psychology, 8% Biological and Biomedical Sciences, 7% Social Sciences
Expenses: 2019-2020: $13,304 in state, $26,409 out of state; room/board: N/A
Financial aid: (313) 593-5300; 69% of undergrads determined to have financial need; average aid package $11,399

University of Michigan–Flint
Flint MI
(810) 762-3300
U.S. News ranking: Nat. U., second tier
Website: www.umflint.edu
Admissions email: admissions@umflint.edu
Public; founded 1956
Freshman admissions: selective; 2018-2019: 4,394 applied, 2,912 accepted. Either SAT or ACT required. SAT 25/75 percentile: 980-1200. High school rank: 15% in top tenth, 40% in top quarter, 78% in top half
Early decision deadline: N/A, notification date: N/A
Early action deadline: N/A, notification date: N/A
Application deadline (fall): 8/22
Undergraduate student body: 3,674 full time, 2,423 part time; 39% male, 61% female; 1% American Indian, 2% Asian, 13% black, 5% Hispanic, 4% multiracial, 0% Pacific Islander, 70% white, 3% international; 98% from in state; 7% live on campus; 1% of students in fraternities, 2% in sororities
Most popular majors: 22% Registered Nursing/Registered Nurse, 7% Health/Health Care Administration/Management, 6% Business Administration and Management, General, 4% Psychology, General, 4% Social Work
Expenses: 2019-2020: $12,406 in state, $23,692 out of state; room/board: $9,116
Financial aid: (810) 762-3444

Walsh College of Accountancy and Business Administration
Troy MI
(248) 823-1600
U.S. News ranking: Business, unranked
Website: www.walshcollege.edu
Admissions email: admissions@walshcollege.edu
Private; founded 1922

Freshman admissions: least selective; 2018-2019: N/A applied, N/A accepted. Neither SAT nor ACT required. SAT 25/75 percentile: N/A. High school rank: N/A
Early decision deadline: N/A, notification date: N/A
Early action deadline: N/A, notification date: N/A
Application deadline (fall): rolling
Undergraduate student body: 65 full time, 737 part time; 49% male, 51% female; 0% American Indian, 5% Asian, 5% black, 3% Hispanic, 2% multiracial, 0% Pacific Islander, 81% white, 1% international; 99% from in state; N/A live on campus; N/A of students in fraternities, N/A in sororities
Most popular majors: 27% Accounting, 20% Business Administration and Management, General, 18% Finance, General, 16% Business/Commerce, General, 10% Information Technology
Expenses: 2019-2020: $18,309; room/board: N/A
Financial aid: (248) 823-1665; 52% of undergrads determined to have financial need

Wayne State University
Detroit MI
(313) 577-2100
U.S. News ranking: Nat. U., No. 246
Website: wayne.edu/
Admissions email: studentservice@wayne.edu
Public; founded 1868
Freshman admissions: selective; 2018-2019: 16,210 applied, 11,533 accepted. Either SAT or ACT required. SAT 25/75 percentile: 1010-1210. High school rank: 18% in top tenth, 45% in top quarter, 78% in top half
Early decision deadline: N/A, notification date: N/A
Early action deadline: N/A, notification date: N/A
Application deadline (fall): 8/1
Undergraduate student body: 12,970 full time, 4,632 part time; 43% male, 57% female; 0% American Indian, 10% Asian, 16% black, 5% Hispanic, 4% multiracial, 0% Pacific Islander, 59% white, 2% international; 98% from in state; 15% live on campus; N/A of students in fraternities, N/A in sororities
Most popular majors: 9% Psychology, General, 5% Biology/Biological Sciences, General, 4% International Business/Trade/Commerce, 4% Organizational Behavior Studies, 4% Registered Nursing/Registered Nurse
Expenses: 2019-2020: $14,629 in state, $31,499 out of state; room/board: $10,748
Financial aid: (313) 577-2100; 72% of undergrads determined to have financial need; average aid package $11,680

Western Michigan University
Kalamazoo MI
(269) 387-2000
U.S. News ranking: Nat. U., No. 246
Website: wmich.edu/
Admissions email: ask-wmu@wmich.edu
Public; founded 1903
Freshman admissions: selective; 2018-2019: 17,051 applied, 13,829 accepted. Either SAT or ACT required. SAT 25/75 percentile: 990-1190. High school rank: 10% in top tenth, 33% in top quarter, 68% in top half
Early decision deadline: N/A, notification date: N/A
Early action deadline: N/A, notification date: N/A
Application deadline (fall): rolling
Undergraduate student body: 14,983 full time, 2,777 part time; 51% male, 49% female; 0% American Indian, 2% Asian, 12% black, 7% Hispanic, 4% multiracial, 0% Pacific Islander, 69% white, 5% international; 87% from in state; 27% live on campus; 8% of students in fraternities, 8% in sororities
Most popular majors: 21% Business, Management, Marketing, and Related Support Services, 12% Health Professions and Related Programs, 7% Engineering, 7% Multi/Interdisciplinary Studies, 7% Visual and Performing Arts
Expenses: 2019-2020: $13,017 in state, $16,041 out of state; room/board: $10,567
Financial aid: (269) 387-6000; 41% of undergrads determined to have financial need; average aid package $14,001

MINNESOTA

Augsburg University
Minneapolis MN
(612) 330-1001
U.S. News ranking: Reg. U. (Mid. W), No. 13
Website: www.augsburg.edu
Admissions email: admissions@augsburg.edu
Private; founded 1869
Affiliation: Evangelical Lutheran Church
Freshman admissions: selective; 2018-2019: 3,564 applied, 1,451 accepted. Neither SAT nor ACT required. ACT 25/75 percentile: 19-24. High school rank: N/A
Early decision deadline: N/A, notification date: N/A
Early action deadline: N/A, notification date: N/A
Application deadline (fall): 8/1
Undergraduate student body: 1,992 full time, 351 part time; 46% male, 54% female; 1% American Indian, 10% Asian, 16% black, 9% Hispanic, 5% multiracial, 0% Pacific Islander, 46% white, 3% international; N/A from in state; 36% live on campus; N/A of students in fraternities, N/A in sororities

Most popular majors: 22% Business, Management, Marketing, and Related Support Services, 14% Health Professions and Related Programs, 8% Education, 7% Social Sciences, 7% Visual and Performing Arts
Expenses: 2019-2020: $39,945; room/board: $10,556
Financial aid: (612) 330-1046

Bemidji State University
Bemidji MN
(218) 755-2040
U.S. News ranking: Reg. U. (Mid. W), No. 92
Website: www.bemidjistate.edu
Admissions email: admissions@bemidjistate.edu
Public; founded 1919
Freshman admissions: selective; 2018-2019: 4,025 applied, 2,609 accepted. Either SAT or ACT required. ACT 25/75 percentile: 19-24. High school rank: 6% in top tenth, 24% in top quarter, 60% in top half
Early decision deadline: N/A, notification date: N/A
Early action deadline: N/A, notification date: N/A
Application deadline (fall): rolling
Undergraduate student body: 3,298 full time, 1,422 part time; 43% male, 57% female; 3% American Indian, 1% Asian, 2% black, 3% Hispanic, 4% multiracial, 0% Pacific Islander, 83% white, 2% international; 87% from in state; 26% live on campus; N/A of students in fraternities, N/A in sororities
Most popular majors: 22% Business, Management, Marketing, and Related Support Services, 17% Health Professions and Related Programs, 10% Education, 6% Psychology, 5% Homeland Security, Law Enforcement, Firefighting and Related Protective Services
Expenses: 2019-2020: $8,696 in state, $8,696 out of state; room/board: $8,660
Financial aid: (218) 755-2034; 62% of undergrads determined to have financial need; average aid package $10,122

Bethany Lutheran College
Mankato MN
(507) 344-7331
U.S. News ranking: Nat. Lib. Arts, second tier
Website: www.blc.edu
Admissions email: admiss@blc.edu
Private; founded 1927
Affiliation: Other
Freshman admissions: selective; 2018-2019: 497 applied, 387 accepted. Either SAT or ACT required. ACT 25/75 percentile: 19-25. High school rank: 4% in top tenth, 40% in top quarter, 71% in top half
Early decision deadline: N/A, notification date: N/A
Early action deadline: N/A, notification date: N/A
Application deadline (fall): 7/1

Undergraduate student body: 593 full time, 146 part time; 48% male, 52% female; 0% American Indian, 2% Asian, 3% black, 4% Hispanic, 2% multiracial, 0% Pacific Islander, 78% white, 10% international; 69% from in state; 67% live on campus; N/A of students in fraternities, N/A in sororities
Most popular majors: 22% Business, Management, Marketing, and Related Support Services, 17% Communication, Journalism, and Related Programs, 11% Biological and Biomedical Sciences, 10% Psychology, 9% English Language and Literature/ Letters
Expenses: 2019-2020: $28,080; room/board: $8,150
Financial aid: (507) 344-7328; 76% of undergrads determined to have financial need; average aid package $23,391

Bethel University
St. Paul MN
(800) 255-8706
U.S. News ranking: Nat. U., No. 197
Website: www.bethel.edu
Admissions email: undergrad-admissions@bethel.edu
Private; founded 1871
Affiliation: Baptist
Freshman admissions: more selective; 2018-2019: 2,184 applied, 1,540 accepted. Either SAT or ACT required. ACT 25/75 percentile: 22-28. High school rank: 25% in top tenth, 55% in top quarter, 84% in top half
Early decision deadline: N/A, notification date: N/A
Early action deadline: N/A, notification date: N/A
Application deadline (fall): rolling
Undergraduate student body: 2,417 full time, 440 part time; 38% male, 62% female; 0% American Indian, 4% Asian, 5% black, 5% Hispanic, 4% multiracial, 0% Pacific Islander, 78% white, 1% international; 82% from in state; 66% live on campus; N/A of students in fraternities, N/A in sororities
Most popular majors: 23% Business, Management, Marketing, and Related Support Services, 21% Health Professions and Related Programs, 11% Education, 7% Communication, Journalism, and Related Programs, 5% Biological and Biomedical Sciences
Expenses: 2019-2020: $38,460; room/board: $10,780
Financial aid: (651) 638-6241; 75% of undergrads determined to have financial need; average aid package $30,734

Capella University[1]
Minneapolis MN
(866) 283-7921
U.S. News ranking: Nat. U., unranked
Website: www.capella.edu
Admissions email: admissionsoffice@capella.edu
For-profit
Application deadline (fall): N/A

Undergraduate student body: N/A full time, N/A part time
Expenses: N/A
Financial aid: N/A

Carleton College
Northfield MN
(507) 222-4190
U.S. News ranking: Nat. Lib. Arts, No. 7
Website: www.carleton.edu
Admissions email: admissions@carleton.edu
Private; founded 1866
Freshman admissions: most selective; 2018-2019: 7,092 applied, 1,407 accepted. Either SAT or ACT required. ACT 25/75 percentile: 31-34. High school rank: 79% in top tenth, 96% in top quarter, 100% in top half
Early decision deadline: 11/15, notification date: 12/15
Early action deadline: N/A, notification date: N/A
Application deadline (fall): 1/15
Undergraduate student body: 2,077 full time, 20 part time; 50% male, 50% female; 0% American Indian, 8% Asian, 5% black, 8% Hispanic, 7% multiracial, 0% Pacific Islander, 60% white, 11% international; 15% from in state; 96% live on campus; N/A of students in fraternities, N/A in sororities
Most popular majors: 18% Social Sciences, 15% Physical Sciences, 11% Computer and Information Sciences and Support Services, 9% Biological and Biomedical Sciences, 9% Mathematics and Statistics
Expenses: 2019-2020: $57,111; room/board: $14,658
Financial aid: (507) 222-4138; 55% of undergrads determined to have financial need; average aid package $49,658

College of St. Benedict
St. Joseph MN
(320) 363-5060
U.S. News ranking: Nat. Lib. Arts, No. 82
Website: www.csbsju.edu
Admissions email: admissions@csbsju.edu
Private; founded 1913
Affiliation: Roman Catholic
Freshman admissions: more selective; 2018-2019: 1,931 applied, 1,610 accepted. Either SAT or ACT required. ACT 25/75 percentile: 22-27. High school rank: 32% in top tenth, 64% in top quarter, 92% in top half
Early decision deadline: N/A, notification date: N/A
Early action deadline: 12/15, notification date: 1/15
Application deadline (fall): rolling
Undergraduate student body: 1,764 full time, 18 part time; 0% male, 100% female; 1% American Indian, 5% Asian, 3% black, 8% Hispanic, 0% multiracial, 0% Pacific Islander, 79% white, 4% international; 83% from in state; 93% live on campus; 0% of students in fraternities, 0% in sororities

Most popular majors: 12% Psychology, General, 12% Rhetoric and Composition, 10% Biology/Biological Sciences, General, 9% Elementary Education and Teaching, 9% Registered Nursing/Registered Nurse
Expenses: 2019-2020: $46,820; room/board: $11,068
Financial aid: (320) 363-5388; 75% of undergrads determined to have financial need; average aid package $38,456

College of St. Scholastica
Duluth MN
(218) 723-6046
U.S. News ranking: Nat. U., No. 254
Website: www.css.edu
Admissions email: admissions@css.edu
Private; founded 1912
Affiliation: Roman Catholic
Freshman admissions: selective; 2018-2019: 3,808 applied, 2,520 accepted. Either SAT or ACT required. ACT 25/75 percentile: 20-26. High school rank: 17% in top tenth, 47% in top quarter, 79% in top half
Early decision deadline: N/A, notification date: N/A
Early action deadline: N/A, notification date: N/A
Application deadline (fall): rolling
Undergraduate student body: 2,062 full time, 417 part time; 29% male, 71% female; 1% American Indian, 3% Asian, 3% black, 4% Hispanic, 3% multiracial, 0% Pacific Islander, 83% white, 2% international; 85% from in state; 51% live on campus; N/A of students in fraternities, N/A in sororities
Most popular majors: 49% Health Professions and Related Programs, 13% Business, Management, Marketing, and Related Support Services, 11% Public Administration and Social Service Professions, 9% Biological and Biomedical Sciences, 5% Psychology
Expenses: 2019-2020: $38,282; room/board: $10,088
Financial aid: (218) 723-7027; 81% of undergrads determined to have financial need; average aid package $26,816

Concordia College–Moorhead
Moorhead MN
(800) 699-9897
U.S. News ranking: Nat. Lib. Arts, No. 132
Website: www.concordiacollege.edu
Admissions email: admissions@cord.edu
Private; founded 1891
Affiliation: Evangelical Lutheran Church
Freshman admissions: more selective; 2018-2019: 4,160 applied, 2,545 accepted. Either SAT or ACT required. ACT 25/75 percentile: 21-27. High school rank: 22% in top tenth, 47% in top quarter, 81% in top half

Early decision deadline: N/A, notification date: N/A
Early action deadline: N/A, notification date: N/A
Undergraduate student body: 2,040 full time, 56 part time; 42% male, 58% female; 1% American Indian, 1% Asian, 2% black, 2% Hispanic, 2% multiracial, 0% Pacific Islander, 83% white, 4% international; 79% from in state; 61% live on campus; 0% of students in fraternities, 0% in sororities
Most popular majors: 16% Business, Management, Marketing, and Related Support Services, 13% Biological and Biomedical Sciences, 12% Education, 8% Communication, Journalism, and Related Programs, 8% Foreign Languages, Literatures, and Linguistics
Expenses: 2019-2020: $41,566; room/board: $8,610
Financial aid: (218) 299-3010; 74% of undergrads determined to have financial need; average aid package $30,984

Concordia University–St. Paul
St. Paul MN
(651) 641-8230
U.S. News ranking: Reg. U. (Mid. W), No. 76
Website: www.csp.edu
Admissions email: admissions@csp.edu
Private; founded 1893
Affiliation: Lutheran Church–Missouri Synod
Freshman admissions: less selective; 2018-2019: 901 applied, 873 accepted. Neither SAT nor ACT required. ACT 25/75 percentile: 18-24. High school rank: N/A
Early decision deadline: N/A, notification date: N/A
Early action deadline: N/A, notification date: N/A
Application deadline (fall): 8/1
Undergraduate student body: 1,673 full time, 1,421 part time; 40% male, 60% female; 1% American Indian, 9% Asian, 11% black, 5% Hispanic, 4% multiracial, 0% Pacific Islander, 63% white, 4% international; 75% from in state; 19% live on campus; N/A of students in fraternities, N/A in sororities
Most popular majors: 18% Business Administration and Management, General, 14% Kinesiology and Exercise Science, 8% Psychology, General, 5% Biology/Biological Sciences, General, 5% Nursing Practice
Expenses: 2019-2020: $22,800; room/board: $9,200
Financial aid: (651) 603-6300; 75% of undergrads determined to have financial need; average aid package $15,543

Crown College[1]
St. Bonifacius MN
(952) 446-4142
U.S. News ranking: Reg. U. (Mid. W), second tier
Website: www.crown.edu
Admissions email: admissions@crown.edu
Private; founded 1916
Affiliation: Christ and Missionary Alliance Church
Application deadline (fall): 8/20
Undergraduate student body: N/A full time, N/A part time
Expenses: 2018-2019: $26,200; room/board: $8,660
Financial aid: (952) 446-4177

Dunwoody College of Technology
Minneapolis MN
(800) 292-4625
U.S. News ranking: Reg. Coll. (Mid. W), No. 24
Website: www.dunwoody.edu
Admissions email: info@dunwoody.edu
Private; founded 1914
Freshman admissions: less selective; 2018-2019: 614 applied, 380 accepted. Either SAT or ACT required for some. SAT 25/75 percentile: N/A. High school rank: 8% in top tenth, 31% in top quarter, 66% in top half
Early decision deadline: N/A, notification date: N/A
Early action deadline: N/A, notification date: N/A
Application deadline (fall): rolling
Undergraduate student body: 1,053 full time, 252 part time; 83% male, 17% female; 0% American Indian, 7% Asian, 5% black, 3% Hispanic, 5% multiracial, 0% Pacific Islander, 71% white, 0% international; 3% from in state; 1% live on campus; N/A of students in fraternities, N/A in sororities
Most popular majors: 37% Manufacturing Engineering, 33% Business Administration and Management, General, 15% Interior Design, 10% Architecture, 5% Computer Systems Analysis/Analyst
Expenses: 2019-2020: $23,119; room/board: N/A
Financial aid: (612) 381-3347; 73% of undergrads determined to have financial need; average aid package $11,611

Gustavus Adolphus College
St. Peter MN
(507) 933-7676
U.S. News ranking: Nat. Lib. Arts, No. 89
Website: gustavus.edu
Admissions email: admission@gustavus.edu
Private; founded 1862
Affiliation: Evangelical Lutheran Church
Freshman admissions: more selective; 2018-2019: 5,168 applied, 3,419 accepted. Neither SAT nor ACT required. ACT 25/75 percentile: 24-30. High school

rank: 32% in top tenth, 61% in top quarter, 94% in top half
Early decision deadline: N/A, notification date: N/A
Early action deadline: 11/1, notification date: 11/15
Application deadline (fall): 5/1
Undergraduate student body: 2,213 full time, 27 part time; 42% male, 58% female; 0% American Indian, 6% Asian, 3% black, 5% Hispanic, 4% multiracial, 0% Pacific Islander, 77% white, 4% international; 81% from in state; 93% live on campus; 16% of students in fraternities, 15% in sororities
Most popular majors: 13% Social Sciences, 11% Business, Management, Marketing, and Related Support Services, 10% Psychology, 9% Biological and Biomedical Sciences, 7% Education
Expenses: 2019-2020: $46,720; room/board: $10,150
Financial aid: (507) 933-7527; 72% of undergrads determined to have financial need; average aid package $41,099

Hamline University
St. Paul MN
(651) 523-2207
U.S. News ranking: Reg. U. (Mid. W), No. 17
Website: www.hamline.edu
Admissions email: admission@hamline.edu
Private; founded 1854
Affiliation: United Methodist
Freshman admissions: selective; 2018-2019: 4,794 applied, 3,219 accepted. Either SAT or ACT required. ACT 25/75 percentile: 20-27. High school rank: 17% in top tenth, 49% in top quarter, 83% in top half
Early decision deadline: 11/1, notification date: 11/15
Early action deadline: 12/1, notification date: N/A
Application deadline (fall): rolling
Undergraduate student body: 2,028 full time, 78 part time; 38% male, 62% female; 0% American Indian, 8% Asian, 9% black, 10% Hispanic, 6% multiracial, 0% Pacific Islander, 65% white, 1% international; 82% from in state; 38% live on campus; N/A of students in fraternities, N/A in sororities
Most popular majors: 19% Social Sciences, 18% Business, Management, Marketing, and Related Support Services, 8% Multi/Interdisciplinary Studies, 7% English Language and Literature/Letters, 7% Psychology
Expenses: 2019-2020: $42,774; room/board: $10,592
Financial aid: (651) 523-2933; 85% of undergrads determined to have financial need; average aid package $31,667

Macalester College
St. Paul MN
(651) 696-6357
U.S. News ranking: Nat. Lib. Arts, No. 25
Website: www.macalester.edu
Admissions email: admissions@macalester.edu
Private; founded 1874
Freshman admissions: more selective; 2018-2019: 5,985 applied, 2,468 accepted. Either SAT or ACT required. ACT 25/75 percentile: 29-33. High school rank: 63% in top tenth, 91% in top quarter, 99% in top half
Early decision deadline: 11/15, notification date: 12/15
Early action deadline: N/A, notification date: N/A
Application deadline (fall): 1/15
Undergraduate student body: 2,140 full time, 34 part time; 40% male, 60% female; 0% American Indian, 8% Asian, 3% black, 8% Hispanic, 6% multiracial, 0% Pacific Islander, 58% white, 16% international; 18% from in state; 60% live on campus; 0% of students in fraternities, 0% in sororities
Most popular majors: 28% Social Sciences, 11% Biological and Biomedical Sciences, 9% Foreign Languages, Literatures, and Linguistics, 8% Mathematics and Statistics, 7% Psychology
Expenses: 2019-2020: $56,292; room/board: $12,592
Financial aid: (651) 696-6214; 68% of undergrads determined to have financial need; average aid package $47,763

Metropolitan State University[1]
St. Paul MN
(651) 772-7600
U.S. News ranking: Nat. U., second tier
Website: www.metrostate.edu
Admissions email: admissions@metrostate.edu
Public
Application deadline (fall): N/A
Undergraduate student body: N/A full time, N/A part time
Expenses: N/A
Financial aid: N/A

Minneapolis College of Art and Design
Minneapolis MN
(612) 874-3800
U.S. News ranking: Arts, unranked
Website: www.mcad.edu
Admissions email: admissions@mcad.edu
Private; founded 1886
Freshman admissions: selective; 2018-2019: 653 applied, 409 accepted. Either SAT or ACT required. ACT 25/75 percentile: 19-26. High school rank: N/A
Early decision deadline: N/A, notification date: N/A
Early action deadline: 12/1, notification date: 12/15
Application deadline (fall): 4/1
Undergraduate student body: 717 full time, 24 part time; 31% male, 69% female; 3% American Indian, 9% Asian, 6% black, 8% Hispanic, 1% multiracial, 1% Pacific Islander, 66% white, 2% international; N/A from in state; 37% live on campus; 0% of students in fraternities, 0% in sororities
Most popular majors: 66% Visual and Performing Arts, 15% Communications Technologies/Technicians and Support Services, 11% Business, Management, Marketing, and Related Support Services, 5% Precision Production, 3% Communication, Journalism, and Related Programs
Expenses: 2018-2019: $39,210; room/board: N/A
Financial aid: (612) 874-3733

Minnesota State University–Mankato
Mankato MN
(507) 389-1822
U.S. News ranking: Reg. U. (Mid. W), No. 84
Website: mankato.mnsu.edu/
Admissions email: admissions@mnsu.edu
Public; founded 1868
Freshman admissions: selective; 2018-2019: 11,317 applied, 6,895 accepted. ACT required. ACT 25/75 percentile: 19-24. High school rank: 8% in top tenth, 26% in top quarter, 65% in top half
Early decision deadline: N/A, notification date: N/A
Early action deadline: N/A, notification date: N/A
Application deadline (fall): rolling
Undergraduate student body: 10,545 full time, 1,947 part time; 47% male, 53% female; 0% American Indian, 4% Asian, 5% black, 5% Hispanic, 3% multiracial, 0% Pacific Islander, 73% white, 9% international
Most popular majors: 20% Business, Management, Marketing, and Related Support Services, 13% Health Professions and Related Programs, 7% Communication, Journalism, and Related Programs, 7% Education, 5% Psychology
Expenses: 2018-2019: $8,184 in state, $16,235 out of state; room/board: N/A
Financial aid: (507) 389-1419; 52% of undergrads determined to have financial need; average aid package $9,549

Minnesota State University–Moorhead
Moorhead MN
(800) 593-7246
U.S. News ranking: Reg. U. (Mid. W), No. 92
Website: www.mnstate.edu
Admissions email: admissions@mnstate.edu
Public; founded 1887
Freshman admissions: selective; 2018-2019: 4,204 applied, 2,533 accepted. Either SAT or ACT required. ACT 25/75 percentile: 20-25. High school rank: 11% in top tenth, 31% in top quarter, 66% in top half
Early decision deadline: N/A, notification date: N/A
Early action deadline: N/A, notification date: N/A
Application deadline (fall): rolling
Undergraduate student body: 3,895 full time, 933 part time; 39% male, 61% female; 1% American Indian, 1% Asian, 4% black, 3% Hispanic, 4% multiracial, 0% Pacific Islander, 79% white, 6% international; 67% from in state; 25% live on campus; 1% of students in fraternities, 2% in sororities
Most popular majors: 19% Education, 18% Business, Management, Marketing, and Related Support Services, 12% Health Professions and Related Programs, 9% Visual and Performing Arts, 6% Public Administration and Social Service Professions
Expenses: 2019-2020: $8,572 in state, $15,982 out of state; room/board: $9,560
Financial aid: (218) 477-2251; 62% of undergrads determined to have financial need; average aid package $3,284

North Central University
Minneapolis MN
(800) 289-6222
U.S. News ranking: Reg. Coll. (Mid. W), No. 53
Website: www.northcentral.edu
Admissions email: admissions@northcentral.edu
Private; founded 1930
Affiliation: Assemblies of God Church
Freshman admissions: selective; 2018-2019: 770 applied, 488 accepted. Either SAT or ACT required. ACT 25/75 percentile: 19-24. High school rank: N/A
Early decision deadline: N/A, notification date: N/A
Early action deadline: 12/1, notification date: 8/1
Application deadline (fall): rolling
Undergraduate student body: 898 full time, 28 part time; 45% male, 55% female; 0% American Indian, 4% Asian, 5% black, 9% Hispanic, 4% multiracial, 0% Pacific Islander, 70% white, 1% international; 56% from in state; 81% live on campus; 0% of students in fraternities, 0% in sororities
Most popular majors: 8% Youth Ministry, 7% Business Administration and Management, General, 7% Elementary Education and Teaching, 7% Religious/Sacred Music, 6% Marketing/Marketing Management, General
Expenses: 2019-2020: $25,090; room/board: $8,010
Financial aid: (612) 343-4485; 85% of undergrads determined to have financial need; average aid package $18,964

Southwest Minnesota State University
Marshall MN
(507) 537-6286
U.S. News ranking: Reg. U. (Mid. W), No. 114
Website: www.smsu.edu
Admissions email: smsu.admissions@smsu.edu
Public; founded 1963
Freshman admissions: selective; 2018-2019: 2,133 applied, 1,287 accepted. Either SAT or ACT required. ACT 25/75 percentile: 7% in top tenth, 21% in top quarter, 56% in top half
Early decision deadline: N/A, notification date: N/A
Early action deadline: N/A, notification date: N/A
Application deadline (fall): 9/1
Undergraduate student body: 1,773 full time, 4,671 part time; 41% male, 59% female; 0% American Indian, 2% Asian, 7% black, 4% Hispanic, 4% multiracial, 0% Pacific Islander, 76% white, 6% international
Most popular majors: 24% Business, Management, Marketing, and Related Support Services, 18% Education, 12% Parks, Recreation, Leisure, and Fitness Studies, 7% Health Professions and Related Programs, 7% Psychology
Expenses: 2019-2020: $8,648 in state, $8,648 out of state; room/board: $8,790
Financial aid: (507) 537-6281; 66% of undergrads determined to have financial need; average aid package $9,589

St. Catherine University[7]
St. Paul MN
(800) 945-4599
U.S. News ranking: Nat. U., No. 228
Website: www.stkate.edu
Admissions email: admissions@stkate.edu
Private; founded 1905
Affiliation: Roman Catholic
Freshman admissions: selective; 2018-2019: N/A applied, N/A accepted. Either SAT or ACT required. ACT 25/75 percentile: 20-26. High school rank: 24% in top tenth, 66% in top quarter, 92% in top half
Early decision deadline: N/A, notification date: N/A
Early action deadline: N/A, notification date: N/A
Application deadline (fall): rolling
Undergraduate student body: 2,143 full time, 1,140 part time
Most popular majors: 44% Health Professions and Related Programs, 12% Business, Management, Marketing, and Related Support Services, 6% Parks, Recreation, Leisure, and Fitness Studies, 5% Psychology, 5% Public Administration and Social Service Professions
Expenses: 2019-2020: $41,614; room/board: $9,300

Financial aid: (651) 690-6061; 84% of undergrads determined to have financial need; average aid package $37,551

St. Cloud State University

St. Cloud MN
(320) 308-2244
U.S. News ranking: Reg. U. (Mid. W), No. 105
Website: www.stcloudstate.edu
Admissions email: scsu4u@stcloudstate.edu
Public; founded 1869
Freshman admissions: selective; 2018-2019: 5,415 applied, 4,668 accepted. Either SAT or ACT required. ACT 25/75 percentile: 18-24. High school rank: 6% in top tenth, 20% in top quarter, 64% in top half
Early decision deadline: N/A, notification date: N/A
Early action deadline: N/A, notification date: N/A
Application deadline (fall): 8/11
Undergraduate student body: 7,840 full time, 3,841 part time; 46% male, 54% female; 0% American Indian, 6% Asian, 9% black, 4% Hispanic, 4% multiracial, 0% Pacific Islander, 66% white, 11% international; 84% from in state; 17% live on campus; 2% of students in fraternities, 2% in sororities
Most popular majors: 22% Business, Management, Marketing, and Related Support Services, 10% Education, 9% Health Professions and Related Programs, 8% Psychology, 7% Communication, Journalism, and Related Programs
Expenses: 2019-2020: $8,656 in state, $16,948 out of state; room/board: $8,882
Financial aid: (320) 308-2047; 59% of undergrads determined to have financial need; average aid package $11,459

St. John's University

Collegeville MN
(320) 363-5060
U.S. News ranking: Nat. Lib. Arts, No. 92
Website: www.twocolleges.com
Admissions email: admissions@csbsju.edu
Private; founded 1857
Affiliation: Roman Catholic
Freshman admissions: selective; 2018-2019: 1,552 applied, 1,241 accepted. Either SAT or ACT required. ACT 25/75 percentile: 22-28. High school rank: 12% in top tenth, 44% in top quarter, 74% in top half
Early decision deadline: N/A, notification date: N/A
Early action deadline: 12/15, notification date: 1/15
Application deadline (fall): rolling
Undergraduate student body: 1,646 full time, 21 part time; 100% male, 0% female; 1% American Indian, 3% Asian, 5% black, 8% Hispanic, 0% multiracial, 0% Pacific Islander, 78% white, 5% international; 80% from in

state; 88% live on campus; 0% of students in fraternities, 0% in sororities
Most popular majors: 21% Business Administration and Management, General, 12% Accounting, 8% Rhetoric and Composition, 7% Economics, General, 6% Biology/Biological Sciences, General
Expenses: 2019-2020: $46,546; room/board: $10,528
Financial aid: (320) 363-3664; 68% of undergrads determined to have financial need; average aid package $35,625

St. Mary's University of Minnesota

Winona MN
(507) 457-1700
U.S. News ranking: Reg. U. (Mid. W), No. 33
Website: www.smumn.edu
Admissions email: admission@smumn.edu
Private; founded 1912
Affiliation: Roman Catholic
Freshman admissions: selective; 2018-2019: 1,641 applied, 1,502 accepted. Either SAT or ACT required. ACT 25/75 percentile: 20-26. High school rank: N/A
Early decision deadline: N/A, notification date: N/A
Early action deadline: N/A, notification date: N/A
Application deadline (fall): 5/1
Undergraduate student body: 1,118 full time, 324 part time; 43% male, 57% female; 0% American Indian, 3% Asian, 9% black, 8% Hispanic, 0% multiracial, 0% Pacific Islander, 68% white, 3% international; 54% from in state; 85% live on campus; 4% of students in fraternities, 3% in sororities
Most popular majors: 16% Business Administration and Management, General, 8% Accounting, 7% Marketing/Marketing Management, 6% Health/Health Care Administration/Management, 6% Psychology, General
Expenses: 2019-2020: $36,670; room/board: $9,350
Financial aid: (612) 238-4552; 73% of undergrads determined to have financial need; average aid package $27,072

St. Olaf College

Northfield MN
(507) 786-3025
U.S. News ranking: Nat. Lib. Arts, No. 62
Website: wp.stolaf.edu/
Admissions email: admissions@stolaf.edu
Private; founded 1874
Freshman admissions: more selective; 2018-2019: 5,496 applied, 2,743 accepted. Either SAT or ACT required. ACT 25/75 percentile: 25-32. High school rank: 41% in top tenth, 72% in top quarter, 96% in top half
Early decision deadline: 11/15, notification date: 12/15

Early action deadline: N/A, notification date: N/A
Application deadline (fall): 1/15
Undergraduate student body: 3,023 full time, 25 part time; 43% male, 57% female; 0% American Indian, 7% Asian, 3% black, 7% Hispanic, 4% multiracial, 0% Pacific Islander, 69% white, 10% international; N/A from in state; 94% live on campus; N/A of students in fraternities, N/A in sororities
Most popular majors: 16% Social Sciences, 11% Biological and Biomedical Sciences, 11% Visual and Performing Arts, 10% Mathematics and Statistics, 9% Foreign Languages, Literatures, and Linguistics
Expenses: 2019-2020: $49,710; room/board: $11,270
Financial aid: (507) 786-3019; 75% of undergrads determined to have financial need; average aid package $42,091

University of Minnesota–Crookston

Crookston MN
(800) 232-6466
U.S. News ranking: Reg. Coll. (Mid. W), No. 39
Website: www.crk.umn.edu
Admissions email: UMCinfo@umn.edu
Public; founded 1966
Freshman admissions: selective; 2018-2019: 1,297 applied, 855 accepted. Either SAT or ACT required. ACT 25/75 percentile: 19-24. High school rank: 9% in top tenth, 34% in top quarter, 61% in top half
Early decision deadline: N/A, notification date: N/A
Early action deadline: N/A, notification date: N/A
Application deadline (fall): rolling
Undergraduate student body: 1,206 full time, 1,604 part time; 45% male, 55% female; 1% American Indian, 3% Asian, 6% black, 4% Hispanic, 3% multiracial, 0% Pacific Islander, 76% white, 4% international; 70% from in state; 24% live on campus; N/A of students in fraternities, N/A in sororities
Most popular majors: 38% Business, Management, Marketing, and Related Support Services, 15% Agriculture, Agriculture Operations, and Related Sciences, 13% Health Professions and Related Programs, 8% Natural Resources and Conservation, 6% Communication, Journalism, and Related Programs
Expenses: 2019-2020: $12,021 in state, $12,021 out of state; room/board: $8,800
Financial aid: (218) 281-8564; 68% of undergrads determined to have financial need; average aid package $12,358

University of Minnesota–Duluth

Duluth MN
(218) 726-7171
U.S. News ranking: Reg. U. (Mid. W), No. 39
Website: www.d.umn.edu
Admissions email: umdadmis@d.umn.edu
Public; founded 1947
Freshman admissions: selective; 2018-2019: 9,204 applied, 6,843 accepted. Either SAT or ACT required. ACT 25/75 percentile: 21-26. High school rank: 20% in top tenth, 47% in top quarter, 87% in top half
Early decision deadline: N/A, notification date: N/A
Early action deadline: N/A, notification date: N/A
Application deadline (fall): 8/1
Undergraduate student body: 8,799 full time, 1,178 part time; 52% male, 48% female; 1% American Indian, 4% Asian, 2% black, 3% Hispanic, 3% multiracial, 0% Pacific Islander, 84% white, 1% international; 87% from in state; 33% live on campus; N/A of students in fraternities, N/A in sororities
Most popular majors: 19% Business, Management, Marketing, and Related Support Services, 14% Engineering, 8% Biological and Biomedical Sciences, 8% Social Sciences, 7% Education
Expenses: 2019-2020: $13,681 in state, $18,881 out of state; room/board: $8,374
Financial aid: (218) 726-8000; 58% of undergrads determined to have financial need; average aid package $12,897

University of Minnesota–Morris

Morris MN
(888) 866-3382
U.S. News ranking: Nat. Lib. Arts, No. 148
Website: www.morris.umn.edu
Admissions email: admissions@morris.umn.edu
Public; founded 1959
Freshman admissions: more selective; 2018-2019: 3,139 applied, 1,971 accepted. Either SAT or ACT required. ACT 25/75 percentile: 22-27. High school rank: 31% in top tenth, 57% in top quarter, 90% in top half
Early decision deadline: N/A, notification date: N/A
Early action deadline: N/A, notification date: N/A
Application deadline (fall): 8/1
Undergraduate student body: 1,463 full time, 91 part time; 43% male, 57% female; 8% American Indian, 3% Asian, 2% black, 5% Hispanic, 13% multiracial, 0% Pacific Islander, 58% white, 11% international; 85% from in state; 52% live on campus; N/A of students in fraternities, N/A in sororities
Most popular majors: 13% Biology/Biological Sciences, General, 12% Psychology, General, 5% Business

Administration and Management, General, 5% Chemistry, General, 5% Computer Science
Expenses: 2019-2020: $13,578 in state, $15,632 out of state; room/board: $8,632
Financial aid: (320) 589-6046; 65% of undergrads determined to have financial need; average aid package $12,936

University of Minnesota–Twin Cities

Minneapolis MN
(800) 752-1000
U.S. News ranking: Nat. U., No. 70
Website: twin-cities.umn.edu/
Admissions email: N/A
Public; founded 1851
Freshman admissions: more selective; 2018-2019: 43,444 applied, 22,525 accepted. Either SAT or ACT required. ACT 25/75 percentile: 26-31. High school rank: 50% in top tenth, 85% in top quarter, 100% in top half
Early decision deadline: N/A, notification date: N/A
Early action deadline: 11/1, notification date: 1/31
Application deadline (fall): rolling
Undergraduate student body: 30,001 full time, 4,632 part time; 47% male, 53% female; 0% American Indian, 10% Asian, 5% black, 4% Hispanic, 4% multiracial, 0% Pacific Islander, 67% white, 8% international; 72% from in state; 22% live on campus; N/A of students in fraternities, N/A in sororities
Most popular majors: 12% Biological and Biomedical Sciences, 11% Engineering, 11% Social Sciences, 10% Business, Management, Marketing, and Related Support Services, 7% Psychology
Expenses: 2019-2020: $15,027 in state, $33,325 out of state; room/board: $10,358
Financial aid: (800) 400-8636; 48% of undergrads determined to have financial need; average aid package $13,482

University of Northwestern–St. Paul

St. Paul MN
(800) 692-4020
U.S. News ranking: Reg. U. (Mid. W), No. 53
Website: www.unwsp.edu
Admissions email: admissions@unwsp.edu
Private; founded 1902
Affiliation: Undenominational
Freshman admissions: selective; 2018-2019: 930 applied, 840 accepted. Either SAT or ACT required. ACT 25/75 percentile: 21-27. High school rank: 22% in top tenth, 45% in top quarter, 80% in top half
Early decision deadline: N/A, notification date: N/A
Early action deadline: N/A, notification date: N/A
Application deadline (fall): 8/1
Undergraduate student body: 2,097 full time, 1,346 part time; 38%

male, 62% female; 0% American Indian, 4% Asian, 4% black, 6% Hispanic, 4% multiracial, 0% Pacific Islander, 80% white, 1% international; 78% from in state; 56% live on campus; 0% of students in fraternities, 0% in sororities
Most popular majors: 9% Psychology, General, 8% Registered Nursing/Registered Nurse, 7% Business Administration and Management, General, 6% Kinesiology and Exercise Science, 4% Biology/ Biological Sciences, General
Expenses: 2019-2020: $32,210; room/board: $9,660
Financial aid: (651) 631-5321; 80% of undergrads determined to have financial need; average aid package $22,956

University of St. Thomas
St. Paul MN
(651) 962-6150
U.S. News ranking: Nat. U., No. 139
Website: www.stthomas.edu
Admissions email: admissions@stthomas.edu
Private; founded 1885
Affiliation: Roman Catholic
Freshman admissions: more selective; 2018-2019: 6,819 applied, 5,583 accepted. Either SAT or ACT required. ACT 25/75 percentile: 24-29. High school rank: 21% in top tenth, 51% in top quarter, 85% in top half
Early decision deadline: N/A, notification date: N/A
Early action deadline: 11/1, notification date: 12/15
Application deadline (fall): rolling
Undergraduate student body: 6,162 full time, 233 part time; 53% male, 47% female; 0% American Indian, 4% Asian, 3% black, 5% Hispanic, 3% multiracial, 0% Pacific Islander, 78% white, 3% international; 77% from in state; 42% live on campus; N/A of students in fraternities, N/A in sororities
Most popular majors: 41% Business, Management, Marketing, and Related Support Services, 8% Engineering, 7% Biological and Biomedical Sciences, 6% Philosophy and Religious Studies, 6% Social Sciences
Expenses: 2018-2019: $42,736; room/board: $10,412
Financial aid: (651) 962-6168; 56% of undergrads determined to have financial need; average aid package $29,751

Walden University[1]
Minneapolis MN
(866) 492-5336
U.S. News ranking: Nat. U., unranked
Website: www.waldenu.edu/
Admissions email: N/A
For-profit; founded 1970
Application deadline (fall): N/A
Undergraduate student body: N/A full time, N/A part time
Expenses: N/A
Financial aid: (443) 537-1719

Winona State University
Winona MN
(507) 457-5100
U.S. News ranking: Reg. U. (Mid. W), No. 66
Website: www.winona.edu
Admissions email: admissions@winona.edu
Public; founded 1858
Freshman admissions: selective; 2018-2019: 7,744 applied, 5,089 accepted. Either SAT or ACT required. ACT 25/75 percentile: 20-24. High school rank: 9% in top tenth, 29% in top quarter, 66% in top half
Early decision deadline: N/A, notification date: N/A
Early action deadline: N/A, notification date: N/A
Application deadline (fall): 7/16
Undergraduate student body: 6,313 full time, 915 part time; 36% male, 64% female; 0% American Indian, 2% Asian, 3% black, 4% Hispanic, 3% multiracial, 0% Pacific Islander, 85% white, 2% international; 71% from in state; 35% live on campus; N/A of students in fraternities, N/A in sororities
Most popular majors: 22% Business, Management, Marketing, and Related Support Services, 15% Health Professions and Related Programs, 13% Education, 8% Parks, Recreation, Leisure, and Fitness Studies, 6% Biological and Biomedical Sciences
Expenses: 2018-2019: $9,425 in state, $15,348 out of state; room/board: $9,010
Financial aid: (507) 457-2800

MISSISSIPPI

Alcorn State University
Lorman MS
(601) 877-6147
U.S. News ranking: Reg. U. (S), No. 82
Website: www.alcorn.edu
Admissions email: ksampson@alcorn.edu
Public; founded 1871
Freshman admissions: less selective; 2018-2019: 4,314 applied, 3,853 accepted. Either SAT or ACT required. ACT 25/75 percentile: 17-22. High school rank: 0% in top tenth, 0% in top quarter, 80% in top half
Early decision deadline: N/A, notification date: N/A
Early action deadline: N/A, notification date: N/A
Application deadline (fall): rolling
Undergraduate student body: 2,855 full time, 318 part time; 39% male, 61% female; 0% American Indian, 0% Asian, 91% black, 1% Hispanic, 0% multiracial, 0% Pacific Islander, 2% white, 5% international
Most popular majors: 15% Biological and Biomedical Sciences, 12% Business, Management, Marketing, and Related Support Services, 10% Health Professions and Related

Programs, 10% Liberal Arts and Sciences, General Studies and Humanities, 9% Education
Expenses: 2019-2020: $7,320 in state, $7,320 out of state; room/ board: $10,788
Financial aid: (601) 877-6672; 53% of undergrads determined to have financial need; average aid package $7,343

Belhaven University
Jackson MS
(601) 968-5940
U.S. News ranking: Reg. U. (S), No. 47
Website: www.belhaven.edu
Admissions email: admission@belhaven.edu
Private; founded 1883
Affiliation: Presbyterian
Freshman admissions: selective; 2018-2019: 1,961 applied, 1,012 accepted. Either SAT or ACT required. ACT 25/75 percentile: 17-24. High school rank: 9% in top tenth, 41% in top quarter, 72% in top half
Early decision deadline: N/A, notification date: N/A
Early action deadline: N/A, notification date: N/A
Application deadline (fall): rolling
Undergraduate student body: 1,155 full time, 1,153 part time; 35% male, 65% female; 0% American Indian, 1% Asian, 42% black, 5% Hispanic, 3% multiracial, 0% Pacific Islander, 40% white, 2% international; 32% from in state; 24% live on campus; N/A of students in fraternities, N/A in sororities
Most popular majors: 30% Business Administration and Management, General, 8% Health/ Health Care Administration/ Management, 8% Social Sciences, General, 6% Applied Psychology, 5% Sport and Fitness Administration/Management
Expenses: 2019-2020: $26,202; room/board: $8,800
Financial aid: (601) 968-5933; 78% of undergrads determined to have financial need; average aid package $16,154

Blue Mountain College
Blue Mountain MS
(662) 685-4161
U.S. News ranking: Reg. Coll. (S), No. 14
Website: bmc.edu/
Admissions email: admissions@bmc.edu
Private; founded 1873
Affiliation: Southern Baptist
Freshman admissions: selective; 2018-2019: 283 applied, 263 accepted. Either SAT or ACT required. ACT 25/75 percentile: 19-25. High school rank: 23% in top tenth, 47% in top quarter, 79% in top half
Early decision deadline: N/A, notification date: N/A
Early action deadline: N/A, notification date: N/A
Application deadline (fall): rolling
Undergraduate student body: 583 full time, 48 part time; 47% male,

53% female; 0% American Indian, 0% Asian, 11% black, 2% Hispanic, 2% multiracial, 0% Pacific Islander, 82% white, 3% international; 81% from in state; 59% live on campus; 0% of students in fraternities, 0% in sororities
Most popular majors: 19% Psychology, General, 16% Elementary Education and Teaching, 13% Business Administration and Management, General, 9% Bible/Biblical Studies, 9% Kinesiology and Exercise Science
Expenses: 2019-2020: $14,100; room/board: $7,100
Financial aid: (662) 685-4771; 79% of undergrads determined to have financial need; average aid package $12,407

Delta State University
Cleveland MS
(662) 846-4020
U.S. News ranking: Reg. U. (S), No. 79
Website: deltastate.edu
Admissions email: admissions@deltastate.edu
Public; founded 1924
Freshman admissions: selective; 2018-2019: 905 applied, 771 accepted. Either SAT or ACT required. ACT 25/75 percentile: 18-24. High school rank: 17% in top tenth, 39% in top quarter, 71% in top half
Early decision deadline: N/A, notification date: N/A
Early action deadline: 4/15, notification date: 9/1
Application deadline (fall): rolling
Undergraduate student body: 1,989 full time, 1,086 part time; 41% male, 59% female; 0% American Indian, 1% Asian, 31% black, 3% Hispanic, 2% multiracial, 0% Pacific Islander, 58% white, 6% international; 79% from in state; 35% live on campus; 13% of students in fraternities, 21% in sororities
Most popular majors: 12% Registered Nursing/Registered Nurse, 10% Physical Education Teaching and Coaching, 9% Family and Consumer Sciences/ Human Sciences, General, 6% Biology/Biological Sciences, General, 6% Elementary Education and Teaching
Expenses: 2019-2020: $7,671 in state, $7,671 out of state; room/ board: $7,908
Financial aid: (662) 846-4670

Jackson State University
Jackson MS
(601) 979-2100
U.S. News ranking: Nat. U., second tier
Website: www.jsums.edu
Admissions email: admappl@jsums.edu
Public; founded 1877
Freshman admissions: less selective; 2018-2019: 7,680 applied, 5,294 accepted. Either

SAT or ACT required. ACT 25/75 percentile: 17-22. High school rank: N/A
Early decision deadline: N/A, notification date: N/A
Early action deadline: N/A, notification date: N/A
Application deadline (fall): 9/19
Undergraduate student body: 4,840 full time, 491 part time; 36% male, 64% female; 0% American Indian, 0% Asian, 92% black, 1% Hispanic, 2% multiracial, 0% Pacific Islander, 3% white, 2% international; 9% from in state; 41% live on campus; 1% of students in fraternities, 2% in sororities
Most popular majors: 8% Biological and Biomedical Sciences, 7% Multi/Interdisciplinary Studies, 6% Public Administration and Social Service Professions, 5% Health Professions and Related Programs, 5% Homeland Security, Law Enforcement, Firefighting and Related Protective Services
Expenses: 2019-2020: $8,620 in state, $19,620 out of state; room/ board: N/A
Financial aid: (601) 979-2227; 92% of undergrads determined to have financial need; average aid package $11,485

Millsaps College
Jackson MS
(601) 974-1050
U.S. News ranking: Nat. Lib. Arts, No. 124
Website: www.millsaps.edu
Admissions email: admissions@millsaps.edu
Private; founded 1890
Affiliation: United Methodist
Freshman admissions: selective; 2018-2019: 4,161 applied, 2,468 accepted. Either SAT or ACT required. ACT 25/75 percentile: 22-28. High school rank: N/A
Early decision deadline: N/A, notification date: N/A
Early action deadline: 11/15, notification date: 1/15
Application deadline (fall): 7/1
Undergraduate student body: 790 full time, 8 part time; 48% male, 52% female; 1% American Indian, 4% Asian, 20% black, 5% Hispanic, 0% multiracial, 0% Pacific Islander, 63% white, 5% international; 47% from in state; 89% live on campus; 58% of students in fraternities, 49% in sororities
Most popular majors: 45% Business, Management, Marketing, and Related Support Services, 19% Biological and Biomedical Sciences, 8% Psychology, 7% Social Sciences, 4% Physical Sciences
Expenses: 2019-2020: $41,314; room/board: $14,210
Financial aid: (601) 974-1220; 70% of undergrads determined to have financial need; average aid package $35,745

Mississippi College

Clinton MS
(601) 925-3800
U.S. News ranking: Nat. U., second tier
Website: www.mc.edu
Admissions email: admissions@mc.edu
Private; founded 1826
Affiliation: Southern Baptist
Freshman admissions: selective; 2018-2019: 2,216 applied, 851 accepted. Either SAT or ACT required. ACT 25/75 percentile: 21-28. High school rank: 33% in top tenth, 58% in top quarter, 80% in top half
Early decision deadline: N/A, notification date: N/A
Early action deadline: N/A, notification date: N/A
Application deadline (fall): rolling
Undergraduate student body: 2,772 full time, 460 part time; 38% male, 62% female; 1% American Indian, 2% Asian, 20% black, 3% Hispanic, 0% multiracial, 0% Pacific Islander, 70% white, 4% international; 69% from in state; 58% live on campus; 23% of students in fraternities, 32% in sororities
Most popular majors: 13% Registered Nursing/Registered Nurse, 9% Biomedical Sciences, General, 7% Accounting, 5% Business Administration and Management, General, 5% Elementary Education and Teaching
Expenses: 2019-2020: $18,610; room/board: $10,610
Financial aid: (601) 925-3212; 55% of undergrads determined to have financial need; average aid package $17,360

Mississippi State University

Mississippi State MS
(662) 325-2224
U.S. News ranking: Nat. U., No. 211
Website: www.msstate.edu
Admissions email: admit@admissions.msstate.edu
Public; founded 1878
Freshman admissions: more selective; 2018-2019: 17,363 applied, 9,893 accepted. Either SAT or ACT required. ACT 25/75 percentile: 22-29. High school rank: 29% in top tenth, 55% in top quarter, 82% in top half
Early decision deadline: N/A, notification date: N/A
Early action deadline: N/A, notification date: N/A
Application deadline (fall): rolling
Undergraduate student body: 16,839 full time, 1,651 part time; 50% male, 50% female; 1% American Indian, 1% Asian, 19% black, 3% Hispanic, 2% multiracial, 0% Pacific Islander, 72% white, 1% international; 65% from in state; 27% live on campus; 24% of students in fraternities, 18% in sororities
Most popular majors: 18% Business, Management, Marketing, and Related Support Services, 17% Engineering, 7% Education, 7% Parks, Recreation, Leisure, and Fitness

Studies, 5% Biological and Biomedical Sciences
Expenses: 2019-2020: $8,910 in state, $23,950 out of state; room/board: $10,435
Financial aid: (662) 325-2450; 65% of undergrads determined to have financial need; average aid package $14,609

Mississippi University for Women

Columbus MS
(662) 329-7106
U.S. News ranking: Reg. U. (S), No. 42
Website: www.muw.edu
Admissions email: admissions@muw.edu
Public; founded 1884
Freshman admissions: selective; 2018-2019: 585 applied, 572 accepted. Either SAT or ACT required. ACT 25/75 percentile: 18-24. High school rank: 27% in top tenth, 56% in top quarter, 80% in top half
Early decision deadline: N/A, notification date: N/A
Early action deadline: N/A, notification date: N/A
Application deadline (fall): rolling
Undergraduate student body: 2,002 full time, 503 part time; 20% male, 80% female; 1% American Indian, 1% Asian, 39% black, 0% Hispanic, 0% multiracial, 0% Pacific Islander, 57% white, 2% international; 84% from in state; 25% live on campus; 9% of students in fraternities, 18% in sororities
Most popular majors: 52% Registered Nursing/Registered Nurse, 12% Business Administration and Management, General, 6% Public Health Education and Promotion, 4% Health and Physical Education/Fitness, General, 3% Speech-Language Pathology/Pathologist
Expenses: 2019-2020: $7,525 in state, $7,525 out of state; room/board: $7,648
Financial aid: (662) 329-7114; 76% of undergrads determined to have financial need; average aid package $8,706

Mississippi Valley State University[1]

Itta Bena MS
(662) 254-3344
U.S. News ranking: Reg. U. (S), second tier
Website: www.mvsu.edu
Admissions email: admsn@mvsu.edu
Public; founded 1950
Application deadline (fall): 8/17
Undergraduate student body: N/A full time, N/A part time
Expenses: N/A
Financial aid: N/A

Rust College

Holly Springs MS
(662) 252-8000
U.S. News ranking: Nat. Lib. Arts, second tier
Website: www.rustcollege.edu
Admissions email: admissions@rustcollege.edu
Private; founded 1866
Affiliation: United Methodist
Freshman admissions: least selective; 2018-2019: 5,558 applied, 2,958 accepted. ACT required. ACT 25/75 percentile: 14-15. High school rank: N/A
Early decision deadline: N/A, notification date: N/A
Early action deadline: N/A, notification date: N/A
Application deadline (fall): rolling
Undergraduate student body: 761 full time, 85 part time; 41% male, 59% female; 0% American Indian, 0% Asian, 94% black, 0% Hispanic, 0% multiracial, 0% Pacific Islander, 0% white, 2% international; N/A from in state; 82% live on campus; N/A of students in fraternities, N/A in sororities
Most popular majors: 26% Biological and Biomedical Sciences, 19% Education, 17% Communication, Journalism, and Related Programs, 15% Public Administration and Social Service Professions, 9% Business, Management, Marketing, and Related Support Services
Expenses: 2019-2020: $9,900; room/board: $4,300
Financial aid: (662) 252-8000

Tougaloo College

Tougaloo MS
(601) 977-7768
U.S. News ranking: Nat. Lib. Arts, second tier
Website: www.tougaloo.edu
Admissions email: admission@tougaloo.edu
Private; founded 1869
Affiliation: United Church of Christ
Freshman admissions: less selective; 2018-2019: 1,934 applied, 1,769 accepted. Either SAT or ACT required. ACT 25/75 percentile: 16-23. High school rank: 28% in top tenth, 30% in top quarter, 78% in top half
Early decision deadline: N/A, notification date: N/A
Early action deadline: N/A, notification date: N/A
Application deadline (fall): 7/1
Undergraduate student body: 696 full time, 30 part time; 32% male, 68% female; 0% American Indian, 0% Asian, 98% black, 0% Hispanic, 0% multiracial, 0% Pacific Islander, 0% white, 1% international; N/A from in state; N/A live on campus; 0% of students in fraternities, 0% in sororities
Most popular majors: 20% Sociology, 15% Biology/Biological Sciences, General, 9% Health and Physical Education/Fitness, Other, 7% English Language and Literature, General, 7% Psychology, General
Expenses: 2019-2020: $10,854; room/board: $6,330

Financial aid: (601) 977-7769; 94% of undergrads determined to have financial need; average aid package $12,500

University of Mississippi

University MS
(662) 915-7226
U.S. News ranking: Nat. U., No. 162
Website: www.olemiss.edu
Admissions email: admissions@olemiss.edu
Public; founded 1848
Freshman admissions: more selective; 2018-2019: 15,371 applied, 13,535 accepted. Either SAT or ACT required for some. ACT 25/75 percentile: 21-29. High school rank: 25% in top tenth, 52% in top quarter, 78% in top half
Early decision deadline: N/A, notification date: N/A
Early action deadline: N/A, notification date: N/A
Application deadline (fall): rolling
Undergraduate student body: 16,636 full time, 1,371 part time; 44% male, 56% female; 0% American Indian, 2% Asian, 12% black, 4% Hispanic, 2% multiracial, 0% Pacific Islander, 78% white, 2% international; 56% from in state; 25% live on campus; 32% of students in fraternities, 43% in sororities
Most popular majors: 7% Accounting, 6% Digital Communication and Media/Multimedia, 6% General Studies, 6% Psychology, General, 5% Marketing/Marketing Management, General
Expenses: 2019-2020: $8,818 in state, $25,090 out of state; room/board: $10,734
Financial aid: (662) 915-5788; 50% of undergrads determined to have financial need; average aid package $11,150

University of Southern Mississippi

Hattiesburg MS
(601) 266-5000
U.S. News ranking: Nat. U., second tier
Website: www.usm.edu/admissions
Admissions email: admissions@usm.edu
Public; founded 1910
Freshman admissions: selective; 2018-2019: 8,550 applied, 8,369 accepted. Either SAT or ACT required. ACT 25/75 percentile: 19-26. High school rank: N/A
Early decision deadline: N/A, notification date: N/A
Early action deadline: N/A, notification date: N/A
Application deadline (fall): rolling
Undergraduate student body: 9,846 full time, 2,074 part time; 37% male, 63% female; 0% American Indian, 1% Asian, 29% black, 3% Hispanic, 4% multiracial, 0% Pacific Islander, 61% white, 2% international; N/A from in state; 21% live on campus; 10% of students in fraternities, 14% in sororities

Most popular majors: 6% Business Administration and Management, General, 6% Elementary Education and Teaching, 6% Psychology, General, 6% Registered Nursing/Registered Nurse, 5% Liberal Arts and Sciences/Liberal Studies
Expenses: 2019-2020: $8,879 in state, $10,879 out of state; room/board: $10,937
Financial aid: (601) 266-4774; 75% of undergrads determined to have financial need; average aid package $10,385

William Carey University

Hattiesburg MS
(601) 318-6103
U.S. News ranking: Nat. U., No. 281
Website: www.wmcarey.edu
Admissions email: admissions@wmcarey.edu
Private; founded 1892
Affiliation: Southern Baptist
Freshman admissions: selective; 2018-2019: 607 applied, 412 accepted. Either SAT or ACT required. ACT 25/75 percentile: 21-29. High school rank: 27% in top tenth, 63% in top quarter, 85% in top half
Early decision deadline: N/A, notification date: N/A
Early action deadline: N/A, notification date: N/A
Application deadline (fall): rolling
Undergraduate student body: 1,575 full time, 1,616 part time; 31% male, 69% female; 0% American Indian, 1% Asian, 31% black, 2% Hispanic, 0% multiracial, 0% Pacific Islander, 59% white, 5% international; 80% from in state; 23% live on campus; 0% of students in fraternities, 2% in sororities
Most popular majors: 24% Educational Leadership and Administration, General, 16% Osteopathic Medicine/Osteopathy, 15% Registered Nursing/Registered Nurse, 10% General Studies, 8% Elementary Education and Teaching
Expenses: 2019-2020: $12,750; room/board: $4,395
Financial aid: (601) 318-6153; 96% of undergrads determined to have financial need; average aid package $16,900

MISSOURI

Avila University[1]

Kansas City MO
(816) 501-2400
U.S. News ranking: Reg. U. (Mid. W), second tier
Website: www.Avila.edu
Admissions email: admissions@mail.avila.edu
Private
Application deadline (fall): N/A
Undergraduate student body: N/A full time, N/A part time
Expenses: N/A
Financial aid: N/A

Central Methodist University
Fayette MO
(660) 248-6251
U.S. News ranking: Reg. U. (Mid. W), No. 78
Website: www.centralmethodist.edu
Admissions email: admissions@centralmethodist.edu
Private; founded 1854
Affiliation: United Methodist
Freshman admissions: selective; 2018-2019: 1,280 applied, 1,195 accepted. Either SAT or ACT required. ACT 25/75 percentile: 20-24. High school rank: 14% in top tenth, 42% in top quarter, 72% in top half
Early decision deadline: N/A, notification date: N/A
Early action deadline: N/A, notification date: N/A
Application deadline (fall): 8/15
Undergraduate student body: 1,131 full time, 17 part time; 47% male, 53% female; 1% American Indian, 1% Asian, 9% black, 7% Hispanic, 3% multiracial, 0% Pacific Islander, 70% white, 6% international; N/A from in state; 66% live on campus, 19% of students in fraternities, 26% in sororities
Most popular majors: 15% Education, 15% Health Professions and Related Programs, 14% Biological and Biomedical Sciences, 13% Business, Management, Marketing, and Related Support Services, 9% Homeland Security, Law Enforcement, Firefighting and Related Protective Services
Expenses: 2018-2019: $24,420; room/board: $7,940
Financial aid: (660) 248-6245

College of the Ozarks
Point Lookout MO
(800) 222-0525
U.S. News ranking: Reg. Coll. (Mid. W), No. 3
Website: www.cofo.edu
Admissions email: admissions@cofo.edu
Private; founded 1906
Affiliation: Interdenominational
Freshman admissions: more selective; 2018-2019: 2,874 applied, 331 accepted. Either SAT or ACT required. ACT 25/75 percentile: 21-26. High school rank: 23% in top tenth, 46% in top quarter, 95% in top half
Early decision deadline: N/A, notification date: N/A
Early action deadline: N/A, notification date: N/A
Application deadline (fall): 7/31
Undergraduate student body: 1,533 full time, 32 part time; 45% male, 55% female; 0% American Indian, 1% Asian, 1% black, 3% Hispanic, 2% multiracial, 0% Pacific Islander, 89% white, 2% international; 72% from in state; 87% live on campus; 0% of students in fraternities, 0% in sororities
Most popular majors: 12% Business Administration and Management, General, 6% Accounting, 6% Registered

Nursing/Registered Nurse, 4% Animal Sciences, General, 4% Criminal Justice/Police Science
Expenses: 2019-2020: $19,660; room/board: $7,600
Financial aid: (417) 690-3292; 92% of undergrads determined to have financial need; average aid package $18,900

Columbia College[1]
Columbia MO
(573) 875-7352
U.S. News ranking: Reg. U. (Mid. W), unranked
Website: www.ccis.edu
Admissions email: admissions@ccis.edu
Private; founded 1851
Application deadline (fall): rolling
Undergraduate student body: N/A full time, N/A part time
Expenses: N/A
Financial aid: (573) 875-7390

Cottey College
Nevada MO
(888) 526-8839
U.S. News ranking: Reg. Coll. (Mid. W), No. 2
Website: www.cottey.edu
Admissions email: admit@cottey.edu
Private; founded 1884
Freshman admissions: selective; 2018-2019: 362 applied, 352 accepted. Either SAT or ACT required. ACT 25/75 percentile: 19-25. High school rank: 16% in top tenth, 53% in top quarter, 74% in top half
Early decision deadline: N/A, notification date: N/A
Early action deadline: N/A, notification date: N/A
Application deadline (fall): rolling
Undergraduate student body: 268 full time, 9 part time; 0% male, 100% female; 1% American Indian, 0% Asian, 6% black, 10% Hispanic, 4% multiracial, 0% Pacific Islander, 67% white, 12% international; 22% from in state; 87% live on campus; 0% of students in fraternities, 0% in sororities
Most popular majors: 18% Business, Management, Marketing, and Related Support Services, 18% Psychology, 15% Biological and Biomedical Sciences, 15% English Language and Literature/Letters, 11% Business, Management, Marketing, and Related Support Services
Expenses: 2019-2020: $21,750; room/board: $7,700
Financial aid: (417) 667-8181; 76% of undergrads determined to have financial need; average aid package $21,715

Culver-Stockton College
Canton MO
(800) 537-1883
U.S. News ranking: Reg. Coll. (Mid. W), No. 33
Website: www.culver.edu
Admissions email: admission@culver.edu
Private; founded 1853

Affiliation: Christian Church (Disciples of Christ)
Freshman admissions: selective; 2018-2019: 4,784 applied, 2,220 accepted. Either SAT or ACT required. ACT 25/75 percentile: 18-23. High school rank: 7% in top tenth, 27% in top quarter, 58% in top half
Early decision deadline: N/A, notification date: N/A
Early action deadline: N/A, notification date: N/A
Application deadline (fall): rolling
Undergraduate student body: 919 full time, 103 part time; 51% male, 49% female; 1% American Indian, 1% Asian, 13% black, 5% Hispanic, 3% multiracial, 0% Pacific Islander, 72% white, 5% international; 55% from in state; 74% live on campus; 39% of students in fraternities, 47% in sororities
Most popular majors: 16% Business Administration and Management, General, 15% Criminal Justice/Law Enforcement Administration, 9% Psychology, General, 8% Sport and Fitness Administration/Management, 7% Elementary Education and Teaching
Expenses: 2019-2020: $27,205; room/board: $8,695
Financial aid: (573) 288-6307; 83% of undergrads determined to have financial need; average aid package $20,849

Drury University
Springfield MO
(417) 873-7205
U.S. News ranking: Reg. U. (Mid. W), No. 20
Website: www.drury.edu
Admissions email: druryad@drury.edu
Private; founded 1873
Affiliation: Christian Church (Disciples of Christ)
Freshman admissions: more selective; 2018-2019: 1,739 applied, 1,190 accepted. Either SAT or ACT required. ACT 25/75 percentile: 22-29. High school rank: 30% in top tenth, 63% in top quarter, 88% in top half
Early decision deadline: N/A, notification date: N/A
Early action deadline: N/A, notification date: N/A
Application deadline (fall): 8/30
Undergraduate student body: 1,462 full time, 27 part time; 42% male, 58% female; 1% American Indian, 1% Asian, 3% black, 2% Hispanic, 4% multiracial, 0% Pacific Islander, 81% white, 7% international; 80% from in state; 61% live on campus; 20% of students in fraternities, 26% in sororities
Most popular majors: 16% Biological and Biomedical Sciences, 15% Business, Management, Marketing, and Related Support Services, 11% Visual and Performing Arts, 8% Architecture and Related Services, 7% Education
Expenses: 2019-2020: $29,515; room/board: $9,046

Financial aid: (417) 873-7312; 68% of undergrads determined to have financial need; average aid package $23,196

Evangel University
Springfield MO
(800) 382-6435
U.S. News ranking: Reg. U. (Mid. W), second tier
Website: www.evangel.edu
Admissions email: admissions@evangel.edu
Private; founded 1955
Affiliation: Assemblies of God Church
Freshman admissions: selective; 2018-2019: 1,142 applied, 904 accepted. Neither SAT nor ACT required. ACT 25/75 percentile: 19-25. High school rank: N/A
Early decision deadline: N/A, notification date: N/A
Early action deadline: N/A, notification date: N/A
Application deadline (fall): rolling
Undergraduate student body: 1,442 full time, 202 part time; 44% male, 56% female; 0% American Indian, 1% Asian, 4% black, 6% Hispanic, 2% multiracial, 0% Pacific Islander, 82% white, 1% international
Most popular majors: Information not available
Expenses: 2019-2020: $24,202; room/board: $8,522
Financial aid: (417) 865-2811; 85% of undergrads determined to have financial need; average aid package $19,362

Fontbonne University
St. Louis MO
(314) 889-1400
U.S. News ranking: Reg. U. (Mid. W), No. 53
Website: www.fontbonne.edu
Admissions email: admissions@fontbonne.edu
Private; founded 1923
Affiliation: Roman Catholic
Freshman admissions: selective; 2018-2019: 706 applied, 575 accepted. Either SAT or ACT required. ACT 25/75 percentile: 18-24. High school rank: N/A
Early decision deadline: N/A, notification date: N/A
Early action deadline: N/A, notification date: N/A
Application deadline (fall): rolling
Undergraduate student body: 781 full time, 110 part time; 39% male, 61% female; 0% American Indian, 2% Asian, 16% black, 5% Hispanic, 4% multiracial, 0% Pacific Islander, 68% white, 2% international
Most popular majors: 10% Business Administration and Management, General, 9% Psychology, General, 8% Liberal Arts and Sciences/Liberal Studies, 7% Social Work, 7% Speech-Language Pathology/Pathologist
Expenses: 2019-2020: $27,260; room/board: $10,280
Financial aid: (314) 889-1414; 75% of undergrads determined to have financial need

Hannibal-LaGrange University[1]
Hannibal MO
(800) 454-1119
U.S. News ranking: Reg. Coll. (Mid. W), No. 51
Website: www.hlg.edu
Admissions email: admissions@hlg.edu
Private; founded 1858
Affiliation: Southern Baptist
Application deadline (fall): 8/27
Undergraduate student body: N/A full time, N/A part time
Expenses: N/A
Financial aid: N/A

Harris-Stowe State University
St. Louis MO
(314) 340-3300
U.S. News ranking: Reg. Coll. (Mid. W), second tier
Website: www.hssu.edu
Admissions email: admissions@hssu.edu
Public; founded 1857
Freshman admissions: least selective; 2018-2019: 6,248 applied, 3,480 accepted. Either SAT or ACT required. ACT 25/75 percentile: 15-19. High school rank: N/A
Early decision deadline: N/A, notification date: N/A
Early action deadline: N/A, notification date: N/A
Application deadline (fall): rolling
Undergraduate student body: 1,398 full time, 318 part time; 33% male, 67% female; 0% American Indian, 0% Asian, 82% black, 3% Hispanic, 3% multiracial, 0% Pacific Islander, 5% white, 1% international; N/A from in state; 33% live on campus; 1% of students in fraternities, N/A in sororities
Most popular majors: 36% Business, Management, Marketing, and Related Support Services, 21% Homeland Security, Law Enforcement, Firefighting and Related Protective Services, 14% Education, 12% Biological and Biomedical Sciences, 6% Social Sciences
Expenses: 2019-2020: $5,388 in state, $10,020 out of state; room/board: $9,491
Financial aid: (314) 340-3502

Kansas City Art Institute[1]
Kansas City MO
(816) 472-4852
U.S. News ranking: Arts, unranked
Website: www.kcai.edu
Admissions email: admiss@kcai.edu
Private; founded 1885
Application deadline (fall): N/A
Undergraduate student body: N/A full time, N/A part time
Expenses: N/A
Financial aid: (816) 802-3448

Lincoln University

Jefferson City MO
(573) 681-5102
U.S. News ranking: Reg. Coll. (Mid. W), second tier
Website: www.lincolnu.edu
Admissions email: admissions@lincolnu.edu
Public; founded 1866
Freshman admissions: least selective; 2018-2019: N/A applied, N/A accepted. Either SAT or ACT required. ACT 25/75 percentile: 14-19. High school rank: 5% in top tenth, 16% in top quarter, 40% in top half
Early decision deadline: N/A, notification date: N/A
Early action deadline: N/A, notification date: N/A
Application deadline (fall): rolling
Undergraduate student body: 1,693 full time, 684 part time; 42% male, 58% female; 0% American Indian, 1% Asian, 57% black, 3% Hispanic, 2% multiracial, 0% Pacific Islander, 30% white, 3% international; 72% from in state; 49% live on campus; N/A of students in fraternities, N/A in sororities
Most popular majors: 11% Business Administration and Management, General, 11% Registered Nursing/Registered Nurse, 8% Criminal Justice/Law Enforcement Administration, 7% Health-Related Knowledge and Skills, Other, 7% Liberal Arts and Sciences/Liberal Studies
Expenses: 2018-2019: $7,632 in state, $14,172 out of state; room/board: $7,068
Financial aid: (573) 681-5032; 56% of undergrads determined to have financial need; average aid package $9,953

Lindenwood University

St. Charles MO
(636) 949-4949
U.S. News ranking: Nat. U., second tier
Website: www.lindenwood.edu
Admissions email: admissions@lindenwood.edu
Private; founded 1827
Freshman admissions: selective; 2018-2019: 3,420 applied, 3,014 accepted. Either SAT or ACT required for some. ACT 25/75 percentile: 20-25. High school rank: N/A
Early decision deadline: N/A, notification date: N/A
Early action deadline: N/A, notification date: N/A
Application deadline (fall): rolling
Undergraduate student body: 5,969 full time, 560 part time; 46% male, 54% female; 0% American Indian, 1% Asian, 13% black, 5% Hispanic, 3% multiracial, 0% Pacific Islander, 56% white, 12% international; 57% from in state; N/A live on campus; N/A of students in fraternities, N/A in sororities
Most popular majors: 18% Business/Commerce, General, 9% Criminal Justice/Safety Studies, 5% Kinesiology and Exercise Science, 5% Psychology,

General, 4% Human Resources Management/Personnel Administration, General
Expenses: 2019-2020: $18,100; room/board: $9,200
Financial aid: (636) 949-4106; 64% of undergrads determined to have financial need; average aid package $14,800

Maryville University of St. Louis

St Louis MO
(800) 627-9855
U.S. News ranking: Nat. U., No. 202
Website: www.maryville.edu
Admissions email: admissions@maryville.edu
Private; founded 1872
Freshman admissions: selective; 2018-2019: 2,074 applied, 1,960 accepted. Either SAT or ACT required for some. ACT 25/75 percentile: 20-26. High school rank: 24% in top tenth, 56% in top quarter, 89% in top half
Early decision deadline: N/A, notification date: N/A
Early action deadline: N/A, notification date: N/A
Application deadline (fall): 8/15
Undergraduate student body: 2,594 full time, 1,084 part time; 34% male, 66% female; 0% American Indian, 3% Asian, 10% black, 5% Hispanic, 3% multiracial, 0% Pacific Islander, 70% white, 4% international; 31% from in state; 26% live on campus; N/A of students in fraternities, N/A in sororities
Most popular majors: 41% Health Professions and Related Programs, 19% Business, Management, Marketing, and Related Support Services, 11% Psychology, 5% Biological and Biomedical Sciences, 5% Visual and Performing Arts
Expenses: 2019-2020: $28,470; room/board: $10,088
Financial aid: (314) 529-9361; 68% of undergrads determined to have financial need; average aid package $21,040

Missouri Baptist University[1]

St. Louis MO
(314) 434-2290
U.S. News ranking: Reg. U. (Mid. W), second tier
Website: www.mobap.edu
Admissions email: admissions@mobap.edu
Private; founded 1964
Application deadline (fall): rolling
Undergraduate student body: N/A full time, N/A part time
Expenses: N/A
Financial aid: (314) 744-7639

Missouri Southern State University

Joplin MO
(417) 781-6778
U.S. News ranking: Reg. Coll. (Mid. W), second tier
Website: www.mssu.edu
Admissions email: admissions@mssu.edu
Public; founded 1937

Freshman admissions: selective; 2018-2019: 2,304 applied, 2,203 accepted. Either SAT or ACT required. ACT 25/75 percentile: 18-24. High school rank: 15% in top tenth, 38% in top quarter, 73% in top half
Early decision deadline: N/A, notification date: N/A
Early action deadline: N/A, notification date: N/A
Application deadline (fall): rolling
Undergraduate student body: 4,172 full time, 1,679 part time; 38% male, 62% female; 3% American Indian, 2% Asian, 6% black, 7% Hispanic, 2% multiracial, 0% Pacific Islander, 73% white, 3% international; 75% from in state; 16% live on campus; 3% of students in fraternities, 3% in sororities
Most popular majors: 26% Business/Commerce, General, 16% Health Professions and Related Clinical Sciences, Other, 10% Liberal Arts and Sciences, General Studies and Humanities, Other, 8% Criminal Justice/Law Enforcement Administration, 8% Elementary Education and Teaching
Expenses: 2019-2020: $7,289 in state, $14,578 out of state; room/board: $6,410
Financial aid: (417) 659-5422; 78% of undergrads determined to have financial need; average aid package $9,904

Missouri State University

Springfield MO
(800) 492-7900
U.S. News ranking: Nat. U., second tier
Website: www.missouristate.edu
Admissions email: info@missouristate.edu
Public; founded 1906
Freshman admissions: selective; 2018-2019: 8,988 applied, 7,637 accepted. Either SAT or ACT required. ACT 25/75 percentile: 21-26. High school rank: 22% in top tenth, 52% in top quarter, 85% in top half
Early decision deadline: N/A, notification date: N/A
Early action deadline: N/A, notification date: N/A
Undergraduate student body: 14,924 full time, 5,214 part time; 42% male, 58% female; 0% American Indian, 1% Asian, 5% black, 4% Hispanic, 4% multiracial, 0% Pacific Islander, 82% white, 3% international; N/A from in state; 22% live on campus; 33% of students in fraternities, 31% in sororities
Most popular majors: 27% Business, Management, Marketing, and Related Support Services, 12% Education, 7% Social Sciences, 6% Communication, Journalism, and Related Programs, 6% Psychology
Expenses: 2019-2020: $7,750 in state, $15,910 out of state; room/board: $8,808
Financial aid: (417) 836-5262; 59% of undergrads determined to have financial need; average aid package $11,600

Missouri University of Science & Technology–Rolla

Rolla MO
(573) 341-4165
U.S. News ranking: Nat. U., No. 179
Website: www.mst.edu
Admissions email: admissions@mst.edu
Public; founded 1870
Freshman admissions: more selective; 2018-2019: 4,333 applied, 3,647 accepted. Either SAT or ACT required. ACT 25/75 percentile: 25-31. High school rank: 40% in top tenth, 71% in top quarter, 94% in top half
Early decision deadline: N/A, notification date: N/A
Early action deadline: N/A, notification date: N/A
Application deadline (fall): 7/1
Undergraduate student body: 6,065 full time, 783 part time; 76% male, 24% female; 0% American Indian, 4% Asian, 3% black, 4% Hispanic, 3% multiracial, 0% Pacific Islander, 81% white, 3% international; N/A from in state; N/A live on campus; 21% of students in fraternities, 24% in sororities
Most popular majors: 70% Engineering, 9% Computer and Information Sciences and Support Services, 5% Engineering Technologies and Engineering-Related Fields, 4% Biological and Biomedical Sciences, 4% Physical Sciences
Expenses: 2019-2020: $10,653 in state, $29,601 out of state; room/board: $10,402
Financial aid: (573) 341-4282; 58% of undergrads determined to have financial need; average aid package $12,480

Missouri Valley College

Marshall MO
(660) 831-4114
U.S. News ranking: Reg. Coll. (Mid. W), second tier
Website: www.moval.edu
Admissions email: admissions@moval.edu
Private; founded 1889
Affiliation: Presbyterian
Freshman admissions: less selective; 2018-2019: 2,516 applied, 1,489 accepted. Either SAT or ACT required. ACT 25/75 percentile: 16-21. High school rank: 6% in top tenth, 21% in top quarter, 50% in top half
Early decision deadline: N/A, notification date: N/A
Early action deadline: N/A, notification date: N/A
Application deadline (fall): rolling
Undergraduate student body: 1,397 full time, 451 part time; 54% male, 46% female; N/A American Indian, N/A Asian, N/A black, N/A Hispanic, N/A multiracial, N/A Pacific Islander, N/A white, N/A international; N/A from in state; 70% live on campus; 5% of students in fraternities, 5% in sororities

Most popular majors: 24% Business, Management, Marketing, and Related Support Services, 18% Parks, Recreation, Leisure, and Fitness Studies, 14% Education, 8% Homeland Security, Law Enforcement, Firefighting and Related Protective Services, 8% Psychology
Expenses: 2019-2020: $21,100; room/board: $9,400
Financial aid: N/A

Missouri Western State University[1]

St. Joseph MO
(816) 271-4266
U.S. News ranking: Reg. U. (Mid. W), second tier
Website: www.missouriwestern.edu
Admissions email: admission@missouriwestern.edu
Public; founded 1969
Application deadline (fall): rolling
Undergraduate student body: N/A full time, N/A part time
Expenses: N/A
Financial aid: (816) 271-4361

Northwest Missouri State University

Maryville MO
(800) 633-1175
U.S. News ranking: Reg. U. (Mid. W), No. 95
Website: www.nwmissouri.edu
Admissions email: admissions@nwmissouri.edu
Public; founded 1905
Freshman admissions: selective; 2018-2019: 6,048 applied, 4,788 accepted. Either SAT or ACT required. ACT 25/75 percentile: 19-24. High school rank: 14% in top tenth, 38% in top quarter, 73% in top half
Early decision deadline: N/A, notification date: N/A
Early action deadline: N/A, notification date: N/A
Application deadline (fall): rolling
Undergraduate student body: 4,928 full time, 726 part time; 43% male, 57% female; 0% American Indian, 1% Asian, 6% black, 4% Hispanic, 4% multiracial, 0% Pacific Islander, 81% white, 3% international; 70% from in state; 33% live on campus; 12% of students in fraternities, 16% in sororities
Most popular majors: 23% Business, Management, Marketing, and Related Support Services, 16% Education, 10% Agriculture, Agriculture Operations, and Related Sciences, 10% Psychology, 7% Communication, Journalism, and Related Programs
Expenses: 2019-2020: $10,298 in state, $17,525 out of state; room/board: $9,022
Financial aid: (660) 562-1138; 66% of undergrads determined to have financial need; average aid package $9,815

Park University

Parkville MO
(877) 505-1059
U.S. News ranking: Reg. U.
(Mid. W), unranked
Website: www.park.edu
Admissions email:
enrollmentservices@park.edu
Private; founded 1875
Freshman admissions: less
selective; 2018-2019: N/A
applied, N/A accepted. Neither
SAT nor ACT required. ACT 25/75
percentile: 16-23. High school
rank: N/A
Early decision deadline: N/A,
notification date: N/A
Early action deadline: N/A,
notification date: N/A
Application deadline (fall): rolling
Undergraduate student body: 4,011
full time, 5,558 part time; 56%
male, 44% female; 0% American
Indian, 2% Asian, 19% black,
21% Hispanic, 4% multiracial,
1% Pacific Islander, 45% white,
2% international
Most popular majors: 24%
Business Administration and
Management, General, 15%
Social Psychology, 9% Computer
and Information Sciences,
General, 9% Criminal Justice/Law
Enforcement Administration, 9%
Human Resources Management/
Personnel Administration, General
Expenses: 2018-2019: $12,650;
room/board: $8,200
Financial aid: (816) 584-6250;
67% of undergrads determined to
have financial need; average aid
package $8,569

Ranken Technical College[1]

Saint Louis MO
(314) 371-0236
U.S. News ranking: Reg. Coll.
(Mid. W), unranked
Website: www.ranken.edu
Admissions email: N/A
Private
Application deadline (fall): N/A
Undergraduate student body: N/A
full time, N/A part time
Expenses: N/A
Financial aid: N/A

Rockhurst University

Kansas City MO
(816) 501-4100
U.S. News ranking: Reg. U.
(Mid. W), No. 13
Website: www.rockhurst.edu
Admissions email:
admission@rockhurst.edu
Private; founded 1910
Affiliation: Roman Catholic
Freshman admissions: more
selective; 2018-2019: 3,746
applied, 2,477 accepted. Either
SAT or ACT required. ACT 25/75
percentile: 22-27. High school
rank: 27% in top tenth, 60% in
top quarter, 87% in top half
Early decision deadline: N/A,
notification date: N/A
Early action deadline: N/A,
notification date: N/A
Application deadline (fall): rolling
Undergraduate student body: 1,456
full time, 889 part time; 40%
male, 60% female; 1% American

Indian, 3% Asian, 6% black,
10% Hispanic, 2% multiracial,
0% Pacific Islander, 71% white,
1% international; 71% from in
state; 48% live on campus; 38%
of students in fraternities, 41%
in sororities
Most popular majors: 24% Health
Professions and Related Programs,
22% Business, Management,
Marketing, and Related Support
Services, 11% Biological and
Biomedical Sciences, 8%
Psychology, 7% Parks, Recreation,
Leisure, and Fitness Studies
Expenses: 2019-2020: $38,760;
room/board: $9,690
Financial aid: (816) 501-4600;
70% of undergrads determined to
have financial need; average aid
package $32,757

Saint Louis University

St. Louis MO
(314) 977-2500
U.S. News ranking: Nat. U., No. 97
Website: www.slu.edu
Admissions email:
admission@slu.edu
Private; founded 1818
Affiliation: Roman Catholic
Freshman admissions: more
selective; 2018-2019: 15,120
applied, 8,698 accepted. Either
SAT or ACT required. ACT 25/75
percentile: 25-31. High school
rank: 48% in top tenth, 77% in
top quarter, 94% in top half
Early decision deadline: N/A,
notification date: N/A
Early action deadline: N/A,
notification date: N/A
Undergraduate student body: 6,560
full time, 607 part time; 40%
male, 60% female; 0% American
Indian, 11% Asian, 6% black,
6% Hispanic, 3% multiracial,
0% Pacific Islander, 68% white,
5% international; 41% from in
state; 53% live on campus; 12%
of students in fraternities, 29%
in sororities
Most popular majors: 27% Health
Professions and Related Programs,
23% Business, Management,
Marketing, and Related Support
Services, 7% Engineering, 7%
Parks, Recreation, Leisure, and
Fitness Studies, 6% Biological
and Biomedical Sciences
Expenses: 2019-2020: $45,424;
room/board: $12,600
Financial aid: (314) 977-2350;
60% of undergrads determined to
have financial need; average aid
package $33,452

Southeast Missouri State University

Cape Girardeau MO
(573) 651-2590
U.S. News ranking: Reg. U.
(Mid. W), No. 78
Website: www.semo.edu
Admissions email:
admissions@semo.edu
Public; founded 1873
Freshman admissions: selective;
2018-2019: 4,638 applied,
3,883 accepted. Either SAT or
ACT required. ACT 25/75

percentile: 20-25. High school
rank: 20% in top tenth, 51% in
top quarter, 71% in top half
Early decision deadline: N/A,
notification date: N/A
Early action deadline: N/A,
notification date: N/A
Application deadline (fall): 7/1
Undergraduate student body: 7,296
full time, 2,745 part time; 41%
male, 59% female; 0% American
Indian, 1% Asian, 9% black, 2%
Hispanic, 2% multiracial, 0%
Pacific Islander, 80% white, 5%
international; N/A from in state;
31% live on campus; 19% of
students in fraternities, 19% in
sororities
Most popular majors: 15%
Business, Management,
Marketing, and Related Support
Services, 10% Education, 9%
Liberal Arts and Sciences, General
Studies and Humanities, 8%
Health Professions and Related
Programs, 7% Communication,
Journalism, and Related Programs
Expenses: 2019-2020: $7,800 in
state, $13,830 out of state; room/
board: $8,282
Financial aid: (573) 651-2253;
63% of undergrads determined to
have financial need; average aid
package $9,928

Southwest Baptist University

Bolivar MO
(417) 328-1810
U.S. News ranking: Reg. U.
(Mid. W), second tier
Website: www.sbuniv.edu
Admissions email:
admissions@sbuniv.edu
Private; founded 1878
Affiliation: Southern Baptist
Freshman admissions: selective;
2018-2019: 2,064 applied,
1,456 accepted. Either SAT
or ACT required. ACT 25/75
percentile: 19-26. High school
rank: 23% in top tenth, 48% in
top quarter, 80% in top half
Early decision deadline: N/A,
notification date: N/A
Early action deadline: N/A,
notification date: N/A
Application deadline (fall): rolling
Undergraduate student body: 1,780
full time, 883 part time; 37%
male, 63% female; 1% American
Indian, 1% Asian, 5% black,
3% Hispanic, 1% multiracial,
0% Pacific Islander, 83% white,
2% international; 74% from in
state; 42% live on campus; 0%
of students in fraternities, 0% in
sororities
Most popular majors: 19%
Registered Nursing/Registered
Nurse, 8% Business
Administration and Management,
General, 8% Elementary
Education and Teaching,
8% Psychology, General, 6%
Kinesiology and Exercise Science
Expenses: 2019-2020: $24,510;
room/board: $7,820
Financial aid: (417) 328-1823;
81% of undergrads determined to
have financial need; average aid
package $18,181

Stephens College

Columbia MO
(800) 876-7207
U.S. News ranking: Reg. U.
(Mid. W), No. 66
Website: www.stephens.edu
Admissions email:
apply@stephens.edu
Private; founded 1833
Freshman admissions: selective;
2018-2019: N/A applied, N/A
accepted. Either SAT or ACT
required. ACT 25/75 percentile:
20-26. High school rank: 17%
in top tenth, 37% in top quarter,
80% in top half
Early decision deadline: 12/31,
notification date: 11/1
Early action deadline: 12/31,
notification date: 12/31
Application deadline (fall): rolling
Undergraduate student body:
459 full time, 92 part time; 1%
male, 99% female; 1% American
Indian, 1% Asian, 14% black,
6% Hispanic, 7% multiracial, 0%
Pacific Islander, 67% white, 0%
international
Most popular majors: 27%
Visual and Performing Arts,
23% Business, Management,
Marketing, and Related Support
Services, 20% Health Professions
and Related Programs, 6%
Biological and Biomedical
Sciences, 5% Family and
Consumer Sciences/Human
Sciences
Expenses: 2018-2019: $30,950;
room/board: $10,632
Financial aid: (573) 876-7106

Truman State University

Kirksville MO
(660) 785-4114
U.S. News ranking: Reg. U.
(Mid. W), No. 7
Website: www.truman.edu
Admissions email:
admissions@truman.edu
Public; founded 1867
Freshman admissions: more
selective; 2018-2019: 4,568
applied, 2,983 accepted. Either
SAT or ACT required. ACT 25/75
percentile: 24-30. High school
rank: 53% in top tenth, 83% in
top quarter, 98% in top half
Early decision deadline: N/A,
notification date: N/A
Early action deadline: N/A,
notification date: N/A
Application deadline (fall): rolling
Undergraduate student body: 4,771
full time, 733 part time; 41%
male, 59% female; 0% American
Indian, 3% Asian, 4% black, 3%
Hispanic, 4% multiracial, 0%
Pacific Islander, 78% white, 7%
international; 76% from in state;
45% live on campus; 21% of
students in fraternities, 18% in
sororities
Most popular majors: 12%
Business Administration and
Management, General, 10%
Biology/Biological Sciences,
General, 9% Psychology, General,
7% Kinesiology and Exercise
Science, 7% Public Health
Education and Promotion
Expenses: 2019-2020: $8,120 in
state, $15,314 out of state; room/
board: $9,012

Financial aid: (660) 785-4130;
52% of undergrads determined to
have financial need; average aid
package $12,543

University of Central Missouri

Warrensburg MO
(660) 543-4290
U.S. News ranking: Reg. U.
(Mid. W), No. 78
Website: www.ucmo.edu
Admissions email:
admit@ucmo.edu
Public; founded 1871
Freshman admissions: selective;
2018-2019: 4,867 applied,
4,184 accepted. Either SAT or
ACT required for some. ACT 25/75
percentile: 19-24. High school
rank: 12% in top tenth, 36% in
top quarter, 70% in top half
Early decision deadline: N/A,
notification date: N/A
Early action deadline: N/A,
notification date: N/A
Application deadline (fall): rolling
Undergraduate student body: 7,293
full time, 2,007 part time; 45%
male, 55% female; 0% American
Indian, 1% Asian, 10% black,
5% Hispanic, 4% multiracial,
0% Pacific Islander, 76% white,
2% international; 88% from in
state; 33% live on campus; 12%
of students in fraternities, 11%
in sororities
Most popular majors: 16% Health
Professions and Related Programs,
13% Education, 12% Business,
Management, Marketing, and
Related Support Services, 8%
Engineering Technologies and
Engineering-Related Fields,
8% Homeland Security, Law
Enforcement, Firefighting and
Related Protective Services
Expenses: 2019-2020: $8,043 in
state, $15,171 out of state; room/
board: $8,962
Financial aid: (660) 543-8266;
59% of undergrads determined to
have financial need; average aid
package $8,542

University of Missouri

Columbia MO
(573) 882-7786
U.S. News ranking: Nat. U.,
No. 139
Website: www.missouri.edu
Admissions email:
mu4u@missouri.edu
Public; founded 1839
Freshman admissions: more
selective; 2018-2019: 18,948
applied, 14,750 accepted. Either
SAT or ACT required. ACT 25/75
percentile: 23-29. High school
rank: 30% in top tenth, 61% in
top quarter, 90% in top half
Early decision deadline: N/A,
notification date: N/A
Early action deadline: N/A,
notification date: N/A
Application deadline (fall): rolling
Undergraduate student body:
20,720 full time, 1,783 part
time; 48% male, 52% female;
0% American Indian, 3% Asian,
8% black, 4% Hispanic, 4%
multiracial, 0% Pacific Islander,

78% white, 3% international; 80% from in state; 25% live on campus; 24% of students in fraternities, 33% in sororities
Most popular majors: 18% Business, Management, Marketing, and Related Support Services, 14% Health Professions and Related Programs, 11% Communication, Journalism, and Related Programs, 8% Engineering, 5% Biological and Biomedical Sciences
Expenses: 2019-2020: $10,477 in state, $28,348 out of state; room/board: $11,618
Financial aid: (573) 882-7506; 49% of undergrads determined to have financial need; average aid package $12,822

University of Missouri–Kansas City
Kansas City MO
(816) 235-1111
U.S. News ranking: Nat. U., No. 263
Website: www.umkc.edu
Admissions email: admissions@umkc.edu
Public; founded 1933
Freshman admissions: more selective; 2018-2019: 6,378 applied, 3,602 accepted. Either SAT or ACT required. ACT 25/75 percentile: 21-28. High school rank: 33% in top tenth, 61% in top quarter, 86% in top half
Early decision deadline: N/A, notification date: N/A
Early action deadline: N/A, notification date: N/A
Application deadline (fall): rolling
Undergraduate student body: 6,606 full time, 4,731 part time; 43% male, 57% female; 0% American Indian, 8% Asian, 12% black, 10% Hispanic, 4% multiracial, 0% Pacific Islander, 57% white, 5% international; 80% from in state; 14% live on campus; 2% of students in fraternities, 4% in sororities
Most popular majors: 18% Business, Management, Marketing, and Related Support Services, 16% Health Professions and Related Programs, 8% Liberal Arts and Sciences, General Studies and Humanities, 7% Biological and Biomedical Sciences, 7% Psychology
Expenses: 2019-2020: $10,396 in state, $26,134 out of state; room/board: $10,890
Financial aid: (816) 235-1154; 64% of undergrads determined to have financial need; average aid package $10,397

University of Missouri–St. Louis
St. Louis MO
(314) 516-5451
U.S. News ranking: Nat. U., No. 281
Website: www.umsl.edu
Admissions email: admissions@umsl.edu
Public; founded 1963
Freshman admissions: more selective; 2018-2019: 2,466 applied, 1,793 accepted. Either

SAT or ACT required. ACT 25/75 percentile: 21-27. High school rank: 26% in top tenth, 59% in top quarter, 88% in top half
Early decision deadline: N/A, notification date: N/A
Early action deadline: N/A, notification date: N/A
Application deadline (fall): 8/19
Undergraduate student body: 5,383 full time, 8,107 part time; 44% male, 56% female; 0% American Indian, 5% Asian, 17% black, 3% Hispanic, 3% multiracial, 0% Pacific Islander, 64% white, 3% international; 89% from in state; 12% live on campus; 1% of students in fraternities, 1% in sororities
Most popular majors: 27% Business, Management, Marketing, and Related Support Services, 13% Health Professions and Related Programs, 8% Psychology, 8% Social Sciences, 7% Education
Expenses: 2019-2020: $11,079 in state, $29,295 out of state; room/board: $9,550
Financial aid: (314) 516-5526; 72% of undergrads determined to have financial need; average aid package $11,595

Washington University in St. Louis
St. Louis MO
(800) 638-0700
U.S. News ranking: Nat. U., No. 19
Website: www.wustl.edu
Admissions email: admissions@wustl.edu
Private; founded 1853
Freshman admissions: most selective; 2018-2019: 31,320 applied, 4,708 accepted. Either SAT or ACT required. ACT 25/75 percentile: 32-35. High school rank: 80% in top tenth, 97% in top quarter, 99% in top half
Early decision deadline: 11/1, notification date: 12/15
Early action deadline: N/A, notification date: N/A
Application deadline (fall): 1/2
Undergraduate student body: 7,146 full time, 605 part time; 47% male, 53% female; 0% American Indian, 16% Asian, 9% black, 9% Hispanic, 5% multiracial, 0% Pacific Islander, 51% white, 7% international; 10% from in state; 74% live on campus; 26% of students in fraternities, 38% in sororities
Most popular majors: 15% Business, Management, Marketing, and Related Support Services, 15% Engineering, 13% Social Sciences, 11% Biological and Biomedical Sciences, 7% Psychology
Expenses: 2019-2020: $55,292; room/board: $16,900
Financial aid: (888) 547-6670; 42% of undergrads determined to have financial need; average aid package $50,010

Webster University
St. Louis MO
(314) 246-7800
U.S. News ranking: Reg. U. (Mid. W), No. 17
Website: www.webster.edu
Admissions email: admit@webster.edu
Private; founded 1915
Freshman admissions: more selective; 2018-2019: 2,498 applied, 1,423 accepted. Either SAT or ACT required. ACT 25/75 percentile: 21-27. High school rank: 21% in top tenth, 47% in top quarter, 78% in top half
Early decision deadline: N/A, notification date: N/A
Early action deadline: N/A, notification date: N/A
Application deadline (fall): 8/1
Undergraduate student body: 2,185 full time, 311 part time; 45% male, 55% female; 0% American Indian, 3% Asian, 11% black, 6% Hispanic, 4% multiracial, 0% Pacific Islander, 66% white, 3% international; 83% from in state; 65% live on campus; 0% of students in fraternities, 2% in sororities
Most popular majors: 34% Business, Management, Marketing, and Related Support Services, 14% Visual and Performing Arts, 11% Communication, Journalism, and Related Programs, 8% Social Sciences, 6% Psychology
Expenses: 2019-2020: $28,700; room/board: $11,120
Financial aid: (800) 983-4623; 74% of undergrads determined to have financial need; average aid package $23,880

Westminster College
Fulton MO
(800) 475-3361
U.S. News ranking: Nat. Lib. Arts, No. 157
Website: www.wcmo.edu/
Admissions email: admissions@westminster-mo.edu
Private; founded 1851
Affiliation: Presbyterian
Freshman admissions: selective; 2018-2019: 885 applied, 836 accepted. Either SAT or ACT required. ACT 25/75 percentile: 20-25. High school rank: 20% in top tenth, 45% in top quarter, 78% in top half
Early decision deadline: N/A, notification date: N/A
Early action deadline: N/A, notification date: N/A
Application deadline (fall): rolling
Undergraduate student body: 692 full time, 25 part time; 56% male, 44% female; 2% American Indian, 1% Asian, 8% black, 3% Hispanic, 1% multiracial, 0% Pacific Islander, 72% white, 7% international; 19% from in state; 81% live on campus; 51% of students in fraternities, 39% in sororities
Most popular majors: 29% Business, Management, Marketing, and Related Support Services, 13% Biological and Biomedical Sciences, 11% Education, 9% Social Sciences,

8% Parks, Recreation, Leisure, and Fitness Studies
Expenses: 2018-2019: $27,600; room/board: $10,140
Financial aid: (573) 592-5364

William Jewell College
Liberty MO
(888) 253-9355
U.S. News ranking: Reg. Coll. (Mid. W), No. 9
Website: www.jewell.edu
Admissions email: admission@william.jewell.edu
Private; founded 1849
Freshman admissions: more selective; 2018-2019: 1,316 applied, 605 accepted. Neither SAT nor ACT required. ACT 25/75 percentile: 22-29. High school rank: 31% in top tenth, 56% in top quarter, 90% in top half
Early decision deadline: N/A, notification date: N/A
Early action deadline: N/A, notification date: N/A
Application deadline (fall): 8/15
Undergraduate student body: 779 full time, 24 part time; 45% male, 55% female; 0% American Indian, 1% Asian, 5% black, 6% Hispanic, 4% multiracial, 0% Pacific Islander, 79% white, 3% international; 62% from in state; 85% live on campus; 40% of students in fraternities, 46% in sororities
Most popular majors: 33% Registered Nursing/Registered Nurse, 17% Business Administration and Management, General, 9% Biology/Biological Sciences, General, 8% Psychology, General, 6% Political Science and Government, General
Expenses: 2019-2020: $34,450; room/board: $10,130
Financial aid: (816) 415-5977; 65% of undergrads determined to have financial need; average aid package $31,003

William Woods University
Fulton MO
(800) 995-3159
U.S. News ranking: Nat. U., second tier
Website: www.williamwoods.edu
Admissions email: admissions@williamwoods.edu
Private; founded 1870
Affiliation: Christian Church (Disciples of Christ)
Freshman admissions: selective; 2018-2019: 885 applied, 566 accepted. Either SAT or ACT required. ACT 25/75 percentile: 19-25. High school rank: 6% in top tenth, 19% in top quarter, 55% in top half
Early decision deadline: N/A, notification date: N/A
Early action deadline: N/A, notification date: N/A
Application deadline (fall): rolling
Undergraduate student body: 770 full time, 165 part time; 29% male, 71% female; 1% American Indian, 0% Asian, 4% black, 4% Hispanic, 2% multiracial, 0% Pacific Islander, 81% white,

5% international; 61% from in state; 61% live on campus; 26% of students in fraternities, 31% in sororities
Most popular majors: 23% Foreign Languages, Literatures, and Linguistics, 18% Business, Management, Marketing, and Related Support Services, 11% Agriculture, Agriculture Operations, and Related Sciences, 8% Biological and Biomedical Sciences, 7% Parks, Recreation, Leisure, and Fitness Studies
Expenses: 2019-2020: $24,830; room/board: $9,890
Financial aid: (573) 592-1793; 71% of undergrads determined to have financial need; average aid package $18,567

MONTANA

Carroll College
Helena MT
(406) 447-4384
U.S. News ranking: Reg. Coll. (W), No. 1
Website: www.carroll.edu
Admissions email: admission@carroll.edu
Private; founded 1909
Affiliation: Roman Catholic
Freshman admissions: more selective; 2018-2019: 2,709 applied, 2,122 accepted. Either SAT or ACT required. ACT 25/75 percentile: 22-28. High school rank: 31% in top tenth, 57% in top quarter, 84% in top half
Early decision deadline: N/A, notification date: N/A
Early action deadline: 12/1, notification date: 1/1
Application deadline (fall): 5/1
Undergraduate student body: 1,195 full time, 127 part time; 42% male, 58% female; 0% American Indian, 1% Asian, 1% black, 4% Hispanic, 4% multiracial, 0% Pacific Islander, 81% white, 2% international; 43% from in state; 56% live on campus; 0% of students in fraternities, 0% in sororities
Most popular majors: 30% Health Professions and Related Programs, 13% Biological and Biomedical Sciences, 10% Business, Management, Marketing, and Related Support Services, 7% Psychology, 5% Communication, Journalism, and Related Programs
Expenses: 2019-2020: $36,280; room/board: $10,036
Financial aid: (406) 447-5425; 65% of undergrads determined to have financial need; average aid package $28,457

Montana State University
Bozeman MT
(406) 994-2452
U.S. News ranking: Nat. U., No. 246
Website: www.montana.edu
Admissions email: admissions@montana.edu
Public; founded 1893
Freshman admissions: selective; 2018-2019: 18,637 applied, 15,226 accepted. Either SAT or ACT required. ACT 25/75

percentile: 21-28. High school rank: 21% in top tenth, 46% in top quarter, 75% in top half
Early decision deadline: N/A, notification date: N/A
Early action deadline: N/A, notification date: N/A
Application deadline (fall): rolling
Undergraduate student body: 12,475 full time, 2,378 part time; 54% male, 46% female; 1% American Indian, 1% Asian, 1% black, 4% Hispanic, 5% multiracial, 0% Pacific Islander, 84% white, 3% international
Most popular majors: 18% Engineering, 12% Business, Management, Marketing, and Related Support Services, 9% Health Professions and Related Programs, 8% Biological and Biomedical Sciences, 8% Family and Consumer Sciences/Human Sciences
Expenses: 2019-2020: $7,472 in state, $25,708 out of state; room/board: $10,300
Financial aid: (406) 994-2845; 46% of undergrads determined to have financial need; average aid package $11,887

Montana State University–Billings
Billings MT
(406) 657-2158
U.S. News ranking: Reg. U. (W), second tier
Website: www.msubillings.edu
Admissions email: admissions@msubillings.edu
Public; founded 1927
Freshman admissions: selective; 2018-2019: 1,335 applied, 1,334 accepted. Either SAT or ACT required for some. ACT 25/75 percentile: 18-23. High school rank: 13% in top tenth, 33% in top quarter, 60% in top half
Early decision deadline: N/A, notification date: N/A
Early action deadline: N/A, notification date: N/A
Application deadline (fall): rolling
Undergraduate student body: 2,303 full time, 1,657 part time; 36% male, 64% female; 5% American Indian, 1% Asian, 1% black, 6% Hispanic, 4% multiracial, 0% Pacific Islander, 81% white, 2% international; 91% from in state; 9% live on campus; N/A of students in fraternities, N/A in sororities
Most popular majors: 28% Business, Management, Marketing, and Related Support Services, 18% Education, 7% Liberal Arts and Sciences, General Studies and Humanities, 7% Psychology, 5% Multi/Interdisciplinary Studies
Expenses: 2019-2020: $5,928 in state, $19,121 out of state; room/board: $7,240
Financial aid: (406) 657-2188; 60% of undergrads determined to have financial need; average aid package $10,254

Montana State University–Northern[1]
Havre MT
(406) 265-3704
U.S. News ranking: Reg. Coll. (W), second tier
Website: www.msun.edu
Admissions email: admissions@msun.edu
Public
Application deadline (fall): N/A
Undergraduate student body: N/A full time, N/A part time
Expenses: N/A
Financial aid: N/A

Montana Technological University
Butte MT
(406) 496-4256
U.S. News ranking: Reg. U. (W), No. 27
Website: www.mtech.edu/
Admissions email: enrollment@mtech.edu
Public; founded 1893
Freshman admissions: selective; 2018-2019: 1,008 applied, 905 accepted. Either SAT or ACT required. ACT 25/75 percentile: 22-27. High school rank: 23% in top tenth, 57% in top quarter, 82% in top half
Early decision deadline: N/A, notification date: N/A
Early action deadline: N/A, notification date: N/A
Application deadline (fall): rolling
Undergraduate student body: 1,818 full time, 512 part time; 60% male, 40% female; 2% American Indian, 1% Asian, 1% black, 2% Hispanic, 0% multiracial, 0% Pacific Islander, 78% white, 9% international; N/A from in state; 14% live on campus; N/A of students in fraternities, N/A in sororities
Most popular majors: 18% Petroleum Engineering, 16% Engineering, General, 12% Mechanical Engineering, 9% Business/Commerce, General, 8% Registered Nursing/Registered Nurse
Expenses: 2019-2020: $7,431 in state, $22,594 out of state; room/board: $9,996
Financial aid: (406) 496-4223; 52% of undergrads determined to have financial need; average aid package $10,983

Rocky Mountain College
Billings MT
(406) 657 1026
U.S. News ranking: Reg. U. (W), No. 37
Website: www.rocky.edu
Admissions email: admissions@rocky.edu
Private; founded 1878
Affiliation: Presbyterian Church (USA)
Freshman admissions: selective; 2018-2019: 1,521 applied, 889 accepted. Either SAT or ACT required. ACT 25/75 percentile: 20-25. High school rank: 17% in top tenth, 46% in top quarter, 76% in top half

Early decision deadline: N/A, notification date: N/A
Early action deadline: N/A, notification date: N/A
Application deadline (fall): rolling
Undergraduate student body: 867 full time, 30 part time; 51% male, 49% female; 3% American Indian, 0% Asian, 3% black, 6% Hispanic, 5% multiracial, 1% Pacific Islander, 78% white, 3% international; 53% from in state; 51% live on campus; N/A of students in fraternities, N/A in sororities
Most popular majors: 16% Business, Management, Marketing, and Related Support Services, 15% Parks, Recreation, Leisure, and Fitness Studies, 10% Biological and Biomedical Sciences, 9% Transportation and Materials Moving, 6% Education
Expenses: 2019-2020: $29,552; room/board: $8,452
Financial aid: (406) 657-1031; 78% of undergrads determined to have financial need; average aid package $24,815

University of Montana
Missoula MT
(800) 462-8636
U.S. News ranking: Nat. U., No. 254
Website: www.umt.edu
Admissions email: admiss@umontana.edu
Public; founded 1893
Freshman admissions: selective; 2018-2019: 5,475 applied, 4,829 accepted. Either SAT or ACT required. ACT 25/75 percentile: 20-26. High school rank: 16% in top tenth, 38% in top quarter, 71% in top half
Early decision deadline: N/A, notification date: N/A
Early action deadline: N/A, notification date: N/A
Application deadline (fall): 8/26
Undergraduate student body: 6,752 full time, 1,554 part time; 45% male, 55% female; 3% American Indian, 1% Asian, 1% black, 5% Hispanic, 4% multiracial, 0% Pacific Islander, 77% white, 1% international; N/A from in state; 33% live on campus; 6% of students in fraternities, 6% in sororities
Most popular majors: 22% Business, Management, Marketing, and Related Support Services, 12% Education, 12% Social Sciences, 9% Natural Resources and Conservation, 8% Psychology
Expenses: 2019-2020: $7,426 in state, $26,218 out of state; room/board: $9,966
Financial aid: (406) 243-5504; 60% of undergrads determined to have financial need; average aid package $11,663

University of Montana–Western
Dillon MT
(877) 683-7331
U.S. News ranking: Reg. Coll. (W), No. 9
Website: w.umwestern.edu/
Admissions email: admissions@umwestern.edu
Public; founded 1893
Freshman admissions: less selective; 2018-2019: 722 applied, 435 accepted. Either SAT or ACT required. ACT 25/75 percentile: 17-22. High school rank: 5% in top tenth, 20% in top quarter, 50% in top half
Early decision deadline: N/A, notification date: N/A
Early action deadline: N/A, notification date: N/A
Application deadline (fall): rolling
Undergraduate student body: 1,176 full time, 336 part time; 35% male, 65% female; 4% American Indian, 0% Asian, 1% black, 5% Hispanic, 2% multiracial, 1% Pacific Islander, 85% white, 0% international
Most popular majors: 20% Business Administration and Management, General, 20% Elementary Education and Teaching, 8% Early Childhood Education and Teaching, 8% Health and Physical Education/Fitness, General, 7% Environmental Science
Expenses: 2019-2020: $5,725 in state, $17,115 out of state; room/board: $8,184
Financial aid: (406) 683-7893; 82% of undergrads determined to have financial need; average aid package $6,900

University of Providence[1]
Great Falls MT
(406) 791-5210
U.S. News ranking: Reg. Coll. (W), unranked
Website: www.uprovidence.edu
Admissions email: melanie.houge@uprovidence.edu
Private; founded 1932
Affiliation: Roman Catholic
Application deadline (fall): 9/1
Undergraduate student body: N/A full time, N/A part time
Expenses: 2018-2019: $25,318; room/board: $9,200
Financial aid: (406) 791 5235

NEBRASKA

Bellevue University[1]
Bellevue NE
(402) 293-2000
U.S. News ranking: Reg. U. (Mid. W), unranked
Website: www.bellevue.edu
Admissions email: info@bellevue.edu
Private
Application deadline (fall): N/A
Undergraduate student body: N/A full time, N/A part time
Expenses: N/A
Financial aid: (402) 557-7095

Chadron State College[1]
Chadron NE
(308) 432-6000
U.S. News ranking: Reg. U. (Mid. W), unranked
Website: www.csc.edu
Admissions email: inquire@csc.edu
Public; founded 1911
Application deadline (fall): N/A
Undergraduate student body: N/A full time, N/A part time
Expenses: N/A
Financial aid: N/A

College of St. Mary
Omaha NE
(402) 399-2407
U.S. News ranking: Reg. U. (Mid. W), No. 53
Website: www.csm.edu
Admissions email: enroll@csm.edu
Private; founded 1923
Affiliation: Roman Catholic
Freshman admissions: selective; 2018-2019: 428 applied, 223 accepted. Either SAT or ACT required. ACT 25/75 percentile: 20-25. High school rank: 15% in top tenth, 40% in top quarter, 72% in top half
Early decision deadline: N/A, notification date: N/A
Early action deadline: N/A, notification date: N/A
Application deadline (fall): rolling
Undergraduate student body: 794 full time, 67 part time; 1% male, 99% female; 1% American Indian, 3% Asian, 8% black, 12% Hispanic, 6% multiracial, 0% Pacific Islander, 69% white, 1% international; 76% from in state; 35% live on campus; N/A of students in fraternities, N/A in sororities
Most popular majors: 32% Registered Nursing/Registered Nurse, 27% Rehabilitation Science, 15% Biology/Biological Sciences, General, 6% Elementary Education and Teaching, 6% Psychology, General
Expenses: 2019-2020: $20,750; room/board: $7,850
Financial aid: (402) 399-2362; 81% of undergrads determined to have financial need; average aid package $15,771

Concordia University
Seward NE
(800) 535-5494
U.S. News ranking: Reg. U. (Mid. W), No. 33
Website: www.cune.edu
Admissions email: admiss@cune.edu
Private; founded 1894
Affiliation: Lutheran Church–Missouri Synod
Freshman admissions: selective; 2018-2019: 1,963 applied, 1,333 accepted. Either SAT or ACT required. ACT 25/75 percentile: 20-26. High school rank: 18% in top tenth, 48% in top quarter, 79% in top half
Early decision deadline: N/A, notification date: N/A
Early action deadline: N/A, notification date: N/A
Application deadline (fall): 8/1

Undergraduate student body: 1,260 full time, 576 part time; 45% male, 55% female; 0% American Indian, 1% Asian, 2% black, 6% Hispanic, 1% multiracial, 0% Pacific Islander, 73% white, 3% international; N/A from in state; 69% live on campus; N/A of students in fraternities, N/A in sororities
Most popular majors: 30% Education, 11% Theology and Religious Vocations, 10% Business, Management, Marketing, and Related Support Services, 9% Psychology, 7% Biological and Biomedical Sciences
Expenses: 2019-2020: $33,490; room/board: $8,850
Financial aid: (402) 643-7270; 78% of undergrads determined to have financial need; average aid package $26,006

Creighton University

Omaha NE
(800) 282-5835
U.S. News ranking: Nat. U., No. 104
Website: www.creighton.edu
Admissions email: admissions@creighton.edu
Private; founded 1878
Affiliation: Roman Catholic
Freshman admissions: more selective; 2018-2019: 10,112 applied, 7,224 accepted. Either SAT or ACT required. ACT 25/75 percentile: 24-30. High school rank: 37% in top tenth, 70% in top quarter, 93% in top half
Early decision deadline: N/A, notification date: N/A
Early action deadline: 11/1, notification date: N/A
Application deadline (fall): 2/15
Undergraduate student body: 4,291 full time, 155 part time; 43% male, 57% female; 0% American Indian, 9% Asian, 2% black, 8% Hispanic, 5% multiracial, 0% Pacific Islander, 71% white, 2% international; 22% from in state; 55% live on campus; 46% of students in fraternities, 30% in sororities
Most popular majors: 29% Business, Management, Marketing, and Related Support Services, 20% Health Professions and Related Programs, 16% Biological and Biomedical Sciences, 8% Social Sciences, 5% Psychology
Expenses: 2019-2020: $41,400; room/board: $11,274
Financial aid: (402) 280-2731; 53% of undergrads determined to have financial need; average aid package $28,839

Doane University

Crete NE
(402) 826-8222
U.S. News ranking: Nat. Lib. Arts, unranked
Website: www.doane.edu
Admissions email: admissions@doane.edu
Private; founded 1872
Freshman admissions: selective; 2018-2019: 2,761 applied, 1,885 accepted. Neither SAT nor ACT required. ACT 25/75 percentile: 19-25. High school rank: 11% in top tenth, 33% in top quarter, 89% in top half
Early decision deadline: N/A, notification date: N/A
Early action deadline: N/A, notification date: N/A
Application deadline (fall): rolling
Undergraduate student body: 994 full time, 17 part time; 55% male, 45% female; 0% American Indian, 1% Asian, 3% black, 8% Hispanic, 4% multiracial, 0% Pacific Islander, 81% white, 2% international; 76% from in state; 78% live on campus; 22% of students in fraternities, 35% in sororities
Most popular majors: 23% Education, 13% Biological and Biomedical Sciences, 10% Business, Management, Marketing, and Related Support Services, 8% Psychology, 8% Social Sciences
Expenses: 2019-2020: $35,300; room/board: $9,800
Financial aid: (402) 826-8260; 75% of undergrads determined to have financial need; average aid package $25,910

Hastings College

Hastings NE
(800) 532-7642
U.S. News ranking: Reg. Coll. (Mid. W), No. 21
Website: www.hastings.edu
Admissions email: hcadmissions@hastings.edu
Private; founded 1882
Affiliation: Presbyterian
Freshman admissions: selective; 2018-2019: 1,946 applied, 1,249 accepted. Either SAT or ACT required. ACT 25/75 percentile: 19-25. High school rank: 18% in top tenth, 45% in top quarter, 71% in top half
Early decision deadline: N/A, notification date: N/A
Early action deadline: N/A, notification date: N/A
Application deadline (fall): 8/1
Undergraduate student body: 950 full time, 98 part time; 50% male, 50% female; 0% American Indian, 1% Asian, 5% black, 10% Hispanic, 3% multiracial, 0% Pacific Islander, 77% white, 4% international
Most popular majors: 29% Business, Management, Marketing, and Related Support Services, 16% Social Sciences, 15% Education, 10% Biological and Biomedical Sciences, 7% Visual and Performing Arts
Expenses: 2019-2020: $31,560; room/board: $9,990
Financial aid: (402) 461-7431; 77% of undergrads determined to have financial need; average aid package $24,257

Midland University[1]

Fremont NE
(402) 941-6501
U.S. News ranking: Reg. U. (Mid. W), second tier
Website: www.midlandu.edu/
Admissions email: admissions@midlandu.edu
Private; founded 1883

Application deadline (fall): rolling
Undergraduate student body: N/A full time, N/A part time
Expenses: N/A
Financial aid: N/A

Nebraska Wesleyan University

Lincoln NE
(402) 465-2218
U.S. News ranking: Reg. U. (Mid. W), No. 11
Website: www.nebrwesleyan.edu/
Admissions email: admissions@nebrwesleyan.edu
Private; founded 1887
Affiliation: United Methodist
Freshman admissions: more selective; 2018-2019: 2,178 applied, 1,570 accepted. Either SAT or ACT required. ACT 25/75 percentile: 21-28. High school rank: 26% in top tenth, 55% in top quarter, 86% in top half
Early decision deadline: N/A, notification date: N/A
Early action deadline: 10/15, notification date: N/A
Application deadline (fall): 8/15
Undergraduate student body: 1,676 full time, 173 part time; 40% male, 60% female; 0% American Indian, 2% Asian, 3% black, 7% Hispanic, 3% multiracial, 0% Pacific Islander, 81% white, 1% international; 87% from in state; 60% live on campus; 21% of students in fraternities, 23% in sororities
Most popular majors: 19% Health Professions and Related Programs, 15% Business, Management, Marketing, and Related Support Services, 11% Biological and Biomedical Sciences, 10% Parks, Recreation, Leisure, and Fitness Studies, 8% Education
Expenses: 2019-2020: $35,444; room/board: $10,172
Financial aid: (402) 465-2167; 75% of undergrads determined to have financial need; average aid package $24,765

Peru State College[1]

Peru NE
(402) 872-3815
U.S. News ranking: Reg. U. (Mid. W), unranked
Website: www.peru.edu
Admissions email: admissions@peru.edu
Public
Application deadline (fall): N/A
Undergraduate student body: N/A full time, N/A part time
Expenses: N/A
Financial aid: N/A

Union College

Lincoln NE
(800) 228-4600
U.S. News ranking: Reg. Coll. (Mid. W), No. 32
Website: www.ucollege.edu
Admissions email: enroll@ucollege.edu
Private; founded 1891
Affiliation: Seventh Day Adventist

Freshman admissions: selective; 2018-2019: 1,345 applied, 831 accepted. Either SAT or ACT required. ACT 25/75 percentile: 18-24. High school rank: N/A
Early decision deadline: N/A, notification date: N/A
Early action deadline: N/A, notification date: N/A
Application deadline (fall): 8/26
Undergraduate student body: 672 full time, 48 part time; 41% male, 59% female; 1% American Indian, 6% Asian, 8% black, 22% Hispanic, 4% multiracial, 1% Pacific Islander, 50% white, 7% international; N/A from in state; 67% live on campus; 0% of students in fraternities, 0% in sororities
Most popular majors: 27% Health Professions and Related Programs, 14% Business, Management, Marketing, and Related Support Services, 10% Biological and Biomedical Sciences, 9% Education, 5% Liberal Arts and Sciences, General Studies and Humanities
Expenses: 2019-2020: $24,620; room/board: $7,170
Financial aid: (402) 486-2505; 75% of undergrads determined to have financial need; average aid package $18,238

University of Nebraska–Kearney

Kearney NE
(800) 532-7639
U.S. News ranking: Reg. U. (Mid. W), No. 46
Website: www.unk.edu
Admissions email: admissionsug@unk.edu
Public; founded 1903
Freshman admissions: selective; 2018-2019: 5,559 applied, 5,205 accepted. Either SAT or ACT required. ACT 25/75 percentile: 19-26. High school rank: 20% in top tenth, 45% in top quarter, 79% in top half
Early decision deadline: N/A, notification date: N/A
Early action deadline: N/A, notification date: N/A
Application deadline (fall): 9/1
Undergraduate student body: 3,941 full time, 543 part time; 41% male, 59% female; 0% American Indian, 1% Asian, 2% black, 12% Hispanic, 2% multiracial, 0% Pacific Islander, 77% white, 5% international; 89% from in state; 37% live on campus; 13% of students in fraternities, 16% in sororities
Most popular majors: 14% Business Administration and Management, General, 12% Elementary Education and Teaching, 8% Operations Management and Supervision, 8% Parks, Recreation and Leisure Studies, 5% Psychology, General
Expenses: 2018-2019: $7,513 in state, $14,503 out of state; room/board: $9,878
Financial aid: (308) 865-8520; 68% of undergrads determined to have financial need; average aid package $11,820

University of Nebraska–Lincoln

Lincoln NE
(800) 742-8800
U.S. News ranking: Nat. U., No. 139
Website: www.unl.edu
Admissions email: Admissions@unl.edu
Public; founded 1869
Freshman admissions: more selective; 2018-2019: 14,956 applied, 11,906 accepted. Either SAT or ACT required. ACT 25/75 percentile: 22-29. High school rank: 26% in top tenth, 54% in top quarter, 86% in top half
Early decision deadline: N/A, notification date: N/A
Early action deadline: N/A, notification date: N/A
Application deadline (fall): 5/1
Undergraduate student body: 19,466 full time, 1,364 part time; 53% male, 47% female; 0% American Indian, 3% Asian, 3% black, 7% Hispanic, 3% multiracial, 0% Pacific Islander, 74% white, 9% international; 76% from in state; 34% live on campus; 18% of students in fraternities, 26% in sororities
Most popular majors: 23% Business, Management, Marketing, and Related Support Services, 11% Engineering, 8% Agriculture, Agriculture Operations, and Related Sciences, 8% Communication, Journalism, and Related Programs, 8% Family and Consumer Sciences/Human Sciences
Expenses: 2019-2020: $9,522 in state, $25,828 out of state; room/board: $11,830
Financial aid: (402) 472-2030; 47% of undergrads determined to have financial need; average aid package $14,746

University of Nebraska–Omaha

Omaha NE
(402) 554-2393
U.S. News ranking: Nat. U., second tier
Website: www.unomaha.edu/
Admissions email: unoadmissions@unomaha.edu
Public; founded 1908
Freshman admissions: selective; 2018-2019: 8,170 applied, 6,673 accepted. Either SAT or ACT required. ACT 25/75 percentile: 19-26. High school rank: 17% in top tenth, 40% in top quarter, 72% in top half
Early decision deadline: N/A, notification date: N/A
Early action deadline: N/A, notification date: N/A
Application deadline (fall): 8/1
Undergraduate student body: 9,868 full time, 2,562 part time; 47% male, 53% female; 0% American Indian, 4% Asian, 6% black, 14% Hispanic, 5% multiracial, 0% Pacific Islander, 65% white, 4% international; 91% from in state; 16% live on campus; 2% of students in fraternities, 2% in sororities

Most popular majors: 12%
Criminal Justice/Safety Studies,
6% Business Administration
and Management, General,
6% Psychology, General, 5%
Accounting, 5% Biology/Biological
Sciences, General
Expenses: 2019-2020: $7,980 in
state, $21,244 out of state; room/
board: $9,920
Financial aid: (402) 554-3408;
61% of undergrads determined to
have financial need; average aid
package $10,056

Wayne State College
Wayne NE
(800) 228-9972
U.S. News ranking: Reg. U.
(Mid. W), No. 95
Website: www.wsc.edu/
Admissions email:
admit1@wsc.edu
Public; founded 1909
Freshman admissions: selective;
2018-2019: 2,023 applied,
2,023 accepted. ACT Required
for some. ACT 25/75 percentile:
18-24. High school rank: 10%
in top tenth, 28% in top quarter,
60% in top half
Early decision deadline: N/A,
notification date: N/A
Early action deadline: N/A,
notification date: N/A
Application deadline (fall): 8/20
Undergraduate student body: 2,572
full time, 403 part time; 44%
male, 56% female; 1% American
Indian, 1% Asian, 4% black,
8% Hispanic, 3% multiracial,
0% Pacific Islander, 80% white,
2% international; 85% from in
state; 44% live on campus; N/A of
students in fraternities, N/A in
sororities
Most popular majors: 25%
Education, 17% Business,
Management, Marketing, and
Related Support Services,
9% Homeland Security, Law
Enforcement, Firefighting and
Related Protective Services, 9%
Psychology, 7% Parks, Recreation,
Leisure, and Fitness Studies
Expenses: 2019-2020: $7,206 in
state, $12,651 out of state; room/
board: $7,930
Financial aid: (402) 375-7230;
71% of undergrads determined to
have financial need; average aid
package $9,745

York College
York NE
(800) 950-9675
U.S. News ranking: Reg. Coll.
(Mid. W), No. 36
Website: www.york.edu
Admissions email: enroll@york.edu
Private; founded 1890
Affiliation: Churches of Christ
Freshman admissions: selective;
2018-2019: 445 applied, 222
accepted. Either SAT or ACT
required. ACT 25/75 percentile:
17-22. High school rank: 4% in
top tenth, 17% in top quarter,
47% in top half
Early decision deadline: N/A,
notification date: N/A
Early action deadline: N/A,
notification date: N/A

Application deadline (fall): 8/31
Undergraduate student body: 375
full time, 30 part time; 52%
male, 48% female; 0% American
Indian, 1% Asian, 12% black,
17% Hispanic, 0% multiracial,
1% Pacific Islander, 57% white,
8% international; 30% from in
state; 85% live on campus; 50%
of students in fraternities, 50%
in sororities
Most popular majors: 22%
Business Administration and
Management, General, 16%
Psychology, General, 10% General
Studies, 9% Criminal Justice/
Law Enforcement Administration,
7% Speech Communication and
Rhetoric
Expenses: 2019-2020: $19,310;
room/board: $8,450
Financial aid: (402) 363-5624,
78% of undergrads determined to
have financial need; average aid
package $26,261

NEVADA

College of Southern Nevada[1]
Las Vegas NV
(702) 651-5000
U.S. News ranking: Reg. Coll. (W),
unranked
Website: www.csn.edu
Admissions email: N/A
Public; founded 1971
Application deadline (fall): N/A
Undergraduate student body: N/A
full time, N/A part time
Expenses: N/A
Financial aid: N/A

Great Basin College[1]
Elko NV
(775) 738-8493
U.S. News ranking: Reg. Coll. (W),
unranked
Website: www.gbcnv.edu
Admissions email: N/A
Public
Application deadline (fall): N/A
Undergraduate student body: N/A
full time, N/A part time
Expenses: N/A
Financial aid: N/A

Nevada State College[1]
Henderson NV
(702) 992-2130
U.S. News ranking: Reg. Coll. (W),
unranked
Website: nsc.nevada.edu
Admissions email: N/A
Public; founded 2002
Application deadline (fall): rolling
Undergraduate student body: N/A
full time, N/A part time
Expenses: N/A
Financial aid: N/A

Sierra Nevada College[1]
Incline Village NV
(866) 412-4636
U.S. News ranking: Reg. U. (W),
second tier
Website: www.sierranevada.edu
Admissions email:
admissions@sierranevada.edu
Private; founded 1969

Application deadline (fall): 8/26
Undergraduate student body: N/A
full time, N/A part time
Expenses: N/A
Financial aid: (775) 831-1314

University of Nevada–Las Vegas
Las Vegas NV
(702) 774-8658
U.S. News ranking: Nat. U.,
second tier
Website: www.unlv.edu
Admissions email:
admissions@unlv.edu
Public; founded 1957
Freshman admissions: selective;
2018-2019: 11,613 applied,
9,527 accepted. Either SAT
or ACT required. ACT 25/75
percentile: 19-24. High school
rank: 22% in top tenth, 52% in
top quarter, 83% in top half
Early decision deadline: N/A,
notification date: N/A
Early action deadline: N/A,
notification date: N/A
Application deadline (fall): 7/1
Undergraduate student body:
18,764 full time, 6,518 part
time; 44% male, 56% female;
0% American Indian, 16% Asian,
8% black, 30% Hispanic, 11%
multiracial, 1% Pacific Islander,
30% white, 3% international;
88% from in state; N/A live
on campus; 6% of students in
fraternities, 6% in sororities
Most popular majors: 26%
Business, Management,
Marketing, and Related Support
Services, 8% Psychology,
7% Homeland Security, Law
Enforcement, Firefighting and
Related Protective Services,
6% Health Professions and
Related Programs, 6% Visual and
Performing Arts
Expenses: 2019-2020: $7,852 in
state, $22,904 out of state; room/
board: $10,892
Financial aid: (833) 318-1228;
64% of undergrads determined to
have financial need; average aid
package $13,397

University of Nevada–Reno
Reno NV
(775) 784-4700
U.S. News ranking: Nat. U.,
No. 240
Website: www.unr.edu
Admissions email:
asknevada@unr.edu
Public; founded 1874
Freshman admissions: selective;
2018-2019: 9,531 applied,
8,402 accepted. Either SAT
or ACT required. ACT 25/75
percentile: 21-26. High school
rank: 27% in top tenth, 58% in
top quarter, 87% in top half
Early decision deadline: N/A,
notification date: N/A
Early action deadline: 11/1,
notification date: 11/15
Application deadline (fall): 4/7
Undergraduate student body:
15,200 full time, 2,730 part
time; 48% male, 52% female; 1%
American Indian, 8% Asian,

3% black, 21% Hispanic, 7%
multiracial, 1% Pacific Islander,
57% white, 1% international
Most popular majors: 17%
Business, Management,
Marketing, and Related Support
Services, 14% Health Professions
and Related Programs, 12%
Engineering, 10% Biological and
Biomedical Sciences, 9% Social
Sciences
Expenses: 2019-2020: $8,024 in
state, $23,075 out of state; room/
board: $10,868
Financial aid: (775) 784-4666;
53% of undergrads determined to
have financial need; average aid
package $9,020

Western Nevada College[1]
Carson City NV
(775) 445-3000
U.S. News ranking: Reg. Coll. (W),
unranked
Website: www.wnc.edu
Admissions email: N/A
Public; founded 1971
Application deadline (fall): N/A
Undergraduate student body: N/A
full time, N/A part time
Expenses: N/A
Financial aid: N/A

NEW HAMPSHIRE

Colby-Sawyer College
New London NH
(800) 272-1015
U.S. News ranking: Reg. Coll. (N),
No. 8
Website: colby-sawyer.edu/
Admissions email:
admissions@colby-sawyer.edu
Private; founded 1837
Freshman admissions: selective;
2018-2019: 2,568 applied,
2,307 accepted. Either SAT or
ACT required for some. SAT 25/75
percentile: 1030-1210. High
school rank: N/A
Early decision deadline: N/A,
notification date: N/A
Early action deadline: 12/1,
notification date: 12/15
Application deadline (fall): rolling
Undergraduate student body: 821
full time, 37 part time; 31%
male, 69% female; 1% American
Indian, 3% Asian, 5% black,
2% Hispanic, 0% multiracial,
0% Pacific Islander, 78% white,
3% international; 39% from in
state; 78% live on campus; 0%
of students in fraternities, 0% in
sororities
Most popular majors: 17%
Registered Nursing/Registered
Nurse, 15% Business
Administration and Management,
General, 10% Kinesiology and
Exercise Science, 9% Biology/
Biological Sciences, General, 7%
Psychology, General
Expenses: 2019-2020: $43,646;
room/board: $14,978
Financial aid: (603) 526-3717;
79% of undergrads determined to
have financial need; average aid
package $35,094

Dartmouth College
Hanover NH
(603) 646-2875
U.S. News ranking: Nat. U., No. 12
Website: www.dartmouth.edu
Admissions email:
admissions.office@dartmouth.edu
Private; founded 1769
Freshman admissions: most
selective; 2018-2019: 22,033
applied, 1,925 accepted. Either
SAT or ACT required. SAT 25/75
percentile: 1420-1560. High
school rank: 95% in top tenth,
99% in top quarter, 100% in
top half
Early decision deadline: 11/1,
notification date: 12/15
Early action deadline: N/A,
notification date: N/A
Application deadline (fall): 1/2
Undergraduate student body: 4,357
full time, 60 part time; 51%
male, 49% female; 2% American
Indian, 15% Asian, 6% black,
10% Hispanic, 5% multiracial,
0% Pacific Islander, 51% white,
9% international; 3% from in
state; 87% live on campus; 35%
of students in fraternities, 42%
in sororities
Most popular majors: 34%
Social Sciences, 8% Biological
and Biomedical Sciences, 8%
Engineering, 7% Computer and
Information Sciences and Support
Services, 5% History
Expenses: 2019-2020: $57,204;
room/board: $16,374
Financial aid: (800) 443-3605;
51% of undergrads determined to
have financial need; average aid
package $52,357

Franklin Pierce University
Rindge NH
(800) 437-0048
U.S. News ranking: Reg. U. (N),
second tier
Website: www.franklinpierce.edu/
Admissions email:
admissions@franklinpierce.edu
Private; founded 1962
Freshman admissions: less
selective; 2018-2019: 5,435
applied, 4,217 accepted. Either
SAT or ACT required for some.
SAT 25/75 percentile: 970-1160.
High school rank: 8% in top
tenth, 19% in top quarter, 56%
in top half
Early decision deadline: N/A,
notification date: N/A
Early action deadline: N/A,
notification date: N/A
Application deadline (fall): rolling
Undergraduate student body: 1,412
full time, 216 part time; 45%
male, 55% female; 1% American
Indian, 3% Asian, 9% black,
8% Hispanic, 0% multiracial,
0% Pacific Islander, 73% white,
0% international; 20% from in
state; 89% live on campus; N/A
of students in fraternities, N/A in
sororities
Most popular majors: 31% Health
Professions and Related Programs,
21% Business, Management,
Marketing, and Related Support
Services, 12% Homeland Security,
Law Enforcement, Firefighting and

Related Protective Services, 7% Parks, Recreation, Leisure, and Fitness Studies, 5% Psychology **Expenses:** 2019-2020: $38,200; room/board: $13,900 **Financial aid:** (877) 372-7347; 90% of undergrads determined to have financial need; average aid package $27,022

Granite State College

Concord NH
(603) 513-1391
U.S. News ranking: Reg. U. (N), unranked
Website: www.granite.edu
Admissions email: gsc.admissions@granite.edu
Public; founded 1972
Freshman admissions: least selective; 2018-2019: 263 applied, 263 accepted. Neither SAT nor ACT required. SAT 25/75 percentile: N/A. High school rank: N/A
Early decision deadline: N/A, notification date: N/A
Early action deadline: N/A, notification date: N/A
Application deadline (fall): rolling
Undergraduate student body: 853 full time, 883 part time; 30% male, 70% female; 0% American Indian, 1% Asian, 3% black, 4% Hispanic, 2% multiracial, 0% Pacific Islander, 83% white, 0% international; 80% from in state; 0% live on campus; 0% of students in fraternities, 0% in sororities
Most popular majors: 27% Business, Management, Marketing, and Related Support Services, 15% Health Professions and Related Programs, 15% Multi/Interdisciplinary Studies, 15% Psychology, 9% Education
Expenses: 2019-2020: $9,645 in state, $10,875 out of state; room/board: N/A
Financial aid: (603) 513-1392; 68% of undergrads determined to have financial need; average aid package $7,157

Keene State College

Keene NH
(603) 358-2276
U.S. News ranking: Reg. Coll. (N), No. 10
Website: www.keene.edu
Admissions email: admissions@keene.edu
Public; founded 1909
Freshman admissions: less selective; 2018-2019: 4,958 applied, 4,034 accepted. Neither SAT nor ACT required. SAT 25/75 percentile: 960-1140. High school rank: 6% in top tenth, 19% in top quarter, 54% in top half
Early decision deadline: N/A, notification date: N/A
Early action deadline: N/A, notification date: N/A
Application deadline (fall): 4/1
Undergraduate student body: 3,400 full time, 103 part time; 45% male, 55% female; 0% American Indian, 1% Asian, 2% black, 4% Hispanic, 2% multiracial,

0% Pacific Islander, 85% white, 0% international; 44% from in state; 56% live on campus; 5% of students in fraternities, 7% in sororities
Most popular majors: 13% Engineering Technologies and Engineering-Related Fields, 11% Education, 11% Health Professions and Related Programs, 8% History, 8% Psychology
Expenses: 2019-2020: $14,568 in state, $23,756 out of state; room/board: $11,560
Financial aid: (603) 358-2280; 68% of undergrads determined to have financial need; average aid package $13,125

New England College

Henniker NH
(603) 428-2223
U.S. News ranking: Reg. U. (N), second tier
Website: www.nec.edu
Admissions email: admission@nec.edu
Private; founded 1946
Freshman admissions: least selective; 2018-2019: 8,616 applied, 8,608 accepted. Neither SAT nor ACT required. SAT 25/75 percentile: 870-950. High school rank: 10% in top tenth, 34% in top quarter, 58% in top half
Early decision deadline: N/A, notification date: N/A
Early action deadline: N/A, notification date: N/A
Application deadline (fall): rolling
Undergraduate student body: 1,815 full time, 25 part time; 42% male, 58% female; 1% American Indian, 2% Asian, 24% black, 8% Hispanic, 4% multiracial, 0% Pacific Islander, 51% white, 4% international; 18% from in state; 41% live on campus; 0% of students in fraternities, 0% in sororities
Most popular majors: 32% Business, Management, Marketing, and Related Support Services, 13% Psychology, 10% Health-Related Knowledge and Skills, 10% Homeland Security, Law Enforcement, Firefighting and Related Protective Services, 6% Computer and Information Sciences and Support Services
Expenses: 2019-2020: $39,120; room/board: $14,176
Financial aid: (603) 428-2436; 83% of undergrads determined to have financial need; average aid package $20,100

New Hampshire Institute of Art[1]

Manchester NH
U.S. News ranking: Arts, unranked
Admissions email: N/A
Private
Application deadline (fall): N/A
Undergraduate student body: N/A full time, N/A part time
Expenses: N/A
Financial aid: N/A

Plymouth State University

Plymouth NH
(603) 535-2237
U.S. News ranking: Reg. U. (N), No. 119
Website: www.plymouth.edu
Admissions email: admissions@plymouth.edu
Public; founded 1871
Freshman admissions: less selective; 2018-2019: 6,646 applied, 5,475 accepted. Neither SAT nor ACT required. SAT 25/75 percentile: 815-1203. High school rank: 4% in top tenth, 17% in top quarter, 47% in top half
Early decision deadline: N/A, notification date: N/A
Early action deadline: N/A, notification date: N/A
Application deadline (fall): 4/1
Undergraduate student body: 4,052 full time, 170 part time; 51% male, 49% female; 0% American Indian, 2% Asian, 2% black, 3% Hispanic, 2% multiracial, 0% Pacific Islander, 83% white, 1% international; 53% from in state; 53% live on campus; 1% of students in fraternities, 3% in sororities
Most popular majors: 24% Business, Management, Marketing, and Related Support Services, 12% Education, 8% Homeland Security, Law Enforcement, Firefighting and Related Protective Services, 8% Parks, Recreation, Leisure, and Fitness Studies, 7% Communication, Journalism, and Related Programs
Expenses: 2019-2020: $14,440 in state, $23,330 out of state; room/board: $11,350
Financial aid: (603) 535-2338; 70% of undergrads determined to have financial need; average aid package $13,066

Rivier University[1]

Nashua NH
(603) 888-1311
U.S. News ranking: Reg. U. (N), second tier
Website: rivier.edu
Admissions email: admissions@rivier.edu
Private
Application deadline (fall): rolling
Undergraduate student body: N/A full time, N/A part time
Expenses: N/A
Financial aid: N/A

Southern New Hampshire University

Manchester NH
(603) 645-9611
U.S. News ranking: Reg. U. (N), No. 92
Website: www.snhu.edu
Admissions email: admission@snhu.edu
Private; founded 1932
Freshman admissions: less selective; 2018-2019: 4,402 applied, 3,995 accepted. Neither SAT nor ACT required. SAT 25/75

percentile: 990-1160. High school rank: 10% in top tenth, 23% in top quarter, 55% in top half
Early decision deadline: N/A, notification date: N/A
Early action deadline: 11/15, notification date: 12/15
Application deadline (fall): rolling
Undergraduate student body: 2,887 full time, 234 part time; 50% male, 50% female; 0% American Indian, 2% Asian, 3% black, 4% Hispanic, 2% multiracial, 0% Pacific Islander, 75% white, 6% international; 51% from in state; 59% live on campus; 3% of students in fraternities, 4% in sororities
Most popular majors: 45% Business, Management, Marketing, and Related Support Services, 9% Education, 8% Psychology, 7% Computer and Information Sciences and Support Services, 6% Homeland Security, Law Enforcement, Firefighting and Related Protective Services
Expenses: 2019-2020: $31,136; room/board: $12,800
Financial aid: (877) 455-7648; 73% of undergrads determined to have financial need; average aid package $22,675

St. Anselm College

Manchester NH
(603) 641-7500
U.S. News ranking: Nat. Lib. Arts, No. 114
Website: www.anselm.edu
Admissions email: admission@anselm.edu
Private; founded 1889
Affiliation: Roman Catholic
Freshman admissions: selective; 2018-2019: 3,896 applied, 2,986 accepted. Either SAT or ACT required for some. SAT 25/75 percentile: 1120-1310. High school rank: 27% in top tenth, 55% in top quarter, 83% in top half
Early decision deadline: 12/1, notification date: 1/1
Early action deadline: 11/15, notification date: 1/15
Application deadline (fall): 2/1
Undergraduate student body: 2,019 full time, 31 part time; 39% male, 61% female; 0% American Indian, 1% Asian, 2% black, 4% Hispanic, 2% multiracial, 0% Pacific Islander, 87% white, 1% international; 22% from in state; 91% live on campus; 0% of students in fraternities, 0% in sororities
Most popular majors: 22% Business, Management, Marketing, and Related Support Services, 22% Health Professions and Related Programs, 15% Social Sciences, 7% Communication, Journalism, and Related Programs, 5% Biological and Biomedical Sciences
Expenses: 2019-2020: $41,800; room/board: $14,750
Financial aid: (603) 641-7110; 68% of undergrads determined to have financial need; average aid package $29,735

Thomas More College of Liberal Arts

Merrimack NH
(603) 880-8308
U.S. News ranking: Nat. Lib. Arts, unranked
Website: www.thomasmorecollege.edu
Admissions email: admissions@thomasmorecollege.edu
Private; founded 1978
Affiliation: Roman Catholic
Freshman admissions: least selective; 2018-2019: 73 applied, 73 accepted. Neither SAT nor ACT required. SAT 25/75 percentile: N/A. High school rank: N/A
Early decision deadline: N/A, notification date: N/A
Early action deadline: N/A, notification date: N/A
Application deadline (fall): N/A
Undergraduate student body: 90 full time, 0 part time; 42% male, 58% female; N/A American Indian, N/A Asian, N/A black, N/A Hispanic, N/A multiracial, N/A Pacific Islander, N/A white, N/A international
Most popular majors: Information not available
Expenses: 2019-2020: $21,600; room/board: $9,700
Financial aid: (603) 880-8308

University of New Hampshire

Durham NH
(603) 862-1360
U.S. News ranking: Nat. U., No. 125
Website: www.unh.edu
Admissions email: admissions@unh.edu
Public; founded 1866
Freshman admissions: selective; 2018-2019: 20,096 applied, 15,430 accepted. Either SAT or ACT required. SAT 25/75 percentile: 1090-1280. High school rank: 20% in top tenth, 48% in top quarter, 85% in top half
Early decision deadline: N/A, notification date: N/A
Early action deadline: 11/15, notification date: 1/1
Application deadline (fall): 2/1
Undergraduate student body: 12,477 full time, 302 part time; 45% male, 55% female; 0% American Indian, 3% Asian, 1% black, 3% Hispanic, 2% multiracial, 0% Pacific Islander, 82% white, 4% international; 46% from in state; 56% live on campus; 14% of students in fraternities, 19% in sororities
Most popular majors: 19% Business Administration and Management, General, 8% Psychology, General, 6% Speech Communication and Rhetoric, 4% Biomedical Sciences, General, 4% Parks, Recreation and Leisure Facilities Management, General
Expenses: 2019-2020: $18,879 in state, $35,409 out of state; room/board: $11,942
Financial aid: (603) 862-3600; 68% of undergrads determined to have financial need; average aid package $24,654

NEW JERSEY

Berkeley College
Woodland Park NJ
(800) 446-5400
U.S. News ranking: Reg. Coll. (N),
unranked
Website: berkeleycollege.edu/
Admissions email: admissions@
berkeleycollege.edu
For-profit; founded 1931
Freshman admissions: least
selective; 2018-2019: N/A
applied, N/A accepted. Neither
SAT nor ACT required. SAT 25/75
percentile: N/A. High school
rank: N/A
Early decision deadline: N/A,
notification date: N/A
Early action deadline: N/A,
notification date: N/A
Application deadline (fall): 8/27
Undergraduate student body: 2,431
full time, 893 part time; 28%
male, 72% female; 0% American
Indian, 1% Asian, 18% black,
41% Hispanic, 0% multiracial,
0% Pacific Islander, 11% white,
1% international; 96% from in
state; 0% live on campus; N/A
of students in fraternities, N/A in
sororities
Most popular majors: 24%
Business Administration and
Management, General, 21%
Criminal Justice/Law Enforcement
Administration, 11% Accounting,
11% Health/Health Care
Administration/Management, 10%
Auctioneering
Expenses: 2019-2020: $26,500;
room/board: N/A
Financial aid: (973) 278-5400

Bloomfield College[1]
Bloomfield NJ
(973) 748-9000
U.S. News ranking: Nat. Lib. Arts,
second tier
Website: www.bloomfield.edu
Admissions email:
admission@bloomfield.edu
Private; founded 1868
Affiliation: Presbyterian Church
(USA)
Application deadline (fall): 8/1
Undergraduate student body: N/A
full time, N/A part time
Expenses: 2018-2019: $29,550;
room/board: $11,950
Financial aid: (973) 748-9000

Caldwell University
Caldwell NJ
(973) 618-3600
U.S. News ranking: Reg. U. (N),
No. 75
Website: www.caldwell.edu
Admissions email:
admissions@caldwell.edu
Private; founded 1939
Affiliation: Roman Catholic
Freshman admissions: selective;
2018-2019: 4,456 applied,
2,949 accepted. Either SAT
or ACT required. SAT 25/75
percentile: 960-1145. High
school rank: 7% in top tenth, 29%
in top quarter, 67% in top half
Early decision deadline: N/A,
notification date: N/A
Early action deadline: 12/1,
notification date: 12/31

Application deadline (fall): 4/1
Undergraduate student body: 1,515
full time, 131 part time; 33%
male, 67% female; 0% American
Indian, 3% Asian, 14% black,
27% Hispanic, 2% multiracial,
0% Pacific Islander, 32% white,
12% international; 83% from in
state; 36% live on campus; 1%
of students in fraternities, 4% in
sororities
Most popular majors: 26% Health
Professions and Related Programs,
18% Business, Management,
Marketing, and Related Support
Services, 16% Psychology,
7% Biological and Biomedical
Sciences, 6% Communication,
Journalism, and Related Programs
Expenses: 2019-2020: $35,740;
room/board: $12,415
Financial aid: (973) 618-3221;
79% of undergrads determined to
have financial need; average aid
package $30,301

Centenary University
Hackettstown NJ
(800) 236-8679
U.S. News ranking: Reg. U. (N),
No. 119
Website:
www.centenaryuniversity.edu
Admissions email: admissions@
centenaryuniversity.edu
Private; founded 1867
Affiliation: United Methodist
Freshman admissions: less
selective; 2018-2019: 1,546
applied, 1,033 accepted. Either
SAT or ACT required. SAT 25/75
percentile: 870-1090. High
school rank: N/A
Early decision deadline: N/A,
notification date: N/A
Early action deadline: N/A,
notification date: N/A
Application deadline (fall): 8/15
Undergraduate student body: 1,058
full time, 208 part time; 36%
male, 64% female; 0% American
Indian, 2% Asian, 12% black,
13% Hispanic, 2% multiracial,
0% Pacific Islander, 57% white,
2% international; 85% from in
state; 53% live on campus; 2%
of students in fraternities, 4% in
sororities
Most popular majors: 38%
Business, Management,
Marketing, and Related Support
Services, 10% Visual and
Performing Arts, 7% Agriculture,
Agriculture Operations, and
Related Sciences, 6% Public
Administration and Social Service
Professions, 6% Social Sciences
Expenses: 2018-2019: $32,998;
room/board: $11,444
Financial aid: (908) 852-1400

College of New Jersey
Ewing NJ
(609) 771-2131
U.S. News ranking: Reg. U. (N),
No. 4
Website: www.tcnj.edu
Admissions email:
admiss@tcnj.edu
Public; founded 1855
Freshman admissions: more
selective; 2018-2019: 13,625
applied, 6,785 accepted. Either
SAT or ACT required. SAT 25/75

percentile: 1160-1350. High
school rank: 37% in top tenth,
75% in top quarter, 97% in
top half
Early decision deadline: 11/1,
notification date: 12/1
Early action deadline: N/A,
notification date: N/A
Application deadline (fall): 2/1
Undergraduate student body: 6,823
full time, 225 part time; 43%
male, 57% female; 0% American
Indian, 12% Asian, 6% black,
13% Hispanic, 0% multiracial,
0% Pacific Islander, 64% white,
0% international; 6% from in
state; 54% live on campus; 15%
of students in fraternities, 13%
in sororities
Most popular majors: 20%
Business Administration,
Management and Operations,
16% Teacher Education and
Professional Development,
Specific Levels and Methods,
8% Registered Nursing, Nursing
Administration, Nursing Research
and Clinical Nursing, 7%
Psychology, General, 6% Biology,
General
Expenses: 2019-2020: $16,923
in state, $28,901 out of state;
room/board: $14,048
Financial aid: (609) 771-2211;
52% of undergrads determined to
have financial need; average aid
package $11,321

College of St. Elizabeth[1]
Morristown NJ
(973) 290-4700
U.S. News ranking: Reg. U. (N),
second tier
Website: www.cse.edu
Admissions email: apply@cse.edu
Private; founded 1899
Affiliation: Roman Catholic
Application deadline (fall): rolling
Undergraduate student body: N/A
full time, N/A part time
Expenses: 2018-2019: $33,613;
room/board: $12,744
Financial aid: (973) 290-4393

Drew University
Madison NJ
(973) 408-3739
U.S. News ranking: Nat. Lib. Arts,
No. 117
Website: www.drew.edu
Admissions email: cadm@drew.edu
Private; founded 1867
Affiliation: United Methodist
Freshman admissions: more
selective; 2018-2019: 3,788
applied, 2,622 accepted. Neither
SAT nor ACT required. SAT
25/75 percentile: 1110-1310.
High school rank: 21% in top
tenth, 47% in top quarter, 82%
in top half
Early decision deadline: 11/15,
notification date: 12/15
Early action deadline: 12/15,
notification date: 1/25
Application deadline (fall): 2/1
Undergraduate student body: 1,634
full time, 34 part time; 42%
male, 58% female; 0% American
Indian, 5% Asian, 7% black,
15% Hispanic, 3% multiracial,
0% Pacific Islander, 52% white,

11% international; N/A from in
state; 80% live on campus; N/A
of students in fraternities, N/A in
sororities
Most popular majors: 23%
Social Sciences, 15% Biological
and Biomedical Sciences,
11% Business, Management,
Marketing, and Related Support
Services, 10% Visual and
Performing Arts, 8% Psychology
Expenses: 2019-2020: $40,960;
room/board: $14,672
Financial aid: (973) 408-3112;
70% of undergrads determined to
have financial need; average aid
package $36,295

Fairleigh Dickinson University
Teaneck NJ
(800) 338-8803
U.S. News ranking: Reg. U. (N),
No. 56
Website: www.fdu.edu
Admissions email:
admissions@fdu.edu
Private; founded 1942
Freshman admissions: selective;
2018-2019: 9,541 applied,
8,280 accepted. Either SAT
or ACT required for some. SAT
25/75 percentile: 1030-1210.
High school rank: 15% in top
tenth, 46% in top quarter, 77%
in top half
Early decision deadline: N/A,
notification date: N/A
Early action deadline: N/A,
notification date: N/A
Application deadline (fall): rolling
Undergraduate student body: 4,872
full time, 3,718 part time; 42%
male, 58% female; 0% American
Indian, 5% Asian, 9% black,
31% Hispanic, 2% multiracial,
0% Pacific Islander, 39% white,
3% international; 85% from in
state; 40% live on campus; N/A
of students in fraternities, N/A in
sororities
Most popular majors: 30%
Liberal Arts and Sciences,
General Studies and Humanities,
18% Business, Management,
Marketing, and Related Support
Services, 11% Psychology,
6% Biological and Biomedical
Sciences, 5% Visual and
Performing Arts
Expenses: 2019-2020: $42,775;
room/board: $13,661
Financial aid: (973) 443-8700;
82% of undergrads determined to
have financial need; average aid
package $33,836

Felician University
Lodi NJ
(201) 355-1457
U.S. News ranking: Reg. U. (N),
second tier
Website: www.felician.edu
Admissions email:
admissions@felician.edu
Private; founded 1942
Affiliation: Roman Catholic
Freshman admissions: less
selective; 2018-2019: 2,267
applied, 1,826 accepted. Either
SAT or ACT required. SAT 25/75
percentile: 920-1080. High
school rank: 9% in top tenth, 20%
in top quarter, 58% in top half

Early decision deadline: N/A,
notification date: N/A
Early action deadline: 11/15,
notification date: 12/23
Application deadline (fall): rolling
Undergraduate student body: 1,457
full time, 167 part time; 30%
male, 70% female; 0% American
Indian, 5% Asian, 21% black,
30% Hispanic, 1% multiracial,
1% Pacific Islander, 29% white,
2% international; N/A from in
state; 30% live on campus; 3%
of students in fraternities, 1% in
sororities
Most popular majors: 44% Health
Professions and Related Programs,
18% Business, Management,
Marketing, and Related Support
Services, 8% Biological and
Biomedical Sciences, 7%
Homeland Security, Law
Enforcement, Firefighting and
Related Protective Services, 4%
Multi/Interdisciplinary Studies
Expenses: 2019-2020: $35,000;
room/board: $13,140
Financial aid: (201) 559-6040;
91% of undergrads determined to
have financial need; average aid
package $28,342

Georgian Court University
Lakewood NJ
(800) 458-8422
U.S. News ranking: Reg. U. (N),
No. 108
Website: georgian.edu
Admissions email:
admissions@georgian.edu
Private; founded 1908
Affiliation: Roman Catholic
Freshman admissions: selective;
2018-2019: 2,087 applied,
1,513 accepted. Either SAT
or ACT required. SAT 25/75
percentile: 935-1130. High
school rank: 9% in top tenth, 31%
in top quarter, 65% in top half
Early decision deadline: N/A,
notification date: N/A
Early action deadline: 12/1,
notification date: N/A
Application deadline (fall): 8/1
Undergraduate student body: 1,417
full time, 366 part time; 30%
male, 70% female; 0% American
Indian, 2% Asian, 10% black,
14% Hispanic, 2% multiracial,
0% Pacific Islander, 63% white,
2% international; 93% from in
state; 26% live on campus; N/A
of students in fraternities, N/A in
sororities
Most popular majors: 23%
Psychology, General, 13%
Registered Nursing/Registered
Nurse, 12% Business
Administration and Management,
General, 9% English Language
and Literature, General, 8%
Elementary Education and
Teaching
Expenses: 2019-2020: $33,610;
room/board: $11,200
Financial aid: (732) 987-2258;
84% of undergrads determined to
have financial need; average aid
package $28,852

Kean University

Union NJ
(908) 737-7100
U.S. News ranking: Reg. U. (N), second tier
Website: www.kean.edu
Admissions email: admitme@kean.edu
Public; founded 1855
Freshman admissions: less selective; 2018-2019: 9,082 applied, 7,809 accepted. Either SAT or ACT required. SAT 25/75 percentile: 890-1080. High school rank: N/A
Early decision deadline: N/A, notification date: N/A
Early action deadline: 12/1, notification date: 1/1
Application deadline (fall): 8/15
Undergraduate student body: 9,609 full time, 2,215 part time; 40% male, 60% female; 0% American Indian, 5% Asian, 21% black, 30% Hispanic, 2% multiracial, 0% Pacific Islander, 31% white, 2% international; N/A from in state; 16% live on campus; N/A of students in fraternities, N/A in sororities
Most popular majors: 17% Psychology, General, 7% Biology/Biological Sciences, General, 7% Business Administration and Management, General, 7% Criminal Justice/Law Enforcement Administration, 6% Speech Communication and Rhetoric
Expenses: 2019-2020: $12,595 in state, $19,771 out of state; room/board: $14,802
Financial aid: (908) 737-3190; 75% of undergrads determined to have financial need; average aid package $11,118

Monmouth University

West Long Branch NJ
(800) 543-9671
U.S. News ranking: Reg. U. (N), No. 28
Website: www.monmouth.edu
Admissions email: admission@monmouth.edu
Private; founded 1933
Freshman admissions: selective; 2018-2019: 9,226 applied, 7,105 accepted. Either SAT or ACT required. SAT 25/75 percentile: 1040-1190. High school rank: 20% in top tenth, 42% in top quarter, 77% in top half
Early decision deadline: N/A, notification date: N/A
Early action deadline: 12/1, notification date: 1/15
Application deadline (fall): 3/1
Undergraduate student body: 4,448 full time, 182 part time; 42% male, 58% female; 0% American Indian, 3% Asian, 5% black, 14% Hispanic, 3% multiracial, 0% Pacific Islander, 71% white, 1% international; 83% from in state; 41% live on campus; 14% of students in fraternities, 18% in sororities
Most popular majors: 27% Business, Management, Marketing, and Related Support Services, 11% Health Professions

and Related Programs, 8% Communication, Journalism, and Related Programs, 7% Education, 6% Psychology
Expenses: 2019-2020: $39,592; room/board: $14,734
Financial aid: (732) 571-3463; 73% of undergrads determined to have financial need; average aid package $27,929

Montclair State University

Montclair NJ
(973) 655-4444
U.S. News ranking: Nat. U., No. 166
Website: www.montclair.edu
Admissions email: undergraduate.admissions@montclair.edu
Public; founded 1908
Freshman admissions: selective; 2018-2019: 14,324 applied, 10,157 accepted. Neither SAT nor ACT required. SAT 25/75 percentile: 990-1170. High school rank: 11% in top tenth, 34% in top quarter, 75% in top half
Early decision deadline: N/A, notification date: N/A
Early action deadline: 11/15, notification date: 12/15
Application deadline (fall): 3/1
Undergraduate student body: 15,133 full time, 1,855 part time; 39% male, 61% female; 0% American Indian, 6% Asian, 13% black, 29% Hispanic, 3% multiracial, 0% Pacific Islander, 40% white, 1% international; 97% from in state; 30% live on campus; N/A of students in fraternities, N/A in sororities
Most popular majors: 20% Business, Management, Marketing, and Related Support Services, 11% Family and Consumer Sciences/Human Sciences, 11% Psychology, 11% Visual and Performing Arts, 6% Social Sciences
Expenses: 2019-2020: $13,073 in state, $21,033 out of state; room/board: $15,674
Financial aid: (973) 655-7020; 73% of undergrads determined to have financial need; average aid package $10,297

New Jersey City University

Jersey City NJ
(888) 441-6528
U.S. News ranking: Reg. U. (N), second tier
Website: www.njcu.edu/
Admissions email: admissions@njcu.edu
Public; founded 1927
Freshman admissions: least selective; 2018-2019: 4,315 applied, 4,136 accepted. Either SAT or ACT required. SAT 25/75 percentile: 850-1060. High school rank: 9% in top tenth, 25% in top quarter, 57% in top half
Early decision deadline: N/A, notification date: N/A
Early action deadline: N/A, notification date: N/A
Undergraduate student body: 5,087 full time, 1,144 part time; 41% male, 59% female; 0% American

Indian, 8% Asian, 23% black, 40% Hispanic, 2% multiracial, 1% Pacific Islander, 20% white, 1% international; 99% from in state; 9% live on campus; N/A of students in fraternities, N/A in sororities
Most popular majors: 20% Registered Nursing/Registered Nurse, 10% Psychology, General, 8% Criminal Justice/Safety Studies, 7% Business Administration and Management, General, 6% Homeland Security, Other
Expenses: 2019-2020: $12,414 in state, $22,220 out of state; room/board: $14,574
Financial aid: (201) 200-3171; 87% of undergrads determined to have financial need; average aid package $11,241

New Jersey Institute of Technology

Newark NJ
(973) 596-3300
U.S. News ranking: Nat. U., No. 97
Website: www.njit.edu
Admissions email: admissions@njit.edu
Public; founded 1881
Freshman admissions: more selective; 2018-2019: 8,123 applied, 5,171 accepted. Either SAT or ACT required. SAT 25/75 percentile: 1190-1380. High school rank: 36% in top tenth, 63% in top quarter, 91% in top half
Early decision deadline: N/A, notification date: N/A
Early action deadline: 11/11, notification date: 12/16
Application deadline (fall): 3/1
Undergraduate student body: 6,827 full time, 1,705 part time; 75% male, 25% female; 0% American Indian, 23% Asian, 8% black, 22% Hispanic, 3% multiracial, 0% Pacific Islander, 34% white, 5% international; 96% from in state; 24% live on campus; 5% of students in fraternities, 2% in sororities
Most popular majors: 22% Computer and Information Sciences and Support Services, 13% Engineering Technologies and Engineering-Related Fields, 6% Architecture and Related Services, 6% Biological and Biomedical Sciences, 5% Business, Management, Marketing, and Related Support Services
Expenses: 2019-2020: $17,338 in state, $32,750 out of state; room/board: $13,600
Financial aid: (973) 596-3476; 70% of undergrads determined to have financial need; average aid package $13,930

Princeton University

Princeton NJ
(609) 258-3060
U.S. News ranking: Nat. U., No. 1
Website: www.princeton.edu
Admissions email: uaoffice@princeton.edu
Private; founded 1746

Freshman admissions: most selective; 2018-2019: 35,370 applied, 1,940 accepted. Either SAT or ACT required. SAT 25/75 percentile: 1440-1570. High school rank: N/A
Early decision deadline: N/A, notification date: N/A
Early action deadline: 11/1, notification date: 12/15
Application deadline (fall): 1/1
Undergraduate student body: 5,321 full time, 107 part time; 51% male, 49% female; 0% American Indian, 21% Asian, 8% black, 10% Hispanic, 5% multiracial, 0% Pacific Islander, 42% white, 12% international; 18% from in state; 94% live on campus; N/A of students in fraternities, N/A in sororities
Most popular majors: 18% Social Sciences, 17% Engineering, 13% Computer and Information Sciences and Support Services, 10% Biological and Biomedical Sciences, 9% Public Administration and Social Service Professions
Expenses: 2019-2020: $51,870; room/board: $17,150
Financial aid: (609) 258-3330; 61% of undergrads determined to have financial need; average aid package $55,602

Ramapo College of New Jersey

Mahwah NJ
(201) 684-7300
U.S. News ranking: Reg. U. (N), No. 32
Website: www.ramapo.edu
Admissions email: admissions@ramapo.edu
Public; founded 1969
Freshman admissions: selective; 2018-2019: 6,945 applied, 4,368 accepted. Either SAT or ACT required. SAT 25/75 percentile: 1050-1230. High school rank: 15% in top tenth, 39% in top quarter, 76% in top half
Early decision deadline: 11/1, notification date: 12/5
Early action deadline: N/A, notification date: N/A
Application deadline (fall): 2/1
Undergraduate student body: 4,821 full time, 788 part time; 44% male, 56% female; 1% American Indian, 8% Asian, 5% black, 18% Hispanic, 0% multiracial, 0% Pacific Islander, 62% white, 2% international; 95% from in state; 45% live on campus; 6% of students in fraternities, 4% in sororities
Most popular majors: 17% Business, Management, Marketing, and Related Support Services, 12% Psychology, 9% Communication, Journalism, and Related Programs, 7% Biological and Biomedical Sciences, 6% Health Professions and Related Programs
Expenses: 2019-2020: $14,769 in state, $24,367 out of state; room/board: $12,792
Financial aid: (201) 684-7549; 56% of undergrads determined to have financial need; average aid package $11,032

Rider University

Lawrenceville NJ
(609) 896-5042
U.S. News ranking: Reg. U. (N), No. 38
Website: www.rider.edu
Admissions email: admissions@rider.edu
Private; founded 1865
Freshman admissions: selective; 2018-2019: 9,429 applied, 6,569 accepted. Either SAT or ACT required. SAT 25/75 percentile: 1000-1190. High school rank: 15% in top tenth, 38% in top quarter, 71% in top half
Early decision deadline: N/A, notification date: N/A
Early action deadline: 11/15, notification date: 12/15
Application deadline (fall): rolling
Undergraduate student body: 3,534 full time, 364 part time; 42% male, 58% female; 0% American Indian, 5% Asian, 13% black, 16% Hispanic, 4% multiracial, 0% Pacific Islander, 58% white, 3% international
Most popular majors: 33% Business Administration and Management, General, 12% Education, General, 12% Visual and Performing Arts, General, 9% Communication, Journalism, and Related Programs, 8% Psychology, General
Expenses: 2019-2020: $42,860; room/board: $15,280
Financial aid: (609) 896-5188; 78% of undergrads determined to have financial need; average aid package $32,185

Rowan University

Glassboro NJ
(856) 256-4200
U.S. News ranking: Nat. U., No. 166
Website: www.rowan.edu
Admissions email: admissions@rowan.edu
Public; founded 1923
Freshman admissions: selective; 2018-2019: 13,993 applied, 10,194 accepted. Either SAT or ACT required. SAT 25/75 percentile: 1005-1225. High school rank: N/A
Early decision deadline: N/A, notification date: N/A
Early action deadline: N/A, notification date: N/A
Application deadline (fall): 3/1
Undergraduate student body: 14,043 full time, 2,077 part time; 55% male, 45% female; 0% American Indian, 5% Asian, 10% black, 10% Hispanic, 4% multiracial, 0% Pacific Islander, 66% white, 1% international; 94% from in state; 63% live on campus; 3% of students in fraternities, 4% in sororities
Most popular majors: 18% Business, Management, Marketing, and Related Support Services, 9% Engineering, 9% Psychology, 8% Education, 7% Communication, Journalism, and Related Programs
Expenses: 2019-2020: $14,000 in state, $22,832 out of state; room/board: $12,904

Financial aid: (856) 256-4281; 68% of undergrads determined to have financial need; average aid package $10,308

Rutgers University–Camden

Camden NJ
(856) 225-6104
U.S. News ranking: Nat. U., No. 166
Website: www.camden.rutgers.edu/
Admissions email: admissions@camden.rutgers.edu
Public; founded 1926
Freshman admissions: selective; 2018-2019: 9,479 applied, 6,766 accepted. Either SAT or ACT required. SAT 25/75 percentile: 1000-1180. High school rank: 15% in top tenth, 43% in top quarter, 80% in top half
Early decision deadline: N/A, notification date: N/A
Early action deadline: 11/1, notification date: 1/31
Application deadline (fall): rolling
Undergraduate student body: 4,764 full time, 1,012 part time; 39% male, 61% female; 0% American Indian, 10% Asian, 19% black, 17% Hispanic, 4% multiracial, 0% Pacific Islander, 46% white, 2% international; N/A from in state; 17% live on campus; N/A of students in fraternities, N/A in sororities
Most popular majors: 18% Registered Nursing/Registered Nurse, 13% Business Administration and Management, 8% Psychology, General, 7% Criminal Justice/Safety Studies, 6% Accounting
Expenses: 2019-2020: $15,264 in state, $31,500 out of state; room/board: $12,691
Financial aid: (856) 225-6039; 82% of undergrads determined to have financial need; average aid package $15,120

Rutgers University–Newark

Newark NJ
(973) 353-5205
U.S. News ranking: Nat. U., No. 132
Website: www.newark.rutgers.edu/
Admissions email: newark@admissions.rutgers.edu
Public; founded 1908
Freshman admissions: selective; 2018-2019: 13,259 applied, 8,319 accepted. Either SAT or ACT required. SAT 25/75 percentile: 1020-1190. High school rank: 22% in top tenth, 48% in top quarter, 84% in top half
Early decision deadline: N/A, notification date: N/A
Early action deadline: 11/1, notification date: 1/31
Application deadline (fall): rolling
Undergraduate student body: 7,726 full time, 1,416 part time; 45% male, 55% female; 0% American Indian, 18% Asian, 20% black, 29% Hispanic, 3% multiracial, 0% Pacific Islander, 22% white, 6% international; N/A from in

state; 17% live on campus; N/A of students in fraternities, N/A in sororities
Most popular majors: 13% Accounting, 13% Psychology, General, 11% Criminal Justice/Safety Studies, 9% Finance, General, 8% Biology/Biological Sciences, General
Expenses: 2019-2020: $14,826 in state, $31,608 out of state; room/board: $13,929
Financial aid: (973) 353-5151; 80% of undergrads determined to have financial need; average aid package $14,692

Rutgers University– New Brunswick

Piscataway NJ
(732) 445-4636
U.S. News ranking: Nat. U., No. 62
Website: newbrunswick.rutgers.edu
Admissions email: admissions@ugadm.rutgers.edu
Public; founded 1766
Freshman admissions: more selective; 2018-2019: 41,348 applied, 24,854 accepted. Either SAT or ACT required. SAT 25/75 percentile: 1190-1410. High school rank: 38% in top tenth, 72% in top quarter, 95% in top half
Early decision deadline: N/A, notification date: N/A
Early action deadline: 11/1, notification date: 1/31
Application deadline (fall): rolling
Undergraduate student body: 34,052 full time, 1,987 part time; 50% male, 50% female; 0% American Indian, 28% Asian, 7% black, 13% Hispanic, 4% multiracial, 0% Pacific Islander, 38% white, 9% international; N/A from in state; 43% live on campus; N/A of students in fraternities, N/A in sororities
Most popular majors: 6% Psychology, General, 4% Biology/ Biological Sciences, General, 4% Computer and Information Sciences, General, 4% Economics, General, 4% Information Science/ Studies
Expenses: 2019-2020: $15,407 in state, $32,189 out of state; room/board: $13,075
Financial aid: (848) 932-2695; 54% of undergrads determined to have financial need, average aid package $13,999

Saint Peter's University

Jersey City NJ
(201) 761-7100
U.S. News ranking: Reg. U. (N), No. 86
Website: www.saintpeters.edu
Admissions email: admissions@saintpeters.edu
Private; founded 1872
Affiliation: Roman Catholic
Freshman admissions: selective; 2018-2019: 4,040 applied, 2,999 accepted. Either SAT or ACT required for some. SAT 25/75 percentile: 940-1120. High school rank: 14% in top tenth, 42% in top quarter, 73% in top half

Early decision deadline: N/A, notification date: N/A
Early action deadline: 12/15, notification date: 1/30
Application deadline (fall): rolling
Undergraduate student body: 2,353 full time, 288 part time; 36% male, 64% female; 0% American Indian, 8% Asian, 21% black, 46% Hispanic, 2% multiracial, 0% Pacific Islander, 14% white, 3% international; N/A from in state; 30% live on campus; 0% of students in fraternities, 0% in sororities
Most popular majors: 27% Business, Management, Marketing, and Related Support Services, 12% Biological and Biomedical Sciences, 10% Homeland Security, Law Enforcement, Firefighting and Related Protective Services, 9% Health Professions and Related Programs, 8% Psychology
Expenses: 2019-2020: $38,700; room/board: $15,950
Financial aid: (201) 761-6060; 91% of undergrads determined to have financial need; average aid package $35,098

Seton Hall University

South Orange NJ
(800) 843-4255
U.S. News ranking: Nat. U., No. 139
Website: www.shu.edu
Admissions email: thehall@shu.edu
Private; founded 1856
Affiliation: Roman Catholic
Freshman admissions: more selective; 2018-2019: 19,260 applied, 13,552 accepted. Either SAT or ACT required. SAT 25/75 percentile: 1150-1310. High school rank: 29% in top tenth, 61% in top quarter, 88% in top half
Early decision deadline: N/A, notification date: N/A
Early action deadline: 12/15, notification date: 1/31
Application deadline (fall): rolling
Undergraduate student body: 5,777 full time, 359 part time; 47% male, 53% female; 0% American Indian, 10% Asian, 8% black, 17% Hispanic, 4% multiracial, 0% Pacific Islander, 49% white, 4% international
Most popular majors: 14% Biology/ Biological Sciences, General, 10% Humanities/Humanistic Studies, 10% Registered Nursing/ Registered Nurse, 6% Finance, General, 5% Marketing/Marketing Management, General
Expenses: 2019-2020: $43,780; room/board: $14,924
Financial aid: (973) 761-9350

Stevens Institute of Technology

Hoboken NJ
(201) 216-5194
U.S. News ranking: Nat. U., No. 74
Website: www.stevens.edu
Admissions email: admissions@stevens.edu
Private; founded 1870

Freshman admissions: most selective; 2018-2019: 9,265 applied, 3,838 accepted. Either SAT or ACT required for some. SAT 25/75 percentile: 1330-1480. High school rank: 72% in top tenth, 96% in top quarter, 100% in top half
Early decision deadline: 11/15, notification date: 12/15
Early action deadline: N/A, notification date: N/A
Application deadline (fall): 1/15
Undergraduate student body: 3,197 full time, 33 part time; 70% male, 30% female; 0% American Indian, 15% Asian, 2% black, 11% Hispanic, 0% multiracial, 0% Pacific Islander, 64% white, 4% international; 62% from in state; 60% live on campus; 29% of students in fraternities, 42% in sororities
Most popular majors: 23% Mechanical Engineering, 11% Computer Science, 9% Bioengineering and Biomedical Engineering, 9% Business Administration and Management, General, 9% Chemical Engineering
Expenses: 2019-2020: $54,014; room/board: $15,770
Financial aid: (201) 216-3400; 64% of undergrads determined to have financial need; average aid package $31,859

Stockton University

Galloway NJ
(609) 652-4261
U.S. News ranking: Reg. U. (N), No. 32
Website: www.stockton.edu
Admissions email: admissions@stockton.edu
Public; founded 1969
Freshman admissions: selective; 2018-2019: 6,084 applied, 5,133 accepted. Either SAT or ACT required. SAT 25/75 percentile: 1000-1190. High school rank: 18% in top tenth, 44% in top quarter, 77% in top half
Early decision deadline: N/A, notification date: N/A
Early action deadline: N/A, notification date: N/A
Application deadline (fall): 5/1
Undergraduate student body: 8,136 full time, 468 part time; 42% male, 58% female; 0% American Indian, 6% Asian, 8% black, 14% Hispanic, 2% multiracial, 0% Pacific Islander, 67% white, 1% international; 98% from in state; 37% live on campus; 8% of students in fraternities, 8% in sororities
Most popular majors: 17% Business Administration and Management, General, 14% Health Professions and Related Programs, 10% Psychology, General, 8% Biology/Biological Sciences, General, 8% Criminology
Expenses: 2018-2019: $13,739 in state, $20,866 out of state; room/board: $12,282
Financial aid: (609) 652-4203; 73% of undergrads determined to have financial need; average aid package $17,064

Thomas Edison State University

Trenton NJ
(609) 777-5680
U.S. News ranking: Reg. U. (N), unranked
Website: www.tesu.edu
Admissions email: admissions@tesu.edu
Public; founded 1972
Freshman admissions: least selective; 2018-2019: N/A applied, N/A accepted. Neither SAT nor ACT required. SAT 25/75 percentile: N/A. High school rank: N/A
Early decision deadline: N/A, notification date: N/A
Early action deadline: N/A, notification date: N/A
Application deadline (fall): rolling
Undergraduate student body: 76 full time, 14,201 part time; 58% male, 42% female; 1% American Indian, 4% Asian, 14% black, 11% Hispanic, 2% multiracial, 1% Pacific Islander, 51% white, 1% international
Most popular majors: Information not available
Expenses: 2018-2019: $7,519 in state, $9,967 out of state; room/ board: N/A
Financial aid: (609) 633-9658

William Paterson University of New Jersey

Wayne NJ
(973) 720-2125
U.S. News ranking: Reg. U. (N), No. 94
Website: www.wpunj.edu/
Admissions email: admissions@wpunj.edu
Public; founded 1855
Freshman admissions: less selective; 2018-2019: 8,150 applied, 7,606 accepted. Either SAT or ACT required for some. SAT 25/75 percentile: 890-1090. High school rank: N/A
Early decision deadline: N/A, notification date: N/A
Early action deadline: N/A, notification date: N/A
Application deadline (fall): 6/1
Undergraduate student body: 7,269 full time, 1,461 part time; 45% male, 55% female; 0% American Indian, 7% Asian, 19% black, 32% Hispanic, 3% multiracial, 0% Pacific Islander, 37% white, 0% international; 98% from in state; 25% live on campus; 1% of students in fraternities, 2% in sororities
Most popular majors: 19% Business, Management, Marketing, and Related Support Services, 10% Communication, Journalism, and Related Programs, 10% Psychology, 8% Homeland Security, Law Enforcement, Firefighting and Related Protective Services, 8% Social Sciences
Expenses: 2019-2020: $13,370 in state, $21,768 out of state; room/board: $11,900
Financial aid: (973) 720-3945; 77% of undergrads determined to have financial need; average aid package $11,517

NEW MEXICO

Eastern New Mexico University
Portales NM
(575) 562-2178
U.S. News ranking: Reg. U. (W), second tier
Website: www.enmu.edu
Admissions email: admissions.office@enmu.edu
Public; founded 1934
Freshman admissions: less selective; 2018-2019: 2,645 applied, 1,597 accepted. Either SAT or ACT required. ACT 25/75 percentile: 17-22. High school rank: 11% in top tenth, 32% in top quarter, 67% in top half
Early decision deadline: N/A, notification date: N/A
Early action deadline: N/A, notification date: N/A
Application deadline (fall): rolling
Undergraduate student body: 2,488 full time, 2,218 part time; 45% male, 55% female; 2% American Indian, 1% Asian, 6% black, 41% Hispanic, 3% multiracial, 1% Pacific Islander, 42% white, 2% international; 72% from in state; 18% live on campus; 8% of students in fraternities, 4% in sororities
Most popular majors: 13% General Studies, 9% Audiology/Audiologist and Speech-Language Pathology/Pathologist, 9% Liberal Arts and Sciences/Liberal Studies, 6% Criminal Justice/Safety Studies, 6% Registered Nursing/Registered Nurse
Expenses: 2019-2020: $6,450 in state, $8,448 out of state; room/board: $7,300
Financial aid: (575) 562-2708; 70% of undergrads determined to have financial need; average aid package $12,215

New Mexico Highlands University[7]
Las Vegas NM
(505) 454-3434
U.S. News ranking: Reg. U. (W), unranked
Website: www.nmhu.edu
Admissions email: admissions@nmhu.edu
Public; founded 1893
Freshman admissions: less selective; 2018-2019: 1,322 applied, 842 accepted. Neither SAT nor ACT required. ACT 25/75 percentile: 18-19. High school rank: 4% in top tenth, 15% in top quarter, 42% in top half
Early decision deadline: N/A, notification date: N/A
Early action deadline: N/A, notification date: N/A
Application deadline (fall): rolling
Undergraduate student body: 1,245 full time, 679 part time
Most popular majors: 34% Health Professions and Related Programs, 20% Education, 14% Business, Management, Marketing, and Related Support Services, 7% Psychology, 4% Biological and Biomedical Sciences

Expenses: 2019-2020: $6,278 in state, $10,590 out of state; room/board: $8,126
Financial aid: (505) 454-3430; 73% of undergrads determined to have financial need; average aid package $9,706

New Mexico Institute of Mining and Technology
Socorro NM
(575) 835-5424
U.S. News ranking: Reg. U. (W), No. 22
Website: www.nmt.edu
Admissions email: Admission@nmt.edu
Public; founded 1889
Freshman admissions: more selective; 2018-2019: 1,740 applied, 403 accepted. Either SAT or ACT required. ACT 25/75 percentile: 23-29. High school rank: 40% in top tenth, 68% in top quarter, 92% in top half
Early decision deadline: N/A, notification date: N/A
Early action deadline: N/A, notification date: N/A
Application deadline (fall): 8/1
Undergraduate student body: 1,269 full time, 143 part time; 70% male, 30% female; 4% American Indian, 3% Asian, 2% black, 32% Hispanic, 4% multiracial, 0% Pacific Islander, 52% white, 2% international; 90% from in state; 50% live on campus; 0% of students in fraternities, 0% in sororities
Most popular majors: 22% Mechanical Engineering, 16% Petroleum Engineering, 8% Chemical Engineering, 7% Computer and Information Sciences, General, 6% Electrical and Electronics Engineering
Expenses: 2019-2020: $8,156 in state, $23,524 out of state; room/board: $8,624
Financial aid: (575) 835-5333; 55% of undergrads determined to have financial need; average aid package $13,069

New Mexico State University
Las Cruces NM
(575) 646-3121
U.S. News ranking: Nat. U., No. 263
Website: www.nmsu.edu
Admissions email: admissions@nmsu.edu
Public; founded 1888
Freshman admissions: selective; 2018-2019: 9,635 applied, 6,326 accepted. Either SAT or ACT required. ACT 25/75 percentile: 17-23. High school rank: 22% in top tenth, 52% in top quarter, 84% in top half
Early decision deadline: N/A, notification date: N/A
Early action deadline: N/A, notification date: N/A
Application deadline (fall): rolling
Undergraduate student body: 9,712 full time, 1,975 part time; 45% male, 55% female; 2% American

Indian, 1% Asian, 2% black, 61% Hispanic, 2% multiracial, 0% Pacific Islander, 26% white, 4% international; 74% from in state; 22% live on campus; 3% of students in fraternities, 2% in sororities
Most popular majors: 17% Business, Management, Marketing, and Related Support Services, 12% Engineering, 10% Health Professions and Related Programs, 7% Liberal Arts and Sciences, General Studies and Humanities, 6% Education
Expenses: 2019-2020: $7,809 in state, $24,917 out of state; room/board: $9,538
Financial aid: (575) 646-4105; 70% of undergrads determined to have financial need; average aid package $15,477

Northern New Mexico College[1]
Espanola NM
(505) 747-2100
U.S. News ranking: Reg. Coll. (W), unranked
Website: www.nnmc.edu
Admissions email: N/A
Public
Application deadline (fall): N/A
Undergraduate student body: N/A full time, N/A part time
Expenses: N/A
Financial aid: N/A

St. John's College
Santa Fe NM
(505) 984-6060
U.S. News ranking: Nat. Lib. Arts, No. 72
Website: www.sjc.edu
Admissions email: santafe.admissions@sjc.edu
Private; founded 1696
Freshman admissions: more selective; 2018-2019: 358 applied, 240 accepted. Either SAT or ACT required for some. SAT 25/75 percentile: 1200-1410. High school rank: 27% in top tenth, 50% in top quarter, 73% in top half
Early decision deadline: 11/1, notification date: 12/1
Early action deadline: 11/15, notification date: 12/15
Application deadline (fall): rolling
Undergraduate student body: 306 full time, 14 part time; 56% male, 44% female; 0% American Indian, 3% Asian, 0% black, 13% Hispanic, 6% multiracial, 0% Pacific Islander, 53% white, 23% international; 13% from in state; 81% live on campus; 0% of students in fraternities, 0% in sororities
Most popular majors: 100% Liberal Arts and Sciences/Liberal Studies
Expenses: 2019-2020: $36,410; room/board: $12,860
Financial aid: (505) 984-6058; 94% of undergrads determined to have financial need; average aid package $46,357

University of New Mexico
Albuquerque NM
(505) 277-8900
U.S. News ranking: Nat. U., No. 218
Website: www.unm.edu
Admissions email: apply@unm.edu
Public; founded 1889
Freshman admissions: selective; 2018-2019: 10,912 applied, 5,629 accepted. Either SAT or ACT required. ACT 25/75 percentile: 19-25. High school rank: N/A
Early decision deadline: N/A, notification date: N/A
Early action deadline: N/A, notification date: N/A
Application deadline (fall): rolling
Undergraduate student body: 13,591 full time, 4,268 part time; 44% male, 56% female; 6% American Indian, 4% Asian, 2% black, 49% Hispanic, 3% multiracial, 0% Pacific Islander, 32% white, 2% international; N/A from in state; 9% live on campus; 5% of students in fraternities, 6% in sororities
Most popular majors: 16% Business, Management, Marketing, and Related Support Services, 11% Health Professions and Related Programs, 11% Psychology, 7% Biological and Biomedical Sciences, 7% Social Sciences
Expenses: 2019-2020: $7,322 in state, $24,490 out of state; room/board: $9,864
Financial aid: (505) 277-8900; 87% of undergrads determined to have financial need

University of the Southwest[1]
Hobbs NM
(575) 392-6563
U.S. News ranking: Reg. U. (W), second tier
Website: www.usw.edu
Admissions email: admissions@usw.edu
Private; founded 1962
Application deadline (fall): rolling
Undergraduate student body: N/A full time, N/A part time
Expenses: N/A
Financial aid: N/A

Western New Mexico University[1]
Silver City NM
(575) 538-6011
U.S. News ranking: Reg. U. (W), unranked
Website: www.wnmu.edu
Admissions email: admissions@wnmu.edu
Public; founded 1893
Application deadline (fall): N/A
Undergraduate student body: N/A full time, N/A part time
Expenses: N/A
Financial aid: N/A

NEW YORK

Adelphi University
Garden City NY
(800) 233-5744
U.S. News ranking: Nat. U., No. 166
Website: www.adelphi.edu
Admissions email: admissions@adelphi.edu
Private; founded 1896
Freshman admissions: selective; 2018-2019: 13,006 applied, 9,649 accepted. Either SAT or ACT required for some. SAT 25/75 percentile: 1080-1270. High school rank: 26% in top tenth, 59% in top quarter, 89% in top half
Early decision deadline: N/A, notification date: N/A
Early action deadline: 12/1, notification date: 12/31
Application deadline (fall): rolling
Undergraduate student body: 5,056 full time, 335 part time; 32% male, 68% female; 0% American Indian, 11% Asian, 9% black, 18% Hispanic, 2% multiracial, 0% Pacific Islander, 50% white, 3% international; 90% from in state; 22% live on campus; 10% of students in fraternities, 13% in sororities
Most popular majors: 34% Registered Nursing/Registered Nurse, 6% Biology/Biological Sciences, General, 6% Business Administration and Management, General, 5% Psychology, General, 3% Communication and Media Studies, Other
Expenses: 2018-2019: $38,660; room/board: $16,030
Financial aid: (516) 877-3080; 68% of undergrads determined to have financial need; average aid package $22,900

Alfred University
Alfred NY
(800) 541-9229
U.S. News ranking: Reg. U. (N), No. 38
Website: www.alfred.edu
Admissions email: admissions@alfred.edu
Private; founded 1836
Freshman admissions: selective; 2018-2019: 4,296 applied, 2,693 accepted. Either SAT or ACT required. SAT 25/75 percentile: 970-1200. High school rank: 13% in top tenth, 34% in top quarter, 67% in top half
Early decision deadline: 12/1, notification date: N/A
Early action deadline: N/A, notification date: N/A
Application deadline (fall): rolling
Undergraduate student body: 1,572 full time, 99 part time; 50% male, 50% female; 0% American Indian, 1% Asian, 11% black, 9% Hispanic, 3% multiracial, 0% Pacific Islander, 62% white, 3% international; 79% from in state; 71% live on campus; 0% of students in fraternities, 0% in sororities
Most popular majors: 18% Fine/Studio Arts, General, 13% Mechanical Engineering, 12%

Psychology, General, 7% Business Administration and Management, General, 6% Elementary Education and Teaching
Expenses: 2019-2020: $34,770; room/board: $12,718
Financial aid: (607) 871-2150; 83% of undergrads determined to have financial need; average aid package $29,512

Bard College
Annandale on Hudson NY
(845) 758-7472
U.S. News ranking: Nat. Lib. Arts, No. 62
Website: www.bard.edu
Admissions email: admissions@bard.edu
Private; founded 1860
Freshman admissions: more selective; 2018-2019: 5,141 applied, 3,319 accepted. Neither SAT nor ACT required. SAT 25/75 percentile: 1248-1420. High school rank: 41% in top tenth, 69% in top quarter, 94% in top half
Early decision deadline: 11/1, notification date: 1/1
Early action deadline: 11/1, notification date: 1/1
Application deadline (fall): 1/1
Undergraduate student body: 1,828 full time, 65 part time; 40% male, 60% female; 0% American Indian, 4% Asian, 6% black, 10% Hispanic, 5% multiracial, 0% Pacific Islander, 57% white, 11% international
Most popular majors: 32% Social Sciences, 30% Visual and Performing Arts, 19% English Language and Literature/Letters, 19% Multi/Interdisciplinary Studies
Expenses: 2019-2020: $56,036; room/board: $15,876
Financial aid: (845) 758-7526; 72% of undergrads determined to have financial need; average aid package $48,432

Barnard College
New York NY
(212) 854-2014
U.S. News ranking: Nat. Lib. Arts, No. 25
Website: www.barnard.edu
Admissions email: admissions@barnard.edu
Private; founded 1889
Freshman admissions: most selective; 2018-2019: 7,897 applied, 1,099 accepted. Either SAT or ACT required. SAT 25/75 percentile: 1330-1500. High school rank: 84% in top tenth, 97% in top quarter, 100% in top half
Early decision deadline: 11/1, notification date: 12/15
Early action deadline: N/A, notification date: N/A
Application deadline (fall): 1/1
Undergraduate student body: 2,519 full time, 43 part time; 0% male, 100% female; 0% American Indian, 15% Asian, 6% black, 12% Hispanic, 6% multiracial, 0% Pacific Islander, 52% white, 10% international; 72% from in state; 91% live on campus; N/A of students in fraternities, N/A in sororities

Most popular majors: 32% Social Sciences, 11% Biological and Biomedical Sciences, 10% Psychology, 9% English Language and Literature/Letters, 9% Visual and Performing Arts
Expenses: 2019-2020: $57,668; room/board: $17,856
Financial aid: (212) 854-2154; 38% of undergrads determined to have financial need; average aid package $53,297

Berkeley College
New York NY
(800) 446-5400
U.S. News ranking: Business, unranked
Website: www.berkeleycollege.edu
Admissions email: admissions@berkeleycollege.edu
For-profit; founded 1931
Freshman admissions: least selective; 2018-2019: N/A applied, N/A accepted. Neither SAT nor ACT required. SAT 25/75 percentile: N/A. High school rank: N/A
Early decision deadline: N/A, notification date: N/A
Early action deadline: N/A, notification date: N/A
Application deadline (fall): 8/27
Undergraduate student body: 2,834 full time, 862 part time; 36% male, 64% female; 0% American Indian, 3% Asian, 23% black, 23% Hispanic, 0% multiracial, 0% Pacific Islander, 5% white, 9% international; 80% from in state; 4% live on campus; N/A of students in fraternities, N/A in sororities
Most popular majors: 24% Business Administration and Management, General, 17% Criminal Justice/Law Enforcement Administration, 15% Fashion Merchandising, 12% Health/Health Care Administration/Management, 8% Accounting
Expenses: 2019-2020: $26,500; room/board: $9,400
Financial aid: (212) 986-4343

Binghamton University–SUNY
Binghamton NY
(607) 777-2171
U.S. News ranking: Nat. U., No. 79
Website: www.binghamton.edu
Admissions email: admit@binghamton.edu
Public; founded 1946
Freshman admissions: more selective; 2018-2019: 38,755 applied, 15,429 accepted. Either SAT or ACT required. SAT 25/75 percentile: 1310-1440. High school rank: 54% in top tenth, 86% in top quarter, 98% in top half
Early decision deadline: N/A, notification date: N/A
Early action deadline: 11/1, notification date: 1/15
Application deadline (fall): rolling
Undergraduate student body: 13,630 full time, 391 part time; 50% male, 50% female; 0% American Indian, 14% Asian, 5% black, 11% Hispanic, 2% multiracial, 0% Pacific Islander,

57% white, 8% international; 88% from in state; 50% live on campus; 14% of students in fraternities, 11% in sororities
Most popular majors: 8% Psychology, General, 7% Neuroscience, 6% Biology/Biological Sciences, General, 6% Economics, General, 5% Registered Nursing/Registered Nurse
Expenses: 2019-2020: $10,201 in state, $27,791 out of state; room/board: $16,068
Financial aid: (607) 777-6358; 52% of undergrads determined to have financial need; average aid package $14,129

Boricua College[7]
New York NY
(212) 694-1000
U.S. News ranking: Reg. Coll. (N), unranked
Website: www.boricuacollege.edu/
Admissions email: isanchez@boricuacollege.edu
Private; founded 1973
Freshman admissions: least selective; 2018-2019: N/A applied, N/A accepted. Neither SAT nor ACT required. SAT 25/75 percentile: N/A. High school rank: N/A
Early decision deadline: N/A, notification date: N/A
Early action deadline: N/A, notification date: N/A
Application deadline (fall): rolling
Undergraduate student body: 639 full time, 0 part time
Most popular majors: Information not available
Expenses: 2018-2019: $11,025; room/board: N/A
Financial aid: N/A

Canisius College
Buffalo NY
(800) 843-1517
U.S. News ranking: Reg. U. (N), No. 19
Website: www.canisius.edu
Admissions email: admissions@canisius.edu
Private; founded 1870
Affiliation: Roman Catholic
Freshman admissions: selective; 2018-2019: 3,549 applied, 2,793 accepted. Either SAT or ACT required. SAT 25/75 percentile: 1050-1270. High school rank: 20% in top tenth, 45% in top quarter, 73% in top half
Early decision deadline: N/A, notification date: N/A
Early action deadline: 11/1, notification date: 12/15
Application deadline (fall): rolling
Undergraduate student body: 2,166 full time, 90 part time; 52% male, 48% female; 0% American Indian, 3% Asian, 9% black, 6% Hispanic, 2% multiracial, 0% Pacific Islander, 73% white, 4% international; 89% from in state; 42% live on campus; 1% of students in fraternities, 1% in sororities
Most popular majors: 38% Business, Management, Marketing, and Related Support Services, 16% Biological and

Biomedical Sciences, 16% Social Sciences, 13% Psychology, 12% Communication, Journalism, and Related Programs
Expenses: 2019-2020: $29,428; room/board: $11,416
Financial aid: (716) 888-2300; 72% of undergrads determined to have financial need; average aid package $22,679

Cazenovia College
Cazenovia NY
(800) 654-3210
U.S. News ranking: Reg. Coll. (N), No. 15
Website: www.cazenovia.edu
Admissions email: admission@cazenovia.edu
Private; founded 1824
Freshman admissions: less selective; 2018-2019: 1,789 applied, 1,294 accepted. Neither SAT nor ACT required. SAT 25/75 percentile: 935-1142. High school rank: 8% in top tenth, 24% in top quarter, 45% in top half
Early decision deadline: N/A, notification date: N/A
Early action deadline: N/A, notification date: N/A
Application deadline (fall): rolling
Undergraduate student body: 708 full time, 162 part time; 26% male, 74% female; 1% American Indian, 2% Asian, 12% black, 3% Hispanic, 3% multiracial, 0% Pacific Islander, 68% white, 0% international; 9% from in state; N/A live on campus; N/A of students in fraternities, N/A in sororities
Most popular majors: 16% Public Administration and Social Service Professions, 16% Visual and Performing Arts, 15% Business, Management, Marketing, and Related Support Services, 11% Homeland Security, Law Enforcement, Firefighting and Related Protective Services, 6% Psychology
Expenses: 2019-2020: $35,634; room/board: $14,344
Financial aid: (315) 655-7000

Clarkson University
Potsdam NY
(800) 527-6577
U.S. News ranking: Nat. U., No. 117
Website: www.clarkson.edu/
Admissions email: admissions@clarkson.edu
Private; founded 1896
Freshman admissions: more selective; 2018-2019: 6,885 applied, 4,894 accepted. Either SAT or ACT required. SAT 25/75 percentile: 1160-1350. High school rank: 35% in top tenth, 69% in top quarter, 95% in top half
Early decision deadline: 12/1, notification date: 1/1
Early action deadline: N/A, notification date: N/A
Application deadline (fall): 1/15
Undergraduate student body: 3,016 full time, 75 part time; 69% male, 31% female; 0% American Indian, 4% Asian, 2% black, 5% Hispanic, 4% multiracial,

0% Pacific Islander, 81% white, 2% international; 69% from in state; 80% live on campus; 15% of students in fraternities, 13% in sororities
Most popular majors: 60% Engineering, General, 19% Purchasing, Procurement/Acquisitions and Contracts Management, 7% Biology/Biological Sciences, General, 3% Computer Science, 2% Mathematics, General
Expenses: 2019-2020: $51,128; room/board: $15,580
Financial aid: (315) 268-6413; 82% of undergrads determined to have financial need; average aid package $45,326

Colgate University
Hamilton NY
(315) 228-7401
U.S. News ranking: Nat. Lib. Arts, No. 17
Website: www.colgate.edu
Admissions email: admission@colgate.edu
Private; founded 1819
Freshman admissions: most selective; 2018-2019: 9,716 applied, 2,422 accepted. Either SAT or ACT required. ACT 25/75 percentile: 31-34. High school rank: 77% in top tenth, 94% in top quarter, 100% in top half
Early decision deadline: 11/15, notification date: 12/15
Early action deadline: N/A, notification date: N/A
Application deadline (fall): 1/15
Undergraduate student body: 2,936 full time, 22 part time; 45% male, 55% female; 0% American Indian, 5% Asian, 5% black, 9% Hispanic, 4% multiracial, 0% Pacific Islander, 65% white, 9% international; 24% from in state; 92% live on campus; N/A of students in fraternities, N/A in sororities
Most popular majors: 9% Economics, General, 7% Political Science and Government, General, 7% Psychology, General, 6% English Language and Literature, General, 5% Neuroscience
Expenses: 2019-2020: $58,045; room/board: $14,540
Financial aid: (315) 228-7431; 35% of undergrads determined to have financial need; average aid package $55,110

College at Brockport–SUNY
Brockport NY
(585) 395-2751
U.S. News ranking: Reg. U. (N), No. 80
Website: www.brockport.edu
Admissions email: admit@brockport.edu
Public; founded 1835
Freshman admissions: selective; 2018-2019: 10,535 applied, 5,617 accepted. Either SAT or ACT required. SAT 25/75 percentile: 1020-1180. High school rank: 8% in top tenth, 33% in top quarter, 76% in top half
Early decision deadline: N/A, notification date: N/A

Early action deadline: N/A, notification date: N/A
Application deadline (fall): 8/1
Undergraduate student body: 6,343 full time, 714 part time; 43% male, 57% female; 0% American Indian, 2% Asian, 11% black, 8% Hispanic, 3% multiracial, 0% Pacific Islander, 70% white, 1% international; 99% from in state; 37% live on campus; 1% of students in fraternities, 1% in sororities
Most popular majors: 21% Health Professions and Related Programs, 16% Business, Management, Marketing, and Related Support Services, 13% Parks, Recreation, Leisure, and Fitness Studies, 7% Psychology, 6% Homeland Security, Law Enforcement, Firefighting and Related Protective Services
Expenses: 2019-2020: $8,670 in state, $18,580 out of state; room/board: $13,758
Financial aid: (585) 395-2501; 76% of undergrads determined to have financial need; average aid package $11,390

College of Mount St. Vincent
Bronx NY
(718) 405-3267
U.S. News ranking: Reg. U. (N), No. 108
Website: www.mountsaintvincent.edu
Admissions email: admissions.office@mountsaintvincent.edu
Private; founded 1847
Affiliation: Roman Catholic
Freshman admissions: less selective; 2018-2019: 3,019 applied, 2,352 accepted. Either SAT or ACT required. SAT 25/75 percentile: 930-1100. High school rank: 1% in top tenth, 29% in top quarter, 66% in top half
Early decision deadline: N/A, notification date: N/A
Early action deadline: 11/15, notification date: 12/15
Application deadline (fall): rolling
Undergraduate student body: 1,562 full time, 74 part time; 29% male, 71% female; 0% American Indian, 8% Asian, 16% black, 44% Hispanic, 4% multiracial, 0% Pacific Islander, 22% white, 1% international; N/A from in state; 51% live on campus; 0% of students in fraternities, 0% in sororities
Most popular majors: 36% Health Professions and Related Programs, 19% Business, Management, Marketing, and Related Support Services, 13% Psychology, 7% Communication, Journalism, and Related Programs, 6% Social Sciences
Expenses: 2019-2020: $40,980; room/board: $11,000
Financial aid: (718) 405-3289; 78% of undergrads determined to have financial need; average aid package $30,042

College of New Rochelle[1]
New Rochelle NY
(800) 933-5923
U.S. News ranking: Reg. U. (N), second tier
Website: www.cnr.edu
Admissions email: admission@cnr.edu
Private; founded 1904
Application deadline (fall): rolling
Undergraduate student body: N/A full time, N/A part time
Expenses: N/A
Financial aid: (914) 654-5225

College of Saint Rose
Albany NY
(518) 454-5150
U.S. News ranking: Reg. U. (N), No. 86
Website: www.strose.edu
Admissions email: admit@strose.edu
Private; founded 1920
Freshman admissions: less selective; 2018-2019: 6,408 applied, 5,597 accepted. Either SAT or ACT required for some. SAT 25/75 percentile: 1010-1190. High school rank: 12% in top tenth, 38% in top quarter, 71% in top half
Early decision deadline: N/A, notification date: N/A
Early action deadline: 12/1, notification date: 12/15
Application deadline (fall): 5/1
Undergraduate student body: 2,402 full time, 87 part time; 33% male, 67% female; 0% American Indian, 3% Asian, 17% black, 7% Hispanic, 12% multiracial, 0% Pacific Islander, 55% white, 3% international; 88% from in state; 49% live on campus; N/A of students in fraternities, N/A in sororities
Most popular majors: 20% Business, Management, Marketing, and Related Support Services, 20% Education, 9% Homeland Security, Law Enforcement, Firefighting and Related Protective Services, 9% Visual and Performing Arts, 8% Communication, Journalism, and Related Programs
Expenses: 2019-2020: $33,386; room/board: $12,968
Financial aid: (518) 337-4915; 84% of undergrads determined to have financial need; average aid package $23,717

The College of Westchester[1]
White Plains NY
U.S. News ranking: Reg. Coll. (N), unranked
Admissions email: N/A
For-profit
Application deadline (fall): N/A
Undergraduate student body: N/A full time, N/A part time
Expenses: N/A
Financial aid: N/A

Columbia University
New York NY
(212) 854-2522
U.S. News ranking: Nat. U., No. 3
Website: www.columbia.edu
Admissions email: ugrad-ask@columbia.edu
Private; founded 1754
Freshman admissions: most selective; 2018-2019: 40,203 applied, 2,260 accepted. Either SAT or ACT required. SAT 25/75 percentile: 1450-1560. High school rank: 96% in top tenth, 99% in top quarter, 100% in top half
Early decision deadline: 11/1, notification date: 12/15
Early action deadline: N/A, notification date: N/A
Application deadline (fall): 1/1
Undergraduate student body: 6,202 full time, 0 part time; 51% male, 49% female; 2% American Indian, 22% Asian, 10% black, 13% Hispanic, 2% multiracial, 0% Pacific Islander, 33% white, 16% international; 22% ffom in state; 92% live on campus; 19% of students in fraternities, 16% in sororities
Most popular majors: 22% Social Sciences, 16% Engineering, 10% Computer and Information Sciences and Support Services, 6% Biological and Biomedical Sciences, 6% Psychology
Expenses: 2019-2020: $61,850; room/board: $14,490
Financial aid: (212) 854-3711; 50% of undergrads determined to have financial need; average aid package $60,205

Concordia College
Bronxville NY
(800) 937-2655
U.S. News ranking: Reg. U. (N), second tier
Website: www.concordia-ny.edu
Admissions email: admission@concordia-ny.edu
Private; founded 1881
Affiliation: Lutheran Church–Missouri Synod
Freshman admissions: less selective; 2018-2019: 1,326 applied, 1,076 accepted. Either SAT or ACT required for some. SAT 25/75 percentile: 950-1118. High school rank: N/A
Early decision deadline: N/A, notification date: N/A
Early action deadline: 11/15, notification date: 12/15
Application deadline (fall): 8/15
Undergraduate student body: 1,112 full time, 114 part time; 22% male, 78% female; 0% American Indian, 5% Asian, 12% black, 18% Hispanic, 0% multiracial, 0% Pacific Islander, 53% white, 10% international
Most popular majors: 26% Registered Nursing/Registered Nurse, 22% Business Administration and Management, General, 11% Social Sciences, General
Expenses: 2019-2020: $34,600; room/board: $13,470
Financial aid: (914) 337-9300; 70% of undergrads determined to have financial need

Cooper Union
New York NY
(212) 353-4120
U.S. News ranking: Reg. Coll. (N), No. 1
Website: cooper.edu
Admissions email: admissions@cooper.edu
Private; founded 1859
Freshman admissions: more selective; 2018-2019: 2,447 applied, 392 accepted. Either SAT or ACT required. SAT 25/75 percentile: 1283-1510. High school rank: N/A
Early decision deadline: 12/1, notification date: 12/22
Early action deadline: N/A, notification date: N/A
Application deadline (fall): 1/7
Undergraduate student body: 856 full time, 2 part time; 61% male, 39% female; 0% American Indian, 21% Asian, 3% black, 10% Hispanic, 6% multiracial, 0% Pacific Islander, 32% white, 20% international; 47% from in state; 1% live on campus; N/A of students in fraternities, N/A in sororities
Most popular majors: 54% Engineering, 34% Fine/Studio Arts, General, 12% Architecture
Expenses: 2019-2020: $46,700; room/board: $17,017
Financial aid: (212) 353-4113; 54% of undergrads determined to have financial need; average aid package $46,001

Cornell University
Ithaca NY
(607) 255-5241
U.S. News ranking: Nat. U., No. 17
Website: www.cornell.edu
Admissions email: admissions@cornell.edu
Private; founded 1865
Freshman admissions: most selective; 2018-2019: 51,324 applied, 5,448 accepted. Either SAT or ACT required. SAT 25/75 percentile: 1390-1540. High school rank: 83% in top tenth, 97% in top quarter, 100% in top half
Early decision deadline: 11/1, notification date: 12/15
Early action deadline: N/A, notification date: N/A
Application deadline (fall): 1/2
Undergraduate student body: 15,182 full time, 0 part time; 47% male, 53% female; 0% American Indian, 19% Asian, 7% black, 14% Hispanic, 5% multiracial, 0% Pacific Islander, 37% white, 11% international; 41% from in state; 52% live on campus; 26% of students in fraternities, 24% in sororities
Most popular majors: 17% Engineering, 14% Business, Management, Marketing, and Related Support Services, 12% Agriculture, Agriculture Operations, and Related Sciences, 12% Biological and Biomedical Sciences, 11% Computer and Information Sciences and Support Services
Expenses: 2019-2020: $57,222; room/board: $15,296

Financial aid: (607) 255-5145; 47% of undergrads determined to have financial need; average aid package $48,835

CUNY–Baruch College
New York NY
(646) 312-1400
U.S. News ranking: Reg. U. (N), No. 16
Website: www.baruch.cuny.edu
Admissions email: admissions@baruch.cuny.edu
Public; founded 1919
Freshman admissions: more selective; 2018-2019: 21,469 applied, 8,436 accepted. Either SAT or ACT required. SAT 25/75 percentile: 1220-1390. High school rank: 50% in top tenth, 77% in top quarter, 95% in top half
Early decision deadline: 12/13, notification date: 1/7
Early action deadline: N/A, notification date: N/A
Application deadline (fall): 2/1
Undergraduate student body: 11,495 full time, 3,529 part time; 53% male, 47% female; 0% American Indian, 32% Asian, 9% black, 26% Hispanic, 1% multiracial, 0% Pacific Islander, 20% white, 11% international; N/A from in state; 2% live on campus; 0% of students in fraternities, 0% in sororities
Most popular majors: 77% Business, Management, Marketing, and Related Support Services, 5% Computer and Information Sciences and Support Services, 4% Social Sciences
Expenses: 2019-2020: $7,921 in state, $18,971 out of state; room/board: $15,499
Financial aid: (646) 312-1399; 67% of undergrads determined to have financial need; average aid package $5,368

CUNY–Brooklyn College
Brooklyn NY
(718) 951-5001
U.S. News ranking: Reg. U. (N), No. 59
Website: www.brooklyn.cuny.edu
Admissions email: adminqry@brooklyn.cuny.edu
Public; founded 1930
Freshman admissions: selective; 2018-2019: 20,936 applied, 9,267 accepted. Either SAT or ACT required. SAT 25/75 percentile: 1040-1220. High school rank: N/A
Early decision deadline: N/A, notification date: N/A
Early action deadline: N/A, notification date: N/A
Application deadline (fall): N/A
Undergraduate student body: 11,142 full time, 3,836 part time; 43% male, 57% female; 0% American Indian, 22% Asian, 20% black, 24% Hispanic, 2% multiracial, 0% Pacific Islander, 29% white, 3% international; 98% from in state; 0% live on campus; 3% of students in fraternities, 3% in sororities

Most popular majors: 18% Psychology, General, 16% Business Administration and Management, General, 10% Accounting, 4% Biology/Biological Sciences, General, 4% Elementary Education and Teaching
Expenses: 2019-2020: $7,240 in state, $18,510 out of state; room/board: N/A
Financial aid: (718) 951-5051; 80% of undergrads determined to have financial need; average aid package $8,987

CUNY–City College
New York NY
(212) 650-7000
U.S. News ranking: Nat. U., No. 228
Website: admissions@ccny.cuny.edu
Admissions email: admissions@ccny.cuny.edu
Public; founded 1847
Freshman admissions: selective; 2018-2019: 27,193 applied, 10,340 accepted. Either SAT or ACT required. SAT 25/75 percentile: 950-1190. High school rank: N/A
Early decision deadline: N/A, notification date: N/A
Early action deadline: N/A, notification date: N/A
Application deadline (fall): rolling
Undergraduate student body: 10,695 full time, 2,971 part time; 49% male, 51% female; 0% American Indian, 26% Asian, 23% black, 32% Hispanic, 2% multiracial, 0% Pacific Islander, 10% white, 6% international; 94% from in state; N/A live on campus; N/A of students in fraternities, N/A in sororities
Most popular majors: 16% Engineering, 16% Psychology, 12% Social Sciences, 10% Biological and Biomedical Sciences, 9% Visual and Performing Arts
Expenses: 2019-2020: $7,205 in state, $18,475 out of state; room/board: N/A
Financial aid: (212) 650-5824; 80% of undergrads determined to have financial need; average aid package $9,140

CUNY–College of Staten Island
Staten Island NY
(718) 982-2010
U.S. News ranking: Reg. U. (N), second tier
Website: www.csi.cuny.edu
Admissions email: admissions@csi.cuny.edu
Public; founded 1976
Freshman admissions: selective; 2018-2019: 14,804 applied, 14,770 accepted. Either SAT or ACT required. SAT 25/75 percentile: 990-1170. High school rank: N/A
Early decision deadline: N/A, notification date: N/A
Early action deadline: N/A, notification date: N/A
Application deadline (fall): rolling
Undergraduate student body: 9,567 full time, 2,644 part time; 46%

male, 54% female; 0% American Indian, 11% Asian, 15% black, 27% Hispanic, 2% multiracial, 0% Pacific Islander, 42% white, 3% international; 99% from in state; 4% live on campus; 0% of students in fraternities, 0% in sororities
Most popular majors: 19% Business, Management, Marketing, and Related Support Services, 19% Psychology, 11% Social Sciences, 7% English Language and Literature/Letters, 6% Biological and Biomedical Sciences
Expenses: 2019-2020: $7,480 in state, $19,150 out of state; room/board: $18,695
Financial aid: (718) 982-2030; 74% of undergrads determined to have financial need; average aid package $8,276

CUNY–Graduate Center[1]
New York NY
U.S. News ranking: Nat. U., unranked
Admissions email: N/A
Public
Application deadline (fall): N/A
Undergraduate student body: N/A full time, N/A part time
Expenses: N/A
Financial aid: N/A

CUNY–Hunter College
New York NY
(212) 772-4490
U.S. News ranking: Reg. U. (N), No. 23
Website: www.hunter.cuny.edu
Admissions email: admissions@hunter.cuny.edu
Public; founded 1870
Freshman admissions: more selective; 2018-2019: 31,030 applied, 11,300 accepted. Either SAT or ACT required. SAT 25/75 percentile: 1090-1260. High school rank: 24% in top tenth, 57% in top quarter, 87% in top half
Early decision deadline: N/A, notification date: N/A
Early action deadline: N/A, notification date: N/A
Application deadline (fall): 3/15
Undergraduate student body: 13,111 full time, 3,138 part time; 35% male, 65% female; 0% American Indian, 31% Asian, 12% black, 23% Hispanic, 0% multiracial, 0% Pacific Islander, 29% white, 6% international
Most popular majors: Information not available
Expenses: 2019-2020: $7,180 in state, $18,450 out of state; room/board: $11,332
Financial aid: (212) 772-4804; 76% of undergrads determined to have financial need; average aid package $8,126

CUNY–John Jay College of Criminal Justice
New York NY
(212) 237-8866
U.S. News ranking: Reg. U. (N), No. 100
Website: www.jjay.cuny.edu/
Admissions email: admissions@jjay.cuny.edu
Public; founded 1965
Freshman admissions: less selective; 2018-2019: 16,502 applied, 6,696 accepted. Either SAT or ACT required. SAT 25/75 percentile: 920-1060. High school rank: N/A
Early decision deadline: N/A, notification date: N/A
Early action deadline: N/A, notification date: N/A
Application deadline (fall): rolling
Undergraduate student body: 10,740 full time, 2,579 part time; 42% male, 58% female; 0% American Indian, 12% Asian, 19% black, 45% Hispanic, 0% multiracial, 0% Pacific Islander, 20% white, 3% international; N/A from in state; 1% live on campus; N/A of students in fraternities, N/A in sororities
Most popular majors: 53% Criminal Justice/Law Enforcement Administration, 15% Forensic Psychology, 15% Social Sciences, 4% Legal Professions and Studies, 3% Public Administration
Expenses: 2019-2020: $4,200 in state, $18,270 out of state; room/board: N/A
Financial aid: (212) 237-8897; 77% of undergrads determined to have financial need; average aid package $8,697

CUNY–Lehman College
Bronx NY
(718) 960-8700
U.S. News ranking: Reg. U. (N), No. 100
Website: www.lehman.cuny.edu
Admissions email: undergraduate.admissions@lehman.cuny.edu
Public; founded 1968
Freshman admissions: less selective; 2018-2019: 15,782 applied, 6,261 accepted. Either SAT or ACT required. SAT 25/75 percentile: 920-1040. High school rank: N/A
Early decision deadline: N/A, notification date: N/A
Early action deadline: N/A, notification date: N/A
Application deadline (fall): 2/1
Undergraduate student body: 7,794 full time, 4,845 part time; 32% male, 68% female; 0% American Indian, 6% Asian, 26% black, 58% Hispanic, 1% multiracial, 0% Pacific Islander, 5% white, 3% international; N/A from in state; N/A live on campus; 1% of students in fraternities, 1% in sororities
Most popular majors: 28% Health Professions and Related Programs, 17% Business, Management, Marketing, and Related Support Services, 14% Social Sciences,

8% Psychology, 6% Public Administration and Social Service Professions
Expenses: 2019-2020: $7,210 in state, $18,480 out of state; room/board: N/A
Financial aid: (718) 960-8545; 89% of undergrads determined to have financial need; average aid package $7,828

CUNY–Medgar Evers College
Brooklyn NY
(718) 270-6024
U.S. News ranking: Reg. Coll. (N), second tier
Website: ares.mec.cuny.edu/admissions/admissions/
Admissions email: mecadmissions@mec.cuny.edu
Public; founded 1970
Freshman admissions: least selective; 2018-2019: 10,147 applied, 10,007 accepted. Neither SAT nor ACT required. SAT 25/75 percentile: 740-920. High school rank: N/A
Early decision deadline: N/A, notification date: N/A
Early action deadline: N/A, notification date: N/A
Application deadline (fall): rolling
Undergraduate student body: 4,705 full time, 1,933 part time; 30% male, 70% female; 0% American Indian, 2% Asian, 62% black, 15% Hispanic, 0% multiracial, 0% Pacific Islander, 1% white, 1% international
Most popular majors: 24% Business, Management, Marketing, and Related Support Services, 21% Biological and Biomedical Sciences, 19% Psychology, 10% Public Administration and Social Service Professions, 9% Health Professions and Related Programs
Expenses: 2019-2020: $6,930 in state, $18,200 out of state; room/board: N/A
Financial aid: (718) 270-6038; 91% of undergrads determined to have financial need; average aid package $7,548

CUNY–New York City College of Technology
Brooklyn NY
(718) 260-5500
U.S. News ranking: Reg. Coll. (N), No. 35
Website: www.citytech.cuny.edu
Admissions email: admissions@citytech.cuny.edu
Public; founded 1946
Freshman admissions: less selective; 2018-2019: 18,980 applied, 14,245 accepted. Either SAT or ACT required for some. SAT 25/75 percentile: N/A. High school rank: N/A
Early decision deadline: N/A, notification date: N/A
Early action deadline: N/A, notification date: N/A
Application deadline (fall): 2/1
Undergraduate student body: 10,902 full time, 6,367 part time; 56% male, 44% female; 0% American Indian, 20% Asian, 28% black, 35% Hispanic, 1%

multiracial, 0% Pacific Islander, 10% white, 5% international; N/A from in state; 0% live on campus; 0% of students in fraternities, 0% in sororities
Most popular majors: 17% Engineering Technologies and Engineering-Related Fields, 16% Computer and Information Sciences and Support Services, 16% Health Professions and Related Programs, 13% Business, Management, Marketing, and Related Support Services, 9% Public Administration and Social Service Professions
Expenses: 2018-2019: $7,120 in state, $14,790 out of state; room/board: N/A
Financial aid: N/A

CUNY–Queens College
Queens NY
(718) 997-5600
U.S. News ranking: Reg. U. (N), No. 52
Website: www.qc.cuny.edu/
Admissions email: admissions@qc.cuny.edu
Public; founded 1937
Freshman admissions: selective; 2018-2019: 18,862 applied, 8,987 accepted. Either SAT or ACT required. SAT 25/75 percentile: 1060-1220. High school rank: N/A
Early decision deadline: N/A, notification date: N/A
Early action deadline: N/A, notification date: N/A
Application deadline (fall): 2/1
Undergraduate student body: 12,201 full time, 4,419 part time; 46% male, 54% female; 0% American Indian, 29% Asian, 9% black, 30% Hispanic, 2% multiracial, 0% Pacific Islander, 25% white, 6% international; 99% from in state; 2% live on campus; 1% of students in fraternities, 1% in sororities
Most popular majors: 20% Psychology, General, 13% Accounting, 10% Economics, General, 6% Sociology, 4% Computer Science
Expenses: 2019-2020: $7,338 in state, $18,608 out of state; room/board: $15,998
Financial aid: (718) 997-5102; 71% of undergrads determined to have financial need; average aid package $6,590

CUNY–York College
Jamaica NY
(718) 262-2165
U.S. News ranking: Reg. Coll. (N), second tier
Website: www.york.cuny.edu
Admissions email: admissions@york.cuny.edu
Public; founded 1966
Freshman admissions: less selective; 2018-2019: 14,176 applied, 7,479 accepted. Either SAT or ACT required. SAT 25/75 percentile: 880-1040. High school rank: N/A
Early decision deadline: N/A, notification date: N/A
Early action deadline: N/A, notification date: N/A

Application deadline (fall): 6/1
Undergraduate student body: 5,085 full time, 3,410 part time; 36% male, 64% female; 1% American Indian, 22% Asian, 38% black, 27% Hispanic, 2% multiracial, 1% Pacific Islander, 5% white, 4% international; 99% from in state; 0% live on campus; 0% of students in fraternities, 0% in sororities
Most popular majors: 21% Health Professions and Related Programs, 19% Business, Management, Marketing, and Related Support Services, 17% Psychology, 9% Public Administration and Social Service Professions, 6% Computer and Information Sciences and Support Services
Expenses: 2019-2020: $7,157 in state, $18,427 out of state; room/board: N/A
Financial aid: (718) 262-2230; 85% of undergrads determined to have financial need; average aid package $7,226

Daemen College
Amherst NY
(716) 839-8225
U.S. News ranking: Nat. U., No. 263
Website: www.daemen.edu/
Admissions email: admissions@daemen.edu
Private; founded 1947
Freshman admissions: selective; 2018-2019: 3,249 applied, 1,752 accepted. Neither SAT nor ACT required. SAT 25/75 percentile: 1040-1230. High school rank: 21% in top tenth, 50% in top quarter, 84% in top half
Early decision deadline: N/A, notification date: N/A
Early action deadline: N/A, notification date: N/A
Application deadline (fall): rolling
Undergraduate student body: 1,495 full time, 244 part time; 30% male, 70% female; 0% American Indian, 3% Asian, 10% black, 7% Hispanic, 1% multiracial, 0% Pacific Islander, 76% white, 2% international; 93% from in state; 35% live on campus; 3% of students in fraternities, 4% in sororities
Most popular majors: 45% Health Professions and Related Programs, 21% Multi/Interdisciplinary Studies, 11% Business, Management, Marketing, and Related Support Services, 6% Visual and Performing Arts, 4% Public Administration and Social Service Professions
Expenses: 2019-2020: $29,430; room/board: $13,010
Financial aid: (716) 839-8254; 82% of undergrads determined to have financial need; average aid package $24,852

Dominican College
Orangeburg NY
(845) 848-7901
U.S. News ranking: Reg. U. (N), second tier
Website: www.dc.edu
Admissions email: admissions@dc.edu
Private; founded 1952

Freshman admissions: less selective; 2018-2019: 2,101 applied, 1,613 accepted. Neither SAT nor ACT required. SAT 25/75 percentile: 940-1120. High school rank: N/A
Early decision deadline: N/A, notification date: N/A
Early action deadline: N/A, notification date: N/A
Application deadline (fall): rolling
Undergraduate student body: 1,304 full time, 146 part time; 34% male, 66% female; 0% American Indian, 6% Asian, 16% black, 33% Hispanic, 3% multiracial, 1% Pacific Islander, 33% white, 2% international; 74% from in state; 63% live on campus; N/A of students in fraternities, N/A in sororities
Most popular majors: 22% Physical Therapy/Therapist, 19% Occupational Therapy/Therapist, 16% Registered Nursing/Registered Nurse, 13% Social Sciences, General, 6% Criminal Justice/Law Enforcement Administration
Expenses: 2019-2020: $29,844; room/board: $13,414
Financial aid: (845) 848-7818; 85% of undergrads determined to have financial need; average aid package $22,960

D'Youville College
Buffalo NY
(716) 829-7600
U.S. News ranking: Nat. U., No. 254
Website: www.dyc.edu
Admissions email: admissions@dyc.edu
Private; founded 1908
Freshman admissions: selective; 2018-2019: 1,254 applied, 1,249 accepted. Either SAT or ACT required. SAT 25/75 percentile: 1030-1200. High school rank: N/A
Early decision deadline: N/A, notification date: N/A
Early action deadline: N/A, notification date: N/A
Application deadline (fall): rolling
Undergraduate student body: 1,262 full time, 437 part time; 26% male, 74% female; 1% American Indian, 5% Asian, 10% black, 5% Hispanic, 2% multiracial, 0% Pacific Islander, 72% white, 1% international; 91% from in state; 16% live on campus; 0% of students in fraternities, 0% in sororities
Most popular majors: 73% Health Professions and Related Programs, 12% Multi/Interdisciplinary Studies, 6% Business, Management, Marketing, and Related Support Services, 4% Biological and Biomedical Sciences, 1% Psychology
Expenses: 2019-2020: $27,940; room/board: $12,652
Financial aid: (716) 829-7500; 92% of undergrads determined to have financial need; average aid package $16,617

Elmira College
Elmira NY
(800) 935-6472
U.S. News ranking: Reg. Coll. (N), No. 6
Website: www.elmira.edu
Admissions email: admissions@elmira.edu
Private; founded 1855
Freshman admissions: selective; 2018-2019: 2,110 applied, 1,782 accepted. Neither SAT nor ACT required. SAT 25/75 percentile: 1070-1210. High school rank: N/A
Early decision deadline: N/A, notification date: N/A
Early action deadline: 10/15, notification date: 10/31
Application deadline (fall): rolling
Undergraduate student body: 746 full time, 73 part time; 32% male, 68% female; 1% American Indian, 2% Asian, 5% black, 5% Hispanic, 2% multiracial, 0% Pacific Islander, 76% white, 4% international; 66% from in state; 85% live on campus; 0% of students in fraternities, 0% in sororities
Most popular majors: 27% Registered Nursing/Registered Nurse, 18% Business, Management, Marketing, and Related Support Services, 11% Psychology, General, 9% Biology/Biological Sciences, General, 9% Education
Expenses: 2019-2020: $35,400; room/board: $12,500
Financial aid: (607) 735-1728; 86% of undergrads determined to have financial need; average aid package $33,285

Excelsior College[1]
Albany NY
(518) 464-8500
U.S. News ranking: Reg. U. (N), unranked
Website: www.excelsior.edu
Admissions email: admissions@excelsior.edu
Private; founded 1971
Application deadline (fall): N/A
Undergraduate student body: N/A full time, N/A part time
Expenses: N/A
Financial aid: N/A

Farmingdale State College–SUNY
Farmingdale NY
(631) 420-2200
U.S. News ranking: Reg. Coll. (N), No. 21
Website: www.farmingdale.edu
Admissions email: admissions@farmingdale.edu
Public; founded 1912
Freshman admissions: selective; 2018-2019: 7,500 applied, 3,455 accepted. Either SAT or ACT required. SAT 25/75 percentile: 1010-1160. High school rank: 9% in top tenth, 31% in top quarter, 71% in top half
Early decision deadline: N/A, notification date: N/A
Early action deadline: N/A, notification date: N/A
Application deadline (fall): 5/1

Undergraduate student body: 7,689 full time, 2,227 part time; 57% male, 43% female; 0% American Indian, 9% Asian, 9% black, 22% Hispanic, 3% multiracial, 0% Pacific Islander, 55% white, 2% international; 99% from in state; 6% live on campus; 4% of students in fraternities, 5% in sororities
Most popular majors: 24% Business, Management, Marketing, and Related Support Services, 13% Engineering Technologies and Engineering-Related Fields, 13% Multi/Interdisciplinary Studies, 10% Health Professions and Related Programs, 10% Homeland Security, Law Enforcement, Firefighting and Related Protective Services
Expenses: 2019-2020: $8,538 in state, $18,448 out of state; room/board: $13,318
Financial aid: (631) 420-2578; 58% of undergrads determined to have financial need; average aid package $8,154

Fashion Institute of Technology
New York NY
(212) 217-3760
U.S. News ranking: Reg. U. (N), unranked
Website: www.fitnyc.edu
Admissions email: FITinfo@fitnyc.edu
Public; founded 1944
Freshman admissions: least selective; 2018-2019: 4,507 applied, 2,374 accepted. Neither SAT nor ACT required. SAT 25/75 percentile: N/A. High school rank: N/A
Early decision deadline: N/A, notification date: N/A
Early action deadline: N/A, notification date: N/A
Application deadline (fall): 1/1
Undergraduate student body: 7,246 full time, 1,309 part time; 17% male, 83% female; 0% American Indian, 11% Asian, 9% black, 21% Hispanic, 4% multiracial, 0% Pacific Islander, 43% white, 12% international; N/A from in state; 21% live on campus; N/A of students in fraternities, N/A in sororities
Most popular majors: 41% Business, Management, Marketing, and Related Support Services, 37% Visual and Performing Arts, 17% Communication, Journalism, and Related Programs, 4% Family and Consumer Sciences/Human Sciences, 1% Communications Technologies/Technicians and Support Services
Expenses: 2019-2020: $6,110 in state, $16,490 out of state; room/board: $14,556
Financial aid: (212) 217-3560; 51% of undergrads determined to have financial need; average aid package $12,023

Five Towns College[1]
Dix Hills NY
(631) 424-7000
U.S. News ranking: Reg. Coll. (N), second tier
Website: www.ftc.edu
Admissions email: admissions@ftc.edu
For-profit; founded 1972
Application deadline (fall): rolling
Undergraduate student body: N/A full time, N/A part time
Expenses: N/A
Financial aid: (631) 656-2168

Fordham University
New York NY
(800) 367-3426
U.S. News ranking: Nat. U., No. 74
Website: www.fordham.edu
Admissions email: enroll@fordham.edu
Private; founded 1841
Affiliation: Roman Catholic
Freshman admissions: more selective; 2018-2019: 46,308 applied, 21,313 accepted. Either SAT or ACT required. SAT 25/75 percentile: 1250-1430. High school rank: 44% in top tenth, 76% in top quarter, 97% in top half
Early decision deadline: 11/1, notification date: 12/20
Early action deadline: 11/1, notification date: 12/20
Application deadline (fall): 1/1
Undergraduate student body: 9,149 full time, 496 part time; 43% male, 57% female; 0% American Indian, 11% Asian, 4% black, 14% Hispanic, 4% multiracial, 0% Pacific Islander, 56% white, 9% international; 42% from in state; 50% live on campus; N/A of students in fraternities, N/A in sororities
Most popular majors: 9% Speech Communication and Rhetoric, 8% Economics, General, 8% Finance, General, 7% Business Administration and Management, General, 6% Psychology, General
Expenses: 2019-2020: $54,093; room/board: $18,508
Financial aid: (718) 817-3800; 59% of undergrads determined to have financial need; average aid package $38,093

Hamilton College
Clinton NY
(800) 843-2655
U.S. News ranking: Nat. Lib. Arts, No. 14
Website: www.hamilton.edu
Admissions email: admission@hamilton.edu
Private; founded 1812
Freshman admissions: most selective; 2018-2019: 6,240 applied, 1,328 accepted. Either SAT or ACT required. SAT 25/75 percentile: 1350-1510. High school rank: 81% in top tenth, 98% in top quarter, 100% in top half
Early decision deadline: 11/15, notification date: 12/15
Early action deadline: N/A, notification date: N/A
Application deadline (fall): 1/1

Undergraduate student body:
1,907 full time, 8 part time; 47% male, 53% female; 0% American Indian, 7% Asian, 4% black, 10% Hispanic, 5% multiracial, 0% Pacific Islander, 63% white, 7% international; 26% from in state; 100% live on campus; 17% of students in fraternities, 8% in sororities
Most popular majors: 16% Economics, General, 8% Mathematics, General, 6% Political Science and Government, General, 5% International Relations and Affairs, 4% Biology/Biological Sciences, General
Expenses: 2019-2020: $56,530; room/board: $14,360
Financial aid: (800) 859-4413; 52% of undergrads determined to have financial need; average aid package $49,164

Hartwick College
Oneonta NY
(607) 431-4150
U.S. News ranking: Nat. Lib. Arts, No. 160
Website: www.hartwick.edu
Admissions email: admissions@hartwick.edu
Private; founded 1797
Freshman admissions: selective; 2018-2019: 4,443 applied, 3,552 accepted. Either SAT or ACT required for some. SAT 25/75 percentile: 1070-1190. High school rank: N/A
Early decision deadline: 11/1, notification date: 11/15
Early action deadline: N/A, notification date: N/A
Application deadline (fall): rolling
Undergraduate student body: 1,156 full time, 20 part time; 41% male, 59% female; 2% American Indian, 3% Asian, 10% black, 5% Hispanic, 0% multiracial, 0% Pacific Islander, 63% white, 2% international; 79% from in state; 87% live on campus; 4% of students in fraternities, 7% in sororities
Most popular majors: 17% Business Administration and Management, General, 17% Registered Nursing/Registered Nurse, 15% Sociology, 13% Biology/Biological Sciences, General, 5% Political Science and Government, General
Expenses: 2019-2020: $46,926; room/board: $12,834
Financial aid: (607) 431-4130; 83% of undergrads determined to have financial need; average aid package $38,054

Hilbert College[1]
Hamburg NY
(716) 649-7900
U.S. News ranking: Reg. Coll. (N), unranked
Website: www.hilbert.edu/
Admissions email: admissions@hilbert.edu
Private
Application deadline (fall): N/A
Undergraduate student body: N/A full time, N/A part time
Expenses: N/A
Financial aid: N/A

Hobart and William Smith Colleges
Geneva NY
(315) 781-3622
U.S. News ranking: Nat. Lib. Arts, No. 72
Website: www.hws.edu
Admissions email: admissions@hws.edu
Private; founded 1822
Freshman admissions: more selective; 2018-2019: 4,526 applied, 2,576 accepted. Either SAT or ACT required for some. SAT 25/75 percentile: 1203-1360. High school rank: 34% in top tenth, 65% in top quarter, 91% in top half
Early decision deadline: 11/15, notification date: 12/15
Early action deadline: N/A, notification date: N/A
Application deadline (fall): 2/1
Undergraduate student body: 2,208 full time, 21 part time; 49% male, 51% female; 1% American Indian, 4% Asian, 6% black, 5% Hispanic, 0% multiracial, 0% Pacific Islander, 74% white, 6% international; 40% from in state; 90% live on campus; 15% of students in fraternities, 4% in sororities
Most popular majors: 13% Economics, General, 9% Political Science and Government, General, 8% Mass Communication/Media Studies, 7% Biology/Biological Sciences, General, 7% Psychology, General
Expenses: 2019-2020: $57,058; room/board: $14,565
Financial aid: (315) 781-3315; 66% of undergrads determined to have financial need; average aid package $41,843

Hofstra University
Hempstead NY
(516) 463-6700
U.S. News ranking: Nat. U., No. 162
Website: www.hofstra.edu
Admissions email: admission@hofstra.edu
Private; founded 1935
Freshman admissions: more selective; 2018-2019: 27,620 applied, 17,456 accepted. Neither SAT nor ACT required. SAT 25/75 percentile: 1150-1330. High school rank: 28% in top tenth, 59% in top quarter, 90% in top half
Early decision deadline: N/A, notification date: N/A
Early action deadline: 11/15, notification date: 12/15
Application deadline (fall): rolling
Undergraduate student body: 6,329 full time, 372 part time; 45% male, 55% female; 0% American Indian, 11% Asian, 9% black, 12% Hispanic, 3% multiracial, 0% Pacific Islander, 56% white, 6% international; 62% from in state; 43% live on campus; 8% of students in fraternities, 10% in sororities
Most popular majors: 6% Marketing/Marketing Management, General, 6% Psychology, General, 5% Accounting, 5% Finance,

General, 4% Community Health and Preventive Medicine
Expenses: 2019-2020: $47,510; room/board: $16,428
Financial aid: (516) 463-8000; 64% of undergrads determined to have financial need; average aid package $32,000

Houghton College
Houghton NY
(800) 777-2556
U.S. News ranking: Nat. Lib. Arts, No. 124
Website: www.houghton.edu
Admissions email: admission@houghton.edu
Private; founded 1883
Affiliation: Wesleyan
Freshman admissions: selective; 2018-2019: 762 applied, 722 accepted. Neither SAT nor ACT required. SAT 25/75 percentile: 1030-1280. High school rank: 29% in top tenth, 50% in top quarter, 75% in top half
Early decision deadline: N/A, notification date: N/A
Early action deadline: N/A, notification date: N/A
Application deadline (fall): rolling
Undergraduate student body: 926 full time, 62 part time; 40% male, 60% female; 0% American Indian, 4% Asian, 6% black, 2% Hispanic, 5% multiracial, 0% Pacific Islander, 72% white, 5% international; N/A from in state; 89% live on campus; 0% of students in fraternities, 0% in sororities
Most popular majors: 10% Biology/Biological Sciences, General, 10% Business Administration and Management, General, 8% Speech Communication and Rhetoric, 7% Elementary Education and Teaching, 7% Psychology, General
Expenses: 2019-2020: $33,458; room/board: $9,568
Financial aid: (585) 567-9328; 84% of undergrads determined to have financial need; average aid package $20,371

Iona College
New Rochelle NY
(914) 633-2502
U.S. News ranking: Reg. U. (N), No. 56
Website: www.iona.edu
Admissions email: admissions@iona.edu
Private; founded 1940
Affiliation: Roman Catholic
Freshman admissions: selective; 2018-2019: 10,062 applied, 8,871 accepted. Either SAT or ACT required. SAT 25/75 percentile: 990-1170. High school rank: 11% in top tenth, 32% in top quarter, 61% in top half
Early decision deadline: N/A, notification date: N/A
Early action deadline: 12/1, notification date: 12/15
Application deadline (fall): 2/15
Undergraduate student body: 2,961 full time, 326 part time; 49% male, 51% female; 1% American Indian, 3% Asian, 11% black, 25% Hispanic, 1% multiracial, 0% Pacific Islander, 53% white,

3% international; 77% from in state; 45% live on campus; 11% of students in fraternities, 21% in sororities
Most popular majors: 39% Business, Management, Marketing, and Related Support Services, 15% Communication, Journalism, and Related Programs, 9% Homeland Security, Law Enforcement, Firefighting and Related Protective Services, 8% Psychology, 6% Health Professions and Related Programs
Expenses: 2019-2020: $40,172; room/board: $15,736
Financial aid: (914) 633-2497; 86% of undergrads determined to have financial need; average aid package $26,735

Ithaca College
Ithaca NY
(800) 429-4274
U.S. News ranking: Reg. U. (N), No. 8
Website: www.ithaca.edu
Admissions email: admission@ithaca.edu
Private; founded 1892
Freshman admissions: selective; 2018-2019: 15,278 applied, 10,472 accepted. Neither SAT nor ACT required. SAT 25/75 percentile: 1160-1338. High school rank: 24% in top tenth, 56% in top quarter, 91% in top half
Early decision deadline: 11/1, notification date: 12/15
Early action deadline: 12/1, notification date: 2/1
Application deadline (fall): 2/1
Undergraduate student body: 5,991 full time, 110 part time; 43% male, 57% female; 0% American Indian, 4% Asian, 6% black, 9% Hispanic, 3% multiracial, 0% Pacific Islander, 73% white, 2% international; 45% from in state; 71% live on campus; 1% of students in fraternities, 1% in sororities
Most popular majors: 24% Communication, Journalism, and Related Programs, 16% Visual and Performing Arts, 15% Health Professions and Related Programs, 11% Business, Management, Marketing, and Related Support Services, 5% Social Sciences
Expenses: 2019-2020: $45,274; room/board: $15,856
Financial aid: (607) 274-3131; 68% of undergrads determined to have financial need; average aid package $38,845

Jamestown Business College[1]
Jamestown NY
U.S. News ranking: Business, unranked
Admissions email: N/A
For-profit
Application deadline (fall): N/A
Undergraduate student body: N/A full time, N/A part time
Expenses: N/A
Financial aid: N/A

Juilliard School[1]
New York NY
(212) 799-5000
U.S. News ranking: Arts, unranked
Website: www.juilliard.edu
Admissions email: admissions@juilliard.edu
Private; founded 1905
Application deadline (fall): 12/1
Undergraduate student body: N/A full time, N/A part time
Expenses: 2019-2020: $47,620; room/board: $17,970
Financial aid: (212) 799-5000; 74% of undergrads determined to have financial need; average aid package $36,562

Keuka College
Keuka Park NY
(315) 279-5254
U.S. News ranking: Reg. U. (N), No. 119
Website: www.keuka.edu
Admissions email: admissions@keuka.edu
Private; founded 1890
Affiliation: American Baptist
Freshman admissions: less selective; 2018-2019: 2,291 applied, 1,961 accepted. Neither SAT nor ACT required. SAT 25/75 percentile: 980-1140. High school rank: N/A
Early decision deadline: N/A, notification date: N/A
Early action deadline: N/A, notification date: N/A
Application deadline (fall): rolling
Undergraduate student body: 1,374 full time, 299 part time; 26% male, 74% female; 1% American Indian, 1% Asian, 7% black, 5% Hispanic, 3% multiracial, 0% Pacific Islander, 78% white, 1% international; N/A from in state; 66% live on campus; N/A of students in fraternities, N/A in sororities
Most popular majors: 29% Public Administration and Social Service Professions, 26% Health Professions and Related Programs, 19% Business, Management, Marketing, and Related Support Services, 8% Homeland Security, Law Enforcement, Firefighting and Related Protective Services, 4% Education
Expenses: 2019-2020: $33,048; room/board: $12,144
Financial aid: (315) 279-5232; 78% of undergrads determined to have financial need; average aid package $19,184

The King's College
New York NY
(212) 659-3610
U.S. News ranking: Nat. Lib. Arts, second tier
Website: www.tkc.edu/
Admissions email: admissions@tkc.edu
Private; founded 1938
Affiliation: Undenominational
Freshman admissions: more selective; 2018-2019: 1,943 applied, 1,078 accepted. Either SAT or ACT required. SAT 25/75 percentile: 1120-1310. High school rank: N/A
Early decision deadline: N/A, notification date: N/A

Early action deadline: 11/15, notification date: 12/15
Application deadline (fall): rolling
Undergraduate student body: 535 full time, 19 part time; 34% male, 66% female; 1% American Indian, 4% Asian, 5% black, 10% Hispanic, 0% multiracial, 0% Pacific Islander, 65% white, 4% international; 9% from in state; N/A live on campus; 0% of students in fraternities, 0% in sororities
Most popular majors: 34% Humanities/Humanistic Studies, 33% Liberal Arts and Sciences, General Studies and Humanities, Other, 22% Business Administration and Management, General, 6% Finance, General, 2% Religion/Religious Studies
Expenses: 2019-2020: $37,690; room/board: $17,184
Financial aid: (646) 237-8902; 68% of undergrads determined to have financial need; average aid package $28,046

Le Moyne College
Syracuse NY
(315) 445-4300
U.S. News ranking: Reg. U. (N), No. 14
Website: www.lemoyne.edu
Admissions email: admission@lemoyne.edu
Private; founded 1946
Affiliation: Roman Catholic
Freshman admissions: selective; 2018-2019: 7,158 applied, 4,925 accepted. Either SAT or ACT required for some. SAT 25/75 percentile: 1080-1270. High school rank: 20% in top tenth, 54% in top quarter, 87% in top half
Early decision deadline: N/A, notification date: N/A
Early action deadline: 11/15, notification date: 12/15
Application deadline (fall): rolling
Undergraduate student body: 2,353 full time, 394 part time; 40% male, 60% female; 0% American Indian, 3% Asian, 6% black, 7% Hispanic, 3% multiracial, 0% Pacific Islander, 77% white, 1% international; 76% from in state; 58% live on campus; 0% of students in fraternities, 0% in sororities
Most popular majors: 13% Psychology, General, 12% Biology/Biological Sciences, General, 10% Registered Nursing/Registered Nurse, 8% Marketing/Marketing Management, General, 6% Finance, General
Expenses: 2019-2020: $35,230; room/board: $14,120
Financial aid: (315) 445-4400; 83% of undergrads determined to have financial need; average aid package $27,819

LIM College
New York NY
(800) 677-1323
U.S. News ranking: Business, unranked
Website: www.limcollege.edu
Admissions email: admissions@limcollege.edu
For-profit; founded 1939

Freshman admissions: less selective; 2018-2019: 1,348 applied, 1,125 accepted. Neither SAT nor ACT required. SAT 25/75 percentile: 970-1150. High school rank: N/A
Early decision deadline: N/A, notification date: N/A
Early action deadline: 11/15, notification date: 12/15
Application deadline (fall): rolling
Undergraduate student body: 1,391 full time, 112 part time; 11% male, 89% female; 1% American Indian, 11% Asian, 19% black, 12% Hispanic, 0% multiracial, 1% Pacific Islander, 46% white, 1% international; N/A from in state; 24% live on campus; N/A of students in fraternities, N/A in sororities
Most popular majors: 91% Business, Management, Marketing, and Related Support Services, 9% Visual and Performing Arts
Expenses: 2019-2020: $27,810; room/board: $20,840
Financial aid: (212) 310-0689

Long Island University
Brookville NY
(516) 299-2900
U.S. News ranking: Nat. U., No. 240
Website: www.liu.edu
Admissions email: admissions@liu.edu
Private; founded 1926
Freshman admissions: selective; 2018-2019: 14,540 applied, 10,983 accepted. Either SAT or ACT required. SAT 25/75 percentile: 1050-1250. High school rank: 15% in top tenth, 42% in top quarter, 72% in top half
Early decision deadline: N/A, notification date: N/A
Early action deadline: 12/1, notification date: 12/15
Application deadline (fall): rolling
Undergraduate student body: 5,688 full time, 4,230 part time; 36% male, 64% female; 0% American Indian, 11% Asian, 15% black, 14% Hispanic, 2% multiracial, 0% Pacific Islander, 35% white, 4% international; 87% from in state; 22% live on campus; 9% of students in fraternities, 14% in sororities
Most popular majors: 16% Registered Nursing/Registered Nurse, 12% Business Administration and Management, General, 9% Health Professions and Related Clinical Sciences, Other, 7% Psychology, General, 5% Biology/Biological Sciences, General
Expenses: 2019-2020: $38,368; room/board: $14,350
Financial aid: N/A; 77% of undergrads determined to have financial need; average aid package $26,065

Manhattan College
Riverdale NY
(718) 862-7200
U.S. News ranking: Reg. U. (N), No. 13
Website: www.manhattan.edu
Admissions email: admit@manhattan.edu
Private; founded 1853
Affiliation: Roman Catholic
Freshman admissions: selective; 2018-2019: 7,929 applied, 5,905 accepted. Either SAT or ACT required. SAT 25/75 percentile: 1070-1260. High school rank: 23% in top tenth, 54% in top quarter, 79% in top half
Early decision deadline: 11/15, notification date: 12/15
Early action deadline: N/A, notification date: N/A
Application deadline (fall): rolling
Undergraduate student body: 3,455 full time, 199 part time; 55% male, 45% female; 0% American Indian, 5% Asian, 6% black, 23% Hispanic, 2% multiracial, 0% Pacific Islander, 55% white, 3% international
Most popular majors: Information not available
Expenses: 2018-2019: $42,608; room/board: $16,220
Financial aid: (718) 862-7178

Manhattan School of Music[1]
New York NY
(917) 493-4436
U.S. News ranking: Arts, unranked
Website: msmnyc.edu/
Admissions email: admission@msmnyc.edu
Private; founded 1917
Application deadline (fall): N/A
Undergraduate student body: N/A full time, N/A part time
Expenses: N/A
Financial aid: (917) 493-4809

Manhattanville College
Purchase NY
(914) 323-5464
U.S. News ranking: Reg. U. (N), No. 73
Website: www.mville.edu
Admissions email: admissions@mville.edu
Private; founded 1841
Freshman admissions: selective; 2018-2019: 3,577 applied, 3,216 accepted. Either SAT or ACT required for some. SAT 25/75 percentile: 1030-1180. High school rank: 14% in top tenth, 34% in top quarter, 77% in top half
Early decision deadline: N/A, notification date: N/A
Early action deadline: 12/1, notification date: 1/1
Application deadline (fall): rolling
Undergraduate student body: 1,513 full time, 75 part time; 40% male, 60% female; 0% American Indian, 2% Asian, 10% black, 27% Hispanic, 3% multiracial, 0% Pacific Islander, 47% white, 7% international; 73% from in state; 60% live on campus; 0% of students in fraternities, 0% in sororities

Most popular majors: 22% Business Administration and Management, General, 12% Speech Communication and Rhetoric, 10% Psychology, General, 8% Social Sciences, General, 6% Education, General
Expenses: 2019-2020: $39,570; room/board: $14,520
Financial aid: (914) 323-5357; 69% of undergrads determined to have financial need; average aid package $28,115

Marist College
Poughkeepsie NY
(845) 575-3226
U.S. News ranking: Reg. U. (N), No. 10
Website: www.marist.edu
Admissions email: admissions@marist.edu
Private; founded 1929
Freshman admissions: more selective; 2018-2019: 11,207 applied, 5,181 accepted. Neither SAT nor ACT required. SAT 25/75 percentile: 1140-1320. High school rank: 22% in top tenth, 51% in top quarter, 85% in top half
Early decision deadline: 11/15, notification date: 12/15
Early action deadline: 11/15, notification date: 1/15
Application deadline (fall): 2/1
Undergraduate student body: 5,139 full time, 531 part time; 42% male, 58% female; 0% American Indian, 3% Asian, 4% black, 10% Hispanic, 3% multiracial, 0% Pacific Islander, 76% white, 2% international; 47% from in state; 61% live on campus; 3% of students in fraternities, 3% in sororities
Most popular majors: 35% Business, Management, Marketing, and Related Support Services, 18% Communication, Journalism, and Related Programs, 10% Psychology, 8% Computer and Information Sciences and Support Services, 4% Biological and Biomedical Sciences
Expenses: 2019-2020: $40,525; room/board: $17,970
Financial aid: (845) 575-3230; 57% of undergrads determined to have financial need; average aid package $25,864

Marymount Manhattan College
New York NY
(212) 517-0430
U.S. News ranking: Nat. Lib. Arts, second tier
Website: www.mmm.edu
Admissions email: admissions@mmm.edu
Private; founded 1936
Freshman admissions: selective; 2018-2019: 5,705 applied, 4,450 accepted. Either SAT or ACT required. SAT 25/75 percentile: 1030-1220. High school rank: N/A
Early decision deadline: N/A, notification date: N/A
Early action deadline: N/A, notification date: N/A

Undergraduate student body: 1,861 full time, 202 part time; 22% male, 78% female; 0% American Indian, 3% Asian, 9% black, 16% Hispanic, 4% multiracial, 0% Pacific Islander, 58% white, 4% international; 37% from in state; 38% live on campus; N/A of students in fraternities, N/A in sororities
Most popular majors: 58% Visual and Performing Arts, 13% Communication, Journalism, and Related Programs, 10% Business, Management, Marketing, and Related Support Services, 7% Psychology, 3% English Language and Literature/Letters
Expenses: 2019-2020: $35,628; room/board: $17,976
Financial aid: (212) 517-0500; 68% of undergrads determined to have financial need; average aid package $18,930

Medaille College[1]
Buffalo NY
(716) 880-2200
U.S. News ranking: Reg. U. (N), second tier
Website: www.medaille.edu
Admissions email: admissionsug@medaille.edu
Private; founded 1937
Application deadline (fall): rolling
Undergraduate student body: N/A full time, N/A part time
Expenses: N/A
Financial aid: (716) 880-2256

Mercy College
Dobbs Ferry NY
(877) 637-2946
U.S. News ranking: Reg. U. (N), second tier
Website: www.mercy.edu
Admissions email: admissions@mercy.edu
Private; founded 1950
Freshman admissions: less selective; 2018-2019: 6,851 applied, 5,443 accepted. Neither SAT nor ACT required. SAT 25/75 percentile: N/A. High school rank: N/A
Early decision deadline: N/A, notification date: N/A
Early action deadline: N/A, notification date: N/A
Application deadline (fall): rolling
Undergraduate student body: 5,001 full time, 1,610 part time; 34% male, 66% female; 0% American Indian, 4% Asian, 22% black, 41% Hispanic, 1% multiracial, 0% Pacific Islander, 21% white, 1% international; 92% from in state; 12% live on campus; N/A of students in fraternities, N/A in sororities
Most popular majors: 23% Health Professions and Related Programs, 21% Business, Management, Marketing, and Related Support Services, 19% Social Sciences, 11% Psychology, 6% Homeland Security, Law Enforcement, Firefighting and Related Protective Services
Expenses: 2019-2020: $19,594; room/board: $14,400
Financial aid: (888) 464-6737; 87% of undergrads determined to have financial need; average aid package $15,347

Metropolitan College of New York[1]
New York NY
(212) 343-1234
U.S. News ranking: Reg. U. (N), second tier
Website: www.mcny.edu
Admissions email: admissions@mcny.edu
Private; founded 1964
Application deadline (fall): rolling
Undergraduate student body: N/A full time, N/A part time
Expenses: 2018-2019: $19,454; room/board: N/A
Financial aid: (212) 343-1234

Molloy College
Rockville Centre NY
(516) 323-4000
U.S. News ranking: Reg. U. (N), No. 23
Website: www.molloy.edu
Admissions email: admissions@molloy.edu
Private; founded 1955
Freshman admissions: selective; 2018-2019: 4,427 applied, 3,587 accepted. Either SAT or ACT required. SAT 25/75 percentile: 1020-1210. High school rank: 17% in top tenth, 56% in top quarter, 84% in top half
Early decision deadline: N/A, notification date: N/A
Early action deadline: 12/1, notification date: 12/15
Application deadline (fall): rolling
Undergraduate student body: 2,762 full time, 677 part time; 27% male, 73% female; 0% American Indian, 8% Asian, 9% black, 17% Hispanic, 2% multiracial, 0% Pacific Islander, 61% white, 0% international; 96% from in state; 8% live on campus; N/A of students in fraternities, N/A in sororities
Most popular majors: 53% Health Professions and Related Programs, 13% Business, Management, Marketing, and Related Support Services, 7% Education, 5% Psychology, 4% Homeland Security, Law Enforcement, Firefighting and Related Protective Services
Expenses: 2019-2020: $32,600; room/board: $15,560
Financial aid: (516) 323-4200; 80% of undergrads determined to have financial need; average aid package $17,046

Monroe College
Bronx NY
(800) 556-6676
U.S. News ranking: Reg. U. (N), No. 80
Website: www.monroecollege.edu
Admissions email: admissions@monroecollege.edu
For-profit; founded 1933
Freshman admissions: least selective; 2018-2019: 6,717 applied, 2,947 accepted. Neither SAT nor ACT required. SAT 25/75 percentile: 650-1053. High school rank: N/A
Early decision deadline: N/A, notification date: N/A

Early action deadline: 12/15, notification date: 1/31
Application deadline (fall): rolling
Undergraduate student body: 4,265 full time, 1,303 part time; 39% male, 61% female; 0% American Indian, 2% Asian, 41% black, 42% Hispanic, 0% multiracial, 0% Pacific Islander, 3% white, 11% international; 83% from in state; 17% live on campus; 0% of students in fraternities, 0% in sororities
Most popular majors: 38% Business, Management, Marketing, and Related Support Services, 24% Health Professions and Related Programs, 19% Homeland Security, Law Enforcement, Firefighting and Related Protective Services, 4% Computer and Information Sciences and Support Services, 3% Personal and Culinary Services
Expenses: 2019-2020: $15,860; room/board: $10,950
Financial aid: (718) 933-6700; 89% of undergrads determined to have financial need; average aid package $11,768

Mount St. Mary College
Newburgh NY
(845) 569-3488
U.S. News ranking: Reg. U. (N), No. 113
Website: www.msmc.edu
Admissions email: admissions@msmc.edu
Private; founded 1959
Freshman admissions: selective; 2018-2019: 3,588 applied, 3,365 accepted. Either SAT or ACT required. SAT 25/75 percentile: 1020-1170. High school rank: 9% in top tenth, 34% in top quarter, 66% in top half
Early decision deadline: N/A, notification date: N/A
Early action deadline: N/A, notification date: N/A
Application deadline (fall): 8/15
Undergraduate student body: 1,675 full time, 330 part time; 29% male, 71% female; 1% American Indian, 2% Asian, 7% black, 17% Hispanic, 1% multiracial, 0% Pacific Islander, 56% white, 1% international; 87% from in state; 48% live on campus; N/A of students in fraternities, N/A in sororities
Most popular majors: 33% Health Professions and Related Programs, 20% Business, Management, Marketing, and Related Support Services, 10% Psychology, 6% Social Sciences, 5% Biological and Biomedical Sciences
Expenses: 2019-2020: $32,772; room/board: $15,864
Financial aid: (845) 569-3394; 80% of undergrads determined to have financial need; average aid package $22,048

Nazareth College
Rochester NY
(585) 389-2860
U.S. News ranking: Reg. U. (N), No. 32
Website: www.naz.edu
Admissions email: admissions@naz.edu
Private; founded 1924
Freshman admissions: more selective; 2018-2019: 4,273 applied, 2,719 accepted. Neither SAT nor ACT required. SAT 25/75 percentile: 1090-1270. High school rank: 25% in top tenth, 58% in top quarter, 88% in top half
Early decision deadline: 11/15, notification date: 12/15
Early action deadline: N/A, notification date: N/A
Application deadline (fall): 2/1
Undergraduate student body: 2,176 full time, 93 part time; 26% male, 74% female; 0% American Indian, 3% Asian, 5% black, 6% Hispanic, 2% multiracial, 0% Pacific Islander, 78% white, 1% international; 89% from in state; 57% live on campus; 0% of students in fraternities, 0% in sororities
Most popular majors: 31% Health Professions and Related Programs, 12% Business, Management, Marketing, and Related Support Services, 10% Psychology, 10% Visual and Performing Arts, 8% Education
Expenses: 2019-2020: $35,416; room/board: $14,230
Financial aid: (585) 389-2310; 83% of undergrads determined to have financial need; average aid package $28,092

The New School
New York NY
(800) 292-3040
U.S. News ranking: Nat. U., No. 153
Website: www.newschool.edu
Admissions email: admission@newschool.edu
Private; founded 1919
Freshman admissions: selective; 2018-2019: 9,911 applied, 5,611 accepted. Neither SAT nor ACT required. SAT 25/75 percentile: 1150-1360. High school rank: 17% in top tenth, 43% in top quarter, 83% in top half
Early decision deadline: N/A, notification date: N/A
Early action deadline: 11/1, notification date: 12/20
Application deadline (fall): 8/1
Undergraduate student body: 6,646 full time, 796 part time; 25% male, 75% female; 0% American Indian, 10% Asian, 5% black, 12% Hispanic, 4% multiracial, 0% Pacific Islander, 33% white, 31% international; 19% from in state; 25% live on campus; 0% of students in fraternities, 0% in sororities
Most popular majors: 19% Fashion/Apparel Design, 10% Fine and Studio Arts Management, 9% Web Page, Digital/Multimedia and Information Resources Design, 8% Liberal Arts and Sciences/Liberal Studies, 5% Fine/Studio Arts, General

Expenses: 2019-2020: $50,954; room/board: $17,600
Financial aid: (212) 229-8930; 40% of undergrads determined to have financial need; average aid package $28,653

New York Institute of Technology
Old Westbury NY
(800) 345-6948
U.S. News ranking: Reg. U. (N), No. 42
Website: www.nyit.edu
Admissions email: admissions@nyit.edu
Private; founded 1955
Freshman admissions: selective; 2018-2019: 9,145 applied, 6,927 accepted. Either SAT or ACT required. SAT 25/75 percentile: 1050-1270. High school rank: N/A
Early decision deadline: N/A, notification date: N/A
Early action deadline: N/A, notification date: N/A
Application deadline (fall): rolling
Undergraduate student body: 3,250 full time, 398 part time; 62% male, 38% female; 0% American Indian, 18% Asian, 10% black, 17% Hispanic, 5% multiracial, 0% Pacific Islander, 26% white, 16% international; 85% from in state; 16% live on campus; 3% of students in fraternities, 4% in sororities
Most popular majors: 16% Biological and Biomedical Sciences, 15% Computer and Information Sciences and Support Services, 13% Architecture and Related Services, 13% Engineering, 12% Business, Management, Marketing, and Related Support Services
Expenses: 2019-2020: $38,010; room/board: $14,470
Financial aid: (516) 686-7680; 73% of undergrads determined to have financial need; average aid package $27,482

New York School of Interior Design[1]
New York NY
(212) 472-1500
U.S. News ranking: Arts, unranked
Website: www.nysid.edu
Admissions email: N/A
Private
Application deadline (fall): N/A
Undergraduate student body: N/A full time, N/A part time
Expenses: N/A
Financial aid: N/A

New York University
New York NY
(212) 998-4500
U.S. News ranking: Nat. U., No. 29
Website: www.nyu.edu
Admissions email: admissions@nyu.edu
Private; founded 1831
Freshman admissions: most selective; 2018-2019: 71,834 applied, 14,359 accepted. Neither

SAT nor ACT required. SAT 25/75 percentile: 1310-1510. High school rank: 71% in top tenth, 100% in top quarter, 100% in top half
Early decision deadline: 11/1, notification date: 12/15
Early action deadline: N/A, notification date: N/A
Application deadline (fall): 1/1
Undergraduate student body: 25,725 full time, 1,008 part time; 42% male, 58% female; 0% American Indian, 19% Asian, 7% black, 15% Hispanic, 4% multiracial, 0% Pacific Islander, 28% white, 20% international; 33% from in state; 42% live on campus; 4% of students in fraternities, 7% in sororities
Most popular majors: 18% Visual and Performing Arts, 14% Social Sciences, 13% Business, Management, Marketing, and Related Support Services, 9% Liberal Arts and Sciences, General Studies and Humanities, 8% Health Professions and Related Programs
Expenses: 2019-2020: $53,308; room/board: $18,684
Financial aid: (212) 998-4444, 50% of undergrads determined to have financial need; average aid package $36,209

Niagara University
Niagara University NY
(716) 286-8700
U.S. News ranking: Reg. U. (N), No. 32
Website: www.niagara.edu
Admissions email: admissions@niagara.edu
Private; founded 1856
Affiliation: Roman Catholic
Freshman admissions: selective; 2018-2019: 3,105 applied, 2,690 accepted. Either SAT or ACT required for some. SAT 25/75 percentile: 1020-1200. High school rank: 16% in top tenth, 40% in top quarter, 77% in top half
Early decision deadline: N/A, notification date: N/A
Early action deadline: 12/15, notification date: 1/3
Application deadline (fall): 8/30
Undergraduate student body: 2,670 full time, 148 part time; 37% male, 63% female; 1% American Indian, 2% Asian, 5% black, 5% Hispanic, 3% multiracial, 0% Pacific Islander, 68% white, 15% international; N/A from in state; 40% live on campus; 1% of students in fraternities, 6% in sororities
Most popular majors: 27% Business, Management, Marketing, and Related Support Services, 21% Education, 14% Health Professions and Related Programs, 10% Social Sciences, 6% Biological and Biomedical Sciences
Expenses: 2019-2020: $34,510; room/board: $11,700
Financial aid: (716) 286-8686; 69% of undergrads determined to have financial need; average aid package $27,511

Nyack College

Nyack NY
(845) 675-4400
U.S. News ranking: Reg. U. (N), second tier
Website: www.nyack.edu
Admissions email: admissions@nyack.edu
Private; founded 1882
Affiliation: Christ and Missionary Alliance Church
Freshman admissions: least selective; 2018-2019: 470 applied, 462 accepted. Either SAT or ACT required for some. SAT 25/75 percentile: 868-1108. High school rank: 11% in top tenth, 24% in top quarter, 51% in top half
Early decision deadline: N/A, notification date: N/A
Early action deadline: N/A, notification date: N/A
Application deadline (fall): rolling
Undergraduate student body: 1,090 full time, 249 part time; 44% male, 56% female; 1% American Indian, 6% Asian, 29% black, 30% Hispanic, 3% multiracial, 1% Pacific Islander, 21% white, 7% international; N/A from in state; 67% live on campus; N/A of students in fraternities, N/A in sororities
Most popular majors: 31% Business, Management, Marketing, and Related Support Services, 13% Theology and Religious Vocations, 8% Multi/Interdisciplinary Studies, 8% Public Administration and Social Service Professions, 7% Psychology
Expenses: 2019-2020: $25,500; room/board: $10,000
Financial aid: (845) 675-4737

Pace University

New York NY
(800) 874-7223
U.S. News ranking: Nat. U., No. 202
Website: www.pace.edu
Admissions email: undergradadmission@pace.edu
Private; founded 1906
Freshman admissions: selective; 2018-2019: 21,520 applied, 16,327 accepted. Either SAT or ACT required for some. SAT 25/75 percentile: 1060-1220. High school rank: 15% in top tenth, 41% in top quarter, 77% in top half
Early decision deadline: 11/1, notification date: 12/1
Early action deadline: 11/1, notification date: 12/1
Application deadline (fall): 2/15
Undergraduate student body: 7,943 full time, 1,017 part time; 38% male, 62% female; 0% American Indian, 8% Asian, 11% black, 12% Hispanic, 5% multiracial, 0% Pacific Islander, 51% white, 10% international; 51% from in state; 42% live on campus; 5% of students in fraternities, 6% in sororities
Most popular majors: 30% Business, Management, Marketing, and Related Support Services, 15% Visual and Performing Arts, 10% Health

Professions and Related Programs, 6% Psychology, 5% Computer and Information Sciences and Support Services
Expenses: 2019-2020: $46,446; room/board: $19,634
Financial aid: (877) 672-1830; 68% of undergrads determined to have financial need; average aid package $33,739

Paul Smith's College

Paul Smiths NY
(888) 873-6570
U.S. News ranking: Reg. Coll. (N), No. 20
Website: www.paulsmiths.edu
Admissions email: admissions@paulsmiths.edu
Private; founded 1946
Freshman admissions: less selective; 2018-2019: 1,302 applied, 752 accepted. Neither SAT nor ACT required. SAT 25/75 percentile: N/A. High school rank: N/A
Early decision deadline: N/A, notification date: N/A
Early action deadline: N/A, notification date: N/A
Application deadline (fall): rolling
Undergraduate student body: 731 full time, 14 part time; 67% male, 33% female; 1% American Indian, 2% Asian, 3% black, 4% Hispanic, 1% multiracial, 0% Pacific Islander, 84% white, 0% international; 68% from in state; 89% live on campus; 0% of students in fraternities, 0% in sororities
Most popular majors: 53% Natural Resources and Conservation, 11% Personal and Culinary Services, 8% Parks, Recreation, Leisure, and Fitness Studies, 4% Multi/Interdisciplinary Studies, 3% Business, Management, Marketing, and Related Support Services
Expenses: 2018-2019: $28,452; room/board: $12,240
Financial aid: (518) 327-6119

Plaza College[1]

Forest Hills NY
(718) 779-1430
U.S. News ranking: Reg. Coll. (N), unranked
Website: www.plazacollege.edu
Admissions email: N/A
For-profit; founded 1916
Application deadline (fall): N/A
Undergraduate student body: N/A full time, N/A part time
Expenses: N/A
Financial aid: N/A

Pratt Institute

Brooklyn NY
(718) 636-3514
U.S. News ranking: Arts, unranked
Website: www.pratt.edu
Admissions email: admissions@pratt.edu
Private; founded 1887
Freshman admissions: more selective; 2018-2019: 7,941 applied, 3,060 accepted. Either SAT or ACT required. SAT 25/75 percentile: 1110-1330. High school rank: N/A

Early decision deadline: N/A, notification date: N/A
Early action deadline: 11/1, notification date: 12/22
Application deadline (fall): 1/5
Undergraduate student body: 3,338 full time, 97 part time; 30% male, 70% female; 0% American Indian, 12% Asian, 4% black, 9% Hispanic, 3% multiracial, 0% Pacific Islander, 38% white, 32% international; 27% from in state; 59% live on campus; N/A of students in fraternities, N/A in sororities
Most popular majors: 17% Architecture, 11% Graphic Design, 11% Interior Design, 10% Illustration, 8% Industrial and Product Design
Expenses: 2019-2020: $53,824; room/board: $13,294
Financial aid: (718) 636-3599; 44% of undergrads determined to have financial need; average aid package $30,615

Purchase College–SUNY

Purchase NY
(914) 251-6300
U.S. News ranking: Nat. Lib. Arts, second tier
Website: www.purchase.edu
Admissions email: admissions@purchase.edu
Public; founded 1967
Freshman admissions: selective; 2018-2019: 3,421 applied, 1,453 accepted. Neither SAT nor ACT required. SAT 25/75 percentile: 1060-1270. High school rank: N/A
Early decision deadline: N/A, notification date: N/A
Early action deadline: 11/15, notification date: 1/1
Application deadline (fall): 5/1
Undergraduate student body: 3,834 full time, 330 part time; 42% male, 58% female; 0% American Indian, 4% Asian, 12% black, 23% Hispanic, 5% multiracial, 0% Pacific Islander, 52% white, 3% international; 87% from in state; 68% live on campus; 0% of students in fraternities, 0% in sororities
Most popular majors: 10% Liberal Arts and Sciences/Liberal Studies, 7% Speech Communication and Rhetoric, 6% Psychology, General, 5% Dance, General, 4% Drama and Dramatics/Theatre Arts, General
Expenses: 2019-2020: $8,698 in state, $18,478 out of state; room/board: $13,764
Financial aid: (914) 251-6354; 67% of undergrads determined to have financial need; average aid package $10,976

Rensselaer Polytechnic Institute

Troy NY
(518) 276-6216
U.S. News ranking: Nat. U., No. 50
Website: www.rpi.edu
Admissions email: admissions@rpi.edu
Private; founded 1824

Freshman admissions: most selective; 2018-2019: 20,402 applied, 8,770 accepted. Either SAT or ACT required. SAT 25/75 percentile: 1330-1500. High school rank: 64% in top tenth, 92% in top quarter, 98% in top half
Early decision deadline: 11/1, notification date: 12/15
Early action deadline: N/A, notification date: N/A
Application deadline (fall): 1/15
Undergraduate student body: 6,607 full time, 21 part time; 68% male, 32% female; 0% American Indian, 14% Asian, 4% black, 9% Hispanic, 6% multiracial, 0% Pacific Islander, 51% white, 15% international; N/A from in state; 57% live on campus; 30% of students in fraternities, 16% in sororities
Most popular majors: 52% Engineering, 17% Computer and Information Sciences and Support Services, 6% Business, Management, Marketing, and Related Support Services, 5% Engineering Technologies and Engineering-Related Fields, 4% Biological and Biomedical Sciences
Expenses: 2019-2020: $55,378; room/board: $15,580
Financial aid: (518) 276-6813; 58% of undergrads determined to have financial need; average aid package $41,327

Roberts Wesleyan College

Rochester NY
(585) 594-6400
U.S. News ranking: Reg. U. (N), No. 73
Website: www.roberts.edu
Admissions email: admissions@roberts.edu
Private; founded 1866
Affiliation: Free Methodist
Freshman admissions: selective; 2018-2019: 1,509 applied, 975 accepted. Neither SAT nor ACT required. SAT 25/75 percentile: 1010-1230. High school rank: 15% in top tenth, 44% in top quarter, 81% in top half
Early decision deadline: N/A, notification date: N/A
Early action deadline: 11/15, notification date: 12/6
Application deadline (fall): 8/20
Undergraduate student body: 1,201 full time, 134 part time; 29% male, 71% female; 0% American Indian, 2% Asian, 8% black, 6% Hispanic, 4% multiracial, 0% Pacific Islander, 73% white, 5% international; N/A from in state; 62% live on campus; 0% of students in fraternities, 0% in sororities
Most popular majors: 37% Health Professions and Related Programs, 14% Business, Management, Marketing, and Related Support Services, 12% Education, 6% Public Administration and Social Service Professions, 5% Homeland Security, Law Enforcement, Firefighting and Related Protective Services

Expenses: 2019-2020: $32,494; room/board: $10,898
Financial aid: (585) 594-6150; 82% of undergrads determined to have financial need; average aid package $22,494

Rochester Institute of Technology

Rochester NY
(585) 475-6631
U.S. News ranking: Nat. U., No. 104
Website: www.rit.edu
Admissions email: admissions@rit.edu
Private; founded 1829
Freshman admissions: more selective; 2018-2019: 18,948 applied, 12,504 accepted. Either SAT or ACT required. SAT 25/75 percentile: 1200-1400. High school rank: 37% in top tenth, 73% in top quarter, 97% in top half
Early decision deadline: 11/1, notification date: 12/15
Early action deadline: N/A, notification date: N/A
Application deadline (fall): rolling
Undergraduate student body: 12,486 full time, 1,027 part time; 68% male, 32% female; 0% American Indian, 10% Asian, 4% black, 8% Hispanic, 4% multiracial, 0% Pacific Islander, 66% white, 7% international; 53% from in state; 51% live on campus; 4% of students in fraternities, 2% in sororities
Most popular majors: 24% Engineering, 15% Computer and Information Sciences and Support Services, 11% Engineering Technologies and Engineering-Related Fields, 11% Visual and Performing Arts, 10% Business, Management, Marketing, and Related Support Services
Expenses: 2019-2020: $45,890; room/board: $13,540
Financial aid: (585) 475-2186; 74% of undergrads determined to have financial need; average aid package $32,078

The Sage Colleges

Troy NY
(518) 244-2217
U.S. News ranking: Nat. U., No. 228
Website: www.sage.edu
Admissions email: admission@sage.edu
Private; founded 1916
Freshman admissions: less selective; 2018-2019: 2,413 applied, 2,249 accepted. Either SAT or ACT required for some. SAT 25/75 percentile: 940-1140. High school rank: 11% in top tenth, 39% in top quarter, 72% in top half
Early decision deadline: N/A, notification date: N/A
Early action deadline: N/A, notification date: N/A
Application deadline (fall): N/A
Undergraduate student body: 1,360 full time, 117 part time; 21% male, 79% female; 0% American Indian, 4% Asian, 11% black,

10% Hispanic, 4% multiracial, 0% Pacific Islander, 61% white, 1% international; 90% from in state; 48% live on campus; N/A of students in fraternities, N/A in sororities
Most popular majors: 29% Health Professions and Related Programs, 14% Business, Management, Marketing, and Related Support Services, 11% Visual and Performing Arts, 10% Biological and Biomedical Sciences, 10% Social Sciences
Expenses: 2019-2020: $31,883; room/board: $12,835
Financial aid: (518) 244-4525; 90% of undergrads determined to have financial need

Sarah Lawrence College
Bronxville NY
(914) 395-2510
U.S. News ranking: Nat. Lib. Arts. No. 68
Website: www.slc.edu
Admissions email: slcadmit@sarahlawrence.edu
Private; founded 1926
Freshman admissions: more selective; 2018-2019: 3,325 applied, 1,857 accepted. Neither SAT nor ACT required. SAT 25/75 percentile: 1240-1420. High school rank: 33% in top tenth, 63% in top quarter, 91% in top half
Early decision deadline: 11/1, notification date: 12/15
Early action deadline: 11/1, notification date: 12/15
Application deadline (fall): 1/15
Undergraduate student body: 1,396 full time, 14 part time; 27% male, 73% female; 0% American Indian, 5% Asian, 5% black, 10% Hispanic, 7% multiracial, 0% Pacific Islander, 54% white, 12% international; 21% from in state; 87% live on campus; 0% of students in fraternities, 0% in sororities
Most popular majors: 100% Liberal Arts and Sciences, General Studies and Humanities
Expenses: 2019-2020: $57,520; room/board: $16,120
Financial aid: (914) 395-2570; 63% of undergrads determined to have financial need; average aid package $39,024

School of Visual Arts
New York NY
(212) 592-2100
U.S. News ranking: Arts, unranked
Website: www.sva.edu/admissions/undergraduate
Admissions email: admissions@sva.edu
For profit; founded 1947
Freshman admissions: selective; 2018-2019: 4,364 applied, 3,055 accepted. Neither SAT nor ACT required. SAT 25/75 percentile: 1053-1320. High school rank: N/A
Early decision deadline: N/A, notification date: N/A
Early action deadline: N/A, notification date: N/A
Application deadline (fall): N/A

Undergraduate student body: 3,610 full time, 104 part time; 30% male, 70% female; 0% American Indian, 14% Asian, 4% black, 10% Hispanic, 0% multiracial, 0% Pacific Islander, 22% white, 46% international; 56% from in state; 31% live on campus; 0% of students in fraternities, 0% in sororities
Most popular majors: 26% Web Page, Digital/Multimedia and Information Resources Design, 13% Illustration, 12% Photography, 9% Computer Graphics, 9% Film/Video and Photographic Arts, Other
Expenses: 2019-2020: $41,900; room/board: $21,200
Financial aid: (212) 592-2043; 38% of undergrads determined to have financial need; average aid package $20,517

Siena College
Loudonville NY
(888) 287-4362
U.S. News ranking: Reg. U. (N), No. 16
Website: www.siena.edu
Admissions email: admissions@siena.edu
Private; founded 1937
Affiliation: Roman Catholic
Freshman admissions: selective; 2018-2019: 7,371 applied, 5,907 accepted. Either SAT or ACT required for some. SAT 25/75 percentile: 1070-1270. High school rank: 19% in top tenth, 51% in top quarter, 84% in top half
Early decision deadline: 12/1, notification date: 1/1
Early action deadline: 12/1, notification date: 1/7
Application deadline (fall): 3/1
Undergraduate student body: 3,026 full time, 141 part time; 44% male, 56% female; 0% American Indian, 4% Asian, 4% black, 8% Hispanic, 2% multiracial, 0% Pacific Islander, 78% white, 3% international; 80% from in state; 75% live on campus; 0% of students in fraternities, 0% in sororities
Most popular majors: 16% Marketing/Marketing Management, General, 14% Accounting, 12% Psychology, General, 9% Finance, General, 6% Economics, General
Expenses: 2019-2020: $38,355; room/board: $15,415
Financial aid: (518) 783-2427; 74% of undergrads determined to have financial need; average aid package $31,870

Skidmore College
Saratoga Springs NY
(518) 580-5570
U.S. News ranking: Nat. Lib. Arts. No. 39
Website: www.skidmore.edu
Admissions email: admissions@skidmore.edu
Private; founded 1903
Freshman admissions: more selective; 2018-2019: 10,796 applied, 2,907 accepted. Either SAT or ACT required for some. SAT 25/75 percentile: 1223-

1400. High school rank: 38% in top tenth, 78% in top quarter, 96% in top half
Early decision deadline: 11/15, notification date: 12/15
Early action deadline: N/A, notification date: N/A
Application deadline (fall): 1/15
Undergraduate student body: 2,585 full time, 27 part time; 39% male, 61% female; 0% American Indian, 5% Asian, 5% black, 9% Hispanic, 5% multiracial, 0% Pacific Islander, 62% white, 12% international; 35% from in state; 90% live on campus; 0% of students in fraternities, 0% in sororities
Most popular majors: 16% Social Sciences, 14% Business, Management, Marketing, and Related Support Services, 11% Visual and Performing Arts, 10% Biological and Biomedical Sciences, 8% English Language and Literature/Letters
Expenses: 2019-2020: $56,172; room/board: $15,000
Financial aid: (518) 580-5750; 42% of undergrads determined to have financial need; average aid package $49,600

St. Bonaventure University
St. Bonaventure NY
(800) 462-5050
U.S. News ranking: Reg. U. (N), No. 19
Website: www.sbu.edu
Admissions email: admissions@sbu.edu
Private; founded 1858
Affiliation: Roman Catholic
Freshman admissions: selective; 2018-2019: 3,163 applied, 2,304 accepted. Either SAT or ACT required. SAT 25/75 percentile: 1040-1240. High school rank: 13% in top tenth, 35% in top quarter, 73% in top half
Early decision deadline: N/A, notification date: N/A
Early action deadline: N/A, notification date: N/A
Application deadline (fall): 7/1
Undergraduate student body: 1,727 full time, 85 part time; 53% male, 47% female; 0% American Indian, 4% Asian, 6% black, 7% Hispanic, 2% multiracial, 0% Pacific Islander, 72% white, 3% international; 74% from in state; 83% live on campus; 0% of students in fraternities, 0% in sororities
Most popular majors: 9% Accounting, 8% Biology/Biological Sciences, General, 8% Finance, General, 8% Sport and Fitness Administration/Management, 7% Business Administration and Management, General
Expenses: 2019-2020: $35,431; room/board: $13,160
Financial aid: (716) 375-2020; 73% of undergrads determined to have financial need; average aid package $27,546

St. Francis College
Brooklyn Heights NY
(718) 489-5200
U.S. News ranking: Reg. Coll. (N). No. 13
Website: www.sfc.edu
Admissions email: admissions@sfc.edu
Private; founded 1859
Freshman admissions: less selective; 2018-2019: 2,795 applied, 2,142 accepted. Either SAT or ACT required for some. SAT 25/75 percentile: 850-1120. High school rank: N/A
Early decision deadline: N/A, notification date: N/A
Early action deadline: N/A, notification date: N/A
Application deadline (fall): 9/15
Undergraduate student body: 2,230 full time, 133 part time; 39% male, 61% female; 1% American Indian, 4% Asian, 19% black, 24% Hispanic, 3% multiracial, 1% Pacific Islander, 35% white, 8% international
Most popular majors: 24% Registered Nursing, Nursing Administration, Nursing Research and Clinical Nursing, 18% Business Administration, Management and Operations, 9% Communication and Media Studies, 8% Criminal Justice and Corrections, 8% Economics
Expenses: 2019-2020: $26,298; room/board: $17,200
Financial aid: (718) 489-5259; 93% of undergrads determined to have financial need; average aid package $19,888

St. John Fisher College
Rochester NY
(585) 385-8064
U.S. News ranking: Nat. U., No. 166
Website: www.sjfc.edu
Admissions email: admissions@sjfc.edu
Private; founded 1948
Affiliation: Roman Catholic
Freshman admissions: selective; 2018-2019: 4,594 applied, 2,961 accepted. Either SAT or ACT required. SAT 25/75 percentile: 1080-1250. High school rank: 24% in top tenth, 56% in top quarter, 85% in top half
Early decision deadline: 12/1, notification date: 1/15
Early action deadline: N/A, notification date: N/A
Application deadline (fall): rolling
Undergraduate student body: 2,623 full time, 129 part time; 41% male, 59% female; 0% American Indian, 3% Asian, 4% black, 5% Hispanic, 2% multiracial, 0% Pacific Islander, 85% white, 0% international; 96% from in state; 52% live on campus; 0% of students in fraternities, 0% in sororities
Most popular majors: 32% Business, Management, Marketing, and Related Support Services, 28% Health Professions and Related Programs, 7% Biological and Biomedical Sciences, 6% Social Sciences, 5% Psychology

Expenses: 2019-2020: $35,150; room/board: $12,650
Financial aid: (585) 385-8042; 80% of undergrads determined to have financial need; average aid package $23,459

St. John's University
Queens NY
(718) 990-2000
U.S. News ranking: Nat. U., No. 179
Website: www.stjohns.edu/
Admissions email: admhelp@stjohns.edu
Private; founded 1870
Affiliation: Roman Catholic
Freshman admissions: selective; 2018-2019: 27,276 applied, 19,929 accepted. Either SAT or ACT required for some. SAT 25/75 percentile: 1070-1270. High school rank: 21% in top tenth, 46% in top quarter, 77% in top half
Early decision deadline: 11/15, notification date: 12/15
Early action deadline: 12/15, notification date: 1/1
Application deadline (fall): rolling
Undergraduate student body: 11,741 full time, 5,143 part time; 42% male, 58% female; 0% American Indian, 15% Asian, 16% black, 11% Hispanic, 5% multiracial, 0% Pacific Islander, 41% white, 5% international; 73% from in state; 26% live on campus; 5% of students in fraternities, 9% in sororities
Most popular majors: 26% Business, Management, Marketing, and Related Support Services, 11% Communication, Journalism, and Related Programs, 10% Health Professions and Related Programs, 8% Biological and Biomedical Sciences, 8% Homeland Security, Law Enforcement, Firefighting and Related Protective Services
Expenses: 2019-2020: $43,000; room/board: $17,720
Financial aid: (718) 990-2000; 76% of undergrads determined to have financial need; average aid package $29,457

St. Joseph's College New York
Brooklyn NY
(631) 687-4500
U.S. News ranking: Reg. U. (N), No. 59
Website: www.sjcny.edu
Admissions email: longislandas@sjcny.edu
Private; founded 1916
Freshman admissions: selective; 2018-2019: 3,833 applied, 2,791 accepted. Either SAT or ACT required. SAT 25/75 percentile: 1020-1200. High school rank: N/A
Early decision deadline: N/A, notification date: N/A
Early action deadline: N/A, notification date: N/A
Application deadline (fall): rolling
Undergraduate student body: 3,485 full time, 606 part time; 32% male, 68% female; 0% American Indian, 3% Asian, 9% black, 17% Hispanic, 2% multiracial,

0% Pacific Islander, 58% white, 0% international; 98% from in state; N/A live on campus; N/A of students in fraternities, N/A in sororities
Most popular majors: 15% Special Education and Teaching, General, 11% Business Administration and Management, General, 7% Accounting, 6% Psychology, General, 6% Rhetoric and Composition
Expenses: 2019-2020: $29,200; room/board: N/A
Financial aid: (631) 687-2600; 79% of undergrads determined to have financial need; average aid package $15,823

St. Lawrence University
Canton NY
(315) 229-5261
U.S. News ranking: Nat. Lib. Arts, No. 58
Website: www.stlawu.edu
Admissions email: admissions@stlawu.edu
Private; founded 1856
Freshman admissions: more selective; 2018-2019: 6,458 applied, 2,975 accepted. Neither SAT nor ACT required. SAT 25/75 percentile: 1180-1350. High school rank: 36% in top tenth, 73% in top quarter, 93% in top half
Early decision deadline: 11/1, notification date: N/A
Early action deadline: N/A, notification date: N/A
Application deadline (fall): 2/1
Undergraduate student body: 2,407 full time, 34 part time; 45% male, 55% female; 0% American Indian, 1% Asian, 3% black, 5% Hispanic, 2% multiracial, 0% Pacific Islander, 78% white, 9% international; 35% from in state; 98% live on campus; 12% of students in fraternities, 18% in sororities
Most popular majors: 31% Social Sciences, 16% Business, Management, Marketing, and Related Support Services, 10% Biological and Biomedical Sciences, 8% Psychology, 6% Communication, Journalism, and Related Programs
Expenses: 2018-2019: $54,846; room/board: $14,134
Financial aid: (315) 229-5265; 62% of undergrads determined to have financial need; average aid package $46,622

Stony Brook University–SUNY
Stony Brook NY
(631) 632-6868
U.S. News ranking: Nat. U., No. 91
Website: www.stonybrook.edu
Admissions email: enroll@stonybrook.edu
Public; founded 1957
Freshman admissions: more selective; 2018-2019: 37,828 applied, 15,880 accepted. Either SAT or ACT required. SAT 25/75 percentile: 1230-1420. High school rank: 47% in top tenth, 80% in top quarter, 97% in top half

Early decision deadline: N/A, notification date: N/A
Early action deadline: N/A, notification date: N/A
Application deadline (fall): 1/15
Undergraduate student body: 16,341 full time, 1,181 part time; 52% male, 48% female; 0% American Indian, 26% Asian, 7% black, 12% Hispanic, 3% multiracial, 0% Pacific Islander, 32% white, 14% international; 94% from in state; 53% live on campus; 2% of students in fraternities, 2% in sororities
Most popular majors: 18% Health Professions and Related Programs, 13% Biological and Biomedical Sciences, 10% Business, Management, Marketing, and Related Support Services, 9% Engineering, 9% Psychology
Expenses: 2019-2020: $10,076 in state, $28,528 out of state; room/board: $14,196
Financial aid: (631) 632-6840; 56% of undergrads determined to have financial need; average aid package $14,200

St. Thomas Aquinas College
Sparkill NY
(845) 398-4100
U.S. News ranking: Reg. U. (N), No. 119
Website: www.stac.edu
Admissions email: admissions@stac.edu
Private; founded 1952
Affiliation: Roman Catholic
Freshman admissions: less selective; 2018-2019: 1,758 applied, 1,336 accepted. Either SAT or ACT required. SAT 25/75 percentile: 910-1120. High school rank: 10% in top tenth, 23% in top quarter, 53% in top half
Early decision deadline: N/A, notification date: N/A
Early action deadline: N/A, notification date: N/A
Application deadline (fall): rolling
Undergraduate student body: 1,164 full time, 698 part time; 48% male, 52% female; 0% American Indian, 3% Asian, 11% black, 24% Hispanic, 1% multiracial, 0% Pacific Islander, 50% white, 5% international; 82% from in state; 51% live on campus; 0% of students in fraternities, 0% in sororities
Most popular majors: 19% Business Administration and Management, General, 12% Criminal Justice/Law Enforcement Administration, 11% Special Education and Teaching, General, 10% Psychology, General, 6% Sport and Fitness Administration/Management
Expenses: 2019-2020: $33,050; room/board: $13,650
Financial aid: (845) 398-4097; 70% of undergrads determined to have financial need; average aid package $18,500

SUNY Buffalo State
Buffalo NY
(716) 878-4017
U.S. News ranking: Reg. U. (N), No. 104
Website: www.buffalostate.edu
Admissions email: admissions@buffalostate.edu
Public; founded 1871
Freshman admissions: less selective; 2018-2019: 15,815 applied, 9,583 accepted. Either SAT or ACT required. SAT 25/75 percentile: 860-1130. High school rank: N/A
Early decision deadline: N/A, notification date: N/A
Early action deadline: N/A, notification date: N/A
Application deadline (fall): rolling
Undergraduate student body: 7,278 full time, 804 part time; 43% male, 57% female; 0% American Indian, 4% Asian, 34% black, 13% Hispanic, 4% multiracial, 0% Pacific Islander, 44% white, 1% international; 99% from in state; 30% live on campus; 1% of students in fraternities, 1% in sororities
Most popular majors: 17% Business, Management, Marketing, and Related Support Services, 9% Education, 8% Homeland Security, Law Enforcement, Firefighting and Related Protective Services, 7% Liberal Arts and Sciences, General Studies and Humanities, 7% Social Sciences
Expenses: 2019-2020: $8,447 in state, $18,357 out of state; room/board: $13,970
Financial aid: (716) 878-4902; 89% of undergrads determined to have financial need; average aid package $9,122

SUNY College–Cortland
Cortland NY
(607) 753-4711
U.S. News ranking: Reg. U. (N), No. 63
Website: www2.cortland.edu/home/
Admissions email: admissions@cortland.edu
Public; founded 1868
Freshman admissions: selective; 2018-2019: 13,289 applied, 5,881 accepted. Either SAT or ACT required for some. SAT 25/75 percentile: 1060-1200. High school rank: 12% in top tenth, 47% in top quarter, 87% in top half
Early decision deadline: N/A, notification date: N/A
Early action deadline: 11/15, notification date: 1/1
Application deadline (fall): rolling
Undergraduate student body: 6,218 full time, 125 part time; 44% male, 56% female; 0% American Indian, 1% Asian, 6% black, 13% Hispanic, 2% multiracial, 0% Pacific Islander, 73% white, 1% international
Most popular majors: 23% Education, 20% Parks, Recreation, Leisure, and Fitness Studies, 10% Health Professions and Related Programs, 10%

Social Sciences, 7% Business, Management, Marketing, and Related Support Services
Expenses: 2019-2020: $8,782 in state, $18,692 out of state; room/board: $12,700
Financial aid: (607) 753-4717; 65% of undergrads determined to have financial need; average aid package $13,591

SUNY College of Agriculture and Technology–Cobleskill
Cobleskill NY
(518) 255-5525
U.S. News ranking: Reg. Coll. (N), No. 19
Website: www.cobleskill.edu
Admissions email: admissionsoffice@cobleskill.edu
Public; founded 1911
Freshman admissions: less selective; 2018-2019: 3,549 applied, 2,736 accepted. Either SAT or ACT required for some. SAT 25/75 percentile: 800-1030. High school rank: 5% in top tenth, 17% in top quarter, 54% in top half
Early decision deadline: N/A, notification date: N/A
Early action deadline: N/A, notification date: N/A
Application deadline (fall): rolling
Undergraduate student body: 2,174 full time, 118 part time; 47% male, 53% female; 0% American Indian, 1% Asian, 12% black, 12% Hispanic, 0% multiracial, 0% Pacific Islander, 67% white, 2% international; 91% from in state; 59% live on campus; N/A of students in fraternities, N/A in sororities
Most popular majors: 15% Business, Management, Marketing, and Related Support Services, Other, 14% Agricultural Animal Breeding, 9% Child Care and Support Services Management, 8% Wildlife, Fish and Wildlands Science and Management, 6% Agribusiness/Agricultural Business Operations
Expenses: 2019-2020: $8,456 in state, $18,236 out of state; room/board: $13,350
Financial aid: (518) 255-5637; 78% of undergrads determined to have financial need; average aid package $7,041

SUNY College of Environmental Science and Forestry
Syracuse NY
(315) 470-6600
U.S. News ranking: Nat. U., No. 121
Website: www.esf.edu
Admissions email: esfinfo@esf.edu
Public; founded 1911
Freshman admissions: more selective; 2018-2019: 2,018 applied, 1,239 accepted. Either SAT or ACT required. SAT 25/75 percentile: 1120-1310. High school rank: 25% in top tenth, 63% in top quarter, 95% in top half

Early decision deadline: 12/1, notification date: 1/15
Early action deadline: N/A, notification date: N/A
Application deadline (fall): 2/1
Undergraduate student body: 1,730 full time, 49 part time; 52% male, 48% female; 0% American Indian, 4% Asian, 2% black, 6% Hispanic, 3% multiracial, 0% Pacific Islander, 78% white, 3% international; 81% from in state; 35% live on campus; 2% of students in fraternities, 2% in sororities
Most popular majors: 35% Biological and Biomedical Sciences, 29% Natural Resources and Conservation, 14% Engineering, 6% Multi/Interdisciplinary Studies, 5% Business, Management, Marketing, and Related Support Services
Expenses: 2019-2020: $8,864 in state, $18,644 out of state; room/board: $16,600
Financial aid: (315) 470-6670; 60% of undergrads determined to have financial need; average aid package $10,160

SUNY College of Technology–Alfred
Alfred NY
(800) 425-3733
U.S. News ranking: Reg. Coll. (N), No. 10
Website: www.alfredstate.edu
Admissions email: admissions@alfredstate.edu
Public; founded 1908
Freshman admissions: selective; 2018-2019: 7,065 applied, 4,449 accepted. Either SAT or ACT required for some. SAT 25/75 percentile: 950-1170. High school rank: N/A
Early decision deadline: N/A, notification date: N/A
Early action deadline: N/A, notification date: N/A
Application deadline (fall): rolling
Undergraduate student body: 3,456 full time, 281 part time; 62% male, 38% female; 0% American Indian, 1% Asian, 12% black, 9% Hispanic, 3% multiracial, 0% Pacific Islander, 71% white, 1% international; 97% from in state; 63% live on campus; 5% of students in fraternities, 9% in sororities
Most popular majors: 18% Business, Management, Marketing, and Related Support Services, 16% Health Professions and Related Programs, 15% Mechanic and Repair Technologies/Technicians, 13% Engineering Technologies and Engineering-Related Fields, 9% Construction Trades
Expenses: 2019-2020: $8,570 in state, $12,440 out of state; room/board: $12,570
Financial aid: (607) 587-4253; 83% of undergrads determined to have financial need; average aid package $11,337

SUNY College of Technology–Canton

Canton NY
(800) 388-7123
U.S. News ranking: Reg. Coll. (N), No. 23
Website: www.canton.edu/
Admissions email: admissions@canton.edu
Public; founded 1906
Freshman admissions: least selective; 2018-2019: 4,485 applied, 3,499 accepted. Either SAT or ACT required for some. SAT 25/75 percentile: 900-1080. High school rank: 2% in top tenth, 14% in top quarter, 48% in top half
Early decision deadline: N/A, notification date: N/A
Early action deadline: N/A, notification date: N/A
Application deadline (fall): rolling
Undergraduate student body: 2,743 full time, 470 part time; 43% male, 57% female; 1% American Indian, 1% Asian, 15% black, 11% Hispanic, 2% multiracial, 0% Pacific Islander, 65% white, 1% international; 97% from in state; 39% live on campus; 1% of students in fraternities, 1% in sororities
Most popular majors: 11% Corrections and Criminal Justice, Other, 11% Health/Health Care Administration/Management, 11% Registered Nursing/Registered Nurse, 8% Business Administration and Management, General, 7% Veterinary/Animal Health Technology/Technician and Veterinary Assistant
Expenses: 2019-2020: $8,605 in state, $18,515 out of state; room/board: $13,000
Financial aid: (315) 386-7616; 86% of undergrads determined to have financial need; average aid package $11,054

SUNY College of Technology–Delhi

Delhi NY
(607) 746-4550
U.S. News ranking: Reg. Coll. (N), No. 15
Website: www.delhi.edu/
Admissions email: enroll@delhi.edu
Public; founded 1913
Freshman admissions: less selective; 2018-2019: 5,935 applied, 3,775 accepted. Either SAT or ACT required for some. SAT 25/75 percentile: 920-1090. High school rank: 4% in top tenth, 16% in top quarter, 49% in top half
Early decision deadline: N/A, notification date: N/A
Early action deadline: 12/1, notification date: 12/15
Application deadline (fall): 8/15
Undergraduate student body: 2,514 full time, 664 part time; 46% male, 54% female; 1% American Indian, 2% Asian, 16% black, 15% Hispanic, 3% multiracial, 0% Pacific Islander, 60% white, 1% international; 96% from in state; 52% live on campus; N/A of students in fraternities, N/A in sororities

Most popular majors: 44% Health Professions and Related Programs, 33% Business, Management, Marketing, and Related Support Services, 9% Homeland Security, Law Enforcement, Firefighting and Related Protective Services, 5% Physical Sciences, 4% Personal and Culinary Services
Expenses: 2019-2020: $8,610 in state, $12,380 out of state; room/board: $12,900
Financial aid: (607) 746-4570; 79% of undergrads determined to have financial need; average aid package $11,226

SUNY College– Old Westbury

Old Westbury NY
(516) 876-3200
U.S. News ranking: Reg. U. (N), second tier
Website: www.oldwestbury.edu
Admissions email: enroll@oldwestbury.edu
Public; founded 1965
Freshman admissions: less selective; 2018-2019: 4,749 applied, 3,703 accepted. Either SAT or ACT required. SAT 25/75 percentile: 970-1120. High school rank: N/A
Early decision deadline: N/A, notification date: N/A
Early action deadline: N/A, notification date: N/A
Application deadline (fall): rolling
Undergraduate student body: 4,759 full time, 670 part time; 41% male, 59% female; 0% American Indian, 11% Asian, 28% black, 26% Hispanic, 3% multiracial, 0% Pacific Islander, 28% white, 1% international; 99% from in state; 18% live on campus; 2% of students in fraternities, 2% in sororities
Most popular majors: 16% Psychology, 11% Business, Management, Marketing, and Related Support Services, 7% Philosophy and Religious Studies
Expenses: 2018-2019: $8,143 in state, $17,923 out of state; room/board: $11,530
Financial aid: N/A

SUNY College– Oneonta[1]

Oneonta NY
(607) 436-2524
U.S. News ranking: Reg. U. (N), No. 52
Website: suny.oneonta.edu/
Admissions email: admissions@oneonta.edu
Public; founded 1889
Application deadline (fall): rolling
Undergraduate student body: N/A full time, N/A part time
Expenses: 2018-2019: $8,421 in state, $17,871 out of state; room/board: $13,205
Financial aid: N/A

SUNY College– Potsdam

Potsdam NY
(315) 267-2180
U.S. News ranking: Reg. U. (N), No. 66
Website: www.potsdam.edu
Admissions email: admissions@potsdam.edu
Public; founded 1816
Freshman admissions: selective; 2018-2019: 6,423 applied, 4,130 accepted. Neither SAT nor ACT required. SAT 25/75 percentile: 1040-1230. High school rank: 15% in top tenth, 23% in top quarter, 85% in top half
Early decision deadline: N/A, notification date: N/A
Early action deadline: N/A, notification date: N/A
Application deadline (fall): rolling
Undergraduate student body: 3,221 full time, 77 part time; 40% male, 60% female; 2% American Indian, 2% Asian, 13% black, 15% Hispanic, 3% multiracial, 0% Pacific Islander, 61% white, 0% international; 96% from in state; 59% live on campus; 8% of students in fraternities, 11% in sororities
Most popular majors: 15% Education, 14% Visual and Performing Arts, 10% Social Sciences, 9% Business, Management, Marketing, and Related Support Services, 8% Psychology
Expenses: 2019-2020: $8,711 in state, $18,621 out of state; room/board: $13,900
Financial aid: (315) 267-2162; 79% of undergrads determined to have financial need; average aid package $15,257

SUNY Empire State College

Saratoga Springs NY
(518) 587-2100
U.S. News ranking: Reg. U. (N), unranked
Website: www.esc.edu
Admissions email: admissions@esc.edu
Public; founded 1971
Freshman admissions: least selective; 2018-2019: 726 applied, 574 accepted. Neither SAT nor ACT required. SAT 25/75 percentile: N/A. High school rank: N/A
Early decision deadline: N/A, notification date: N/A
Early action deadline: N/A, notification date: N/A
Application deadline (fall): rolling
Undergraduate student body: 3,599 full time, 5,708 part time; 38% male, 62% female; 0% American Indian, 2% Asian, 17% black, 14% Hispanic, 2% multiracial, 0% Pacific Islander, 58% white, 0% international
Most popular majors: 35% Business, Management, Marketing, and Related Support Services, 25% Public Administration and Social

Service Professions, 8% Health Professions and Related Programs, 8% Psychology, 6% Physical Sciences
Expenses: 2019-2020: $7,405 in state, $17,185 out of state; room/board: N/A
Financial aid: N/A

SUNY–Fredonia

Fredonia NY
(800) 252-1212
U.S. News ranking: Reg. U. (N), No. 56
Website: www.fredonia.edu
Admissions email: admissions@fredonia.edu
Public; founded 1826
Freshman admissions: selective; 2018-2019: 6,183 applied, 4,711 accepted. Either SAT or ACT required. SAT 25/75 percentile: 970-1170. High school rank: 17% in top tenth, 43% in top quarter, 76% in top half
Early decision deadline: N/A, notification date: N/A
Early action deadline: N/A, notification date: N/A
Application deadline (fall): rolling
Undergraduate student body: 4,314 full time, 119 part time; 43% male, 57% female; 0% American Indian, 2% Asian, 9% black, 10% Hispanic, 3% multiracial, 0% Pacific Islander, 72% white, 2% international; 95% from in state; 52% live on campus; 1% of students in fraternities, 1% in sororities
Most popular majors: 16% Business, Management, Marketing, and Related Support Services, 16% Education, 13% Visual and Performing Arts, 9% Communication, Journalism, and Related Programs, 5% Multi/Interdisciplinary Studies
Expenses: 2019-2020: $8,688 in state, $18,268 out of state; room/board: $12,790
Financial aid: (716) 673-3253; 74% of undergrads determined to have financial need; average aid package $12,199

SUNY–Geneseo

Geneseo NY
(585) 245-5571
U.S. News ranking: Reg. U. (N), No. 14
Website: www.geneseo.edu
Admissions email: admissions@geneseo.edu
Public; founded 1871
Freshman admissions: more selective; 2018-2019: 10,548 applied, 6,836 accepted. Either SAT or ACT required. SAT 25/75 percentile: 1120-1300. High school rank: 26% in top tenth, 60% in top quarter, 93% in top half
Early decision deadline: 11/15, notification date: 12/15
Early action deadline: N/A, notification date: N/A
Application deadline (fall): 1/1
Undergraduate student body: 5,304 full time, 143 part time; 39% male, 61% female; 0% American Indian, 6% Asian, 3% black,

9% Hispanic, 3% multiracial, 0% Pacific Islander, 76% white, 1% international; 97% from in state; 55% live on campus; 20% of students in fraternities, 21% in sororities
Most popular majors: 21% Social Sciences, 13% Business, Management, Marketing, and Related Support Services, 13% Psychology, 12% Biological and Biomedical Sciences, 9% Education
Expenses: 2019-2020: $8,927 in state, $18,837 out of state; room/board: $14,018
Financial aid: (585) 245-5731; 54% of undergrads determined to have financial need; average aid package $10,010

SUNY Maritime College

Throggs Neck NY
(718) 409-7221
U.S. News ranking: Reg. U. (N), No. 66
Website: www.sunymaritime.edu
Admissions email: admissions@sunymaritime.edu
Public; founded 1874
Freshman admissions: selective; 2018-2019: 1,355 applied, 971 accepted. Either SAT or ACT required. SAT 25/75 percentile: 1075-1260. High school rank: 50% in top tenth, 50% in top quarter, 100% in top half
Early decision deadline: 11/1, notification date: 12/15
Early action deadline: N/A, notification date: N/A
Application deadline (fall): 1/31
Undergraduate student body: 1,542 full time, 44 part time; 88% male, 12% female; 0% American Indian, 4% Asian, 5% black, 14% Hispanic, 3% multiracial, 0% Pacific Islander, 69% white, 2% international; N/A from in state; 83% live on campus; N/A of students in fraternities, N/A in sororities
Most popular majors: 38% Marine Science/Merchant Marine Officer, 20% Mechanical Engineering, 16% Business, Management, Marketing, and Related Support Services, Other, 10% Naval Architecture and Marine Engineering, 6% Atmospheric Sciences and Meteorology, General
Expenses: 2019-2020: $8,504 in state, $18,414 out of state; room/board: $13,340
Financial aid: (718) 409-7400; 53% of undergrads determined to have financial need; average aid package $8,523

SUNY–Morrisville

Morrisville NY
(315) 684-6046
U.S. News ranking: Reg. Coll. (N), No. 29
Website: www.morrisville.edu
Admissions email: admissions@morrisville.edu
Public; founded 1908
Freshman admissions: less selective; 2018-2019: 5,346 applied, 3,793 accepted. Either SAT or ACT required for some.

SAT 25/75 percentile: 930-1080. High school rank: 2% in top tenth, 11% in top quarter, 50% in top half
Early decision deadline: N/A, notification date: N/A
Early action deadline: N/A, notification date: N/A
Application deadline (fall): 8/17
Undergraduate student body: 2,508 full time, 478 part time; 51% male, 49% female; 0% American Indian, 1% Asian, 22% black, 8% Hispanic, 3% multiracial, 0% Pacific Islander, 64% white, 1% international; 95% from in state; 16% live on campus; 0% of students in fraternities, 0% in sororities
Most popular majors: 23% Agriculture, Agriculture Operations, and Related Sciences, 19% Homeland Security, Law Enforcement, Firefighting and Related Protective Services, 15% Business, Management, Marketing, and Related Support Services, 11% Mechanic and Repair Technologies/Technicians, 9% Computer and Information Sciences and Support Services
Expenses: 2019-2020: $8,670 in state, $13,740 out of state; room/board: $15,600
Financial aid: (315) 684-6289; 84% of undergrads determined to have financial need; average aid package $10,611

SUNY–New Paltz
New Paltz NY
(845) 257-3200
U.S. News ranking: Reg. U. (N), No. 28
Website: www.newpaltz.edu
Admissions email: admissions@newpaltz.edu
Public; founded 1828
Freshman admissions: more selective; 2018-2019: 15,419 applied, 6,375 accepted. Either SAT or ACT required. SAT 25/75 percentile: 1090-1270. High school rank: 22% in top tenth, 61% in top quarter, 90% in top half
Early decision deadline: N/A, notification date: N/A
Early action deadline: 11/15, notification date: 12/15
Application deadline (fall): 4/1
Undergraduate student body: 6,190 full time, 502 part time; 39% male, 61% female; 0% American Indian, 5% Asian, 6% black, 21% Hispanic, 3% multiracial, 0% Pacific Islander, 59% white, 2% international; N/A from in state; 47% live on campus; 5% of students in fraternities, 5% in sororities
Most popular majors: 17% Business, Management, Marketing, and Related Support Services, 13% Social Sciences, 12% Communication, Journalism, and Related Programs, 11% Visual and Performing Arts, 9% Education
Expenses: 2019-2020: $8,502 in state, $18,412 out of state; room/board: $13,928
Financial aid: (845) 257-3256; 63% of undergrads determined to have financial need; average aid package $11,606

SUNY–Oswego
Oswego NY
(315) 312-2250
U.S. News ranking: Reg. U. (N), No. 52
Website: www.oswego.edu
Admissions email: admiss@oswego.edu
Public; founded 1861
Freshman admissions: selective; 2018-2019: 13,414 applied, 7,192 accepted. Either SAT or ACT required. SAT 25/75 percentile: 1040-1210. High school rank: 11% in top tenth, 50% in top quarter, 84% in top half
Early decision deadline: N/A, notification date: N/A
Early action deadline: 11/30, notification date: 12/15
Application deadline (fall): rolling
Undergraduate student body: 6,767 full time, 314 part time; 50% male, 50% female; 0% American Indian, 3% Asian, 10% black, 12% Hispanic, 3% multiracial, 0% Pacific Islander, 69% white, 3% international; 97% from in state; 97% live on campus; 8% of students in fraternities, 11% in sororities
Most popular majors: 26% Business, Management, Marketing, and Related Support Services, 15% Communication, Journalism, and Related Programs, 7% Biological and Biomedical Sciences, 7% Education, 6% Health Professions and Related Programs
Expenses: 2019-2020: $8,640 in state, $18,220 out of state; room/board: $14,140
Financial aid: (315) 312-2248; 70% of undergrads determined to have financial need; average aid package $11,359

SUNY–Plattsburgh
Plattsburgh NY
(888) 673-0012
U.S. News ranking: Reg. U. (N), No. 63
Website: www.plattsburgh.edu
Admissions email: admissions@plattsburgh.edu
Public; founded 1889
Freshman admissions: selective; 2018-2019: 9,202 applied, 4,992 accepted. Either SAT or ACT required. SAT 25/75 percentile: 1050-1230. High school rank: 18% in top tenth, 43% in top quarter, 84% in top half
Early decision deadline: N/A, notification date: N/A
Early action deadline: N/A, notification date: N/A
Application deadline (fall): rolling
Undergraduate student body: 4,853 full time, 444 part time; 43% male, 57% female; 1% American Indian, 3% Asian, 10% black, 11% Hispanic, 2% multiracial, 0% Pacific Islander, 64% white, 6% international; 97% from in state; 55% live on campus; 15% of students in fraternities, 15% in sororities
Most popular majors: 19% Business, Management, Marketing, and Related Support

Services, 10% Health Professions and Related Programs, 8% Communication, Journalism, and Related Programs, 8% Psychology, 7% Homeland Security, Law Enforcement, Firefighting and Related Protective Services
Expenses: 2019-2020: $8,530 in state, $18,310 out of state; room/board: $13,630
Financial aid: (518) 564-2072; 68% of undergrads determined to have financial need; average aid package $14,248

SUNY Polytechnic Institute–Albany/Utica
Utica NY
(315) 792-7500
U.S. News ranking: Reg. U. (N), No. 12
Website: www.sunypoly.edu
Admissions email: admissions@sunypoly.edu
Public; founded 1966
Freshman admissions: selective; 2018-2019: 3,373 applied, 2,187 accepted. Either SAT or ACT required. SAT 25/75 percentile: 1000-1350. High school rank: 45% in top tenth, 68% in top quarter, 96% in top half
Early decision deadline: N/A, notification date: N/A
Early action deadline: 11/15, notification date: 12/15
Application deadline (fall): 6/1
Undergraduate student body: 1,930 full time, 330 part time; 65% male, 35% female; 0% American Indian, 8% Asian, 7% black, 9% Hispanic, 3% multiracial, 0% Pacific Islander, 72% white, 1% international; 97% from in state; 34% live on campus; 0% of students in fraternities, 0% in sororities
Most popular majors: 23% Engineering Technologies and Engineering-Related Fields, 19% Business, Management, Marketing, and Related Support Services, 17% Computer and Information Sciences and Support Services, 14% Health Professions and Related Programs, 9% Engineering
Expenses: 2019-2020: $8,561 in state, $17,811 out of state; room/board: $14,025
Financial aid: (315) 792-7210; 71% of undergrads determined to have financial need; average aid package $11,220

Syracuse University
Syracuse NY
(315) 443-3611
U.S. News ranking: Nat. U., No. 54
Website: www.syracuse.edu
Admissions email: orange@syr.edu
Private; founded 1870
Freshman admissions: more selective; 2018-2019: 34,981 applied, 17,443 accepted. Either SAT or ACT required. SAT 25/75 percentile: 1180-1370. High school rank: 39% in top tenth, 71% in top quarter, 94% in top half

Early decision deadline: 11/15, notification date: 12/15
Early action deadline: N/A, notification date: N/A
Application deadline (fall): 1/1
Undergraduate student body: 14,655 full time, 571 part time; 46% male, 54% female; 1% American Indian, 7% Asian, 7% black, 9% Hispanic, 3% multiracial, 0% Pacific Islander, 57% white, 14% international; 39% from in state; 53% live on campus; 26% of students in fraternities, 41% in sororities
Most popular majors: 15% Communication, Journalism, and Related Programs, 13% Social Sciences, 11% Business, Management, Marketing, and Related Support Services, 10% Visual and Performing Arts, 8% Engineering
Expenses: 2019-2020: $53,849; room/board: $15,910
Financial aid: (315) 443-1513; 43% of undergrads determined to have financial need; average aid package $40,030

Touro College
New York NY
(212) 463-0400
U.S. News ranking: Nat. U., second tier
Website: www.touro.edu/
Admissions email: admissions.nyscas@touro.edu
Private; founded 1971
Freshman admissions: selective; 2018-2019: 1,928 applied, 1,360 accepted. Neither SAT nor ACT required. SAT 25/75 percentile: 1085-1350. High school rank: N/A
Early decision deadline: N/A, notification date: N/A
Early action deadline: N/A, notification date: N/A
Application deadline (fall): rolling
Undergraduate student body: 3,934 full time, 2,048 part time; 28% male, 72% female; 0% American Indian, 3% Asian, 14% black, 9% Hispanic, 1% multiracial, 0% Pacific Islander, 60% white, 4% international; 86% from in state; N/A live on campus; N/A of students in fraternities, N/A in sororities
Most popular majors: 23% Psychology, 17% Multi/Interdisciplinary Studies, 16% Health Professions and Related Programs, 9% Biological and Biomedical Sciences, 6% Business, Management, Marketing, and Related Support Services
Expenses: 2019-2020: $20,550; room/board: $10,650
Financial aid: (646) 565-6000; 75% of undergrads determined to have financial need; average aid package $12,906

Union College
Schenectady NY
(518) 388-6112
U.S. News ranking: Nat. Lib. Arts, No. 45
Website: www.union.edu
Admissions email: admissions@union.edu
Private; founded 1795

Freshman admissions: more selective; 2018-2019: 6,716 applied, 2,598 accepted. Either SAT or ACT required for some. SAT 25/75 percentile: 1270-1430. High school rank: 61% in top tenth, 80% in top quarter, 94% in top half
Early decision deadline: 11/15, notification date: 12/15
Early action deadline: 11/1, notification date: N/A
Application deadline (fall): 1/15
Undergraduate student body: 2,195 full time, 11 part time; 54% male, 46% female; 0% American Indian, 5% Asian, 4% black, 8% Hispanic, 3% multiracial, 0% Pacific Islander, 70% white, 9% international; 40% from in state; 88% live on campus; 28% of students in fraternities, 34% in sororities
Most popular majors: 12% Economics, General, 9% Mechanical Engineering, 6% Biology/Biological Sciences, General, 6% Neuroscience, 6% Political Science and Government, General
Expenses: 2019-2020: $57,324; room/board: $14,061
Financial aid: (518) 388-6123; 50% of undergrads determined to have financial need; average aid package $46,068

United States Merchant Marine Academy
Kings Point NY
(866) 546-4778
U.S. News ranking: Reg. Coll. (N), No. 3
Website: www.usmma.edu
Admissions email: admissions@usmma.edu
Public; founded 1943
Freshman admissions: more selective; 2018-2019: 1,863 applied, 280 accepted. Either SAT or ACT required. ACT 25/75 percentile: 25-29. High school rank: 28% in top tenth, 66% in top quarter, 93% in top half
Early decision deadline: N/A, notification date: N/A
Early action deadline: N/A, notification date: N/A
Application deadline (fall): 2/1
Undergraduate student body: 996 full time, 0 part time; 82% male, 18% female; 1% American Indian, 7% Asian, 2% black, 8% Hispanic, 0% multiracial, 1% Pacific Islander, 77% white, 1% international; 10% from in state; 100% live on campus; 0% of students in fraternities, 0% in sororities
Most popular majors: Engineering, Other, Marine Science/Merchant Marine Officer, Systems Engineering
Expenses: 2019-2020: $1,050 in state, $1,050 out of state; room/board: N/A
Financial aid: (516) 726-5638

United States Military Academy[1]
West Point NY
(845) 938-4041
U.S. News ranking: Nat. Lib. Arts, No. 21
Website: www.usma.edu/SitePages/Home.aspx
Admissions email: admissions-info@usma.edu
Public; founded 1802
Application deadline (fall): 2/28
Undergraduate student body: N/A full time, N/A part time
Expenses: 2018-2019: $0 in state, $0 out of state; room/board: $0
Financial aid: N/A

University at Albany–SUNY
Albany NY
(518) 442-5435
U.S. News ranking: Nat. U., No. 147
Website: www.albany.edu
Admissions email: ugadmissions@albany.edu
Public; founded 1844
Freshman admissions: more selective; 2018-2019: 27,679 applied, 14,416 accepted. Either SAT or ACT required. SAT 25/75 percentile: 1100-1260. High school rank: 20% in top tenth, 55% in top quarter, 85% in top half
Early decision deadline: N/A, notification date: N/A
Early action deadline: 11/1, notification date: 1/15
Application deadline (fall): 3/1
Undergraduate student body: 12,899 full time, 699 part time; 49% male, 51% female; 0% American Indian, 8% Asian, 19% black, 18% Hispanic, 3% multiracial, 0% Pacific Islander, 44% white, 5% international; 91% from in state; 46% live on campus; 3% of students in fraternities, 3% in sororities
Most popular majors: 31% Social Sciences, 14% Business, Management, Marketing, and Related Support Services, 10% Psychology, 9% Communication, Journalism, and Related Programs, 7% Biological and Biomedical Sciences
Expenses: 2019-2020: $10,026 in state, $26,666 out of state; room/board: $14,240
Financial aid: (518) 442-3202; 68% of undergrads determined to have financial need; average aid package $11,395

University at Buffalo–SUNY
Buffalo NY
(716) 645-6900
U.S. News ranking: Nat. U., No. 79
Website: www.buffalo.edu
Admissions email: ub-admissions@buffalo.edu
Public; founded 1846
Freshman admissions: more selective; 2018-2019: 31,196 applied, 17,423 accepted. Either SAT or ACT required. SAT 25/75 percentile: 1160-1330. High school rank: 35% in top tenth, 70% in top quarter, 97% in top half
Early decision deadline: N/A, notification date: N/A
Early action deadline: 11/15, notification date: N/A
Application deadline (fall): rolling
Undergraduate student body: 19,941 full time, 1,666 part time; 56% male, 44% female; 0% American Indian, 15% Asian, 8% black, 7% Hispanic, 2% multiracial, 0% Pacific Islander, 47% white, 15% international; 98% from in state; 35% live on campus; 2% of students in fraternities, 2% in sororities
Most popular majors: 18% Business, Management, Marketing, and Related Support Services, 16% Engineering, 15% Social Sciences, 11% Psychology, 9% Biological and Biomedical Sciences
Expenses: 2019-2020: $10,180 in state, $27,850 out of state; room/board: $14,134
Financial aid: (716) 645-8232; 59% of undergrads determined to have financial need; average aid package $10,385

University of Rochester
Rochester NY
(585) 275-3221
U.S. News ranking: Nat. U., No. 29
Website: www.rochester.edu
Admissions email: admit@admissions.rochester.edu
Private; founded 1850
Freshman admissions: most selective; 2018-2019: 21,253 applied, 6,253 accepted. Neither SAT nor ACT required. SAT 25/75 percentile: 1320-1500. High school rank: 75% in top tenth, 94% in top quarter, 100% in top half
Early decision deadline: 11/1, notification date: 12/15
Early action deadline: N/A, notification date: N/A
Application deadline (fall): 1/5
Undergraduate student body: 6,293 full time, 242 part time; 50% male, 50% female; 0% American Indian, 11% Asian, 5% black, 7% Hispanic, 3% multiracial, 0% Pacific Islander, 42% white, 27% international; 46% from in state; 78% live on campus; 19% of students in fraternities, 19% in sororities
Most popular majors: 15% Engineering, 14% Social Sciences, 12% Health Professions and Related Programs, 11% Biological and Biomedical Sciences, 9% Visual and Performing Arts
Expenses: 2019-2020: $56,026; room/board: $16,546
Financial aid: (585) 275-3226; 55% of undergrads determined to have financial need; average aid package $49,022

Utica College
Utica NY
(315) 792-3006
U.S. News ranking: Reg. U. (N), No. 86
Website: www.utica.edu
Admissions email: admiss@utica.edu
Private; founded 1946
Freshman admissions: selective; 2018-2019: 4,224 applied, 3,566 accepted. Either SAT or ACT required for some. SAT 25/75 percentile: 1030-1220. High school rank: 13% in top tenth, 35% in top quarter, 66% in top half
Early decision deadline: 11/15, notification date: 12/15
Early action deadline: 11/15, notification date: 12/15
Application deadline (fall): rolling
Undergraduate student body: 2,909 full time, 813 part time; 40% male, 60% female; 0% American Indian, 4% Asian, 10% black, 9% Hispanic, 2% multiracial, 0% Pacific Islander, 69% white, 1% international; 88% from in state; 39% live on campus; 2% of students in fraternities, 2% in sororities
Most popular majors: 52% Health Professions and Related Programs, 21% Homeland Security, Law Enforcement, Firefighting and Related Protective Services, 6% Business, Management, Marketing, and Related Support Services, 5% Psychology, 4% Communication, Journalism, and Related Programs
Expenses: 2019-2020: $22,110; room/board: $11,670
Financial aid: (315) 792-3215; 83% of undergrads determined to have financial need; average aid package $14,592

Vassar College
Poughkeepsie NY
(845) 437-7300
U.S. News ranking: Nat. Lib. Arts, No. 14
Website: www.vassar.edu
Admissions email: admissions@vassar.edu
Private; founded 1861
Freshman admissions: most selective; 2018-2019: 8,312 applied, 2,043 accepted. Either SAT or ACT required. SAT 25/75 percentile: 1370-1510. High school rank: 61% in top tenth, 91% in top quarter, 98% in top half
Early decision deadline: 11/15, notification date: 12/15
Early action deadline: N/A, notification date: N/A
Application deadline (fall): 1/1
Undergraduate student body: 2,442 full time, 14 part time; 41% male, 59% female; 0% American Indian, 12% Asian, 4% black, 11% Hispanic, 8% multiracial, 0% Pacific Islander, 56% white, 9% international; 28% from in state; 97% live on campus; N/A of students in fraternities, N/A in sororities
Most popular majors: Information not available
Expenses: 2019-2020: $58,770; room/board: $14,720

Vaughn College of Aeronautics and Technology
Flushing NY
(718) 429-6600
U.S. News ranking: Reg. Coll. (N), No. 12
Website: www.vaughn.edu
Admissions email: admitme@vaughn.edu
Private; founded 1932
Freshman admissions: less selective; 2018-2019: 674 applied, 550 accepted. Either SAT or ACT required. SAT 25/75 percentile: 940-1147. High school rank: N/A
Early decision deadline: N/A, notification date: N/A
Early action deadline: N/A, notification date: N/A
Application deadline (fall): rolling
Undergraduate student body: 1,294 full time, 244 part time; 88% male, 12% female; 0% American Indian, 11% Asian, 18% black, 34% Hispanic, 2% multiracial, 1% Pacific Islander, 13% white, 6% international; 88% from in state; 12% live on campus; 11% of students in fraternities, 0% in sororities
Most popular majors: 58% Engineering Technologies and Engineering-Related Fields, 42% Transportation and Materials Moving
Expenses: 2019-2020: $26,640; room/board: $14,725
Financial aid: (718) 429-6600; 68% of undergrads determined to have financial need; average aid package $9,062

Villa Maria College[1]
Buffalo NY
U.S. News ranking: Reg. Coll. (N), unranked
Admissions email: N/A
Private
Application deadline (fall): N/A
Undergraduate student body: N/A full time, N/A part time
Expenses: 2018-2019: $23,280; room/board: N/A
Financial aid: (716) 961-1849; 82% of undergrads determined to have financial need; average aid package $16,831

Wagner College
Staten Island NY
(718) 390-3411
U.S. News ranking: Reg. U. (N), No. 32
Website: www.wagner.edu
Admissions email: admissions@wagner.edu
Private; founded 1883
Freshman admissions: selective; 2018-2019: 2,898 applied, 2,023 accepted. Either SAT or ACT required for some. SAT 25/75 percentile: 1070-1270. High school rank: 20% in top tenth, 49% in top quarter, 80% in top half

Financial aid: (845) 437-5320; 63% of undergrads determined to have financial need; average aid package $54,947

Early decision deadline: N/A, notification date: N/A
Early action deadline: 12/1, notification date: 1/5
Application deadline (fall): 2/15
Undergraduate student body: 1,723 full time, 39 part time; 35% male, 65% female; 0% American Indian, 5% Asian, 8% black, 13% Hispanic, 3% multiracial, 0% Pacific Islander, 62% white, 4% international; 42% from in state; 63% live on campus; 10% of students in fraternities, 11% in sororities
Most popular majors: 33% Health Professions and Related Programs, 16% Business, Management, Marketing, and Related Support Services, 15% Visual and Performing Arts, 8% Psychology
Expenses: 2019-2020: $48,280; room/board: $14,575
Financial aid: (718) 390-3122; 68% of undergrads determined to have financial need; average aid package $31,881

Webb Institute
Glen Cove NY
(516) 671-8355
U.S. News ranking: Engineering, unranked
Website: www.webb.edu
Admissions email: admissions@webb.edu
Private; founded 1889
Freshman admissions: more selective; 2018-2019: 99 applied, 33 accepted. Either SAT or ACT required. SAT 25/75 percentile: 1400-1550. High school rank: 78% in top tenth, 100% in top quarter, 100% in top half
Early decision deadline: 10/15, notification date: 12/15
Early action deadline: N/A, notification date: N/A
Application deadline (fall): 2/1
Undergraduate student body: 104 full time, 0 part time; 76% male, 24% female; 0% American Indian, 11% Asian, 0% black, 2% Hispanic, 6% multiracial, 0% Pacific Islander, 81% white, 0% international; 28% from in state; 100% live on campus; 0% of students in fraternities, 0% in sororities
Most popular majors: 100% Naval Architecture and Marine Engineering
Expenses: 2019-2020: $51,690; room/board: $15,400
Financial aid: (516) 403-5928; 14% of undergrads determined to have financial need; average aid package $3,000

Wells College
Aurora NY
(800) 952-9355
U.S. News ranking: Nat. Lib. Arts, No. 124
Website: www.wells.edu/
Admissions email: admissions@wells.edu
Private; founded 1868
Freshman admissions: selective; 2018-2019: 1,856 applied, 1,461 accepted. Neither SAT nor ACT required. SAT 25/75 percentile: 1000-1230. High

school rank: 21% in top tenth, 40% in top quarter, 78% in top half
Early decision deadline: 12/15, notification date: 1/1
Early action deadline: 12/15, notification date: 1/15
Application deadline (fall): 3/1
Undergraduate student body: 465 full time, 5 part time; 36% male, 64% female; 1% American Indian, 2% Asian, 15% black, 7% Hispanic, 10% multiracial, 0% Pacific Islander, 58% white, 1% international; 76% from in state; 93% live on campus; 0% of students in fraternities, 0% in sororities
Most popular majors: 21% Biological and Biomedical Sciences, 15% Psychology, 14% Business, Management, Marketing, and Related Support Services, 6% Natural Resources and Conservation, 6% Social Sciences
Expenses: 2019-2020: $30,900; room/board: $14,100
Financial aid: (315) 364-3289; 93% of undergrads determined to have financial need; average aid package $35,797

Yeshiva University
New York NY
(212) 960-5277
U.S. News ranking: Nat. U., No. 97
Website: www.yu.edu
Admissions email: yuadmit@ymail.yu.edu
Private; founded 1886
Freshman admissions: more selective; 2018-2019: 1,508 applied, 909 accepted. Either SAT or ACT required. ACT 25/75 percentile: 22-30. High school rank: N/A
Early decision deadline: 11/1, notification date: 12/15
Early action deadline: N/A, notification date: N/A
Application deadline (fall): 2/1
Undergraduate student body: 2,633 full time, 49 part time; 52% male, 48% female; 0% American Indian, 0% Asian, 0% black, 0% Hispanic, 0% multiracial, 0% Pacific Islander, 94% white, 6% international; 35% from in state; 68% live on campus; N/A of students in fraternities, N/A in sororities
Most popular majors: 18% Biology/Biological Sciences, General, 13% Accounting, 12% Psychology, General, 8% Finance, General, 7% Marketing/Marketing Management, General
Expenses: 2019-2020: $44,900; room/board: $12,500
Financial aid: (212) 960-5399; 54% of undergrads determined to have financial need; average aid package $39,554

NORTH CAROLINA

Appalachian State University
Boone NC
(828) 262-2120
U.S. News ranking: Reg. U. (S), No. 6
Website: www.appstate.edu
Admissions email: admissions@appstate.edu
Public; founded 1899
Freshman admissions: selective; 2018-2019: 16,154 applied, 11,221 accepted. Either SAT or ACT required. ACT 25/75 percentile: 22-26. High school rank: 19% in top tenth, 59% in top quarter, 93% in top half
Early decision deadline: N/A, notification date: N/A
Early action deadline: 11/1, notification date: 1/25
Application deadline (fall): 3/1
Undergraduate student body: 16,421 full time, 960 part time; 44% male, 56% female; 0% American Indian, 2% Asian, 3% black, 6% Hispanic, 4% multiracial, 0% Pacific Islander, 83% white, 0% international; N/A from in state; 33% live on campus; 8% of students in fraternities, 12% in sororities
Most popular majors: 21% Business, Management, Marketing, and Related Support Services, 12% Health Professions and Related Programs, 9% Education, 8% Communication, Journalism, and Related Programs, 7% Parks, Recreation, Leisure, and Fitness Studies
Expenses: 2019-2020: $7,397 in state, $22,204 out of state; room/board: $8,826
Financial aid: (828) 262-2190; 54% of undergrads determined to have financial need; average aid package $9,717

Barton College
Wilson NC
(800) 345-4973
U.S. News ranking: Reg. Coll. (S), No. 10
Website: www.barton.edu
Admissions email: enroll@barton.edu
Private; founded 1902
Affiliation: Christian Church (Disciples of Christ)
Freshman admissions: selective; 2018-2019: 3,486 applied, 1,381 accepted. Either SAT or ACT required. SAT 25/75 percentile: 920-1120. High school rank: 12% in top tenth, 34% in top quarter, 69% in top half
Early decision deadline: N/A, notification date: N/A
Early action deadline: N/A, notification date: N/A
Application deadline (fall): rolling
Undergraduate student body: 932 full time, 44 part time; 37% male, 63% female; 1% American Indian, 1% Asian, 20% black, 9% Hispanic, 3% multiracial, 0% Pacific Islander, 57% white, 5% international; 76% from in state; 51% live on campus; 13% of students in fraternities, 13% in sororities

Most popular majors: 24% Health Professions and Related Programs, 17% Business, Management, Marketing, and Related Support Services, 13% Public Administration and Social Service Professions, 8% Parks, Recreation, Leisure, and Fitness Studies, 6% Visual and Performing Arts
Expenses: 2019-2020: $31,730; room/board: $10,420
Financial aid: (252) 399-6371; 85% of undergrads determined to have financial need; average aid package $23,908

Belmont Abbey College
Belmont NC
(888) 222-0110
U.S. News ranking: Reg. Coll. (S), No. 22
Website: www.belmontabbeycollege.edu
Admissions email: admissions@bac.edu
Private; founded 1876
Affiliation: Roman Catholic
Freshman admissions: selective; 2018-2019: 2,107 applied, 1,681 accepted. Either SAT or ACT required for some. SAT 25/75 percentile: 950-1180. High school rank: 9% in top tenth, 11% in top quarter, 55% in top half
Early decision deadline: N/A, notification date: N/A
Early action deadline: N/A, notification date: N/A
Application deadline (fall): 8/1
Undergraduate student body: 1,440 full time, 116 part time; 50% male, 50% female; 1% American Indian, 2% Asian, 13% black, 1% Hispanic, 0% multiracial, 0% Pacific Islander, 58% white, 2% international
Most popular majors: 32% Business Administration and Management, General, 11% Elementary Education and Teaching, 10% Accounting, 8% Sport and Fitness Administration/Management
Expenses: 2019-2020: $18,500; room/board: $10,354
Financial aid: (704) 461-6895; 66% of undergrads determined to have financial need; average aid package $13,951

Bennett College
Greensboro NC
(336) 370-8624
U.S. News ranking: Nat. Lib. Arts, second tier
Website: www.bennett.edu
Admissions email: admiss@bennett.edu
Private; founded 1873
Affiliation: United Methodist
Freshman admissions: least selective; 2018-2019: 3,938 applied, 3,794 accepted. Either SAT or ACT required. SAT 25/75 percentile: 800-1000. High school rank: 3% in top tenth, 32% in top quarter, 60% in top half
Early decision deadline: N/A, notification date: N/A
Early action deadline: N/A, notification date: N/A
Application deadline (fall): rolling

Undergraduate student body: 463 full time, 71 part time; 0% male, 100% female; 0% American Indian, 0% Asian, 86% black, 2% Hispanic, 5% multiracial, 0% Pacific Islander, 0% white, 0% international; 50% from in state; 78% live on campus; N/A of students in fraternities, N/A in sororities
Most popular majors: 21% Business Administration and Management, General, 17% Psychology, General, 15% Journalism, Other, 14% Biology/Biological Sciences, General, 8% Social Work
Expenses: 2019-2020: $18,513; room/board: $8,114
Financial aid: (336) 517-2209; 99% of undergrads determined to have financial need

Brevard College
Brevard NC
(828) 884-8300
U.S. News ranking: Reg. Coll. (S), No. 24
Website: www.brevard.edu
Admissions email: admissions@brevard.edu
Private; founded 1853
Affiliation: United Methodist
Freshman admissions: less selective; 2018-2019: 2,619 applied, 1,207 accepted. Neither SAT nor ACT required. ACT 25/75 percentile: 18-22. High school rank: 4% in top tenth, 18% in top quarter, 50% in top half
Early decision deadline: N/A, notification date: N/A
Early action deadline: N/A, notification date: N/A
Application deadline (fall): rolling
Undergraduate student body: 687 full time, 15 part time; 57% male, 43% female; 1% American Indian, 1% Asian, 12% black, 7% Hispanic, 6% multiracial, 0% Pacific Islander, 68% white, 1% international; 58% from in state; 80% live on campus; N/A of students in fraternities, N/A in sororities
Most popular majors: 15% Business Administration and Management, General, 12% Criminal Justice/Law Enforcement Administration, 9% Multi-/Interdisciplinary Studies, Other, 7% Health and Wellness, General, 7% Kinesiology and Exercise Science
Expenses: 2019-2020: $30,250; room/board: $10,400
Financial aid: (828) 884-8287; 82% of undergrads determined to have financial need; average aid package $31,319

Campbell University
Buies Creek NC
(910) 893-1200
U.S. News ranking: Nat. U., No. 272
Website: www.campbell.edu
Admissions email: admissions@campbell.edu
Private; founded 1887
Freshman admissions: selective; 2018-2019: 6,240 applied, 4,761 accepted. Either SAT or ACT required. ACT 25/75 percentile: 19-25. High school

rank: 26% in top tenth, 55% in top quarter, 87% in top half
Early decision deadline: N/A, notification date: N/A
Early action deadline: N/A, notification date: N/A
Application deadline (fall): rolling
Undergraduate student body: 3,471 full time, 771 part time; 48% male, 52% female; 1% American Indian, 2% Asian, 15% black, 9% Hispanic, 5% multiracial, 0% Pacific Islander, 59% white, 2% international; 83% from in state; 40% live on campus; 3% of students in fraternities, 4% in sororities
Most popular majors: 11% Business Administration and Management, General, 8% Science Technologies/Technicians, Other, 7% Kinesiology and Exercise Science, 6% Biology/Biological Sciences, General, 6% Finance and Financial Management Services, Other
Expenses: 2019-2020: $33,880; room/board: $12,190
Financial aid: (910) 893-1232; 74% of undergrads determined to have financial need; average aid package $38,323

Catawba College
Salisbury NC
(800) 228-2922
U.S. News ranking: Reg. Coll. (S), No. 8
Website: www.catawba.edu
Admissions email: admission@catawba.edu
Private; founded 1851
Affiliation: United Church of Christ
Freshman admissions: less selective; 2018-2019: 3,061 applied, 1,580 accepted. Either SAT or ACT required for some. SAT 25/75 percentile: 910-1140. High school rank: 12% in top tenth, 36% in top quarter, 63% in top half
Early decision deadline: N/A, notification date: N/A
Early action deadline: N/A, notification date: N/A
Application deadline (fall): rolling
Undergraduate student body: 1,277 full time, 48 part time; 46% male, 54% female; 0% American Indian, 1% Asian, 21% black, 7% Hispanic, 4% multiracial, 0% Pacific Islander, 62% white, 4% international; N/A from in state; 60% live on campus; N/A of students in fraternities, N/A in sororities
Most popular majors: 22% Business, Management, Marketing, and Related Support Services, 13% Education, 12% Parks, Recreation, Leisure, and Fitness Studies, 11% Visual and Performing Arts, 8% Biological and Biomedical Sciences
Expenses: 2019-2020: $30,520; room/board: $10,488
Financial aid: (704) 637-4416; 82% of undergrads determined to have financial need; average aid package $27,250

Chowan University

Murfreesboro NC
(252) 398-1236
U.S. News ranking: Nat. Lib. Arts, second tier
Website: chowan.edu/
Admissions email: admissions@chowan.edu
Private; founded 1848
Affiliation: Baptist
Freshman admissions: least selective; 2018-2019: 3,567 applied, 2,115 accepted. Either SAT or ACT required. SAT 25/75 percentile: 810-1000. High school rank: 2% in top tenth, 7% in top quarter, 31% in top half
Early decision deadline: N/A, notification date: N/A
Early action deadline: N/A, notification date: N/A
Application deadline (fall): rolling
Undergraduate student body: 1,356 full time, 39 part time; 49% male, 51% female; 1% American Indian, 0% Asian, 66% black, 3% Hispanic, 2% multiracial, 0% Pacific Islander, 18% white, 3% international; 54% from in state; 89% live on campus; 3% of students in fraternities, 3% in sororities
Most popular majors: 17% Homeland Security, Law Enforcement, Firefighting and Related Protective Services, 15% Business, Management, Marketing, and Related Support Services, 15% Multi/Interdisciplinary Studies, 15% Psychology, 14% Parks, Recreation, Leisure, and Fitness Studies
Expenses: 2019-2020: $25,480; room/board: $9,500
Financial aid: (252) 398-6269; 93% of undergrads determined to have financial need; average aid package $22,553

Davidson College

Davidson NC
(800) 768-0380
U.S. News ranking: Nat. Lib. Arts, No. 17
Website: davidson.edu
Admissions email: admission@davidson.edu
Private; founded 1837
Affiliation: Presbyterian Church (USA)
Freshman admissions: most selective; 2018-2019: 5,724 applied, 1,116 accepted. Either SAT or ACT required. SAT 25/75 percentile: 1290-1450. High school rank: 73% in top tenth, 97% in top quarter, 100% in top half
Early decision deadline: 11/15, notification date: 12/15
Early action deadline: N/A, notification date: N/A
Application deadline (fall): 1/7
Undergraduate student body: 1,843 full time, 0 part time; 52% male, 48% female; 0% American Indian, 5% Asian, 7% black, 8% Hispanic, 4% multiracial, 0% Pacific Islander, 67% white, 7% international; N/A from in state; 95% live on campus; 30% of students in fraternities, 49% in sororities

Most popular majors: 17% Political Science and Government, General, 13% Economics, General, 11% Biology/Biological Sciences, General, 10% English Language and Literature, General, 8% Psychology, General
Expenses: 2019-2020: $53,049; room/board: $14,803
Financial aid: (800) 768-0380; 50% of undergrads determined to have financial need; average aid package $49,192

Duke University

Durham NC
(919) 684-3214
U.S. News ranking: Nat. U., No. 10
Website: www.duke.edu/
Admissions email: undergrad-admissions@duke.edu
Private; founded 1838
Freshman admissions: most selective; 2018-2019: 35,767 applied, 3,189 accepted. Either SAT or ACT required. ACT 25/75 percentile: 33-35. High school rank: 95% in top tenth, 98% in top quarter, 100% in top half
Early decision deadline: 11/1, notification date: 12/15
Early action deadline: N/A, notification date: N/A
Application deadline (fall): 1/3
Undergraduate student body: 6,659 full time, 23 part time; 50% male, 50% female; 1% American Indian, 22% Asian, 10% black, 9% Hispanic, 2% multiracial, 0% Pacific Islander, 42% white, 10% international
Most popular majors: 12% Computer Science, 10% Econometrics and Quantitative Economics, 9% Public Policy Analysis, General, 8% Biology/Biological Sciences, General, 7% Psychology, General
Expenses: 2019-2020: $58,198; room/board: $17,000
Financial aid: (919) 684-6225; 47% of undergrads determined to have financial need; average aid package $54,672

East Carolina University

Greenville NC
(252) 328-6640
U.S. News ranking: Nat. U., No. 228
Website: www.ecu.edu
Admissions email: admis@ecu.edu
Public; founded 1907
Freshman admissions: selective; 2018-2019: 17,498 applied, 14,383 accepted. Either SAT or ACT required. SAT 25/75 percentile: 1030-1180. High school rank: 13% in top tenth, 38% in top quarter, 76% in top half
Early decision deadline: N/A, notification date: N/A
Early action deadline: N/A, notification date: N/A
Application deadline (fall): 3/1
Undergraduate student body: 19,562 full time, 3,509 part time; 43% male, 57% female; 1% American Indian, 3% Asian, 16% black, 7% Hispanic, 4% multiracial, 0% Pacific Islander, 67% white, 0% international;

90% from in state; 23% live on campus; 5% of students in fraternities, 8% in sororities
Most popular majors: 18% Business, Management, Marketing, and Related Support Services, 17% Health Professions and Related Programs, 7% Education, 6% Communication, Journalism, and Related Programs, 6% Engineering Technologies and Engineering-Related Fields
Expenses: 2019-2020: $7,239 in state, $23,516 out of state; room/board: $10,030
Financial aid: (252) 328-6610; 60% of undergrads determined to have financial need; average aid package $10,817

Elizabeth City State University

Elizabeth City NC
(252) 335-3305
U.S. News ranking: Reg. Coll. (S), No. 26
Website: www.ecsu.edu
Admissions email: admissions@mail.ecsu.edu
Public; founded 1891
Freshman admissions: least selective; 2018-2019: 2,461 applied, 1,462 accepted. Either SAT or ACT required. SAT 25/75 percentile: 860-990. High school rank: 2% in top tenth, 5% in top quarter, 33% in top half
Early decision deadline: N/A, notification date: N/A
Early action deadline: N/A, notification date: N/A
Application deadline (fall): 8/1
Undergraduate student body: 1,423 full time, 214 part time; 43% male, 57% female; 1% American Indian, 1% Asian, 71% black, 4% Hispanic, 4% multiracial, 0% Pacific Islander, 16% white, 0% international
Most popular majors: Information not available
Expenses: 2019-2020: $3,980 in state, $7,980 out of state; room/board: $8,316
Financial aid: (252) 335-4850; 96% of undergrads determined to have financial need; average aid package $11,145

Elon University

Elon NC
(800) 334-8448
U.S. News ranking: Nat. U., No. 84
Website: www.elon.edu
Admissions email: admissions@elon.edu
Private; founded 1889
Freshman admissions: more selective; 2018-2019: 10,729 applied, 7,740 accepted. Either SAT or ACT required. SAT 25/75 percentile: 1150-1330. High school rank: 25% in top tenth, 57% in top quarter, 87% in top half
Early decision deadline: 11/1, notification date: 12/1
Early action deadline: 11/1, notification date: 12/20
Application deadline (fall): 1/10
Undergraduate student body: 6,029 full time, 167 part time; 40% male, 60% female; 0% American Indian, 2% Asian, 6% black,

6% Hispanic, 3% multiracial, 0% Pacific Islander, 80% white, 2% international; 19% from in state; 68% live on campus; 20% of students in fraternities, 39% in sororities
Most popular majors: 33% Business/Commerce, General, 19% Communication and Media Studies, 7% Health and Physical Education/Fitness, 7% Public Administration, 7% Social Sciences, General
Expenses: 2019-2020: $36,571; room/board: $12,685
Financial aid: (336) 278-7640; 34% of undergrads determined to have financial need; average aid package $20,456

Fayetteville State University

Fayetteville NC
(910) 672-1371
U.S. News ranking: Reg. U (S), No. 87
Website: www.uncfsu.edu/fsu-admissions/undergraduate-admissions
Admissions email: admissions@uncfsu.edu
Public; founded 1867
Freshman admissions: less selective; 2018-2019: 4,130 applied, 2,803 accepted. Either SAT or ACT required. SAT 25/75 percentile: 890-1030. High school rank: 7% in top tenth, 26% in top quarter, 63% in top half
Early decision deadline: N/A, notification date: N/A
Early action deadline: N/A, notification date: N/A
Application deadline (fall): 6/30
Undergraduate student body: 4,058 full time, 1,415 part time; 32% male, 68% female; 2% American Indian, 2% Asian, 62% black, 8% Hispanic, 3% multiracial, 0% Pacific Islander, 19% white, 1% international; 94% from in state; 27% live on campus; 1% of students in fraternities, 1% in sororities
Most popular majors: 20% Registered Nursing/Registered Nurse, 13% Psychology, General, 10% Business Administration and Management, General, 10% Criminal Justice/Safety Studies, 6% Biology/Biological Sciences, General
Expenses: 2018-2019: $4,915 in state, $16,523 out of state; room/board: $8,236
Financial aid: (910) 672-1325; 84% of undergrads determined to have financial need; average aid package $11,153

Gardner-Webb University

Boiling Springs NC
(800) 253-6472
U.S. News ranking: Nat. U., No. 281
Website: www.gardner-webb.edu
Admissions email: admissions@gardner-webb.edu
Private; founded 1905
Freshman admissions: selective, 2018-2019: 4,206 applied, 2,024 accepted. Either SAT or ACT required. SAT 25/75

percentile: 970-1180. High school rank: 17% in top tenth, 42% in top quarter, 75% in top half
Early decision deadline: N/A, notification date: N/A
Early action deadline: N/A, notification date: N/A
Application deadline (fall): rolling
Undergraduate student body: 1,641 full time, 387 part time; 36% male, 64% female; 1% American Indian, 1% Asian, 14% black, 4% Hispanic, 2% multiracial, 0% Pacific Islander, 65% white, 0% international
Most popular majors: 25% Business, Management, Marketing, and Related Support Services, 20% Health Professions and Related Programs, 17% Psychology, 6% Biological and Biomedical Sciences, 5% Homeland Security, Law Enforcement, Firefighting and Related Protective Services
Expenses: 2019-2020: $31,460; room/board: $10,390
Financial aid: (704) 406-4247; 74% of undergrads determined to have financial need; average aid package $26,016

Greensboro College

Greensboro NC
(336) 272-7102
U.S. News ranking: Reg. Coll. (S), No. 36
Website: www.gborocollege.edu
Admissions email: admissions@gborocollege.edu
Private; founded 1838
Affiliation: United Methodist
Freshman admissions: selective; 2018-2019: 1,977 applied, 879 accepted. Either SAT or ACT required. SAT 25/75 percentile: 910-1140. High school rank: 7% in top tenth, 20% in top quarter, 53% in top half
Early decision deadline: N/A, notification date: N/A
Early action deadline: N/A, notification date: N/A
Application deadline (fall): 8/28
Undergraduate student body: 740 full time, 164 part time; 49% male, 51% female; 1% American Indian, 1% Asian, 26% black, 4% Hispanic, 6% multiracial, 0% Pacific Islander, 54% white, 0% international; 79% from in state; 3% live on campus; 0% of students in fraternities, 3% in sororities
Most popular majors: 14% Business, Management, Marketing, and Related Support Services, 13% Liberal Arts and Sciences, General Studies and Humanities, 12% Social Sciences, 11% Health Professions and Related Programs, 10% Biological and Biomedical Sciences
Expenses: 2019-2020: $18,500; room/board: $10,800
Financial aid: (336) 272-7102; 86% of undergrads determined to have financial need; average aid package $12,445

Guilford College

Greensboro NC
(800) 992-7759
U.S. News ranking: Nat. Lib. Arts, No. 154
Website: www.guilford.edu
Admissions email: admission@guilford.edu
Private; founded 1837
Affiliation: Friends
Freshman admissions: selective; 2018-2019: 3,211 applied, 2,070 accepted. Either SAT or ACT required for some. ACT 25/75 percentile: 17-24. High school rank: 12% in top tenth, 33% in top quarter, 65% in top half
Early decision deadline: N/A, notification date: N/A
Early action deadline: 12/1, notification date: 12/15
Application deadline (fall): 8/10
Undergraduate student body: 1,388 full time, 179 part time; 49% male, 51% female; 0% American Indian, 3% Asian, 26% black, 10% Hispanic, 4% multiracial, 0% Pacific Islander, 56% white, 1% international; 71% from in state; 59% live on campus; 0% of students in fraternities, 0% in sororities
Most popular majors: 13% Crafts/Craft Design, Folk Art and Artisanry, 13% Psychology, General, 8% Criminal Justice and Corrections, 8% Health and Physical Education/Fitness, 7% Accounting and Related Services
Expenses: 2019-2020: $38,410; room/board: $11,800
Financial aid: (336) 316-2354; 65% of undergrads determined to have financial need; average aid package $27,702

High Point University

High Point NC
(800) 345-6993
U.S. News ranking: Reg. Coll. (S), No. 1
Website: www.highpoint.edu
Admissions email: admiss@highpoint.edu
Private; founded 1924
Affiliation: United Methodist
Freshman admissions: selective; 2018-2019: 10,098 applied, 7,770 accepted. Neither SAT nor ACT required. SAT 25/75 percentile: 1090-1250. High school rank: 15% in top tenth, 43% in top quarter, 74% in top half
Early decision deadline: 11/1, notification date: 11/27
Early action deadline: 11/15, notification date: 12/15
Application deadline (fall): 3/1
Undergraduate student body: 4,504 full time, 41 part time; 43% male, 57% female; 0% American Indian, 2% Asian, 5% black, 5% Hispanic, 6% multiracial, 0% Pacific Islander, 78% white, 2% international; 24% from in state; 95% live on campus; 9% of students in fraternities, 26% in sororities
Most popular majors: 35% Business, Management, Marketing, and Related Support Services, 21% Communication, Journalism, and Related Programs, 8% Parks, Recreation, Leisure,

and Fitness Studies, 6% Biological and Biomedical Sciences, 6% Visual and Performing Arts
Expenses: 2019-2020: $36,268; room/board: $14,702
Financial aid: (336) 841-9128; 42% of undergrads determined to have financial need; average aid package $17,947

Johnson C. Smith University

Charlotte NC
(704) 378-1010
U.S. News ranking: Nat. Lib. Arts, second tier
Website: www.jcsu.edu
Admissions email: admissions@jcsu.edu
Private; founded 1867
Freshman admissions: least selective; 2018-2019: 6,369 applied, 2,919 accepted. SAT or ACT required. SAT 25/75 percentile: 810-980. High school rank: N/A
Early decision deadline: N/A, notification date: N/A
Early action deadline: N/A, notification date: N/A
Application deadline (fall): rolling
Undergraduate student body: 1,428 full time, 52 part time; 39% male, 61% female; 0% American Indian, 0% Asian, 85% black, 3% Hispanic, 1% multiracial, 0% Pacific Islander, 1% white, 1% international; 40% from in state; 50% live on campus; N/A of students in fraternities, N/A in sororities
Most popular majors: 20% Business Administration and Management, General, 13% Social Work, 12% Sport and Fitness Administration/Management, 10% Criminology, 9% Biology/Biological Sciences, General
Expenses: 2019-2020: $18,236; room/board: $7,100
Financial aid: (704) 378-1291; 93% of undergrads determined to have financial need; average aid package $15,432

Lees-McRae College[7]

Banner Elk NC
(828) 898-5241
U.S. News ranking: Reg. Coll. (S), No. 33
Website: www.lmc.edu
Admissions email: admissions@lmc.edu
Private; founded 1900
Affiliation: Presbyterian Church (USA)
Freshman admissions: less selective; 2018-2019: 1,462 applied, 836 accepted. Either SAT or ACT required for some. ACT 25/75 percentile: 17-23. High school rank: N/A
Early decision deadline: 11/1, notification date: 11/15
Early action deadline: 12/1, notification date: 12/15
Application deadline (fall): rolling
Undergraduate student body: 915 full time, 51 part time
Most popular majors: 26% Health Professions and Related Programs, 19% Biological and Biomedical Sciences, 15% Legal Professions

and Studies, 12% Education, 6% Business, Management, Marketing, and Related Support Services
Expenses: 2018-2019: $26,198; room/board: $11,078
Financial aid: (828) 898-8740

Lenoir-Rhyne University

Hickory NC
(828) 328-7300
U.S. News ranking: Reg. U. (S), No. 43
Website: www.lr.edu
Admissions email: admission@lr.edu
Private; founded 1891
Affiliation: Evangelical Lutheran Church
Freshman admissions: less selective; 2018-2019: 5,087 applied, 3,759 accepted. Either SAT or ACT required. SAT 25/75 percentile: 960-1180. High school rank: N/A
Early decision deadline: N/A, notification date: N/A
Early action deadline: 11/7, notification date: 11/21
Application deadline (fall): rolling
Undergraduate student body: 1,566 full time, 259 part time; 40% male, 60% female; 1% American Indian, 2% Asian, 11% black, 8% Hispanic, 4% multiracial, 0% Pacific Islander, 68% white, 3% international; 81% from in state; 54% live on campus; 7% of students in fraternities, 12% in sororities
Most popular majors: 21% Health Professions and Related Programs, 18% Parks, Recreation, Leisure, and Fitness Studies, 12% Business, Management, Marketing, and Related Support Services, 7% Biological and Biomedical Sciences, 7% Psychology
Expenses: 2019-2020: $37,400; room/board: $12,510
Financial aid: (828) 328-7300; 86% of undergrads determined to have financial need; average aid package $31,172

Livingstone College

Salisbury NC
(704) 216-6001
U.S. News ranking: Reg. Coll. (S), second tier
Website: www.livingstone.edu/
Admissions email: admissions@livingstone.edu
Private; founded 1879
Affiliation: African Methodist Episcopal Zion Church
Freshman admissions: least selective; 2018-2019: 6,873 applied, 2,862 accepted. Either SAT or ACT required. SAT 25/75 percentile: 770-930. High school rank: 2% in top tenth, 6% in top quarter, 23% in top half
Early decision deadline: N/A, notification date: N/A
Early action deadline: N/A, notification date: N/A
Application deadline (fall): rolling
Undergraduate student body: 1,139 full time, 9 part time; 50% male, 50% female; 0% American

Indian, 0% Asian, 83% black, 0% Hispanic, 3% multiracial, 0% Pacific Islander, 2% white, 1% international; 65% from in state; 82% live on campus; 30% of students in fraternities, 30% in sororities
Most popular majors: 16% Business Administration and Management, General, 13% Criminal Justice/Safety Studies, 13% Sport and Fitness Administration/Management, 11% Biology/Biological Sciences, General, 6% Social Work
Expenses: 2019-2020: $17,763; room/board: $6,596
Financial aid: (704) 216-6069; 97% of undergrads determined to have financial need; average aid package $14,815

Mars Hill University

Mars Hill NC
(866) 642-4968
U.S. News ranking: Reg. Coll. (S), No. 22
Website: www.mhu.edu
Admissions email: admissions@mhu.edu
Private; founded 1856
Freshman admissions: selective; 2018-2019: 2,008 applied, 1,152 accepted. Either SAT or ACT required. ACT 25/75 percentile: 16-22. High school rank: 5% in top tenth, 27% in top quarter, 60% in top half
Early decision deadline: N/A, notification date: N/A
Early action deadline: N/A, notification date: N/A
Application deadline (fall): rolling
Undergraduate student body: 1,079 full time, 53 part time; 46% male, 54% female; 2% American Indian, 2% Asian, 19% black, 6% Hispanic, 4% multiracial, 0% Pacific Islander, 59% white, 5% international; 71% from in state; 69% live on campus; 7% of students in fraternities, 11% in sororities
Most popular majors: 20% Business, Management, Marketing, and Related Support Services, 16% Education, 14% Health Professions and Related Programs, 11% Public Administration and Social Service Professions, 6% Homeland Security, Law Enforcement, Firefighting and Related Protective Services
Expenses: 2019-2020: $34,118; room/board: $9,878
Financial aid: (828) 689-1103; 67% of undergrads determined to have financial need; average aid package $24,724

Meredith College

Raleigh NC
(919) 760-8581
U.S. News ranking: Nat. Lib. Arts, No. 148
Website: www.meredith.edu
Admissions email: admissions@meredith.edu
Private; founded 1891
Freshman admissions: selective; 2018-2019: 1,897 applied, 1,187 accepted. Either SAT or ACT required. SAT 25/75

percentile: 1000-1200. High school rank: 17% in top tenth, 48% in top quarter, 79% in top half
Early decision deadline: 10/30, notification date: 11/15
Early action deadline: 12/1, notification date: 12/15
Application deadline (fall): 2/15
Undergraduate student body: 1,531 full time, 72 part time; 0% male, 100% female; 1% American Indian, 3% Asian, 8% black, 9% Hispanic, 3% multiracial, 0% Pacific Islander, 69% white, 1% international; 81% from in state; 55% live on campus; 0% of students in fraternities, 0% in sororities
Most popular majors: 12% Psychology, General, 11% Biology/Biological Sciences, General, 6% Business Administration and Management, General, 5% Interior Design, 4% Social Work
Expenses: 2019-2020: $38,620; room/board: $11,364
Financial aid: (919) 760-8565; 73% of undergrads determined to have financial need; average aid package $33,279

Methodist University

Fayetteville NC
(910) 630-7027
U.S. News ranking: Reg. U. (S), No. 71
Website: www.methodist.edu
Admissions email: admissions@methodist.edu
Private; founded 1956
Affiliation: United Methodist
Freshman admissions: selective; 2018-2019: 3,633 applied, 1,987 accepted. Either SAT or ACT required. ACT 25/75 percentile: 18-23. High school rank: 12% in top tenth, 37% in top quarter, 73% in top half
Early decision deadline: N/A, notification date: N/A
Early action deadline: N/A, notification date: N/A
Application deadline (fall): rolling
Undergraduate student body: 1,580 full time, 192 part time; 52% male, 48% female; 1% American Indian, 1% Asian, 17% black, 7% Hispanic, 2% multiracial, 0% Pacific Islander, 42% white, 10% international
Most popular majors: Information not available
Expenses: 2019-2020: $34,522; room/board: $12,828
Financial aid: (910) 630-7000; 76% of undergrads determined to have financial need; average aid package $22,560

Montreat College

Montreat NC
(800) 622-6968
U.S. News ranking: Reg. U. (S), second tier
Website: www.montreat.edu
Admissions email: admissions@montreat.edu
Private; founded 1916
Freshman admissions: selective; 2018-2019: 940 applied, 519 accepted. Either SAT or ACT required. SAT 25/75 percentile: 920-1140. High school rank: N/A

Early decision deadline: N/A, notification date: N/A
Early action deadline: N/A, notification date: N/A
Application deadline (fall): rolling
Undergraduate student body: 569 full time, 145 part time; 51% male, 49% female; 2% American Indian, 1% Asian, 15% black, 6% Hispanic, 3% multiracial, 1% Pacific Islander, 64% white, 3% international
Most popular majors: 24% Psychology, Other, 22% Business Administration and Management, General, 8% Communication and Media Studies, 8% Theology/Theological Studies, 7% Business Administration, Management and Operations, Other
Expenses: 2019-2020: $27,850; room/board: $9,400
Financial aid: (828) 669-8012; 82% of undergrads determined to have financial need; average aid package $22,206

North Carolina A&T State University

Greensboro NC
(336) 334-7946
U.S. News ranking: Nat. U., No. 281
Website: www.ncat.edu
Admissions email: uadmit@ncat.edu
Public; founded 1891
Freshman admissions: selective; 2018-2019: 11,088 applied, 6,807 accepted. Either SAT or ACT required. SAT 25/75 percentile: 950-1110. High school rank: 12% in top tenth, 36% in top quarter, 76% in top half
Early decision deadline: N/A, notification date: N/A
Early action deadline: N/A, notification date: N/A
Application deadline (fall): 6/30
Undergraduate student body: 9,591 full time, 1,038 part time; 43% male, 57% female; 0% American Indian, 1% Asian, 82% black, 4% Hispanic, 4% multiracial, 0% Pacific Islander, 5% white, 1% international; 76% from in state; 28% live on campus; 1% of students in fraternities, 1% in sororities
Most popular majors: 12% Engineering, 9% Communication, Journalism, and Related Programs, 9% Parks, Recreation, Leisure, and Fitness Studies, 8% Liberal Arts and Sciences, General Studies and Humanities, 6% Homeland Security, Law Enforcement, Firefighting and Related Protective Services
Expenses: 2019-2020: $6,657 in state, $20,167 out of state; room/board: $7,930
Financial aid: (336) 334-7973; 86% of undergrads determined to have financial need; average aid package $11,794

North Carolina Central University

Durham NC
(919) 530-6298
U.S. News ranking: Reg. U. (S), No. 54
Website: www.nccu.edu
Admissions email: admissions@nccu.edu
Public; founded 1910
Freshman admissions: less selective; 2018-2019: 13,019 applied, 6,072 accepted. Either SAT or ACT required. SAT 25/75 percentile: 900-1050. High school rank: 7% in top tenth, 21% in top quarter, 60% in top half
Early decision deadline: N/A, notification date: N/A
Early action deadline: N/A, notification date: N/A
Application deadline (fall): rolling
Undergraduate student body: 5,328 full time, 1,106 part time; 32% male, 68% female; 0% American Indian, 1% Asian, 81% black, 5% Hispanic, 5% multiracial, 0% Pacific Islander, 6% white, 0% international; 16% from in state; 34% live on campus; N/A of students in fraternities, N/A in sororities
Most popular majors: 12% Criminal Justice/Safety Studies, 11% Business Administration and Management, General, 8% Family and Consumer Sciences/Human Sciences, General, 8% Psychology, General, 6% Social Sciences, General
Expenses: 2019-2020: $6,534 in state, $19,241 out of state; room/board: $8,954
Financial aid: (919) 530-6180; 82% of undergrads determined to have financial need; average aid package $9,744

North Carolina State University–Raleigh

Raleigh NC
(919) 515-2434
U.S. News ranking: Nat. U., No. 84
Website: admissions.ncsu.edu
Admissions email: undergrad-admissions@ncsu.edu
Public; founded 1887
Freshman admissions: more selective; 2018-2019: 30,193 applied, 14,058 accepted. Either SAT or ACT required. SAT 25/75 percentile: 1250-1390. High school rank: 48% in top tenth, 85% in top quarter, 99% in top half
Early decision deadline: N/A, notification date: N/A
Early action deadline: 11/1, notification date: 1/30
Application deadline (fall): 1/15
Undergraduate student body: 22,317 full time, 2,882 part time; 53% male, 47% female; 0% American Indian, 7% Asian, 6% black, 6% Hispanic, 4% multiracial, 0% Pacific Islander, 69% white, 4% international; 91% from in state; 38% live on campus; 13% of students in fraternities, 17% in sororities
Most popular majors: 27% Engineering, 15% Business,

Management, Marketing, and Related Support Services, 8% Biological and Biomedical Sciences, 7% Agriculture, Agriculture Operations, and Related Sciences, 4% Communication, Journalism, and Related Programs
Expenses: 2019-2020: $9,101 in state, $29,220 out of state; room/board: $11,359
Financial aid: N/A; 49% of undergrads determined to have financial need; average aid package $12,946

North Carolina Wesleyan College

Rocky Mount NC
(800) 488-6292
U.S. News ranking: Reg. Coll. (S), No. 43
Website: www.ncwc.edu
Admissions email: adm@ncwc.edu
Private; founded 1956
Affiliation: United Methodist
Freshman admissions: less selective; 2018-2019: 3,136 applied, 1,969 accepted. SAT required for some. SAT 25/75 percentile: 870-1090. High school rank: 9% in top tenth, 22% in top quarter, 57% in top half
Early decision deadline: N/A, notification date: N/A
Early action deadline: N/A, notification date: N/A
Application deadline (fall): rolling
Undergraduate student body: 1,677 full time, 331 part time; 44% male, 56% female; 1% American Indian, 1% Asian, 42% black, 3% Hispanic, 3% multiracial, 0% Pacific Islander, 29% white, 7% international; 75% from in state; 71% live on campus; 1% of students in fraternities, 2% in sororities
Most popular majors: 24% Business Administration and Management, General, 19% Organizational Leadership, 15% Criminal Justice/Law Enforcement Administration, 11% Psychology, General, 7% Accounting
Expenses: 2019-2020: $32,050; room/board: $11,150
Financial aid: (252) 985-5200; 83% of undergrads determined to have financial need; average aid package $23,497

Pfeiffer University

Misenheimer NC
(800) 338-2060
U.S. News ranking: Reg. U. (S), No. 58
Website: www.pfeiffer.edu
Admissions email: admissions@pfeiffer.edu
Private; founded 1885
Affiliation: United Methodist
Freshman admissions: selective; 2018-2019: 2,701 applied, 1,743 accepted. Neither SAT nor ACT required. SAT 25/75 percentile: 900-1130. High school rank: 10% in top tenth, 31% in top quarter, 64% in top half
Early decision deadline: N/A, notification date: N/A
Early action deadline: N/A, notification date: N/A
Application deadline (fall): rolling

Undergraduate student body: 845 full time, 55 part time; 42% male, 58% female; 0% American Indian, 1% Asian, 26% black, 9% Hispanic, 4% multiracial, 0% Pacific Islander, 59% white, 1% international; 85% from in state; 61% live on campus; 8% of students in fraternities, 9% in sororities
Most popular majors: 25% Business, Management, Marketing, and Related Support Services, 17% Health Professions and Related Programs, 14% Parks, Recreation, Leisure, and Fitness Studies, 9% Family and Consumer Sciences/Human Sciences, 7% Homeland Security, Law Enforcement, Firefighting and Related Protective Services
Expenses: 2019-2020: $31,050; room/board: $11,508
Financial aid: (704) 463-3060

Queens University of Charlotte

Charlotte NC
(800) 849-0202
U.S. News ranking: Reg. U. (S), No. 13
Website: www.queens.edu
Admissions email: admissions@queens.edu
Private; founded 1857
Affiliation: Presbyterian
Freshman admissions: selective; 2018-2019: 2,419 applied, 1,900 accepted. Either SAT or ACT required. SAT 25/75 percentile: 1033-1218. High school rank: 15% in top tenth, 46% in top quarter, 80% in top half
Early decision deadline: 11/1, notification date: 12/1
Early action deadline: 12/1, notification date: 12/31
Application deadline (fall): 9/5
Undergraduate student body: 1,552 full time, 214 part time; 33% male, 67% female; 1% American Indian, 2% Asian, 16% black, 10% Hispanic, 1% multiracial, 0% Pacific Islander, 57% white, 9% international; N/A from in state; 68% live on campus; 5% of students in fraternities, 17% in sororities
Most popular majors: 33% Health Professions and Related Programs, 18% Business, Management, Marketing, and Related Support Services, 11% Biological and Biomedical Sciences, 7% Parks, Recreation, Leisure, and Fitness Studies, 6% Communication, Journalism, and Related Programs
Expenses: 2019-2020: $35,720; room/board: $11,222
Financial aid: (704) 337-2225; 68% of undergrads determined to have financial need; average aid package $26,996

Salem College

Winston-Salem NC
(336) 721-2621
U.S. News ranking: Nat. Lib. Arts, No. 132
Website: www.salem.edu
Admissions email: admissions@salem.edu
Private; founded 1772

Affiliation: Moravian Church
Freshman admissions: more selective; 2018-2019: 665 applied, 270 accepted. Either SAT or ACT required. ACT 25/75 percentile: 21-28. High school rank: 44% in top tenth, 67% in top quarter, 92% in top half
Early decision deadline: N/A, notification date: N/A
Early action deadline: N/A, notification date: N/A
Application deadline (fall): rolling
Undergraduate student body: 552 full time, 151 part time; 3% male, 97% female; 0% American Indian, 2% Asian, 18% black, 16% Hispanic, 5% multiracial, 0% Pacific Islander, 57% white, 0% international; 72% from in state; 60% live on campus; 0% of students in fraternities, 0% in sororities
Most popular majors: 12% Education, General, 11% Business Administration and Management, General, 11% Criminal Justice/Safety Studies, 11% Psychology, General, 9% Biology/Biological Sciences, General
Expenses: 2019-2020: $30,266; room/board: $12,000
Financial aid: (336) 721-2808; 85% of undergrads determined to have financial need; average aid package $27,708

Shaw University

Raleigh NC
(800) 214-6683
U.S. News ranking: Reg. Coll. (S), second tier
Website: www.shawu.edu
Admissions email: admissions@shawu.edu
Private; founded 1865
Affiliation: Baptist
Freshman admissions: least selective; 2018-2019: 12,156 applied, 6,364 accepted. Either SAT or ACT required. SAT 25/75 percentile: 780-910. High school rank: 1% in top tenth, 5% in top quarter, 26% in top half
Early decision deadline: N/A, notification date: N/A
Early action deadline: N/A, notification date: N/A
Application deadline (fall): 7/30
Undergraduate student body: 1,247 full time, 58 part time; 42% male, 58% female; 0% American Indian, 6% Asian, 65% black, 3% Hispanic, 9% multiracial, 1% Pacific Islander, 1% white, 5% international; 58% from in state; 55% live on campus; N/A of students in fraternities, N/A in sororities
Most popular majors: 14% Business Administration and Management, General, 13% Social Work, 7% Mass Communication/Media Studies, 6% Kinesiology and Exercise Science, 5% Education, Other
Expenses: 2018-2019: $16,480; room/board: $8,158
Financial aid: (919) 546-8565

Southeastern Baptist Theological Seminary[1]

Wake Forest NC
(919) 761-2246
U.S. News ranking: Reg. U. (S), unranked
Website: www.sebts.edu/
Admissions email: admissions@sebts.edu
Private; founded 1950
Affiliation: Southern Baptist
Application deadline (fall): 8/1
Undergraduate student body: N/A full time, N/A part time
Expenses: N/A
Financial aid: N/A

St. Augustine's University

Raleigh NC
(919) 516-4012
U.S. News ranking: Reg. Coll. (S), No. 55
Website: www.st-aug.edu
Admissions email: admissions@st-aug.edu
Private; founded 1867
Affiliation: Episcopal Church, Reformed
Freshman admissions: least selective; 2018-2019: 4,663 applied, 2,957 accepted. Either SAT or ACT required. SAT 25/75 percentile: 768-940. High school rank: N/A
Early decision deadline: N/A, notification date: N/A
Early action deadline: N/A, notification date: N/A
Application deadline (fall): rolling
Undergraduate student body: 750 full time, 17 part time; 51% male, 49% female; 0% American Indian, 0% Asian, 91% black, 1% Hispanic, 0% multiracial, 0% Pacific Islander, 2% white, 5% international; 65% from in state; 81% live on campus; N/A of students in fraternities, N/A in sororities
Most popular majors: 13% Kinesiology and Exercise Science, 12% Business Administration and Management, General, 12% Sport and Fitness Administration/Management, 9% Business Administration, Management and Operations, Other, 9% Sociology
Expenses: 2019-2020: $17,890; room/board: $7,692
Financial aid: (919) 516-4309

University of Mount Olive[1]

Mount Olive NC
(919) 658-2502
U.S. News ranking: Reg. U. (S), No. 65
Website: www.umo.edu/
Admissions email: admissions@umo.edu
Private; founded 1951
Affiliation: Original Free Will Baptist
Application deadline (fall): rolling
Undergraduate student body: N/A full time, N/A part time
Expenses: N/A
Financial aid: (919) 658-2502

University of North Carolina–Asheville

Asheville NC
(828) 251-6481
U.S. News ranking: Nat. Lib. Arts, No. 148
Website: www.unca.edu
Admissions email: admissions@unca.edu
Public; founded 1927
Freshman admissions: selective; 2018-2019: 3,163 applied, 2,601 accepted. Either SAT or ACT required. SAT 25/75 percentile: 1060-1250. High school rank: 17% in top tenth, 42% in top quarter, 80% in top half
Early decision deadline: N/A, notification date: N/A
Early action deadline: N/A, notification date: N/A
Application deadline (fall): 8/1
Undergraduate student body: 3,232 full time, 511 part time; 43% male, 57% female; 1% American Indian, 2% Asian, 5% black, 8% Hispanic, 4% multiracial, 0% Pacific Islander, 76% white, 1% international; 87% from in state; 45% live on campus; 3% of students in fraternities, 4% in sororities
Most popular majors: 11% Psychology, General, 9% Business Administration and Management, General, 6% Environmental Studies, 6% Mass Communication/Media Studies, 5% Public Health Education and Promotion
Expenses: 2019-2020: $7,145 in state, $23,868 out of state; room/board: $9,380
Financial aid: (828) 251-6535; 60% of undergrads determined to have financial need; average aid package $12,879

University of North Carolina–Chapel Hill

Chapel Hill NC
(919) 966-3621
U.S. News ranking: Nat. U., No. 29
Website: www.unc.edu
Admissions email: unchelp@admissions.unc.edu
Public; founded 1789
Freshman admissions: most selective; 2018-2019: 43,473 applied, 9,524 accepted. Either SAT or ACT required. ACT 25/75 percentile: 27-33. High school rank: 78% in top tenth, 96% in top quarter, 99% in top half
Early decision deadline: N/A, notification date: N/A
Early action deadline: 10/15, notification date: 1/31'
Application deadline (fall): 1/15
Undergraduate student body: 18,526 full time, 591 part time; 41% male, 59% female; 1% American Indian, 11% Asian, 8% black, 8% Hispanic, 5% multiracial, 0% Pacific Islander, 60% white, 3% international; 82% from in state; 51% live on campus; 20% of students in fraternities, 20% in sororities

University of North Carolina–Greensboro

Greensboro NC
(336) 334-5243
U.S. News ranking: Nat. U., No. 272
Website: www.uncg.edu/
Admissions email: admissions@uncg.edu
Public; founded 1891
Freshman admissions: selective; 2018-2019: 8,170 applied, 6,846 accepted. Either SAT or ACT required. SAT 25/75 percentile: 990-1160. High school rank: 14% in top tenth, 38% in top quarter, 76% in top half

Most popular majors: 17% Social Sciences, 9% Biological and Biomedical Sciences, 9% Communication, Journalism, and Related Programs, 8% Psychology, 7% Business, Management, Marketing, and Related Support Services
Expenses: 2019-2020: $9,043 in state, $36,222 out of state; room/board: $11,526
Financial aid: (919) 962-8396; 44% of undergrads determined to have financial need; average aid package $18,872

University of North Carolina–Charlotte

Charlotte NC
(704) 687-5507
U.S. News ranking: Nat. U., No. 228
Website: www.uncc.edu/
Admissions email: admissions@uncc.edu
Public; founded 1946
Freshman admissions: selective; 2018-2019: 17,119 applied, 11,500 accepted. Either SAT or ACT required. ACT 25/75 percentile: 21-26. High school rank: 17% in top tenth, 47% in top quarter, 86% in top half
Early decision deadline: N/A, notification date: N/A
Early action deadline: 11/1, notification date: 1/30
Application deadline (fall): 6/1
Undergraduate student body: 21,025 full time, 3,362 part time; 53% male, 47% female; 0% American Indian, 7% Asian, 16% black, 10% Hispanic, 5% multiracial, 0% Pacific Islander, 57% white, 2% international; 92% from in state; 25% live on campus; 6% of students in fraternities, 10% in sororities
Most popular majors: 19% Business, Management, Marketing, and Related Support Services, 9% Engineering, 8% Psychology, 8% Social Sciences, 7% Communication, Journalism, and Related Programs
Expenses: 2019-2020: $6,854 in state, $20,288 out of state; room/board: $13,224
Financial aid: (704) 687-5504; 62% of undergrads determined to have financial need; average aid package $9,499

University of North Carolina–Pembroke

Pembroke NC
(910) 521-6262
U.S. News ranking: Reg. U. (S), No. 87
Website: www.uncp.edu
Admissions email: admissions@uncp.edu
Public; founded 1887
Freshman admissions: less selective; 2018-2019: 4,316 applied, 3,506 accepted. Either SAT or ACT required. ACT 25/75 percentile: 17-21. High school rank: 10% in top tenth, 35% in top quarter, 72% in top half
Early decision deadline: N/A, notification date: N/A
Early action deadline: N/A, notification date: N/A
Application deadline (fall): 6/30
Undergraduate student body: 4,945 full time, 1,124 part time; 39% male, 61% female; 15% American Indian, 2% Asian, 33% black, 6% Hispanic, 4% multiracial, 0% Pacific Islander, 36% white, 1% international; 96% from in state; 34% live on campus; 7% of students in fraternities, 4% in sororities
Most popular majors: 14% Homeland Security, Law Enforcement, Firefighting and Related Protective Services, 12% Biological and Biomedical Sciences, 10% Business, Management, Marketing, and Related Support Services, 9% Parks, Recreation, Leisure, and Fitness Studies, 9% Social Sciences
Expenses: 2019-2020: $3,490 in state, $7,490 out of state; room/board: $8,924
Financial aid: (910) 521-6255; 78% of undergrads determined to have financial need; average aid package $9,295

Early decision deadline: N/A, notification date: N/A
Early action deadline: N/A, notification date: N/A
Application deadline (fall): rolling
Undergraduate student body: 14,265 full time, 2,376 part time; 34% male, 66% female; 0% American Indian, 5% Asian, 30% black, 11% Hispanic, 5% multiracial, 0% Pacific Islander, 47% white, 2% international; 79% from in state; 34% live on campus; 2% of students in fraternities, 3% in sororities
Most popular majors: 7% Business Administration and Management, General, 4% Psychology, General, 4% Public Health Education and Promotion, 4% Registered Nursing/Registered Nurse, 3% Elementary Education and Teaching
Expenses: 2019-2020: $7,404 in state, $22,564 out of state; room/board: $9,264
Financial aid: (336) 334-5702; 85% of undergrads determined to have financial need; average aid package $11,741

University of North Carolina School of the Arts

Winston-Salem NC
(336) 770-3291
U.S. News ranking: Arts, unranked
Website: www.uncsa.edu
Admissions email: admissions@uncsa.edu
Public; founded 1963
Freshman admissions: selective; 2018-2019: 1,180 applied, 442 accepted. Either SAT or ACT required. SAT 25/75 percentile: 1090-1280. High school rank: 11% in top tenth, 39% in top quarter, 81% in top half
Early decision deadline: N/A, notification date: N/A
Early action deadline: N/A, notification date: N/A
Application deadline (fall): 3/15
Undergraduate student body: 884 full time, 6 part time; 47% male, 53% female; 1% American Indian, 2% Asian, 9% black, 8% Hispanic, 5% multiracial, 0% Pacific Islander, 71% white, 3% international; 52% from in state; 60% live on campus; 0% of students in fraternities, 0% in sororities
Most popular majors: 100% Visual and Performing Arts
Expenses: 2019-2020: $9,358 in state, $25,901 out of state; room/board: $9,156
Financial aid: (336) 770-3297; 56% of undergrads determined to have financial need; average aid package $13,845

University of North Carolina–Wilmington

Wilmington NC
(910) 962-3243
U.S. News ranking: Nat. U., No. 185
Website: www.uncw.edu
Admissions email: admissions@uncw.edu
Public; founded 1947
Freshman admissions: more selective; 2018-2019: 13,117 applied, 8,034 accepted. Either SAT or ACT required. ACT 25/75 percentile: 23-27. High school rank: 24% in top tenth, 60% in top quarter, 92% in top half
Early decision deadline: N/A, notification date: N/A
Early action deadline: 11/1, notification date: 1/20
Application deadline (fall): 2/1
Undergraduate student body: 12,157 full time, 2,295 part time; 38% male, 62% female; 0% American Indian, 2% Asian, 4% black, 7% Hispanic, 4% multiracial, 0% Pacific Islander, 78% white, 1% international; 89% from in state; 27% live on campus; 10% of students in fraternities, 10% in sororities
Most popular majors: 19% Business Administration and Management, General, 16% Registered Nursing/Registered Nurse, 6% Psychology, General, 5% Biology/Biological Sciences, General, 5% Speech Communication and Rhetoric

Expenses: 2019-2020: $7,181 in state; $21,246 out of state; room/board: $10,897
Financial aid: (910) 962-3177; 58% of undergrads determined to have financial need; average aid package $9,155

Wake Forest University
Winston-Salem NC
(336) 758-5201
U.S. News ranking: Nat. U., No. 27
Website: www.wfu.edu
Admissions email: admissions@wfu.edu
Private; founded 1834
Freshman admissions: most selective; 2018-2019: 12,937 applied, 3,803 accepted. Neither SAT nor ACT required. ACT 25/75 percentile: 29-33. High school rank: 76% in top tenth, 92% in top quarter, 97% in top half
Early decision deadline: 11/15, notification date: N/A
Early action deadline: N/A, notification date: N/A
Application deadline (fall): 1/1
Undergraduate student body: 5,171 full time, 54 part time; 47% male, 53% female; 0% American Indian, 4% Asian, 6% black, 7% Hispanic, 3% multiracial, 0% Pacific Islander, 69% white, 10% international; N/A from in state; 75% live on campus; 33% of students in fraternities, 59% in sororities
Most popular majors: 24% Social Sciences, 19% Business, Management, Marketing, and Related Support Services, 9% Biological and Biomedical Sciences, 8% Communication, Journalism, and Related Programs, 8% Psychology
Expenses: 2019-2020: $55,440; room/board: $16,740
Financial aid: (336) 758-5154; 30% of undergrads determined to have financial need; average aid package $50,514

Warren Wilson College
Asheville NC
(800) 934-3536
U.S. News ranking: Nat. Lib. Arts, No. 160
Website: www.warren-wilson.edu/
Admissions email: admit@warren-wilson.edu
Private; founded 1894
Freshman admissions: selective; 2018-2019: 1,133 applied, 946 accepted. Neither SAT nor ACT required. ACT 25/75 percentile: 22-28. High school rank: 13% in top tenth, 38% in top quarter, 72% in top half
Early decision deadline: 11/1, notification date: 12/1
Early action deadline: 11/15, notification date: 12/1
Application deadline (fall): rolling
Undergraduate student body: 638 full time, 19 part time; 35% male, 65% female; 1% American Indian, 1% Asian, 7% black, 7% Hispanic, 4% multiracial, 0% Pacific Islander, 76% white, 2% international; 38% from in

state; 86% live on campus; 0% of students in fraternities, 0% in sororities
Most popular majors: 19% Environmental Studies, 9% History, General, 9% Social Sciences, Other, 9% Visual and Performing Arts, General, 8% Psychology, General
Expenses: 2019-2020: $37,364; room/board: $11,300
Financial aid: (828) 771-2082

Western Carolina University
Cullowhee NC
(828) 227-7317
U.S. News ranking: Reg. U. (S), No. 23
Website: www.wcu.edu
Admissions email: admiss@email.wcu.edu
Public; founded 1889
Freshman admissions: selective; 2018-2019: 19,341 applied, 7,667 accepted. Either SAT or ACT required. ACT 25/75 percentile: 20-25. High school rank: 14% in top tenth, 41% in top quarter, 77% in top half
Early decision deadline: N/A, notification date: N/A
Early action deadline: 11/15, notification date: 12/15
Application deadline (fall): 3/1
Undergraduate student body: 8,617 full time, 1,410 part time; 45% male, 55% female; 1% American Indian, 1% Asian, 5% black, 7% Hispanic, 4% multiracial, 0% Pacific Islander, 79% white, 1% international; 91% from in state; 48% live on campus; N/A of students in fraternities, N/A in sororities
Most popular majors: 22% Business, Management, Marketing, and Related Support Services, 19% Health Professions and Related Programs, 9% Education, 7% Homeland Security, Law Enforcement, Firefighting and Related Protective Services, 5% Public Administration and Social Service Professions
Expenses: 2019-2020: $4,220 in state, $8,220 out of state; room/board: 9,682
Financial aid: (828) 227-7290; 65% of undergrads determined to have financial need; average aid package $9,921

William Peace University
Raleigh NC
(919) 508-2214
U.S. News ranking: Reg. Coll. (S), No. 26
Website: www.peace.edu
Admissions email: admissions@peace.edu
Private; founded 1857
Affiliation: Presbyterian Church (USA)
Freshman admissions: selective; 2018-2019: 1,876 applied, 1,074 accepted. Either SAT or ACT required. SAT 25/75 percentile: 920-1080. High school rank: 7% in top tenth, 25% in top quarter, 67% in top half

Early decision deadline: N/A, notification date: N/A
Early action deadline: N/A, notification date: N/A
Application deadline (fall): rolling
Undergraduate student body: 832 full time, 78 part time; 47% male, 53% female; 1% American Indian, 2% Asian, 28% black, 12% Hispanic, 4% multiracial, 0% Pacific Islander, 47% white, 0% international; 89% from in state; 54% live on campus; 0% of students in fraternities, 0% in sororities
Most popular majors: 37% Business, Management, Marketing, and Related Support Services, 14% Psychology, 10% Social Sciences, 9% Communication, Journalism, and Related Programs, 7% Biological and Biomedical Sciences
Expenses: 2019-2020: $31,700; room/board: $11,640
Financial aid: (919) 508-2394; 87% of undergrads determined to have financial need; average aid package $23,876

Wingate University
Wingate NC
(800) 755-5550
U.S. News ranking: Nat. U., second tier
Website: www.wingate.edu/
Admissions email: admit@wingate.edu
Private; founded 1896
Freshman admissions: selective; 2018-2019: 14,784 applied, 12,530 accepted. Either SAT or ACT required. SAT 25/75 percentile: 960-1170. High school rank: 15% in top tenth, 40% in top quarter, 76% in top half
Early decision deadline: N/A, notification date: N/A
Early action deadline: N/A, notification date: N/A
Application deadline (fall): rolling
Undergraduate student body: 2,683 full time, 43 part time; 40% male, 60% female; 0% American Indian, 2% Asian, 18% black, 4% Hispanic, 8% multiracial, 0% Pacific Islander, 57% white, 4% international; 74% from in state; 75% live on campus; 6% of students in fraternities, 15% in sororities
Most popular majors: 15% Business, Management, Marketing, and Related Support Services, 13% Biological and Biomedical Sciences, 12% Public Administration and Social Service Professions, 11% Parks, Recreation, Leisure, and Fitness Studies, 10% Communication, Journalism, and Related Programs
Expenses: 2019-2020: $35,910; room/board: $10,280
Financial aid: (704) 233-8010, 87% of undergrads determined to have financial need; average aid package $31,901

Winston-Salem State University[1]
Winston-Salem NC
(336) 750-2070
U.S. News ranking: Reg. U. (S), No. 61
Website: www.wssu.edu
Admissions email: admissions@wssu.edu
Public; founded 1892
Application deadline (fall): 3/15
Undergraduate student body: N/A full time, N/A part time
Expenses: N/A
Financial aid: N/A

NORTH DAKOTA

Bismarck State College
Bismarck ND
(701) 224-2459
U.S. News ranking: Reg. Coll. (Mid. W), second tier
Website: bismarckstate.edu/
Admissions email: bsc.admissions@bismarckstate.edu
Public; founded 1939
Freshman admissions: less selective; 2018-2019: N/A applied, N/A accepted. Neither SAT nor ACT required. SAT 25/75 percentile: N/A. High school rank: N/A
Early decision deadline: N/A, notification date: N/A
Early action deadline: N/A, notification date: N/A
Application deadline (fall): rolling
Undergraduate student body: 2,025 full time, 1,753 part time; 57% male, 43% female; N/A American Indian, N/A Asian, N/A black, N/A Hispanic, N/A multiracial, N/A Pacific Islander, N/A white, N/A international
Most popular majors: Information not available
Expenses: 2018-2019: $3,992 in state, $5,588 out of state; room/board: $6,284
Financial aid: (701) 224-5441

Dickinson State University
Dickinson ND
(701) 483-2175
U.S. News ranking: Reg. Coll. (Mid. W), No. 48
Website: www.dickinsonstate.edu/
Admissions email: dsu.hawks@dsu.nodak.edu
Public; founded 1918
Freshman admissions: less selective; 2018-2019: 530 applied, 352 accepted. Either SAT or ACT required for some. ACT 25/75 percentile: 18-23. High school rank: N/A
Early decision deadline: N/A, notification date: N/A
Early action deadline: N/A, notification date: N/A
Application deadline (fall): 8/15
Undergraduate student body: 900 full time, 475 part time; 40% male, 60% female; 1% American Indian, 1% Asian, 4% black, 6% Hispanic, 3% multiracial, 0% Pacific Islander, 78% white, 5% international; 77% from in state; N/A live on campus; N/A

of students in fraternities, N/A in sororities
Most popular majors: 50% Business, Management, Marketing, and Related Support Services, 12% Multi/Interdisciplinary Studies, 9% Education, 6% Health Professions and Related Programs, 4% Computer and Information Sciences and Support Services
Expenses: 2019-2020: $7,888 in state, $11,150 out of state; room/board: $7,686
Financial aid: (701) 483-2371; 56% of undergrads determined to have financial need; average aid package $10,591

Mayville State University
Mayville ND
(701) 788-4667
U.S. News ranking: Reg. Coll. (Mid. W), No. 50
Website: www.mayvillestate.edu
Admissions email: masuadmissions@mayvillestate.edu
Public; founded 1889
Freshman admissions: selective; 2018-2019: N/A applied, N/A accepted. Either SAT or ACT required. ACT 25/75 percentile: 18-23. High school rank: N/A
Early decision deadline: N/A, notification date: N/A
Early action deadline: N/A, notification date: N/A
Application deadline (fall): rolling
Undergraduate student body: 604 full time, 473 part time; 38% male, 62% female; 2% American Indian, 1% Asian, 6% black, 7% Hispanic, 5% multiracial, 1% Pacific Islander, 79% white, 0% international; N/A from in state; 10% live on campus; 0% of students in fraternities, 0% in sororities
Most popular majors: Information not available
Expenses: 2019-2020: $8,498 in state, $9,946 out of state; room/board: $6,875
Financial aid: (701) 788-4767; 65% of undergrads determined to have financial need; average aid package $11,369

Minot State University
Minot ND
(701) 858-3350
U.S. News ranking: Reg. U., (Mid. W), No. 111
Website: www.minotstateu.edu
Admissions email: askmsu@minotstateu.edu
Public; founded 1913
Freshman admissions: selective; 2018-2019: 818 applied, 494 accepted. Either SAT or ACT required. ACT 25/75 percentile: 18-23. High school rank: 11% in top tenth, 20% in top quarter, 64% in top half
Early decision deadline: N/A, notification date: N/A
Early action deadline: N/A, notification date: N/A
Application deadline (fall): rolling
Undergraduate student body: 1,979 full time, 936 part time; 40%

male, 60% female; 3% American Indian, 1% Asian, 5% black, 7% Hispanic, 4% multiracial, 0% Pacific Islander, 68% white, 10% international; 70% from in state; 17% live on campus; N/A of students in fraternities, N/A in sororities
Most popular majors: 11% Business Administration and Management, General, 10% Social Work, 9% Registered Nursing/Registered Nurse, 7% Elementary Education and Teaching, 5% Finance, General
Expenses: 2019-2020: $7,288 in state, $7,288 out of state; room/board: $7,144
Financial aid: (701) 858-3375; 49% of undergrads determined to have financial need; average aid package $10,538

North Dakota State University
Fargo ND
(701) 231-8643
U.S. News ranking: Nat. U., No. 281
Website: www.ndsu.edu
Admissions email: NDSU.Admission@ndsu.edu
Public; founded 1890
Freshman admissions: selective; 2018-2019: 5,599 applied, 5,181 accepted. Either SAT or ACT required. ACT 25/75 percentile: 21-26. High school rank: 16% in top tenth, 43% in top quarter, 77% in top half
Early decision deadline: N/A, notification date: N/A
Early action deadline: N/A, notification date: N/A
Application deadline (fall): 8/1
Undergraduate student body: 10,237 full time, 1,188 part time; 54% male, 46% female; 1% American Indian, 1% Asian, 3% black, 2% Hispanic, 3% multiracial, 0% Pacific Islander, 87% white, 1% international; 41% from in state; 35% live on campus; 8% of students in fraternities, 8% in sororities
Most popular majors: 15% Business, Management, Marketing, and Related Support Services, 15% Health Professions and Related Programs, 13% Engineering, 11% Agriculture, Agriculture Operations, and Related Sciences, 6% Family and Consumer Sciences/Human Sciences
Expenses: 2019-2020: $10,516 in state, $13,628 out of state; room/board: $9,088
Financial aid: (701) 231-6221; 52% of undergrads determined to have financial need; average aid package $12,047

University of Jamestown
Jamestown ND
(701) 252-3467
U.S. News ranking: Reg. Coll. (Mid. W), No. 39
Website: www.uj.edu
Admissions email: admissions@uj.edu
Private; founded 1883

Affiliation: Presbyterian Church (USA)
Freshman admissions: selective; 2018-2019: 1,356 applied, 834 accepted. Either SAT or ACT required. ACT 25/75 percentile: 19-24. High school rank: 13% in top tenth, 30% in top quarter, 67% in top half
Early decision deadline: N/A, notification date: N/A
Early action deadline: N/A, notification date: N/A
Application deadline (fall): 9/10
Undergraduate student body: 868 full time, 25 part time; 51% male, 49% female; 0% American Indian, 1% Asian, 5% black, 10% Hispanic, 3% multiracial, 1% Pacific Islander, 73% white, 7% international; 42% from in state; 74% live on campus; 0% of students in fraternities, 0% in sororities
Most popular majors: 18% Registered Nursing/Registered Nurse, 17% Business Administration and Management, General, 11% Kinesiology and Exercise Science, 8% Elementary Education and Teaching, 6% Biology/Biological Sciences, General
Expenses: 2019-2020: $22,428; room/board: $7,886
Financial aid: (701) 252-3467; 69% of undergrads determined to have financial need; average aid package $17,481

University of Mary
Bismarck ND
(701) 355-8030
U.S. News ranking: Nat. U., second tier
Website: www.umary.edu
Admissions email: marauder@umary.edu
Private; founded 1959
Affiliation: Roman Catholic
Freshman admissions: selective; 2018-2019: 1,294 applied, 1,134 accepted. Either SAT or ACT required. ACT 25/75 percentile: 20-26. High school rank: N/A
Early decision deadline: N/A, notification date: N/A
Early action deadline: N/A, notification date: N/A
Application deadline (fall): rolling
Undergraduate student body: 1,846 full time, 688 part time; 40% male, 60% female; 2% American Indian, 1% Asian, 2% black, 4% Hispanic, 1% multiracial, 0% Pacific Islander, 78% white, 0% international; 48% from in state; 40% live on campus; N/A of students in fraternities, N/A in sororities
Most popular majors: 30% Health Professions and Related Programs, 21% Business, Management, Marketing, and Related Support Services, 13% Education, 6% Liberal Arts and Sciences, General Studies and Humanities, 4% Parks, Recreation, Leisure, and Fitness Studies
Expenses: 2019-2020: $19,074; room/board: $7,540
Financial aid: (701) 355-8226; 64% of undergrads determined to have financial need; average aid package $13,816

University of North Dakota
Grand Forks ND
(800) 225-5863
U.S. News ranking: Nat. U., No. 263
Website: und.edu
Admissions email: admissions@und.edu
Public; founded 1883
Freshman admissions: selective; 2018-2019: 5,021 applied, 4,128 accepted. Either SAT or ACT required. ACT 25/75 percentile: 21-27. High school rank: 18% in top tenth, 43% in top quarter, 74% in top half
Early decision deadline: N/A, notification date: N/A
Early action deadline: N/A, notification date: N/A
Application deadline (fall): rolling
Undergraduate student body: 8,184 full time, 2,334 part time; 56% male, 44% female; 1% American Indian, 2% Asian, 2% black, 4% Hispanic, 4% multiracial, 0% Pacific Islander, 81% white, 5% international; 39% from in state; 27% live on campus; 12% of students in fraternities, 13% in sororities
Most popular majors: 6% Psychology, General, 6% Registered Nursing/Registered Nurse, 6% Speech Communication and Rhetoric, 5% General Studies, 5% Mechanical Engineering
Expenses: 2019-2020: $9,736 in state, $13,842 out of state; room/board: $9,424
Financial aid: (701) 777-3121; 49% of undergrads determined to have financial need; average aid package $14,144

Valley City State University
Valley City ND
(701) 845-7101
U.S. News ranking: Reg. Coll. (Mid. W), No. 43
Website: www.vcsu.edu
Admissions email: enrollment.services@vcsu.edu
Public; founded 1890
Freshman admissions: selective; 2018-2019: 460 applied, 339 accepted. Either SAT or ACT required. ACT 25/75 percentile: 18-23. High school rank: N/A
Early decision deadline: N/A, notification date: N/A
Early action deadline: N/A, notification date: N/A
Application deadline (fall): rolling
Undergraduate student body: 862 full time, 542 part time; 42% male, 58% female; 1% American Indian, 0% Asian, 3% black, 6% Hispanic, 4% multiracial, 0% Pacific Islander, 81% white, 2% international; 63% from in state; 29% live on campus; 1% of students in fraternities, 1% in sororities
Most popular majors: 66% Education, 8% Business, Management, Marketing, and Related Support Services, 4% Natural Resources and Conservation, 4% Parks,

Recreation, Leisure, and Fitness Studies, 3% Public Administration and Social Service Professions
Expenses: 2019-2020: $7,707 in state, $12,119 out of state; room/board: $6,500
Financial aid: (701) 845-7541; 61% of undergrads determined to have financial need; average aid package $11,871

NORTHERN MARIANA ISLANDS

Northern Marianas College[1]
Saipan MP
(670) 237-6700
U.S. News ranking: Reg. Coll. (W), unranked
Website: www.hiwassee.edu
Admissions email: N/A
Public
Application deadline (fall): N/A
Undergraduate student body: N/A full time, N/A part time
Expenses: N/A
Financial aid: N/A

OHIO

Antioch University[1]
Yellow Springs OH
(937) 769-1818
U.S. News ranking: Reg. U. (Mid. W), unranked
Website: midwest.antioch.edu
Admissions email: admission.aum@antioch.edu
Private; founded 1852
Application deadline (fall): rolling
Undergraduate student body: N/A full time, N/A part time
Expenses: 2018-2019: $18,972; room/board: N/A
Financial aid: N/A

Art Academy of Cincinnati
Cincinnati OH
(513) 562-6262
U.S. News ranking: Arts, unranked
Website: www.artacademy.edu
Admissions email: admissions@artacademy.edu
Private; founded 1869
Freshman admissions: least selective; 2018-2019: 1,114 applied, 1,113 accepted. Either SAT or ACT required. SAT 25/75 percentile: N/A. High school rank: N/A
Early decision deadline: N/A, notification date: N/A
Early action deadline: N/A, notification date: N/A
Application deadline (fall): N/A
Undergraduate student body: 174 full time, 9 part time; 30% male, 70% female; 1% American Indian, 2% Asian, 11% black, 6% Hispanic, 5% multiracial, 1% Pacific Islander, 73% white, 0% international
Most popular majors: 32% Illustration, 26% Design and Visual Communications, General, 16% Photography, 11% Painting, 8% Sculpture
Expenses: 2019-2020: $34,335; room/board: $6,600

Ashland University
Ashland OH
(419) 289-5052
U.S. News ranking: Reg. U. (Mid. W), No. 53
Website: www.ashland.edu/admissions
Admissions email: enrollme@ashland.edu
Private; founded 1878
Freshman admissions: selective; 2018-2019: 4,656 applied, 3,169 accepted. Either SAT or ACT required. ACT 25/75 percentile: 20-25. High school rank: 17% in top tenth, 41% in top quarter, 73% in top half
Early decision deadline: N/A, notification date: N/A
Early action deadline: N/A, notification date: N/A
Application deadline (fall): rolling
Undergraduate student body: 3,489 full time, 1,530 part time; 53% male, 47% female; 1% American Indian, 1% Asian, 15% black, 3% Hispanic, 2% multiracial, 0% Pacific Islander, 70% white, 4% international; 91% from in state; 72% live on campus; 1% of students in fraternities, 1% in sororities
Most popular majors: 20% Health Professions and Related Programs, 17% Education, 13% Business, Management, Marketing, and Related Support Services, 6% Biological and Biomedical Sciences, 5% Homeland Security, Law Enforcement, Firefighting and Related Protective Services
Expenses: 2019-2020: $21,980; room/board: $10,340
Financial aid: (419) 289-5944; 79% of undergrads determined to have financial need; average aid package $16,553

Baldwin Wallace University
Berea OH
(440) 826-2222
U.S. News ranking: Reg. U. (Mid. W), No. 10
Website: www.bw.edu
Admissions email: admission@bw.edu
Private; founded 1845
Freshman admissions: selective; 2018-2019: 3,926 applied, 2,915 accepted. Either SAT or ACT required for some. ACT 25/75 percentile: 21-27. High school rank: 18% in top tenth, 46% in top quarter, 78% in top half
Early decision deadline: N/A, notification date: N/A
Early action deadline: N/A, notification date: N/A
Application deadline (fall): rolling
Undergraduate student body: 2,923 full time, 213 part time; 46% male, 54% female; 0% American Indian, 1% Asian, 9% black, 6% Hispanic, 5% multiracial, 0% Pacific Islander, 78% white, 1% international; 76% from in state; 57% live on campus; 15% of students in fraternities, 19% in sororities

Financial aid: (513) 562-8757; 75% of undergrads determined to have financial need; average aid package $20,118

Most popular majors: 24% Business, Management, Marketing, and Related Support Services, 14% Visual and Performing Arts, 13% Health Professions and Related Programs, 8% Biological and Biomedical Sciences, 7% Psychology
Expenses: 2019-2020: $33,530; room/board: $10,110
Financial aid: (440) 826-2108; 76% of undergrads determined to have financial need; average aid package $25,129

Bluffton University
Bluffton OH
(800) 488-3257
U.S. News ranking: Reg. Coll. (Mid. W), No. 26
Website: www.bluffton.edu
Admissions email: admissions@bluffton.edu
Private; founded 1899
Affiliation: Mennonite Church
Freshman admissions: selective; 2018-2019: 2,175 applied, 914 accepted. Either SAT or ACT required. ACT 25/75 percentile: 18-25. High school rank: 13% in top tenth, 31% in top quarter, 61% in top half
Early decision deadline: N/A, notification date: N/A
Early action deadline: N/A, notification date: N/A
Application deadline (fall): rolling
Undergraduate student body: 605 full time, 95 part time; 55% male, 45% female; 0% American Indian, 1% Asian, 10% black, 3% Hispanic, 4% multiracial, 0% Pacific Islander, 75% white, 2% international; N/A from in state; 81% live on campus; N/A of students in fraternities, N/A in sororities
Most popular majors: 26% Business, Management, Marketing, and Related Support Services, 15% Education, 10% Parks, Recreation, Leisure, and Fitness Studies, 9% Public Administration and Social Service Professions, 6% Psychology
Expenses: 2019-2020: $33,736; room/board: $11,124
Financial aid: (419) 358-3266; 83% of undergrads determined to have financial need; average aid package $27,811

Bowling Green State University
Bowling Green OH
(419) 372-2478
U.S. News ranking: Nat. U., No. 246
Website: www.bgsu.edu
Admissions email: choosebgsu@bgsu.edu
Public; founded 1910
Freshman admissions: selective; 2018-2019: 17,028 applied, 12,303 accepted. Either SAT or ACT required. ACT 25/75 percentile: 20-25. High school rank: 15% in top tenth, 38% in top quarter, 70% in top half
Early decision deadline: N/A, notification date: N/A
Early action deadline: N/A, notification date: N/A
Application deadline (fall): 7/15

Undergraduate student body: 12,987 full time, 1,871 part time; 45% male, 55% female; 0% American Indian, 1% Asian, 9% black, 4% Hispanic, 4% multiracial, 0% Pacific Islander, 78% white, 2% international; 86% from in state; 40% live on campus; 11% of students in fraternities, 10% in sororities
Most popular majors: 4% Biology/Biological Sciences, General, 4% Education, Other, 4% Education/Teaching of Individuals in Early Childhood Special Education Programs, 4% Psychology, General, 3% Special Education and Teaching, General
Expenses: 2019-2020: $11,318 in state, $19,305 out of state; room/board: $10,396
Financial aid: (419) 372-2651; 65% of undergrads determined to have financial need; average aid package $14,344

Capital University
Columbus OH
(866) 544-6175
U.S. News ranking: Reg. U. (Mid. W), No. 28
Website: www.capital.edu
Admissions email: admission@capital.edu
Private; founded 1830
Affiliation: Evangelical Lutheran Church
Freshman admissions: selective; 2018-2019: 3,958 applied, 2,890 accepted. Either SAT or ACT required. ACT 25/75 percentile: 21-26. High school rank: 22% in top tenth, 51% in top quarter, 87% in top half
Early decision deadline: N/A, notification date: N/A
Early action deadline: N/A, notification date: N/A
Application deadline (fall): 5/1
Undergraduate student body: 2,316 full time, 178 part time; 37% male, 63% female; 0% American Indian, 2% Asian, 10% black, 4% Hispanic, 5% multiracial, 0% Pacific Islander, 74% white, 2% international; 92% from in state; 58% live on campus; 6% of students in fraternities, 11% in sororities
Most popular majors: 17% Health Professions and Related Programs, 15% Business, Management, Marketing, and Related Support Services, 10% Education, 10% Social Sciences, 9% Visual and Performing Arts
Expenses: 2019-2020: $36,872; room/board: $11,264
Financial aid: (614) 236-6771; 80% of undergrads determined to have financial need; average aid package $30,081

Case Western Reserve University
Cleveland OH
(216) 368-4450
U.S. News ranking: Nat. U., No. 40
Website: www.case.edu
Admissions email: admission@case.edu
Private; founded 1826
Freshman admissions: most selective; 2018-2019: 26,642

applied, 7,794 accepted. Either SAT or ACT required. ACT 25/75 percentile: 30-34. High school rank: 70% in top tenth, 93% in top quarter, 99% in top half
Early decision deadline: 11/1, notification date: 12/15
Early action deadline: 11/1, notification date: 12/15
Application deadline (fall): 1/15
Undergraduate student body: 5,096 full time, 166 part time; 55% male, 45% female; 0% American Indian, 21% Asian, 4% black, 8% Hispanic, 5% multiracial, 0% Pacific Islander, 47% white, 14% international; 28% from in state; 80% live on campus; 28% of students in fraternities, 36% in sororities
Most popular majors: 10% Bioengineering and Biomedical Engineering, 7% Biology/Biological Sciences, General, 7% Mechanical Engineering, 6% Computer Science, 6% Registered Nursing/Registered Nurse
Expenses: 2019-2020: $50,904; room/board: $15,614
Financial aid: (216) 368-4530; 48% of undergrads determined to have financial need; average aid package $44,441

Cedarville University
Cedarville OH
(800) 233-2784
U.S. News ranking: Reg. U. (Mid. W), No. 25
Website: www.cedarville.edu
Admissions email: admissions@cedarville.edu
Private; founded 1887
Affiliation: Baptist
Freshman admissions: more selective; 2018-2019: 3,755 applied, 2,969 accepted. Either SAT or ACT required. ACT 25/75 percentile: 23-29. High school rank: 29% in top tenth, 60% in top quarter, 88% in top half
Early decision deadline: N/A, notification date: N/A
Early action deadline: N/A, notification date: N/A
Application deadline (fall): 8/1
Undergraduate student body: 3,278 full time, 481 part time; 47% male, 53% female; 0% American Indian, 2% Asian, 1% black, 2% Hispanic, 4% multiracial, 0% Pacific Islander, 88% white, 2% international; 43% from in state; 82% live on campus; 0% of students in fraternities, 0% in sororities
Most popular majors: 22% Health Professions and Related Programs, 14% Business, Management, Marketing, and Related Support Services, 8% Education, 8% Engineering, 7% Visual and Performing Arts
Expenses: 2019-2020: $31,322; room/board: $7,618
Financial aid: (937) 766-7866; 70% of undergrads determined to have financial need; average aid package $22,873

Central State University
Wilberforce OH
(937) 376-6348
U.S. News ranking: Reg. Coll. (Mid. W), second tier
Website: www.centralstate.edu
Admissions email: admissions@centralstate.edu
Public; founded 1887
Freshman admissions: least selective; 2018-2019: 12,353 applied, 7,051 accepted. Neither SAT nor ACT required. ACT 25/75 percentile: 14-18. High school rank: 7% in top tenth, 23% in top quarter, 59% in top half
Early decision deadline: N/A, notification date: N/A
Early action deadline: N/A, notification date: N/A
Application deadline (fall): rolling
Undergraduate student body: 2,029 full time, 70 part time; 40% male, 60% female; 0% American Indian, 0% Asian, 88% black, 1% Hispanic, 2% multiracial, 0% Pacific Islander, 1% white, 4% international; 50% from in state; 24% live on campus; 1% of students in fraternities, 1% in sororities
Most popular majors: 22% Business, Management, Marketing, and Related Support Services, 13% Homeland Security, Law Enforcement, Firefighting and Related Protective Services, 13% Psychology, 9% Biological and Biomedical Sciences, 8% Communication, Journalism, and Related Programs
Expenses: 2018-2019: $6,346 in state, $8,346 out of state; room/board: $10,232
Financial aid: (937) 376-6574

Cleveland Institute of Art
Cleveland OH
(216) 421-7418
U.S. News ranking: Arts, unranked
Website: www.cia.edu
Admissions email: admissions@cia.edu
Private; founded 1882
Freshman admissions: selective; 2018-2019: 1,025 applied, 753 accepted. Neither SAT nor ACT required. ACT 25/75 percentile: 19-25. High school rank: 9% in top tenth, 32% in top quarter, 64% in top half
Early decision deadline: N/A, notification date: N/A
Early action deadline: 12/1, notification date: 12/15
Application deadline (fall): rolling
Undergraduate student body: 649 full time, 21 part time; 33% male, 67% female; 0% American Indian, 3% Asian, 11% black, 8% Hispanic, 5% multiracial, 0% Pacific Islander, 67% white, 6% international; N/A from in state; 49% live on campus; 1% of students in fraternities, 1% in sororities
Most popular majors: 21% Industrial and Product Design, 20% Illustration, 11% Graphic Design, 7% Animation, Interactive Technology, Video Graphics and

Special Effects, 6% Medical Illustration/Medical Illustrator
Expenses: 2019-2020: $43,305; room/board: $11,330
Financial aid: (216) 421-7425; 79% of undergrads determined to have financial need; average aid package $27,398

Cleveland Institute of Music
Cleveland OH
(216) 795-3107
U.S. News ranking: Arts, unranked
Website: www.cim.edu/
Admissions email: admission@cim.edu
Private; founded 1920
Freshman admissions: least selective; 2018-2019: 504 applied, 185 accepted. Neither SAT nor ACT required. SAT 25/75 percentile: N/A. High school rank: N/A
Early decision deadline: N/A, notification date: N/A
Early action deadline: N/A, notification date: N/A
Application deadline (fall): 12/1
Undergraduate student body: 231 full time, 0 part time; 49% male, 51% female; 0% American Indian, 10% Asian, 1% black, 0% Hispanic, 0% multiracial, 0% Pacific Islander, 27% white, 22% international
Most popular majors: 100% Music
Expenses: 2018-2019: $41,487; room/board: $15,048
Financial aid: (216) 795-3192

Cleveland State University
Cleveland OH
(216) 687-5411
U.S. News ranking: Nat. U., second tier
Website: www.csuohio.edu
Admissions email: admissions@csuohio.edu
Public; founded 1964
Freshman admissions: selective; 2018-2019: 9,918 applied, 8,762 accepted. Either SAT or ACT required. ACT 25/75 percentile: 19-25. High school rank: 15% in top tenth, 38% in top quarter, 69% in top half
Early decision deadline: N/A, notification date: N/A
Early action deadline: 5/1, notification date: N/A
Application deadline (fall): 8/16
Undergraduate student body: 9,357 full time, 2,887 part time; 47% male, 53% female; 0% American Indian, 3% Asian, 15% black, 7% Hispanic, 4% multiracial, 0% Pacific Islander, 63% white, 6% international; 90% from in state; 8% live on campus; 1% of students in fraternities, 1% in sororities
Most popular majors: 9% Psychology, General, 8% Clinical/Medical Laboratory Science and Allied Professions, Other, 4% Biology/Biological Sciences, General, 4% Mechanical Engineering, 4% Social Work
Expenses: 2019-2020: $10,880 in state, $15,054 out of state; room/board: $11,576

Financial aid: (216) 687-5594; 71% of undergrads determined to have financial need; average aid package $9,163

College of Wooster
Wooster OH
(330) 263-2322
U.S. News ranking: Nat. Lib. Arts, No. 66
Website: www.wooster.edu/
Admissions email: admissions@wooster.edu
Private; founded 1866
Freshman admissions: more selective; 2018-2019: 6,244 applied, 3,383 accepted. Either SAT or ACT required. ACT 25/75 percentile: 25-30. High school rank: 45% in top tenth, 71% in top quarter, 87% in top half
Early decision deadline: 11/1, notification date: 11/15
Early action deadline: 11/15, notification date: 12/31
Application deadline (fall): 2/15
Undergraduate student body: 1,996 full time, 8 part time; 46% male, 54% female; 1% American Indian, 5% Asian, 10% black, 5% Hispanic, 0% multiracial, 0% Pacific Islander, 63% white, 15% international; 36% from in state; 99% live on campus; N/A of students in fraternities, N/A in sororities
Most popular majors: 9% Political Science and Government, General, 8% Biology/Biological Sciences, General, 8% Psychology, General, 7% English Language and Literature, General, 7% History, General
Expenses: 2019-2020: $52,000; room/board: $12,250
Financial aid: (330) 263-2317; 66% of undergrads determined to have financial need; average aid package $45,235

Columbus College of Art and Design
Columbus OH
(614) 222-3261
U.S. News ranking: Arts, unranked
Website: www.ccad.edu
Admissions email: admissions@ccad.edu
Private; founded 1879
Freshman admissions: selective; 2018-2019: 805 applied, 709 accepted. Neither SAT nor ACT required. ACT 25/75 percentile: 19-25. High school rank: N/A
Early decision deadline: N/A, notification date: N/A
Early action deadline: 12/1, notification date: 12/15
Application deadline (fall): 8/1
Undergraduate student body: 1,008 full time, 24 part time; 30% male, 70% female; 0% American Indian, 3% Asian, 9% black, 7% Hispanic, 5% multiracial, 0% Pacific Islander, 66% white, 6% international
Most popular majors: 23% Commercial and Advertising Art, 21% Illustration, 20% Animation, Interactive Technology, Video Graphics and Special Effects, 8% Fine Arts and Art Studies, Other, 8% Industrial and Product Design

Expenses: 2019-2020: $36,750; room/board: $9,680
Financial aid: (614) 222-3274; 81% of undergrads determined to have financial need; average aid package $25,750

Defiance College
Defiance OH
(419) 783-2359
U.S. News ranking: Reg. Coll. (Mid. W), No. 46
Website: www.defiance.edu
Admissions email: admissions@defiance.edu
Private; founded 1850
Affiliation: United Church of Christ
Freshman admissions: less selective; 2018-2019: 1,502 applied, 787 accepted. Either SAT or ACT required. ACT 25/75 percentile: 17-23. High school rank: 2% in top tenth, 21% in top quarter, 52% in top half
Early decision deadline: N/A, notification date: N/A
Early action deadline: N/A, notification date: N/A
Application deadline (fall): rolling
Undergraduate student body: 474 full time, 51 part time; 53% male, 47% female; 1% American Indian, 1% Asian, 14% black, 9% Hispanic, 1% multiracial, 0% Pacific Islander, 72% white, 2% international
Most popular majors: 13% Criminal Justice/Police Science, 11% Business/Commerce, General, 11% Social Work, 7% Kinesiology and Exercise Science, 7% Sport and Fitness Administration/Management
Expenses: 2019-2020: $33,260; room/board: $10,540
Financial aid: (419) 783-2376; 92% of undergrads determined to have financial need; average aid package $24,462

Denison University
Granville OH
(740) 587-6276
U.S. News ranking: Nat. Lib. Arts, No. 43
Website: www.denison.edu
Admissions email: admission@denison.edu
Private; founded 1831
Freshman admissions: more selective; 2018-2019: 8,042 applied, 2,727 accepted. Neither SAT nor ACT required. SAT 25/75 percentile: 1210-1380. High school rank: 64% in top tenth, 85% in top quarter, 100% in top half
Early decision deadline: 11/15, notification date: 12/15
Early action deadline: N/A, notification date: N/A
Application deadline (fall): 1/15
Undergraduate student body: 2,256 full time, 29 part time; 46% male, 54% female; 0% American Indian, 4% Asian, 6% black, 9% Hispanic, 3% multiracial, 0% Pacific Islander, 62% white, 12% international; 26% from in state; 99% live on campus; 48% of students in fraternities, 27% in sororities

Most popular majors: 25% Social Sciences, 12% Biological and Biomedical Sciences, 11% Communication, Journalism, and Related Programs, 8% Psychology, 7% English Language and Literature/Letters
Expenses: 2019-2020: $53,830; room/board: $13,050
Financial aid: (740) 587-6276; 52% of undergrads determined to have financial need; average aid package $48,802

Franciscan University of Steubenville
Steubenville OH
(740) 283-6226
U.S. News ranking: Reg. U. (Mid. W), No. 17
Website: www.franciscan.edu
Admissions email: admissions@franciscan.edu
Private; founded 1946
Affiliation: Roman Catholic
Freshman admissions: more selective; 2018-2019: 2,100 applied, 1,619 accepted. Either SAT or ACT required. SAT 25/75 percentile: 1060-1280. High school rank: 24% in top tenth, 59% in top quarter, 83% in top half
Early decision deadline: N/A, notification date: N/A
Early action deadline: N/A, notification date: N/A
Application deadline (fall): rolling
Undergraduate student body: 2,039 full time, 202 part time; 40% male, 60% female; 0% American Indian, 2% Asian, 1% black, 12% Hispanic, 2% multiracial, 0% Pacific Islander, 81% white, 1% international; 78% from in state; 80% live on campus; 0% of students in fraternities, 0% in sororities
Most popular majors: 25% Theology/Theological Studies, 14% Business Administration and Management, General, 8% Registered Nursing/Registered Nurse, 7% Multicultural Education, 7% Psychology, General
Expenses: 2019-2020: $28,880; room/board: $8,680
Financial aid: (740) 284-5216; 67% of undergrads determined to have financial need; average aid package $18,093

Franklin University[1]
Columbus OH
(888) 341-6237
U.S. News ranking: Business, unranked
Website: www.franklin.edu
Admissions email: info@franklin.edu
Private; founded 1902
Application deadline (fall): N/A
Undergraduate student body: N/A full time, N/A part time
Expenses: N/A
Financial aid: N/A

Heidelberg University
Tiffin OH
(419) 448-2330
U.S. News ranking: Reg. Coll. (Mid. W), No. 18
Website: www.heidelberg.edu
Admissions email: adminfo@heidelberg.edu
Private; founded 1850
Affiliation: United Church of Christ
Freshman admissions: selective; 2018-2019: 1,827 applied, 1,228 accepted. Either SAT or ACT required. ACT 25/75 percentile: 19-25. High school rank: N/A
Early decision deadline: N/A, notification date: N/A
Early action deadline: N/A, notification date: N/A
Application deadline (fall): 8/1
Undergraduate student body: 1,028 full time, 11 part time; 51% male, 49% female; 0% American Indian, 1% Asian, 9% black, 3% Hispanic, 4% multiracial, 0% Pacific Islander, 81% white, 1% international
Most popular majors: Information not available
Expenses: 2019-2020: $31,700; room/board: $10,700
Financial aid: (419) 448-2293; 87% of undergrads determined to have financial need; average aid package $27,083

Hiram College
Hiram OH
(330) 569-5169
U.S. News ranking: Reg. Coll. (Mid. W), No. 14
Website: www.hiram.edu
Admissions email: admission@hiram.edu
Private; founded 1850
Freshman admissions: selective; 2018-2019: 2,687 applied, 1,548 accepted. Either SAT or ACT required for some. ACT 25/75 percentile: 18-25. High school rank: 13% in top tenth, 39% in top quarter, 71% in top half
Early decision deadline: N/A, notification date: N/A
Early action deadline: N/A, notification date: N/A
Application deadline (fall): rolling
Undergraduate student body: 824 full time, 420 part time; 43% male, 57% female; 0% American Indian, 2% Asian, 17% black, 6% Hispanic, 4% multiracial, 0% Pacific Islander, 61% white, 1% international; 80% from in state; 80% live on campus; 0% of students in fraternities, 0% in sororities
Most popular majors: 34% Business, Management, Marketing, and Related Support Services, 12% Social Sciences, 11% Biological and Biomedical Sciences, 11% Health Professions and Related Programs, 6% Psychology
Expenses: 2019-2020: $37,710; room/board: $10,290
Financial aid: (330) 569-5441; 90% of undergrads determined to have financial need; average aid package $28,530

John Carroll University
University Heights OH
(888) 335-6800
U.S. News ranking: Reg. U. (Mid. W), No. 2
Website: sites.jcu.edu/
Admissions email: enrollment@jcu.edu
Private; founded 1886
Affiliation: Roman Catholic
Freshman admissions: more selective; 2018-2019: 4,007 applied, 3,336 accepted. Either SAT or ACT required. ACT 25/75 percentile: 22-28. High school rank: 24% in top tenth, 53% in top quarter, 87% in top half
Early decision deadline: N/A, notification date: N/A
Early action deadline: 12/1, notification date: 12/15
Application deadline (fall): rolling
Undergraduate student body: 2,996 full time, 80 part time; 52% male, 48% female; 0% American Indian, 2% Asian, 4% black, 4% Hispanic, 2% multiracial, 0% Pacific Islander, 85% white, 2% international; 66% from in state; 53% live on campus; 9% of students in fraternities, 21% in sororities
Most popular majors: 40% Business, Management, Marketing, and Related Support Services, 9% Social Sciences, 8% Communication, Journalism, and Related Programs, 7% Biological and Biomedical Sciences, 7% Psychology
Expenses: 2019-2020: $42,910; room/board: $12,232
Financial aid: (888) 335-6800; 71% of undergrads determined to have financial need; average aid package $33,943

Kent State University
Kent OH
(330) 672-2444
U.S. News ranking: Nat. U., No. 211
Website: www.kent.edu
Admissions email: kentadm@kent.edu
Public; founded 1910
Freshman admissions: selective; 2018-2019: 16,337 applied, 13,946 accepted. Either SAT or ACT required. ACT 25/75 percentile: 20-25. High school rank: 15% in top tenth, 39% in top quarter, 75% in top half
Early decision deadline: N/A, notification date: N/A
Early action deadline: N/A, notification date: N/A
Application deadline (fall): 5/1
Undergraduate student body: 20,044 full time, 2,513 part time; 39% male, 61% female; 0% American Indian, 2% Asian, 9% black, 4% Hispanic, 4% multiracial, 0% Pacific Islander, 75% white, 4% international; N/A from in state; 30% live on campus; N/A of students in fraternities, N/A in sororities
Most popular majors: 22% Business, Management, Marketing, and Related Support Services, 16% Health Professions and Related Programs, 8%

Communication, Journalism, and Related Programs, 8% Education, 6% Visual and Performing Arts
Expenses: 2019-2020: $10,916 in state, $19,792 out of state; room/board: $11,682
Financial aid: (330) 672-2972; 63% of undergrads determined to have financial need; average aid package $10,909

Kenyon College
Gambier OH
(740) 427-5776
U.S. News ranking: Nat. Lib. Arts, No. 27
Website: www.kenyon.edu
Admissions email: admissions@kenyon.edu
Private; founded 1824
Freshman admissions: more selective; 2018-2019: 6,152 applied, 2,204 accepted. Either SAT or ACT required. ACT 25/75 percentile: 29-33. High school rank: 55% in top tenth, 79% in top quarter, 96% in top half
Early decision deadline: 11/15, notification date: 12/18
Early action deadline: N/A, notification date: N/A
Application deadline (fall): 1/15
Undergraduate student body: 1,719 full time, 15 part time; 45% male, 55% female; 0% American Indian, 4% Asian, 4% black, 8% Hispanic, 5% multiracial, 0% Pacific Islander, 70% white, 7% international; 13% from in state; 99% live on campus; 27% of students in fraternities, 32% in sororities
Most popular majors: 14% English Language and Literature, General, 12% Economics, General, 7% History, General, 7% Psychology, General, 5% Political Science and Government, General
Expenses: 2019-2020: $58,570; room/board: $12,580
Financial aid: (740) 427-5430; 42% of undergrads determined to have financial need; average aid package $46,004

Lake Erie College[1]
Painesville OH
(855) 467-8676
U.S. News ranking: Reg. U. (Mid. W), No. 114
Website: www.lec.edu
Admissions email: admissions@lec.edu
Private; founded 1856
Application deadline (fall): 8/1
Undergraduate student body: N/A full time, N/A part time
Expenses: 2019-2020: $32,322; room/board: $9,908
Financial aid: (440) 375-7100; 83% of undergrads determined to have financial need; average aid package $26,063

Lourdes University
Sylvania OH
(419) 885-5291
U.S. News ranking: Reg. U. (Mid. W), second tier
Website: www.lourdes.edu
Admissions email: luadmits@lourdes.edu
Private; founded 1958
Affiliation: Roman Catholic

Freshman admissions: selective; 2018-2019: 946 applied, 849 accepted. Either SAT or ACT required. ACT 25/75 percentile: 18-24. High school rank: 12% in top tenth, 40% in top quarter, 67% in top half
Early decision deadline: N/A, notification date: N/A
Early action deadline: N/A, notification date: N/A
Application deadline (fall): rolling
Undergraduate student body: 842 full time, 243 part time; 40% male, 60% female; 0% American Indian, 1% Asian, 12% black, 10% Hispanic, 4% multiracial, 0% Pacific Islander, 70% white, 0% international; 68% from in state; 40% live on campus; 0% of students in fraternities, 0% in sororities
Most popular majors: 39% Registered Nursing/Registered Nurse, 10% Business Administration and Management, General, 7% Criminal Justice/Safety Studies, 7% Social Work, 6% Multi-/Interdisciplinary Studies, Other
Expenses: 2019-2020: $23,550; room/board: $10,590
Financial aid: (419) 824-3504; 82% of undergrads determined to have financial need; average aid package $16,739

Malone University
Canton OH
(330) 471-8145
U.S. News ranking: Reg. U. (Mid. W), No. 53
Website: www.malone.edu
Admissions email: admissions@malone.edu
Private; founded 1892
Affiliation: Friends
Freshman admissions: selective; 2018-2019: 2,039 applied, 1,421 accepted. Either SAT or ACT required. ACT 25/75 percentile: 19-25. High school rank: 13% in top tenth, 35% in top quarter, 72% in top half
Early decision deadline: N/A, notification date: N/A
Early action deadline: N/A, notification date: N/A
Application deadline (fall): rolling
Undergraduate student body: 1,044 full time, 244 part time; 42% male, 58% female; 0% American Indian, 0% Asian, 12% black, 3% Hispanic, 3% multiracial, 0% Pacific Islander, 77% white, 2% international; 88% from in state; 61% live on campus; 0% of students in fraternities, 0% in sororities
Most popular majors: 12% Business Administration and Management, General, 12% Registered Nursing/Registered Nurse, 4% Accounting, 4% Communication, Journalism, and Related Programs, Other, 4% Early Childhood Education and Teaching
Expenses: 2019-2020: $31,800; room/board: $9,800
Financial aid: (330) 471-8161; 85% of undergrads determined to have financial need; average aid package $26,785

Marietta College
Marietta OH
(800) 331-7896
U.S. News ranking: Reg. Coll. (Mid. W), No. 10
Website: www.marietta.edu
Admissions email: admit@marietta.edu
Private; founded 1835
Freshman admissions: selective; 2018-2019: 2,850 applied, 1,967 accepted. Either SAT or ACT required. ACT 25/75 percentile: 20-26. High school rank: 24% in top tenth, 47% in top quarter, 76% in top half
Early decision deadline: N/A, notification date: N/A
Early action deadline: 11/1, notification date: 11/15
Application deadline (fall): rolling
Undergraduate student body: 992 full time, 60 part time; 59% male, 41% female; 0% American Indian, 0% Asian, 4% black, 3% Hispanic, 3% multiracial, 0% Pacific Islander, 73% white, 13% international; 33% from in state; 79% live on campus; 4% of students in fraternities, 7% in sororities
Most popular majors: 25% Petroleum Engineering, 6% Finance, General, 5% Geological and Earth Sciences/Geosciences, Other, 4% Business Administration and Management, General, 4% Early Childhood Education and Teaching
Expenses: 2019-2020: $36,040; room/board: $11,320
Financial aid: (740) 376 4712; 72% of undergrads determined to have financial need; average aid package $36,541

Miami University–Oxford
Oxford OH
(513) 529-2531
U.S. News ranking: Nat. U., No. 91
Website: www.MiamiOH.edu
Admissions email: admission@MiamiOH.edu
Public; founded 1809
Freshman admissions: more selective; 2018-2019: 30,126 applied, 22,459 accepted. Either SAT or ACT required. ACT 25/75 percentile: 26-31. High school rank: 34% in top tenth, 66% in top quarter, 92% in top half
Early decision deadline: 11/15, notification date: 12/15
Early action deadline: 12/1, notification date: 2/1
Application deadline (fall): 2/1
Undergraduate student body: 16,714 full time, 612 part time; 50% male, 50% female; 0% American Indian, 2% Asian, 3% black, 5% Hispanic, 4% multiracial, 0% Pacific Islander, 71% white, 14% international; 51% from in state; 45% live on campus; 19% of students in fraternities, 29% in sororities
Most popular majors: 26% Business, Management, Marketing, and Related Support Services, 10% Social Sciences, 9% Communication, Journalism,

and Related Programs, 7% Health Professions and Related Programs, 6% Education
Expenses: 2019-2020: $15,232 in state, $34,307 out of state; room/board: $13,397
Financial aid: (513) 529-8734; 34% of undergrads determined to have financial need; average aid package $15,185

Mount St. Joseph University
Cincinnati OH
(513) 244-4531
U.S. News ranking: Reg. U. (Mid. W), No. 83
Website: www.msj.edu
Admissions email: admission@mail.msj.edu
Private; founded 1920
Affiliation: Roman Catholic
Freshman admissions: selective; 2018-2019: 1,832 applied, 1,105 accepted. Either SAT or ACT required. ACT 25/75 percentile: 20-25. High school rank: 11% in top tenth, 33% in top quarter, 72% in top half
Early decision deadline: N/A, notification date: N/A
Early action deadline: N/A, notification date: N/A
Application deadline (fall): 8/17
Undergraduate student body: 1,006 full time, 442 part time; 41% male, 59% female; 0% American Indian, 1% Asian, 12% black, 3% Hispanic, 4% multiracial, 0% Pacific Islander, 79% white, 0% international; 82% from in state; N/A live on campus; N/A of students in fraternities, N/A in sororities
Most popular majors: 20% Health Professions and Related Programs, 17% Business, Management, Marketing, and Related Support Services, 9% Education, 8% Biological and Biomedical Sciences, 8% Psychology
Expenses: 2019-2020: $31,100; room/board: $9,720
Financial aid: (513) 244-4418; 80% of undergrads determined to have financial need; average aid package $22,736

Mount Vernon Nazarene University
Mount Vernon OH
(866) 462-6868
U.S. News ranking: Reg. U. (Mid. W), No. 66
Website: www.mvnu.edu/
Admissions email: admissions@mvnu.edu
Private; founded 1968
Affiliation: Church of the Nazarene
Freshman admissions: selective; 2018-2019: 1,427 applied, 1,081 accepted. Either SAT or ACT required. ACT 25/75 percentile: 19-28. High school rank: 22% in top tenth, 48% in top quarter, 82% in top half
Early decision deadline: N/A, notification date: N/A
Early action deadline: N/A, notification date: N/A
Application deadline (fall): 7/15
Undergraduate student body: 1,518 full time, 320 part time; 37% male, 63% female; 0% American

Indian, 0% Asian, 3% black, 3% Hispanic, 3% multiracial, 0% Pacific Islander, 86% white, 1% international; 87% from in state; 55% live on campus; 0% of students in fraternities, 0% in sororities
Most popular majors: 27% Business Administration and Management, General, 13% Registered Nursing/Registered Nurse, 10% Biology/Biological Sciences, General, 9% Early Childhood Education and Teaching, 9% Social Work
Expenses: 2018-2019: $29,244; room/board: $8,170
Financial aid: (740) 397-9000

Muskingum University
New Concord OH
(740) 826-8137
U.S. News ranking: Reg. U. (Mid. W), No. 46
Website: www.muskingum.edu
Admissions email: adminfo@muskingum.edu
Private; founded 1837
Affiliation: Presbyterian Church (USA)
Freshman admissions: selective; 2018-2019: 2,175 applied, 1,570 accepted. Either SAT or ACT required. ACT 25/75 percentile: 19-24. High school rank: 12% in top tenth, 35% in top quarter, 71% in top half
Early decision deadline: N/A, notification date: N/A
Early action deadline: N/A, notification date: N/A
Application deadline (fall): 8/1
Undergraduate student body: 1,353 full time, 263 part time; 44% male, 56% female; 0% American Indian, 1% Asian, 5% black, 2% Hispanic, 4% multiracial, 0% Pacific Islander, 80% white, 3% international; 91% from in state; 64% live on campus; 26% of students in fraternities, 37% in sororities
Most popular majors: 24% Health Professions and Related Programs, 16% Business, Management, Marketing, and Related Support Services, 8% Biological and Biomedical Sciences, 8% Education, 7% Psychology
Expenses: 2019-2020: $29,128; room/board: $11,590
Financial aid: (740) 826-8139; 85% of undergrads determined to have financial need; average aid package $26,039

Notre Dame College of Ohio[1]
Cleveland OH
(216) 373-5355
U.S. News ranking: Reg. U. (Mid. W), second tier
Website: www.notredamecollege.edu
Admissions email: admissions@ndc.edu
Private; founded 1922
Application deadline (fall): rolling
Undergraduate student body: N/A full time, N/A part time
Expenses: N/A
Financial aid: (216) 373-5263

Oberlin College

Oberlin OH
(440) 775-8411
U.S. News ranking: Nat. Lib. Arts, No. 33
Website: www.oberlin.edu
Admissions email: college.admissions@oberlin.edu
Private; founded 1833
Freshman admissions: more selective; 2018-2019: 7,525 applied, 2,725 accepted. Either SAT or ACT required. SAT 25/75 percentile: 1280-1490. High school rank: 53% in top tenth, 85% in top quarter, 96% in top half
Early decision deadline: 11/15, notification date: 12/15
Early action deadline: N/A, notification date: N/A
Application deadline (fall): 1/15
Undergraduate student body: 2,758 full time, 27 part time; 43% male, 57% female; 0% American Indian, 4% Asian, 5% black, 8% Hispanic, 8% multiracial, 0% Pacific Islander, 62% white, 11% international; 6% from in state; 90% live on campus; 0% of students in fraternities, 0% in sororities
Most popular majors: 13% Music, 9% Political Science and Government, Other, 8% Biological and Biomedical Sciences, 7% Applied Economics, 4% Psychology
Expenses: 2019-2020: $56,818; room/board: $16,826
Financial aid: (440) 775-8142; 51% of undergrads determined to have financial need; average aid package $45,020

Ohio Christian University[1]

Circleville OH
(877) 762-8669
U.S. News ranking: Reg. U. (Mid. W), second tier
Website: www.ohiochristian.edu/
Admissions email: enroll@ohiochristian.edu
Private; founded 1948
Affiliation: Churches of Christ
Application deadline (fall): N/A
Undergraduate student body: N/A full time, N/A part time
Expenses: N/A
Financial aid: N/A

Ohio Dominican University

Columbus OH
(614) 251-4500
U.S. News ranking: Reg. U. (Mid. W), No. 84
Website: www.ohiodominican.edu
Admissions email: admissions@ohiodominican.edu
Private; founded 1911
Affiliation: Roman Catholic
Freshman admissions: selective; 2018-2019: 1,550 applied, 1,168 accepted. Either SAT or ACT required for some. ACT 25/75 percentile: 19-24. High school rank: 12% in top tenth, 33% in top quarter, 71% in top half
Early decision deadline: N/A, notification date: N/A

Early action deadline: N/A, notification date: N/A
Application deadline (fall): rolling
Undergraduate student body: 952 full time, 236 part time; 46% male, 54% female; 1% American Indian, 1% Asian, 26% black, 4% Hispanic, 5% multiracial, 0% Pacific Islander, 53% white, 3% international; 94% from in state; 43% live on campus; 0% of students in fraternities, 0% in sororities
Most popular majors: 12% Business Administration and Management, General, 11% Biology/Biological Sciences, General, 10% Kinesiology and Exercise Science, 7% Sport and Fitness Administration/ Management, 6% Early Childhood Education and Teaching
Expenses: 2019-2020: $31,680; room/board: $11,220
Financial aid: (614) 251-4778; 83% of undergrads determined to have financial need; average aid package $25,204

Ohio Northern University

Ada OH
(888) 408-4668
U.S. News ranking: Reg. Coll. (Mid. W), No. 5
Website: www.onu.edu
Admissions email: admissions-ug@onu.edu
Private; founded 1871
Affiliation: United Methodist
Freshman admissions: more selective; 2018-2019: 4,331 applied, 2,959 accepted. Either SAT or ACT required. ACT 25/75 percentile: 22-27. High school rank: 26% in top tenth, 62% in top quarter, 90% in top half
Early decision deadline: N/A, notification date: N/A
Early action deadline: N/A, notification date: N/A
Application deadline (fall): 8/15
Undergraduate student body: 2,118 full time, 179 part time; 55% male, 45% female; 0% American Indian, 1% Asian, 4% black, 1% Hispanic, 2% multiracial, 0% Pacific Islander, 79% white, 2% international; 83% from in state; 75% live on campus; 14% of students in fraternities, 23% in sororities
Most popular majors: Information not available
Expenses: 2019-2020: $33,440; room/board: $12,040
Financial aid: (419) 772-2271; 83% of undergrads determined to have financial need; average aid package $27,794

Ohio State University–Columbus

Columbus OH
(614) 292-3980
U.S. News ranking: Nat. U., No. 54
Website: www.osu.edu
Admissions email: askabuckeye@osu.edu
Public; founded 1870
Freshman admissions: more selective; 2018-2019: 48,077 applied, 24,988 accepted. Either SAT or ACT required. ACT 25/75

percentile: 27-32. High school rank: 63% in top tenth, 94% in top quarter, 99% in top half
Early decision deadline: N/A, notification date: N/A
Early action deadline: 11/1, notification date: 1/31
Application deadline (fall): 2/1
Undergraduate student body: 42,831 full time, 3,989 part time; 51% male, 49% female; 0% American Indian, 7% Asian, 6% black, 4% Hispanic, 4% multiracial, 0% Pacific Islander, 67% white, 9% international; 75% from in state; 32% live on campus; 8% of students in fraternities, 12% in sororities
Most popular majors: 5% Finance, General, 5% Psychology, General, 4% Biology/Biological Sciences, General, 4% Marketing/Marketing Management, General, 4% Speech Communication and Rhetoric
Expenses: 2019-2020: $11,084 in state, $32,061 out of state; room/board: $12,708
Financial aid: (614) 292-0300; 47% of undergrads determined to have financial need; average aid package $14,537

Ohio University

Athens OH
(740) 593-4100
U.S. News ranking: Nat. U., No. 185
Website: www.ohio.edu
Admissions email: admissions@ohio.edu
Public; founded 1804
Freshman admissions: selective; 2018-2019: 23,385 applied, 18,311 accepted. Either SAT or ACT required. ACT 25/75 percentile: 21-26. High school rank: 17% in top tenth, 44% in top quarter, 82% in top half
Early decision deadline: N/A, notification date: N/A
Early action deadline: 12/1, notification date: N/A
Application deadline (fall): 2/1
Undergraduate student body: 17,041 full time, 5,234 part time; 40% male, 60% female; 0% American Indian, 1% Asian, 6% black, 3% Hispanic, 4% multiracial, 0% Pacific Islander, 83% white, 2% international; 82% from in state; 43% live on campus; 6% of students in fraternities, 8% in sororities
Most popular majors: 36% Registered Nursing/Registered Nurse, 4% Business Administration and Management, General, 4% Liberal Arts and Sciences, General Studies and Humanities, Other, 3% Journalism, 3% Speech Communication and Rhetoric
Expenses: 2019-2020: $12,612 in state, $22,406 out of state; room/board: $13,332
Financial aid: (740) 593-4141; 57% of undergrads determined to have financial need; average aid package $8,977

Ohio Wesleyan University

Delaware OH
(740) 368-3020
U.S. News ranking: Nat. Lib. Arts, No. 92
Website: www.owu.edu
Admissions email: owuadmit@owu.edu
Private; founded 1842
Affiliation: United Methodist
Freshman admissions: more selective; 2018-2019: 4,705 applied, 3,246 accepted. Either SAT or ACT required for some. ACT 25/75 percentile: 22-28. High school rank: 25% in top tenth, 53% in top quarter, 81% in top half
Early decision deadline: 11/15, notification date: 11/30
Early action deadline: 12/1, notification date: 12/15
Application deadline (fall): 3/1
Undergraduate student body: 1,547 full time, 14 part time; 46% male, 54% female; 0% American Indian, 3% Asian, 9% black, 6% Hispanic, 5% multiracial, 0% Pacific Islander, 68% white, 6% international; N/A from in state; 88% live on campus; 35% of students in fraternities, 31% in sororities
Most popular majors: 17% Business, Management, Marketing, and Related Support Services, 13% Social Sciences, 12% Biological and Biomedical Sciences, 9% Parks, Recreation, Leisure, and Fitness Studies, 9% Psychology
Expenses: 2019-2020: $47,130; room/board: $12,800
Financial aid: (740) 368-3050; 73% of undergrads determined to have financial need; average aid package $38,634

Otterbein University

Westerville OH
(614) 823-1500
U.S. News ranking: Reg. U. (Mid. W), No. 20
Website: www.otterbein.edu
Admissions email: UOtterB@Otterbein.edu
Private; founded 1847
Affiliation: United Methodist
Freshman admissions: selective; 2018-2019: 2,911 applied, 2,401 accepted. Either SAT or ACT required. ACT 25/75 percentile: 21-27. High school rank: 24% in top tenth, 54% in top quarter, 85% in top half
Early decision deadline: N/A, notification date: N/A
Early action deadline: N/A, notification date: N/A
Application deadline (fall): rolling
Undergraduate student body: 2,284 full time, 211 part time; 38% male, 62% female; 0% American Indian, 2% Asian, 7% black, 4% Hispanic, 5% multiracial, 0% Pacific Islander, 77% white, 1% international; 87% from in state; 61% live on campus; N/A of students in fraternities, N/A in sororities
Most popular majors: 18% Health Professions and Related Programs, 14% Business, Management,

Marketing, and Related Support Services, 11% Visual and Performing Arts, 9% Education, 8% Communication, Journalism, and Related Programs
Expenses: 2019-2020: $32,474; room/board: $11,186
Financial aid: (614) 823-1502; 74% of undergrads determined to have financial need; average aid package $22,280

Shawnee State University

Portsmouth OH
(740) 347-1749
U.S. News ranking: Reg. U. (Mid. W), second tier
Website: www.shawnee.edu
Admissions email: To_SSU@shawnee.edu
Public; founded 1986
Freshman admissions: selective; 2018-2019: 3,019 applied, 2,233 accepted. Either SAT or ACT required for some. ACT 25/75 percentile: 19-24. High school rank: 18% in top tenth, 42% in top quarter, 76% in top half
Early decision deadline: N/A, notification date: N/A
Early action deadline: N/A, notification date: N/A
Application deadline (fall): rolling
Undergraduate student body: 2,571 full time, 526 part time; 45% male, 55% female; 0% American Indian, 1% Asian, 5% black, 1% Hispanic, 3% multiracial, 0% Pacific Islander, 87% white, 1% international
Most popular majors: Information not available
Expenses: 2019-2020: $8,265 in state, $14,189 out of state; room/board: $10,570
Financial aid: (740) 351-4243; 75% of undergrads determined to have financial need; average aid package $9,135

Tiffin University

Tiffin OH
(419) 448-3423
U.S. News ranking: Reg. U. (Mid. W), No. 114
Website: www.tiffin.edu
Admissions email: admiss@tiffin.edu
Private; founded 1888
Freshman admissions: less selective; 2018-2019: 3,977 applied, 2,753 accepted. Either SAT or ACT required for some. ACT 25/75 percentile: 17-22. High school rank: N/A
Early decision deadline: N/A, notification date: N/A
Early action deadline: N/A, notification date: N/A
Application deadline (fall): rolling
Undergraduate student body: 1,724 full time, 499 part time; 51% male, 49% female; 0% American Indian, 0% Asian, 9% black, 3% Hispanic, 2% multiracial, 0% Pacific Islander, 34% white, 11% international; N/A from in state; 50% live on campus; 3% of students in fraternities, 3% in sororities
Most popular majors: 35% Business, Management, Marketing, and Related Support

Services, 34% Homeland Security, Law Enforcement, Firefighting and Related Protective Services, 10% Psychology, 6% Computer and Information Sciences and Support Services, 5% Health Professions and Related Programs
Expenses: 2018-2019: $25,000; room/board: $11,200
Financial aid: (419) 448-3279

Union Institute and University[1]
Cincinnati OH
(800) 861-6400
U.S. News ranking: Nat. U., unranked
Website: www.myunion.edu
Admissions email: admissions@myunion.edu
Private; founded 1964
Affiliation: Other
Application deadline (fall): rolling
Undergraduate student body: N/A full time, N/A part time
Expenses: 2018-2019: $16,526; room/board: N/A
Financial aid: (513) 487-1126

University of Akron
Akron OH
(330) 972-7077
U.S. News ranking: Nat. U., second tier
Website: www.uakron.edu
Admissions email: admissions@uakron.edu
Public; founded 1870
Freshman admissions: selective; 2018-2019: 16,088 applied, 11,089 accepted. Either SAT or ACT required. ACT 25/75 percentile: 19-26. High school rank: 16% in top tenth, 41% in top quarter, 77% in top half
Early decision deadline: N/A, notification date: N/A
Early action deadline: 11/1, notification date: 12/15
Application deadline (fall): 7/1
Undergraduate student body: 12,408 full time, 3,225 part time; 53% male, 47% female; 0% American Indian, 3% Asian, 11% black, 3% Hispanic, 4% multiracial, 0% Pacific Islander, 75% white, 2% international; 94% from in state; 20% live on campus; 4% of students in fraternities, 4% in sororities
Most popular majors: 19% Marketing/Marketing Management, General, 16% Chiropractic, 15% Engineering, General, 8% Education, General, 5% Speech Communication and Rhetoric
Expenses: 2019-2020: $11,636 in state, $17,784 out of state; room/board: $12,200
Financial aid: (330) 972-5860; 68% of undergrads determined to have financial need; average aid package $8,797

University of Cincinnati
Cincinnati OH
(513) 556-1100
U.S. News ranking: Nat. U., No. 139
Website: www.uc.edu
Admissions email: admissions@uc.edu
Public; founded 1819
Freshman admissions: more selective; 2018-2019: 23,296 applied, 17,033 accepted. Either SAT or ACT required. ACT 25/75 percentile: 24-29. High school rank: 24% in top tenth, 52% in top quarter, 84% in top half
Early decision deadline: N/A, notification date: N/A
Early action deadline: 12/1, notification date: N/A
Application deadline (fall): 3/1
Undergraduate student body: 23,103 full time, 3,807 part time; 51% male, 49% female; 0% American Indian, 4% Asian, 7% black, 3% Hispanic, 4% multiracial, 0% Pacific Islander, 74% white, 4% international; 83% from in state; 24% live on campus; 10% of students in fraternities, 10% in sororities
Most popular majors: 21% Business, Management, Marketing, and Related Support Professions and Related Programs, 12% Engineering, 7% Visual and Performing Arts, 6% Communication, Journalism, and Related Programs
Expenses: 2019-2020: $11,660 in state, $26,994 out of state; room/board: $11,668
Financial aid: (513) 556-6982; 48% of undergrads determined to have financial need; average aid package $8,278

University of Cincinnati–UC Blue Ash College[1]
Cincinnati OH
(513) 745-5600
U.S. News ranking: Reg. Coll. (Mid. W), unranked
Website: www.rwc.uc.edu/
Admissions email: N/A
Public
Application deadline (fall): N/A
Undergraduate student body: N/A full time, N/A part time
Expenses: N/A
Financial aid: N/A

University of Dayton
Dayton OH
(937) 229-4411
U.S. News ranking: Nat. U., No. 132
Website: www.udayton.edu
Admissions email: admission@udayton.edu
Private; founded 1850
Affiliation: Roman Catholic
Freshman admissions: selective; 2018-2019: 16,693 applied, 12,016 accepted. Either SAT or ACT required. ACT 25/75 percentile: 25-30. High school rank: 25% in top tenth, 60% in top quarter, 87% in top half

Early decision deadline: N/A, notification date: N/A
Early action deadline: 11/1, notification date: 12/15
Application deadline (fall): 3/1
Undergraduate student body: 8,162 full time, 455 part time; 52% male, 48% female; 0% American Indian, 1% Asian, 3% black, 6% Hispanic, 5% multiracial, 0% Pacific Islander, 79% white, 5% international; 49% from in state; 75% live on campus; 12% of students in fraternities, 21% in sororities
Most popular majors: 32% Business, Management, Marketing, and Related Support Services, 17% Engineering, 7% Communication, Journalism, and Related Programs, 7% Education, 7% Health Professions and Related Programs
Expenses: 2019-2020: $44,100; room/board: $14,050
Financial aid: (800) 427-5029; 58% of undergrads determined to have financial need; average aid package $31,910

University of Findlay
Findlay OH
(419) 434-4732
U.S. News ranking: Nat. U., No. 240
Website: www.findlay.edu
Admissions email: admissions@findlay.edu
Private; founded 1882
Affiliation: Church of God
Freshman admissions: selective; 2018-2019: 3,525 applied, 2,587 accepted. Either SAT or ACT required. ACT 25/75 percentile: 21-26. High school rank: 25% in top tenth, 58% in top quarter, 85% in top half
Early decision deadline: N/A, notification date: N/A
Early action deadline: N/A, notification date: N/A
Application deadline (fall): rolling
Undergraduate student body: 2,434 full time, 1,180 part time; 33% male, 67% female; 0% American Indian, 1% Asian, 4% black, 4% Hispanic, 2% multiracial, 0% Pacific Islander, 79% white, 6% international; N/A from in state; 45% live on campus; 1% of students in fraternities, 2% in sororities
Most popular majors: 30% Health Professions and Related Programs, 23% Business, Management, Marketing, and Related Support Services, 10% Agriculture, Agriculture Operations, and Related Sciences, 10% Biological and Biomedical Sciences, 4% Education
Expenses: 2019-2020: $35,410; room/board: $10,200
Financial aid: (419) 434-4791; 69% of undergrads determined to have financial need; average aid package $29,297

University of Mount Union
Alliance OH
(330) 823-2590
U.S. News ranking: Reg. Coll. (Mid. W), No. 13
Website: www.mountunion.edu/
Admissions email: admission@mountunion.edu
Private; founded 1846
Affiliation: United Methodist
Freshman admissions: selective; 2018-2019: 2,396 applied, 2,310 accepted. Either SAT or ACT required. ACT 25/75 percentile: 20-26. High school rank: 20% in top tenth, 45% in top quarter, 78% in top half
Early decision deadline: N/A, notification date: N/A
Early action deadline: N/A, notification date: N/A
Application deadline (fall): rolling
Undergraduate student body: 2,074 full time, 42 part time; 53% male, 47% female; 0% American Indian, 1% Asian, 8% black, 4% Hispanic, 4% multiracial, 0% Pacific Islander, 78% white, 1% international; 81% from in state; 68% live on campus; N/A of students in fraternities, N/A in sororities
Most popular majors: 22% Business, Management, Marketing, and Related Support Services, 12% Parks, Recreation, Leisure, and Fitness Studies, 8% Education, 5% Biological and Biomedical Sciences, 5% Engineering
Expenses: 2019-2020: $31,700; room/board: $10,500
Financial aid: (330) 823-2674; 81% of undergrads determined to have financial need; average aid package $23,530

University of Northwestern Ohio[1]
Lima OH
(419) 998-3120
U.S. News ranking: Reg. Coll. (Mid. W), unranked
Website: www.unoh.edu/
Admissions email: info@unoh.edu
Private
Application deadline (fall): N/A
Undergraduate student body: N/A full time, N/A part time
Expenses: N/A
Financial aid: N/A

University of Rio Grande[1]
Rio Grande OH
(740) 245-7208
U.S. News ranking: Reg. Coll. (Mid. W), unranked
Website: www.rio.edu
Admissions email: admissions@rio.edu
Private; founded 1876
Application deadline (fall): rolling
Undergraduate student body: N/A full time, N/A part time
Expenses: N/A
Financial aid: (740) 245-7285

University of Toledo
Toledo OH
(419) 530-8888
U.S. News ranking: Nat. U., second tier
Website: www.utoledo.edu
Admissions email: enroll@utoledo.edu
Public; founded 1872
Freshman admissions: selective; 2018-2019: 10,792 applied, 10,107 accepted. Either SAT or ACT required. ACT 25/75 percentile: 20-26. High school rank: 20% in top tenth, 43% in top quarter, 75% in top half
Early decision deadline: N/A, notification date: N/A
Early action deadline: N/A, notification date: N/A
Application deadline (fall): rolling
Undergraduate student body: 12,941 full time, 3,124 part time; 51% male, 49% female; 0% American Indian, 2% Asian, 11% black, 5% Hispanic, 4% multiracial, 0% Pacific Islander, 69% white, 6% international; N/A from in state; 23% live on campus; N/A of students in fraternities, N/A in sororities
Most popular majors: 24% Business, Management, Marketing, and Related Support Services, 16% Health Professions and Related Programs, 15% Engineering, 5% Multi/Interdisciplinary Studies, 4% Biological and Biomedical Sciences
Expenses: 2019-2020: $10,634 in state, $19,994 out of state; room/board: $12,470
Financial aid: (419) 530-8700; 63% of undergrads determined to have financial need; average aid package $11,469

Urbana University[1]
Urbana OH
(937) 484-1400
U.S. News ranking: Reg. U. (Mid. W), second tier
Website: www.urbana.edu
Admissions email: admiss@urbana.edu
Private
Application deadline (fall): N/A
Undergraduate student body: N/A full time, N/A part time
Expenses: N/A
Financial aid: N/A

Ursuline College
Pepper Pike OH
(440) 449-4203
U.S. News ranking: Reg. U. (Mid. W), No. 43
Website: www.ursuline.edu
Admissions email: admission@ursuline.edu
Private; founded 1871
Affiliation: Roman Catholic
Freshman admissions: selective; 2018-2019: 528 applied, 477 accepted. Either SAT or ACT required. ACT 25/75 percentile: 19-24. High school rank: 12% in top tenth, 39% in top quarter, 77% in top half
Early decision deadline: N/A, notification date: N/A
Early action deadline: N/A, notification date: N/A

Application deadline (fall): rolling
Undergraduate student body: 494 full time, 137 part time; 7% male, 93% female; 0% American Indian, 2% Asian, 21% black, 2% Hispanic, 5% multiracial, 0% Pacific Islander, 61% white, 2% international; 9% from in state; 26% live on campus; 0% of students in fraternities, 0% in sororities
Most popular majors: 56% Health Professions and Related Programs, 13% Business, Management, Marketing, and Related Support Services, 6% Psychology, 4% Biological and Biomedical Sciences, 4% Visual and Performing Arts
Expenses: 2019-2020: $33,440; room/board: $11,126
Financial aid: (440) 646-8309; 83% of undergrads determined to have financial need; average aid package $24,154

Walsh University
North Canton OH
(800) 362-9846
U.S. News ranking: Reg. U. (Mid. W), No. 46
Website: www.walsh.edu
Admissions email: admissions@walsh.edu
Private; founded 1958
Affiliation: Roman Catholic
Freshman admissions: selective; 2018-2019: 1,756 applied, 1,366 accepted. Either SAT or ACT required for some. ACT 25/75 percentile: 19-26. High school rank: N/A
Early decision deadline: N/A, notification date: N/A
Early action deadline: N/A, notification date: N/A
Application deadline (fall): rolling
Undergraduate student body: 1,715 full time, 312 part time; 41% male, 59% female; 0% American Indian, 1% Asian, 6% black, 4% Hispanic, 3% multiracial, 0% Pacific Islander, 60% white, 5% international
Most popular majors: 32% Business, Management, Marketing, and Related Support Services, 16% Health Professions and Related Programs, 11% Education, 8% Psychology, 7% Biological and Biomedical Sciences
Expenses: 2019-2020: $30,830; room/board: $10,900
Financial aid: (330) 490-7146; 75% of undergrads determined to have financial need; average aid package $24,192

Wilberforce University[1]
Wilberforce OH
(800) 367-8568
U.S. News ranking: Reg. Coll. (Mid. W), second tier
Website: www.wilberforce.edu
Admissions email: admissions@wilberforce.edu
Private
Application deadline (fall): N/A
Undergraduate student body: N/A full time, N/A part time
Expenses: N/A
Financial aid: N/A

Wilmington College
Wilmington OH
(937) 481-2260
U.S. News ranking: Reg. Coll. (Mid. W), No. 24
Website: www.wilmington.edu/
Admissions email: admission@wilmington.edu
Private; founded 1870
Affiliation: Friends
Freshman admissions: selective; 2018-2019: 1,694 applied, 1,433 accepted. Either SAT or ACT required. ACT 25/75 percentile: 18-23. High school rank: 13% in top tenth, 33% in top quarter, 66% in top half
Early decision deadline: N/A, notification date: N/A
Early action deadline: N/A, notification date: N/A
Application deadline (fall): 8/1
Undergraduate student body: 1,165 full time, 95 part time; 49% male, 51% female; 1% American Indian, 0% Asian, 11% black, 2% Hispanic, 3% multiracial, 0% Pacific Islander, 76% white, 1% international; 87% from in state; 61% live on campus; 17% of students in fraternities, 31% in sororities
Most popular majors: 23% Business Administration and Management, General, 22% Agricultural Business and Management, General, 8% Education, General, 7% Accounting, 6% Sport and Fitness Administration/Management
Expenses: 2019-2020: $26,775; room/board: $10,100
Financial aid: (937) 481-2337

Wittenberg University
Springfield OH
(937) 327-6314
U.S. News ranking: Nat. Lib. Arts, No. 160
Website: www.wittenberg.edu/
Admissions email: admission@wittenberg.edu
Private; founded 1845
Affiliation: Evangelical Lutheran Church
Freshman admissions: selective; 2018-2019: 6,040 applied, 5,451 accepted. Neither SAT nor ACT required. ACT 25/75 percentile: 22-28. High school rank: 16% in top tenth, 40% in top quarter, 73% in top half
Early decision deadline: 11/15, notification date: 12/1
Early action deadline: 12/1, notification date: 1/1
Application deadline (fall): rolling
Undergraduate student body: 1,681 full time, 76 part time; 45% male, 55% female; 0% American Indian, 1% Asian, 10% black, 4% Hispanic, 5% multiracial, 0% Pacific Islander, 77% white, 1% international; 77% from in state; 88% live on campus; 27% of students in fraternities, 29% in sororities
Most popular majors: 20% Business, Management, Marketing, and Related Support Services, 14% Biological and Biomedical Sciences, 11% Social Sciences, 7% Psychology, 6% Education

Expenses: 2019-2020: $40,280; room/board: $10,564
Financial aid: (937) 327-7318; 80% of undergrads determined to have financial need; average aid package $32,183

Wright State University
Dayton OH
(937) 775-5700
U.S. News ranking: Nat. U., second tier
Website: www.wright.edu
Admissions email: admissions@wright.edu
Public; founded 1967
Freshman admissions: selective; 2018-2019: 5,820 applied, 5,523 accepted. Either SAT or ACT required. ACT 25/75 percentile: 18-25. High school rank: 17% in top tenth, 38% in top quarter, 67% in top half
Early decision deadline: N/A, notification date: N/A
Early action deadline: N/A, notification date: N/A
Application deadline (fall): 8/20
Undergraduate student body: 8,449 full time, 2,476 part time; 48% male, 52% female; 0% American Indian, 3% Asian, 11% black, 4% Hispanic, 4% multiracial, 0% Pacific Islander, 75% white, 3% international; N/A from in state; 19% live on campus; N/A of students in fraternities, N/A in sororities
Most popular majors: 27% Business, Management, Marketing, and Related Support Services, 13% Education, 13% Engineering, 11% Health Professions and Related Programs, 6% Psychology
Expenses: 2019-2020: $9,578 in state, $18,996 out of state; room/board: $12,084
Financial aid: (937) 775-4000; 63% of undergrads determined to have financial need; average aid package $10,997

Xavier University
Cincinnati OH
(877) 982-3648
U.S. News ranking: Reg. U. (Mid. W), No. 5
Website: www.xavier.edu
Admissions email: xuadmit@xavier.edu
Private; founded 1831
Affiliation: Roman Catholic
Freshman admissions: selective; 2018-2019: 15,100 applied, 11,143 accepted. Either SAT or ACT required. ACT 25/75 percentile: 22-28. High school rank: 19% in top tenth, 50% in top quarter, 81% in top half
Early decision deadline: N/A, notification date: N/A
Early action deadline: N/A, notification date: N/A
Application deadline (fall): rolling
Undergraduate student body: 4,782 full time, 215 part time; 46% male, 54% female; 0% American Indian, 3% Asian, 9% black, 6% Hispanic, 4% multiracial, 0% Pacific Islander, 76% white, 2% international; 44% from in

state; 49% live on campus; N/A of students in fraternities, N/A in sororities
Most popular majors: 28% Business, Management, Marketing, and Related Support Services, 13% Health Professions and Related Programs, 9% Liberal Arts and Sciences, General Studies and Humanities, 6% Biological and Biomedical Sciences, 6% Social Sciences
Expenses: 2019-2020: $40,450; room/board: $13,310
Financial aid: (513) 745-3142; 57% of undergrads determined to have financial need; average aid package $24,585

Youngstown State University
Youngstown OH
(877) 468-6978
U.S. News ranking: Reg. U. (Mid. W), second tier
Website: www.ysu.edu
Admissions email: enroll@ysu.edu
Public; founded 1908
Freshman admissions: selective; 2018-2019: 10,541 applied, 7,148 accepted. Either SAT or ACT required. ACT 25/75 percentile: 18-24. High school rank: 13% in top tenth, 36% in top quarter, 69% in top half
Early decision deadline: N/A, notification date: N/A
Early action deadline: N/A, notification date: N/A
Application deadline (fall): 8/1
Undergraduate student body: 9,070 full time, 2,454 part time; 47% male, 53% female; 0% American Indian, 1% Asian, 9% black, 4% Hispanic, 3% multiracial, 0% Pacific Islander, 75% white, 3% international; 84% from in state; 11% live on campus; 3% of students in fraternities, 3% in sororities
Most popular majors: 6% Registered Nursing/Registered Nurse, 5% Criminal Justice/Safety Studies, 5% General Studies, 5% Social Work, 4% Biology/Biological Sciences, General
Expenses: 2019-2020: $9,461 in state, $15,101 out of state; room/board: $9,700
Financial aid: (330) 941-3505; 68% of undergrads determined to have financial need; average aid package $9,677

OKLAHOMA

Bacone College[1]
Muskogee OK
(888) 682-5514
U.S. News ranking: Reg. Coll. (W), second tier
Website: www.bacone.edu/
Admissions email: admissions@bacone.edu
Private
Application deadline (fall): rolling
Undergraduate student body: N/A full time, N/A part time
Expenses: N/A
Financial aid: N/A

Cameron University
Lawton OK
(580) 581-2289
U.S. News ranking: Reg. U. (W), second tier
Website: www.cameron.edu
Admissions email: admissions@cameron.edu
Public; founded 1908
Freshman admissions: less selective; 2018-2019: 1,123 applied, 1,123 accepted. Either SAT or ACT required for some. ACT 25/75 percentile: 16-21. High school rank: 3% in top tenth, 14% in top quarter, 39% in top half
Early decision deadline: N/A, notification date: N/A
Early action deadline: N/A, notification date: N/A
Application deadline (fall): rolling
Undergraduate student body: 2,713 full time, 1,231 part time; 38% male, 62% female; 6% American Indian, 2% Asian, 12% black, 15% Hispanic, 9% multiracial, 0% Pacific Islander, 49% white, 3% international; 88% from in state; 9% live on campus; 2% of students in fraternities, 2% in sororities
Most popular majors: 11% Business Administration and Management, General, 8% Psychology, General, 7% Corrections and Criminal Justice, Other, 7% Health and Physical Education/Fitness, General, 6% Computer Science
Expenses: 2019-2020: $6,450 in state, $15,870 out of state; room/board: $5,452
Financial aid: (580) 581-2293; 70% of undergrads determined to have financial need; average aid package $9,537

East Central University
Ada OK
(580) 559-5628
U.S. News ranking: Reg. U. (W), second tier
Website: www.ecok.edu
Admissions email: admissions@ecok.edu
Public; founded 1909
Freshman admissions: selective; 2018-2019: 812 applied, 671 accepted. ACT required. ACT 25/75 percentile: 18-23. High school rank: 22% in top tenth, 44% in top quarter, 78% in top half
Early decision deadline: N/A, notification date: N/A
Early action deadline: N/A, notification date: N/A
Application deadline (fall): rolling
Undergraduate student body: 2,309 full time, 656 part time; 41% male, 59% female; 13% American Indian, 0% Asian, 4% black, 6% Hispanic, 7% multiracial, 0% Pacific Islander, 59% white, 9% international; 91% from in state; 35% live on campus; 3% of students in fraternities, 3% in sororities
Most popular majors: 15% Health Professions and Related Programs, 14% Business, Management, Marketing, and Related

Support Services, 11% Public Administration and Social Service Professions, 7% Biological and Biomedical Sciences, 7% Parks, Recreation, Leisure, and Fitness Studies
Expenses: 2019-2020: $6,810 in state, $16,020 out of state; room/board: $6,848
Financial aid: (580) 559-5243; 84% of undergrads determined to have financial need; average aid package $6,423

Langston University

Langston OK
(405) 466-3231
U.S. News ranking: Reg. U. (W), second tier
Website: www.langston.edu/
Admissions email: admissions@langston.edu
Public, founded 1897
Freshman admissions: less selective; 2018-2019: 12,354 applied, 6,837 accepted. Either SAT or ACT required. ACT 25/75 percentile: 17-26. High school rank: N/A
Early decision deadline: N/A, notification date: N/A
Early action deadline: N/A, notification date: N/A
Application deadline (fall): rolling
Undergraduate student body: 1,720 full time, 225 part time; 37% male, 63% female; 1% American Indian, 0% Asian, 58% black, 2% Hispanic, 7% multiracial, 0% Pacific Islander, 4% white, 1% international
Most popular majors: 12% Psychology, General, 11% Registered Nursing/Registered Nurse, 9% Liberal Arts and Sciences/Liberal Studies, 8% Teacher Education and Professional Development, Specific Subject Areas, Other, 6% Agriculture, Agriculture Operations, and Related Sciences
Expenses: 2018-2019: $6,232 in state, $13,950 out of state; room/board: $10,597
Financial aid: (405) 466-3357

Mid-America Christian University[1]

Oklahoma City OK
(405) 691-3800
U.S. News ranking: Reg. U. (W), unranked
Website: www.macu.edu
Admissions email: info@macu.edu
Private
Application deadline (fall): N/A
Undergraduate student body: N/A full time, N/A part time
Expenses: N/A
Financial aid: N/A

Northeastern State University

Tahlequah OK
(918) 444-2200
U.S. News ranking: Reg. U. (W), No. 77
Website: www.nsuok.edu
Admissions email: nsuinfo@nsuok.edu
Public; founded 1846

Freshman admissions: selective; 2018-2019: 1,474 applied, 1,431 accepted. ACT required. ACT 25/75 percentile: 18-23. High school rank: 24% in top tenth, 48% in top quarter, 82% in top half
Early decision deadline: N/A, notification date: N/A
Early action deadline: N/A, notification date: N/A
Application deadline (fall): rolling
Undergraduate student body: 4,687 full time, 2,054 part time; 38% male, 62% female; 18% American Indian, 2% Asian, 4% black, 6% Hispanic, 22% multiracial, 0% Pacific Islander, 45% white, 2% international; 95% from in state; 17% live on campus; 2% of students in fraternities, 4% in sororities
Most popular majors: 9% Research and Experimental Psychology, Other, 7% Criminal Justice/Law Enforcement Administration, 6% Accounting, 6% General Studies, 5% Elementary Education and Teaching
Expenses: 2019-2020: $6,650 in state, $14,720 out of state, room/board: $7,638
Financial aid: (918) 444-3410; 67% of undergrads determined to have financial need; average aid package $13,552

Northwestern Oklahoma State University

Alva OK
(580) 327-8545
U.S. News ranking: Reg. U. (W), second tier
Website: www.nwosu.edu
Admissions email: recruit@nwosu.edu
Public; founded 1897
Freshman admissions: selective; 2018-2019: 1,544 applied, 1,145 accepted. Either SAT or ACT required. ACT 25/75 percentile: 17-22. High school rank: 11% in top tenth, 30% in top quarter, 64% in top half
Early decision deadline: N/A, notification date: N/A
Early action deadline: N/A, notification date: N/A
Application deadline (fall): rolling
Undergraduate student body: 1,448 full time, 357 part time; 40% male, 60% female; 8% American Indian, 1% Asian, 8% black, 10% Hispanic, 2% multiracial, 0% Pacific Islander, 64% white, 2% international; 78% from in state; 52% live on campus; N/A of students in fraternities, N/A in sororities
Most popular majors: 16% Registered Nursing/Registered Nurse, 10% Agribusiness/Agricultural Business Operations, 10% Business Administration and Management, General, 10% Psychology, General, 8% Parks, Recreation, Leisure, and Fitness Studies, Other
Expenses: 2018-2019: $7,471 in state, $14,558 out of state; room/board: N/A
Financial aid: N/A

Oklahoma Baptist University

Shawnee OK
(405) 585-5000
U.S. News ranking: Reg. Coll. (W), No. 7
Website: www.okbu.edu
Admissions email: admissions@okbu.edu
Private; founded 1910
Affiliation: Southern Baptist
Freshman admissions: selective; 2018-2019: 4,334 applied, 2,787 accepted. Either SAT or ACT required. ACT 25/75 percentile: 20-26. High school rank: 22% in top tenth, 49% in top quarter, 80% in top half
Early decision deadline: N/A, notification date: N/A
Early action deadline: N/A, notification date: N/A
Application deadline (fall): 8/1
Undergraduate student body: 1,778 full time, 30 part time; 40% male, 60% female; 5% American Indian, 1% Asian, 6% black, 2% Hispanic, 14% multiracial, 0% Pacific Islander, 68% white, 3% international
Most popular majors: Information not available
Expenses: 2019-2020: $29,864; room/board: $7,490
Financial aid: (405) 585-5020; 76% of undergrads determined to have financial need; average aid package $24,192

Oklahoma Christian University

Oklahoma City OK
(405) 425-5050
U.S. News ranking: Reg. U. (W), No. 34
Website: www.oc.edu/
Admissions email: admissions@oc.edu
Private; founded 1950
Affiliation: Churches of Christ
Freshman admissions: selective; 2018-2019: 2,452 applied, 1,588 accepted. Either SAT or ACT required. ACT 25/75 percentile: 20-27. High school rank: 21% in top tenth, 52% in top quarter, 83% in top half
Early decision deadline: N/A, notification date: N/A
Early action deadline: N/A, notification date: N/A
Application deadline (fall): rolling
Undergraduate student body: 1,767 full time, 138 part time; 50% male, 50% female; 2% American Indian, 1% Asian, 5% black, 7% Hispanic, 7% multiracial, 0% Pacific Islander, 73% white, 5% international; 46% from in state; 77% live on campus; 30% of students in fraternities, 37% in sororities
Most popular majors: 19% Business, Management, Marketing, and Related Support Services, 13% Engineering, 13% Health Professions and Related Programs, 9% Visual and Performing Arts, 7% Education
Expenses: 2019-2020: $23,950; room/board: $8,550
Financial aid: (405) 425-5190; 67% of undergrads determined to have financial need; average aid package $24,125

Oklahoma City University

Oklahoma City OK
(405) 208-5050
U.S. News ranking: Nat. U., No. 240
Website: www.okcu.edu
Admissions email: uadmissions@okcu.edu
Private; founded 1904
Affiliation: United Methodist
Freshman admissions: selective; 2018-2019: 1,748 applied, 1,330 accepted. Either SAT or ACT required. ACT 25/75 percentile: 23-29. High school rank: 31% in top tenth, 56% in top quarter, 87% in top half
Early decision deadline: N/A, notification date: N/A
Early action deadline: N/A, notification date: N/A
Application deadline (fall): rolling
Undergraduate student body: 1,544 full time, 70 part time; 32% male, 68% female; 2% American Indian, 2% Asian, 5% black, 11% Hispanic, 9% multiracial, 0% Pacific Islander, 65% white, 6% international; 48% from in state; 57% live on campus; 20% of students in fraternities, 28% in sororities
Most popular majors: 31% Adult Health Nurse/Nursing, 16% General Studies, 8% Music Performance, General, 6% Dance, General, 5% Acting
Expenses: 2019-2020: $32,594; room/board: $11,236
Financial aid: (405) 208-5211; 61% of undergrads determined to have financial need; average aid package $21,913

Oklahoma Panhandle State University

Goodwell OK
(580) 349-1370
U.S. News ranking: Reg. Coll. (W), second tier
Website: www.opsu.edu
Admissions email: opsu.admissions@opsu.edu
Public; founded 1909
Freshman admissions: less selective; 2018-2019: N/A applied, N/A accepted. Neither SAT nor ACT required. SAT 25/75 percentile: N/A. High school rank: N/A
Early decision deadline: N/A, notification date: N/A
Early action deadline: N/A, notification date: N/A
Application deadline (fall): rolling
Undergraduate student body: 946 full time, 316 part time; 49% male, 51% female; 3% American Indian, 1% Asian, 6% black, 27% Hispanic, 3% multiracial, 0% Pacific Islander, 39% white, 3% international
Most popular majors: Information not available
Expenses: 2018-2019: $7,930 in state, $8,674 out of state; room/board: $5,302
Financial aid: N/A

Oklahoma State University

Stillwater OK
(405) 744-5358
U.S. News ranking: Nat. U., No. 192
Website: go.okstate.edu
Admissions email: admissions@okstate.edu
Public; founded 1890
Freshman admissions: more selective; 2018-2019: 14,405 applied, 10,629 accepted. Either SAT or ACT required. ACT 25/75 percentile: 22-28. High school rank: 27% in top tenth, 55% in top quarter, 84% in top half
Early decision deadline: N/A, notification date: N/A
Early action deadline: N/A, notification date: N/A
Application deadline (fall): rolling
Undergraduate student body: 17,684 full time, 2,890 part time; 51% male, 49% female; 4% American Indian, 2% Asian, 4% black, 8% Hispanic, 10% multiracial, 0% Pacific Islander, 68% white, 4% international; N/A from in state; 43% live on campus; 17% of students in fraternities, 25% in sororities
Most popular majors: 28% Business, Management, Marketing, and Related Support Services, 13% Engineering, 9% Agriculture, Agriculture Operations, and Related Sciences, 6% Biological and Biomedical Sciences, 6% Family and Consumer Sciences/Human Sciences
Expenses: 2019-2020: $9,019 in state, $24,539 out of state; room/board: $9,106
Financial aid: (405) 744-6604; 54% of undergrads determined to have financial need; average aid package $15,272

Oklahoma State University Institute of Technology–Okmulgee

Okmulgee OK
(918) 293-4680
U.S. News ranking: Reg. Coll. (W), No. 23
Website: osuit.edu/admissions
Admissions email: osuit.admissions@okstate.edu
Public; founded 1946
Freshman admissions: less selective; 2018-2019: 8,244 applied, 995 accepted. Either SAT or ACT required. ACT 25/75 percentile: 16-21. High school rank: 8% in top tenth, 22% in top quarter, 57% in top half
Early decision deadline: N/A, notification date: N/A
Early action deadline: N/A, notification date: N/A
Application deadline (fall): rolling
Undergraduate student body: 1,687 full time, 716 part time; 64% male, 36% female; 10% American Indian, 1% Asian, 4% black, 7% Hispanic, 12% multiracial, 0% Pacific Islander, 55% white, 1% international; 94% from in

state; 30% live on campus; 0% of students in fraternities, 0% in sororities
Most popular majors: 51% Information Technology, 38% Instrumentation Technology/Technician, 11% Civil Engineering Technology/Technician
Expenses: 2019-2020: $5,550 in state, $11,160 out of state; room/board: $6,988
Financial aid: (918) 293-5222; 75% of undergrads determined to have financial need; average aid package $10,027

Oklahoma State University–Oklahoma City[1]
Oklahoma City OK
(405) 945-3224
U.S. News ranking: Reg. Coll. (W), unranked
Website: www.osuokc.edu/
Admissions email: admissions@osuokc.edu
Public; founded 1961
Application deadline (fall): rolling
Undergraduate student body: N/A full time, N/A part time
Expenses: 2018-2019: $4,478 in state, $11,558 out of state; room/board: N/A
Financial aid: (405) 945-3211

Oklahoma Wesleyan University[1]
Bartlesville OK
(866) 222-8226
U.S. News ranking: Reg. U. (W), No. 82
Website: www.okwu.edu
Admissions email: admissions@okwu.edu
Private; founded 1972
Affiliation: Wesleyan
Application deadline (fall): rolling
Undergraduate student body: N/A full time, N/A part time
Expenses: 2018-2019: $26,956; room/board: $8,344
Financial aid: (918) 335-6282

Oral Roberts University
Tulsa OK
(800) 678-8876
U.S. News ranking: Reg. Coll. (W), No. 5
Website: www.oru.edu
Admissions email: admissions@oru.edu
Private; founded 1963
Affiliation: Interdenominational
Freshman admissions: selective; 2018-2019: 2,872 applied, 2,313 accepted. Either SAT or ACT required. ACT 25/75 percentile: 19-25. High school rank: 17% in top tenth, 40% in top quarter, 77% in top half
Early decision deadline: N/A, notification date: N/A
Early action deadline: N/A, notification date: N/A
Application deadline (fall): rolling
Undergraduate student body: 2,850 full time, 673 part time; 40% male, 60% female; 2% American Indian, 2% Asian, 12% black,

13% Hispanic, 5% multiracial, 0% Pacific Islander, 39% white, 10% international; N/A from in state; 60% live on campus; N/A of students in fraternities, N/A in sororities
Most popular majors: 22% Business, Management, Marketing, and Related Support Services, 15% Theology and Religious Vocations, 10% Communication, Journalism, and Related Programs, 7% Engineering, 6% Visual and Performing Arts
Expenses: 2019-2020: $30,070; room/board: $8,450
Financial aid: (918) 495-6510; 71% of undergrads determined to have financial need; average aid package $27,727

Rogers State University
Claremore OK
(918) 343-7545
U.S. News ranking: Reg. Coll. (W), second tier
Website: www.rsu.edu/
Admissions email: admissions@rsu.edu
Public; founded 1909
Freshman admissions: less selective; 2018-2019: 1,257 applied, 1,057 accepted. Either SAT or ACT required. ACT 25/75 percentile: 18-19. High school rank: 14% in top tenth, 21% in top quarter, 63% in top half
Early decision deadline: N/A, notification date: N/A
Early action deadline: N/A, notification date: N/A
Application deadline (fall): rolling
Undergraduate student body: 2,262 full time, 1,374 part time; 40% male, 60% female; 13% American Indian, 2% Asian, 4% black, 6% Hispanic, 16% multiracial, 0% Pacific Islander, 57% white, 0% international; 95% from in state; 26% live on campus; 0% of students in fraternities, 1% in sororities
Most popular majors: 30% Business Administration and Management, General, 10% Biology/Biological Sciences, General, 9% Registered Nursing/Registered Nurse, 9% Social Sciences, General, 8% Multi-/Interdisciplinary Studies, Other
Expenses: 2019-2020: $7,200 in state, $15,540 out of state; room/board: $9,814
Financial aid: (918) 343-7553; 87% of undergrads determined to have financial need; average aid package $10,049

Southeastern Oklahoma State University[1]
Durant OK
(580) 745-2060
U.S. News ranking: Reg. U. (W), second tier
Website: www.se.edu
Admissions email: admissions@se.edu
Public; founded 1909
Affiliation: Other
Application deadline (fall): rolling

Undergraduate student body: N/A full time, N/A part time
Expenses: N/A
Financial aid: (580) 745-2186

Southern Nazarene University[1]
Bethany OK
(405) 491-6324
U.S. News ranking: Reg. U. (W), second tier
Website: www.snu.edu
Admissions email: admissions@snu.edu
Private; founded 1899
Application deadline (fall): 8/6
Undergraduate student body: N/A full time, N/A part time
Expenses: N/A
Financial aid: (405) 491-6310

Southwestern Christian University
Bethany OK
(405) 789-7661
U.S. News ranking: Reg. Coll. (W), No. 23
Website: www.swcu.edu/
Admissions email: admissions@swcu.edu
Private; founded 1946
Affiliation: Pentecostal Holiness Church
Freshman admissions: less selective; 2018-2019: 558 applied, 325 accepted. Either SAT or ACT required. ACT 25/75 percentile: 16-21. High school rank: N/A
Early decision deadline: N/A, notification date: N/A
Early action deadline: N/A, notification date: N/A
Application deadline (fall): rolling
Undergraduate student body: 487 full time, 73 part time; 56% male, 44% female; 5% American Indian, 1% Asian, 21% black, 11% Hispanic, 4% multiracial, 1% Pacific Islander, 39% white, 15% international; 58% from in state; 36% live on campus; 0% of students in fraternities, 6% in sororities
Most popular majors: 40% Business Administration and Management, General, 22% Sport and Fitness Administration/Management, 18% Psychology, General, 7% Theology and Religious Vocations, Other, 3% Early Childhood Education and Teaching
Expenses: 2019-2020: $18,630; room/board: $8,400
Financial aid: (405) 789-7661; 98% of undergrads determined to have financial need; average aid package $16,443

Southwestern Oklahoma State University
Weatherford OK
(580) 774-3782
U.S. News ranking: Reg. U. (W), No. 82
Website: www.swosu.edu
Admissions email: admissions@swosu.edu
Public; founded 1901

Freshman admissions: selective; 2018-2019: 2,505 applied, 2,301 accepted. Neither SAT nor ACT required. ACT 25/75 percentile: 18-24. High school rank: 29% in top tenth, 49% in top quarter, 75% in top half
Early decision deadline: N/A, notification date: N/A
Early action deadline: N/A, notification date: N/A
Application deadline (fall): rolling
Undergraduate student body: 3,593 full time, 857 part time; 40% male, 60% female; 4% American Indian, 2% Asian, 4% black, 11% Hispanic, 9% multiracial, 0% Pacific Islander, 62% white, 5% international; 91% from in state; 27% live on campus; 1% of students in fraternities, 1% in sororities
Most popular majors: 27% Registered Nursing/Registered Nurse, 17% Business Administration and Management, General, 6% Elementary Education and Teaching, 5% Parks, Recreation and Leisure Facilities Management, General, 4% Kinesiology and Exercise Science
Expenses: 2018-2019: $7,335 in state, $14,235 out of state; room/board: $5,840
Financial aid: (580) 774-3786

University of Central Oklahoma
Edmond OK
(405) 974-2727
U.S. News ranking: Reg. U. (W), No. 62
Website: www.uco.edu/
Admissions email: onestop@uco.edu
Public; founded 1890
Freshman admissions: selective; 2018-2019: 5,359 applied, 4,204 accepted. Either SAT or ACT required. ACT 25/75 percentile: 19-24. High school rank: 15% in top tenth, 38% in top quarter, 72% in top half
Early decision deadline: N/A, notification date: N/A
Early action deadline: N/A, notification date: N/A
Application deadline (fall): rolling
Undergraduate student body: 10,110 full time, 3,644 part time; 41% male, 59% female; 4% American Indian, 4% Asian, 9% black, 12% Hispanic, 10% multiracial, 0% Pacific Islander, 54% white, 5% international; 92% from in state; 11% live on campus; 1% of students in fraternities, 2% in sororities
Most popular majors: 23% Business, Management, Marketing, and Related Support Services, 10% Health Professions and Related Programs, 9% Homeland Security, Law Enforcement, Firefighting and Related Protective Services, 9% Liberal Arts and Sciences, General Studies and Humanities, 7% Communication, Journalism, and Related Programs
Expenses: 2019-2020: $7,753 in state, $18,640 out of state; room/board: $8,130

Financial aid: (405) 974-2727; 64% of undergrads determined to have financial need; average aid package $10,191

University of Oklahoma
Norman OK
(405) 325-2252
U.S. News ranking: Nat. U., No. 132
Website: www.ou.edu
Admissions email: admrec@ou.edu
Public; founded 1890
Freshman admissions: more selective; 2018-2019: 15,811 applied, 12,283 accepted. Either SAT or ACT required. ACT 25/75 percentile: 23-29. High school rank: 32% in top tenth, 63% in top quarter, 90% in top half
Early decision deadline: N/A, notification date: N/A
Early action deadline: N/A, notification date: N/A
Application deadline (fall): 2/1
Undergraduate student body: 19,033 full time, 3,119 part time; 50% male, 50% female; 4% American Indian, 7% Asian, 5% black, 10% Hispanic, 9% multiracial, 0% Pacific Islander, 61% white, 4% international; N/A from in state; 32% live on campus; 28% of students in fraternities, 33% in sororities
Most popular majors: 22% Business, Management, Marketing, and Related Support Services, 14% Engineering, 8% Communication, Journalism, and Related Programs, 8% Liberal Arts and Sciences, General Studies and Humanities, 7% Social Sciences
Expenses: 2019-2020: $11,763 in state, $27,144 out of state; room/board: $10,994
Financial aid: (405) 325-9000; 48% of undergrads determined to have financial need; average aid package $14,869

University of Science and Arts of Oklahoma[1]
Chickasha OK
(405) 574-1357
U.S. News ranking: Nat. Lib. Arts, second tier
Website: www.usao.edu
Admissions email: usao-admissions@usao.edu
Public; founded 1908
Application deadline (fall): 8/30
Undergraduate student body: N/A full time, N/A part time
Expenses: 2019-2020: $8,040 in state, $18,900 out of state; room/board: $6,150
Financial aid: (405) 574-1350; 71% of undergrads determined to have financial need; average aid package $12,801

University of Tulsa
Tulsa OK
(918) 631-2307
U.S. News ranking: Nat. U., No. 121
Website: utulsa.edu
Admissions email: admission@utulsa.edu
Private; founded 1894

OREGON

Affiliation: Presbyterian Church (USA)
Freshman admissions: more selective; 2018-2019: 8,526 applied, 3,476 accepted. Either SAT or ACT required. ACT 25/75 percentile: 25-32. High school rank: 65% in top tenth, 83% in top quarter, 95% in top half
Early decision deadline: N/A, notification date: N/A
Early action deadline: 11/1, notification date: 12/15
Application deadline (fall): rolling
Undergraduate student body: 3,161 full time, 135 part time; 55% male, 45% female; 3% American Indian, 5% Asian, 6% black, 8% Hispanic, 5% multiracial, 0% Pacific Islander, 56% white, 16% international; 58% from in state; 40% live on campus; 6% of students in fraternities, 12% in sororities
Most popular majors: 29% Engineering, 22% Business, Management, Marketing, and Related Support Services, 6% Social Sciences, 5% Biological and Biomedical Sciences, 5% Health Professions and Related Programs
Expenses: 2019-2020: $42,238; room/board: $11,450
Financial aid: (918) 631-2526; 51% of undergrads determined to have financial need; average aid package $39,628

OREGON

Art Institute of Portland[1]
Portland OR
(503) 228-6528
U.S. News ranking: Arts, unranked
Website: www.artinstitutes.edu/portland/
Admissions email: N/A
For-profit
Application deadline (fall): N/A
Undergraduate student body: N/A full time, N/A part time
Expenses: N/A
Financial aid: N/A

Corban University[1]
Salem OR
(800) 845-3005
U.S. News ranking: Reg. Coll. (W), No. 7
Website: www.corban.edu
Admissions email: admissions@corban.edu
Private; founded 1935
Affiliation: Evangelical Christian
Application deadline (fall): 8/1
Undergraduate student body: N/A full time, N/A part time
Expenses: 2019-2020: $33,378; room/board: $10,316
Financial aid: (503) 375-7106; 79% of undergrads determined to have financial need; average aid package $23,624

Eastern Oregon University
La Grande OR
(541) 962-3393
U.S. News ranking: Reg. U. (W), No. 77
Website: www.eou.edu
Admissions email: admissions@eou.edu
Public; founded 1929
Freshman admissions: less selective; 2018-2019: 1,010 applied, 994 accepted. Either SAT or ACT required. SAT 25/75 percentile: 940-1133. High school rank: 9% in top tenth, 32% in top quarter, 77% in top half
Early decision deadline: N/A, notification date: N/A
Early action deadline: 2/1, notification date: N/A
Application deadline (fall): 9/1
Undergraduate student body: 1,689 full time, 1,055 part time; 40% male, 60% female; 2% American Indian, 2% Asian, 2% black, 11% Hispanic, 5% multiracial, 3% Pacific Islander, 72% white, 1% international; N/A from in state; 15% live on campus; N/A of students in fraternities, N/A in sororities
Most popular majors: 33% Business, Management, Marketing, and Related Support Services, 12% Education, 10% Parks, Recreation, Leisure, and Fitness Studies, 8% Multi/Interdisciplinary Studies, 6% Liberal Arts and Sciences, General Studies and Humanities
Expenses: 2019-2020: $9,084 in state, $21,729 out of state; room/board: $9,852
Financial aid: (541) 962-3550; 74% of undergrads determined to have financial need; average aid package $10,406

George Fox University
Newberg OR
(800) 765-4369
U.S. News ranking: Nat. U., No. 246
Website: www.georgefox.edu
Admissions email: admissions@georgefox.edu
Private; founded 1891
Affiliation: Friends
Freshman admissions: selective; 2018-2019: 2,888 applied, 2,377 accepted. Either SAT or ACT required. SAT 25/75 percentile: 1020-1230. High school rank: 32% in top tenth, 63% in top quarter, 89% in top half
Early decision deadline: N/A, notification date: N/A
Early action deadline: 11/1, notification date: 12/9
Application deadline (fall): rolling
Undergraduate student body: 2,487 full time, 209 part time; 42% male, 58% female; 1% American Indian, 4% Asian, 1% black, 13% Hispanic, 8% multiracial, 1% Pacific Islander, 69% white, 1% international; 58% from in state; 54% live on campus; N/A of students in fraternities, N/A in sororities

Most popular majors: 15% Business Administration, Management and Operations, 11% Engineering, General, 7% Registered Nursing, Nursing Administration, Nursing Research and Clinical Nursing, 6% Teacher Education and Professional Development, Specific Levels and Methods, 4% Biology, General
Expenses: 2019-2020: $37,280; room/board: $11,650
Financial aid: (503) 554-2302; 74% of undergrads determined to have financial need; average aid package $22,703

Lewis & Clark College
Portland OR
(800) 444-4111
U.S. News ranking: Nat. Lib. Arts, No. 72
Website: www.lclark.edu
Admissions email: admissions@lclark.edu
Private; founded 1867
Freshman admissions: more selective; 2018-2019: 6,139 applied, 4,528 accepted. Either SAT or ACT required for some. SAT 25/75 percentile: 1230-1390. High school rank: 37% in top tenth, 72% in top quarter, 96% in top half
Early decision deadline: 11/1, notification date: 12/15
Early action deadline: 11/1, notification date: 12/31
Application deadline (fall): 1/15
Undergraduate student body: 2,058 full time, 29 part time; 39% male, 61% female; 1% American Indian, 5% Asian, 3% black, 12% Hispanic, 7% multiracial, 0% Pacific Islander, 63% white, 5% international; 20% from in state; 69% live on campus; 0% of students in fraternities, 0% in sororities
Most popular majors: 30% Psychology, General, 10% Biology/Biological Sciences, General, 7% English Language and Literature, General, 7% International Relations and Affairs, 7% Sociology and Anthropology
Expenses: 2019-2020: $52,780; room/board: $13,000
Financial aid: (503) 768-7090; 56% of undergrads determined to have financial need; average aid package $42,683

Linfield College
McMinnville OR
(800) 640-2287
U.S. News ranking: Nat. Lib. Arts, No. 117
Website: www.linfield.edu
Admissions email: admission@linfield.edu
Private; founded 1858
Affiliation: American Baptist
Freshman admissions: selective; 2018-2019: 2,199 applied, 1,782 accepted. Either SAT or ACT required for some. SAT 25/75 percentile: 1020-1200. High school rank: N/A
Early decision deadline: N/A, notification date: N/A
Early action deadline: 11/1, notification date: 1/15

Application deadline (fall): rolling
Undergraduate student body: 1,334 full time, 42 part time; 39% male, 61% female; 1% American Indian, 5% Asian, 2% black, 18% Hispanic, 8% multiracial, 1% Pacific Islander, 60% white, 3% international; 58% from in state; 73% live on campus; 28% of students in fraternities, 27% in sororities
Most popular majors: 20% Business, Management, Marketing, and Related Support Services, 11% Social Sciences, 10% Education, 10% Library Science, 9% Parks, Recreation, Leisure, and Fitness Studies
Expenses: 2019-2020: $44,062; room/board: $12,670
Financial aid: (503) 883-2225; 77% of undergrads determined to have financial need; average aid package $36,593

Northwest Christian University
Eugene OR
(541) 684-7201
U.S. News ranking: Reg. U. (W), No. 72
Website: www.nwcu.edu
Admissions email: admissions@nwcu.edu
Private; founded 1895
Affiliation: Christian Church (Disciples of Christ)
Freshman admissions: selective; 2018-2019: 479 applied, 299 accepted. Either SAT or ACT required. SAT 25/75 percentile: 935-1170. High school rank: 13% in top tenth, 42% in top quarter, 79% in top half
Early decision deadline: N/A, notification date: N/A
Early action deadline: N/A, notification date: N/A
Application deadline (fall): rolling
Undergraduate student body: 418 full time, 175 part time; 39% male, 61% female; 2% American Indian, 2% Asian, 5% black, 6% Hispanic, 10% multiracial, 1% Pacific Islander, 72% white, 1% international; 71% from in state; 32% live on campus; N/A of students in fraternities, N/A in sororities
Most popular majors: 24% Business, Management, Marketing, and Related Support Services, 18% Health Professions and Related Programs, 15% Education, 12% Multi/Interdisciplinary Studies, 10% Psychology
Expenses: 2019-2020: $31,410; room/board: $9,700
Financial aid: (541) 684-7201; 80% of undergrads determined to have financial need; average aid package $24,320

Oregon Institute of Technology
Klamath Falls OR
(541) 885-1150
U.S. News ranking: Reg. Coll. (W), No. 6
Website: www.oit.edu
Admissions email: oit@oit.edu
Public; founded 1947

Freshman admissions: selective; 2018-2019: 939 applied, 900 accepted. Either SAT or ACT required. SAT 25/75 percentile: 1030-1240. High school rank: 28% in top tenth, 57% in top quarter, 90% in top half
Early decision deadline: N/A, notification date: N/A
Early action deadline: N/A, notification date: N/A
Application deadline (fall): 9/4
Undergraduate student body: 2,311 full time, 2,901 part time; 52% male, 48% female; 1% American Indian, 6% Asian, 2% black, 10% Hispanic, 5% multiracial, 0% Pacific Islander, 64% white, 2% international
Most popular majors: 45% Health Professions and Related Programs, 22% Engineering, 14% Engineering Technologies and Engineering-Related Fields, 6% Business, Management, Marketing, and Related Support Services, 4% Psychology
Expenses: 2018-2019: $9,987 in state, $28,055 out of state; room/board: $9,640
Financial aid: (541) 885-1280; 66% of undergrads determined to have financial need; average aid package $11,089

Oregon State University
Corvallis OR
(541) 737-4411
U.S. News ranking: Nat. U., No. 139
Website: oregonstate.edu
Admissions email: osuadmit@oregonstate.edu
Public; founded 1868
Freshman admissions: more selective; 2018-2019: 14,890 applied, 12,006 accepted. Either SAT or ACT required. SAT 25/75 percentile: 1080-1310. High school rank: 28% in top tenth, 58% in top quarter, 89% in top half
Early decision deadline: N/A, notification date: N/A
Early action deadline: 11/1, notification date: 12/15
Application deadline (fall): 9/1
Undergraduate student body: 18,591 full time, 7,108 part time; 54% male, 46% female; 1% American Indian, 8% Asian, 1% black, 10% Hispanic, 7% multiracial, 0% Pacific Islander, 64% white, 7% international; 66% from in state; 17% live on campus; 11% of students in fraternities, 15% in sororities
Most popular majors: 10% Computer Science, 7% Business Administration, Management and Operations, 6% Human Development, Family Studies, and Related Services, 5% Health and Physical Education/Fitness, 4% Mechanical Engineering
Expenses: 2019-2020: $11,709 in state, $31,314 out of state; room/board: $13,485
Financial aid: (541) 737-2241; 51% of undergrads determined to have financial need; average aid package $12,883

Pacific Northwest College of Art[1]

Portland OR
(503) 226-4391
U.S. News ranking: Arts, unranked
Website: www.pnca.edu
Admissions email:
admissions@pnca.edu
Private
Application deadline (fall): N/A
Undergraduate student body: N/A
full time, N/A part time
Expenses: N/A
Financial aid: N/A

Pacific University

Forest Grove OR
(800) 677-6712
U.S. News ranking: Nat. U.,
No. 185
Website: www.pacificu.edu
Admissions email:
admissions@pacificu.edu
Private; founded 1849
Freshman admissions: selective;
2018-2019: 2,491 applied,
2,125 accepted. Either SAT
or ACT required. SAT 25/75
percentile: 1060-1250. High
school rank: N/A
Early decision deadline: N/A,
notification date: N/A
Early action deadline: N/A,
notification date: N/A
Application deadline (fall): 8/15
Undergraduate student body: 1,809
full time, 85 part time; 38%
male, 62% female; 1% American
Indian, 11% Asian, 2% black,
16% Hispanic, 12% multiracial,
2% Pacific Islander, 50% white,
1% international; N/A from in
state; 54% live on campus; 1%
of students in fraternities, 6% in
sororities
Most popular majors: 19% Health
Professions and Related Programs,
13% Business, Management,
Marketing, and Related Support
Services, 11% Parks, Recreation,
Leisure, and Fitness Studies,
10% Biological and Biomedical
Sciences, 8% Education
Expenses: 2019-2020: $46,402;
room/board: $12,904
Financial aid: (503) 352-2871;
81% of undergrads determined to
have financial need; average aid
package $34,684

Portland State University

Portland OR
(800) 547-8887
U.S. News ranking: Nat. U.,
second tier
Website: www.pdx.edu
Admissions email:
admissions@pdx.edu
Public; founded 1946
Freshman admissions: selective;
2018-2019: 6,743 applied,
6,082 accepted. Either SAT
or ACT required for some. SAT
25/75 percentile: 1010-1230.
High school rank: 16% in top
tenth, 47% in top quarter, 87%
in top half
Early decision deadline: N/A,
notification date: N/A
Early action deadline: N/A,
notification date: N/A
Application deadline (fall): rolling

Undergraduate student body:
14,292 full time, 6,675 part
time; 46% male, 54% female;
1% American Indian, 9% Asian,
4% black, 16% Hispanic, 7%
multiracial, 1% Pacific Islander,
54% white, 5% international; N/A
from in state; 9% live on campus;
1% of students in fraternities,
1% in sororities
Most popular majors: 22%
Business, Management,
Marketing, and Related Support
Services, 12% Social Sciences,
8% Health Professions and
Related Programs, 7% Psychology,
6% Visual and Performing Arts
Expenses: 2019-2020: $9,578 in
state, $28,410 out of state; room/
board: $11,172
Financial aid: (503) 725-3461;
67% of undergrads determined to
have financial need; average aid
package $11,153

Reed College[1]

Portland OR
(503) 777-7511
U.S. News ranking: Nat. Lib. Arts,
No. 68
Website: www.reed.edu/
Admissions email:
admission@reed.edu
Private
Application deadline (fall): N/A
Undergraduate student body: N/A
full time, N/A part time
Expenses: N/A
Financial aid: N/A

Southern Oregon University

Ashland OR
(541) 552-6411
U.S. News ranking: Reg. U. (W),
second tier
Website: www.sou.edu
Admissions email:
admissions@sou.edu
Public; founded 1926
Freshman admissions: less
selective; 2018-2019: 2,779
applied, 2,125 accepted. Either
SAT or ACT required. SAT 25/75
percentile: 920-1150. High
school rank: N/A
Early decision deadline: N/A,
notification date: N/A
Early action deadline: N/A,
notification date: N/A
Application deadline (fall): rolling
Undergraduate student body: 3,391
full time, 1,865 part time; 39%
male, 61% female; 1% American
Indian, 2% Asian, 3% black,
12% Hispanic, 9% multiracial,
1% Pacific Islander, 60% white,
2% international; 60% from in
state; 17% live on campus; N/A
of students in fraternities, N/A in
sororities
Most popular majors: 17%
Business, Management,
Marketing, and Related Support
Services, 13% Visual and
Performing Arts, 10% Education,
10% Psychology, 8% Social
Sciences
Expenses: 2018-2019: $9,615 in
state, $25,545 out of state; room/
board: $14,199
Financial aid: N/A

University of Oregon

Eugene OR
(800) 232-3825
U.S. News ranking: Nat. U.,
No. 104
Website: www.uoregon.edu
Admissions email:
uoadmit@uoregon.edu
Public; founded 1876
Freshman admissions: selective;
2018-2019: 24,474 applied,
20,404 accepted. Either SAT
or ACT required. SAT 25/75
percentile: 1080-1290. High
school rank: 22% in top tenth,
55% in top quarter, 87% in
top half
Early decision deadline: N/A;
notification date: N/A
Early action deadline: 11/1,
notification date: 12/15
Application deadline (fall): 1/15
Undergraduate student body:
17,550 full time, 1,551 part
time; 46% male, 54% female;
1% American Indian, 6% Asian,
2% black, 13% Hispanic, 8%
multiracial, 0% Pacific Islander,
58% white, 10% international;
56% from in state; 22% live
on campus; 16% of students in
fraternities, 20% in sororities
Most popular majors: 11%
Business/Commerce, General,
8% Economics, General, 8%
Social Sciences, General,
7% Psychology, General, 5%
Advertising
Expenses: 2019-2020: $12,720
in state, $36,615 out of state;
room/board: $13,482
Financial aid: (541) 346-3221;
45% of undergrads determined to
have financial need; average aid
package $11,022

University of Portland

Portland OR
(888) 627-5601
U.S. News ranking: Reg. U. (W),
No. 2
Website: www.up.edu
Admissions email:
admissions@up.edu
Private; founded 1901
Affiliation: Roman Catholic
Freshman admissions: more
selective; 2018-2019: 10,666
applied, 8,046 accepted. Either
SAT or ACT required. SAT 25/75
percentile: 1140-1320. High
school rank: 38% in top tenth,
72% in top quarter, 94% in
top half
Early decision deadline: N/A,
notification date: N/A
Early action deadline: N/A,
notification date: N/A
Application deadline (fall): 1/15
Undergraduate student body: 3,703
full time, 85 part time; 40%
male, 60% female; 0% American
Indian, 14% Asian, 1% black,
13% Hispanic, 8% multiracial,
2% Pacific Islander, 57% white,
3% international; 27% from in
state; 55% live on campus; 0%
of students in fraternities, 0% in
sororities
Most popular majors: 17% Health
Professions and Related Programs,
13% Business, Management,
Marketing, and Related Support
Services, 12% Engineering,
11% Biological and Biomedical
Sciences, 6% Psychology

Expenses: 2019-2020: $47,818;
room/board: $13,684
Financial aid: (503) 943-7311;
59% of undergrads determined to
have financial need; average aid
package $32,606

Warner Pacific University

Portland OR
(503) 517-1020
U.S. News ranking: Reg. Coll. (W),
No. 12
Website: www.warnerpacific.edu
Admissions email:
admissions@warnerpacific.edu
Private; founded 1937
Affiliation: Church of God
Freshman admissions: least
selective; 2018-2019: 508
applied, 495 accepted. Either
SAT or ACT required. SAT 25/75
percentile: 870-1060. High
school rank: 6% in top tenth, 17%
in top quarter, 65% in top half
Early decision deadline: N/A,
notification date: N/A
Early action deadline: N/A,
notification date: N/A
Application deadline (fall): rolling
Undergraduate student body:
359 full time, 5 part time; 46%
male, 54% female; 1% American
Indian, 6% Asian, 12% black,
36% Hispanic, 9% multiracial,
2% Pacific Islander, 33% white,
1% international; 72% from in
state; 41% live on campus; 0%
of students in fraternities, 0% in
sororities
Most popular majors: 15% Family
and Consumer Sciences/Human
Sciences, 15% Parks, Recreation,
Leisure, and Fitness Studies,
13% Business, Management,
Marketing, and Related
Support Services, 13% Public
Administration and Social Service
Professions, 12% Biological and
Biomedical Sciences
Expenses: 2019-2020: $18,660;
room/board: $10,020
Financial aid: (503) 517-1091;
83% of undergrads determined to
have financial need; average aid
package $17,382

Western Oregon University

Monmouth OR
(503) 838-8211
U.S. News ranking: Reg. U. (W),
No. 66
Website: www.wou.edu
Admissions email:
wolfgram@wou.edu
Public; founded 1856
Freshman admissions: less
selective; 2018-2019: 3,201
applied, 2,704 accepted. Neither
SAT nor ACT required. SAT 25/75
percentile: 940-1150. High school
rank: 13% in top tenth, 34% in
top quarter, 74% in top half
Early decision deadline: N/A,
notification date: N/A
Early action deadline: N/A,
notification date: N/A
Application deadline (fall): rolling
Undergraduate student body: 3,906
full time, 742 part time; 36%
male, 64% female; 1% American
Indian, 4% Asian, 4% black,

17% Hispanic, 3% multiracial,
3% Pacific Islander, 60% white,
6% international; N/A from in
state; 25% live on campus; 1%
of students in fraternities, 1% in
sororities
Most popular majors: 12%
Business, Management,
Marketing, and Related Support
Services, 12% Education,
12% Psychology, 10% Multi/
Interdisciplinary Studies,
9% Homeland Security, Law
Enforcement, Firefighting and
Related Protective Services
Expenses: 2019-2020: $9,540 in
state, $26,415 out of state; room/
board: $10,415
Financial aid: (503) 838-8475;
79% of undergrads determined to
have financial need; average aid
package $10,164

Willamette University

Salem OR
(877) 542-2787
U.S. News ranking: Nat. Lib. Arts,
No. 68
Website: www.willamette.edu
Admissions email:
bearcat@willamette.edu
Private; founded 1842
Freshman admissions: more
selective; 2018-2019: 4,204
applied, 3,516 accepted. Neither
SAT nor ACT required. SAT
25/75 percentile: 1170-1350.
High school rank: 46% in top
tenth, 73% in top quarter, 96%
in top half
Early decision deadline: 11/15,
notification date: 12/30
Early action deadline: 11/15,
notification date: 12/30
Application deadline (fall): 1/15
Undergraduate student body: 1,759
full time, 49 part time; 42%
male, 58% female; 1% American
Indian, 7% Asian, 2% black, 14%
Hispanic, 8% multiracial, 0%
Pacific Islander, 63% white, 1%
international; N/A from in state;
60% live on campus; 26% of
students in fraternities, 19% in
sororities
Most popular majors: 24% Social
Sciences, 8% Physical Sciences,
7% Biological and Biomedical
Sciences, 6% Communication,
Journalism, and Related Programs,
6% Parks, Recreation, Leisure,
and Fitness Studies
Expenses: 2019-2020: $52,074;
room/board: $12,940
Financial aid: (503) 370-6273;
64% of undergrads determined to
have financial need; average aid
package $37,658

PENNSYLVANIA

Albright College

Reading PA
(800) 252-1856
U.S. News ranking: Nat. Lib. Arts,
second tier
Website: www.albright.edu/
Admissions email:
admission@albright.edu
Private; founded 1856
Affiliation: United Methodist
Freshman admissions: selective;
2018-2019: 6,757 applied,
4,188 accepted. Neither SAT

nor ACT required. SAT 25/75 percentile: 1023-1200. High school rank: 14% in top tenth, 40% in top quarter, 76% in top half
Early decision deadline: N/A, notification date: N/A
Early action deadline: N/A, notification date: N/A
Application deadline (fall): rolling
Undergraduate student body: 1,887 full time, 25 part time; 40% male, 60% female; 1% American Indian, 2% Asian, 23% black, 15% Hispanic, 2% multiracial, 0% Pacific Islander, 50% white, 2% international; 57% from in state; 80% live on campus; 10% of students in fraternities, 13% in sororities
Most popular majors: 27% Business, Management, Marketing, and Related Support Services, 16% Psychology, 14% Visual and Performing Arts, 11% Social Sciences, 7% Biological and Biomedical Sciences
Expenses: 2019-2020: $25,642; room/board: $12,480
Financial aid: (610) 921-7515; 92% of undergrads determined to have financial need; average aid package $39,431

Allegheny College
Meadville PA
(800) 521-5293
U.S. News ranking: Nat. Lib. Arts, No. 82
Website: allegheny.edu
Admissions email: admissions@allegheny.edu
Private; founded 1815
Affiliation: United Methodist
Freshman admissions: more selective; 2018-2019: 5,479 applied, 3,485 accepted. Neither SAT nor ACT required. SAT 25/75 percentile: 1120-1340. High school rank: 28% in top tenth, 66% in top quarter, 90% in top half
Early decision deadline: 11/1, notification date: 11/15
Early action deadline: 12/1, notification date: 1/1
Application deadline (fall): 2/15
Undergraduate student body: 1,721 full time, 46 part time; 45% male, 55% female; 0% American Indian, 4% Asian, 9% black, 9% Hispanic, 5% multiracial, 0% Pacific Islander, 67% white, 4% international; 51% from in state; 95% live on campus; 22% of students in fraternities, 23% in sororities
Most popular majors: 14% Psychology, General, 11% Biology/Biological Sciences, General, 11% Economics, General, 9% Speech Communication and Rhetoric, 8% Environmental Science
Expenses: 2019-2020: $49,260, room/board: $12,640
Financial aid: (800) 835-7780; 78% of undergrads determined to have financial need; average aid package $43,273

Alvernia University
Reading PA
(610) 796-8220
U.S. News ranking: Reg. U. (N), No. 94
Website: www.alvernia.edu/
Admissions email: admissions@alvernia.edu
Private; founded 1958
Affiliation: Roman Catholic
Freshman admissions: selective; 2018-2019: 2,628 applied, 1,797 accepted. Either SAT or ACT required. SAT 25/75 percentile: 950-1130. High school rank: N/A
Early decision deadline: N/A, notification date: N/A
Early action deadline: N/A, notification date: N/A
Application deadline (fall): rolling
Undergraduate student body: 1,690 full time, 506 part time; 30% male, 70% female; 0% American Indian, 2% Asian, 12% black, 11% Hispanic, 3% multiracial, 0% Pacific Islander, 68% white, 0% international; 74% from in state; 65% live on campus; 0% of students in fraternities, 0% in sororities
Most popular majors: 50% Health Professions and Related Programs, 14% Business, Management, Marketing, and Related Support Services, 11% Homeland Security, Law Enforcement, Firefighting and Related Protective Services, 6% Psychology, 4% Education
Expenses: 2018-2019: $35,100; room/board: $12,340
Financial aid: (610) 796-8356

American College of Financial Services[1]
Bryn Mawr PA
(610) 526-1000
U.S. News ranking: Business, unranked
Website: www.pqc.edu
Admissions email: N/A
Private
Application deadline (fall): N/A
Undergraduate student body: N/A full time, N/A part time
Expenses: N/A
Financial aid: N/A

Arcadia University
Glenside PA
(215) 572-2910
U.S. News ranking: Reg. U. (N), No. 42
Website: www.arcadia.edu
Admissions email: admiss@arcadia.edu
Private; founded 1853
Freshman admissions: selective; 2018-2019: 9,243 applied, 5,930 accepted. Either SAT or ACT required. SAT 25/75 percentile: 1050-1250. High school rank: 21% in top tenth, 50% in top quarter, 83% in top half
Early decision deadline: N/A, notification date: N/A
Early action deadline: N/A, notification date: N/A
Application deadline (fall): rolling
Undergraduate student body: 1,951 full time, 209 part time; 32%

male, 68% female; 0% American Indian, 5% Asian, 9% black, 10% Hispanic, 5% multiracial, 0% Pacific Islander, 65% white; 4% international; 59% from in state; 52% live on campus; 0% of students in fraternities, 0% in sororities
Most popular majors: 15% Biology/Biological Sciences, General, 12% Psychology, General, 7% International Business/Trade/Commerce, 6% Health/Health Care Administration/Management, 4% Criminology
Expenses: 2019-2020: $44,440; room/board: $13,900
Financial aid: (215) 572-2980; 81% of undergrads determined to have financial need; average aid package $34,971

The Art Institute of Philadelphia[1]
Philadelphia PA
U.S. News ranking: Arts, unranked
Admissions email: N/A
Private
Application deadline (fall): N/A
Undergraduate student body: N/A full time, N/A part time
Expenses: N/A
Financial aid: N/A

Art Institute of Pittsburgh[1]
Pittsburgh PA
(412) 263-6600
U.S. News ranking: Arts, unranked
Website: www.artinstitutes.edu/pittsburgh/Admissions
Admissions email: aip@aii.edu
For-profit
Application deadline (fall): N/A
Undergraduate student body: N/A full time, N/A part time
Expenses: N/A
Financial aid: N/A

Bloomsburg University of Pennsylvania
Bloomsburg PA
(570) 389-4316
U.S. News ranking: Reg. U. (N), No. 113
Website: www.bloomu.edu
Admissions email: buadmiss@bloomu.edu
Public; founded 1839
Freshman admissions: selective; 2018-2019: 8,749 applied, 6,718 accepted. Either SAT or ACT required. SAT 25/75 percentile: 990-1150. High school rank: 8% in top tenth, 29% in top quarter, 62% in top half
Early decision deadline: N/A, notification date: N/A
Early action deadline: N/A, notification date: N/A
Application deadline (fall): rolling
Undergraduate student body: 7,512 full time, 741 part time; 43% male, 57% female; 0% American Indian, 1% Asian, 7% black, 7% Hispanic, 2% multiracial, 0% Pacific Islander, 78% white; 0% international; 91% from in state; 42% live on campus; N/A of students in fraternities, N/A in sororities

Most popular majors: 19% Business Administration and Management, General, 6% Criminal Justice/Safety Studies, 5% Mass Communication/Media Studies, 5% Organizational Communication, General, 5% Psychology, General
Expenses: 2019-2020: $10,958 in state, $22,532 out of state; room/board: $10,468
Financial aid: (570) 389-4297; 67% of undergrads determined to have financial need; average aid package $9,347

Bryn Athyn College of the New Church
Bryn Athyn PA
(267) 502-6000
U.S. News ranking: Nat. Lib. Arts, second tier
Website: www.brynathyn.edu
Admissions email: admissions@brynathyn.edu
Private; founded 1877
Affiliation: Other
Freshman admissions: selective; 2018-2019: 250 applied, 222 accepted. Either SAT or ACT required. SAT 25/75 percentile: 996-1203. High school rank: N/A
Early decision deadline: N/A, notification date: N/A
Early action deadline: N/A, notification date: N/A
Application deadline (fall): rolling
Undergraduate student body: 285 full time, 11 part time; 48% male, 52% female; 1% American Indian, 2% Asian, 15% black, 8% Hispanic, 1% multiracial, 0% Pacific Islander, 64% white, 6% international; N/A from in state; 44% live on campus; N/A of students in fraternities, N/A in sororities
Most popular majors: 30% Business, Management, Marketing, and Related Support Services, 21% Psychology, 17% Biological and Biomedical Sciences, 11% History, 9% English Language and Literature/Letters
Expenses: 2019-2020: $24,471; room/board: $12,240
Financial aid: (267) 502-6000

Bryn Mawr College
Bryn Mawr PA
(610) 526-5152
U.S. News ranking: Nat. Lib. Arts, No. 27
Website: www.brynmawr.edu
Admissions email: admissions@brynmawr.edu
Private; founded 1885
Freshman admissions: more selective; 2018-2019: 3,166 applied, 1,079 accepted. Neither SAT nor ACT required. SAT 25/75 percentile: 1300-1500. High school rank: 59% in top tenth, 91% in top quarter, 99% in top half
Early decision deadline: 11/15, notification date: 12/15
Early action deadline: N/A, notification date: N/A
Application deadline (fall): 1/15

Undergraduate student body: 1,350 full time, 10 part time; 0% male, 100% female; 0% American Indian, 13% Asian, 6% black, 10% Hispanic, 6% multiracial, 0% Pacific Islander, 39% white, 22% international
Most popular majors: 26% Social Sciences, 11% Biological and Biomedical Sciences, 11% Foreign Languages, Literatures, and Linguistics, 11% Mathematics and Statistics, 9% Physical Sciences
Expenses: 2019-2020: $54,440; room/board: $17,100
Financial aid: (610) 526-5245; 53% of undergrads determined to have financial need; average aid package $51,553

Bucknell University
Lewisburg PA
(570) 577-3000
U.S. News ranking: Nat. Lib. Arts, No. 35
Website: www.bucknell.edu
Admissions email: admissions@bucknell.edu
Private; founded 1846
Freshman admissions: more selective; 2018-2019: 10,144 applied, 3,352 accepted. Either SAT or ACT required. SAT 25/75 percentile: 1250-1420. High school rank: 58% in top tenth, 85% in top quarter, 98% in top half
Early decision deadline: 11/15, notification date: 12/15
Early action deadline: N/A, notification date: N/A
Application deadline (fall): 1/15
Undergraduate student body: 3,581 full time, 16 part time; 49% male, 51% female; 0% American Indian, 6% Asian, 4% black, 7% Hispanic, 4% multiracial, 0% Pacific Islander, 72% white, 7% international; 21% from in state; 92% live on campus; 35% of students in fraternities, 40% in sororities
Most popular majors: 13% Economics, General, 7% Accounting and Finance, 6% Biology/Biological Sciences, General, 6% Political Science and Government, General, 6% Psychology, General
Expenses: 2019-2020: $58,196; room/board: $14,174
Financial aid: (570) 577-1331; 38% of undergrads determined to have financial need; average aid package $34,500

Cabrini University
Radnor PA
(610) 902-8552
U.S. News ranking: Reg. U. (N), No. 116
Website: www.cabrini.edu
Admissions email: admit@cabrini.edu
Private; founded 1957
Affiliation: Roman Catholic
Freshman admissions: less selective; 2018-2019: 3,565 applied, 2,563 accepted. Neither SAT nor ACT required. SAT 25/75 percentile: 990-1170. High school rank: N/A

Early decision deadline: N/A, notification date: N/A
Early action deadline: N/A, notification date: N/A
Application deadline (fall): 9/5
Undergraduate student body: 1,486 full time, 223 part time; 39% male, 61% female; 0% American Indian, 2% Asian, 22% black, 14% Hispanic, 3% multiracial, 0% Pacific Islander, 54% white, 0% international; N/A from in state; 66% live on campus; N/A of students in fraternities, N/A in sororities
Most popular majors: Information not available
Expenses: 2019-2020: $32,775; room/board: $12,590
Financial aid: (610) 902-8424

Cairn University[7]
Langhorne PA
(215) 702-4235
U.S. News ranking: Reg. U. (N), No. 126
Website: cairn.edu/
Admissions email: admissions@cairn.edu
Private; founded 1913
Affiliation: Undenominational
Freshman admissions: less selective; 2018-2019: 578 applied, 517 accepted. Either SAT or ACT required. SAT 25/75 percentile: 890-1130. High school rank: N/A
Early decision deadline: N/A, notification date: N/A
Early action deadline: N/A, notification date: N/A
Application deadline (fall): rolling
Undergraduate student body: 756 full time, 49 part time
Most popular majors: Information not available
Expenses: 2018-2019: $27,279; room/board: $10,294
Financial aid: (215) 702-4243

California University of Pennsylvania
California PA
(724) 938-4404
U.S. News ranking: Reg. U. (N), second tier
Website: www.calu.edu/
Admissions email: inquiry@calu.edu
Public; founded 1852
Affiliation: Episcopal Church, Reformed
Freshman admissions: less selective; 2018-2019: 2,909 applied, 2,820 accepted. Either SAT or ACT required. SAT 25/75 percentile: 900-1100. High school rank: 5% in top tenth, 22% in top quarter, 55% in top half
Early decision deadline: N/A, notification date: N/A
Early action deadline: N/A, notification date: N/A
Application deadline (fall): 8/21
Undergraduate student body: 4,212 full time, 962 part time; 46% male, 54% female; 0% American Indian, 1% Asian, 13% black, 3% Hispanic, 4% multiracial, 0% Pacific Islander, 75% white, 1% international; N/A from in state; 48% live on campus; 5% of students in fraternities, 6% in sororities

Most popular majors: 19% Health Professions and Related Programs, 12% Business, Management, Marketing, and Related Support Services, 11% Parks, Recreation, Leisure, and Fitness Studies, 7% Social Sciences, 6% Homeland Security, Law Enforcement, Firefighting and Related Protective Services
Expenses: 2018-2019: $10,840 in state, $14,586 out of state; room/board: $10,344
Financial aid: (724) 938-4415; 76% of undergrads determined to have financial need; average aid package $9,364

Carlow University
Pittsburgh PA
(412) 578-6059
U.S. News ranking: Reg. U. (N), No. 75
Website: www.carlow.edu
Admissions email: admissions@carlow.edu
Private; founded 1929
Affiliation: Roman Catholic
Freshman admissions: selective; 2018-2019: 898 applied, 778 accepted. Either SAT or ACT required. SAT 25/75 percentile: 1000-1180. High school rank: 19% in top tenth, 50% in top quarter, 85% in top half
Early decision deadline: N/A, notification date: N/A
Early action deadline: N/A, notification date: N/A
Application deadline (fall): rolling
Undergraduate student body: 1,071 full time, 262 part time; 18% male, 82% female; 0% American Indian, 3% Asian, 17% black, 3% Hispanic, 4% multiracial, 0% Pacific Islander, 68% white, 0% international; 5% from in state; 32% live on campus; 0% of students in fraternities, 5% in sororities
Most popular majors: 33% Registered Nursing/Registered Nurse, 9% Biology/Biological Sciences, General, 8% Early Childhood Education and Teaching, 7% Psychology, General, 6% Social Work
Expenses: 2019-2020: $30,528; room/board: $11,902
Financial aid: (412) 578-6171

Carnegie Mellon University
Pittsburgh PA
(412) 268-2082
U.S. News ranking: Nat. U., No. 25
Website: www.cmu.edu
Admissions email: admission@andrew.cmu.edu
Private; founded 1900
Freshman admissions: most selective; 2018-2019: 24,351 applied, 4,170 accepted. Either SAT or ACT required. SAT 25/75 percentile: 1450-1550. High school rank: 87% in top tenth, 97% in top quarter, 100% in top half
Early decision deadline: 11/1, notification date: 12/15
Early action deadline: N/A, notification date: N/A
Application deadline (fall): 1/1

Undergraduate student body: 6,680 full time, 267 part time; 50% male, 50% female; 0% American Indian, 30% Asian, 4% black, 9% Hispanic, 4% multiracial, 0% Pacific Islander, 26% white, 22% international; 14% from in state; 58% live on campus; 16% of students in fraternities, 11% in sororities
Most popular majors: 25% Engineering, 13% Computer and Information Sciences and Support Services, 10% Business, Management, Marketing, and Related Support Services, 10% Mathematics and Statistics, 10% Multi/Interdisciplinary Studies
Expenses: 2019-2020: $57,119; room/board: $14,972
Financial aid: (412) 268-8981; 40% of undergrads determined to have financial need; average aid package $46,595

Cedar Crest College
Allentown PA
(800) 360-1222
U.S. News ranking: Reg. U. (N), No. 86
Website: www.cedarcrest.edu
Admissions email: admissions@cedarcrest.edu
Private; founded 1867
Freshman admissions: selective; 2018-2019: 1,343 applied, 768 accepted. Either SAT or ACT required. SAT 25/75 percentile: 940-1170. High school rank: 15% in top tenth, 43% in top quarter, 82% in top half
Early decision deadline: N/A, notification date: N/A
Early action deadline: N/A, notification date: N/A
Application deadline (fall): rolling
Undergraduate student body: 929 full time, 394 part time; 11% male, 89% female; 0% American Indian, 2% Asian, 9% black, 16% Hispanic, 1% multiracial, 0% Pacific Islander, 59% white, 9% international; 82% from in state; 34% live on campus; N/A of students in fraternities, N/A in sororities
Most popular majors: 29% Registered Nursing/Registered Nurse, 12% Business Administration and Management, General, 6% Psychology, General, 6% Social Work, 5% Health Communication
Expenses: 2019-2020: $40,374; room/board: $11,891
Financial aid: (610) 606-4666; 92% of undergrads determined to have financial need; average aid package $30,400

Central Penn College
Summerdale PA
(717) 728-2401
U.S. News ranking: Reg. Coll. (N), second tier
Website: www.centralpenn.edu
Admissions email: admissions@centralpenn.edu
For-profit; founded 1881
Freshman admissions: less selective; 2018-2019: 279 applied, 202 accepted. Neither SAT nor ACT required. SAT 25/75 percentile: N/A. High school rank: N/A

Early decision deadline: N/A, notification date: N/A
Early action deadline: N/A, notification date: N/A
Application deadline (fall): rolling
Undergraduate student body: 243 full time, 780 part time; 35% male, 65% female; 3% American Indian, 3% Asian, 20% black, 3% Hispanic, 4% multiracial, 0% Pacific Islander, 65% white, 0% international
Most popular majors: 41% Business Administration and Management, General, 19% Criminal Justice/Safety Studies, 10% Computer Science, 9% Accounting, 9% Legal Professions and Studies, Other
Expenses: 2019-2020: $18,714; room/board: $8,094
Financial aid: (717) 728-2261

Chatham University
Pittsburgh PA
(800) 837-1290
U.S. News ranking: Nat. U., No. 185
Website: www.chatham.edu
Admissions email: admissions@chatham.edu
Private; founded 1869
Freshman admissions: selective; 2018-2019: 2,761 applied, 1,529 accepted. Neither SAT nor ACT required. SAT 25/75 percentile: 1040-1250. High school rank: 29% in top tenth, 56% in top quarter, 83% in top half
Early decision deadline: N/A, notification date: N/A
Early action deadline: N/A, notification date: N/A
Application deadline (fall): 8/1
Undergraduate student body: 1,020 full time, 85 part time; 28% male, 72% female; 0% American Indian, 3% Asian, 6% black, 3% Hispanic, 2% multiracial, 0% Pacific Islander, 79% white, 3% international
Most popular majors: 24% Health Professions and Related Programs, 14% Biological and Biomedical Sciences, 10% Business, Management, Marketing, and Related Support Services, 10% Psychology, 7% Social Sciences
Expenses: 2019-2020: $38,738; room/board: $12,505
Financial aid: (412) 365-1849; 74% of undergrads determined to have financial need; average aid package $36,742

Chestnut Hill College
Philadelphia PA
(215) 248-7001
U.S. News ranking: Reg. U. (N), No. 94
Website: www.chc.edu
Admissions email: admissions@chc.edu
Private; founded 1924
Affiliation: Roman Catholic
Freshman admissions: less selective; 2018-2019: 1,008 applied, 968 accepted. Either SAT or ACT required. SAT 25/75 percentile: 940-1120. High school rank: 6% in top tenth, 23% in top quarter, 51% in top half

Early decision deadline: N/A, notification date: N/A
Early action deadline: N/A, notification date: N/A
Application deadline (fall): rolling
Undergraduate student body: 1,022 full time, 271 part time; 39% male, 61% female; 0% American Indian, 2% Asian, 33% black, 11% Hispanic, 4% multiracial, 0% Pacific Islander, 39% white, 2% international; N/A from in state; 49% live on campus; N/A of students in fraternities, N/A in sororities
Most popular majors: 24% Business, Management, Marketing, and Related Support Services, 22% Public Administration and Social Service Professions, 11% Homeland Security, Law Enforcement, Firefighting and Related Protective Services, 10% Education, 8% Psychology
Expenses: 2019-2020: $37,200; room/board: $11,000
Financial aid: (215) 248-7182; 84% of undergrads determined to have financial need; average aid package $25,925

Cheyney University of Pennsylvania[1]
Cheyney PA
(610) 399-2275
U.S. News ranking: Nat. Lib. Arts, second tier
Website: www.cheyney.edu
Admissions email: admissions@cheyney.edu
Public; founded 1837
Application deadline (fall): N/A
Undergraduate student body: N/A full time, N/A part time
Expenses: N/A
Financial aid: N/A

Clarion University of Pennsylvania
Clarion PA
(814) 393-2306
U.S. News ranking: Reg. U. (N), No. 113
Website: www.clarion.edu
Admissions email: admissions@clarion.edu
Public; founded 1867
Freshman admissions: less selective; 2018-2019: 2,373 applied, 2,233 accepted. Either SAT or ACT required. SAT 25/75 percentile: 950-1130. High school rank: 10% in top tenth, 32% in top quarter, 69% in top half
Early decision deadline: N/A, notification date: N/A
Early action deadline: N/A, notification date: N/A
Application deadline (fall): rolling
Undergraduate student body: 3,132 full time, 810 part time; 33% male, 67% female; 0% American Indian, 1% Asian, 7% black, 3% Hispanic, 2% multiracial, 0% Pacific Islander, 83% white, 0% international; 92% from in state; 35% live on campus; 6% of students in fraternities, 12% in sororities

Most popular majors: 27% Health Professions and Related Programs, 20% Business, Management, Marketing, and Related Support Services, 9% Liberal Arts and Sciences, General Studies and Humanities, 6% Education, 4% Communication, Journalism, and Related Programs
Expenses: 2019-2020: $11,149 in state, $15,007 out of state; room/board: $12,668
Financial aid: (814) 393-2315; 82% of undergrads determined to have financial need; average aid package $10,864

Curtis Institute of Music[1]
Philadelphia PA
(215) 893-5252
U.S. News ranking: Arts, unranked
Website: www.curtis.edu
Admissions email: admissions@curtis.edu
Private; founded 1924
Application deadline (fall): N/A
Undergraduate student body: N/A full time, N/A part time
Expenses: N/A
Financial aid: (215) 717-3188

Delaware Valley University
Doylestown PA
(215) 489-2211
U.S. News ranking: Reg. U. (N), No. 119
Website: www.delval.edu
Admissions email: admitme@delval.edu
Private; founded 1896
Freshman admissions: selective; 2018-2019: 2,423 applied, 1,591 accepted. Either SAT or ACT required. SAT 25/75 percentile: 970-1160. High school rank: 10% in top tenth, 33% in top quarter, 64% in top half
Early decision deadline: N/A, notification date: N/A
Early action deadline: N/A, notification date: N/A
Application deadline (fall): rolling
Undergraduate student body: 1,744 full time, 238 part time; 41% male, 59% female; 1% American Indian, 1% Asian, 9% black, 7% Hispanic, 2% multiracial, 0% Pacific Islander, 69% white, 1% international; 66% from in state; 49% live on campus; 0% of students in fraternities, 0% in sororities
Most popular majors: 41% Agriculture, Agriculture Operations, and Related Sciences, 16% Biological and Biomedical Sciences, 16% Business, Management, Marketing, and Related Support Services, 11% Natural Resources and Conservation, 6% Homeland Security, Law Enforcement, Firefighting and Related Protective Services
Expenses: 2019-2020: $40,620; room/board: $14,620
Financial aid: (215) 489-2975; 82% of undergrads determined to have financial need; average aid package $28,570

DeSales University
Center Valley PA
(610) 282-4443
U.S. News ranking: Reg. U. (N), No. 59
Website: www.desales.edu
Admissions email: admiss@desales.edu
Private; founded 1964
Affiliation: Roman Catholic
Freshman admissions: selective; 2018-2019: 3,190 applied, 2,505 accepted. Either SAT or ACT required. SAT 25/75 percentile: 1010-1230. High school rank: 24% in top tenth, 43% in top quarter, 64% in top half
Early decision deadline: N/A, notification date: N/A
Early action deadline: N/A, notification date: N/A
Application deadline (fall): 8/1
Undergraduate student body: 1,959 full time, 540 part time; 36% male, 64% female; 0% American Indian, 3% Asian, 4% black, 13% Hispanic, 3% multiracial, 0% Pacific Islander, 70% white, 0% international; 67% from in state; 41% live on campus; N/A of students in fraternities, N/A in sororities
Most popular majors: 22% Registered Nursing/Registered Nurse, 8% Accounting, 7% Criminal Justice/Safety Studies, 6% Drama and Dramatics/Theatre Arts, General, 6% Health Professions and Related Clinical Sciences, Other
Expenses: 2019-2020: $38,700; room/board: $13,000
Financial aid: (610) 282-1100; 78% of undergrads determined to have financial need; average aid package $26,116

Dickinson College
Carlisle PA
(800) 644-1773
U.S. News ranking: Nat. Lib. Arts, No. 46
Website: www.dickinson.edu
Admissions email: admissions@dickinson.edu
Private; founded 1783
Freshman admissions: more selective; 2018-2019: 6,248 applied, 3,070 accepted. Neither SAT nor ACT required. SAT 25/75 percentile: 1200-1390. High school rank: 41% in top tenth, 74% in top quarter, 96% in top half
Early decision deadline: 11/15, notification date: 12/15
Early action deadline: 12/1, notification date: 2/15
Application deadline (fall): 1/15
Undergraduate student body: 2,361 full time, 38 part time; 42% male, 58% female; 0% American Indian, 4% Asian, 5% black, 9% Hispanic, 3% multiracial, 0% Pacific Islander, 64% white, 14% international; 20% from in state; 100% live on campus; 4% of students in fraternities, 25% in sororities
Most popular majors: 10% International Business/Trade/Commerce, 8% Economics, General, 8% Political Science and Government, General,

6% International Relations and Affairs, 5% Psychology, General
Expenses: 2019-2020: $56,498; room/board: $14,176
Financial aid: (717) 245-1308; 61% of undergrads determined to have financial need; average aid package $48,116

Drexel University
Philadelphia PA
(800) 237-3935
U.S. News ranking: Nat. U., No. 97
Website: www.drexel.edu
Admissions email: enroll@drexel.edu
Private; founded 1891
Freshman admissions: more selective; 2018-2019: 30,242 applied, 23,267 accepted. Either SAT or ACT required. SAT 25/75 percentile: 1170-1380. High school rank: 33% in top tenth, 64% in top quarter, 90% in top half
Early decision deadline: 11/1, notification date: N/A
Early action deadline: 11/1, notification date: 12/15
Application deadline (fall): 1/15
Undergraduate student body: 11,768 full time, 1,722 part time; 50% male, 50% female; 0% American Indian, 17% Asian, 7% black, 7% Hispanic, 4% multiracial, 0% Pacific Islander, 52% white, 11% international; 51% from in state; 22% live on campus; 11% of students in fraternities, 10% in sororities
Most popular majors: 25% Business, Management, Marketing, and Related Support Services, 21% Health Professions and Related Programs, 20% Engineering, 9% Visual and Performing Arts, 4% Computer and Information Sciences and Support Services
Expenses: 2019-2020: $54,516; room/board: $14,241
Financial aid: (215) 895-1600; 65% of undergrads determined to have financial need; average aid package $38,636

Duquesne University
Pittsburgh PA
(412) 396-6222
U.S. News ranking: Nat. U., No. 132
Website: www.duq.edu
Admissions email: admissions@duq.edu
Private; founded 1878
Affiliation: Roman Catholic
Freshman admissions: more selective; 2018-2019: 7,505 applied, 5,392 accepted. Either SAT or ACT required for some. SAT 25/75 percentile: 1140-1280. High school rank: 26% in top tenth, 57% in top quarter, 87% in top half
Early decision deadline: 11/1, notification date: 11/15
Early action deadline: 12/1, notification date: 1/15
Application deadline (fall): 7/1
Undergraduate student body: 5,896 full time, 117 part time; 36% male, 64% female; 0% American Indian, 3% Asian, 5% black,

4% Hispanic, 3% multiracial, 0% Pacific Islander, 80% white, 3% international; 72% from in state; 60% live on campus; 17% of students in fraternities, 24% in sororities
Most popular majors: 20% Nursing Science, 5% Biology/Biological Sciences, General, 4% Accounting, 4% Early Childhood Education and Teaching, 4% Finance, General
Expenses: 2019-2020: $39,992; room/board: $13,088
Financial aid: (412) 396-6607; 67% of undergrads determined to have financial need; average aid package $27,227

Eastern University
St. Davids PA
(800) 452-0996
U.S. News ranking: Reg. U. (N), No. 63
Website: www.eastern.edu
Admissions email: ugadm@eastern.edu
Private; founded 1952
Affiliation: American Baptist
Freshman admissions: selective; 2018-2019: 1,761 applied, 1,205 accepted. Neither SAT nor ACT required. SAT 25/75 percentile: 1030-1190. High school rank: 12% in top tenth, 40% in top quarter, 70% in top half
Early decision deadline: N/A, notification date: N/A
Early action deadline: N/A, notification date: N/A
Application deadline (fall): rolling
Undergraduate student body: 1,463 full time, 422 part time; 32% male, 68% female; 0% American Indian, 2% Asian, 20% black, 19% Hispanic, 2% multiracial, 0% Pacific Islander, 50% white, 2% international; 41% from in state; 79% live on campus; N/A of students in fraternities, N/A in sororities
Most popular majors: 16% Early Childhood Education and Teaching, 11% Business Administration and Management, General, 9% Registered Nursing/Registered Nurse, 7% Social Work, 6% Organizational Leadership
Expenses: 2019-2020: $33,854; room/board: $11,536
Financial aid: (610) 225-5102; 82% of undergrads determined to have financial need; average aid package $26,684

East Stroudsburg University of Pennsylvania
East Stroudsburg PA
(570) 422-3542
U.S. News ranking: Reg. U. (N), second tier
Website: www.esu.edu/admissions/index.cfm
Admissions email: admission@esu.edu
Public; founded 1893
Freshman admissions: less selective; 2018-2019: 9,712 applied, 6,986 accepted. Neither SAT nor ACT required. SAT 25/75

percentile: 910-1120. High school rank: 8% in top tenth, 24% in top quarter, 58% in top half
Early decision deadline: N/A, notification date: N/A
Early action deadline: N/A, notification date: N/A
Application deadline (fall): 5/1
Undergraduate student body: 5,243 full time, 470 part time; 44% male, 56% female; 0% American Indian, 2% Asian, 20% black, 12% Hispanic, 4% multiracial, 0% Pacific Islander, 58% white, 0% international; 79% from in state; 48% live on campus; N/A of students in fraternities, N/A in sororities
Most popular majors: 16% Athletic Training/Trainer, 15% Business Administration and Management, General, 11% Parks, Recreation and Leisure Facilities Management, General, 9% Biology/Biological Sciences, General, 9% Education
Expenses: 2019-2020: $11,418 in state, $24,318 out of state; room/board: $11,760
Financial aid: (570) 422-2800; 75% of undergrads determined to have financial need; average aid package $8,191

Edinboro University of Pennsylvania
Edinboro PA
(888) 846-2676
U.S. News ranking: Reg. U. (N), second tier
Website: www.edinboro.edu
Admissions email: admissions@edinboro.edu
Public; founded 1857
Freshman admissions: selective; 2018-2019: 2,327 applied, 1,861 accepted. Either SAT or ACT required. SAT 25/75 percentile: 960-1140. High school rank: 9% in top tenth, 29% in top quarter, 65% in top half
Early decision deadline: N/A, notification date: N/A
Early action deadline: N/A, notification date: N/A
Application deadline (fall): rolling
Undergraduate student body: 3,201 full time, 371 part time; 42% male, 58% female; 0% American Indian, 1% Asian, 6% black, 4% Hispanic, 4% multiracial, 0% Pacific Islander, 82% white, 1% international; 87% from in state; 30% live on campus; 5% of students in fraternities, 7% in sororities
Most popular majors: 12% Fine/Studio Arts, General, 9% Business Administration and Management, General, 8% Registered Nursing/Registered Nurse, 7% Early Childhood Education and Teaching, 7% Research and Experimental Psychology, Other
Expenses: 2019-2020: $10,543 in state, $14,401 out of state; room/board: $9,800
Financial aid: (814) 732-3500; 79% of undergrads determined to have financial need; average aid package $9,053

Elizabethtown College

Elizabethtown PA
(717) 361-1400
U.S. News ranking: Nat. Lib. Arts, No. 105
Website: www.etown.edu
Admissions email: admissions@etown.edu
Private; founded 1899
Affiliation: Church of Brethren
Freshman admissions: more selective; 2018-2019: 2,010 applied, 1,522 accepted. Either SAT or ACT required. SAT 25/75 percentile: 1070-1290. High school rank: 30% in top tenth, 63% in top quarter, 90% in top half
Early decision deadline: N/A, notification date: N/A
Early action deadline: N/A, notification date: N/A
Application deadline (fall): rolling
Undergraduate student body: 1,593 full time, 38 part time; 39% male, 61% female; 0% American Indian, 3% Asian, 3% black, 3% Hispanic, 2% multiracial, 0% Pacific Islander, 86% white, 2% international; 69% from in state; 84% live on campus; 0% of students in fraternities, 0% in sororities
Most popular majors: 18% Business, Management, Marketing, and Related Support Services, 13% Health Professions and Related Programs, 11% Biological and Biomedical Sciences, 9% Engineering, 8% Education
Expenses: 2019-2020: $32,000; room/board: $11,710
Financial aid: N/A; 77% of undergrads determined to have financial need; average aid package $34,766

Franklin and Marshall College

Lancaster PA
(717) 358-3953
U.S. News ranking: Nat. Lib. Arts, No. 38
Website: www.fandm.edu
Admissions email: admission@fandm.edu
Private; founded 1787
Freshman admissions: more selective; 2018-2019: 6,557 applied, 2,316 accepted. Neither SAT nor ACT required. SAT 25/75 percentile: 1260-1440. High school rank: 59% in top tenth, 84% in top quarter, 97% in top half
Early decision deadline: 11/15, notification date: 12/15
Early action deadline: N/A, notification date: N/A
Application deadline (fall): 1/15
Undergraduate student body: 2,290 full time, 19 part time; 45% male, 55% female; 0% American Indian, 5% Asian, 6% black, 10% Hispanic, 2% multiracial, 0% Pacific Islander, 56% white, 18% international; 28% from in state; 99% live on campus; 20% of students in fraternities, 27% in sororities
Most popular majors: 10% Business Administration and Management, General, 8% Economics, General, 8% Political

Science and Government, General, 5% Biology/Biological Sciences, General, 5% Psychology, General
Expenses: 2019-2020: $58,795; room/board: $14,455
Financial aid: (717) 358-3991; 54% of undergrads determined to have financial need; average aid package $52,703

Gannon University

Erie PA
(814) 871-7240
U.S. News ranking: Nat. U., No. 218
Website: www.gannon.edu
Admissions email: admissions@gannon.edu
Private; founded 1925
Affiliation: Roman Catholic
Freshman admissions: selective; 2018-2019: 5,124 applied, 4,143 accepted. Either SAT or ACT required. SAT 25/75 percentile: 1020-1220. High school rank: 20% in top tenth, 48% in top quarter, 78% in top half
Early decision deadline: N/A, notification date: N/A
Early action deadline: N/A, notification date: N/A
Application deadline (fall): rolling
Undergraduate student body: 2,653 full time, 638 part time; 41% male, 59% female; 0% American Indian, 2% Asian, 5% black, 4% Hispanic, 3% multiracial, 0% Pacific Islander, 72% white, 9% international; N/A from in state; 48% live on campus; 15% of students in fraternities, 14% in sororities
Most popular majors: 30% Health Professions and Related Programs, 13% Engineering, 12% Business, Management, Marketing, and Related Support Services, 8% Biological and Biomedical Sciences, 6% Homeland Security, Law Enforcement, Firefighting and Related Protective Services
Expenses: 2019-2020: $33,226; room/board: $13,530
Financial aid: (814) 871-7337; 78% of undergrads determined to have financial need; average aid package $26,463

Geneva College

Beaver Falls PA
(724) 847-6500
U.S. News ranking: Reg. U. (N), No. 92
Website: www.geneva.edu
Admissions email: admissions@geneva.edu
Private; founded 1848
Affiliation: Reformed Presbyterian Church
Freshman admissions: selective; 2018-2019: 1,941 applied, 1,229 accepted. Either SAT or ACT required. SAT 25/75 percentile: 1000-1240. High school rank: 19% in top tenth, 43% in top quarter, 71% in top half
Early decision deadline: N/A, notification date: N/A
Early action deadline: N/A, notification date: N/A
Application deadline (fall): rolling

Undergraduate student body: 1,180 full time, 196 part time; 53% male, 47% female; 0% American Indian, 1% Asian, 7% black, 2% Hispanic, 3% multiracial, 0% Pacific Islander, 81% white, 2% international; 73% from in state; 60% live on campus; 0% of students in fraternities, 0% in sororities
Most popular majors: 14% Engineering, General, 8% Business Administration and Management, General, 6% Teacher Education, Multiple Levels, 5% Accounting, 5% Public Administration and Social Service Professions, Other
Expenses: 2019-2020: $28,190; room/board: $10,530
Financial aid: (724) 847-6532; 83% of undergrads determined to have financial need; average aid package $22,163

Gettysburg College

Gettysburg PA
(800) 431-0803
U.S. News ranking: Nat. Lib. Arts, No. 53
Website: www.gettysburg.edu/
Admissions email: admiss@gettysburg.edu
Private; founded 1832
Freshman admissions: more selective; 2018-2019: 6,269 applied, 2,847 accepted. Either SAT or ACT required. SAT 25/75 percentile: 1270-1420. High school rank: 62% in top tenth, 83% in top quarter, 99% in top half
Early decision deadline: 11/15, notification date: 12/15
Early action deadline: N/A, notification date: N/A
Application deadline (fall): 1/15
Undergraduate student body: 2,427 full time, 6 part time; 48% male, 52% female; 0% American Indian, 2% Asian, 4% black, 9% Hispanic, 2% multiracial, 0% Pacific Islander, 74% white, 6% international; 27% from in state; 95% live on campus; 33% of students in fraternities, 33% in sororities
Most popular majors: 27% Social Sciences, 14% Biological and Biomedical Sciences, 9% Business, Management, Marketing, and Related Support Services, 7% Psychology, 6% English Language and Literature/Letters
Expenses: 2019-2020: $56,390; room/board: $13,460
Financial aid: (717) 337-6611; 60% of undergrads determined to have financial need; average aid package $42,219

Grove City College

Grove City PA
(724) 458-2100
U.S. News ranking: Nat. Lib. Arts, No. 114
Website: www.gcc.edu
Admissions email: admissions@gcc.edu
Private; founded 1876
Affiliation: Undenominational
Freshman admissions: more selective; 2018-2019: 1,814 applied, 1,434 accepted. Either

SAT or ACT required. SAT 25/75 percentile: 1085-1275. High school rank: 33% in top tenth, 81% in top quarter, 90% in top half
Early decision deadline: 11/1, notification date: 12/15
Early action deadline: N/A, notification date: N/A
Application deadline (fall): 3/20
Undergraduate student body: 2,280 full time, 58 part time; 52% male, 48% female; 0% American Indian, 2% Asian, 1% black, 1% Hispanic, 3% multiracial, 0% Pacific Islander, 91% white, 1% international; 45% from in state; 96% live on campus; N/A of students in fraternities, N/A in sororities
Most popular majors: 10% Mechanical Engineering, 7% Biology/Biological Sciences, General, 7% Speech Communication and Rhetoric, 6% Accounting, 6% Business Administration and Management, General
Expenses: 2019-2020: $18,470; room/board: $10,060
Financial aid: (724) 458-3300; 47% of undergrads determined to have financial need; average aid package $7,999

Gwynedd Mercy University

Gwynedd Valley PA
(215) 641-5510
U.S. News ranking: Reg. U. (N), No. 104
Website: www.gmercyu.edu/
Admissions email: admissions@gmercyu.edu
Private; founded 1948
Affiliation: Roman Catholic
Freshman admissions: less selective; 2018-2019: 1,213 applied, 1,116 accepted. Either SAT or ACT required. SAT 25/75 percentile: 940-1110. High school rank: 10% in top tenth, 32% in top quarter, 65% in top half
Early decision deadline: N/A, notification date: N/A
Early action deadline: N/A, notification date: N/A
Application deadline (fall): 8/20
Undergraduate student body: 1,898 full time, 135 part time; 24% male, 76% female; 1% American Indian, 6% Asian, 22% black, 5% Hispanic, 3% multiracial, 0% Pacific Islander, 60% white, 0% international; 86% from in state; 22% live on campus; 0% of students in fraternities, 0% in sororities
Most popular majors: 70% Health Professions and Related Programs, 15% Business, Management, Marketing, and Related Support Services, 5% Education, 3% Psychology, 2% Biological and Biomedical Sciences
Expenses: 2019-2020: $34,580; room/board: $12,470
Financial aid: (215) 646-7300; 85% of undergrads determined to have financial need; average aid package $22,739

Harrisburg University of Science and Technology

Harrisburg PA
(717) 901-5150
U.S. News ranking: Reg. U. (N), second tier
Website: www.harrisburgu.edu
Admissions email: admissions@harrisburgu.edu
Private; founded 2001
Freshman admissions: less selective; 2018-2019: N/A applied, N/A accepted. Neither SAT nor ACT required. SAT 25/75 percentile: N/A. High school rank: N/A
Early decision deadline: N/A, notification date: N/A
Early action deadline: N/A, notification date: N/A
Application deadline (fall): rolling
Undergraduate student body: 525 full time, 460 part time; 53% male, 47% female; 1% American Indian, 4% Asian, 40% black, 14% Hispanic, 5% multiracial, 0% Pacific Islander, 34% white, 1% international
Most popular majors: Information not available
Expenses: 2018-2019: $23,900; room/board: $6,800
Financial aid: (717) 901-5115

Haverford College

Haverford PA
(610) 896-1350
U.S. News ranking: Nat. Lib. Arts, No. 11
Website: www.haverford.edu
Admissions email: admission@haverford.edu
Private; founded 1833
Freshman admissions: most selective; 2018-2019: 4,672 applied, 878 accepted. Either SAT or ACT required. SAT 25/75 percentile: 1370-1530. High school rank: 95% in top tenth, 97% in top quarter, 100% in top half
Early decision deadline: 11/15, notification date: 12/15
Early action deadline: N/A, notification date: N/A
Application deadline (fall): 1/15
Undergraduate student body: 1,308 full time, 2 part time; 49% male, 51% female; 0% American Indian, 13% Asian, 7% black, 10% Hispanic, 3% multiracial, 0% Pacific Islander, 53% white, 11% international; 12% from in state; 98% live on campus; 0% of students in fraternities, 0% in sororities
Most popular majors: 27% Social Sciences, General, 13% Physical Sciences, 10% Psychology, General, 9% Biology/Biological Sciences, General, 8% Mathematics, General
Expenses: 2019-2020: $56,698; room/board: $16,770
Financial aid: (610) 896-1350; 46% of undergrads determined to have financial need; average aid package $54,861

Holy Family University[1]

Philadelphia PA
(215) 637-3050
U.S. News ranking: Reg. U. (N), second tier
Website: www.holyfamily.edu
Admissions email: admissions@holyfamily.edu
Private; founded 1954
Affiliation: Roman Catholic
Application deadline (fall): rolling
Undergraduate student body: N/A full time, N/A part time
Expenses: 2019-2020: $31,040; room/board: $14,140
Financial aid: (267) 341-3233

Immaculata University

Immaculata PA
(610) 647-4400
U.S. News ranking: Nat. U., No. 211
Website: www.immaculata.edu
Admissions email: admiss@immaculata.edu
Private; founded 1920
Affiliation: Roman Catholic
Freshman admissions: selective; 2018-2019: 1,639 applied, 1,330 accepted. Either SAT or ACT required for some. SAT 25/75 percentile: 1018-1223. High school rank: 9% in top tenth, 28% in top quarter, 65% in top half
Early decision deadline: N/A, notification date: N/A
Early action deadline: N/A, notification date: N/A
Application deadline (fall): rolling
Undergraduate student body: 823 full time, 681 part time; 27% male, 73% female; 0% American Indian, 2% Asian, 16% black, 7% Hispanic, 2% multiracial, 0% Pacific Islander, 70% white, 2% international; N/A from in state; 29% live on campus; 1% of students in fraternities, 5% in sororities
Most popular majors: 47% Health Professions and Related Programs, 24% Business, Management, Marketing, and Related Support Services, 8% Parks, Recreation, Leisure, and Fitness Studies, 4% Education, 4% Homeland Security, Law Enforcement, Firefighting and Related Protective Services
Expenses: 2019-2020: $27,350; room/board: $12,620
Financial aid: (610) 647-4400; 77% of undergrads determined to have financial need; average aid package $17,396

Indiana University of Pennsylvania

Indiana PA
(724) 357-2230
U.S. News ranking: Nat. U., second tier
Website: www.iup.edu
Admissions email: admissions-inquiry@iup.edu
Public; founded 1875
Freshman admissions: less selective; 2018-2019: 9,522 applied, 8,878 accepted. Either SAT or ACT required. SAT 25/75 percentile: 910-1120. High

school rank: 8% in top tenth, 23% in top quarter, 57% in top half
Early decision deadline: N/A, notification date: N/A
Early action deadline: N/A, notification date: N/A
Application deadline (fall): rolling
Undergraduate student body: 8,359 full time, 856 part time; 42% male, 58% female; 0% American Indian, 1% Asian, 12% black, 5% Hispanic, 5% multiracial, 0% Pacific Islander, 73% white, 3% international; 92% from in state; 30% live on campus; 10% of students in fraternities, 9% in sororities
Most popular majors: 28% Business, Management, Marketing, and Related Support Services, 14% Social Sciences, 11% Health Professions and Related Programs, 6% Family and Consumer Sciences/Human Sciences, 5% Visual and Performing Arts
Expenses: 2019-2020: $13,354 in state, $17,674 out of state; room/board: $12,744
Financial aid: (724) 357-2218; 74% of undergrads determined to have financial need; average aid package $10,458

Juniata College

Huntingdon PA
(877) 586-4282
U.S. News ranking: Nat. Lib. Arts, No. 82
Website: www.juniata.edu
Admissions email: admissions@juniata.edu
Private, founded 1876
Freshman admissions: more selective; 2018-2019: 2,437 applied, 1,710 accepted. Neither SAT nor ACT required. SAT 25/75 percentile: 1080-1320. High school rank: 31% in top tenth, 67% in top quarter, 93% in top half
Early decision deadline: 11/15, notification date: 12/1
Early action deadline: 1/5, notification date: 2/15
Application deadline (fall): 3/15
Undergraduate student body: 1,339 full time, 84 part time; 43% male, 57% female; 0% American Indian, 3% Asian, 3% black, 5% Hispanic, 3% multiracial, 0% Pacific Islander, 76% white, 7% international; 63% from in state; 87% live on campus; N/A of students in fraternities, N/A in sororities
Most popular majors: 22% Biological and Biomedical Sciences, 20% Business, Management, Marketing, and Related Support Services, 10% Natural Resources and Conservation, 7% Education, 5% Communication, Journalism, and Related Programs
Expenses: 2019-2020: $47,075; room/board: $12,800
Financial aid: (814) 641-3144; 75% of undergrads determined to have financial need; average aid package $38,359

Keystone College

La Plume PA
(570) 945-8111
U.S. News ranking: Reg. Coll. (N), No. 32
Website: www.keystone.edu
Admissions email: admissions@keystone.edu
Private; founded 1868
Freshman admissions: least selective; 2018-2019: 2,912 applied, 2,056 accepted. Neither SAT nor ACT required. SAT 25/75 percentile: 820-1125. High school rank: N/A
Early decision deadline: N/A, notification date: N/A
Early action deadline: N/A, notification date: N/A
Application deadline (fall): rolling
Undergraduate student body: 1,077 full time, 263 part time; 30% male, 62% female; 0% American Indian, 1% Asian, 10% black, 8% Hispanic, 2% multiracial, 0% Pacific Islander, 74% white, 0% international; 83% from in state; 35% live on campus; 0% of students in fraternities, 0% in sororities
Most popular majors: 21% Business, Management, Marketing, and Related Support Services, 10% Homeland Security, Law Enforcement, Firefighting and Related Protective Services, 10% Psychology, 9% Computer and Information Sciences and Support Services, 9% Education
Expenses: 2019-2020: $26,720; room/board: $11,900
Financial aid: N/A

King's College

Wilkes-Barre PA
(888) 546-4772
U.S. News ranking: Reg. U. (N), No. 48
Website: www.kings.edu
Admissions email: admissions@kings.edu
Private; founded 1946
Affiliation: Roman Catholic
Freshman admissions: selective; 2018-2019: 4,292 applied, 3,330 accepted. Neither SAT nor ACT required. SAT 25/75 percentile: 1010-1200. High school rank: 18% in top tenth, 41% in top quarter, 68% in top half
Early decision deadline: 12/1, notification date: 12/15
Early action deadline: 12/1, notification date: 12/15
Application deadline (fall): rolling
Undergraduate student body: 2,066 full time, 203 part time; 52% male, 48% female; 0% American Indian, 3% Asian, 4% black, 8% Hispanic, 2% multiracial, 0% Pacific Islander, 71% white, 9% international; 72% from in state; 48% live on campus; 0% of students in fraternities, 0% in sororities
Most popular majors: 15% Accounting, 14% Health Professions and Related Clinical Sciences, Other, 9% Business Administration and Management, General, 7% Criminal Justice/Safety Studies, 5% Psychology, General

Expenses: 2019-2020: $38,724; room/board: $13,464
Financial aid: (570) 208-5900; 77% of undergrads determined to have financial need; average aid package $27,254

Kutztown University of Pennsylvania

Kutztown PA
(610) 683-4060
U.S. News ranking: Reg. U. (N), No. 126
Website: www.kutztown.edu
Admissions email: admissions@kutztown.edu
Public; founded 1866
Freshman admissions: selective; 2018-2019: 8,371 applied, 6,741 accepted. Either SAT or ACT required. SAT 25/75 percentile: 970-1140. High school rank: 8% in top tenth, 23% in top quarter, 57% in top half
Early decision deadline: N/A, notification date: N/A
Early action deadline: N/A, notification date: N/A
Application deadline (fall): rolling
Undergraduate student body: 6,953 full time, 438 part time; 47% male, 53% female; 0% American Indian, 2% Asian, 8% black, 9% Hispanic, 3% multiracial, 0% Pacific Islander, 75% white, 1% international; 88% from in state; 49% live on campus; 5% of students in fraternities, 11% in sororities
Most popular majors: 20% Business Administration and Management, General, 9% Psychology, General, 8% Communication and Media Studies, 7% Criminal Justice/Safety Studies, 5% Parks, Recreation and Leisure Studies
Expenses: 2019-2020: $10,950 in state, $14,808 out of state; room/board: $11,576
Financial aid: (610) 683-4077; 73% of undergrads determined to have financial need; average aid package $9,158

Lackawanna College

Scranton PA
(570) 961-7898
U.S. News ranking: Reg. Coll. (N), unranked
Website: www.lackawanna.edu
Admissions email: admissions@lackawanna.edu
Private
Freshman admissions: least selective; 2018-2019: 1,840 applied, 572 accepted. Neither SAT nor ACT required. SAT 25/75 percentile: N/A. High school rank: N/A
Early decision deadline: N/A, notification date: N/A
Early action deadline: N/A, notification date: N/A
Application deadline (fall): rolling
Undergraduate student body: 1,326 full time, 547 part time; 47% male, 53% female; 1% American Indian, 1% Asian, 14% black, 13% Hispanic, 2% multiracial, 0% Pacific Islander, 58% white,

0% international; N/A from in state; 17% live on campus; N/A of students in fraternities, N/A in sororities
Most popular majors: 35% Business, Management, Marketing, and Related Support Services, 20% Health Professions and Related Programs, 18% Liberal Arts and Sciences, General Studies and Humanities, 11% Homeland Security, Law Enforcement, Firefighting and Related Protective Services, 8% Engineering Technologies and Engineering-Related Fields
Expenses: 2018-2019: $15,660; room/board: $10,300
Financial aid: N/A

Lafayette College

Easton PA
(610) 330-5100
U.S. News ranking: Nat. Lib. Arts, No. 39
Website: www.lafayette.edu/
Admissions email: admissions@lafayette.edu
Private; founded 1826
Freshman admissions: more selective; 2018-2019: 9,237 applied, 2,715 accepted. Either SAT or ACT required. SAT 25/75 percentile: 1250-1435. High school rank: 52% in top tenth, 78% in top quarter, 96% in top half
Early decision deadline: 11/15, notification date: 12/15
Early action deadline: N/A, notification date: N/A
Application deadline (fall): 1/15
Undergraduate student body: 2,603 full time, 39 part time; 48% male, 52% female; 0% American Indian, 4% Asian, 5% black, 7% Hispanic, 3% multiracial, 0% Pacific Islander, 66% white, 10% international; 19% from in state; 92% live on campus; 24% of students in fraternities, 34% in sororities
Most popular majors: 36% Social Sciences, 22% Engineering, 10% Biological and Biomedical Sciences, 6% Psychology, 4% Visual and Performing Arts
Expenses: 2019-2020: $55,002; room/board: $16,264
Financial aid: (610) 330-5055; 33% of undergrads determined to have financial need; average aid package $50,594

Lancaster Bible College

Lancaster PA
(717) 569-7071
U.S. News ranking: Reg. U. (N), second tier
Website: www.lbc.edu/
Admissions email: admissions@lbc.edu
Private; founded 1933
Affiliation: Other
Freshman admissions: selective; 2018-2019: 716 applied, 408 accepted. Either SAT or ACT required. SAT 25/75 percentile: 1000-1200. High school rank: N/A
Early decision deadline: N/A, notification date: N/A

Early action deadline: N/A, notification date: N/A
Application deadline (fall): N/A
Undergraduate student body: 986 full time, 702 part time; 48% male, 52% female; 0% American Indian, 1% Asian, 25% black, 5% Hispanic, 9% multiracial, 0% Pacific Islander, 46% white, 0% international
Most popular majors: Information not available
Expenses: 2019-2020: $26,170; room/board: $9,100
Financial aid: (717) 560-8254; 79% of undergrads determined to have financial need; average aid package $20,271

La Roche University

Pittsburgh PA
(800) 838-4572
U.S. News ranking: Reg. U. (N), second tier
Website: www.laroche.edu
Admissions email: admissions@laroche.edu
Private; founded 1963
Affiliation: Roman Catholic
Freshman admissions: less selective; 2018-2019: 1,309 applied, 1,301 accepted. Either SAT or ACT required. SAT 25/75 percentile: 910-1110. High school rank: 6% in top tenth, 29% in top quarter, 60% in top half
Early decision deadline: N/A, notification date: N/A
Early action deadline: N/A, notification date: N/A
Application deadline (fall): rolling
Undergraduate student body: 1,118 full time, 171 part time; 44% male, 56% female; 0% American Indian, 1% Asian, 9% black, 5% Hispanic, 3% multiracial, 0% Pacific Islander, 62% white, 15% international; 90% from in state; 40% live on campus; 0% of students in fraternities, 0% in sororities
Most popular majors: 9% Psychology, General, 8% Criminal Justice/Safety Studies, 7% Health Professions and Related Clinical Sciences, Other, 7% Information Technology, 7% Registered Nursing/Registered Nurse
Expenses: 2019-2020: $29,464; room/board: $11,910
Financial aid: (412) 536-1120; 69% of undergrads determined to have financial need; average aid package $31,921

La Salle University

Philadelphia PA
(215) 951-1500
U.S. News ranking: Reg. U. (N), No. 38
Website: www.lasalle.edu
Admissions email: admiss@lasalle.edu
Private; founded 1863
Affiliation: Roman Catholic
Freshman admissions: selective; 2018-2019: 6,642 applied, 5,392 accepted. Either SAT or ACT required for some. SAT 25/75 percentile: 970-1160. High school rank: 11% in top tenth, 30% in top quarter, 67% in top half
Early decision deadline: N/A, notification date: N/A

Early action deadline: 11/15, notification date: 12/15
Application deadline (fall): rolling
Undergraduate student body: 3,360 full time, 537 part time; 38% male, 62% female; 0% American Indian, 5% Asian, 20% black, 20% Hispanic, 3% multiracial, 0% Pacific Islander, 48% white, 2% international; 69% from in state; 46% live on campus; 16% of students in fraternities, 17% in sororities
Most popular majors: 12% Registered Nursing/Registered Nurse, 8% Psychology, General, 7% Communication and Media Studies, Other, 7% Finance, General, 7% Marketing/Marketing Management, General
Expenses: 2019-2020: $31,650; room/board: $15,150
Financial aid: (215) 951-1070; 77% of undergrads determined to have financial need; average aid package $22,572

Lebanon Valley College

Annville PA
(717) 867-6181
U.S. News ranking: Reg. U. (N), No. 28
Website: www.lvc.edu
Admissions email: admission@lvc.edu
Private; founded 1866
Affiliation: United Methodist
Freshman admissions: selective; 2018-2019: 2,731 applied, 2,136 accepted. Neither SAT nor ACT required. SAT 25/75 percentile: 1068-1280. High school rank: 22% in top tenth, 48% in top quarter, 80% in top half
Early decision deadline: N/A, notification date: N/A
Early action deadline: N/A, notification date: N/A
Application deadline (fall): rolling
Undergraduate student body: 1,651 full time, 93 part time; 46% male, 54% female; 0% American Indian, 2% Asian, 3% black, 5% Hispanic, 3% multiracial, 0% Pacific Islander, 84% white, 1% international; 80% from in state; 77% live on campus; 10% of students in fraternities, 10% in sororities
Most popular majors: 16% Business, Management, Marketing, and Related Support Services, 16% Education, 12% Social Sciences, 9% Biological and Biomedical Sciences, 9% Health Professions and Related Programs
Expenses: 2019-2020: $44,910; room/board: $12,200
Financial aid: (717) 867-6126; 87% of undergrads determined to have financial need; average aid package $34,567

Lehigh University

Bethlehem PA
(610) 758-3100
U.S. News ranking: Nat. U., No. 50
Website: www1.lehigh.edu
Admissions email: admissions@lehigh.edu
Private; founded 1865

Freshman admissions: more selective; 2018-2019: 15,622 applied, 3,488 accepted. Either SAT or ACT required. SAT 25/75 percentile: 1270-1450. High school rank: 58% in top tenth, 88% in top quarter, 99% in top half
Early decision deadline: 11/1, notification date: 12/15
Early action deadline: N/A, notification date: N/A
Application deadline (fall): 1/1
Undergraduate student body: 4,982 full time, 65 part time; 54% male, 46% female; 0% American Indian, 8% Asian, 3% black, 10% Hispanic, 3% multiracial, 0% Pacific Islander, 63% white, 9% international; 27% from in state; 63% live on campus; 30% of students in fraternities, 39% in sororities
Most popular majors: 13% Finance, General, 9% Mechanical Engineering, 6% Accounting, 6% Marketing/Marketing Management, General, 5% Chemical Engineering
Expenses: 2019-2020: $55,240; room/board: $14,160
Financial aid: (610) 758-3181; 42% of undergrads determined to have financial need; average aid package $50,425

Lincoln University

Lincoln University PA
(800) 790-0191
U.S. News ranking: Reg. U. (N), No. 119
Website: www.lincoln.edu
Admissions email: admissions@lincoln.edu
Public; founded 1854
Freshman admissions: least selective; 2018-2019: 4,521 applied, 3,661 accepted. Either SAT or ACT required. SAT 25/75 percentile: 860-1020. High school rank: 10% in top tenth, 25% in top quarter, 52% in top half
Early decision deadline: N/A, notification date: N/A
Early action deadline: N/A, notification date: N/A
Application deadline (fall): 5/1
Undergraduate student body: 1,963 full time, 159 part time; 34% male, 66% female; 0% American Indian, 0% Asian, 85% black, 4% Hispanic, 3% multiracial, 0% Pacific Islander, 1% white, 3% international; 49% from in state; 84% live on campus; N/A of students in fraternities, N/A in sororities
Most popular majors: 16% Public Administration and Social Service Professions, 13% Business, Management, Marketing, and Related Support Services, 11% Health Professions and Related Programs, 11% Social Sciences, 10% Communication, Journalism, and Related Programs
Expenses: 2019-2020: $11,266 in state, $16,636 out of state; room/board: $9,828
Financial aid: (800) 561-2606; 90% of undergrads determined to have financial need; average aid package $12,656

Lock Haven University of Pennsylvania

Lock Haven PA
(570) 484-2011
U.S. News ranking: Reg. U. (N), No. 94
Website: www.lockhaven.edu
Admissions email: admissions@lockhaven.edu
Public; founded 1870
Freshman admissions: less selective; 2018-2019: 2,560 applied, 2,415 accepted. Either SAT or ACT required. SAT 25/75 percentile: 920-1110. High school rank: 11% in top tenth, 29% in top quarter, 63% in top half
Early decision deadline: N/A, notification date: N/A
Early action deadline: N/A, notification date: N/A
Application deadline (fall): rolling
Undergraduate student body: 2,798 full time, 269 part time; 42% male, 58% female; 1% American Indian, 1% Asian, 8% black, 4% Hispanic, 1% multiracial, 0% Pacific Islander, 83% white, 1% international; 95% from in state; 31% live on campus; 3% of students in fraternities, 4% in sororities
Most popular majors: 13% Health Professions and Related Clinical Sciences, Other, 11% Criminal Justice/Law Enforcement Administration, 9% Sport and Fitness Administration/Management, 8% Business Administration and Management, General, 5% Parks, Recreation and Leisure Facilities Management, General
Expenses: 2019-2020: $10,878 in state, $20,452 out of state; room/board: $10,368
Financial aid: (570) 484-2452; 75% of undergrads determined to have financial need; average aid package $9,869

Lycoming College

Williamsport PA
(800) 345-3920
U.S. News ranking: Nat. Lib. Arts, No. 117
Website: www.lycoming.edu
Admissions email: admissions@lycoming.edu
Private; founded 1812
Freshman admissions: selective; 2018-2019: 2,433 applied, 1,596 accepted. Neither SAT nor ACT required. SAT 25/75 percentile: 1010-1198. High school rank: 21% in top tenth, 46% in top quarter, 79% in top half
Early decision deadline: 11/15, notification date: 12/1
Early action deadline: 12/1, notification date: 12/15
Application deadline (fall): rolling
Undergraduate student body: 1,135 full time, 7 part time; 47% male, 53% female; 0% American Indian, 1% Asian, 13% black, 12% Hispanic, 3% multiracial, 0% Pacific Islander, 60% white, 6% international; 59% from in state; 87% live on campus; 14% of students in fraternities, 21% in sororities

Most popular majors: 20% Social Sciences, 18% Business, Management, Marketing, and Related Support Services, 13% Psychology, 10% Biological and Biomedical Sciences, 9% Visual and Performing Arts
Expenses: 2019-2020: $41,626; room/board: $13,008
Financial aid: (570) 321-4140; 86% of undergrads determined to have financial need; average aid package $40,139

Mansfield University of Pennsylvania

Mansfield PA
(800) 577-6826
U.S. News ranking: Nat. Lib. Arts, second tier
Website: www.mansfield.edu
Admissions email: admissns@mansfield.edu
Public; founded 1857
Freshman admissions: less selective; 2018-2019: 1,595 applied, 1,464 accepted. Either SAT or ACT required for some. SAT 25/75 percentile: 950-1130. High school rank: 8% in top tenth, 27% in top quarter, 67% in top half
Early decision deadline: N/A, notification date: N/A
Early action deadline: N/A, notification date: N/A
Application deadline (fall): rolling
Undergraduate student body: 1,453 full time, 146 part time; 39% male, 61% female; 0% American Indian, 1% Asian, 10% black, 3% Hispanic, 3% multiracial, 0% Pacific Islander, 80% white, 0% international; 17% from in state; 53% live on campus; N/A of students in fraternities, N/A in sororities
Most popular majors: 12% Health Professions and Related Programs, 12% Visual and Performing Arts, 8% Public Administration and Social Service Professions, 7% Homeland Security, Law Enforcement, Firefighting and Related Protective Services, 7% Liberal Arts and Sciences, General Studies and Humanities
Expenses: 2018-2019: $12,330 in state, $21,780 out of state; room/board: $11,928
Financial aid: N/A; 67% of undergrads determined to have financial need; average aid package $1,733

Marywood University

Scranton PA
(866) 279-9663
U.S. News ranking: Reg. U. (N), No. 42
Website: www.marywood.edu
Admissions email: YourFuture@marywood.edu
Private; founded 1915
Affiliation: Roman Catholic
Freshman admissions: selective; 2018-2019: 2,137 applied, 1,607 accepted. Either SAT or ACT required. SAT 25/75 percentile: 1010-1190. High school rank: 17% in top tenth, 45% in top quarter, 82% in top half

Early decision deadline: N/A, notification date: N/A
Early action deadline: N/A, notification date: N/A
Application deadline (fall): rolling
Undergraduate student body: 1,756 full time, 194 part time; 32% male, 68% female; 0% American Indian, 2% Asian, 3% black, 8% Hispanic, 2% multiracial, 0% Pacific Islander, 77% white, 2% international; 72% from in state; 35% live on campus; 6% of students in fraternities, 8% in sororities
Most popular majors: 34% Health Professions and Related Programs, 14% Business, Management, Marketing, and Related Support Services, 7% Architecture and Related Services, 7% Education, 6% Visual and Performing Arts
Expenses: 2019-2020: $35,900, room/board: $13,957
Financial aid: (570) 348-4500; 82% of undergrads determined to have financial need; average aid package $26,557

Mercyhurst University
Erie PA
(814) 824-2202
U.S. News ranking: Reg. U. (N), No. 48
Website: www.mercyhurst.edu
Admissions email: admug@mercyhurst.edu
Private; founded 1926
Affiliation: Roman Catholic
Freshman admissions: selective; 2018-2019: 3,084 applied, 2,676 accepted. Neither SAT nor ACT required. SAT 25/75 percentile: 1020-1210. High school rank: N/A
Early decision deadline: N/A, notification date: N/A
Early action deadline: N/A, notification date: N/A
Application deadline (fall): rolling
Undergraduate student body: 2,328 full time, 73 part time; 41% male, 59% female; 1% American Indian, 2% Asian, 5% black, 4% Hispanic, 2% multiracial, 0% Pacific Islander, 76% white, 7% international; 43% from in state; 74% live on campus; 0% of students in fraternities, 0% in sororities
Most popular majors: Information not available
Expenses: 2019-2020: $40,170; room/board: $12,880
Financial aid: (814) 824-2288; 76% of undergrads determined to have financial need; average aid package $39,703

Messiah College
Mechanicsburg PA
(717) 691-6000
U.S. News ranking: Reg. U. (N), No. 16
Website: www.messiah.edu
Admissions email: admissions@messiah.edu
Private; founded 1909
Affiliation: Interdenominational
Freshman admissions: more selective; 2018-2019: 2,530 applied, 1,996 accepted. Either SAT or ACT required. SAT 25/75 percentile: 1080-1310. High

school rank: 37% in top tenth, 61% in top quarter, 90% in top half
Early decision deadline: N/A, notification date: N/A
Early action deadline: N/A, notification date: N/A
Application deadline (fall): rolling
Undergraduate student body: 2,598 full time, 136 part time; 39% male, 61% female; 0% American Indian, 2% Asian, 2% black, 5% Hispanic, 3% multiracial, 0% Pacific Islander, 81% white, 5% international; 64% from in state; 88% live on campus; N/A of students in fraternities, N/A in sororities
Most popular majors: 11% Engineering, General, 6% Business Administration and Management, General, 6% Registered Nursing/Registered Nurse, 5% Health Professions and Related Programs, 4% Family and Community Services
Expenses: 2019-2020: $36,120; room/board: $10,580
Financial aid: (717) 691-6007; 72% of undergrads determined to have financial need; average aid package $25,358

Millersville University of Pennsylvania
Millersville PA
(717) 871-4625
U.S. News ranking: Reg. U. (N), No. 94
Website: www.millersville.edu
Admissions email: Admissions@millersville.edu
Public; founded 1855
Freshman admissions: selective; 2018-2019: 6,585 applied, 5,134 accepted. Either SAT or ACT required. SAT 25/75 percentile: 990-1180. High school rank: 10% in top tenth, 30% in top quarter, 68% in top half
Early decision deadline: N/A, notification date: N/A
Early action deadline: N/A, notification date: N/A
Application deadline (fall): rolling
Undergraduate student body: 5,557 full time, 1,222 part time; 43% male, 57% female; 0% American Indian, 3% Asian, 9% black, 11% Hispanic, 1% multiracial, 0% Pacific Islander, 74% white, 1% international; 92% from in state; 32% live on campus; 4% of students in fraternities, 4% in sororities
Most popular majors: 12% Business, Management, Marketing, and Related Support Services, 11% Education, 10% Social Sciences, 8% Health Professions and Related Programs, 8% Psychology
Expenses: 2019-2020: $12,250 in state, $21,970 out of state; room/board: $12,980
Financial aid: (717) 871-5100; 69% of undergrads determined to have financial need; average aid package $8,902

Misericordia University
Dallas PA
(570) 674-6264
U.S. News ranking: Nat. U., No. 192
Website: www.misericordia.edu/
Admissions email: admiss@misericordia.edu
Private; founded 1924
Affiliation: Roman Catholic
Freshman admissions: selective; 2018-2019: 1,652 applied, 1,365 accepted. Either SAT or ACT required. SAT 25/75 percentile: 1040-1200. High school rank: 20% in top tenth, 53% in top quarter, 82% in top half
Early decision deadline: N/A, notification date: N/A
Early action deadline: N/A, notification date: N/A
Application deadline (fall): rolling
Undergraduate student body: 1,614 full time, 416 part time; 31% male, 69% female; 0% American Indian, 1% Asian, 3% black, 3% Hispanic, 3% multiracial, 0% Pacific Islander, 86% white, 0% international; 73% from in state; 46% live on campus; 0% of students in fraternities, 0% in sororities
Most popular majors: 50% Health Professions and Related Programs, 15% Business, Management, Marketing, and Related Support Services, 7% Social Sciences, 6% Biological and Biomedical Sciences, 5% Psychology
Expenses: 2019-2020: $34,560; room/board: $14,220
Financial aid: (570) 674-6222; 82% of undergrads determined to have financial need; average aid package $24,707

Moore College of Art & Design[1]
Philadelphia PA
(215) 965-4015
U.S. News ranking: Arts; unranked
Website: www.moore.edu
Admissions email: admiss@moore.edu
Private; founded 1848
Application deadline (fall): rolling
Undergraduate student body: N/A full time, N/A part time
Expenses: N/A
Financial aid: N/A

Moravian College
Bethlehem PA
(610) 861-1320
U.S. News ranking: Nat. Lib. Arts, No. 136
Website: www.moravian.edu
Admissions email: admission@moravian.edu
Private; founded 1742
Affiliation: Moravian Church
Freshman admissions: selective; 2018-2019: 2,443 applied, 1,779 accepted. Either SAT or ACT required. SAT 25/75 percentile: 1050-1200. High school rank: 17% in top tenth, 48% in top quarter, 85% in top half

Early decision deadline: N/A, notification date: N/A
Early action deadline: N/A, notification date: N/A
Application deadline (fall): 3/1
Undergraduate student body: 1,919 full time, 220 part time; 39% male, 61% female; 0% American Indian, 2% Asian, 3% black, 11% Hispanic, 2% multiracial, 0% Pacific Islander, 72% white, 4% international; 73% from in state; 61% live on campus; 11% of students in fraternities, 11% in sororities
Most popular majors: 27% Health Professions and Related Programs, 19% Business, Management, Marketing, and Related Support Services, 14% Social Sciences, 8% Psychology, 6% Biological and Biomedical Sciences
Expenses: 2019-2020: $45,312; room/board: $13,914
Financial aid: (610) 861-1330; 82% of undergrads determined to have financial need; average aid package $30,917

Mount Aloysius College[7]
Cresson PA
(814) 886-6383
U.S. News ranking: Reg. Coll. (N), No. 34
Website: www.mtaloy.edu
Admissions email: admissions@mtaloy.edu
Private; founded 1853
Freshman admissions: less selective; 2018-2019: 2,453 applied, 1,117 accepted. Either SAT or ACT required. SAT 25/75 percentile: 943-1120. High school rank: N/A
Early decision deadline: N/A, notification date: N/A
Early action deadline: N/A, notification date: N/A
Application deadline (fall): rolling
Undergraduate student body: 992 full time, 741 part time
Most popular majors: 40% Health Professions and Related Programs, 19% Business, Management, Marketing, and Related Support Services, 10% Biological and Biomedical Sciences, 6% Computer and Information Sciences and Support Services, 6% Homeland Security, Law Enforcement, Firefighting and Related Protective Services
Expenses: 2019-2020: $23,680; room/board: $10,966
Financial aid: (814) 886-6357; 87% of undergrads determined to have financial need; average aid package $13,900

Muhlenberg College
Allentown PA
(484) 664-3200
U.S. News ranking: Nat. Lib. Arts, No. 72
Website: www.muhlenberg.edu
Admissions email: admissions@muhlenberg.edu
Private; founded 1848
Affiliation: Lutheran Church in America
Freshman admissions: more selective; 2018-2019: 4,146 applied, 2,562 accepted. Either

SAT or ACT required for some. SAT 25/75 percentile: 1170-1360. High school rank: 40% in top tenth, 70% in top quarter, 94% in top half
Early decision deadline: 11/15, notification date: 12/15
Early action deadline: N/A, notification date: N/A
Application deadline (fall): 2/1
Undergraduate student body: 2,248 full time, 92 part time; 39% male, 61% female; 0% American Indian, 3% Asian, 4% black, 8% Hispanic, 2% multiracial, 0% Pacific Islander, 72% white, 4% international; 30% from in state; 91% live on campus; 4% of students in fraternities, 11% in sororities
Most popular majors: 11% Business Administration and Management, General, 9% Drama and Dramatics/Theatre Arts, General, 9% Mass Communication/Media Studies, 8% Finance, General, 7% Psychology, General
Expenses: 2019-2020: $54,600; room/board: $12,165
Financial aid: (484) 664-3175; 61% of undergrads determined to have financial need; average aid package $37,874

Neumann University
Aston PA
(610) 558-5616
U.S. News ranking: Reg. U. (N), second tier
Website: www.neumann.edu
Admissions email: neumann@neumann.edu
Private; founded 1965
Affiliation: Roman Catholic
Freshman admissions: less selective; 2018-2019: 3,112 applied, 2,148 accepted. Either SAT or ACT required. SAT 25/75 percentile: 910-1090. High school rank: N/A
Early decision deadline: N/A, notification date: N/A
Early action deadline: 12/1, notification date: 12/25
Application deadline (fall): rolling
Undergraduate student body: 1,432 full time, 563 part time; 34% male, 66% female; 0% American Indian, 2% Asian, 26% black, 6% Hispanic, 3% multiracial, 0% Pacific Islander, 55% white, 1% international; 68% from in state; 52% live on campus; N/A of students in fraternities, N/A in sororities
Most popular majors: 19% Registered Nursing, Nursing Administration, Nursing Research and Clinical Nursing, Other, 15% Homeland Security, Law Enforcement, Firefighting and Related Protective Services, Other, 14% Liberal Arts and Sciences/Liberal Studies, 9% Business Administration and Management, General, 7% Psychology, General
Expenses: 2019-2020: $32,960; room/board: $13,680
Financial aid: (610) 558-5521; 85% of undergrads determined to have financial need; average aid package $22,378

Peirce College

Philadelphia PA
(888) 467-3472
U.S. News ranking: Reg. Coll. (N), unranked
Website: www.peirce.edu
Admissions email: info@peirce.edu
Private; founded 1865
Freshman admissions: least selective; 2018-2019: N/A applied, N/A accepted. Neither SAT nor ACT required. SAT 25/75 percentile: N/A. High school rank: N/A
Early decision deadline: N/A, notification date: N/A
Early action deadline: N/A, notification date: N/A
Application deadline (fall): rolling
Undergraduate student body: 278 full time, 993 part time; 28% male, 72% female; 0% American Indian, 3% Asian, 62% black, 7% Hispanic, 2% multiracial, 0% Pacific Islander, 18% white, 1% international
Most popular majors: 42% Business, Management, Marketing, and Related Support Services, 24% Computer and Information Sciences and Support Services, 16% Health Professions and Related Programs, 14% Legal Professions and Studies, 4% Homeland Security, Law Enforcement, Firefighting and Related Protective Services
Expenses: 2018-2019: $15,060; room/board: N/A
Financial aid: N/A

Pennsylvania Academy of the Fine Arts[1]

Philadelphia PA
(215) 972-7625
U.S. News ranking: Arts, unranked
Website: www.pafa.edu
Admissions email: admissions@pafa.edu
Private; founded 1805
Application deadline (fall): 8/29
Undergraduate student body: N/A full time, N/A part time
Expenses: 2019-2020: $40,376; room/board: $12,010
Financial aid: N/A; 100% of undergrads determined to have financial need

Pennsylvania College of Art and Design

Lancaster PA
(800) 689-0379
U.S. News ranking: Arts, unranked
Website: pcad.edu
Admissions email: admissions@pcad.edu
Private; founded 1982
Freshman admissions: less selective; 2018-2019: 302 applied, 131 accepted. Neither SAT nor ACT required. SAT 25/75 percentile: 856-1166. High school rank: 10% in top tenth, 17% in top quarter, 52% in top half
Early decision deadline: N/A, notification date: N/A
Early action deadline: N/A, notification date: N/A
Application deadline (fall): rolling

Undergraduate student body: 242 full time, 9 part time; 33% male, 67% female; 1% American Indian, 5% Asian, 6% black, 4% Hispanic, 6% multiracial, 0% Pacific Islander, 73% white, 0% international; N/A from in state; 23% live on campus; N/A of students in fraternities, N/A in sororities
Most popular majors: 39% Illustration, 22% Graphic Design, 17% Game and Interactive Media Design, 11% Fine/Studio Arts, General, 1% Photography
Expenses: 2018-2019: $25,850; room/board: $10,225
Financial aid: N/A

Pennsylvania College of Technology

Williamsport PA
(570) 327-4761
U.S. News ranking: Reg. Coll. (N), No. 14
Website: www.pct.edu
Admissions email: admissions@pct.edu
Public; founded 1914
Freshman admissions: less selective; 2018-2019: 3,921 applied, 3,224 accepted. Neither SAT nor ACT required. SAT 25/75 percentile: 980-1180. High school rank: 4% in top tenth, 21% in top quarter, 54% in top half
Early decision deadline: N/A, notification date: N/A
Early action deadline: N/A, notification date: N/A
Application deadline (fall): 7/1
Undergraduate student body: 4,378 full time, 944 part time; 63% male, 37% female; 0% American Indian, 1% Asian, 3% black, 4% Hispanic, 2% multiracial, 0% Pacific Islander, 88% white, 0% international; 90% from in state; 31% live on campus; 1% of students in fraternities, N/A in sororities
Most popular majors: 30% Engineering Technologies and Engineering-Related Fields, 22% Health Professions and Related Programs, 15% Business, Management, Marketing, and Related Support Services, 10% Computer and Information Sciences and Support Services, 9% Construction Trades
Expenses: 2019-2020: $17,400 in state, $24,840 out of state; room/board: $10,896
Financial aid: (570) 327-4766; 78% of undergrads determined to have financial need

Pennsylvania State University–Erie, The Behrend College

Erie PA
(814) 898-6100
U.S. News ranking: Unranked
Website: behrend.psu.edu/
Admissions email: behrend.admissions@psu.edu
Public; founded 1948
Freshman admissions: N/A; 2018-2019: 3,392 applied, 3,023 accepted. Either SAT or ACT

required. SAT 25/75 percentile: 1050-1280. High school rank: 19% in top tenth, 45% in top quarter, 83% in top half
Early decision deadline: N/A, notification date: N/A
Early action deadline: N/A, notification date: N/A
Application deadline (fall): rolling
Undergraduate student body: 3,964 full time, 188 part time; 66% male, 34% female; 0% American Indian, 4% Asian, 3% black, 3% Hispanic, 3% multiracial, 0% Pacific Islander, 78% white, 9% international; N/A from in state; 38% live on campus; N/A of students in fraternities, N/A in sororities
Most popular majors: 36% Business, Management, Marketing, and Related Support Services, 27% Engineering, 6% Biological and Biomedical Sciences, 5% Engineering Technologies and Engineering-Related Fields, 5% Health Professions and Related Programs
Expenses: 2018-2019: $15,198 in state, $24,450 out of state; room/board: $11,570
Financial aid: (814) 865-6301

Pennsylvania State University–Harrisburg[1]

Middletown PA
(717) 948-6250
U.S. News ranking: Unranked
Website: www.hbg.psu.edu/
Admissions email: hbgadmit@psu.edu
Public
Application deadline (fall): N/A
Undergraduate student body: N/A full time, N/A part time
Expenses: N/A
Financial aid: N/A

Pennsylvania State University–University Park

University Park PA
(814) 865-5471
U.S. News ranking: Nat. U., No. 57
Website: www.psu.edu
Admissions email: admissions@psu.edu
Public; founded 1855
Freshman admissions: more selective; 2018-2019: 52,742 applied, 29,793 accepted. Either SAT or ACT required. SAT 25/75 percentile: 1160-1360. High school rank: 43% in top tenth, 76% in top quarter, 96% in top half
Early decision deadline: N/A, notification date: N/A
Early action deadline: 11/1, notification date: 12/24
Application deadline (fall): rolling
Undergraduate student body: 39,321 full time, 1,042 part time; 53% male, 47% female; 0% American Indian, 6% Asian, 4% black, 7% Hispanic, 3% multiracial, 0% Pacific Islander, 66% white, 12% international; N/A from in state; 35% live on campus; 17% of students in fraternities, 20% in sororities

Most popular majors: 18% Engineering, 16% Business, Management, Marketing, and Related Support Services, 9% Computer and Information Sciences and Support Services, 8% Social Sciences, 7% Communication, Journalism, and Related Programs
Expenses: 2019-2020: $18,450 in state, $35,514 out of state; room/board: $11,884
Financial aid: (814) 865-6301; 48% of undergrads determined to have financial need; average aid package $10,939

Pittsburgh Technical College[1]

Oakdale PA
(412) 809-5100
U.S. News ranking: Reg. Coll. (N), unranked
Website: www.btc.edu
Admissions email: N/A
Private
Application deadline (fall): N/A
Undergraduate student body: N/A full time, N/A part time
Expenses: N/A
Financial aid: N/A

Point Park University

Pittsburgh PA
(800) 321-0129
U.S. News ranking: Reg. U. (N), No. 80
Website: www.pointpark.edu
Admissions email: enroll@pointpark.edu
Private; founded 1960
Freshman admissions: selective; 2018-2019: 5,834 applied, 3,796 accepted. Either SAT or ACT required. SAT 25/75 percentile: 980-1190. High school rank: 10% in top tenth, 32% in top quarter, 68% in top half
Early decision deadline: N/A, notification date: N/A
Early action deadline: N/A, notification date: N/A
Application deadline (fall): rolling
Undergraduate student body: 2,749 full time, 447 part time; 40% male, 60% female; 0% American Indian, 2% Asian, 13% black, 6% Hispanic, 4% multiracial, 0% Pacific Islander, 72% white, 4% international
Most popular majors: 11% Business, Management, Marketing, and Related Support Services, Other, 10% Drama and Dramatics/Theatre Arts, General, 9% Dance, General, 7% Business Administration and Management, General, 6% Cinematography and Film/Video Production
Expenses: 2019-2020: $32,750; room/board: $12,440
Financial aid: (412) 392-3930; 93% of undergrads determined to have financial need; average aid package $25,601

Robert Morris University

Moon Township PA
(412) 397-5200
U.S. News ranking: Nat. U., No. 202
Website: www.rmu.edu
Admissions email: admissions@rmu.edu
Private; founded 1921
Freshman admissions: selective; 2018-2019: 6,638 applied, 5,641 accepted. Either SAT or ACT required. SAT 25/75 percentile: 1030-1200. High school rank: 15% in top tenth, 42% in top quarter, 76% in top half
Early decision deadline: N/A, notification date: N/A
Early action deadline: N/A, notification date: N/A
Application deadline (fall): rolling
Undergraduate student body: 3,683 full time, 322 part time; 56% male, 44% female; 0% American Indian, 1% Asian, 6% black, 3% Hispanic, 3% multiracial, 0% Pacific Islander, 74% white, 11% international; 86% from in state; 48% live on campus; 10% of students in fraternities, 14% in sororities
Most popular majors: 14% Engineering, Other, 9% Registered Nursing/Registered Nurse, 8% Accounting, 6% Business Administration and Management, General, 5% Manufacturing Engineering
Expenses: 2019-2020: $31,200; room/board: $11,780
Financial aid: (412) 397-6250; 71% of undergrads determined to have financial need; average aid package $24,222

Rosemont College

Rosemont PA
(610) 526-2966
U.S. News ranking: Reg. U. (N), second tier
Website: www.rosemont.edu
Admissions email: admissions@rosemont.edu
Private; founded 1921
Affiliation: Roman Catholic
Freshman admissions: less selective; 2018-2019: 1,221 applied, 797 accepted. Either SAT or ACT required. SAT 25/75 percentile: 910-1140. High school rank: N/A
Early decision deadline: N/A, notification date: N/A
Early action deadline: N/A, notification date: N/A
Application deadline (fall): 8/27
Undergraduate student body: 462 full time, 110 part time; 36% male, 64% female; 0% American Indian, 2% Asian, 44% black, 6% Hispanic, 3% multiracial, 0% Pacific Islander, 39% white, 2% international
Most popular majors: 40% Business, Management, Marketing, and Related Support Services, 23% Social Sciences, 10% Biological and Biomedical Sciences, 9% English Language and Literature/Letters, 6% Visual and Performing Arts

Expenses: 2018-2019: $19,900; room/board: $12,438 ·
Financial aid: (610) 527-0200

Saint Vincent College
Latrobe PA
(800) 782-5549
U.S. News ranking: Nat. Lib. Arts, No. 132
Website: www.stvincent.edu
Admissions email: admission@stvincent.edu
Private; founded 1846
Freshman admissions: selective; 2018-2019: 2,354 applied, 1,609 accepted. Either SAT or ACT required. SAT 25/75 percentile: 1030-1230. High school rank: 22% in top tenth, 38% in top quarter, 75% in top half
Early decision deadline: N/A, notification date: N/A
Early action deadline: N/A, notification date: N/A
Application deadline (fall): 5/1
Undergraduate student body: 1,595 full time, 81 part time; 55% male, 45% female; 0% American Indian, 1% Asian, 6% black, 3% Hispanic, 2% multiracial, 0% Pacific Islander, 83% white, 1% international; 77% from in state; 72% live on campus; N/A of students in fraternities, N/A in sororities
Most popular majors: 29% Business, Management, Marketing, and Related Support Services, 14% Biological and Biomedical Sciences, 11% Social Sciences, 7% Psychology, 6% Communication, Journalism, and Related Programs
Expenses: 2019-2020: $36,914; room/board: $11,802
Financial aid: (724) 805-2555; 78% of undergrads determined to have financial need; average aid package $31,951

Seton Hill University
Greensburg PA
(724) 838-4255
U.S. News ranking: Reg. U. (N), No. 48
Website: www.setonhill.edu
Admissions email: admit@setonhill.edu
Private; founded 1883
Affiliation: Roman Catholic
Freshman admissions: selective; 2018-2019: 2,471 applied, 1,853 accepted. Neither SAT nor ACT required. SAT 25/75 percentile: 1020-1240. High school rank: 19% in top tenth, 45% in top quarter, 77% in top half
Early decision deadline: N/A, notification date: N/A
Early action deadline: N/A, notification date: N/A
Application deadline (fall): 8/15
Undergraduate student body: 1,592 full time, 118 part time; 36% male, 64% female; 0% American Indian, 1% Asian, 9% black, 4% Hispanic, 3% multiracial, 0% Pacific Islander, 81% white, 2% international; N/A from in state; 55% live on campus; N/A of students in fraternities, N/A in sororities

Most popular majors: 26% Business, Management, Marketing, and Related Support Services, 11% Visual and Performing Arts, 10% Health Professions and Related Programs, 7% Biological and Biomedical Sciences, 7% Parks, Recreation, Leisure, and Fitness Studies
Expenses: 2019-2020: $36,856; room/board: $12,212
Financial aid: (724) 830-1010; 82% of undergrads determined to have financial need; average aid package $27,989

Shippensburg University of Pennsylvania
Shippensburg PA
(717) 477-1231
U.S. News ranking: Reg. U. (N), No. 100
Website: www.ship.edu
Admissions email: admiss@ship.edu
Public; founded 1871
Freshman admissions: selective; 2018-2019: 5,540 applied, 4,854 accepted. Either SAT or ACT required. SAT 25/75 percentile: 970-1170. High school rank: 9% in top tenth, 27% in top quarter, 59% in top half
Early decision deadline: N/A, notification date: N/A
Early action deadline: N/A, notification date: N/A
Application deadline (fall): rolling
Undergraduate student body: 5,018 full time, 483 part time; 48% male, 52% female; 0% American Indian, 2% Asian, 11% black, 6% Hispanic, 4% multiracial, 0% Pacific Islander, 75% white, 1% international; 93% from in state; 33% live on campus; 10% of students in fraternities, 10% in sororities
Most popular majors: 9% Psychology, General, 8% Business Administration and Management, General, 7% Criminal Justice/Safety Studies, 6% Journalism, 6% Marketing/Marketing Management, General
Expenses: 2019-2020: $12,744 in state, $20,536 out of state; room/board: $13,114
Financial aid: (717) 477-1131; 71% of undergrads determined to have financial need; average aid package $9,929

Slippery Rock University of Pennsylvania
Slippery Rock PA
(800) 929-4778
U.S. News ranking: Reg. U. (N), No. 75
Website: www.sru.edu/admissions
Admissions email: asktherock@sru.edu
Public; founded 1889
Freshman admissions: selective; 2018-2019: 5,369 applied, 3,928 accepted. Either SAT or ACT required. SAT 25/75 percentile: 1010-1170. High school rank: 11% in top tenth, 35% in top quarter, 71% in top half

Early decision deadline: N/A, notification date: N/A
Early action deadline: N/A, notification date: N/A
Application deadline (fall): rolling
Undergraduate student body: 7,032 full time, 506 part time; 44% male, 56% female; 0% American Indian, 1% Asian, 5% black, 3% Hispanic, 4% multiracial, 0% Pacific Islander, 85% white, 1% international; 91% from in state; 36% live on campus; 6% of students in fraternities, 7% in sororities
Most popular majors: 24% Health Professions and Related Programs, 10% Business, Management, Marketing, and Related Support Services, 9% Education, 9% Engineering Technologies and Engineering-Related Fields, 9% Parks, Recreation, Leisure, and Fitness Studies
Expenses: 2019-2020: $10,498 in state, $14,356 out of state; room/board: $10,530
Financial aid: (724) 738-2044; 70% of undergrads determined to have financial need; average aid package $9,246

St. Francis University
Loretto PA
(814) 472-3100
U.S. News ranking: Reg. U. (N), No. 23
Website: www.francis.edu/undergraduate_admissions
Admissions email: admissions@francis.edu
Private; founded 1847
Affiliation: Roman Catholic
Freshman admissions: selective; 2018-2019: 1,706 applied, 1,286 accepted. Either SAT or ACT required. SAT 25/75 percentile: 1040-1250. High school rank: 31% in top tenth, 60% in top quarter, 87% in top half
Early decision deadline: N/A, notification date: N/A
Early action deadline: N/A, notification date: N/A
Application deadline (fall): rolling
Undergraduate student body: 1,485 full time, 626 part time; 35% male, 65% female; 0% American Indian, 2% Asian, 8% black, 2% Hispanic, 2% multiracial, 0% Pacific Islander, 81% white, 1% international; 80% from in state; 61% live on campus; 1% of students in fraternities, 2% in sororities
Most popular majors: 13% Physician Assistant, 8% Occupational Therapy/Therapist, 7% Registered Nursing/Registered Nurse, 4% Physical Therapy/Therapist, 4% Psychology, General
Expenses: 2018-2019: $36,410; room/board: $12,290
Financial aid: (814) 472-3010

St. Joseph's University
Philadelphia PA
(610) 660-1300
U.S. News ranking: Reg. U. (N), No. 10
Website: www.sju.edu
Admissions email: admit@sju.edu
Private; founded 1851

Affiliation: Roman Catholic
Freshman admissions: more selective; 2018-2019: 8,843 applied, 6,749 accepted. Neither SAT nor ACT required. SAT 25/75 percentile: 1120-1290. High school rank: 19% in top tenth, 50% in top quarter, 79% in top half
Early decision deadline: 11/1, notification date: 12/20
Early action deadline: 11/1, notification date: 12/20
Application deadline (fall): rolling
Undergraduate student body: 4,350 full time, 554 part time; 45% male, 55% female; 0% American Indian, 3% Asian, 6% black, 7% Hispanic, 3% multiracial, 0% Pacific Islander, 78% white, 2% international; 47% from in state; 48% live on campus; 7% of students in fraternities, 24% in sororities
Most popular majors: 56% Business, Management, Marketing, and Related Support Services, 8% Education, 7% Social Sciences, 5% Communication, Journalism, and Related Programs, 5% Psychology
Expenses: 2019-2020: $46,550; room/board: $14,840
Financial aid: (610) 660-1346; 62% of undergrads determined to have financial need; average aid package $31,086

Susquehanna University
Selinsgrove PA
(800) 326-9672
U.S. News ranking: Nat. Lib. Arts, No. 117
Website: www.susqu.edu
Admissions email: suadmiss@susqu.edu
Private; founded 1858
Affiliation: Evangelical Lutheran Church
Freshman admissions: selective; 2018-2019: 5,690 applied, 4,116 accepted. Neither SAT nor ACT required. SAT 25/75 percentile: 1098-1260. High school rank: 21% in top tenth, 51% in top quarter, 85% in top half
Early decision deadline: 11/15, notification date: 12/1
Early action deadline: 11/1, notification date: 12/1
Application deadline (fall): rolling
Undergraduate student body: 2,215 full time, 82 part time; 44% male, 56% female; 0% American Indian, 2% Asian, 6% black, 7% Hispanic, 3% multiracial, 0% Pacific Islander, 79% white, 2% international; N/A from in state; 93% live on campus; 21% of students in fraternities, 18% in sororities
Most popular majors: 20% Business, Management, Marketing, and Related Support Services, 14% Biological and Biomedical Sciences, 10% Communication, Journalism, and Related Programs, 10% English Language and Literature/Letters, 8% Psychology
Expenses: 2019-2020: $49,180; room/board: $13,140

Financial aid: (570) 372-4450; 84% of undergrads determined to have financial need; average aid package $37,730

Swarthmore College
Swarthmore PA
(610) 328-8300
U.S. News ranking: Nat. Lib. Arts, No. 3
Website: www.swarthmore.edu
Admissions email: admissions@swarthmore.edu
Private; founded 1864
Freshman admissions: most selective; 2018-2019: 10,749 applied, 1,020 accepted. Either SAT or ACT required. SAT 25/75 percentile: 1380-1550. High school rank: 90% in top tenth, 99% in top quarter, 100% in top half
Early decision deadline: 11/15, notification date: 12/15
Early action deadline: N/A, notification date: N/A
Application deadline (fall): 1/1
Undergraduate student body: 1,554 full time, 5 part time; 49% male, 51% female; 0% American Indian, 17% Asian, 8% black, 13% Hispanic, 7% multiracial, 0% Pacific Islander, 39% white, 13% international; 37% from in state; 96% live on campus; 0% of students in fraternities, 0% in sororities
Most popular majors: 27% Social Sciences, 13% Computer and Information Sciences and Support Services, 12% Biological and Biomedical Sciences, 7% Engineering, 7% Mathematics and Statistics
Expenses: 2019-2020: $54,656; room/board: $16,088
Financial aid: (610) 328-8358; 56% of undergrads determined to have financial need; average aid package $52,814

Temple University
Philadelphia PA
(215) 204-7200
U.S. News ranking: Nat. U., No. 104
Website: www.temple.edu
Admissions email: askanowl@temple.edu
Public; founded 1884
Freshman admissions: more selective; 2018-2019: 35,501 applied, 20,771 accepted. Neither SAT nor ACT required. SAT 25/75 percentile: 1130-1320. High school rank: 23% in top tenth, 56% in top quarter, 91% in top half
Early decision deadline: N/A, notification date: N/A
Early action deadline: 11/1, notification date: 1/10
Application deadline (fall): 2/1
Undergraduate student body: 26,784 full time, 2,700 part time; 47% male, 53% female; 0% American Indian, 12% Asian, 13% black, 7% Hispanic, 3% multiracial, 0% Pacific Islander, 56% white, 6% international; 79% from in state; 20% live on campus; 2% of students in fraternities, 3% in sororities

Most popular majors: 26% Business, Management, Marketing, and Related Support Services, 13% Communication, Journalism, and Related Programs, 7% Visual and Performing Arts, 6% Health Professions and Related Programs, 6% Parks, Recreation, Leisure, and Fitness Studies
Expenses: 2019-2020: $19,748 in state, $34,126 out of state; room/board: $12,188
Financial aid: (215) 204-2244; 68% of undergrads determined to have financial need; average aid package $12,383

Thiel College
Greenville PA
(800) 248-4435
U.S. News ranking: Reg. Coll. (N), No. 29
Website: www.thiel.edu
Admissions email: admission@thiel.edu
Private; founded 1866
Affiliation: Evangelical Lutheran Church
Freshman admissions: least selective; 2018-2019: 1,821 applied, 1,386 accepted. Either SAT or ACT required. SAT 25/75 percentile: 860-1080. High school rank: 5% in top tenth, 22% in top quarter, 53% in top half
Early decision deadline: N/A, notification date: N/A
Early action deadline: N/A, notification date: N/A
Application deadline (fall): rolling
Undergraduate student body: 730 full time, 4 part time; 57% male, 43% female; 0% American Indian, 2% Asian, 17% black, 4% Hispanic, 4% multiracial, 0% Pacific Islander, 72% white, 0% international
Most popular majors: Information not available
Expenses: 2019-2020: $32,596; room/board: $13,040
Financial aid: (724) 589-2178; 92% of undergrads determined to have financial need; average aid package $25,806

Thomas Jefferson University
Philadelphia PA
(800) 951-7287
U.S. News ranking: Nat. U., No. 153
Website: www.jefferson.edu/
Admissions email: admissions@PhilaU.edu
Private; founded 1824
Freshman admissions: selective; 2018-2019: 4,522 applied, 2,635 accepted. Either SAT or ACT required. SAT 25/75 percentile: 1060-1240. High school rank: 25% in top tenth, 51% in top quarter, 82% in top half
Early decision deadline: N/A, notification date: N/A
Early action deadline: N/A, notification date: 11/15
Application deadline (fall): rolling
Undergraduate student body: 2,942 full time, 662 part time; 27% male, 73% female; 0% American Indian, 8% Asian, 15% black,

8% Hispanic, 3% multiracial, 0% Pacific Islander, 56% white, 3% international
Most popular majors: Architecture, Business Administration and Management, General, Diagnostic Medical Sonography/Sonographer and Ultrasound Technician, Family Practice Nurse/Nursing, Fashion Merchandising
Expenses: 2019-2020: $41,715; room/board: $13,881
Financial aid: (215) 951-2940; 83% of undergrads determined to have financial need; average aid package $28,738

University of Pennsylvania
Philadelphia PA
(215) 898-7507
U.S. News ranking: Nat. U., No. 6
Website: www.upenn.edu
Admissions email: info@admissions.upenn.edu
Private; founded 1740
Freshman admissions: most selective; 2018-2019: 44,491 applied, 3,740 accepted. Either SAT or ACT required. SAT 25/75 percentile: 1440-1560. High school rank: 96% in top tenth, 99% in top quarter, 100% in top half
Early decision deadline: 11/1, notification date: 12/15
Early action deadline: N/A, notification date: N/A
Application deadline (fall): 1/5
Undergraduate student body: 9,931 full time, 252 part time; 48% male, 52% female; 0% American Indian, 21% Asian, 7% black, 10% Hispanic, 5% multiracial, 0% Pacific Islander, 41% white, 13% international; N/A from in state; 51% live on campus; 30% of students in fraternities, 28% in sororities
Most popular majors: 20% Business, Management, Marketing, and Related Support Services, 15% Social Sciences, 11% Biological and Biomedical Sciences, 10% Engineering, 10% Health Professions and Related Programs
Expenses: 2019-2020: $57,770; room/board: $16,190
Financial aid: (215) 898-1988; 46% of undergrads determined to have financial need; average aid package $51,860

University of Pittsburgh
Pittsburgh PA
(412) 624-7488
U.S. News ranking: Nat. U., No. 57
Website: www.oafa.pitt.edu/
Admissions email: oafa@pitt.edu
Public; founded 1787
Freshman admissions: more selective; 2018-2019: 29,857 applied, 17,696 accepted. Either SAT or ACT required. SAT 25/75 percentile: 1270-1430. High school rank: 55% in top tenth, 88% in top quarter, 99% in top half
Early decision deadline: N/A, notification date: N/A
Early action deadline: N/A, notification date: N/A

Application deadline (fall): rolling
Undergraduate student body: 18,421 full time, 909 part time; 48% male, 52% female; 0% American Indian, 10% Asian, 5% black, 4% Hispanic, 4% multiracial, 0% Pacific Islander, 70% white, 5% international; 73% from in state; 43% live on campus; 9% of students in fraternities, 11% in sororities
Most popular majors: 16% Business, Management, Marketing, and Related Support Services, 14% Engineering, 12% Health Professions and Related Programs, 10% Social Sciences, 9% Biological and Biomedical Sciences
Expenses: 2019-2020: $19,718 in state, $33,746 out of state; room/board: $11,250
Financial aid: (412) 624-7180; 51% of undergrads determined to have financial need; average aid package $12,443

University of Scranton
Scranton PA
(570) 941-7540
U.S. News ranking: Reg. U. (N), No. 6
Website: www.scranton.edu
Admissions email: admissions@scranton.edu
Private; founded 1888
Affiliation: Roman Catholic
Freshman admissions: more selective; 2018-2019: 9,968 applied, 7,296 accepted. Either SAT or ACT required. SAT 25/75 percentile: 1120-1280. High school rank: 30% in top tenth, 65% in top quarter, 90% in top half
Early decision deadline: N/A, notification date: N/A
Early action deadline: 11/15, notification date: 12/15
Application deadline (fall): 3/1
Undergraduate student body: 3,565 full time, 164 part time; 43% male, 57% female; 0% American Indian, 3% Asian, 2% black, 10% Hispanic, 2% multiracial, 0% Pacific Islander, 79% white, 1% international; 60% from in state; 65% live on campus; N/A of students in fraternities, N/A in sororities
Most popular majors: 21% Business, Management, Marketing, and Related Support Services, 21% Health Professions and Related Programs, 14% Biological and Biomedical Sciences, 7% Parks, Recreation, Leisure, and Fitness Studies, 6% Communication, Journalism, and Related Programs
Expenses: 2019-2020: $45,790; room/board: $15,366
Financial aid: (570) 941-7701; 76% of undergrads determined to have financial need; average aid package $31,744

University of the Arts[1]
Philadelphia PA
(215) 717-6049
U.S. News ranking: Arts, unranked
Website: www.uarts.edu
Admissions email: admissions@uarts.edu
Private; founded 1876
Application deadline (fall): rolling
Undergraduate student body: N/A full time, N/A part time
Expenses: N/A
Financial aid: (215) 717-6170

University of Valley Forge
Phoenixville PA
(800) 432-8322
U.S. News ranking: Reg. Coll. (N), No. 32
Website: www.valleyforge.edu/
Admissions email: admissions@valleyforge.edu
Private; founded 1939
Affiliation: Assemblies of God Church
Freshman admissions: selective; 2018-2019: 374 applied, 221 accepted. Neither SAT nor ACT required. SAT 25/75 percentile: 960-1148. High school rank: 7% in top tenth, 23% in top quarter, 58% in top half
Early decision deadline: N/A, notification date: N/A
Early action deadline: N/A, notification date: N/A
Application deadline (fall): 8/1
Undergraduate student body: 491 full time, 118 part time; 48% male, 52% female; 0% American Indian, 2% Asian, 16% black, 16% Hispanic, 5% multiracial, 0% Pacific Islander, 56% white, 1% international; 48% from in state; 74% live on campus; 0% of students in fraternities, 0% in sororities
Most popular majors: 20% Divinity/Ministry, 15% Digital Communication and Media/Multimedia, 13% Psychology, General, 11% Youth Ministry, 6% Social Work
Expenses: 2019-2020: $22,000; room/board: $9,130
Financial aid: (610) 917-1475; 85% of undergrads determined to have financial need; average aid package $16,402

Ursinus College
Collegeville PA
(610) 409-3200
U.S. News ranking: Nat. Lib. Arts, No. 82
Website: www.ursinus.edu
Admissions email: admission@ursinus.edu
Private; founded 1869
Freshman admissions: more selective; 2018-2019: 3,361 applied, 2,382 accepted. Either SAT or ACT required for some. SAT 25/75 percentile: 1140-1320. High school rank: 20% in top tenth, 51% in top quarter, 78% in top half
Early decision deadline: 12/1, notification date: 12/15
Early action deadline: 11/1, notification date: 12/15
Application deadline (fall): 2/1

Undergraduate student body: 1,408 full time, 27 part time; 49% male, 51% female; 0% American Indian, 4% Asian, 8% black, 8% Hispanic, 3% multiracial, 0% Pacific Islander, 73% white, 2% international; 60% from in state; 93% live on campus; N/A of students in fraternities, N/A in sororities
Most popular majors: 35% Biological and Biomedical Sciences, 18% Social Sciences, 8% Psychology, 7% Communication, Journalism, and Related Programs, 7% English Language and Literature/Letters
Expenses: 2019-2020: $53,610; room/board: $13,120
Financial aid: (610) 409-3600; 76% of undergrads determined to have financial need; average aid package $42,001

Villanova University
Villanova PA
(610) 519-4000
U.S. News ranking: Nat. U., No. 46
Website: www.villanova.edu
Admissions email: gotovu@villanova.edu
Private; founded 1842
Affiliation: Roman Catholic
Freshman admissions: most selective; 2018-2019: 22,741 applied, 6,645 accepted. Either SAT or ACT required. SAT 25/75 percentile: 1300-1470. High school rank: 72% in top tenth, 93% in top quarter, 99% in top half
Early decision deadline: 11/1, notification date: 12/20
Early action deadline: 11/1, notification date: 1/15
Application deadline (fall): 1/15
Undergraduate student body: 6,565 full time, 352 part time; 47% male, 53% female; 0% American Indian, 6% Asian, 5% black, 8% Hispanic, 3% multiracial, 0% Pacific Islander, 75% white, 2% international; 21% from in state; 67% live on campus; 19% of students in fraternities, 39% in sororities
Most popular majors: 26% Business, Management, Marketing, and Related Support Services, 15% Engineering, 13% Health Professions and Related Programs, 12% Social Sciences, 8% Communication, Journalism, and Related Programs
Expenses: 2019-2020: $55,430; room/board: $14,444
Financial aid: (610) 519-4010; 48% of undergrads determined to have financial need; average aid package $40,651

Washington and Jefferson College
Washington PA
(724) 223-6025
U.S. News ranking: Nat. Lib. Arts, No. 92
Website: www.washjeff.edu
Admissions email: admission@washjeff.edu
Private; founded 1781
Freshman admissions: more selective; 2018-2019: N/A applied, N/A accepted. Neither

SAT nor ACT required. SAT 25/75 percentile: 1130-1320. High school rank: 32% in top tenth, 62% in top quarter, 89% in top half
Early decision deadline: 12/1, notification date: 12/15
Early action deadline: 1/15, notification date: 2/15
Application deadline (fall): 3/1
Undergraduate student body: 1,350 full time, 6 part time; 51% male, 49% female; 0% American Indian, 2% Asian, 5% black, 5% Hispanic, 4% multiracial, 0% Pacific Islander, 74% white, 3% international; 23% from in state; 93% live on campus; 38% of students in fraternities, 32% in sororities
Most popular majors: 15% Business/Commerce, General, 9% Psychology, General, 7% Accounting, 6% Political Science and Government, General, 5% Biology/Biological Sciences, General
Expenses: 2019-2020: $49,338; room/board: $12,776
Financial aid: (724) 223-6019; 79% of undergrads determined to have financial need; average aid package $39,176

Waynesburg University

Waynesburg PA
(800) 225-7393
U.S. News ranking: Reg. U. (N), No. 66
Website: www.waynesburg.edu/
Admissions email: admissions@waynesburg.edu
Private; founded 1849
Affiliation: Presbyterian Church (USA)
Freshman admissions: selective; 2018-2019: 1,590 applied, 1,454 accepted. Either SAT or ACT required. SAT 25/75 percentile: 980-1150. High school rank: 11% in top tenth, 36% in top quarter, 72% in top half
Early decision deadline: N/A, notification date: N/A
Early action deadline: N/A, notification date: N/A
Application deadline (fall): rolling
Undergraduate student body: 1,287 full time, 43 part time; 43% male, 57% female; 0% American Indian, 1% Asian, 4% black, 2% Hispanic, 3% multiracial, 0% Pacific Islander, 86% white, 0% international; 78% from in state; 80% live on campus; N/A of students in fraternities, N/A in sororities
Most popular majors: 21% Nursing Practice, 14% Business Administration and Management, General, 12% Criminal Justice/Law Enforcement Administration, 7% Psychology, General, 7% Speech Communication and Rhetoric
Expenses: 2019-2020: $25,570; room/board: $10,520
Financial aid: (724) 852-3208; 82% of undergrads determined to have financial need; average aid package $20,639

West Chester University of Pennsylvania

West Chester PA
(610) 436-3414
U.S. News ranking: Reg. U. (N), No. 55
Website: www.wcupa.edu/
Admissions email: ugadmiss@wcupa.edu
Public; founded 1871
Freshman admissions: selective; 2018-2019: 12,002 applied, 8,934 accepted. Either SAT or ACT required. SAT 25/75 percentile: 1050-1200. High school rank: 9% in top tenth, 32% in top quarter, 70% in top half
Early decision deadline: N/A, notification date: N/A
Early action deadline: N/A, notification date: N/A
Application deadline (fall): rolling
Undergraduate student body: 13,060 full time, 1,507 part time; 41% male, 59% female; 0% American Indian, 2% Asian, 11% black, 6% Hispanic, 4% multiracial, 0% Pacific Islander, 75% white, 0% international; 89% from in state; 36% live on campus; 12% of students in fraternities, 12% in sororities
Most popular majors: 25% Business, Management, Marketing, and Related Support Services, 16% Health Professions and Related Programs, 10% Education, 8% English Language and Literature/Letters, 7% Psychology
Expenses: 2019-2020: $9,943 in state, $21,517 out of state; room/board: $9,326
Financial aid: (610) 436-2627; 59% of undergrads determined to have financial need; average aid package $8,402

Westminster College

New Wilmington PA
(724) 946-7100
U.S. News ranking: Nat. Lib. Arts, No. 114
Website: www.westminster.edu
Admissions email: admis@westminster.edu
Private; founded 1852
Affiliation: Presbyterian Church (USA)
Freshman admissions: selective; 2018-2019: 3,011 applied, 2,000 accepted. Either SAT or ACT required. SAT 25/75 percentile: 1000-1225. High school rank: 13% in top tenth, 26% in top quarter, 61% in top half
Early decision deadline: N/A, notification date: N/A
Early action deadline: 11/15, notification date: 12/1
Application deadline (fall): 5/1
Undergraduate student body: 1,155 full time, 41 part time; 48% male, 52% female; 1% American Indian, 0% Asian, 5% black, 2% Hispanic, 1% multiracial, 0% Pacific Islander, 70% white, 0% international; N/A from in state; 75% live on campus; N/A of students in fraternities, N/A in sororities

Most popular majors: 29% Business, Management, Marketing, and Related Support Services, 13% Biological and Biomedical Sciences, 11% Education, 8% Social Sciences, 7% Psychology
Expenses: 2019-2020: $37,300; room/board: $11,450
Financial aid: (724) 946-7102; 87% of undergrads determined to have financial need; average aid package $30,623

Widener University

Chester PA
(610) 499-4126
U.S. News ranking: Nat. U., No. 202
Website: www.widener.edu
Admissions email: admissions.office@widener.edu
Private; founded 1821
Freshman admissions: selective; 2018-2019: 6,422 applied, 4,444 accepted. Either SAT or ACT required. SAT 25/75 percentile: 1020-1200. High school rank: N/A
Early decision deadline: N/A, notification date: N/A
Early action deadline: N/A, notification date: N/A
Application deadline (fall): rolling
Undergraduate student body: 2,910 full time, 435 part time; 43% male, 57% female; 0% American Indian, 3% Asian, 13% black, 5% Hispanic, 4% multiracial, 0% Pacific Islander, 71% white, 2% international; 60% from in state; 47% live on campus; 10% of students in fraternities, 14% in sororities
Most popular majors: 28% Health Professions and Related Programs, 17% Business, Management, Marketing, and Related Support Services, 15% Engineering, 9% Psychology, 5% Computer and Information Sciences and Support Services
Expenses: 2019-2020: $47,328; room/board: $14,736
Financial aid: (610) 499-4161; 79% of undergrads determined to have financial need; average aid package $34,073

Wilkes University

Wilkes-Barre PA
(570) 408-4400
U.S. News ranking: Nat. U., No. 211
Website: www.wilkes.edu
Admissions email: admissions@wilkes.edu
Private; founded 1933
Freshman admissions: selective; 2018-2019: 3,932 applied, 2,942 accepted. Either SAT or ACT required. SAT 25/75 percentile: 1050-1240. High school rank: 23% in top tenth, 60% in top quarter, 84% in top half
Early decision deadline: N/A, notification date: N/A
Early action deadline: N/A, notification date: N/A
Application deadline (fall): rolling
Undergraduate student body: 2,212 full time, 243 part time; 53% male, 47% female; 0% American

Indian, 2% Asian, 5% black, 7% Hispanic, 3% multiracial, 0% Pacific Islander, 72% white, 7% international; 79% from in state; 44% live on campus; 0% of students in fraternities, 0% in sororities
Most popular majors: 20% Business, Management, Marketing, and Related Support Services, 18% Health Professions and Related Programs, 15% Engineering, 7% Social Sciences, 6% Psychology
Expenses: 2019-2020: $37,622; room/board: $15,108
Financial aid: (570) 408-4512; 79% of undergrads determined to have financial need; average aid package $28,186

Wilson College

Chambersburg PA
(800) 421-8402
U.S. News ranking: Reg. U. (N), second tier
Website: www.wilson.edu
Admissions email: admissions@wilson.edu
Private; founded 1869
Affiliation: Presbyterian Church (USA)
Freshman admissions: less selective; 2018-2019: 824 applied, 757 accepted. Either SAT or ACT required for some. SAT 25/75 percentile: 950-1130. High school rank: 8% in top tenth, 30% in top quarter, 75% in top half
Early decision deadline: N/A, notification date: N/A
Early action deadline: N/A, notification date: N/A
Application deadline (fall): rolling
Undergraduate student body: 675 full time, 369 part time; 21% male, 79% female; 0% American Indian, 1% Asian, 4% black, 4% Hispanic, 2% multiracial, 0% Pacific Islander, 61% white, 4% international; 71% from in state; 47% live on campus; 0% of students in fraternities, 0% in sororities
Most popular majors: 23% Veterinary/Animal Health Technology/Technician and Veterinary Assistant, 8% Business Administration and Management, General, 7% Animal-Assisted Therapy, 6% Accounting, 6% Animal Sciences, Other
Expenses: 2019-2020: $25,300; room/board: $11,594
Financial aid: (717) 264-3787; 82% of undergrads determined to have financial need; average aid package $20,272

York College of Pennsylvania

York PA
(717) 849-1600
U.S. News ranking: Reg. U. (N), No. 80
Website: www.ycp.edu
Admissions email: admissions@ycp.edu
Private; founded 1787
Freshman admissions: selective; 2018-2019: 5,644 applied, 3,931 accepted. Either SAT or ACT required. SAT 25/75

percentile: 1020-1220. High school rank: 13% in top tenth, 40% in top quarter, 75% in top half
Early decision deadline: 12/15, notification date: 10/1
Early action deadline: N/A, notification date: N/A
Application deadline (fall): 9/5
Undergraduate student body: 3,707 full time, 343 part time; 46% male, 54% female; 0% American Indian, 2% Asian, 5% black, 7% Hispanic, 4% multiracial, 0% Pacific Islander, 79% white, 1% international; N/A from in state; 57% live on campus; 3% of students in fraternities, 5% in sororities
Most popular majors: 24% Business, Management, Marketing, and Related Support Services, 14% Health Professions and Related Programs, 8% Education, 8% Homeland Security, Law Enforcement, Firefighting and Related Protective Services, 7% Parks, Recreation, Leisure, and Fitness Studies
Expenses: 2019-2020: $20,886; room/board: $11,540
Financial aid: (717) 815-6539; 68% of undergrads determined to have financial need; average aid package $13,866

PUERTO RICO

American University of Puerto Rico–Bayamon[1]

Bayamon PR
U.S. News ranking: Reg. Coll. (S), unranked
Website: www.clark.edu
Admissions email: N/A
Private
Application deadline (fall): N/A
Undergraduate student body: N/A full time, N/A part time
Expenses: N/A
Financial aid: N/A

American University of Puerto Rico–Manati[1]

Bayamon PR
(787) 620-2040
U.S. News ranking: Reg. Coll. (S), unranked
Website: www.aupr.edu/
Admissions email: N/A
Private
Application deadline (fall): N/A
Undergraduate student body: N/A full time, N/A part time
Expenses: N/A
Financial aid: N/A

Bayamon Central University[1]

Bayamon PR
(787) 786-3030
U.S. News ranking: Reg. U. (S), unranked
Website: www.ucb.edu.pr/
Admissions email: N/A
Private
Application deadline (fall): N/A

Undergraduate student body: N/A full time, N/A part time
Expenses: N/A
Financial aid: N/A

Caribbean University[1]
Bayamon PR
(787) 780-0070
U.S. News ranking: Reg. U. (S), unranked
Website: www.caribbean.edu/
Admissions email: N/A
Private
Application deadline (fall): N/A
Undergraduate student body: N/A full time, N/A part time
Expenses: N/A
Financial aid: N/A

Colegio Universitario de San Juan[1]
San Juan PR
(787) 480-2400
U.S. News ranking: Reg. Coll. (S), unranked
Website: www.pierce.ctc.edu
Admissions email: N/A
Public
Application deadline (fall): N/A
Undergraduate student body: N/A full time, N/A part time
Expenses: N/A
Financial aid: N/A

EDP University of Puerto Rico Inc–San Juan[1]
San Juan PR
U.S. News ranking: Reg. U. (S), unranked
Website: www.greenriver.edu/
Admissions email: N/A
Private
Application deadline (fall): N/A
Undergraduate student body: N/A full time, N/A part time
Expenses: N/A
Financial aid: N/A

Escuela de Artes Plasticas de Puerto Rico[1]
San Juan PR
(787) 725-8120
U.S. News ranking: Arts, unranked
Website: www.eap.edu
Admissions email: N/A
Public
Application deadline (fall): N/A
Undergraduate student body: N/A full time, N/A part time
Expenses: N/A
Financial aid: N/A

Ponce Health Sciences University[1]
Ponce PR
U.S. News ranking: Nat. U., unranked
Website: www.ghc.edu
Admissions email: N/A
For-profit
Application deadline (fall): N/A
Undergraduate student body: N/A full time, N/A part time
Expenses: N/A
Financial aid: N/A

Pontifical Catholic University of Puerto Rico–Arecibo[1]
Arecibo PR
U.S. News ranking: Reg. U. (S), unranked
Website: www.edcc.edu
Admissions email: N/A
Private
Undergraduate student body: N/A full time, N/A part time
Expenses: N/A
Financial aid: N/A

Pontifical Catholic University of Puerto Rico–Ponce
Ponce PR
(787) 841-2000
U.S. News ranking: Nat. U., unranked
Website: www.pucpr.edu
Admissions email: admisiones@pucpr.edu
Private; founded 1948
Affiliation: Roman Catholic
Freshman admissions: least selective; 2018-2019: 2,570 applied, 2,357 accepted. Either SAT or ACT required for some. SAT 25/75 percentile: N/A. High school rank: N/A
Early decision deadline: N/A, notification date: N/A
Early action deadline: N/A, notification date: N/A
Application deadline (fall): 8/19
Undergraduate student body: 4,699 full time, 592 part time; 39% male, 61% female; 0% American Indian, 0% Asian, 0% black, 99% Hispanic, 0% multiracial, 0% Pacific Islander, 0% white, 0% international
Most popular majors: 14% Biomedical Sciences, General, 12% Registered Nursing/ Registered Nurse, 9% Liberal Arts and Sciences/Liberal Studies, 6% Psychology, General, 6% Social Work
Expenses: 2019-2020: $5,580; room/board: $5,091
Financial aid: (787) 841-2000; 89% of undergrads determined to have financial need; average aid package $8,286

Puerto Rico Conservatory of Music[1]
San Juan PR
(787) 751-0160
U.S. News ranking: Arts, unranked
Website: www.cmpr.edu
Admissions email: cmpr.edu/admisiones
Public
Application deadline (fall): N/A
Undergraduate student body: N/A full time, N/A part time
Expenses: N/A
Financial aid: N/A

Universidad Adventista de las Antillas[1]
Mayaguez PR
(787) 834-9595
U.S. News ranking: Reg. Coll. (S), unranked
Website: www.uaa.edu/esp/
Admissions email: N/A
Private
Application deadline (fall): N/A
Undergraduate student body: N/A full time, N/A part time
Expenses: N/A
Financial aid: N/A

Universidad del Este[1]
Carolina PR
U.S. News ranking: Reg. U. (S), unranked
Website: www.suagm.edu/une/
Admissions email: N/A
Private; founded 1949
Application deadline (fall): rolling
Undergraduate student body: N/A full time, N/A part time
Expenses: N/A
Financial aid: N/A

Universidad del Turabo[1]
Gurabo PR
(787) 743-7979
U.S. News ranking: Nat. U., unranked
Website: www.ut.suagm.edu
Admissions email: admisiones-ut@suagm.edu
Private; founded 1972
Application deadline (fall): rolling
Undergraduate student body: N/A full time, N/A part time
Expenses: N/A
Financial aid: N/A

Universidad Metropolitana[1]
Rio Piedras PR
(787) 766-1717
U.S. News ranking: Reg. U. (S), unranked
Website: www.suagm.edu/
Admissions email: N/A
Private
Application deadline (fall): rolling
Undergraduate student body: N/A full time, N/A part time
Expenses: N/A
Financial aid: N/A

Universidad Politecnica de Puerto Rico
Hato Rey PR
(787) 622-8000
U.S. News ranking: Engineering, unranked
Website: www.pupr.edu
Admissions email: admisiones@pupr.edu
Private; founded 1966
Freshman admissions: least selective; 2018-2019: 841 applied, 740 accepted. Neither SAT nor ACT required. SAT 25/75 percentile: N/A. High school rank: N/A
Early decision deadline: N/A, notification date: N/A

Early action deadline: N/A, notification date: N/A
Application deadline (fall): rolling
Undergraduate student body: 1,659 full time, 1,855 part time; 77% male, 23% female; 0% American Indian, 0% Asian, 0% black, 100% Hispanic, 0% multiracial, 0% Pacific Islander, 0% white, 0% international; 99% from in state; N/A live on campus; N/A of students in fraternities, N/A in sororities
Most popular majors: 27% Mechanical Engineering, 10% Computer Engineering, General, 10% Electrical and Electronics Engineering, 9% Architecture, 9% Civil Engineering, General
Expenses: 2018-2019: $8,610; room/board: $11,928
Financial aid: N/A

University of Puerto Rico–Aguadilla
Aguadilla PR
(787) 890-2681
U.S. News ranking: Reg. Coll. (S), unranked
Website: www.uprag.edu/
Admissions email: melba.serrano@upr.edu
Public; founded 1972
Freshman admissions: selective; 2018-2019: 2,909 applied, 809 accepted. SAT required. SAT 25/75 percentile: 927-1130. High school rank: N/A
Early decision deadline: N/A, notification date: N/A
Early action deadline: N/A, notification date: N/A
Application deadline (fall): 5/31
Undergraduate student body: 2,848 full time, 291 part time; 45% male, 55% female; 0% American Indian, 0% Asian, 0% black, 100% Hispanic, 0% multiracial, 0% Pacific Islander, 0% white, 0% international
Most popular majors: 30% Biology/ Biological Sciences, General, 10% Marketing/Marketing Management, General, 9% Electrical, Electronic and Communications Engineering Technology/Technician, 9% Executive Assistant/Executive Secretary, 8% Human Resources Management/Personnel Administration, General
Expenses: 2019-2020: $4,684 in state, $6,639 out of state; room/board: $11,161
Financial aid: (787) 890-2681

University of Puerto Rico–Arecibo
Arecibo PR
(787) 815-0000
U.S. News ranking: Reg. Coll. (S), unranked
Website: www.upra.edu/
Admissions email: admisiones.arecibo@upr.edu
Public; founded 1967
Freshman admissions: least selective; 2018-2019: 1,868 applied, 848 accepted. Neither SAT nor ACT required. SAT 25/75 percentile: N/A. High school rank: N/A
Early decision deadline: 3/31, notification date: 3/31

Early action deadline: N/A, notification date: N/A
Application deadline (fall): 1/31
Undergraduate student body: 3,385 full time, 275 part time; 40% male, 60% female; 0% American Indian, 0% Asian, 0% black, 100% Hispanic, 0% multiracial, 0% Pacific Islander, 0% white, 0% international; 100% from in state; N/A live on campus; N/A of students in fraternities, N/A in sororities
Most popular majors: 16% Microbiology, General, 15% Radio and Television Broadcasting Technology/Technician, 13% Registered Nursing/Registered Nurse, 12% Industrial and Organizational Psychology, 8% Accounting
Expenses: 2018-2019: $4,284 in state, $6,239 out of state; room/ board: $11,161
Financial aid: (787) 815-0000

University of Puerto Rico–Bayamon
Bayamon PR
(787) 993-8952
U.S. News ranking: Reg. Coll. (S), unranked
Website: www.uprb.edu/
Admissions email: N/A
Public; founded 1971
Freshman admissions: least selective; 2018-2019: 1,564 applied, 1,093 accepted. Neither SAT nor ACT required. SAT 25/75 percentile: N/A. High school rank: N/A
Early decision deadline: N/A, notification date: N/A
Early action deadline: N/A, notification date: N/A
Application deadline (fall): 2/15
Undergraduate student body: 3,643 full time, 546 part time; 49% male, 51% female; 0% American Indian, 0% Asian, 0% black, 100% Hispanic, 0% multiracial, 0% Pacific Islander, 0% white, 0% international
Most popular majors: Information not available
Expenses: 2019-2020: $4,089 in state, $7,999 out of state; room/ board: N/A
Financial aid: (787) 993-8953

University of Puerto Rico–Cayey
Cayey PR
(787) 738-2161
U.S. News ranking: Nat. Lib. Arts, unranked
Website: cayey.upr.edu/ oficina-de-admisiones/
Admissions email: admisiones.cayey@upr.edu
Public; founded 1967
Freshman admissions: least selective; 2018-2019: 910 applied, 658 accepted. Neither SAT nor ACT required. SAT 25/75 percentile: N/A. High school rank: N/A
Early decision deadline: N/A, notification date: N/A
Early action deadline: N/A, notification date: N/A
Application deadline (fall): N/A

Undergraduate student body: 3,108 full time, 0 part time; 35% male, 65% female; N/A% American Indian, N/A% Asian, N/A% black, 100% Hispanic, N/A% multiracial, N/A% Pacific Islander, N/A% white, N/A% international
Most popular majors: 18% Construction Trades, Other, 17% Biology/Biological Sciences, General, 16% Biology/Biological Sciences, General, 9% Accounting, 7% Psychology, General
Expenses: 2018-2019: $4,904 in state, $6,394 out of state; room/board: $11,161
Financial aid: (787) 738-2161; 78% of undergrads determined to have financial need

University of Puerto Rico–Humacao

Humacao PR
(787) 850-9301
U.S. News ranking: Reg. Coll. (S), unranked
Website: www.uprh.edu/~admision/
Admissions email: elizabeth.gerena@upr.edu
Public; founded 1962
Freshman admissions: least selective; 2018-2019: 1,698 applied, 711 accepted. Neither SAT nor ACT required. SAT 25/75 percentile: N/A. High school rank: N/A
Early decision deadline: N/A, notification date: N/A
Early action deadline: N/A, notification date: N/A
Application deadline (fall): 1/31
Undergraduate student body: 3,007 full time, 293 part time; 37% male, 63% female; 0% American Indian, 0% Asian, 2% black, 90% Hispanic, 0% multiracial, 0% Pacific Islander, 1% white, 0% international; 100% from in state; N/A live on campus; N/A of students in fraternities, N/A in sororities
Most popular majors: 12% Accounting, 11% Social Work, 8% Biology/Biological Sciences, General, 8% Registered Nursing/Registered Nurse
Expenses: 2018-2019: $4,094 in state, $6,049 out of state; room/board: N/A
Financial aid: N/A

University of Puerto Rico–Mayaguez

Mayaguez PR
(787) 832-4040
U.S. News ranking: Reg. U. (S), unranked
Website: www.uprm.edu
Admissions email: admisiones@uprm.edu
Public; founded 1911
Affiliation: Undenominational
Freshman admissions: least selective; 2018-2019: 3,524 applied, 2,238 accepted. Neither SAT nor ACT required. SAT 25/75 percentile: N/A. High school rank: N/A
Early decision deadline: N/A, notification date: N/A

Early action deadline: N/A, notification date: N/A
Application deadline (fall): 6/11
Undergraduate student body: 11,307 full time, 980 part time; 54% male, 46% female; 0% American Indian, 0% Asian, 0% black, 94% Hispanic, 0% multiracial, 0% Pacific Islander, 0% white, 0% international
Most popular majors: Information not available
Expenses: 2018-2019: $4,094 in state, $6,049 out of state; room/board: $11,161
Financial aid: (787) 265-3863; 81% of undergrads determined to have financial need; average aid package $6,743

University of Puerto Rico–Ponce

Ponce PR
(787) 844-8181
U.S. News ranking: Nat. Lib. Arts, unranked
Website: www.uprp.edu
Admissions email: admi.ponce@upr.edu
Public; founded 1970
Freshman admissions: least selective; 2018-2019: 1,971 applied, 695 accepted. SAT required. SAT 25/75 percentile: N/A. High school rank: N/A
Early decision deadline: N/A, notification date: N/A
Early action deadline: N/A, notification date: N/A
Application deadline (fall): 1/31
Undergraduate student body: 2,615 full time, 213 part time; 42% male, 58% female; 0% American Indian, 0% Asian, 0% black, 100% Hispanic, 0% multiracial, 0% Pacific Islander, 0% white, 0% international
Most popular majors: 17% Biological and Biomedical Sciences, Other, 12% Forensic Psychology, 11% Elementary Education and Teaching, 9% Accounting, 9% Psychology, Other
Expenses: 2019-2020: $4,394 in state, $6,536 out of state; room/board: N/A
Financial aid: (787) 844-8181

University of Puerto Rico– Rio Piedras

Rio Piedras PR
(787) 764-3680
U.S. News ranking: Nat. U., unranked
Website: www.uprrp.edu/
Admissions email: N/A
Public; founded 1903
Freshman admissions: least selective; 2018-2019: 5,950 applied, 2,539 accepted. Neither SAT nor ACT required. SAT 25/75 percentile: N/A. High school rank: N/A
Early decision deadline: N/A, notification date: N/A
Early action deadline: N/A, notification date: N/A
Application deadline (fall): 1/31
Undergraduate student body: 10,238 full time, 1,419 part time; 38% male, 62% female; 0% American Indian, 0% Asian,

3% black, 84% Hispanic, 0% multiracial, 0% Pacific Islander, 1% white, 0% international
Most popular majors: 15% Biology/Biological Sciences, General, 9% Psychology, General, 6% Accounting, 4% Foreign Languages and Literatures, General, 3% Natural Sciences
Expenses: 2018-2019: $4,054 in state, $6,009 out of state; room/board: $11,161
Financial aid: (787) 552-1324; 73% of undergrads determined to have financial need; average aid package $4,047

University of Puerto Rico–Utuado

Utuado PR
(787) 894-2316
U.S. News ranking: Reg. Coll. (S), unranked
Website: www.uprutuado.edu
Admissions email: admisiones.utuado@upr.edu
Public; founded 1978
Freshman admissions: least selective; 2018-2019: 941 applied, 380 accepted. Neither SAT nor ACT required. SAT 25/75 percentile: N/A. High school rank: N/A
Early decision deadline: N/A, notification date: N/A
Early action deadline: N/A, notification date: N/A
Application deadline (fall): 1/31
Undergraduate student body: 792 full time, 50 part time; 48% male, 52% female; 0% American Indian, 0% Asian, 4% black, 87% Hispanic, 0% multiracial, 0% Pacific Islander, 1% white, 0% international; 100% from in state; N/A live on campus; N/A of students in fraternities, N/A in sororities
Most popular majors: 37% Executive Assistant/Executive Secretary, 34% Accounting, 29% Elementary Education and Teaching
Expenses: 2018-2019: $4,278 in state, $6,049 out of state; room/board: N/A
Financial aid: (787) 894-3810; 100% of undergrads determined to have financial need

University of the Sacred Heart

Santurce PR
(787) 728-1515
U.S. News ranking: Reg. U. (S), unranked
Website: www.sagrado.edu/
Admissions email: admision@sagrado.edu
Private; founded 1935
Affiliation: Roman Catholic
Freshman admissions: least selective, 2018-2019: N/A applied, N/A accepted. Neither SAT nor ACT required. SAT 25/75 percentile: N/A. High school rank: N/A
Early decision deadline: N/A, notification date: N/A
Early action deadline: N/A, notification date: N/A
Application deadline (fall): N/A

Undergraduate student body: 3,483 full time, 756 part time; 38% male, 62% female; 0% American Indian, 0% Asian, 0% black, 100% Hispanic, 0% multiracial, 0% Pacific Islander, 0% white, 0% international
Most popular majors: Information not available
Expenses: 2018-2019: $5,343; room/board: $9,400
Financial aid: (787) 728-1515

RHODE ISLAND

Brown University

Providence RI
(401) 863-2378
U.S. News ranking: Nat. U., No. 14
Website: www.brown.edu/admission/undergraduate/
Admissions email: admission@brown.edu
Private; founded 1764
Freshman admissions: most selective; 2018-2019: 35,437 applied, 2,718 accepted. Either SAT or ACT required. SAT 25/75 percentile: 1420-1550. High school rank: 96% in top tenth, 98% in top quarter, 100% in top half
Early decision deadline: 11/1, notification date: 12/15
Early action deadline: N/A, notification date: N/A
Application deadline (fall): 1/1
Undergraduate student body: 6,735 full time, 308 part time; 46% male, 54% female; 0% American Indian, 15% Asian, 6% black, 11% Hispanic, 6% multiracial, 0% Pacific Islander, 43% white, 11% international; 5% from in state; 72% live on campus; 14% of students in fraternities, 10% in sororities
Most popular majors: 11% Computer Science, 10% Econometrics and Quantitative Economics, 6% Biology/Biological Sciences, General, 6% Entrepreneurship/Entrepreneurial Studies, 5% Engineering, General
Expenses: 2019-2020: $58,504; room/board: $15,332
Financial aid: (401) 863-2721; 41% of undergrads determined to have financial need; average aid package $52,141

Bryant University

Smithfield RI
(800) 622-7001
U.S. News ranking: Reg. U. (N), No. 7
Website: www.bryant.edu
Admissions email: admission@bryant.edu
Private; founded 1863
Freshman admissions: more selective; 2018-2019: 7,235 applied, 5,475 accepted. Neither SAT nor ACT required. SAT 25/75 percentile: 1130-1300. High school rank: 26% in top tenth, 55% in top quarter, 88% in top half
Early decision deadline: 11/1, notification date: 12/1
Early action deadline: 11/15, notification date: 1/15
Application deadline (fall): 2/1

Undergraduate student body: 3,453 full time, 46 part time; 62% male, 38% female; 0% American Indian, 4% Asian, 3% black, 7% Hispanic, 2% multiracial, 0% Pacific Islander, 75% white, 8% international; N/A from in state; 81% live on campus; 7% of students in fraternities, 15% in sororities
Most popular majors: 76% Business, Management, Marketing, and Related Support Services, 5% Communication, Journalism, and Related Programs, 5% Mathematics and Statistics, 3% Computer and Information Sciences and Support Services, 3% Social Sciences
Expenses: 2019-2020: $45,395; room/board: $15,705
Financial aid: (401) 232-6020; 60% of undergrads determined to have financial need; average aid package $25,821

Johnson & Wales University

Providence RI
(800) 342-5598
U.S. News ranking: Reg. U. (N), No. 80
Website: www.jwu.edu/
Admissions email: pvd@admissions.jwu.edu
Private; founded 1914
Freshman admissions: less selective; 2018-2019: 11,802 applied, 10,740 accepted. Either SAT or ACT required for some. SAT 25/75 percentile: 990-1190. High school rank: 4% in top tenth, 27% in top quarter, 76% in top half
Early decision deadline: N/A, notification date: N/A
Early action deadline: 11/1, notification date: 11/15
Application deadline (fall): rolling
Undergraduate student body: 6,263 full time, 418 part time; 40% male, 60% female; 1% American Indian, 2% Asian, 13% black, 13% Hispanic, 4% multiracial, 0% Pacific Islander, 55% white, 7% international
Most popular majors: 42% Business, Management, Marketing, and Related Support Services, 20% Family and Consumer Sciences/Human Sciences, 10% Parks, Recreation, Leisure, and Fitness Studies, 8% Personal and Culinary Services, 6% Homeland Security, Law Enforcement, Firefighting and Related Protective Services
Expenses: 2019-2020: $33,404; room/board: $12,582
Financial aid: (401) 598-1857; 76% of undergrads determined to have financial need; average aid package $24,546

New England Institute of Technology[1]
East Greenwich RI
(800) 736-7744
U.S. News ranking: Reg. Coll. (N), second tier
Website: www.neit.edu/
Admissions email: NEITAdmissions@neit.edu
Private; founded 1940
Affiliation: Other
Application deadline (fall): rolling
Undergraduate student body: N/A full time, N/A part time
Expenses: N/A
Financial aid: (401) 739-5000

Providence College
Providence RI
(401) 865-2535
U.S. News ranking: Reg. U. (N), No. 1
Website: www.providence.edu
Admissions email: pcadmiss@providence.edu
Private; founded 1917
Affiliation: Roman Catholic
Freshman admissions: more selective; 2018-2019: 11,421 applied, 5,593 accepted. Neither SAT nor ACT required. SAT 25/75 percentile: 1210-1360. High school rank: 40% in top tenth, 73% in top quarter, 93% in top half
Early decision deadline: 11/15, notification date: 1/1
Early action deadline: 11/1, notification date: 1/1
Application deadline (fall): 1/15
Undergraduate student body: 4,148 full time, 231 part time; 45% male, 55% female; 0% American Indian, 1% Asian, 4% black, 10% Hispanic, 2% multiracial, 0% Pacific Islander, 77% white, 2% international; 11% from in state; 81% live on campus; 0% of students in fraternities, 0% in sororities
Most popular majors: 40% Business, Management, Marketing, and Related Support Services, 12% Social Sciences, 9% Biological and Biomedical Sciences, 7% Psychology, 6% Education
Expenses: 2019-2020: $52,438; room/board: $15,140
Financial aid: (401) 865-2286; 47% of undergrads determined to have financial need; average aid package $35,421

Rhode Island College
Providence RI
(800) 669-5760
U.S. News ranking: Reg. U. (N), No. 116
Website: www.ric.edu
Admissions email: admissions@ric.edu
Public; founded 1854
Freshman admissions: less selective; 2018-2019: 4,613 applied, 3,360 accepted. Either SAT or ACT required. SAT 25/75 percentile: 890-1100. High school rank: 19% in top tenth, 40% in top quarter, 74% in top half
Early decision deadline: N/A, notification date: N/A

Early action deadline: N/A, notification date: N/A
Application deadline (fall): 3/15
Undergraduate student body: 5,108 full time, 1,580 part time; 31% male, 69% female; 0% American Indian, 3% Asian, 10% black, 21% Hispanic, 2% multiracial, 0% Pacific Islander, 56% white, 0% international; 85% from in state; 14% live on campus; N/A of students in fraternities, N/A in sororities
Most popular majors: 22% Health Professions and Related Programs, 17% Business, Management, Marketing, and Related Support Services, 11% Education, 9% Public Administration and Social Service Professions, 8% Psychology
Expenses: 2019-2020: $10,068 in state, $22,831 out of state; room/board: $11,829
Financial aid: (401) 456-8033; 71% of undergrads determined to have financial need; average aid package $9,185

Rhode Island School of Design
Providence RI
(401) 454-6300
U.S. News ranking: Arts, unranked
Website: www.risd.edu
Admissions email: admissions@risd.edu
Private; founded 1877
Freshman admissions: more selective; 2018-2019: 3,913 applied, 934 accepted. Either SAT or ACT required. SAT 25/75 percentile: 1180-1440. High school rank: N/A
Early decision deadline: 11/1, notification date: 12/7
Early action deadline: N/A, notification date: N/A
Application deadline (fall): 2/1
Undergraduate student body: 1,994 full time, 0 part time; 32% male, 68% female; 0% American Indian, 18% Asian, 4% black, 9% Hispanic, 5% multiracial, 0% Pacific Islander, 30% white, 30% international; 5% from in state; 60% live on campus; N/A of students in fraternities, N/A in sororities
Most popular majors: 16% Illustration, 15% Industrial and Product Design, 13% Graphic Design, 8% Film/Video and Photographic Arts, Other, 7% Painting
Expenses: 2019-2020: $52,860; room/board: $13,720
Financial aid: (401) 454-6661; 40% of undergrads determined to have financial need; average aid package $35,064

Roger Williams University
Bristol RI
(401) 254-3500
U.S. News ranking: Reg. U. (N), No. 28
Website: www.rwu.edu
Admissions email: admit@rwu.edu
Private; founded 1956
Freshman admissions: selective; 2018-2019: 9,147 applied, 7,875 accepted. Either SAT

or ACT required for some. SAT 25/75 percentile: 1080-1250. High school rank: 13% in top tenth, 35% in top quarter, 72% in top half
Early decision deadline: N/A, notification date: N/A
Early action deadline: 11/15, notification date: 12/1
Application deadline (fall): 2/1
Undergraduate student body: 3,962 full time, 575 part time; 48% male, 52% female; 0% American Indian, 2% Asian, 2% black, 7% Hispanic, 2% multiracial, 0% Pacific Islander, 79% white, 2% international; 21% from in state; 75% live on campus; N/A of students in fraternities, N/A in sororities
Most popular majors: 28% Business, Management, Marketing, and Related Support Services, 12% Homeland Security, Law Enforcement, Firefighting and Related Protective Services, 7% Biological and Biomedical Sciences, 7% Communication, Journalism, and Related Programs, 7% Science Technologies/Technicians
Expenses: 2019-2020: $36,978; room/board: $15,390
Financial aid: (401) 254-3100; 65% of undergrads determined to have financial need; average aid package $22,916

Salve Regina University
Newport RI
(888) 467-2583
U.S. News ranking: Reg. U. (N), No. 23
Website: www.salve.edu
Admissions email: admissions@salve.edu
Private; founded 1934
Affiliation: Roman Catholic
Freshman admissions: selective; 2018-2019: 4,721 applied, 3,596 accepted. Either SAT or ACT required for some. SAT 25/75 percentile: 1090-1250. High school rank: 11% in top tenth, 34% in top quarter, 73% in top half
Early decision deadline: N/A, notification date: N/A
Early action deadline: 11/1, notification date: 1/1
Application deadline (fall): rolling
Undergraduate student body: 1,957 full time, 64 part time; 33% male, 67% female; 0% American Indian, 1% Asian, 2% black, 7% Hispanic, 3% multiracial, 0% Pacific Islander, 81% white, 2% international; 18% from in state; 60% live on campus; 0% of students in fraternities, 0% in sororities
Most popular majors: 25% Business Administration and Management, General, 18% Registered Nursing/Registered Nurse, 11% Education, 9% Psychology, General, 7% Criminal Justice/Law Enforcement Administration
Expenses: 2019-2020: $41,450; room/board: $14,960
Financial aid: (401) 341-2901; 76% of undergrads determined to have financial need; average aid package $28,323

University of Rhode Island
Kingston RI
(401) 874-7100
U.S. News ranking: Nat. U., No. 166
Website: www.uri.edu
Admissions email: admission@uri.edu
Public; founded 1892
Freshman admissions: selective; 2018-2019: 22,779 applied, 16,257 accepted. Either SAT or ACT required. SAT 25/75 percentile: 1090-1260. High school rank: 18% in top tenth, 47% in top quarter, 83% in top half
Early decision deadline: N/A, notification date: N/A
Early action deadline: 12/1, notification date: 1/31
Application deadline (fall): 2/1
Undergraduate student body: 12,475 full time, 1,390 part time; 44% male, 56% female; 0% American Indian, 3% Asian, 5% black, 10% Hispanic, 3% multiracial, 0% Pacific Islander, 73% white, 1% international; 52% from in state; 40% live on campus; 16% of students in fraternities, 22% in sororities
Most popular majors: 11% Registered Nursing/Registered Nurse, 6% Psychology, General, 6% Speech Communication and Rhetoric, 4% Kinesiology and Exercise Science, 3% Human Development and Family Studies, General
Expenses: 2019-2020: $14,566 in state, $31,686 out of state; room/board: $12,688
Financial aid: (401) 874-9500; 85% of undergrads determined to have financial need; average aid package $16,753

SOUTH CAROLINA

Allen University[1]
Columbia SC
(803) 376-5735
U.S. News ranking: Nat. Lib. Arts, second tier
Website: www.allenuniversity.edu
Admissions email: admissions@allenuniversity.edu
Private; founded 1870
Application deadline (fall): rolling
Undergraduate student body: 1,957 full time, 64 part time; 33% male, 67% female; 0% American Indian, 1% Asian, 2% black, 7% Hispanic, 3% multiracial, 0% Pacific Islander, 81% white, 2% international; 18% from in state; 60% live on campus; 0% of students in fraternities, 0% in sororities
Expenses: N/A
Financial aid: (803) 376-5930

Anderson University
Anderson SC
(864) 231-5607
U.S. News ranking: Reg. U. (S), No. 50
Website: www.andersonuniversity.edu
Admissions email: admission@andersonuniversity.edu
Private; founded 1911
Affiliation: Southern Baptist
Freshman admissions: more selective; 2018-2019: 3,325 applied, 2,071 accepted. Either SAT or ACT required. ACT 25/75 percentile: 20-26. High school

rank: 42% in top tenth, 61% in top quarter, 87% in top half
Early decision deadline: N/A, notification date: N/A
Early action deadline: N/A, notification date: N/A
Application deadline (fall): rolling
Undergraduate student body: 2,526 full time, 355 part time; 31% male, 69% female; 0% American Indian, 1% Asian, 5% black, 3% Hispanic, 2% multiracial, 0% Pacific Islander, 84% white, 1% international; 79% from in state; 48% live on campus; N/A of students in fraternities, N/A in sororities
Most popular majors: 24% Health Professions and Related Programs, 17% Business, Management, Marketing, and Related Support Services, 14% Education, 9% Visual and Performing Arts, 7% Homeland Security, Law Enforcement, Firefighting and Related Protective Services
Expenses: 2019-2020: $29,230; room/board: $10,280
Financial aid: (864) 231-2181; 79% of undergrads determined to have financial need; average aid package $20,554

Benedict College[1]
Columbia SC
(803) 253-5143
U.S. News ranking: Reg. Coll. (S), second tier
Website: www.benedict.edu
Admissions email: admissions@benedict.edu
Private; founded 1870
Application deadline (fall): rolling
Undergraduate student body: N/A full time, N/A part time
Expenses: N/A
Financial aid: N/A

Bob Jones University
Greenville SC
(800) 252-6363
U.S. News ranking: Reg. U. (S), No. 34
Website: www.bju.edu/admission
Admissions email: admission@bju.edu
Private; founded 1927
Affiliation: Evangelical Christian
Freshman admissions: selective; 2018-2019: 1,234 applied, 960 accepted. Either SAT or ACT required. ACT 25/75 percentile: 20-27. High school rank: 14% in top tenth, 38% in top quarter, 67% in top half
Early decision deadline: N/A, notification date: N/A
Early action deadline: N/A, notification date: N/A
Application deadline (fall): rolling
Undergraduate student body: 2,273 full time, 374 part time; 45% male, 55% female; 0% American Indian, 2% Asian, 2% black, 2% Hispanic, 8% multiracial, 0% Pacific Islander, 72% white, 7% international; 46% from in state; 72% live on campus; N/A of students in fraternities, N/A in sororities
Most popular majors: 11% Business Administration and Management, General, 5% Counseling Psychology,

5% Registered Nursing/Registered Nurse, 4% Accounting, 4% Criminal Justice/Safety Studies
Expenses: 2019-2020: $19,100; room/board: $7,580
Financial aid: (864) 242-5100; 71% of undergrads determined to have financial need; average aid package $13,059

Charleston Southern University
Charleston SC
(843) 863-7050
U.S. News ranking: Reg. U. (S), No. 58
Website: www.charlestonsouthern.edu/
Admissions email: enroll@csuniv.edu
Private; founded 1964
Affiliation: Baptist
Freshman admissions: selective; 2018-2019: 4,431 applied, 2,287 accepted. Either SAT or ACT required. SAT 25/75 percentile: 1020-1190. High school rank: 21% in top tenth, 46% in top quarter, 75% in top half
Early decision deadline: N/A, notification date: N/A
Early action deadline: N/A, notification date: N/A
Application deadline (fall): rolling
Undergraduate student body: 2,729 full time, 216 part time; 37% male, 63% female; 0% American Indian, 1% Asian, 21% black, 4% Hispanic, 4% multiracial, 0% Pacific Islander, 58% white, 1% international; 82% from in state; 42% live on campus; N/A of students in fraternities, N/A in sororities
Most popular majors: 12% Registered Nursing/Registered Nurse, 7% Biology/Biological Sciences, General, 7% Kinesiology and Exercise Science, 7% Psychology, General, 6% Criminal Justice/Law Enforcement Administration
Expenses: 2018-2019: $25,540; room/board: $10,200
Financial aid: (843) 863-7050

The Citadel
Charleston SC
(843) 953-5230
U.S. News ranking: Reg. U. (S), No. 2
Website: www.citadel.edu
Admissions email: admissions@citadel.edu
Public; founded 1842
Affiliation: Other
Freshman admissions: selective; 2018-2019: 2,672 applied, 2,159 accepted. Either SAT or ACT required. SAT 25/75 percentile: 1030-1220. High school rank: 8% in top tenth, 31% in top quarter, 64% in top half
Early decision deadline: N/A, notification date: N/A
Early action deadline: N/A, notification date: N/A
Application deadline (fall): rolling
Undergraduate student body: 2,654 full time, 257 part time; 89% male, 11% female; 0% American Indian, 2% Asian, 9% black,

7% Hispanic, 5% multiracial, 0% Pacific Islander, 75% white, 1% international; 68% from in state; 100% live on campus; 0% of students in fraternities, 0% in sororities
Most popular majors: 32% Business Administration and Management, General, 21% Engineering, General, 15% Criminal Justice/Law Enforcement Administration, 9% Social Sciences, General, 5% Kinesiology and Exercise Science
Expenses: 2018-2019: $12,056 in state, $34,988 out of state; room/board: $6,904
Financial aid: (843) 953-5187; 58% of undergrads determined to have financial need; average aid package $18,477

Claflin University
Orangeburg SC
(800) 922-1276
U.S. News ranking: Reg. Coll. (S), No. 9
Website: www.claflin.edu
Admissions email: admissions@claflin.edu
Private; founded 1869
Affiliation: United Methodist
Freshman admissions: less selective; 2018-2019: 9,684 applied, 5,458 accepted. Either SAT or ACT required. ACT 25/75 percentile: 18-20. High school rank: 11% in top tenth, 32% in top quarter, 74% in top half
Early decision deadline: N/A, notification date: N/A
Early action deadline: N/A, notification date: N/A
Application deadline (fall): 8/1
Undergraduate student body: 1,984 full time, 96 part time; 32% male, 68% female; 1% American Indian, 1% Asian, 94% black, 0% Hispanic, 0% multiracial, 0% Pacific Islander, 1% white, 1% international; 85% from in state; 65% live on campus; 15% of students in fraternities, 11% in sororities
Most popular majors: 13% Business Administration and Management, General, 12% Criminal Justice/Safety Studies, 10% Psychology, General, 8% Mass Communication/Media Studies, 7% Biology/Biological Sciences, General
Expenses: 2018-2019: $16,722; room/board: $9,294
Financial aid: (803) 535-5720

Clemson University
Clemson SC
(864) 656-2287
U.S. News ranking: Nat. U., No. 70
Website: www.clemson.edu
Admissions email: cuadmissions@clemson.edu
Public; founded 1889
Freshman admissions: more selective; 2018-2019: 28,845 applied, 13,613 accepted. Either SAT or ACT required. ACT 25/75 percentile: 27-32. High school rank: 56% in top tenth, 87% in top quarter, 98% in top half
Early decision deadline: N/A, notification date: N/A

Early action deadline: N/A, notification date: N/A
Application deadline (fall): 5/1
Undergraduate student body: 18,971 full time, 698 part time; 51% male, 49% female; 0% American Indian, 3% Asian, 6% black, 5% Hispanic, 3% multiracial, 0% Pacific Islander, 82% white, 1% international; 66% from in state; 41% live on campus; 16% of students in fraternities, 31% in sororities
Most popular majors: 20% Engineering, 19% Business, Management, Marketing, and Related Support Services, 10% Biological and Biomedical Sciences, 7% Health Professions and Related Programs, 6% Social Sciences
Expenses: 2019-2020: $15,120 in state, $38,112 out of state; room/board: $11,414
Financial aid: (864) 656-2280; 46% of undergrads determined to have financial need; average aid package $11,743

Coastal Carolina University
Conway SC
(843) 349-2170
U.S. News ranking: Reg. U. (S), No. 41
Website: www.coastal.edu
Admissions email: admissions@coastal.edu
Public; founded 1954
Freshman admissions: selective; 2018-2019: 14,057 applied, 9,777 accepted. Either SAT or ACT required. ACT 25/75 percentile: 19-24. High school rank: 11% in top tenth, 33% in top quarter, 69% in top half
Early decision deadline: N/A, notification date: N/A
Early action deadline: N/A, notification date: N/A
Application deadline (fall): 8/1
Undergraduate student body: 8,941 full time, 976 part time; 46% male, 54% female; 0% American Indian, 1% Asian, 19% black, 5% Hispanic, 5% multiracial, 0% Pacific Islander, 66% white, 1% international; 47% from in state; 44% live on campus; 3% of students in fraternities, 5% in sororities
Most popular majors: 9% Business Administration and Management, General, 8% Kinesiology and Exercise Science, 8% Marine Biology and Biological Oceanography, 8% Speech Communication and Rhetoric, 6% Marketing/Marketing Management, General
Expenses: 2019-2020: $11,640 in state, $27,394 out of state; room/board: $9,290
Financial aid: (843) 349-2313; 68% of undergrads determined to have financial need; average aid package $11,175

Coker College
Hartsville SC
(843) 383-8050
U.S. News ranking: Reg. U. (S), No. 43
Website: www.coker.edu
Admissions email: admissions@coker.edu
Private; founded 1908
Freshman admissions: selective; 2018-2019: 1,546 applied, 967 accepted. Either SAT or ACT required. ACT 25/75 percentile: 17-22. High school rank: 35% in top tenth, 42% in top quarter, 75% in top half
Early decision deadline: N/A, notification date: N/A
Early action deadline: 12/1, notification date: 12/15
Undergraduate student body: 1,001 full time, 128 part time; 45% male, 55% female; 1% American Indian, 1% Asian, 32% black, 3% Hispanic, 8% multiracial, 0% Pacific Islander, 51% white, 4% international; 75% from in state; 60% live on campus; 0% of students in fraternities, 0% in sororities
Most popular majors: 13% Business Administration and Management, General, 13% Business/Commerce, General, 10% Health and Physical Education/Fitness, General, 8% Criminology, 6% Biology/Biological Sciences, General
Expenses: 2019-2020: $30,196; room/board: $9,604
Financial aid: (843) 383-8050; 87% of undergrads determined to have financial need; average aid package $24,281

College of Charleston
Charleston SC
(843) 953-5670
U.S. News ranking: Reg. U. (S), No. 8
Website: www.cofc.edu
Admissions email: admissions@cofc.edu
Public; founded 1770
Freshman admissions: selective; 2018-2019: 11,675 applied, 9,254 accepted. Either SAT or ACT required. SAT 25/75 percentile: 1070-1250. High school rank: 20% in top tenth, 51% in top quarter, 87% in top half
Early decision deadline: 11/1, notification date: 12/1
Early action deadline: 12/1, notification date: 1/1
Application deadline (fall): 2/15
Undergraduate student body: 9,103 full time, 777 part time; 36% male, 64% female; 0% American Indian, 2% Asian, 8% black, 6% Hispanic, 4% multiracial, 0% Pacific Islander, 78% white, 1% international; N/A from in state; 32% live on campus; 11% of students in fraternities, 24% in sororities
Most popular majors: 28% Business, Management, Marketing, and Related Support Services, 12% Biological and Biomedical Sciences, 9% Visual and Performing Arts, 8% Social

Sciences, 6% Communication, Journalism, and Related Programs
Expenses: 2019-2020: $12,978 in state, $33,308 out of state; room/board: $12,123
Financial aid: (843) 953-5540; 51% of undergrads determined to have financial need; average aid package $14,110

Columbia College
Columbia SC
(800) 277-1301
U.S. News ranking: Reg. U. (S), No. 54
Website: www.columbiasc.edu
Admissions email: admissions@columbiasc.edu
Private; founded 1854
Affiliation: United Methodist
Freshman admissions: least selective; 2018-2019: 877 applied, 841 accepted. Neither SAT nor ACT required. ACT 25/75 percentile: 15-19. High school rank: 13% in top tenth, 30% in top quarter, 69% in top half
Early decision deadline: N/A, notification date: N/A
Early action deadline: N/A, notification date: N/A
Application deadline (fall): rolling
Undergraduate student body: 765 full time, 400 part time; 20% male, 80% female; 0% American Indian, 1% Asian, 37% black, 4% Hispanic, 3% multiracial, 0% Pacific Islander, 46% white, 1% international; 92% from in state; 35% live on campus; 0% of students in fraternities, 2% in sororities
Most popular majors: 35% Criminal Justice/Safety Studies, 10% Crisis/Emergency/Disaster Management, 10% Social Work, 6% Psychology, General, 4% Biology/Biological Sciences, General
Expenses: 2019-2020: $19,890; room/board: $7,900
Financial aid: (803) 786-3612; 86% of undergrads determined to have financial need; average aid package $15,428

Columbia International University
Columbia SC
(800) 777-2227
U.S. News ranking: Reg. U. (S), No. 38
Website: www.ciu.edu
Admissions email: yesciu@ciu.edu
Private; founded 1923
Affiliation: Multiple Protestant Denominations
Freshman admissions: selective; 2018-2019: 611 applied, 204 accepted. Either SAT or ACT required. SAT 25/75 percentile: 940-1120. High school rank: 9% in top tenth, 32% in top quarter, 58% in top half
Early decision deadline: N/A, notification date: N/A
Early action deadline: N/A, notification date: N/A
Application deadline (fall): 8/1
Undergraduate student body: 540 full time, 51 part time; 48% male, 52% female; 0% American Indian, 1% Asian, 19% black,

5% Hispanic, 1% multiracial, 0% Pacific Islander, 58% white, 4% international
Most popular majors: 65% Theology and Religious Vocations, 12% Liberal Arts and Sciences, General Studies and Humanities, 6% Psychology, 5% Business, Management, Marketing, and Related Support Services, 4% Education
Expenses: 2019-2020: $23,940; room/board: $8,850
Financial aid: (803) 807-5037; 83% of undergrads determined to have financial need; average aid package $19,928

Converse College
Spartanburg SC
(864) 596-9040
U.S. News ranking: Reg. U. (S), No. 22
Website: www.converse.edu
Admissions email: admissions@converse.edu
Private; founded 1889
Freshman admissions: selective; 2018-2019: 1,808 applied, 1,058 accepted. Either SAT or ACT required. ACT 25/75 percentile: 20-25. High school rank: 17% in top tenth, 45% in top quarter, 79% in top half
Early decision deadline: N/A, notification date: N/A
Early action deadline: N/A, notification date: N/A
Application deadline (fall): 8/1
Undergraduate student body: 842 full time, 51 part time; 1% male, 99% female; 0% American Indian, 1% Asian, 11% black, 4% Hispanic, 3% multiracial, 0% Pacific Islander, 63% white, 6% international
Most popular majors: Information not available
Expenses: 2019-2020: $19,240; room/board: $11,260
Financial aid: (864) 596-9019; 80% of undergrads determined to have financial need; average aid package $15,981

Erskine College
Due West SC
(864) 379-8838
U.S. News ranking: Reg. Coll. (S), No. 6
Website: www.erskine.edu
Admissions email: admissions@erskine.edu
Private; founded 1839
Affiliation: Presbyterian
Freshman admissions: selective; 2018-2019: 910 applied, 530 accepted. Either SAT or ACT required. SAT 25/75 percentile: 930-1140. High school rank: 15% in top tenth, 28% in top quarter, 70% in top half
Early decision deadline: N/A, notification date: N/A
Early action deadline: N/A, notification date: N/A
Application deadline (fall): rolling
Undergraduate student body: 564 full time, 10 part time; 56% male, 44% female; 1% American Indian, 2% Asian, 12% black, 5% Hispanic, 0% multiracial, 1% Pacific Islander, 62% white,

0% international; 71% from in state; 87% live on campus; N/A of students in fraternities, N/A in sororities
Most popular majors: 24% Business, Management, Marketing, and Related Support Services, 15% Biological and Biomedical Sciences, 12% Parks, Recreation, Leisure, and Fitness Studies, 9% Business, Management, Marketing, and Related Support Services, 9% Psychology
Expenses: 2019-2020: $36,150; room/board: $11,350
Financial aid: (864) 379-8886; 100% of undergrads determined to have financial need; average aid package $25,500

Francis Marion University
Florence SC
(843) 661-1231
U.S. News ranking: Reg. U. (S), No. 61
Website: www.fmarion.edu
Admissions email: admissions@fmarion.edu
Public; founded 1970
Freshman admissions: selective; 2018-2019: 5,029 applied, 3,211 accepted. Either SAT or ACT required. ACT 25/75 percentile: 17-22. High school rank: 13% in top tenth, 44% in top quarter, 80% in top half
Early decision deadline: N/A, notification date: N/A
Early action deadline: N/A, notification date: N/A
Application deadline (fall): rolling
Undergraduate student body: 2,883 full time, 602 part time; 31% male, 69% female; 0% American Indian, 1% Asian, 38% black, 3% Hispanic, 3% multiracial, 0% Pacific Islander, 52% white, 2% international; 95% from in state; 43% live on campus; 2% of students in fraternities, 6% in sororities
Most popular majors: 26% Health Professions and Related Programs, 18% Business, Management, Marketing, and Related Support Services, 13% Biological and Biomedical Sciences, 10% Psychology, 7% Social Sciences
Expenses: 2019-2020: $11,160 in state, $21,544 out of state; room/board: $8,344
Financial aid: (843) 661-1190; 79% of undergrads determined to have financial need; average aid package $12,267

Furman University
Greenville SC
(864) 294-2034
U.S. News ranking: Nat. Lib. Arts, No. 46
Website: www.furman.edu/
Admissions email: admissions@furman.edu
Private; founded 1826
Freshman admissions: more selective; 2018-2019: 5,469 applied, 3,339 accepted. Neither SAT nor ACT required. ACT 25/75 percentile: 28-32. High school rank: 41% in top tenth, 71% in top quarter, 92% in top half

Early decision deadline: 11/1, notification date: 11/15
Early action deadline: 11/1, notification date: 12/20
Application deadline (fall): 1/15
Undergraduate student body: 2,663 full time, 91 part time; 41% male, 59% female; 0% American Indian, 2% Asian, 7% black, 6% Hispanic, 3% multiracial, 0% Pacific Islander, 77% white, 4% international; 32% from in state; 88% live on campus; 32% of students in fraternities, 61% in sororities
Most popular majors: 10% Health Professions and Related Clinical Sciences, Other, 8% Business Administration and Management, General, 8% Political Science and Government, General, 8% Speech Communication and Rhetoric, 6% Psychology, General
Expenses: 2019-2020: $50,844; room/board: $13,034
Financial aid: (864) 294-2030; 46% of undergrads determined to have financial need; average aid package $41,883

Lander University
Greenwood SC
(864) 388-8307
U.S. News ranking: Reg. Coll. (S), No. 29
Website: www.lander.edu
Admissions email: admissions@lander.edu
Public; founded 1872
Freshman admissions: selective; 2018-2019: 5,450 applied, 2,320 accepted. Either SAT or ACT required. SAT 25/75 percentile: 930-1120. High school rank: 14% in top tenth, 38% in top quarter, 74% in top half
Early decision deadline: N/A, notification date: N/A
Early action deadline: N/A, notification date: N/A
Application deadline (fall): rolling
Undergraduate student body: 2,764 full time, 206 part time; 32% male, 68% female; 1% American Indian, 1% Asian, 28% black, 3% Hispanic, 0% multiracial, 0% Pacific Islander, 61% white, 3% international
Most popular majors: 25% Business Administration and Management, General, 8% Kinesiology and Exercise Science, 8% Registered Nursing/Registered Nurse, 7% Psychology, General, 6% Early Childhood Education and Teaching
Expenses: 2018-2019: $11,700 in state, $21,300 out of state; room/board: $9,100
Financial aid: (864) 388-8340

Limestone College
Gaffney SC
(864) 488-4554
U.S. News ranking: Reg. Coll. (S), No. 49
Website: www.limestone.edu
Admissions email: admiss@limestone.edu
Private; founded 1845
Affiliation: Undenominational
Freshman admissions: selective; 2018-2019: 2,876 applied,

394 accepted. Either SAT or ACT required for some. SAT 25/75 percentile: 860-1090. High school rank: N/A
Early decision deadline: N/A, notification date: N/A
Early action deadline: N/A, notification date: N/A
Application deadline (fall): 8/22
Undergraduate student body: 1,796 full time, 578 part time; 44% male, 56% female; 1% American Indian, 1% Asian, 45% black, 4% Hispanic, 0% multiracial, 0% Pacific Islander, 45% white, 4% international; 80% from in state; 19% live on campus; 1% of students in fraternities, 1% in sororities
Most popular majors: 31% Business, Management, Marketing, and Related Support Services, 16% Public Administration and Social Service Professions, 8% Computer and Information Sciences and Support Services, 7% Health Professions and Related Programs, 7% Homeland Security, Law Enforcement, Firefighting and Related Protective Services
Expenses: 2019-2020: $26,300; room/board: $9,900
Financial aid: (864) 488-8251; 96% of undergrads determined to have financial need; average aid package $12,593

Morris College[1]
Sumter SC
(803) 934-3225
U.S. News ranking: Reg. Coll. (S), second tier
Website: www.morris.edu
Admissions email: admissions@morris.edu
Private; founded 1908
Affiliation: Baptist
Application deadline (fall): rolling
Undergraduate student body: N/A full time, N/A part time
Expenses: 2018-2019: $13,886; room/board: $6,033
Financial aid: N/A

Newberry College
Newberry SC
(800) 845-4955
U.S. News ranking: Reg. Coll. (S), No. 16
Website: www.newberry.edu/
Admissions email: admission@newberry.edu
Private; founded 1856
Affiliation: Lutheran Church in America
Freshman admissions: less selective; 2018-2019: 2,264 applied, 1,502 accepted. Either SAT or ACT required. ACT 25/75 percentile: 17-23. High school rank: 9% in top tenth, 30% in top quarter, 61% in top half
Early decision deadline: N/A, notification date: N/A
Early action deadline: N/A, notification date: N/A
Application deadline (fall): rolling
Undergraduate student body: 1,190 full time, 18 part time; 57% male, 43% female; 1% American Indian, 0% Asian, 27% black, 3% Hispanic, 5% multiracial,

0% Pacific Islander, 51% white, 5% international; 79% from in state; 82% live on campus; 13% of students in fraternities, 30% in sororities
Most popular majors: 18% Business Administration and Management, General, 17% Parks, Recreation and Leisure Studies, 13% Education, General, 8% Biology/Biological Sciences, General, 6% Registered Nursing/Registered Nurse
Expenses: 2019-2020: $27,400; room/board: $11,000
Financial aid: (803) 321-5127; 86% of undergrads determined to have financial need; average aid package $23,191

North Greenville University
Tigerville SC
(864) 977-7001
U.S. News ranking: Reg. U. (S), No. 50
Website: www.ngu.edu
Admissions email: admissions@ngu.edu
Private; founded 1892
Affiliation: Southern Baptist
Freshman admissions: selective; 2018-2019: 2,021 applied, 1,205 accepted. Either SAT or ACT required. ACT 25/75 percentile: 21-30. High school rank: 22% in top tenth, 44% in top quarter, 72% in top half
Early decision deadline: N/A, notification date: N/A
Early action deadline: N/A, notification date: N/A
Application deadline (fall): 8/22
Undergraduate student body: 2,025 full time, 383 part time; 47% male, 53% female; N/A American Indian, N/A Asian, N/A black, N/A Hispanic, N/A multiracial, N/A Pacific Islander, N/A white, N/A international
Most popular majors: 13% Business Administration and Management, General, 7% Health and Wellness, General, 6% Bible/Biblical Studies, 6% Sport and Fitness Administration/Management, 5% Elementary Education and Teaching
Expenses: 2019-2020: $21,120; room/board: $10,240
Financial aid: (864) 977-7057; 82% of undergrads determined to have financial need; average aid package $18,233

Presbyterian College
Clinton SC
(800) 476-7272
U.S. News ranking: Nat. Lib. Arts, No. 140
Website: www.presby.edu
Admissions email: mfox@presby.edu
Private; founded 1880
Affiliation: Presbyterian Church (USA)
Freshman admissions: selective; 2018-2019: 2,462 applied, 1,695 accepted. Either SAT or ACT required for some. SAT 25/75 percentile: 1010-1210. High school rank: 21% in top tenth, 52% in top quarter, 89% in top half

Early decision deadline: N/A, notification date: N/A
Early action deadline: 11/15, notification date: 12/15
Application deadline (fall): 6/30
Undergraduate student body: 994 full time, 86 part time; 48% male, 53% female; 0% American Indian, 1% Asian, 15% black, 4% Hispanic, 4% multiracial, 0% Pacific Islander, 71% white, 4% international; 70% from in state; 95% live on campus; 33% of students in fraternities, 44% in sororities
Most popular majors: 24% History, 14% Biological and Biomedical Sciences, 13% Psychology, 9% History, 9% Social Sciences
Expenses: 2019-2020: $39,460; room/board: $10,680
Financial aid: (864) 833-8287; 76% of undergrads determined to have financial need; average aid package $37,073

South Carolina State University[7]

Orangeburg SC
(803) 536-7185
U.S. News ranking: Reg. U. (S), No. 82
Website: www.scsu.edu
Admissions email: admissions@scsu.edu
Public; founded 1896
Freshman admissions: less selective; 2018-2019: 3,415 applied, 1,818 accepted. Either SAT or ACT required. ACT 25/75 percentile: 15-18. High school rank: 4% in top tenth, 39% in top quarter, 52% in top half
Early decision deadline: N/A, notification date: N/A
Early action deadline: N/A, notification date: N/A
Application deadline (fall): 7/31
Undergraduate student body: 2,152 full time, 278 part time
Most popular majors: 14% Biological and Biomedical Sciences, 14% Business, Management, Marketing, and Related Support Services, 12% Education, 10% Family and Consumer Sciences/Human Sciences, 7% Engineering Technologies and Engineering-Related Fields
Expenses: 2018-2019: $1,532 in state, $21,750 out of state; room/board: $9,890
Financial aid: (803) 536-7067

Southern Wesleyan University[1]

Central SC
(864) 644-5550
U.S. News ranking: Reg. U. (S), No. 75
Website: www.swu.edu
Admissions email: admissions@swu.edu
Private
Application deadline (fall): N/A
Undergraduate student body: N/A full time, N/A part time
Expenses: N/A
Financial aid: N/A

University of South Carolina

Columbia SC
(803) 777-7700
U.S. News ranking: Nat. U., No. 104
Website: www.sc.edu
Admissions email: admissions-ugrad@sc.edu
Public; founded 1801
Freshman admissions: more selective; 2018-2019: 30,889 applied, 19,480 accepted. Either SAT or ACT required. SAT 25/75 percentile: 1190-1360. High school rank: 29% in top tenth, 62% in top quarter, 91% in top half
Early decision deadline: N/A, notification date: N/A
Early action deadline: 10/15, notification date: 12/20
Application deadline (fall): 12/1
Undergraduate student body: 25,633 full time, 1,100 part time; 47% male, 53% female; 0% American Indian, 3% Asian, 9% black, 5% Hispanic, 4% multiracial, 0% Pacific Islander, 76% white, 2% international; 62% from in state; 27% live on campus; 22% of students in fraternities, 34% in sororities
Most popular majors: 7% Finance and Financial Management Services, 5% Public Health, 4% Biology, General, 4% Business Administration, Management and Operations, 4% Physiology, Pathology and Related Sciences
Expenses: 2019-2020: $12,688 in state, $33,928 out of state; room/board: $10,670
Financial aid: (803) 777-8134; 50% of undergrads determined to have financial need; average aid package $12,025

University of South Carolina–Aiken

Aiken SC
(803) 641-3366
U.S. News ranking: Reg. Coll. (S), No. 13
Website: www.usca.edu/
Admissions email: admit@sc.edu
Public; founded 1961
Freshman admissions: selective; 2018-2019: 3,115 applied, 1,587 accepted. Either SAT or ACT required. SAT 25/75 percentile: 950-1140. High school rank: 15% in top tenth, 40% in top quarter, 75% in top half
Early decision deadline: N/A, notification date: N/A
Early action deadline: N/A, notification date: N/A
Application deadline (fall): 7/1
Undergraduate student body: 2,671 full time, 673 part time; 35% male, 65% female; 0% American Indian, 1% Asian, 26% black, 5% Hispanic, 4% multiracial, 0% Pacific Islander, 58% white, 3% international; 88% from in state; 27% live on campus; 9% of students in fraternities, 9% in sororities
Most popular majors: 26% Business, Management, Marketing, and Related Support Services, 14% Health Professions and Related Programs, 10%

Parks, Recreation, Leisure, and Fitness Studies, 9% Education, 7% Biological and Biomedical Sciences
Expenses: 2019-2020: $10,760 in state, $21,218 out of state; room/board: $7,946
Financial aid: (803) 641-3476; 67% of undergrads determined to have financial need; average aid package $11,898

University of South Carolina–Beaufort[1]

Bluffton SC
(843) 208-8000
U.S. News ranking: Nat. Lib. Arts, second tier
Website: www.uscb.edu
Admissions email: admissions@uscb.edu
Public; founded 1959
Application deadline (fall): 7/1
Undergraduate student body: N/A full time, N/A part time
Expenses: N/A
Financial aid: (843) 521-4117

University of South Carolina–Upstate

Spartanburg SC
(864) 503-5246
U.S. News ranking: Reg. Coll. (S), No. 11
Website: www.uscupstate.edu/
Admissions email: admissions@uscupstate.edu
Public; founded 1967
Freshman admissions: selective; 2018-2019: 4,467 applied, 2,296 accepted. Either SAT or ACT required. ACT 25/75 percentile: 17-22. High school rank: 12% in top tenth, 35% in top quarter, 73% in top half
Early decision deadline: N/A, notification date: N/A
Early action deadline: N/A, notification date: N/A
Application deadline (fall): rolling
Undergraduate student body: 4,250 full time, 1,786 part time; 34% male, 66% female; 0% American Indian, 3% Asian, 33% black, 6% Hispanic, 4% multiracial, 0% Pacific Islander, 51% white, 2% international; 94% from in state; 17% live on campus; 1% of students in fraternities, 3% in sororities
Most popular majors: 29% Registered Nursing/Registered Nurse, 16% Business Administration and Management, General, 9% Education, General, 8% Liberal Arts and Sciences/Liberal Studies, 7% Psychology, General
Expenses: 2019-2020: $11,868 in state, $23,536 out of state; room/board: $9,764
Financial aid: (864) 503-5340; 76% of undergrads determined to have financial need; average aid package $9,830

Voorhees College

Denmark SC
(803) 780-1030
U.S. News ranking: Reg. Coll. (S), No. 55
Website: www.voorhees.edu
Admissions email: admissions@voorhees.edu
Private; founded 1897
Affiliation: Protestant Episcopal
Freshman admissions: least selective; 2018-2019: 7,212 applied, 4,720 accepted. Neither SAT nor ACT required. Average composite ACT score: 17. High school rank: N/A
Early decision deadline: N/A, notification date: N/A
Early action deadline: N/A, notification date: N/A
Application deadline (fall): N/A
Undergraduate student body: 482 full time, 9 part time; 43% male, 57% female; 0% American Indian, 0% Asian, 97% black, 0% Hispanic, 0% multiracial, 0% Pacific Islander, 1% white, 2% international; 62% from in state; N/A live on campus; N/A of students in fraternities, N/A in sororities
Most popular majors: Information not available
Expenses: 2019-2020: $12,630; room/board: $7,346
Financial aid: (803) 780-1234; 96% of undergrads determined to have financial need; average aid package $13,708

Winthrop University

Rock Hill SC
(803) 323-2191
U.S. News ranking: Reg. U. (S), No. 17
Website: www.winthrop.edu
Admissions email: admissions@winthrop.edu
Public; founded 1886
Affiliation: Other
Freshman admissions: selective; 2018-2019: 5,190 applied, 3,492 accepted. Either SAT or ACT required. SAT 25/75 percentile: 950-1160. High school rank: 13% in top tenth, 42% in top quarter, 80% in top half
Early decision deadline: N/A, notification date: N/A
Early action deadline: N/A, notification date: N/A
Application deadline (fall): rolling
Undergraduate student body: 4,331 full time, 556 part time; 30% male, 70% female; 0% American Indian, 1% Asian, 30% black, 6% Hispanic, 4% multiracial, 0% Pacific Islander, 57% white, 1% international; 91% from in state; 48% live on campus; N/A of students in fraternities, 2% in sororities
Most popular majors: Biological and Biomedical Sciences, Business, Management, Marketing, and Related Support Services, Education, Parks, Recreation, Leisure, and Fitness Studies, Psychology
Expenses: 2019-2020: $15,806 in state, $30,116 out of state; room/board: $9,340
Financial aid: (803) 323-2189; 76% of undergrads determined to have financial need; average aid package $13,642

Wofford College

Spartanburg SC
(864) 597-4130
U.S. News ranking: Nat. Lib. Arts, No. 72
Website: www.wofford.edu
Admissions email: admissions@wofford.edu
Private; founded 1854
Affiliation: United Methodist
Freshman admissions: more selective; 2018-2019: 3,520 applied, 2,238 accepted. Neither SAT nor ACT required. SAT 25/75 percentile: 1180-1350. High school rank: 38% in top tenth, 64% in top quarter, 91% in top half
Early decision deadline: 11/1, notification date: 12/1
Early action deadline: 11/15, notification date: 2/1
Application deadline (fall): 1/15
Undergraduate student body: 1,588 full time, 20 part time; 47% male, 53% female; 0% American Indian, 2% Asian, 9% black, 4% Hispanic, 3% multiracial, 0% Pacific Islander, 80% white, 2% international; 56% from in state; 97% live on campus; 47% of students in fraternities, 55% in sororities
Most popular majors: 24% Business, Management, Marketing, and Related Support Services, 14% Biological and Biomedical Sciences, 14% Social Sciences, 8% Psychology, 7% English Language and Literature/Letters
Expenses: 2019-2020: $45,710; room/board: $13,225
Financial aid: (864) 597-4160; 63% of undergrads determined to have financial need; average aid package $38,257

SOUTH DAKOTA

Augustana University

Sioux Falls SD
(605) 274-5516
U.S. News ranking: Reg. U. (Mid. W), No. 9
Website: www.augie.edu
Admissions email: admission@augie.edu
Private; founded 1860
Affiliation: Evangelical Lutheran Church
Freshman admissions: more selective; 2018-2019: 2,201 applied, 1,440 accepted. Either SAT or ACT required. ACT 25/75 percentile: 23-28. High school rank: 31% in top tenth, 64% in top quarter, 90% in top half
Early decision deadline: N/A, notification date: N/A
Early action deadline: N/A, notification date: N/A
Application deadline (fall): rolling
Undergraduate student body: 1,717 full time, 75 part time; 37% male, 63% female; 0% American Indian, 1% Asian, 3% black, 2% Hispanic, 2% multiracial, 0% Pacific Islander, 84% white, 8% international; 51% from in state; 70% live on campus; N/A of students in fraternities, N/A in sororities

Most popular majors: 16% Health Professions and Related Programs, 14% Business, Management, Marketing, and Related Support Services, 12% Education, 11% Biological and Biomedical Sciences, 8% Parks, Recreation, Leisure, and Fitness Studies
Expenses: 2019-2020: $33,960; room/board: $8,378
Financial aid: (605) 274-5216; 62% of undergrads determined to have financial need; average aid package $27,248

Black Hills State University
Spearfish SD
(800) 255-2478
U.S. News ranking: Reg. U. (Mid. W), second tier
Website: www.bhsu.edu
Admissions email: admissions@bhsu.edu
Public; founded 1883
Freshman admissions: selective; 2018-2019: 1,890 applied, 1,669 accepted. Either SAT or ACT required. ACT 25/75 percentile: 18-24. High school rank: N/A
Early decision deadline: N/A, notification date: N/A
Early action deadline: N/A, notification date: N/A
Application deadline (fall): rolling
Undergraduate student body: 2,029 full time, 1,716 part time; 36% male, 64% female; 4% American Indian, 1% Asian, 1% black, 6% Hispanic, 5% multiracial, 0% Pacific Islander, 81% white, 1% international
Most popular majors: Information not available
Expenses: 2019-2020: $9,009 in state, $12,155 out of state; room/board: $7,142
Financial aid: (605) 642-6145

Dakota State University
Madison SD
(888) 378-9988
U.S. News ranking: Reg. U. (Mid. W), No. 84
Website: www.dsu.edu
Admissions email: admissions@dsu.edu
Public; founded 1881
Freshman admissions: selective; 2018-2019: 1,056 applied, 879 accepted. Either SAT or ACT required. ACT 25/75 percentile: 20-26. High school rank: 8% in top tenth, 23% in top quarter, 54% in top half
Early decision deadline: N/A, notification date: N/A
Early action deadline: N/A, notification date: N/A
Application deadline (fall): rolling
Undergraduate student body: 1,448 full time, 1,545 part time; 59% male, 41% female; 1% American Indian, 2% Asian, 3% black, 4% Hispanic, 4% multiracial, 0% Pacific Islander, 84% white, 1% international; N/A from in state; 36% live on campus; N/A of students in fraternities, N/A in sororities

Most popular majors: 56% Computer and Information Sciences and Support Services, 12% Education, 11% Business, Management, Marketing, and Related Support Services, 5% Health Professions and Related Programs, 4% Visual and Performing Arts
Expenses: 2019-2020: $9,535 in state, $12,606 out of state; room/board: $7,033
Financial aid: (605) 256-5152; 67% of undergrads determined to have financial need; average aid package $8,362

Dakota Wesleyan University
Mitchell SD
(800) 333-8506
U.S. News ranking: Reg. Coll. (Mid. W), No. 26
Website: www.dwu.edu
Admissions email: admissions@dwu.edu
Private; founded 1885
Affiliation: United Methodist
Freshman admissions: selective; 2018-2019: 639 applied, 470 accepted. Either SAT or ACT required. ACT 25/75 percentile: 19-24. High school rank: 9% in top tenth, 28% in top quarter, 66% in top half
Early decision deadline: N/A, notification date: N/A
Early action deadline: N/A, notification date: N/A
Application deadline (fall): rolling
Undergraduate student body: 675 full time, 124 part time; 44% male, 56% female; 2% American Indian, 1% Asian, 2% black, 7% Hispanic, 3% multiracial, 0% Pacific Islander, 84% white, 2% international
Most popular majors: 47% Registered Nursing/Registered Nurse, 15% Business Administration and Management, General, 11% Elementary Education and Teaching, 5% Biology/Biological Sciences, General, 5% Sport and Fitness Administration/Management
Expenses: 2019-2020: $28,750; room/board: $7,100
Financial aid: (605) 995-2663; 83% of undergrads determined to have financial need; average aid package $18,619

Mount Marty College
Yankton SD
(855) 686-2789
U.S. News ranking: Reg. U. (Mid. W), No. 84
Website: www.mtmc.edu
Admissions email: mmcadmit@mtmc.edu
Private; founded 1936
Freshman admissions: selective; 2018-2019: 523 applied, 362 accepted. Either SAT or ACT required. ACT 25/75 percentile: 18-24. High school rank: N/A
Early decision deadline: N/A, notification date: N/A
Early action deadline: N/A, notification date: N/A
Application deadline (fall): 8/30

Undergraduate student body: 497 full time, 365 part time; 43% male, 57% female; 3% American Indian, 1% Asian, 3% black, 11% Hispanic, 1% multiracial, 0% Pacific Islander, 76% white, 3% international; 53% from in state; 75% live on campus; N/A of students in fraternities, N/A in sororities
Most popular majors: 20% Registered Nursing/Registered Nurse, 12% Business Administration and Management, General, 10% Education, General, 10% Kinesiology and Exercise Science, 8% Criminal Justice/Safety Studies
Expenses: 2019-2020: $28,126; room/board: $8,146
Financial aid: (605) 668-1589; 79% of undergrads determined to have financial need; average aid package $27,555

National American University[1]
Rapid City SD
(605) 394-4827
U.S. News ranking: Reg. Coll. (Mid. W), unranked
Website: www.national.edu/rc
Admissions email: N/A
For-profit
Application deadline (fall): N/A
Undergraduate student body: N/A full time, N/A part time
Expenses: N/A
Financial aid: N/A

Northern State University
Aberdeen SD
(800) 678-5330
U.S. News ranking: Reg. U. (Mid. W), No. 84
Website: www.northern.edu
Admissions email: admissions@northern.edu
Public; founded 1901
Freshman admissions: selective; 2018-2019: 1,066 applied, 939 accepted. Either SAT or ACT required. ACT 25/75 percentile: 19-24. High school rank: 9% in top tenth, 29% in top quarter, 63% in top half
Early decision deadline: N/A, notification date: N/A
Early action deadline: N/A, notification date: N/A
Application deadline (fall): rolling
Undergraduate student body: 1,333 full time, 1,718 part time; 42% male, 58% female; 3% American Indian, 2% Asian, 2% black, 4% Hispanic, 3% multiracial, 0% Pacific Islander, 81% white, 4% international; 70% from in state; 37% live on campus; 0% of students in fraternities, 0% in sororities
Most popular majors: 30% Business, Management, Marketing, and Related Support Services, 25% Education, 14% Biological and Biomedical Sciences, 7% Parks, Recreation, Leisure, and Fitness Studies, 7% Social Sciences
Expenses: 2019-2020: $8,750 in state, $11,821 out of state; room/board: $8,925

Financial aid: (605) 626-2640; 64% of undergrads determined to have financial need; average aid package $11,007

South Dakota School of Mines and Technology[7]
Rapid City SD
(605) 394-1979
U.S. News ranking: Engineering, unranked
Website: www.sdsmt.edu
Admissions email: admissions@sdsmt.edu
Public; founded 1885
Freshman admissions: selective; 2018-2019: 1,451 applied, 1,209 accepted. Either SAT or ACT required. ACT 25/75 percentile: 24-29. High school rank: 24% in top tenth, 56% in top quarter, 86% in top half
Early decision deadline: N/A, notification date: N/A
Early action deadline: N/A, notification date: N/A
Application deadline (fall): rolling
Undergraduate student body: 1,873 full time, 431 part time
Most popular majors: Information not available
Expenses: 2018-2019: $10,560 in state, $14,820 out of state; room/board: $8,440
Financial aid: (605) 394-2274

South Dakota State University
Brookings SD
(800) 952-3541
U.S. News ranking: Nat. U., No. 272
Website: www.sdstate.edu
Admissions email: SDSU_Admissions@sdstate.edu
Public; founded 1881
Freshman admissions: selective; 2018-2019: 5,390 applied, 4,982 accepted. Either SAT or ACT required. ACT 25/75 percentile: 20-26. High school rank: 16% in top tenth, 39% in top quarter, 73% in top half
Early decision deadline: N/A, notification date: N/A
Early action deadline: N/A, notification date: N/A
Undergraduate student body: 8,169 full time, 2,378 part time; 47% male, 53% female; 1% American Indian, 1% Asian, 2% black, 3% Hispanic, 2% multiracial, 0% Pacific Islander, 87% white, 4% international
Most popular majors: 23% Health Professions and Related Programs, 17% Agriculture, Agriculture Operations, and Related Sciences, 8% Engineering, 7% Social Sciences, 6% Education
Expenses: 2019-2020: $9,115 in state, $12,590 out of state; room/board: $8,145
Financial aid: (605) 688-4695; 54% of undergrads determined to have financial need; average aid package $8,504

University of Sioux Falls
Sioux Falls SD
(605) 331-6600
U.S. News ranking: Reg. U. (Mid. W), No. 102
Website: www.usiouxfalls.edu
Admissions email: admissions@usiouxfalls.edu
Private; founded 1883
Affiliation: American Baptist
Freshman admissions: selective; 2018-2019: 2,157 applied, 1,965 accepted. Either SAT or ACT required. ACT 25/75 percentile: 20-25. High school rank: 13% in top tenth, 37% in top quarter, 71% in top half
Early decision deadline: N/A, notification date: N/A
Early action deadline: N/A, notification date: N/A
Application deadline (fall): rolling
Undergraduate student body: 1,137 full time, 182 part time; 38% male, 62% female; 0% American Indian, 1% Asian, 6% black, 2% Hispanic, 6% multiracial, 0% Pacific Islander, 83% white, 1% international; 58% from in state; 44% live on campus; N/A of students in fraternities, N/A in sororities
Most popular majors: 22% Business, Management, Marketing, and Related Support Services, 20% Health Professions and Related Programs, 12% Education, 8% Psychology, 6% Parks, Recreation, Leisure, and Fitness Studies
Expenses: 2019-2020: $18,910; room/board: $7,550
Financial aid: (605) 331-6623; 69% of undergrads determined to have financial need; average aid package $12,765

University of South Dakota
Vermillion SD
(605) 658-6200
U.S. News ranking: Nat. U., No. 263
Website: www.usd.edu
Admissions email: admissions@usd.edu
Public; founded 1862
Freshman admissions: selective; 2018-2019: 4,119 applied, 3,534 accepted. Either SAT or ACT required. ACT 25/75 percentile: 20-25. High school rank: 13% in top tenth, 37% in top quarter, 68% in top half
Early decision deadline: N/A, notification date: N/A
Early action deadline: N/A, notification date: N/A
Application deadline (fall): N/A
Undergraduate student body: 4,969 full time, 2,621 part time; 37% male, 63% female; N/A American Indian, N/A Asian, N/A black, N/A Hispanic, N/A multiracial, N/A Pacific Islander, N/A white, N/A international
Most popular majors: Information not available
Expenses: 2019-2020: $9,332 in state, $12,807 out of state; room/board: $8,409
Financial aid: N/A

TENNESSEE

Austin Peay State University
Clarksville TN
(931) 221-7661
U.S. News ranking: Reg. U. (S), No. 58
Website: www.apsu.edu
Admissions email: admissions@apsu.edu
Public; founded 1927
Freshman admissions: selective; 2018-2019: 7,710 applied, 7,231 accepted. Either SAT or ACT required for some. ACT 25/75 percentile: 19-24. High school rank: 12% in top tenth, 34% in top quarter, 72% in top half
Early decision deadline: N/A, notification date: N/A
Early action deadline: N/A, notification date: N/A
Application deadline (fall): 8/8
Undergraduate student body: 6,993 full time, 2,878 part time, 41% male, 59% female; 0% American Indian, 1% Asian, 23% black, 8% Hispanic, 7% multiracial, 0% Pacific Islander, 58% white, 0% international; N/A from in state; 16% live on campus; 6% of students in fraternities, 7% in sororities
Most popular majors: 14% Health Professions and Related Programs, 12% Parks, Recreation, Leisure, and Fitness Studies, 10% Business, Management, Marketing, and Related Support Services, 8% Homeland Security, Law Enforcement, Firefighting and Related Protective Services, 7% Psychology
Expenses: 2018-2019: $8,471 in state, $24,467 out of state; room/board: $9,600
Financial aid: (931) 221-7907; 82% of undergrads determined to have financial need; average aid package $11,444

Belmont University
Nashville TN
(615) 460-6785
U.S. News ranking: Nat. U., No. 166
Website: www.Belmont.edu
Admissions email: buadmission@belmont.edu
Private; founded 1890
Affiliation: Interdenominational
Freshman admissions: more selective; 2018-2019: 8,210 applied, 6,771 accepted. Either SAT or ACT required. ACT 25/75 percentile: 24-29. High school rank: 30% in top tenth, 59% in top quarter, 89% in top half
Early decision deadline: N/A, notification date: N/A
Early action deadline: N/A, notification date: N/A
Application deadline (fall): 8/1
Undergraduate student body: 6,367 full time, 289 part time; 35% male, 65% female; 0% American Indian, 2% Asian, 5% black, 6% Hispanic, 4% multiracial, 0% Pacific Islander, 81% white, 1% international; 31% from in state; 54% live on campus; 2% of students in fraternities, 14% in sororities

Most popular majors: 41% Visual and Performing Arts, 13% Business, Management, Marketing, and Related Support Services, 11% Health Professions and Related Programs, 6% Communication, Journalism, and Related Programs, 5% Communications Technologies/Technicians and Support Services
Expenses: 2019-2020: $35,650; room/board: $12,520
Financial aid: (615) 460-6403; 53% of undergrads determined to have financial need; average aid package $20,334

Bethel University
McKenzie TN
(731) 352-4030
U.S. News ranking: Reg. U. (S), second tier
Website: www.bethelu.edu
Admissions email: N/A
Private; founded 1842
Affiliation: Cumberland Presbyterian
Freshman admissions: selective; 2018-2019: 1,889 applied, 1,260 accepted. Either SAT or ACT required for some. ACT 25/75 percentile: 16-25. High school rank: 5% in top tenth, 19% in top quarter, 47% in top half
Early decision deadline: N/A, notification date: N/A
Early action deadline: N/A, notification date: N/A
Application deadline (fall): 8/16
Undergraduate student body: 2,981 full time, 1,579 part time; 44% male, 56% female; 0% American Indian, 0% Asian, 37% black, 2% Hispanic, 5% multiracial, 0% Pacific Islander, 52% white, 2% international; 84% from in state; 26% live on campus; 5% of students in fraternities, 2% in sororities
Most popular majors: 49% Business, Management, Marketing, and Related Support Services, 31% Homeland Security, Law Enforcement, Firefighting and Related Protective Services, 8% Health Professions and Related Programs, 2% Parks, Leisure, and Fitness Studies, 2% Visual and Performing Arts
Expenses: 2019-2020: $17,010; room/board: $9,198
Financial aid: (731) 352-8412; 93% of undergrads determined to have financial need; average aid package $15,789

Bryan College
Dayton TN
(800) 277-9522
U.S. News ranking: Reg. U. (S), No. 47
Website: www.bryan.edu
Admissions email: admissions@bryan.edu
Private; founded 1930
Affiliation: Evangelical Christian
Freshman admissions: selective; 2018-2019: 902 applied, 463 accepted. Either SAT or ACT required for some. ACT 25/75 percentile: 21-26. High school rank: 15% in top tenth, 44% in top quarter, 85% in top half

Early decision deadline: N/A, notification date: N/A
Early action deadline: N/A, notification date: N/A
Application deadline (fall): rolling
Undergraduate student body: 673 full time, 568 part time; 45% male, 55% female; 1% American Indian, 1% Asian, 5% black, 3% Hispanic, 2% multiracial, 0% Pacific Islander, 84% white, 3% international; N/A from in state; 73% live on campus; N/A of students in fraternities, N/A in sororities
Most popular majors: 51% Business, Management, Marketing, and Related Support Services, 10% Education, 10% Psychology, 7% Parks, Recreation, Leisure, and Fitness Studies, 4% Theology and Religious Vocations
Expenses: 2019-2020: $28,000; room/board: $7,800
Financial aid: (423) 775-7339; 80% of undergrads determined to have financial need; average aid package $23,310

Carson-Newman University
Jefferson City TN
(800) 678-9061
U.S. News ranking: Nat. U., second tier
Website: www.cn.edu
Admissions email: admitme@cn.edu
Private; founded 1851
Affiliation: Baptist
Freshman admissions: selective; 2018-2019: 3,736 applied, 2,467 accepted. Either SAT or ACT required. ACT 25/75 percentile: 20-26. High school rank: N/A
Early decision deadline: N/A, notification date: N/A
Early action deadline: N/A, notification date: N/A
Application deadline (fall): rolling
Undergraduate student body: 1,661 full time, 113 part time; 41% male, 59% female; 1% American Indian, 1% Asian, 9% black, 3% Hispanic, 3% multiracial, 0% Pacific Islander, 79% white, 3% international; 81% from in state; 49% live on campus; N/A of students in fraternities, N/A in sororities
Most popular majors: 18% Business, Management, Marketing, and Related Support Services, 16% Health Professions and Related Programs, 13% Education, 10% Parks, Recreation, Leisure, and Fitness Studies, 8% Psychology
Expenses: 2019-2020: $28,900; room/board: $8,724
Financial aid: (865) 471-3247; 85% of undergrads determined to have financial need; average aid package $22,336

Christian Brothers University
Memphis TN
(901) 321-3205
U.S. News ranking: Reg. U. (S), No. 25
Website: www.cbu.edu
Admissions email: admissions@cbu.edu
Private; founded 1871
Affiliation: Roman Catholic
Freshman admissions: more selective; 2018-2019: 2,793 applied, 1,552 accepted. Either SAT or ACT required. ACT 25/75 percentile: 22-27. High school rank: 28% in top tenth, 61% in top quarter, 85% in top half
Early decision deadline: N/A, notification date: N/A
Early action deadline: N/A, notification date: N/A
Application deadline (fall): rolling
Undergraduate student body: 1,437 full time, 109 part time; 49% male, 51% female; 1% American Indian, 5% Asian, 26% black, 8% Hispanic, 5% multiracial, 0% Pacific Islander, 34% white, 4% international; 75% from in state; 44% live on campus; N/A of students in fraternities, N/A in sororities
Most popular majors: 20% Business Administration and Management, General, 9% Computer Engineering, General, 9% Psychology, General, 5% Biology/Biological Sciences, General, 5% Natural Sciences
Expenses: 2019-2020: $33,840; room/board: $7,700
Financial aid: (901) 321-3305; 68% of undergrads determined to have financial need; average aid package $25,538

Cumberland University
Lebanon TN
(615) 444-2562
U.S. News ranking: Reg. U. (S), No. 84
Website: www.cumberland.edu
Admissions email: admissions@cumberland.edu
Private; founded 1842
Freshman admissions: selective; 2018-2019: 2,308 applied, 1,423 accepted. Either SAT or ACT required. ACT 25/75 percentile: 19-23. High school rank: N/A
Early decision deadline: N/A, notification date: N/A
Early action deadline: N/A, notification date: N/A
Application deadline (fall): rolling
Undergraduate student body: 1,694 full time, 399 part time; 44% male, 56% female; 1% American Indian, 1% Asian, 12% black, 4% Hispanic, 0% multiracial, 0% Pacific Islander, 58% white, 3% international
Most popular majors: 43% Registered Nursing/Registered Nurse, 9% Physical Education Teaching and Coaching, 7% Business Administration and Management, General, 4% Criminal Justice/Law Enforcement Administration, 4% Management Science

Expenses: 2018-2019: $22,890; room/board: $9,290
Financial aid: (615) 547-1399

East Tennessee State University[1]
Johnson City TN
(423) 439-4213
U.S. News ranking: Nat. U., second tier
Website: www.etsu.edu
Admissions email: go2etsu@etsu.edu
Public; founded 1911
Application deadline (fall): 8/15
Undergraduate student body: N/A full time, N/A part time
Expenses: N/A
Financial aid: (423) 439 4300

Fisk University
Nashville TN
(888) 702-0022
U.S. News ranking: Nat. Lib. Arts, second tier
Website: www.fisk.edu
Admissions email: admissions@fisk.edu
Private; founded 1866
Freshman admissions: selective; 2018-2019: 1,885 applied, 1,348 accepted. Either SAT or ACT required. ACT 25/75 percentile: 17-23. High school rank: 19% in top tenth, 43% in top quarter, 71% in top half
Early decision deadline: N/A, notification date: N/A
Early action deadline: 11/1, notification date: 12/31
Application deadline (fall): rolling
Undergraduate student body: 716 full time, 27 part time; 30% male, 70% female; 0% American Indian, 0% Asian, 86% black, 1% Hispanic, 2% multiracial, 0% Pacific Islander, 1% white, 5% international
Most popular majors: 24% Business Administration, Management and Operations, 21% Psychology, General, 14% Biology, General, 5% English Language and Literature, General, 5% Political Science and Government
Expenses: 2018-2019: $21,480; room/board: $10,790
Financial aid: (615) 329-8585

Freed-Hardeman University
Henderson TN
(731) 348-3481
U.S. News ranking: Reg. U. (S), No. 31
Website: www.fhu.edu
Admissions email: admissions@fhu.edu
Private; founded 1869
Affiliation: Churches of Christ
Freshman admissions: selective; 2018-2019: 866 applied, 804 accepted. Either SAT or ACT required. ACT 25/75 percentile: 21-28. High school rank: 30% in top tenth, 51% in top quarter, 78% in top half
Early decision deadline: N/A, notification date: N/A
Early action deadline: N/A, notification date: N/A
Application deadline (fall): rolling

Undergraduate student body: 1,270 full time, 278 part time; 43% male, 57% female; 1% American Indian, 0% Asian, 4% black, 0% Hispanic, 1% multiracial, 0% Pacific Islander, 86% white, 2% international; 66% from in state; 82% live on campus; 0% of students in fraternities, 0% in sororities
Most popular majors: 18% Business, Management, Marketing, and Related Support Services, 12% Health Professions and Related Programs, 8% Education, 8% Public Administration and Social Service Professions, 8% Theology and Religious Vocations
Expenses: 2019-2020: $22,950; room/board: $7,950
Financial aid: (731) 989-6662; 74% of undergrads determined to have financial need; average aid package $19,118

Hiwassee College[1]
Madisonville TN
(423) 442-2001
U.S. News ranking: Reg. Coll. (S), second tier
Website: www.highline.edu
Admissions email: N/A
Private
Application deadline (fall): N/A
Undergraduate student body: N/A full time, N/A part time
Expenses: N/A
Financial aid: N/A

King University
Bristol TN
(423) 652-4861
U.S. News ranking: Reg. U. (S), No. 65
Website: www.king.edu
Admissions email: admissions@king.edu
Private; founded 1867
Affiliation: Presbyterian
Freshman admissions: selective; 2018-2019: 1,046 applied, 608 accepted. Neither SAT nor ACT required. ACT 25/75 percentile: 19-25. High school rank: 12% in top tenth, 26% in top quarter, 64% in top half
Early decision deadline: N/A, notification date: N/A
Early action deadline: N/A, notification date: N/A
Application deadline (fall): rolling
Undergraduate student body: 1,460 full time, 119 part time; 38% male, 62% female; 0% American Indian, 1% Asian, 6% black, 4% Hispanic, 1% multiracial, 0% Pacific Islander, 73% white, 3% international; 57% from in state; 21% live on campus; N/A of students in fraternities, N/A in sororities
Most popular majors: 38% Health Professions and Related Programs, 29% Business, Management, Marketing, and Related Support Services, 8% Computer and Information Sciences and Support Services, 7% Psychology, 3% Homeland Security, Law Enforcement, Firefighting and Related Protective Services
Expenses: 2018-2019: $15,617; room/board: $8,762

Financial aid: (423) 652-4726; 83% of undergrads determined to have financial need; average aid package $16,476

Lane College
Jackson TN
(731) 426-7533
U.S. News ranking: Nat. Lib. Arts, second tier
Website: www.lanecollege.edu
Admissions email: admissions@lanecollege.edu
Private; founded 1882
Affiliation: Christian Methodist Episcopal
Freshman admissions: less selective; 2018-2019: N/A applied, N/A accepted. Neither SAT nor ACT required. SAT 25/75 percentile: N/A. High school rank: N/A
Early decision deadline: N/A, notification date: N/A
Early action deadline: N/A, notification date: N/A
Application deadline (fall): 7/1
Undergraduate student body: 1,184 full time, 48 part time; 51% male, 49% female; 0% American Indian, 0% Asian, 91% black, 1% Hispanic, 3% multiracial, 0% Pacific Islander, 0% white, 0% international
Most popular majors: Information not available
Expenses: 2018-2019: $11,500; room/board: $7,350
Financial aid: N/A

Lee University
Cleveland TN
(423) 614-8500
U.S. News ranking: Reg. U. (S), No. 34
Website: www.leeuniversity.edu
Admissions email: admissions@leeuniversity.edu
Private; founded 1918
Affiliation: Church of God
Freshman admissions: selective; 2018-2019: 2,443 applied, 2,029 accepted. Either SAT or ACT required. ACT 25/75 percentile: 21-28. High school rank: 24% in top tenth, 49% in top quarter, 78% in top half
Early decision deadline: N/A, notification date: N/A
Early action deadline: N/A, notification date: N/A
Application deadline (fall): rolling
Undergraduate student body: 3,780 full time, 1,103 part time; 39% male, 61% female; 0% American Indian, 1% Asian, 5% black, 2% Hispanic, 3% multiracial, 0% Pacific Islander, 82% white, 3% international; 43% from in state; 47% live on campus; 8% of students in fraternities, 8% in sororities
Most popular majors: 18% Theology and Religious Vocations, 14% Education, 12% Communication, Journalism, and Related Programs, 11% Business, Management, Marketing, and Related Support Services, 10% Health Professions and Related Programs
Expenses: 2019-2020: $18,770; room/board: $8,325

Financial aid: (423) 614-8300; 68% of undergrads determined to have financial need; average aid package $14,010

LeMoyne-Owen College
Memphis TN
(901) 435-1500
U.S. News ranking: Reg. Coll. (S), second tier
Website: www.loc.edu/
Admissions email: admission@loc.edu
Private; founded 1862
Affiliation: United Church of Christ
Freshman admissions: least selective; 2018-2019: 419 applied, 389 accepted. ACT required. ACT 25/75 percentile: 15-17. High school rank: N/A
Early decision deadline: N/A, notification date: N/A
Early action deadline: N/A, notification date: N/A
Application deadline (fall): 8/1
Undergraduate student body: 761 full time, 124 part time; 31% male, 69% female; 0% American Indian, 0% Asian, 98% black, 0% Hispanic, 0% multiracial, 0% Pacific Islander, 0% white, 2% international
Most popular majors: 40% Business Administration and Management, General, 15% Criminal Justice/Safety Studies, 9% Education, General, 8% Biology/Biological Sciences, General, 8% Social Work
Expenses: 2019-2020: $11,216; room/board: $6,100
Financial aid: (901) 435-1550

Lincoln Memorial University
Harrogate TN
(423) 869-6280
U.S. News ranking: Nat. U., No. 254
Website: www.lmunet.edu
Admissions email: admissions@lmunet.edu
Private; founded 1897
Freshman admissions: selective; 2018-2019: 1,836 applied, 795 accepted. Neither SAT nor ACT required. ACT 25/75 percentile: 19-25. High school rank: 26% in top tenth, 55% in top quarter, 83% in top half
Early decision deadline: N/A, notification date: N/A
Early action deadline: N/A, notification date: N/A
Application deadline (fall): rolling
Undergraduate student body: 1,395 full time, 558 part time; 28% male, 72% female; 2% American Indian, 1% Asian, 6% black, 0% Hispanic, 0% multiracial, 0% Pacific Islander, 85% white, 0% international; 60% from in state; 43% live on campus; 1% of students in fraternities, 1% in sororities
Most popular majors: 51% Health Professions and Related Programs, 14% Business, Management, Marketing, and Related Support Services, 9% Biological and Biomedical Sciences, 8% Education, 4% Psychology

Expenses: 2019-2020: $22,740; room/board: $8,250
Financial aid: (423) 869-6336; 85% of undergrads determined to have financial need; average aid package $22,394

Lipscomb University
Nashville TN
(615) 966-1776
U.S. News ranking: Nat. U., No. 218
Website: www.lipscomb.edu
Admissions email: admissions@lipscomb.edu
Private; founded 1891
Affiliation: Churches of Christ
Freshman admissions: more selective; 2018-2019: 3,638 applied, 2,165 accepted. Either SAT or ACT required. ACT 25/75 percentile: 22-29. High school rank: 30% in top tenth, 58% in top quarter, 87% in top half
Early decision deadline: N/A, notification date: N/A
Early action deadline: N/A, notification date: N/A
Application deadline (fall): rolling
Undergraduate student body: 2,738 full time, 200 part time; 39% male, 61% female; 0% American Indian, 3% Asian, 7% black, 8% Hispanic, 3% multiracial, 0% Pacific Islander, 75% white, 3% international; 61% from in state; 47% live on campus; 23% of students in fraternities, 24% in sororities
Most popular majors: 24% Business, Management, Marketing, and Related Support Services, 11% Biological and Biomedical Sciences, 8% Education, 6% Engineering, 6% Psychology
Expenses: 2019-2020: $33,424; room/board: $13,280
Financial aid: (615) 966-6205; 62% of undergrads determined to have financial need; average aid package $29,133

Martin Methodist College
Pulaski TN
(931) 363-9800
U.S. News ranking: Reg. Coll. (S), No. 34
Website: www.martinmethodist.edu
Admissions email: info@martinmethodist.edu
Private; founded 1870
Affiliation: United Methodist
Freshman admissions: selective; 2018-2019: 772 applied, 769 accepted. Either SAT or ACT required. ACT 25/75 percentile: 18-24. High school rank: N/A
Early decision deadline: N/A, notification date: N/A
Early action deadline: N/A, notification date: N/A
Application deadline (fall): rolling
Undergraduate student body: 769 full time, 132 part time; 39% male, 61% female; 0% American Indian, 1% Asian, 10% black, 3% Hispanic, 2% multiracial, 0% Pacific Islander, 72% white, 4% international; 75% from in

state; 43% live on campus; 0% of students in fraternities, 0% in sororities
Most popular majors: 28% Business Administration and Management, General, 18% Health and Physical Education/Fitness, General, 16% Behavioral Sciences, 10% Registered Nursing/Registered Nurse, 5% Biology/Biological Sciences, General
Expenses: 2018-2019: $23,496; room/board: $8,400
Financial aid: (931) 424-7366

Maryville College
Maryville TN
(865) 981-8092
U.S. News ranking: Reg. Coll. (S), No. 3
Website: www.maryvillecollege.edu
Admissions email: admissions@maryvillecollege.edu
Private; founded 1819
Affiliation: Presbyterian Church (USA)
Freshman admissions: selective; 2018-2019: 2,346 applied, 1,279 accepted. Either SAT or ACT required. ACT 25/75 percentile: 21-27. High school rank: 24% in top tenth, 42% in top quarter, 74% in top half
Early decision deadline: N/A, notification date: N/A
Early action deadline: N/A, notification date: N/A
Application deadline (fall): 5/1
Undergraduate student body: 1,102 full time, 44 part time; 45% male, 55% female; 0% American Indian, 1% Asian, 11% black, 4% Hispanic, 4% multiracial, 0% Pacific Islander, 76% white, 2% international; 75% from in state; 68% live on campus; N/A of students in fraternities, N/A in sororities
Most popular majors: 21% Business, Management, Marketing, and Related Support Services, 14% Social Sciences, 11% Biological and Biomedical Sciences, 11% Parks, Recreation, Leisure, and Fitness Studies, 9% Education
Expenses: 2019-2020: $35,578; room/board: $11,710
Financial aid: (865) 981-8100; 82% of undergrads determined to have financial need; average aid package $32,852

Memphis College of Art[1]
Memphis TN
(800) 727-1088
U.S. News ranking: Arts, unranked
Website: www.mca.edu
Admissions email: info@mca.edu
Private; founded 1936
Application deadline (fall): rolling
Undergraduate student body: N/A full time, N/A part time
Expenses: N/A
Financial aid: (901) 272-5138

Middle Tennessee State University

Murfreesboro TN
(615) 898-2233
U.S. News ranking: Nat. U., second tier
Website: www.mtsu.edu
Admissions email: admissions@mtsu.edu
Public; founded 1911
Freshman admissions: selective; 2018-2019: 8,055 applied, 7,534 accepted. Either SAT or ACT required. ACT 25/75 percentile: 20-26. High school rank: N/A
Early decision deadline: N/A, notification date: N/A
Early action deadline: N/A, notification date: N/A
Application deadline (fall): rolling
Undergraduate student body: 15,511 full time, 3,740 part time; 46% male, 54% female; 0% American Indian, 3% Asian, 20% black, 6% Hispanic, 4% multiracial, 0% Pacific Islander, 63% white, 3% international; 91% from in state; 17% live on campus; 5% of students in fraternities, 9% in sororities
Most popular majors: 16% Business, Management, Marketing, and Related Support Services, 12% Liberal Arts and Sciences, General Studies and Humanities, 9% Visual and Performing Arts, 6% Communication, Journalism, and Related Programs, 5% Health Professions and Related Programs
Expenses: 2019-2020: $9,424 in state, $29,038 out of state; room/board: $9,772
Financial aid: (615) 898-5454; 69% of undergrads determined to have financial need; average aid package $9,879

Milligan College

Milligan College TN
(423) 461-8730
U.S. News ranking: Reg. U. (S), No. 13
Website: www.milligan.edu
Admissions email: admissions@milligan.edu
Private; founded 1866
Affiliation: Christian Churches and Churches of Christ
Freshman admissions: selective; 2018-2019: 482 applied, 402 accepted. Either SAT or ACT required. ACT 25/75 percentile: 22-28. High school rank: N/A
Early decision deadline: N/A, notification date: N/A
Early action deadline: N/A, notification date: N/A
Application deadline (fall): rolling
Undergraduate student body: 734 full time, 95 part time; 43% male, 57% female; 0% American Indian, 2% Asian, 4% black, 5% Hispanic, 2% multiracial, 0% Pacific Islander, 82% white, 5% international; 64% from in state; 75% live on campus; 0% of students in fraternities, 0% in sororities
Most popular majors: 15% Business Administration and Management, General, 10% Communication and Media

Studies, 10% Health and Physical Education/Fitness, General, 10% Psychology, General, 9% Registered Nursing/Registered Nurse
Expenses: 2019-2020: $34,650; room/board: $7,300
Financial aid: (423) 461-8968; 81% of undergrads determined to have financial need; average aid package $25,278

Rhodes College

Memphis TN
(800) 844-5969
U.S. News ranking: Nat. Lib. Arts, No. 53
Website: www.rhodes.edu
Admissions email: adminfo@rhodes.edu
Private; founded 1848
Affiliation: Presbyterian
Freshman admissions: more selective; 2018-2019: 5,093 applied, 2,269 accepted. Either SAT or ACT required. ACT 25/75 percentile: 28-31. High school rank: 54% in top tenth, 85% in top quarter, 99% in top half
Early decision deadline: 11/1, notification date: 9/15
Early action deadline: 11/15, notification date: 1/1
Application deadline (fall): 1/15
Undergraduate student body: 1,992 full time, 16 part time; 44% male, 56% female; 0% American Indian, 6% Asian, 9% black, 6% Hispanic, 5% multiracial, 0% Pacific Islander, 69% white, 4% international; 29% from in state; 69% live on campus; 34% of students in fraternities, 40% in sororities
Most popular majors: 22% Social Sciences, 20% Biological and Biomedical Sciences, 14% Business, Management, Marketing, and Related Support Services, 7% Physical Sciences, 7% Psychology
Expenses: 2019-2020: $49,198; room/board: $11,524
Financial aid: (800) 844-5969; 50% of undergrads determined to have financial need; average aid package $40,793

Southern Adventist University

Collegedale TN
(423) 236-2835
U.S. News ranking: Reg. U. (S), No. 50
Website: www.southern.edu
Admissions email: admissions@southern.edu
Private; founded 1892
Affiliation: Seventh Day Adventist
Freshman admissions: selective; 2018-2019: 1,658 applied, 1,549 accepted. Either SAT or ACT required. ACT 25/75 percentile: 19-26. High school rank: N/A
Early decision deadline: N/A, notification date: N/A
Early action deadline: N/A, notification date: N/A
Application deadline (fall): rolling
Undergraduate student body: 2,139 full time, 392 part time; 42% male, 58% female; 0% American

Indian, 11% Asian, 10% black, 25% Hispanic, 7% multiracial, 1% Pacific Islander, 41% white, 6% international; 34% from in state; N/A live on campus; 0% of students in fraternities, 0% in sororities
Most popular majors: 39% Health Professions and Related Programs, 10% Business, Management, Marketing, and Related Support Services, 7% Biological and Biomedical Sciences, 7% Education, 5% Visual and Performing Arts
Expenses: 2019-2020: $22,520; room/board: $7,240
Financial aid: (423) 236-2535; 68% of undergrads determined to have financial need; average aid package $16,910

Tennessee State University

Nashville TN
(615) 963-5101
U.S. News ranking: Nat. U., second tier
Website: www.tnstate.edu
Admissions email: jcade@tnstate.edu
Public; founded 1912
Freshman admissions: less selective; 2018-2019: 8,910 applied, 4,609 accepted. Either SAT or ACT required. ACT 25/75 percentile: 17-21. High school rank: N/A
Early decision deadline: N/A, notification date: N/A
Early action deadline: N/A, notification date: N/A
Application deadline (fall): 7/1
Undergraduate student body: 5,029 full time, 1,092 part time; 38% male, 62% female; 0% American Indian, 1% Asian, 76% black, 1% Hispanic, 2% multiracial, 0% Pacific Islander, 11% white, 7% international
Most popular majors: 16% Health Professions and Related Programs, 15% Business, Management, Marketing, and Related Support Services, 8% Education, 8% Homeland Security, Law Enforcement, Firefighting and Related Protective Services, 8% Psychology
Expenses: 2019-2020: $7,251 in state, $20,607 out of state; room/board: $7,500
Financial aid: (615) 963-5701; 91% of undergrads determined to have financial need; average aid package $11,850

Tennessee Technological University

Cookeville TN
(800) 255-8881
U.S. News ranking: Nat. U., No. 272
Website: www.tntech.edu
Admissions email: admissions@tntech.edu
Public; founded 1915
Freshman admissions: more selective; 2018-2019: 6,913 applied, 5,237 accepted. Either SAT or ACT required. ACT 25/75

percentile: 21-27. High school rank: 27% in top tenth, 59% in top quarter, 86% in top half
Early decision deadline: N/A, notification date: N/A
Early action deadline: N/A, notification date: N/A
Application deadline (fall): rolling
Undergraduate student body: 7,999 full time, 1,007 part time; 55% male, 45% female; 0% American Indian, 2% Asian, 4% black, 3% Hispanic, 4% multiracial, 0% Pacific Islander, 84% white, 3% international; 94% from in state; 26% live on campus; 9% of students in fraternities, 9% in sororities
Most popular majors: 8% Mechanical Engineering, 8% Teacher Education, Multiple Levels, 7% Business Administration and Management, General, 7% Liberal Arts and Sciences/Liberal Studies, 6% Registered Nursing/Registered Nurse
Expenses: 2019-2020: $8,900 in state, $17,373 out of state; room/board: $8,850
Financial aid: (931) 372-3070; 71% of undergrads determined to have financial need; average aid package $11,044

Tennessee Wesleyan University

Athens TN
(423) 746-5286
U.S. News ranking: Reg. Coll. (S), No. 16
Website: www.tnwesleyan.edu
Admissions email: admissions@tnwesleyan.edu
Private; founded 1857
Affiliation: United Methodist
Freshman admissions: selective; 2018-2019: 758 applied, 472 accepted. Either SAT or ACT required. ACT 25/75 percentile: 19-24. High school rank: 16% in top tenth, 35% in top quarter, 74% in top half
Early decision deadline: N/A, notification date: N/A
Early action deadline: N/A, notification date: N/A
Application deadline (fall): rolling
Undergraduate student body: 886 full time, 97 part time; 37% male, 63% female; 0% American Indian, 1% Asian, 7% black, 3% Hispanic, 2% multiracial, 0% Pacific Islander, 54% white, 7% international; N/A from in state; 30% live on campus; 6% of students in fraternities, 7% in sororities
Most popular majors: 44% Business, Management, Marketing, and Related Support Services, 24% Health Professions and Related Programs, 8% Parks, Recreation, Leisure, and Fitness Studies, 6% Education, 3% Psychology
Expenses: 2019-2020: $25,150; room/board: $8,050
Financial aid: (423) 746-5209; 84% of undergrads determined to have financial need; average aid package $14,763

Trevecca Nazarene University

Nashville TN
(615) 248-1320
U.S. News ranking: Nat. U., second tier
Website: www.trevecca.edu
Admissions email: admissions_und@trevecca.edu
Private; founded 1901
Affiliation: Church of the Nazarene
Freshman admissions: selective; 2018-2019: 1,671 applied, 1,070 accepted. Either SAT or ACT required. ACT 25/75 percentile: 19-25. High school rank: 22% in top tenth, 30% in top quarter, 69% in top half
Early decision deadline: N/A, notification date: N/A
Early action deadline: N/A, notification date: N/A
Application deadline (fall): 8/1
Undergraduate student body: 1,886 full time, 425 part time; 38% male, 62% female; 0% American Indian, 1% Asian, 13% black, 9% Hispanic, 3% multiracial, 0% Pacific Islander, 61% white, 6% international; N/A from in state; 39% live on campus; N/A of students in fraternities, N/A in sororities
Most popular majors: 35% Business, Management, Marketing, and Related Support Services, 11% Health Professions and Related Programs, 10% Theology and Religious Vocations, 6% Communication, Journalism, and Related Programs, 6% Psychology
Expenses: 2019-2020: $26,098; room/board: $8,900
Financial aid: (615) 248-1242

Tusculum University[1]

Greeneville TN
(800) 729-0256
U.S. News ranking: Reg. U. (S), No. 84
Website: www.tusculum.edu
Admissions email: admissions@tusculum.edu
Private; founded 1794
Affiliation: Presbyterian
Application deadline (fall): rolling
Undergraduate student body: N/A full time, N/A part time
Expenses: N/A
Financial aid: (423) 636-5377

Union University

Jackson TN
(800) 338-6466
U.S. News ranking: Nat. U., No. 185
Website: www.uu.edu
Admissions email: admissions@uu.edu
Private; founded 1823
Affiliation: Southern Baptist
Freshman admissions: more selective; 2018-2019: 2,663 applied, 1,529 accepted. Either SAT or ACT required. ACT 25/75 percentile: 23-30. High school rank: 34% in top tenth, 62% in top quarter, 90% in top half
Early decision deadline: N/A, notification date: N/A
Early action deadline: N/A, notification date: N/A

Application deadline (fall): rolling
Undergraduate student body: 1,780 full time, 411 part time; 33% male, 67% female; 1% American Indian, 2% Asian, 17% black, 2% Hispanic, 0% multiracial, 0% Pacific Islander, 74% white, 2% international; 71% from in state; 74% live on campus; 29% of students in fraternities, 31% in sororities
Most popular majors: 31% Health Professions and Related Programs, 26% Business, Management, Marketing, and Related Support Services, 6% Education, 6% Psychology, 6% Public Administration and Social Service Professions
Expenses: 2019-2020: $33,900; room/board: $10,400
Financial aid: (731) 661-5015; 80% of undergrads determined to have financial need; average aid package $26,846

University of Memphis

Memphis TN
(901) 678-2111
U.S. News ranking: Nat. U., No. 272
Website: www.memphis.edu
Admissions email: recruitment@memphis.edu
Public; founded 1912
Freshman admissions: selective; 2018-2019: 14,160 applied, 11,923 accepted. Either SAT or ACT required. ACT 25/75 percentile: 19-26. High school rank: 14% in top tenth, 37% in top quarter, 69% in top half
Early decision deadline: N/A, notification date: N/A
Early action deadline: N/A, notification date: N/A
Application deadline (fall): 7/1
Undergraduate student body: 12,064 full time, 5,169 part time; 41% male, 59% female; 0% American Indian, 4% Asian, 37% black, 6% Hispanic, 4% multiracial, 0% Pacific Islander, 47% white, 2% international; N/A from in state; 14% live on campus; 6% of students in fraternities, 8% in sororities
Most popular majors: 18% Business, Management, Marketing, and Related Support Services, 11% Health Professions and Related Programs, 10% Multi/Interdisciplinary Studies, 5% Liberal Arts and Sciences, General Studies and Humanities, 5% Psychology
Expenses: 2019-2020: $9,701 in state, $16,037 out of state; room/board: $10,175
Financial aid: (901) 678-4825; 76% of undergrads determined to have financial need; average aid package $7,491

University of Tennessee

Knoxville TN
(865) 974-1111
U.S. News ranking: Nat. U., No. 104
Website: utk.edu
Admissions email: admissions@utk.edu
Public; founded 1794

Freshman admissions: more selective; 2018-2019: 20,457 applied, 15,912 accepted. Either SAT or ACT required. ACT 25/75 percentile: 25-31. High school rank: 36% in top tenth, 66% in top quarter, 90% in top half
Early decision deadline: N/A, notification date: N/A
Early action deadline: 11/1, notification date: 12/15
Application deadline (fall): rolling
Undergraduate student body: 21,489 full time, 1,326 part time; 49% male, 51% female; 0% American Indian, 4% Asian, 6% black, 4% Hispanic, 3% multiracial, 0% Pacific Islander, 78% white, 1% international; 82% from in state; 32% live on campus; 18% of students in fraternities, 31% in sororities
Most popular majors: 24% Business, Management, Marketing, and Related Support Services, 11% Engineering, 8% Parks, Recreation, Leisure, and Fitness Studies, 7% Communication, Journalism, and Related Programs, 7% Social Sciences
Expenses: 2019-2020: $13,264 in state, $31,454 out of state; room/board: $11,482
Financial aid: (865) 974-1111; 56% of undergrads determined to have financial need; average aid package $13,685

University of Tennessee–Chattanooga

Chattanooga TN
(423) 425-4662
U.S. News ranking: Nat. U., second tier
Website: www.utc.edu
Admissions email: utcmocs@utc.edu
Public; founded 1886
Freshman admissions: selective; 2018-2019: 8,854 applied, 6,695 accepted. Either SAT or ACT required. ACT 25/75 percentile: 21-27. High school rank: N/A
Early decision deadline: N/A, notification date: N/A
Early action deadline: N/A, notification date: N/A
Application deadline (fall): 5/1
Undergraduate student body: 9,099 full time, 1,140 part time; 44% male, 56% female; 0% American Indian, 2% Asian, 10% black, 5% Hispanic, 3% multiracial, 0% Pacific Islander, 76% white, 1% international; 93% from in state; 30% live on campus; 14% of students in fraternities, 16% in sororities
Most popular majors: 20% Business, Management, Marketing, and Related Support Services, 10% Parks, Recreation, Leisure, and Fitness Studies, 9% Education, 8% Engineering, 7% Health Professions and Related Programs
Expenses: 2019-2020: $9,656 in state, $25,774 out of state; room/board: $10,159

Financial aid: (423) 425-4677; 63% of undergrads determined to have financial need; average aid package $10,411

University of Tennessee–Martin

Martin TN
(800) 829-8861
U.S. News ranking: Reg. U. (S), No. 28
Website: www.utm.edu
Admissions email: admitme@utm.edu
Public; founded 1900
Freshman admissions: selective; 2018-2019: 8,048 applied, 5,544 accepted. ACT required. ACT 25/75 percentile: 21-26. High school rank: 17% in top tenth, 43% in top quarter, 78% in top half
Early decision deadline: N/A, notification date: N/A
Early action deadline: N/A, notification date: N/A
Application deadline (fall): rolling
Undergraduate student body: 4,748 full time, 1,946 part time; 40% male, 60% female; 0% American Indian, 1% Asian, 14% black, 3% Hispanic, 2% multiracial, 0% Pacific Islander, 78% white, 2% international; 90% from in state; 30% live on campus; 13% of students in fraternities, 14% in sororities
Most popular majors: 19% Business, Management, Marketing, and Related Support Services, 15% Agriculture, Agriculture Operations, and Related Sciences, 10% Parks, Recreation, Leisure, and Fitness Studies, 9% Multi/Interdisciplinary Studies, 8% Education
Expenses: 2019-2020: $9,748 in state, $15,788 out of state; room/board: $6,396
Financial aid: (731) 881-7040; 75% of undergrads determined to have financial need; average aid package $11,535

The University of the South

Sewanee TN
(800) 522-2234
U.S. News ranking: Nat. Lib. Arts, No. 43
Website: www.sewanee.edu
Admissions email: admiss@sewanee.edu
Private; founded 1857
Affiliation: Protestant Episcopal
Freshman admissions: more selective; 2018-2019: 3,465 applied, 2,258 accepted. Neither SAT nor ACT required. ACT 25/75 percentile: 25-31. High school rank: 30% in top tenth, 61% in top quarter, 92% in top half
Early decision deadline: 11/15, notification date: 12/15
Early action deadline: 12/1, notification date: 2/15
Application deadline (fall): 2/1
Undergraduate student body: 1,678 full time, 20 part time; 49% male, 51% female; 0% American Indian, 2% Asian, 5% black, 5% Hispanic, 3% multiracial, 0% Pacific Islander, 81% white,

3% international; 22% from in state; 99% live on campus; 56% of students in fraternities, 64% in sororities
Most popular majors: 14% Economics, General, 14% Psychology, General, 13% English Language and Literature, General, 10% International/Global Studies, 7% Political Science and Government, General
Expenses: 2019-2020: $46,472; room/board: $13,268
Financial aid: (931) 598-1312; 47% of undergrads determined to have financial need; average aid package $35,337

Vanderbilt University

Nashville TN
(800) 288-0432
U.S. News ranking: Nat. U., No. 15
Website: www.vanderbilt.edu
Admissions email: admissions@vanderbilt.edu
Private; founded 1873
Freshman admissions: most selective; 2018-2019: 34,313 applied, 3,298 accepted. Either SAT or ACT required. ACT 25/75 percentile: 33-35. High school rank: 89% in top tenth, 96% in top quarter, 99% in top half
Early decision deadline: 11/1, notification date: 12/15
Early action deadline: N/A, notification date: N/A
Application deadline (fall): 1/1
Undergraduate student body: 6,789 full time, 72 part time; 49% male, 51% female; 0% American Indian, 14% Asian, 11% black, 10% Hispanic, 6% multiracial, 0% Pacific Islander, 45% white, 9% international; 5% from in state; 94% live on campus; 33% of students in fraternities, 48% in sororities
Most popular majors: 13% Economics, General, 10% Multi-/Interdisciplinary Studies, Other, 10% Social Sciences, General, 5% Mathematics, General, 4% Computer Science
Expenses: 2019-2020: $52,070; room/board: $16,910
Financial aid: (615) 322-3591; 50% of undergrads determined to have financial need; average aid package $51,787

Watkins College of Art, Design & Film[1]

Nashville TN
(615) 383-4848
U.S. News ranking: Arts, unranked
Website: www.watkins.edu
Admissions email: admission@watkins.edu
Private
Application deadline (fall): N/A
Undergraduate student body: N/A full time, N/A part time
Expenses: N/A
Financial aid: N/A

Welch College

Gallatin TN
(615) 675-5359
U.S. News ranking: Reg. Coll. (S), No. 16
Website: www.welch.edu
Admissions email: recruit@welch.edu
Private; founded 1942
Affiliation: Free Will Baptist Church
Freshman admissions: selective; 2018-2019: 188 applied, 148 accepted. Either SAT or ACT required. ACT 25/75 percentile: 19-24. High school rank: 26% in top tenth, 49% in top quarter, 79% in top half
Early decision deadline: N/A, notification date: N/A
Early action deadline: N/A, notification date: N/A
Application deadline (fall): rolling
Undergraduate student body: 239 full time, 134 part time; 44% male, 56% female; 0% American Indian, 1% Asian, 8% black, 3% Hispanic, 1% multiracial, 0% Pacific Islander, 86% white, 0% international; N/A from in state; 51% live on campus; 71% of students in fraternities, 80% in sororities
Most popular majors: 37% Theology and Religious Vocations, 13% Business, Management, Marketing, and Related Support Services, 10% Biological and Biomedical Sciences, 8% Education, 8% Psychology
Expenses: 2019-2020: $19,582; room/board: $7,932
Financial aid: (615) 675-5278; 84% of undergrads determined to have financial need; average aid package $13,871

TEXAS

Abilene Christian University

Abilene TX
(800) 460-6228
U.S. News ranking: Reg. U. (W), No. 12
Website: www.acu.edu
Admissions email: info@admissions.acu.edu
Private; founded 1906
Affiliation: Churches of Christ
Freshman admissions: selective; 2018-2019: 11,569 applied, 6,590 accepted. Either SAT or ACT required. SAT 25/75 percentile: 1040-1230. High school rank: 24% in top tenth, 56% in top quarter, 86% in top half
Early decision deadline: N/A, notification date: N/A
Early action deadline: 11/1, notification date: 11/15
Application deadline (fall): 2/15
Undergraduate student body: 3,407 full time, 137 part time; 40% male, 60% female; 0% American Indian, 1% Asian, 9% black, 17% Hispanic, 5% multiracial, 0% Pacific Islander, 64% white, 4% international; 85% from in state; 45% live on campus; 30% of students in fraternities, 35% in sororities

Most popular majors: 7% Psychology, General, 7% Registered Nursing/Registered Nurse, 7% Sport and Fitness Administration/Management, 6% Accounting, 5% Marketing/Marketing Management, General
Expenses: 2019-2020: $36,300; room/board: $11,485
Financial aid: (325) 674-2300; 66% of undergrads determined to have financial need; average aid package $24,771

Amberton University[1]

Garland TX
(972) 279-6511
U.S. News ranking: Reg. U. (W), unranked
Website: www.amberton.edu
Admissions email: advisor@amberton.edu
Private; founded 1981
Affiliation: Other
Application deadline (fall): rolling
Undergraduate student body: N/A full time, N/A part time
Expenses: N/A
Financial aid: N/A

Angelo State University

San Angelo TX
(325) 942-2041
U.S. News ranking: Reg. U. (W), second tier
Website: www.angelo.edu
Admissions email: admissions@angelo.edu
Public; founded 1928
Freshman admissions: selective; 2018-2019: 4,152 applied, 3,035 accepted. Either SAT or ACT required. ACT 25/75 percentile: 18-24. High school rank: 12% in top tenth, 35% in top quarter, 72% in top half
Early decision deadline: N/A, notification date: N/A
Early action deadline: N/A, notification date: N/A
Application deadline (fall): 8/26
Undergraduate student body: 5,499 full time, 3,253 part time; 43% male, 57% female; 0% American Indian, 1% Asian, 7% black, 37% Hispanic, 3% multiracial, 0% Pacific Islander, 47% white, 4% international; 97% from in state; 34% live on campus; 6% of students in fraternities, 4% in sororities
Most popular majors: 17% Business, Management, Marketing, and Related Support Services, 12% Multi/Interdisciplinary Studies, 9% Health Professions and Related Programs, 9% Parks, Recreation, Leisure, and Fitness Studies, 8% Psychology
Expenses: 2019-2020: $8,721 in state, $21,381 out of state; room/board: $9,130
Financial aid: (325) 942-2246; 69% of undergrads determined to have financial need; average aid package $10,906

Art Institute of Houston[1]

Houston TX
(713) 623-2040
U.S. News ranking: Arts, unranked
Website: www.artinstitute.edu/houston/
Admissions email: N/A
For-profit
Application deadline (fall): N/A
Undergraduate student body: N/A full time, N/A part time
Expenses: N/A
Financial aid: N/A

Austin College

Sherman TX
(800) 526-4276
U.S. News ranking: Nat. Lib. Arts, No. 117
Website: www.austincollege.edu
Admissions email: admission@austincollege.edu
Private; founded 1849
Affiliation: Presbyterian
Freshman admissions: more selective; 2018-2019: 3,832 applied, 2,120 accepted. Either SAT or ACT required for some. SAT 25/75 percentile: 1130-1330. High school rank: 24% in top tenth, 50% in top quarter, 79% in top half
Early decision deadline: 12/1, notification date: 1/15
Early action deadline: 12/1, notification date: 1/15
Application deadline (fall): 3/1
Undergraduate student body: 1,284 full time, 4 part time; 49% male, 51% female; 0% American Indian, 13% Asian, 10% black, 21% Hispanic, 5% multiracial, 0% Pacific Islander, 49% white, 2% international; N/A from in state; 84% live on campus; 18% of students in fraternities, 22% in sororities
Most popular majors: 27% Business/Commerce, General, 17% Biology/Biological Sciences, General, 10% Social Sciences, General, 8% Psychology, General, 6% Physical Sciences
Expenses: 2019-2020: $41,155; room/board: $12,752
Financial aid: (903) 813-2900; 69% of undergrads determined to have financial need; average aid package $35,321

Baylor University

Waco TX
(800) 229-5678
U.S. News ranking: Nat. U., No. 79
Website: www.baylor.edu
Admissions email: Admissions@Baylor.edu
Private; founded 1845
Affiliation: Baptist
Freshman admissions: more selective; 2018-2019: 34,681 applied, 17,910 accepted. Either SAT or ACT required. ACT 25/75 percentile: 26-31. High school rank: 40% in top tenth, 73% in top quarter, 95% in top half
Early decision deadline: N/A, notification date: N/A
Early action deadline: 11/1, notification date: 1/15
Application deadline (fall): 2/1

Undergraduate student body: 13,976 full time, 212 part time; 40% male, 60% female; 0% American Indian, 7% Asian, 6% black, 16% Hispanic, 5% multiracial, 0% Pacific Islander, 63% white, 3% international; 66% from in state; 36% live on campus; 20% of students in fraternities, 34% in sororities
Most popular majors: 8% Biology/Biological Sciences, General, 7% Registered Nursing/Registered Nurse, 5% Accounting, 4% Marketing/Marketing Management, General, 3% Mechanical Engineering
Expenses: 2019-2020: $47,364; room/board: $13,842
Financial aid: (254) 710-2611; 54% of undergrads determined to have financial need; average aid package $31,333

Brazosport College[1]

Lake Jackson TX
(979) 230-3000
U.S. News ranking: Reg. Coll. (W), unranked
Website: www.brazosport.edu
Admissions email: N/A
Public
Application deadline (fall): N/A
Undergraduate student body: N/A full time, N/A part time
Expenses: N/A
Financial aid: N/A

Concordia University Texas[1]

Austin TX
(800) 865-4282
U.S. News ranking: Reg. U. (W), second tier
Website: www.concordia.edu
Admissions email: admissions@concordia.edu
Private; founded 1926
Application deadline (fall): 8/1
Undergraduate student body: N/A full time, N/A part time
Expenses: N/A
Financial aid: (512) 313-4672

Dallas Baptist University

Dallas TX
(214) 333-5360
U.S. News ranking: Nat. U., No. 281
Website: www.dbu.edu
Admissions email: admiss@dbu.edu
Private; founded 1898
Affiliation: Baptist
Freshman admissions: selective; 2018-2019: 2,757 applied, 2,428 accepted. Either SAT or ACT required. ACT 25/75 percentile: 20-24. High school rank: 18% in top tenth, 46% in top quarter, 77% in top half
Early decision deadline: N/A, notification date: N/A
Early action deadline: N/A, notification date: N/A
Application deadline (fall): rolling
Undergraduate student body: 2,364 full time, 650 part time; 42% male, 58% female; 1% American Indian, 2% Asian, 10% black, 18% Hispanic, 1% multiracial,

0% Pacific Islander, 61% white, 8% international; 92% from in state; 64% live on campus; 17% of students in fraternities, 24% in sororities
Most popular majors: 14% Business Administration and Management, General, 12% Multi-/Interdisciplinary Studies, Other, 6% Elementary Education and Teaching, 6% Psychology, General, 5% Finance, General
Expenses: 2019-2020: $30,320; room/board: $8,226
Financial aid: (214) 333-5363; 65% of undergrads determined to have financial need; average aid package $16,668

East Texas Baptist University

Marshall TX
(800) 804-3828
U.S. News ranking: Reg. Coll. (W), No. 19
Website: www.etbu.edu
Admissions email: admissions@etbu.edu
Private; founded 1912
Affiliation: Baptist
Freshman admissions: selective; 2018-2019: 1,849 applied, 1,007 accepted. Either SAT or ACT required. ACT 25/75 percentile: 18-23. High school rank: 13% in top tenth, 36% in top quarter, 71% in top half
Early decision deadline: N/A, notification date: N/A
Early action deadline: N/A, notification date: N/A
Application deadline (fall): 8/27
Undergraduate student body: 1,296 full time, 189 part time; 45% male, 55% female; 0% American Indian, 0% Asian, 16% black, 10% Hispanic, 4% multiracial, 0% Pacific Islander, 67% white, 1% international; 89% from in state; 81% live on campus; 0% of students in fraternities, 0% in sororities
Most popular majors: 17% Business, Management, Marketing, and Related Support Services, 17% Education, 15% Multi/Interdisciplinary Studies, 10% Psychology, 9% Parks, Recreation, Leisure, and Fitness Studies
Expenses: 2019-2020: $27,210; room/board: $9,328
Financial aid: (903) 923-2137; 84% of undergrads determined to have financial need; average aid package $20,063

Hardin-Simmons University

Abilene TX
(325) 670-1206
U.S. News ranking: Reg. U. (W), No. 41
Website: www.hsutx.edu/
Admissions email: enroll@hsutx.edu
Private; founded 1891
Affiliation: Baptist
Freshman admissions: selective; 2018-2019: 1,766 applied, 1,487 accepted. Either SAT or ACT required. ACT 25/75 percentile: 18-24. High school

rank: 16% in top tenth, 38% in top quarter, 68% in top half
Early decision deadline: N/A, notification date: N/A
Early action deadline: N/A, notification date: N/A
Application deadline (fall): rolling
Undergraduate student body: 1,625 full time, 140 part time; 47% male, 53% female; 0% American Indian, 1% Asian, 9% black, 19% Hispanic, 4% multiracial, 0% Pacific Islander, 62% white, 2% international; 3% from in state; 54% live on campus; 7% of students in fraternities, 14% in sororities
Most popular majors: 12% Business, Management, Marketing, and Related Support Services, 12% Health Professions and Related Programs, 11% Psychology, 10% Parks, Recreation, Leisure, and Fitness Studies, 9% Biological and Biomedical Sciences
Expenses: 2019-2020: $30,140; room/board: $9,850
Financial aid: (325) 670-1206; 77% of undergrads determined to have financial need; average aid package $24,415

Houston Baptist University

Houston TX
(281) 649-3211
U.S. News ranking: Reg. U. (W), No. 61
Website: www.hbu.edu
Admissions email: admissions@hbu.edu
Private; founded 1960
Affiliation: Baptist
Freshman admissions: selective; 2018-2019: 7,051 applied, 4,937 accepted. Either SAT or ACT required. SAT 25/75 percentile: 1030-1200. High school rank: 22% in top tenth, 54% in top quarter, 86% in top half
Early decision deadline: N/A, notification date: N/A
Early action deadline: N/A, notification date: N/A
Application deadline (fall): rolling
Undergraduate student body: 1,876 full time, 445 part time; 36% male, 64% female; 1% American Indian, 8% Asian, 17% black, 36% Hispanic, 3% multiracial, 0% Pacific Islander, 24% white, 4% international; 96% from in state; 34% live on campus; 4% of students in fraternities, 7% in sororities
Most popular majors: 28% Health Professions and Related Programs, 16% Business, Management, Marketing, and Related Support Services, 9% Biological and Biomedical Sciences, 8% Multi/Interdisciplinary Studies, 8% Parks, Recreation, Leisure, and Fitness Studies
Expenses: 2019-2020: $33,450; room/board: $8,955
Financial aid: (281) 649-3749; 74% of undergrads determined to have financial need; average aid package $28,187

Howard Payne University

Brownwood TX
(325) 649-8020
U.S. News ranking: Reg. Coll. (W), No. 14
Website: www.hputx.edu
Admissions email: enroll@hputx.edu
Private; founded 1889
Affiliation: Baptist
Freshman admissions: selective; 2018-2019: 1,576 applied, 913 accepted. Either SAT or ACT required. SAT 25/75 percentile: 950-1100. High school rank: N/A
Early decision deadline: N/A, notification date: N/A
Early action deadline: N/A, notification date: N/A
Application deadline (fall): rolling
Undergraduate student body: 812 full time, 150 part time; 54% male, 46% female; 1% American Indian, 1% Asian, 13% black, 25% Hispanic, 3% multiracial, 0% Pacific Islander, 51% white, 0% international
Most popular majors: Information not available
Expenses: 2019-2020: $29,198; room/board: $8,708
Financial aid: (325) 649-8014; 86% of undergrads determined to have financial need; average aid package $21,443

Huston-Tillotson University

Austin TX
(512) 505-3029
U.S. News ranking: Reg. Coll. (W), second tier
Website: htu.edu/
Admissions email: admission@htu.edu
Private
Freshman admissions: least selective; 2018-2019: 3,156 applied, 1,480 accepted. Either SAT or ACT required. SAT 25/75 percentile: 810-980. High school rank: N/A
Early decision deadline: N/A, notification date: N/A
Early action deadline: N/A, notification date: N/A
Application deadline (fall): 5/1
Undergraduate student body: 1,035 full time, 84 part time; 38% male, 62% female; 0% American Indian, 0% Asian, 64% black, 27% Hispanic, 1% multiracial, 0% Pacific Islander, 5% white, 2% international
Most popular majors: 25% Business Administration and Management, General, 16% Kinesiology and Exercise Science, 13% Psychology, General, 8% Biology/Biological Sciences, General, 8% Teacher Education, Multiple Levels
Expenses: 2018-2019: $14,346; room/board: $7,568
Financial aid: N/A

Jarvis Christian College

Hawkins TX
(903) 730-4890
U.S. News ranking: Reg. Coll. (W), second tier
Website: www.jarvis.edu
Admissions email: Recruitment@jarvis.edu
Private; founded 1912
Affiliation: Christian Church (Disciples of Christ)
Freshman admissions: least selective; 2018-2019: 4,397 applied, 615 accepted. Either SAT or ACT required. SAT 25/75 percentile: 800-980. High school rank: N/A
Early decision deadline: N/A, notification date: N/A
Early action deadline: N/A, notification date: N/A
Application deadline (fall): 8/1
Undergraduate student body: 923 full time, 41 part time; 45% male, 55% female; 0% American Indian, 0% Asian, 77% black, 11% Hispanic, 0% multiracial, 0% Pacific Islander, 4% white, 0% international; 85% from in state; 75% live on campus; N/A of students in fraternities, N/A in sororities
Most popular majors: 25% Business Administration and Management, General, 19% Kinesiology and Exercise Science, 15% Criminal Justice/Safety Studies, 7% Biology/Biological Sciences, General, 7% Social Work
Expenses: 2019-2020: $11,720; room/board: $8,574
Financial aid: (903) 730-4890; 96% of undergrads determined to have financial need; average aid package $11,755

Lamar University

Beaumont TX
(409) 880-8888
U.S. News ranking: Nat. U., second tier
Website: www.lamar.edu
Admissions email: admissions@lamar.edu
Public; founded 1923
Freshman admissions: selective; 2018-2019: 5,486 applied, 4,626 accepted. Either SAT or ACT required. SAT 25/75 percentile: 950-1100. High school rank: 15% in top tenth, 39% in top quarter, 71% in top half
Early decision deadline: N/A, notification date: N/A
Early action deadline: N/A, notification date: N/A
Undergraduate student body: 5,735 full time, 3,169 part time; 42% male, 58% female; 1% American Indian, 5% Asian, 28% black, 18% Hispanic, 1% multiracial, 0% Pacific Islander, 45% white, 1% international; 96% from in state; 26% live on campus; N/A of students in fraternities, N/A in sororities
Most popular majors: 20% Health Professions and Related Programs, 13% Business, Management, Marketing, and Related Support Services, 13% Engineering, 13%

Multi/Interdisciplinary Studies, 7% Liberal Arts and Sciences, General Studies and Humanities
Expenses: 2019-2020: $10,342 in state, $23,002 out of state; room/board: $9,158
Financial aid: (409) 880-7011; 64% of undergrads determined to have financial need; average aid package $5,288

LeTourneau University

Longview TX
(903) 233-4300
U.S. News ranking: Reg. U. (W), No. 25
Website: www.letu.edu
Admissions email: admissions@letu.edu
Private; founded 1946
Freshman admissions: more selective; 2018-2019: 1,922 applied, 875 accepted. Either SAT or ACT required for some. SAT 25/75 percentile: 1090-1320. High school rank: 22% in top tenth, 50% in top quarter, 85% in top half
Early decision deadline: N/A, notification date: N/A
Early action deadline: N/A, notification date: N/A
Application deadline (fall): rolling
Undergraduate student body: 1,317 full time, 1,484 part time; 52% male, 48% female; 1% American Indian, 1% Asian, 10% black, 8% Hispanic, 6% multiracial, 0% Pacific Islander, 63% white, 3% international; 67% from in state; 69% live on campus; 0% of students in fraternities, 0% in sororities
Most popular majors: 23% Engineering, 21% Business, Management, Marketing, and Related Support Services, 13% Education, 7% Transportation and Materials Moving, 6% Engineering Technologies and Engineering-Related Fields
Expenses: 2019-2020: $31,270; room/board: $9,970
Financial aid: (903) 233-4350; 72% of undergrads determined to have financial need; average aid package $23,406

Lubbock Christian University

Lubbock TX
(806) 720-7151
U.S. News ranking: Reg. U. (W), No. 66
Website: lcu.edu
Admissions email: admissions@lcu.edu
Private; founded 1957
Affiliation: Churches of Christ
Freshman admissions: selective; 2018-2019: 696 applied, 624 accepted. Either SAT or ACT required. ACT 25/75 percentile: 18-25. High school rank: 22% in top tenth, 47% in top quarter, 78% in top half
Early decision deadline: 10/31, notification date: 12/15
Early action deadline: 6/15, notification date: 7/15
Application deadline (fall): 6/1
Undergraduate student body: 1,272 full time, 167 part time; 40%

male, 60% female; 1% American Indian, 1% Asian, 4% black, 24% Hispanic, 0% multiracial, 0% Pacific Islander, 68% white, 2% international; 90% from in state; 37% live on campus; 20% of students in fraternities, 18% in sororities
Most popular majors: 32% Health Professions and Related Programs, 15% Business, Management, Marketing, and Related Support Services, 12% Education, 7% Parks, Recreation, Leisure, and Fitness Studies, 6% Public Administration and Social Service Professions
Expenses: 2019-2020: $23,330; room/board: $6,790
Financial aid: (806) 720-7176; 74% of undergrads determined to have financial need; average aid package $15,635

McMurry University

Abilene TX
(325) 793-4700
U.S. News ranking: Reg. Coll. (W), No. 18
Website: mcm.edu/
Admissions email: admissions@mcm.edu
Private; founded 1923
Affiliation: United Methodist
Freshman admissions: selective; 2018-2019: 1,826 applied, 753 accepted. Either SAT or ACT required. SAT 25/75 percentile: 950-1150. High school rank: 12% in top tenth, 40% in top quarter, 72% in top half
Early decision deadline: N/A, notification date: N/A
Early action deadline: N/A, notification date: N/A
Application deadline (fall): 8/15
Undergraduate student body: 990 full time, 138 part time; 50% male, 50% female; 1% American Indian, 1% Asian, 13% black, 26% Hispanic, 3% multiracial, 0% Pacific Islander, 49% white, 5% international; 97% from in state; 48% live on campus; 14% of students in fraternities, 17% in sororities
Most popular majors: 20% Business, Management, Marketing, and Related Support Services, 16% Education, 12% Social Sciences, 8% Psychology, 8% Visual and Performing Arts
Expenses: 2019-2020: $27,924; room/board: $8,820
Financial aid: (325) 793-4978; 82% of undergrads determined to have financial need; average aid package $21,901

Midland College[1]

Midland TX
(432) 685-4500
U.S. News ranking: Reg. Coll. (W), unranked
Website: www.midland.edu/
Admissions email: pebensberger@midland.edu
Public
Application deadline (fall): N/A
Undergraduate student body: N/A full time, N/A part time
Expenses: N/A
Financial aid: N/A

Midwestern State University

Wichita Falls TX
(800) 842-1922
U.S. News ranking: Reg. U. (W), No. 70
Website: www.mwsu.edu
Admissions email: admissions@mwsu.edu
Public; founded 1922
Freshman admissions: selective; 2018-2019: 3,630 applied, 2,580 accepted. Either SAT or ACT required for some. SAT 25/75 percentile: 940-1140. High school rank: 12% in top tenth, 41% in top quarter, 72% in top half
Early decision deadline: N/A, notification date: N/A
Early action deadline: N/A, notification date: N/A
Application deadline (fall): 8/1
Undergraduate student body: 4,256 full time, 1,116 part time; 40% male, 60% female; 1% American Indian, 3% Asian, 15% black, 21% Hispanic, 4% multiracial, 0% Pacific Islander, 48% white, 9% international; N/A from in state; 30% live on campus; N/A of students in fraternities, N/A in sororities
Most popular majors: 33% Health Professions and Related Programs, 17% Business, Management, Marketing, and Related Support Services, 13% Multi/Interdisciplinary Studies, 6% Biological and Biomedical Sciences, 5% Engineering
Expenses: 2019-2020: $9,380 in state, $11,330 out of state; room/board: $8,910
Financial aid: (940) 397-4214; 60% of undergrads determined to have financial need; average aid package $15,251

National American University–Austin[1]

Austin TX
(512) 651-4700
U.S. News ranking: Reg. Coll. (W), unranked
Website: www.skagit.edu
Admissions email: N/A
For-profit
Application deadline (fall): N/A
Undergraduate student body: N/A full time, N/A part time
Expenses: N/A
Financial aid: N/A

Our Lady of the Lake University

San Antonio TX
(800) 436-6558
U.S. News ranking: Nat. U., second tier
Website: www.ollusa.edu
Admissions email: admission@lake.ollusa.edu
Private; founded 1895
Affiliation: Roman Catholic
Freshman admissions: less selective; 2018-2019: 4,375 applied, 4,056 accepted. Either SAT or ACT required. SAT 25/75 percentile: 910-1080. High school rank: 14% in top tenth, 38% in top quarter, 73% in top half

Early decision deadline: N/A, notification date: N/A
Early action deadline: N/A, notification date: N/A
Application deadline (fall): 8/1
Undergraduate student body: 1,291 full time, 128 part time; 32% male, 68% female; 1% American Indian, 1% Asian, 8% black, 76% Hispanic, 1% multiracial, 0% Pacific Islander, 11% white, 1% international; N/A from in state; 35% live on campus; 1% of students in fraternities, 3% in sororities
Most popular majors: 17% Psychology, General, 16% Social Work, 14% Business Administration and Management, General, 9% Kinesiology and Exercise Science, 8% Communication Sciences and Disorders, General
Expenses: 2019-2020: $29,218; room/board: $9,730
Financial aid: (210) 434-6711; 86% of undergrads determined to have financial need; average aid package $22,908

Paul Quinn College[1]
Dallas TX
(214) 379-5546
U.S. News ranking: Reg. Coll. (W), unranked
Website: www.rtc.edu
Admissions email: N/A
Private
Application deadline (fall): N/A
Undergraduate student body: N/A full time, N/A part time
Expenses: N/A
Financial aid: N/A

Prairie View A&M University
Prairie View TX
(936) 261-1000
U.S. News ranking: Reg. U. (W), second tier
Website: www.pvamu.edu
Admissions email: admission@pvamu.edu
Public; founded 1876
Freshman admissions: less selective; 2018-2019: 7,158 applied, 5,321 accepted. Either SAT or ACT required. SAT 25/75 percentile: 890-1050. High school rank: 6% in top tenth, 25% in top quarter, 65% in top half
Early decision deadline: N/A, notification date: N/A
Early action deadline: N/A, notification date: N/A
Application deadline (fall): 6/1
Undergraduate student body: 7,953 full time, 571 part time; 36% male, 64% female; 0% American Indian, 2% Asian, 84% black, 9% Hispanic, 2% multiracial, 0% Pacific Islander, 2% white, 1% international; 8% from in state; 45% live on campus; N/A of students in fraternities, N/A in sororities
Most popular majors: 16% Engineering, 16% Health Professions and Related Programs, 10% Business, Management, Marketing, and Related Support Services, 8% Homeland Security, Law Enforcement, Firefighting and

Related Protective Services, 7% Parks, Recreation, Leisure, and Fitness Studies
Expenses: 2019-2020: $10,786 in state, $25,655 out of state; room/board: $8,859
Financial aid: (936) 261-1000; 86% of undergrads determined to have financial need; average aid package $15,438

Rice University
Houston TX
(713) 348-7423
U.S. News ranking: Nat. U., No. 17
Website: www.rice.edu
Admissions email: admission@rice.edu
Private; founded 1912
Freshman admissions: most selective; 2018-2019: 20,923 applied, 2,328 accepted. Either SAT or ACT required. ACT 25/75 percentile: 33-35. High school rank: 87% in top tenth, 96% in top quarter, 99% in top half
Early decision deadline: 11/1, notification date: 12/15
Early action deadline: N/A, notification date: N/A
Application deadline (fall): 1/1
Undergraduate student body: 3,899 full time, 93 part time; 52% male, 48% female; 0% American Indian, 26% Asian, 7% black, 16% Hispanic, 4% multiracial, 0% Pacific Islander, 33% white, 12% international; 42% from in state; 71% live on campus; 0% of students in fraternities, 0% in sororities
Most popular majors: 7% Computer and Information Sciences, General, 6% Chemical Engineering, 6% Economics, General, 6% Kinesiology and Exercise Science, 6% Mechanical Engineering
Expenses: 2019-2020: $49,112; room/board: $14,140
Financial aid: (713) 348-4958; 39% of undergrads determined to have financial need; average aid package $47,654

Sam Houston State University
Huntsville TX
(936) 294-1828
U.S. News ranking: Nat. U., No. 281
Website: www.shsu.edu
Admissions email: admissions@shsu.edu
Public; founded 1879
Freshman admissions: selective; 2018-2019: 11,818 applied, 9,283 accepted. Either SAT or ACT required. SAT 25/75 percentile: 1000-1140. High school rank: N/A
Early decision deadline: N/A, notification date: N/A
Early action deadline: N/A, notification date: N/A
Application deadline (fall): 8/1
Undergraduate student body: 15,063 full time, 3,410 part time; 38% male, 62% female; 1% American Indian, 2% Asian, 18% black, 24% Hispanic, 3% multiracial, 0% Pacific Islander, 50% white, 1%

international; 98% from in state; 21% live on campus; 6% of students in fraternities, 5% in sororities
Most popular majors: 22% Business, Management, Marketing, and Related Support Services, 20% Homeland Security, Law Enforcement, Firefighting and Related Protective Services, 9% Multi/Interdisciplinary Studies, 8% Health Professions and Related Programs, 5% Psychology
Expenses: 2019-2020: $10,483 in state, $22,933 out of state; room/board: $9,670
Financial aid: (936) 294-1774; 68% of undergrads determined to have financial need; average aid package $11,611

Schreiner University
Kerrville TX
(830) 792-7217
U.S. News ranking: Reg. Coll. (W), No. 12
Website: www.schreiner.edu
Admissions email: admissions@schreiner.edu
Private; founded 1923
Affiliation: Presbyterian Church (USA)
Freshman admissions: selective; 2018-2019: 1,184 applied, 1,080 accepted. Either SAT or ACT required. SAT 25/75 percentile: 960-1130. High school rank: 12% in top tenth, 33% in top quarter, 67% in top half
Early decision deadline: N/A, notification date: N/A
Early action deadline: N/A, notification date: N/A
Application deadline (fall): 8/1
Undergraduate student body: 1,110 full time, 209 part time; 43% male, 57% female; 0% American Indian, 1% Asian, 5% black, 42% Hispanic, 2% multiracial, 0% Pacific Islander, 49% white, 1% international; 97% from in state; 65% live on campus; 3% of students in fraternities, 8% in sororities
Most popular majors: 28% Health Professions and Related Programs, 19% Business, Management, Marketing, and Related Support Services, 11% Parks, Recreation, Leisure, and Fitness Studies, 10% Biological and Biomedical Sciences, 8% Psychology
Expenses: 2019-2020: $30,470; room/board: $12,140
Financial aid: (830) 792-7229; 78% of undergrads determined to have financial need; average aid package $22,685

Southern Methodist University
Dallas TX
(800) 323-0672
U.S. News ranking: Nat. U., No. 64
Website: www.smu.edu
Admissions email: ugadmission@smu.edu
Private; founded 1911
Affiliation: United Methodist
Freshman admissions: more selective; 2018-2019: 12,603 applied, 6,457 accepted. Either SAT or ACT required. ACT 25/75 percentile: 29-33. High school

rank: 49% in top tenth, 80% in top quarter, 95% in top half
Early decision deadline: 11/1, notification date: 12/31
Early action deadline: 11/1, notification date: 12/31
Application deadline (fall): 1/15
Undergraduate student body: 6,273 full time, 206 part time; 51% male, 49% female; 0% American Indian, 7% Asian, 5% black, 12% Hispanic, 4% multiracial, 0% Pacific Islander, 64% white, 8% international; 45% from in state; 54% live on campus; 24% of students in fraternities, 37% in sororities
Most popular majors: 26% Business, Management, Marketing, and Related Support Services, 12% Social Sciences, 9% Communication, Journalism, and Related Programs, 9% Engineering, 6% Visual and Performing Arts
Expenses: 2019-2020: $56,560; room/board: $16,750
Financial aid: (214) 768-3417; 31% of undergrads determined to have financial need; average aid package $44,493

South Texas College[1]
McAllen TX
(956) 872-8311
U.S. News ranking: Reg. Coll. (W), unranked
Website: www.southtexascollege.edu/
Admissions email: N/A
Public
Application deadline (fall): N/A
Undergraduate student body: N/A full time, N/A part time
Expenses: N/A
Financial aid: N/A

Southwestern Adventist University
Keene TX
(817) 202-6749
U.S. News ranking: Reg. Coll. (W), No. 11
Website: www.swau.edu
Admissions email: admissions@swau.edu
Private; founded 1893
Affiliation: Seventh Day Adventist
Freshman admissions: less selective; 2018-2019: 1,576 applied, 872 accepted. Either SAT or ACT required. SAT 25/75 percentile: 900-1145. High school rank: 10% in top tenth, 23% in top quarter, 70% in top half
Early decision deadline: N/A, notification date: N/A
Early action deadline: N/A, notification date: N/A
Application deadline (fall): 8/1
Undergraduate student body: 715 full time, 61 part time; 40% male, 60% female; 1% American Indian, 7% Asian, 13% black, 50% Hispanic, 6% multiracial, 3% Pacific Islander, 20% white, 0% international; N/A from in state; 45% live on campus; 0% of students in fraternities, 0% in sororities
Most popular majors: 35% Registered Nursing/Registered Nurse, 9% Education, General,

8% General Studies, 5% Theology/Theological Studies, 4% Computer Science
Expenses: 2019-2020: $22,188; room/board: $7,800
Financial aid: (817) 202-6262

Southwestern Assemblies of God University[1]
Waxahachie TX
(888) 937-7248
U.S. News ranking: Reg. U. (W), second tier
Website: www.sagu.edu/
Admissions email: admissions@sagu.edu
Private; founded 1927
Application deadline (fall): rolling
Undergraduate student body: N/A full time, N/A part time
Expenses: N/A
Financial aid: (972) 825-4730

Southwestern Christian College[1]
Terrell TX
(972) 524-3341
U.S. News ranking: Reg. Coll. (W), unranked
Website: www.swcc.edu
Admissions email: N/A
Private
Application deadline (fall): N/A
Undergraduate student body: N/A full time, N/A part time
Expenses: N/A
Financial aid: N/A

Southwestern University
Georgetown TX
(512) 863-1200
U.S. News ranking: Nat. Lib. Arts, No. 92
Website: www.southwestern.edu
Admissions email: admission@southwestern.edu
Private; founded 1840
Affiliation: United Methodist
Freshman admissions: more selective; 2018-2019: 4,551 applied, 2,049 accepted. Either SAT or ACT required. SAT 25/75 percentile: 1130-1330. High school rank: 34% in top tenth, 70% in top quarter, 94% in top half
Early decision deadline: 11/1, notification date: 12/1
Early action deadline: 12/1, notification date: 3/1
Application deadline (fall): 2/1
Undergraduate student body: 1,416 full time, 14 part time; 45% male, 55% female; 0% American Indian, 3% Asian, 5% black, 24% Hispanic, 4% multiracial, 0% Pacific Islander, 61% white, 1% international; 90% from in state; 78% live on campus; 23% of students in fraternities, 22% in sororities
Most popular majors: 16% Business, Management, Marketing, and Related Support Services, 12% Social Sciences, 11% Biological and Biomedical Sciences, 9% Communication, Journalism, and Related Programs, 9% Psychology

Expenses: 2019-2020: $43,560; room/board: $12,320
Financial aid: (512) 863-1259; 64% of undergrads determined to have financial need; average aid package $37,110

St. Edward's University

Austin TX
(512) 448-8500
U.S. News ranking: Reg. U. (W), No. 8
Website: www.stedwards.edu
Admissions email: seu.admit@stedwards.edu
Private; founded 1885
Affiliation: Roman Catholic
Freshman admissions: selective; 2018-2019: 5,577 applied, 4,818 accepted. Either SAT or ACT required. SAT 25/75 percentile: 1080-1270. High school rank: 21% in top tenth, 55% in top quarter, 88% in top half
Early decision deadline: N/A, notification date: N/A
Early action deadline: N/A, notification date: N/A
Application deadline (fall): 5/1
Undergraduate student body: 3,477 full time, 312 part time; 38% male, 62% female; 1% American Indian, 3% Asian, 4% black, 44% Hispanic, 3% multiracial, 0% Pacific Islander, 36% white, 8% international; N/A from in state; 32% live on campus; N/A of students in fraternities, N/A in sororities
Most popular majors: 25% Business, Management, Marketing, and Related Support Services, 10% Communication, Journalism, and Related Programs, 9% Biological and Biomedical Sciences, 8% Psychology, 7% Visual and Performing Arts
Expenses: 2019-2020: $47,190; room/board: $14,004
Financial aid: (512) 448-8516; 69% of undergrads determined to have financial need; average aid package $36,366

Stephen F. Austin State University[1]

Nacogdoches TX
(936) 468-2504
U.S. News ranking: Nat. U., second tier
Website: www.sfasu.edu
Admissions email: admissions@sfasu.edu
Public; founded 1923
Application deadline (fall): rolling
Undergraduate student body: N/A full time, N/A part time
Expenses: 2018-2019: $10,287 in state, $22,737 out of state; room/board: $8,964
Financial aid: (936) 468-2230

St. Mary's University of San Antonio

San Antonio TX
(210) 436-3126
U.S. News ranking: Reg. U. (W), No. 10
Website: www.stmarytx.edu
Admissions email: uadm@stmarytx.edu
Private; founded 1852
Affiliation: Roman Catholic
Freshman admissions: selective; 2018-2019: 5,350 applied, 4,011 accepted. Either SAT or ACT required. SAT 25/75 percentile: 1050-1250. High school rank: 34% in top tenth, 58% in top quarter, 83% in top half
Early decision deadline: N/A, notification date: N/A
Early action deadline: N/A, notification date: N/A
Application deadline (fall): rolling
Undergraduate student body: 2,262 full time, 111 part time; 45% male, 55% female; 0% American Indian, 2% Asian, 3% black, 67% Hispanic, 1% multiracial, 0% Pacific Islander, 15% white, 8% international; 90% from in state; 55% live on campus; 11% of students in fraternities, 10% in sororities
Most popular majors: 22% Business, Management, Marketing, and Related Support Services, 15% Social Sciences, 11% Biological and Biomedical Sciences, 9% Parks, Recreation, Leisure, and Fitness Studies, 8% Engineering
Expenses: 2019-2020: $32,140; room/board: $10,720
Financial aid: (210) 436-3141; 71% of undergrads determined to have financial need; average aid package $28,040

Sul Ross State University[1]

Alpine TX
(432) 837-8050
U.S. News ranking: Reg. U. (W), second tier
Website: www.sulross.edu
Admissions email: admissions@sulross.edu
Public; founded 1917
Application deadline (fall): rolling
Undergraduate student body: N/A full time, N/A part time
Expenses: N/A
Financial aid: (432) 837-8059

Tarleton State University

Stephenville TX
(800) 687-8236
U.S. News ranking: Reg. U. (W), No. 70
Website: www.tarleton.edu
Admissions email: uadm@tarleton.edu
Public; founded 1899
Freshman admissions: selective; 2018-2019: 7,279 applied, 5,693 accepted. Either SAT or ACT required. SAT 25/75 percentile: 970-1150. High school rank: 9% in top tenth, 24% in top quarter, 67% in top half

Early decision deadline: N/A, notification date: N/A
Early action deadline: 12/1, notification date: N/A
Application deadline (fall): 8/1
Undergraduate student body: 8,379 full time, 2,937 part time; 38% male, 62% female; 0% American Indian, 1% Asian, 8% black, 20% Hispanic, 4% multiracial, 0% Pacific Islander, 65% white, 0% international; 98% from in state; 33% live on campus; N/A of students in fraternities, N/A in sororities
Most popular majors: 20% Business, Management, Marketing, and Related Support Services, 13% Multi/Interdisciplinary Studies, 9% Agriculture, Agriculture Operations, and Related Sciences, 9% Health Professions and Related Programs, 7% Parks, Recreation, Leisure, and Fitness Studies
Expenses: 2019-2020: $11,275 in state, $21,087 out of state; room/board: $10,712
Financial aid: (254) 968-9070; 64% of undergrads determined to have financial need; average aid package $9,196

Texas A&M International University

Laredo TX
(956) 326-2200
U.S. News ranking: Reg. U. (W), No. 58
Website: www.tamiu.edu
Admissions email: enroll@tamiu.edu
Public; founded 1970
Freshman admissions: selective; 2018-2019: 7,432 applied, 3,945 accepted. Either SAT or ACT required. SAT 25/75 percentile: 930-1100. High school rank: 21% in top tenth, 52% in top quarter, 85% in top half
Early decision deadline: N/A, notification date: N/A
Early action deadline: N/A, notification date: N/A
Application deadline (fall): 8/1
Undergraduate student body: 5,235 full time, 1,757 part time; 40% male, 60% female; 0% American Indian, 0% Asian, 0% black, 95% Hispanic, 0% multiracial, 0% Pacific Islander, 2% white, 1% international
Most popular majors: 34% Business, Management, Marketing, and Related Support Services, 25% Education, 14% Homeland Security, Law Enforcement, Firefighting and Related Protective Services, 14% Psychology, 11% Health Professions and Related Programs
Expenses: 2019-2020: $9,474 in state, $22,134 out of state; room/board: $8,618
Financial aid: (956) 326-2225; 88% of undergrads determined to have financial need; average aid package $9,958

Texas A&M University– College Station

College Station TX
(979) 845-3741
U.S. News ranking: Nat. U., No. 70
Website: www.tamu.edu
Admissions email: admissions@tamu.edu
Public; founded 1876
Freshman admissions: more selective; 2018-2019: 36,423 applied, 24,503 accepted. Either SAT or ACT required. SAT 25/75 percentile: 1170-1380. High school rank: 63% in top tenth, 92% in top quarter, 99% in top half
Early decision deadline: N/A, notification date: N/A
Early action deadline: N/A, notification date: N/A
Application deadline (fall): 12/1
Undergraduate student body: 47,399 full time, 6,344 part time; 53% male, 47% female; 0% American Indian, 8% Asian, 3% black, 24% Hispanic, 3% multiracial, 0% Pacific Islander, 61% white, 1% international
Most popular majors: 16% Business, Management, Marketing, and Related Support Services, 16% Engineering, 11% Multi/Interdisciplinary Studies, 9% Agriculture, Agriculture Operations, and Related Sciences, 7% Biological and Biomedical Sciences
Expenses: 2019-2020: $11,232 in state, $37,726 out of state; room/board: $10,400
Financial aid: (979) 845-3236; 48% of undergrads determined to have financial need; average aid package $17,039

Texas A&M University– Commerce

Commerce TX
(903) 886-5000
U.S. News ranking: Nat. U., second tier
Website: www.tamuc.edu/
Admissions email: Admissions@tamuc.edu
Public; founded 1889
Freshman admissions: selective; 2018-2019: 10,333 applied, 3,517 accepted. Either SAT or ACT required. SAT 25/75 percentile: 960-1140. High school rank: 16% in top tenth, 44% in top quarter, 77% in top half
Early decision deadline: N/A, notification date: N/A
Early action deadline: N/A, notification date: N/A
Application deadline (fall): 8/15
Undergraduate student body: 5,671 full time, 2,565 part time; 40% male, 60% female; 1% American Indian, 1% Asian, 22% black, 22% Hispanic, 7% multiracial, 0% Pacific Islander, 44% white, 1% international; 96% from in state; 31% live on campus; 2% of students in fraternities, 2% in sororities
Most popular majors: 26% Business, Management, Marketing, and Related Support Services,

17% Multi/Interdisciplinary Studies, 12% Education, 5% Computer and Information Sciences and Support Services, 4% Parks, Recreation, Leisure, and Fitness Studies
Expenses: 2019-2020: $8,748 in state, $21,198 out of state; room/board: $8,822
Financial aid: (903) 886-5096; 73% of undergrads determined to have financial need; average aid package $9,450

Texas A&M University– Corpus Christi

Corpus Christi TX
(361) 825-2624
U.S. News ranking: Nat. U., second tier
Website: www.tamucc.edu/
Admissions email: admiss@tamucc.edu
Public; founded 1947
Freshman admissions: selective; 2018-2019: 9,053 applied, 7,875 accepted. Either SAT or ACT required. SAT 25/75 percentile: 980-1160. High school rank: 14% in top tenth, 45% in top quarter, 81% in top half
Early decision deadline: N/A, notification date: N/A
Early action deadline: N/A, notification date: N/A
Application deadline (fall): 7/1
Undergraduate student body: 7,713 full time, 2,063 part time; 41% male, 59% female; 0% American Indian, 3% Asian, 5% black, 51% Hispanic, 2% multiracial, 0% Pacific Islander, 36% white, 2% international; 95% from in state; 25% live on campus; 1% of students in fraternities, 3% in sororities
Most popular majors: 20% Health Professions and Related Programs, 15% Business, Management, Marketing, and Related Support Services, 10% Multi/Interdisciplinary Studies, 8% Biological and Biomedical Sciences, 6% Psychology
Expenses: 2018-2019: $9,055 in state, $18,863 out of state; room/board: N/A
Financial aid: (361) 825-2332; 67% of undergrads determined to have financial need; average aid package $11,842

Texas A&M University– Galveston[1]

Galveston TX
U.S. News ranking: Unranked
Admissions email: N/A
Public
Application deadline (fall): N/A
Undergraduate student body: N/A full time, N/A part time
Expenses: N/A
Financial aid: N/A

Texas A&M University–Kingsville
Kingsville TX
(361) 593-2315
U.S. News ranking: Nat. U., second tier
Website: www.tamuk.edu
Admissions email: admissions@tamuk.edu
Public; founded 1925
Freshman admissions: selective; 2018-2019: 7,218 applied, 6,436 accepted. Either SAT or ACT required. SAT 25/75 percentile: 940-1130. High school rank: 14% in top tenth, 42% in top quarter, 75% in top half
Early decision deadline: N/A, notification date: N/A
Early action deadline: N/A, notification date: N/A
Application deadline (fall): 8/20
Undergraduate student body: 5,162 full time, 1,809 part time; 51% male, 49% female; 0% American Indian, 1% Asian, 6% black, 72% Hispanic, 1% multiracial, 0% Pacific Islander, 16% white, 5% international; 95% from in state; 27% live on campus; N/A of students in fraternities, N/A in sororities
Most popular majors: 23% Engineering, 10% Business, Management, Marketing, and Related Support Services, 10% Multi/Interdisciplinary Studies, 7% Parks, Recreation, Leisure, and Fitness Studies, 7% Social Sciences
Expenses: 2019-2020: $8,628 in state, $21,791 out of state; room/board: $8,760
Financial aid: (361) 593-3911; 76% of undergrads determined to have financial need; average aid package $10,427

Texas A&M University–Texarkana[1]
Texarkana TX
(903) 223-3069
U.S. News ranking: Reg. U. (W), No. 75
Website: www.tamut.edu
Admissions email: admissions@tamut.edu
Public; founded 1971
Application deadline (fall): rolling
Undergraduate student body: N/A full time, N/A part time
Expenses: 2019-2020: $7,217 in state, $8,117 out of state; room/board: $8,994
Financial aid: (903) 334-6601; 70% of undergrads determined to have financial need; average aid package $10,906

Texas Christian University
Fort Worth TX
(800) 828-3764
U.S. News ranking: Nat. U., No. 97
Website: www.tcu.edu
Admissions email: frogmail@tcu.edu
Private; founded 1873
Affiliation: Christian Church (Disciples of Christ)
Freshman admissions: more selective; 2018-2019: 20,156 applied, 8,210 accepted. Either SAT or ACT required. ACT 25/75 percentile: 26-30. High school rank: 50% in top tenth, 78% in top quarter, 96% in top half
Early decision deadline: 11/1, notification date: 12/5
Early action deadline: 11/1, notification date: 12/15
Application deadline (fall): 2/1
Undergraduate student body: 9,162 full time, 283 part time; 41% male, 59% female; 1% American Indian, 3% Asian, 6% black, 14% Hispanic, 1% multiracial, 0% Pacific Islander, 69% white, 5% international; 52% from in state; 51% live on campus; 41% of students in fraternities, 58% in sororities
Most popular majors: 24% Business, Management, Marketing, and Related Support Services, 15% Communication, Journalism, and Related Programs, 13% Health Professions and Related Programs, 11% Social Sciences, 4% Psychology
Expenses: 2019-2020: $49,250; room/board: $13,200
Financial aid: (817) 257-7858; 39% of undergrads determined to have financial need; average aid package $32,632

Texas College[1]
Tyler TX
(903) 593-8311
U.S. News ranking: Reg. Coll. (W), unranked
Website: www.texascollege.edu
Admissions email: cmarshall-biggins@texascollege.edu
Private
Application deadline (fall): N/A
Undergraduate student body: N/A full time, N/A part time
Expenses: N/A
Financial aid: N/A

Texas Lutheran University
Seguin TX
(800) 771-8521
U.S. News ranking: Reg. Coll. (W), No. 4
Website: www.tlu.edu
Admissions email: admissions@tlu.edu
Private; founded 1891
Affiliation: Evangelical Lutheran Church
Freshman admissions: selective; 2018-2019: 2,198 applied, 1,193 accepted. Either SAT or ACT required. SAT 25/75 percentile: 990-1160. High school rank: 11% in top tenth, 42% in top quarter, 78% in top half
Early decision deadline: N/A, notification date: N/A
Early action deadline: 12/15, notification date: 2/15
Application deadline (fall): 2/1
Undergraduate student body: 1,337 full time, 73 part time; 50% male, 50% female; 0% American Indian, 1% Asian, 9% black, 37% Hispanic, 0% multiracial, 0% Pacific Islander, 49% white,

0% international; 98% from in state; 55% live on campus; 7% of students in fraternities, 11% in sororities
Most popular majors: 22% Business, Management, Marketing, and Related Support Services, 15% Health Professions and Related Programs, 11% Education, 10% Parks, Recreation, Leisure, and Fitness Studies, 7% Biological and Biomedical Sciences
Expenses: 2019-2020: $30,860; room/board: $10,440
Financial aid: (830) 372-8010; 81% of undergrads determined to have financial need; average aid package $25,868

Texas Southern University
Houston TX
(713) 313-7071
U.S. News ranking: Nat. U., second tier
Website: www.tsu.edu
Admissions email: admissions@tsu.edu
Public; founded 1927
Freshman admissions: least selective; 2018-2019: 13,776 applied, 7,802 accepted. Either SAT or ACT required. SAT 25/75 percentile: 830-990. High school rank: 4% in top tenth, 16% in top quarter, 47% in top half
Early decision deadline: 12/1, notification date: N/A
Early action deadline: N/A, notification date: N/A
Application deadline (fall): 8/1
Undergraduate student body: 6,503 full time, 1,101 part time; 42% male, 58% female; 1% American Indian, 2% Asian, 81% black, 6% Hispanic, 1% multiracial, 0% Pacific Islander, 1% white, 7% international; 90% from in state; 25% live on campus; N/A of students in fraternities, N/A in sororities
Most popular majors: 8% Banking and Financial Support Services, 7% Business Administration and Management, General, 6% Accounting, 5% General Studies, 5% Health/Health Care Administration/Management
Expenses: 2018-2019: $9,173 in state, $21,623 out of state; room/board: $9,664
Financial aid: (713) 313-7071

Texas State University
San Marcos TX
(512) 245-2364
U.S. News ranking: Nat. U., second tier
Website: www.txstate.edu
Admissions email: admissions@txstate.edu
Public; founded 1899
Freshman admissions: selective; 2018-2019: 24,793 applied, 19,320 accepted. Either SAT or ACT required. SAT 25/75 percentile: 1010-1180. High school rank: 13% in top tenth, 47% in top quarter, 91% in top half
Early decision deadline: N/A, notification date: N/A

Early action deadline: N/A, notification date: N/A
Undergraduate student body: 28,042 full time, 6,145 part time; 42% male, 58% female; 0% American Indian, 2% Asian, 10% black, 38% Hispanic, 4% multiracial, 0% Pacific Islander, 44% white, 1% international; 97% from in state; 19% live on campus; 5% of students in fraternities, 5% in sororities
Most popular majors: 8% Multi-/Interdisciplinary Studies, Other, 6% Business Administration and Management, General, 6% Kinesiology and Exercise Science, 6% Psychology, General, 5% Marketing/Marketing Management, General
Expenses: 2019-2020: $11,257 in state, $23,917 out of state; room/board: $10,602
Financial aid: (512) 245-2315; 61% of undergrads determined to have financial need; average aid package $10,990

Texas Tech University
Lubbock TX
(806) 742-1480
U.S. News ranking: Nat. U., No. 218
Website: www.ttu.edu
Admissions email: admissions@ttu.edu
Public; founded 1923
Freshman admissions: selective; 2018-2019: 24,452 applied, 17,280 accepted. Either SAT or ACT required. SAT 25/75 percentile: 1070-1240. High school rank: 19% in top tenth, 51% in top quarter, 84% in top half
Early decision deadline: N/A, notification date: N/A
Early action deadline: N/A, notification date: N/A
Application deadline (fall): 8/1
Undergraduate student body: 27,648 full time, 4,309 part time; 53% male, 47% female; 0% American Indian, 3% Asian, 7% black, 30% Hispanic, 3% multiracial, 0% Pacific Islander, 55% white, 3% international; 9% from in state; 26% live on campus; 15% of students in fraternities, 38% in sororities
Most popular majors: 19% Business, Management, Marketing, and Related Support Services, 14% Engineering, 10% Multi/Interdisciplinary Studies, 7% Communication, Journalism, and Related Programs, 7% Family and Consumer Sciences/Human Sciences
Expenses: 2019-2020: $11,320 in state, $23,770 out of state; room/board: $9,772
Financial aid: (806) 834-1780; 49% of undergrads determined to have financial need; average aid package $10,058

Texas Wesleyan University
Fort Worth TX
(817) 531-4422
U.S. News ranking: Nat. U., second tier
Website: www.txwes.edu
Admissions email: admission@txwes.edu
Private; founded 1890
Affiliation: United Methodist
Freshman admissions: selective; 2018-2019: 4,096 applied, 1,469 accepted. Either SAT or ACT required. SAT 25/75 percentile: 975-1090. High school rank: 10% in top tenth, 31% in top quarter, 66% in top half
Early decision deadline: N/A, notification date: N/A
Early action deadline: N/A, notification date: N/A
Application deadline (fall): rolling
Undergraduate student body: 1,291 full time, 413 part time; 48% male, 52% female; 1% American Indian, 1% Asian, 19% black, 33% Hispanic, 8% multiracial, 0% Pacific Islander, 27% white, 10% international; 83% from in state; 34% live on campus; 5% of students in fraternities, 4% in sororities
Most popular majors: 38% Marketing/Marketing Management, General, 15% Multi-/Interdisciplinary Studies, Other, 8% Criminal Justice/Safety Studies, 7% Psychology, General, 6% Computer Science
Expenses: 2018-2019: $30,300; room/board: N/A
Financial aid: (817) 531-4420

Texas Woman's University
Denton TX
(940) 898-3188
U.S. News ranking: Nat. U., second tier
Website: www.twu.edu
Admissions email: admissions@twu.edu
Public; founded 1901
Freshman admissions: selective; 2018-2019: 5,727 applied, 4,971 accepted. Either SAT or ACT required for some. SAT 25/75 percentile: 970-1160. High school rank: 18% in top tenth, 49% in top quarter, 81% in top half
Early decision deadline: N/A, notification date: N/A
Early action deadline: N/A, notification date: N/A
Application deadline (fall): 8/25
Undergraduate student body: 6,880 full time, 3,510 part time; 12% male, 88% female; 0% American Indian, 9% Asian, 17% black, 31% Hispanic, 4% multiracial, 0% Pacific Islander, 38% white, 1% international; 98% from in state; 19% live on campus; 2% of students in fraternities, 3% in sororities
Most popular majors: 34% Health Professions and Related Programs, 11% Business, Management, Marketing, and Related Support Services, 11% Liberal Arts and Sciences, General Studies and Humanities, 9% Multi/

Interdisciplinary Studies, 7% Family and Consumer Sciences/ Human Sciences
Expenses: 2019-2020: $9,480 in state, $21,930 out of state; room/board: $8,550
Financial aid: (940) 898-3064; 67% of undergrads determined to have financial need; average aid package $14,012

Trinity University
San Antonio TX
(800) 874-6489
U.S. News ranking: Reg. U. (W), No. 1
Website: www.trinity.edu
Admissions email: admissions@trinity.edu
Private; founded 1869
Affiliation: Presbyterian
Freshman admissions: more selective; 2018-2019: 8,654 applied, 2,956 accepted. Either SAT or ACT required. SAT 25/75 percentile: 1260-1430. High school rank: 42% in top tenth, 77% in top quarter, 97% in top half
Early decision deadline: 11/1, notification date: 12/15
Early action deadline: 11/1, notification date: 12/15
Application deadline (fall): 2/1
Undergraduate student body: 2,433 full time, 44 part time; 47% male, 53% female; 1% American Indian, 7% Asian, 4% black, 21% Hispanic, 4% multiracial, 0% Pacific Islander, 57% white, 5% international; 76% from in state; 82% live on campus; 8% of students in fraternities, 15% in sororities
Most popular majors: 23% Business, Management, Marketing, and Related Support Services, 15% Social Sciences, 13% Biological and Biomedical Sciences, 7% Foreign Languages, Literatures, and Linguistics, 6% Communication, Journalism, and Related Programs
Expenses: 2019-2020: $44,680; room/board: $13,584
Financial aid: (210) 999-8005; 47% of undergrads determined to have financial need; average aid package $39,603

Tyler Junior College[1]
Tyler TX
(903) 510-2200
U.S. News ranking: Reg. Coll. (W), unranked
Admissions email: N/A
Public
Application deadline (fall): rolling
Undergraduate student body: N/A full time, N/A part time
Expenses: N/A
Financial aid: N/A

University of Dallas
Irving TX
(800) 628-6999
U.S. News ranking: Reg. U. (W), No. 7
Website: www.udallas.edu
Admissions email: ugadmis@udallas.edu
Private; founded 1956
Affiliation: Roman Catholic

Freshman admissions: more selective; 2018-2019: 4,846 applied, 1,896 accepted. Either SAT or ACT required. SAT 25/75 percentile: 1120-1340. High school rank: 41% in top tenth, 66% in top quarter, 86% in top half
Early decision deadline: N/A, notification date: N/A
Early action deadline: 12/1, notification date: 1/15
Application deadline (fall): 8/1
Undergraduate student body: 1,447 full time, 24 part time; 47% male, 53% female; 0% American Indian, 7% Asian, 2% black, 24% Hispanic, 3% multiracial, 0% Pacific Islander, 59% white, 3% international; 49% from in state; 60% live on campus; N/A of students in fraternities, N/A in sororities
Most popular majors: 20% Business, Management, Marketing, and Related Support Services, 15% Biological and Biomedical Sciences, 15% Social Sciences, 10% English Language and Literature/Letters, 8% Theology and Religious Vocations
Expenses: 2019-2020: $42,680; room/board: $12,760
Financial aid: (972) 721-5266; 62% of undergrads determined to have financial need; average aid package $34,947

University of Houston
Houston TX
(713) 743-1010
U.S. News ranking: Nat. U., No. 185
Website: www.uh.edu
Admissions email: admissions@uh.edu
Public; founded 1927
Freshman admissions: more selective; 2018-2019: 22,461 applied, 14,002 accepted. Either SAT or ACT required. SAT 25/75 percentile: 1130-1310. High school rank: 32% in top tenth, 66% in top quarter, 89% in top half
Early decision deadline: N/A, notification date: N/A
Early action deadline: N/A, notification date: N/A
Application deadline (fall): 6/1
Undergraduate student body: 28,029 full time, 10,319 part time; 50% male, 50% female; 0% American Indian, 22% Asian, 10% black, 36% Hispanic, 3% multiracial, 0% Pacific Islander, 23% white, 4% international; 98% from in state; 17% live on campus; 4% of students in fraternities, 3% in sororities
Most popular majors: 28% Business, Management, Marketing, and Related Support Services, 10% Engineering, 6% Biological and Biomedical Sciences, 6% Psychology, 5% Computer and Information Sciences and Support Services
Expenses: 2019-2020: $11,276 in state, $26,936 out of state; room/board: $9,368
Financial aid: (713) 743-1010; 60% of undergrads determined to have financial need; average aid package $12,979

University of Houston–Clear Lake
Houston TX
(281) 283-2500
U.S. News ranking: Reg. U. (W), No. 43
Website: www.uhcl.edu
Admissions email: admissions@uhcl.edu
Public; founded 1974
Freshman admissions: selective; 2018-2019: 1,830 applied, 823 accepted. Either SAT or ACT required. SAT 25/75 percentile: 1030-1200. High school rank: 14% in top tenth, 41% in top quarter, 74% in top half
Early decision deadline: N/A, notification date: N/A
Early action deadline: N/A, notification date: N/A
Application deadline (fall): 8/1
Undergraduate student body: 3,099 full time, 3,113 part time; 38% male, 62% female; 0% American Indian, 6% Asian, 8% black, 41% Hispanic, 3% multiracial, 0% Pacific Islander, 39% white, 1% international; N/A from in state; 2% live on campus; N/A of students in fraternities, N/A in sororities
Most popular majors: 26% Business, Management, Marketing, and Related Support Services, 22% Multi/Interdisciplinary Studies, 9% Psychology, 5% Health Professions and Related Programs, 5% Social Sciences
Expenses: 2019-2020: $9,786 in state, $26,370 out of state; room/board: $11,180
Financial aid: (281) 283-2482; 66% of undergrads determined to have financial need; average aid package $9,455

University of Houston–Downtown
Houston TX
(713) 221-8522
U.S. News ranking: Reg. U. (W), second tier
Website: www.uhd.edu
Admissions email: uhdadmit@uhd.edu
Public; founded 1974
Freshman admissions: less selective; 2018-2019: 4,416 applied, 3,673 accepted. Either SAT or ACT required. SAT 25/75 percentile: 940-1080. High school rank: 6% in top tenth, 27% in top quarter, 68% in top half
Early decision deadline: N/A, notification date: N/A
Early action deadline: N/A, notification date: N/A
Application deadline (fall): 6/1
Undergraduate student body: 6,201 full time, 6,479 part time; 40% male, 60% female; 0% American Indian, 9% Asian, 19% black, 50% Hispanic, 1% multiracial, 0% Pacific Islander, 15% white, 6% international; 98% from in state; 0% live on campus; 1% of students in fraternities, 1% in sororities
Most popular majors: 30% Business, Management, Marketing, and Related Support Services, 30% Multi/Interdisciplinary Studies,

8% Homeland Security, Law Enforcement, Firefighting and Related Protective Services, 7% Psychology, 4% Communication, Journalism, and Related Programs
Expenses: 2019-2020: $8,186 in state, $20,846 out of state; room/board: N/A
Financial aid: (713) 221-8041; 69% of undergrads determined to have financial need; average aid package $10,277

University of Houston–Victoria[1]
Victoria TX
(877) 970-4848
U.S. News ranking: Reg. U. (W), second tier
Website: www.uhv.edu/
Admissions email: admissions@uhv.edu
Public; founded 1973
Application deadline (fall): 8/1
Undergraduate student body: N/A full time, N/A part time
Expenses: N/A
Financial aid: N/A

University of Mary Hardin-Baylor
Belton TX
(254) 295-4520
U.S. News ranking: Reg. U. (W), No. 43
Website: www.umhb.edu
Admissions email: admission@umhb.edu
Private; founded 1845
Affiliation: Baptist
Freshman admissions: selective; 2018-2019: 11,783 applied, 10,214 accepted. Either SAT or ACT required. SAT 25/75 percentile: 1030-1200. High school rank: 18% in top tenth, 45% in top quarter, 76% in top half
Early decision deadline: N/A, notification date: N/A
Early action deadline: N/A, notification date: N/A
Application deadline (fall): rolling
Undergraduate student body: 3,181 full time, 216 part time; 35% male, 65% female; 1% American Indian, 2% Asian, 14% black, 22% Hispanic, 3% multiracial, 0% Pacific Islander, 55% white, 1% international; 97% from in state; 59% live on campus; N/A of students in fraternities, N/A in sororities
Most popular majors: 28% Health Professions and Related Programs, 16% Business, Management, Marketing, and Related Support Services, 10% Education, 7% Psychology, 6% Parks, Recreation, Leisure, and Fitness Studies
Expenses: 2019-2020: $29,800; room/board: $8,782
Financial aid: (254) 295-4517; 81% of undergrads determined to have financial need; average aid package $18,315

University of North Texas
Denton TX
(940) 565-2681
U.S. News ranking: Nat. U., No. 281
Website: www.unt.edu
Admissions email: undergrad@unt.edu
Public; founded 1890
Freshman admissions: selective; 2018-2019: 19,765 applied, 14,084 accepted. Either SAT or ACT required. SAT 25/75 percentile: 1060-1260. High school rank: 19% in top tenth, 50% in top quarter, 89% in top half
Early decision deadline: N/A, notification date: N/A
Early action deadline: N/A, notification date: N/A
Application deadline (fall): 8/1
Undergraduate student body: 25,443 full time, 5,904 part time; 48% male, 52% female; 0% American Indian, 7% Asian, 14% black, 26% Hispanic, 4% multiracial, 0% Pacific Islander, 44% white, 4% international; 93% from in state; 19% live on campus; 4% of students in fraternities, 6% in sororities
Most popular majors: 19% Business, Management, Marketing, and Related Support Services, 12% Multi/Interdisciplinary Studies, 11% Liberal Arts and Sciences, General Studies and Humanities, 8% Visual and Performing Arts, 7% Communication, Journalism, and Related Programs
Expenses: 2019-2020: $11,251 in state, $23,911 out of state; room/board: $9,610
Financial aid: (940) 565-3901; 62% of undergrads determined to have financial need; average aid package $12,218

University of North Texas–Dallas
Dallas TX
U.S. News ranking: Reg. U. (W), No. 77
Admissions email: N/A
Public; founded 2010
Freshman admissions: less selective; 2018-2019: 1,670 applied, 1,388 accepted. Either SAT or ACT required. SAT 25/75 percentile: 920-1080. High school rank: 16% in top tenth, 38% in top quarter, 71% in top half
Early decision deadline: N/A, notification date: N/A
Early action deadline: N/A, notification date: N/A
Application deadline (fall): 8/10
Undergraduate student body: 1,828 full time, 1,178 part time; 31% male, 69% female; 0% American Indian, 2% Asian, 30% black, 55% Hispanic, 2% multiracial, 0% Pacific Islander, 9% white, 1% international; 0% from in state; N/A live on campus; N/A of students in fraternities, N/A in sororities
Most popular majors: 33% Multi/Interdisciplinary Studies, 26% Business, Management, Marketing, and Related Support

Services, 13% Homeland Security, Law Enforcement, Firefighting and Related Protective Services, 13% Psychology, 7% Social Sciences
Expenses: 2018-2019: $9,139 in state, $21,589 out of state; room/board: $8,948
Financial aid: N/A

University of St. Thomas
Houston TX
(713) 525-3500
U.S. News ranking: Reg. U. (W), No. 19
Website: www.stthom.edu
Admissions email: admissions@stthom.edu
Private; founded 1947
Affiliation: Roman Catholic
Freshman admissions: selective; 2018-2019: 1,216 applied, 1,000 accepted. Either SAT or ACT required. SAT 25/75 percentile: 1060-1250. High school rank: 23% in top tenth, 52% in top quarter, 81% in top half
Early decision deadline: N/A, notification date: N/A
Early action deadline: 12/1, notification date: 12/15
Application deadline (fall): rolling
Undergraduate student body: 1,573 full time, 474 part time; 37% male, 63% female; 0% American Indian, 12% Asian, 7% black, 47% Hispanic, 2% multiracial, 0% Pacific Islander, 21% white, 8% international; 98% from in state; 20% live on campus; N/A of students in fraternities, N/A in sororities
Most popular majors: 23% Business, Management, Marketing, and Related Support Services, 18% Biological and Biomedical Sciences, 11% Liberal Arts and Sciences, General Studies and Humanities, 11% Social Sciences, 10% Health Professions and Related Programs
Expenses: 2019-2020: $31,460; room/board: $9,300
Financial aid: (713) 525-2170; 69% of undergrads determined to have financial need; average aid package $25,607

University of Texas–Arlington
Arlington TX
(817) 272-6287
U.S. News ranking: Nat. U., second tier
Website: www.uta.edu
Admissions email: admissions@uta.edu
Public; founded 1895
Freshman admissions: selective; 2018-2019: 12,335 applied, 9,809 accepted. Either SAT or ACT required. SAT 25/75 percentile: 1060-1260. High school rank: 28% in top tenth, 66% in top quarter, 90% in top half
Early decision deadline: N/A, notification date: N/A
Early action deadline: N/A, notification date: N/A
Application deadline (fall): N/A

Undergraduate student body: 19,326 full time, 15,146 part time; 39% male, 61% female; 0% American Indian, 12% Asian, 15% black, 29% Hispanic, 4% multiracial, 0% Pacific Islander, 35% white, 4% international; 86% from in state; 11% live on campus; 1% of students in fraternities, 1% in sororities
Most popular majors: 44% Health Professions and Related Programs, 15% Business, Management, Marketing, and Related Support Services, 5% Engineering, 4% Biological and Biomedical Sciences, 4% Liberal Arts and Sciences, General Studies and Humanities
Expenses: 2019-2020: $11,040 in state, $28,129 out of state; room/board: $10,290
Financial aid: (817) 272-3568; 70% of undergrads determined to have financial need; average aid package $10,849

University of Texas–Austin
Austin TX
(512) 475-7399
U.S. News ranking: Nat. U., No. 48
Website: www.utexas.edu
Admissions email: N/A
Public; founded 1883
Freshman admissions: most selective; 2018-2019: 50,575 applied, 19,482 accepted. Either SAT or ACT required. SAT 25/75 percentile: 1230-1480. High school rank: 85% in top tenth, 95% in top quarter, 99% in top half
Early decision deadline: N/A, notification date: N/A
Early action deadline: N/A, notification date: N/A
Application deadline (fall): 12/1
Undergraduate student body: 38,097 full time, 2,707 part time; 46% male, 54% female; 0% American Indian, 22% Asian, 4% black, 24% Hispanic, 4% multiracial, 0% Pacific Islander, 40% white, 5% international; N/A from in state; 18% live on campus; 13% of students in fraternities, 20% in sororities
Most popular majors: 13% Engineering, 12% Business, Management, Marketing, and Related Support Services, 12% Communication, Journalism, and Related Programs, 12% Social Sciences, 10% Biological and Biomedical Sciences
Expenses: 2019-2020: $10,818 in state, $38,228 out of state; room/board: $11,812
Financial aid: (512) 475-6282; 40% of undergrads determined to have financial need; average aid package $12,425

University of Texas–Dallas
Richardson TX
(972) 883-2270
U.S. News ranking: Nat. U., No. 147
Website: www.utdallas.edu
Admissions email: interest@utdallas.edu
Public; founded 1969

Freshman admissions: more selective; 2018-2019: 13,123 applied, 10,606 accepted. Either SAT or ACT required. SAT 25/75 percentile: 1220-1440. High school rank: 37% in top tenth, 66% in top quarter, 90% in top half
Early decision deadline: N/A, notification date: N/A
Early action deadline: N/A, notification date: N/A
Application deadline (fall): 5/1
Undergraduate student body: 16,691 full time, 3,181 part time; 57% male, 43% female; 0% American Indian, 33% Asian, 5% black, 18% Hispanic, 4% multiracial, 0% Pacific Islander, 32% white, 4% international; 91% from in state; 25% live on campus; 5% of students in fraternities, 7% in sororities
Most popular majors: 24% Business, Management, Marketing, and Related Support Services, 13% Biological and Biomedical Sciences, 12% Computer and Information Sciences and Support Services, 12% Engineering, 8% Health Professions and Related Programs
Expenses: 2019-2020: $13,442 in state, $38,168 out of state; room/board: $11,532
Financial aid: (972) 883-4020; 52% of undergrads determined to have financial need; average aid package $13,813

University of Texas–El Paso
El Paso TX
(915) 747-5890
U.S. News ranking: Nat. U., second tier
Website: www.utep.edu
Admissions email: futureminer@utep.edu
Public; founded 1914
Freshman admissions: less selective; 2018-2019: 10,456 applied, 10,455 accepted. Either SAT or ACT required for some. SAT 25/75 percentile: 940-1130. High school rank: 18% in top tenth, 39% in top quarter, 67% in top half
Early decision deadline: N/A, notification date: N/A
Early action deadline: N/A, notification date: N/A
Application deadline (fall): 9/5
Undergraduate student body: 14,044 full time, 7,420 part time; 47% male, 53% female; 0% American Indian, 1% Asian, 2% black, 84% Hispanic, 1% multiracial, 0% Pacific Islander, 6% white, 6% international; 90% from in state; N/A live on campus; N/A of students in fraternities, N/A in sororities
Most popular majors: 15% Business, Management, Marketing, and Related Support Services, 12% Health Professions and Related Programs, 11% Engineering, 10% Biological and Biomedical Sciences, 8% Multi-/Interdisciplinary Studies
Expenses: 2018-2019: $7,998 in state, $22,429 out of state; room/board: $9,781

Financial aid: (915) 747-5204; 75% of undergrads determined to have financial need; average aid package $14,564

University of Texas of the Permian Basin
Odessa TX
(432) 552-2605
U.S. News ranking: Reg. U. (W), No. 82
Website: www.utpb.edu
Admissions email: admissions@utpb.edu
Public; founded 1973
Freshman admissions: selective; 2018-2019: 846 applied, 698 accepted. Either SAT or ACT required. SAT 25/75 percentile: 970-1130. High school rank: 23% in top tenth, 52% in top quarter, 85% in top half
Early decision deadline: N/A, notification date: N/A
Early action deadline: N/A, notification date: N/A
Application deadline (fall): 8/26
Undergraduate student body: 711 full time, 4,033 part time; 42% male, 58% female; 0% American Indian, 2% Asian, 7% black, 54% Hispanic, 2% multiracial, 0% Pacific Islander, 32% white, 3% international; 94% from in state; 29% live on campus; N/A of students in fraternities, N/A in sororities
Most popular majors: 22% Business Administration and Management, General, 15% Psychology, General, 10% Petroleum Engineering, 8% Multi-/Interdisciplinary Studies, Other, 7% Registered Nursing/Registered Nurse
Expenses: 2019-2020: $8,465 in state, $10,115 out of state; room/board: $10,944
Financial aid: (432) 552-2620; 73% of undergrads determined to have financial need; average aid package $17,965

University of Texas–Rio Grande Valley
Edinburg TX
(888) 882-4026
U.S. News ranking: Nat. U., second tier
Website: www.utrgv.edu/en-us/index.htm
Admissions email: admissions@utrgv.edu
Public; founded 2013
Freshman admissions: selective; 2018-2019: 11,191 applied, 9,069 accepted. Either SAT or ACT required. ACT 25/75 percentile: 17-22. High school rank: 22% in top tenth, 51% in top quarter, 80% in top half
Early decision deadline: N/A, notification date: N/A
Early action deadline: N/A, notification date: N/A
Application deadline (fall): 7/1
Undergraduate student body: 19,128 full time, 5,550 part time; 43% male, 57% female; 0% American Indian, 1% Asian, 0% black, 91% Hispanic, 0% multiracial, 0% Pacific Islander, 2% white, 2% international

Most popular majors: 13% Business, Management, Marketing, and Related Support Services, 12% Biological and Biomedical Sciences, 11% Health Professions and Related Programs, 10% Psychology, 9% Homeland Security, Law Enforcement, Firefighting and Related Protective Services
Expenses: 2018-2019: $7,813 in state, $17,773 out of state; room/board: $8,124
Financial aid: N/A

University of Texas–San Antonio
San Antonio TX
(210) 458-8000
U.S. News ranking: Nat. U., second tier
Website: www.utsa.edu
Admissions email: prospects@utsa.edu
Public; founded 1969
Freshman admissions: selective; 2018-2019: 16,918 applied, 13,370 accepted. Either SAT or ACT required. SAT 25/75 percentile: 1040-1220. High school rank: 18% in top tenth, 58% in top quarter, 91% in top half
Early decision deadline: N/A, notification date: N/A
Early action deadline: N/A, notification date: N/A
Application deadline (fall): 6/1
Undergraduate student body: 22,542 full time, 5,446 part time; 50% male, 50% female; 0% American Indian, 6% Asian, 9% black, 57% Hispanic, 3% multiracial, 0% Pacific Islander, 22% white, 2% international; 98% from in state; 12% live on campus; 3% of students in fraternities, 5% in sororities
Most popular majors: 20% Business, Management, and Related Support Services, 9% Engineering, 8% Psychology, 7% Biological and Biomedical Sciences, 6% Education
Expenses: 2019-2020: $9,722 in state, $24,722 out of state; room/board: $7,050
Financial aid: (210) 458-8000; 68% of undergrads determined to have financial need; average aid package $9,706

University of Texas–Tyler
Tyler TX
(903) 566-7203
U.S. News ranking: Nat. U., second tier
Website: www.uttyler.edu
Admissions email: admissions@uttyler.edu
Public; founded 1971
Freshman admissions: selective; 2018-2019: 3,086 applied, 2,416 accepted. Either SAT or ACT required. SAT 25/75 percentile: 1080-1280. High school rank: 12% in top tenth, 36% in top quarter, 71% in top half
Early decision deadline: N/A, notification date: N/A

Early action deadline: N/A, notification date: N/A
Application deadline (fall): 8/26
Undergraduate student body: 4,708 full time, 2,625 part time; 44% male, 56% female; 0% American Indian, 4% Asian, 9% black, 20% Hispanic, 3% multiracial, 0% Pacific Islander, 58% white, 3% international; 98% from in state; 22% live on campus; 4% of students in fraternities, 7% in sororities
Most popular majors: 24% Registered Nursing/ Registered Nurse, 12% Multi-/ Interdisciplinary Studies, Other, 6% Psychology, General, 5% Kinesiology and Exercise Science, 5% Mechanical Engineering
Expenses: 2019-2020: $8,742 in state, $22,752 out of state; room/ board: $9,502
Financial aid: (903) 566-7180; 79% of undergrads determined to have financial need; average aid package $11,506

University of the Incarnate Word
San Antonio TX
(210) 829-6005
U.S. News ranking: Nat. U., No. 272
Website: www.uiw.edu
Admissions email: admis@uiwtx.edu
Private; founded 1881
Affiliation: Roman Catholic
Freshman admissions: selective; 2018-2019: 4,894 applied, 4,304 accepted. Either SAT or ACT required. SAT 25/75 percentile: 950-1140. High school rank: 16% in top tenth, 39% in top quarter, 72% in top half
Early decision deadline: N/A, notification date: N/A
Early action deadline: N/A, notification date: N/A
Application deadline (fall): rolling
Undergraduate student body: 4,103 full time, 1,455 part time; 39% male, 61% female; 0% American Indian, 2% Asian, 7% black, 57% Hispanic, 2% multiracial, 0% Pacific Islander, 19% white, 4% international; 94% from in state; 18% live on campus; 1% of students in fraternities, 2% in sororities
Most popular majors: 13% Business Administration and Management, General, 8% Biology/Biological Sciences, General, 6% Psychology, General, 6% Registered Nursing/Registered Nurse, 4% Elementary Education and Teaching
Expenses: 2019-2020: $32,576; room/board: $12,824
Financial aid: (210) 829-6008; 76% of undergrads determined to have financial need; average aid package $21,383

Wade College[1]
Dallas TX
U.S. News ranking: Reg. Coll. (W), unranked
Admissions email: N/A
For-profit
Application deadline (fall): N/A
Undergraduate student body: N/A full time, N/A part time

Expenses: N/A
Financial aid: N/A

Wayland Baptist University
Plainview TX
(806) 291-3500
U.S. News ranking: Reg. U. (W), second tier
Website: www.wbu.edu
Admissions email: admitme@wbu.edu
Private; founded 1908
Affiliation: Baptist
Freshman admissions: less selective; 2018-2019: 663 applied, 650 accepted. Either SAT or ACT required. ACT 25/75 percentile: 16-22. High school rank: 6% in top tenth, 23% in top quarter, 52% in top half
Early decision deadline: N/A, notification date: N/A
Early action deadline: N/A, notification date: N/A
Application deadline (fall): rolling
Undergraduate student body: 945 full time, 2,410 part time; 49% male, 51% female; 1% American Indian, 2% Asian, 18% black, 32% Hispanic, 5% multiracial, 1% Pacific Islander, 36% white, 2% international; 70% from in state; 16% live on campus; N/A of students in fraternities, N/A in sororities
Most popular majors: Information not available
Expenses: 2019-2020: $22,658; room/board: $8,342
Financial aid: (806) 291-3520; 77% of undergrads determined to have financial need; average aid package $14,199

West Texas A&M University
Canyon TX
(806) 651-2020
U.S. News ranking: Reg. U. (W), No. 75
Website: www.wtamu.edu
Admissions email: admissions@wtamu.edu
Public; founded 1910
Freshman admissions: selective; 2018-2019: 5,427 applied, 3,521 accepted. Either SAT or ACT required. ACT 25/75 percentile: 19-24. High school rank: 17% in top tenth, 44% in top quarter, 78% in top half
Early decision deadline: N/A, notification date: N/A
Early action deadline: N/A, notification date: N/A
Application deadline (fall): 8/1
Undergraduate student body: 5,484 full time, 1,892 part time; 42% male, 58% female; 1% American Indian, 2% Asian, 5% black, 30% Hispanic, 3% multiracial, 0% Pacific Islander, 57% white, 2% international; 88% from in state; 26% live on campus; 3% of students in fraternities, 5% in sororities
Most popular majors: 15% Business, Management, Marketing, and Related Support Services, 12% Health Professions and Related Programs, 10% Agri-culture, Agriculture Operations,

and Related Sciences, 10% Liberal Arts and Sciences, General Studies and Humanities, 7% Education
Expenses: 2019-2020: $8,688 in state, $10,274 out of state; room/ board: $7,196
Financial aid: (806) 651-2055; 64% of undergrads determined to have financial need; average aid package $9,534

Wiley College[1]
Marshall TX
(800) 658-6889
U.S. News ranking: Reg. Coll. (W), second tier
Website: www.wileyc.edu
Admissions email: admissions@wileyc.edu
Private; founded 1873
Application deadline (fall): rolling
Undergraduate student body: N/A full time, N/A part time
Expenses: N/A
Financial aid: (903) 927-3216

UTAH

Brigham Young University–Provo
Provo UT
(801) 422-4104
U.S. News ranking: Nat. U., No. 77
Website: www.byu.edu
Admissions email: admissions@byu.edu
Private; founded 1875
Affiliation: Latter Day Saints (Mormon Church)
Freshman admissions: more selective; 2018-2019: 11,205 applied, 7,224 accepted. Either SAT or ACT required. ACT 25/75 percentile: 26-31. High school rank: 54% in top tenth, 85% in top quarter, 98% in top half
Early decision deadline: N/A, notification date: N/A
Early action deadline: N/A, notification date: N/A
Application deadline (fall): 12/15
Undergraduate student body: 28,253 full time, 3,188 part time; 50% male, 50% female; 0% American Indian, 2% Asian, 1% black, 6% Hispanic, 4% multiracial, 1% Pacific Islander, 81% white, 3% international; 65% from in state; 19% live on campus; 0% of students in fraternities, 0% in sororities
Most popular majors: 16% Business, Management, Marketing, and Related Support Services, 10% Biological and Biomedical Sciences, 8% Engineering, 7% Education, 7% Social Sciences
Expenses: 2019-2020: $5,790; room/board: $7,766
Financial aid: (801) 422-4104; 51% of undergrads determined to have financial need; average aid package $7,968

Dixie State University
Saint George UT
(435) 652-7702
U.S. News ranking: Reg. Coll. (W), No. 25
Website: www.dixie.edu
Admissions email: admissions@dixie.edu
Public; founded 1911
Freshman admissions: selective; 2018-2019: 14,504 applied, 14,504 accepted. Either SAT or ACT required for some. ACT 25/75 percentile: 17-24. High school rank: 11% in top tenth, 30% in top quarter, 62% in top half
Early decision deadline: N/A, notification date: N/A
Early action deadline: N/A, notification date: N/A
Application deadline (fall): 8/15
Undergraduate student body: 6,106 full time, 3,822 part time; 43% male, 57% female; 1% American Indian, 1% Asian, 3% black, 12% Hispanic, 4% multiracial, 2% Pacific Islander, 75% white, 2% international; 75% from in state; N/A live on campus; N/A of students in fraternities, N/A in sororities
Most popular majors: 18% Business, Management, Marketing, and Related Support Services, 15% Communication, Journalism, and Related Programs, 15% Health Professions and Related Programs, 9% Homeland Security, Law Enforcement, Firefighting and Related Protective Services, 7% Visual and Performing Arts
Expenses: 2019-2020: $5,516 in state, $15,798 out of state; room/ board: $6,974
Financial aid: (435) 652-7575; 62% of undergrads determined to have financial need; average aid package $10,708

Snow College[1]
Ephraim UT
(435) 283-7159
U.S. News ranking: Reg. Coll. (W), unranked
Website: www.snow.edu/admissions/
Admissions email: admissions@snow.edu
Public; founded 1888
Application deadline (fall): rolling
Undergraduate student body: N/A full time, N/A part time
Expenses: N/A
Financial aid: N/A

Southern Utah University
Cedar City UT
(435) 586-7740
U.S. News ranking: Reg. U. (W), No. 72
Website: www.suu.edu
Admissions email: adminfo@suu.edu
Public; founded 1897
Freshman admissions: selective; 2018-2019: 12,435 applied, 9,846 accepted. Either SAT or ACT required. ACT 25/75 percentile: 21-27. High school rank: 19% in top tenth, 47% in top quarter, 79% in top half

Early decision deadline: N/A, notification date: N/A
Early action deadline: N/A, notification date: N/A
Application deadline (fall): 5/1
Undergraduate student body: 6,808 full time, 2,463 part time; 42% male, 58% female; 1% American Indian, 1% Asian, 3% black, 7% Hispanic, 0% multiracial, 1% Pacific Islander, 74% white, 6% international; N/A from in state; 11% live on campus; N/A of students in fraternities, N/A in sororities
Most popular majors: 14% Business, Management, Marketing, and Related Support Services, 11% Education, 7% Family and Consumer Sciences/ Human Sciences, 7% Health Professions and Related Programs, 6% Liberal Arts and Sciences, General Studies and Humanities
Expenses: 2019-2020: $6,770 in state, $20,586 out of state; room/ board: $7,349
Financial aid: (435) 586-7735; 60% of undergrads determined to have financial need; average aid package $9,688

University of Utah
Salt Lake City UT
(801) 581-8761
U.S. News ranking: Nat. U., No. 104
Website: www.utah.edu
Admissions email: admissions@utah.edu
Public; founded 1850
Freshman admissions: more selective; 2018-2019: 23,096 applied, 15,441 accepted. Either SAT or ACT required. ACT 25/75 percentile: 22-29. High school rank: N/A
Early decision deadline: N/A, notification date: N/A
Early action deadline: 12/1, notification date: 1/15
Application deadline (fall): 4/1
Undergraduate student body: 18,499 full time, 6,244 part time; 53% male, 47% female; 0% American Indian, 6% Asian, 1% black, 13% Hispanic, 6% multiracial, 0% Pacific Islander, 68% white, 4% international; 72% from in state; 14% live on campus; 6% of students in fraternities, 8% in sororities
Most popular majors: 7% Speech Communication and Rhetoric, 6% Psychology, General, 5% Economics, General, 4% Biology/ Biological Sciences, General, 4% Registered Nursing/Registered Nurse
Expenses: 2019-2020: $9,498 in state, $30,132 out of state; room/ board: $10,684
Financial aid: (801) 581-6211; 46% of undergrads determined to have financial need; average aid package $19,812

Utah State University
Logan UT
(435) 797-1079
U.S. News ranking: Nat. U., No. 254
Website: www.usu.edu
Admissions email: admit@usu.edu
Public; founded 1888

Freshman admissions: selective; 2018-2019: 15,099 applied, 13,446 accepted. Either SAT or ACT required. ACT 25/75 percentile: 21-28. High school rank: 21% in top tenth, 46% in top quarter, 77% in top half **Early decision deadline:** N/A, notification date: N/A **Early action deadline:** N/A, notification date: N/A **Application deadline (fall):** rolling **Undergraduate student body:** 17,394 full time, 7,486 part time; 46% male, 54% female; 2% American Indian, 1% Asian, 1% black, 6% Hispanic, 2% multiracial, 0% Pacific Islander, 82% white, 1% international; N/A from in state; N/A live on campus; 3% of students in fraternities, 3% in sororities **Most popular majors:** 8% Communication Sciences and Disorders, General, 8% Economics, General, 4% Business Administration and Management, General, 4% Physical Education Teaching and Coaching, 4% Psychology, General **Expenses:** 2019-2020: $7,659 in state, $22,197 out of state; room/board: $5,770 **Financial aid:** (435) 797-0173; 53% of undergrads determined to have financial need; average aid package $11,579

Utah Valley University
Orem UT
(801) 863-8706
U.S. News ranking: Reg. U. (W), unranked
Website: www.uvu.edu/
Admissions email: admissions@uvu.edu
Public; founded 1941
Freshman admissions: selective; 2018-2019: 10,117 applied, 10,117 accepted. Neither SAT nor ACT required. ACT 25/75 percentile: 18-25. High school rank: 10% in top tenth, 28% in top quarter, 59% in top half **Early decision deadline:** N/A, notification date: N/A **Early action deadline:** N/A, notification date: N/A **Application deadline (fall):** 8/1 **Undergraduate student body:** 19,261 full time, 20,136 part time; 53% male, 47% female; 1% American Indian, 1% Asian, 1% black, 12% Hispanic, 3% multiracial, 1% Pacific Islander, 78% white, 2% international; 87% from in state; 0% live on campus; N/A of students in fraternities, N/A in sororities **Most popular majors:** 21% Business, Management, Marketing, and Related Support Services, 11% Psychology, 8% Education, 7% Computer and Information Sciences and Support Services, 7% Health Professions and Related Programs **Expenses:** 2019-2020: $5,820 in state, $16,570 out of state; room/board: N/A **Financial aid:** (801) 863-6746; 59% of undergrads determined to have financial need; average aid package $7,986

Weber State University
Ogden UT
(801) 626-6743
U.S. News ranking: Reg. U. (W), No. 80
Website: weber.edu
Admissions email: admissions@weber.edu
Public; founded 1889
Freshman admissions: selective; 2018-2019: 7,255 applied, 7,255 accepted. Neither SAT nor ACT required. ACT 25/75 percentile: 18-24. High school rank: 10% in top tenth, 31% in top quarter, 60% in top half **Early decision deadline:** N/A, notification date: N/A **Early action deadline:** N/A, notification date: N/A **Application deadline (fall):** 8/31 **Undergraduate student body:** 11,444 full time, 16,021 part time; 45% male, 55% female; 1% American Indian, 2% Asian, 2% black, 12% Hispanic, 3% multiracial, 1% Pacific Islander, 74% white, 2% international; N/A from in state; 4% live on campus; 3% of students in fraternities, 4% in sororities **Most popular majors:** 16% Registered Nursing/Registered Nurse, 6% Selling Skills and Sales Operations, 4% Clinical/Medical Laboratory Technician, 4% Computer Science, 4% Criminal Justice/Safety Studies **Expenses:** 2019-2020: $6,963 in state, $16,945 out of state; room/board: $9,900 **Financial aid:** (801) 626-7569; 59% of undergrads determined to have financial need; average aid package $6,543

Western Governors University[1]
Salt Lake City UT
(801) 274-3280
U.S. News ranking: Reg. U. (W), unranked
Website: www.wgu.edu/
Admissions email: info@wgu.edu
Private; founded 1996
Application deadline (fall): N/A **Undergraduate student body:** N/A full time, N/A part time **Expenses:** N/A **Financial aid:** (877) 435-7948

Westminster College
Salt Lake City UT
(801) 832-2200
U.S. News ranking: Reg. U. (W), No. 12
Website: www.westminstercollege.edu
Admissions email: admission@westminstercollege.edu
Private; founded 1875
Affiliation: Undenominational
Freshman admissions: selective; 2018-2019: 1,864 applied, 1,732 accepted. Either SAT or ACT required. ACT 25/75 percentile: 21-27. High school rank: 21% in top tenth, 44% in top quarter, 81% in top half **Early decision deadline:** N/A, notification date: N/A

Early action deadline: N/A, notification date: N/A **Application deadline (fall):** rolling **Undergraduate student body:** 1,865 full time, 103 part time; 40% male, 60% female; 1% American Indian, 3% Asian, 2% black, 12% Hispanic, 5% multiracial, 0% Pacific Islander, 70% white, 4% international; 64% from in state; 32% live on campus; 0% of students in fraternities, 0% in sororities **Most popular majors:** 26% Health Professions and Related Programs, 19% Business, Management, Marketing, and Related Support Services, 8% Biological and Biomedical Sciences, 7% Psychology, 6% Visual and Performing Arts **Expenses:** 2019-2020: $34,984; room/board: $9,810 **Financial aid:** (801) 832-2500; 63% of undergrads determined to have financial need; average aid package $28,582

VERMONT

Bennington College
Bennington VT
(800) 833-6845
U.S. News ranking: Nat. Lib. Arts, No. 89
Website: www.bennington.edu
Admissions email: admissions@bennington.edu
Private; founded 1932
Freshman admissions: more selective; 2018-2019: 1,494 applied, 852 accepted. Neither SAT nor ACT required. SAT 25/75 percentile: 1230-1390. High school rank: 55% in top tenth, 79% in top quarter, 92% in top half **Early decision deadline:** 11/15, notification date: 12/14 **Early action deadline:** 12/1, notification date: 2/1 **Application deadline (fall):** 1/15 **Undergraduate student body:** 704 full time, 31 part time; 36% male, 64% female; 0% American Indian, 1% Asian, 4% black, 10% Hispanic, 3% multiracial, 0% Pacific Islander, 59% white, 17% international; 3% from in state; 99% live on campus; 0% of students in fraternities, 0% in sororities **Most popular majors:** 39% Visual and Performing Arts, 11% Social Sciences, 10% English Language and Literature/Letters, 5% Foreign Languages, Literatures, and Linguistics, 4% Mathematics and Statistics **Expenses:** 2019-2020: $55,950; room/board: $16,200 **Financial aid:** (802) 440-4325; 62% of undergrads determined to have financial need; average aid package $45,929

Castleton University
Castleton VT
(800) 639-8521
U.S. News ranking: Reg. Coll. (N), No. 21
Website: www.castleton.edu
Admissions email: info@castleton.edu
Public; founded 1787

Freshman admissions: less selective; 2018-2019: 2,185 applied, 1,895 accepted. Either SAT or ACT required. SAT 25/75 percentile: 930-1170. High school rank: 8% in top tenth, 27% in top quarter, 61% in top half **Early decision deadline:** N/A, notification date: N/A **Early action deadline:** N/A, notification date: N/A **Application deadline (fall):** rolling **Undergraduate student body:** 1,818 full time, 72 part time; 47% male, 53% female; 0% American Indian, 1% Asian, 2% black, 2% Hispanic, 3% multiracial, 0% Pacific Islander, 84% white, 2% international; 70% from in state; 60% live on campus; N/A of students in fraternities, N/A in sororities **Most popular majors:** 15% Registered Nursing/Registered Nurse, 12% Business Administration and Management, General, 5% Health/Medical Preparatory Programs, Other, 5% Multi-/Interdisciplinary Studies, Other, 5% Social Work **Expenses:** 2018-2019: $12,314 in state, $28,322 out of state; room/board: $10,598 **Financial aid:** N/A

Champlain College
Burlington VT
(800) 570-5858
U.S. News ranking: Reg. U. (N), No. 66
Website: www.champlain.edu
Admissions email: admission@champlain.edu
Private; founded 1878
Freshman admissions: selective; 2018-2019: 4,977 applied, 3,753 accepted. Neither SAT nor ACT required. SAT 25/75 percentile: 1090-1280. High school rank: 14% in top tenth, 35% in top quarter, 70% in top half **Early decision deadline:** 11/15, notification date: 12/15 **Early action deadline:** N/A, notification date: N/A **Application deadline (fall):** 1/15 **Undergraduate student body:** 2,047 full time, 82 part time; 62% male, 38% female; 0% American Indian, 3% Asian, 3% black, 7% Hispanic, 4% multiracial, 0% Pacific Islander, 75% white, 1% international; 21% from in state; 71% live on campus; 0% of students in fraternities, 0% in sororities **Most popular majors:** 10% Business Administration and Management, General, 10% Cyber/Computer Forensics and Counterterrorism, 9% Liberal Arts and Sciences/Liberal Studies, 8% Computer and Information Systems Security/Information Assurance, 4% Graphic Design **Expenses:** 2019-2020: $41,828; room/board: $15,766 **Financial aid:** (802) 865-5435; 70% of undergrads determined to have financial need; average aid package $28,783

College of St. Joseph[1]
Rutland VT
(802) 773-5286
U.S. News ranking: Reg. Coll. (N), second tier
Website: www.csj.edu
Admissions email: admissions@csj.edu
Private; founded 1956
Application deadline (fall): 8/15 **Undergraduate student body:** N/A full time, N/A part time **Expenses:** N/A **Financial aid:** (802) 776-5262

Goddard College[1]
Plainfield VT
(800) 906-8312
U.S. News ranking: Reg. U. (N), unranked
Website: www.goddard.edu
Admissions email: admissions@goddard.edu
Private; founded 1863
Application deadline (fall): N/A **Undergraduate student body:** N/A full time, N/A part time **Expenses:** N/A **Financial aid:** (800) 468-4888

Landmark College
Putney VT
(802) 387-6718
U.S. News ranking: Reg. Coll. (N), No. 25
Website: www.landmark.edu
Admissions email: admissions@landmark.edu
Private; founded 1985
Freshman admissions: less selective; 2018-2019: 360 applied, 206 accepted. Neither SAT nor ACT required. SAT 25/75 percentile: N/A. High school rank: N/A **Early decision deadline:** N/A, notification date: N/A **Early action deadline:** N/A, notification date: N/A **Application deadline (fall):** N/A **Undergraduate student body:** 337 full time, 152 part time; 67% male, 33% female; 1% American Indian, 4% Asian, 3% black, 6% Hispanic, 2% multiracial, 0% Pacific Islander, 66% white, 1% international; N/A from in state; 95% live on campus; N/A of students in fraternities, N/A in sororities **Most popular majors:** 88% Liberal Arts and Sciences, General Studies and Humanities, 8% Computer and Information Sciences and Support Services, 4% Visual and Performing Arts **Expenses:** 2019-2020: $59,100; room/board: $12,900 **Financial aid:** (802) 781-6178; 59% of undergrads determined to have financial need; average aid package $36,630

Marlboro College
Marlboro VT
(800) 343-0049
U.S. News ranking: Nat. Lib. Arts, No. 136
Website: www.marlboro.edu
Admissions email: admissions@marlboro.edu
Private; founded 1946

Freshman admissions: selective; 2018-2019: 102 applied, 94 accepted. Neither SAT nor ACT required. SAT 25/75 percentile: 1060-1360. High school rank: N/A
Early decision deadline: 11/15, notification date: 12/1
Early action deadline: 1/15, notification date: 2/1
Application deadline (fall): rolling
Undergraduate student body: 144 full time, 2 part time; 44% male, 56% female; 0% American Indian, 3% Asian, 4% black, 2% Hispanic, 3% multiracial, 0% Pacific Islander, 73% white, 2% international
Most popular majors: 32% Visual and Performing Arts, 19% English Language and Literature/Letters, 18% Social Sciences, 6% Area, Ethnic, Cultural, Gender, and Group Studies, 5% Philosophy and Religious Studies
Expenses: 2019-2020: $27,485; room/board: $12,595
Financial aid: (802) 258-9237; 81% of undergrads determined to have financial need; average aid package $39,397

Marlboro College Graduate & Professional Studies[1]
Marlboro VT
(802) 258-9200
U.S. News ranking: Reg. Coll. (N), unranked
Website: www.scc.spokane.edu
Admissions email: N/A
Private
Application deadline (fall): N/A
Undergraduate student body: N/A full time, N/A part time
Expenses: N/A
Financial aid: N/A

Middlebury College
Middlebury VT
(802) 443-3000
U.S. News ranking: Nat. Lib. Arts, No. 7
Website: www.middlebury.edu
Admissions email: admissions@middlebury.edu
Private; founded 1800
Freshman admissions: most selective; 2018-2019: 9,227 applied, 1,542 accepted. Either SAT or ACT required. SAT 25/75 percentile: 1330-1500. High school rank: 80% in top tenth, 95% in top quarter, 99% in top half
Early decision deadline: 11/1, notification date: 12/15
Early action deadline: N/A, notification date: N/A
Application deadline (fall): 1/1
Undergraduate student body: 2,551 full time, 28 part time; 47% male, 53% female; 0% American Indian, 7% Asian, 4% black, 10% Hispanic, 5% multiracial, 0% Pacific Islander, 62% white, 10% international; 5% from in state; 98% live on campus; 0% of students in fraternities, 0% in sororities
Most popular majors: 13% Economics, General, 8% Environmental Studies, 7% Political

Science and Government, General, 5% Computer Science, 5% Psychology, General
Expenses: 2019-2020: $56,216; room/board: $16,032
Financial aid: (802) 443-5228; 46% of undergrads determined to have financial need; average aid package $52,352

Northern Vermont University[1]
Johnson VT
(800) 635-2356
U.S. News ranking: Reg. U. (N), second tier
Website: www.jsc.edu
Admissions email: JSCAdmissions@jsc.edu
Public; founded 1828
Application deadline (fall): rolling
Undergraduate student body: N/A full time, N/A part time
Expenses: N/A
Financial aid: N/A

Norwich University
Northfield VT
(800) 468-6679
U.S. News ranking: Reg. U. (N), No. 66
Website: www.norwich.edu
Admissions email: nuadm@norwich.edu
Private; founded 1819
Freshman admissions: selective; 2018-2019: 4,344 applied, 2,863 accepted. Either SAT or ACT required for some. SAT 25/75 percentile: 1040-1270. High school rank: 12% in top tenth, 33% in top quarter, 66% in top half
Early decision deadline: N/A, notification date: N/A
Early action deadline: N/A, notification date: N/A
Application deadline (fall): rolling
Undergraduate student body: 2,581 full time, 601 part time; 76% male, 24% female; 1% American Indian, 3% Asian, 5% black, 10% Hispanic, 4% multiracial, 0% Pacific Islander, 72% white, 2% international; 12% from in state; 69% live on campus; N/A of students in fraternities, N/A in sororities
Most popular majors: 27% Military Science, Leadership and Operational Art, 17% Homeland Security, Law Enforcement, Firefighting and Related Protective Services, 10% Business, Management, Marketing, and Related Support Services, 8% Engineering, 8% Social Sciences
Expenses: 2018-2019: $40,016; room/board: $13,840
Financial aid: (802) 485-3015

Sterling College[1]
Craftsbury Common VT
(802) 586-7711
U.S. News ranking: Nat. Lib. Arts, unranked
Website: www.sterlingcollege.edu
Admissions email: admissions@sterlingcollege.edu
Private; founded 1958
Application deadline (fall): N/A

Undergraduate student body: N/A full time, N/A part time
Expenses: N/A
Financial aid: N/A

St. Michael's College
Colchester VT
(800) 762-8000
U.S. News ranking: Nat. Lib. Arts, No. 124
Website: www.smcvt.edu
Admissions email: admission@smcvt.edu
Private; founded 1904
Affiliation: Roman Catholic
Freshman admissions: selective; 2018-2019: 4,040 applied, 3,339 accepted. Neither SAT nor ACT required. SAT 25/75 percentile: 1140-1320. High school rank: 24% in top tenth, 53% in top quarter, 82% in top half
Early decision deadline: N/A, notification date: N/A
Early action deadline: 11/1, notification date: 12/21
Application deadline (fall): 2/1
Undergraduate student body: 1,669 full time, 25 part time; 46% male, 54% female; 0% American Indian, 2% Asian, 2% black, 6% Hispanic, 2% multiracial, 0% Pacific Islander, 82% white, 3% international; 15% from in state; 93% live on campus; N/A of students in fraternities, N/A in sororities
Most popular majors: 17% Social Sciences, 16% Business, Management, Marketing, and Related Support Services, 10% Biological and Biomedical Sciences, 8% Education, 8% Psychology
Expenses: 2019-2020: $47,045; room/board: $12,950
Financial aid: (802) 654-3243; 65% of undergrads determined to have financial need; average aid package $31,371

University of Vermont
Burlington VT
(802) 656-3370
U.S. News ranking: Nat. U., No. 121
Website: www.uvm.edu
Admissions email: admissions@uvm.edu
Public; founded 1791
Freshman admissions: more selective; 2018-2019: 21,263 applied, 14,365 accepted. Either SAT or ACT required. SAT 25/75 percentile: 1180-1360. High school rank: 37% in top tenth, 73% in top quarter, 94% in top half
Early decision deadline: N/A, notification date: N/A
Early action deadline: 11/1, notification date: 12/15
Application deadline (fall): 1/15
Undergraduate student body: 10,434 full time, 894 part time; 41% male, 59% female; 0% American Indian, 3% Asian, 1% black, 4% Hispanic, 3% multiracial, 0% Pacific Islander, 82% white, 5% international; 29% from in state; 51% live on campus; 8% of students in fraternities, 7% in sororities

Most popular majors: 9% Business Administration and Management, General, 6% Psychology, General, 5% Environmental Studies, 4% Mechanical Engineering, 4% Registered Nursing/Registered Nurse
Expenses: 2019-2020: $18,802 in state, $43,690 out of state; room/board: $12,916
Financial aid: (802) 656-5700; 56% of undergrads determined to have financial need; average aid package $26,752

Vermont Technical College
Randolph Center VT
(802) 728-1244
U.S. News ranking: Reg. Coll. (N), No. 23
Website: www.vtc.edu
Admissions email: admissions@vtc.edu
Public; founded 1866
Freshman admissions: less selective; 2018-2019: 1,039 applied, 718 accepted. Either SAT or ACT required for some. ACT 25/75 percentile: 19-27. High school rank: 7% in top tenth, 26% in top quarter, 60% in top half
Early decision deadline: N/A, notification date: N/A
Early action deadline: N/A, notification date: N/A
Application deadline (fall): rolling
Undergraduate student body: 1,069 full time, 541 part time; 52% male, 48% female; 0% American Indian, 1% Asian, 2% black, 2% Hispanic, 9% multiracial, 0% Pacific Islander, 82% white, 2% international; 84% from in state; 31% live on campus; N/A of students in fraternities, N/A in sororities
Most popular majors: Information not available
Expenses: 2019-2020: $15,971 in state, $29,003 out of state; room/board: $11,420
Financial aid: (802) 728-1248; 80% of undergrads determined to have financial need; average aid package $12,000

VIRGIN ISLANDS

University of the Virgin Islands
St. Thomas VI
(340) 693-1150
U.S. News ranking: Reg. Coll. (S), unranked
Website: www.uvi.edu
Admissions email: admit@uvi.edu
Public; founded 1962
Freshman admissions: least selective; 2018-2019: 749 applied, 713 accepted. Neither SAT nor ACT required. SAT 25/75 percentile: 815-1125. High school rank: 15% in top tenth, 37% in top quarter, 67% in top half
Early decision deadline: N/A, notification date: N/A
Early action deadline: N/A, notification date: N/A
Application deadline (fall): 4/30
Undergraduate student body: 1,223 full time, 511 part time; 34% male, 66% female; 0% American Indian, 1% Asian, 71% black,

11% Hispanic, 1% multiracial, 0% Pacific Islander, 5% white, 5% international; 90% from in state; N/A live on campus; N/A of students in fraternities, N/A in sororities
Most popular majors: 16% Registered Nursing/Registered Nurse, 13% Accounting, 13% Business Administration and Management, General, 10% Biology/Biological Sciences, General, 9% Criminal Justice/Police Science
Expenses: 2019-2020: $5,235 in state, $14,496 out of state; room/board: $9,900
Financial aid: (340) 692-4192; 67% of undergrads determined to have financial need; average aid package $9,250

VIRGINIA

Averett University
Danville VA
(434) 791-5600
U.S. News ranking: Reg. Coll. (S), No. 15
Website: www.averett.edu
Admissions email: admit@averett.edu
Private; founded 1859
Affiliation: Other
Freshman admissions: less selective; 2018-2019: 2,833 applied, 1,717 accepted. Either SAT or ACT required. SAT 25/75 percentile: 890-1090. High school rank: 8% in top tenth, 27% in top quarter, 56% in top half
Early decision deadline: N/A, notification date: N/A
Early action deadline: N/A, notification date: N/A
Application deadline (fall): rolling
Undergraduate student body: 934 full time, 31 part time; 57% male, 43% female; 0% American Indian, 1% Asian, 29% black, 4% Hispanic, 4% multiracial, 0% Pacific Islander, 56% white, 6% international; 44% from in state; 58% live on campus; 1% of students in fraternities, 0% in sororities
Most popular majors: 17% Health Professions and Related Programs, 14% Business, Management, Marketing, and Related Support Services, 14% Parks, Recreation, Leisure, and Fitness Studies, 9% Education, 9% Psychology
Expenses: 2019-2020: $35,600; room/board: $10,560
Financial aid: (434) 791-5646; 86% of undergrads determined to have financial need; average aid package $27,059

Bluefield College
Bluefield VA
(276) 326-4231
U.S. News ranking: Reg. Coll. (S), No. 46
Website: www.bluefield.edu
Admissions email: admissions@bluefield.edu
Private; founded 1922
Affiliation: Baptist
Freshman admissions: least selective; 2018-2019: 1,153 applied, 1,087 accepted. Either

SAT or ACT required. SAT 25/75 percentile: 898-1063. High school rank: 4% in top tenth, 16% in top quarter, 45% in top half
Early decision deadline: N/A, notification date: N/A
Early action deadline: N/A, notification date: N/A
Application deadline (fall): rolling
Undergraduate student body: 822 full time, 125 part time; 50% male, 50% female; 0% American Indian, 0% Asian, 25% black, 5% Hispanic, 4% multiracial, 0% Pacific Islander, 60% white, 3% international; 70% from in state; 68% live on campus; 6% of students in fraternities, 6% in sororities
Most popular majors: 24% Public Administration and Social Service Professions, 17% Criminal Justice/Safety Studies, 14% Organizational Leadership, 14% Public Health/Community Nurse/Nursing, 8% Kinesiology and Exercise Science
Expenses: 2019-2020: $27,036; room/board: $9,356
Financial aid: (276) 326-4280; 89% of undergrads determined to have financial need; average aid package $16,950

Bridgewater College
Bridgewater VA
(800) 759-8328
U.S. News ranking: Nat. Lib. Arts, second tier
Website: www.bridgewater.edu
Admissions email: admissions@bridgewater.edu
Private; founded 1880
Affiliation: Church of Brethren
Freshman admissions: selective; 2018-2019: 6,360 applied, 4,203 accepted. Either SAT or ACT required. SAT 25/75 percentile: 980-1170. High school rank: 14% in top tenth, 38% in top quarter, 72% in top half
Early decision deadline: N/A, notification date: N/A
Early action deadline: N/A, notification date: N/A
Application deadline (fall): 5/1
Undergraduate student body: 1,832 full time, 7 part time; 44% male, 56% female; 0% American Indian, 1% Asian, 16% black, 7% Hispanic, 5% multiracial, 0% Pacific Islander, 65% white, 2% international; 75% from in state; 82% live on campus; 0% of students in fraternities, 0% in sororities
Most popular majors: 25% Business, Management, Marketing, and Related Support Services, 12% Social Sciences, 9% Parks, Recreation, Leisure, and Fitness Studies, 7% Biological and Biomedical Sciences, 7% Liberal Arts and Sciences, General Studies and Humanities
Expenses: 2019-2020: $36,600; room/board: $12,970
Financial aid: (540) 828-5376; 83% of undergrads determined to have financial need; average aid package $32,671

Christopher Newport University
Newport News VA
(757) 594-7015
U.S. News ranking: Reg. U. (S), No. 6
Website: www.cnu.edu
Admissions email: admit@cnu.edu
Public; founded 1960
Freshman admissions: more selective; 2018-2019: 7,430 applied, 5,035 accepted. Either SAT or ACT required for some. SAT 25/75 percentile: 1110-1280. High school rank: 17% in top tenth, 51% in top quarter, 87% in top half
Early decision deadline: 11/15, notification date: 12/15
Early action deadline: 12/1, notification date: 1/15
Application deadline (fall): 2/1
Undergraduate student body: 4,789 full time, 68 part time; 44% male, 56% female; 0% American Indian, 3% Asian, 6% black, 6% Hispanic, 5% multiracial, 0% Pacific Islander, 75% white, 0% international; 91% from in state; 79% live on campus; 23% of students in fraternities, 32% in sororities
Most popular majors: 17% Business Administration and Management, General, 15% Psychology, General, 13% Biology/Biological Sciences, General, 10% Speech Communication and Rhetoric, 6% Political Science and Government, General
Expenses: 2019-2020: $14,924 in state, $27,458 out of state; room/board: $11,760
Financial aid: (757) 594-7170; 46% of undergrads determined to have financial need; average aid package $10,107

College of William and Mary
Williamsburg VA
(757) 221-4223
U.S. News ranking: Nat. U., No. 40
Website: www.wm.edu
Admissions email: admission@wm.edu
Public; founded 1693
Freshman admissions: most selective; 2018-2019: 14,644 applied, 5,406 accepted. Either SAT or ACT required. SAT 25/75 percentile: 1310-1490. High school rank: 77% in top tenth, 95% in top quarter, 99% in top half
Early decision deadline: 11/1, notification date: 12/1
Early action deadline: N/A, notification date: N/A
Application deadline (fall): 1/1
Undergraduate student body: 6,300 full time, 77 part time; 42% male, 58% female; 0% American Indian, 8% Asian, 7% black, 9% Hispanic, 5% multiracial, 0% Pacific Islander, 59% white, 6% international; 69% from in state; 71% live on campus; 28% of students in fraternities, 29% in sororities
Most popular majors: 23% Social Sciences, 11% Biological and Biomedical Sciences, 11% Business, Management, Marketing, and Related Support Services, 8% Multi/Interdisciplinary Studies, 7% Parks, Recreation, Leisure, and Fitness Studies
Expenses: 2019-2020: $22,922 in state, $46,283 out of state; room/board: $12,926
Financial aid: (757) 221-2420; 38% of undergrads determined to have financial need; average aid package $24,726

Eastern Mennonite University
Harrisonburg VA
(800) 368-2665
U.S. News ranking: Reg. U. (S), No. 31
Website: www.emu.edu
Admissions email: admiss@emu.edu
Private; founded 1917
Affiliation: Mennonite Church
Freshman admissions: selective; 2018-2019: 1,245 applied, 737 accepted. Either SAT or ACT required. SAT 25/75 percentile: 1000-1230. High school rank: N/A
Early decision deadline: N/A, notification date: N/A
Early action deadline: N/A, notification date: N/A
Application deadline (fall): rolling
Undergraduate student body: 849 full time, 191 part time; 36% male, 64% female; 0% American Indian, 3% Asian, 9% black, 7% Hispanic, 4% multiracial, 0% Pacific Islander, 69% white, 4% international; 62% from in state; 44% live on campus; N/A of students in fraternities, N/A in sororities
Most popular majors: 46% Health Professions and Related Programs, 10% Business, Management, Marketing, and Related Support Services, 7% Liberal Arts and Sciences, General Studies and Humanities, 6% Biological and Biomedical Sciences, 4% Psychology
Expenses: 2019-2020: $38,230; room/board: $11,380
Financial aid: (540) 432-4137; 74% of undergrads determined to have financial need; average aid package $33,641

ECPI University
Virginia Beach VA
(866) 499-0336
U.S. News ranking: Reg. U. (S), second tier
Website: www.ecpi.edu/
Admissions email: request@ecpi.edu
For-profit; founded 1966
Freshman admissions: less selective; 2018-2019: 5,548 applied, 4,006 accepted. Neither SAT nor ACT required. SAT 25/75 percentile: N/A. High school rank: N/A
Early decision deadline: N/A, notification date: N/A
Early action deadline: N/A, notification date: N/A
Application deadline (fall): rolling
Undergraduate student body: 12,567 full time, 137 part time; 42% male, 58% female; 1% American Indian, 3% Asian, 39% black, 9% Hispanic, 3% multiracial, 1% Pacific Islander, 39% white, 0% international
Most popular majors: 15% Licensed Practical/Vocational Nurse Training, 15% Medical/Clinical Assistant, 11% Network and System Administration/Administrator, 10% Computer and Information Systems Security/Information Assurance, 10% Registered Nursing/Registered Nurse
Expenses: 2019-2020: $15,811; room/board: N/A
Financial aid: N/A

Emory and Henry College
Emory VA
(800) 848-5493
U.S. News ranking: Nat. Lib. Arts, No. 148
Website: www.ehc.edu
Admissions email: ehadmiss@ehc.edu
Private; founded 1836
Affiliation: United Methodist
Freshman admissions: selective; 2018-2019: 1,705 applied, 1,172 accepted. Either SAT or ACT required. SAT 25/75 percentile: 980-1160. High school rank: 17% in top tenth, 43% in top quarter, 78% in top half
Early decision deadline: 11/15, notification date: 12/15
Early action deadline: N/A, notification date: N/A
Application deadline (fall): rolling
Undergraduate student body: 956 full time, 23 part time; 47% male, 53% female; 0% American Indian, 1% Asian, 9% black, 4% Hispanic, 4% multiracial, 0% Pacific Islander, 77% white, 0% international; 65% from in state; 76% live on campus; N/A of students in fraternities, N/A in sororities
Most popular majors: 15% Social Sciences, 11% Business, Management, Marketing, and Related Support Services, 10% Psychology, 8% Communication, Journalism, and Related Programs, 8% Visual and Performing Arts
Expenses: 2019-2020: $35,100; room/board: $12,100
Financial aid: (276) 944-6105; 89% of undergrads determined to have financial need; average aid package $32,909

Ferrum College
Ferrum VA
(800) 868-9797
U.S. News ranking: Reg. Coll. (S), No. 36
Website: www.ferrum.edu
Admissions email: admissions@ferrum.edu
Private; founded 1913
Freshman admissions: least selective; 2018-2019: 3,927 applied, 2,961 accepted. Either SAT or ACT required for some. SAT 25/75 percentile: 870-1053. High school rank: 1% in top tenth, 1% in top quarter, 42% in top half
Early decision deadline: N/A, notification date: N/A
Early action deadline: N/A, notification date: N/A
Application deadline (fall): rolling
Undergraduate student body: 1,104 full time, 20 part time; 56% male, 44% female; 1% American Indian, 1% Asian, 33% black, 5% Hispanic, 6% multiracial, 0% Pacific Islander, 51% white, 1% international; 76% from in state; 90% live on campus; N/A of students in fraternities, N/A in sororities
Most popular majors: 16% Business Administration and Management, General, 13% Health/Medical Preparatory Programs, Other, 9% Criminal Justice/Safety Studies, 9% Physical Education Teaching and Coaching, 9% Social Sciences, General
Expenses: 2018-2019: $34,175; room/board: $11,570
Financial aid: N/A

George Mason University
Fairfax VA
(703) 993-2400
U.S. News ranking: Nat. U., No. 153
Website: www2.gmu.edu
Admissions email: admissions@gmu.edu
Public; founded 1972
Freshman admissions: more selective; 2018-2019: 19,557 applied, 15,852 accepted. Either SAT or ACT required for some. SAT 25/75 percentile: 1120-1320. High school rank: 18% in top tenth, 50% in top quarter, 87% in top half
Early decision deadline: N/A, notification date: N/A
Early action deadline: 11/1, notification date: 12/15
Application deadline (fall): 1/15
Undergraduate student body: 21,213 full time, 4,979 part time; 50% male, 50% female; 0% American Indian, 20% Asian, 11% black, 15% Hispanic, 5% multiracial, 0% Pacific Islander, 39% white, 5% international; 90% from in state; 23% live on campus; 5% of students in fraternities, 8% in sororities
Most popular majors: 6% Criminal Justice/Police Science, 6% Psychology, General, 5% Accounting, 5% Biology/Biological Sciences, General, 5% Information Technology
Expenses: 2019-2020: $12,564 in state, $36,024 out of state; room/board: $11,705
Financial aid: (703) 993-2353; 57% of undergrads determined to have financial need; average aid package $14,000

Hampden-Sydney College
Hampden-Sydney VA
(800) 755-0733
U.S. News ranking: Nat. Lib. Arts, No. 111
Website: www.hsc.edu
Admissions email: hsapp@hsc.edu
Private; founded 1775
Affiliation: Presbyterian
Freshman admissions: selective; 2018-2019: 3,240 applied, 1,912 accepted. Either SAT or ACT required. SAT 25/75

percentile: 1050-1250. High school rank: 11% in top tenth, 22% in top quarter, 64% in top half
Early decision deadline: 11/1, notification date: 12/1
Early action deadline: 1/15, notification date: 2/15
Application deadline (fall): 3/1
Undergraduate student body: 1,072 full time, 0 part time; 100% male, 0% female; 0% American Indian, 1% Asian, 5% black, 4% Hispanic, 3% multiracial, 0% Pacific Islander, 86% white, 0% international; 70% from in state; 95% live on campus; 33% of students in fraternities, N/A in sororities
Most popular majors: 28% Business/Managerial Economics, 11% Biology/Biological Sciences, General, 9% Economics, General, 9% Political Science and Government, General, 8% History, General
Expenses: 2019-2020: $46,890; room/board: $13,712
Financial aid: (434) 223-6265; 68% of undergrads determined to have financial need; average aid package $33,849

Hampton University
Hampton VA
(757) 727-5328
U.S. News ranking: Nat. U., No. 218
Website: www.hamptonu.edu
Admissions email: admissions@hamptonu.edu
Private; founded 1868
Freshman admissions: selective; 2018-2019: 13,028 applied, 4,690 accepted. Either SAT or ACT required for some. ACT 25/75 percentile: 19-24. High school rank: 13% in top tenth, 22% in top quarter, 61% in top half
Early decision deadline: N/A, notification date: N/A
Early action deadline: 11/1, notification date: 12/31
Application deadline (fall): 3/1
Undergraduate student body: 3,510 full time, 162 part time; 34% male, 66% female; 0% American Indian, 0% Asian, 96% black, 1% Hispanic, 0% multiracial, 0% Pacific Islander, 1% white, 1% international; 25% from in state; 61% live on campus; 5% of students in fraternities, 4% in sororities
Most popular majors: 11% Biology/Biological Sciences, General, 9% Psychology, General, 8% Business Administration and Management, General, 7% Liberal Arts and Sciences/Liberal Studies, 7% Organizational Communication, General
Expenses: 2019-2020: $28,024; room/board: $12,366
Financial aid: (757) 727-5635; 62% of undergrads determined to have financial need; average aid package $6,161

Hollins University
Roanoke VA
(800) 456-9595
U.S. News ranking: Nat. Lib. Arts, No. 102
Website: www.hollins.edu
Admissions email: huadm@hollins.edu
Private; founded 1842
Freshman admissions: more selective; 2018-2019: 3,667 applied, 2,344 accepted. Either SAT or ACT required. SAT 25/75 percentile: 1070-1280. High school rank: 23% in top tenth, 55% in top quarter, 82% in top half
Early decision deadline: 11/1, notification date: 11/15
Early action deadline: 11/15, notification date: 12/1
Application deadline (fall): N/A
Undergraduate student body: 666 full time, 10 part time; 0% male, 100% female; 1% American Indian, 2% Asian, 10% black, 8% Hispanic, 7% multiracial, 0% Pacific Islander, 64% white, 7% international; N/A from in state; 89% live on campus; N/A of students in fraternities, N/A in sororities
Most popular majors: 20% Visual and Performing Arts, 14% Social Sciences, 11% Biological and Biomedical Sciences, 11% English Language and Literature/Letters, 9% Psychology
Expenses: 2019-2020: $40,010; room/board: $13,930
Financial aid: (540) 362-6332; 77% of undergrads determined to have financial need; average aid package $37,488

James Madison University
Harrisonburg VA
(540) 568-5681
U.S. News ranking: Reg. U. (S), No. 3
Website: www.jmu.edu
Admissions email: admissions@jmu.edu
Public; founded 1908
Freshman admissions: selective; 2018-2019: 23,149 applied, 16,467 accepted. Neither SAT nor ACT required. SAT 25/75 percentile: 1120-1290. High school rank: 18% in top tenth, 36% in top quarter, 93% in top half
Early decision deadline: N/A, notification date: N/A
Early action deadline: 11/1, notification date: 1/15
Application deadline (fall): 1/15
Undergraduate student body: 18,881 full time, 1,042 part time; 42% male, 58% female; 0% American Indian, 5% Asian, 5% black, 7% Hispanic, 5% multiracial, 0% Pacific Islander, 75% white, 2% international; N/A from in state; 31% live on campus; 4% of students in fraternities, 8% in sororities
Most popular majors: 19% Health Professions and Related Programs, 18% Business, Management, Marketing, and Related Support Services, 8% Communication,

Journalism, and Related Programs, 8% Social Sciences, 6% Liberal Arts and Sciences, General Studies and Humanities
Expenses: 2019-2020: $11,576 in state, $28,790 out of state; room/board: $10,582
Financial aid: (540) 568-7820; 43% of undergrads determined to have financial need; average aid package $8,755

Liberty University
Lynchburg VA
(800) 543-5317
U.S. News ranking: Nat. U., second tier
Website: www.liberty.edu
Admissions email: admissions@liberty.edu
Private; founded 1971
Affiliation: Evangelical Christian
Freshman admissions: selective; 2018-2019: 29,021 applied, 16,127 accepted. Either SAT or ACT required. SAT 25/75 percentile: 980-1180. High school rank: 24% in top tenth, 52% in top quarter, 82% in top half
Early decision deadline: N/A, notification date: N/A
Early action deadline: N/A, notification date: N/A
Application deadline (fall): rolling
Undergraduate student body: 27,401 full time, 18,534 part time; 42% male, 58% female; 0% American Indian, 1% Asian, 11% black, 6% Hispanic, 2% multiracial, 0% Pacific Islander, 53% white, 1% international; 39% from in state; 57% live on campus; N/A of students in fraternities, N/A in sororities
Most popular majors: 17% Business, Management, Marketing, and Related Support Services, 9% Health Professions and Related Programs, 9% Visual and Performing Arts, 8% Psychology, 7% Parks, Recreation, Leisure, and Fitness Studies
Expenses: 2019-2020: $24,906; room/board: $10,540
Financial aid: (434) 582-2270; 73% of undergrads determined to have financial need; average aid package $14,818

Longwood University
Farmville VA
(434) 395-2060
U.S. News ranking: Reg. U. (S), No. 13
Website: www.longwood.edu/
Admissions email: admissions@longwood.edu
Public; founded 1839
Freshman admissions: selective; 2018-2019: 5,162 applied, 4,601 accepted. Either SAT or ACT required. SAT 25/75 percentile: 980-1150. High school rank: 9% in top tenth, 28% in top quarter, 65% in top half
Early decision deadline: N/A, notification date: N/A
Early action deadline: 12/1, notification date: 1/15
Application deadline (fall): rolling
Undergraduate student body: 3,793 full time, 531 part time; 32% male, 68% female; 0% American Indian, 1% Asian, 10% black,

6% Hispanic, 4% multiracial, 0% Pacific Islander, 74% white, 1% international; 95% from in state; 65% live on campus; 14% of students in fraternities, 15% in sororities
Most popular majors: 15% Liberal Arts and Sciences, General Studies and Humanities, 14% Business, Management, Marketing, and Related Support Services, 10% Health Professions and Related Programs, 8% Homeland Security, Law Enforcement, Firefighting and Related Protective Services, 8% Social Sciences
Expenses: 2019-2020: $13,760 in state, $29,720 out of state; room/board: $12,076
Financial aid: (434) 395-2077; 62% of undergrads determined to have financial need; average aid package $11,373

Mary Baldwin University
Staunton VA
(800) 468-2262
U.S. News ranking: Nat. U., No. 272
Website: www.marybaldwin.edu
Admissions email: admit@marybaldwin.edu
Private; founded 1842
Freshman admissions: less selective; 2018-2019: 6,371 applied, 6,365 accepted. Either SAT or ACT required. SAT 25/75 percentile: 950-1130. High school rank: 11% in top tenth, 34% in top quarter, 63% in top half
Early decision deadline: N/A, notification date: N/A
Early action deadline: N/A, notification date: N/A
Application deadline (fall): rolling
Undergraduate student body: 960 full time, 367 part time; 14% male, 86% female; 1% American Indian, 1% Asian, 24% black, 9% Hispanic, 5% multiracial, 0% Pacific Islander, 53% white, 1% international; 73% from in state; 50% live on campus; N/A of students in fraternities, N/A in sororities
Most popular majors: 15% Business Administration and Management, General, 11% Liberal Arts and Sciences/Liberal Studies, 11% Social Work, 10% Psychology, General, 9% Registered Nursing/Registered Nurse
Expenses: 2019-2020: $31,085; room/board: $9,730
Financial aid: (540) 887-7025; 91% of undergrads determined to have financial need; average aid package $27,093

Marymount University
Arlington VA
(703) 284-1500
U.S. News ranking: Reg. U. (S), No. 37
Website: www.marymount.edu
Admissions email: admissions@marymount.edu
Private; founded 1950
Affiliation: Roman Catholic
Freshman admissions: less selective; 2018-2019: 2,873 applied, 2,611 accepted. Either

SAT or ACT required for some. SAT 25/75 percentile: 950-1180. High school rank: 8% in top tenth, 25% in top quarter, 61% in top half
Early decision deadline: N/A, notification date: N/A
Early action deadline: 11/15, notification date: 12/14
Application deadline (fall): rolling
Undergraduate student body: 2,070 full time, 217 part time; 36% male, 64% female; 0% American Indian, 8% Asian, 14% black, 19% Hispanic, 3% multiracial, 0% Pacific Islander, 35% white, 17% international; 60% from in state; 30% live on campus; N/A of students in fraternities, N/A in sororities
Most popular majors: 23% Registered Nursing/Registered Nurse, 17% Business Administration and Management, General, 9% Information Technology, 7% Health Professions and Related Programs, 7% Psychology, General
Expenses: 2019-2020: $32,850; room/board: $13,575
Financial aid: (703) 284-1530; 62% of undergrads determined to have financial need; average aid package $21,642

Norfolk State University
Norfolk VA
(757) 823-8396
U.S. News ranking: Reg. U. (S), No. 91
Website: www.nsu.edu
Admissions email: admissions@nsu.edu
Public; founded 1935
Freshman admissions: least selective; 2018-2019: 7,442 applied, 6,675 accepted. Either SAT or ACT required. SAT 25/75 percentile: 860-1030. High school rank: 6% in top tenth, 15% in top quarter, 43% in top half
Early decision deadline: N/A, notification date: N/A
Early action deadline: N/A, notification date: N/A
Undergraduate student body: 4,133 full time, 527 part time; 35% male, 65% female; 0% American Indian, 1% Asian, 85% black, 4% Hispanic, 5% multiracial, 0% Pacific Islander, 3% white, 0% international
Most popular majors: Information not available
Expenses: 2019-2020: $9,622 in state, $24,742 out of state; room/board: $10,844
Financial aid: (757) 823-8381

Old Dominion University
Norfolk VA
(757) 683-3685
U.S. News ranking: Nat. U., No. 263
Website: www.odu.edu
Admissions email: admissions@odu.edu
Public; founded 1930
Freshman admissions: selective; 2018-2019: 13,335 applied, 11,600 accepted. Either SAT or ACT required for some. SAT

25/75 percentile: 990-1200. High school rank: 9% in top tenth, 30% in top quarter, 71% in top half
Early decision deadline: N/A, notification date: N/A
Early action deadline: 12/1, notification date: 1/15
Application deadline (fall): 2/1
Undergraduate student body: 15,003 full time, 4,369 part time; 45% male, 55% female; 0% American Indian, 5% Asian, 32% black, 9% Hispanic, 7% multiracial, 0% Pacific Islander, 44% white, 1% international; 92% from in state; 25% live on campus; 8% of students in fraternities, 5% in sororities
Most popular majors: 19% Health Professions and Related Programs, 16% Business, Management, Marketing, and Related Support Services, 12% Social Sciences, 8% Engineering, 8% English Language and Literature/Letters
Expenses: 2019-2020: $11,212 in state, $30,652 out of state; room/board: $12,708
Financial aid: (757) 683-3683; 69% of undergrads determined to have financial need; average aid package $10,655

Radford University

Radford VA
(540) 831-5371
U.S. News ranking: Reg. U. (S), No. 28
Website: www.radford.edu
Admissions email: admissions@radford.edu
Public; founded 1910
Freshman admissions: less selective; 2018-2019: 14,161 applied, 10,561 accepted. Neither SAT nor ACT required. SAT 25/75 percentile: 940-1130. High school rank: 5% in top tenth, 16% in top quarter, 49% in top half
Early decision deadline: N/A, notification date: N/A
Early action deadline: 12/1, notification date: 1/15
Application deadline (fall): rolling
Undergraduate student body: 7,556 full time, 370 part time; 43% male, 57% female; 0% American Indian, 2% Asian, 17% black, 7% Hispanic, 5% multiracial, 0% Pacific Islander, 66% white, 1% international; 94% from in state; 45% live on campus; 10% of students in fraternities, 10% in sororities
Most popular majors: 10% Multi-/Interdisciplinary Studies, Other, 9% Psychology, General, 8% Criminal Justice/Safety Studies, 7% Business Administration and Management, General, 7% Physical Education Teaching and Coaching
Expenses: 2019-2020: $11,350 in state, $22,985 out of state; room/board: $9,637
Financial aid: (540) 831-5408; 66% of undergrads determined to have financial need; average aid package $10,794

Randolph College

Lynchburg VA
(800) 745-7692
U.S. News ranking: Nat. Lib. Arts, No. 132
Website: www.randolphcollege.edu/
Admissions email: admissions@randolphcollege.edu
Private; founded 1891
Affiliation: United Methodist
Freshman admissions: selective; 2018-2019: 1,576 applied, 1,366 accepted. Either SAT or ACT required. SAT 25/75 percentile: 960-1190. High school rank: 12% in top tenth, 33% in top quarter, 70% in top half
Early decision deadline: N/A, notification date: N/A
Early action deadline: 11/15, notification date: N/A
Application deadline (fall): rolling
Undergraduate student body: 586 full time, 14 part time; 37% male, 63% female; 0% American Indian, 3% Asian, 16% black, 7% Hispanic, 6% multiracial, 0% Pacific Islander, 64% white, 3% international; N/A from in state; 77% live on campus; N/A of students in fraternities, N/A in sororities
Most popular majors: 16% Social Sciences, 13% Biological and Biomedical Sciences, 10% Visual and Performing Arts, 9% Health Professions and Related Programs, 8% Psychology
Expenses: 2019-2020: $41,131; room/board: $13,580
Financial aid: (434) 947-8128; 83% of undergrads determined to have financial need; average aid package $35,000

Randolph-Macon College

Ashland VA
(800) 888-1762
U.S. News ranking: Nat. Lib. Arts, No. 111
Website: www.rmc.edu
Admissions email: admissions@rmc.edu
Private; founded 1830
Affiliation: United Methodist
Freshman admissions: selective; 2018-2019: 2,907 applied, 1,951 accepted. Either SAT or ACT required. SAT 25/75 percentile: 1020-1240. High school rank: 15% in top tenth, 40% in top quarter, 73% in top half
Early decision deadline: N/A, notification date: N/A
Early action deadline: 11/15, notification date: 1/1
Application deadline (fall): 3/1
Undergraduate student body: 1,464 full time, 24 part time; 47% male, 53% female; 0% American Indian, 1% Asian, 10% black, 4% Hispanic, 4% multiracial, 0% Pacific Islander, 76% white, 2% international; N/A from in state; 82% live on campus; 29% of students in fraternities, 25% in sororities
Most popular majors: 16% Business/Commerce, General, 9% Biology/Biological Sciences, General, 8% Communication and Media Studies, 8% Psychology,

General, 7% Political Science and Government, General
Expenses: 2019-2020: $42,550; room/board: $12,220
Financial aid: (804) 752-7259; 71% of undergrads determined to have financial need; average aid package $30,349

Regent University

Virginia Beach VA
(888) 718-1222
U.S. News ranking: Nat. U., No. 281
Website: www.regent.edu/
Admissions email: admissions@regent.edu
Private; founded 1978
Affiliation: Undenominational
Freshman admissions: less selective; 2018-2019: 2,854 applied, 2,405 accepted. Either SAT or ACT required. SAT 25/75 percentile: 950-1170. High school rank: 11% in top tenth, 40% in top quarter, 64% in top half
Early decision deadline: N/A, notification date: N/A
Early action deadline: N/A, notification date: N/A
Application deadline (fall): 8/1
Undergraduate student body: 2,402 full time, 2,244 part time; 38% male, 62% female; 0% American Indian, 1% Asian, 27% black, 9% Hispanic, 5% multiracial, 0% Pacific Islander, 55% white, 1% international; 42% from in state; 15% live on campus; N/A of students in fraternities, N/A in sororities
Most popular majors: 24% Business Administration, Management and Operations, 18% Communication and Media Studies, 15% Psychology, General, 15% Theological and Ministerial Studies, 6% Education, General
Expenses: 2019-2020: $19,280; room/board: $9,033
Financial aid: (757) 352-4125; 81% of undergrads determined to have financial need; average aid package $11,444

Roanoke College

Salem VA
(540) 375-2270
U.S. News ranking: Nat. Lib. Arts, No. 130
Website: www.roanoke.edu
Admissions email: admissions@roanoke.edu
Private; founded 1842
Affiliation: Evangelical Lutheran Church
Freshman admissions: selective; 2018-2019: 5,122 applied, 3,713 accepted. Either SAT or ACT required. SAT 25/75 percentile: 1040-1230. High school rank: 18% in top tenth, 41% in top quarter, 80% in top half
Early decision deadline: 11/15, notification date: 12/15
Early action deadline: N/A, notification date: N/A
Application deadline (fall): 3/15
Undergraduate student body: 1,956 full time, 61 part time, 42% male, 58% female; 0% American Indian, 1% Asian, 5% black, 5% Hispanic, 4% multiracial,

0% Pacific Islander, 81% white, 2% international; 56% from in state; 77% live on campus; 18% of students in fraternities, 19% in sororities
Most popular majors: 18% Business Administration and Management, General, 8% Communication and Media Studies, 8% Psychology, General, 7% Biology/Biological Sciences, General, 7% Kinesiology and Exercise Science
Expenses: 2019-2020: $45,176; room/board: $14,134
Financial aid: (540) 375-2235; 75% of undergrads determined to have financial need; average aid package $38,206

Shenandoah University

Winchester VA
(540) 665-4581
U.S. News ranking: Nat. U., No. 263
Website: www.su.edu
Admissions email: admit@su.edu
Private; founded 1875
Affiliation: United Methodist
Freshman admissions: selective; 2018-2019: 2,225 applied, 1,564 accepted. Either SAT or ACT required. SAT 25/75 percentile: 980-1190. High school rank: 25% in top tenth, 52% in top quarter, 80% in top half
Early decision deadline: N/A, notification date: N/A
Early action deadline: N/A, notification date: N/A
Application deadline (fall): rolling
Undergraduate student body: 1,967 full time, 67 part time; 40% male, 60% female; 1% American Indian, 3% Asian, 10% black, 6% Hispanic, 1% multiracial, 0% Pacific Islander, 59% white, 2% international; 59% from in state; 47% live on campus; 0% of students in fraternities, 0% in sororities
Most popular majors: 25% Registered Nursing/Registered Nurse, 10% Business Administration and Management, General, 7% Exercise Physiology, 7% Psychology, General, 6% Biology/Biological Sciences, General
Expenses: 2019-2020: $33,242; room/board: $10,570
Financial aid: (540) 665-4538; 77% of undergrads determined to have financial need; average aid package $21,297

Southern Virginia University[1]

Buena Vista VA
U.S. News ranking: Nat. Lib. Arts, second tier
Admissions email: N/A
Private
Application deadline (fall): N/A
Undergraduate student body: N/A full time, N/A part time
Expenses: 2019-2020: $17,290; room/board: $8,040
Financial aid: (540) 261-8463

Sweet Briar College

Sweet Briar VA
(800) 381-6142
U.S. News ranking: Nat. Lib. Arts, No. 154
Website: www.sbc.edu
Admissions email: admissions@sbc.edu
Private; founded 1901
Freshman admissions: selective; 2018-2019: 654 applied, 494 accepted. Either SAT or ACT required for some. SAT 25/75 percentile: 990-1210. High school rank: 22% in top tenth, 47% in top quarter, 65% in top half
Early decision deadline: N/A, notification date: N/A
Early action deadline: 11/1, notification date: 11/16
Application deadline (fall): rolling
Undergraduate student body: 331 full time, 5 part time; 3% male, 97% female; 0% American Indian, 2% Asian, 10% black, 8% Hispanic, 3% multiracial, 0% Pacific Islander, 72% white, 3% international; 47% from in state; 94% live on campus; N/A of students in fraternities, N/A in sororities
Most popular majors: 11% Business/Commerce, General, 11% Psychology, General, 8% Biology/Biological Sciences, General, 8% Engineering Science, 8% History, General
Expenses: 2019-2020: $22,020; room/board: $13,200
Financial aid: (434) 381-6156; 74% of undergrads determined to have financial need; average aid package $19,418

University of Lynchburg

Lynchburg VA
(434) 544-8300
U.S. News ranking: Reg. U. (S), No. 20
Website: www.lynchburg.edu
Admissions email: admissions@lynchburg.edu
Private; founded 1903
Affiliation: Christian Church (Disciples of Christ)
Freshman admissions: selective; 2018-2019: 3,937 applied, 3,812 accepted. Either SAT or ACT required. SAT 25/75 percentile: 980-1185. High school rank: 13% in top tenth, 22% in top quarter, 69% in top half
Early decision deadline: 11/15, notification date: 12/15
Early action deadline: N/A, notification date: N/A
Application deadline (fall): rolling
Undergraduate student body: 1,930 full time, 156 part time; 39% male, 61% female; 1% American Indian, 2% Asian, 11% black, 5% Hispanic, 3% multiracial, 0% Pacific Islander, 76% white, 1% international; 71% from in state; 74% live on campus; 12% of students in fraternities, 12% in sororities
Most popular majors: 23% Health Professions and Related Programs, 17% Social Sciences, 13% Biological and Biomedical Sciences, 12% Business, Management, Marketing, and Related Support Services

Expenses: 2018-2019: $37,690; room/board: $10,680
Financial aid: (800) 426-8101; 80% of undergrads determined to have financial need; average aid package $29,919

University of Mary Washington

Fredericksburg VA
(540) 654-2000
U.S. News ranking: Reg. U. (S), No. 16
Website: www.umw.edu
Admissions email: admit@umw.edu
Public; founded 1908
Freshman admissions: selective; 2018-2019: 5,909 applied, 4,240 accepted. Either SAT or ACT required for some. SAT 25/75 percentile: 1050-1269. High school rank: 16% in top tenth, 46% in top quarter, 81% in top half
Early decision deadline: 11/1, notification date: 12/10
Early action deadline: 11/15, notification date: 1/31
Application deadline (fall): 2/1
Undergraduate student body: 3,876 full time, 534 part time; 36% male, 64% female; 0% American Indian, 4% Asian, 8% black, 10% Hispanic, 6% multiracial, 0% Pacific Islander, 68% white, 1% international; 91% from in state; 56% live on campus; N/A of students in fraternities, N/A in sororities
Most popular majors: 16% Business, Management, and Related Support Services, 15% Social Sciences, 11% Liberal Arts and Sciences, General Studies and Humanities, 10% English Language and Literature/Letters, 10% Psychology
Expenses: 2018-2019: $11,630 in state, $26,220 out of state; room/board: $11,118
Financial aid: (540) 654-2468

University of Richmond

Univ. of Richmond VA
(804) 289-8640
U.S. News ranking: Nat. Lib. Arts, No. 23
Website: www.richmond.edu
Admissions email: admission@richmond.edu
Private; founded 1830
Freshman admissions: more selective; 2018-2019: 11,882 applied, 3,585 accepted. Either SAT or ACT required. SAT 25/75 percentile: 1290-1460. High school rank: 56% in top tenth, 86% in top quarter, 96% in top half
Early decision deadline: 11/1, notification date: 12/15
Early action deadline: 11/1, notification date: 1/20
Application deadline (fall): 1/15
Undergraduate student body: 3,019 full time, 208 part time; 48% male, 52% female; 0% American Indian, 7% Asian, 8% black, 8% Hispanic, 4% multiracial, 0% Pacific Islander, 58% white, 9% international; 23% from in

state; 91% live on campus; 22% of students in fraternities, 30% in sororities
Most popular majors: 36% Business, Management, Marketing, and Related Support Services, 15% Social Sciences, 10% Biological and Biomedical Sciences, 6% Multi/Interdisciplinary Studies, 5% Psychology
Expenses: 2019-2020: $54,690; room/board: $12,900
Financial aid: (804) 289-8438; 40% of undergrads determined to have financial need; average aid package $49,423

University of Virginia

Charlottesville VA
(434) 982-3200
U.S. News ranking: Nat. U., No. 28
Website: www.virginia.edu
Admissions email: undergradadmission@virginia.edu
Public; founded 1819
Freshman admissions: most selective; 2018-2019: 37,182 applied, 9,828 accepted. Either SAT or ACT required. SAT 25/75 percentile: 1330-1500. High school rank: 90% in top tenth, 98% in top quarter, 100% in top half
Early decision deadline: N/A, notification date: N/A
Early action deadline: 11/1, notification date: 1/31
Application deadline (fall): 1/1
Undergraduate student body: 16,007 full time, 770 part time; 45% male, 55% female; 0% American Indian, 15% Asian, 7% black, 6% Hispanic, 5% multiracial, 0% Pacific Islander, 57% white, 4% international; 69% from in state; 38% live on campus; N/A of students in fraternities, N/A in sororities
Most popular majors: 9% Economics, General, 8% Biology/Biological Sciences, General, 8% Business/Commerce, General, 6% International Relations and Affairs, 6% Psychology, General
Expenses: 2019-2020: $17,891 in state, $50,920 out of state; room/board: $11,950
Financial aid: (434) 982-6000; 35% of undergrads determined to have financial need; average aid package $28,986

University of Virginia–Wise

Wise VA
(888) 282-9324
U.S. News ranking: Nat. Lib. Arts, second tier
Website: www.uvawise.edu
Admissions email: admissions@uvawise.edu
Public; founded 1954
Freshman admissions: selective; 2018-2019: 828 applied, 641 accepted. Either SAT or ACT required. SAT 25/75 percentile: 950-1130. High school rank: 17% in top tenth, 43% in top quarter, 75% in top half
Early decision deadline: N/A, notification date: N/A
Early action deadline: 12/1, notification date: 12/15

Application deadline (fall): 8/15
Undergraduate student body: 1,154 full time, 911 part time; 38% male, 62% female; 0% American Indian, 1% Asian, 10% black, 1% Hispanic, 0% multiracial, 0% Pacific Islander, 78% white, 0% international; 91% from in state; 38% live on campus; 1% of students in fraternities, 2% in sororities
Most popular majors: 22% Education, 13% Social Sciences, 11% Psychology, 9% Business, Management, Marketing, and Related Support Services, 8% History
Expenses: 2019-2020: $10,252 in state, $27,987 out of state; room/board: $10,751
Financial aid: (276) 376-7130; 86% of undergrads determined to have financial need; average aid package $16,027

Virginia Commonwealth University

Richmond VA
(800) 841-3638
U.S. News ranking: Nat. U., No. 162
Website: www.vcu.edu
Admissions email: ugrad@vcu.edu
Public; founded 1838
Freshman admissions: selective; 2018-2019: 17,915 applied, 13,858 accepted. Either SAT or ACT required for some. SAT 25/75 percentile: 1070-1260. High school rank: 17% in top tenth, 44% in top quarter, 80% in top half
Early decision deadline: N/A, notification date: N/A
Early action deadline: N/A, notification date: N/A
Application deadline (fall): 1/16
Undergraduate student body: 20,508 full time, 3,550 part time; 40% male, 60% female; 0% American Indian, 14% Asian, 19% black, 10% Hispanic, 7% multiracial, 0% Pacific Islander, 44% white, 3% international; 91% from in state; 28% live on campus; N/A of students in fraternities, N/A in sororities
Most popular majors: 9% Psychology, 7% Business, Management, Marketing, and Related Support Services, 6% Biological and Biomedical Sciences, 6% Education, 5% Communication, Journalism, and Related Programs
Expenses: 2019-2020: $14,596 in state, $35,244 out of state; room/board: $10,995
Financial aid: (804) 828-6076; 62% of undergrads determined to have financial need; average aid package $12,230

Virginia Military Institute

Lexington VA
(800) 767-4207
U.S. News ranking: Nat. Lib. Arts, No. 72
Website: www.vmi.edu
Admissions email: admissions@vmi.edu
Public; founded 1839

Freshman admissions: selective; 2018-2019: 1,768 applied, 907 accepted. Either SAT or ACT required. SAT 25/75 percentile: 1100-1310. High school rank: 20% in top tenth, 44% in top quarter, 82% in top half
Early decision deadline: 11/15, notification date: 12/15
Early action deadline: N/A, notification date: N/A
Application deadline (fall): 2/1
Undergraduate student body: 1,685 full time, 0 part time; 87% male, 13% female; 0% American Indian, 4% Asian, 6% black, 7% Hispanic, 2% multiracial, 0% Pacific Islander, 77% white, 2% international; 63% from in state; 100% live on campus; N/A of students in fraternities, N/A in sororities
Most popular majors: 14% Civil Engineering, General, 14% International Relations and Affairs, 13% Economics, General, 9% Biology/Biological Sciences, General, 9% Mechanical Engineering
Expenses: 2019-2020: $19,118 in state, $45,962 out of state; room/board: $9,766
Financial aid: (540) 464-7208

Virginia State University[7]

Petersburg VA
(804) 524-5902
U.S. News ranking: Reg. U. (S), No. 61
Website: www.vsu.edu
Admissions email: admiss@vsu.edu
Public; founded 1882
Freshman admissions: least selective; 2018-2019: 7,007 applied, 6,383 accepted. Either SAT or ACT required. SAT 25/75 percentile: 840-1010. High school rank: 8% in top tenth, 17% in top quarter, 50% in top half
Early decision deadline: N/A, notification date: N/A
Early action deadline: N/A, notification date: N/A
Application deadline (fall): 5/1
Undergraduate student body: 3,862 full time, 134 part time
Most popular majors: Information not available
Expenses: 2018-2019: $9,056 in state, $19,576 out of state; room/board: $11,208
Financial aid: (800) 823-7214; 92% of undergrads determined to have financial need; average aid package $12,250

Virginia Tech

Blacksburg VA
(540) 231-6267
U.S. News ranking: Nat. U., No. 74
Website: www.vt.edu
Admissions email: admissions@vt.edu
Public; founded 1872
Freshman admissions: more selective; 2018-2019: 31,936 applied, 20,709 accepted. Either SAT or ACT required. SAT 25/75 percentile: 1180-1390. High school rank: 38% in top tenth, 77% in top quarter, 97% in top half

Early decision deadline: 11/1, notification date: 12/15
Early action deadline: 12/1, notification date: 2/22
Application deadline (fall): 1/15
Undergraduate student body: 27,180 full time, 631 part time; 57% male, 43% female; 0% American Indian, 10% Asian, 4% black, 6% Hispanic, 5% multiracial, 0% Pacific Islander, 65% white, 7% international; N/A from in state; 33% live on campus; 13% of students in fraternities, 19% in sororities
Most popular majors: 23% Engineering, 21% Business, Management, Marketing, and Related Support Services, 9% Family and Consumer Sciences/Human Sciences, 8% Biological and Biomedical Sciences, 8% Social Sciences
Expenses: 2019-2020: $13,691 in state, $32,835 out of state; room/board: $5,518
Financial aid: (540) 231-5179; 42% of undergrads determined to have financial need; average aid package $10,980

Virginia Union University

Richmond VA
(804) 257-5600
U.S. News ranking: Nat. Lib. Arts, second tier
Website: www.vuu.edu/
Admissions email: admissions@vuu.edu
Private; founded 1865
Affiliation: Baptist
Freshman admissions: least selective; 2018-2019: 5,837 applied, 3,345 accepted. Neither SAT nor ACT required. SAT 25/75 percentile: 782-970. High school rank: 7% in top tenth, 15% in top quarter, 46% in top half
Early decision deadline: N/A, notification date: N/A
Early action deadline: N/A, notification date: N/A
Application deadline (fall): 6/30
Undergraduate student body: 1,109 full time, 77 part time; 47% male, 53% female; 0% American Indian, 0% Asian, 90% black, 1% Hispanic, 0% multiracial, 0% Pacific Islander, 1% white, 0% international
Most popular majors: Information not available
Expenses: 2019-2020: $17,448; room/board: $8,598
Financial aid: (804) 257-5882; 94% of undergrads determined to have financial need; average aid package $15,065

Virginia Wesleyan University

Norfolk VA
(757) 455-3208
U.S. News ranking: Nat. Lib. Arts, second tier
Website: www.vwu.edu
Admissions email: enrollment@vwu.edu
Private; founded 1961
Affiliation: United Methodist
Freshman admissions: selective; 2018-2019: 2,656 applied, 1,870 accepted. Either SAT or ACT required. SAT 25/75

percentile: 980-1180. High school rank: 10% in top tenth, 32% in top quarter, 61% in top half
Early decision deadline: N/A, notification date: N/A
Early action deadline: N/A, notification date: N/A
Application deadline (fall): rolling
Undergraduate student body: 1,262 full time, 89 part time; 41% male, 59% female; 1% American Indian, 1% Asian, 26% black, 8% Hispanic, 6% multiracial, 1% Pacific Islander, 53% white, 1% international; 76% from in state; 66% live on campus; 10% of students in fraternities, 9% in sororities
Most popular majors: 13% Social Sciences, 12% Business, Management, Marketing, and Related Support Services, 12% Homeland Security, Law Enforcement, Firefighting and Related Protective Services, 7% Biological and Biomedical Sciences, 7% Psychology
Expenses: 2019-2020: $36,660; room/board: $9,988
Financial aid: (757) 455-3345; 85% of undergrads determined to have financial need; average aid package $24,610

Washington and Lee University
Lexington VA
(540) 458-8710
U.S. News ranking: Nat. Lib. Arts, No. 10
Website: www.wlu.edu
Admissions email: admissions@wlu.edu
Private; founded 1749
Freshman admissions: most selective; 2018-2019: 5,855 applied, 1,239 accepted. Either SAT or ACT required. ACT 25/75 percentile: 31-34. High school rank: 83% in top tenth, 97% in top quarter, 100% in top half
Early decision deadline: 11/1, notification date: 12/15
Early action deadline: N/A, notification date: N/A
Application deadline (fall): 1/1
Undergraduate student body: 1,825 full time, 4 part time; 50% male, 50% female; 0% American Indian, 4% Asian, 3% black, 5% Hispanic, 4% multiracial, 0% Pacific Islander, 81% white, 4% international; 15% from in state; 76% live on campus; 75% of students in fraternities, 75% in sororities
Most popular majors: 12% Business Administration and Management, General, 11% Economics, General, 10% Accounting and Business/ Management, 10% Political Science and Government, General, 4% Mathematics, General
Expenses: 2019-2020: $54,830; room/board: $14,845
Financial aid: (540) 458-8717; 46% of undergrads determined to have financial need; average aid package $53,443

WASHINGTON

Art Institute of Seattle[1]
Seattle WA
(206) 448-0900
U.S. News ranking: Arts, unranked
Website: www.ais.edu
Admissions email: N/A
For-profit
Application deadline (fall): N/A
Undergraduate student body: N/A full time, N/A part time
Expenses: N/A
Financial aid: N/A

Bellevue College[1]
Bellevue WA
(425) 564-1000
U.S. News ranking: Reg. Coll. (W), unranked
Website: www.bellevuecollege.edu
Admissions email: N/A
Public
Application deadline (fall): N/A
Undergraduate student body: N/A full time, N/A part time
Expenses: N/A
Financial aid: N/A

Bellingham Technical College[1]
Bellingham WA
(360) 752-7000
U.S. News ranking: Reg. Coll. (W), unranked
Website: www.spokanefalls.edu
Admissions email: N/A
Public
Application deadline (fall): N/A
Undergraduate student body: N/A full time, N/A part time
Expenses: N/A
Financial aid: N/A

Cascadia College
Bothell WA
(425) 352-8000
U.S. News ranking: Reg. Coll. (W), unranked
Website: www.national.edu/ locations/campuses/austin/
Admissions email: admissions@cascadia.edu
Public; founded 2000
Freshman admissions: least selective; 2018-2019: N/A applied, N/A accepted. Neither SAT nor ACT required. SAT 25/75 percentile: N/A. High school rank: N/A
Early decision deadline: N/A, notification date: N/A
Early action deadline: N/A, notification date: N/A
Application deadline (fall): rolling
Undergraduate student body: 1,740 full time, 1,593 part time; 49% male, 51% female; 0% American Indian, 9% Asian, 2% black, 11% Hispanic, 10% multiracial, 0% Pacific Islander, 49% white, 6% international
Most popular majors: Information not available
Expenses: 2018-2019: $3,931 in state, $9,297 out of state; room/board: N/A
Financial aid: N/A

Centralia College[1]
Centralia WA
U.S. News ranking: Reg. Coll. (W), unranked
Admissions email: N/A
Public
Application deadline (fall): N/A
Undergraduate student body: N/A full time, N/A part time
Expenses: N/A
Financial aid: N/A

Central Washington University
Ellensburg WA
(509) 963-1211
U.S. News ranking: Reg. U. (W), No. 55
Website: www.cwu.edu
Admissions email: admissions@cwu.edu
Public; founded 1891
Freshman admissions: less selective; 2018-2019: 10,321 applied, 8,033 accepted. Either SAT or ACT required. SAT 25/75 percentile: 930-1130. High school rank: N/A
Early decision deadline: N/A, notification date: N/A
Early action deadline: N/A, notification date: N/A
Application deadline (fall): rolling
Undergraduate student body: 9,963 full time, 1,125 part time; 48% male, 52% female; 1% American Indian, 4% Asian, 4% black, 16% Hispanic, 8% multiracial, 1% Pacific Islander, 51% white, 3% international; 94% from in state; 7% live on campus; 0% of students in fraternities, 0% in sororities
Most popular majors: 23% Education, 18% Business, Management, Marketing, and Related Support Services, 8% Computer and Information Sciences and Support Services, 8% Social Sciences, 6% Psychology
Expenses: 2019-2020: $7,484 in state, $22,738 out of state; room/board: $12,637
Financial aid: (509) 963-1611; 68% of undergrads determined to have financial need; average aid package $4,026

City University of Seattle[1]
Seattle WA
(888) 422-4898
U.S. News ranking: Reg. U. (W), unranked
Website: www.cityu.edu
Admissions email: info@cityu.edu
Private; founded 1973
Application deadline (fall): N/A
Undergraduate student body: N/A full time, N/A part time
Expenses: N/A
Financial aid: N/A

Clark College[1]
Vancouver WA
(360) 992-2000
U.S. News ranking: Reg. Coll. (W), unranked
Website: www.tacomacc.edu
Admissions email: N/A
Public
Application deadline (fall): N/A

Undergraduate student body: N/A full time, N/A part time
Expenses: N/A
Financial aid: N/A

Clover Park Technical College[7]
Lakewood WA
(253) 589-5800
U.S. News ranking: Reg. Coll. (W), unranked
Website: www.cptc.edu
Admissions email: admissions@cptc.edu
Public
Freshman admissions: least selective; 2018-2019: N/A applied, N/A accepted. Neither SAT nor ACT required. SAT 25/75 percentile: N/A. High school rank: N/A
Early decision deadline: N/A, notification date: N/A
Early action deadline: N/A, notification date: N/A
Application deadline (fall): N/A
Undergraduate student body: 2,388 full time, 1,671 part time
Most popular majors: Information not available
Expenses: N/A
Financial aid: N/A

Columbia Basin College[1]
Pasco WA
U.S. News ranking: Reg. Coll. (W), unranked
Admissions email: N/A
Public
Application deadline (fall): N/A
Undergraduate student body: N/A full time, N/A part time
Expenses: N/A
Financial aid: N/A

Cornish College of the Arts
Seattle WA
(800) 726-2787
U.S. News ranking: Arts, unranked
Website: www.cornish.edu
Admissions email: admission@cornish.edu
Private; founded 1914
Freshman admissions: least selective; 2018-2019: 870 applied, 674 accepted. Neither SAT nor ACT required. SAT 25/75 percentile: N/A. High school rank: N/A
Early decision deadline: N/A, notification date: N/A
Early action deadline: 12/1, notification date: 12/15
Application deadline (fall): N/A
Undergraduate student body: 617 full time, 6 part time; 32% male, 68% female; N/A American Indian, N/A Asian, N/A black, N/A Hispanic, N/A multiracial, N/A Pacific Islander, N/A white, N/A international
Most popular majors: Information not available
Expenses: 2019-2020: $33,360; room/board: $12,664
Financial aid: (206) 726-5063; 75% of undergrads determined to have financial need; average aid package $26,922

Eastern Washington University
Cheney WA
(509) 359-2397
U.S. News ranking: Reg. U. (W), No. 62
Website: www.ewu.edu
Admissions email: admissions@ewu.edu
Public; founded 1882
Freshman admissions: less selective; 2018-2019: 8,367 applied, 5,310 accepted. Either SAT or ACT required. SAT 25/75 percentile: 870-1080. High school rank: N/A
Early decision deadline: N/A, notification date: N/A
Early action deadline: N/A, notification date: N/A
Application deadline (fall): 5/15
Undergraduate student body: 9,012 full time, 1,498 part time; 46% male, 54% female; 1% American Indian, 3% Asian, 4% black, 17% Hispanic, 7% multiracial, 0% Pacific Islander, 61% white, 4% international; N/A from in state; 17% live on campus; 6% of students in fraternities, 5% in sororities
Most popular majors: 18% Business, Management, Marketing, and Related Support Services, 10% Social Sciences, 9% Biological and Biomedical Sciences, 9% Health Professions and Related Programs, 8% Psychology
Expenses: 2019-2020: $7,460 in state, $24,958 out of state; room/board: $12,406
Financial aid: (509) 359-2314; 63% of undergrads determined to have financial need; average aid package $13,581

Edmonds Community College[1]
Lynnwood WA
(425) 640-1459
U.S. News ranking: Reg. Coll. (W), unranked
Website: www.wvc.edu
Admissions email: N/A
Public
Application deadline (fall): N/A
Undergraduate student body: N/A full time, N/A part time
Expenses: N/A
Financial aid: N/A

Evergreen State College
Olympia WA
(360) 867-6170
U.S. News ranking: Reg. U. (W), No. 37
Website: www.evergreen.edu
Admissions email: admissions@evergreen.edu
Public; founded 1967
Freshman admissions: selective; 2018-2019: 1,194 applied, 1,137 accepted. Either SAT or ACT required. SAT 25/75 percentile: 1000-1220. High school rank: 19% in top tenth, 24% in top quarter, 60% in top half
Early decision deadline: N/A, notification date: N/A

Early action deadline: N/A, notification date: N/A
Application deadline (fall): rolling
Undergraduate student body: 2,781 full time, 237 part time; 42% male, 58% female; 3% American Indian, 3% Asian, 5% black, 12% Hispanic, 7% multiracial, 1% Pacific Islander, 65% white, 0% international
Most popular majors: 83% Liberal Arts and Sciences/Liberal Studies, 17% Biological and Physical Sciences
Expenses: 2018-2019: $7,944 in state, $26,460 out of state; room/board: $11,346
Financial aid: (360) 867-6205

Gonzaga University
Spokane WA
(800) 322-2584
U.S. News ranking: Nat. U., No. 79
Website: www.gonzaga.edu
Admissions email: admissions@gonzaga.edu
Private; founded 1887
Affiliation: Roman Catholic
Freshman admissions: more selective; 2018-2019: 8,400 applied, 5,512 accepted. Either SAT or ACT required. SAT 25/75 percentile: 1183-1350. High school rank: 41% in top tenth, 76% in top quarter, 97% in top half
Early decision deadline: N/A, notification date: N/A
Early action deadline: 11/15, notification date: 1/15
Application deadline (fall): 2/1
Undergraduate student body: 5,244 full time, 73 part time; 47% male, 53% female; 1% American Indian, 5% Asian, 1% black, 11% Hispanic, 6% multiracial, 0% Pacific Islander, 72% white, 1% international; 48% from in state; 52% live on campus; 0% of students in fraternities, 0% in sororities
Most popular majors: 27% Business, Management, Marketing, and Related Support Services, 13% Social Sciences, 12% Engineering, 11% Biological and Biomedical Sciences, 6% Psychology
Expenses: 2019-2020: $45,140; room/board: $12,330
Financial aid: (509) 313-6562; 52% of undergrads determined to have financial need; average aid package $30,697

Grays Harbor College[1]
Aberdeen WA
(360) 532-9020
U.S. News ranking: Reg. Coll. (W), unranked
Website: www.yvcc.edu
Admissions email: N/A
Public
Application deadline (fall): N/A
Undergraduate student body: N/A full time, N/A part time
Expenses: N/A
Financial aid: N/A

Green River College[1]
Auburn WA
(253) 833-9111
U.S. News ranking: Reg. Coll. (W), unranked
Website: uwc.edu
Admissions email: N/A
Public
Application deadline (fall): N/A
Undergraduate student body: N/A full time, N/A part time
Expenses: N/A
Financial aid: N/A

Heritage University[1]
Toppenish WA
(509) 865-8500
U.S. News ranking: Reg. U. (W), unranked
Website: www.heritage.edu
Admissions email: admissions@heritage.edu
Private
Application deadline (fall): N/A
Undergraduate student body: N/A full time, N/A part time
Expenses: N/A
Financial aid: N/A

Highline College[1]
Des Moines WA
(206) 878-3710
U.S. News ranking: Reg. Coll. (W), unranked
Website: www.marianas.edu/
Admissions email: N/A
Public
Application deadline (fall): N/A
Undergraduate student body: N/A full time, N/A part time
Expenses: N/A
Financial aid: N/A

Lake Washington Institute of Technology
Kirkland WA
(425) 739-8104
U.S. News ranking: Reg. Coll. (W), unranked
Website: www.lwtech.edu/
Admissions email: admissions@lwtech.edu
Public; founded 1949
Freshman admissions: least selective; 2018-2019: 150 applied, 150 accepted. Neither SAT nor ACT required. SAT 25/75 percentile: N/A. High school rank: N/A
Early decision deadline: N/A, notification date: N/A
Early action deadline: N/A, notification date: N/A
Application deadline (fall): rolling
Undergraduate student body: 2,254 full time, 2,135 part time; 39% male, 61% female; 1% American Indian, 14% Asian, 4% black, 2% Hispanic, 7% multiracial, 1% Pacific Islander, 61% white, 0% international; 99% from in state; 0% live on campus; 0% of students in fraternities, 0% in sororities
Most popular majors: 3% Dental Hygiene/Hygienist, 2% Design and Visual Communications, General, 1% Logistics, Materials, and Supply Chain Management, 1% Public Health, General

Expenses: 2019-2020: $7,743 in state, $19,288 out of state; room/board: N/A
Financial aid: (425) 739-8106

North Seattle College[1]
Seattle WA
U.S. News ranking: Reg. Coll. (W), unranked
Admissions email: N/A
Public
Application deadline (fall): N/A
Undergraduate student body: N/A full time, N/A part time
Expenses: N/A
Financial aid: N/A

Northwest University
Kirkland WA
(425) 889-5231
U.S. News ranking: Reg. U. (W), No. 55
Website: www.northwestu.edu
Admissions email: admissions@northwestu.edu
Private; founded 1934
Affiliation: Assemblies of God Church
Freshman admissions: selective; 2018-2019: 501 applied, 477 accepted. Either SAT or ACT required. SAT 25/75 percentile: 1030-1225. High school rank: N/A
Early decision deadline: N/A, notification date: N/A
Early action deadline: 11/15, notification date: 12/15
Application deadline (fall): rolling
Undergraduate student body: 936 full time, 39 part time; 34% male, 66% female; 2% American Indian, 5% Asian, 4% black, 9% Hispanic, 7% multiracial, 2% Pacific Islander, 67% white, 5% international
Most popular majors: 12% Registered Nursing/Registered Nurse, 7% Psychology, General, 5% Business Administration and Management, General, 5% Organizational Communication, General, 4% Missions/Missionary Studies and Missiology
Expenses: 2019-2020: $32,960; room/board: $9,000
Financial aid: (425) 889-5336; 78% of undergrads determined to have financial need; average aid package $25,275

Olympic College[1]
Bremerton WA
(360) 792-6050
U.S. News ranking: Reg. Coll. (W), unranked
Website: www.olympic.edu
Admissions email: N/A
Public
Application deadline (fall): N/A
Undergraduate student body: N/A full time, N/A part time
Expenses: N/A
Financial aid: N/A

Pacific Lutheran University
Tacoma WA
(800) 274-6758
U.S. News ranking: Reg. U. (W), No. 20
Website: www.plu.edu
Admissions email: admission@plu.edu
Private; founded 1890
Affiliation: Lutheran Church in America
Freshman admissions: selective; 2018-2019: 3,742 applied, 2,986 accepted. Either SAT or ACT required. SAT 25/75 percentile: 1070-1270. High school rank: N/A
Early decision deadline: N/A, notification date: N/A
Early action deadline: N/A, notification date: N/A
Application deadline (fall): rolling
Undergraduate student body: 2,712 full time, 57 part time; 36% male, 64% female; 1% American Indian, 10% Asian, 4% black, 12% Hispanic, 10% multiracial, 1% Pacific Islander, 59% white, 3% international; 76% from in state; 48% live on campus; 0% of students in fraternities, 0% in sororities
Most popular majors: 16% Business, Management, Marketing, and Related Support Services, 13% Health Professions and Related Programs, 10% Social Sciences, 8% Biological and Biomedical Sciences, 8% Parks, Recreation, Leisure, and Fitness Studies
Expenses: 2019-2020: $43,674; room/board: $10,876
Financial aid: (253) 535-7161; 75% of undergrads determined to have financial need; average aid package $39,174

Peninsula College[1]
Port Angeles WA
(360) 452-9277
U.S. News ranking: Reg. Coll. (W), unranked
Website: www.pencol.edu
Admissions email: N/A
Public
Application deadline (fall): N/A
Undergraduate student body: N/A full time, N/A part time
Expenses: N/A
Financial aid: N/A

Pierce College–Fort Steilacoom[1]
Lakewood WA
(253) 964-6500
U.S. News ranking: Reg. Coll. (W), unranked
Website: www.whatcom.ctc.edu
Admissions email: N/A
Public
Application deadline (fall): N/A
Undergraduate student body: N/A full time, N/A part time
Expenses: N/A
Financial aid: N/A

Renton Technical College[1]
Renton WA
(425) 235-2352
U.S. News ranking: Reg. Coll. (W), unranked
Website: aupr.edu
Admissions email: N/A
Public
Application deadline (fall): N/A
Undergraduate student body: N/A full time, N/A part time
Expenses: N/A
Financial aid: N/A

Saint Martin's University
Lacey WA
(800) 368-8803
U.S. News ranking: Reg. U. (W), No. 27
Website: www.stmartin.edu
Admissions email: admissions@stmartin.edu
Private; founded 1895
Affiliation: Roman Catholic
Freshman admissions: selective; 2018-2019: 1,125 applied, 1,074 accepted. Either SAT or ACT required for some. SAT 25/75 percentile: 1020-1220. High school rank: 27% in top tenth, 57% in top quarter, 85% in top half
Early decision deadline: N/A, notification date: N/A
Early action deadline: N/A, notification date: N/A
Application deadline (fall): 7/12
Undergraduate student body: 1,172 full time, 172 part time; 52% male, 48% female; 2% American Indian, 8% Asian, 5% black, 14% Hispanic, 8% multiracial, 5% Pacific Islander, 50% white, 5% international; 80% from in state; 39% live on campus; 0% of students in fraternities, 0% in sororities
Most popular majors: 22% Business, Management, Marketing, and Related Support Services, 15% Psychology, 14% Engineering, 8% Biological and Biomedical Sciences, 8% Homeland Security, Law Enforcement, Firefighting and Related Protective Services
Expenses: 2019-2020: $38,560; room/board: $12,000
Financial aid: (360) 486-8868; 76% of undergrads determined to have financial need; average aid package $29,759

Seattle Central College[1]
Seattle WA
(206) 934-5450
U.S. News ranking: Reg. Coll. (W), unranked
Website: www.seattlecentral.edu/
Admissions email: Admissions.Central@seattlecolleges.edu
Public; founded 1966
Application deadline (fall): rolling
Undergraduate student body: N/A full time, N/A part time
Expenses: N/A
Financial aid: N/A

Seattle Pacific University

Seattle WA
(800) 366-3344
U.S. News ranking: Nat. U.,
No. 192
Website: www.spu.edu
Admissions email:
admissions@spu.edu
Private; founded 1891
Affiliation: Free Methodist
Freshman admissions: selective;
2018-2019: 4,172 applied,
3,758 accepted. Either SAT
or ACT required. SAT 25/75
percentile: 1030-1240. High
school rank: 1% in top tenth, 2%
in top quarter, 12% in top half
Early decision deadline: N/A,
notification date: N/A
Early action deadline: 11/15,
notification date: 1/5
Application deadline (fall): 2/1
Undergraduate student body: 2,781
full time, 95 part time; 33%
male, 67% female; 0% American
Indian, 13% Asian, 5% black,
13% Hispanic, 8% multiracial,
1% Pacific Islander, 51% white,
6% international; N/A from in
state; 55% live on campus; N/A
of students in fraternities, N/A in
sororities
Most popular majors: 16%
Business, Management,
Marketing, and Related Support
Services, 12% Social Sciences,
11% Health Professions and
Related Programs, 9% Visual and
Performing Arts, 8% Biological
and Biomedical Sciences
Expenses: 2019-2020: $45,078;
room/board: $12,285
Financial aid: (206) 281-2061;
69% of undergrads determined to
have financial need; average aid
package $38,601

Seattle University

Seattle WA
(206) 296-2000
U.S. News ranking: Nat. U.,
No. 139
Website: www.seattleu.edu
Admissions email:
admissions@seattleu.edu
Private; founded 1891
Affiliation: Roman Catholic
Freshman admissions: more
selective; 2018-2019: 8,640
applied, 6,536 accepted. Either
SAT or ACT required. SAT 25/75
percentile: 1130-1320. High
school rank: 27% in top tenth,
64% in top quarter, 94% in
top half
Early decision deadline: N/A,
notification date: N/A
Early action deadline: 11/15,
notification date: 12/23
Application deadline (fall): rolling
Undergraduate student body: 4,519
full time, 245 part time; 39%
male, 61% female; 0% American
Indian, 16% Asian, 3% black,
12% Hispanic, 8% multiracial,
1% Pacific Islander, 42% white,
11% international; N/A from in
state; 50% live on campus; N/A
of students in fraternities, N/A in
sororities
Most popular majors: 25%
Business, Management,
Marketing, and Related Support
Services, 14% Health Professions

and Related Programs, 7%
Engineering, 6% Psychology, 6%
Social Sciences
Expenses: 2019-2020: $46,590;
room/board: $12,531
Financial aid: (206) 296-5852;
58% of undergrads determined to
have financial need; average aid
package $37,437

Skagit Valley College[1]

Mount Vernon WA
(360) 416-7600
U.S. News ranking: Reg. Coll. (W),
unranked
Website: www.pucpr.edu/arecibo
Admissions email: N/A
Public
Application deadline (fall): N/A
Undergraduate student body: N/A
full time, N/A part time
Expenses: N/A
Financial aid: N/A

South Seattle College[1]

Seattle WA
(206) 764-5300
U.S. News ranking: Reg. Coll. (W),
unranked
Website: www.southseattle.edu
Admissions email: N/A
Public
Application deadline (fall): N/A
Undergraduate student body: N/A
full time, N/A part time
Expenses: N/A
Financial aid: N/A

Spokane Community College[1]

Spokane WA
(509) 533-7000
U.S. News ranking: Reg. Coll. (W),
unranked
Website: www.cunisanjuan.edu
Admissions email: N/A
Public
Application deadline (fall): N/A
Undergraduate student body: N/A
full time, N/A part time
Expenses: N/A
Financial aid: N/A

Spokane Falls Community College[1]

Spokane WA
(509) 533-3500
U.S. News ranking: Reg. Coll. (W),
unranked
Website: www.psm.edu
Admissions email: N/A
Public
Application deadline (fall): N/A
Undergraduate student body: N/A
full time, N/A part time
Expenses: N/A
Financial aid: N/A

Tacoma Community College[1]

Tacoma WA
(253) 566-5000
U.S. News ranking: Reg. Coll. (W),
unranked
Website: www.edpuniversity.edu
Admissions email: N/A
Public
Application deadline (fall): N/A

Undergraduate student body: N/A
full time, N/A part time
Expenses: N/A
Financial aid: N/A

University of Puget Sound

Tacoma WA
(253) 879-3211
U.S. News ranking: Nat. Lib. Arts,
No. 89
Website: www.pugetsound.edu
Admissions email:
admission@pugetsound.edu
Private; founded 1888
Freshman admissions: more
selective; 2018-2019: 5,730
applied, 5,060 accepted. Neither
SAT nor ACT required. SAT
25/75 percentile: 1130-1350.
High school rank: 28% in top
tenth, 58% in top quarter, 91%
in top half
Early decision deadline: 11/15,
notification date: 12/15
Early action deadline: 11/15,
notification date: 1/15
Application deadline (fall): 1/15
Undergraduate student body: 2,348
full time, 16 part time; 40%
male, 60% female; 0% American
Indian, 6% Asian, 2% black, 9%
Hispanic, 9% multiracial, 1%
Pacific Islander, 69% white, 0%
international; 23% from in state;
66% live on campus; 26% of
students in fraternities, 27% in
sororities
Most popular majors: 18%
Social Sciences, 12% Business,
Management, Marketing, and
Related Support Services, 10%
Biological and Biomedical
Sciences, 9% Psychology, 5%
Foreign Languages, Literatures,
and Linguistics
Expenses: 2019-2020: $51,740;
room/board: $13,000
Financial aid: (253) 879-3214;
54% of undergrads determined to
have financial need; average aid
package $35,216

University of Washington

Seattle WA
(206) 543-9686
U.S. News ranking: Nat. U., No. 62
Website: www.washington.edu
Admissions email:
pseegert@uw.edu
Public; founded 1861
Freshman admissions: more
selective; 2018-2019: 45,907
applied, 22,350 accepted. Either
SAT or ACT required. SAT 25/75
percentile: 1220-1460. High
school rank: 58% in top tenth,
88% in top quarter, 99% in
top half
Early decision deadline: N/A,
notification date: N/A
Early action deadline: N/A,
notification date: N/A
Application deadline (fall): 11/15
Undergraduate student body:
29,496 full time, 2,603 part
time; 47% male, 53% female;
0% American Indian, 25% Asian,
3% black, 8% Hispanic, 7%
multiracial, 0% Pacific Islander,
39% white, 16% international;

69% from in state; 29% live
on campus; N/A of students in
fraternities, N/A in sororities
Most popular majors: 15%
Social Sciences, 11% Biological
and Biomedical Sciences,
11% Business, Management,
Marketing, and Related Support
Services, 9% Engineering, 7%
Computer and Information
Sciences and Support Services
Expenses: 2019-2020: $11,465
in state, $38,796 out of state;
room/board: $13,296
Financial aid: (206) 543-6101;
42% of undergrads determined to
have financial need; average aid
package $16,658

Walla Walla University[1]

College Place WA
(509) 527-2327
U.S. News ranking: Reg. U. (W),
No. 49
Website: www.wallawalla.edu
Admissions email:
info@wallawalla.edu
Private; founded 1892
Affiliation: Seventh Day Adventist
Application deadline (fall): rolling
Undergraduate student body: N/A
full time, N/A part time
Expenses: 2018-2019: $28,035;
room/board: $7,845
Financial aid: (509) 527-2815

Washington State University

Pullman WA
(888) 468-6978
U.S. News ranking: Nat. U.,
No. 166
Website: www.wsu.edu
Admissions email:
admissions@wsu.edu
Public; founded 1890
Freshman admissions: selective;
2018-2019: 22,773 applied,
17,579 accepted. Either SAT
or ACT required. SAT 25/75
percentile: 1020-1210. High
school rank: N/A
Early decision deadline: N/A,
notification date: N/A
Early action deadline: N/A,
notification date: N/A
Application deadline (fall): rolling
Undergraduate student body:
22,877 full time, 3,221 part
time; 47% male, 53% female;
1% American Indian, 6% Asian,
3% black, 15% Hispanic, 7%
multiracial, 0% Pacific Islander,
61% white, 4% international;
82% from in state; 25% live
on campus; 17% of students in
fraternities, 21% in sororities
Most popular majors: 21%
Business, Management,
Marketing, and Related Support
Services, 11% Engineering, 10%
Social Sciences, 8% Health
Professions and Related Programs,
7% Psychology
Expenses: 2019-2020: $11,841
in state, $26,419 out of state;
room/board: $11,648
Financial aid: (509) 335-9711;
58% of undergrads determined to
have financial need; average aid
package $13,110

Wenatchee Valley College[1]

Wenatchee WA
(509) 682-6800
U.S. News ranking: Reg. Coll. (W),
unranked
Website: www.cascadia.edu
Admissions email: N/A
Public
Application deadline (fall): N/A
Undergraduate student body: N/A
full time, N/A part time
Expenses: N/A
Financial aid: N/A

Western Washington University

Bellingham WA
(360) 650-3440
U.S. News ranking: Reg. U. (W),
No. 17
Website: www.wwu.edu
Admissions email: admit@wwu.edu
Public; founded 1893
Freshman admissions: selective;
2018-2019: 11,124 applied,
9,751 accepted. Either SAT
or ACT required. SAT 25/75
percentile: 1080-1280. High
school rank: 24% in top tenth,
56% in top quarter, 86% in
top half
Early decision deadline: N/A,
notification date: N/A
Early action deadline: 11/1,
notification date: 12/31
Application deadline (fall): 1/31
Undergraduate student body:
13,893 full time, 1,277 part
time; 43% male, 57% female;
0% American Indian, 6% Asian,
2% black, 9% Hispanic, 9%
multiracial, 0% Pacific Islander,
71% white, 1% international;
86% from in state; 26% live
on campus; 0% of students in
fraternities, 0% in sororities
Most popular majors: 15%
Business, Management,
Marketing, and Related Support
Services, 12% Social Sciences,
7% Multi/Interdisciplinary Studies,
7% Natural Resources and
Conservation, 6% Education
Expenses: 2019-2020: N/A in
state, N/A out of state; room/
board: $12,036
Financial aid: (360) 650-2422;
49% of undergrads determined to
have financial need; average aid
package $16,294

Whatcom Community College[1]

Bellingham WA
(360) 383-3000
U.S. News ranking: Reg. Coll. (W),
unranked
Website: www.marlboro.edu/
academics/graduate
Admissions email: N/A
Public
Application deadline (fall): N/A
Undergraduate student body: N/A
full time, N/A part time
Expenses: N/A
Financial aid: N/A

Whitman College

Walla Walla WA
(509) 527-5176
U.S. News ranking: Nat. Lib. Arts,
No. 46
Website: www.whitman.edu
Admissions email:
admission@whitman.edu
Private; founded 1883
Freshman admissions: more
selective; 2018-2019: 5,064
applied, 2,551 accepted. Either
SAT or ACT required for some.
ACT 25/75 percentile: 29-32.
High school rank: 52% in top
tenth, 83% in top quarter, 99%
in top half
Early decision deadline: 11/15,
notification date: 12/20
Early action deadline: N/A,
notification date: N/A
Application deadline (fall): 1/15
Undergraduate student body: 1,436
full time, 28 part time; 42%
male, 58% female; 1% American
Indian, 6% Asian, 2% black, 8%
Hispanic, 7% multiracial, 1%
Pacific Islander, 66% white, 8%
international; 32% from in state;
66% live on campus; 35% of
students in fraternities, 34% in
sororities
Most popular majors: 24% Social
Sciences, 17% Biological and
Biomedical Sciences, 12% Visual
and Performing Arts, 9% Physical
Sciences, 7% Psychology
Expenses: 2019-2020: $53,820;
room/board: $13,512
Financial aid: (509) 527-5178;
45% of undergrads determined to
have financial need; average aid
package $43,371

Whitworth University

Spokane WA
(800) 533-4668
U.S. News ranking: Reg. U. (W),
No. 3
Website: www.whitworth.edu
Admissions email:
admissions@whitworth.edu
Private; founded 1890
Affiliation: Presbyterian Church
(USA)
Freshman admissions: more
selective; 2018-2019: 3,731
applied, 3,387 accepted. Either
SAT or ACT required for some.
SAT 25/75 percentile: 1090-
1290. High school rank: 34% in
top tenth, 64% in top quarter,
91% in top half
Early decision deadline: N/A,
notification date: N/A
Early action deadline: 1/15,
notification date: 2/15
Application deadline (fall): 8/1
Undergraduate student body: 2,304
full time, 51 part time; 40%
male, 60% female; 1% American
Indian, 5% Asian, 2% black,
10% Hispanic, 9% multiracial,
1% Pacific Islander, 68% white,
4% international; 74% from in
state; 45% live on campus; 0%
of students in fraternities, 0% in
sororities
Most popular majors: 12%
Business, Management,
Marketing, and Related
Support Services, 11% Multi/
Interdisciplinary Studies, 9%
Social Sciences, 8% Education,
6% Health Professions and
Related Programs

Expenses: 2019-2020: $44,940;
room/board: $11,800
Financial aid: (509) 777-3215;
71% of undergrads determined to
have financial need; average aid
package $38,637

Yakima Valley College[1]

Yakima WA
(509) 574-4600
U.S. News ranking: Reg. Coll. (W),
unranked
Website: usfsm.edu/
Admissions email: N/A
Public
Application deadline (fall): N/A
Undergraduate student body: N/A
full time, N/A part time
Expenses: N/A
Financial aid: N/A

WEST VIRGINIA

Alderson Broaddus University

Philippi WV
(800) 263-1549
U.S. News ranking: Reg. Coll. (S),
No. 39
Website: www.ab.edu
Admissions email:
admissions@ab.edu
Private; founded 1871
Affiliation: American Baptist
Freshman admissions: selective;
2018-2019: 3,988 applied,
1,696 accepted. Either SAT
or ACT required. SAT 25/75
percentile: 920-1100. High
school rank: 3% in top tenth, 19%
in top quarter, 57% in top half
Early decision deadline: N/A,
notification date: N/A
Early action deadline: N/A,
notification date: N/A
Application deadline (fall): 8/25
Undergraduate student body: 791
full time, 45 part time; 54%
male, 46% female; 1% American
Indian, 1% Asian, 23% black,
5% Hispanic, 1% multiracial,
0% Pacific Islander, 63% white,
5% international; 36% from in
state; 83% live on campus; N/A
of students in fraternities, N/A in
sororities
Most popular majors: Information
not available
Expenses: 2019-2020: $29,220;
room/board: $9,400
Financial aid: (304) 457-6354;
88% of undergrads determined to
have financial need; average aid
package $29,356

American Public University System

Charles Town WV
(877) 777-9081
U.S. News ranking: Reg. U. (S),
unranked
Website: www.apus.edu
Admissions email: N/A
For-profit; founded 1991
Freshman admissions: least
selective; 2018-2019: N/A
applied, N/A accepted. Neither
SAT nor ACT required. SAT 25/75
percentile: N/A. High school
rank: N/A

Early decision deadline: N/A,
notification date: N/A
Early action deadline: N/A,
notification date: N/A
Application deadline (fall): rolling
Undergraduate student body: 2,324
full time, 35,422 part time; 64%
male, 36% female; 1% American
Indian, 2% Asian, 16% black,
13% Hispanic, 4% multiracial,
1% Pacific Islander, 55% white,
1% international
Most popular majors: 19%
Business Administration and
Management, General, 8%
Criminal Justice/Safety Studies,
6% International/Global Studies,
5% Kinesiology and Exercise
Science, 5% Logistics, Materials,
and Supply Chain Management
Expenses: 2019-2020: $8,600;
room/board: N/A
Financial aid: (855) 731-9218

Bethany College

Bethany WV
(304) 829-7611
U.S. News ranking: Nat. Lib. Arts,
second tier
Website: www.bethanywv.edu
Admissions email:
enrollment@bethanywv.edu
Private; founded 1840
Affiliation: Christian Church
(Disciples of Christ)
Freshman admissions: less
selective; 2018-2019: 1,094
applied, 993 accepted. Either
SAT or ACT required. SAT 25/75
percentile: 890-1130. High
school rank: 5% in top tenth, 20%
in top quarter, 53% in top half
Early decision deadline: N/A,
notification date: N/A
Early action deadline: N/A,
notification date: N/A
Application deadline (fall): rolling
Undergraduate student body:
556 full time, 4 part time; 60%
male, 40% female; 2% American
Indian, 1% Asian, 19% black,
5% Hispanic, 0% multiracial, 1%
Pacific Islander, 51% white, 4%
international
Most popular majors: 16%
Psychology, General, 8% Political
Science and Government, Other,
7% History, General, 7% Physical
Education Teaching and Coaching,
6% Speech Communication and
Rhetoric
Expenses: 2019-2020: $30,666;
room/board: $11,108
Financial aid: (304) 829-7601;
87% of undergrads determined to
have financial need; average aid
package $34,056

Bluefield State College

Bluefield WV
(304) 327-4065
U.S. News ranking: Reg. Coll. (S),
No. 52
Website: bluefieldstate.edu/
Admissions email:
bscadmit@bluefieldstate.edu
Public; founded 1895
Freshman admissions: selective;
2018-2019: 625 applied, 478
accepted. Either SAT or ACT
required. ACT 25/75 percentile:
17-22. High school rank: N/A

Early decision deadline: N/A,
notification date: N/A
Early action deadline: N/A,
notification date: N/A
Application deadline (fall): rolling
Undergraduate student body: 985
full time, 290 part time; 36%
male, 64% female; N/A American
Indian, N/A Asian, N/A black, N/A
Hispanic, N/A multiracial, N/A
Pacific Islander, N/A white, N/A
international
Most popular majors: Information
not available
Expenses: 2019-2020: $10,584
in state, $14,352 out of state;
room/board: N/A
Financial aid: (304) 327-4020

Concord University

Athens WV
(888) 384-5249
U.S. News ranking: Reg. U. (S),
second tier
Website: www.concord.edu
Admissions email: admissions@
concord.edu
Public; founded 1872
Freshman admissions: selective;
2018-2019: 1,673 applied,
1,489 accepted. Either SAT
or ACT required. ACT 25/75
percentile: 18-23. High school
rank: 16% in top tenth, 43% in
top quarter, 71% in top half
Early decision deadline: N/A,
notification date: N/A
Early action deadline: N/A,
notification date: N/A
Application deadline (fall): rolling
Undergraduate student body: 1,577
full time, 152 part time; 41%
male, 59% female; 0% American
Indian, 1% Asian, 6% black,
1% Hispanic, 2% multiracial,
0% Pacific Islander, 82% white,
5% international; 84% from in
state; 43% live on campus; N/A
of students in fraternities, N/A in
sororities
Most popular majors: 19%
Business, Management,
Marketing, and Related Support
Services, 17% Education,
16% Liberal Arts and
Sciences, General Studies and
Humanities, 7% Biological and
Biomedical Sciences, 7% Public
Administration and Social Service
Professions
Expenses: 2019-2020: $8,385 in
state, $18,037 out of state; room/
board: $9,304
Financial aid: (304) 384-5358;
78% of undergrads determined to
have financial need; average aid
package $8,491

Davis and Elkins College[1]

Elkins WV
(304) 637-1230
U.S. News ranking: Reg. Coll. (S),
No. 41
Website: www.davisandelkins.edu
Admissions email:
admiss@davisandelkins.edu
Private
Application deadline (fall): N/A
Undergraduate student body: N/A
full time, N/A part time
Expenses: N/A
Financial aid: N/A

Fairmont State University

Fairmont WV
(304) 367-4010
U.S. News ranking: Reg. U. (S),
second tier
Website: www.fairmontstate.edu
Admissions email:
admit@fairmontstate.edu
Public; founded 1865
Freshman admissions: selective;
2018-2019: 2,442 applied,
2,325 accepted. Either SAT
or ACT required. ACT 25/75
percentile: 18-23. High school
rank: 11% in top tenth, 34% in
top quarter, 67% in top half
Early decision deadline: N/A,
notification date: N/A
Early action deadline: N/A,
notification date: N/A
Application deadline (fall): 8/1
Undergraduate student body: 3,114
full time, 559 part time; 43%
male, 57% female; 0% American
Indian, 0% Asian, 5% black,
2% Hispanic, 3% multiracial,
0% Pacific Islander, 87% white,
2% international; N/A from in
state; 29% live on campus; N/A
of students in fraternities, N/A in
sororities
Most popular majors: 14%
Business, Management,
Marketing, and Related Support
Services, 14% Engineering
Technologies and Engineering-
Related Fields, 12% Homeland
Security, Law Enforcement,
Firefighting and Related Protective
Services, 10% Health Professions
and Related Programs, 8% Liberal
Arts and Sciences, General
Studies and Humanities
Expenses: 2019-2020: $7,890 in
state, $17,140 out of state; room/
board: $10,064
Financial aid: (304) 367-4826;
72% of undergrads determined to
have financial need; average aid
package $9,254

Glenville State College

Glenville WV
(304) 462-4128
U.S. News ranking: Reg. Coll. (S),
No. 60
Website: www.glenville.edu
Admissions email:
admissions@glenville.edu
Public; founded 1872
Freshman admissions: less
selective; 2018-2019: 2,526
applied, 1,797 accepted. Either
SAT or ACT required. ACT 25/75
percentile: 16-22. High school
rank: 9% in top tenth, 23% in top
quarter, 51% in top half
Early decision deadline: N/A,
notification date: N/A
Early action deadline: N/A,
notification date: N/A
Application deadline (fall): rolling
Undergraduate student body: 1,013
full time, 573 part time; 56%
male, 44% female; 1% American
Indian, 1% Asian, 16% black,
2% Hispanic, 0% multiracial, 0%
Pacific Islander, 75% white, 0%
international
Most popular majors: 18%
Homeland Security, Law
Enforcement, Firefighting and
Related Protective Services,

18% Natural Resources and Conservation, 11% Education, 8% Liberal Arts and Sciences, General Studies and Humanities, 7% Psychology
Expenses: 2019-2020: $7,308 in state, $14,872 out of state; room/board: $9,942
Financial aid: (304) 462-6171; 85% of undergrads determined to have financial need; average aid package $11,570

Marshall University
Huntington WV
(800) 642-3499
U.S. News ranking: Nat. U., second tier
Website: www.marshall.edu
Admissions email: admissions@marshall.edu
Public; founded 1837
Freshman admissions: selective; 2018-2019: 4,987 applied, 4,519 accepted. Either SAT or ACT required. ACT 25/75 percentile: 19-25. High school rank: N/A
Early decision deadline: N/A, notification date: N/A
Early action deadline: N/A, notification date: N/A
Undergraduate student body: 7,460 full time, 2,133 part time; 42% male, 58% female; 0% American Indian, 1% Asian, 6% black, 2% Hispanic, 3% multiracial, 0% Pacific Islander, 84% white, 2% international; 18% from in state; N/A live on campus; N/A of students in fraternities, N/A in sororities
Most popular majors: 22% Health Professions and Related Programs, 15% Business, Management, Marketing, and Related Support Services, 11% Liberal Arts and Sciences, General Studies and Humanities, 10% Education, 6% Psychology
Expenses: 2019-2020: $8,412 in state, $19,266 out of state; room/board: $9,580
Financial aid: (304) 696-3162; 72% of undergrads determined to have financial need; average aid package $11,290

Ohio Valley University
Vienna WV
(877) 446-8668
U.S. News ranking: Reg. Coll. (S), No. 44
Website: www.ovu.edu
Admissions email: admissions@ovu.edu
Private; founded 1958
Affiliation: Churches of Christ
Freshman admissions: selective; 2018-2019: 820 applied, 292 accepted. Either SAT or ACT required. ACT 25/75 percentile: 17-24. High school rank: N/A
Early decision deadline: N/A, notification date: N/A
Early action deadline: N/A, notification date: N/A
Application deadline (fall): 8/15
Undergraduate student body: 374 full time, 107 part time; 49% male, 51% female; 0% American Indian, 1% Asian, 9% black, 4% Hispanic, 2% multiracial,

0% Pacific Islander, 60% white, 17% international; 30% from in state; 46% live on campus; 33% of students in fraternities, 52% in sororities
Most popular majors: 48% Business, Management, Marketing, and Related Support Services, 15% Education, 12% Psychology, 7% Multi/Interdisciplinary Studies, 5% Homeland Security, Law Enforcement, Firefighting and Related Protective Services
Expenses: 2019-2020: $21,900; room/board: $7,980
Financial aid: (304) 865-6077; 54% of undergrads determined to have financial need; average aid package $16,043

Salem University[1]
Salem WV
(304) 326-1109
U.S. News ranking: Reg. U. (S), unranked
Website: www.salemu.edu
Admissions email: admissions@salemu.edu
For-profit
Application deadline (fall): N/A
Undergraduate student body: N/A full time, N/A part time
Expenses: N/A
Financial aid: N/A

Shepherd University
Shepherdstown WV
(304) 876-5212
U.S. News ranking: Nat. Lib. Arts, second tier
Website: www.shepherd.edu
Admissions email: admission@shepherd.edu
Public; founded 1871
Freshman admissions: selective; 2018-2019: 1,565 applied, 1,400 accepted. Either SAT or ACT required. SAT 25/75 percentile: 970-1160. High school rank: N/A
Early decision deadline: N/A, notification date: N/A
Early action deadline: 11/15, notification date: 12/1
Application deadline (fall): rolling
Undergraduate student body: 2,543 full time, 837 part time; 44% male, 56% female; 0% American Indian, 2% Asian, 9% black, 6% Hispanic, 4% multiracial, 0% Pacific Islander, 77% white, 1% international; 67% from in state; 34% live on campus; 3% of students in fraternities, 4% in sororities
Most popular majors: 16% General Studies, 12% Business Administration and Management, General, 12% Registered Nursing/Registered Nurse, 8% Parks, Recreation and Leisure Studies, 5% Secondary Education and Teaching
Expenses: 2019-2020: $7,784 in state, $18,224 out of state; room/board: $10,776
Financial aid: (304) 876-5470; 66% of undergrads determined to have financial need; average aid package $12,813

University of Charleston
Charleston WV
(800) 995-4682
U.S. News ranking: Nat. U., second tier
Website: www.ucwv.edu
Admissions email: admissions@ucwv.edu
Private; founded 1888
Freshman admissions: less selective; 2018-2019: 2,283 applied, 1,151 accepted. Neither SAT nor ACT required. ACT 25/75 percentile: 18-23. High school rank: N/A
Early decision deadline: N/A, notification date: N/A
Early action deadline: N/A, notification date: N/A
Application deadline (fall): rolling
Undergraduate student body: 1,205 full time, 725 part time; 56% male, 44% female; N/A American Indian, N/A Asian, N/A black, N/A Hispanic, N/A multiracial, N/A Pacific Islander, N/A white, N/A international
Most popular majors: Information not available
Expenses: 2019-2020: $30,600; room/board: $9,400
Financial aid: (304) 357-4944; 70% of undergrads determined to have financial need; average aid package $28,418

West Liberty University
West Liberty WV
(304) 336-8076
U.S. News ranking: Reg. U. (S), No. 75
Website: www.westliberty.edu
Admissions email: admissions@westliberty.edu
Public; founded 1837
Freshman admissions: less selective; 2018-2019: 1,857 applied, 1,288 accepted. Either SAT or ACT required. ACT 25/75 percentile: 17-23. High school rank: 14% in top tenth, 35% in top quarter, 70% in top half
Early decision deadline: N/A, notification date: N/A
Early action deadline: N/A, notification date: N/A
Application deadline (fall): rolling
Undergraduate student body: 1,871 full time, 354 part time; 37% male, 63% female; 0% American Indian, 0% Asian, 3% black, 1% Hispanic, 2% multiracial, 0% Pacific Islander, 75% white, 3% international; 71% from in state; 39% live on campus; 3% of students in fraternities, 4% in sororities
Most popular majors: 18% Business Administration and Management, General, 12% General Studies, 8% Dental Hygiene/Hygienist, 8% Elementary Education and Teaching, 6% Biology/Biological Sciences, General
Expenses: 2018-2019: $7,730 in state, $15,670 out of state; room/board: $9,406
Financial aid: (304) 336-8016

West Virginia University Institute of Technology
Beckley WV
(304) 442-3146
U.S. News ranking: Unranked
Website: www.wvutech.edu
Admissions email: tech-admissions@mail.wvu.edu
Public; founded 1895
Freshman admissions: N/A; 2018-2019: 1,517 applied, 920 accepted. Either SAT or ACT required. ACT 25/75 percentile:

West Virginia State University[1]
Institute WV
(304) 766-4345
U.S. News ranking: Reg. Coll. (S), No. 46
Website: www.wvstateu.edu
Admissions email: admissions@wvstateu.edu
Public; founded 1891
Application deadline (fall): 8/17
Undergraduate student body: N/A full time, N/A part time
Expenses: 2018-2019: $8,212 in state, $17,666 out of state; room/board: $12,366
Financial aid: (304) 204-4361

West Virginia University
Morgantown WV
(304) 442-3146
U.S. News ranking: Nat. U., No. 228
Website: www.wvu.edu
Admissions email: go2wvu@mail.wvu.edu
Public; founded 1867
Freshman admissions: selective; 2018-2019: 18,639 applied, 15,211 accepted. Either SAT or ACT required. ACT 25/75 percentile: 21-27. High school rank: 23% in top tenth, 48% in top quarter, 78% in top half
Early decision deadline: N/A, notification date: N/A
Early action deadline: N/A, notification date: N/A
Application deadline (fall): 8/1
Undergraduate student body: 19,568 full time, 1,587 part time; 51% male, 49% female; 0% American Indian, 2% Asian, 4% black, 4% Hispanic, 4% multiracial, 0% Pacific Islander, 80% white, 6% international; 48% from in state; 22% live on campus; 2% of students in fraternities, 1% in sororities
Most popular majors: 16% Engineering, 13% Business, Management, Marketing, and Related Support Services, 7% Communication, Journalism, and Related Programs, 7% Health Professions and Related Programs, 7% Social Sciences
Expenses: 2019-2020: $8,976 in state, $25,320 out of state; room/board: $11,062
Financial aid: (304) 293-8571; 52% of undergrads determined to have financial need; average aid package $7,488

21-27. High school rank: 21% in top tenth, 51% in top quarter, 87% in top half
Early decision deadline: N/A, notification date: N/A
Early action deadline: N/A, notification date: N/A
Application deadline (fall): rolling
Undergraduate student body: 1,175 full time, 580 part time; 54% male, 46% female; 0% American Indian, 1% Asian, 6% black, 3% Hispanic, 6% multiracial, 0% Pacific Islander, 76% white, 7% international; 86% from in state; 23% live on campus; N/A of students in fraternities, N/A in sororities
Most popular majors: 38% Engineering, 16% Liberal Arts and Sciences, General Studies and Humanities, 10% Business, Management, Marketing, and Related Support Services, 8% Health Professions and Related Programs, 7% Public Administration and Social Service Professions
Expenses: 2019-2020: $7,560 in state, $18,912 out of state; room/board: $11,628
Financial aid: (304) 293-8571; 66% of undergrads determined to have financial need; average aid package $7,441

West Virginia University–Parkersburg[1]
Parkersburg WV
(304) 424-8000
U.S. News ranking: Reg. Coll. (S), unranked
Website: www.wvup.edu
Admissions email: info@mail.wvup.edu
Public
Application deadline (fall): N/A
Undergraduate student body: N/A full time, N/A part time
Expenses: N/A
Financial aid: N/A

West Virginia Wesleyan College
Buckhannon WV
(800) 722-9933
U.S. News ranking: Reg. U. (S), No. 54
Website: www.wvwc.edu
Admissions email: admissions@wvwc.edu
Private; founded 1890
Affiliation: United Methodist
Freshman admissions: selective; 2018-2019: 2,159 applied, 1,515 accepted. Either SAT or ACT required. ACT 25/75 percentile: 19-25. High school rank: 22% in top tenth, 50% in top quarter, 83% in top half
Early decision deadline: N/A, notification date: N/A
Early action deadline: N/A, notification date: N/A
Application deadline (fall): 8/15
Undergraduate student body: 1,162 full time, 18 part time; 46% male, 54% female; 0% American Indian, 0% Asian, 10% black, 3% Hispanic, 4% multiracial, 0% Pacific Islander, 75% white,

6% international; 63% from in state; 78% live on campus; 30% of students in fraternities, 30% in sororities
Most popular majors: 14% Parks, Recreation, Leisure, and Fitness Studies, 13% Health Professions and Related Programs, 12% Business, Management, Marketing, and Related Support Services, 11% Education, 9% Physical Sciences
Expenses: 2019-2020: $31,944; room/board: $9,298
Financial aid: (304) 473-8080; 79% of undergrads determined to have financial need; average aid package $29,728

Wheeling Jesuit University
Wheeling WV
(304) 243-2359
U.S. News ranking: Reg. U. (S), No. 47
Website: www.wju.edu/admissions/
Admissions email: admiss@wju.edu
Private; founded 1954
Affiliation: Roman Catholic
Freshman admissions: selective; 2018-2019: 1,621 applied, 1,468 accepted. Either SAT or ACT required. ACT 25/75 percentile: 19-24. High school rank: 7% in top tenth, 32% in top quarter, 60% in top half
Early decision deadline: N/A, notification date: N/A
Early action deadline: N/A, notification date: N/A
Application deadline (fall): rolling
Undergraduate student body: 755 full time, 106 part time; 54% male, 46% female; 0% American Indian, 0% Asian, 12% black, 3% Hispanic, 2% multiracial, 1% Pacific Islander, 67% white, 2% international; 31% from in state; 76% live on campus; 0% of students in fraternities, 0% in sororities
Most popular majors: 25% Health Professions and Related Programs, 22% Business, Management, Marketing, and Related Support Services, 9% Psychology, 7% Biological and Biomedical Sciences, 6% Homeland Security, Law Enforcement, Firefighting and Related Protective Services
Expenses: 2019-2020: $29,290; room/board: $9,900
Financial aid: (304) 243-2304; 78% of undergrads determined to have financial need; average aid package $26,835

WISCONSIN

Alverno College
Milwaukee WI
(414) 382-6100
U.S. News ranking: Reg. U. (Mid. W), No. 53
Website: www.alverno.edu
Admissions email: admissions@alverno.edu
Private; founded 1887
Affiliation: Roman Catholic
Freshman admissions: less selective; 2018-2019: 747 applied, 501 accepted. Either

SAT or ACT required. ACT 25/75 percentile: 17-21. High school rank: N/A
Early decision deadline: N/A, notification date: N/A
Early action deadline: N/A, notification date: N/A
Application deadline (fall): rolling
Undergraduate student body: 995 full time, 224 part time; 1% male, 99% female; 1% American Indian, 5% Asian, 14% black, 30% Hispanic, 5% multiracial, 0% Pacific Islander, 46% white, 0% international; 93% from in state; 17% live on campus; 0% of students in fraternities, 0% in sororities
Most popular majors: 35% Health Professions and Related Programs, 18% Business, Management, Marketing, and Related Support Services, 9% Psychology, 7% Liberal Arts and Sciences, General Studies and Humanities, 6% Communication, Journalism, and Related Programs
Expenses: 2019-2020: $29,456; room/board: $8,800
Financial aid: (414) 382-6040; 89% of undergrads determined to have financial need; average aid package $24,196

Beloit College
Beloit WI
(608) 363-2500
U.S. News ranking: Nat. Lib. Arts, No. 82
Website: www.beloit.edu
Admissions email: admiss@beloit.edu
Private; founded 1846
Freshman admissions: selective; 2018-2019: 4,200 applied, 2,369 accepted. Either SAT or ACT required for some. ACT 25/75 percentile: 21-29. High school rank: 15% in top tenth, 56% in top quarter, 87% in top half
Early decision deadline: 11/1, notification date: 12/1
Early action deadline: 12/1, notification date: 1/1
Application deadline (fall): rolling
Undergraduate student body: 1,228 full time, 47 part time; 45% male, 55% female; 0% American Indian, 4% Asian, 7% black, 11% Hispanic, 4% multiracial, 0% Pacific Islander, 52% white, 17% international; N/A from in state; 85% live on campus; 16% of students in fraternities, 15% in sororities
Most popular majors: 24% Social Sciences, 10% English Language and Literature/Letters, 10% Physical Sciences, 10% Psychology, 7% Business, Management, Marketing, and Related Support Services
Expenses: 2019-2020: $51,532; room/board: $9,360
Financial aid: (608) 363-2696; 61% of undergrads determined to have financial need; average aid package $46,286

Cardinal Stritch University
Milwaukee WI
(414) 410-4040
U.S. News ranking: Nat. U., second tier
Website: www.stritch.edu
Admissions email: admissions@stritch.edu
Private; founded 1937
Affiliation: Roman Catholic
Freshman admissions: selective; 2018-2019: 943 applied, 669 accepted. Either SAT or ACT required for some. ACT 25/75 percentile: 18-22. High school rank: 8% in top tenth, 44% in top quarter, 72% in top half
Early decision deadline: N/A, notification date: N/A
Early action deadline: N/A, notification date: N/A
Application deadline (fall): rolling
Undergraduate student body: 807 full time, 650 part time; 30% male, 70% female; 1% American Indian, 3% Asian, 21% black, 18% Hispanic, 3% multiracial, 0% Pacific Islander, 38% white, 15% international; 88% from in state; 22% live on campus; 0% of students in fraternities, 0% in sororities
Most popular majors: Information not available
Expenses: 2019-2020: $31,798; room/board: $8,946
Financial aid: (414) 410-4016; 68% of undergrads determined to have financial need; average aid package $24,575

Carroll University
Waukesha WI
(262) 524-7220
U.S. News ranking: Reg. U. (Mid. W), No. 66
Website: www.carrollu.edu/
Admissions email: info@carrollu.edu
Private; founded 1846
Affiliation: Presbyterian
Freshman admissions: selective; 2018-2019: 3,769 applied, 2,587 accepted. Either SAT or ACT required. ACT 25/75 percentile: 21-26. High school rank: N/A
Early decision deadline: N/A, notification date: N/A
Early action deadline: N/A, notification date: N/A
Application deadline (fall): rolling
Undergraduate student body: 2,690 full time, 211 part time; 34% male, 66% female; 0% American Indian, 4% Asian, 2% black, 8% Hispanic, 3% multiracial, 0% Pacific Islander, 80% white, 2% international
Most popular majors: 20% Health Professions and Related Programs, 17% Parks, Recreation, Leisure, and Fitness Studies, 15% Business, Management, Marketing, and Related Support Services, 8% Biological and Biomedical Sciences, 8% Education
Expenses: 2019-2020: $32,960; room/board: $9,760
Financial aid: (262) 524-7296; 78% of undergrads determined to have financial need; average aid package $25,956

Carthage College
Kenosha WI
(262) 551-6000
U.S. News ranking: Reg. Coll. (Mid. W), No. 14
Website: www.carthage.edu
Admissions email: admissions@carthage.edu
Private; founded 1847
Freshman admissions: selective; 2018-2019: 8,109 applied, 5,500 accepted. Neither SAT nor ACT required. ACT 25/75 percentile: 21-27. High school rank: 21% in top tenth, 47% in top quarter, 81% in top half
Early decision deadline: N/A, notification date: N/A
Early action deadline: N/A, notification date: N/A
Application deadline (fall): rolling
Undergraduate student body: 2,649 full time, 127 part time; 44% male, 56% female; 0% American Indian, 2% Asian, 6% black, 13% Hispanic, 3% multiracial, 0% Pacific Islander, 68% white, 1% international; 36% from in state; 66% live on campus; 6% of students in fraternities, 10% in sororities
Most popular majors: 31% Business, Management, Marketing, and Related Support Services, 9% Visual and Performing Arts, 7% Biological and Biomedical Sciences, 7% Communication, Journalism, and Related Programs, 7% Psychology
Expenses: 2019-2020: $45,100; room/board: $12,400
Financial aid: (262) 551-6001; 80% of undergrads determined to have financial need; average aid package $35,096

Concordia University Wisconsin
Mequon WI
(262) 243-4300
U.S. News ranking: Nat. U., No. 281
Website: www.cuw.edu
Admissions email: admissions@cuw.edu
Private; founded 1881
Affiliation: Lutheran Church–Missouri Synod
Freshman admissions: selective; 2018-2019: 3,380 applied, 2,188 accepted. Either SAT or ACT required. ACT 25/75 percentile: 20-26. High school rank: 26% in top tenth, 51% in top quarter, 84% in top half
Early decision deadline: N/A, notification date: N/A
Early action deadline: N/A, notification date: N/A
Application deadline (fall): N/A
Undergraduate student body: 2,410 full time, 1,083 part time; 35% male, 65% female; 1% American Indian, 2% Asian, 10% black, 1% Hispanic, 3% multiracial, 0% Pacific Islander, 71% white, 8% international; N/A from in state; 37% live on campus; N/A of students in fraternities, N/A in sororities
Most popular majors: 30% Health Professions and Related Programs, 28% Business, Management, Marketing, and Related Support

Services, 9% Biological and Biomedical Sciences, 8% Education, 4% Homeland Security, Law Enforcement, Firefighting and Related Protective Services
Expenses: 2019-2020: $30,352; room/board: $11,170
Financial aid: (262) 243-2025

Edgewood College
Madison WI
(608) 663-2294
U.S. News ranking: Nat. U., No. 202
Website: www.edgewood.edu
Admissions email: admissions@edgewood.edu
Private; founded 1927
Affiliation: Roman Catholic
Freshman admissions: selective; 2018-2019: 1,560 applied, 1,137 accepted. Either SAT or ACT required. ACT 25/75 percentile: 20-25. High school rank: 17% in top tenth, 50% in top quarter, 83% in top half
Early decision deadline: N/A, notification date: N/A
Early action deadline: N/A, notification date: N/A
Application deadline (fall): 8/15
Undergraduate student body: 1,281 full time, 207 part time; 27% male, 73% female; 0% American Indian, 3% Asian, 4% black, 7% Hispanic, 3% multiracial, 0% Pacific Islander, 77% white, 3% international; 91% from in state; 35% live on campus; N/A of students in fraternities, N/A in sororities
Most popular majors: 28% Registered Nursing/Registered Nurse, 11% Business/Commerce, General, 10% Psychology, General, 6% Biology/Biological Sciences, General, 5% Communication and Media Studies
Expenses: 2019-2020: $30,600; room/board: $11,350
Financial aid: (608) 663-4300; 75% of undergrads determined to have financial need; average aid package $22,680

Herzing University[1]
Madison WI
(800) 596-0724
U.S. News ranking: Reg. U. (Mid. W), second tier
Website: www.herzing.edu/
Admissions email: info@msn.herzing.edu
For-profit; founded 1965
Affiliation: Other
Application deadline (fall): N/A
Undergraduate student body: N/A full time, N/A part time
Expenses: N/A
Financial aid: N/A

Lakeland University[1]
Plymouth WI
(920) 565-1226
U.S. News ranking: Reg. U. (Mid. W), second tier
Website: www.lakeland.edu
Admissions email: admissions@lakeland.edu
Private; founded 1862
Application deadline (fall): rolling

WISCONSIN

Undergraduate student body: N/A full time, N/A part time
Expenses: N/A
Financial aid: N/A

Lawrence University
Appleton WI
(800) 227-0982
U.S. News ranking: Nat. Lib. Arts, No. 58
Website: www.lawrence.edu
Admissions email: admissions@lawrence.edu
Private; founded 1847
Freshman admissions: more selective; 2018-2019: 3,502 applied, 2,188 accepted. Neither SAT nor ACT required. ACT 25/75 percentile: 27-31. High school rank: 35% in top tenth, 69% in top quarter, 91% in top half
Early decision deadline: 11/1, notification date: 12/1
Early action deadline: 11/1, notification date: 12/15
Application deadline (fall): 1/15
Undergraduate student body: 1,420 full time, 52 part time; 47% male, 53% female; 0% American Indian, 5% Asian, 5% black, 10% Hispanic, 4% multiracial, 0% Pacific Islander, 63% white, 13% international; 27% from in state; 94% live on campus; 8% of students in fraternities, 10% in sororities
Most popular majors: 22% Visual and Performing Arts, 19% Social Sciences, 14% Biological and Biomedical Sciences, 9% Psychology, 6% Foreign Languages, Literatures, and Linguistics
Expenses: 2019-2020: $49,122; room/board: $10,719
Financial aid: (920) 832-6584; 61% of undergrads determined to have financial need; average aid package $41,150

Maranatha Baptist University
Watertown WI
(920) 206-2327
U.S. News ranking: Reg. Coll. (Mid. W), No. 46
Website: www.mbu.edu
Admissions email: admissions@mbu.edu
Private; founded 1968
Freshman admissions: selective; 2018-2019: 250 applied, 190 accepted. Either SAT or ACT required. ACT 25/75 percentile: 20-26. High school rank: 15% in top tenth, 39% in top quarter, 75% in top half
Early decision deadline: N/A, notification date: N/A
Early action deadline: N/A, notification date: N/A
Application deadline (fall): rolling
Undergraduate student body: 533 full time, 252 part time; 45% male, 55% female; 0% American Indian, 2% Asian, 1% black, 4% Hispanic, 4% multiracial, 0% Pacific Islander, 87% white, 1% international
Most popular majors: 20% Education, 17% Theology and Religious Vocations, 16% Business, Management, Marketing, and Related Support Services, 12% Liberal Arts

and Sciences, General Studies and Humanities, 7% Health Professions and Related Programs
Expenses: 2018-2019: $15,410; room/board: $7,100
Financial aid: (920) 206-2318

Marian University[1]
Fond du Lac WI
(920) 923-7650
U.S. News ranking: Reg. U. (Mid. W), No. 105
Website: www.marianuniversity.edu/
Admissions email: admissions@marianuniversity.edu
Private; founded 1936
Affiliation: Roman Catholic
Application deadline (fall): rolling
Undergraduate student body: N/A full time, N/A part time
Expenses: 2018-2019: $27,400; room/board: $7,222
Financial aid: (920) 923-8737

Marquette University
Milwaukee WI
(800) 222-6544
U.S. News ranking: Nat. U., No. 84
Website: www.marquette.edu
Admissions email: admissions@marquette.edu
Private; founded 1881
Affiliation: Roman Catholic
Freshman admissions: more selective; 2018-2019: 15,574 applied, 12,717 accepted. Either SAT or ACT required. ACT 25/75 percentile: 24-30. High school rank: 36% in top tenth, 69% in top quarter, 95% in top half
Early decision deadline: N/A, notification date: N/A
Early action deadline: N/A, notification date: N/A
Application deadline (fall): 12/1
Undergraduate student body: 8,121 full time, 314 part time; 46% male, 54% female; 0% American Indian, 7% Asian, 4% black, 13% Hispanic, 3% multiracial, 0% Pacific Islander, 69% white, 3% international; 31% from in state; 54% live on campus; N/A of students in fraternities, N/A in sororities
Most popular majors: 28% Business, Management, Marketing, and Related Support Services, 12% Biological and Biomedical Sciences, 10% Engineering, 9% Communication, Journalism, and Related Programs, 8% Social Sciences
Expenses: 2019-2020: $43,936; room/board: $13,200
Financial aid: (414) 288-4000; 59% of undergrads determined to have financial need; average aid package $30,471

Milwaukee Institute of Art and Design[1]
Milwaukee WI
(414) 291-8070
U.S. News ranking: Arts, unranked
Website: www.miad.edu
Admissions email: admissions@miad.edu
Private; founded 1974
Application deadline (fall): 8/15

Undergraduate student body: N/A full time, N/A part time
Expenses: 2018-2019: $37,360; room/board: $9,300
Financial aid: (414) 847-3270

Milwaukee School of Engineering
Milwaukee WI
(800) 332-6763
U.S. News ranking: Reg. U. (Mid. W), No. 8
Website: www.msoe.edu
Admissions email: explore@msoe.edu
Private; founded 1903
Freshman admissions: more selective; 2018-2019: 3,294 applied, 2,079 accepted. Either SAT or ACT required. ACT 25/75 percentile: 25-30. High school rank: N/A
Early decision deadline: N/A, notification date: N/A
Early action deadline: N/A, notification date: N/A
Application deadline (fall): rolling
Undergraduate student body: 2,489 full time, 106 part time; 74% male, 26% female; 0% American Indian, 5% Asian, 2% black, 7% Hispanic, 3% multiracial, 0% Pacific Islander, 68% white, 8% international; 64% from in state; 43% live on campus; 3% of students in fraternities, 11% in sororities
Most popular majors: 73% Engineering, 14% Health Professions and Related Programs, 11% Business, Management, Marketing, and Related Support Services, 1% Engineering Technologies and Engineering-Related Fields, 1% Multi/Interdisciplinary Studies
Expenses: 2019-2020: $42,162; room/board: $10,107
Financial aid: (414) 277-7224; 79% of undergrads determined to have financial need; average aid package $30,233

Mount Mary University
Milwaukee WI
(414) 930-3024
U.S. News ranking: Reg. U. (Mid. W), No. 78
Website: www.mtmary.edu
Admissions email: mmu-admiss@mtmary.edu
Private; founded 1913
Affiliation: Roman Catholic
Freshman admissions: less selective; 2018-2019: 739 applied, 458 accepted. Either SAT or ACT required. ACT 25/75 percentile: 16-21. High school rank: 12% in top tenth, 44% in top quarter, 80% in top half
Early decision deadline: N/A, notification date: N/A
Early action deadline: N/A, notification date: N/A
Application deadline (fall): rolling
Undergraduate student body: 648 full time, 78 part time; 0% male, 100% female; 0% American Indian, 8% Asian, 20% black, 24% Hispanic, 4% multiracial, 0% Pacific Islander, 43% white, 2% international

Most popular majors: 22% Health Professions and Related Programs, 18% Business, Management, Marketing, and Related Support Services, 10% Communication, Journalism, and Related Programs, 10% Visual and Performing Arts, 8% Psychology
Expenses: 2019-2020: $31,160; room/board: $9,180
Financial aid: (414) 930-3163; 83% of undergrads determined to have financial need; average aid package $25,352

Northland College
Ashland WI
(715) 682-1224
U.S. News ranking: Reg. Coll. (Mid. W), No. 22
Website: www.northland.edu
Admissions email: admit@northland.edu
Private; founded 1892
Affiliation: United Church of Christ
Freshman admissions: selective; 2018-2019: 2,506 applied, 1,277 accepted. Either SAT or ACT required for some. ACT 25/75 percentile: 18-25. High school rank: 9% in top tenth, 30% in top quarter, 73% in top half
Early decision deadline: N/A, notification date: N/A
Early action deadline: N/A, notification date: N/A
Application deadline (fall): rolling
Undergraduate student body: 558 full time, 24 part time; 46% male, 54% female; 4% American Indian, 1% Asian, 3% black, 4% Hispanic, 3% multiracial, 0% Pacific Islander, 74% white, 5% international; 49% from in state; 65% live on campus; 0% of students in fraternities, 0% in sororities
Most popular majors: 21% Natural Resources and Conservation, 15% Biological and Biomedical Sciences, 11% Parks, Recreation, Leisure, and Fitness Studies, 8% Education, 8% Physical Sciences
Expenses: 2019-2020: $37,516; room/board: $9,406
Financial aid: (715) 682-1255; 88% of undergrads determined to have financial need; average aid package $30,675

Ripon College
Ripon WI
(920) 748-8115
U.S. News ranking: Nat. Lib. Arts, No. 105
Website: www.ripon.edu
Admissions email: adminfo@ripon.edu
Private; founded 1851
Freshman admissions: selective; 2018-2019: 2,619 applied, 1,807 accepted. Either SAT or ACT required for some. ACT 25/75 percentile: 20-27. High school rank: 17% in top tenth, 38% in top quarter, 81% in top half
Early decision deadline: N/A, notification date: N/A
Early action deadline: N/A, notification date: N/A
Application deadline (fall): rolling
Undergraduate student body: 788 full time, 19 part time; 47% male, 53% female; 0% American Indian, 1% Asian, 4% black,

9% Hispanic, 3% multiracial, 0% Pacific Islander, 79% white, 3% international; 71% from in state; 93% live on campus; 41% of students in fraternities, 30% in sororities
Most popular majors: 17% Business/Commerce, General, 13% Psychology, General, 12% English Language and Literature, General, 9% Biology/Biological Sciences, General, 8% Chemistry, Other
Expenses: 2019-2020: $45,113; room/board: $8,653
Financial aid: (920) 748-8301; 87% of undergrads determined to have financial need; average aid package $36,917

Silver Lake College[1]
Manitowoc WI
(920) 686-6175
U.S. News ranking: Reg. U. (Mid. W), second tier
Website: www.sl.edu
Admissions email: admissions@sl.edu
Private; founded 1935
Affiliation: Roman Catholic
Application deadline (fall): rolling
Undergraduate student body: N/A full time, N/A part time
Expenses: N/A
Financial aid: (920) 686-6175

St. Norbert College
De Pere WI
(800) 236-4878
U.S. News ranking: Nat. Lib. Arts, No. 145
Website: www.snc.edu
Admissions email: admit@snc.edu
Private; founded 1898
Affiliation: Roman Catholic
Freshman admissions: more selective; 2018-2019: 4,118 applied, 3,199 accepted. Either SAT or ACT required. ACT 25/75 percentile: 22-27. High school rank: 26% in top tenth, 57% in top quarter, 85% in top half
Early decision deadline: N/A, notification date: N/A
Early action deadline: N/A, notification date: N/A
Application deadline (fall): rolling
Undergraduate student body: 2,083 full time, 49 part time; 41% male, 59% female; 1% American Indian, 1% Asian, 2% black, 5% Hispanic, 1% multiracial, 0% Pacific Islander, 88% white, 2% international; 79% from in state; 82% live on campus; 10% of students in fraternities, 10% in sororities
Most popular majors: 17% Business/Commerce, General, 14% Biology/Biological Sciences, General, 11% Elementary Education and Teaching, 10% Speech Communication and Rhetoric, 6% Psychology, General
Expenses: 2019-2020: $39,529; room/board: $10,435
Financial aid: (920) 403-3071; 73% of undergrads determined to have financial need; average aid package $26,998

University of Wisconsin Colleges[1]

Madison WI
(877) 895-3276
U.S. News ranking: Reg. Coll. (Mid. W), unranked
Website: www.gmc.edu/
Admissions email: N/A
Public
Application deadline (fall): N/A
Undergraduate student body: N/A full time, N/A part time
Expenses: N/A
Financial aid: N/A

University of Wisconsin–Eau Claire

Eau Claire WI
(715) 836-5415
U.S. News ranking: Reg. U. (Mid. W), No. 33
Website: www.uwec.edu
Admissions email: admissions@uwec.edu
Public; founded 1916
Freshman admissions: selective; 2018-2019: 5,855 applied, 5,037 accepted. Either SAT or ACT required. ACT 25/75 percentile: 21-26. High school rank: 17% in top tenth, 48% in top quarter, 93% in top half
Early decision deadline: N/A, notification date: N/A
Early action deadline: N/A, notification date: N/A
Application deadline (fall): 8/20
Undergraduate student body: 9,448 full time, 665 part time; 38% male, 62% female; 0% American Indian, 3% Asian, 1% black, 3% Hispanic, 2% multiracial, 0% Pacific Islander, 88% white, 2% international; 68% from in state; 35% live on campus; N/A of students in fraternities, N/A in sororities
Most popular majors: 26% Business, Management, Marketing, and Related Support Services, 15% Health Professions and Related Programs, 8% Education, 6% Psychology, 5% Parks, Recreation, Leisure, and Fitness Studies
Expenses: 2019-2020: $8,840 in state, $17,116 out of state; room/board: $8,216
Financial aid: (715) 836-3000; 50% of undergrads determined to have financial need; average aid package $9,794

University of Wisconsin–Green Bay[1]

Green Bay WI
(920) 465-2111
U.S. News ranking: Reg. U. (Mid. W), No. 95
Website: www.uwgb.edu
Admissions email: uwgb@uwgb.edu
Public; founded 1965
Application deadline (fall): rolling
Undergraduate student body: N/A full time, N/A part time
Expenses: 2018-2019: $7,878 in state, $15,728 out of state; room/board: $7,306
Financial aid: (920) 465-2111

University of Wisconsin–La Crosse

La Crosse WI
(608) 785-8939
U.S. News ranking: Reg. U. (Mid. W), No. 28
Website: www.uwlax.edu
Admissions email: admissions@uwlax.edu
Public; founded 1909
Freshman admissions: more selective; 2018-2019: 6,048 applied, 4,730 accepted. Either SAT or ACT required. ACT 25/75 percentile: 23-27. High school rank: 21% in top tenth, 57% in top quarter, 96% in top half
Early decision deadline: N/A, notification date: N/A
Early action deadline: N/A, notification date: N/A
Application deadline (fall): rolling
Undergraduate student body: 9,130 full time, 546 part time; 44% male, 56% female; 0% American Indian, 2% Asian, 1% black, 3% Hispanic, 3% multiracial, 0% Pacific Islander, 90% white, 1% international; 82% from in state; 35% live on campus; N/A of students in fraternities, N/A in sororities
Most popular majors: 21% Business, Management, Marketing, and Related Support Services, 14% Biological and Biomedical Sciences, 12% Health Professions and Related Programs, 10% Parks, Recreation, Leisure, and Fitness Studies, 10% Psychology
Expenses: 2018-2019: $8,933 in state, $17,602 out of state; room/board: $6,331
Financial aid: (608) 785-8604; 45% of undergrads determined to have financial need; average aid package $8,621

University of Wisconsin–Madison

Madison WI
(608) 262-3961
U.S. News ranking: Nat. U., No. 46
Website: www.wisc.edu
Admissions email: onwisconsin@admissions.wisc.edu
Public; founded 1848
Freshman admissions: more selective; 2018-2019: 42,741 applied, 22,099 accepted. Either SAT or ACT required. ACT 25/75 percentile: 27-32. High school rank: 54% in top tenth, 90% in top quarter, 99% in top half
Early decision deadline: N/A, notification date: N/A
Early action deadline: 11/1, notification date: 12/31
Application deadline (fall): 2/1
Undergraduate student body: 29,412 full time, 3,236 part time; 49% male, 51% female; 0% American Indian, 6% Asian, 2% black, 5% Hispanic, 3% multiracial, 0% Pacific Islander, 71% white, 10% international; 65% from in state; 25% live on campus; 8% of students in fraternities, 8% in sororities
Most popular majors: 8% Economics, General, 7% Biology/Biological Sciences, General, 6% Computer and Information

Sciences, General, 5% Psychology, General, 4% Finance, General
Expenses: 2019-2020: $10,725 in state, $37,785 out of state; room/board: $11,558
Financial aid: (608) 262-3060; 37% of undergrads determined to have financial need; average aid package $18,194

University of Wisconsin–Milwaukee

Milwaukee WI
(414) 229-2222
U.S. News ranking: Nat. U., second tier
Website: www.uwm.edu
Admissions email: uwmlook@uwm.edu
Public; founded 1956
Freshman admissions: selective; 2018-2019: 8,280 applied, 7,325 accepted. Either SAT or ACT required for some. ACT 25/75 percentile: 20-25. High school rank: 10% in top tenth, 22% in top quarter, 71% in top half
Early decision deadline: N/A, notification date: N/A
Early action deadline: N/A, notification date: N/A
Application deadline (fall): 8/1
Undergraduate student body: 16,669 full time, 3,587 part time; 47% male, 53% female; 0% American Indian, 7% Asian, 7% black, 12% Hispanic, 4% multiracial, 0% Pacific Islander, 66% white, 3% international; N/A from in state; 20% live on campus; N/A of students in fraternities, N/A in sororities
Most popular majors: 24% Business, Management, Marketing, and Related Support Services, 12% Health Professions and Related Programs, 7% Engineering, 6% Education, 6% Visual and Performing Arts
Expenses: 2018-2019: $9,588 in state, $20,867 out of state; room/board: $10,728
Financial aid: N/A

University of Wisconsin–Oshkosh

Oshkosh WI
(920) 424-3164
U.S. News ranking: Reg. U. (Mid. W), second tier
Website: www.uwosh.edu
Admissions email: admissions@uwosh.edu
Public; founded 1871
Freshman admissions: selective; 2018-2019: 6,310 applied, 4,328 accepted. Either SAT or ACT required. ACT 25/75 percentile: 20-24. High school rank: 10% in top tenth, 33% in top quarter, 76% in top half
Early decision deadline: N/A, notification date: N/A
Early action deadline: N/A, notification date: N/A
Application deadline (fall): rolling
Undergraduate student body: 7,821 full time, 4,948 part time; 39% male, 61% female; 0% American Indian, 4% Asian, 3% black, 5% Hispanic, 3% multiracial, 0% Pacific Islander, 83% white,

0% international; 91% from in state; 33% live on campus; 3% of students in fraternities, 3% in sororities
Most popular majors: 17% Business, Management, Marketing, and Related Support Services, 14% Health Professions and Related Programs, 13% Education, 7% Communication, Journalism, and Related Programs, 7% Social Sciences
Expenses: 2018-2019: $7,621 in state, $15,194 out of state; room/board: $8,092
Financial aid: (920) 424-3377

University of Wisconsin–Parkside

Kenosha WI
(262) 595-2355
U.S. News ranking: Nat. Lib. Arts, second tier
Website: www.uwp.edu
Admissions email: admissions@uwp.edu
Public; founded 1968
Freshman admissions: selective; 2018-2019: 1,651 applied, 1,443 accepted. Either SAT or ACT required for some. ACT 25/75 percentile: 18-23. High school rank: 12% in top tenth, 36% in top quarter, 74% in top half
Early decision deadline: N/A, notification date: N/A
Early action deadline: N/A, notification date: N/A
Application deadline (fall): rolling
Undergraduate student body: 3,197 full time, 893 part time; 47% male, 53% female; 0% American Indian, 4% Asian, 9% black, 18% Hispanic, 4% multiracial, 0% Pacific Islander, 64% white, 2% international; 82% from in state; 18% live on campus; N/A of students in fraternities, N/A in sororities
Most popular majors: 26% Business, Management, Marketing, and Related Support Services, 11% Homeland Security, Law Enforcement, Firefighting and Related Protective Services, 10% Psychology, 7% Visual and Performing Arts, 6% Biological and Biomedical Sciences
Expenses: 2019-2020: $7,649 in state, $15,638 out of state; room/board: $8,026
Financial aid: (262) 595-2574; 66% of undergrads determined to have financial need; average aid package $9,321

University of Wisconsin–Platteville[1]

Platteville WI
(608) 342-1125
U.S. News ranking: Reg. U. (Mid. W), No. 95
Website: www.uwplatt.edu
Admissions email: admit@uwplatt.edu
Public; founded 1866
Application deadline (fall): rolling
Undergraduate student body: N/A full time, N/A part time
Expenses: N/A
Financial aid: (608) 342-6188

University of Wisconsin–River Falls

River Falls WI
(715) 425-3500
U.S. News ranking: Reg. U. (Mid. W), No. 84
Website: www.uwrf.edu
Admissions email: admissions@uwrf.edu
Public; founded 1874
Freshman admissions: selective; 2018-2019: 3,209 applied, 2,409 accepted. Either SAT or ACT required. ACT 25/75 percentile: 20-25. High school rank: 11% in top tenth, 34% in top quarter, 71% in top half
Early decision deadline: N/A, notification date: N/A
Early action deadline: N/A, notification date: N/A
Application deadline (fall): rolling
Undergraduate student body: 5,206 full time, 519 part time; 37% male, 63% female; 0% American Indian, 3% Asian, 1% black, 4% Hispanic, 3% multiracial, 0% Pacific Islander, 88% white, 1% international; 50% from in state; 47% live on campus; 7% of students in fraternities, 3% in sororities
Most popular majors: 21% Business, Management, Marketing, and Related Support Services, 18% Agriculture, Agriculture Operations, and Related Sciences, 15% Education, 7% Biological and Biomedical Sciences, 7% Social Sciences
Expenses: 2018-2019: $8,025 in state, $15,598 out of state; room/board: $7,760
Financial aid: (715) 425-3141; 59% of undergrads determined to have financial need; average aid package $7,196

University of Wisconsin–Stevens Point

Stevens Point WI
(715) 346-2441
U.S. News ranking: Reg. U. (Mid. W), No. 53
Website: www.uwsp.edu
Admissions email: admiss@uwsp.edu
Public; founded 1894
Freshman admissions: selective; 2018-2019: 3,930 applied, 3,246 accepted. Either SAT or ACT required for some. ACT 25/75 percentile: 20-25. High school rank: 9% in top tenth, 33% in top quarter, 72% in top half
Early decision deadline: N/A, notification date: N/A
Early action deadline: N/A, notification date: N/A
Application deadline (fall): rolling
Undergraduate student body: 6,725 full time, 660 part time; 47% male, 53% female; 0% American Indian, 3% Asian, 2% black, 4% Hispanic, 2% multiracial, 0% Pacific Islander, 86% white, 1% international; 88% from in state; 28% live on campus; 5% of students in fraternities, 5% in sororities
Most popular majors: 9% Business Administration and Management, General, 6% Biology/Biological Sciences, General, 5% Natural

Resources Management and Policy, 5% Psychology, General, 4% Elementary Education and Teaching
Expenses: 2019-2020: $8,318 in state, $16,585 out of state; room/board: $7,428
Financial aid: (715) 346-4771; 60% of undergrads determined to have financial need; average aid package $9,814

University of Wisconsin–Stout
Menomonie WI
(715) 232-1232
U.S. News ranking: Reg. U. (Mid. W), No. 72
Website: www.uwstout.edu
Admissions email: admissions@uwstout.edu
Public; founded 1891
Freshman admissions: selective; 2018-2019: 2,871 applied, 2,628 accepted. Either SAT or ACT required. ACT 25/75 percentile: 20-25. High school rank: 8% in top tenth, 28% in top quarter, 64% in top half
Early decision deadline: N/A, notification date: N/A
Early action deadline: N/A, notification date: N/A
Application deadline (fall): rolling
Undergraduate student body: 6,140 full time, 1,415 part time; 57% male, 43% female; 0% American Indian, 4% Asian, 2% black, 3% Hispanic, 3% multiracial, 0% Pacific Islander, 87% white, 2% international; N/A from in state; 39% live on campus; 2% of students in fraternities, 3% in sororities
Most popular majors: 35% Business, Management, Marketing, and Related Support Services, 11% Visual and Performing Arts, 8% Family and Consumer Sciences/Human Sciences, 7% Computer and Information Sciences and Support Services, 7% Engineering Technologies and Engineering-Related Fields
Expenses: 2019-2020: $9,463 in state, $17,430 out of state; room/board: $6,944
Financial aid: (715) 232-1363; 55% of undergrads determined to have financial need; average aid package $11,013

University of Wisconsin–Superior
Superior WI
(715) 394-8230
U.S. News ranking: Nat. Lib. Arts, second tier
Website: www.uwsuper.edu
Admissions email: admissions@uwsuper.edu
Public; founded 1893
Freshman admissions: selective; 2018-2019: 936 applied, 690 accepted. Either SAT or ACT required. ACT 25/75 percentile: 19-24. High school rank: 8% in top tenth, 25% in top quarter, 60% in top half
Early decision deadline: N/A, notification date: N/A
Early action deadline: N/A, notification date: N/A
Application deadline (fall): 8/1
Undergraduate student body: 1,793 full time, 501 part time; 38% male, 62% female; 1% American Indian, 1% Asian, 2% black, 3% Hispanic, 4% multiracial, 0% Pacific Islander, 79% white, 10% international; N/A from in state; 31% live on campus; N/A of students in fraternities, N/A in sororities
Most popular majors: 15% Business, Management, Marketing, and Related Support Services, 14% Multi/Interdisciplinary Studies, 13% Biological and Biomedical Sciences, 13% Education, 7% Communication, Journalism, and Related Programs
Expenses: 2019-2020: $8,132 in state, $15,705 out of state; room/board: $7,280
Financial aid: (715) 394-8200; 62% of undergrads determined to have financial need; average aid package $11,210

University of Wisconsin–Whitewater
Whitewater WI
(262) 472-1440
U.S. News ranking: Reg. U. (Mid. W), No. 61
Website: www.uww.edu
Admissions email: uwwadmit@uww.edu
Public; founded 1868
Freshman admissions: selective; 2018-2019: 4,960 applied, 4,324 accepted. Either SAT or ACT required. ACT 25/75 percentile: 20-24. High school rank: 9% in top tenth, 30% in top quarter, 70% in top half
Early decision deadline: N/A, notification date: N/A
Early action deadline: N/A, notification date: N/A
Application deadline (fall): 5/1
Undergraduate student body: 9,497 full time, 1,250 part time; 51% male, 49% female; 0% American Indian, 2% Asian, 4% black, 7% Hispanic, 5% multiracial, 0% Pacific Islander, 82% white, 1% international; N/A from in state; 37% live on campus; 4% of students in fraternities, 6% in sororities
Most popular majors: 34% Business, Management, Marketing, and Related Support Services, 14% Education, 8% Communication, Journalism, and Related Programs, 7% Social Sciences, 6% Public Administration and Social Service Professions
Expenses: 2019-2020: $7,695 in state, $16,416 out of state; room/board: $6,908
Financial aid: (262) 472-1130; 58% of undergrads determined to have financial need; average aid package $8,590

Viterbo University
La Crosse WI
(608) 796-3010
U.S. News ranking: Reg. U. (Mid. W), No. 61
Website: www.viterbo.edu
Admissions email: admission@viterbo.edu
Private; founded 1890
Affiliation: Roman Catholic
Freshman admissions: selective; 2018-2019: 1,372 applied, 1,040 accepted. Either SAT or ACT required. ACT 25/75 percentile: 21-26. High school rank: 23% in top tenth, 51% in top quarter, 84% in top half
Early decision deadline: N/A, notification date: N/A
Early action deadline: N/A, notification date: N/A
Application deadline (fall): rolling
Undergraduate student body: 1,394 full time, 320 part time; 26% male, 74% female; 0% American Indian, 1% Asian, 0% black, 3% Hispanic, 5% multiracial, 0% Pacific Islander, 87% white, 2% international; 62% from in state; 35% live on campus; 0% of students in fraternities, 0% in sororities
Most popular majors: 50% Health Professions and Related Programs, 21% Business, Management, Marketing, and Related Support Services, 6% Visual and Performing Arts, 4% Education, 4% Psychology
Expenses: 2019-2020: $28,650; room/board: $9,295
Financial aid: (608) 796-3900; 78% of undergrads determined to have financial need; average aid package $21,777

Wisconsin Lutheran College
Milwaukee WI
(414) 443-8811
U.S. News ranking: Reg. Coll. (Mid. W), No. 17
Website: www.wlc.edu
Admissions email: admissions@wlc.edu
Private; founded 1973
Affiliation: Wisconsin Evangelical Lutheran Synod
Freshman admissions: selective; 2018-2019: 969 applied, 779 accepted. Either SAT or ACT required. ACT 25/75 percentile: 20-26. High school rank: 21% in top tenth, 47% in top quarter, 74% in top half
Early decision deadline: N/A, notification date: N/A
Early action deadline: N/A, notification date: N/A
Application deadline (fall): rolling
Undergraduate student body: 951 full time, 134 part time; 44% male, 56% female; 0% American Indian, 2% Asian, 6% black, 7% Hispanic, 3% multiracial, 0% Pacific Islander, 81% white, 1% international; 73% from in state; 65% live on campus; N/A of students in fraternities, N/A in sororities
Most popular majors: 32% Business, Management, Marketing, and Related Support Services, 10% Health Professions and Related Programs, 9% Education, 8% Communication, Journalism, and Related Programs, 7% Biological and Biomedical Sciences
Expenses: 2019-2020: $30,850; room/board: $10,496
Financial aid: (414) 443-8856; 83% of undergrads determined to have financial need; average aid package $23,597

WYOMING

University of Wyoming
Laramie WY
(307) 766-5160
U.S. News ranking: Nat. U., No. 228
Website: www.uwyo.edu
Admissions email: admissions@uwyo.edu
Public; founded 1886
Freshman admissions: selective; 2018-2019: 5,293 applied, 5,083 accepted. Either SAT or ACT required. ACT 25/75 percentile: 22-28. High school rank: 21% in top tenth, 48% in top quarter, 80% in top half
Early decision deadline: N/A, notification date: N/A
Early action deadline: N/A, notification date: N/A
Application deadline (fall): 8/10
Undergraduate student body: 8,457 full time, 1,541 part time; 49% male, 51% female; 1% American Indian, 1% Asian, 1% black, 7% Hispanic, 4% multiracial, 0% Pacific Islander, 72% white, 4% international; N/A from in state; 25% live on campus; 8% of students in fraternities, 7% in sororities
Most popular majors: 16% Business, Management, Marketing, and Related Support Services, 12% Engineering, 11% Health Professions and Related Programs, 10% Education, 7% Biological and Biomedical Sciences
Expenses: 2019-2020: $5,581 in state, $18,151 out of state; room/board: $10,437
Financial aid: (307) 766-2116; 47% of undergrads determined to have financial need; average aid package $10,356

More @ usnews.com/bestcolleges